THIRTEENTH EDITION

Educational Psychology

ANITA WOOLFOLK

The Ohio State University

PEARSON

Boston   Columbus   Indianapolis   New York   San Francisco   Hoboken
Amsterdam   Cape Town   Dubai   London   Madrid   Milan   Munich   Paris   Montreal   Toronto
Delhi   Mexico City   São Paulo   Sydney   Hong Kong   Seoul   Singapore   Taipei   Tokyo

Vice President and Editorial Director: Jeffery W. Johnston
Vice President and Publisher: Kevin M. Davis
Development Editor: Gail Gottfried
Editorial Assistant: Caitlin Griscom
Executive Field Marketing Manager: Krista Clark
Senior Product Marketing Manager: Christopher Barry
Project Manager: Lauren Carlson
Procurement Specialist: Carol Melville
Senior Art Director: Diane Lorenzo
Cover Designer: Jennifer Hart
Cover Art: Anita Woolfolk Hoy
Media Project Manager: Tammy Walters
Full-Service Project Management: Roxanne Klaas, S4Carlisle Publishing Services
Composition: S4Carlisle Publishing Services
Printer/Binder: Courier - Kendallville
Cover Printer: Courier - Kendallville
Text Font: 10/13 Adobe Garamond Pro

Credits and acknowledgments for material borrowed from other sources and reproduced, with permission, in this textbook appear on the appropriate page within the text.

Every effort has been made to provide accurate and current Internet information in this book. However, the Internet and information posted on it are constantly changing, so it is inevitable that some of the Internet addresses listed in this textbook will change.

Library of Congress Cataloging-in-Publication Data

Hoy, Anita Woolfolk,
 Educational psychology / Anita Woolfolk.—Thirteenth edition.
  pages cm
 Includes bibliographical references and index.
 ISBN 978-0-13-354992-8—ISBN 0-13-354992-5
 1. Educational psychology—Textbooks. I. Title.
LB1051.W743 2014
                           370.15—dc23

2014024281

10 9 8 7 6 5 4 3 2 1

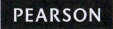

ISBN 10:   0-13-354992-5
ISBN 13: 978-0-13-354992-8

To my mother,

Marion Wieckert Pratt.

A remarkable educator,
An adventurous world traveler,
A courageous advocate for all in need,
And a wonderful guide in life—

Thank you.

About the Author

So you will know your author a bit better, here is some information.

Anita Woolfolk Hoy was born in Fort Worth, Texas, where her mother taught child development at TCU and her father was an early worker in the computer industry. She is a Texas Longhorn—all her degrees are from the University of Texas, Austin, the last one a PhD. After graduating, she was a psychologist working with children in elementary and secondary schools in 15 counties of central Texas. She began her career in higher education as a professor of educational psychology at Rutgers University, and then moved to The Ohio State University in 1994. Today she is Professor Emerita at Ohio State. Anita's research focuses on motivation and cognition, specifically, students' and teachers' sense of efficacy and teachers' beliefs about education. For many years she was the editor of *Theory Into Practice,* a journal that brings the best ideas from research to practicing educators. With students and colleagues, she has published over 80 books, book chapters, and research articles. Anita has served as Vice-President for Division K (Teaching & Teacher Education) of the American Educational Research Association and President of Division 15 (Educational Psychology) of the American Psychological Association. Just before completing this thirteenth edition of *Educational Psychology,* she collaborated with Nancy Perry, University of British Columbia, to write the second edition of *Child Development* (Pearson, 2015), a book for all those who work with and love children.

Preface

Many of you reading this book are enrolled in an educational psychology course as part of your professional preparation for teaching, counseling, speech therapy, nursing, or psychology. The material in this text should be of interest to everyone who is concerned about education and learning, from the nursery school volunteer to the instructor in a community program for adults with disabilities. No background in psychology or education is necessary to understand this material. It is as free of jargon and technical language as possible, and many people have worked to make this edition clear, relevant, and interesting.

Since the first edition of *Educational Psychology* appeared, there have been many exciting developments in the field. The thirteenth edition continues to emphasize the educational implications and applications of research on child development, cognitive science, learning, motivation, teaching, and assessment. Theory and practice are not separated in the text, but are considered together. The book is written to show how information and ideas drawn from research in educational psychology can be applied to solve the everyday problems of teaching. To help you explore the connections between research and practice, you will find in these pages a wealth of examples, lesson segments, case studies, guidelines, and even practical tips from experienced teachers. As you read this book, I believe you will see the immense value and usefulness of educational psychology. The field offers unique and crucial knowledge to any who dare to teach and to all who love to learn.

NEW CONTENT IN THE THIRTEENTH EDITION

Across the book, there is increased coverage of a number of important topics. Some of these include:

- New explorations of current research on teaching and models of **expert teaching**, introduced in Chapter 1 and continued throughout the book.
- Increased coverage of the **brain, neuroscience, and teaching** emphasized in Chapter 2 and also integrated into several other chapters.
- Increased coverage of **the impact of technology and virtual learning environments** on the lives of students and teachers today.
- Increased emphasis on **diversity in today's classrooms** (see especially Chapters 1 to 6). Portraits of students in educational settings make diversity real and human for readers.

Key content changes in each chapter include:

- Chapter 1: My goal is that this text will provide the knowledge and skills that will enable you to build a solid foundation for an authentic sense of teaching efficacy in every context and for every student, so there is new information about **three models of good teaching**: Charlotte Danielson's Framework for Teaching, TeachingWorks from the University of Michigan, and the Gates Foundation Measure of Effective Teaching. Also, the section on research now examines different kinds of **qualitative and quantitative research** and what you can learn from each kind (see Table 1.2).
- Chapter 2: New information on the **brain**, **synaptic plasticity**, **executive functioning**, and **implications for teaching**, including an approach based on Vygotsky called *Tools of the Mind*.
- Chapter 3: New sections on **cultural differences in play**, **physical activity and students with disabilities**, **eating disorders** and the Web sites that promote them, **self-concept**, and Jonathan Haidt's **model of moral psychology**.
- Chapter 4: New sections on **nine possible multiple intelligences**, **accommodations under Section 504**, **autism spectrum disorders**, **student drug use**, and ways to **identify students who are gifted and talented**.

- Chapter 5: New information on **learning to read**, **emergent literacy and language diversity**, **sheltered instruction**, and **student-led conferences**.
- Chapter 6: New coverage of **homeless and highly mobile students**, expanded coverage of **poverty and school achievement**, **opportunity gaps**, and **stereotype threat**.
- Chapter 7: Expanded coverage of **teaching implications** of behavioral learning.
- Chapter 8: Updated coverage of **working memory**, **developmental differences**, and **teaching implications** of cognitive learning theories.
- Chapter 9: Updated sections on **metacognition** and **learning strategies**, **creativity**, and **transfer**, and a new section on **Paul and Elder's model of critical thinking**.
- Chapter 10: New material on **inquiry learning** and **teaching in a digital world**, including **Betty's Brain**—an example of a virtual learning environment, the **use of games** in teaching, and the initiative to teach **computational thinking and coding**.
- Chapter 11: Updated coverage of **self-efficacy**, **self-regulated learning**, and new material on **emotional self-regulation**.
- Chapter 12: Updated treatment of **self-determination theory** and **goal theory**, expanded coverage of **helping students cope with anxiety**, and new material on **flow** and **motivation**.
- Chapter 13: New sections on understanding your **beliefs about classroom management**, **creating caring relationships**, **bullying**, **restorative justice**, **and** Marvin Marshall's views on **consequences and penalties**.
- Chapter 14: Recent **research on teaching**, as well as new sections on the **Common Core** and **Understanding by Design**.
- Chapter 15: New sections on **what teachers think** about high-stakes testing, **value-added assessment**, and **PARCC tests**.

A CRYSTAL CLEAR PICTURE OF THE FIELD AND WHERE IT IS HEADED

The thirteenth edition maintains the lucid writing style for which the book is renowned. The text provides accurate, up-to-date coverage of the foundational areas within educational psychology: learning, development, motivation, teaching, and assessment, combined with intelligent examinations of emerging trends in the field and society that affect student learning, such as student diversity, inclusion of students with special learning needs, education and neuroscience, educational policy, and technology.

FEATURES OF THE BOOK

Advances in Digital Technologies Reflected in the Book's Pedagogy

Resources available in the etext enable readers to observe development in context and to apply and assess their understanding of the concepts in the book. These resources include (a) embedded assessments with feedback and (b) content extensions and examples.

EMBEDDED ASSESSMENTS WITH FEEDBACK. In every chapter, readers will find three types of assessments: Self-check quizzes, application exercises, and a licensure practice exercise.

- Short self-check quizzes appear at the end of each major text section. The quizzes are designed to help readers assess their mastery of the learning outcome or outcomes covered in the sections they've just read. When readers of the etext click on a highlighted link in the Pearson etext, an interactive multiple-choice quiz is displayed. Readers may answer the questions and then submit their quizzes to be scored, after which they can see the questions they've answered correctly, the questions they've answered incorrectly, and written feedback that includes rationales for the correct and incorrect answers.

ENHANCEDetext *self-check*

- Application exercises, titled *Practice Using What You Have Learned,* are included after the summary in every chapter. Clicking on the "play" button in the Pearson etext opens the exercise, allowing readers to view a video and answer open-ended questions that encourage application of chapter content to teaching and learning in real classrooms. After readers submit their answers to these questions, they receive feedback in the form of model answers written by experts.

- Licensure practice exercises, titled *Connect and Extend to Licensure,* are modeled after the types of questions found on teacher licensure exams. At the end of each chapter, these exercises include multiple-choice questions on key concepts presented in the chapter and constructed-response questions based on a short written case. Clicking on the licensure exam link allows readers to enter their responses and receive expert feedback.

CONTENT EXTENSIONS AND EXAMPLES. This enhanced etext includes both videos and podcasts that extend and expand on the chapter content.

- The video examples allow readers to see many concepts and principles *in action*—for instance, in students' behaviors and verbal reflections, in teachers' classroom strategies, and in adult–child interactions.

Video 1.1
A bilingual teacher conducts a discussion with immigrant high school students. She asks students to discuss what teachers can do to help English learners and students from different cultures.

ENHANCEDetext *video example*

- The *Anita Talks* podcasts are direct links to relevant selections from *Anita Talks about Teaching,* a series of podcasts in which Dr. Woolfolk discusses how chapters of this text relate to the profession of teaching.

PODCAST 1.1
In this podcast, textbook author Anita Woolfolk talks about the importance of teachers in students' lives. Did you know that "teacher involvement and caring is the most significant predictor of a student's engagement in school from 1st grade through 12th grade?" Listen to learn more.

ENHANCEDetext *podcast*

Additional Text Features

With an unswerving emphasis on educational psychology's practical relevance for teachers and students in classrooms, the text is replete with current issues and debates, examples, lesson segments, case studies, and practical ideas from experienced teachers.

POINT/COUNTERPOINT
What Should Schools Do to Encourage Students' Self-Esteem?

There are over 2,000 books describing how to increase self-esteem. Schools and mental health facilities continue to develop self-esteem programs (Slater, 2002). The attempts to improve students' self-esteem have taken three main forms: personal development activities such as sensitivity training; self-esteem programs where the curriculum focuses directly on improving self-esteem; and structural changes in schools that place greater emphasis on cooperation, student participation, community involvement, and ethnic pride. Are these efforts valuable?

POINT The self-esteem movement has big problems. Some people have accused schools of developing programs where the main objective is "to dole out a huge heaping of praise, regardless of actual accomplishments" (Slater, 2002, p. 45). Frank Pajares and Dale Schunk (2002) point to another problem. "[W]hen what is communicated to children from an early age is that nothing matters quite as much as how they feel or how confident they should be, one can rest assured that the world will sooner or later teach a lesson in humility that may not easily be learned. An obsession with one's sense of self is responsible for an alarming increase in depression and other mental difficulties" (p. 16). Sensitivity training and self-esteem courses assume that we encourage self-esteem by changing the individual's beliefs,

Self-Esteem," suggests that we rethink self-esteem and move toward honest self-appraisal that will lead to self-control. She suggests, "Maybe self-control should replace self-esteem as a primary peg to reach for" (p. 47).

COUNTERPOINT The self-esteem movement has promise Erik Erikson (1980) warned years ago: "Children cannot be fooled by empty praise and condescending encouragement. They may have to accept artificial bolstering of their self-esteem in lieu of something better. . . ." Erikson explained that a strong and positive identity comes only from "wholehearted and consistent recognition of real accomplishment, that is, achievement that has meaning in their culture" (p. 95). A study that followed 322 sixth-grade students for 2 years found that students' satisfaction with school, their sense that classes were interesting and teachers cared, and teacher feedback and evaluations influenced students' self-esteem. In PE, teachers' opinions were especially powerful in shaping students' conceptions of their athletic abilities (Hoge, Smit, & Hanson, 1990). Being placed in a low-ability group or being held back in school seems to have a negative impact on students' self-esteem, but learning in collaborative and cooperative settings seems to have a positive effect (Covington, 1992; Deci & Ryan, 1985). Interestingly, special pro-

Point/Counterpoint sections in each chapter present two perspectives on a controversial question related to the field; topics include debates on the kinds of research that should guide education (p. 19), brain-based education (p. 40), the self-esteem movement (p. 104), pills or skills for students with ADHD (p. 144), the best way to teach English language learners (p. 193), tracking (p. 220), using rewards to encourage student learning (p. 280), what's wrong with memorization (p. 318), teaching critical thinking and problem solving (p. 358), problem-based education (p. 383), teacher efficacy (p. 423), the value of trying to make learning entertaining (p. 464), zero tolerance (p. 514), homework (p. 546), and holding children back (p. 590).

GUIDELINES
Helping Children of Divorce

Take note of any sudden changes in behavior that might indicate problems at home.
Examples
1. Be alert to physical symptoms such as repeated headaches or stomach pains, rapid weight gain or loss, fatigue, or excess energy.
2. Be aware of signs of emotional distress such as moodiness, temper tantrums, or difficulty in paying attention or concentrating.
3. Let parents know about the students' signs of stress.

Talk individually to students about their attitude or behavior changes. This gives you a chance to find out about unusual stress such as divorce.
Examples
1. Be a good listener. Students may have no other adult willing to hear their concerns.
2. Let students know you are available to talk, and let the student set the agenda.

Watch your language to make sure you avoid stereotypes

3. The student may be angry with his or her parents, but may direct the anger at teachers. Don't take the student's anger personally.

Find out what resources are available at your school.
Examples
1. Talk to the school psychologist, guidance counselor, social worker, or principal about students who seem to need outside help.
2. Consider establishing a discussion group, led by a trained adult, for students whose parents are going through a divorce.

Be sensitive to both parents' rights to information.
Examples
1. When parents have joint custody, both are entitled to receive information and attend parent–teacher conferences.
2. The noncustodial parent may still be concerned about the child's school progress. Check with your principal about state laws regarding the noncustodial parent's rights.

Guidelines appear throughout each chapter, providing concrete applications of theories or principles discussed. See, for example, pages 85, 198, 320.

GUIDELINES
Family and Community Partnerships

Promoting Transfer

Keep families informed about their child's curriculum so they can support learning.
Examples
1. At the beginning of units or major projects, send a letter summarizing the key goals, a few of the major assignments, and some common problems students have in learning the material for that unit.
2. Ask parents for suggestions about how their child's interests could be connected to the curriculum topics.
3. Invite parents to school for an evening of "strategy learning." Have the students teach their family members one of the strategies they have learned in school.

Give families ideas for how they might encourage their children to practice, extend, or apply learning from school.
Examples
1. To extend writing, ask parents to encourage their children to write letters or e-mails to companies or civic organizations asking for information or free products. Provide a shell letter form for structure and ideas, and include addresses of companies that provide free samples or information.
2. Ask family members to include their children in some projects that require measurement, halving or doubling recipes, or estimating costs.

3. Suggest that students work with grandparents to do a family memory book. Combine historical research and writing.

Show connections between learning in school and life outside school.
Examples
1. Ask families to talk about and show how they use the skills their children are learning in their jobs, hobbies, or community involvement projects.
2. Ask family members to come to class to demonstrate how they use reading, writing, science, math, or other knowledge in their work.

Make families partners in practicing learning strategies.
Examples
1. Focus on one learning strategy at a time. Ask families to simply remind their children to use a particular strategy with homework that week.
2. Develop a lending library of books and videotapes to teach families about learning strategies.
3. Give parents a copy of the *Guidelines: Becoming an Expert Student* on page XXX, rewritten for your grade level.

Guidelines: Family and Community Partnerships sections offer specific guidelines for involving all families in their children's learning—especially relevant now, when demand for parental involvement is at an all-time high and the need for cooperation between home and school is critical. See, for example, pages 49, 200, 362.

Teachers' Casebook sections present students with realistic classroom scenarios at the beginning of each chapter and ask "What Would You Do?"—giving students the opportunity to apply all the important topics of the chapter to these scenarios via application questions. Students may then compare their responses to those of veteran teachers appearing at the end of each chapter. See, for example, pages 30, 208, 410.

> ### TEACHERS' **CASEBOOK**
> **WHAT WOULD YOU DO?** UNCRITICAL THINKING
>
> This year's class is worse than any you've ever had. You assigned a research paper, and you find more and more students are using the Web for their information. In itself, using the Web is not bad, but the students appear to be completely uncritical about what they find on the Internet. "If it is on the Web, it must be right" is the attitude of most students. Their first drafts are filled with quotes that seem very biased to you, but there are no sources cited or listed. It is not just that students don't know how to reference their
>
> work. You are more concerned that they cannot critically evaluate what they are reading. And all they are reading is the Net!
>
> **CRITICAL THINKING**
> - How would you help your students evaluate the information they are finding on the Web?
> - Beyond this immediate issue, how will you help students think more critically about the subjects you are teaching?
> - How will you take into account the cultural beliefs and values of your students as you support their critical thinking?

Reaching Every Student sections present ideas for assessing, teaching, and motivating ALL of the students in today's inclusive classrooms. See, for example on page 65.

> ### Reaching Every Student: Teaching in the "Magic Middle"
>
> Both Piaget and Vygotsky probably would agree that students need to be taught in the magic middle (Berger, 2012), or the place of the "match" (J. Hunt, 1961)—where they are neither bored nor frustrated. Students should be put in situations where they have to reach to understand but where support from other students, learning materials, or the teacher is also available. Sometimes the best teacher is another student who has just figured out how to solve the problem, because this student is probably operating in the learner's ZPD. Having a student work with someone who is just a bit better at the activity would be a good idea because both students benefit in the exchange of explanations, elaborations, and questions. In addition, students should be encouraged to use language to organize their thinking and to talk about what they are trying to accomplish. Dialogue and discussion are important avenues to learning (Karpov & Bransford, 1995; Kozulin & Presseisen, 1995; Wink & Putney, 2002). The *Guidelines: Applying Vygotsky's Ideas in Teaching* on the next page gives more ideas for applying Vygotsky's insights.

Lessons for Teachers are succinct and usable principles for teaching based on the research. See, for example, on page 66.

> ### Cognitive Development: Lessons for Teachers
>
> In spite of cross-cultural differences in cognitive development and the different theories of development, there are some convergences. Piaget, Vygotsky, and more recent researchers studying cognitive development and the brain probably would agree with the following big ideas:
>
> 1. Cognitive development requires both physical and social stimulation.
> 2. To develop thinking, children have to be mentally, physically, and linguistically active. They need to experiment, talk, describe, reflect, write, and solve problems. But they also benefit from teaching, guidance, questions, explanations, demonstrations, and challenges to their thinking.
> 3. Teaching students what they already know is boring. Trying to teach what the student isn't ready to learn is frustrating and ineffective.
> 4. Challenge with support will keep students engaged but not fearful.

SUPPLEMENTS

This thirteenth edition of *Educational Psychology* provides a comprehensive and integrated collection of supplements to assist students and professors alike in maximizing learning and instruction. Together, these materials immerse students in the content of the text, allowing them and their instructors to benefit from a deeper and more meaningful learning experience. The following resources are available for instructors to download from www.pearsonhighered.com/educator. Enter the author, title of the text, or the ISBN number, then select this text, and click on the "Resources" tab. Download the supplement you need. If you require assistance in downloading any resources, contact your Pearson representative.

INSTRUCTOR'S RESOURCE MANUAL. The *Instructor's Resource Manual* synthesizes all of the resources available for each chapter and sifts through the materials to match the delivery method (e.g., semester, quarter) and areas of emphasis for the course. This manual includes activities and strategies designed to help prospective teachers—and others seeking a career working with children or adolescents—to apply the developmental concepts and strategies they have learned.

POWERPOINT® SLIDES. Slide sets for each chapter include chapter objectives, key concepts, summaries of content, and graphic aids, each designed to support class lectures and help students organize, synthesize, and remember core content. All PowerPoint® slides have been updated for consistency and reflect current content in this new edition.

TEST BANK. Built from the course objectives, the test bank questions offer both lower-level questions that ask students to identify or explain concepts, principles, and theories about development and higher-level questions that require students to apply concepts, principles, and theories to student behavior and teaching strategies.

TESTGEN®. TestGen is a powerful test generator available exclusively from Pearson Education publishers. You install TestGen on your personal computer (Windows or Macintosh) and create your own tests for classroom testing and for other specialized delivery options, such as over a local area network or on the Web. A test bank, which is also called a Test Item File (TIF), typically contains a large set of test items, organized by chapter and ready for your use in creating a test, based on the associated textbook material. Assessments may be created for both print and testing online.

The tests can be downloaded in the following formats:

TestGen Testbank file—PC
TestGen Testbank file—MAC
TestGen Testbank—Blackboard 9 TIF
TestGen Testbank—Blackboard CE/Vista (WebCT) TIF
Angel Test Bank (zip)
D2L Test Bank (zip)
Moodle Test Bank
Sakai Test Bank (zip)

ACKNOWLEDGMENTS

During the years I have worked on this book, from initial draft to this most recent revision, many people have supported the project. Without their help, this text simply could not have been written.

Many educators contributed to this edition and previous editions. Carol Weinstein wrote the section in Chapter 13 on spaces for learning. Nancy Perry (University of British Columbia) and Philip Winne (Simon Frasier University) wrote sections of Chapter 11 on self-regulation. Brad Henry (The Ohio State University) crafted sections on technology in two chapters. Michael Yough (Purdue University) looked over several chapters including Chapter 5, "Language Development, Language Diversity, and Immigrant Education." Chapter 5 was also improved by suggestions from Alan Hirvela, The Ohio State University. Jerrell Cassady, Ball State University, provided invaluable guidance for Chapter 11, "Social Cognitive Views of Learning and Motivation," and Chapter 12, "Motivation in Learning and Teaching." The portraits of students in Chapters 1 and 6 were provided by Nancy Knapp (University of Georgia). Raye Lakey is responsible for the media integration and for updating the *Test Bank, PowerPoint® Presentations*, and the *Instructor's Resource Manual*.

As I made decisions about how to revise this edition, I benefited from the ideas of colleagues around the country who took the time to complete surveys, answer my questions, and review chapters.

For their revision reviews, thanks to Gregg Schraw, University of Nevada—Las Vegas; Theresa M. Stahler, Kutztown University; Kate Niehaus, University of South Carolina; Nithya Iyer, The State University of New York at Oneonta; and Alan Hirvela, The Ohio State University.

Many classroom teachers across the country and around the world contributed their experience, creativity, and expertise to the *Teachers' Casebook*. I have thoroughly enjoyed my association with these master teachers, and I am grateful for the perspective they brought to the book:

AIMEE FREDETTE • Second-Grade Teacher
Fisher Elementary School, Walpole, MA
ALLAN OSBORNE • Assistant Principal
Snug Harbor Community School, Quincy, MA
BARBARA PRESLEY • Transition/Work Study Coordinator—High School Level,
BESTT Program (Baldwinsville Exceptional Student Training and Transition Program)
C. W. Baker High School, Baldwinsville, NY

CARLA S. HIGGINS • K–5 Literacy Coordinator
Legend Elementary School, Newark, OH
DAN DOYLE • History Teacher, Grade 11
St. Joseph's Academy, Hoffman, IL
DANIELLE HARTMAN • Second Grade
Claymont Elementary School, Ballwin, MO
DR. NANCY SHEEHAN-MELZACK • Art and Music Teacher
Snug Harbor Community School, Quincy, MA
JACALYN D. WALKER • Eighth-Grade Science Teacher
Treasure Mountain Middle School, Park City, UT
JANE W. CAMPBELL • Second-Grade Teacher
John P. Faber Elementary School, Dunellen, NJ
JENNIFER L. MATZ • Sixth Grade
Williams Valley Elementary, Tower City, PA
JENNIFER PINCOSKI • Learning Resource Teacher, K–12
Lee County School District, Fort Myers, FL
JESSICA N. MAHTABAN • Eighth-Grade Math
Woodrow Wilson Middle School, Clifton, NJ
JOLITA HARPER • Third Grade
Preparing Academic Leaders Academy, Maple Heights, OH
KAREN BOYARSKY • Fifth-Grade Teacher
Walter C. Black Elementary School, Hightstown, NJ
KATIE CHURCHILL • Third-Grade Teacher
Oriole Parke Elementary School, Chicago, IL
KATIE PIEL • Kindergarten to Sixth-Grade Teacher
West Park School, Moscow, ID
KEITH J. BOYLE • English Teacher, Grades 9–12
Dunellen High School, Dunellen, NJ
KELLEY CROCKETT
Meadowbrook Elementary School, Fort Worth, TX
KELLY L. HOY • Fifth Grade
The Phillips Brooks School, Menlo Park, CA
KELLY MCELROY BONIN • High School Counselor
Klein Oak High School, Spring, TX
LAUREN ROLLINS • First Grade
Boulevard Elementary School, Shaker Heights, OH
LINDA GLISSON AND SUE MIDDLETON • Fifth-Grade Team Teachers
St. James Episcopal Day School, Baton Rouge, LA
LINDA SPARKS • First Grade
John F. Kennedy School, Billerica, MA
LOU DE LAURO • Fifth-Grade Language Arts
John P. Faber School, Dunellen, NJ
M. DENISE LUTZ • Technology Coordinator
Grandview Heights High School, Columbus, OH
MADYA AYALA • High School Teacher of Preperatoria
Eugenio Garza Lagüera, Campus Garza Sada, Monterrey, N. L. Mexico
MARIE HOFFMAN HURT • Eighth-Grade Foreign Language Teacher
(German and French)
Pickerington Local Schools, Pickerington, OH
MICHAEL YASIS
L. H. Tanglen Elementary School, Minnetonka, MN
NANCY SCHAEFER • Grades 9–12

Cincinnati Hills Christian Academy High School, Cincinnati, OH
PAM GASKILL • Second Grade
Riverside Elementary School, Dublin, OH
PATRICIA A. SMITH • High School Math
Earl Warren High School, San Antonio, TX
PAUL DRAGIN • English as a Second Language, Grades 9–12
Columbus East High School, Columbus, OH
PAULA COLEMERE • Special Education Teacher—English, History
McClintock High School, Tempe, AZ
SARA VINCENT • Special Education
Langley High School, McLean, VA
THOMAS NAISMITH • Science Teacher Grades 7–12
Slocum Independent School District, Elkhart, TX
VALERIE A. CHILCOAT • 5th-/6th-Grade Advanced Academics
Glenmount School, Baltimore, MD

In a project of this size, so many people make essential contributions. Carrie Mollette, Jorgensen Fernandez, and Janet Woods worked diligently, often through weekends, to obtain permissions for the material reproduced in this text and the supplements. The text designer, Diane Lorenzo, made the look of this book the best yet—hard to do after 12 editions. Project Managers Roxanne Klaas from S4Carlisle and Lauren Carlson from Pearson kept all aspects of the project moving forward with amazing skill, grace, and good humor. Somehow they brought sanity to what could have been chaos and fun to what might have been drudgery. Now the book is in the able hands of marketing managers Christopher Barry and Krista Clark. I can't wait to see what they are planning for me now! What a talented and creative group—I am honored to work with them all.

On this edition, I was again privileged to work with an outstanding editorial group. Their intelligence, creativity, sound judgment, style, and enduring commitment to quality can be seen on every page of this text. Kevin Davis, Publisher, guided the project from reviews to completion with the eye of an artist, the mind of a scholar, and the logistical capacity of a high-powered computer. He proved to be an excellent collaborator with a wise grasp of the field and a sense of the future. Caitlin Griscom, Editorial Assistant, kept everything running smoothly and kept my e-mail humming. Luanne Dreyer Elliott carefully and expertly copy edited every page—who knew I could invent such "creative" spellings! On this edition I was fortunate to have the help of Gail Gottfried, an outstanding developmental editor with the perfect combination of vast knowledge, organizational ability, and creative thinking. The text features, *Teachers' Casebook,* and excellent pedagogical supports would not exist without her tireless efforts.

Finally, I want to thank my family and friends for their kindness and support during the long days and nights that I worked on this book. To my family, Marion, Bob, Eric, Suzie, Lizzie, Wayne K., Marie, Kelly, Tom, Lisa, Lauren, Mike, and the newest member, Amaya—you are amazing.

And of course, to Wayne Hoy, my friend, colleague, inspiration, passion, husband—you are simply the best.

—ANITA WOOLFOLK HOY

Brief Contents

PART III: TEACHING AND ASSESSING

Contents

3 The Self, Social, and Moral Development 72

PART II: LEARNING AND MOTIVATION

7 Behavioral Views of Learning 250

8 Cognitive Views of Learning 288

9 Complex Cognitive Processes 326

10 The Learning Sciences and Constructivism 368

11 Social Cognitive Views of Learning and Motivation 410

12 Motivation in Learning and Teaching 442

PART III: TEACHING AND ASSESSING

13 Creating Learning Environments 486

14 Teaching Every Student 528

15 Classroom Assessment, Grading, and Standardized Testing 568

Special Features

POINT/COUNTERPOINT

1 | LEARNING, TEACHING, AND EDUCATIONAL PSYCHOLOGY

TEACHERS' CASEBOOK

WHAT WOULD YOU DO? LEAVING NO STUDENT BEHIND

It is your second year as a teacher in the Davis East school district. Over the last 4 years, the number of students from immigrant families has increased dramatically in your school. In your class, you have two students who speak Somali, one Hmong, one Farsi, and three Spanish speakers. Some of them know a little English, but many have very few words other than "OK." If there had been more students from each of the language groups, the district would have given your school additional resources and special programs in each language, providing you extra help, but there are not quite enough students speaking most of the languages to meet the requirements. In addition, you have several students with special needs; learning disabilities, particularly problems in reading, seem to be the most common. Your state and district require you to prepare *all* your students for the achievement tests in the spring, and the national emphasis is on readiness for college and career by the end of high school—*for everyone*. Your only possible extra resource is a student intern from the local college.

CRITICAL THINKING

- What would you do to help all your students to progress and prepare for the achievement tests?
- How would you make use of the intern so that both she and your students learn?
- How could you involve the families of your non-English–speaking students and students with learning disabilities to support their children's learning?

OVERVIEW AND OBJECTIVES

Like many students, you may begin this course with a mixture of anticipation and wariness. Perhaps you are required to take educational psychology as part of a program in teacher education, speech therapy, nursing, or counseling. You may have chosen this class as an elective. Whatever your reason for enrolling, you probably have questions about teaching, schools, students—or even about yourself—that you hope this course may answer. I have written the 13th edition of *Educational Psychology* with questions such as these in mind.

In this first chapter, we begin with the state of education in today's world. Teachers have been both criticized as ineffective and lauded as the best hope for young people. Do teachers make a difference in students' learning? What characterizes good teaching—how do truly effective teachers think and act? What do they believe about student, learning, and themselves? Only when you are aware of the challenges and possibilities of teaching and learning today can you appreciate the contributions of educational psychology.

After a brief introduction to the world of the teacher, we turn to a discussion of educational psychology itself. How can principles identified by educational psychologists benefit teachers, therapists, parents, and others who are interested in teaching and learning? What exactly is the content of educational psychology, and where does this information come from? Finally, we consider an overview of a model that organizes research in educational psychology to identify the key student and school factors related to student learning (J. Lee & Shute, 2010). My goal is that you will become a confident and competent beginning teacher, so by the time you have completed this chapter, you should be able to:

Objective 1.1	Describe the key elements of and changes to the No Child Left Behind Act.
Objective 1.2	Discuss the essential features of effective teaching, including different frameworks describing what good teachers do.
Objective 1.3	Describe the methods used to conduct research in the field of educational psychology and the kinds of questions each method can address.
Objective 1.4	Recognize how theories and research in development and learning are related to educational practice.

LEARNING AND TEACHING TODAY

Welcome to my favorite topic—educational psychology—the study of development, learning, motivation, teaching, and assessment in and out of schools. I believe this is the most important course you will take to prepare for your future as an educator in the classroom or the consulting office, whether your "students" are children or adults learning how to read or individuals discovering how to improve their diets. In fact, there is evidence that new teachers who have course work in development and learning are twice as likely to stay in teaching (National Commission on Teaching and America's Future, 2003). This may be a required course for you, so let me make the case for educational psychology, first by introducing you to classrooms today.

Students Today: Dramatic Diversity and Remarkable Technology

Who are the students in American classrooms today? Here are a few statistics about the United States and Canada (Children's Defense Fund, 2012; Dewan, 2010; Freisen, 2010; Meece & Kurtz-Costes, 2001; National Center for Child Poverty, 2013; National Center for Education Statistics, 2013; U.S. Census Bureau, 2010a).

- In 2010, 13% of the people living in the United States were born outside of the United States, and 20% spoke a language other than English at home—about 60% of these families spoke Spanish. Today, about 22% of children under the age of 18 are Latino. By 2050, Latinos will comprise about one quarter of the U.S. population (U.S. Census Bureau, 2010b).
  - In Canada, projections are that by 2031, one in three Canadians will belong to a visible minority, with South Asians being the largest group represented. About 17% of the population report that their first language is not French or English but instead is one of over 100 other languages.
  - In the 2011–2012 school year, about 60% of students with disabilities spent most of their time in general education classrooms.
  - In America, more than 16 million children—about 22% of all children—live in poverty, defined in 2013 by the U.S. Department of Health and Human Services as an income of $23,550 for a family of four ($29,440 in Alaska and $27,090 in Hawaii). Of those over 16 million, over 7 million live in extreme poverty. The United States has the *second highest* rate of child poverty among the economically advantaged countries of the world. Only Romania has a higher rate of child poverty. Iceland, the Scandinavian countries, Cyprus, and the Netherlands have the lowest rates of child poverty, about 7% or less (UNICEF, 2012; U.S. Census Bureau, 2011a).
  - The average wealth of White households is 18 times the wealth of Hispanic households and 20 times higher than Black households. These are the largest gaps observed since these data were first published a quarter century ago (Children's Defense Fund, 2012).
  - About one in six American children have a mild-to-severe developmental disability such as speech and language impairments, intellectual disabilities, cerebral palsy, or autism (Centers for Disease Control, 2013).
  - Out of 100 graduates in the high school class of 2013, about 71 had experienced physical assault; 51 had used alcohol, cigarettes, or illicit drugs in the previous 30 days, and 7 smoked marijuana every day; 48 were sexually active, but only 27 used condoms the last time they had sex; 39 had been bullied physically or emotionally; 20 watched 4 hours or more of television every day; 17 were employed; 16 had carried a weapon in the previous year; 12 had attention-deficit hyperactivity disorder (ADHD); and 4 had an eating disorder (Child Trends, 2013).

In contrast, because of the effects of mass media, these diverse students share many similarities today, particularly the fact that most are far more technologically literate than their teachers. For example:

- Infants to 8-year-olds spend an average of almost 2 hours each day watching TV or videos, 29 minutes listening to music, and 25 minutes working with

computers or computer games. In 2013, 75% of homes with children under age 8 had a smartphone, tablet, or other mobile device (Common Sense Media, 2012, 2013).
- Among teens, 77% have a cell phone; about one third of these are smartphones. And 90% of 13- to 17-year-olds use social media (Common Sense Media, 2012).

These statistics are dramatic but a bit impersonal. As a teacher, counselor, recreational worker, speech therapist, or family member, you will encounter real children. In this book, you will meet many individuals such as Felipe, a fifth-grade boy from a Spanish-speaking family who is working to learn school subjects and make friends in a language that is new to him; Ternice, an outspoken African American girl in an urban middle school who is hiding her giftedness; Benjamin, a good high school athlete diagnosed with ADHD whose wealthy parents have very high expectations for him and his teachers; Trevor, a second-grade student who has trouble with the meaning of *symbol*; Allison, head of a popular clique and tormentor of the outcast Stephanie; Davy, a shy, struggling reader who is already falling behind in all his second-grade work; Eliot, a bright sixth-grade student with severe learning disabilities; and Jessie, a student in a rural high school who just doesn't seem to care about her sinking grade-point average (GPA) or school in general.

Even though students in classrooms are increasingly diverse in race, ethnicity, language, and economic level, teachers are much less diverse—the percentage of White teachers is increasing (now about 91%), while the percentage of Black teachers is falling, down to about 7%. Clearly, it is important for all teachers to know and be able to work effectively with all their students. Several chapters in this book are devoted to understanding these diverse students. In addition, many times within each chapter, we will explore student diversity and inclusion through research, cases, and practical applications.

Confidence in Every Context

Schools are about teaching and learning; all other activities are secondary to these basic goals. But teaching and learning in the contexts just described can be challenging for both teachers and students. This book is about understanding the complex processes of development, learning, motivation, teaching, and assessment so that you can become a capable and confident teacher.

Much of my own research has focused on **teachers' sense of efficacy**, defined as a teacher's belief that he or she can reach even difficult students to help them learn. This confident belief appears to be one of the few personal characteristics of teachers that predict student achievement (Çakıroğlu, Aydın, & Woolfolk Hoy, 2012; Tschannen-Moran & Woolfolk Hoy, 2001; Tschannen-Moran, Woolfolk Hoy, & Hoy, 1998; Woolfolk & Hoy, 1990; Woolfolk Hoy, Hoy, & Davis, 2009). Teachers with a high sense of efficacy work harder and persist longer even when students are difficult to teach, in part because these teachers believe in themselves and in their students. Also, they are less likely to experience burnout and more likely to be satisfied with their jobs (Fernet, Guay, Senécal, & Austin, 2012; Fives, Hamman, & Olivarez, 2005; Klassen & Chiu, 2010).

I have found that prospective teachers tend to increase in their personal sense of efficacy as a consequence of completing student teaching. But sense of efficacy may decline after the first year as a teacher, perhaps because the support that was there for you in student teaching is gone (Woolfolk Hoy & Burke-Spero, 2005). Teachers' sense of efficacy is higher in schools when the other teachers and administrators have high expectations for students and the teachers receive help from their principals in solving instructional and management problems (Capa, 2005). Another important conclusion from our research is that efficacy grows from real success with students, not just from the moral support or cheerleading of professors and colleagues. Any experience or training that helps you succeed in the day-to-day tasks of teaching will give you a foundation for developing a sense of efficacy in your career. This book was written to provide the knowledge and skills that form a solid foundation for an authentic sense of efficacy in teaching.

High Expectations for Teachers and Students

On January 8, 2002, President George W. Bush signed into law the No Child Left Behind (NCLB) Act. Actually, NCLB was the most recent authorization of the Elementary and Secondary Education Act (ESEA), first passed in 1965. In a nutshell, NCLB required that all students in grades 3 through 8 and once more in high school must take annual standardized achievement tests in reading and mathematics. In addition, they must be tested in science—one test a year in each of three grade spans (3 to 5, 6 to 9, 10 to 12). Based on these test scores, schools were judged to determine if their students were making adequate yearly progress (AYP) toward becoming proficient in the subjects tested. States had some say in defining proficiency and in setting AYP standards. But no matter how states defined these standards, NCLB required that all students must reach proficiency by the end of the 2013–2014 school year. Schools also had to develop AYP goals and report scores separately for several groups, including racial and ethnic minority students, students with disabilities, students whose first language is not English, and students from low-income homes.

For a while, NCLB dominated education. Testing expanded. Often schools and teachers were punished if they did not perform; NCLB was widely criticized. "To date, NCLB's test based accountability and status bar, 100% proficiency targets have been blunt instruments, generating inaccurate performance results, perverse incentives, and unintended negative consequences" (Hopkins et al., 2013, p. 101). For example, expecting students whose first language is not English to perform at the same level as native speakers on tests given in English set the students up for failure and frustration. Under NCLB, too many schools were labeled as failing. Many educators suggested that accountability measures should focus on growth, not a narrow definition of achievement (McEachin & Polikoff, 2012).

NCLB was supposed to be reauthorized in 2007 or 2008. On March 13, 2010, the Obama Administration released *A Blueprint for Reform: The Reauthorization of the Elementary and Secondary Education Act* (2.ed.gov/policy/elsec/leg/blueprint/publicationtoc.html) to describe a vision for the reauthorization of NCLB. One of the major changes suggested was to move from a punishment-based system to one that rewards excellent teaching and student growth. The Blueprint described five priorities (U.S. Department of Education, 2010):

1. *College- and career-ready students.* Regardless of their income, race, ethnic or language background, or disability status, every student should graduate from high school ready for college or a career. To accomplish this goal, the Blueprint recommends *improved assessments* and *turnaround grants* to transform schools. In addition, Arne Duncan, the Secretary of Education, waived the requirement to reach 100% proficiency for states that can demonstrate they have adopted their own testing and accountability programs and are making progress toward the goal of college or career readiness for all their high school graduates (Dillon, 2011).

2. *Great teachers and leaders in every school.* "Research shows that top-performing teachers can make a dramatic difference in the achievement of their students, and suggests that the impact of being assigned to top-performing teachers year after year is enough to significantly narrow achievement gaps" (U.S. Department of Education, 2010, p. 13). To support this goal, the Blueprint proposed a Teacher and Leader Improvement Fund of competitive grants and new pathways for preparing educators. The focus of this book is to create great leaders in every school.

3. *Equity and opportunity for all students.* All students will be included in an accountability system that builds on college- and career-ready standards, rewards progress and success, and requires rigorous interventions in the lowest performing schools.

4. *Raise the bar and reward excellence.* Race to the Top, a series of competitive grants for schools, provided incentives for excellence by encouraging state and local leaders to work together on ambitious reforms, make tough choices, and develop comprehensive plans that change policies and practices to improve outcomes for students.

5. *Promote innovation and continuous improvement.* In addition to the Race to the Top grants, an Investing in Innovation Fund will support local and nonprofit leaders as they develop and scale up programs that have demonstrated success and discover the next generation of innovative solutions.

Time will tell how these proposals unfold, especially in the challenging economic environment we have experienced lately. One possible change in the next reauthorization of the law may be to focus on the bottom 5% of schools, those that have low achievement year after year (McEachin & Polikoff, 2012).

It seems likely that capable and confident teachers will be required to reach these goals. Is that true? But do teachers really make a difference? Good question.

Do Teachers Make a Difference?

You saw in the statistics presented earlier that in America many children are growing up in poverty. For a while, some researchers concluded that wealth and social status, not teaching, were the major factors determining who learned in schools (e.g., Coleman, 1966). In fact, much of the early research on teaching was conducted by educational psychologists who refused to accept these claims that teachers were powerless in the face of poverty and societal problems (Wittrock, 1986).

How can you decide whether teaching makes a difference? Perhaps one of your teachers influenced your decision to become an educator. Even if you had such a teacher, and I hope you did, one of the purposes of educational psychology in general and this text in particular is to go beyond individual experiences and testimonies, powerful as they are, to examine larger groups. The results of many studies speak to the power of teachers in the lives of students. You will see several examples next.

TEACHER–STUDENT RELATIONSHIPS. Bridgett Hamre and Robert Pianta (2001) followed all the children who entered kindergarten one year in a small school district and continued in that district through the eighth grade. The researchers concluded that the quality of the teacher–student relationship in kindergarten (defined in terms of level of conflict with the child, the child's dependency on the teacher, and the teacher's affection for the child) predicted a number of academic and behavioral outcomes *through the eighth grade*, particularly for students with many behavior problems. Even when the gender, ethnicity, cognitive ability, and behavior ratings of the student were accounted for, the relationship with the teacher still predicted aspects of school success. So students with significant behavior problems in the early years are less likely to have problems later in school if their first teachers are sensitive to their needs and provide frequent, consistent feedback. In another study that followed children from third through fifth grade, Pianta and his colleagues found that two factors helped children with lower skills in mathematics begin to close the achievement gap. The factors were higher-level (not just basic skills) instruction and positive relationships with teachers (Crosnoe, Morrison, Burchinal, Pianta, Keating, Friedman, & Clarke-Stewart, 2010).

It appears that the connection between teacher relationships and student outcomes is widespread. Deborah Roorda and her colleagues (2011) reviewed research from 99 studies around the world that examined the connections between teacher–student relationships and student engagement. Positive teacher relationships predicted positive student engagement at every grade, but the relationships were especially strong for students who were at risk academically and for older students. So evidence is mounting for a strong association between the quality of teacher–child relationships and school performance.

THE COST OF POOR TEACHING. In a widely publicized study, researchers examined how students are affected by having several effective or ineffective teachers in a row (Sanders & Rivers, 1996). They looked at fifth graders in two large metropolitan school systems in Tennessee. Students who had highly effective teachers for third, fourth, and fifth grades scored at the 83rd percentile on average on a standardized mathematics achievement test in one district and at the 96th percentile in the other (99th percentile is the highest possible score). In contrast, students who had the least effective teachers 3 years in a row averaged at the 29th percentile in math achievement in one district and 44th percentile in the other—a difference of over 50 percentile points in both cases! Students who had average teachers or a mixture of teachers with low, average, and high effectiveness for the 3 years had math scores between these extremes. Sanders and Rivers concluded that the best teachers encouraged good-to-excellent gains in achievement for all students, but lower-achieving students were the first to benefit from good teaching. The effects of teaching were cumulative and residual; that is, better teaching in a later grade could partially make up for less effective teaching in earlier grades, but could not erase all the deficits. In fact, one study found that at least 7% of the differences in test score gains for students could be traced to their teachers (Hanushek, Rivkin, & Kain, 2005; Rivkin, Hanushek, & Kain, 2001).

PODCAST 1.1
In this podcast, textbook author Anita Woolfolk talks about the importance of teachers in students' lives. Did you know that "teacher involvement and caring is the most significant predictor of a student's engagement in school from 1st grade through 12th grade?" Listen to learn more.

ENHANCEDetext *podcast*

Video 1.1
A bilingual teacher conducts a discussion with immigrant high school students. She asks students to discuss what teachers can do to help English learners and students from different cultures.

ENHANCEDetext *video example*

Another study about test score gains from the Los Angeles public schools may be especially interesting to you. Robert Gordon and his colleagues (2006) measured the test performance of elementary school students in *beginning teachers'* classes. Teachers were ranked into quartiles based on how well their students performed during the teachers' first 2 years. Then the researchers looked at the test performance of students in classes with the top 25% of the teachers and the bottom 25% during their third year of teaching. After controlling for the effects of students' prior test scores, their families' wealth, and other factors, the students working with the top 25% of the teachers gained an average of 5 percentile points more compared to students with similar beginning of the year test scores, while students in the bottom 25% lost an average of 5 percentile points. So students working with a less effective teacher could be an average of 10 percentile points behind the students working with an effective teacher. If these losses accumulate, then students working with poorer teachers would fall farther and farther behind. In fact, the researchers speculated that ". . . having a top-quartile teacher four years in a row would be enough to close the black-white test score gap" [of about 34 percentile points] (R. Gordon, Kane, & Staiger, 2006, p. 8).

Effective teachers who establish positive relationships with their students appear to be a powerful force in those students' lives. Students who have problems seem to benefit the most from good teaching. So an important question is, "What makes a teacher effective? What is good teaching?"

ENHANCEDetext *self-check*

WHAT IS GOOD TEACHING?

Connect and Extend to PRAXIS II®

Teacher Professionalism (IV, A2)
Begin your own development by reading educational publications. One widely read periodical is *Education Week*. You can access it online at edweek.com.

Educators, psychologists, philosophers, novelists, journalists, filmmakers, mathematicians, scientists, historians, policy makers, and parents, to name only a few groups, have examined this question; there are hundreds of answers. And good teaching is not confined to classrooms. It occurs in homes and hospitals, museums and sales meetings, therapists' offices, and summer camps. In this book, we are primarily concerned with teaching in classrooms, but much of what you will learn applies to other settings as well.

Inside Three Classrooms

To begin our examination of good teaching, let's step inside the classrooms of three outstanding teachers. The three situations are real. The first two teachers worked with my student teachers in local elementary and middle schools and were studied by one of my colleagues, Carol Weinstein (Weinstein & Romano, 2015). The third teacher became an expert at helping students with severe learning difficulties, with the guidance of a consultant.

A BILINGUAL FIRST GRADE. Most of the 25 students in Viviana's class have recently emigrated from the Dominican Republic; the rest come from Nicaragua, Mexico, Puerto Rico, and Honduras. Even though the children speak little or no English when they begin school, by the time they leave in June, Viviana has helped them master the normal first-grade curriculum for their district. She accomplishes this by teaching in Spanish early in the year to aid understanding and then gradually introducing English as the students are ready. Viviana does not want her students segregated or labeled as disadvantaged. She encourages them to take pride in their Spanish-speaking heritage and uses every available opportunity to support their developing English proficiency.

Both Viviana's expectations for her students and her commitment to them are high. She has an optimism that reveals her dedication: "I always hope that there's somebody out there that I will reach and that I'll make a difference" (Weinstein & Romano, 2015, p. 15). For Viviana, teaching is not just a job; it is a way of life.

A SUBURBAN FIFTH GRADE. Ken teaches fifth grade in a suburban school in central New Jersey. Students in the class represent a range of racial, ethnic, family income, and language backgrounds. Ken emphasizes "process writing." His students complete first drafts, discuss them with others in the class, revise, edit, and "publish" their work. The students also keep daily journals and often use them to share personal concerns with Ken. They tell him of problems at home, fights, and fears; he always takes the time to respond in writing. Ken also uses technology to connect lessons to real life. Students learn about ocean ecosystems by using a special interactive software program. For social studies, the class plays two simulation games that focus on history. One is about coming of age in Native American cultures, and the other focuses on the colonization of America.

Throughout the year, Ken is very interested in the social and emotional development of his students; he wants them to learn about responsibility and fairness as well as science and social studies. This concern is evident in the way he develops his class rules at the beginning of the year. Rather than specifying dos and don'ts, Ken and his students devise a "Bill of Rights" for the class, describing the rights of the students. These rights cover most of the situations that might need a "rule."

AN INCLUSIVE CLASS. Eliot was bright and articulate. He easily memorized stories as a child, but he could not read by himself. His problems stemmed from severe learning difficulties with auditory and visual integration and long-term visual memory. When he tried to write, everything got jumbled. Dr. Nancy White worked with Eliot's teacher, Mia Russell, to tailor intensive tutoring that specifically focused on Eliot's individual learning patterns and his errors. With his teachers' help, over the next years, Eliot became an expert on his own learning and was transformed into an independent learner; he knew which strategies he had to use and when to use them. According to Eliot, "Learning that stuff is not fun, but it works!" (Hallahan & Kauffman, 2006, pp. 184–185).

What do you see in these three classrooms? The teachers are confident and committed to their students. They must deal with a wide range of students: different languages, different home situations, and different abilities and learning challenges. They must adapt instruction and assessment to students' needs. They must make the most abstract concepts, such as ecosystems, real and understandable for their particular students. The whole time that these experts are navigating through the academic material, they also are taking care of the emotional needs of their students, propping up sagging self-esteem, and encouraging responsibility. If we followed these teachers from the first day of class, we would see that they carefully plan and teach the basic procedures for living and learning in their classes. They can efficiently collect and correct homework, regroup students, give directions, distribute materials, and deal with disruptions—and do all of this while also making a mental note to find out why one of their students is so tired. Finally, they are **reflective**—they constantly think back over situations to analyze what they did and why, and to consider how they might improve learning for their students.

SO WHAT IS GOOD TEACHING? Is good teaching science or art, the application of research-based theories or the creative invention of specific practices? Is a good teacher an expert explainer—"a sage on the stage" or a great coach—"a guide by the side"? These debates have raged for years. In your other education classes, you probably will encounter criticisms of the scientific, teacher-centered sages. You will be encouraged to be inventive, student-centered guides. *But beware of either/or choices.* Teachers must be both knowledgeable and inventive. They must be able to use a range of strategies, and they must also be capable of inventing new strategies. They must have some basic research-based routines for managing classes, but they must also be willing and able to break from the routine when the situation calls for change. They must know the research on student development, and they also need to know their own particular students who are unique combinations of culture, gender, and geography. Personally, I hope you all become teachers who are both sages and guides, wherever you stand.

Another answer to "What is good teaching?" involves considering what different models and frameworks for teaching have to offer. We look at this next.

MODELS OF GOOD TEACHING. In the last few years, educators, policy makers, government agencies, and philanthropists have spent millions of dollars identifying what works in teaching and specifically how to identify good teaching. These efforts have led to a number of models for teaching and teacher evaluation systems. We will briefly examine three to help answer the question, "What is good teaching?" Another reason to consider these models is that when you become a teacher, you

Video 1.2
Teachers must be both knowledgeable and inventive. They must be able to use a range of strategies, and they must also be capable of inventing new strategies. In this video, the teacher knows her students and uses strategies that help each student learn. Observe how she supports students who are English language learners, and observe her method of grouping students to meet diverse needs.

ENHANCEDetext *video example*

may be evaluated based on one of these approaches, or something like them—teacher evaluation is a very hot topic these days! We will look at Charlotte Danielson's Framework for Teaching, the high-leverage practices identified by TeachingWorks at the University of Michigan, and the Measures of Effective Teaching project sponsored by the Bill and Melinda Gates Foundation.

Danielson's Frameworks for Teaching. The Framework for Teaching was first published in 1996 and has been revised three times since then, the latest in 2013 (see danielsongroup.org for information about Charlotte Danielson and the Framework for Teaching). According to Charlotte Danielson (2013):

> The Framework for Teaching identifies those aspects of a teacher's responsibilities that have been documented through empirical studies and theoretical research as promoting improved student learning. While the Framework is not the only possible description of practice, these responsibilities seek to define what teachers should know and be able to do in the exercise of their profession. (p. 3)

Danielson's Framework has four domains or areas of responsibility: Planning and Preparation, Classroom Environment, Instruction, and Professional Responsibilities. Each domain is further divided into components, as you can see in Figure 1.1.

When the Framework is used for teacher evaluation, each of these 22 components is further divided into elements (76 in all), and several indicators are specified for each component. For example, component 1b, demonstrating knowledge of students, includes the elements describing knowledge of

- child and adolescent development
- the learning process
- students' skills, knowledge, and language proficiency
- students' interests and cultural heritage
- students' special needs (p. 13)

Indicators of this knowledge of students includes the formal and informal information about students that the teacher gathers in planning instruction, the student interests and needs the teacher

---

FIGURE 1.1

CHARLOTTE DANIELSON'S FRAMEWORK FOR TEACHING

Danielson's Framework for Teaching divides the complex task of teaching into the 22 components shown here, clustered into four domains of teaching responsibility: Planning and Preparation, Classroom Environment, Instruction, and Professional Responsibilities. The two domains of Classroom Environment and Instruction can be observed as teachers work with their classes, but success in all four domains is necessary for distinguished teaching.

Domain 1: Planning and Preparation
1a Demonstrating Knowledge of Content and Pedagogy
1b Demonstrating Knowledge of Students
1c Setting Instructional Outcomes
1d Demonstrating Knowledge of Resources
1e Designing Coherent Instruction
1f Designing Student Assessments

Domain 2: Classroom Environment
2a Creating an Environment of Respect and Rapport
2b Establishing a Culture for Learning
2c Managing Classroom Procedures
2d Managing Student Behavior
2e Organizing Physical Space

Domain 3: Instruction
3a Communicating with Students
3b Using Questioning and Discussion Techniques
3c Engaging Students in Learning
3d Using Assessment in Instruction
3e Demonstrating Flexibility and Responsiveness

Domain 4: Professional Responsibilities
4a Reflecting on Teaching
4b Maintaining Accurate Records
4c Communicating with Families
4d Participating in a Professional Community
4e Growing and Developing Professionally
4f Showing Professionalism

Source: Reprinted with permission from Danielson, C. (2013). The Framework for Teaching Evaluation Instrument: 2013 Edition. Princeton, NJ: The Danielson Group. Retrieved from http://www.danielsongroup.org/article.aspx?page=frameworkforteaching

identifies, the teacher's participation in community cultural events, opportunities the teacher has designed for families to share their cultural heritages, and any databases the teacher has for students with special needs (Danielson, 2013).

The evaluation system further defines four levels of proficiency for each of the 22 components: unsatisfactory, basic, proficient, and distinguished, with a definition, critical attributes, and possible examples of what each level might look like in action. Two examples of distinguished knowledge of students are teachers who plan lessons with three different follow-up activities designed to match different students' abilities and a teacher who attends a local Mexican heritage event to meet members of her students' extended families. Many other examples are possible, but these two give a sense of distinguished knowledge of students (component 1b).

You can see that it would take extensive training to use this framework well for teacher evaluation. When you become a teacher, you may learn more about this conception of good teaching because your school district is using it. For now, be assured that you will gain knowledge and skills in all 22 components in this text. For example, you will gain knowledge of students (component 1b) in Chapters 2 through 6.

TeachingWorks. TeachingWorks is a national project based at the University of Michigan and dedicated to improving teaching practice. Project members working with experienced teachers have identified 19 high-leverage teaching practices, defined as actions that are central to teaching and useful across most grades levels, academic subjects, and teaching situations. The TeachingWorks researchers call these practices "a set of 'best bets,' warranted by research evidence, wisdom of practice, and logic" (teachingworks.org/work-of-teaching/high-leverage-practices). These practices are specific enough to be taught and observed, so they can be a basis for teacher education and evaluation. See Figure 1.2 for these 19 practices. Again, you will develop skills and knowledge about all of these practices in this text. (For a more complete description of the 19 high-leverage practices, see teachingworks.org/work-of-teaching/high-leverage-practices.)

FIGURE 1.2

TEACHINGWORKS 19 HIGH-LEVERAGE TEACHING PRACTICES

These practices are based on research evidence, the wisdom of practice, and logic.

1. Making content (e.g., specific texts, problems, ideas, theories, processes) explicit through explanation, modeling, representations, and examples
2. Leading a whole-class discussion
3. Eliciting and interpreting individual students' thinking
4. Establishing norms and routines for classroom discourse and work that are central to the subject-matter domain
5. Recognizing particular common patterns of student thinking and development in a subject-matter domain
6. Identifying and implementing an instructional response or strategy in response to common patterns of student thinking
7. Teaching a lesson or segment of instruction
8. Implementing organizational routines, procedures, and strategies to support a learning environment
9. Setting up and managing small group work
10. Engaging in strategic relationship-building conversations with student
11. Setting long- and short-term learning goals for students referenced to external benchmarks
12. Appraising, choosing, and modifying tasks and texts for a specific learning goal
13. Designing a sequence of lessons toward a specific learning goal
14. Selecting and using particular methods to check understanding and monitor student learning during and across lessons
15. Composing, selecting, and interpreting and using information from quizzes, tests, and other methods of summative assessment
16. Providing oral and written feedback to students on their work
17. Communicating about a student with a parent or guardian
18. Analyzing instruction for the purpose of improving it
19. Communicating with other professionals

Source: Reprinted with permission from TeachingWorks (2014), High-leverage practices. Retrieved from http://www.teachingworks.org/work-of-teaching/high-leverage-practices

When you compare the 19 high-leverage practices in Figure 1.2 with the 22 Danielson components in Figure 1.1, do you see similarities and overlaps?

MEASURES OF EFFECTIVE TEACHING. In 2009, the Bill and Melinda Gates Foundation launched the Measures of Teaching Effectiveness (MET) Project, a research partnership between 3,000 teachers and research teams at dozens of institutions. The goal was clear from the title—to build and test measures of effective teaching. The Gates Foundation tackled this problem because research shows that teachers matter; they matter more than technology or funding or school facilities. In pursuing the goal, the project members made a key assumption. Teaching is complex; multiple measures will be needed to capture effective teaching and provide useful feedback for personnel decisions and professional development. In addition to using student achievement gains on state tests, the MET researchers examined many established and newer measures of effectiveness including the Tripod Student Perception Survey developed by Ron Ferguson at Harvard University (R. F. Ferguson, 2008), the Content Knowledge for Teaching (CKT) test from the University of Michigan (Ball, Thames, & Phelps, 2008), and several classroom observations systems, the Danielson (2013) Framework for Teaching described earlier, and the Classroom Assessment Scoring System (CLASS, Pianta, LaParo, & Hamre, 2008) described in Chapter 14. The MET researchers also examined several other observation approaches specific to certain subjects such as the Stanford University's Protocol for Language Arts Teaching Observations (PLATO) (Stanford University, 2013) and the University of Texas UTeach Teacher Observation Protocol (UTOP) (Marder & Walkington, 2010) for assessing math and science instruction. The final report of the project (MET Project, 2013) identified the following three measures used together as a valid and reliable way of assessing teaching that leads to student learning:

1. Student *gains on state tests.*
2. Surveys of *student perceptions* of their teachers. The Tripod Student Perception Survey asks students to agree or disagree with statements such as "My teacher takes time to help us remember what we learn" (for K–2 students), "In class we learn to correct our mistakes (upper elementary students), and "In this class, my teacher accepts nothing less than our full effort" (secondary students) (from Cambridge Education, tripodproject.org/student-perception-surveys/sample-questions/; for more information about the Tripod Student Perception Survey, go to tripodproject.org/student-perception-surveys).
3. *Classroom observations* from the Danielson (2013) Framework for Teaching.

Remember, teaching is complex. To capture effective teaching, these measures have to be used accurately and together. Also, the best combination of reliability and prediction of student gains in both state tests and tests of higher-level thinking comes when gains on standardized tests are weighted between 33% and 50% in assessing effectiveness, with student perception and class observation results providing the rest of the information (MET Project, 2013).

Are you surprised that teacher's content knowledge for the subject taught did not make the cut in measuring teacher effectiveness? So far math seems to be the one area where teacher knowledge is related to student learning, but with better measures of teacher knowledge, we may find more relationships (Gess-Newsome, 2013; Goe, 2013; MET Project, 2013).

Is all this talk about expert teachers and effective teaching making you a little nervous? Viviana, Ken, and Mia are experts at the science and art of teaching, but they have years of experience. What about you?

Beginning Teachers

STOP & THINK Imagine walking into your first day of teaching. List the concerns, fears, and worries you have. What assets do you bring to the job? What would build your confidence to teach? •

Beginning teachers everywhere share many concerns, including maintaining classroom discipline, motivating students, accommodating differences among students, evaluating students' work, dealing

TABLE 1.1 • **Advice for Student Teachers from Their Students**

> The students in Ms. Amato's first-grade class gave this advice as a gift to their student teacher on her last day.
>
> 1. Teach us as much as you can.
> 2. Give us homework.
> 3. Help us when we have problems with our work.
> 4. Help us to do the right thing.
> 5. Help us make a family in school.
> 6. Read books to us.
> 7. Teach us to read.
> 8. Help us write about faraway places.
> 9. Give us lots of compliments, like "Oh, that's so beautiful."
> 10. Smile at us.
> 11. Take us for walks and on trips.
> 12. Respect us.
> 13. Help us get our education.

Source: Nieto, Sonia, Affirming Diversity: The Sociopolitical Context of Multicultural Education, MyLabSchool Edition, 4th edition, © 2004. Reprinted by permission of Pearson Education, Inc. Upper Saddle River, NJ.

with parents, and getting along with other teachers (Conway & Clark, 2003; Melnick & Meister, 2008; Veenman, 1984). Many teachers also experience what has been called "reality shock" when they take their first job because they really cannot ease into their responsibilities. On the first day of their first job, beginning teachers face the same tasks as teachers with years of experience. Student teaching, while a critical element, does not really prepare prospective teachers for starting off a school year with a new class. If you listed any of these concerns in your response to the *Stop & Think* question, you shouldn't be troubled. They come with the job of being a beginning teacher (Borko & Putnam, 1996; Cooke & Pang, 1991).

With experience, hard work, and good support, seasoned teachers can focus on the students' needs and judge their success by the accomplishments of their students (Fuller, 1969; Pigge & Marso, 1997). One experienced teacher described the shift from concerns about yourself to concerns about your students: "The difference between a beginning teacher and an experienced one is that the beginning teacher asks, 'How am I doing?' and the experienced teacher asks, 'How are the children doing?'" (Codell, 2001, p. 191).

My goal in writing this book is to give you the foundation for becoming an expert as you gain experience. One thing experts do is listen to their students. Table 1.1 shows some advice a first-grade class gave to their student teacher: It looks like the students know about good teaching, too.

I began this chapter claiming that educational psychology is the most important course you will take. OK, maybe I am a bit biased—I have been teaching the subject for over four decades! So let me tell you more about my favorite topic.

ENHANCEDetext *self-check*

THE ROLE OF EDUCATIONAL PSYCHOLOGY

For as long as the formal study of educational psychology has existed—over 100 years—there have been debates about what it really is. Some people believe educational psychology is simply knowledge gained from psychology and applied to the activities of the classroom. Others believe it involves applying the methods of psychology to study classroom and school life (Brophy, 2003). A quick look at history shows that educational psychology and teaching have been closely linked since the beginning.

In the Beginning: Linking Educational Psychology and Teaching

In one sense, educational psychology is very old. Issues Plato and Aristotle discussed—the role of the teacher, the relationship between teacher and student, methods of teaching, the nature and

Connect and Extend to PRAXIS II®

Teacher Professionalism (IV, A1)
Your professional growth relies on your becoming a member of a community of practice. The national organizations listed here have hundreds of affiliations and chapters across the country with regular conferences, conventions, and meetings to advance instruction in their areas. Take a look at their Web sites to get a feel for their approaches to issues related to professionalism.

- National Council of Teachers of English (ncte.org)
- International Reading Association (reading.org)
- National Science Teachers Association (nsta.org)
- National Council for the Social Studies (ncss.org)
- National Council of Teachers of Mathematics (nctm.org)

order of learning, the role of emotion in learning—are still topics in educational psychology today. But let's fast forward to recent history. From the beginning, psychology in the United States was linked to teaching. At Harvard in 1890, William James founded the field of psychology and developed a lecture series for teachers entitled *Talks to Teachers about Psychology*. These lectures were given in summer schools for teachers around the country and then published in 1899. James's student, G. Stanley Hall, founded the American Psychological Association. His dissertation was about children's understandings of the world; teachers helped him collect data. Hall encouraged teachers to make detailed observations to study their students' development—as his mother had done when she was a teacher. Hall's student John Dewey founded the Laboratory School at the University of Chicago and is considered the father of the progressive education movement (Berliner, 2006; Hilgard, 1996; Pajares, 2003). Another of William James's students, E. L. Thorndike, wrote the first educational psychology text in 1903 and founded the *Journal of Educational Psychology* in 1910.

In the 1940s and 1950s, the study of educational psychology concentrated on individual differences, assessment, and learning behaviors. In the 1960s and 1970s, the focus of research shifted to the study of cognitive development and learning, with attention to how students learn concepts and remember. More recently, educational psychologists have investigated how culture and social factors affect learning and development and the role of educational psychology in shaping public policy (Anderman, 2011; Pressley & Roehrig, 2003).

Educational Psychology Today

What is educational psychology today? The view generally accepted is that **educational psychology** is a distinct discipline with its own theories, research methods, problems, and techniques. Educational psychologists do research on learning and teaching and, at the same time, work to improve educational policy and practice (Anderman, 2011; Pintrich, 2000). To understand as much as possible about learning and teaching, educational psychologists examine what happens when someone (a teacher or parent or software designer) teaches something (math or weaving or dancing) to someone else (student or co-worker or team) in some setting (classroom or theater or gym) (Berliner, 2006; Schwab, 1973). So educational psychologists study child and adolescent development; learning and motivation—including how people learn different academic subjects such as reading or mathematics; social and cultural influences on learning; teaching and teachers; and assessment, including testing (Alexander & Winne, 2006).

But even with all this research on so many topics, are the findings of educational psychologists really that helpful for teachers? After all, most teaching is just common sense, isn't it? Let's take a few minutes to examine these questions.

Is It Just Common Sense?

In many cases, the principles set forth by educational psychologists—after spending much thought, time, and money—sound pathetically obvious. People are tempted to say, and usually do say, "Everyone knows that!" Consider these examples.

HELPING STUDENTS. When should teachers provide help for lower-achieving students as they do class work?

Commonsense Answer. Teachers should offer help often. After all, these lower-achieving students may not know when they need help or they may be too embarrassed to ask for help.

ANSWER BASED ON RESEARCH. Sandra Graham (1996) found that when teachers provide help before students ask, the students and others watching are more likely to conclude that the helped student does not have the ability to succeed. The student is more likely to attribute failures to lack of ability instead of lack of effort, so motivation suffers.

SKIPPING GRADES. Should a school encourage exceptionally bright students to skip grades or to enter college early?

Commonsense Answer. No! Very intelligent students who are several years younger than their classmates are likely to be social misfits. They are neither physically nor emotionally ready for dealing with older students and would be miserable in the social situations that are so important in school, especially in the later grades.

ANSWER BASED ON RESEARCH. Maybe. The first two conclusions in the report *A Nation Deceived: How Schools Hold Back America's Brightest Children* are: (1) Acceleration is the most effective curriculum intervention for children who are gifted, and (2) for students who are bright, acceleration has long-term beneficial effects, both academically and socially (Colangelo, Assouline, & Gross, 2004). One example of the positive long-term effects is that mathematically talented students who skipped grades in elementary or secondary school were more likely to go on to earn advanced degrees and publish widely cited articles in scientific journals (Park, Lubinski, & Benbow, 2013). Whether acceleration is the best solution for a student depends on many specific individual characteristics, including the intelligence and maturity of the student as well as the other available options. For some students, moving quickly through the material and working in advanced courses with older students is a very good idea. See Chapter 4 for more on adapting teaching to students' abilities.

STUDENTS IN CONTROL. Does giving students more control over their own learning—more choices—help them learn?

Commonsense Answer. Of course! Students who choose their own learning materials and tasks will be more engaged and thus learn more.

ANSWER BASED ON RESEARCH. Not so fast! Sometimes giving students more control and choice can support learning, but sometimes not. For example, giving lower-ability students choice in learning tasks sometimes means the students just keep practicing what they already do well instead of tackling tougher assignments. This happened when hairdressing students were given choices. The lower-ability students kept practicing easy tasks such as washing hair but were reluctant to try more difficult projects such as giving permanents. When they developed portfolios to monitor their progress and received regular coaching and advice from their teachers, the students made better choices—so guided choice and some teacher control may be useful in some situations (Kicken, Brand-Gruwel, van Merriënboer, & Slot, 2009).

OBVIOUS ANSWERS? Years ago, Lily Wong (1987) demonstrated that just seeing research results in writing can make them seem obvious. She selected 12 findings from research on teaching. She presented 6 of the findings in their correct form and 6 in exactly the opposite form to both college students and experienced teachers. Both the college students and the teachers rated about half of the wrong findings as "obviously" correct. In a follow-up study, another group of subjects was shown the 12 findings and their opposites and was asked to pick which ones were correct. For 8 of the 12 findings, the subjects chose the wrong result more often than the right one.

Recently, Paul Kirschner and Joren van Merriënboer (2013) made a similar point when they challenged several "urban legends" in education about the assertion that learners (like the hairdressing students just described) know best how to learn. These strongly held beliefs about students today as self-educating digital natives who can multitask, have unique learning styles, and always make good choices about how to learn *have no strong basis in research*, but they are embraced nonetheless.

You may have thought that educational psychologists spend their time discovering the obvious. The preceding examples point out the danger of this kind of thinking. When a principle is stated in simple terms, it can sound simplistic. A similar phenomenon takes place when we see a professional dancer or athlete perform; the well-trained performer makes it look easy. But we see only the results of the training, not all the work that went into mastering the individual movements. And bear in mind that any research finding—or its opposite—may sound like common sense. The issue is not what *sounds* sensible, but what is *demonstrated* when the principle is put to the test in research—our next topic (Gage, 1991).

ENHANCEDetext *self-check*

Using Research to Understand and Improve Learning

STOP & THINK Quickly, list all the different research methods you can think of. •

Educational psychologists design and conduct many different kinds of research studies. Some of these are **descriptive studies**—their purpose is simply to describe events in a particular class or several classes.

CORRELATION STUDIES.   Often, the results of descriptive studies include reports of correlations. We will take a minute to examine this concept, because you will encounter many correlations in the coming chapters. A **correlation** is a number that indicates both the strength and the direction of a relationship between two events or measurements. Correlations range from 1.00 to −1.00. The closer the correlation is to either 1.00 or −1.00, the stronger the relationship. For example, the correlation between weight and height is about .70 (a strong relationship); the correlation between weight and number of languages spoken is about .00 (no relationship at all).

The sign of the correlation tells the direction of the relationship. A **positive correlation** indicates that the two factors increase or decrease together. As one gets larger, so does the other. Weight and height are positively correlated because greater weight tends to be associated with greater height. A **negative correlation** means that increases in one factor are related to *decreases* in the other, for example, the less you pay for a theater or concert ticket, the greater your distance from the stage. It is important to note that correlations do not prove cause and effect (see Figure 1.3). For example, weight and height are correlated—heavier people tend to be taller than lighter people. But gaining weight obviously does not cause you to grow taller. Knowing a person's weight simply allows you to make a general prediction about that person's height. Educational psychologists identify correlations so they can make predictions about important events in the classroom.

EXPERIMENTAL STUDIES.   A second type of research—**experimentation**—allows educational psychologists to go beyond predictions and actually study cause and effect. Instead of just observing and describing an existing situation, the investigators introduce changes and note the results. First, a number of comparable groups of participants are created. In psychological research, the term **participants** (also called **subjects**) generally refers to the people being studied—such as teachers or eighth graders. One common way to make sure that groups of participants are essentially the same is to assign each person to a group using a random procedure. **Random** means each participant has

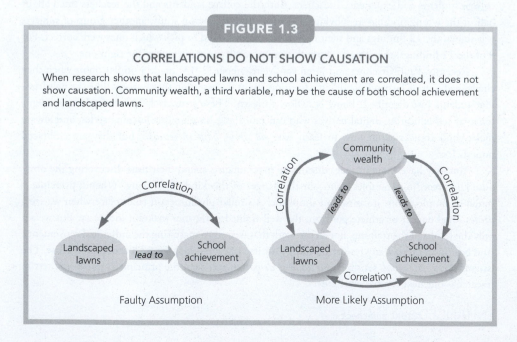

FIGURE 1.3

CORRELATIONS DO NOT SHOW CAUSATION

When research shows that landscaped lawns and school achievement are correlated, it does not show causation. Community wealth, a third variable, may be the cause of both school achievement and landscaped lawns.

Faulty Assumption

More Likely Assumption

an equal chance of being in any group. **Quasi-experimental studies** meet most of the criteria for true experiments, with the important exception that the participants are not assigned to groups at random. Instead, existing groups such as classes or schools participate in the experiments.

In experiments or quasi-experiments, for one or more of the groups studied, the experimenters change some aspect of the situation to see if this change or "treatment" has an expected effect. The results in each group are then compared. Usually, statistical tests are conducted. When differences are described as **statistically significant**, it means that they probably did not happen simply by chance. For example, if you see $p < .05$ in a study, this indicates that the result reported could happen by chance less than 5 times out of 100, and $p < .01$ means less than 1 time in 100.

A number of the studies we will examine attempt to identify cause-and-effect relationships by asking questions such as this: If some teachers receive training in how to teach spelling using word parts (*cause*), will their students become better spellers than students whose teachers did not receive training (*effect*)? This actually was a *field experiment* because it took place in real classrooms and not a simulated laboratory situation. In addition, it was a *quasi-experiment* because the students were in existing classes and had not been randomly assigned to teachers, so we cannot be certain the experimental and control groups were the same before the teachers received their training. The researchers handled this by looking at improvement in spelling, not just final achievement level, and the results showed that the training worked (Hurry et al., 2005).

SINGLE-SUBJECT EXPERIMENTAL DESIGNS. The goal of **single-subject experimental studies** is to determine the effects of a therapy, teaching method, or other intervention. One common approach is to observe the individual for a baseline period (A) and assess the behavior of interest; try an intervention (B) and note the results; then remove the intervention and go back to baseline conditions (A); and finally reinstate the intervention (B). This form of single-subject design is called an ABAB experiment. For example, a teacher might record how much time students are out of their seats without permission during a week-long baseline period (A), and then try ignoring those who are out of their seats, but praising those who are seated and record how many are wandering out of their seats for the week (B). Next, the teacher returns to baseline conditions (A) and records results, and then reinstates the praise-and-ignore strategy (B) (Landrum & Kauffman, 2006). When this intervention was first tested, the praise-and-ignore strategy proved effective in increasing the time students spent in their seats (C. H. Madsen, Becker, Thomas, Koser, & Plager, 1968).

CLINICAL INTERVIEWS AND CASE STUDIES. Jean Piaget pioneered an approach called the *clinical interview* to understand children's thinking. The clinical interview uses open-ended questioning to probe responses and to follow up on answers. Questions go wherever the child's responses lead. Here is an example of a clinical interview with a 7-year-old. Piaget is trying to understand the child's thinking about lies and truth, so he asks, "What is a lie?"

> "What is a lie?—*What isn't true. What they say that they haven't done.*—Guess how old I am.—*Twenty.* No, I'm thirty.—Was that a lie you told me?—*I didn't do it on purpose.*—I know. But is it a lie all the same, or not?—*Yes, it is the same, because I didn't say how old you were.*—Is it a lie?—*Yes, because I didn't speak the truth.*—Ought you be punished?—*No.*—Was it naughty or not naughty?—*Not so naughty.*—Why?—*Because I spoke the truth afterwards!*" (Piaget, 1965, p. 144).

Researchers also may employ case studies. A **case study** investigates one person or situation in depth. For example, Benjamin Bloom and his colleagues conducted in-depth studies of highly accomplished concert pianists, sculptors, Olympic swimmers, tennis players, mathematicians, and neurologists to try to understand what factors supported the development of outstanding talent. The researchers interviewed family members, teachers, friends, and coaches to build an extensive case study of each of these highly accomplished individuals (B. S. Bloom et al., 1985). Some educators recommend case study methods to identify students for gifted programs because the information gathered is richer than just test scores.

ETHNOGRAPHY. **Ethnographic methods**, borrowed from anthropology, involve studying the naturally occurring events in the life of a group to understand the meaning of these events to the people involved. In educational psychology research, ethnographies might study how students in different cultural groups are viewed by their peers or how teachers' beliefs about students' abilities affect classroom interactions. In some studies the researcher uses **participant observation**, actually participating in the group, to understand the actions from the perspectives of the people in the situation. Teachers can do their own informal ethnographies to understand life in their classrooms.

THE ROLE OF TIME IN RESEARCH. Many things that psychologists want to study, such as cognitive development (Chapter 2), happen over several months or years. Ideally, researchers would study the development by observing their subjects over many years as changes occur. These are called *longitudinal studies*. They are informative, but time-consuming, expensive, and not always practical: Keeping up with participants over a number of years as they grow up and move can be impossible. As a consequence, much research is *cross-sectional*, focusing on groups of students at different ages. For example, to study how children's conceptions of numbers change from ages 3 to 16, researchers can interview children of several different ages, rather than following the same children for 14 years.

Longitudinal and cross-sectional research examines change over long periods of time. The goal of **microgenetic studies** is to intensively study cognitive processes in the midst of change—while the change is actually occurring. For example, researchers might analyze how children learn a particular strategy for adding two-digit numbers over the course of several weeks. The microgenetic approach has three basic characteristics: the researchers (a) observe the entire period of the change—from when it starts to the time it is relatively stable; (b) make many observations, often using videotape recordings, interviews, and transcriptions of the exact words of the individuals being studied; (c) put the observed behavior "under a microscope," that is, they examine it moment by moment or trial by trial. The goal is to explain the underlying mechanisms of change—for example, what new knowledge or skills are developing to allow change to take place (Siegler & Crowley, 1991). This kind of research is expensive and time-consuming, so often only one or two children are studied.

QUANTITATIVE VERSUS QUALITATIVE RESEARCH. There is a distinction that you will encounter in your journey through educational psychology—the contrast between **qualitative** and **quantitative research**. These are large categories, and, like many categories, a bit fuzzy at the edges, but here are some simplified differences.

Qualitative Research. Case studies and ethnographies are examples of qualitative research. This type of research uses words, dialogue, events, themes, and images as data. Interviews and observations are key procedures. The goal is not to discover general principles, but rather to explore specific situations or people in depth and to understand the meaning of the events to the people involved in order to tell their story. Qualitative researchers assume that no process of understanding meaning can be completely objective. They are more interested in interpreting subjective, personal, or socially constructed meanings.

Quantitative Research. Both correlational and experimental types of research generally are quantitative because measurements are taken and computations are made. Quantitative research uses numbers, measurement, and statistics to assess levels or sizes of relationships among variables or differences between groups. Quantitative researchers try to be as objective as possible and remove their own biases from their results. One advantage of good quantitative research is that results from one study can be generalized or applied to other similar situations or people.

One of the requirements of the landmark NCLB Act was that educational programs and practices receiving federal money had to be consistent with "*scientifically based research*." Specifically, the NCLB Act stated that scientifically based research:

- Uses observations or experiments to systematically gather valid and reliable data.
- Involves rigorous and appropriate procedures for analyzing the data.
- Is clearly described so it can be repeated by others.
- Has been rigorously reviewed by appropriate, independent experts.

This description of scientifically based research fits the quantitative experimental approach described earlier better than qualitative methods such as ethnographic research or case studies, but there is continuing debate about what this means, as you will see in the *Point/Counterpoint*.

POINT/COUNTERPOINT
What Kind of Research Should Guide Education?

In the past decade, policies in both health care and in the treatment of psychological problems have emphasized evidence-based practices (McHugh & Barlow, 2010). The American Psychological Association defines **evidence-based practice in psychology (EBPP)** as "the integration of the best available research with clinical expertise in the context of patient characteristics, culture, and preferences" (American Psychological Association Task Force on Evidence-Based Practice for Children and Adolescents, 2008, p. 5). What does this mean in education?

POINT Research should be scientific; educational reforms should be based on solid evidence.

According to Robert Slavin (2002), tremendous progress has occurred in fields such as medicine, agriculture, transportation, and technology because:

In each of these fields, processes of development, rigorous evaluation, and dissemination have produced a pace of innovation and improvement that is unprecedented in history. . . . These innovations have transformed the world. Yet education has failed to embrace this dynamic, and as a result, education moves from fad to fad. Educational practice does change over time, but the change process more resembles the pendulum swings of taste characteristic of art or fashion (think hemlines) rather than the progressive improvements characteristic of science and technology. (2002, p. 16)

The major reason for extraordinary advances in medicine and agriculture, according to Slavin, is that these fields base their practices on scientific evidence. Randomized clinical trials and replicated experiments are the sources of the evidence.

In his Presidential Address to the First Conference of the International Mind, Brain, and Education Society, Kurt Fischer (2009, pp. 3–4) said:

What happened to education? If research produces useful knowledge for most of the industries and businesses of the world, then shouldn't it be serving the same function for education? Somehow education has been mostly exempt from this grounding in research. Dewey (1896) proposed the establishment of laboratory schools to ground education in research through combining research with practice in schools, ensuring both formative evaluation and democratic feedback. Unfortunately, his vision has never been realized. There is no infrastructure in education that routinely studies learning and teaching to assess effectiveness. If Revlon and Toyota can spend millions on research to create better products, how can schools continue to use alleged "best practices" without collecting evidence about what really works?

A recent article in the *New York Times* suggests lack of evidence is still a problem.

Most [educational] programs that had been sold as effective had no good evidence behind them. And when rigorous studies were done, as many as 90 percent of programs that seemed promising in small, unscientific studies had no effect on achievement or actually made achievement scores worse. For example, Michael Garet, the vice president of the American Institutes for Research, a behavioral and social science research group, led a study that instructed seventh-grade math teachers in a summer institute, helping them understand the math they teach—like why, when dividing fractions, do you invert and multiply? The teachers' knowledge of math improved, but student achievement did not. (Kolata, 2013, p. 3)

COUNTERPOINT Experiments are not the only or even the best source of evidence for education.

David Olson (2004) disagrees strongly with Slavin's position. He claims that we cannot use medicine as an analogy to education. "Treatments" in education are much more complex and unpredictable than administering one drug or another in medicine. And every educational program is changed by classroom conditions and the way it is implemented. Patti Lather, a colleague of mine at Ohio State, says, "In improving the quality of practice, complexity and the messiness of practice-in-context cannot be fantasized away. To try to do so yields impoverishment rather than improvement. That loss is being borne by the children, teachers, and administrators in our schools" (Lather, 2004, p. 30). David Berliner (2002) makes a similar point:

Doing science and implementing scientific findings are so difficult in education because humans in schools are embedded in complex and changing networks of social interaction. The participants in those networks have variable power to affect each other from day to day, and the ordinary events of life (a sick child, a messy divorce, a passionate love affair, migraine headaches, hot flashes, a birthday party, alcohol abuse, a new principal, a new child in the classroom, rain that keeps the children from a recess outside the school building) all affect doing science in school settings by limiting the generalizability of educational research findings. Compared to designing bridges and circuits or splitting either atoms or genes, the science to help change schools and classrooms is harder to do because context cannot be controlled (p. 19).

Berliner concludes that "A single method is not what the government should be promoting for educational researchers" (Berliner, 2002, p. 20).

BEWARE OF EITHER/OR: WHAT CAN YOU LEARN?

Complex problems in education need a whole range of methods for study. *Qualitative* research tells us specifically what happened in one or a few situations. Conclusions can be applied deeply, but only to what was studied. *Quantitative* research can tell us what generally happens under certain conditions. Conclusions can be applied more broadly. Today many researchers are using *mixed methods* or *complementary methods*—both qualitative and quantitative—to study questions both broadly and deeply. In the final analysis, the methods used—quantitative, qualitative, or a mixture of both—should fit the questions asked. Different approaches to research can ask different questions and provide different kinds of answers, as you can see in Table 1.2.

TABLE 1.2 • What Can We Learn?
Different approaches to research can ask and answer different questions.

RESEARCH METHOD	PURPOSES/QUESTIONS ADDRESSED	EXAMPLE
Correlational	To assess the strength and direction of the relation between two variables; to make predictions.	Is average amount of homework completed weekly related to student performance on unit tests? If so, is the relation positive or negative?
Experimental	To identify cause-and-effect relations; to test possible explanations for effects.	Will giving more homework cause students to learn more in science class?
Single-Subject Experiment	To identify the effects of a treatment or intervention for one individual.	When Emily records the number of pages she reads each night, will she read more pages? If she stops recording, will her amount of reading return to the previous levels?
Case Studies	To understand one or a few individuals or situations in depth.	How does one boy make the transition from a small rural elementary school to a large middle school? What are his main problems, concerns, issues, accomplishments, fears, supports, etc.?
Ethnography	To understand experiences from the participants' point of view: what is their meaning?	How do new teachers make sense of the norms, expectations, and culture of their new school, and how do they respond?
Mixed Methods	To ask complex questions involving causes, meanings, and relations among variables; to pursue both depth and breadth in research questions.	Based on an in-depth study of 10 classrooms, select the classes with the fewest behavior problems, then explore how teachers in those classes established a positive learning climate by interviewing teachers and students and analyzing videotapes made at the beginning of school.

TEACHERS AS RESEARCHERS. Research also can be a way to improve teaching in one classroom or one school. The same kind of careful observation, intervention, data gathering, and analysis that occurs in large research projects can be applied in any classroom to answer questions such as "Which writing prompts seem to encourage the most creative writing in my class?" "When does Kenyon seem to have the greatest difficulty concentrating on academic tasks?" "Would assigning task roles in science groups lead to more equitable participation of girls and boys in the work?" This kind of problem-solving investigation is called **action research**. By focusing on a specific problem and making careful observations, teachers can learn a great deal about both their teaching and their students.

You can find reports of the findings from all types of studies in journals that are referenced in this book. I have published articles in many of these journals and also have reviewed manuscripts to decide what will be published. For years I was editor of the *Theory Into Practice* journal (tip.ehe.osu .edu). I think this is a terrific journal to inspire and guide action research in classrooms. For a great overview of the past 50 years in educational research and practice, see the Special 50th Anniversary issue of *Theory Into Practice* (Gaskill, 2013).

Theories for Teaching

As we saw earlier, the major goal of educational psychology is to understand what happens when someone teaches something to someone else in some setting (Berliner, 2006; Schwab, 1973). Reaching this goal is a slow process. There are very few landmark studies that answer a question once and for all. There are so many different kinds of students, teachers, tasks, and settings; and besides, human beings are pretty complicated. To deal with this complexity, research in educational psychology examines limited aspects of a situation—perhaps a few variables at a time or life in one or two classrooms. If enough studies are completed in a certain area and findings repeatedly point to the same conclusions, we eventually arrive at a principle. This is the term for an established relationship between two or more factors—between a certain teaching strategy, for example, and student achievement.

Another tool for building a better understanding of the teaching and learning processes is *theory*. The commonsense notion of theory (as in "Oh well, it was only a theory") is "a guess or hunch." But the scientific meaning of *theory* is quite different. "A theory in science is an inter-related set of concepts that is used to explain a body of data and to make predictions about the results of future experiments" (Stanovich, 1992, p. 21). Given a number of established principles, educational psychologists have developed explanations for the relationships among many variables and even whole systems of relationships. There are theories to explain how language develops, how differences in intelligence occur, and, as noted earlier, how people learn.

You will encounter many theories of development, learning, and motivation in this book. Theories are based on systematic research, and they are the beginning and ending points of the research cycle. In the beginning, theories provide the research *hypotheses* to be tested or the questions examined. A hypothesis is a prediction of what will happen in a research study based on theory and previous research. For example, two different theories might suggest two competing predictions that could be tested. Piaget's theory might suggest that instruction cannot teach young children to think more abstractly, whereas Vygotsky's theory might suggest that this is possible. Of course, at times, psychologists don't know enough to make predictions, so they just ask *research questions*. An example question might be: "Is there a difference in Internet usage by male and female adolescents from different ethnic groups?"

Research is a continuing cycle that involves:

- Clear specification of hypotheses, problems, or questions based on current understandings or theories
- Systematic gathering and analyzing of all kinds of information (data) about the questions from well-chosen research participants in carefully selected situations
- Interpreting and analyzing the data gathered using appropriate methods to answer the questions or solve the problems
- Modification and improvement of explanatory theories based on the results of those analyses, and
- Formulation of new and better questions based on the improved theories . . . and on and on.

This empirical process of collecting data to test and improve theories is repeated over and over. Empirical means "based on data." When researchers say that identifying an effective antibiotic or choosing a successful way to teach reading is an "empirical question," they mean that you

Video 1.3
A Spanish teacher conducts research in her classroom and explains the results and the impact on her students. Notice the types of changes her students reported after the teacher implemented formative assessments.

ENHANCEDetext *video example*

need data and evidence to make the call. Constructing decisions from empirical analyses protects psychologists from developing theories based on personal biases, rumors, fears, faulty information, or preferences (Mertler & Charles, 2005). Answering questions with carefully gathered data means that research is self-correcting. If predictions do not play out or if answers to carefully formulated questions do not support current best understandings (theories), then the theories have to be changed. You can use the same kind of systematic and self-correcting thinking in your work with students.

Few theories explain and predict perfectly. In this book, you will see many examples of educational psychologists taking different theoretical positions and disagreeing on the overall explanations of such broad topics as learning and motivation. Because no one theory offers all the answers, it makes sense to consider what each has to offer.

So why, you may ask, is it necessary to deal with theories? Why not just stick to principles? The answer is that both are useful. Principles of classroom management, for example, will give you help with specific problems. A good theory of classroom management, on the other hand, will give you a new way of thinking about discipline problems; it will give you cognitive tools for creating solutions to many different problems and for predicting what might work in new situations. A major goal of this book is to provide you with the best and the most useful theories of development, learning, motivation, and teaching—those that have solid evidence behind them. Although you may prefer some theories to others, consider them all as ways of understanding the challenges teachers face.

I began this chapter by asserting that Educational Psychology is my favorite topic, as well as a key source of knowledge and skills for teaching. I end this chapter with one more bit of evidence for my enthusiasm. Educational psychology will help you support student learning—the goal of all teaching.

Supporting Student Learning

In an article in the *Educational Psychologist,* a major journal in our field, Jihyun Lee and Valerie Shute (2010) reported sifting through thousands of studies of student learning conducted over the course of 60 years, seeking to identify those that had direct measures of student achievement in reading and mathematics. Then they narrowed their focus to studies with strong effects. About 150 studies met all their rigorous criteria. Using the results from these studies, Lee and Shute identified about a dozen variables that were directly linked to K–12 student achievement. The researchers grouped these factors into two categories: *student personal factors* and *school and social-contextual factors*, as you can see in Table 1.3. When I read this article, I was pleased to see that my favorite subject, educational psychology, provides a base for developing knowledge and skills in virtually every area except principal leadership (for that subject you have to consult a book I wrote with my husband on principals as instructional leaders—Woolfolk Hoy & Hoy, 2013).

As you can see in Table 1.3, this text should help you become a capable and confident teacher who can get students engaged in the classroom learning community—a community that respects its members. This book will guide you toward becoming a teacher who helps students develop into interested, motivated, self-regulated, and confident learners. As a consequence, you will be able to set high expectations for your students, rally the support of parents, and build your own sense of efficacy as a teacher.

ENHANCEDetext *self-check*

TABLE 1.3 • **Research-Based Personal and Social-Contextual Factors that Support Student Achievement in K–12 Classrooms**

STUDENT PERSONAL FACTORS	EXAMPLES	WHERE IN THIS TEXT
Student Engagement		
Engaging Students' Behavior	Make sure students attend classes, follow rules, and participate in school activities.	Chapters 5–7, 13
Engaging Students' Minds and Motivations	Design challenging tasks, tap intrinsic motivation, support student investment in learning, and nurture student self-efficacy and other positive academic beliefs.	Chapters 2, 3, 10, 12
Engaging Students' Emotions	Connect to student interest, pique curiosity, foster a sense of belonging and class connections, diminish anxiety, and increase enjoyment in learning.	Chapters 3, 5, 6, 10, 12
Learning Strategies		
Cognitive Strategies	Directly teach knowledge and skills that support student learning and deep processing of valuable information (e.g., summarizing, inferring, applying, and reasoning).	Chapters 7–9, 14
Metacognitive Strategies	Directly teach students to monitor, regulate, and evaluate their own cognitive processes, strengths, and weaknesses as learners; teach them about when, where, why, and how to use specific strategies.	Chapters 7–9, 11
Behavioral Strategies	Directly teach students strategies and tactics for managing, monitoring, and evaluating their action, motivation, affect, and environment, such as skills in: time management test taking help seeking note taking homework management	Chapters 7–14

SOCIAL-CONTEXTUAL FACTORS	EXAMPLES	WHERE IN THIS TEXT
School Climate		
Academic Emphasis	Set high expectations for your students, and encourage the whole school to do the same; emphasize positive relations with the school community.	Chapters 11–13
Teacher Variables	If possible, teach in a school with the positive qualities of collective efficacy, teacher empowerment, and sense of affiliation.	Chapters 1, 11, 13
Principal Leadership	If possible, teach in a school with the positive qualities of collegiality, high morale, and clearly conveyed goals.	See Woolfolk Hoy and Hoy (2013).
Social-Familial Influences		
Parental Involvement	Support parents in supporting their children's learning.	Chapters 3–6, 12
Peer Influences	Create class and school norms that honor achievement, encourage peer support, and discourage peer conflict.	Chapters 3, 10, 13, 15

Source: Based on Lee, J., & Shute, V. J. (2010). Personal and social-contextual factors in K–12 academic performance: An integrative perspective on student learning. Educational Psychologist, 45, 185–202.

SUMMARY

- **Learning and Teaching Today (pp. 4–8)**

  What are classrooms like today? In 2010, 13% of the people living in the United States were born in another country, and 20% spoke a language other than English at home—half of these families speak Spanish. By 2050, there will be no majority race or ethnic group in the United States; every American will be a member of a minority group. About 22% of American children currently live in poverty. In the 2009–2010 school year, about 60% of school-age students with disabilities received most of their education in general education classrooms. Even though students in classrooms are increasingly diverse in race, ethnicity, language, and economic level, teachers are less diverse—the percentage of White teachers is increasing, while the percentage of Black teachers is falling. This book is about understanding the complex processes of development, learning, motivation, teaching, and assessment so that you can become a capable and confident teacher with a high but authentic sense of efficacy.

  What is NCLB? The No Child Left Behind Act of 2002 required standardized achievement testing in reading and mathematics every year for all students in grades 3 through 8, and once more in high school. Science was tested once in each grade span: elementary, middle, and high school. Based on these test scores, schools were judged to determine if their students are making adequate yearly progress (AYP) toward becoming proficient in the subjects tested. The NCLB Act required that all students in the schools must reach proficiency by the end of the 2013–2014 school year; it didn't happen. NCLB was supposed to be reauthorized in 2007 or 2008. On March 13, 2010, The Obama Administration released *ESEA Blueprint for Reform* to describe a vision for the reauthorization of NCLB (U.S. Department of Education, 2010). Two ideas are for tests to assess growth, not absolute achievement, and to focus on the bottom 5% of schools.

  What evidence is there that teachers make a difference? Several studies speak to the power of teachers in the lives of students. The first found that the quality of the teacher–student relationship in kindergarten predicted several aspects of school success through the eighth grade. The second study found similar results for students from preschool through fifth grade, a finding confirmed by almost 100 students in countries around the world. The third study examined math achievement for students in two large school districts as they moved through third, fourth, and fifth grades. Again, the quality of the teacher made a difference: Students who had three high-quality teachers in a row were way ahead of peers who spent 1 or more years with less-competent teachers. In a study that followed children from third through fifth grade, two factors helped children with lower skills in mathematics begin to close the achievement gap: higher-level (not just basic skills) instruction and positive relationships with teachers. Similar findings hold for beginning teachers.

- **What Is Good Teaching? (pp. 8–13)**

  Good teachers are committed to their students. They must deal with a wide range of student abilities and challenges: different languages, different home situations, and different abilities and disabilities. They must adapt instruction and assessment to students' needs. The whole time that these experts are navigating through the academic material, they also are taking care of the emotional needs of their students, propping up sagging self-esteem, and encouraging responsibility. From the first day of class, they carefully plan and teach the basic procedures for living and learning in their classes.

  What are some research-based models of effective teaching? Charlotte Danielson describes a Framework for Teaching, which has 22 components organized into four domains or areas of teaching responsibility: Planning and Preparation, Classroom Environment, Instruction, and Professional Responsibilities. This framework is the basis for a widely used system of teacher evaluation. TeachingWorks, a national project based at the University of Michigan and dedicated to improving teaching practice, has identified 19 high-leverage teaching practices, defined as actions that are central to teaching and useful across most grade levels, academic subjects, and teaching situations. Finally, the Bill and Melinda Gates Foundation launched the Measures of Teaching Effectiveness (MET) Project, a research partnership between 3,000 teachers and research teams at dozens of institutions, that has identified a three-part system for evaluating good teaching that includes gains on state achievement tests (weighted at about 33% to 50%), student perceptions of teachers, and classroom observations using the Danielson Framework for Teaching. The latter two make up the 66% to 50% of the weighting in the evaluations.

  What are the concerns of beginning teachers? Learning to teach is a gradual process. The concerns and problems of teachers change as they grow in their ability. During the beginning years, attention tends to be focused on maintaining discipline, motivating students, accommodating differences among students, evaluating students' work, dealing with parents, and getting along with other teachers. Even with these concerns, many beginning teachers bring creativity and energy to their teaching and improve every year. The more experienced teacher can move on to concerns about professional growth and effectiveness in teaching a wide range of students.

- **The Role of Educational Psychology (pp. 13–23)**

What is educational psychology? Educational psychology has been linked to teaching since it began in the United States over a century ago. The goals of educational psychology are to understand and to improve the teaching and learning processes. Educational psychologists develop knowledge and methods; they also use the knowledge and methods of psychology and other related disciplines to study learning and teaching in everyday situations. Educational psychologists examine what happens when someone/something (a teacher or parent or computer) teaches something (math or weaving or dancing) to someone else (student or co-worker or team) in some setting (classroom or theater or gym).

What are the research methods in educational psychology? Correlational methods identify relationships and allow predictions. A correlation is a number that indicates both the strength and the direction of a relationship between two events or measurements. The closer the correlation is to either 1.00 or –1.00, the stronger the relationship. Experimental studies allow researchers to detect causes, not just make predictions. Experimental studies should help teachers implement useful changes. Instead of just observing and describing an existing situation, the investigators introduce changes and note the results. Quasi-experimental studies meet most of the criteria for true experiments, with the important exception being that the participants are not assigned to groups at random. Instead, existing groups such as classes or schools participate in the experiments. In single-subject experimental designs, researchers examine the effects of treatments on one person, often by using a baseline/intervention/baseline/intervention, or ABAB, approach. Clinical interviews, case studies, and ethnographies look in detail at the experiences of a few individuals or groups. If participants are studied over time, the research is called *longitudinal*. If researchers intensively study cognitive processes in the midst of change—as the change is actually happening—over several sessions or weeks, then the research is *microgenetic*. No matter what method is used, results from the research are used to further develop and improve theories, so that even better hypotheses and questions can be developed to guide future research.

What is the difference between qualitative and quantitative research? There is a general distinction between qualitative and quantitative research. These are large categories and, like many categories, a bit fuzzy at the edges. Case studies and ethnographies are examples of qualitative research. This type of research uses words, dialogue, events, themes, and images as data. Interviews and observations are key procedures. The goal is not to discover general principles, but rather to explore specific situations or people in depth and to understand the meaning of the events to the people involved in order to tell their story. Both correlational and experimental types of research generally are quantitative because measurements are taken and computations are made. Quantitative research uses numbers, measurement, and statistics to assess levels or sizes of relationships among variables or differences between groups. Different types of research can answer different questions.

Scientifically based research, which is more consistent with quantitative research, systematically uses observations or experiments to gather valid and reliable data; involves rigorous and appropriate procedures for gathering and analyzing the data; is clearly described so it can be repeated by others; and has been rigorously reviewed by appropriate, independent experts. When teachers or schools make systematic observations or test out methods to improve teaching and learning for their students, they are conducting action research.

Distinguish between principles and theories. A principle is an established relationship between two or more factors—between a certain teaching strategy, for example, and student achievement. A theory is an interrelated set of concepts that is used to explain a body of data and to make predictions. The principles from research offer a number of possible answers to specific problems, and the theories offer perspectives for analyzing almost any situation that may arise. Research is a continuing cycle that involves clear specification of hypotheses or questions based on good theory, systematic gathering and analyzing of data, modification and improvement of explanatory theories based on the results, and the formulation of new, better questions based on the improved theories.

What key factors support student learning? A synthesis of about 150 studies of student learning found two broad categories of influence: *student personal factors* and *school and social-contextual factors*. When I read this article, I was pleased to see that my favorite subject, educational psychology, provides a base for developing knowledge and skills in virtually every area except principal leadership.

PRACTICE USING WHAT YOU HAVE LEARNED

To access and complete the exercises, click the link under the images below.

Using Research to Understand and Improve Teaching

Effective Teaching

ENHANCEDetext *application exercise*

ENHANCEDetext *application exercise*

KEY TERMS

Action research   20
Case study   17
Correlations   16
Descriptive studies   16
Educational psychology   14
Empirical   21
Ethnography   17
Evidence-based practice in psychology
    (EBPP)   19

Experimentation   16
Hypothesis/hypotheses   21
Microgenetic studies   18
Negative correlation   16
Participant observation   18
Participants/subjects   16
Positive correlation   16
Principle   21
Qualitative research   18

Quantitative research   18
Quasi-experimental studies   17
Random   16
Reflective   9
Single-subject experimental studies   17
Statistically significant   17
Teachers' sense of efficacy   5
Theory   21

CONNECT AND EXTEND TO LICENSURE

MULTIPLE-CHOICE QUESTIONS

1. Novice teachers face numerous tasks and scenarios with which they have little prior experience. For teachers currently entering the field, which of the following is not a challenge they are apt to encounter?
   A. Students who may exhibit superior technology skills as compared to their teachers
   B. An increasingly diverse population of students and families
   C. Inadequate resources to ensure the safety of their students while using technology in the classroom
   D. Students who face the challenges associated with living in poverty

2. Both students and teachers work harder and persist longer when they have a high sense of efficacy. Which of the

following does not enhance self-efficacy in both students and teachers?
   A. Formal school relationships that focus solely on skills
   B. Day-to-day success in achieving tasks
   C. High expectations from those in the environment
   D. Assistance from more knowledgeable partners

3. All the students in Ms. Clare's third-grade class engage in weekly test reviews. Ms. Clare believes that these reviews will enhance student retention when standardized testing occurs in the spring. Which of Ms. Clare's students under the No Child Left Behind Act will have his or her scores reported separately?
   A. Susan Frasier, who was recently identified with a learning disability
   B. Brendan Kincaid, who must wear corrected lenses in order to read

C. Miranda Ruiz, whose English is excellent even though her parents moved to the United States from Mexico 10 years ago

D. Lauren Stone, who is a member of the third grade's cohort of students who are gifted and talented

CONSTRUCTED-RESPONSE QUESTIONS

Case

Sandra Chapman was determined to add to her repertoire of teaching skills as she entered her second year of teaching. Her first year as a high school teacher proved to be more of a challenge than she expected. Her school, located in the heart of the city, drew students from all walks of life and economic circumstances. Last year, she initially hoped that all of her students would master the history curriculum that she had inherited, but by midyear several of her students were not attending class on a regular basis. In an effort to increase attendance, she took points off students' grades when they missed class and intentionally ignored them when they returned. She believed that by not taking an interest in where they were, she would not reinforce their "skipping" behavior. She also thought that by continually reminding students of how much they did not know, she would encourage them to study. Sadly, these methods did not work well, and attendance only further declined. She is now in the process of designing some new strategies.

4. Identify the methods Sandra Chapman uses to encourage attendance, and explain why these methods might have been unsuccessful.

5. What advice would you offer Sandra Chapman as she prepares to develop new methods?

ENHANCEDetext *licensure exam*

TEACHERS' CASEBOOK

WHAT WOULD THEY DO? LEAVING NO STUDENT BEHIND

Here is how several expert teachers said they would prepare a highly diverse group of students for spring achievement tests and readiness for college and career.

BARBARA PRESLEY—Transition/Work Study Coordinator— High School Level

BESTT Program (Baldwinsville Exceptional Student Training and Transition Program), C. W. Baker High School, Baldwinsville, NY

As the Transition/Work Study Coordinator and the originator of the BESTT Program, my responsibility was to prepare students who are severely disabled for life post high school. The philosophy of the Baldwinsville School District supported an employment model for training. Employment sites at local businesses were developed, and Job Coaches were hired to work 1:1 with students in a "real-life" work environment with real work assignments and expectations.

While some, but not all, of our students had to sit for exams, we found that the confidence they developed while at "work" and the work ethic they learned in that environment gave them the skills they needed to do their best in the testing situation. Job Coaches (interns) were invaluable in the "community classroom" not only because they taught our students the skills they needed to succeed, but also because they taught the community to recognize and appreciate our students for their capabilities rather than their disabilities. It is education that works two ways.

JENNIFER PINCOSKI—Learning Resource Teacher: K–12
Lee County School District, Fort Myers, FL

One of the advantages for teachers in this situation is that many of the strategies that are effective for students with learning disabilities are also effective for second-language learners. Even students who are meeting benchmarks will benefit from these supports. Some of these strategies include labeling items throughout the classroom for language/vocabulary acquisition, providing visual supports whenever possible, and using a variety of graphic organizers. Cooperative learning groups and the total physical response (TPR) method can also help in the development of both language skills and content knowledge. Activities can be tiered to match students' levels of understanding, and, to demonstrate their learning, students can be offered multiple assignment options from which to choose.

Exposing students to new vocabulary and content through auditory, visual, AND hands-on instruction will yield the best results. Broken down to its most basic level, this philosophy can be summarized by the proverb, "Tell me and I'll forget; show me and I'll remember; involve me and I'll understand." Students should be active participants in the learning process, not spectators.

JESSICA N. MAHTABAN—Eighth-Grade Math Teacher
Woodrow Wilson Middle School, Clifton, NJ

The first thing to address is survival. Each student must learn his/her name, address, and phone number. It is crucial for all students to know this information in case of any type of emergency. Afterward, the students will become familiar with the classroom routines and expectations. Once the students are comfortable with the routines and expectations, they will be able to focus on language. The intern, administration, parents, and I must meet frequently to work cooperatively on making projects and goals for each student.

During any lesson I would provide visual cues (gestures, pictures, objects) with verbal instruction. I would speak to the students in short sentences and give clear examples of what is expected from them. The intern and I will interact with students as they work independently or cooperatively during an activity. We will also check comprehension frequently, so that we can help any student that does not understand.

LAUREN ROLLINS—First-Grade Teacher
Boulevard Elementary School, Shaker Heights, OH

As a teacher, my job is to do my best to meet the needs of every student in my classroom, regardless of what resources are available to me. This situation, while challenging, is no exception. If resources will not be provided to me by the school, it is my job to find them on my own or make them myself. Outside of the classroom, the first thing I would do is to contact any local agencies, community centers, or religious institutions that may be able to help me put together learning materials for the students from immigrant families. In the meantime, I would create labels for the classroom and for the homes of my students to expose them to as much English print as possible. I would use translation Web sites to include the words in both English and their native languages. I would organize after school/evening meetings for these students and their families to provide as much additional exposure to the English language as possible. The role of the college intern would be to assist me in the differentiation of instruction to meet the individual/small-group needs of my students. Together, the intern and I could create and implement skill-based lessons to help all of the students make meaningful progress with the curriculum and with test preparation.

PAUL DRAGIN—ESL Teacher, Grades 9–12
Columbus East High School, Columbus, OH

Multiple obstacles are posed in this situation. The scenario presents two pieces of information that I would key in on. One is that problems in reading seem to be the most common. This is the challenge I would place as the number one priority due to its preeminence in terms of predicting future academic success. Scoring well on the achievement tests and doing well in college are not realistic expectations without reading success. The other piece of information that is advantageous is the student intern from the local college. With reading as the focus, I would instruct the intern on some basic reading diagnostics to get a clearer picture of each student's reading level. From there, we could choose texts that would be appropriate to increase comprehension and fluency. With two instructors in the room, we would be better equipped for small-group instruction to target the various reading levels. This targeted reading instruction would be

a benefit to the intern as well as the students, because the intern's services would be vital to instruction and together we would assist the students in their reading comprehension and subsequent language acquisition.

PAULA COLEMERE—Special Education Teacher– English, History
McClintock High School, Tempe, AZ

Before even beginning to teach this group of students, I would set my room up for success. Students can be distracted by too many things on the walls; therefore, everything I choose to display would be very deliberate. To do this, I would start with a blank slate and take everything off of the walls. I would label objects, such as the door, pencil sharpener, desks, and so on, with signs to help the students who are English language learners (ELLs) to build vocabulary. I would save an area to create a "word wall" for content area vocabulary; this will aid both the students who are ELLs and the students with special needs. It would be important to me to educate myself on the background of my students and where they come from. This would help me to make a personal connection with each student and it would help me to understand cultural differences when making contact with the family. It is also important to have an understanding of what is happening in their home countries to try to make connections to learning based on their experiences. Finally, graphic organizers would be a key part of my lesson planning because they help students to organize information.

SARA VINCENT—Special Education Teacher
Langley High School, McLean, VA

The classroom situation described requires the teacher to be creative. She must differentiate her lesson plans to accommodate the language barriers and the different learning styles. Because many of the students know a little English and others have reading troubles, a teacher can provide pictures with each lesson. For example, an assistive technology consultant can provide a teacher with computer programs, such as BoardMaker and PixWrite, which allow the teacher to compose lesson plans, and accompanying assessments using words and pictures to convey ideas needed to help the students pass the end of the year achievement tests. As students become more proficient in English, some of the supports may be faded. The teacher should use the intern for students who are struggling and for those students who are achieving to move to a faster-paced curriculum. The most important factors for this teacher are vigilance, flexibility, and creativity. A teacher with these characteristics will ensure that the needs of the students are met.

LINDA SPARKS—First Grade Teacher,
John F. Kennedy School, Billerica, MA

I have found through the years that all students can learn, no matter what their backgrounds are, as long as they are given the right tools. I always start the new school year with all concrete, visual, and hands-on lessons. This way everyone is being introduced to the same skills in the same manner. During this time, I am trying to pick out each student's learning style and/or assessment needs. I have had many student teachers through the years, and in the beginning I use them as my extra pair of eyes and hands and for assistance. Once trust has developed among the students, my student teachers, and me, I find I can begin to separate the students into smaller groups where I can better meet their needs. I also open the doors to families, offering them times to come in, whether it is before school, after school, or lunch times (adapting to their schedules) to help them better understand what is going on in the classroom and to help them help their children at home. I have found this to be very helpful to the student, and it provides me with a better understanding of the family. I show them materials I am using (Unifix® cubes for place value, pictures, models, symbols, etc.). Once the students are placed in groups, we can continue to teach according to their specific needs. I like to keep heterogeneous groups. That way, the students are more confident, and they don't have time to think about why they are in a specific group. My student teacher and I work together as a team to meet the needs of all of the students. I find that as long as the doors of communication are kept open, learning is possible for all students.

2 | COGNITIVE DEVELOPMENT

TEACHERS' CASEBOOK

WHAT WOULD YOU DO? SYMBOLS AND CYMBALS

The district curriculum guide calls for a unit on poetry, including lessons on *symbolism* in poems. You are concerned that many of your fourth-grade students may not be ready to understand this abstract concept. To test the waters, you ask a few students what a *symbol* is.

"It's sorta like a big metal thing that you bang together." Tracy waves her hands like a drum major.

"Yeah," Sean adds, "My sister plays one in the high school band."

You realize they are on the wrong track here, so you try again. "I was thinking of a different kind of symbol, like a ring as a symbol of marriage or a heart as a symbol of love, or. . . ."

You are met with blank stares.

Trevor ventures, "You mean like the Olympic torch?"

"And what does that symbolize, Trevor?" you ask.

"Like I said, a torch." Trevor wonders how you could be so dense.

CRITICAL THINKING

- What do these students' reactions tell you about children's thinking?
- How would you approach this unit?
- What more would you do to "listen" to your students' thinking so you could match your teaching to their level of thinking?
- How would you give your students concrete experiences with symbolism?
- How will you decide if the students are not developmentally ready for this material?

Tursunbaev Ruslan/Shutterstock

OVERVIEW AND OBJECTIVES

What is going on with Trevor? In this chapter, you will find out. We begin with a definition of *development* and examine three questions about development that psychologists have debated for many years: nature versus nurture, continuity versus discontinuity, and critical versus sensitive periods for development. Next we look at general principles of human development that most psychologists affirm. To understand cognitive development, we begin by studying how the brain works and then explore the ideas of two of the most influential cognitive developmental theorists, Jean Piaget and Lev Vygotsky. Piaget's ideas have implications for teachers about how their students think and what they can learn. We will consider criticisms of his ideas as well. The work of Lev Vygotsky, a Russian psychologist, highlights the important role teachers and parents play in the cognitive development of the child. Vygotsky's theory is becoming more and more influential in the field of child development. By the time you have completed this chapter, you should be able to:

Objective 2.1	Provide a definition of development that takes into account three agreed-upon principles and describe three continuing debates about development, along with current consensus on these questions.
Objective 2.2	Summarize some current research on the physical development of the brain and possible implications for teaching.
Objective 2.3	Explain the principles and stages presented in Piaget's theory of cognitive development.
Objective 2.4	Explain the principles presented in Vygotsky's theory of development.
Objective 2.5	Discuss how the ideas of Piaget and Vygotsky influence current educational research and practice.

A DEFINITION OF DEVELOPMENT

In the next few chapters, as we explore how children develop, we will encounter some surprising situations.

- Leah, a 5-year-old, is certain that rolling out a ball of clay into a snake creates more clay.
- A 9-year-old child in Geneva, Switzerland, firmly insists that it is impossible to be Swiss and Genevan at the same time: "I'm already Swiss. I can't also be Genevan."
- Jamal, a very bright elementary school student, cannot answer the question, "How would life be different if people did not sleep?" because he insists, "People HAVE TO SLEEP!"
- A young girl who once said her *feet* hurt suddenly begins to refer to her *foots,* and then describes her *footses,* before she finally returns to talking about her *feet.*
- A 2-year-old brings his own mother to comfort a friend who is crying, even though the friend's mother is available, too.

What explains these interesting events? You will soon find out, because you are entering the world of child and adolescent development.

The term **development** in its most general psychological sense refers to certain changes that occur in human beings (or animals) between conception and death. The term is not applied to all changes, but rather to those that appear in orderly ways and remain for a reasonably long period of time. A temporary change caused by a brief illness, for example, is not considered a part of development. Human development can be divided into a number of different aspects. **Physical development**, as you might guess, deals with changes in the body. **Personal development** is the term generally used for changes in an individual's personality. **Social development** refers to changes in the way an individual relates to others. And **cognitive development** refers to changes in thinking, reasoning, and decision making.

Many changes during development are simply matters of growth and maturation. **Maturation** refers to changes that occur naturally and spontaneously and that are, to a large extent, genetically programmed. Such changes emerge over time and are relatively unaffected by environment, except in cases of malnutrition or severe illness. Much of a person's physical development falls into this category. Other changes are brought about through learning, as individuals interact with their environment. Such changes make up a large part of a person's social development. But what about the development of thinking and personality? Most psychologists agree that in these areas, both maturation and interaction with the environment (or *nature* and *nurture,* as they are sometimes called) are important, but they disagree about the amount of emphasis to place on each one. Nature versus nurture is one of three continuing discussions in theories of development.

Three Questions Across the Theories

Because there are many different approaches to research and theory, there are some continuing debates about key questions surrounding development.

WHAT IS THE SOURCE OF DEVELOPMENT? NATURE VERSUS NURTURE. Which is more important in development, the "nature" of an individual (heredity, genes, biological processes, maturation, etc.) or the "nurture" of environmental contexts (education, parenting, culture, social policies, etc.)? This debate has raged for at least 2,000 years and has accumulated many labels along the way, including "heredity versus environment," "biology versus culture," "maturation versus learning," and "innate versus acquired abilities." In earlier centuries, philosophers, poets, religious leaders, and politicians argued the question. Today scientists bring new tools to the discussion as they can map genes or trace the effects of drugs on brain activity, for example (Gottlieb, Wahlsten, & Lickliter, 2006). Even in scientific explanations, the pendulum has swung back and forth between nature and nurture (Cairns & Cairns, 2006; Overton, 2006).

Today the environment is seen as critical to development, but so are biological factors and individual differences. In fact, some psychologists assert that behaviors are determined 100% by biology and 100% by environment—they can't be separated (P. H. Miller, 2011). Current views emphasize complex **coactions** (joint actions) of nature and nurture. For example, a child born with a very easygoing, calm disposition will likely elicit different reactions from parents, playmates, and teachers than a child who is often upset and difficult to soothe; this shows that individuals are active in constructing their own environments. But environments shape individuals as well—if not, what good would education be? So today, the *either/or* debates about nature and nurture are of less interest to educational and developmental psychologists. As a pioneering developmental psychologist said over 100 years ago, the more exciting questions involve understanding how "both causes work together" (Baldwin, 1895, p. 77).

WHAT IS THE SHAPE OF DEVELOPMENT? CONTINUITY VERSUS DISCONTINUITY. Is human development a continuous process of increasing abilities, or are there leaps to new stages when abilities actually change? A continuous process would be like gradual improvement in your running endurance through systematic exercise. A discontinuous change (also called *qualitative*) would be like many of the changes in humans during puberty, such as the ability to reproduce—an entirely different ability. Qualitative changes are contrasted with purely quantitative change, such as the adolescent growing taller.

You can think of continuous or quantitative change like walking up a ramp to go higher and higher: Progress is steady. A discontinuous or qualitative change is more like walking up stairs: There are level periods, and then you ascend the next step all at once. Piaget's theory of cognitive development, described in the next section, is an example of *qualitative,* discontinuous change in children's thinking abilities. But other explanations of cognitive development based on learning theories emphasize gradual, continuous, *quantitative* change.

TIMING: IS IT TOO LATE? CRITICAL VERSUS SENSITIVE PERIODS. Are there critical periods during which certain abilities, such as language, need to develop? If those opportunities are missed, can the child still "catch up"? These are questions about timing and development. Many earlier psychologists, particularly those influenced by Freud, believed that early childhood experiences were critical, especially for emotional/social and cognitive development. But does early toilet training really set all of us on a particular life path? Probably not. More recent research shows that later experiences are powerful, too, and can change the direction of development (J. Kagan & Herschkowitz, 2005). Most psychologists today talk about sensitive periods—not critical periods. There are times when a person is especially ready for or responsive to certain experiences.

BEWARE OF EITHER/OR. As you might imagine, these debates about development proved too complicated to be settled by splitting alternatives into either/or possibilities (Griffins & Gray, 2005). Today, most psychologists view human development, learning, and motivation as a set of interacting and coacting contexts, from the inner biological structures and processes that influence development such as genes, cells, nutrition, and disease, to the external factors of families, neighborhoods, social relationships, educational and health institutions, public policies, time periods, historical events, and so on. So the effects of a childhood disease on the cognitive development of a child born in the 16th century to a poor family and treated by bloodletting or leeches will be quite different than the effect of the same disease on a child born in 2016 to a wealthy family and given the best treatment available for that time period. Throughout the rest of this book, we will try to make sense of development, learning, motivation, and teaching without falling into the *either/or trap.*

General Principles of Development

Although there is disagreement about exactly how development takes place, there are a few general principles almost all theorists would support.

1. *People develop at different rates.* In your own classroom, you will have a whole range of examples of different developmental rates. Some students will be larger, better coordinated, or more mature in their thinking and social relationships. Others will be much slower to mature in these areas. Except in rare cases of very rapid or very slow development, such differences are normal and should be expected in any large group of students.

2. *Development is relatively orderly.* People develop abilities in a logical order. In infancy, they sit before they walk, babble before they talk, and see the world through their own eyes before they can begin to imagine how others see it. In school, they will master addition before algebra, Harry Potter before Shakespeare, and so on. But "orderly" does not necessarily mean linear or predictable—people might advance, stay the same for a period of time, or even go backward.

3. *Development takes place gradually.* Very rarely do changes appear overnight. A student who cannot manipulate a pencil or answer a hypothetical question may well develop this ability, but the change is likely to take time.

ENHANCEDetext *self-check*

THE BRAIN AND COGNITIVE DEVELOPMENT

If you have taken an introductory psychology class, you have read about the brain and nervous system. You probably remember that there are several different areas of the brain and that certain areas are involved in particular functions. For example, the feathery-looking *cerebellum* coordinates and orchestrates balance and smooth, skilled movements—from the graceful gestures of the dancer to the everyday action of eating without stabbing yourself in the nose with a fork. The cerebellum may also play a role in higher cognitive functions such as learning. The *hippocampus* is critical in recalling new information and recent experiences, while the *amygdala* directs emotions. The *thalamus* is involved in our ability to learn new information, *particularly* if it is verbal. Figure 2.1 shows the various regions of the brain.

Advances in brain imaging techniques have allowed scientists remarkable access to the functioning brain. For example, functional magnetic resonance imaging (fMRI) shows how blood flows within the brain when children or adults do different cognitive tasks. Event-related potential (ERP)

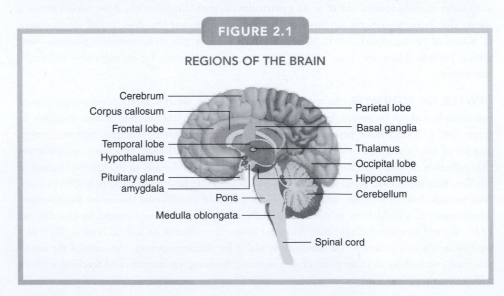

FIGURE 2.1

REGIONS OF THE BRAIN

measurements assess electrical activity of the brain through the skull or scalp as people perform activities such as reading or learning vocabulary words. **Positron emission tomography (PET)** scans can track brain activity under different conditions.

Let's begin our look at the brain by examining its tiny components: neurons, synapses, and glial cells.

The Developing Brain: Neurons

A newborn baby's brain weighs about 1 pound, barely one third of the weight of an adult brain. But this infant brain has billions of **neurons**, the specialized nerve cells that accumulate and transmit information (in the form of electrical activity) in the brain and other parts of the nervous system. Neurons are a grayish color, so they sometimes are called the *gray matter* of the brain. One neuron has the information processing capacity of a small computer. That means the processing power of one 3-pound human brain is likely greater than all the computers in the world. Of course, computers do many things, like calculate square roots of large numbers, much faster than humans can (J. R. Anderson, 2010). These incredibly important neuron cells are tiny; about 30,000 could fit on the head of a pin (Sprenger, 2010). Scientists once believed that all the neurons a person would ever have were present at birth, but now we know that the production of new neurons, **neurogenesis**, continues into adulthood, especially in the hippocampus region (Koehl & Abrous, 2011).

Neuron cells send out long arm- and branch-like fibers called *axons* and *dendrites* to connect with other neuron cells. The fiber ends from different neurons don't actually touch; there are tiny spaces between them, about one billionth of a meter in length, called **synapses**. Neurons share information by using electrical signals and by releasing chemicals that jump across the synapses. Axons transmit information out to muscles, glands, or other neurons; dendrites receive information and transmit it to the neuron cells themselves. Communication between neurons by these synaptic transmissions is strengthened or weakened, depending on patterns of use. So the strength of these synaptic connections is dynamic—always changing. This is called **synaptic plasticity**, or just **plasticity**, a very important concept for educators, as you will see soon. Connections between neurons become stronger with use or practice and weaker when not used (Dubinsky, Roehrig, & Varma, 2013). Figure 2.2 on the next page shows these components of the neuron system (J. R. Anderson, 2010).

At birth, each of the child's 100 to 200 billion neurons has about 2,500 synapses. However, the fibers that reach out from the neurons and the synapses between the fiber ends increase during the first years of life, perhaps into adolescence or longer. By ages 2 to 3, each neuron has around 15,000 synapses; children this age have many more synapses than they will have as adults. In fact, they are *oversupplied* with the neurons and synapses that they will need to adapt to their environments. However, only those neurons that are used will survive, and unused neurons will be "pruned." This pruning is necessary and supports cognitive development. Researchers have found that some developmental disabilities are associated with a gene defect that interferes with pruning (Bransford, Brown, & Cocking, 2000; J. L. Cook & Cook, 2014).

Two kinds of overproduction and pruning processes take place. One is called *experience-expectant* because synapses are overproduced in certain parts of the brain during specific developmental periods, awaiting (expecting) stimulation. For example, during the first months of life, the brain expects visual and auditory stimulation. If a normal range of sights and sounds occurs, then the visual and auditory areas of the brain develop. But children who are born completely deaf receive no auditory stimulation and, as a result, the auditory processing area of their brains becomes devoted to processing visual information. Similarly, the visual processing area of the brain for children blind from birth becomes devoted to auditory processing (C. A. Nelson, 2001; Neville, 2007).

Experience-expectant overproduction and pruning processes are responsible for general development in large areas of the brain and may explain why adults have difficulty with pronunciations that are not part of their native language. For example, the distinction between the sounds of *r* and *l* is important in English but not in Japanese, so by about 10 months, Japanese infants lose the

FIGURE 2.2

A SINGLE NEURON

Each neuron (nerve cell) includes dendrites that bring in messages and an axon that sends out messages. This is a single neuron, but each neuron is in a network with many others.

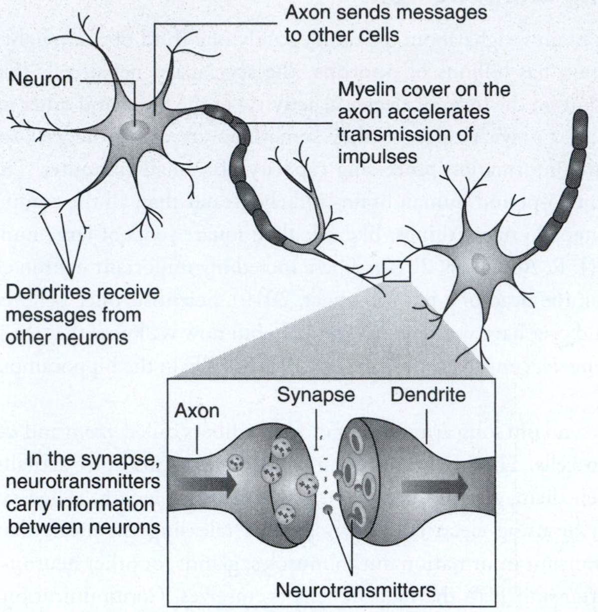

Axon sends messages to other cells

Neuron

Myelin cover on the axon accelerates transmission of impulses

Dendrites receive messages from other neurons

Axon   Synapse   Dendrite

In the synapse, neurotransmitters carry information between neurons

Neurotransmitters

ability to discriminate between *r* and *1; those neurons are pruned away.* As a result, Japanese adults learning these sounds require intense instruction and practice (Bransford et al., 2000; Hinton, Miyamoto, & Della-Chiesa, 2008).

The second kind of synaptic overproduction and pruning is called *experience-dependent.* Here, synaptic connections are formed based on the individual's experiences. New synapses are formed in response to neural activity in very localized areas of the brain. Examples are learning to ride a bike or use a spreadsheet. The brain does not "expect" these behaviors, so new synapses form stimulated by these experiences. Again, more synapses are produced than will be kept after "pruning." Experience-dependent processes are involved in individual learning, such as mastering unfamiliar sound pronunciations in a second language you are studying.

Stimulating environments may help in the pruning process in early life (experience-expectant period) and also may support increased synapse development in adulthood (experience-dependent period) (J. L. Cook & Cook, 2014). In fact, animal studies have shown that rats raised in stimulating environments (with toys, tasks for learning, other rats, and human handling) develop and retain 25% more synapses than rats who are raised with little stimulation. Even though the research with rats may not apply directly to humans, it is clear that extreme deprivation can have negative effects on human brain development. But extra stimulation will not necessarily improve development for young children who are getting adequate or typical amounts (Byrnes & Fox, 1998; Kolb & Whishaw, 1998). So spending money on expensive toys or baby education programs probably offers more stimulation than is necessary. Pots and pans, blocks and books, sand and water all provide excellent stimulation—especially if accompanied by caring conversations with parents or teachers.

Look back at Figure 2.2. It appears that there is nothing between the neurons but air. Actually, this is wrong. The spaces are filled with **glial cells**, the *white matter* of the brain. There are trillions of these cells; they greatly outnumber neurons. Glial cells appear to have many functions, such as fighting infections, controlling blood flow and communication among neurons, and providing the *myelin* coating (see Figure 2.2) around axon fibers (Ormrod, 2012). **Myelination**, the coating of axon neuron fibers with an insulating fatty glial covering, influences thinking and learning. This process is something like coating bare electrical wires with rubber or plastic. This myelin coating makes message transmission faster and more efficient. Myelination happens quickly in the early years but continues gradually into adolescence, with the child's brain doubling in volume in the first year of life and doubling again around puberty (J. R. Anderson, 2010).

The Developing Brain: Cerebral Cortex

Let's move from the neuron level to the brain itself. The outer 1/8-inch-thick covering is the cerebral cortex—the largest area of the brain. It is a thin sheet of neurons, but it is almost 3 square feet in area for adults. To get all that area in your head, the sheet is crumpled together with many folds and wrinkles (J. R. Anderson, 2010). In humans, this area of the brain is much larger than it is in lower animals. The cerebral cortex accounts for about 85% of the brain's weight in adulthood and contains the greatest number of neurons. The cerebral cortex allows the greatest human accomplishments, such as complex problem solving and language.

The cortex is the last part of the brain to develop, so it is believed to be more susceptible to environmental influences than other areas of the brain (Gluck, Mercado, & Myers, 2008; Schacter, Gilbert, & Wenger, 2009). Parts of the cortex mature at different rates. The region of the cortex that controls physical motor movement matures first, then the areas that control complex senses such as vision and hearing, and last, the frontal lobe that controls higher-order thinking processes. The temporal lobes of the cortex that play major roles in emotions, judgment, and language do not develop fully until the high school years and maybe later.

Different areas of the cortex seem to have distinct functions, as shown in Figure 2.3. Even though different functions are found in particular areas of the brain, these specialized functions are quite specific and elementary. To accomplish more complex functions such as speaking or reading, the various areas of the cortex must communicate and work together (J. R. Anderson, 2010; Byrnes & Fox, 1998).

Another aspect of brain functioning that has implications for cognitive development is lateralization, or the specialization of the two hemispheres of the brain. We know that each half of the brain controls the opposite side of the body. Damage to the right side of the brain will affect movement of the left side of the body and vice versa. In addition, certain areas of the brain affect

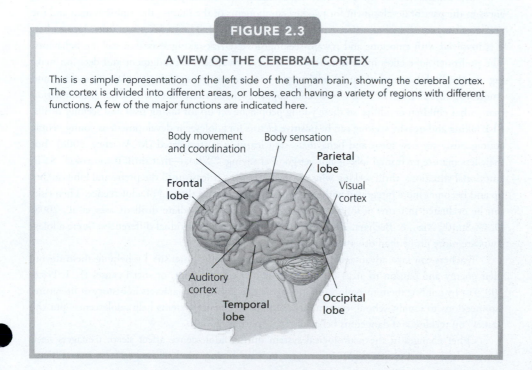

FIGURE 2.3

A VIEW OF THE CEREBRAL CORTEX

This is a simple representation of the left side of the human brain, showing the cerebral cortex. The cortex is divided into different areas, or lobes, each having a variety of regions with different functions. A few of the major functions are indicated here.

Body movement and coordination

Body sensation

Parietal lobe

Frontal lobe

Visual cortex

Auditory cortex

Temporal lobe

Occipital lobe

particular behaviors. For most of us, the left hemisphere of the brain is a major factor in language processing, and the right hemisphere handles much of our spatial-visual information and emotions (nonverbal information). For some left-handed people, the relationship may be reversed, but for most left-handers, and for females on average, there is less hemispheric specialization altogether (J. R. Anderson, 2010; O'Boyle & Gill, 1998). The brains of young children show more plasticity (adaptability) because they are not as specialized or lateralized as the brains of older children and adults. Young children with damage to the left side of the brain are somewhat able to overcome the damage, which allows language development to proceed. Different areas of the brain take over the functions of the damaged area. But in older children and adults, this compensation is less likely to occur after damage to the left brain hemisphere.

These differences in performance by the brain's hemispheres, however, are more relative than absolute; one hemisphere is just more efficient than the other in performing certain functions. Language is processed "differently, but simultaneously" by the left and right hemispheres (Alferink & Farmer-Dougan, 2010, p. 44). Nearly any task, particularly the complex skills and abilities that concern teachers, requires simultaneous participation of many different areas of the brain in constant communication with each other. For example, the right side of the brain is better at figuring out the meaning of a story, but the left side is where grammar and syntax are understood, so both sides of the brain have to work together in reading. Remember, no mental activity is exclusively the work of a single part of the brain, so there is no such thing as a "right-brained student" unless that individual has had the left hemisphere removed—a rare and radical treatment for some forms of epilepsy.

Adolescent Development and the Brain

The brain continues to develop throughout childhood and adolescence. During adolescence, changes in the brain increase individuals' abilities to control their behavior in both low-stress and high-stress situations, to be more purposeful and organized, and to inhibit impulsive behavior (Wigfield et al., 2006). But these abilities are not fully developed until the early 20s, so adolescents may "seem" like adults, at least in low-stress situations, but their brains are not mature. They often have trouble avoiding risks and controlling impulses. This is why adolescents' brains have been described as "high horse power, poor steering" (Organisation for Economic Co-operation and Development [OECD], 2007, p. 6).

One explanation for this problem with avoiding risks and impulsive behavior looks to differences in the pace of development for two key components of the brain—the limbic system and the prefrontal cortex of the brain (Casey, Getz, & Galvan, 2008). The limbic system develops earlier; it is involved with emotions and reward-seeking/novelty/risk-taking/sensation-seeking behaviors. The prefrontal lobe takes more time to develop; it is involved with judgment and decision making. As the limbic system matures, adolescents become more responsive to pleasure seeking and emotional stimulation. In fact, adolescents appear to need more intense emotional stimulation than either children or adults, so these young people are set up for taking risks and seeking thrills. Risk taking and novelty seeking can be positive factors for adolescent development as young people courageously try new ideas and behaviors—and learning is stimulated (McAnarney, 2008). But their less mature prefrontal lobe is not yet good at saying, "Whoa—that thrill is too risky!" So in emotional situations, thrill seeking wins out over caution, at least until the prefrontal lobe catches up and becomes more integrated with the limbic system toward the end of adolescence. Then risks can be evaluated in terms of long-term consequences, not immediate thrills (Casey et al., 2008; D. G. Smith, Xiao, & Bechara, 2012). In addition, there are individual differences: Some adolescents are more prone than others to engage in risky behaviors.

Teachers can take advantage of their adolescent students' intensity by helping them devote their energy and passion to areas such as politics, the environment, or social causes (L. F. Price, 2005) or by guiding them to explore emotional connections with characters in history or literature. Connections to family, school, community, and positive belief systems help adolescents "put the brakes" on reckless and dangerous behaviors (McAnarney, 2008).

Other changes in the neurological system during adolescence affect sleep; teenagers need about 9 hours of sleep per night, but many students' biological clocks are reset so it is difficult for them to fall asleep before midnight. Yet in many school districts, high school begins by 7:30, so 9 hours of sleep are impossible to get, and students are continually sleep deprived. Classes that keep students in their seats taking notes for the full period may literally "put the students to sleep." With no time for breakfast and little for lunch, these students' nutritional needs are often deprived as well (Sprenger, 2005).

Putting It All Together: How the Brain Works

What is your conception of the brain? Is the brain a culture-free container that holds knowledge the same way for everyone? Is the brain like a library of facts or a computer filled with information? Do you wake up in the morning, download what you need for the day, and then go merrily on your way? Is the brain like a pipe that transfers information from one person to another—a teacher to a student, for example? Kurt Fischer (2009)—a developmental psychologist and Harvard professor—offers a different view, based on neuroscience research. Knowing is actively constructing understandings and actions. Knowledge is based in our activities, and the brain is constantly changing:

> When animals and people do things in their worlds, they shape their behavior. Based on brain research, we know that likewise they literally shape the anatomy and physiology of their brains (and bodies). When we actively control our experience, that experience sculpts the way that our brains work, changing neurons, synapses, and brain activity. (p. 5)

All experiences sculpt the brain—play and deliberate practice, formal and informal learning (Dubinsky et al., 2013). You encountered the term earlier that describes the brain's capacity for constant change in neurons, synapses, and activity—*plasticity*. Cultural differences in brain activity provide examples of how interactions in the world shape the brain through plasticity. For example, in one study, when Chinese speakers added and compared Arabic numbers, they showed brain activity in the motor (movement) areas of their brains, whereas English speakers performing the same tasks had activity in the language areas of their brains (Tang et al., 2006). One explanation is that Chinese children are taught arithmetic using an abacus—a calculation tool that involves movement and spatial positions. As adults, these children retain a kind of visual-motor sense of numbers (Varma, McCandliss, & Schwartz, 2008). There also are cultural differences in how languages affect reading. For example, when they read, native Chinese speakers activate additional parts of their brain associated with spatial information processing, probably because the language characters used in written Chinese are pictures. But Chinese speakers also activate these spatial areas of the brain when they read English, demonstrating that reading proficiency can be reached through different neural pathways (Hinton, Miyamoto, & Della-Chiesa, 2008).

So thanks to plasticity, the brain is ever changing, shaped by activity, culture, and context. We build knowledge as we do things, as we manipulate objects and ideas mentally and physically. As you can imagine, educators have looked for applications of neuroscience research for their instruction. This has led to vigorous debate between the enthusiastic educational advocates of brain-based education and the skeptical neuroscience researchers who caution that studies of the brain do not really address major educational questions. Many publications for parents and teachers have useful ideas about the brain and education, but beware of suggestions that oversimplify. The jury still is out on many of these "brain-based" programs (Beauchamp & Beauchamp, 2013). See the *Point/ Counterpoint* on the next page for a slice of this debate.

So what can teachers learn from neuroscience? We turn to this next.

Neuroscience, Learning, and Teaching

First let's be clear about what neuroscience does not tell teachers. There are many popular neuro-myths (myths about the brain), as you can see in Table 2.1 on page 42. We have to be careful about what we encounter in the media.

It is *not* a myth that teaching can change the organization and structure of the brain. For example, individuals who are deaf and use sign language have different patterns of electrical activity in their brains than people who are deaf and do not use sign language (Varma, McCandliss, & Schwartz, 2008). What are some other effects of instruction on the brain?

PODCAST 2.1
Listen as textbook author Anita Woolfolk talks about brain-based education. What does this mean? Are there some clear implications for teachers or is it still too early to say?

ENHANCEDetext *podcast*

POINT/COUNTERPOINT
Brain-Based Education

Educators are hearing more and more about brain-based education, the importance of early stimulation for brain development, the "Mozart effect," and right- and left-brain activities. In fact, based on some research findings that listening to 10 minutes of Mozart can briefly improve spatial reasoning (Rauscher & Shaw, 1998; K. M. Steele, Bass, & Crook, 1999), a former governor of Georgia established a program to give a Mozart CD to every newborn. The scientists who had done the work couldn't believe how their research had been "applied" (Katzir & Paré-Blagoev, 2006). In fact, the governor apparently had confused experiments on infant brain development with studies of adults (Pinker, 2002). Are there clear educational implications from the neuroscience research on the brain?

POINT **No, the implications are not clear.** Catherine and Miriam Beauchamp (2013) note that the application of neuroscience to education actually has been plagued by misapplications because the findings have been treated in isolation, without attention to knowledge from other disciplines such as cognitive science or educational psychology that place the findings in context. To further complicate the problem of misapplications, educators and neuroscience researchers have different meanings for "learning" and don't have an appreciation for each others' reality; neuroscientists don't understand schools, and few educators have a background in neurobiology.

John Bruer, president of the James S. McDonnell Foundation, has written articles that are critical of the brain-based education craze (Bruer, 1999, 2002). He notes that many so-called applications of brain research begin with solid science, but then move to unwarranted speculation, and end in a sort of appealing folk tale about the brain and learning. He suggests that for each claim, the educator should ask, "Where does the science end and the speculation begin?" For example, one claim that Bruer questions is the notion of right-brain, left-brain learning.

> "Right brain versus left brain" is one of those popular ideas that will not die. Speculations about the educational significance of brain laterality have been circulating in the education literature for 30 years. Although repeatedly criticized and dismissed by psychologists and brain scientists, the speculation continues. David Sousa devotes a chapter of *How the Brain Learns* to explaining brain laterality and presents classroom strategies that teachers might use to ensure that both hemispheres are involved

in learning. . . . Now let's consider the brain sciences and how or whether they offer support for some of the particular teaching strategies Sousa recommends. To involve the right hemisphere in learning, Sousa writes, teachers should encourage students to generate and use mental imagery. . . . What brain scientists currently know about spatial reasoning and mental imagery provides counter examples to such simplistic claims as these. Such claims arise out of a folk theory about brain laterality, not a neuroscientific one. . . . Different brain areas are specialized for different tasks, but that specialization occurs at a finer level of analysis than "using visual imagery." Using visual imagery may be a useful learning strategy, but if it is useful it is not because it involves an otherwise underutilized right hemisphere in learning. (Bruer, 1999, pp. 653–654)

Ten years later, Kurt Fischer (2009), president of the International Mind, Brain, and Education Society, lamented:

> Expectations for neuroscience and genetics to shape educational practice and policy have exploded far beyond what is merited by the state of the emerging field of MBE [mind body education] and the level of knowledge about how brains and genetics function. . . . Many neuromyths "have entered popular discourse—beliefs about how the brain and body work that are widely accepted but blatantly wrong" (OECD, 2007). Most of what is put forward as "brain based education" builds on these scientifically inaccurate myths: The one small way that neuroscience relates to most brain-based education is that the students have brains. There is no grounding for these claims in the young field of neuroscience.

No teacher doubts that the brain is important in learning. As Steven Pinker (2002), professor of psychology at Harvard University, observed, does anyone really think learning takes place somewhere else, like the pancreas? But knowing that learning affects the brain does not tell us how to teach. All learning affects the brain; "this should be obvious, but nowadays any banality about learning can be dressed up in neurospeak and treated like a great revelation of science" (Pinker, 2002, p. 86). Virtually all of the so-called best practices for brain-based education are simple restatements of good teaching based on understandings of how people learn, not how their brain works. For example, we have known for over 100 years that it is more effective to learn in many shorter practice sessions as opposed to one long cramming session. To tie that fact to building more dendrites does not give teachers new strategies (Alferink & Farmer-Dougan, 2010). Finally, Richard Haier and Rex Jung (2008) look to the future: "Someday, we believe that our educational system will be informed by neuroscience knowledge, especially concerning intelligence, but how we get from here to there remains unclear" (p. 177).

COUNTERPOINT Yes, teaching should be brain-based.

Articles in popular magazines such as *Newsweek* assert, " . . . it's naive to say that brain discoveries have no consequences for understanding how humans learn" (Begley, 2007). Do scientists agree? In their article on "Applying Cognitive Neuroscience Research to Education" in the *Educational Psychologist*, Tami Katzir and Juliana Paré-Blagoev (2006) concluded, "When applied correctly, brain science may serve as a vehicle for advancing the application of our understanding of learning and development. . . . Brain research can challenge common-sense views about teaching and learning by suggesting additional systems that are involved in particular tasks and activities" (p. 70). If we are to guard against overstating the links between brain research and education, then we should not ask if to teach, but instead "how best to teach neuroscience concepts to pre-service teachers" (Dubinsky et al., 2013, p. 325). A number of universities, including Harvard, Cambridge, Dartmouth, the University of Texas at Arlington, University of Minnesota, University of Southern California, Beijing Normal University, Southeast University in Nanjing, and Johns Hopkins are pioneering this process. They have established training programs for educators in brain-education studies (Dubinsky et al., 2013; K. Fischer, 2009; Wolfe, 2010). Other educational psychologists have called for a new professional specialty—neuro-educators (Beauchamp & Beauchamp, 2013).

Brain research is leading to much better understandings about learning disabilities. For example, neuroscience studies of people with reading disabilities have found that these individuals may have trouble with sounds and sound patterns or with retrieving the names of very familiar letters, so there may be different bases for the reading disabilities (Katzir & Paré-Blagoev, 2006).

There are examples of applying knowledge of brain research to education. A reading improvement product called *FastForword* was developed by two neuroscientists, Dr. Michael Merzenich and Dr. Paula Tallal, and is already in use today in classrooms around the country (see scilearn.com/results/success-stories/index.php). It specifically uses discoveries in neural plasticity to change the brain's ability to read the printed word (Tallal & Miller, 2003).

In his presidential address for the First Conference of the International Mind, Brain, and Education Society, Kurt Fischer noted:

> The primary goal of the emerging field of Mind, Brain, and Education is to join biology, cognitive science, development, and education in order to create a sound grounding of education in research. The growing, worldwide movement needs to avoid the myths and distortions of popular conceptions of brain and genetics and build on the best integration of research with practice, creating a strong infrastructure that joins scientists with educators to study effective learning and teaching in educational settings. (2009, pp. 3–16)

Fischer makes the point that we can go from understanding how the brain works to understanding cognitive processes, and then to developing educational practices. But jumping directly from knowledge about the brain to educational practices probably involves too much speculation.

BEWARE OF EITHER/OR

Schools should not be run on curricula based solely on the biology of the brain. However, to ignore what we do know about the brain would be equally irresponsible. Brain-based learning offers some direction for educators who want more purposeful, informed teaching. At the very least, the neuroscience research is helping us to understand why effective teaching strategies, such as distributed practice, work.

Resources: Podcast on understanding the brain: http://www.oecd.org/edu/ceri/understandingthebrainthebirthofalearningscience.htm

INSTRUCTION AND BRAIN DEVELOPMENT. Several studies have shown differences in brain activity associated with instruction. For example, the intensive instruction and practice provided to rehabilitate stroke victims can help them regain functioning by forming new connections and using new areas of the brain (Bransford, Brown, & Cocking, 2000; McKinley, 2011). In another example, Margarete Delazer and her colleagues (2005) compared students' brain activity as they learned new arithmetic operations, either by just memorizing the answers or by learning an algorithm strategy. Using fMRI, the researchers found that students who simply memorized answers showed greater activity in the area of the brain that specializes in retrieving verbal information, whereas the students who used a strategy showed greater activity in the visual-spatial processing portion of the brain.

TABLE 2.1 • **Myths About the Brain**

COMMON MYTHS	TRUTH
1. You use only 10% of your brain.	1. You use all your brain. That is why strokes are so devastating.
2. Listening to Mozart will make children smarter.	2. Listening won't, but learning to play a musical instrument is associated with increased cognitive achievement.
3. Some people are more "right brained," and others are more "left brained."	3. It takes both sides of your brain to do most things.
4. A young child's brain can only manage to learn one language at a time.	4. Children all over the world can and do learn two languages at once.
5. You can't change your brain.	5. Our brains are changing all the time.
6. Damage to the brain is permanent.	6. Most people recover well from minor brain injuries.
7. Playing games like Sudoku keeps your brain from aging.	7. Playing Sudoku makes you better at playing Sudoku and similar games. Physical exercise is a better bet to prevent decline.
8. The human brain is the biggest brain.	8. Sperm whales have brains five times heavier than those of humans.
9. Alcoholic beverages kill brain cells.	9. Heavy drinking does not kill brain cells, but it can damage the nerve ends called dendrites, and this causes problems with communicating messages in the brain. This damage is mostly reversible.
10. The adolescent's brain is the same as that of an adult.	10. There are critical differences between adolescents' and adults' brains: Adolescents' brains have "high horsepower, but poor steering" (K. Fischer, 2009).

Source: Based on Aamodt & Wang (2008); K. W. Fischer (2009); Freeman (2011); OECD (2007).

In another dramatic example of how teaching can affect brain development, K. W. Fischer (2009) describes two children who each had one brain hemisphere removed as a treatment for severe epilepsy. Nico's right hemisphere was removed when he was 3, and his parents were told he would never have good visual-spatial skills. With strong and constant support and teaching, Nico grew up to be a skilled artist! Brooke's left hemisphere was removed when he was 11. His parents were told he would lose his ability to talk. Again, with strong support, he regained enough speaking and reading ability to finish high school and attend community college.

THE BRAIN AND LEARNING TO READ. Brain imaging research is revealing interesting differences among skilled and less-skilled readers as they learn new vocabulary. For example, one imaging study showed that less-skilled readers had trouble establishing high-quality representations of new vocabulary words in their brains, as indicated by ERP measurements of electrical activity of the brain. When they encountered the new word later, less-skilled readers' brains often didn't recognize that they had seen the word before, even though they had learned the words in an earlier lesson. If words you have learned seem unfamiliar later, you can see how it would be hard to understand what you read (Balass, Nelson, & Perfetti, 2010).

In another study, Bennett Shaywitz and his colleagues (2004) studied 28 children ages 6 to 9 who were good readers and 49 children who were poor readers. Differences in the brain activity of the two groups showed on fMRIs. The poor readers underused parts of their brains' left hemisphere and sometimes overused their right hemispheres. After over 100 hours of intensive instruction in letter–sound combinations, reading ability improved; the brains of the poor readers started to function more like those of the good readers and continued this functioning a year later. Poor readers who received the standard school remediation did not show the brain function changes.

Reading is not innate or automatic—every brain has to be taught to read (Frey & Fisher, 2010). Reading is a complex integration of the systems in the brain that recognize sounds, written symbols, meanings, and sequences, and then connect with what the reader already knows. This has to happen quickly and automatically (Wolf et al., 2009).

Will brain research help us teach reading more effectively? Judith Willis (2009), a neurobiologist who became a science teacher, cautions that "Neuroimaging and the other brain monitoring systems used for reading research offer *suggestive* rather than completely empirical links between how the brain learns and metabolizes oxygen or glucose, conducts electricity, or changes its cellular density." (p. 333)

Although the strategies for teaching reading that are consistent with brain research are not completely new, the research may help us understand *why* these strategies work. What are some strategies suggested? Use multiple approaches that teach sounds, spelling, meanings, sequencing, and vocabulary through reading, writing, discussing, explaining, drawing, and modeling. Different students may learn in different ways, but all need practice in literacy.

EMOTIONS, LEARNING, AND THE BRAIN. Finally, another clear connection between the brain and classroom learning is in the area of emotions and stress. Let's step inside a high school math classroom described by Hinton, Miyamoto, and Della-Chiesa (2008, p. 91) for an example:

> Patricia, a high school student, struggles with mathematics. The last few times she answered a mathematics question she got it wrong and felt terribly embarrassed, which formed an association between mathematics . . . and negative emotions. . . . Her teacher had just asked her to come to the blackboard to solve a problem. This caused an immediate transfer of this emotionally-charged association to the amygdala, which elicits fear. Meanwhile, a slower, cortically-driven cognitive appraisal of the situation is occurring: she remembers her difficulty completing her mathematics homework last night, notices the problem on the board contains complicated graphs, and realizes that the boy she has a crush on is watching her from a front-row seat. These various thoughts converge to a cognitive confirmation that this is a threatening situation, which reinforces her progressing fear response and disrupts her ability to concentrate on solving the mathematics problem.

In Chapter 7 you will learn about how emotions can become paired with particular situations; and in Chapter 12, you will see that anxiety interferes with learning, whereas challenge, interest, and curiosity can support learning. If students feel unsafe and anxious, they are not likely to be able to focus attention on academics (Sylvester, 2003). But if students are not challenged or interested, learning suffers too. Keeping the level of challenge and support "just right" is a challenge for teachers. And helping students learn to regulate their own emotions and motivation is an important goal for education (see Chapter 11). Simply put, learning will be more effective "if educators help to minimize stress and fear at school, teach students emotional regulation strategies, and provide a positive learning environment that is motivating to students" (Hinton, Miyamoto, & Della-Chiesa, 2008).

- -

STOP & THINK As a teacher, you don't want to fall for overly simplistic "brain-based" teaching slogans. But obviously, the brain and learning are intimately related—this is not a surprise. So how can you be a savvy, "neuroscientific" teacher (Murphy & Benton, 2010)? •

- -

Lessons for Teachers: General Principles

What can we learn from neuroscience? One overarching idea is that teachers and students should transform the notion of learning from "using your brain" to "changing your brain"—embrace the amazing plasticity of the brain (Dubinsky et al., 2013). Here are some general teaching implications drawn from Driscoll (2005), Dubinsky and colleagues (2013), Murphy and Benton (2010), Sprenger (2010), and Wolfe (2010):

1. Human capabilities—intelligence, communication, problem solving, and so on—emerge from each person's unique synaptic activity overlaid on his or her genetically endowed brain anatomy; nature and nurture are in constant activity together. The brain can place some limits on learning in the form of genetic brain anomalies in neural wiring or structure, but learning can occur through alternate pathways in the brain (as Nico and Brooke demonstrate). So, there are multiple ways both to teach and to learn a skill, depending on the student.

2. Many cognitive functions are differentiated; they are associated with different parts of the brain. So, learners are likely to have preferred modes of processing (e.g., visual or verbal) as well as varying capabilities in these modes. Using a range of modalities for instruction and activities that draw on different senses may support learning—for example, using maps and songs to teach geography. Assessment should be differentiated, too.

3. The brain is relatively plastic, so enriched, active environments and flexible instructional strategies are likely to support cognitive development in young children and learning in adults.

4. Some learning disorders may have a neurological basis; neurological testing may assist in diagnosing and treating these disorders, as well as in evaluating the effects of various treatments.

5. The brain can change, but it takes time, so teachers must be consistent, patient, and compassionate in teaching and reteaching in different ways, as Nico's and Brooke's parents and teachers could tell you.

6. Learning from real-life problems and concrete experiences helps students construct knowledge and also gives them multiple pathways for learning and retrieving information.

7. The brain seeks meaningful patterns and connections with existing networks, so teachers should tie new information to what students already understand and help them form new connections. Information that is not linked to existing knowledge will be easily forgotten.

8. It takes a long time to build and consolidate knowledge. Numerous visits in different contexts over time (not all at once) help to form strong, multiple connections.

9. Large, general concepts should be emphasized over small specific facts so students can build enduring, useful knowledge categories and associations that are not constantly changing.

10. Stories should be used in teaching. Stories engage many areas of the brain—memories, experiences, feelings, and beliefs. Stories also are organized and have a sequence—beginning, middle, end—so they are easier to remember than unrelated or unorganized information.

11. Helping students understand how activity (practice, problem solving, making connections, inquiry, etc.) changes their brain and how emotions and stress affect attention and memory can be motivating, leading to greater self-efficacy and self-regulated learning (we talk more about this in Chapter 11). One important message to students is that they are responsible for doing what it takes to change their own brains; you have to work (and play) to learn.

For the rest of the chapter, we turn from the brain and cognitive development to examine several major theories of cognitive development, the first offered by a biologist turned psychologist, Jean Piaget.

ENHANCEDetext *self-check*

PIAGET'S THEORY OF COGNITIVE DEVELOPMENT

Swiss psychologist Jean Piaget was a real prodigy. In fact, in his teens, he published so many scientific papers on mollusks (marine animals such as oysters, clams, octopuses, snails, and squid) that he was offered a job as the curator of the mollusk collection at the Museum of Natural History in Geneva. He told the museum officials that he wanted to finish high school first. For a while, Piaget worked in Alfred Binet's laboratory in Paris developing intelligence tests for children. The reasons children gave for their wrong answers fascinated him, and this prompted him to study the thinking behind their answers. This question intrigued him for the rest of his life (Green & Piel, 2010). He continued to write until his death at the age of 84 (P. H. Miller, 2011).

During his long career, Piaget devised a model describing how humans go about making sense of their world by gathering and organizing information (Piaget, 1954, 1963, 1970a, 1970b). We will examine Piaget's ideas closely, because they provide an explanation of the development of thinking from infancy to adulthood.

- -

STOP & THINK Can you be in Pittsburgh, Pennsylvania, and the United States all at the same time? Is this a difficult question for you? How long did it take you to answer? •

- -

According to Piaget (1954), certain ways of thinking that are quite simple for an adult, such as the Pittsburgh question in *Stop & Think*, are not so simple for a child. For example, do you remember the 9-year-old child at the beginning of the chapter who was asked if he could be a Genevan? He answered, *"No, that's not possible. I'm already Swiss. I can't also be Genevan"* (Piaget, 1965/1995, p. 252). Imagine teaching this student geography. The student has trouble with classifying one concept (Geneva) as a subset of another (Switzerland). There are other differences between adult and child thinking. Children's concepts of time may be different from your own. They may think, for example, that they will some day catch up to a sibling in age, or they may confuse the past and the future. Let's examine why.

Influences on Development

Cognitive development is much more than the addition of new facts and ideas to an existing store of information. According to Piaget, our thinking processes change radically, though slowly, from birth to maturity because we constantly strive to make sense of the world. Piaget identified four factors—biological maturation, activity, social experiences, and equilibration—that interact to influence changes in thinking (Piaget, 1970a). Let's briefly examine the first three factors. We'll return to a discussion of equilibration in the next section.

One of the most important influences on the way we make sense of the world is *maturation,* the unfolding of the biological changes that are genetically programmed. Parents and teachers have little impact on this aspect of cognitive development, except to be sure that children get the nourishment and care they need to be healthy.

Activity is another influence. With physical maturation comes the increasing ability to act on the environment and learn from it. When a young child's coordination is reasonably developed, for example, the child can discover principles about balance by experimenting with a seesaw. Thus, as we act on the environment—as we explore, test, observe, and eventually organize information—we are likely to alter our thinking processes at the same time.

As we develop, we are also interacting with the people around us. According to Piaget, our cognitive development is influenced by *social transmission,* or learning from others. Without social transmission, we would need to reinvent all the knowledge already offered by our culture. The amount people can learn from social transmission varies according to their stage of cognitive development.

Maturation, activity, and social transmission all work together to influence cognitive development. How do we respond to these influences?

Basic Tendencies in Thinking

As a result of his early research in biology, Piaget concluded that all species inherit two basic tendencies, or "invariant functions." The first of these tendencies is toward organization—the combining, arranging, recombining, and rearranging of behaviors and thoughts into coherent systems. The second tendency is toward adaptation, or adjusting to the environment.

ORGANIZATION. People are born with a tendency to organize their thinking processes into psychological structures. These psychological structures are our systems for understanding and interacting with the world. Simple structures are continually combined and coordinated to become more sophisticated and thus more effective. Very young infants, for example, can either look at an object or grasp it when it comes in contact with their hands. They cannot coordinate looking and grasping at the same time. As they develop, however, infants organize these two separate behavioral structures into a coordinated higher-level structure of looking at, reaching for, and grasping the object. They can, of course, still use each structure separately (Flavell, Miller, & Miller, 2002; P. H. Miller, 2011).

Piaget gave a special name to these structures: schemes. In his theory, schemes are the basic building blocks of thinking. They are organized systems of actions or thought that allow us to mentally represent or "think about" the objects and events in our world. Schemes can be very small and specific, for example, the sucking-through-a-straw scheme or the recognizing-a-rose scheme.

Or they can be larger and more general, for example, the drinking scheme or the gardening scheme. As a person's thinking processes become more organized and new schemes develop, behavior also becomes more sophisticated and better suited to the environment.

ADAPTATION. In addition to the tendency to organize psychological structures, people also inherit the tendency to adapt to their environment. Two basic processes are involved in adaptation: assimilation and accommodation.

Assimilation takes place when we use our existing schemes to make sense of events in our world. Assimilation involves trying to understand something new by fitting it into what we already know. At times, we may have to distort the new information to make it fit. For example, the first time many children see a raccoon, they call it a "kitty." They try to match the new experience with an existing scheme for identifying animals.

Accommodation occurs when we must change existing schemes to respond to a new situation. If we cannot make new data fit any existing schemes, then we must develop more appropriate structures. We adjust our thinking to fit the new information, instead of adjusting the information to fit our thinking. Children demonstrate accommodation when they add the scheme for recognizing raccoons to their other systems for identifying animals.

People adapt to their increasingly complex environments by using existing schemes whenever these schemes work (assimilation) and by modifying and adding to their schemes when something new is needed (accommodation). In fact, both processes are required most of the time. Even using an established pattern such as sucking through a straw requires some accommodation if the straw is of a different size or length than the type you are used to. If you have tried drinking juice from box packages, you know that you have to add a new skill to your sucking-through-a-straw scheme: don't squeeze the box or you will shoot juice through the straw, straight up into the air and into your lap. Whenever new experiences are assimilated into an existing scheme, the scheme is enlarged and changed somewhat, so assimilation involves some accommodation (Mascolo & Fischer, 2005).

There are also times when neither assimilation nor accommodation is used. If people encounter something that is too unfamiliar, they may ignore it. Experience is filtered to fit the kind of thinking a person is doing at a given time. For example, if you overhear a conversation in a foreign language, you probably will not try to make sense of the exchange unless you have some knowledge of the language.

EQUILIBRATION. According to Piaget, organizing, assimilating, and accommodating can be viewed as a kind of complex balancing act. In his theory, the actual changes in thinking take place through the process of **equilibration**—the act of searching for a balance. Piaget assumed that people continually test the adequacy of their thinking processes in order to achieve that balance. Briefly, the process of equilibration works like this: If we apply a particular scheme to an event or situation and the scheme works, then equilibrium exists. If the scheme does not produce a satisfying result, then **disequilibrium** exists, and we become uncomfortable. This motivates us to keep searching for a solution through assimilation and accommodation, and thus our thinking changes and moves ahead. Of course, the level of disequilibrium must be just right or optimal—too little and we aren't interested in changing, too much and we may be discouraged or anxious and not change.

Four Stages of Cognitive Development

Now we turn to the actual differences that Piaget hypothesized for children as they grow. Piaget believed that all people pass through the same four stages in exactly the same order. The stages are generally associated with specific ages, as shown in Table 2.2, but these are only general guidelines, not labels for all children of a certain age. Piaget noted that individuals may go through long periods of transition between stages and that a person may show characteristics of one stage in one situation, but traits of a higher or lower stage in other situations. Therefore, remember that knowing a student's age is never a guarantee you will know how the child thinks (Orlando & Machado, 1996).

INFANCY: THE SENSORIMOTOR STAGE. The earliest period is called the **sensorimotor** stage, because the child's thinking involves seeing, hearing, moving, touching, tasting, and so on.

Video 2.1
The children in this video are learning something new about growth by observing a tadpole as it changes from day to day. They can assimilate the idea that the tadpole grows legs, but they need to accommodate their concept of growth to understand why the tadpole's tail gets smaller.

ENHANCEDetext *video example*

TABLE 2.2 • **Piaget's Stages of Cognitive Development**

STAGE	APPROXIMATE AGE	CHARACTERISTICS
Sensorimotor	0–2 years	Learns through reflexes, senses, and movement—actions on the environment. Begins to imitate others and remember events; shifts to symbolic thinking. Comes to understand that objects do not cease to exist when they are out of sight—object permanence. Moves from reflexive actions to intentional activity.
Preoperational	Begins about the time the child starts talking, to about 7 years old	Develops language and begins to use symbols to represent objects. Has difficulty with past and future—thinks in the present. Can think through operations logically in one direction. Has difficulties understanding the point of view of another person.
Concrete Operational	Begins about first grade, to early adolescence, around 11 years old	Can think logically about concrete (hands-on) problems. Understands conservation and organizes things into categories and in series. Can reverse thinking to mentally "undo" actions. Understands past, present, and future.
Formal Operational	Adolescence to adulthood	Can think hypothetically and deductively. Thinking becomes more scientific. Solves abstract problems in logical fashion. Can consider multiple perspectives and develops concerns about social issues, personal identity, and justice.

During this period, infants develop **object permanence**, the understanding that objects exist in the environment whether they perceive them or not. This is the beginning of the important ability to construct a mental representation. As most parents discover, before infants develop object permanence, it is relatively easy to take something away from them. The trick is to distract them and remove the object while they are not looking—"out of sight, out of mind." The older infant who searches for the ball that has rolled out of sight is indicating an understanding that objects still exist even when they are not in view (M. K. Moore & Meltzoff, 2004). Some researchers suggest that infants as young as 3 to 4 months may know that an object still exists, but they do not have either the memory skills to "hold on" to the location of the object or the motor skills to coordinate a search (Baillargeon, 1999; Flavell et al., 2002).

A second major accomplishment in the sensorimotor period is the beginning of logical, **goal-directed actions**. Think of the familiar clear plastic container baby toy with a lid and several colorful items inside that can be dumped out and replaced. A 6-month-old baby is likely to become frustrated trying to get to the toys inside. An older child who has mastered the basics of the sensorimotor stage will probably be able to deal with the toy in an orderly fashion by building a "container toy" scheme: (1) get the lid off, (2) turn the container upside down, (3) shake if the items jam, and (4) watch the items fall. Separate lower-level schemes have been organized into a higher-level scheme to achieve a goal.

The child is soon able to reverse this action by refilling the container. Learning to reverse actions is a basic accomplishment of the sensorimotor stage. As we will soon see, however, learning to reverse thinking—that is, learning to imagine the reverse of a sequence of actions—takes much longer.

EARLY CHILDHOOD TO THE EARLY ELEMENTARY YEARS: THE PREOPERATIONAL STAGE. By the end of the sensorimotor stage, the child can use many action schemes. However, as long as these schemes remain tied to physical actions, they are of no use in recalling the past,

Family Circus © 2002 Bil Keane, Inc. King Features Syndicate.

"I can't tell you 'cause I'm wearin' my mittens."

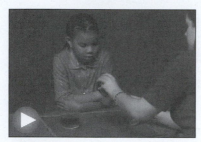

Video 2.2
In this video, children participate in tasks that show their understanding of conservation of volume and conservation of number. Compare the responses, and identify each child's stage of cognitive development, according to Piaget's theory.

ENHANCEDetext *video example*

keeping track of information, or planning. For this, children need what Piaget called **operations**, or actions that are carried out and reversed *mentally* rather than physically. At the **preoperational** stage the child is moving toward mastery, but has not yet mastered these mental operations (so thinking is *pre*operational).

According to Piaget, the first type of thinking that is separate from action involves making action schemes symbolic. The ability to form and use symbols—words, gestures, signs, images, and so on—is thus a major accomplishment of the preoperational period and moves children closer to mastering the mental operations of the next stage. This ability to work with symbols to represent an object that is not present, such as using the word *horse* or a picture of a horse or even pretending to ride a broomstick horse, is called the **semiotic function**. In fact, the child's earliest use of symbols is in pretending. Children who are not yet able to talk will often use action symbols—pretending to drink from an empty cup or touching a comb to their hair, showing that they know what each object is for. This behavior also shows that their schemes are becoming more general and less tied to specific actions. The eating scheme, for example, can be used in playing house. During the preoperational stage, there is also rapid development of that very important symbol system, language. Between the ages of 2 and 4, most children enlarge their vocabulary from about 200 to 2,000 words.

As the child moves through the preoperational stage, the developing ability to think about objects in symbolic form remains somewhat limited to thinking in one direction only, or using one-way logic. It is very difficult for the child to "think backward," or imagine how to reverse the steps in a task. **Reversible thinking** is involved in many tasks that are difficult for the preoperational child, such as the conservation of matter.

Conservation is the principle that the amount or number of something remains the same even if the arrangement or appearance is changed, as long as nothing is added and nothing is taken away. You know that if you tear a piece of paper into several pieces, you will still have the same amount of paper. To prove this, you know that you can reverse the process by taping the pieces back together, but a child using preoperational thinking can't think that way. Here is a classic example of difficulty with conservation. Leah, a 5-year-old, is shown two identical glasses, both short and wide in shape. Both have exactly the same amount of colored water in them. She agrees that the amounts are "the same." The experimenter then pours the water from one of the glasses into a taller, narrower glass and asks, "Now, does one glass have more water, or are they the same?" Leah responds that the tall glass has more because "It goes up more here" (she points to higher level on taller glass).

Piaget's explanation for Leah's answer is that she is focusing, or *centering*, attention on the dimension of height. She has difficulty considering more than one aspect of the situation at a time, or **decentering**. The preoperational child cannot understand that decreased diameter compensates for increased height, because this would require taking into account two dimensions at once. Thus, children at the preoperational stage have trouble freeing themselves from their own immediate perceptions of how the world appears.

This brings us to another important characteristic of the preoperational stage. Preoperational children, according to Piaget, have a tendency to be **egocentric**, to see the world and the experiences of others from their own viewpoint. The concept of egocentrism, as Piaget intended it, does not mean selfish; it simply means children often assume that everyone else shares their feelings, reactions, and perspectives. For example, if a little boy at this stage is afraid of dogs, he may assume that all children share this fear. The 2-year-old at the beginning of this chapter who brought his own mother to comfort a distressed friend—even though the friend's mother was available—was simply seeing the situation through his own eyes. Very young children center on their own perceptions and on the way the situation appears to them. This is one reason it is difficult for preoperational children to understand that *your* right hand is not on the same side as theirs when you are facing them.

Research has shown that young children are not totally egocentric in every situation, however. Children as young as 2 describe more details about a situation to a parent who was not present than they provide to a parent who experienced the situation with them. So young children do seem quite able to take the needs and different perspectives of others into account, at least in certain situations (Flavell et al., 2002). And in fairness to young children, even adults can make assumptions that others feel or think like they do—think about all the politicians who believe "the people agree with

GUIDELINES
Family and Community Partnerships

Helping Families Care for Preoperational Children

Encourage families to use concrete props and visual aids whenever possible.

Examples

1. When family members use words such as *part, whole,* or *one half,* encourage them to demonstrate using objects in the house such as cutting an apple or pizza into parts.
2. Let children add and subtract with sticks, rocks, or colored chips. This technique also is helpful for early concrete-operational students.

Make instructions relatively short—not too many steps at once. Use actions as well as words.

Examples

1. When giving instructions such as how to feed a pet, first model the process, then ask the child to try it.
2. Explain a game by acting out one of the parts.

Help children develop their ability to see the world from someone else's point of view.

Examples

1. Ask children to imagine "how your sister felt when you broke her toy."

2. Be clear about rules for sharing or use of material. Help children understand the value of the rules, and help them develop empathy by asking them to think about how they would like to be treated. Avoid long lectures on "sharing" or being "nice."

Give children a great deal of hands-on practice with the skills that serve as building blocks for more complex skills such as reading comprehension or collaboration.

Examples

1. Provide cut-out letters or letter magnets for the refrigerator to build words.
2. Do activities that require measuring and simple calculations—cooking, dividing a batch of popcorn equally.

Provide a wide range of experiences in order to build a foundation for concept learning and language.

Examples

1. Take trips to zoos, gardens, theaters, and concerts; encourage storytelling.
2. Give children words to describe what they are doing, hearing, seeing, touching, tasting, and smelling.

---

me!" The *Guidelines: Family and Community Partnerships* gives ideas for working with preoperational thinkers and for guiding families in supporting the cognitive development of their children.

LATER ELEMENTARY TO THE MIDDLE SCHOOL YEARS: THE CONCRETE-OPERATIONAL STAGE. Piaget coined the term **concrete operations** to describe this stage of "hands-on" thinking. The basic characteristics of the stage are the recognition of the logical stability of the physical world; the realization that elements can be changed or transformed and still conserve many of their original characteristics; and the understanding that these changes can be reversed.

Look at Figure 2.4 on the next page to see examples of the different tasks given to children to assess conservation and the approximate age ranges when most children can solve these problems. According to Piaget, the ability to solve conservation problems depends on having an understanding of three basic aspects of reasoning: identity, compensation, and reversibility. With a complete mastery of **identity**, the student knows that if nothing is added or taken away, the material remains the same. With an understanding of **compensation**, the student knows that an apparent change in one direction can be compensated for by a change in another direction. That is, if the glass is narrower, the liquid will rise higher in the glass. And with an understanding of **reversibility**, the student can mentally cancel out the change that has been made. Leah apparently knew it was the same water (identity), but she lacked compensation and reversibility, so she was still moving toward conservation.

Another important operation mastered at this stage is **classification**. Classification depends on a student's abilities to focus on a single characteristic of objects in a set (e.g., color) and group the objects according to that characteristic. More advanced classification at this stage involves recognizing that one class fits into another. A city can be in a particular state or province and also in a particular country, as you probably knew when I asked you earlier about Pittsburgh, Pennsylvania, USA. As children apply this advanced classification to locations, they often become fascinated with "complete" addresses such as Lee Jary, 5116 Forest Hill Drive, Richmond Hill, Ontario, Canada, North America, Northern Hemisphere, Earth, Solar System, Milky Way, Universe.

FIGURE 2.4

SOME PIAGETIAN CONSERVATION TASKS

In addition to the tasks shown here, other tasks involve the conservation of number, length, weight, and volume. These tasks are all achieved over the concrete-operational period.

	Suppose you start with this	➡	Then you change the situation to this	➡	The question you would ask a child is
(a) conservation of mass	A B	Roll out clay ball B	A B		Which is bigger, A or B?
(b) conservation of weight	A B	Roll out clay ball B	A B		Which will weigh more, A or B?
(c) conservation of volume	A B	Take clay ball out of water and roll out clay ball B	A B		When I put the clay back into the water beakers, in which beaker will the water be higher?
(d) conservation of continuous quantity	A B C	Pour water in beaker A into beaker C	A B C		Which beaker has more liquid, B or C?
(e) conservation of number	A B	Break candy bar B into pieces	A B		Which is more candy? A or B

Source: Woolfolk, A., & Perry, N. E., Child Development (2nd ed.), © 2015 by Pearson Education, Inc. Reproduced by permission of Pearson Education, Inc. All rights reserved.

Classification is also related to reversibility. The ability to reverse a process mentally allows the concrete-operational student to see that there is more than one way to classify a group of objects. The student understands, for example, that buttons can be classified by color, and then reclassified by size or by the number of holes.

Seriation is the process of making an orderly arrangement from large to small or vice versa. This understanding of sequential relationships permits a student to construct a logical series in which A < B < C (A is less than B is less than C) and so on. Unlike the preoperational child, the concrete-operational child can grasp the notion that B can be larger than A but still smaller than C.

With the abilities to handle operations such as conservation, classification, and seriation, the student at the concrete-operational stage has finally developed a complete and very logical system of thinking. However, this system of thinking is still tied to physical reality. The logic is based on concrete situations that can be organized, classified, or manipulated. Thus, children at this stage can imagine several different arrangements for the furniture in their rooms. They do not have to solve the problem strictly through trial and error by actually moving the furniture. However, the concrete-operational child is not yet able to reason about hypothetical, abstract problems that involve the coordination of many factors at once. This kind of coordination is part of Piaget's next and final stage of cognitive development.

In any grade you teach, knowledge of concrete-operational thinking will be helpful (see *Guidelines: Teaching the Concrete-Operational Child*). In the early grades, the students are moving toward this logical system of thought. In the middle grades, it is in full flower, ready to be applied and extended by your teaching. Students in high school and even adults still commonly use concrete-operational thinking, especially in areas that are new or unfamiliar.

HIGH SCHOOL AND COLLEGE: FORMAL OPERATIONS. Some students remain at the concrete-operational stage throughout their school years, even throughout life. However, new experiences, usually those that take place in school, eventually present most students with problems that they cannot solve using concrete operations.

STOP & THINK You are packing for a long trip, but want to pack light. How many different three-piece outfits (slacks, shirt, jacket) will you have if you include three shirts, three slacks, and three jackets (assuming of course that they all go together in fashion perfection)? Time yourself to see how long it takes to arrive at the answer. •

GUIDELINES
Teaching the Concrete-Operational Child

Continue to use concrete props and visual aids, especially when dealing with sophisticated material.
Examples
1. Use timelines in history and three-dimensional models in science.
2. Use diagrams to illustrate hierarchical relationships such as branches of government and the agencies under each branch.

Continue to give students a chance to manipulate and test objects.
Examples
1. Set up simple scientific experiments such as the following involving the relationship between fire and oxygen. What happens to a flame when you blow on it from a distance? (If you don't blow it out, the flame gets larger briefly, because it has more oxygen to burn.) What happens when you cover the flame with a jar?
2. Have students make candles by dipping wicks in wax, weave cloth on a simple loom, bake bread, set type by hand, or do other craft work that illustrates the daily occupations of people in the colonial period.

Make sure presentations and readings are brief and well organized.
Examples
1. Assign stories or books with short, logical chapters, moving to longer reading assignments only when students are ready.
2. Break up a presentation, giving students an opportunity to practice the first steps before introducing the next steps.

Use familiar examples to explain more complex ideas.
Examples
1. Compare students' lives with those of characters in a story. After reading *Island of the Blue Dolphins* (the true story of a girl who grew up alone on a deserted island), ask, "Have you ever had to stay alone for a long time? How did you feel?"
2. Teach the concept of area by having students measure two schoolrooms that are different sizes.

Give opportunities to classify and group objects and ideas on increasingly complex levels.
Examples
1. Give students slips of paper with individual sentences written on each paper, and ask the students to group the sentences into paragraphs.
2. Compare the systems of the human body to other kinds of systems: the brain to a computer, the heart to a pump. Break down stories into components, from the broad to the specific: author, story, characters, plot, theme, place, time.

Present problems that require logical, analytical thinking.
Examples
1. Discuss open-ended questions that stimulate thinking: "Are the brain and the mind the same thing?" "How should the city deal with stray animals?" "What is the largest number?"
2. Use sports photos or pictures of crisis situations (Red Cross helping in disasters, victims of poverty or war, senior citizens who need assistance) to stimulate problem-solving discussions.

What happens when a number of variables interact, as in a laboratory experiment or the question in *Stop & Think?* A mental system for controlling sets of variables and working through a set of possibilities is needed. These are the abilities Piaget called **formal operations**.

At the level of formal operations, the focus of thinking can shift from what is to what might be. Situations do not have to be experienced to be imagined. You met Jamal at the beginning of this chapter. Even though he is a bright elementary school student, he could not answer the question, "How would life be different if people did not have to sleep?" because he insisted, "People HAVE TO SLEEP!" In contrast, the adolescent who has mastered formal operations can consider contrary-to-fact questions. In answering, the adolescent demonstrates the hallmark of formal operations—**hypothetico-deductive reasoning**. The formal-operational thinker can consider a hypothetical situation (people do not sleep) and reason *deductively* (from the general assumption to specific implications, such as longer workdays, more money spent on energy and lighting, smaller houses without bedrooms, or new entertainment industries). Formal operations also include *inductive* reasoning, or using specific observations to identify general principles. For example, the economist observes many specific changes in the stock market and attempts to identify general principles about economic cycles from this information.

Connect and Extend to PRAXIS II®

Reasoning (II, A1)
Be able to distinguish between inductive and deductive reasoning. Explain the role that each plays in the learning of concepts.

Using formal operations is a new way of reasoning that involves "thinking about thinking" or "mental operations on mental operations" (Inhelder & Piaget, 1958). For example, the child using concrete operations can categorize animals by their physical characteristics or by their habitats, but a child using formal operations can perform "second-order" operations on these category operations to *infer relationships between* habitat and physical characteristics—such as understanding that the physical characteristic of thick fur on animals is related to their arctic habitats (Kuhn & Franklin, 2006). Abstract formal-operational thinking is necessary for success in many advanced high school and college courses. For example, most math is concerned with hypothetical situations, assumptions, and givens: "Let $x = 10$," or "Assume $x2 + y2 = z2$," or "Given two sides and an adjacent angle. . . ." Work in social studies and literature requires abstract thinking, too: "What did Wilson mean when he called World War I the 'war to end all wars'?" "What are some metaphors for hope and despair in Shakespeare's sonnets?" "What symbols of old age does T. S. Eliot use in *The Waste Land?*" "How do animals symbolize human character traits in Aesop's fables?"

The organized, scientific thinking of formal operations requires that students systematically generate different possibilities for a given situation. For example, if asked, "How many different shirt/slacks/jacket outfits can you make using three of each kind of clothing?" the child using formal operations can systematically identify the 27 possible combinations. (Did you get it right?) A concrete-operational thinker might name just a few combinations, using each piece of clothing only once. The underlying system of combinations is not yet available.

Another characteristic of this stage is **adolescent egocentrism**. Unlike egocentric young children, adolescents do not deny that other people may have different perceptions and beliefs; the adolescents just become very focused on their own ideas. They spend much time examining their own beliefs and attitudes. This leads to what Elkind (1981) calls the sense of an *imaginary audience*—the feeling that everyone is watching. Thus, adolescents believe that others are analyzing them: "Everyone noticed that I wore this shirt twice this week." "The whole class thought my answer was dumb!" You can see that social blunders or imperfections in appearance can be devastating if "everybody is watching." Luckily, this feeling of being "on stage" seems to peak in early adolescence by age 14 or 15, although in unfamiliar situations we all may feel our mistakes are being noticed.

The ability to think hypothetically, consider alternatives, identify all possible combinations, and analyze their own thinking has some interesting consequences for adolescents. Because they can think about worlds that do not exist, they often become interested in science fiction. Because they can reason from general principles to specific actions, they often are critical of people whose actions seem to contradict their principles. Adolescents can deduce the set of "best" possibilities and imagine ideal worlds (or ideal parents and teachers, for that matter). This explains why many students at this age develop interests in utopias, political causes, and social issues. They want to design better worlds, and their thinking allows them to do so. Adolescents also can imagine many possible futures for themselves and may try to decide which is best. Feelings about any of these ideals may be strong.

DO WE ALL REACH THE FOURTH STAGE? Most psychologists agree that there is a level of thinking more sophisticated than concrete operations. But there is a debate about how universal formal-operational thinking actually is, even among adults. The first three stages of Piaget's theory are forced on most people by physical realities. Objects really are permanent. The amount of water doesn't change when it is poured into another glass. Formal operations, however, are not so closely tied to the physical environment. Being able to use formal operations may be the result of practice in solving hypothetical problems and using formal scientific reasoning—abilities that are valued and taught in literate cultures, particularly in college. Even so, not all high school students can perform Piaget's formal-operational tasks (Shayer, 2003). The *Guidelines: Helping Students to Use Formal Operations* will help you support the development of formal operations in your students.

Piaget himself (1974) suggested that most adults might only be able to use formal-operational thought in a few areas where they have the greatest experience or interest. Taking a college class fosters formal-operational abilities in that subject, but not necessarily in others (Lehman & Nisbett, 1990). Expect many students in your middle school or high school classes to have trouble thinking hypothetically, especially when they are learning something new. Students sometimes find shortcuts for dealing with problems that are beyond their grasp; they may memorize formulas or lists of steps. These systems may be helpful for passing tests, but real understanding will take place only if students can go beyond this superficial use of memorization.

Information Processing, Neo-Piagetian, and Neuroscience Views of Cognitive Development

As you will see in Chapter 8, there are explanations for why children have trouble with conservation and other Piagetian tasks. These explanations focus on the development of information processing skills, such as attention, memory capacity, and learning strategies. As children mature and their brains develop, they are better able to focus their attention, process information more quickly, hold more information in memory, and use thinking strategies more easily and flexibly (Siegler, 2000, 2004). One critical development is improvement in executive functioning. **Executive functioning** involves all those processes that we use to organize, coordinate, and perform goal-directed, intentional actions. Executive functioning skills include focusing attention, inhibiting impulsive responses,

---

GUIDELINES
Helping Students to Use Formal Operations

Continue to use concrete-operational teaching strategies and materials.

Examples

1. Use visual aids such as charts and illustrations as well as somewhat more sophisticated graphs and diagrams, especially when the material is new.
2. Compare the experiences of characters in stories to students' experiences.

Give students the opportunity to explore many hypothetical questions.

Examples

1. Have students write position papers, then exchange these papers with the opposing side and debate topical social issues such as the environment, the economy, and national health insurance.
2. Ask students to write about their personal vision of a utopia; write a description of a universe that has no sex differences; write a description of Earth after humans are extinct.

Give students opportunities to solve problems and reason scientifically.

Examples

1. Set up group discussions in which students design experiments to answer questions.
2. Ask students to justify two different positions on animal rights, with logical arguments for each position.

Whenever possible, teach broad concepts, not just facts, using materials and ideas relevant to the students' lives (Delpit, 1995).

Examples

1. When discussing the Civil War, consider racism or other issues that have divided the United States since then.
2. When teaching about poetry, let students find lyrics from popular songs that illustrate poetic devices, and talk about how these devices do or don't work well to communicate the meanings and feelings the songwriters intended.

making and changing plans, and using memory to hold and manipulate information (Best & Miller, 2010; Raj & Bell, 2010). As children develop more sophisticated and effective executive functioning skills, they are active in advancing their own development; they are constructing, organizing, and improving their own knowledge and strategies (Siegler & Alibali, 2005). For example, one classic Piagetian task is to show children 10 daisies and 2 roses, then ask if there are more daisies or more flowers. Young children see more daisies and jump to the answer, "daisies." As they mature, children are better at resisting (inhibiting) that first response based on appearances and can answer based on the fact that both daisies and roses are flowers. But even adults have to take a fraction of a second to resist the obvious, so inhibiting impulsive responses is important for developing complex knowledge throughout life (Borst, Poirel, Pineau, Cassotti, & Houdé, 2013).

Some developmental psychologists have formulated **neo-Piagetian theories** that retain Piaget's insights about children's construction of knowledge and the general trends in children's thinking but add findings from information processing theories about the role of attention, memory, and strategies (Croker, 2012). Perhaps the best-known neo-Piagetian theory was developed by Robbie Case (1992, 1998). He devised an explanation of cognitive development suggesting that children develop in stages within specific domains such as numerical concepts, spatial concepts, social tasks, storytelling, reasoning about physical objects, and motor development. As children practice using the schemes in a particular domain (e.g., using counting schemes in the number concept area), accomplishing the schemes requires less attention. The schemes become more automatic because the child does not have to "think so hard." This frees up mental resources and memory to do more, so the child can combine simple schemes into more complex ones and invent new schemes when needed (assimilation and accommodation in action).

Kurt Fischer (2009) connected cognitive development in different domains to research on the brain. He also examined development in different domains such as reading or math. You may remember Nico and Brooke, the remarkable children we met earlier in the chapter who each had one side of their brain removed to treat severe epilepsy, yet both still developed other pathways in their brains to recover lost spatial and verbal abilities. We have seen that one of the implications of research on the brain is that there are multiple pathways for learning.

Fischer (2009) has found, however, that even though their brains follow different pathways as they master skills in speaking, reading, and mathematics, children's growth patterns show a similar series of spurts and they go through predictable levels of development. When learning a new skill, children move through three tiers—from *actions* to *representations* to *abstractions*. Within each tier, the pattern is moving from accomplishing a single action to mapping or coordinating two actions together, such as coordinating addition and multiplication in math, to creating whole systems of understanding. At the level of abstractions, children finally move to constructing explanatory principles. This may remind you of sensorimotor, concrete operations, and formal operations in Piaget's theory. Look at Table 2.3, which shows the movement through the tiers of *actions* to *representations* to *abstractions*.

For each skill level, the brain reorganizes itself, too. Table 2.3 shows this progression between birth and 45 years. Notice the column that says "Age of Emergence of Optimal Level." This column shows the ages at which the skills will develop if the individuals have *quality support and the chance to practice*. The age the skill emerges without support and practice is shown in the last column. Support and practice are keys in another explanation of cognitive development we will discuss soon—Vygotsky's theory.

Some Limitations of Piaget's Theory

Although most psychologists agree with Piaget's insightful descriptions of *how* children think, many disagree with his explanations of *why* thinking develops as it does.

THE TROUBLE WITH STAGES. Some psychologists have questioned the existence of four separate stages of thinking, even though they agree that children do go through the changes that Piaget described (Mascolo & Fischer, 2005; P. H. Miller, 2011). One problem with the stage model is the lack of consistency in children's thinking. For example, children can conserve number (the

TABLE 2.3 • A Pattern of Cognitive Development over 45 Years

As children develop skills in speaking, reading, and mathematics, their growth patterns show a similar series of spurts. In learning a new skill, children move from *actions* to *representations* to *abstractions*.

TIERS	LEVELS	AGE OF EMERGENCE OF OPTIMAL LEVEL	AGE OF FUNCTIONAL LEVEL
		23–25 years	30–45 years
Abstraction	Ab4. Principles	18–20 years	23–40 years
	Ab3. Systems		
	Ab2. Mappings	14–16 years	17–30 years
	Rp4./Ab1. Single Abstraction	10–12 years	13–20 years
Representations	Rp3 Systems	6–7 years	7–12 years
	Rp2 Mappings	3½–4½ years	4–8 years
	Sm4./Rp1. Single Representations	2 years	2–5 years
Actions	Sm3. Systems	11–13 months	11–24 months
	Sm2. Mappings	7–8 months	7–13 months
	Sm1. Single Actions	3–4 months	3–9 months

Source: Reprinted with permission from Fischer, K. W. (2009). Mind, brain, and education: Building a scientific groundwork for learning and teaching. Mind, Brain, and Education, 3, p. 10.

number of blocks does not change when they are rearranged) a year or two before they can conserve weight (a ball of clay does not change when you flatten it). Why can't they use conservation consistently in every situation? In fairness, we should note that in his later work, even Piaget put less emphasis on stages of cognitive development and gave more attention to how thinking *changes* through equilibration (P. H. Miller, 2011).

Another problem with the idea of separate stages is that the processes may be more continuous than they seem. Changes may seem like discontinuous, qualitative leaps when we look across longer time periods. The 3-year-old persistently searching for a lost toy seems qualitatively different from the infant who doesn't miss a toy or search when the toy rolls under a sofa. But if we watched a developing child very closely and observed moment-to-moment or hour-to-hour changes, we might see that indeed there are gradual, continuous changes. Rather than appearing all at once, the knowledge that a hidden toy still exists may be a product of the older child's more fully developed memory: He knows that the toy is under the sofa because he remembers seeing it roll there, whereas the infant can't hold on to that memory. The longer you require children to wait before searching—the longer you make them remember the object—the older they have to be to succeed (Siegler & Alibali, 2005).

Change can be both continuous and discontinuous, as described by a branch of mathematics called *catastrophe theory*. Changes that appear suddenly, like the collapse of a bridge, are preceded by many slowly developing changes such as gradual, continuous corrosion of the metal structures. Similarly, gradually developing changes in children can lead to large changes in abilities that seem abrupt (Dawson-Tunik, Fischer, & Stein, 2004; Siegler & Alibali, 2005).

UNDERESTIMATING CHILDREN'S ABILITIES. It now appears that Piaget underestimated the cognitive abilities of children, particularly younger ones. The problems he gave young children may have been too difficult and the directions too confusing. His subjects may have understood more than they could demonstrate when solving these problems. For example, work by Gelman and her colleagues (Gelman, 2000; Gelman & Cordes, 2001) shows that preschool children know much more about the concept of number than Piaget thought, even if they sometimes make mistakes or get confused. As long as preschoolers work with only 3 or 4 objects at a time, they can tell that the number remains the same, even if the objects are spread far apart or clumped close together. Mirjam Ebersbach (2009) demonstrated that most of the German kindergartners in her study considered all three dimensions—width, height, and length—when they estimated the volume of a wooden block (actually, how many small cubes it would take to make bigger blocks of different sizes). In other words, we may be born with a greater store of cognitive tools than Piaget suggested. Some basic understandings or core knowledge, such as the permanence of objects or the sense of number, may be part of our evolutionary equipment, ready for use in our cognitive development (Geary & Bjorklund, 2000; Woodward & Needham, 2009).

Piaget's theory does not explain how even young children can perform at an advanced level in certain areas where they have highly developed knowledge and expertise. An expert 9-year-old chess player may think abstractly about chess moves, whereas a novice 20-year-old player may have to resort to more concrete strategies to plan and remember moves (Siegler, 1998).

Finally, Piaget argued that the development of cognitive operations such as conservation or abstract thinking cannot be accelerated. He believed that children had to be developmentally ready to learn. Quite a bit of research, however, has shown that with effective instruction, children can learn to perform cognitive operations such as conservation. They do not have to naturally discover these ways of thinking on their own. Knowledge and experience in a situation affect the kind of thinking that students can do (Brainerd, 2003).

COGNITIVE DEVELOPMENT AND CULTURE. One final criticism of Piaget's theory is that it overlooks the important effects of the child's cultural and social group. Research across different cultures has generally confirmed that although Piaget was accurate about the sequence of the stages in children's thinking, the age ranges for the stages vary. Western children typically move to the next stage about 2 to 3 years earlier than children in non-Western societies. But careful research has shown that these differences across cultures depend on the subject or domain tested and whether the culture values and teaches knowledge in that domain. For example, children in Brazil who sell candy in the streets instead of attending school appear to fail a certain kind of Piagetian task—class inclusion (Are there more daisies, more tulips, or more flowers in the picture?). But when the tasks are phrased within concepts they understand—selling candy—then these children perform better than Brazilian children the same age who attend school (Saxe, 1999). When a culture or context emphasizes a cognitive ability, children growing up in that culture tend to acquire that ability sooner. In a study that compared Chinese first-, third-, and fifth-grade students to American students in the same grades, the Chinese students mastered a Piagetian task that involved distance, time, and speed relationships about 2 years ahead of American students, most likely because the Chinese education system puts more emphasis on math and science in the early grades (Zhou, Peverly, Beohm, & Chongde, 2001).

Even concrete operations such as classification may develop differently in different cultures. For example, when individuals from the Kpelle people of Africa were asked to sort 20 objects, they created groups that made sense to them—a hoe with a potato, a knife with an orange. The experimenter could not get the Kpelle to change their categories; they said this way of sorting is how a wise man would do it. Finally, the experimenter asked in desperation, "Well, how would a fool do it?" Then the subjects promptly created the four neat classification piles the experimenter had expected—food, tools, and so on (Rogoff & Morelli, 1989).

There is another increasingly influential view of cognitive development. Proposed years ago by Lev Vygotsky and recently rediscovered, this theory ties cognitive development to culture.

ENHANCEDetext *self-check*

VYGOTSKY'S SOCIOCULTURAL PERSPECTIVE

Psychologists today recognize that culture shapes cognitive development by determining what and how the child will learn about the world—the content and processes of thinking. For example, young Zinacanteco Indian girls of southern Mexico learn complicated ways of weaving cloth through informal instruction by adults in their communities. Cultures that prize cooperation and sharing teach these abilities early, whereas cultures that encourage competition nurture competitive skills in their children. The stages observed by Piaget are not necessarily "natural" for all children because to some extent they reflect the expectations and activities of Western cultures, as the Kpelle people just described have taught us (Kozulin, 2003; Kozulin et al., 2003; Rogoff, 2003).

A major spokesperson for this **sociocultural theory** (also called *sociohistoric*) was a Russian psychologist who died in 1934. Lev Semenovich Vygotsky was only 38 when he died of tuberculosis, but during his brief life he produced over 100 books and articles. Some of the translations are now available (e.g., Vygotsky, 1978, 1986, 1987a, 1987b, 1987c, 1993, 1997). Vygotsky began studying learning and development to improve his own teaching. He went on to write about language and thought, the psychology of art, learning and development, and educating students with special needs. His work was banned in Russia for many years because he referenced Western psychologists. But in the past 50 years, with the rediscovery of his writings, Vygotsky's ideas have become major influences in psychology and education and have provided alternatives to many of Piaget's theories (Gredler, 2009a, 2009b, 2012; Kozulin, 2003; Kozulin et al., 2003; Van Der Veer, 2007; Wink & Putney, 2002).

Vygotsky believed that human activities take place in cultural settings and that they cannot be understood apart from these settings. One of his key ideas was that our specific mental structures and processes can be traced to our interactions with others. These social interactions are more than simple influences on cognitive development—they actually create our cognitive structures and thinking processes (Palincsar, 1998). In fact, "Vygotsky conceptualized development as the transformation of socially shared activities into internalized processes" (John-Steiner & Mahn, 1996, p. 192). We will examine three themes in Vygotsky's writings that explain how social processes form learning and thinking: the social sources of individual thinking; the role of cultural tools in learning and development, especially the tool of language; and the zone of proximal development (Driscoll, 2005; Gredler, 2012; Wertsch & Tulviste, 1992).

The Social Sources of Individual Thinking

Vygotsky assumed that

> Every function in a child's cultural development appears twice: first, on the social level and later on the individual level; first between people (interpsychological) and then inside the child (intrapsychological). This applies equally to voluntary attention, to logical memory, and to the formation of concepts. All the higher functions originate as actual relations between human individuals. (Vygotsky, 1978, p. 57)

In other words, higher mental processes, such as directing your own attention and thinking through problems, first are *co-constructed* during shared activities between the child and another person. Then these **co-constructed processes** are internalized by the child and become part of that child's cognitive development (Gredler, 2009a, 2009b; Mercer, 2013). For example, children first use language in activities with others, to regulate the behavior of the others ("No nap!" or "I wanna cookie."). Later, however, the child can regulate her own behavior using private speech ("careful—don't spill"), as you will see in a later section. So, for Vygotsky, social interaction was more than influence; it was the origin of higher mental processes such as problem solving. Consider this example:

> A six-year-old has lost a toy and asks her father for help. The father asks her where she last saw the toy; the child says "I can't remember." He asks a series of questions—did you have it in your room? Outside? Next door? To each question, the child answers, "no." When he says "in the car?" she says "I think so" and goes to retrieve the toy. (Tharp & Gallimore, 1988, p. 14)

Who remembered? The answer is really neither the father nor the daughter, but the two together. The remembering and problem solving were co-constructed—between people—in the interaction. But the child (and the father) may have internalized strategies to use next time something is lost. At some point, the child will be able to function independently to solve this kind of problem. So, like the strategy for finding the toy, higher functions appear first between a child and a "teacher" before they exist within the individual child (Kozulin, 1990, 2003; Kozulin et al., 2003).

Here is another example of the social sources of individual thinking. Richard Anderson and his colleagues (2001) studied how fourth graders in small-group classroom discussions *appropriate* (take for themselves and use) argument stratagems that occur in the discussions. An *argument stratagem* is a particular form such as "I think [POSITION] because [REASON]," where the student fills in the position and the reason. For example, a student might say, "I think that the wolves should be left alone because they are not hurting anyone." Another strategy form is "If [ACTION], then [BAD CONSEQUENCE]," as in "If they don't trap the wolves, then the wolves will eat the cows." Other forms manage participation, for example, "What do you think [NAME]?" or "Let [NAME] talk."

Anderson's research identified 13 forms of talk and argument that helped to manage the discussion, get everyone to participate, present and defend positions, and handle confusion. The use of these different forms of talking and thinking *snowballed:* Once a useful argument was employed by one student, it spread to other students, and the argument stratagem form appeared more and more in the discussions. Open discussions—students asking and answering each other's questions—were better than teacher-dominated discussion for the development of these argument forms. Over time, these ways of presenting, attacking, and defending positions could be internalized as mental reasoning and decision making for the individual students.

Both Piaget and Vygotsky emphasized the importance of social interactions in cognitive development, but Piaget saw a different role for interaction. He believed that interaction encouraged development by creating disequilibrium—that is, cognitive conflict motivated change. Thus, Piaget believed that the most helpful interactions were those between peers, because peers are on an equal basis and can challenge each other's thinking. Vygotsky, on the other hand, suggested that children's cognitive development is fostered by interactions with people who are more capable or advanced in their thinking—people such as parents and teachers (Moshman, 1997; Palincsar, 1998). Of course, students can learn from both adults and peers, and today, computers can play a role in supporting communication across distances or in different languages.

Cultural Tools and Cognitive Development

Vygotsky believed that cultural tools, including technical tools (e.g., printing presses, plows, rulers, abacuses, graph paper—today, we would add mobile devices, computers, the Internet, real-time translators for mobile devices and chats, search engines, digital organizers and calendars, assistive technologies for students with learning challenges, etc.) and psychological tools (signs and symbol systems, e.g., numbers and mathematical systems, Braille and sign language, maps, works of art, codes, and language) play very important roles in cognitive development. For example, as long as the culture provides only Roman numerals for representing quantity, certain ways of thinking mathematically—from long division to calculus—are difficult or impossible. But if a number system has a zero, fractions, positive and negative values, and an infinite quantity of numbers, then much more is possible. The number system is a psychological tool that supports learning and cognitive development—it changes the thinking process. This symbol system is passed from adult to child and from child to child through formal and informal interactions and teachings.

TECHNICAL TOOLS IN A DIGITAL AGE. The use of technical tools such as calculators and spell checkers has been somewhat controversial in education. Technology is increasingly "checking up" on us. I rely on the spell checker in my word processing program to protect me from embarrassment. But I also read student papers with spelling replacements that must have come from decisions made by the word processing program—without a "sense check" by the writer. Is student learning harmed or helped by these technology supports? Just because students learned mathematics in the past with paper-and-pencil procedures and practice does not mean that this is the best way to learn. For example, in the Third International Mathematics and Science Study (Trends in International Mathematics and Science Study [TIMSS], 1998), on every test at the advanced level, students who said that they used calculators in their daily math course work performed much better than students who rarely or never used calculators. In fact, the research on calculators has found that rather than eroding basic skills, calculator use has positive effects on students' problem-solving skills and attitudes toward math (Ellington, 2003, 2013; Waits & Demana, 2000). There is a catch, however. On simple math problems it probably is better to attempt recalling or calculating the answer first before turning to a calculator. Self-generating answers before resorting to calculators supports math fact learning and fluency in arithmetic (Pyke & LeFevre, 2011).

PSYCHOLOGICAL TOOLS. Vygotsky believed that all higher-order mental processes such as reasoning and problem solving are *mediated* by (accomplished through and with the help of) psychological tools. These tools allow children to transform their thinking by enabling them to gain greater and greater mastery of their own cognitive processes; they advance their own development as they use the tools. Vygotsky believed the essence of cognitive development is mastering the use of psychological tools such as language to accomplish the kind of advanced thinking and problem solving that could not be accomplished without those tools (Gredler, 2012; Karpov & Haywood, 1998). The process is something like this: As children engage in activities with adults or more capable peers, they exchange ideas and ways of thinking about or representing concepts—drawing maps, for example, as a way to represent spaces and places. Children internalize these co-created ideas. Children's knowledge, ideas, attitudes, and values develop through *appropriating* or "taking for themselves" the ways of acting and thinking provided by both their culture and other members of their group (Wertsch, 2007).

In this exchange of signs and symbols and explanations, children begin to develop a "cultural tool kit" to make sense of and learn about their world (Wertsch, 1991). The kit is filled with technical tools such as graphing calculators or rulers directed toward the external world and psychological tools for acting mentally such as concepts, problem-solving strategies, and (as we saw earlier) argument stratagems. Children do not just receive the tools, however. They transform the tools as they construct their own representations, symbols, patterns, and understandings. These understandings are gradually changed as the children continue to engage in social activities and try to make sense of their world (John-Steiner & Mahn, 1996; Wertsch, 1991). In Vygotsky's theory, language is the most important symbol system in the tool kit, and it is the one that helps to fill the kit with other tools.

The Role of Language and Private Speech

Language is critical for cognitive development because it provides a way to express ideas and ask questions, the categories and concepts for thinking, and the links between the past and the future. Language frees us from the immediate situation to think about what was and what might be (Driscoll, 2005; Mercer, 2013). Vygotsky thought that:

> the specifically human capacity for language enables children to provide for auxiliary tools in the solution of difficult tasks, to overcome impulsive action, to plan a solution to a problem prior to its execution, and to master their own behavior. (Vygotsky, 1978, p. 28)

Vygotsky placed more emphasis than Piaget on the role of learning and language in cognitive development. He believed that "thinking depends on speech, on the means of thinking, and on the child's socio-cultural experience" (Vygotsky, 1987a, p. 120). And Vygotsky believed that language in the form of private speech (talking to yourself) guides cognitive development.

PRIVATE SPEECH: VYGOTSKY'S AND PIAGET'S VIEWS COMPARED. If you have spent much time around young children, you know that they often talk to themselves as they play. This can happen when the child is alone or, even more often, in a group of children—each child talks enthusiastically, without any real interaction or conversation. Piaget called this the **collective monologue**, and he labeled all of the children's self-directed talk "egocentric speech." He assumed that this egocentric speech is another indication that young children can't see the world through the eyes of others, so they chat away without taking into account the needs or interests of their listeners. As they mature, and especially as they have disagreements with peers, Piaget believed, children develop *socialized speech*. They learn to listen and exchange (or argue) ideas.

Vygotsky had very different ideas about young children's **private speech**. He suggested that, rather than being a sign of cognitive immaturity, these mutterings play an important role in cognitive development because they move children in stages toward *self-regulation:* the ability to plan, monitor, and guide your own thinking and problem solving. First the child's behavior is regulated by others using language and other signs such as gestures. For example, the parent says, "No!" when the child reaches toward a candle flame. Next, the child learns to regulate the behavior of others using the same language tools. The child says "No!" to another child who is trying to take away a toy, often even imitating the parent's voice tone. The child also begins to use private speech to regulate her own behavior, saying "no" quietly to herself as she is tempted to touch the flame. Finally, the child learns to regulate her own behavior by using silent inner speech (Karpov & Haywood, 1998).

For example, in any preschool room you might hear 4- or 5-year-olds saying, "No, it won't fit. Try it here. Turn. Turn. Maybe this one!" while they do puzzles. Around the age of 7, children's self-directed speech goes underground, changing from spoken to whispered speech and then to silent lip movements. Finally, the children just "think" the guiding words. The use of private speech peaks at around age 9 and then decreases, although one study found that some students from ages 11 to 17 still spontaneously muttered to themselves during problem solving (McCafferty, 2004; Winsler, Carlton, & Barry, 2000; Winsler & Naglieri, 2003). Vygotsky called this inner speech "an internal plane of verbal thinking" (Vygotsky, 1934/1987c, p. 279)—a critical accomplishment on the road to higher-order thinking.

This series of steps from spoken words to silent inner speech is another example of how higher mental functions first appear between people as they communicate and regulate each other's behavior, and then emerge again within the individual as cognitive processes. Through this fundamental process, the child is using language to accomplish important cognitive activities such as directing attention, solving problems, planning, forming concepts, and gaining self-control. Research supports Vygotsky's ideas (Berk & Spuhl, 1995; Emerson & Miyake, 2003). Children and adults tend to use more private speech when they are confused, having difficulties, or making mistakes (R. M. Duncan & Cheyne, 1999). Have you ever thought to yourself something like, "Let's see, the first step is" or "Where did I use my glasses last?" or "If I read to the end of this page, then I can . . ."? You were using inner speech to remind, cue, encourage, or guide yourself.

This internal verbal thinking is not stable until about age 12, so children in elementary school may need to continue talking through problems and explaining their reasoning in order to develop their abilities to control their thinking (Gredler, 2012). Because private speech helps students regulate their thinking, it makes sense to allow, and even encourage, students to use private speech in school. Teachers' insisting on total silence when young students are working on difficult problems may make the work even harder for them. Take note when muttering increases in your class—this could be a sign that students need help.

Table 2.4 contrasts Piaget's and Vygotsky's theories of private speech. We should note that Piaget accepted many of Vygotsky's arguments and came to agree that language could be used in both egocentric and problem-solving ways (Piaget, 1962).

TABLE 2.4 • **Differences Between Piaget's and Vygotsky's Theories of Egocentric, or Private, Speech**

	PIAGET	VYGOTSKY
	Represents an inability to take the perspective of another and engage in reciprocal communication.	Represents externalized thought; its function is to communicate with the self for the purpose of self-guidance and self-direction.
Course of Development	Declines with age.	Increases at younger ages and then gradually loses its audible quality to become internal verbal thought.
Relationship to Social Speech	Negative; least socially and cognitively mature children use more egocentric speech.	Positive; private speech develops out of social interaction with others.
Relationship to Environmental Contexts		Increases with task difficulty. Private speech serves a helpful self-guiding function in situations where more cognitive effort is needed to reach a solution.

Source: From "Development of Private Speech among Low-Income Appalachian Children," by L. E. Berk and R. A. Garvin, 1984, Developmental Psychology, 20, p. 272. Copyright © 1984 by the American Psychological Association. Adapted with permission.

The Zone of Proximal Development

According to Vygotsky, at any given point in development, a child is on the verge of solving certain problems—"processes that have not matured at the time but are in a period of maturation" (Vygotsky, 1930–1931/1998, p. 201). The child just needs some structure, demonstrations, clues, reminders, help with remembering details or steps, encouragement to keep trying, and so on. Some problems, of course, are beyond the child's capabilities, even if every step is explained clearly. The **zone of proximal development (ZPD)** is the area between the child's current performance (the problems the child can solve independently without any support) and the level of performance that the child could achieve with adult guidance or by working with "a more fully developed child" (p. 202). It is a dynamic and changing space as student and teacher interact and understandings are exchanged. This is the area where instruction can succeed. Kathleen Berger (2012) called this area the "magic middle"—somewhere between what the student already knows and what the student isn't ready to learn.

PRIVATE SPEECH AND THE ZONE. We can see how Vygotsky's beliefs about the role of private speech in cognitive development fit with the notion of the ZPD. Often, an adult uses verbal prompts and structuring to help a child solve a problem or accomplish a task. We will see later that this type of support has been called *scaffolding*. This support can be gradually reduced as the child takes over the guidance, perhaps first by giving the prompts as private speech and finally as inner speech. As an example, think of the young girl described earlier who had lost her toy. Let's move forward several years in her life and listen to her *thoughts* as an older student when she realizes that a schoolbook is missing. They might sound something like this:

"Where's my math book? Used it in class. Thought I put it in my book bag after class. Dropped my bag on the bus. That dope Larry kicked my stuff, so maybe. . . ."

The girl can now systematically search for ideas about the lost book without help from anyone.

THE ROLE OF LEARNING AND DEVELOPMENT. Piaget defined *development* as the active construction of knowledge and *learning* as the passive formation of associations (Siegler, 2000). He was interested in knowledge construction and believed that cognitive development has to come before learning—the child had to be cognitively "ready" to learn. He said that "learning is subordinated to development and not vice-versa" (Piaget, 1964, p. 17). Students can memorize, for example, that Geneva is in Switzerland, but still insist that they cannot be Genevan and Swiss at the same time. True understanding will take place only when the child has developed the operation of *class inclusion*—that one category can be included within another. But as we saw earlier, research has not supported Piaget's position on the need for cognitive development to precede learning (Brainerd, 2003).

In contrast, Vygotsky believed that learning is an active process that does not have to wait for readiness. In fact, "properly organized learning results in mental development and sets in motion a variety of developmental processes that would be impossible apart from learning" (Vygotsky, 1978, p. 90). He saw learning as a tool in development; learning pulls development up to higher levels, and social interaction is a key in learning. In other words, what develops next is what is affected by learning (Bodrova & Leong, 2012; Gredler, 2012; Wink & Putney, 2002). Vygotsky's belief that learning pulls development to higher levels and more advanced thinking means that other people, including teachers, play a significant role in cognitive development. This does not mean that Vygotsky believed memorization is learning. When teachers try to directly communicate their understanding, the result can be a "meaningless acquisition of words" and "mere verbalization" (Vygotsky 1934/1987b, p. 356) that actually hides an understanding vacuum (Gredler, 2012). In Vygotsky's words, the teacher "explains, informs, inquires, corrects, and forces the child to explain" (p. 216).

Limitations of Vygotsky's Theory

Vygotsky's theory added important considerations by highlighting the role of culture and social processes in cognitive development, but he may have gone too far. As you have seen in this chapter, we may be born with a greater store of cognitive tools than either Piaget or Vygotsky suggested.

Video 2.3
In this video, one teacher guides young children in putting together puzzles and another guides a boy to create a pattern by organizing toy trucks based on color. Is the process of organizing toys in a pattern based on color a skill that is in the boy's zone of proximal development, or is it still too advanced for a child at his developmental level?

ENHANCEDetext *video example*

Some basic understandings, such as the idea that adding increases quantity, may be part of our biological predispositions, ready for use to guide our cognitive development. Young children appear to figure out much about the world before they have the chance to learn from either their culture or teachers (Schunk, 2012; Woodward & Needham, 2009). The major limitation of Vygotsky's theory, however, is that it consists mostly of general ideas; Vygotsky died before he could expand and elaborate on his ideas and pursue his research. His students continued to investigate his ideas, but much of that work was suppressed by Stalin's regime until the 1950s and 1960s (Gredler, 2005, 2009b; Kozulin, 1990, 2003; Kozulin et al., 2003). A final limitation might be that Vygotsky did not have time to detail the applications of his theories for teaching, even though he was very interested in instruction. So, most of the applications described today have been created by others—and we don't even know if Vygotsky would agree with them. It is clear that some of his concepts, like ZPD, have been misrepresented at times (Gredler, 2012).

ENHANCEDetext *self-check*

IMPLICATIONS OF PIAGET'S AND VYGOTSKY'S THEORIES FOR TEACHERS

Piaget did not make specific educational recommendations, and Vygotsky did not have enough time to develop a complete set of applications. But we can glean some guidance from both men.

Piaget: What Can We Learn?

Piaget was more interested in understanding children's thinking than in guiding teachers. He did express some general ideas about educational philosophy, however. He believed that the main goal of education should be to help children learn how to learn, and that education should "form not furnish" the minds of students (Piaget, 1969, p. 70). Piaget has taught us that we can learn a great deal about how children think by listening carefully and by paying close attention to their ways of solving problems. If we understand children's thinking, we will be better able to match teaching methods to children's current knowledge and abilities; in other words, we will be better able to differentiate instruction.

Even though Piaget did not design programs of education based on his ideas, his influence on current educational practice is huge (Hindi & Perry, 2007). For example, the National Association for the Education of Young Children has guidelines for developmentally appropriate practice (DAP) that incorporate Piaget's findings (Bredekamp, 2011; Bredekamp & Copple, 1997).

Connect and Extend to PRAXIS II®

Implications of Piaget's Theory (I, A2)
The music, physical education, and art teachers in a rural, pre-K-to-8 school district work with students who characterize several of Piaget's stages. How should these three teachers adjust their teaching from level to level over the course of a week?

UNDERSTANDING AND BUILDING ON STUDENTS' THINKING. The students in any class will vary greatly in both their level of cognitive development and their academic knowledge. As a teacher, how can you determine whether students are having trouble because they lack the necessary thinking abilities or because they simply have not learned the basic facts? To do this, Case (1985) suggests you observe your students carefully as they try to solve the problems you have presented. What kind of logic do they use? Do they focus on only one aspect of the situation? Are they fooled by appearances? Do they suggest solutions systematically or by guessing and forgetting what they have already tried? Ask your students how they tried to solve the problem. Listen to their strategies. What kind of thinking is behind repeated mistakes or problems? Students are the best sources of information about their own thinking (Confrey, 1990).

An important implication of Piaget's theory for teaching is what J. Hunt years ago (1961) called, "the problem of the match." Students must be neither bored by work that is too simple nor left behind by teaching they cannot understand. According to Hunt, disequilibrium must be kept "just right" to encourage growth. Setting up situations that lead to unexpected results can help create an appropriate level of disequilibrium. When students experience some conflict between what they think should happen (a piece of wood should sink because it is big) and what actually happens (it floats!), they may rethink the situation, and new knowledge may develop.

Many materials and lessons can be understood at several levels and can be "just right" for a range of cognitive abilities. Classics such as *Alice in Wonderland,* myths, and fairy tales can be enjoyed at both concrete and symbolic levels. It is also possible for a group of students to be introduced to a topic together, and then work individually on follow-up activities matched to their learning needs. Using multilevel lessons is called *differentiated instruction* (Hipsky, 2011; Tomlinson, 2005b). We will look at this approach more closely in Chapter 14.

ACTIVITY AND CONSTRUCTING KNOWLEDGE. Piaget's fundamental insight was that individuals construct their own understanding; learning is a constructive process. At every level of cognitive development, you will also want to see that students are actively engaged in the learning process. In Piaget's words:

> Knowledge is not a copy of reality. To know an object, to know an event, is not simply to look at it and make a mental copy or image of it. To know an object is to act on it. To know is to modify, to transform the object, and to understand the process of this transformation, and as a consequence to understand the way the object is constructed. (Piaget, 1964, p. 8)

For example, research in teaching mathematics indicates that students from kindergarten to college remember basic facts better when they have learned using manipulatives versus using abstract symbols only (Carbonneau, Marley, & Selig, 2012). But this active experience, even at the earliest school levels, should not be limited to the physical manipulation of objects. It should also include mental manipulation of ideas that arise out of class projects or experiments (Gredler, 2005, 2012). For example, after a social studies lesson on different jobs, a primary-grade teacher might show students a picture of a woman and ask, "What could this person be?" After answers such as "teacher," "doctor," "secretary," "lawyer," "saleswoman," and so on, the teacher could suggest, "How about a daughter?" Answers such as "sister," "mother," "aunt," and "granddaughter" may follow. This should help the children switch dimensions in their classification and center on another aspect of the situation. Next, the teacher might suggest "American," "jogger," or "blonde." With older children, hierarchical classification might be involved: It is a picture of a woman, who is a human being; a human being is a primate, which is a mammal, which is an animal, which is a life form.

All students need to interact with teachers and peers in order to test their thinking, to be challenged, to receive feedback, and to watch how others work out problems. Disequilibrium is often set in motion quite naturally when the teacher or another student suggests a new way of thinking about something. As a general rule, students should act on, manipulate, observe, and then talk and/or write about (to the teacher and each other) what they have experienced. Concrete experiences provide the raw materials for thinking. Communicating with others makes students use, test, and sometimes change their thinking strategies.

Vygotsky: What Can We Learn?

Like Piaget, Vygotsky believed that the main goal of education was the development of higher mental functions, not simply filling students' memories with facts. So Vygotsky probably would oppose educational curricula that are an inch deep and a mile wide or seem like "trivial pursuit." As an example of this trivial pursuit curriculum, Margaret Gredler (2009a) described a set of materials for a 9-week science unit that had 61 glossary terms such as *aqueous solution, hydrogen bonding,* and *fractional crystallization*—many terms described with only one or two sentences.

There are at least three ways that higher mental functions can be developed through cultural tools and passed from one individual to another: *imitative* learning (one person tries to imitate the other), *instructed* learning (learners internalize the instructions of the teacher and use these

Connect and Extend to PRAXIS II®

Implications of Vygotsky's Theory (I, A2)
Make a list of scaffolding techniques that would be appropriate with different instructional levels and content areas. Think of scaffolding techniques that others have used when you learned things outside of school (e.g., sports, hobbies).

instructions to self-regulate), and *collaborative* learning (a group of peers strives to understand each other and learning occurs in the process) (Tomasello, Kruger, & Ratner, 1993). Vygotsky was most concerned with the second type, *instructed* learning through direct teaching or by structuring experiences that encourage another's learning, but his theory supports learning through *imitation* or *collaboration* as well. Thus, Vygotsky's ideas are relevant for educators who teach directly, intentionally use modeling to teach, or create collaborative learning environments (Das, 1995; Wink & Putney, 2002). That pretty much includes all of us.

THE ROLE OF ADULTS AND PEERS. Vygotsky believed the child is not alone in the world "discovering" the cognitive operations of conservation or classification. This discovery is assisted or mediated by family members, teachers, peers, and even software tools (Puntambekar & Hubscher, 2005). Most of this guidance is communicated through language, at least in Western cultures. In some cultures, observing a skilled performance, not talking about it, guides the child's learning (Rogoff, 1990). Some people have called this adult assistance **scaffolding**, taken from Wood, Bruner, and Ross (1976). The idea is that children use the help for support while they build a firm understanding that will eventually allow them to solve the problems on their own. Actually, when Wood and his colleagues introduced the term *scaffolding,* they were talking about how teachers set up or structure learning environments, but Vygotsky's theory implies more dynamic exchanges between student and teacher that allow the teacher to support students in the parts of the task they cannot do alone—the interactions of assisted learning, as you will see next (Schunk, 2012).

Video 2.4
The children in this class are learning about earthworms. How does the teacher guide the students to encourage them to make their own discoveries?

ENHANCEDetext *video example*

ASSISTED LEARNING. Vygotsky's theory suggests that teachers need to do more than just arrange the environment so that students can discover on their own. Children cannot and should not be expected to reinvent or rediscover knowledge already available in their cultures. Rather, they should be guided and assisted in their learning (Karpov & Haywood, 1998).

Assisted learning, or guided participation, requires first learning from the student what is needed; then giving information, prompts, reminders, and encouragement at the right time and in the right amounts; and gradually allowing the students to do more and more on their own. Teachers can assist learning by adapting materials or problems to students' current levels; demonstrating skills or thought processes; walking students through the steps of a complicated problem; doing part of the problem (e.g., in algebra, the students set up the equation and the teacher does the calculations or vice versa); giving detailed feedback and allowing revisions; or asking questions that refocus students' attention (Rosenshine & Meister, 1992). Cognitive apprenticeships (Chapter 10) are examples. Look at Table 2.5 for examples of strategies that can be used in any lesson.

An Example Curriculum: Tools of the Mind

Deborah Leong and Elena Bodrova (2012) worked for years to develop a curriculum for preschool through second-grade children based on Vygotsky's theory. In Russia, Dr. Bodrova had studied with students and colleagues of Vygotsky and wanted to bring his ideas to teachers. The result is the *Tools*

TABLE 2.5 • Strategies to Provide Scaffolding

- Model the thought process for the students: Think out loud as you solve the problem or outline an essay, for example.
- Provide organizers or starters such as *who, what, why, how, what next?*
- Do part of the problem.
- Give hints and cues.
- Encourage students to set short-term goals and take small steps.
- Connect new learning to students' interests or prior learning.
- Use graphic organizers: timelines, charts, tables, categories, checklists, and graphs.
- Simplify the task, clarify the purpose, and give clear directions.
- Teach key vocabulary and provide examples.

FIGURE 2.5

BRANDON'S PLAY PLANS

At the beginning of age three, Brandon's play plans show that he wants to go to the art center. By the end of age four, Brandon plans to pretend to be a king. He is beginning to use sounds in writing.

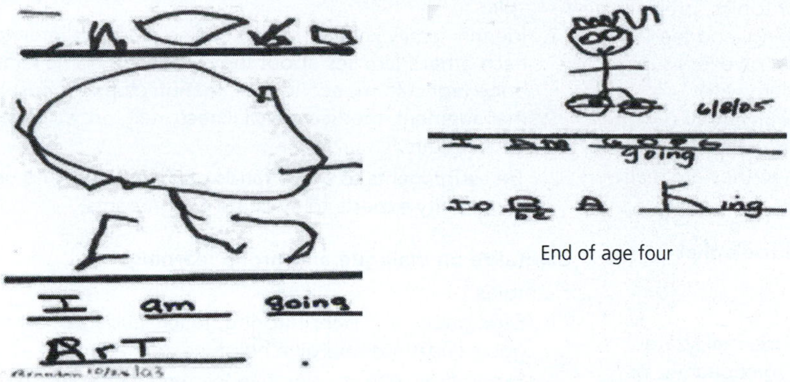

End of age four

Beginning of age three

Source: "Brandon's Plan, Beginning Age 3 Preschool". Tools of the Mind. http://www.toolsofthemind .org/curriculum/preschool. Used by permission.

of the Mind project that includes curriculum ideas for preschool, kindergarten, and special needs (see toolsofthemind.org). One key idea taken from Vygotsky is that as children develop mental tools such as strategies for focusing attention, they cease being prisoners of their environment—having their attention "grabbed away" by any new sight or sound. They learn to control their attention. A second key idea is that play, particularly dramatic pretend play, is the most important activity supporting the development of young children. Through dramatic play children learn to focus attention, control impulses, follow rules, use symbols, regulate their own behaviors, and cooperate with others. So a key element of the *Tools of the Mind* curriculum for young children is play plans, created by the students themselves. Children draw a picture of how they plan to play that day, and then describe it to the teacher, who may make notes on the page and thus model literacy activities. Plans become more complex and detailed as children become better planners. Figure 2.5 shows Brandon's simple play plan at the beginning of age three and then another plan at the end of age four. His later plan shows better fine motor control, more mature drawing, increased imagination, and greater use of language.

Reaching Every Student: Teaching in the "Magic Middle"

Both Piaget and Vygotsky probably would agree that students need to be taught in the magic middle (Berger, 2012), or the place of the "match" (J. Hunt, 1961)—where they are neither bored nor frustrated. Students should be put in situations where they have to reach to understand but where support from other students, learning materials, or the teacher is also available. Sometimes the best teacher is another student who has just figured out how to solve the problem, because this student is probably operating in the learner's ZPD. Having a student work with someone who is just a bit better at the activity would be a good idea because both students benefit in the exchange of explanations, elaborations, and questions. In addition, students should be encouraged to use language to organize their thinking and to talk about what they are trying to accomplish. Dialogue and discussion are important avenues to learning (Karpov & Bransford, 1995; Kozulin & Presseisen, 1995; Wink & Putney, 2002). The *Guidelines: Applying Vygotsky's Ideas in Teaching* on the next page gives more ideas for applying Vygotsky's insights.

Connect and Extend to PRAXIS II®

Distinctions Between Piaget's and Vygotsky's Theories (I, A2)
Consider how two teachers—one based in Vygotskian theory and one based in Piagetian theory—might differ in their concepts of learning and teaching and the instructional techniques that they might prefer.

GUIDELINES
Applying Vygotsky's Ideas in Teaching

Tailor scaffolding to the needs of students.

Examples

1. When students are beginning new tasks or topics, provide models, prompts, sentence starters, coaching, and feedback. As the students grow in competence, give less support and more opportunities for independent work.
2. Give students choices about the level of difficulty or degree of independence in projects; encourage them to challenge themselves but to seek help when they are really stuck.

Make sure students have access to powerful tools that support thinking.

Examples

1. Teach students to use learning and organizational strategies, research tools, language tools (wikis, dictionaries, or computer searches), spreadsheets, and word-processing programs.
2. Model the use of tools; show students how you use an appointment book or electronic notebook to make plans and manage time, for example.

Build on the students' cultural funds of knowledge (N. Gonzalez, Moll, & Amanti, 2005; Moll et al., 1992).

Examples

1. Identify family knowledge by having students interview each other's families about their work and home knowledge (agriculture, economics, manufacturing, household management, medicine and illness, religion, child care, cooking, etc.).
2. Tie assignments to these funds of knowledge, and use community experts to evaluate assignments.

Capitalize on dialogue and group learning.

Examples

1. Experiment with peer tutoring; teach students how to ask good questions and give helpful explanations.
2. Experiment with cooperative learning strategies described in Chapter 10.

Source: For more information about Vygotsky and his theories, see tip.psychology.org/vygotsky.html

Cognitive Development: Lessons for Teachers

In spite of cross-cultural differences in cognitive development and the different theories of development, there are some convergences. Piaget, Vygotsky, and more recent researchers studying cognitive development and the brain probably would agree with the following big ideas:

1. Cognitive development requires both physical and social stimulation.
2. To develop thinking, children have to be mentally, physically, and linguistically active. They need to experiment, talk, describe, reflect, write, and solve problems. But they also benefit from teaching, guidance, questions, explanations, demonstrations, and challenges to their thinking.
3. Teaching students what they already know is boring. Trying to teach what the student isn't ready to learn is frustrating and ineffective.
4. Challenge with support will keep students engaged but not fearful.

ENHANCEDetext *self-check*

SUMMARY

- **A Definition of Development (pp. 32–34)**

  What are the different kinds of development? Human development can be divided into physical development (changes in the body), personal development (changes in an individual's personality), social development (changes in the way an individual relates to others), and cognitive development (changes in thinking).

  What are three questions about development and three general principles? For decades, psychologists and the public have debated whether development is shaped more by nature or nurture, whether change is a continuous process or involves qualitative differences or stages, and whether there are critical times for the development of certain abilities. We know today that these simple either/or distinctions cannot capture the complexities of human development where coactions and interactions are the rule. Theorists generally agree that people develop at different rates, that development is an orderly process, and that development takes place gradually.

- **The Brain and Cognitive Development (pp. 34–44)**

What part of the brain is associated with higher mental functions? The cortex is a crumpled sheet of neurons that serves three major functions: receiving signals from sense organs (such as visual or auditory signals), controlling voluntary movement, and forming connections. The part of the cortex that controls physical motor movement develops or matures first, then the areas that control complex senses such as vision and hearing, and last, the frontal lobe, which controls higher-order thinking processes.

What is lateralization, and why is it important? Lateralization is the specialization of the two sides, or hemispheres, of the brain. For most people, the left hemisphere is the major factor in language, and the right hemisphere is prominent in spatial and visual processing. Even though certain functions are associated with particular parts of the brain, the various parts and systems of the brain work together to learn and perform complex activities such as reading and constructing understanding.

What are some implications for teachers? Recent advances in both methods and findings in the neurosciences provide exciting information about brain activity during learning and brain activity differences among people with varying abilities and challenges and from different cultures. These findings have some basic implications for teaching, but many of the strategies offered by "brain-based" advocates are simply good teaching. Perhaps we now know more about why these strategies work.

- **Piaget's Theory of Cognitive Development (pp. 44–56)**

What are the main influences on cognitive development? Piaget's theory of cognitive development is based on the assumption that people try to make sense of the world and actively create knowledge through direct experiences with objects, people, and ideas. Maturation, activity, social transmission, and the need for equilibrium all influence the way thinking processes and knowledge develop. In response to these influences, thinking processes and knowledge develop through changes in the organization of thought (the development of schemes) and through adaptation—including the complementary processes of assimilation (incorporating into existing schemes) and accommodation (changing existing schemes).

What is a scheme? Schemes are the basic building blocks of thinking. They are organized systems of actions or thought that allow us to mentally represent or "think about" the objects and events in our world. Schemes may be very small and specific (grasping, recognizing a square), or they may be larger and more general (using a map in a new city). People adapt to their environment as they increase and organize their schemes.

As children move from sensorimotor to formal-operational thinking, what are the major changes? Piaget believed that young people pass through four stages as they develop: sensorimotor, preoperational, concrete-operational, and formal-operational. In the sensorimotor stage, infants explore the world through their senses and motor activity, and they work toward mastering object permanence and performing goal-directed activities. In the preoperational stage, symbolic thinking and logical operations begin. Children in the stage of concrete operations can think logically about tangible situations and can demonstrate conservation, reversibility, classification, and seriation. The ability to perform hypothetico-deductive reasoning, coordinate a set of variables, and imagine other worlds marks the stage of formal operations.

How do neo-Piagetian and information processing views explain changes in children's thinking over time? Information processing theories focus on attention, memory capacity, learning strategies, and other processing skills to explain how children develop rules and strategies for making sense of the world and solving problems. Neo-Piagetian approaches also look at attention, memory, and strategies and at how thinking develops in different domains such as numbers or spatial relations. Research in neuroscience suggests that when learning a new skill, children move through three tiers—from *actions* to *representations* to *abstractions*. Within each tier, the pattern is moving from accomplishing a single action to mapping or coordinating two actions together such as coordinating addition and multiplication in math, to creating whole systems of understanding.

What are some limitations of Piaget's theory? Piaget's theory has been criticized because children and adults often think in ways that are inconsistent with the notion of invariant stages. It also appears that Piaget underestimated children's cognitive abilities; he insisted that children could not be taught the operations of the next stage but had to develop them on their own. Alternative explanations place greater emphasis on students' developing information processing skills and ways teachers can enhance their development. Piaget's work is also criticized for overlooking cultural factors in child development.

- **Vygotsky's Sociocultural Perspective (pp. 56–62)**

  According to Vygotsky, what are three main influences on cognitive development? Vygotsky believed that human activities must be understood in their cultural settings. He believed that our specific mental structures and processes can be traced to our interactions with others; that the tools of the culture, especially the tool of language, are key factors in development; and that the ZPD is where learning and development are possible.

  What are psychological tools and why are they important? Psychological tools are signs and symbol systems such as numbers and mathematical systems, codes, and language that support learning and cognitive development. They change the thinking process by enabling and shaping thinking. Many of these tools are passed from adult to child through formal and informal interactions and teachings.

  Explain how interpsychological development becomes intrapsychological development. Higher mental processes appear first between people as they are co-constructed during shared activities. As children engage in activities with adults or more capable peers, they exchange ideas and ways of thinking about or representing concepts. Children internalize these co-created ideas. Children's knowledge, ideas, attitudes, and values develop through appropriating, or "taking for themselves," the ways of acting and thinking provided by their culture and by the more capable members of their group.

  What are the differences between Piaget's and Vygotsky's perspectives on private speech and its role in development? Vygotsky's sociocultural view asserts that cognitive development hinges on social interaction and the development of language. As an example, Vygotsky describes the role of children's self-directed talk in guiding and monitoring thinking and problem solving, whereas Piaget suggests that private speech is an indication of the child's egocentrism. Vygotsky, more than Piaget, emphasized the significant role played by adults and more-able peers in children's learning. This adult assistance provides early support while students build the understanding necessary to solve problems on their own later.

  What is a student's ZPD? At any given point in development, there are certain problems that a child is on the verge of being able to solve and others that are beyond the child's capabilities. The ZPD is where the child cannot solve a problem alone but can succeed under adult guidance or in collaboration with a more advanced peer.

  What are two criticisms or limitations of Vygotsky's theory? Vygotsky may have overemphasized the role of social interaction in cognitive development; children figure out quite a bit on their own. Also, because he died so young, Vygotsky was not able to develop and elaborate on his theories. His students and others since have taken up that work.

- **Implications of Piaget's and Vygotsky's Theories for Teachers (pp. 62–66)**

  What is the "problem of the match" described by Hunt? The "problem of the match" is that students must be neither bored by work that is too simple nor left behind by teaching they cannot understand. According to Hunt, disequilibrium must be carefully balanced to encourage growth. Situations that lead to errors can help create an appropriate level of disequilibrium.

  What is active learning? Why is Piaget's theory of cognitive development consistent with active learning? Piaget's fundamental insight was that individuals construct their own understanding; learning is a constructive process. At every level of cognitive development, students must be able to incorporate information into their own schemes. To do this, they must act on the information in some way. This active experience, even at the earliest school levels, should include both physical manipulation of objects and mental manipulation of ideas. As a general rule, students should act, manipulate, observe, and then talk and/or write about what they have experienced. Concrete experiences provide the raw materials for thinking. Communicating with others makes students use, test, and sometimes change their thinking abilities.

  What is assisted learning, and what role does scaffolding play? Assisted learning, or guided participation in the classroom, requires scaffolding—understanding the students' needs; giving information, prompts, reminders, and encouragement at the right time and in the right amounts; and then gradually allowing the students to do more and more on their own. Teachers can assist learning by adapting materials or problems to students' current levels, demonstrating skills or thought processes, walking students through the steps of a complicated problem, doing part of the problem, giving detailed feedback and allowing revisions, or asking questions that refocus students' attention.

PRACTICE USING WHAT YOU HAVE LEARNED

To access and complete the exercises, click the link under the images below.

Zone of Proximal Development

ENHANCEDetext *application exercise*

Developmental Differences

ENHANCEDetext *application exercise*

KEY TERMS

CONNECT AND EXTEND TO LICENSURE

MULTIPLE-CHOICE QUESTIONS

1. Mr. Winstel was worried about his former star student, Ramon. As the seventh-grade year progressed, Ramon was frequently being called into the principal's office for skateboard stunts that broke school rules and bordered on dangerous. Recently, Ramon's parents contacted Mr. Winstel to alert him to the fact that Ramon had been skipping school to hang out with some older boys in the neighborhood. Which of the following answers would typically best describe what is happening with Ramon?
   A. Ramon's culture demands that boys of his age begin to engage in behaviors that reflect fearlessness.
   B. Ramon's limbic system is maturing, but his prefrontal lobe has not yet caught up.
   C. Ramon is engaging in deviant behaviors as a cry for attention from his parents.
   D. Ramon is undergoing a period of synaptic pruning, which causes adolescents to engage in risk-taking behavior.

2. Miss McClintock discovered that five of the children in her class were developmentally advanced. All of the students' language skills were exploding! Although many of the students still had trouble sharing, a few appeared to understand that by sharing, everyone could be happy. Finally, there was even one child who could solve conservation problems. According to Piagetian theory, in what stage are the students in Miss McClintock's class?
   A. Formal Operations
   B. Concrete Operations
   C. Preoperational
   D. Sensorimotor

3. In introducing students to persuasive advertising methods, which of the following approaches would be most apt to lead to student retention?
   A. Determine what students already know about the topic, and connect new information to their prior knowledge.
   B. Have students initially watch several commercials and take notes.
   C. Lecture students on the major persuasive techniques, and have a quiz to assess learning.
   D. Have students form groups to research persuasive techniques.

4. Research studies involving the brain and learning indicate all but which one of the following statements is true?
   A. There is no such thing as "left-brain" and "right-brain" thinking.
   B. The production of new neurons continues into adulthood.
   C. Using different modalities for instruction and activities that draw on different senses may support learning.
   D. Pruning can damage heavily used cognitive pathways.

CONSTRUCTED-RESPONSE QUESTIONS

Case

When planning for instruction, Mr. Gething remembered that students should be neither bored nor frustrated. Although this made sense to him, he was unsure how he would compensate for the diverse group of students he had in his second-period language arts class. Some students had difficulty with the English language, and other students planned to participate in the school's annual Shakespearean play. He knew that by grouping students of mixed ability, he could occasionally draw on the talents of his knowledgeable students to assist the less-advanced students. He also understood that without guidelines, students might not accomplish anything.

5. Explain the theory of learning Mr. Gething is initially drawing on, and identify the individual credited with it.
6. What is the term for the assistance that the more knowledgeable class members may provide to the less-advanced students in order for them to succeed? List some strategies these students might use to assist their peers.

ENHANCEDetext *licensure exam*

TEACHERS' CASEBOOK

WHAT WOULD THEY DO? SYMBOLS AND CYMBALS

Here is how several expert teachers said they would help their students understand abstract concepts.

LINDA GLISSON AND SUE MIDDLETON—Fifth-Grade Team Teachers

St. James Episcopal Day School, Baton Rouge, LA

To begin the lesson, I would have the students use a dictionary to define the word *symbolism* (root word—*symbol*) to discover that it means "something that stands for or represents something else." I would then give them a brief "across the curriculum" exercise in ways they incorporate symbols and symbolism into their thinking every day. Examples follow. *Social studies, American history:* The American flag is just a piece of cloth. Why then do we recite a pledge to it? Stand at attention when it passes in a parade? What does it stand for? *English, literature—fables and fairy tales:* What does the wolf usually represent (stand for)? The lion? The lamb? *Art:* What color stands for a glorious summer day? Evil? Goodness and purity? I would continue with math symbols, scientific symbols, and music symbols and lead the students toward contributing other examples such as symbols representing holidays. I would then tell them about their own examples of symbolism that I had recorded. The students' participation in and enthusiasm for the exercises would serve to determine whether they were ready for the material.

DR. NANCY SHEEHAN-MELZACK—Art and Music Teacher
Snug Harbor Community School, Quincy, MA

Even very young children can recognize symbols if the symbol is presented first and the explanation required second. A drawing of an octagon on a pole has always elicited the answer, "A stop sign," whenever I have shown it. Children recognize symbols, but the teacher needs to work from their concrete knowledge to the more abstract concept, and there are a great many symbols in their daily life on which one can draw. Children as young as first-graders can recognize traffic sign shapes, letters of the alphabet, and numbers, and further can recognize that they stand for directions, sounds, and how many. When they talk about these very common symbols, they can also realize they all use them for the same meaning.

VALERIE A. CHILCOAT—Fifth/Sixth-Grade
Advanced Academics
Glenmount School, Baltimore, MD

Concrete examples of symbolism must come from the students' own world. Street signs, especially those with pictures and not words, are a great example. These concrete symbols, however, are not exactly the same as symbolism used in poetry. The link has to be made from the concrete to the abstract. Silly poetry is one way to do this. It is motivating to the students to read or listen to, and it can provide many examples of one thing acting as another. This strategy can also be used in lower grades to simply expose children to poetry containing symbolism.

KAREN BOYARSKY—Fifth-Grade Teacher
Walter C. Black Elementary School, Hightstown, NJ

You can tell a lot about students' thinking simply by interpreting their reactions. Knowing how to interpret students' reactions is just as important as any other assessment tool you might use. In this case, it is clear that the students are confused about the concept of symbolism. This is a difficult concept even for many fifth-graders to understand and should be approached slowly. One approach to this topic would be to present students with pictures of familiar symbols, such as McDonald's Golden Arches, the Nike Swoosh, or the Target logo. Students could attempt to explain what each of these symbols mean. A discussion about why manufacturers choose to use symbols instead of words would follow. Another approach would be to have the students interpret comparisons that use *like* or *as*. For example, "Sue is as pretty as a flower." The teacher would guide the student to see that the author is using a flower to symbolize Sue's looks.

3 | THE SELF, SOCIAL, AND MORAL DEVELOPMENT

TEACHERS' CASEBOOK

WHAT WOULD YOU DO? MEAN GIRLS

You have seen it before, but this year the situation in your middle school classroom seems especially vicious. A clique of popular girls has made life miserable for several of their former friends—who are now "rejects." The discarded friends have committed the social sins of not fitting in—they wear the wrong clothes or aren't "pretty" enough or aren't interested in boys yet. To keep the status distinctions clear between themselves and "the others," the popular girls spread gossip about their former friends, often disclosing the intimate secrets revealed when the "out" girls and the "in" girls were *best* friends—only a few months ago.

Today, you discover that Stephanie, one of the rejected girls, has written a long, heart-baring e-mail to her former best friend, Alison, asking why Alison is "acting so mean." The now-popular Alison forwarded the e-mail to the entire school, and Stephanie is humiliated. She has been absent for 3 days since the incident.

CRITICAL THINKING

- How would you respond to each of the girls?
- What—if anything—would you say to your other students?
- Are there ways you can address the issues raised by this situation in your classes?
- Reflecting on your years in school, were your experiences more like those of Alison or Stephanie?

OVERVIEW AND OBJECTIVES

Schooling involves more than cognitive development. As you think back on your years in school, what stands out—highlights of academic knowledge or memories of feelings, friendships, and fears? In this chapter, we examine the latter, which comprise personal, social, and moral development.

We begin by looking at a basic aspect of development that affects all the others—physical changes as students mature. Then we explore Urie Bronfenbrenner's bioecological theory and use it as a framework for examining three major influences on children's personal and social development: families, peers, and teachers. Families today have gone through many transitions, and these changes affect the roles of teachers. Next, we explore ideas about how we come to understand ourselves by looking at self-concept and identity, including racial-ethnic identity. Erikson's psychosocial theory provides a lens for viewing these developments. Finally, we consider moral development. What factors determine our views about morality? What can teachers do to foster such personal qualities as honesty and cooperation? Why do students cheat in their academic work, and what can be done?

By the time you have completed this chapter, you should be able to:

Objective 3.1 Describe general trends, group differences, and challenges in physical development through childhood and adolescence.

Objective 3.2 Discuss how the components of Bronfenbrenner's bioecological model influence development, especially the impact of families, parenting styles, peers, and teachers.

Objective 3.3 Describe general trends and group differences in the development of identity and self-concept.

Objective 3.4 Explain theories of moral development including those of Kohlberg, Gilligan, Nucci, and Haidt, and how teachers can deal with one moral challenge for students—cheating.

PHYSICAL DEVELOPMENT

This chapter is about personal and social development, but we begin with a kind of development that is a basic concern of all individuals and families—physical development.

- -

STOP & THINK How tall are you? What grade were you in when you reached that height? Were you one of the tallest or shortest students in your middle or high school, or were you about average? Did you know students who were teased because of something about their physical appearance? How important was your physical development to your feelings about yourself? •

- -

Physical and Motor Development

For most children, at least in the early years, growing up means getting bigger and stronger, and becoming more coordinated. It also can be a frightening, disappointing, exciting, and puzzling time.

YOUNG CHILDREN. Preschool children are very active. Their *gross-motor* (large muscle) skills improve greatly during these early years. Between ages 2 and about 4 or 5, preschoolers' muscles grow stronger, their brains develop to better integrate information about movements, their balance improves, and their center of gravity moves lower, so they are able to run, jump, climb, and hop. By age 2, most children stop "toddling." Their awkward, wide-legged gait becomes smooth and rhythmic; they have perfected walking. During their third year, most children learn to run, throw, and jump, but these activities are not well controlled until age 4 or 5. Most of these movements develop naturally if the child has normal physical abilities and the opportunity to play. Children with physical problems, however, may need special training to develop these skills. And because they can't always judge when to stop, many preschoolers need interludes of rest scheduled after periods of physical exertion (Darcey & Travers, 2006; Thomas & Thomas, 2008).

Fine-motor skills such as tying shoes or fastening buttons, which require the coordination of small movements, also improve greatly during the preschool years. Children should be given the chance to work with large paintbrushes, fat pencils and crayons, large pieces of drawing paper, large Legos, and soft clay or play dough to accommodate their current skills. During this time, children will begin to develop a lifelong preference for their right or left hand. By age 5, about 90% of students prefer their right hand for most skilled work, and 10% or so prefer their left hand, with more boys than girls being left-handed (R. S. Feldman, 2004; E. L. Hill & Khanem, 2009). Handedness is a genetically based preference, so don't try to make children switch.

ELEMENTARY SCHOOL YEARS. During the elementary school years, physical development is fairly steady for most children. They become taller, leaner, and stronger, so they are better able to master sports and games. There is tremendous variation among children, however. A particular child can be much larger or smaller than average and still be perfectly healthy. Because children at this age are very aware of physical differences but are not the most tactful people, you may overhear comments such as "You're too little to be in fifth grade. What's wrong with you?" or "How come you're so fat?"

Throughout elementary school, many of the girls are likely to be as large as or larger than the boys in their classes. Between the ages of 11 and 14, girls are, on average, taller and heavier than boys of the same age. This size discrepancy can give girls an advantage in physical activities, but some girls may feel conflict over this and, as a result, downplay their physical abilities (Woolfolk & Perry, 2015).

THE ADOLESCENT YEARS. Puberty marks the beginning of sexual maturity. It is not a single event, but a series of changes involving almost every part of the body. The sex differences in physical development observed during the later elementary years become even more pronounced at the beginning of puberty. But these changes take time. The earliest visible signs of puberty in girls are the growth of nipples and budding of their breasts at around age 10 for European American and Canadian adolescents. At about the same time, boys' testes and scrotum begin to grow larger. On average, between ages 12 and 13, girls have their first menstrual period (called menarche), but the range is from age 10 to 16½. Boys have their first sperm ejaculation (called spermarche) between the ages of 12 to 14. Boys develop facial hair over the next several years, reaching their final beard potential by about age 18 or 19—with some exceptions who take longer to develop their final facial hair. Less-welcome changes in puberty are increases in skin oiliness, skin acne, and body odor.

Girls reach their final height by age 15 or 16, several years ahead of boys, so there is a time in middle school, as in late elementary school, when many girls are taller than their male classmates. Most boys continue growing until about age 19, but both boys and girls can continue to grow slightly until about age 25 (Thomas & Thomas, 2008; Wigfield, Byrnes, & Eccles, 2006). The ages for reaching maximum height are a bit younger for African American and Latino/a adolescents and a bit older for Asian Americans.

EARLY AND LATER MATURING. Psychologists have been particularly interested in the academic, social, and emotional differences between adolescents who mature early and those who mature later. For girls, maturing way ahead of classmates can be a definite disadvantage. Being larger and more "developed" than everyone else your age is not a valued characteristic for girls in many cultures (D. C. Jones, 2004; Mendle & Ferrero, 2012). Early maturation is associated with emotional difficulties such as depression, anxiety, lower achievement in school, drug and alcohol abuse, unplanned pregnancy, suicide, greater risk of breast cancer in later life, and eating disorders, especially in societies that define thinness as attractive, at least for European American girls. Researchers have found fewer problems for early-maturing African American girls, but studies of these girls are limited (DeRose, Shiyko, Foster, & Brooks-Gunn, 2011; Stattin, Kerr, & Skoog, 2011). The timing of maturation is not the only factor affecting girls; social influences are powerful too. In a study of Native American (United States) and First Nations (Canada) girls, Melissa Walls and Les Whitbeck (2011) found early-maturating girls were more likely to abuse alcohol and drugs, but this association was influenced by social factors such as early dating and the attitudes of peers toward drugs. Maturing early can place girls in dating and friendship contexts where it is difficult to say no to drugs. Also, at least one study has found that the problems of early-maturing girls were present before puberty, so it is possible that life stresses cause both early maturation and emotional difficulties (DeRose et al., 2011).

Researchers also have found a correlation between age at menarche and adult body mass index (BMI), a measure of body fat; the younger the girl was when she had her first period, the greater her adult BMI, on average (M. A. Harris, Prior, & Koehoom, 2008). Later-maturing girls seem to have fewer problems, but they may worry that something is wrong with them, so adult reassurance and support are important.

Early maturity in males is associated with popularity. The early-maturer's taller, broad-shouldered body type fits the cultural stereotype for the male ideal; late-maturing boys may experience lower self-esteem because they are smaller and less muscular than the "ideal" for men (Harter, 2006). Even so, recent research points to more disadvantages than advantages for early maturation in boys. Early maturing boys tend to engage in more delinquent behavior—and this is true for White, African American, and Mexican American boys. They also appear to be at greater risk for depression, victimization by bullies, eating disorders, early sexual activity, and for abusing alcohol, illicit drugs, and cigarettes (Cota-Robles, Neiss, & Rowe, 2002; Mendle & Ferrero, 2012; Westling, Andrews, Hampson, & Peterson, 2008).

Boys who mature late may have a more difficult time initially. However, some studies show that in adulthood, males who matured later tend to be more creative, tolerant, and perceptive. Perhaps the trials and anxieties of maturing late teach some boys to be better problem solvers

Connect and Extend to PRAXIS II®

Human Development (I, A2)
Explain how development in one domain (e.g., physical, emotional) can affect development in other domains.

Video 3.1
Teenager Josh articulately describes some of the challenges that adolescents face, including his early maturation, a friend's eating disorder, peer pressure, sexual relationships, and his after-school job.

ENHANCEDetext *video example*

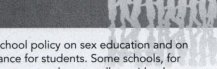

GUIDELINES
Dealing with Physical Differences in the Classroom

Address students' physical differences in ways that do not call unnecessary attention to the variations.

Examples

1. Try to seat smaller students so they can see and participate in class activities, but avoid seating arrangements that are obviously based on height.
2. Balance sports and games that rely on size and strength with games that reflect cognitive, artistic, social, or musical abilities, such as charades or drawing games.
3. Don't use, and don't allow students to use, nicknames based on physical traits.
4. In preschool classes, keep a good supply of left-handed scissors.

Help students obtain factual information on differences in physical development.

Examples

1. Set up science projects on sex differences in growth rates.
2. Have readings available that focus on differences between early and late maturers. Make sure that you present the positives and the negatives of each.

3. Find out the school policy on sex education and on informal guidance for students. Some schools, for example, encourage teachers to talk to girls who are upset about their first menstrual period, while other schools expect teachers to send the girls to talk to the school nurse (if your school still has one—budget cuts have eliminated many).
4. Give the students models in literature or in their community of accomplished and caring individuals who do not fit the culture's ideal physical stereotypes.

Accept that concerns about appearance and the opposite sex will occupy much time and energy for adolescents.

Examples

1. Allow some time at the end of class for socializing.
2. Deal with some of these issues in curriculum-related materials.

For more information about accommodations for physical differences in your classroom, see dos.claremontmckenna.edu/ PhysicalLearningDiff.asp.

(Brooks-Gunn, 1988; Steinberg, 2005). All adolescents can benefit from knowing that there is a very wide range for timing and rates in "normal" maturation and that there are challenges for both early and late maturers. See the *Guidelines: Dealing with Physical Differences in the Classroom*.

Play, Recess, and Physical Activity

Maria Montessori once noted, "Play is children's work," and Piaget and Vygotsky would agree. The American Academy of Pediatrics stated, "Play is essential to development because it contributes to the cognitive, physical, social, and emotional well-being of children and youth" (Ginsburg, 2007, p. 182). The brain develops with stimulation, and play provides some of that stimulation at every age. In fact, some neuroscientists suggest that play might help in the important process of pruning brain synapses during childhood (Pellis, 2006). Other psychologists believe play allows children to experiment safely as they learn about their environment, try out new behaviors, solve problems, and adapt to new situations (Pellegrini, Dupuis, & Smith, 2007). Babies in the sensorimotor stage learn by exploring, sucking, pounding, shaking, throwing—acting on their environments. Preoperational preschoolers love make-believe play and use pretending to form symbols, explore language, and interact with others. They are beginning to play simple games with predictable rules. Elementary-school-age children also like fantasy, but this fantasy play becomes more complex as children create characters and rules, for example, rules about how to bow to and obey the "Queen of everything." They also are beginning to play more complex games and sports, and thus learn cooperation, fairness, negotiation, and winning and losing as well as developing more sophisticated language. As children grow into adolescents, play continues to be part of their physical and social development (Woolfolk & Perry, 2015).

CULTURAL DIFFERENCES IN PLAY. Consistent with so many other topics, there are cultural differences in play, as Vygotsky probably would emphasize. In some cultures, such as American or Turkish, adults, particularly mothers, often are play partners with their children. But in other cultures such as East Indian, Indonesian, or Mayan, adults are not seen as appropriate play partners for children; siblings and peers are the ones who teach younger children how to participate in play activities (Callaghan et al., 2011; Vandermass-Peler, 2002). In some families and cultures, children spend more time helping with chores and less time in solitary or group play. Different materials and "toys" are used as available in different cultural groups—everything from expensive video games to sticks, rocks, and banana leaves. Children use what their culture provides to play. In addition, there are cultural differences in how children resolve conflicts in play. For example, compared to Canadian children, Chinese children in one study were more assertive in requesting a toy but also more willing to share and more likely to spontaneously offer a toy to another child (French et al., 2011). Also, teachers in the United States and Australia may place less emphasis on the value of play for children's learning compared to teachers in other countries such as Norway, Sweden, New Zealand, and Japan, where a "play pedagogy" may be part of the curriculum (Lillemyr, Søbstad, Marder, & Flowerday, 2011; Synodi, 2010).

EXERCISE AND RECESS. Physical activity and participation in athletics has benefits for all students' health, well-being, leadership skills, and their social relationships. Because most teens do not get much physical activity in their daily lives today, schools have a role in promoting active play. There are good, academic reasons for recess and exercise. Phillip Tomporowski and his colleagues (2008) reviewed the research on physical activity and cognitive development and concluded "systematic exercise programs may actually enhance the development of specific types of mental processing known to be important for meeting challenges encountered both in academics and throughout the lifespan" (p. 127). Other researchers note that students in Asian countries, who consistently outperform U.S. students on international reading, science, and mathematics tests, have more frequent recess breaks throughout the school day. One study of 11,000 students who were 8 and 9 years old found that students who had daily recess of 15 minutes or longer every day were better behaved in class than students who had little or no recess. This was true even after controlling for student gender and ethnicity, public or private school setting, and class size (Barros, Silver, & Stein, 2009). Unfortunately, physical education (PE) time in the United States is being cut to allow for more academic time focused on test preparation (Ginsburg, 2007; Pellegrini & Bohn, 2005).

PHYSICAL ACTIVITY AND STUDENTS WITH DISABILITIES. The sports participation of students with disabilities is limited in most schools. Recess breaks may be especially important for students with attention-deficit hyperactive disorder (ADHD). If more breaks were provided, fewer students, especially boys, might be diagnosed with ADHD (Pellegrini & Bohn, 2005). But this could change. Federal laws state that students in all grades have equal opportunities to participate in PE classes and extracurricular sports. Specifically, schools have the legal obligation "to provide students with disabilities an equal opportunity to participate alongside their peers in after-school athletics and clubs. . . . [S]chools may not exclude students who have an intellectual, developmental, physical, or any other disability from trying out and playing on a team, if they are otherwise qualified" (Duncan, 2013). Schools are not expected to change their standards for making or staying on a team, but they are expected to make reasonable accommodations, such as using a visual starter instead of a starting gun in races where a participant is deaf. Also, some disabled sports participation such as wheelchair basketball could be added to the extracurricular options.

One reason for concern about physical activity for children is the increase in childhood obesity, as you will see next.

Challenges in Physical Development

Physical development is public. Everyone sees how tall, short, heavy, thin, muscular, or coordinated you are. As students move into adolescence, they feel "on stage," as if everyone is evaluating them; and physical development is part of what is being evaluated. So physical development also has psychological consequences (Thomas & Thomas, 2008).

OBESITY. If you have seen the news lately, you know that obesity is a growing problem in America, especially for children. In fact, since 1971, the incidence of childhood obesity has doubled in every age group from ages 2 to 19 (Centers for Disease Control, 2009). Obesity usually is defined as

Video 3.2
As this video suggests, recess, school sports, and lessons that include physical activity help to foster not only motor development but also social and cognitive skills. Physical activity and participation in athletics has benefits for all students' health, well-being, academic success, leadership skills, and their social relationships.

ENHANCEDetext *video example*

FIGURE 3.1

2009–2011 OBESITY PREVALENCE AMONG LOW-INCOME CHILDREN AGE 2 TO 4 YEARS BY COUNTIES IN THE UNITED STATES

0–5%   >5–10%   >10–15%   >15–20%   >20%   No Data

Source: Centers for Disease Control and Prevention. Data retrieved from http://www.cdc.gov/obesity/ downloads/pednssfactsheet.pdf. Map retrieved from http://www.cdc.gov/obesity/childhood/lowincome.html

being more than 20% heavier than average compared to others of the same age, sex, and body build. Obesity rates are particularly high among children from low-income families; one in seven preschool children in these families is obese. Figure 3.1 shows county-by-county rates of obesity in the United States.

The consequences of obesity are serious for children and adolescents: diabetes, strain on bones and joints, respiratory problems, and a greater chance of heart problems as adults. Playing with friends or participating in sports can be affected negatively. In addition, children with obesity often are the targets of cruel teasing. Like everything else involving children's development, this increase in obesity rates probably has many interacting causes including poor diet, genetic factors, increased hours sitting in front of televisions and playing video games, and lack of exercise (Woolfolk & Perry, 2015).

Another challenge in physical development for many children involves not too much weight, but too little.

EATING DISORDERS. As children grow and their bodies change, many become very concerned about their appearance. This has always been true, but today, the emphasis on fitness and beauty makes young people even more likely to worry about how their bodies "measure up." Both boys and girls can become dissatisfied with their bodies because they don't match the cultural ideals in magazines and films. New York City acknowledged this widespread problem in 2013 with its Girls Project, geared toward girls ages 7 to 12 (Hartocollis, 2013; nyc.gov/html/girls/). Another project, GirlsHealth.gov sponsored by the US Office on Women's Health, provides posters like those in Figure 3.2. Their motto is "Be healthy. Be happy. Be you. Beautiful."

Excessive concern with body image can be a factor in developing eating disorders such as **bulimia** (binge eating followed by purging, fasting, or excessive exercise) and **anorexia nervosa** (self-starvation).

FIGURE 3.2

POSTERS FROM THE GIRLS HEALTH PROJECT

The U.S. Office of Women's Health launched an initiative to promote healthy, positive behaviors in girls ages 10–16.

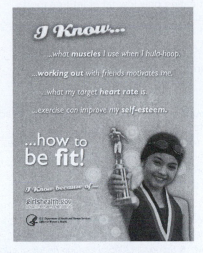

Source: http://www.girlshealth.gov/

Individuals with bulimia often binge, eating an entire gallon of ice cream or a whole cake. Then, to avoid gaining weight, they force themselves to vomit or they use strong laxatives to purge themselves of the extra calories. Students with bulimia are hard to detect because they tend to maintain a normal weight, but their digestive systems can be permanently damaged. About 2% of the people in the United States have bulimia (Downs & Blow, 2013). Anorexia is an even more dangerous disorder, for anorexics either refuse to eat or eat practically nothing while often exercising obsessively. In the process, they may lose 20% to 25% of their body weight, and some (about 5%) literally starve themselves to death (Crow et al., 2009). Anorexia most often affects adolescents and young adults; a little over 1% of people in the United States have anorexia (Downs & Blow, 2013). Anorexic students become very thin, and may appear pale, have brittle fingernails, and develop fine dark hairs all over their bodies. They are easily chilled because they have so little fat to insulate their bodies. They often are depressed, insecure, moody, and lonely. Girls may stop having their menstrual period.

The latest *Diagnostic and Statistical Manual* (*DSM-5*) of the American Psychiatric Association added *binge eating* as a disorder defined by two indicators: "recurring episodes of eating significantly more food in a short period of time than most people would eat under similar circumstances, with episodes marked by feelings of lack of control" (American Psychiatric Association, 2013b). Binge eating is a more severe problem than simply overeating because it is associated with significant physical and psychological problems. About 5% to 6% of the people in the United States suffer from binge eating disorders (Downs & Blow, 2013).

Eating disorders are becoming more common, sometimes encouraged and supported by pro-ana (pro-anorexia nervosa) and pro-ima (pro-bulimia) social networks, blogs, and Web sites. The pro-ana and pro-ima movements often are militant in their support of the "choice" of anorexia or bulimia as a "lifestyle" (Casilli, Tubaro, & Araya, 2012). The related digital media supports eating disorders by providing photographs of very thin models, ideas for rapid unhealthy weight loss and ways of concealing it, motivational statements and social support, virtual communities and online discussions, and a sense of belonging to a special group that understands you and combats your

GUIDELINES
Supporting Positive Body Images in Adolescents

Listen to adolescents talk about their health.

Examples

1. If they mention wanting to lose weight, seize the opportunity to talk about healthy weight, body image, and cultural influences on youth.
2. It they mention diets they or their friends are trying, provide them with nutritionally sound information about myths, misinformation, and dangers related to fad diets.
3. In general, be attentive. An adolescent may make a brief comment that could serve as a terrific entrance into a valuable conversation about body image.

Ask questions.

Examples

1. Are you concerned about your weight (or shape or size) at all? Do you think your friends are concerned about their weight? Do you or your friends talk a lot about your weight?
2. Do you know that diets are the worst way to lose or maintain weight? Have you ever dieted? Why?

3. Do you know that eating only low-fat or fat-free foods is NOT healthy eating? Do you know that you need fat in your diet and that without it you can have all kinds of health problems?

Make available resources for adolescents who have body image issues.

Examples

1. Have accurate, youth-oriented resources available to read, look up on the Internet, or find in a library.
2. Encourage youth to continue conversations about these issues with you, their parents, a health professional, a trusted teacher, or a caring, knowledgeable adult.
3. Deal with some of these issues in curriculum-related materials.

For more information about adolescents and body image, see epi.umn.edu/let/pubs/img/adol_ch13.pdf

Source: Based on Story, M., & Stang, J. (2005). Nutrition needs of adolescents. In J. S. M. Story (Ed.), Guidelines for adolescent nutritional services *(pp. 158–159). Minneapolis, MN: University of Minnesota.*

feelings of loneliness and isolation (Rodgers, Skowron, & Chabrol, 2011). Pro-ana Web sites are available in many countries and languages; for example, almost 300 sites exist in 2012 in the French language alone (Casilli, Pailler, & Tubaro, 2013).

Unfortunately, adolescents obsessed with body images and constantly trying to control their weight may encounter these Web sites as they search the Internet for diets and weight loss strategies. People who frequent the Web sites may feel that others in the virtual community are the only ones who truly understand and accept them—the only place they can be "real" (Peebles et al., 2012). Some social networking sites are acknowledging the problem. In 2012, Tumblr and Pinterest decided to ban all "thinspiration" content—the sharing of motivational images and messages about unhealthy weight loss (Casilli et al., 2013).

All these students usually require professional help. Don't ignore the warning signs: less than one third of people with eating disorders actually receive treatment (Stice & Shaw, 2004). A teacher may be the person who begins the chain of help for students with these tragic problems. See the *Guidelines: Supporting Positive Body Images in Adolescents.*

People certainly are more than physical bodies. The rest of this chapter is about personal and moral development, beginning with a theoretical frame to put that development in context.

ENHANCEDetext *self-check*

BRONFENBRENNER: THE SOCIAL CONTEXT FOR DEVELOPMENT

We put the developing person in context by exploring the work of Urie Bronfenbrenner (1917–2005), who was born in Moscow, Russia, but moved with his family to the United States when he was 6. Bronfenbrenner completed a double major in psychology and music at Cornell in 1938 and a PhD in psychology from the University of Michigan in 1942. Over his long career in psychology, he worked as a clinical psychologist in the U.S. Army and as a professor at the University of Michigan and at Cornell. He also helped to found the Head Start early childhood program.

The Importance of Context and the Bioecological Model

"Students typically do not learn alone but rather in collaboration with their teachers, in company with their peers, and with encouragement of their families" (Durlak, Weissberg, Dymnicki, Taylor, & Schellinger, 2011, p. 405). Teachers, families, and peers are part of the students' context. **Context** is the total situation that surrounds and interacts with an individual's thoughts, feelings, and actions to shape development and learning. Contextual effects on the developing individual are both internal and external. For example, hormone levels within the body are contexts for developing organs, including the brain, as well as for adolescents' self-concepts during puberty. The focus of this book, however, is the contexts outside the person. Children grow up in families and are members of particular ethnic, language, religious, and economic communities. They live in neighborhoods, attend schools, and are members of classes, teams, or glee clubs. The social and educational programs, along with the policies of governments, affect their lives. These contexts influence the development of behaviors, beliefs, and knowledge by providing resources, supports, incentives and punishments, expectations, teachers, models, tools—all the building blocks of learning and development (Dodge, 2011; Lerner, Theokas, & Bobek, 2005).

Contexts also affect how actions are interpreted. For example, if a stranger approaches a 7-month-old infant, the baby is likely to cry if the setting is unfamiliar, but she may not cry if the stranger is in her home. Adults are more likely to help a stranger in need in small towns as opposed to larger cities (J. Kagan & Herschkowitz, 2005). Think about hearing a telephone ring. Is it 3:00 in the afternoon or 3:00 in the morning? Did you just call someone and leave a message asking for a return call? Has the phone been ringing off the hook, or is this the first call in days? Did you just sit down to dinner? The meaning of the ring and the feelings you have will vary, depending on the context.

Urie Bronfenbrenner's **bioecological model** of development (Bronfenbrenner, 1989; Bronfenbrenner & Morris, 2006) recognizes that the physical and social contexts in which we develop are *ecosystems* because they are constantly interacting with and influencing each other. Look at Figure 3.3 on the next page. Every person lives within a microsystem, inside a mesosystem, embedded in an exosystem, all of which are a part of the macrosystem—like a set of Russian painted dolls, nested one inside the other. In addition, all development occurs in and is influenced by the time period—the chronosystem.

In the microsystem are the person's immediate relationships and activities. For a child, the microsystem might be the immediate family, friends, or teachers and the activities of play and school. Relationships in the microsystem are reciprocal; they flow in both directions. The child affects the parent, and the parent influences the child, for example. The mesosystem is the set of interactions and relationships among all the elements of the microsystem—the family members interacting with each other or with the teacher. Again, all relationships are reciprocal; the teacher influences the parents, and the parents affect the teacher, and these interactions affect the child. The exosystem includes all the social settings that affect the child, even though the child is not a direct member of these systems. Examples are the teachers' relations with administrators and the school board; the parents' jobs; the community resources for health, employment, or recreation; or the family's religious affiliation. The macrosystem is the larger society—its values, laws, policies, conventions, and traditions.

Families

The first context for child development is the mother's womb. Scientists are learning more about the effects of this first environment—the role of the expectant mother's level of stress, nutrition, smoking, alcohol and drug intake, exercise, and general health in her infant's development. Clearly, the influence of the family begins before birth, but many new influences follow (Woolfolk & Perry, 2015).

FAMILY STRUCTURE. In the United States, the proportion of children growing up in a home with just one parent has doubled since the 1970s. About 10% of children have parents who never married, and most of these children (89%) live with their mothers. In fact, projections are that

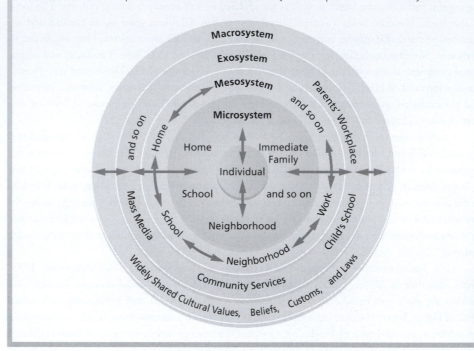

FIGURE 3.3

URIE BRONFENBRENNER'S BIOECOLOGICAL MODEL OF HUMAN DEVELOPMENT

Every person develops within a *microsystem* (family, friends, school activities, teacher, etc.) inside a *mesosystem* (the interactions among all the microsystem elements), embedded in an *exosystem* (social settings that affect the child, even though the child is not a direct member—community resources, parents' workplace, etc.); all are part of the *macrosystem* (the larger society with its laws, customs, values, etc.). All development occurs in and is influenced by the time period—the *chronosystem*.

only about half of all children will grow up with two parents who stay married (P. R. Amato, 2006; Schoen & Canudas-Romo, 2006). Increasingly, children today may be part of **blended families**, with stepbrothers or stepsisters who move in and out of their lives. Some children live with an aunt, with grandparents, with one parent, in foster or adoptive homes, or with an older brother or sister. In some cultures such as Asian, Latin American, or African, children are more likely to grow up in **extended families**, with grandparents, aunts, uncles, and cousins living in the same household or at least in daily contact with each other. In addition, there are several million gay and lesbian parents in the United States (estimates are hard to determine because some parents conceal details about their sexual orientation to protect their children from bias and prejudice). The best advice is to avoid the phrases "your parents" and "your mother and father" and instead to speak of "your family" when talking to students.

No matter who is doing the parenting, research has identified characteristic differences in parents' styles.

PARENTING STYLES. One well-known description of **parenting styles** is based on the research of Diane Baumrind (1991, 1996, 2005). Her early work focused on a careful longitudinal study of 100 (mostly European American, middle-class) preschool children. Through observation of children and parents and interviews with parents, Baumrind and the other researchers who built on her findings identified four parenting styles based on the parents' high or low levels of warmth and control:

- *Authoritative parents* (high warmth, high control) set clear limits, enforce rules, and expect mature behavior. But they are warm with their children. They listen to concerns, give reasons for rules, and allow more democratic decision making. There is less strict punishment and more guidance. Parents help children think through the consequences of their actions (Hoffman, 2001).

- *Authoritarian parents* (low warmth, high control) seem cold and controlling in their interactions with their children. The children are expected to be mature and to do what the parent says, "Because I said so!" There is not much talk about emotions. Punishments are strict, but not abusive. The parents love their children, but they are not openly affectionate.
- *Permissive parents* (high warmth, low control) are warm and nurturing, but they have few rules or consequences for their children and expect little in the way of mature behavior because "They're just kids."
- *Rejecting/Neglecting/Uninvolved parents* (low warmth, low control) don't seem to care at all and can't be bothered with controlling, communicating, or teaching their children.

Authoritarian, authoritative, and permissive parents love their children and are trying to do their best; they simply have different ideas about the best ways to parent. In broad strokes, there are differences in children's feelings and behavior associated with these three parenting styles. At least in European American, middle-class families, children of *authoritative* parents are more likely to do well in school, be happy with themselves, and relate well to others. Children of *authoritarian* parents are more likely to feel guilty or depressed, and children of *permissive* parents may have trouble interacting with peers—they are used to having their way (Berger, 2006; Spera, 2005).

Of course, the extreme of permissiveness becomes indulgence. Indulgent parents cater to their children's every whim—perhaps it is easier than being the adult who must make unpopular decisions. Both indulgent and rejecting/neglecting/uninvolved parenting styles can be harmful.

CULTURE AND PARENTING. Parenting that is strict and directive, with clear rules and consequences, combined with high levels of warmth and emotional support, is associated with higher academic achievement and greater emotional maturity for inner-city children (P. W. Garner & Spears, 2000; Jarrett, 1995). Differences in cultural values and in the danger level of some urban neighborhoods may make tighter parental control appropriate, and even necessary (Smetana, 2000). In addition, in cultures that have a greater respect for elders and a more group-centered rather than individualist philosophy, it may be a misreading of the parents' actions to perceive their demand for obedience as "authoritarian" (Lamb & Lewis, 2005; Nucci, 2001). In fact, research by Ruth Chao (2001; Chao & Tseng, 2002) has challenged Baumrind's conclusions for Asian families. Chao finds that an alternative parenting style of *chiao shun* (a Chinese term that Chao translates as "training") better characterizes parenting in Asian and Asian American families.

Research with Latino parents also questions whether studies of parenting styles based on European American families are helpful in understanding Latino families. Using a carefully designed observation system, Melanie Domenech Rodríguez and her colleagues included a third dimension of parenting—giving children more or less autonomy (freedom to make decisions). They found that almost all of the Latino parents they studied could be characterized as *protective* (high on warmth, high on control/demand, and low on granting autonomy) or *authoritative* (high on all three—warmth, control/demand, and granting autonomy). Also, these Latino parents tended to be more demanding and less likely to grant autonomy to their female children (Domenech Rodríguez, Donovick, & Crowley, 2009).

Whatever the structure of the families you work with, see the *Guidelines: Family and Community Partnerships* on the next page for making connections.

ATTACHMENT. The emotional bond that forms between people is called attachment. The first attachment is between the child and parents or other caregivers. The quality of this bond appears to have implications for forming relationships throughout life (R. A. Thompson & Raikes, 2003). Children who form what are called secure attachments with caregivers receive comfort when needed and are more confident to explore their world, perhaps because they know they can count on the caregiver. Children who form insecure or disorganized attachments can be fearful, sad, anxious, clinging, rejecting, or angry in interactions with the caregivers. Some research indicates that authoritarian parenting styles are related to forming insecure attachments, but as we saw earlier, many factors influence the effects of parenting styles (Roeser, Peck, & Nasir, 2006).

Connect and Extend to PRAXIS II®

Families (I, B6)
Understand the influence of families, their culture, and values on student learning.

GUIDELINES
Family and Community Partnerships

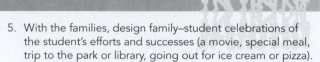

Connecting with families.

1. Work with families to co-create methods for family involvement. Offer a range of possible participation methods. Make sure the plans are realistic and fit the lives of the families you are dealing with.

2. Remember that some students' families have had negative experiences with schools or may fear or mistrust schools and teachers. Find other places to collaborate: before or after ball games, or at a local church or recreation center. Go where families go; don't always expect them to come to school.

3. Maintain regular home–school contact through telephone calls or notes. If a family has no telephone, identify a contact person (relative or friend) who can take messages. If literacy is a problem, use pictures, symbols, and codes for written communication.

4. Make all communications positive, emphasizing growth, progress, and accomplishments.

5. With the families, design family–student celebrations of the student's efforts and successes (a movie, special meal, trip to the park or library, going out for ice cream or pizza).

6. On a regular basis, send home a note in word or picture form that describes the student's progress. Ask families to indicate how they celebrated the success and to return the note.

7. Follow up with a telephone call to discuss progress, answer questions, solicit family suggestions, and express appreciation for the families' contributions.

8. Make sure families feel welcome if they visit the classroom.

For more information on family school partnerships, see gse.harvard.edu/hfrp/projects/family.html

Source: From "Effects of Parent Involvement in Isolation or in Combination with Peer Tutoring on Student Self-Concept and Mathematics Achievement," by J. Fantuzzo, G. Davis, and M. Ginsburg, Journal of Educational Psychology, 87, pp. 272–281. Copyright © 1995 by the American Psychological Association. Adapted with permission of the APA.

The quality of attachment has implications for teachers. For example, in preschools, children who have formed secure attachments with parents/caregivers are less dependent on teachers and interact with other children appropriately. Secure attachment is positively related to achievement test scores, teacher assessments of social competence throughout the school years, and even to lower dropout rates (Roeser et al., 2006). As we will see later, researchers are currently examining students' attachment to teachers and schools as a positive force in their lives.

DIVORCE. The divorce rate in the United States is one of the highest in the world. Some analysts estimate that between 40% and 50% of first-time marriages that took place in the 1990s will end in divorce—and the divorce rate is even higher for second and third marriages (P. R. Amato, 2001; Schoen & Canudas-Romo, 2006). And as too many of us know from experiences in our own families, separation and divorce are stressful events for all participants, even under the best circumstances. The actual separation of the parents may have been preceded by years of conflict in the home or may come as a shock to all, including friends and children. During the divorce itself, conflict may increase as property and custody rights are being negotiated. After the divorce, more changes may disrupt the child's life as the custodial parent moves to a new neighborhood or works longer hours. For the child, this can mean leaving behind important friendships in the old neighborhood or school, just when support is needed the most. Even in those rare cases where there are few conflicts, ample resources, and the continuing support of friends and extended family, divorce is never easy for anyone. But it can be a better alternative for children than growing up in a home filled with conflict and discord. "Destructive conflict in any type of family undermines the well-being of parents and children" (Hetherington, 2006, p. 232).

The first 2 years after the divorce seem to be the most difficult period for both boys and girls and especially hard for young adolescents (ages 10 to 14). Recent research also indicates that divorce is harder on boys than girls, maybe because mothers still tend to get custody of children, which leaves boys without a male role model in the house (Fuller-Thomson & Dalton, 2011). Children may have problems in school or just skip school, lose or gain an unusual amount of weight, have trouble sleeping, or experience other difficulties. However, adjustment to divorce is an individual matter; some children respond with increased responsibility, maturity, and coping skills (P. R. Amato, 2006; L. F. Amato, Loomis, & Booth, 1995; American Psychological Association, 2004). Over time, about 75% to 80% of children in divorced families adapt and become reasonably well adjusted (Hetherington & Kelly, 2003). See the *Guidelines: Helping Children of Divorce.*

GUIDELINES
Helping Children of Divorce

Take note of any sudden changes in behavior that might indicate problems at home.

Examples

1. Be alert to physical symptoms such as repeated headaches or stomach pains, rapid weight gain or loss, fatigue, or excess energy.
2. Be aware of signs of emotional distress such as moodiness, temper tantrums, or difficulty in paying attention or concentrating.
3. Let parents know about the students' signs of stress.

Talk individually to students about their attitude or behavior changes. This gives you a chance to find out about unusual stress such as divorce.

Examples

1. Be a good listener. Students may have no other adult willing to hear their concerns.
2. Let students know you are available to talk, and let the student set the agenda.

Watch your language to make sure you avoid stereotypes about "happy" (two-parent) homes.

Examples

1. Simply say "your families" instead of "your mothers and fathers" when addressing the class.
2. Avoid statements such as "We need volunteers for room mother" or "Your father can help you."

Help students maintain self-esteem.

Examples

1. Recognize a job well done.
2. Make sure the student understands the assignment and can handle the workload. This is not the time to pile on new and very difficult work.

3. The student may be angry with his or her parents, but may direct the anger at teachers. Don't take the student's anger personally.

Find out what resources are available at your school.

Examples

1. Talk to the school psychologist, guidance counselor, social worker, or principal about students who seem to need outside help.
2. Consider establishing a discussion group, led by a trained adult, for students whose parents are going through a divorce.

Be sensitive to both parents' rights to information.

Examples

1. When parents have joint custody, both are entitled to receive information and attend parent–teacher conferences.
2. The noncustodial parent may still be concerned about the child's school progress. Check with your principal about state laws regarding the noncustodial parent's rights.

Be aware of long-term problems for students moving between two households.

Examples

1. Books, assignments, and gym clothes may be left at one parent's house when the student is currently on visitation with the other parent.
2. Parents may not show up for their turn to pick up their child at school or may miss a parent–teacher conference because the note never got home.

For ideas about helping children understand divorce, see muextension.missouri.edu/xplor/hesguide/humanrel/gh6600.htm

Peers

Children also develop within peer groups. Rubin and his colleagues (Rubin, Coplan, Chen, Buskirk, & Wojslawowicz, 2005) distinguish between two kinds of peer groups: cliques and crowds.

CLIQUES. *Cliques* are relatively small, friendship-based groups (typically between three and a dozen members); they are more evident in middle childhood and early adolescence. These cliques typically include peers of the same sex and age who share common interests and engage in similar activities. Cliques serve young peoples' emotional and security needs by providing a stable social context in which group members know each other well and form close friendships (B. B. Brown, 2004; Henrich, Brookmeyer, Shrier, & Shahar, 2006).

STOP & THINK Think back to high school—did you have friends in any of these groups: normals, populars, brains, jocks, partyers, druggies, others? What were the main "crowds" at your school? How did your friends influence you? •

CROWDS. *Crowds* are less intimate, more loosely organized groups based on shared interests, activities, attitudes, or reputations. Even though they may go by different names in different schools, the most common crowds are *jocks, brains, nerds, druggies, goths, populars, normals, nobodies,* and *loners.* Students don't necessarily *join* crowds; they are associated with or *assigned to* crowds by other students based on reputations and stereotypes (J. L. Cook & Cook, 2014). In fact, crowd members may or may not interact with one another. Associations with crowds occurs during early and middle adolescence (Rubin et al., 2005). W. Andrew Collins and Laurence Steinberg (2006, p. 1022) call crowds "an identity 'way station' or placeholder during the period between individuation from parents and establishment of a coherent personal identity."

Crowds become far less prominent in late adolescence. Interestingly, adolescents who are relatively more confident in their identity tend not to value crowd affiliations as much as those who are still exploring, and by high school, many adolescents believe affiliations with particular crowds stifle their identity and self-expression (W. A. Collins & Steinberg, 2006).

PEER CULTURES. At any age, students who have a set of "rules"—how to dress, talk, style their hair, and interact with others—are called peer cultures. The group determines which activities, music, or other students are in or out of favor. For example, when Jessica, a popular high school student, was asked to explain the rules that her group lives by, she had no trouble:

> OK. No. 1: clothes. You cannot wear jeans any day but Friday, and you cannot wear a ponytail or sneakers more than once a week. Monday is fancy day—like black pants or maybe you bust out with a skirt. You have to remind people how cute you are in case they forgot over the weekend. No. 2: parties. Of course we sit down and discuss which ones we're going to because there is no point in getting all dressed up for a party that's going to be lame. (Talbot, 2002, p. 28)

These peer cultures encourage conformity to the group rules. When another girl in Jessica's group wore jeans on Monday, Jessica confronted her: "Why are you wearing jeans today? Did you forget it was Monday?" (Talbot, 2002, p. 28). Jessica explained that the group had to suspend this "rebel" several times, not allowing her to sit with them at lunch.

To understand the power of peers, we have to look at situations where the values and interests of parents clash with those of peers, and then see whose influence dominates. In these comparisons, peers usually win in matters of style and socializing. Parents and teachers still are influential in matters of morality, career choice, and religion (J. R. Harris, 1998). Also, not all aspects of peer cultures are bad or cruel. The norms in some groups are positive and support achievement in school.

FRIENDSHIPS. Friendships are central to students' lives at every age. When there has been a falling-out or an argument, when rumors are started and pacts are made to ostracize someone (as with Alison and Stephanie at the beginning of the chapter), the results can be devastating. Beyond the immediate trauma of being "in" or "out" of the group, peer relationships influence students' motivation and achievement in school (A. A. Ryan, 2001). In one study, sixth-grade students without friends showed lower levels of academic achievement and fewer positive social behaviors and were more emotionally distressed, even 2 years later, than students with at least one friend (Wentzel, Barry, & Caldwell, 2004). The characteristics of friends and the quality of the friendships matter, too. Having stable, supportive relationships with friends who are socially competent and mature enhances social development, protects students with emotional problems, and supports students during difficult times such as parents' divorce or transition to new schools (W. A. Collins & Steinberg, 2006).

But the influence of friendships is not always positive. Based on a 3-year study that surveyed 20,000 high school students in Wisconsin and California, Steinberg (1998) found that 1 in every 5 students said that their friends made fun of people who tried to do well in school and about 40% of the students were just going through the motions of learning. About 90% had copied someone else's homework, and 66% had cheated on a test within the last year. This lack of investment was due in part to peer pressure because for many adolescents, "peers—not parents—are the chief determinants of how intensely they are invested in school and how much effort they devote to their education" (p. 331).

POPULARITY. What does it mean to be popular? We could answer this question by observing students or by using ratings from parents or teachers. But the most common way to assess popularity

Video 3.3
Young children often say that their friends are the people they play with. Grade schoolers typically describe friendships by mentioning shared activities. Older children and teens, like the boy shown here, are more likely than younger children to mention specific traits and interests. The young girl and the high school boy both convey that friends support you and are there for you.

ENHANCEDetext *video example*

TABLE 3.1 • **What Does It Take to Be Popular?**

POPULAR CHILDREN
Popular prosocial children: These children are both academically and socially competent. They do well in school and communicate well with peers. When they disagree with other children, they respond appropriately and have effective strategies for working things out.   *Popular antisocial children:* This subgroup of children often includes boys who are aggressive. They may be athletic, and other children tend to think they are "cool" in the ways they bully other children and defy adult authority.
REJECTED CHILDREN
Rejected aggressive children: High rates of conflict and hyperactivity/impulsivity characterize the behaviors of this subgroup. These children have poor perspective-taking skills and self-control. They often misunderstand the intentions of others, assign blame, and act aggressively on their angry or hurt feelings.   *Rejected withdrawn children:* These children are timid and withdrawn, often the targets of bullies. They are often socially awkward and withdraw from social interactions to avoid being scorned or attacked.
CONTROVERSIAL CHILDREN
As the descriptor implies, controversial children have both positive and negative social qualities and, as a result, their social status can change over time. They can be hostile and disruptive in some situations and then engage in positive prosocial behaviors in others. These children have friends and are generally happy with their peer relationships.
NEGLECTED CHILDREN
Perhaps surprisingly, most neglected children are well adjusted and they are not less socially competent than other children. Peers tend to view them as shy, but they don't report being lonely or unhappy about their social lives. Apparently they don't experience the extreme social anxiety and wariness that withdrawn children do.

Source: Woolfolk, A. & Perry, N. E. (2015). Child and adolescent development, 2nd Ed. Reprinted by permisison of Pearson Education.

is to ask the students themselves two questions: Is this child liked? and What is this child like? Based on answers to these questions, we can identify four categories of children (see Table 3.1).

As you can see in Table 3.1, children identified as *popular* (highly rated) may behave in positive or negative ways. Children identified as *rejected* probably merit their low ratings because they are aggressive, immature, socially unskilled, or withdrawn. Children identified as *controversial* get mixed reviews; they display both positive and negative social behaviors. Finally, children identified as *neglected* are almost invisible—their peers simply do not mention them—but there is no consistent evidence that neglected children are anxious or withdrawn (Rubin et al., 2005).

CAUSES AND CONSEQUENCES OF REJECTION. Children and adolescents are not always tolerant of differences. About 5% to 10% of children experience some form of problems with peers—rejection, bullying, and other difficulties (Boivin et al., 2013). In this section we are talking about *rejected* children. We will examine the very real and dangerous problems of bullying and cyberbullying in Chapter 13.

New students who are physically, intellectually, ethnically, racially, economically, or linguistically different may be rejected in classes with established cliques or crowds. Students who are aggressive, withdrawn, and inattentive-hyperactive are more likely to be rejected. But classroom context matters too, especially for aggressive or withdrawn students. In classrooms where the general level of aggression is high, being aggressive is less likely to lead to peer rejection. And in classrooms where solitary play and work are more common, being withdrawn is not as likely to lead to rejection. Thus, part of being rejected is just being too different from the norm. Also, being more attractive or engaging in prosocial behaviors such as sharing, cooperating, and friendly interactions are associated with peer acceptance, no matter what the classroom context. Many aggressive and withdrawn students lack these social skills; inattentive-hyperactive students often misread social cues or have trouble controlling impulses, so their social skills suffer, too (Coplan, Prakash, O'Neil, & Armer, 2004; Stormshak, Bierman, Bruschi, Dodge, & Coie, 1999).

When students are rejected they may develop emotional problems such as depression or thoughts of suicide, behavioral or physical health problems, and difficulties in school (Boivin et al., 2013). Rejected children are less likely to participate in classroom learning activities, so their achievement suffers; they are more likely to drop out of school as adolescents and may even evidence more problems as adults. For example, rejected aggressive students are more likely to commit crimes as they grow older (Buhs, Ladd, & Herald, 2006; Coie & Dodge, 1998; Fredricks, Blumenfeld, & Paris, 2004). A teacher should be aware of how each student gets along with the group. Are there outcasts? Careful adult intervention can often correct such problems, especially at the late elementary and middle school levels, as we will see next (Pearl, Leung, Acker, Farmer, & Rodkin, 2007).

Sometimes rejection becomes aggression.

AGGRESSION. Aggression should not be confused with assertiveness, which means affirming or maintaining a legitimate right. Saying, "You are sitting in my chair!" is assertive. Pushing the invader out of the chair is aggressive. There are several forms of aggression. The most common form is **instrumental aggression**, which is intended to gain an object or privilege, such as shoving to get a chair or snatching a book from another student. The intent is to get what you want, not to hurt the other child, but the hurt may happen anyway. A second kind is **hostile aggression**—inflicting intentional harm. Hostile aggression can take the form of either **overt aggression**, such as threats or physical attacks (as in, "I'm gonna beat you up!"), or **relational aggression**, which involves threatening or damaging social relationships (as in, "I'm never going to speak to you again!"). Boys are more likely to use overt aggression, and girls, like Alison in the opening case, are more likely to use relational aggression, especially in middle school and beyond (Ostrov & Godleski, 2010). A final kind of hostile aggression is a growing concern today, **cyber aggression**—using e-mail, Twitter, Facebook, or other social media to spread rumors, make threats, or otherwise terrorize peers, as Alison did in the case at the beginning of this chapter.

Aggressive students tend to believe that violence will be rewarded, and they use aggression to get what they want. They are more likely to believe that violent retaliation is acceptable: "It's OK to shove people when you're mad" (Egan, Monson, & Perry, 1998). Seeing violent acts go unpunished probably affirms and encourages these beliefs. In addition, some children, particularly boys, have difficulty reading the intentions of others (Dodge & Pettit, 2003; Zelli, Dodge, Lochman, & Laird, 1999). They assume another child "did it on purpose" when their block tower is toppled, they are pushed on the bus, or some other mistake is made. Retaliation follows, and the cycle of aggression continues.

Children with more serious conduct problems often are identified during elementary school. But the problems are not new behaviors; usually they are behaviors the students have not outgrown from their early years (Petitclerc, Boivin, Dionne, Zoccolillo, & Tremblay, 2009). So waiting for children to "outgrow" aggressive behaviors does not work. For example, one study in Finland asked teachers to rate students' aggression by answering "never," "sometimes," or "often" to statements such as "hurts another child when angry." Teacher-rated aggression when students were age 8 predicted school adjustment problems in early adolescence and long-term unemployment in adulthood (Kokko & Pulkkinen, 2000). Similar results were found in a study conducted in Canada, New Zealand, and the United States. Boys (but not girls) who were often physically aggressive in elementary school were at risk for continuing violent and nonviolent forms of delinquency through adolescence (Broidy et al., 2003).

It is clear that helping children handle aggression can make a lasting difference in their lives. One of the best approaches for preventing problems with aggression later in life is to intervene early. For example, one study found that aggressive children whose teachers taught them conflict management strategies were diverted from a life path of aggression and violence (Aber, Brown, & Jones, 2003). Sandra Graham (1996) has successfully experimented with approaches that help aggressive fifth- and sixth-grade boys become better judges of others' intentions. Strategies include engaging in role-play, participating in group discussions of personal experiences, interpreting social cues from photographs, playing pantomime games, making videos, and writing endings to unfinished stories. The boys in the 12-session training group showed clear improvement in reading the intentions of others and responding with less aggression.

RELATIONAL AGGRESSION. Insults, gossip, exclusion, taunts—all are forms of relational aggression, sometimes called *social aggression* because the intent is to harm social connections. After second or third grade, girls tend to engage in relational aggression more than boys, possibly because as girls become aware of gender stereotypes, they push their overt aggression underground into verbal, not physical, attacks. Relational aggression can be even more damaging than overt physical aggression—both to the victim and the aggressor. Victims, like Stephanie in the chapter opening, often are devastated. Teachers and other students may view relational aggressors as even more problematic than physical aggressors (Crick, Casas, & Mosher, 1997; Ostrov & Godleski, 2010). As early as preschool, children need to learn how to negotiate social relations without resorting to any kind of aggression. Interviews with adolescents reveal how much they count on their teachers and other adults in the school to protect them (Garbarino & deLara, 2002). We will examine more specific classroom strategies, especially strategies for handling *bullying* and cyberbullying, in Chapter 13, *Creating Learning Environments*.

MEDIA, MODELING, AND AGGRESSION. Modeling plays an important role in the expression of aggression (Bandura, Ross, & Ross, 1963). Children who grow up in homes filled with harsh punishment and family violence are more likely to use aggression to solve their own problems (G. R. Patterson, 1997).

One very real source of aggressive models is found in almost every home in America—television. From ages 6 to 11, children spend an average of 28 hours a week watching television—more time than any other activity except sleep (Rideout, Foehr, & Roberts, 2010). With all this viewing, the possible influence of television violence is a real concern because in the United States, 82% of TV programs have at least some violence. The rate for children's programs is especially high—an average of 32 violent acts per hour, with cartoons being the worst. And in more than 70% of the violent scenes, the violence goes unpunished (Kirsh, 2005; Mediascope, 1996). Does watching violent TV increase aggression? A panel of experts assembled by the U.S. Surgeon General to study media and violence reached a strong and clear conclusion: "Research on violent television and films, video games, and music reveals unequivocal evidence that media violence increases the likelihood of aggressive and violent behavior in both immediate and long-term contexts" (C. A. Anderson et al., 2003, p. 81).

You can reduce the negative effects of TV violence by stressing three points with your students: (1) most people do not behave in the aggressive ways shown on television; (2) the violent acts on TV are not real, but are created by special effects and stunts; and (3) there are better ways to resolve conflicts, and these are the ways most real people use to solve their problems (Huesmann et al., 2003). Also, avoid using TV viewing as a reward or punishment because that makes television even more attractive to children (Slaby et al., 1995). But television is not the only source of violent models. Students growing up in the inner cities see gang violence. Newspapers, magazines, and the radio are filled with stories of murders, rapes, and robberies. Many popular films are also filled with graphic depictions of violence, often performed by the "hero" who saves the day. And what about those video games?

VIDEO GAMES AND AGGRESSIVE BEHAVIOR. Recently, researchers reviewed 130 reports based on over 130,000 participants from Western countries such as the United States, Australia, Germany, Italy, the Netherlands, Portugal, and the United Kingdom, as well as from Japan (C. A. Anderson et al., 2010). They found that playing violent video games is a causal factor for increased aggressive thoughts, feelings, and actions, along with decreased feelings of empathy. Culture and gender had very little impact on how susceptible players were to the effects of these games. But playing positive video games can increase prosocial behaviors, so it is not that games themselves are bad. It appears that we learn what we play, but there are few prosocial games and many violent ones. So an important issue facing teachers, parents, and our whole society is determining what we should do to limit the risks to children. See the *Guidelines: Dealing with Aggression and Encouraging Cooperation* on the next page (Anderman, Cupp, & Lane, 2009; T. A. Murdock & Anderman, 2006).

Reaching Every Student: Teacher Support

Because they are the main adults in students' lives for many hours each week, teachers have opportunities to play a significant role in students' personal and social development. For students facing emotional or interpersonal problems, teachers are sometimes the best source of help. When

GUIDELINES
Dealing with Aggression and Encouraging Cooperation

Present yourself as a nonaggressive model.

Examples

1. Do not use threats of aggression to win obedience.
2. When problems arise, model nonviolent conflict resolution strategies (see Chapter 13).

Ensure that your classroom has enough space and appropriate materials for every student.

Examples

1. Prevent overcrowding.
2. Make sure prized toys or resources are plentiful.
3. Remove or confiscate materials that encourage personal aggression, such as toy guns.
4. Avoid highly competitive activities and evaluations.

Make sure students do not profit from aggressive behaviors.

Examples

1. Comfort the victim of aggression, and ignore the aggressor.
2. Use reasonable punishment, especially with older students.

Teach directly about positive social behaviors.

Examples

1. Incorporate lessons on social ethics/morality through reading selections and discussions.
2. Discuss the effects of antisocial actions such as stealing, bullying, and spreading rumors.
3. Provide models and encouragement; role-play appropriate conflict resolution.
4. Build self-esteem by building skills and knowledge.
5. Seek help for students who seem especially isolated and victimized.

Provide opportunities for learning tolerance and cooperation.

Examples

1. Emphasize the similarities among people rather than the differences.
2. Set up group projects that encourage cooperation.

For more ideas, see the National Youth Violence Prevention Resource Center: safeyouth.gov/Resources/Prevention/Pages/PreventionHome.aspx

---

students have chaotic and unpredictable home lives, they need a caring, predictable structure in school. They need teachers who set clear limits, are consistent, enforce rules firmly but not punitively, respect students, and show genuine concern. Being liked by teachers can offset the negative effects of peer rejection in middle school. And students who have few friends but are not rejected—simply ignored by other students—can remain well adjusted academically and socially when they are liked and supported by teachers.

As a teacher, you can be available to your students if they want to talk about their personal problems without requiring them to do so. One of my student teachers gave a boy in her class a journal entitled "Very Hard Thoughts" so that he could write about his parents' divorce. Sometimes he talked to her about the journal entries, but at other times, he just recorded his feelings. The student teacher was very careful to respect the boy's privacy about his writings.

ACADEMIC AND PERSONAL CARING. When researchers ask students to describe a "good teacher," three qualities are consistently at the center of their descriptions. Good teachers have positive interpersonal relationships—they care about their students. Second, good teachers keep the classroom organized and maintain authority without being rigid or "mean." Finally, good teachers are good motivators—they can make learning fun by being creative and innovative so students learn something. Authoritative teaching strategies, like authoritative approaches to parenting, appear to lead to positive relationships with students and to enhance motivation for learning (Noguera, 2005; Woolfolk Hoy & Weinstein, 2006). We will look at motivation in Chapter 12 and at management in Chapter 13, so for now let's focus on caring and teaching.

Research has documented the value and importance of positive relationships with teachers for students at every grade level (Allen et al., 2013; R. I. Chapman et al., 2013; Crosnoe et al., 2010; Hamre & Pianta, 2001; Shechtman & Yaman, 2012). Teachers' behaviors that communicate liking and respect, such as eye contact, relaxed body posture, and smiling, are associated with students' liking of teachers, interest in courses, and motivation to achieve (Woolfolk & Perry, 2015). For example, one of my doctoral graduates studied middle school mathematics classes and found that students' perceptions of their teachers' affective support and caring were related to the effort they invested in learning math (Sakiz, Pape, & Woolfolk Hoy, 2008). Tamera Murdock and Angela Miller (2003) found that eighth-grade students' perceptions that their teachers cared about them were significantly related to the students' academic motivation, even after taking into account the motivational influences of parents and peers. In high school, teacher sensitivity to the students' needs and perspectives predicts the students' performance on end-of-year standardized tests (Allen et al., 2013).

Students define caring in two ways. One is *academic caring*—setting high, but reasonable expectations and helping students reach those goals. The second is *personal caring*—being patient, respectful, humorous, willing to listen, interested in students' issues and personal problems. For students who are higher achieving, academic caring is especially important, but for students who are placed at risk and often alienated from school, personal caring is critical (Cothran & Ennis, 2000; Woolfolk Hoy & Weinstein, 2006). In fact, in one study in a Texas high school, the Mexican and Mexican American students saw teacher caring as a prerequisite for their own caring about school; in other words, they needed to be *cared for* before they could *care about* school (Valenzuela, 1999). Unfortunately, in the same school, the mostly non-Latino teachers expected the students to care about school before they would invest their caring in the students. And for many teachers, caring about school meant behaving in more "middle-class" ways.

These contrasting student and teacher views can lead to a downward spiral of mistrust. Students withhold their cooperation until teachers "earn it" with their authentic caring. Teachers withhold caring until students "earn it" with respect for authority and cooperation. Marginalized students expect unfair treatment and behave defensively when they sense any unfairness. Teachers get tough and punish. Students feel correct about their mistrusting and become more guarded and defiant. Teachers feel correct in mistrusting and become more controlling and punitive, and on it goes (Woolfolk Hoy & Weinstein, 2006).

Of course, students need both academic and personal caring. Katz (1999) interviewed eight Latino immigrant students in a middle school and concluded:

> High expectations without caring can result in setting goals that are impossible for the student to reach without adult support and assistance. On the other hand, caring without high expectations can turn dangerously into paternalism in which teachers feel sorry for "underprivileged" youth but never challenge them academically. High expectations and caring in tandem, however, can make a powerful difference in students' lives. (p. 814)

In short, caring means not giving up on students in addition to demonstrating and teaching kindness in the classroom (H. A. Davis, 2003).

Teachers and Child Abuse

Certainly, one critical way to care about students is to protect their welfare and intervene in cases of abuse. Although accurate information about the number of abused children in the United States is difficult to find because many cases go unreported, every year about 3,000,000 cases of abuse and neglect are reported and 900,000 are confirmed. That means a child is abused or neglected every 47 seconds (Children's Defense Fund, 2013b). Of course, parents are not the only people who abuse children. Siblings, other relatives, and even teachers have been responsible for the physical and sexual abuse of children.

As part of your responsibilities as a teacher, you must alert your principal, school psychologist, or school social worker if you suspect abuse. In all 50 states, the District of Columbia, and the U.S. territories, the law requires certain professionals, often including teachers, to report suspected cases of child abuse. The legal definition of *abuse* has been broadened in many states to include neglect and failure to provide proper care and supervision. Be sure that you understand the laws in your state or province on this important issue, as well as your own moral responsibility. At least four children die of abuse or neglect each day in the United States, in many cases because no one would "get involved" (Children's Defense Fund, 2013a). Even children who survive abuse pay a great

TABLE 3.2 • Indicators of Child Abuse

The following are some of the signs of abuse. Not every child with these signs is abused, but these indicators should be investigated. To learn about who must report child abuse, see childwelfare.gov/systemwide/laws_policies/statutes/manda.cfm.

	PHYSICAL INDICATORS	BEHAVIORAL INDICATORS
Physical Abuse	• Unexplained bruises and welts (in various stages of healing), marks in the shape of belt buckles or electrical cords, human bite marks, puncture marks, bald spots, regularly appearing after absences or weekends • Unexplained burns, especially cigarette burns, burns in the shape of irons, rope burns, or immersion-burns (sock-like or glove-like) • Unexplained fractures, lacerations, or abrasions in various stages of healing • Injuries attributed to the child being "clumsy" or "accident prone"	• Awkward movements, complains of soreness • Self-destructive • Withdrawn and aggressive—behavioral extremes • Uncomfortable with physical contact • Arrives at school early or stays late, as if afraid • Chronic runaway (adolescents) • Wears high-neck, long-sleeved clothing, not matching weather, to cover body • Frequent absences
Physical Neglect	• Abandonment • Unattended physical problems or medical needs • Constant fatigue, lack of energy • Little or no supervision • Often hungry, dressed inappropriately for weather, poor hygiene • Lice, distended stomach, emaciation	• Falls asleep in class • Steals food, begs from classmates • Reports that no caretaker is at home • Frequently absent or tardy, or stays as long as possible at school • Self-destructive • Trouble with the law
Sexual Abuse	• Difficulty walking or sitting • Pain or itching in genital area • Torn, stained, or bloodied underclothing • Bruises or bleeding in external genitalia • Venereal disease, especially in preteens • Frequent urinary or yeast infections • Pregnancy	• Doesn't want to change for gym, PE • Withdrawn, chronic depression • Role reversal, overly concerned for siblings • Promiscuity, excessive seductiveness • Peer problems, lack of involvement • Massive weight change • Suicide attempts (especially adolescents) • Inappropriate sex play or premature understanding of sex, frequent masturbation, sexual play with dolls or stuffed animals • Sudden school difficulties

price. In school alone, physically abused children are more likely to be aggressive in the classroom, have difficulty understanding social situations and recognizing emotions in others, and are retained in grades and referred for special education services more often than children who were not abused (Luke & Banerjee, 2013; Roeser et al., 2006). What should you look for as indicators of abuse? Table 3.2 lists possible indicators.

Society and Media

All of the students you will teach are growing up in a world of media, mobility, and machines. Today 75% of children ages 0 to 8 live in homes with at least one mobile device—smartphone, iPad, iPod, tablet—many of these children have their own (Common Sense Media, 2013). In 2010, 75% of adolescents ages 12 to 17 had cell phones. Many had computers, even from early ages. Each year their use of technology increases (Common Sense Media, 2013; Nielsen Company, 2010; Rideout et al., 2010; Turkle, 2011). Figure 3.4 shows the different technologies that 12-, 14-, and 17-year-olds use daily to keep in touch with friends.

Teens are sending or receiving an average of 3,339 text messages per month—over 100 per day (Nielsen Company, 2010). When do they have time for anything else? And these texts demand immediate attention. One high school sophomore told Sherry Turkle (2011) that within his circle of friends, texts had to be answered as soon as possible, within 10 minutes, maximum. As he noted, "Texting is pressure" (p. 266). This pressure means that peers and even parents are always present—their messages demanding a response, even if the student is in class and must text in secret under the desk or with hands inside a backpack. Students and adults are spending more time with technology and less with

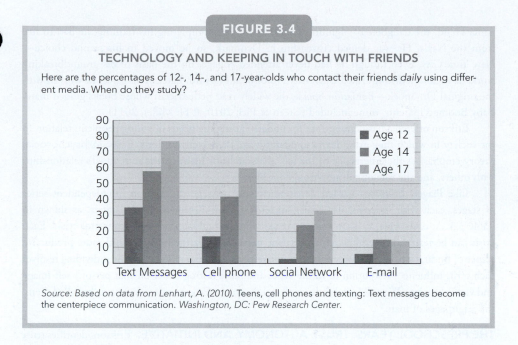

FIGURE 3.4

TECHNOLOGY AND KEEPING IN TOUCH WITH FRIENDS

Here are the percentages of 12-, 14-, and 17-year-olds who contact their friends *daily* using different media. When do they study?

Source: Based on data from Lenhart, A. (2010). Teens, cell phones and texting: Text messages become the centerpiece communication. Washington, DC: Pew Research Center.

each other. But these instant, superficial communications via cell phones, computers, iPads, and other electronic communication devices are not necessarily ties that bind students in deep relationships; instead, they are ties that preoccupy and distract (Turkle, 2011). What will it be like to teach students who send and receive over 100 text messages a day, and who can't focus on your class when a Pinterest posting appears? These are questions you will have to answer when you step into a classroom.

ENHANCEDetext *self-check*

IDENTITY AND SELF-CONCEPT

What is identity? Is identity different from self-concept or self-esteem? How do we come to understand other people and ourselves? In this section we look at the development of identity and sense of self. You will see patterns similar to those noted in Chapter 2 for cognitive development. Children's understandings of themselves are concrete at first. Early views of self and friends are based on immediate behaviors and appearances. Children assume that others share their feelings and perceptions. Their thinking about themselves and others is simple, segmented, and rule-bound, not flexible or integrated into organized systems. In time, children can think abstractly about internal processes—beliefs, intentions, values, and motivations. With these developments in thinking, children can incorporate more abstract qualities into their knowledge of self, others, and situations (Harter, 2003, 2006; Woolfolk & Perry, 2015).

In this section you will encounter the term *identity* along with several *self-* terms: *self-concept, self-esteem,* and *self-worth.* The distinctions among these terms are not always sharp; even psychologists disagree about what each term means (Roeser et al., 2006). In general, *identity* is a broader concept than the *self-* terms. Identity includes people's general sense of themselves along with all their beliefs, emotions, values, commitments, and attitudes. Identity integrates all the different aspects and roles of the self (Wigfield et al., 2006). But it is common for researchers to use *self-concept* and *identity* interchangeably. To make matters easier, I will too. We begin our consideration of identity/self-concept with the framework of Erik Erikson.

Erikson: Stages of Psychosocial Development

Like Piaget, Erik Erikson did not start his career as a psychologist. He skipped college, travelled around Europe, and ended up teaching in Vienna, where he studied psychoanalysis with

Anna Freud, the daughter of Sigmund Freud. Soon after completing his training, he had to flee from the Nazis. He was denied citizenship in Denmark, so he moved to his second choice— New York City. Even though he had never attended college, on the basis of his groundbreaking work, he became a distinguished University Professor at Harvard. Later in his career he worked with the original Dr. Spock—Benjamin Spock, the widely read pediatrician whose books guided many Baby Boomers' parents, mine included (Green & Piel, 2010; P. H. Miller, 2011).

Erikson offered a basic framework for understanding the needs of young people in relation to the society in which they grow, learn, and later make their contributions. Erikson's **psychosocial** theory emphasizes the emergence of the self, the search for identity, the individual's relationships with others, and the role of culture throughout life.

Like Piaget, Erikson regarded development as a passage through an interdependent series of stages, each with its particular goals, concerns, accomplishments, and dangers, as shown in Table 3.3. At each stage, Erikson suggests that the individual faces a **developmental crisis**. Each crisis can be resolved by embracing an extreme position or by the healthier and more productive stance of finding a balance between the extreme responses. The way in which the individual resolves each crisis influences resolution of future crises and has a lasting effect on that person's self-image and view of society. We will look briefly at all eight stages in Erikson's theory—or, as he called them, the "eight ages of man."

THE PRESCHOOL YEARS: TRUST, AUTONOMY, AND INITIATIVE. Erikson identifies trust versus mistrust as the basic conflict of infancy. According to Erikson, the infant will develop a

TABLE 3.3 • Erikson's Eight Stages of Psychosocial Development

STAGES	APPROXIMATE AGE	IMPORTANT EVENT	DESCRIPTION
1. Basic trust versus basic mistrust	Birth to 12–18 months	Feeding	The infant must form a first loving, trusting relationship with the caregiver or develop a sense of mistrust.
2. Autonomy versus shame/doubt	18 months to 3 years	Toilet training	The child's energies are directed toward the development of physical skills, including walking, grasping, controlling the sphincter. The child learns control but may develop shame and doubt if not handled well.
3. Initiative versus guilt	3 to 6 years	Independence	The child continues to become more assertive and to take more initiative but may be too forceful, which can lead to guilt feelings.
4. Industry versus inferiority	6 to 12 years	School	The child must deal with demands to learn new skills or risk a sense of inferiority, failure, and incompetence.
5. Identity versus role confusion	Adolescence	Peer relationships	The teenager must achieve identity in occupation, gender roles, politics, and religion.
6. Intimacy versus isolation	Young adulthood	Love relationships	The young adult must develop intimate relationships or suffer feelings of isolation.
7. Generativity versus stagnation	Middle adulthood	Parenting/Mentoring	Each adult must find some way to satisfy and support the next generation.
8. Ego integrity versus despair	Late adulthood	Reflection on and acceptance of one's life	The culmination is a sense of acceptance of oneself and a sense of fulfillment.

Source: Lefton, Lester A., Psychology, 5th Edition, © 1994. Reprinted by permission of Pearson Education, Inc. Upper Saddle River, NJ.

sense of trust if its needs for food and care are met with comforting regularity and responsiveness from caregivers. In this first year, infants are in Piaget's sensorimotor stage and are just beginning to learn that they are separate from the world around them. This realization is part of what makes trust so important: Infants must trust the aspects of their world that are beyond their control (P. H. Miller, 2011; Posada et al., 2002). Having a secure attachment (described earlier in this chapter) helps young children develop trust and also learn when mistrust is appropriate—either extreme of complete trust or mistrust is dysfunctional.

Erikson's second stage, autonomy *versus shame and doubt,* marks the beginning of self-control and self-confidence as young children begin to assume responsibilities for self-care such as feeding, toileting, and dressing. During this period, parents must tread a fine line in being protective—but not overprotective. If parents do not reinforce their children's efforts to master basic motor and cognitive skills, children may begin to feel shame; they may learn to doubt their abilities to manage the world. Erikson believes that children who experience too much doubt at this stage will lack confidence in their own abilities throughout life. Of course, some doubt is appropriate if the task is too difficult or dangerous—again the need for balance.

For Erikson, the next stage of initiative *versus guilt* "adds to autonomy the quality of undertaking, planning, and attacking a task for the sake of being active and on the move" (Erikson, 1963, p. 255). The challenge of this period is to maintain a balance between zest for activity and an understanding that not every impulse can be acted on. Again, adults must tread a fine line, this time in providing supervision without interference. If children are not allowed to do things on their own, a sense of guilt may develop; they may come to believe that what they want to do is always "wrong." The *Guidelines: Encouraging Initiative and Industry* on the next page suggest ways of encouraging initiative.

Connect and Extend to PRAXIS II®

Erikson's Psychosocial Theory of Development (I, A1, 2)
The school population spans four stages of Erikson's theory. Identify the major crisis of each of these stages. How can teachers support positive resolution of each of these stages? What are the implications for negative resolution of these crises?

THE ELEMENTARY AND MIDDLE SCHOOL YEARS: INDUSTRY VERSUS INFERIORITY. Let's set the stage for the next phase. Between the ages of 5 and 7, when most children start school, cognitive development is proceeding rapidly. Children can process more information faster, and their memory spans are increasing. They are moving from preoperational to concrete-operational thinking. As these internal changes progress, the children are spending hours every weekday in the new physical and social world of school. They must now reestablish Erikson's stages of psychosocial development in the unfamiliar school setting. They must learn to trust new adults, act autonomously in this more complex situation, and initiate actions in ways that fit the new rules of school.

The next psychosocial challenge for the school years is what Erikson calls industry *versus inferiority.* Students are beginning to see the relationship between perseverance and the pleasure of a job completed. In modern societies, children's ability to move between the worlds of home, neighborhood, and school, and to cope with academics, group activities, and friends will lead to a growing sense of competence. Difficulty with these challenges can result in feelings of inferiority. Children must master new skills and work toward new goals, at the same time they are being compared to others and risking failure. Because schools tend to reflect middle-class values and norms, making the transition to school and meeting the challenge of *industry versus inferiority* may be especially difficult for children who differ economically or culturally. The *Guidelines: Encouraging Initiative and Industry* on the next page gives ideas that encourage industry.

After elementary school, in the transition to middle school, students confront an increased focus on grades and performance as well as more competition on all fronts—academic, social, and athletic. Just when they are eager to make decisions and assume more independence, students encounter more rules, required courses, and assignments. They change from a close connection with one teacher all year to more impersonal relations with numerous teachers in many different subjects across the year. They also go from being the most mature and highest status students in a small, familiar elementary school to being the "babies" in a large, impersonal middle school (T. B. Murdock, Hale, & Weber, 2001; Rudolph, Lambert, Clark, & Kurlakowsky, 2001; Wigfield, Eccles, MacIver, Rueman, & Midgley, 1991). In this demanding context, they face the next challenge—identity.

ADOLESCENCE: THE SEARCH FOR IDENTITY. As students move into adolescence, they are developing capabilities for abstract thinking and understanding the perspectives of others. Even

GUIDELINES
Encouraging Initiative and Industry

Encourage children to make and to act on choices.

Examples

1. Have a free-choice time when children can select an activity or game.
2. As much as possible, avoid interrupting children who are very involved in what they are doing.
3. When children suggest an activity, try to follow their suggestions or incorporate their ideas into ongoing activities.
4. Offer positive choices: Instead of saying, "You can't have the cookies now," ask, "Would you like the cookies after lunch or after naptime?"

Make sure that each child has a chance to experience success.

Examples

1. When introducing a new game or skill, teach it in small steps.
2. Avoid competitive games when the range of abilities in the class is great.

Encourage make-believe with a wide variety of roles.

Examples

1. Have costumes and props that go along with stories the children enjoy. Encourage the children to act out the stories or make up new adventures for favorite characters.
2. Monitor the children's play to be sure no one monopolizes playing "teacher," "Mommy," "Daddy," or other heroes.

Be tolerant of accidents and mistakes, especially when children are attempting to do something on their own.

Examples

1. Use cups and pitchers that make it easy to pour and hard to spill.
2. Recognize the attempt, even if the product is unsatisfactory.

3. If mistakes are made, show students how to clean up, repair, or redo.
4. If a student consistently behaves in ways that are highly unusual or unacceptable, seek guidance from the school counselor or psychologist. The best time to help children deal with psychosocial problems is at an early age.

Make sure that students have opportunities to set and work toward realistic goals.

Examples

1. Begin with short assignments, then move on to longer ones. Monitor student progress by setting up progress checkpoints.
2. Teach students to set reasonable goals. Write down goals, and have students keep a journal of progress toward these goals.

Give students a chance to show their independence and responsibility.

Examples

1. Tolerate honest mistakes.
2. Delegate to students tasks such as watering class plants, collecting and distributing materials, monitoring the computer lab, grading homework, keeping records of forms returned, and so on.

Provide support to students who seem discouraged.

Examples

1. Use individual charts and contracts that show student progress.
2. Keep samples of earlier work so students can see their improvements.
3. Have awards for most improved, most helpful, most hardworking.

---

greater physical changes are taking place as the students approach puberty. So, with developing minds and bodies, young adolescents must confront the central issue of constructing an identity that will provide a firm basis for adulthood. The individual has been developing a sense of self since infancy. But adolescence marks the first time that a conscious effort is made to answer the now-pressing question: "Who am I?" The conflict defining this stage is *identity* versus *role confusion*. *Identity* refers to the organization of the individual's drives, abilities, beliefs, and history into a consistent image of self. It involves deliberate choices and decisions, particularly about work, values, ideology, and commitments to people and ideas (P. H. Miller, 2011; Penuel & Wertsch, 1995). If adolescents fail to integrate all these aspects and choices, or if they feel unable to choose at all, role confusion threatens.

- -

STOP & THINK Have you decided on your career? What alternatives did you consider? Who or what was influential in shaping your decision? •

- -

James Marcia (1991, 1994, 1999; Kroger, Martinussen, & Marcia, 2010) expanded on Erikson's theory of identity formation. Specifically, he focused on two essential processes in achieving a mature identity: exploration and commitment. **Exploration** refers to the process by which adolescents consider and try out alternative beliefs, values, and behaviors in an effort to determine which will give them the most satisfaction. **Commitment** refers to individuals' choices concerning political and religious beliefs, for example, usually as a consequence of exploring the options. Then, Marcia identified four categories of *identity status* that arise from four patterns of exploration and commitment.

The first, **identity achievement**, means that after *exploring* the realistic options, the individual has made choices and is *committed* to pursuing them. It appears that few students achieve this status by the end of high school; students who attend college may take even longer to decide. It is not uncommon for the explorations to continue into the early 20s. About 80% of students change their majors at least once (just ask my mom). And some adults may achieve a firm identity at one period in their lives, only to reject that identity and achieve a new one later. So identity, once achieved, may not be unchanging for everyone (Adams, Berzonsky, & Keating, 2006; Kroger et al., 2010; Nurmi, 2004).

Adolescents in the midst of struggling with choices are experiencing what Erikson called a **moratorium**. Erikson used the term *moratorium* to describe exploration with a delay in commitment to personal and occupational choices. This delay is very common, and probably healthy, for modern adolescents. Erikson believed that adolescents in complex societies have an identity crisis during moratorium. Today, the period is no longer referred to as a *crisis* because, for most people, the experience is a gradual exploration rather than a traumatic upheaval (Kroger et al., 2010; Wigfield, Byrnes, & Eccles, 2006). Both identity-achieved and moratorium statuses are considered healthy.

Identity foreclosure is commitment without exploration. Foreclosed adolescents have not experimented with different identities or explored a range of options, but simply have committed themselves to the goals, values, and lifestyles of others—usually their parents, but sometimes cults or extremist groups. Foreclosed adolescents tend to be rigid, intolerant, dogmatic, and defensive (Frank, Pirsch, & Wright, 1990).

Identity diffusion occurs when individuals do not explore any options or commit to any actions. They reach no conclusions about who they are or what they want to do with their lives. Adolescents experiencing identity diffusion may be apathetic and withdrawn, with little hope for the future, or they may be openly rebellious. These adolescents often go along with the crowd, so they are more likely to abuse drugs (Archer & Waterman, 1990; Kroger, 2000).

Schools that give adolescents experiences with community service, real-world work, internships, and mentoring help to foster identity formation (C. R. Cooper, 1998). See the *Guidelines: Supporting Identity Formation* on the next page.

IDENTITY AND TECHNOLOGY. Some scholars of technology have speculated that establishing a separate identity is complicated for adolescents today because they are constantly connected to others. Parents often give a cell phone to their children somewhere between the ages of 7 and 10, or even earlier, with the specific requirement that the children always answer a call from the parent. Sherry Turkle (2011) calls this happy recipient of a new cell phone a "tethered child," now able to participate in activities such as spending time at a mall or on the beach that would not have been allowed without the safety tether of the phone. But the price paid is that these children never navigate social and physical landscapes completely alone—parents and friends always are a speed dial away. The chance to solve problems, experience autonomy, and handle situations on your own is the basis for achieving identity and mature judgment. The tethered child is never alone. Texting means the tether is even shorter. The high school students Turkle interviewed talked about the "big mistake" of teaching their parents to text or instant message. A friend of mine is a physician at a university health center. She describes undergraduate patients who respond to her question, "What are your health concerns today?" with the answer, "My mom is on the phone—she'll tell you" and then the college student hands a cell phone to the doctor. Constant connectivity complicates achieving a separate identity and autonomy.

Connectivity also "offers new possibilities for experimenting with identity, particularly in adolescence, the sense of a free space, what Eric Erikson called the *moratorium*" (Turkle, 2011, p. 152). On Second Life or The Sims Online or other life-simulation sites, adolescents can create

GUIDELINES
Supporting Identity Formation

Give students many models for career choices and other adult roles.

Examples

1. Point out models from literature and history. Have a calendar with the birthdays of eminent women, minority leaders, or people who made a little-known contribution to the subject you are teaching. Briefly discuss the person's accomplishments on his or her birthday.
2. Invite guest speakers to describe how and why they chose their professions. Make sure all kinds of work and workers are represented.

Help students find resources for working out personal problems.

Examples

1. Encourage them to talk to school counselors.
2. Discuss potential outside services.

Be tolerant of teenage fads as long as they don't offend others or interfere with learning.

Examples

1. Discuss the fads of earlier eras (neon hair, powdered wigs, love beads).
2. Don't impose strict dress or hair codes.

Give students realistic feedback about their work and support for improving. Adolescents may need many "second chances."

Examples

1. When students misbehave or perform poorly, make sure they understand the consequences of their behavior—the effects on themselves and others.
2. Give students model answers or show them other students' completed projects from previous years so they can compare their work to good examples.
3. Never use a student's work as a "bad" example. Create negative examples from multiple sources including mistakes you have made.
4. Because students are "trying on" roles, keep the roles separate from the person. Criticize the behavior without criticizing the student.

For more ideas about working with adolescents using Erikson's theory, see cde.ca.gov/ls/cg/pp/documents/erikson.pdf

whole new identities and keep multiple personalities "alive." Some people even talk about their "life mix," a mash up of what they live online and what they live in real life. For some adolescents, the boundaries may be unclear and easily crossed. Is the profile adolescents create on Facebook the "real" person, or as one high school senior described, the identity that you "mold" to present to the world? But with worldwide access to the self-presentation, a critical question arises, "How will the self I present be judged by others?" For connected and tethered adolescents today, Elkind's (1985) imaginary audience (discussed in Chapter 2) is now a real, online audience. The consequences are not all positive, as another senior agonized:

> You have to know that everything you put up will be perused very carefully. And that makes it necessary for you to obsess over what you do put up and how you portray yourself. . . . And when you have to think about what you come across as, that's just another way that . . . you are thinking of yourself in a bad way. (Turkle, 2011, p. 184)

BEYOND THE SCHOOL YEARS. The crises of Erikson's stages of adulthood all involve the quality of human relations. Intimacy *versus isolation* refers to a willingness to relate to another person on a deep level, to have a relationship based on more than mutual need. Someone who has not achieved a sufficiently strong sense of identity tends to fear being overwhelmed or swallowed up by another person and may retreat into isolation. Generativity *versus stagnation* extends the ability to care for another person and involves concern and guidance for both the next generation and future generations. Productivity and creativity are essential features. Achieving integrity *versus despair* means consolidating your sense of self and fully accepting its unique and now unalterable history (Hearn, Saulnier, Strayer, Glenham, Koopman, & Marcia, 2012).

Erikson's work helped start the life-span development approach, and his theories have been especially useful in understanding adolescence and developing concepts of self. But feminists have criticized his notion that identity precedes intimacy, because their research indicates that for women, identity achievement is fused with achieving intimacy (P. H. Miller, 2011). And, as you will see next, recent research has focused on identity issues not fully explored by Erikson—racial and ethnic identity.

Racial-Ethnic Identity

As early as 1903, W. E. B. Du Bois wrote about the "double consciousness" of African Americans. In essence, African Americans, like other ethnic or racial groups, are conscious of their ethnic identity as they negotiate being members of the larger culture as well. Ethnic minority students have to "sift through two sets of cultural values and identity options" to achieve a firm identity, so they may need more time to explore possibilities—a longer moratorium in Erikson's terms (Markstrom-Adams, 1992, p. 177). But the exploration is important; some psychologists consider ethnic identity a "master status," one that dominates all other identity concerns when judging the self (Charmaraman & Grossman, 2010; M. Herman, 2004).

ETHNIC IDENTITIES: OUTCOME AND PROCESS. Jean Phinney (1990, 2003) describes four outcomes for ethnic minority youth in their search for identity. They can try *assimilation,* fully adopting the values and behaviors of the majority culture and rejecting their ethnic culture. At the opposite end, they can be *separated,* associating only with members of their ethnic culture. A third possibility is *marginality,* living in the majority culture, but feeling alienated and uncomfortable in it and disconnected from the minority culture as well. The final alternative is *biculturalism* (sometimes called *integration*), maintaining ties to both cultures. And there are at least three ways to be bicultural. You could alternate between the two cultures, being fully "majority" in your behavior in one situation and fully "minority" in other situations. Or you could blend the two cultures by finding values and behaviors that are common to both and acting on them. Finally, you could fuse the two cultures by truly merging them into a new and complete whole (Phinney & Devich-Navarro, 1997).

No matter what your identity outcome is, having strong positive feelings about your own ethnic group seems to be important for good mental health as well as engagement and success in school (J. L. Cook & Cook, 2014; Steinberg, 2005). In fact, Amy Marks and her colleagues (Marks, Patton, & Coll, 2011) determined that bicultural adolescents who form strong, positive multiethnic identities have higher self-esteem, fewer mental health problems, and higher academic achievement than peers with a single ethnic identity or an undeveloped multiethnic identity.

Some psychologists have used Marcia's identity statuses to understand the process of forming an ethnic identity. Children may begin with an unexamined ethnic identity, either because they have not explored at all (diffusion) or because they have accepted the identity encouraged by others (foreclosure). Many European American adolescents could fit the unexamined category. A period of ethnic identity exploration (moratorium) might be followed by a resolution of the conflict (identity achieved).

RACIAL IDENTITY: OUTCOME AND PROCESS. William Cross (1991; Cross & Cross, 2007; DeCuir-Gunby, 2009) devised a framework that specifically addresses African American racial identity. The process he calls **nigrescence** has five stages:

- *Pre-encounter:* At this stage, Cross says that an African American's attitude may range from ignoring race to feeling neutral about race, to actually being anti-Black. African Americans at this stage may adopt certain beliefs of White Americans, including the tendency to see "Whiteness" as superior. Some level of self-hate is a possible consequence. At the pre-encounter stage, people value other aspects of their identity, such as religion, profession, or social status.
- *Encounter:* This stage is often triggered by encounters with overt, covert, or institutional racism. For instance, when an African American is followed around in an upscale store, is assaulted by police, or sees news reports about such assaults, then his or her eyes are opened to the reality that race matters in society. The African American becomes attuned to his or her Blackness.
- *Immersion/Emersion:* Cross sees this as a transition—an in-between state that may cause people to be anxious about "becoming the 'right kind' of Black person" (Cross, 1991, p. 202). In response to encounters with discrimination, the individuals fill their lives with symbols of

Blackness; they buy books about Black experiences and socialize mainly with other African Americans, for example. They are eager to understand their racial heritage more deeply.

- *Internalization:* Individuals are firmly connected to and secure in their sense of racial identity. They don't worry about what friends or outsiders think—they are confident in their own standards of Blackness.
- *Internalization-Commitment:* This stage is very closely connected with internalization. The main difference is a person's continued interest in and commitment to Black affairs. Such individuals chart their lives to connect to their Black racial identity; for example, a painter dedicates his life to painting Black images or a researcher dedicates her life to studying African American educational experiences.

Determining a racial identity may be even more complicated for biracial or multiracial adolescents. The parent they live with, the make-up of their neighborhood, their appearance, and experiences of discrimination or support can influence these adolescents' decisions about racial identity. Some psychologists think that these challenges help multiracial youth develop stronger and more complex identities, but other researchers argue that the challenges present an extra burden in an already-tough process (M. Herman, 2004). Perhaps the outcome depends in part on the support adolescents receive in facing the challenges.

RACIAL AND ETHNIC PRIDE. For all students, pride in family and community is part of the foundation of a stable identity. Special efforts to encourage racial and ethnic pride are particularly important, so that students examining their identities do not get the message that differences are deficits. In one study, researchers found that African American preschool students whose homes were rich with African American culture had more factual knowledge and better problem-solving skills than students whose homes lacked rich cultural resources. Parents who encouraged their children to be proud of their heritage reported fewer behavior problems with their children than parents who did not encourage racial pride (Caughy, O'Campo, Randolph, & Nickerson, 2002). In other research, positive racial identity was found to be related to higher self-esteem and fewer emotional problems for both African American and White adolescents (DuBois, Burk-Braxton, Swenson, Tevendale, & Hardesty, 2002).

Each of us has an ethnic heritage. Janet Helms (1995) has written about stages in White identity development. H. Richard Milner (2003) has pointed to the importance of racial identity development and awareness, especially in teaching. When majority adolescents are knowledgeable and secure about their own heritage, they are also more respectful of the heritage of others. Thus, exploring the racial and ethnic roots of all students should foster both pride in self and acceptance of others (Rotherham-Borus, 1994).

In the next sections we move from overarching considerations of identity to more specific conceptions of self. In educational psychology, much research is focused on self-concept and self-esteem.

Self-Concept

The term *self-concept* is part of our everyday conversations. We talk about people who have a "low" self-concept or individuals whose self-concept is not "strong," as if self-concept were the oil level in a car or your abdominal muscles. These actually are misuses of the term. In psychology, self-concept generally refers to our perceptions of ourselves—how we see our abilities, attitudes, attributes, beliefs, and expectations (Harter, 2006; Pajares & Schunk, 2001). We could consider self-concept to be our mental picture of who we are. It is our attempt to explain ourselves to ourselves, to build a scheme (in Piaget's terms) that organizes our impressions, attitudes, and beliefs about ourselves. But this model or scheme is not permanent, unified, or unchanging. Our self-perceptions can vary from situation to situation and from one phase of our lives to another.

THE STRUCTURE OF SELF-CONCEPT. Self-concept is multidimensional. A student's overall self-concept is made up of more specific concepts, including academic and nonacademic self-concepts, and these self-concepts are made up of even more specific concepts such as self-concepts in math and languages or appearance and popularity with friends. Herbert Marsh and his colleagues (Marsh, Craven, & Martin, 2006) have identified up to 17 different self-concepts in *academic* areas (verbal, mathematics, problem solving, art, computers) and *nonacademic* areas (e.g., physical appearance, popularity, trustworthiness, relations with parents, emotional stability).

For academic subjects, self-concepts include both perceptions of competence (I am good in science) and affect or attitudes (I like science) (Arens, Yeung, Crave, & Hasselhorn, 2011). For adolescents, both their overall academic self-concept (how quickly they learn or how well they do in school in general) and their subject-specific self-concept (how good they think they are in math, their attitudes toward math) may influence their decisions and motivation. For example, your educational aspirations and goals (e.g., deciding to attend college) are driven by your general academic self-concept. But the major you chose in college is influenced by your subject-specific academic self-concepts (Brunner et al., 2010).

Separate, specific-subject self-concepts are not necessarily integrated into an overall self-concept for adults after they finish their formal education because they are no longer in situations where specific academic subjects are taught and tested. So self-concept probably is more situation-specific in adults (Marsh et al., 2006; Schunk, Meece &, Pintrich 2014).

HOW SELF-CONCEPT DEVELOPS. The self-concept evolves through constant self-evaluation in different situations. Children and adolescents are continually asking themselves, in effect, "How am I doing?" They gauge the verbal and nonverbal reactions of significant people—parents and other family members in the early years, and friends, schoolmates, and teachers later—to make these judgments (Harter, 1998, 2006).

Younger children tend to have positive and optimistic self-concepts. They don't compare themselves to peers; they just compare their current skill level to what they could do earlier in their lives and see improvement. In some ways this confidence protects them from disappointment and maintains persistence—a good thing for developing children (Harter, 2006). Older students are less optimistic, more realistic, and even cynical. In either case, for younger and older students, self-evaluations contribute to a person's self-concept in any given domain and also to an overall sense of self-worth, known as *self-esteem,* which is discussed in a later section.

With experience in school, children make self-concept appraisals based on their own performance. This process begins early in school. Researchers followed 60 students in New Zealand from the time they started school until the middle of their third year (J. W. Chapman, Tunmer, & Prochnow, 2000). In the first 2 months of school, differences in reading self-concept began to develop, based on the ease or difficulty students had learning to read. Students who entered school with good knowledge about sounds and letters learned to read more easily and developed more positive reading self-concepts. Over time, differences in the reading performance of students with high and low reading self-concepts grew even greater. The children's early experiences with the important school task of reading had a strong impact on their self-concept.

As they mature, students become more realistic, but many are not accurate judges of their own abilities. Some students suffer from "illusions of incompetence"; they seriously underestimate their own competence (Phillips & Zimmerman, 1990). As students grow more self-conscious during the middle school years, their self-concepts are tied to physical appearance and social acceptance as well as school achievement. These years can be exceedingly difficult for students such as Stephanie, described at the opening of this chapter (Wigfield, Eccles, & Pintrich, 1996).

For older students, both self and other comparisons shape self-concepts, at least in Western cultures. Students' self-concepts in math are shaped by how their math performance compares to their performance history. They also compare themselves to other math students (Altermatt, Pomerantz, Ruble, Frey, & Greulich, 2002; Schunk et al., 2014). Generally speaking, students who are strong in math in an average school feel better about their math skills than do students of equal ability in high-achieving schools. Marsh and his colleagues (2008) call this the "Big-Fish-Little-Pond Effect (BFLP)." Research that surveyed 265,180 15-year-old students in 10,221 schools across 41 countries around the world found the BFLP effect in every one of these countries (Seaton, Marsh, & Craven, 2009). Another study of almost 400,000 high school students in 57 counties found similar results in science (Nagengast & Marsh, 2012). In an interesting example of the BFLP effect, the academic self-concepts of Belgian middle school students who were moved to a lower track improved, even though their actual achievement decreased (S. Wouters, De Fraine, Colpin, Van Damme, & Verschueren, 2012). Participation in a gifted and talented program seems to have a "Little-Fish-in-a-Big-Pond" effect: Students who participate in gifted programs, compared to similar students who remain in general education classes, tend to show declines in academic self-concepts over time, but no changes in nonacademic self-concepts (Marsh & Craven, 2002; Preckel, Goetz, & Frenzel, 2010).

Before we move on to look at self-concept and achievement, an important caveat is in order. The development of self-concept does not follow the same path in every culture. Most Western and European parents want their children to develop a strong sense of self and a spirit of independence, but Asian parents want their children to develop a strong sense of interdependence and to define themselves in relation to the significant people in their lives—their family, their community/culture (Peterson, Cobas, Bush, Supple, & Wilson, 2004). And not all subcultures within Western societies emphasize independence to the same extent. Many ethnic groups value family or group interdependence over independence. For example, many Latino children are taught that their personal identities are inseparable from the identity of their families, and many Native American families, even in urban areas, often live with or near relatives and operate like a communal village (Parke & Buriel, 2006).

SELF-CONCEPT AND ACHIEVEMENT. Many psychologists consider self-concept to be the foundation of both social and emotional development. Research has linked self-concept to a wide range of accomplishments—from performance in competitive sports to job satisfaction to achievement in school (Byrne, 2002; Goetz, Cronjaeger, Frenzel, Ludtke, & Hall, 2010; Marsh & O'Mara, 2008; Möller & Pohlmann, 2010). Some evidence for the link between self-concept and school achievement is that performance in academic subjects is correlated with specific self-concepts in those areas, but not with social or physical self-concepts. For example, in one study, math self-concept correlated .77 with math test scores, .59 with grades, and .51 with coursework selection (Marsh et al., 2006; O'Mara, Marsh, Craven, & Debus, 2006).

That last correlation of math self-concept with course selection points to an important way self-concept affects learning in school. Think back to high school. When you had a chance to choose courses, did you pick your worst subjects—those where you felt least capable? Probably not. Herbert Marsh and Alexander Yeung (1997) examined how 246 boys in early high school in Sydney, Australia, chose their courses. Academic self-concept for a particular subject (mathematics, science, etc.) was the most important predictor of course selection—more important than previous grades in the subject or overall self-concept. The courses selected in high school put students on a path toward the future, so self-concepts about particular academic subjects can be life-changing influences.

Unfortunately, heavy emphasis on grade point averages (GPAs) for admission to some colleges can affect course choice as well, especially if students avoid classes to protect their GPAs because they see themselves as "no good" in math, science, world languages, or other challenging classes. Of course, we know from Chapter 1 that correlation is not cause; higher self-concept probably can encourage higher achievement, but high achievement likely also leads to higher self-concept, so the causes work in both directions (Pinxten, De Fraine, Van Damme & D'Haenens, 2010).

Sex Differences in Self-Concept of Academic Competence

Do girls and boys differ in their self-concepts? A study followed 761 middle-class, primarily European American students from first grade through high school (Jacobs, Lanza, Osgood, Eccles, & Wigfield, 2002). It is difficult to get longitudinal data, so this is a valuable study. In first grade, girls and boys had comparable perceptions of their own abilities in language arts, but boys felt significantly more competent in math and sports. Competence beliefs declined for both boys and girls across the grades, but boys fell faster in math, so that by high school, math competence beliefs were about the same for boys and girls. In language arts, boys' competence ratings fell more sharply than those of girls after first grade, but both leveled off during high school. In sports, competence ratings for both boys and girls dropped, but boys remained significantly more confident in their competence in sports throughout the entire 12 years.

Other studies have also found that girls tend to see themselves as more able than boys in reading and close friendships; boys are more confident about their abilities in math and athletics. Of course, some of these differences in self-confidence may reflect actual differences in achievement; girls tend to be better readers than boys, for example. As we have seen, many self-beliefs are reciprocally related to achievement—each affects the other (Eccles, Wigfield, & Schiefele, 1998; Pinxten et al., 2010). When these results are examined together with Marsh and Yeung's (1997) findings that academic self-concept influences course selection, it seems that many students make decisions about courses that forever limit their future options.

For most ethnic groups (except African Americans), boys are more confident than girls about their abilities in math and science. Unfortunately, there are no long-term studies of other ethnic groups, so these patterns may be limited to European Americans.

Self-Esteem

STOP & THINK How strongly do you agree or disagree with the following statements?
On the whole, I am satisfied with myself.
I feel that I have a number of good qualities.
I wish I could have more respect for myself.
At times, I think that I am no good at all.
I certainly feel useless at times.
I take a positive attitude toward myself. •

These *Stop & Think* questions are taken from a widely used measure of self-esteem (Hagborg, 1993; Rosenberg, 1979).

Self-esteem is an overall judgment of self-worth that includes feeling proud or ashamed of yourself as a person. If people judge themselves positively—if they "like what they see"—we say that they have high self-esteem (Schunk et al., 2014). Can you see the judgments of self-worth in the *Stop & Think* questions?

The terms *self-concept* and *self-esteem* are often used interchangeably, even though they have distinct meanings. Self-concept is a perception about who you are—for example, the belief that you are a good athlete. Self-esteem is an overall, general sense of value or self-worth. Self-concept is who I am, and self-esteem is how I feel about myself (O'Mara et al., 2006). As you can see in the *Stop & Think* items, the questions are pretty general; no specific areas such as academics or appearance are targeted. Self-esteem is influenced by whether the culture around you values your particular characteristics and capabilities (Bandura, 1997; Schunk et al., 2014).

Over 100 years ago, William James (1890) suggested that self-esteem is determined by how successful we are in accomplishing tasks or reaching goals we value. If a skill or accomplishment is not important, incompetence in that area doesn't threaten self-esteem. The reasons individuals give for their successes or failures also are important. To build self-esteem, students must attribute their successes to their own actions, not to luck or to special assistance.

Do schools affect self-esteem: Is school important? As you can see from the *Point/Counterpoint* on the next page, the school's role in student self-esteem has been hotly debated. Teachers' feedback, grading practices, evaluations, and communication of caring for students can make a difference in how students feel about their abilities in particular subjects. But the greatest increases in self-esteem come when students grow more competent in areas they value—including the social areas that become so important in adolescence. So, a teacher's greatest challenge is to help students achieve important understandings and skills (Osborne & Jones, 2011).

Connect and Extend to PRAXIS II®

Self-Esteem (I, A2)
Understand the bidirectional effects of school life and self-esteem on each other. What can teachers do to enhance students' self-esteem?

ENHANCEDetext *self-check*

POINT/COUNTERPOINT
What Should Schools Do to Encourage Students' Self-Esteem?

There are over 2,000 books describing how to increase self-esteem. Schools and mental health facilities continue to develop self-esteem programs (Slater, 2002). The attempts to improve students' self-esteem have taken three main forms: personal development activities such as sensitivity training; self-esteem programs where the curriculum focuses directly on improving self-esteem; and structural changes in schools that place greater emphasis on cooperation, student participation, community involvement, and ethnic pride. Are these efforts valuable?

POINT **The self-esteem movement has big problems.** Some people have accused schools of developing programs where the main objective is "to dole out a huge heaping of praise, regardless of actual accomplishments" (Slater, 2002, p. 45). Frank Pajares and Dale Schunk (2002) point to another problem. "[W]hen what is communicated to children from an early age is that nothing matters quite as much as how they feel or how confident they should be, one can rest assured that the world will sooner or later teach a lesson in humility that may not easily be learned. An obsession with one's sense of self is responsible for an alarming increase in depression and other mental difficulties" (p. 16). Sensitivity training and self-esteem courses assume that we encourage self-esteem by changing the individual's beliefs, making the young person work harder against the odds. But what if the student's environment is truly unsafe, debilitating, and unsupportive? Some people have overcome tremendous problems, but to expect everyone to do so "ignores the fact that having positive self-esteem is almost impossible for many young people, given the deplorable conditions under which they are forced to live by the inequities in our society" (Beane, 1991, p. 27).

Worse yet, some psychologists are now contending that low self-esteem is not a problem, whereas high self-esteem may be. For example, they contend, people with high self-esteem are more willing to inflict pain and punishment on others (Baumeister, Campbell, Krueger, & Vohs, 2003; Slater, 2002). In addition, high self-esteem does not seem to predict academic learning. In a large study of adolescents, global self-esteem did not correlate with any of the nine academic outcomes measured (Marsh et al., 2006). And when people set self-esteem as a main goal, they may pursue that goal in ways that are harmful over the long run. They may, for example, avoid constructive criticisms or challenging tasks (Crocker & Park, 2004). Psychologist Lauren Slater (2002), in her article "The Trouble with Self-Esteem," suggests that we rethink self-esteem and move toward honest self-appraisal that will lead to self-control. She suggests, "Maybe self-control should replace self-esteem as a primary peg to reach for" (p. 47).

COUNTERPOINT **The self-esteem movement has promise** Erik Erikson (1980) warned years ago: "Children cannot be fooled by empty praise and condescending encouragement. They may have to accept artificial bolstering of their self-esteem in lieu of something better. . . ." Erikson explained that a strong and positive identity comes only from "wholehearted and consistent recognition of real accomplishment, that is, achievement that has meaning in their culture" (p. 95). A study that followed 322 sixth-grade students for 2 years found that students' satisfaction with school, their sense that classes were interesting and teachers cared, and teacher feedback and evaluations influenced students' self-esteem. In PE, teachers' opinions were especially powerful in shaping students' conceptions of their athletic abilities (Hoge, Smit, & Hanson, 1990). Being placed in a low-ability group or being held back in school seems to have a negative impact on students' self-esteem, but learning in collaborative and cooperative settings seems to have a positive effect (Covington, 1992; Deci & Ryan, 1985). Interestingly, special programs such as "Student of the Month" or admission to advanced math classes had little effect on self-esteem.

Beyond the "feel-good psychology" of some aspects of the self-esteem movement is a basic truth: Self-esteem is a basic right of all humans. We deserve to respect ourselves, and neither the society nor its school should undermine that respect. Remember the Girls Project described in Figure 3.2, which reminds young girls that their value, and their self-esteem, should be based on their character, skills, and attributes—not appearance. If we view self-esteem accurately as a product of our thinking and our actions—our values, ideas, and beliefs as well as our interactions with others—then we see a significant role for the school. Practices that allow authentic participation, cooperation, problem solving, and accomplishment should replace policies that damage self-esteem, such as tracking and competitive grading.

BEWARE OF EITHER/OR

Another possibility is to change the focus from self-esteem to more specific self-concepts, because self-concepts in specific areas such as math are related to learning in math

(O'Mara et al., 2006). Because self-concept and achievement probably affect each other, the researchers concluded:

> In summary, whereas the optimal way to improve self-concept over the short-term is to focus interventions directly on self-concept enhancement, interventions that combine direct self-concept enhancement in concert with performance enhancement, coupled with appropriate feedback and praise, are likely to be advantageous when the goals of the intervention are to improve both self-concept and performance. (Marsh et al., 2006, p. 198)

UNDERSTANDING OTHERS AND MORAL DEVELOPMENT

As we seek our own identity and form images of ourselves, we are also learning about right and wrong. One aspect of moral development is understanding our significant others. How do we learn to interpret what others are thinking and feeling?

Theory of Mind and Intention

By the time they are 2 or 3 years old, children are beginning to develop a **theory of mind**, an understanding that other people are people too, with their own minds, thoughts, feelings, beliefs, desires, and perceptions (Astington & Dack, 2008; Flavell, Miller, & Miller, 2002; S. A. Miller, 2009). Children need a theory of mind to make sense of other people's behavior. Why is Sarah crying? Does she feel sad because no one will play with her? Children also need a theory of mind to understand that beliefs can differ from reality and that people can have different views. As you will see in Chapter 4, one explanation for autism is that children with this condition lack a theory of mind to help them understand their own or other people's emotions and behaviors.

Around the age of 2, children have a sense of intention, at least of their own intentions. They will announce, "I wanna peanut butter sandwich." As children develop a theory of mind, they also can understand that other people have intentions of their own. Older preschoolers who get along well with their peers can separate intentional from unintentional actions and react accordingly. For example, they will not get angry when another child accidentally knocks over their block tower. But aggressive children have more trouble assessing intention. They are likely to attack anyone who topples their tower, even accidentally (Dodge & Pettit, 2003). As children mature, they are more able to assess and consider the intentions of others.

With a developing theory of mind, children are increasingly able to understand that other people have different feelings and experiences and therefore may have a different viewpoint or perspective. This **perspective-taking ability** develops over time until it is quite sophisticated in adults. Being able to understand how others might think and feel is important in fostering cooperation and moral development, reducing prejudice, resolving conflicts, and encouraging positive social behaviors in general (Gehlbach, 2004). Some coaching in perspective taking from the teacher ("How would you feel if . . . ?" "Why do you think Charice . . . ?") might help if children mistreat peers and the mistreatment is not part of a deeper emotional or behavioral disorder (Woolfolk & Perry, 2015).

Moral Development

Along with a more advanced theory of mind and an understanding of intention, children also are developing a sense of right and wrong. Until recently, theory and research about moral development focused on children's **moral reasoning**, their thinking about right and wrong. Lately, some new perspectives building on insights from social and evolutionary psychology and neuroscience suggest there is more to morality than thinking (Haidt, 2013), as you will see later in this section. First, let's look at the most famous conception of moral development based on reasoning—Kohlberg's theory.

KOHLBERG'S THEORIES OF MORAL DEVELOPMENT. For years, Lawrence Kohlberg's (1963, 1975, 1981) theory of moral development, which was based in part on Piaget's ideas, dominated psychology and education.

STOP & THINK A man's wife is dying. There is one drug that could save her, but it is very expensive, and the druggist who invented it will not sell it at a price low enough for the man to buy it. Finally, the man becomes desperate and considers stealing the drug for his wife. What should he do, and why? •

Kohlberg evaluated the moral reasoning of both children and adults by presenting them with **moral dilemmas**, or hypothetical situations like the one in *Stop & Think* in which people must make difficult decisions and give their reasons.

Based on their reasoning, Kohlberg proposed a detailed sequence of six stages of moral reasoning, or judgments about right and wrong:

Preconventional Level: Judgment Is Based Solely on a Person's Own Needs and Perceptions

- Stage 1: *Obedience Orientation*—Obey rules to avoid punishments and bad consequences.
- Stage 2: *Rewards/Exchange Orientation*—Right and wrong is determined by personal needs and wants—"If I want it, it is right."

Conventional Level: The Expectations of Society and Laws Are Taken into Account

- Stage 3: *Being Nice/Relationships Orientation*—Being good means being nice and pleasing others.
- Stage 4: *Law and Order Orientation*—Laws and authorities must be obeyed; the social system must be maintained.

Postconventional (Principled) Level: Judgments Are Based on Abstract, More Personal Principles of Justice that Are Not Necessarily Defined by Society's Laws

- Stage 5: *Social Contract Orientation*—The moral choice is determined by socially agreed upon standards—"the greatest good for the greatest number."
- Stage 6: *Universal Ethical Principles Orientation*—There are universal principles of human dignity and social justice that individuals should uphold, regardless of the law and no matter what other people say.

Moral reasoning is related to both cognitive and emotional development. Abstract thinking becomes increasingly important in the higher stages of moral development, as children move from decisions based on absolute rules to those based on abstract principles such as justice and mercy. The ability to see another's perspective, to judge intentions, and use formal-operational thinking to imagine alternative bases for laws and rules also enters into judgments at the higher stages.

Video 3.4
The boy in this video was told a story in which a boy, Mike, finds a wallet filled with money and must decide what to do with it. What stage of moral development best characterizes his response?

ENHANCEDetext *video example*

CRITICISMS OF KOHLBERG'S THEORY. In reality, Kohlberg's stages do not seem to be separate, sequenced, and consistent. People often give reasons for moral choices that reflect several different stages simultaneously. Or a person's choices in one instance may fit one stage, and his or her decisions in a different situation may reflect another stage. One of the most hotly debated criticisms of Kohlberg's theory is that the stages are biased in favor of Western male values that emphasize individualism. His stages do not represent the way moral reasoning develops either in women or in other cultures, because the stage theory was based on a longitudinal study of American men only (Gilligan, 1982; Gilligan & Attanucci, 1988).

Carol Gilligan (1982) proposed a different sequence of moral development, an "ethic of care." Gilligan suggested that individuals move from a focus on self-interest to moral reasoning based on commitment to specific individuals and relationships, and then to the highest level of morality based on the principles of responsibility and care for all people. Some research supports this ethic of care and indicates that it is more typical of women's orientation to moral problem solving, especially when they reason about personal and real-life issues (Garmon, Basinger, Gregg, & Gibbs, 1996). However, a meta-analysis that combined the results of 113 studies found only small differences in moral orientation in line with Gilligan's theory (Jaffee & Hyde, 2000). The meta-analysis suggests both men and women use *care* to reason about interpersonal dilemmas and *justice* to reason about societal dilemmas. It appears that moral reasoning is more strongly influenced by the context and content of the dilemma than by the gender of the reasoner.

Caring for students and helping students learn to care has become a theme for many educators. For example, Nel Noddings (1995) urged that "themes of care" be used to organize the curriculum. Possible themes include "Caring for Self," "Caring for Family and Friends," and "Caring for Strangers and the World." Using the theme of "Caring for Strangers and the World," there could be units on crime, war, poverty, tolerance, ecology, or technology. The events after the massive tornado destruction and hurricanes in the United States or civil wars in the Middle East that left thousands homeless or refugees might be a starting point for these units.

Moral Judgments, Social Conventions, and Personal Choices

STOP & THINK
1. If there were no law against it, would it be OK to blind someone?
2. If there were no rule against it, would it be OK to chew gum in class?
3. Who should decide your favorite vegetable or how to style your hair? •

We probably could agree that it is wrong to blind someone, wrong to break class rules, and wrong to dictate food preferences or hairstyles for other people, but it is a different kind of "wrong" in each case. The first question is about actions that are inherently immoral. The answer to the question is concerned with conceptions of justice, fairness, human rights, and human welfare. Even young children know that it is not OK to hurt other people or steal from them—law or no law. But some rules, like no gum chewing in question 2, are social conventions—agreed-upon rules and ways of doing things in a particular situation. Students (mostly) avoid chewing gum when the class rules (conventions) say so. It is not inherently immoral to chew gum; it is just against the rules. Some classes—in college, for example—work well using different rules. And it is not immoral to dislike lima beans (at least I hope not) or to wear your hair long if you are a male; these are *personal choices*—individual preferences and private issues.

Another criticism of Kohlberg's stages is that they mix up moral judgments with decisions about social conventions and also overlook personal choice. Larry Nucci (2001, 2009; Lagattuta, Nucci, & Bosacki, 2010) offers an explanation of moral development that covers all three domains or areas: *moral judgments, social conventions,* and *personal choice.* Children's thinking and reasoning develop across all domains, but the pace of development may not be the same in every area. Even the cognitive (neurological) processing of judgments in the moral and conventional domains differs (Lahat, Helwig, & Zelazo, 2013). By about age 4, children around the world make fairly firm distinctions between moral and conventions issues (Nucci, 2009).

For teachers, the most common "right and wrong" situations involve the moral and conventional domains.

MORAL VERSUS CONVENTIONAL DOMAINS. In the *moral domain,* two fundamental issues are justice and welfare/compassion (Nucci, 2009). Some of the earliest moral issues in classrooms involve dividing and sharing materials, or distributive justice (Damon, 1994). For young children (ages 5 to 6), fair distribution is based on equality; thus, teachers often hear, "Keshawn got more than I did—that's not fair!" In the next few years, children come to recognize that some people should get more based on merit—they worked harder or performed better. Around age 8, children can take need into account and can reason based on benevolence; they can understand that some students may get more time or resources from the teacher because those students have special needs. So children move through stages in reasoning about moral issues: a sense that justice means equal treatment for all; an appreciation of equity and special needs; a more abstract integration of equity and equality along with a sense of caring in social relations; and finally, as adults, a sense that morality involves both benevolence and fairness and that moral principles are independent of the norms of any particular group (Nucci, 2001, 2009).

In the *conventional domain,* children begin by believing that rules simply exist. For example, if you have spent time with young children, you know that there is a period when you can say, "Eating in front of the TV is not allowed!" and get away with it. Piaget (1965) called this the state of moral realism. At this stage, the child believes that rules about conduct or rules about how to play

---

FIGURE 3.5

AN ALGEBRA LESSON THAT ALSO ENCOURAGES MAKING MORAL JUDGMENTS

Students are given this scenario to discuss in pairs:

> Four kids who are neighbors (John, Mark, Sally, and Mary) decide to work together on a paper route to make some money. John and Mary are both 15 and in high school, while Mark and Sally are both 12 years old and seventh graders. At the end of their first week they earn $48. But now they have a problem. They didn't decide ahead of time how to divide up the money that they had earned.

a. Sally argues that the fairest way is to divide up the money equally.
b. Mary argues that Sally was lazy and only delivered half as many papers as Mary. So Sally should get half as much as Mary and the other kids.
c. Mark argues that he and John were stronger than Mary and Sally, who are girls, and together carried 25% more than the girls did altogether. So the boys should each get 25% more than each of the girls.
d. John agrees that the reason Sally carried fewer papers than Mary is that she is lazy. He also argues that even though Mary isn't as strong as the boys, she worked just as hard. However, he also argues that the older kids (he and Mary) should get 25% more than the younger kids because older kids have more expenses than younger ones do. So, in his mind, he and Mary should get the same amount and 25% more than Mark, but Sally should get half as much as Mark because she was lazy.

The Assignment

1. Please create algebraic equations that would express each solution for the best way to divide the $48.
2. Provide a written answer for the solution you and your partner think is the fairest.
3. Explain why you think that is the fairest solution, and provide your argument as to why the other solutions are not as fair.

Source: Nucci, L. (2009). Nice is not enough: Facilitating moral development (pp. 156–157). Upper Saddle River, NJ: Pearson.

---

a game are absolute and can't be changed. If a rule is broken, the child believes that the punishment should be determined by how much damage is done, not by the intention of the child or by other circumstances. So, accidentally breaking three cups is worse than intentionally breaking one, and in the child's eyes, the punishment for the three-cup offense should be greater.

As children interact with others and see that different people have different rules, there is a gradual shift to a **morality of cooperation**. Children come to understand that people make rules and people can change them. When rules are broken, both the damage done and the intention of the offender are taken into account.

As they mature, children understand that rules, even though they are arbitrary, are made to maintain order and that people in charge make the rules. Then as students move through adolescence, they swing from understanding conventions as the appropriate ways to operate in a social system to viewing them as nothing but society's standards that have become set because they are widely applied and seldom challenged. Finally, adults realize that conventions are useful in coordinating social life, but changeable, too. So, compared to young children, older adolescents and adults generally are more accepting of others who think differently about conventions and customs.

IMPLICATIONS FOR TEACHERS. In his book *Nice Is Not Enough*, Larry Nucci (2009) describes many specific K–12 lessons that integrate academic content with development in three domains of *moral judgments, social conventions,* and *personal choice.* See Figure 3.5 for an algebra lesson.

Nucci also offers several suggestions for creating a moral climate in your classroom. First, it is important to establish a community of mutual respect and warmth with a fair and consistent application of the rules. Without that kind of community, all your attempts to create a moral climate will be undermined. Second, teachers' responses to students should be appropriate to the domain of the behavior—moral or conventional. For example, here are some responses to moral issues (Nucci, 2001, p. 146):

1. When an act is inherently hurtful or unjust, emphasize the harm done to others: "John, that really hurt Jamal."
2. Encourage perspective taking: "Chris, how would you feel if someone stole from you?"

In contrast, here are two responses to rules or conventional issues:

3. Restate the rule: "Lisa, you are not allowed to be out of your seat during announcements."
4. Command: "Howie, stop swearing!"

In all four cases, the teacher's response fits the domain. To create an inappropriate response, just switch responses 1 or 2 with 3 or 4. For example, "Lisa, how would you feel if other people got out of their seat during announcements?" Lisa might feel just fine. And it is a weak response to a moral transgression to say, "John, it is against the rules to hit." It is more than against the rules—it hurts and it is wrong.

In the third domain—personal—children must sort out what decisions and actions are their personal choices and what decisions are outside personal choice. This process is the foundation for developing moral concepts related to individual rights, fairness, and democracy. Here, diverse cultures may have very different understandings about individual choice, privacy, and the role of individuality in the larger society.

Diversity in Moral Reasoning

A number of broad cultural distinctions might influence moral reasoning. Some cultures can be considered more traditional, with greater emphasis on customs and rituals that change slowly over time. In contrast, traditions and customs tend to change more rapidly in modern cultures. Nucci (2009) suggests that in more traditional cultures, customs may become "moralized." For example, not wearing head coverings in some cultures may seem to be in the conventional domain to outsiders, but is closer to the moral domain for members of the culture, especially when religious beliefs are involved. Consider the findings of one study described by Nucci that asked devout Hindus to rate 35 behaviors that violated community norms. An eldest son's getting a haircut and eating chicken a day after his father's death was considered the worst violation. What seem like personal choices (getting a haircut and eating chicken) is a moral issue because the Hindus believed that the son's behavior would put his father's soul in danger—a terrible and eternal fate. So, to understand what is choice, convention, or what is moral, we need to know about the beliefs of the culture.

In cultures that are more family centered or group oriented (often called *collectivist cultures*), the highest moral value might involve putting the opinions of the group before decisions based on individual conscience. Research has found that children's reasoning about moral, conventional, and personal domains is similar across cultures. For example, although Chinese culture encourages deference to authority, Chinese children agree with Western children that adults have no right to dictate how children spend their free time. And people without authority, including children, should be obeyed when what they want you to do is fair and just, but disobeyed when what they dictate is immoral or unjust (Helwig, Arnold, Tan, & Boyd, 2003; K. M. Kim, 1998).

Beyond Reasoning: Haidt's Social Intuitionist Model of Moral Psychology

In everyday life, making moral choices involves more than reasoning. Emotions, instincts, competing goals, relationships, and practical considerations all affect choices. Jonathan Haidt (2012, 2013) believes that Kohlberg overemphasized cognitive reasoning about morality. Haidt's Social Intuitionist Model is based on research in social and evolutionary psychology and neuroscience. There are three key principles:

1. *Intuition comes first, reasoning second.* Moral reasoning is something we do only after a first automatic, emotional response (call it intuition) has pushed us toward a moral judgment of right

Connect and Extend to PRAXIS II®

Moral Development (I, A2)
Moral issues can have an important impact on the classroom. Identify major issues related to moral development, and explain what a teacher can do to appropriately address these issues.

or wrong. We instinctively feel sympathy–disgust, like–dislike, attraction–revulsion, and so on, in response to a situation or dilemma. Then we reason about why our reaction is right as we prepare to defend the choice to others, so reasoning plays a social role of maintaining our position and respect in our group. As we will see several times in this text, current perspectives on cognition decision making based on neuroscience include *dual-process models* with one system that is fast, automatic, and strongly affected by emotions and a second system that is slower, more analytic, and reflective. These dual-processing systems are at work in all human decisions and choices—including moral judgments.

2. *There is more to morality than fairness and harm.* Most theories of moral reasoning are grounded in the moral values of justice (fairness/cheating) and welfare (care/harm). Haidt believes that focusing on only these values reflects a WEIRD moral framework (Western, educated, industrialized, rich, and democratic). In WEIRD cultures, justice and human welfare are central to morality. But Haidt's research with participants around the world has identified four other important moral values or moral foundations:

- *Loyalty/betrayal* underlies self-sacrifice for the good of the group, patriotism, and the ideas of "one for all and all for one" or "no Marine left behind."
- *Authority/subversion* is the foundation of leadership and followership—respect for legitimate authority.
- *Sanctity/degradation* is the foundation for striving to live a more noble and clean life and avoid contamination. Sanctity determines what objects or ideas are sacred and which ones are disgusting.
- One other candidate for a moral foundation is *liberty/oppression,* the basis for resentment and resistance to domination, such as a hatred for bullies and dictators.

These moral foundations are present in all cultures because they evolved over thousands of years as humans lived in social groups and sought to survive. Cultures may have different ways of enacting these moral foundations, however. For example, many people in India believe the cow is sacred, and for many people in the United States the flag is sacred. So, many Indians feel disgust at harming a cow, and many Americans feel disgust when they see the U.S. flag burned. See moralfoundations.org for a description of the moral foundations.

3. *Morality binds and blinds.* When individuals in a group share the same symbols of the sacred, heroes, leaders, beliefs about right and wrong—in short, when they share the same moral beliefs—then the group is bound together. They are loyal to each other—"one for all and all for one." They respect their leaders and each other. But in being bound together (and therefore being more likely to survive), they are blind to the moral beliefs of other groups that seem so "wrong."

The Social Intuitionist Model is quite new, so there are few applications to education. The advantage of the model is that it fits insights from neuroscience, social psychology, and sociobiology. The model reminds us that there is more to morality than reasoning. We have an immediate instinctive reaction about what is right and wrong, and then we "reason" to justify our choice. Justifying our choices maintains our position in our group, which helped humans survive over centuries. Moral education probably needs to acknowledge the foundations of morality beyond justice and welfare and also understand the ways different cultures and groups enact those moral beliefs. Current social emotional learning approaches emphasize feelings as well as valuing and relationships (Shechtman & Yaman, 2012).

Moral Behavior and the Example of Cheating

Three important influences on moral behavior are modeling, internalization, and self-concept. First, children who have been consistently exposed to caring, generous adult models will tend to be more concerned for the rights and feelings of others (Eisenberg & Fabes, 1998; Woolfolk & Perry, 2015). Second, most theories of moral behavior assume that young children's moral behavior is first controlled by others through direct instruction, supervision, rewards and punishments, and correction. But in time, children **internalize** the moral rules and principles of the authority figures who have guided them; that is, children adopt the external standards as their own. If children are given reasons they can understand when they are corrected—particularly reasons that highlight the effects of actions on others—then they are more likely to internalize moral principles. They learn to behave morally even when "no one is watching" (Hoffman, 2000).

Finally, we must integrate moral beliefs and values into our total sense of who we are, our self-concept.

> The tendency for a person to behave morally is largely dependent on the extent to which moral beliefs and values are integrated in the personality, and in one's sense of self. The influence our moral beliefs have on our lives, therefore, is contingent on the personal importance that we as individuals attach to them—we must identify and respect them as our own. (Arnold, 2000, p. 372)

WHO CHEATS? About 80% to 90% of high school and college students cheat at some point in school. In fact, the rates of academic cheating have been rising for the past 30 years, perhaps in response to increased pressures and high-stakes testing (T. A. Murdock & Anderman, 2006).

There are some individual differences in cheating. Most studies of adolescent and college-age students find that males are more likely to cheat than females and lower-achieving students are more likely to cheat than higher achievers. Students focusing on performance goals (making good grades, looking smart) as opposed to learning goals, and students with a low sense of academic self-efficacy (a belief that they probably can't do well in school) are more likely to cheat. Finally, students who are impulsive may be more likely to cheat.

But cheating is not all about individual differences—the situation plays a role as well. In one study, the level of cheating decreased when students moved from math classes that emphasized competition and grades to classes that emphasized understanding and mastery (Anderman & Midgley, 2004). Students are less likely to cheat when they view their teacher as credible. If students trust the teacher as a credible source, they may be more likely to value the content being taught and therefore want to actually learn it (Anderman, Cupp, & Lane, 2009). In addition, students also are particularly likely to cheat when they are behind or "cramming for tests" or when they believe that their teachers do not care about them. For example, Erica had this perspective:

> I am a high school honors student, and I think there are different degrees of cheating. I'm a dedicated student, but when my history teacher bombards me with 50 questions due tomorrow or when a teacher gives me a fill-in-the-blanks worksheet on a night when I have swim practice, church, aerobics—and other homework—I'm going to copy from a friend! . . . Since I only do this when I need to, it isn't a habit. Every kid does this when they're in a pinch. (L. A. Jensen, Arnett, Feldman, & Cauffman, 2002, p. 210)

Tamera Murdock and Eric Anderman (2006) have proposed a model for integrating what we know about cheating and doing research to learn more. They suggest that in deciding to cheat, students ask three questions: What is my goal? Can I do this? What are the costs? See Table 3.4 on the next page for some example answers to these questions that might be associated with decisions about whether to cheat and some example strategies to support *not* cheating.

DEALING WITH CHEATING. The implications for teachers are straightforward. To prevent cheating, try to avoid putting students in high-pressure situations. Make sure they are well prepared for tests, projects, and assignments so they can do reasonably well without cheating. Be a trustworthy and credible source of information. Focus on learning and not on grades. Encourage collaboration on assignments and experiment with open-book, collaborative, or take-home tests. I often tell my students what concepts will be on the test and encourage them to discuss the concepts and their applications before the test. You might also make extra help available for those who need it. Be clear about your policies in regard to cheating, and enforce them consistently. Help students to resist temptation by monitoring them carefully during testing.

TABLE 3.4 • When Do Students Cheat?

Tamera Murdock and Eric Anderman have developed a model of academic cheating based on the answers to three questions.

QUESTIONS	LESS LIKELY TO CHEAT: EXAMPLE ANSWERS	MORE LIKELY TO CHEAT: EXAMPLE ANSWERS	WHAT CAN THE TEACHER DO? EXAMPLE STRATEGIES
What is my goal?	The goal is to learn, get smarter, and be the best I can be. It is my goal.	The goal is to look good, outperform others. The goal is imposed on me.	Communicate that the point of the class is to learn—everyone can get better.
Can I do it?	I can do it with reasonable effort.	I doubt my ability to do it.	Build students' confidence by helping them take small but successful steps. Point out students' past accomplishments.
What are the costs?	I will get caught and punished if I cheat. I will feel morally wrong or dishonored if I cheat.	I probably won't get caught and punished if I cheat. Everyone does it, so it can't be wrong. The pressure is too great—I can't fail. I have to cheat.	Make mistakes an opportunity to learn. Take the pressure out of assignments with the chance to revise. Monitor to prevent cheating, and follow through with reasonable penalties.

Source: Adapted from T. A. Murdock and Anderman (2006).

PERSONAL/SOCIAL DEVELOPMENT: LESSONS FOR TEACHERS

Both Erikson and Bronfenbrenner stress that individuals are influenced by their social and cultural contexts. For example, here are a few big ideas:

1. Students whose parents are divorcing can benefit from authoritative teachers who are both warm and clear about requirements.
2. For all students, self-concepts are increasingly differentiated over time—they may feel competent in one subject, but not in others, or very capable as friends or family members, but not good about work in school.
3. For all students, it is a challenge to forge a meaningful identity that integrates their decisions about career, religion, ethnicity, gender roles, and connection to society. Teachers are in a position to support this quest.
4. Being rejected by peers is harmful for all students. Many students need guidance in developing social skills, in more accurately reading the intentions of others, in resolving conflicts, and in coping with aggression. Again, teachers can provide guidance.
5. When working under high pressure, with unreasonable workloads, and with little chance of being caught, many students will cheat. It is up to teachers and schools to avoid these conditions.

ENHANCEDetext *self-check*

SUMMARY

• **Physical Development (pp. 74–80)**

Describe the changes in physical development of children in the preschool, elementary, and secondary grades. During the preschool years, there is rapid development of children's gross- and fine-motor skills. Physical development continues throughout the elementary school years, with girls often ahead of boys in size. With

adolescence comes puberty and emotional struggles to cope with all the related changes.

What are some of the consequences of early and late maturation for boys and girls? Females mature about 2 years ahead of males. Early-maturing boys are more likely to enjoy high social status; they tend to be popular and to be leaders. But they also tend to engage in more delinquent behavior—this is true for White, African American, and Mexican American boys. Early maturation is not generally beneficial for girls.

What is the role of recess and physical activity in development? Play supports brain development, language, and social development. Children release tensions, learn to solve problems, adapt to new situations, cooperate, and negotiate. The increase in childhood obesity is linked to inactivity and increased time spent watching TV and playing passive games such as video and Internet games.

What are some of the signs of eating disorders? Anorexic students may appear pale, have brittle fingernails, and have fine dark hairs developing all over their bodies. They are easily chilled because they have so little fat to insulate their bodies. They often are depressed, insecure, moody, and lonely. Girls may stop having their menstrual period.

- **Bronfenbrenner: The Social Context for Development (pp. 80–93)**
Describe Bronfenbrenner's bioecological model of development. Bronfenbrenner's model takes into account both the biological aspects internal to the individual and the nested social and cultural contexts that shape development. Every person develops within a microsystem (immediate relationships and activities) inside a mesosystem (relationships among microsystems), embedded in an exosystem (larger social settings such as communities); all of these are part of the macrosystem (culture). In addition, all development occurs in and is influenced by the time period—the chronosystem.

What are some aspects of the family that affect students in school? Students probably have experienced different parenting styles, and these styles can influence their social adjustment. At least in European American, middle-class families, children of authoritative parents are more likely to be happy with themselves and relate well to others, whereas children of authoritarian parents are more likely to feel guilty or depressed, and children of permissive parents may have trouble interacting with peers. But cultures also differ in parenting styles. Research indicates that higher-control parenting is linked to better grades for Asian and African American students.

How does divorce affect students? During the divorce itself, conflict may increase as property and custody rights are being decided. After the divorce, the custodial parent may have to move to a less expensive home, go to work for the first time, or work longer hours. For the child, this can mean leaving behind important friendships just when support is needed the most, having only one parent who has less time than ever to be with them, or adjusting to new family structures when parents remarry.

Why are peer relationships important? Peer relationships play a significant role in healthy personal and social development. Strong evidence shows that adults who had close friends as children have higher self-esteem and are more capable of maintaining intimate relationships than adults who had lonely childhoods. Adults who were rejected as children tend to have more problems, such as dropping out of school or committing crimes.

What are peer cultures? Groups of students develop their own norms for appearance and social behavior. Group loyalties can lead to rejection for some students, leaving them upset and unhappy.

What are the different types of aggression? Peer aggression can be instrumental (intended to gain an object or privilege), or hostile (intended to inflict harm). Hostile aggression can be either overt threats or physical attacks, or relational aggression, which involves threatening or damaging social relationships. Boys are more likely to use overt aggression, and girls are more likely to use relational aggression. Today the many social media applications and sites provide other avenues for relational aggression.

How does ever-present media affect aggression and empathy? The world and the media provide many negative models of behavior. In time, children internalize the moral rules and principles of the authority figures who have guided them. If children are given reasons—particularly reasons that highlight the effects of actions on others—they can understand when they are corrected and are more likely to internalize moral principles. Some schools have adopted programs to increase students' capacity to care for others.

How can teachers' academic and personal caring affect students? Students value caring in teachers. Caring can be expressed as support for academic learning and as concern for personal problems. For students who are higher achieving and have higher socioeconomic status, academic caring may be more important, but for students who are alienated from school, personal caring may be more important.

What are some signs of child abuse? Signs of abuse or neglect include unexplained bruises, burns, bites, or other injuries; fatigue; depression; frequent absences; poor hygiene; inappropriate clothing; problems with peers; and many others. Teachers must report suspected cases of child abuse and can be instrumental in helping students cope with other risks as well.

- **Identity and Self-Concept (pp. 93–105)**
What are Erikson's stages of psychosocial development? Erikson's emphasis on the relationship between

society and the individual is a psychosocial theory of development—a theory that connects personal development (*psycho*) to the social environment (*social*). Erikson believed that people go through eight life stages, each of which involves a central crisis. Adequate resolution of each crisis leads to greater personal and social competence and a stronger foundation for solving future crises. In the first two stages, an infant must develop a sense of trust over mistrust and a sense of autonomy over shame and doubt. In early childhood, the focus of the third stage is on developing initiative and avoiding feelings of guilt. In the child's elementary school years, the fourth stage involves achieving a sense of industry and avoiding feelings of inferiority. In the fifth stage, identity versus role confusion, adolescents consciously attempt to solidify their identity. According to Marcia, these efforts may lead to identity diffusion, foreclosure, moratorium, or achievement. Erikson's three stages of adulthood involve struggles to achieve intimacy, generativity, and integrity.

Describe the formation of ethnic and racial identities. Ethnic and racial minority students are confronted with the challenge of forming an identity while living in two worlds—the values, beliefs, and behaviors of their group and those of the larger culture. Most explanations for identity development describe stages moving from being unaware of differences between minority group and majority cultures, to different ways of negotiating the differences, and finally to an integration of cultures.

How does self-concept change as children develop? Self-concept (definition of self) becomes increasingly complex, differentiated, and abstract as we mature. Self-concept evolves through constant self-reflection, social interaction, and experiences in and out of school. Students develop a self-concept by comparing themselves to personal (internal) standards and social (external) standards. High self-esteem is related to better overall school experience, both academically and socially. Gender and ethnic stereotypes are significant factors as well.

Distinguish between self-concept and self-esteem. Both self-concept and self-esteem are beliefs about the self. Self-concept is our attempt to build a scheme that organizes our impressions, feelings, and attitudes about ourselves. But this model is not permanent. Self-perceptions vary from situation to situation and from one phase of our lives to another. Self-esteem is an evaluation of your self-worth. If people evaluate their worth positively, we say that they have high self-esteem. Self-concept and self-esteem are often used interchangeably, even though they have distinct meanings. Self-concept is a cognitive structure, and self-esteem is an affective evaluation.

Are there differences in self-concepts for girls and boys? From 1st to 12th grade, competence beliefs decline for both boys and girls in math, language arts, and sports. By high school, boys and girls express about the same competence in math, girls are higher in language arts, and boys are higher in sports. In terms of general self-esteem, both boys and girls report declines in the transition to middle school, but boys' self-esteem goes up in high school while girls' self-esteem stays down.

- **Understanding Others and Moral Development (pp. 105–112)**

What is a theory of mind, and why is it important? A theory of mind is an understanding that other people are people too, with their own minds, thoughts, feelings, beliefs, desires, and perceptions. Children need a theory of mind to make sense of other people's behavior. As children develop a theory of mind, they can also understand that other people have intentions of their own.

How do perspective-taking skills change as students mature? An understanding of intentions develops as children mature, but aggressive students often have trouble understanding the intentions of others. Social perspective taking also changes as we mature. Young children believe that everyone has the same thoughts and feelings they do. Later, they learn that others have separate identities and therefore separate feelings and perspectives.

What are the key differences among the preconventional, conventional, and postconventional levels of moral reasoning? Kohlberg's theory of moral development includes three levels: (1) a preconventional level, where judgments are based on self-interest; (2) a conventional level, where judgments are based on traditional family values and social expectations; and (3) a postconventional level, where judgments are based on more abstract and personal ethical principles. Critics suggest that Kohlberg's view does not account for possible cultural differences in moral reasoning or differences between moral reasoning and moral behavior.

Describe Gilligan's levels of moral reasoning. Carol Gilligan has suggested that because Kohlberg's stage theory was based on a longitudinal study of men only, it is very possible that the moral reasoning of women and the stages of women's development were not adequately represented. She has proposed an "ethic of care." Gilligan believes that individuals move from a focus on self-interest to moral reasoning based on commitment to specific individuals and relationships, and then to the highest level of morality based on the principles of responsibility and care for all people. Women are somewhat more likely to use a care orientation, but studies also show that both men and women can use both orientations.

How does thinking in the moral and conventional domains change over time? Beliefs about morality move from the young child's sense that justice means equal treatment for all to the adult's understanding that morality involves beneficence and fairness and that moral principles are independent of the norms of any particular group. In thinking about social conventions, children begin by believing that the regularities they see are real and right. After going through several stages, adults realize that conventions are useful in coordinating social life, but changeable too.

What influences moral behavior? Adults first control young children's moral behavior through direct instruction, supervision, rewards and punishments, and correction. A second important influence on the development of moral behavior is modeling. Children who have been consistently exposed to caring, generous adult models will tend to be more concerned for the rights and feelings of others.

Why do students cheat? In schools, cheating is a common behavior problem that involves moral issues. The decision to cheat is based on three questions: What is my goal? Can I do this? What are the costs? Cheating is caused by both individual and situational factors, but if the pressure is great enough and the chance of getting caught is slim, many students will cheat.

PRACTICE USING WHAT YOU HAVE LEARNED

To access and complete the exercises, click the link under the images below.

Moral Reasoning

ENHANCEDetext *application exercise*

Psychosocial Development

ENHANCEDetext *application exercise*

KEY TERMS

Anorexia nervosa 78
Attachment 83
Autonomy 95
Bioecological model 81
Blended families 82
Body mass index (BMI) 75
Bulimia 78
Commitment 97
Context 81
Cyber aggression 88
Developmental crisis 94

Distributive justice 107
Exploration 97
Extended families 82
Generativity 98
Hostile aggression 88
Identity 93
Identity achievement 97
Identity diffusion 97
Identity foreclosure 97
Industry 95
Initiative 95

Instrumental aggression 88
Integrity 98
Internalize 111
Intimacy 98
Menarche 75
Moral dilemmas 106
Moral realism 107
Moral reasoning 105
Morality of cooperation 108
Moratorium 97
Nigrescence 99

CONNECT AND EXTEND TO LICENSURE

MULTIPLE-CHOICE QUESTIONS

1. Authoritative teaching strategies are associated with what students identify as "good teachers." Identify which one of the following educators is demonstrating authoritative techniques in the classroom.
   A. When Marcus failed to take his seat upon entering the room, Miss Thomas reminded him of the class rules and consequences.
   B. Paulo, a shy new student to the class, was forced by Mr. Hall on his first day in his new school to give a speech about his past experiences in Guatemala.
   C. Dina was allowed by her teacher to skip recess and play inside by herself because she did not have any friends.
   D. Mr. Krall allowed the students to have two free days at the beginning of the year in which to become acquainted with their peers in the classroom.

2. When new students arrive in Ms. Taylor's class, she understands that they may initially have adjustment issues. In addition to pairing new students with a partner to assist them in navigating Central Middle School, she also makes sure she addresses their psychosocial needs. Which one of the following strategies would be appropriate for a new student in Ms. Taylor's middle-school class?
   A. Allow the students to plan what they would like to do during their day at school.
   B. Encourage the students to take responsibility for their own personal needs.
   C. Provide support so that new students can feel a sense of competence and success.
   D. Let students know that the relationships they make in middle school are important to their emotional well-being and happiness later in life.

3. Research suggests that a majority of students cheat at some point in their academic careers. Which one of the following is not a recommendation to reduce cheating in the classroom?
   A. Clear guidelines on what constitutes cheating, accompanied by consequences that, when imposed, will deter other students due to their severity.
   B. Reduce the focus on grades, and provide the material for students with which they must be familiar.
   C. Encourage collaboration with peers on assignments to provide necessary support and decrease anxiety.
   D. Ensure students are well prepared for assignments and tests.

CONSTRUCTED-RESPONSE QUESTIONS

Case

Suzanne Wilson entered Ms. Sullivan's class in the fall without any friends. While many of the third-graders engaged in collaborative games on the playground, Suzanne stood on the periphery, and the other students did not include her. In class her behaviors were more typical of a younger child, sucking her thumb when she became upset and refusing to share during group activities. By December, Ms. Sullivan decided to take steps to intervene. She called Mr. and Mrs. Wilson for a parent meeting. When the Wilsons arrived, Suzanne was with them. What then transpired was shocking to Ms. Sullivan. Suzanne adamantly insisted that her parents not talk with her teacher in private. Yelling above the crying and screaming, the Wilsons apologized and suggested they return on another day when Suzanne was feeling more agreeable.

4. Identify and explain the parenting style the Wilsons appear to practice.
5. What strategies should Ms. Sullivan employ to assist Suzanne with her emotional development?

ENHANCEDetext *licensure exam*

TEACHERS' CASEBOOK

WHAT WOULD THEY DO? MEAN GIRLS

Here is how several expert teachers said they would address the situation with Alison and the clique of "mean girls."

THOMAS NAISMITH—Science Teacher, Grades 7–12
Slocum Independent School District, Elkhart, TX

To bring civility to this classroom, I would address the situation in two stages. First, I would meet individually with the two girls involved in the most recent incident. I would make it very clear to Alison that her behavior was totally inappropriate and that such behavior was far beneath her. I would suggest to her that I was sure that it was just a temporary lapse of good judgment on her part and that I was sure that such an incident would not occur again. I would also ask her to play a role in helping to stop some of the other inappropriate behavior that was occurring in my classroom.

I would explain to Stephanie that she did not need to be embarrassed, because her classmates would appreciate the fact that she had made an effort to restore an old "friendship." I would comment on her positive qualities, explain that she should feel good about herself, and suggest that she seek the companionship of students who are open to her friendship.

The second step would be to address the class as a whole. I would be nonspecific in my comments, but I would make it very clear that the gossip and other "ugly" behavior would need to stop. I would explain that our classroom is a mini-society and that every member has the responsibility of treating others appropriately. I would further explain that they did not have to be "friends" with everyone but should treat everyone with respect and dignity.

JACALYN D. WALKER—Eighth-Grade Science Teacher
Treasure Mountain Middle School, Park City, UT

Never work in a vacuum. This is especially important in a middle school or junior high school. Work with your school counselor, other grade-level teachers, and parents. If you are doing this, you will have several options for dealing with this problem. You cannot fake caring about 12-, 13-, and 14-year-olds. They can spot a fake. You must be working with this age group because you truly like them as people. You appreciate their humor and their abilities. With a caring, trusting, and respectful relationship, students will be open to your help and guidance. Parents are often not involved in the classroom at these grade levels, but there are great programs available to get parents involved.

NANCY SCHAEFER—Grades 9–12
Cincinnati Hills Christian Academy High School, Cincinnati, OH

I would first make a phone call to Stephanie's home. Under the guise of calling about assignments because of the days she has missed, I would talk to one of her parents or guardians. My first goal would be to find out if the parents are aware of the situation. Sometimes girls like Stephanie are too embarrassed to tell their parents the whole story or even any of the real story. If the parents did not know the entire story, I might try to get Stephanie on the phone and help her tell her parents. Letting the adults around her know what has happened can relieve some of the shame she might be feeling.

I would then work with Stephanie and one or more of her parents to plan Stephanie's transition back to school. A school counselor might also be involved in this conversation. The adults would help Stephanie come up with a plan for how to handle possible difficult situations: face-to-face encounters with Alison, encounters with other old "friends," mean messages she might receive during the school day, or comments made to her by other students. We would help her think through these situations and practice how she could respond. I could talk to Stephanie's teachers to work on rearranging groups or seating to move the girls away from each other or to foster other friendships for Stephanie. Because almost every one has stories about unfaithful friends, Stephanie might benefit from talking with a freshman or sophomore about that person's experiences and how he or she made new friends. Finally, I would try to arrange a brief and supervised meeting between Stephanie and Alison. Allowing an encounter to happen in a controlled environment would provide Stephanie an outlet to voice her hurt, without her having to resort to inappropriate actions.

During all of this, I would want to make sure that someone was also working with Alison, to prevent the escalation of events. This may be an administrator responsible for discipline, if school rules were violated; the school counselor; or another teacher with a good relationship with Alison. I would encourage the involvement of Alison's parents, especially if this were not the first vicious episode.

4 | LEARNER DIFFERENCES AND LEARNING NEEDS

TEACHERS' **CASEBOOK**

WHAT WOULD YOU DO? INCLUDING EVERY STUDENT

It is a new school year, and your district has had a change in policy. "Special Education" programs have been discontinued and ALL students will now be included in general education classrooms full time. You knew that you were going to have students with a wide range of abilities, social skills, and motivation for learning in your classroom, but now you also have a student with severe asthma, a fairly high-functioning student with Asperger syndrome, a student with severe learning disabilities, and two students who are on medication for attention-deficit hyperactivity disorder (ADHD). It is not clear what resources will be available to you, but even so, you want to face this challenge with confidence and a sense of efficacy for teaching all students.

CRITICAL THINKING

- How will you design a standards-based curriculum that will allow all of the students to learn to their fullest potential and demonstrate proficiency toward the standards?
- What can you do to address the specific problems of your students who have been identified with special needs?
- How will you remain confident in you new situation?

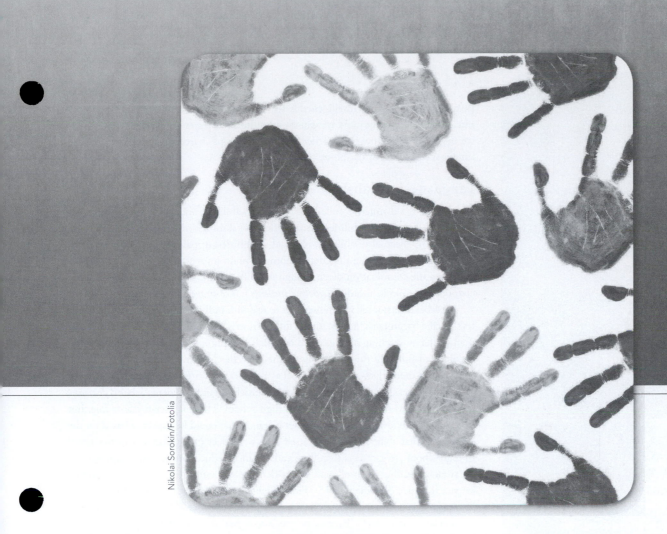

Nikolai Sorokin/Fotolia

OVERVIEW AND OBJECTIVES

To answer the critical thinking questions, you need an understanding of individual differences. So far, we have talked little about individuals. We have discussed principles of development that apply to everyone—stages, processes, conflicts, and tasks. Our development as human beings is similar in many ways, but not in every way. Even among members of the same family, there are marked contrasts in appearance, interests, abilities, and temperament, and these differences have important implications for teaching. We will spend some time analyzing the concepts of intelligence and learning styles because these terms are so often misunderstood. You probably will have at least one student with special needs in your class, whatever grade you teach, so in this chapter we also explore both common and less frequently occurring learning problems that students may have. As we discuss each problem area, we will consider how a teacher might recognize problems, seek help, and plan instruction, including using the approach of response to intervention. By the time you have completed this chapter, you should be able to:

Objective 4.1	Describe current theories of intelligence including the advantages and disadvantages of labeling, hierarchical and multiple theories of intelligence, how intelligence is measured, and what these measurements tell teachers.
Objective 4.2	Discuss the values and limitations of considering students' learning styles.
Objective 4.3	Discuss the implications of the IDEA and Section 504 protections for contemporary education.
Objective 4.4	Understand and address the special educational needs of students with learning challenges.
Objective 4.5	Recognize and respond to the special educational needs of students who are gifted and talented.

INTELLIGENCE

Because the concept of intelligence is so important, so controversial, and so often misunderstood in education, we will spend quite a few pages discussing it. But before we begin, let's examine the practice of labeling people based on differences such as intelligence, ability, or disability.

Language and Labels

Every child is a distinctive collection of talents, abilities, and limitations. Some students have learning disabilities, communication disorders, emotional or behavioral disorders, intellectual disabilities, physical disabilities, impaired vision or difficulties hearing, autism spectrum disorders, traumatic brain injury, remarkable gifts and talents, or some combination. Even though we will use terms like these throughout the chapter, a caution is in order: *Labeling students is a controversial issue.*

A label does not tell which methods to use with individual students. For example, few specific "treatments" automatically follow from a "diagnosis" of behavioral disorder; many different teaching strategies and materials are appropriate. Further, the labels can become self-fulfilling prophecies. Everyone—teachers, parents, classmates, and even the students themselves—may see a label as a stigma that cannot be changed. Evidence indicates, for example, that teachers and counselors guide students labeled *learning disabled* into less-demanding courses in high school. This may seem reasonable, but this guidance to lower-level courses goes beyond what could be expected based on the students' actual abilities. The label itself seems to affect the guidance. Courses taken in high school are gateways to college and advanced education, so lower expectations for students leading to enrollment in less-demanding courses can have a life-changing impact (D. Rice & Muller, 2013). Finally, labels are mistaken for explanations, as in, "Santiago gets into fights because he has a behavior disorder." "How do you know he has a behavior disorder?" "Because he gets into fights" (Friend, 2014).

On the other hand, some educators argue that for younger students, at least, being labeled as "special needs" protects the child. For example, if classmates know a student has an intellectual disability (once called *mental retardation*), they will be more willing to accept his or her behaviors. Of course, diagnostic labels still open doors to some programs, useful information, adaptive technology and equipment, or financial assistance. Labels probably both stigmatize and help students.

DISABILITIES AND HANDICAPS. A disability is just what the word implies—an *inability* to do something specific such as pronounce words or see or walk. A handicap is a *disadvantage* in certain situations. Some disabilities lead to handicaps, but not in all contexts. For example, being blind (a visual disability) is a handicap if you want to drive a car, but not when you are composing music or talking on the telephone. Stephen Hawking, the greatest living physicist, has Lou Gehrig's disease and no longer can walk or talk. He once said that he is lucky that he became a theoretical physicist "because it is all in the mind. So my disability has not been a serious handicap." It is important that we do not create *handicaps* for people by the way we react to their *disabilities*. Some educators have suggested that we drop the word *handicap* altogether because the source of the word is demeaning. *Handicap* came from the phrase "cap-in-hand," used to describe people with disabilities who once were forced to beg just to survive (Hardman, Drew, & Egan, 2014).

We can think of all human characteristics as being on a continuum, for instance, from very acute hearing to complete deafness. We all fall somewhere on that continuum, and our position on the continuum changes over our lifetimes. As we age, for example, we are likely to experience changes in hearing, vision, and even some aspects of intellectual ability, as you will see later in this chapter.

FIGURE 4.1

DISABILITY ETIQUETTE

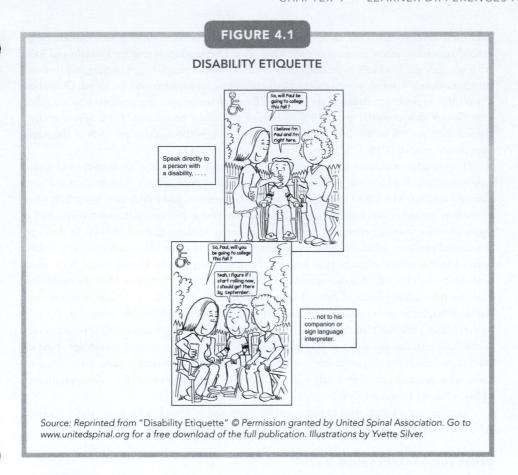

Source: Reprinted from "Disability Etiquette" © Permission granted by United Spinal Association. Go to www.unitedspinal.org for a free download of the full publication. Illustrations by Yvette Silver.

When speaking about a person with a disability, it is important that we avoid the language of pity, as in "confined to a wheelchair" or "victim of AIDS." Wheelchairs are not confining. They allow people to get around. Using "victim of" or "suffering with" makes the person seem powerless. On their resources Web site, the United Spinal Association offers a free pdf booklet with many ideas about disability. Every teacher should read it. See Figure 4.1 for an example.

Another way of showing respect to individuals with disabilities is to use "person-first" language.

PERSON-FIRST LANGUAGE. Because everyone has a range of abilities, it makes sense to avoid labels such as "emotionally disturbed student" or "at-risk student." Describing a complex person with one or two words implies that the condition labeled is the most important aspect of the person. Actually, the individual has many characteristics and abilities, and to focus on the disability is to misrepresent the individual. An alternative is "person-first" language or speaking of "students with a behavior disorder" or "students placed at risk." Here, the emphasis is on the students first.

Students with learning disabilities	NOT	Learning disabled students
Students receiving special education	NOT	Special education students
A person with epilepsy	NOT	An epileptic
A child with a physical disability	NOT	A crippled child
Children diagnosed with autism	NOT	Autistic children or autistics

POSSIBLE BIASES IN THE APPLICATION OF LABELS. Although many good tests and careful procedures are available to identify students with disabilities and to use labels properly, racial and ethnic minority students are *overrepresented* in the disability categories and underrepresented in programs for students with gifts and talents. For example, based on their actual numbers in schools, African American students are about twice as likely to be identified as having a mental health condition and almost three times as likely to be identified as having an intellectual disability.

And these students are more likely than White or Asian students to be placed outside of the general education system for most of their school day. The opposite is true for Latina/o and Asian students; they are less likely to be diagnosed in almost all categories except hearing impairments. Another example involves *underrepresentation* in programs for students who are gifted. Only about 8% of African American students are identified for programs supporting students who are gifted, even though they comprise about 14% to 15% of the school population. For Latino/a students the numbers are 8% to 9% in these programs, even though the students are 16% of the school population (Friend, 2014; U.S. Department of Education, 2011).

For decades, educators have struggled to understand the causes of these over- and under-representations. Explanations include the higher poverty rates among African American and Latina/o families, which lead to poorer prenatal care, nutrition, and health care; systematic biases in teachers' attitudes, curriculum, instruction, and the referral process itself; and teachers' lack of preparation for working effectively with ethnic minority students (Friend, 2014). To deal with the referral problem, educators have recommended gathering more information about a student before a formal referral is made. How long has the student been in the United States? What about proficiency with English? Are there unusual stressors such as being homeless? Does the curriculum build on the student's funds of cultural knowledge (Chapter 5)? Is the classroom culturally compatible (Chapter 6) and engaging (Chapter 12)? Is the teacher knowledgeable about and respectful of the student's culture? Can the student's abilities be assessed through alternative approaches such as creativity tests and portfolios or performances (Chapter 15)? Having more knowledge about the student and his or her circumstances outside of school should help teachers make better decisions about what programs are appropriate (Gonzalez, Brusca-Vega, & Yawkey, 1997; National Alliance of Black School Educators, 2002).

Intelligence is widely used in placement decisions and as a label in life in general. Let's begin with a basic question, . . .

What Does Intelligence Mean?

STOP & THINK Who was the most intelligent person in your high school? Write down a name and the first 4 or 5 words that come to mind when you see that person in your mind's eye. What made you pick this individual? •

The idea that people vary in what we call **intelligence** has been with us for a long time. Plato discussed similar variations more than 2,000 years ago. Most early theories about the nature of intelligence involved one or more of the following three themes: (1) the capacity to learn; (2) the total knowledge a person has acquired; and (3) the ability to adapt successfully to new situations and to the environment in general. A recent definition captures these elements and stresses higher-order thinking: intelligence is "the ability to reason deductively or inductively, think abstractly, use analogies, synthesize information, and apply it to new domains" (Kanazawa, 2010, p. 281).

INTELLIGENCE: ONE ABILITY OR MANY? There are moderate-to-high correlations among scores on *all* mental tests. In fact, this consistent finding "is arguably both the best established and the most striking phenomenon in the psychological study of intelligence" (van der Mass et al., 2006, p. 855). Because of these persistent intercorrelations, some psychologists believe intelligence is a basic ability that affects performance on all cognitively oriented tasks, from solving mathematical problems to analyzing poetry to taking history essay examinations. What could explain these results? Charles Spearman (1927) suggested that individuals use mental energy, which he called g, to perform any mental test. Spearman added that each test also requires some specific abilities as well—so ability to do any mental task is based on g + task-specific abilities. Today, psychologists generally agree that we can mathematically compute a common factor (g) across cognitive tests, but this computed factor is simply an indication or measure of general intelligence; it is not general intelligence itself (Kanazawa, 2010). Just having an overall mathematical indicator of intelligence isn't much help in understanding specific human abilities, so the notion of *g* does not have much explanatory power; it doesn't tell us what intelligence is or where it comes from (Blair, 2006).

Raymond Cattell and John Horn's theory of fluid and crystallized intelligence is more helpful in providing explanations (Cattell, 1963; Horn, 1998; Kanazawa, 2010). **Fluid intelligence** is mental efficiency and the reasoning ability included in Kanazawa's definition of intelligence just quoted (Kanazawa, 2010). The neurophysiological underpinnings of fluid intelligence may be related to changes in brain volume, myelinization (coating of neural fibers that makes processing faster), the density of dopamine receptors, or processing abilities in the prefrontal lobe of the brain such as selective attention and especially *working memory* (Waterhouse, 2006), an aspect of brain functioning we will explore in Chapter 8. This aspect of intelligence increases until late adolescence (about age 22) because it is grounded in brain development, and then declines gradually with age. Fluid intelligence is sensitive to injuries and diseases.

In contrast, **crystallized intelligence** is the ability to apply the problem-solving methods appropriate in your cultural context—the "application to new domains" part of Kanazawa's definition of intelligence. Crystallized intelligence can increase throughout the life span because it includes learned skills and knowledge such as reading, facts, and how to hail a cab, make a quilt, or design a unit on symbolism in poetry. By *investing fluid intelligence* in solving problems, we *develop our crystallized intelligence,* but many tasks in life such as mathematical reasoning draw on both fluid and crystallized intelligence working together (Ferrer & McArdle, 2004; Finkel, Reynolds, McArdle, Gatz, & Pedersen, 2003; Hunt, 2000).

The most widely accepted psychometric view today is that intelligence, like self- concept, has many facets and is a hierarchy of abilities, with general ability at the top and more specific abilities at lower levels of the hierarchy (Schalke et al., 2013; Tucker-Drob, 2009). John Carroll (1997) identifies one general ability, a few broad abilities (e.g., fluid and crystallized abilities, learning and memory, visual and auditory perception, and processing speed), and at least 70 specific abilities such as language development, memory span, and simple reaction time. General ability may be related to the maturation and functioning of the frontal lobe of the brain, while specific abilities may be connected to other parts of the brain (Byrnes & Fox, 1998).

Multiple Intelligences

While Howard Gardner was a developmental psychologist doing research with two very different groups—students who are artistically gifted at Harvard's Project Zero and patients with brain injuries at Boston's Veterans Administration (VA) Medical Center—he started thinking about a new theory of intelligence. Time and time again at the VA Medical Center, Gardner observed brain-injured patients who were lost spatially but could do all kinds of verbal tasks, and other patients who had the opposite set of abilities and problems. He also worked with young children at Project Zero who could draw expertly but not craft a good sentence and vice versa. Gardner concluded that there are several separate mental abilities and developed his now-famous **theory of multiple intelligences (MI)** that describes at least eight separate intelligences (1983, 2003, 2009, 2011).

WHAT ARE THESE INTELLIGENCES? The eight intelligences in MI theory are linguistic (verbal), musical, spatial, logical-mathematical, bodily-kinesthetic (movement), interpersonal (understanding others), intrapersonal (understanding self), and naturalist (observing and understanding natural and human-made patterns and systems). Gardner stresses that there may be more kinds of intelligence—eight is not a magic number. He has speculated that there may be a spiritual intelligence and an existential intelligence—the abilities to contemplate big questions about the meaning of life (Gardner, 2009, 2011). As Gardner witnessed firsthand in his early research with veterans and students, individuals may excel in one of these eight areas, but have no remarkable abilities, or may even have problems, in the other seven. Table 4.1 on the next page summarizes these eight (or nine) intelligences.

Connect and Extend to PRAXIS II®

Multiple Intelligences (I, B1)
Many teachers erroneously assume that they must address each of the eight intelligences in each lesson they design. What are some of the realistic implications of the theory for classroom instruction?

TABLE 4.1 • **Eight (or Nine) Intelligences**
Howard Gardner's theory of multiple intelligences suggests that there are eight or nine kinds of human abilities.
An individual might have strengths or weaknesses in one or several areas.

LOGICAL-MATHEMATICAL Skills: • Sensitivity to, and capacity to discern, logical or numerical patterns. • Ability to handle long chains of reasoning. **Example/Career Paths:** Scientist Mathematician Engineer	**LINGUISTIC** Skills: • Sensitivity to sounds, rhythms, and word meanings. • Sensitivity to different functions of language. **Example/Career Paths:** Poet Journalist Novelist
MUSICAL Skills: • Ability to appreciate and produce rhythm, tone, pitch, and timbre. • Appreciation of forms of musical expression. **Example/Career Paths:** Composer Pianist Drummer	**SPATIAL** Skills: • Ability to perceive the visual and spatial world accurately. • Ability to perform transformations on those perceptions. **Example/Career Paths:** Sculptor Navigator Architect
INTERPERSONAL Skills: • Ability to read the moods and motivations of others. • Ability to understand desires and needs of others and respond appropriately. **Example/Career Paths:** Therapist Salesperson Mediator	**INTRAPERSONAL** Skills: • Knowledge of your own strengths, weaknesses, capabilities, and needs and ability to use these to guide your behavior. • Access to your own feelings. **Example:** Anyone with detailed, accurate knowledge of self
NATURALIST Skills: • Ability to recognize plants and animals. • Ability to use categories and systems to understand the natural world. **Example/Career Paths:** Farmer Gardener Animal tracker	**BODILY-KINESTHETIC** Skills: • Ability to control body movements and know where your body is in space. • Ability to handle objects skillfully. **Example/Career Paths:** Dancer Gymnast Juggler
EXISTENTIAL Skills: • Ability to consider and examine deeper or larger questions about human existence and the meaning of life. • Ability to understand religious and spiritual ideas. **Example/Career Paths:** Philosopher Clergy Life coaches	

Source: Based on "Multiple Intelligences Go to School," by H. Gardner and T. Hatch (1989), Educational Researcher, 18(8), and "Are There Additional Intelligences? The Case for the Naturalist, Spiritual, and Existential Intelligences," by H. Gardner (1999) in J. Kane (Ed.), Educational Information and Transformation, Upper Saddle River, NJ: Prentice-Hall.

Gardner believes that intelligence has a biological base. An intelligence is a "biopsychological potential to process information in certain ways in order to solve problems or create products that are valued in at least one culture or community" (Gardner, 2009, p. 5). Varying cultures and eras of history place different values on the eight intelligences. A naturalist intelligence is critical in farming cultures, whereas verbal and mathematical intelligences are important in technological cultures. In fact, Gardner suggests what industrialized cultures usually label as "intelligence" is just a combination of linguistic and logical-mathematical skills, especially those taught in modern, secular schools (2009).

CRITICS OF MULTIPLE INTELLIGENCES THEORY. Gardner's MI theory has not received wide acceptance in the scientific community, even though many educators embrace it. Lynn Waterhouse (2006) concluded that no published studies validate MI theory. The eight intelligences are not independent; there are correlations among the abilities. In fact, logical-mathematical and spatial intelligences are highly correlated (Sattler, 2008). So, these "separate abilities" may not be so separate after all. Evidence linking musical and spatial abilities has prompted Gardner to consider that there may be connections among the intelligences (Gardner, 1998). In addition, some critics suggest that several intelligences are really talents (bodily-kinesthetic skill, musical ability) or personality traits (interpersonal ability). Other "intelligences" are not new at all. Many researchers have identified verbal and spatial abilities as elements of intelligence. Daniel Willingham (2004) has been even more blunt. "In the end, Gardner's theory is not that helpful. For scientists the theory is almost certainly incorrect. For educators, the daring applications forwarded by others in Gardner's name (and of which he disapproves) are unlikely to help students" (p. 24).

So there is not yet strong research evidence that adopting an MI approach will enhance learning. In one of the few carefully designed evaluations, Callahan, Tomlinson, and Plucker (1997) found no significant gains in either achievement or self-concept for students who participated in START, an MI approach to identifying and promoting talent in students who were at risk of failing.

GARDNER RESPONDS. In response to these criticisms, defenders of MI theory say that the critics have a very narrow view of intelligence and research about intelligence. Gardner based his theory on a set of criteria that integrated a wide range of research in psychology. Gardner's criteria for defining a specific intelligence are:

- Potential [of the intelligence] isolation by brain damage
- The existence of prodigies and other exceptional individuals who are experts in some areas and average or below in others
- An identifiable core operation or set of operations
- A distinctive developmental trajectory, culminating in expert performances
- An evolutionary history and evolutionary plausibility
- Support from experimental psychological tasks
- Evidence from psychometric findings
- Susceptibility to encoding in a symbol system (Gardner, 2009, p. 5)

Gardner's supporters believe newer research methods that look at dynamic models and study intelligence in cultural contexts will support MI theory (J.-Q. Chen, 2004; Gardner & Moran, 2006). In addition, Gardner (2003, 2009) also has responded to critics by identifying a number of myths, misconceptions, and misuses related to MI theory and schooling. For example, he stresses that an intelligence is not the same as a sensory system; there is no "auditory intelligence" or "visual intelligence." Intelligences are not the same as learning styles. (Gardner doesn't believe that people actually have consistent learning styles.) Another misconception is that MI theory disproves the idea of general intelligence. Gardner does not deny the existence of a general ability, but he does question how useful general intelligence is as an explanation for human achievements. Stay tuned for more developments.

MULTIPLE INTELLIGENCES GO TO SCHOOL. First let's consider a few misuses of MI theory in schools. Gardner particularly deplored an educational project in Australia that proclaimed different ethnic groups had certain specific intelligences but lacked others. Gardner went on television in Australia to call this program what it really was—"pseudoscience" and "veiled racism" (Gardner, 2009, p. 7). The project was cancelled. Another misuse is that some teachers embrace a simplistic version of Gardner's theory. They include every "intelligence" in every lesson, no matter how inappropriate.

Video 4.1
In this video, a seventh grade science teacher incorporates several of the multiple intelligences into his assessments. Is this teacher using Gardner's theory to foster effective learning?

ENHANCEDetext *video example*

A better way to use the theory is to focus on six Entry Points—narrative, logical-quantitative, aesthetic, experiential, interpersonal, and existential/foundational—in designing a curriculum (Gardner, 2006; Wares, 2013). For example, to teach about evolution, teachers might use the Entry Points as follows (Kornhaber, Fierros, & Veenema, 2004):

Narrative: Provide rich stories about Darwin's voyage to the Galapagos Islands or traditional folk-tales about the different plants and animals.

Logical-quantitative: Examine Darwin's attempts to map the distributions of the species or pose logical problems about what would happen to the ecosystem if one species disappeared.

Aesthetic: Examine Darwin's drawings of the species he studied on the Galapagos Islands.

Experiential: Do laboratory activities such as breeding fruit flies or completing virtual simulations of evolutionary processes.

Interpersonal: Form research teams or hold debates.

Existential/foundational: Consider questions about why species die out or what the purpose is for variation in species.

Multiple Intelligences: Lessons for Teachers

After years of work on his MI theory, Gardner believes two lessons are most important for teachers (2009). First, teachers should take the individual differences among students seriously and differentiate their instruction to connect with each student. Much of this book will help you do just that. Second, any discipline, skill, or concept should be taught in several appropriate ways (but not eight ways every time). Anything worth knowing has different representations and multiple connections to various ways of thinking. And understandings can be expressed in words, images, movements, tables, charts, numbers, equations, poetry, and on and on. These two big ideas should *guide* educational interventions, but Gardner stresses that his theory itself is not an educational intervention. The MI theory expands our thinking about abilities and avenues for teaching, but learning is still hard work, even if there are multiple paths to knowledge.

Intelligence as a Process

As you can see, the theories of Spearman, Cattell and Horn, Carroll, and Gardner tend to describe how individuals differ in the *content* of intelligence—different abilities. Work in cognitive psychology has emphasized instead the *information processing* that is common to all people. How do humans gather and use information to solve problems and behave intelligently? New views of intelligence are emerging from this work. The debates in the 2006 issue of *Behavioral and Brain Sciences* emphasized working memory capacity, the abilities to focus attention and inhibit impulses, and emotional self-regulation as aspects of fluid cognitive abilities.

Robert Sternberg's triarchic theory of successful intelligence is a cognitive process approach to understanding intelligence (Sternberg, 1985, 2004; Stemler, Sternberg, Grigorenko, Jarvin, & Sharpes, 2009). Sternberg uses the term *successful intelligence* to stress that intelligence is more than what is tested by mental abilities measures: Intelligence is about life success based on your own definition of success in your cultural context.

Sternberg believes the processes involved in intelligence are universal for humans. These processes are defined in terms of components: elementary information processes that are classified by the functions they serve and by how general they are. At least three different functions are served. The first function—higher-order planning, strategy selection, and monitoring—is performed by *metacomponents* (sometimes called *executive processes*—see Chapter 8). A second function—implementing the strategies selected—is handled by *performance components,* such as taking notes to focus attention in class. The third function—gaining new knowledge—is performed by *knowledge-acquisition components,* such as separating relevant from irrelevant information as you try to understand a new concept. Some processes are specific; that is, they are necessary for only one kind of task, such as solving analogies. Other processes, such as monitoring progress and switching strategies, are very general and may be necessary in almost every cognitive task. This may help to explain the persistent correlations among all types of mental tests. People who are effective in selecting good problem-solving strategies, monitoring progress, and moving to a new approach when the first one fails are more likely to succeed on all types of tests.

Applying *metacomponents, performance components,* and *knowledge-acquisition components* allows individuals to solve problems in different situations and to develop three kinds of successful intelligence: analytic, creative, and practical. *Analytic intelligence* involves applying these components to situations with relatively familiar problems. *Creative intelligence* is necessary to cope successfully with new experiences in two ways: (1) using insight, or the ability to deal effectively with novel situations and find new solutions, and (2) using automaticity, the ability to become efficient and automatic in thinking and problem solving—the ability to quickly make the new solutions part of your cognitive tool kit, so to speak.

The third part of the triarchic theory, *practical intelligence,* highlights the importance of choosing an environment in which you can succeed, adapting to that environment, and reshaping it if necessary. People who are successful often seek situations in which their abilities will be valued, then work hard to capitalize on those abilities and compensate for any weaknesses. Thus, intelligence in this third sense involves practical matters such as career choice or social skills. In a field study in Voronezh, Russia, Elena Grigorenko and Robert Sternberg (2001) found that adults with higher practical and analytical intelligence coped better both mentally and physically with the stresses caused by rapid changes in that part of the world.

In recent years, Sternberg has added the concept of "wisdom" to his explanation of successful intelligence to create the WICS theory (Wisdom, Intelligence, Creativity Synthesized). According to WICS theory, the goal of education is to help citizens use: "(a) creativity to generate new ideas and problems as well as possible solutions to the problems, (b) analytical intelligence to evaluate the quality of these solutions, (c) practical intelligence to implement decisions and persuade others of their value, and (d) wisdom to ensure that these decisions help achieve a common good over the long and short terms" (Grigorenko et al., 2009, p. 965).

Even though there are many theories of intelligence, teachers, students, and parents are most familiar with intelligence as a number or score on an intelligence quotient (IQ) test.

Measuring Intelligence

STOP & THINK   How are an inch and a mile alike? What does *obstreperous* mean? Repeat these numbers backwards: 8 5 7 3 0 2 1 9 7. In what two ways is a lamp better than a candle? •

These items, taken from Sattler (2001, p. 222), are similar to the verbal questions from a common individual intelligence test for children. Another part of the test asks the child to copy a design using blocks, find the missing part of a picture, or select from several pictures the two that go together. Even though psychologists do not agree about what intelligence is, they do agree that intelligence, as measured by standardized tests, is related to learning in school. Why is this so? It has to do in part with the way intelligence tests were first developed.

BINET'S DILEMMA.   In 1904, Alfred Binet was confronted with the following problem by the minister of public instruction in Paris: How can students who will need special instruction and extra help be identified early in their school careers, before they fail in general education classes? Binet was also a political activist and very concerned about the rights of children. He believed that having an objective measure of learning ability could protect students living in poverty who might be forced to leave school because they were the victims of discrimination and assumed to be slow learners.

Binet and his collaborator Theodore Simon wanted to measure not merely school achievement but also the intellectual skills students needed to do well in school. After trying many different tests and eliminating items that did not discriminate between successful and unsuccessful students, Binet and Simon finally identified 58 tests, several for each age group from 3 to 13. Binet's tests allowed the examiner to determine a mental age for a child. A child who succeeded on the

Connect and Extend to PRAXIS II®

Intelligence Testing (II, C1, 4)
The public often misunderstands
intelligence testing. Be prepared
to respond to questions about the
appropriate uses of intelligence tests.
What are some inappropriate uses of
these tests?

items passed by most 6-year-olds, for example, was considered to have a mental age of 6, whether the child was actually 4, 5, 6, 7, or 8 years old.

The concept of **intelligence quotient (IQ)** was added after Binet's test was brought to the United States and revised at Stanford University to give us the Stanford-Binet test. An IQ score was computed by comparing the mental-age score to the person's actual chronological age. The formula was:

$$\text{Intelligence Quotient} = \text{Mental Age}/\text{Chronological Age} \times 100$$

The early Stanford-Binet test has been revised five times, most recently in 2003 (Roid, 2003). The practice of computing a mental age has proved to be problematic because IQ scores calculated on the basis of mental age do not have the same meaning as children get older. To cope with this problem, the concept of deviation IQ was introduced. The **deviation IQ** score is a number that tells exactly how much above or below the average a person scored on the test, compared to others in the same age group, as you will see in the next section.

WHAT DOES AN IQ SCORE MEAN? Most intelligence tests are designed so that they have certain statistical characteristics. For example, the average score is 100; 50% of the people from the general population who take the tests will score 100 or below, and 50% will score above 100. About 68% of the general population will earn IQ scores between 85 and 115. Only about 16% will receive scores below 85, and only 16% will score above 115. Note, however, that these figures hold true for White, native-born Americans whose first language is Standard English. Whether IQ tests should even be used with ethnic minority-group students is hotly debated.

GROUP VERSUS INDIVIDUAL IQ TESTS. The Stanford-Binet is an individual intelligence test. It has to be administered to one student at a time by a trained psychologist, and it takes about 2 hours. Most of the questions are asked orally and do not require reading or writing. A student usually pays closer attention and is more motivated to do well when working directly with an adult.

Psychologists also have developed group tests that can be given to whole classes or schools. Compared to an individual test, a group test is much less likely to yield an accurate picture of any one person's abilities. When students take tests in a group, they may do poorly because they do not understand the instructions, because they have trouble reading, because their pencils break or they lose their place on the answer sheet, because other students distract them, or because the answer format confuses them (Sattler, 2008). As a teacher, you should be very wary of IQ scores based on group tests. The *Guidelines: Interpreting IQ Scores* will help you interpret IQ scores realistically.

THE FLYNN EFFECT: ARE WE GETTING SMARTER? Ever since IQ tests were introduced in the early 1900s, scores in 20 different industrialized countries and in some more traditional cultures have been rising. In fact, in a decade, the average score goes up about 3 points on standardized IQ tests—maybe you really are smarter than your parents! At least you probably would score about 10 points higher on an IQ test. This is called the **Flynn effect** after James Flynn, a political scientist who documented the phenomenon (Daley, Whaley, Sigman, Espinosa, & Neumann, 2003; Folger, 2012). So are we getting smarter? James Flynn (2012) answers this way:

> If you mean "Do our brains have more potential at conception than those of our ances-
> tors?" then we are not. If you mean "Are we developing mental abilities that allow us to
> better deal with the complexity of the modern world, including problems of economic
> development?" then we are. (p. 1)

Some explanations include better nutrition and medical care for children and parents, increasing complexity in the environment that stimulates abstract thinking, smaller families who give more attention to their children, increased literacy of parents (particularly better-educated mothers), more and better schooling, and better preparation for taking tests. One result of the Flynn effect is that the norms used to determine scores (you will read more about norms in Chapter 15) have to be continually revised. In other words, to keep a score of 100 as the average, the test questions have to be made more difficult. This increasing difficulty has implications for any program that uses IQ scores as part of its entrance requirements. For example, some "average" students of the previous

GUIDELINES
Interpreting IQ Scores

Check to see if the score is based on an individual or a group test. Be wary of group test scores.

Examples

1. Individual tests include the Wechsler Scales (WPPSI–III, WISC-IV, WAIS-IV), the Stanford-Binet, the McCarthy Scales of Children's Abilities, the Woodcock-Johnson Psycho-Educational Battery, the Naglieri Nonverbal Ability Test—Individual, and the Kaufman Assessment Battery for Children.
2. Group tests include the Otis-Lennon School Abilities Tests, Slosson Intelligence Test, Raven Progressive Matrices, Naglieri Nonverbal Ability Test—Multiform, Differential Abilities Scales, and Wide Range Intelligence Test.

Remember that IQ tests are only estimates of general aptitude for learning.

Examples

1. Ignore small differences in scores among students.
2. Bear in mind that even an individual student's scores may change over time for many reasons, including measurement error.
3. Be aware that a total score is usually an average of scores on several kinds of questions. A score in the middle or average range may mean that the student performed at the average on every kind of question or that the student did quite well in some areas (e.g., on verbal tasks) and rather poorly in other areas (e.g., on quantitative tasks).

Remember that IQ scores reflect a student's past experiences and learning.

Examples

1. Consider these scores to be predictors of school abilities, not measures of innate intellectual abilities.
2. If a student is doing well in your class, do not change your opinion or lower your expectations just because one score seems low.
3. Be wary of IQ scores for minority students and for students whose first language was not English. Even scores on "culture-free" tests are lower for students placed at risk.
4. Remember that both adaptive skills and scores on IQ tests are used to determine intellectual abilities and disabilities.

For more about interpreting IQ scores, see wilderdom.com/personality/L2-1UnderstandingIQ.html

---

generation might be identified today as having intellectual disabilities because the test questions are harder (Folger, 2012; Kanaya, Scullin, & Ceci, 2003).

INTELLIGENCE AND ACHIEVEMENT. Scoring higher on IQ tests is related to academic achievement for children in all ethnic groups. In fact, researchers in England found a strong relationship (.64) between measured IQ at age 8 and achievement on standardized tests in math, English, and science at age 14. These findings came from the *Avon Longitudinal Study of Parents and Children,* an extensive investigation that involved more than 14,000 children born in and around Bristol England between April 1991 and December 1992 (Bornstein, Hahn, & Wolke, 2013). To see the remarkable wealth of data analyzed in this study—not just IQ but also measures of information processing abilities at age 4 months, behavior problems at 36 months, extensive health data for mothers and children, parent education, and so much more—go to bristol.ac.uk/alspac/.

The relations between IQ scores and school achievement are interesting, but standard IQ tests measure only analytic IQ, not practical or creative IQs. Elena Grigorenko and her colleagues (2009) used the usual standardized test scores and grade-point average (GPA) to predict middle school students' achievement in high school but also included tests of students' abilities to manage their own learning and motivation, along with measures of practical and creative intelligence. Using this broader picture of students' abilities, the researchers were able to make better predictions, not only of achievement in high school but also of the rate of growth. In another series of studies, Angela Duckworth and her colleagues (2012) found that IQ scores predict standardized test scores but measures of self-regulation (see Chapter 11) are better predictors of grades in school. So IQ test scores are related to some kinds of academic achievement, but if measures of self-regulated learning skills, practical intelligence, and creativity are included, we can make even better predictions of school success.

But what about life after school? Do people who score high on IQ tests achieve more in life? Here the answer is less clear, because life success and education are intertwined. High school graduates earn over $200,000 more than nongraduates in their lifetime; college graduates earn over $1,100,000 more; graduates with doctoral degrees earn $2,400,000 more; and graduates with professional degrees (physicians, lawyers, etc.), over $3,400,000 more in their lifetime (Cheeseman Day & Newburger, 2002). People with higher intelligence test scores tend to complete more years of school and to have higher-status jobs. However, when the number of years of education is held constant, the correlation decreases between IQ scores, income, and success in later life. Just as Grigorenko and coworkers (2009) found, other factors such as self-regulation, motivation, social skills, and luck may make the difference in life achievement (Alarcon & Edwards, 2013; Neisser et al., 1996).

Gender Differences in Intelligence

From infancy through the preschool years, most studies find few differences between boys and girls in overall mental and motor development or in specific abilities. During the school years and beyond, psychologists find no differences in general intelligence on the standard measures. These tests have been designed and standardized to minimize sex differences. However, scores on some tests of specific abilities show sex differences. Also, the scores of males tend to be slightly more variable in general, so there are more males than females with very high and very low scores on tests (Halpern et al., 2007; Lindberg, Hyde, Peterson, & Linn, 2010). In addition, more boys than girls are diagnosed with learning disabilities, ADHD, and autism. Diane Halpern and her colleagues (2007) summarize the research:

> By the end of grade school and beyond, females perform better on assessments of verbal abilities when assessments are heavily weighted with writing and the language-usage items cover topics with which females are familiar; sex differences favoring females are much larger in these conditions than when assessments of verbal abilities do not include writing. In contrast, males excel on certain visuospatial-ability measures. (p. 40)

There is a caution, however. In most studies of sex differences, race and ethnicity are not taken into account. For example, when researchers studied ethnic groups separately, among White students, very small differences in mathematics performance favored White males in high school and college, but among ethnic minority students, slight differences favored females. Also, research suggested small differences in complex problem-solving skills favoring boys in high school, perhaps because problem solving is taught more in physics classes than in math, and boys are more likely than girls to take physics—another reason to encourage all students to get a good background in science (Lindberg et al., 2010).

Several recent international *meta-analyses* (analyses that combine data from many different studies on the same topic) have found few differences in mathematics achievement for boys and girls. For example, Sara Lindberg and her colleagues analyzed data from 242 studies that included 1.3 million elementary through high school students. Overall, they found that in the United States and some other nations, girls' and boys' performance in mathematics is comparable, but the researchers found some differences by nations: girls scored higher than boys in several countries such as Russia, Bahrain, and Mexico; and boys' scores were higher in other countries such as Switzerland, the Netherlands, and African nations (Else-Quest, Hyde, & Linn, 2010; Lindberg et al., 2010). Also, the International Comparisons in Fourth-Grade Reading Literacy (Mullis, Martin, Gonzalez, & Kennedy, 2003) revealed that in 34 countries, fourth-grade boys scored below girls in reading literacy. Finally, girls in general tend to get higher grades than boys in mathematics classes.

Males on average are better on tests that require mental rotation of a figure in space, prediction of the trajectories of moving objects, and navigating. Some researchers argue that evolution has favored these skills in males (Buss, 1995; Geary, 1995, 1999), but others relate these skills to males' more active play styles, their greater experience with video games and construction toys like Legos, males' greater confidence in spatial tasks, and their participation in athletics. Factors that undermine girl's performance may be stereotypes that girls do not do well and their anxiety while performing timed spatial tests (Else-Quest et al., 2010; Maeda & Yoon, 2012; Stumpf, 1995). Some educational psychologists believe that spatial skills are neglected in school curricula and that even a small amount of instruction can make a big difference for students (Uttal, Hand, & Newcombe, 2009).

The cross-cultural comparisons suggest that much of the difference in mathematics scores between boys and girls comes from learning, not biology. And studies showing that adults rated a math paper attributed to "John T. McKay" a full point higher on a 5-point scale than the same paper attributed to "Joan T. McKay" suggests that discrimination and stereotyped expectations play a role as well (Angier & Chang, 2005). Lindberg and her colleagues sum it up well: "Overall, it is clear that in the United States and some other nations, girls have reached parity with boys in mathematics performance. It is crucial that this information be made widely known to counteract stereotypes about female math inferiority held by gatekeepers such as parents and teachers and by students themselves" (2010, p. 1134). I agree that combating these stereotypes is critical. Melanie Steffens and her colleagues (2010) in Germany found that by age 9, girls already had developed implicit (out of awareness) math-gender stereotypes; the girls associated men with mathematics. These implicit beliefs grew stronger into adolescence, predicted girls' achievement in math, and affected their decisions to take elective math courses.

HEREDITY OR ENVIRONMENT? Nowhere has the nature-versus-nurture debate raged so hard as in the area of intelligence. Should intelligence be seen as a potential, limited by our genetic makeup? Or does intelligence simply refer to an individual's current level of intellectual functioning, as influenced by experience and education?

Beware of either/or comparisons: It is impossible to separate intelligence "in the genes" from intelligence "due to experience." Today, most psychologists believe that differences in intelligence are the result of both heredity and environment, probably in about equal proportions for children (Petrill & Wilkerson, 2000). And environmental influences include everything from the health of a child's mother during pregnancy to the amount of lead in the child's home to the quality of teaching a child receives. For example, Japanese and Chinese students know much more mathematics than American students, but their intelligence test scores are quite similar. This superiority in math probably is related to differences in the way mathematics is taught and studied in the three countries and to the self-motivation skills of many Asian students (Baron, 1998; Stevenson & Stigler, 1992). Also, when German secondary school students participated in an academic track (a high-quality and demanding learning environment) rather than a vocational track in school, their general cognitive abilities (intelligence) improved (Becker, Lüdtke, Trautwein, Köller, & Baumert, 2012).

BEING SMART ABOUT IQ TESTS. We saw that intelligence tests originally were developed, in part, to protect the rights of children from poorer families who might be denied an education on the false grounds that they weren't able to learn. We also saw that intelligence tests predict school success equally accurately for students of different races and income levels. Even so, these tests can never be free of cultural content, so they always will have some biases built in. Keep this in mind when you see your students' scores on any test. Finally, remember that the results of every assessment for every student should be used to support that student's learning and development and to identify effective practices, not to deny the student access to resources or appropriate teaching. For all adults caring for children—parents, teachers, administrators, counselors, medical workers— it is especially important to realize that cognitive skills, like any other skills, are always improvable. *Intelligence is a current state of affairs, affected by past experiences and open to future changes.*

Now that you have a sense of what intelligence means, let's consider another kind of individual difference that often is misunderstood and misused in education—learning styles.

ENHANCEDetext *self-check*

LEARNING AND THINKING STYLES

For many years, researchers have examined individual differences in "styles"—cognitive styles, learning styles, problem-solving styles, thinking styles, decision-making styles . . . the list goes on. Li-fang Zhang and Robert Sternberg (2005) organize the work on individual styles into three traditions. *Cognitive-centered* styles assess the ways people process information, for example, by being reflective or impulsive

Connect and Extend to PRAXIS II®

Learning/Cognitive Styles (I, B1)
Familiarize yourself with the major issues involved with learning and cognitive styles, and understand their implications for classroom practice.

in responding (J. Kagan, 1976). *Personality-centered* styles assess more stable personality traits such as being extroverted versus being introverted or relying on thinking versus feeling (Myers & McCaulley, 1988). *Activity-centered* styles assess a combination of cognition and personality traits that affect how people approach activities, so these styles may be of special interest to teachers.

One theme in activity-centered approaches is the differences between surface and deep approaches to processing information in learning situations (R. E. Snow, Corno, & Jackson, 1996). Students who take a surface-processing approach focus on memorizing the learning materials, not understanding them. These students tend to be motivated by rewards, grades, external standards, and the desire to be evaluated positively by others. Individuals who have a deep-processing approach see the learning activities as a means for understanding some underlying concepts or meanings. They tend to learn for the sake of learning and are less concerned about how their performance is evaluated. Deep processing is associated with greater learning and retention. Of course, the situation can encourage deep or surface processing, but evidence indicates that individuals have tendencies to approach learning situations in characteristic ways (Biggs, 2001; Coffield, Moseley, Hall, & Ecclestone, 2004; Komarraju, Karau, Schmeck, & Avdic, 2011).

Learning Styles/Preferences

Here is another "style" term. You may have heard about learning styles or used the phrase yourself. **Learning style** usually is defined as the way a person approaches learning and studying. But beware—some conceptions of learning styles have little research support; others are based on solid studies. First, the cautions.

CAUTIONS ABOUT LEARNING STYLES. Since the late 1970s, a great deal has been written about differences in students' "learning styles" (Dunn & Dunn, 1978, 1987; Dunn & Griggs, 2003; Gregorc, 1982; Keefe, 1982). But I believe **learning preferences** is a more accurate label because most of the research describes preferences for particular learning environments—for example, where, when, with whom, or with what lighting, food, or music you like to study. A number of instruments assess students' learning preferences, for example, The Learning Style Inventory (Dunn, Dunn, & Price, 1989), Learning Styles Inventory (Revised) (McLeod, 2010), and the Learning Style Profile (Keefe & Monk, 1986).

Are these useful tools? Tests of learning style have been strongly criticized (Pashler, McDaniel, Rohrer, & Bjork, 2009). In fact, in an extensive examination of learning styles instruments, researchers at the Learning Skills Research Centre in England concluded, "with regard to work by Dunn and Dunn, Gregorc, and Riding, our examination of the reliability and validity of their learning style instruments strongly suggests that they should not be used in education or business" (Coffield et al., 2004, p. 127). Most researchers are skeptical about the value of learning preferences. "The reason researchers roll their eyes at learning styles research is the utter failure to find that assessing children's learning styles and matching to instructional methods has any effect on their learning (Stahl, 2002, p. 99). In fact, an experimental study had college students self-assess their learning style as auditory, visual, or kinesthetic and then taught the students in keeping with their professed style (Kratzig & Arbuthnott, 2006). Matching learning with teaching styles did not improve learning. When the researchers examined how people identified their own learning styles, they concluded that people's judgments represented preferences rather than superior skills in using auditory, visual, or kinesthetic modalities. If college students have trouble identifying their own learning style, think about fourth or ninth graders!

In summary, the most recent review of learning styles research ends with these words: "The contrast between the enormous popularity of the learning-styles approach within education and the lack of credible evidence for its utility is, in our opinion, striking and disturbing. If classification of students' learning styles has practical utility, it remains to be demonstrated" (Pashler et al., 2009, p. 117).

So why are these ideas so popular? Part of the answer is that many thriving commercial companies are making large profits by providing advice to teachers, tutors, and managers about learning styles based on "inflated claims and sweeping conclusions which go beyond the current knowledge base" (Coffield et al., 2004, p. 127). Money talks. Also, the idea of multimodal learning is

TABLE 4.2 • Richard Mayer's Three Facets of the Visualizer–Verbalizer Dimension
There are three facets to visual versus verbal learning: ability, style, and preference. Individuals can be high or low on any or all of these facets.

FACET	TYPES OF LEARNERS	DEFINITION
Cognitive Ability	High spatial ability	Good abilities to create, remember, and manipulate images and spatial information
	Low spatial ability	Poor abilities to create, remember, and manipulate images and spatial information
Cognitive Style	Visualizer	Thinks using images and visual information
	Verbalizer	Thinks using words and verbal information
Learning Preference	Visual learner	Prefers instruction using pictures
	Verbal learner	Prefers instruction using words

popular. People like visual materials and animated presentations. But these animations can lead to a phenomenon called an *illusion of understanding*. Students think they understand because the content seems less difficult, they are overly optimistic, and so they don't monitor their learning or use other metacognitive skills to process deeply. Lower-ability learners are especially susceptible to developing illusions of understanding with animated presentations (Paik & Schraw, 2013).

THE VALUE OF CONSIDERING LEARNING STYLES. There is one learning styles distinction that has research support. Richard Mayer (e.g., Mayer & Massa, 2003) has been studying the distinction between visual and verbal learners, with a focus on learning from computer-based multimedia. Here, the assessment of learning styles is carefully done and more valid than assessments based on many of the commercial inventories. Mayer has found a visualizer–verbalizer dimension and that it has three facets: *cognitive spatial ability* (low or high), *cognitive style* (visualizer vs. verbalizer), and *learning preference* (visual learner vs. verbal learner), as shown in Table 4.2. So the picture is more complex than simply being a visual or a verbal learner. A student might have a preference for learning with pictures, but low spatial ability could make using pictures for learning less effective. To complicate matters even more, spatial abilities may be important for learning from static pictures but less important for learning from animation; so the type of learning materials matters, too (Hoeffler & Leutner, 2011). These differences can be reliably measured, but research has not identified the effects of teaching to these styles; certainly, presenting information in multiple modalities might be useful.

So before you try to accommodate all your students' learning styles, remember that students, especially younger ones, may not be the best judges of how they should learn. Preference for a particular style does not guarantee that using the style will be effective. Sometimes students, particularly poorer students, prefer what is easy and comfortable (e.g., animation to explain difficult material); real learning can be hard and uncomfortable. In some cases, students prefer to learn in a certain way because they have no alternatives; it is the only way they know how to approach the task. These students may benefit from developing new—and perhaps more effective—ways to learn. Learning styles probably are a minor factor in learning; factors such as teaching strategies and social connections in classrooms likely play much larger roles (Kratzig & Arbuthnott, 2006).

Beyond Either/Or

Even though much of the work on matching learning styles and preferences to teaching is suspect, with unreliable measures and inflated claims, thinking about learning styles has some value. First, by helping students think about how they learn, you can develop thoughtful self-monitoring and self-awareness. In upcoming chapters, we will look at the value of such self-knowledge for learning and motivation. Second, looking at individual students' approaches to learning might help teachers appreciate, accept, and accommodate student differences and differentiate instruction (Coffield et al., 2004; Rosenfeld & Rosenfeld, 2004).

Schools can make available learning options, such as having quiet, private corners as well as large tables for working; comfortable cushions as well as straight chairs; brightly lighted desks along with darker areas; headphones for listening to music as well as earplugs; structured as well as open-ended assignments; and information available from visuals, podcasts, and DVDs as well as books. Will making these alterations lead to greater learning? Here the answer is not clear. Very bright students appear to need less structure and to prefer quiet, solitary learning (Torrance, 1986), and the visual–verbal distinction seems to be valid. If nothing else, some accommodation of student preferences may make your classroom more inviting and student friendly and communicate to your students that you care about them as individuals.

Thus far, we have focused mostly on the varying abilities and styles of students. For the rest of the chapter, we will consider factors that can interfere with learning. It is important for all teachers to be aware of these issues because laws and policy changes initiated in the mid 1970s continue to expand teachers' responsibilities in working with all students.

ENHANCEDetext *self-check*

INDIVIDUAL DIFFERENCES AND THE LAW

STOP & THINK Have you ever had the experience of being the only one in a group who had trouble doing something? How would you feel if every day in school you faced the same kind of difficulty, while everyone else seemed to find the work easier than you? What kind of support and teaching would you need to keep trying? •

IDEA

Since 1975, in the United States, a series of laws, beginning with PL 94–142 (the Education of All Handicapped Children Act), has led to revolutionary changes in the education of children with disabilities. The legislation, now called the Individuals with Disabilities Education Act (IDEA), was revised in 1990, 1997, and 2004. At the most general level, the law now requires states to provide a free, appropriate public education (FAPE) for all students with disabilities who participate in special education. There are no exceptions—the law requires zero reject. This policy also applies to students with communicable diseases such as AIDS. The expenses of meeting the special needs of these students are considered a public responsibility. Every state in the United States has a *child find* system to alert and educate the public about services for children with disabilities and to distribute useful information.

The definition of *disability* is specific in IDEA. The 13 categories of disabilities covered are listed in Table 4.3, along with the numbers of students in each category during the 2011–2012 school year. In 2011, just over 60% of these students received at least 80% of their instruction in general education settings. Most of these students spend some of their school day in general education classes. You can see that no matter what grade or subject you teach, you will work with students with special needs.

Before we look at the different categories, let's examine the requirements in IDEA. Three major points are of interest to parents and teachers: the concept of "least restrictive placement"; the individualized education program; and the protection of the rights of both students with disabilities and their parents.

LEAST RESTRICTIVE ENVIRONMENT. IDEA requires states to develop procedures for educating each child in the least restrictive environment (LRE), a setting that is as close to the general education class setting as possible. Over the years, recommended approaches to achieve this

TABLE 4.3 • **Students Ages 3 to 21 Served Under IDEA**

Thirteen categories of students are served under IDEA. The table shows the number of students in each category in the 2011–2012 school year.

DISABILITY	NUMBER OF STUDENTS IN 2010–2011
Specific learning disabilities	2,303,000
Speech/language impairments	1,373,000
Other health impairments (not orthopedic)	743,000
Autism spectrum disorders	455,000
Intellectual disability (mental retardation)	435,000
Developmental delay	393,000
Emotional disturbances	373,000
Multiple disabilities	132,000
Hearing impairments	78,000
Orthopedic impairments	61,000
Visual impairments	28,000
Traumatic brain injury	26,000
Deaf-blind	2,000
Total	6,402,000

have moved from **mainstreaming** (including children with special needs in a few general education classes as convenient), to **integration** (fitting the child into existing class structures), to **inclusion** (restructuring educational settings to promote belonging for all students) (Avramidis, Bayliss, & Burden, 2000). Even though the IDEA legislation does not use the word *inclusion,* today the LRE is assumed to be inclusion as much as possible. In the end, successful inclusion probably depends on teachers' being knowledgeable and well prepared, getting the support they need to teach, and being committed to inclusion. However, an emphasis on standardized testing may interfere with good teaching for included students (Friend, 2014; Idol, 2006; Kemp & Carter, 2006).

INDIVIDUALIZED EDUCATION PROGRAM. The drafters of the laws recognized that each student is unique and may need a specially tailored program to make progress. The **Individualized Education Program (IEP)** is an agreement between parents and the school about the services that will be provided to the student. The IEP is written by a team that includes the student's parents or guardians, a general education teacher who works with the student, a special education teacher, a representative of the school district (often the principal), a qualified person who can interpret the student's evaluation results (often a school psychologist), and (if appropriate) the student. For students 16 and older, the team may include representatives from outside agencies who are providing services to help the student make transitions to life and support services after school. If the school and parents agree, the team could add other people who have special knowledge of the child (e.g., a therapist). The program usually is updated each year. For an example IEP, go to education.com/reference/article/individualized-education-program-IEP/, or simply do a web search for "example IEPs."

The IEP must state in writing:

1. The student's present level of academic achievement and functional performance (sometimes referred to as *PLAAFP*).
2. Annual goals—measurable performance goals for the year. Students with significant needs or multiple disabilities may also have *short-term objectives,* or *benchmarks,* to make sure progress

Video 4.2
In this IEP conference, the parent describes the development of her daughter's individualized education program, and the team members discuss her current goals. How do the parents and the child benefit from participation in this type of meeting?

ENHANCEDetext *video example*

is continuous. The plan must tell how progress toward these goals and objectives will be measured. Parents must get progress reports at least as often as report cards are sent home for all students.

3. A statement of specific special education and related services to be provided to the student and details of when and where those services will be initiated and when they will end. This statement can include descriptions of supplementary aids and assistive technologies (e.g., using speech recognition software such as *Dragon*® to dictate answers or compose essays, or writing using a computer).

4. An explanation of how much of the student's program WILL NOT be in general education classroom and school settings.

5. A statement about how the student will participate in state and districtwide assessments, particularly those required by the No Child Left Behind accountability procedures.

6. Beginning at age 14 and by age 16, a statement of needed transitional services to move the student toward further education or work in adult life (Friend, 2014; D. C. Smith, Tyler, & Smith, 2014).

Figure 4.2 is an example of an individual transition planning (ITP) form for employment.

THE RIGHTS OF STUDENTS AND FAMILIES. Several stipulations in IDEA protect the rights of parents and students. Schools must have procedures for maintaining the confidentiality of student records. Testing practices must not discriminate against students from different cultural backgrounds. Parents have the right to see all records relating to the testing, placement, and teaching of their child. If they wish, parents may obtain an independent evaluation of their child. Parents may bring an advocate or representative to the meeting at which the IEP is developed. Students whose parents are unavailable must be assigned a surrogate parent to participate in the planning. Parents must receive written notice (in their native language) before any evaluation or change in placement is made. Finally, parents have the right to challenge the program developed for their child, and they are protected by due process of law. Because teachers often have conferences with these families, I have provided the *Guidelines: Family and Community Partnerships* on page 138 to make the meetings more effective, but be aware that guidelines apply to meetings with all your students and their parents.

Section 504 Protections

Not all students who need special accommodations in school are covered by IDEA or are eligible for the services provided by the law. But these students' educational needs may be covered by other legislation. As a consequence of the civil rights movement in the 1960s and 1970s, the federal government passed the Vocational Rehabilitation Act of 1973. Section 504 of that law prevents discrimination against people with disabilities in any program that receives federal money, such as public schools.

Through Section 504, all school-age children are ensured an equal opportunity to participate in school activities. The definition of *disability* is broad in Section 504. If a student has a condition that substantially limits participation in school, then the school still must develop a plan for giving that student access to education, even though the school gets no extra funds. To get assistance through Section 504, students must be assessed, often by a team, and a plan developed. Unlike IDEA, however, there are fewer rules about how this must happen, so individual schools design their own procedures (Friend, 2014). Look at Table 4.4 on page 138 to see an example of the kinds of accommodations that might be made for a student. Many of these ideas seem to be "just good teaching." But I have been surprised to see how many teachers won't let students use calculators or audio recorders because "they should learn to do it like everyone else!" Two major groups are considered for Section 504 accommodations: students with medical or health needs (e.g., diabetes, drug addiction or alcoholism, severe allergies, communicable diseases, or temporary disabilities resulting from accidents) and students with ADHD, if they are not already covered by IDEA.

The Americans with Disabilities Act of 1990 (ADA) prohibits discrimination against persons with disabilities in employment, transportation, public access, local government, and

Connect and Extend to PRAXIS II®

Individual Education Programs (IEP) (I, B3)
When you sign an IEP, you are signing an important educational and legal document. Be sure that you can explain the purpose of an IEP, identify its components, and describe the kind of information that can be contained in one.

FIGURE 4.2

EXAMPLE OF A TRANSITION PLANNING FORM

This ITP was developed for a student who is moving toward work in a grocery store. The plan describes the needed services so the student can transition into supported employment.

ILLUSTRATIVE TRANSITION PLANNING FORM IN THE AREA OF EMPLOYMENT

Student: _Robert Brown_

Meeting Date: _January 20, 2003_

Graduation Date: _June, 2004_

IEP/Transition Planning Team Members: *Robert Brown (student), Mrs. Brown (parent), Jill Green (teacher), Mike Weatherby (Vocational Education), Dick Rose (Rehabilitation), Susan Marr (Developmental Disabilities Agency)*

TRANSITION PLANNING AREA: *Employment*

Student Preferences and Desired Postschool Goals:	*Robert would like to work in a grocery store as a produce stocker.*
Present Levels of Performance:	*Robert has held several work experience placements in local grocery stores (see attached placement summaries). He requires a self-management checklist using symbols to complete assigned work tasks. His rate of task completion is below the expected employer levels.*
Need Transition Services:	*Robert will require job placement, training, and follow-along services from an employment specialist. In addition, he needs bus training to get to his job.*

ANNUAL GOAL: *Robert will work Monday through Friday from 1:00 to 4:00 p.m. at Smith's Food Center as a produce stocker, completing all assigned tasks without assistance from the employment specialist on ten consecutive weekly performance probes.*

Activities	Person	Completion Date
1. Place Robert on the state supported employment waiting list.	Susan Marr	May 1, 2003
2. Obtain a monthly bus pass.	Mrs. Brown	February 1, 2003
3. Schedule Robert for employee orientation training.		February 16, 2003

Source: McDonnell, J., Hardman, M. L., & McDonnell, A. P. (2003). Introduction to Persons with Moderate and Severe Disabilities: Educational and Social Issues, 2nd Ed. Reprinted by permission of Pearson Education, Inc.

GUIDELINES
Family and Community Partnerships

Productive Conferences

Plan and prepare for a productive conference.

Examples

1. Have a clear purpose, and gather the needed information. If you want to discuss student progress, have work samples available.
2. Send home a list of questions, and ask families to bring the information to the conference. Sample questions from Friend and Bursuck (2012, p. 89) are:
   1. What are your priorities for your child's education this year?
   2. What information would you like me to know that would help me better understand and instruct your child? What are your child's learning strengths? Unique needs?
   3. What are the best ways to communicate with you? Phone or voice mail? E-mail or text message? Face to face? Written notes?
   4. What questions do you have about your child's education?
   5. How could we at school help make this the most successful year ever for your child?
   6. Are there any topics you want to discuss at the conference for which I might need to prepare? If so, please let me know.
   7. Would you like other individuals to participate in the conference? If so, please give me a list of their names so I can invite them.
   8. Would you like me to have particular school information available? If so, please let me know.

During the conference, create and maintain an atmosphere of collaboration and respect.

Examples

1. Arrange the room for private conversation. Put a sign on your door to avoid interruptions. Meet around a conference table for better collaboration. Have tissues available.
2. Address families as "Mr." and "Ms.," not "Mom" and "Dad" or "Grandma." Use students' names.
3. Listen to families' concerns, and build on their suggestions for their children.

After the conference, keep good records and follow up on decisions.

Examples

1. Make notes to yourself, and keep them organized.
2. Summarize any actions or decisions in writing, and send a copy to the family and any other teachers or professionals involved.
3. Communicate with families on other occasions, especially when there is good news to share.

For more information about parent conferences, see:
content.scholastic.com/browse/home.jsp, *and search using* "parent teacher conference."

TABLE 4.4 • **Examples of Accommodations Under Section 504**

The types of accommodations that can be written into a Section 504 plan are almost without limit. Some accommodations may relate to physical changes in the learning environment (e.g., air filters are installed to remove allergens). However, many students who have Section 504 plans have functional impairments related to their learning or behavior, and their needs are somewhat similar to those of students with disabilities. The following is a sample of instructional accommodations that could be incorporated into a Section 504 plan:

- Seat the student nearest to where the teacher leads most instruction.
- Provide clues such as clock faces indicating beginning and ending times for instruction.
- Establish home–school communication systems for monitoring behavior.
- Fold assignments in half so that the student is less overwhelmed by the quantity of work.
- Make directions telegraphic; that is, concise and clear.
- Record lessons so the student can listen to them again.
- Use multisensory presentation techniques, including peer tutors, experiments, games, and cooperative groups.
- Mark right answers instead of wrong answers.
- Send a set of textbooks to be left at home so that the student does not have to remember to bring books to and from school.
- Provide audio books so the student can listen to assignments instead of reading them.

If you review these items, you can see that many just make good instructional sense. They are effective instructional practices that help learners with special needs succeed in your classroom.

Source: From Friend, M. & Bursuck, W. D. (2012) Including Students with Special Needs: A Practical Guide for Classroom Teachers, 6th Ed. Reprinted by permission of Pearson Education, Inc.

telecommunications. This comprehensive legislation extends the protections of Section 504 beyond the school and workplace to libraries, local and state government, restaurants, hotels, theaters, stores, public transportation, and many other settings.

ENHANCEDetext *self-check*

STUDENTS WITH LEARNING CHALLENGES

Before we look at some of the learning challenges children face, let's overview recent work on the neuroscience of learning difficulties. With all of the new technology, the amount of research on the brain and learning disabilities has grown exponentially.

Neuroscience and Learning Challenges

One of the early explanations for learning disabilities was minimal brain dysfunction. We now know that many other factors also are involved in the learning challenges children face, but certainly injuries or diseases of the brain can lead to disabilities in language, mathematics, attention, or behavior. In addition, some evidence indicates that intensive teaching interventions can lead to changes in brain functioning (Simos et al., 2007). Studies of the brains of students with learning disabilities and with attention-deficit disorders show some differences in structure and activity compared to those of students without problems. For example, in people with attention disorders, some areas of the brain may be smaller. The flow of blood appears to be lower than typical in the cerebellum and frontal lobes, and the levels of electrical activity are different in certain brain areas, compared to people without attention deficits (Barkley, 2006). Elementary school students with specific language disabilities appear to have immature auditory systems; their brains process basic auditory information in a way similar to the brains of children 3 to 4 years younger (Goswami, 2004). The implications of these brain differences for instruction are still being worked out. It is difficult to determine exactly which came first, the learning problems or the brain differences (Friend, 2014).

Quite a bit of research on learning problems has focused on working memory (discussed in Chapter 8), partly because working memory capacity is a good predictor of a range of cognitive skills including language understanding, reading and mathematics abilities, and fluid intelligence (Bayliss, Jarrold, Baddeley, Gunn, & Leigh, 2005). In addition, some studies indicate that children who have learning disabilities in reading and mathematics problem solving have considerable difficulties with working memory (Melby-Lervåg & Hulme, 2013; H. L. Swanson & Jerman, 2006; H. L. Swanson, Zheng, & Jerman, 2009). Specifically, some research shows that children with learning disabilities have problems using the system of working memory that holds verbal and auditory information while you work with it. Because children with learning disabilities have trouble holding on to words and sounds, it is difficult for them to put the words together to comprehend the meaning of a sentence or to figure out what a math story problem is really asking about.

An even more serious problem may be difficulties retrieving needed information from long-term memory, so it is hard for these children to simultaneously hold on to information (e.g., the result from the first two figures multiplied in an algebra problem) while they have to transform new incoming information, such as the next numbers to add. Important bits of information keep getting lost. Finally, children with learning disabilities in arithmetic and problem solving seem to have problems holding visual–spatial information such as number lines or quantity comparisons in working memory, so creating mental representations of "less than" and "greater than" problems is challenging (D'Amico & Guarnera, 2005).

As you saw in Table 4.3, more than 40% of all students receiving some kind of special education services in the public schools are diagnosed as having learning disabilities—by far the largest category of students with disabilities. We begin our exploration of learning challenges with these students.

Students with Learning Disabilities

How do you explain a student who struggles to read, write, spell, or learn math, even though the student doesn't have intellectual disabilities, emotional problems, or educational disadvantages and has normal vision, hearing, and language capabilities? The student probably has a **learning disability**, but there is no fully agreed-upon definition of this term. One text on learning disabilities describes 11 definitions (Hallahan et al., 2012), including the definition used in IDEA: "a disorder in one or more of the basic psychological processes involved in understanding or using language, spoken or written, that may manifest itself in imperfect ability to listen, think, speak, read, write, spell, or do mathematical calculation" (p. 138). Most definitions agree that students with learning disabilities perform significantly below what would be expected, given their other abilities.

Most educational psychologists believe that learning disabilities have both physiological and environmental bases, such as neurological dysfunction, exposure to toxins before birth from mothers who smoked or drank while pregnant, premature birth, poor nutrition, lead-based paint in the home, or even poor instruction. Genetics plays a role as well. If parents have a learning disability, their children have a 30% to 50% chance of having a learning disability (Friend, 2014; Hallahan et al., 2012).

STUDENT CHARACTERISTICS. Students with learning disabilities are not all alike. The most common characteristics are specific difficulties in one or more academic areas; poor coordination; problems paying attention; hyperactivity and impulsivity; problems organizing and interpreting visual and auditory information; seeming lack of motivation; and difficulties making and keeping friends (Hallahan et al., 2012; Rosenberg et al., 2011). As you can see, many students with other disabilities (e.g., ADHD) and many normal students may have some of the same characteristics. To complicate the situation even more, not all students with learning disabilities will have these problems, and very few will have all of these characteristics. One student may be 3 years behind in reading but above grade level in math, while another student may have the opposite strengths and weaknesses, and a third may have problems with organizing and studying that affect almost all subject areas.

Most students with learning disabilities have difficulties reading. Table 4.5 lists some of the most common problems, although these problems are not always signs of learning disabilities. For English-speaking students, these difficulties appear to be *phonemic awareness*—problems with

TABLE 4.5 • Reading Problems of Students with Learning Disabilities
Do any of your students show these signs? They could be indications of learning disabilities.

ANXIETY AROUND READING

- Reluctant to read
- Cries or acts out to avoid reading
- Seems tense when reading

DIFFICULTY RECOGNIZING WORDS OR LETTERS

- Inserts an incorrect word, substitutes or skips words
- Reverses letters or numbers—48 for 24, for example
- Mispronounces words—"cape" for "cope"
- Mixes up order of words in sentences: "I can bikes ride" for "I can ride bikes."
- Reads very slowly and with little fluency—starts and stops often

POOR VOCABULARY SKILLS

- Can't read new vocabulary words
- Has limited vocabulary

DIFFICULTY WITH UNDERSTANDING OR REMEMBERING WHAT WAS READ

- Can't recall basic facts from the reading
- Can't make inferences or identify the main idea

relating sounds to letters that make up words, making spelling hard as well (Lyon, Shaywitz, & Shaywitz, 2003; Willcutt et al., 2001). For Chinese speakers, reading disabilities seem to be related to *morphological awareness,* or the ability to combine morphemes into words. Morphemes are the smallest units of meaning that make sense alone. For example, *books* has two morphemes: "book" and "s"—the "s" has meaning because it makes "book" plural. Recognizing units of meaning in Chinese characters is helpful in learning the language (Shu, McBride-Chang, Wu, & Liu, 2006).

Math, both computation and problem solving, is the second most common problem area for students with learning disabilities. Whereas English-speaking students with reading disabilities have trouble associating sounds with letters, students with some math disabilities have difficulty automatically associating numerals (1, 2, 3, etc.) with the correct magnitude—how many is 28, for example. So, before young students learn math computations, some may need extra practice to become automatic in associating numerals with the quantities they represent (Rubinsten & Henik, 2006).

The writing of some students with learning disabilities is virtually unreadable, and their spoken language can be halting and disorganized, as you can see in Figure 4.3. Students with

---

FIGURE 4.3

WRITING SAMPLE FROM A 14-YEAR-OLD STUDENT WITH A LEARNING DISABILITY

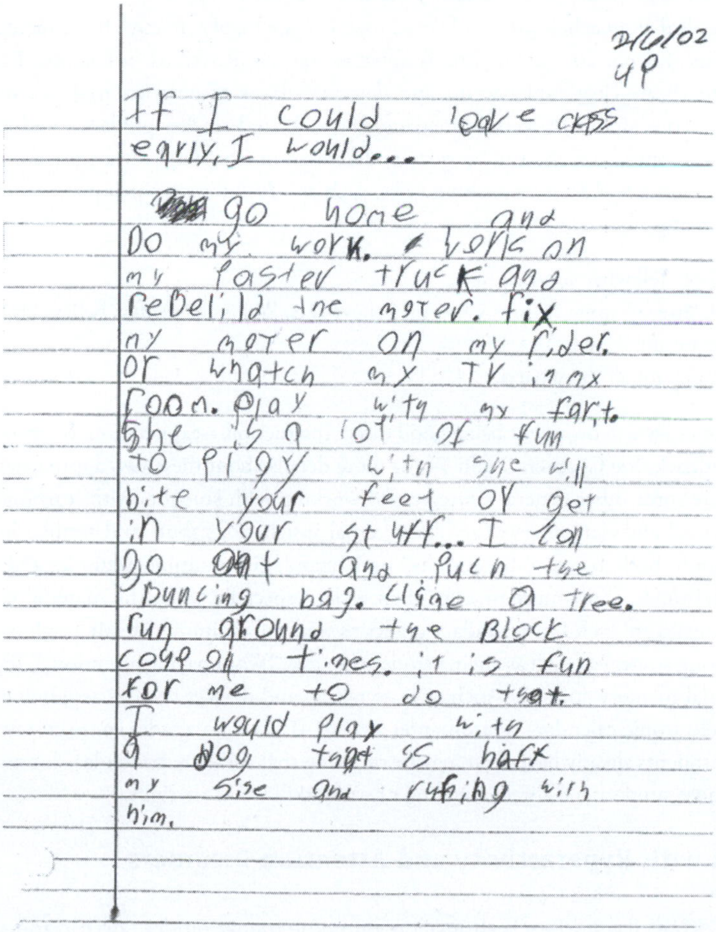

Source: Friend, M. & Bursuck, W. D. (2012) Including Students with Special Needs: A Practical Guide for Classroom Teachers, *6th Ed. Reprinted by permission of Pearson Education, Inc.*

learning disabilities often lack effective ways of approaching academic tasks. They don't know how to focus on the relevant information, get organized, apply learning strategies and study skills, change strategies when the one being used isn't working, or evaluate their learning. They tend to be passive learners, in part because they don't know how to learn—they have failed so often. Working independently is especially trying, so they often leave homework and seatwork incomplete (Hallahan et al., 2012).

TEACHING STUDENTS WITH LEARNING DISABILITIES. Early diagnosis is important so that students with learning disabilities do not become terribly frustrated and discouraged. The students themselves do not understand why they are having such trouble, and they may become victims of learned helplessness. This condition was first identified in learning experiments with animals. The animals were put in situations in which they received punishment (electric shocks) that they could not control. Later, when the situation was changed and they could have escaped the shocks or turned them off, the animals didn't even bother trying (Seligman, 1975). They had learned to be helpless victims. Students with learning disabilities may also come to believe that they cannot control or improve their own learning. This is a powerful belief. The students never exert the effort to discover that they can make a difference in their own learning, so they remain passive and helpless.

Students with learning disabilities may also try to compensate for their problems and develop bad learning habits in the process, or they may begin avoiding certain subjects out of fear of not being able to handle the work. To prevent these things from happening, teachers should refer the students to the appropriate professionals in the school as early as possible.

Two general approaches, preferably used together, are highly effective for students with learning disabilities (Friend, 2014). The first is *direct instruction*, described in Chapter 14. The basics of this approach are clear explanations and demonstrations of new material, teaching in small steps with practice after each step, immediate feedback, and teacher guidance and support. The second general approach is *strategy instruction*, described in Chapter 9. Strategies are specific rules for focusing attention and accomplishing tasks, such as *TREE* for supporting elementary students' persuasive writing.

Topic sentence: Tell what you believe.
Reasons: Tell three or more reasons why you believe this. Will your readers believe this?
Ending: Wrap it up!
Examine: Check for all three parts.

These strategies have to be taught using good direct instruction—explanation, examples, and practice with feedback. See Chapters 9 and 14 for more details about these two approaches.

Here are some other general strategies for working with students with learning disabilities. In the preschool and elementary years, keep verbal instructions short and simple; have students repeat directions back to you to be sure they understand; give multiple examples and repeat main points several times; allow more practice than usual, especially when the material is new. Many of these strategies are useful in secondary grades as well. In addition, directly teach older students self-monitoring strategies, such as cueing students to ask, "Was I paying attention?" Teach students to use external memory strategies such as note taking and devices such as assignment books, to-do lists, or electronic calendars (Hardman et al., 2014). In every grade, connect new material to knowledge students already have. You may be thinking that these are good ideas for many students who need more support and direct teaching of study skills. You are right.

Students with Hyperactivity and Attention Disorders

STOP & THINK If a student is struggling with time management and organization issues, what kind of accommodations would you provide? •

You probably have heard of and may even have used the term *hyperactivity*. The notion is a modern one; there were no "hyperactive children" 50 to 60 years ago. Such children, like Mark Twain's Huckleberry Finn, were seen as rebellious, lazy, or "fidgety" (Nylund, 2000). Today, ADHD is common. In 2010, I opened the newspaper and saw the headline, "ADHD diagnoses soar in 4 years." The Centers for Disease Control (2011) now puts the number of boys ages 3 to 17 in the United States who have ever been diagnosed with ADHD at 12%. For girls the number is almost 5%. But the United States is not alone. A report from the 2nd International Congress on ADHD (Thome & Reddy, 2009) noted evidence is increasing that ADHD is a worldwide problem and that people with ADHD have striking and consistent characteristics in every culture. The rates in different countries vary from 4% to 10% worldwide (Fabiano, Pelham, Coles, Gnagy, Chronis-Tuscano, & O'Connor, 2009; Gerwe et al., 2009). Closer to home, many student teachers in my program have classes that include 5 or 6 students diagnosed as "hyperactive," and in one class, 10 students have that diagnosis. Even closer, several of my immediate family members have ADHD.

DEFINITIONS. Hyperactivity is not one particular condition, but two kinds of problems that may or may not occur together: attention disorders and impulsive-hyperactivity problems. About half the children diagnosed in the United States have both conditions. Today, most psychologists agree that the main problem for children labeled hyperactive is directing and maintaining attention, not simply controlling their physical activity. The American Psychiatric Association has established a diagnostic category called **attention-deficit hyperactivity disorder (ADHD)** to identify children with this problem. The association describes ADHD as a neurodevelopmental disorder affecting both children and adults. It is a persistent or ongoing pattern of inattention and/or hyperactivity-impulsivity that gets in the way of an individual's daily life or typical development (American Psychiatric Association, *DSM-5*, 2013b). Some indicators are:

- **Inattention:** Doesn't pay close attention to class activities, details of work, teacher directions, class discussions; can't organize work, notebooks, desk, assignments; easily distracted and forgetful; loses things.
- **Hyperactivity/impulsivity:** Fidgets, and squirms; can't stay in assigned seat; can't move slowly, seems driven by a motor to go fast; talks excessively; blurts out answers; has trouble waiting for a turn; interrupts.

All children show some of these behaviors some of the time, but children with ADHD are likely to have some of these symptoms before age 7, the symptoms occur across many settings (not just school), and the symptoms lead to problems learning and getting along with others. ADHD usually is diagnosed in elementary school, but research suggests that problems with attention and hyperactivity may begin to show up as early as 3 years old (Friedman-Weieneth, Harvey, Youngswirth, & Goldstein, 2007). Even though about 2 to 3 times more boys than girls are identified as hyperactive, the gap appears to be narrowing. Girls have the same symptoms as boys but tend to show the symptoms in less obvious ways, so they may not be identified as often and thus may miss getting appropriate support (Friend, 2014).

Just a few years ago, most psychologists thought that ADHD diminished as children entered adolescence, but now evidence shows that the problems can persist into adulthood for at least half of those with ADHD (Hirvikoski et al., 2011). Adolescence—with the increased stresses of puberty, transition to middle or high school, more demanding academic work, and more engrossing social relationships—can be an especially difficult time for students with ADHD (E. Taylor, 1998). When children diagnosed with ADHD become adults, about 30% have no more symptoms, 25% have persistent behavioral problems such as drug use or criminal behaviors, and around 25% develop major depression (Rosenberg et al., 2011).

TREATING ADHD WITH DRUGS. Today, drug therapy for ADHD is increasing, but this approach is controversial, as you can see in the *Point/Counterpoint* on the next page.

ALTERNATIVES/ADDITIONS TO DRUG TREATMENTS. Gregory A. Fabiano and his colleagues (2009) identified 174 studies conducted between 1967 and 2006 that included almost

Connect and Extend to PRAXIS II

ADHD (I, B2)
A new student's parent calls you to tell you that a neurologist has diagnosed her child with ADHD. What typical behaviors can you expect from the student? What can you do to support that student's development?

Video 4.3
In this video, two student teachers discuss their observations and experiences with students who have ADHD. They make suggestions about teaching strategies that work and strategies that are ineffective with these students.

ENHANCEDetext *video example*

POINT/COUNTERPOINT
Pills or Skills for Children with ADHD?

About 3% of school-age children in the United States (ages 6 to 18) take some kind of medication for ADHD. Should children with ADHD be given drugs?

POINT **Yes, drugs are helpful in ADHD.** Ritalin and other prescribed drugs such as Adderall, Focalin, Dexadrine, Vyvanse, and Cylert are stimulants, but in particular dosages, they tend to have paradoxical effects on many children with ADHD. Short-term effects include possible improvements in social behaviors such as cooperation, attention, and compliance. Research suggests that about 70% to 80% of children with ADHD are more manageable and better able to benefit from educational and social interventions when on medication (Hutchinson, 2009). In fact, both stimulants such as Adderall and Ritalin and nonstimulant treatments such as Strattera appear to have some helpful effects for many children and adolescents with ADHD (Kratchovil, 2009). Positive results also have been reported with Buspar, usually used to treat anxiety, and even with some supplements such as pycnogenol (Trebaticka et al., 2009). And some evidence indicates that Strattera might have positive effects on working memory, planning, and inhibition—at least for the Chinese children studied (Yang et al., 2009). German researchers studying the effects of longer-acting, once-a-day Concerta concluded that the transition from short-acting stimulants to Concerta was "associated with significant improvements in daily functioning in several areas of life, severity of disease, and in quality of life" (Gerwe et al., 2009, p. 185).

COUNTERPOINT **No, drugs should not be the first treatment tried with ADHD.** Many children experience negative side effects when taking these drugs, such as increased heart rate and higher blood pressure, interference with growth rate, insomnia, weight loss, and nausea (D. C. Smith et al., 2014). For most children, these side effects are mild and can be controlled by adjusting the dosage. However, little is known about the long-term effects of drug therapy. A new drug called Strattera is not a stimulant but may lead to increased thoughts of suicide. As a parent or teacher, you need to keep up with the research on treatments for ADHD.

Many studies have concluded that the improvements in behavior from the drugs *seldom* lead to improvements in academic learning or peer relationships, two areas where children with ADHD have great problems. Because children appear to improve dramatically in their behavior, parents and teachers, relieved to see change, may assume the problem has been cured. It hasn't. The children still need special help in learning, especially interventions focused on how to make *connections* among elements in readings or presentations in order to build coherent, accurate representations of the information (Bailey et al., 2009; Doggett, 2004; Purdie, Hattie, & Carroll, 2002).

BEWARE OF EITHER/OR

The bottom line is that even if students in your class are on medication, it is critical that they also learn the academic and social skills they will need to succeed. They need to learn how and when to apply learning strategies and study skills. Also, they need to be encouraged to persist when challenged by difficult tasks and to see themselves as having control over their learning and behavior. Medication alone will not make this happen, but it may help. For learning to occur, medication needs to be paired with other effective interventions.

3,000 participants in behavioral treatments for ADHD; all studies met rigorous standards of quality research. Behavioral treatments involve the application of methods derived from behavioral learning theories such as contingency management, time-out, shaping, self-regulation, and modeling (see Chapters 7 and 11). The researchers then compared treated with untreated groups or individuals before and after one or more different kinds of treatments. Their conclusion? Findings were clear and impressive. "Based on these results, there is strong and consistent evidence that behavioral treatments are effective for treating ADHD" (Fabiano et al., 2009, p. 129). In an interview, Fabiano said, "Our results suggest that efforts should be redirected from debating the effectiveness of behavioral interventions to dissemination, enhancing and improving the use of these programs in community, school and mental health settings" (Hirvikoski et al., 2011). Researchers working with adults in Sweden also found that behavioral methods stressing a balance between accepting and changing ADHD symptoms and behaviors proved effective.

In sum, one large study in Australia concluded what you might guess—we should attack the problem on all fronts:

> Multimodal approaches to intervention have been found to be most effective in terms of lasting change. For most, but not all children and adolescents, treatment with psychostimulants has beneficial effects, provided that it is accompanied by remedial tuition, counseling, and behavior management by parents/teachers, as required. Thus, advice from several different professions may be necessary. (van Kraayenoord, Rice, Carroll, Fritz, Dillon, & Hill, 2001, p. 7)

Even if students in your class are on medication, it is critical that they also learn the academic and social skills they will need to survive. Again, this will not happen by itself, even if behavior improves with medication (Purdie et al., 2002).

Lessons for Teachers: Learning Disabilities and ADHD

Long assignments may overwhelm students with learning disabilities and attention deficits, so give them a few problems or paragraphs at a time with clear consequences for completion. Another promising approach combines instruction in learning and memory strategies with motivational training. The goal is to help students develop the "skill and will" to improve their achievement. They are also taught to monitor their own behavior and encouraged to be persistent and to see themselves as "in control" (Pfiffner, Barkley, & DuPaul, 2006).

The notion of being in control is part of a therapy strategy for dealing with ADHD, one that stresses personal agency. Rather than treating the problem child, David Nylund's (2000) approach enlists the child's strengths to conquer his or her problems—to put the child in control. New metaphors for the situation are developed. Rather than seeing the problems as inside the child, Nylund helps everyone see ADHD, Trouble, Boredom, and other enemies of learning as outside the child—demons to be conquered or unruly spirits to be enlisted in the service of what the child wants to accomplish. The focus is on solutions.

As a teacher, you can look for times when the student is engaged—even short times. What is different about these times? Discover the student's strengths, and allow yourself to be amazed by them. Make changes in your teaching that support the changes the student is trying to make. Nylund gives the following example: Chris (age 9) and his teacher, Ms. Baker, became partners in putting Chris in control of his concentration in school. Ms. Baker moved Chris's seat to the front of the room. The two designed a subtle signal to get Chris back on track, and Chris organized his messy desk. These sound like some of the Section 504 accommodations in Table 4.4. When Chris's concentration improved, Chris received an award at a party given in his honor. Chris described how he was learning to listen in class: "You just have to have a strong mind and tell ADHD and Boredom not to bother you" (Nylund, 2000, p. 166). Students with ADHD have some suggestions, too, as you can see in Table 4.6 on the next page, taken from Nylund (2000, pp. 202–203).

Students with Communication Disorders

Students with communication disorders who are between the ages of 6 and 21 are the second largest group served by special education. These students may have language disorders, speech disorders, or both. They make up about 19% of students receiving services. Communication disorders can arise from many sources, because so many different aspects of the individual are involved in learning language and using speech. A child with a hearing impairment will not learn to speak normally. Injuries can cause neurological problems that interfere with speech or language. Children who are not listened to, or whose perception of the world is distorted by emotional problems, will reflect these problems in their language development. Because speaking involves movements, any impairment of the motor functions involved with speech can cause language disorders. And because

TABLE 4.6 • **Students with ADHD Give Teachers Advice**

Students with ADHD make these recommendations for their teachers (Nylund, 2000):

- Use lots of pictures (visual clues) to help me learn.
- Recognize cultural and racial identity.
- Know when to bend the rules.
- Notice when I am doing well.
- Don't tell the other kids that I am taking Ritalin.
- Offer us choices.
- Don't just lecture—it's boring!
- Realize that I am intelligent.
- Let me walk around the classroom.
- Don't give tons of homework.
- More recess!
- Be patient.

language development and thinking are so interwoven, any problems in cognitive functioning can affect ability to use language.

SPEECH DISORDERS. Students who cannot produce sounds effectively for speaking are considered to have a speech disorder. About 5% of school-age children have some form of speech impairment. Articulation problems and fluency disorders (stuttering) are the two most common problems.

Articulation disorders include distorting a sound like a lisp (*thumtimes* for *sometimes*), substituting one sound for another (*shairp* for *chair*), adding a sound (*chuch air* for *chair*), or omitting sounds (*chai* for *chair*) (Rosenberg et al., 2011). Keep in mind, however, that most children are 6 to 8 years old before they can successfully pronounce all English sounds in normal conversation. The sounds of the consonants *l, r, y, s, v,* and *z* and the consonant blends *sh, ch, ng, zh,* and *th* are the last to be mastered (Friend, 2014). Also, there are dialect differences based on geography that do not represent articulation problems. A child in your class who is from New England might say "ideer" for "idea," but have no speech impairment.

Stuttering generally appears between the ages of 3 and 4. Causes of stuttering are unknown but might include emotional or neurological problems or learned behavior. If stuttering continues more than a year or so, the child should be referred to a speech therapist. Early intervention can make a big difference (Hardman et al., 2014). When you are working with a student who stutters, speak to the child often, privately, and without hurrying, interrupting, or finishing the child's words and sentences. Pause often, especially after the child finishes speaking. Communicate that it is OK to take time to think before you speak. Notice when the stuttering is more and less frequent. Avoid pressuring the child to speak quickly. In class discussions, call on the child early in the discussion so tension won't build up, and ask a question that can be answered with few words. Speak frankly about the stuttering, but assure the student it is nothing to be ashamed of—many successful people, including kings, have shared the challenge and learned to improve (Friend, 2014; Rosenberg et al., 2011).

Voicing problems, a third type of speech impairment, include speaking with an inappropriate pitch, quality, or loudness, or in a monotone. A student with any of these problems should be referred to a speech therapist. Recognizing the problem is the first step. Be alert for students whose pronunciation, loudness, voice quality, speech fluency, expressive range, or rate is very different from that of their peers. Pay attention also to students who seldom speak. Are they simply shy, or do they have difficulties with language?

LANGUAGE DISORDERS. Language differences are not necessarily language disorders. Students with language disorders are markedly deficient in their ability to understand or express language, compared with other students of their own age and cultural group (Owens, 2012). Students who seldom speak, who use few words or very short sentences, or who rely only on gestures to communicate should be referred to a qualified school professional for observation or testing. Table 4.7 gives ideas for promoting language development for all students.

TABLE 4.7 • **Encouraging Language Development**

- Talk about things that interest children.
- Follow the children's lead. Reply to their initiations and comments. Share their excitement.
- Don't ask too many questions. If you must, use questions such as *how did/do, . . . why did/do, . . .* and *what happened . . .* that result in longer explanatory answers.
- Encourage children to ask questions. Respond openly and honestly. If you don't want to answer a question, say so, and explain why. (*I don't think I want to answer that question; it's very personal.*)
- Use a pleasant tone of voice. You need not be a comedian, but you can be light and humorous. Children love it when adults are a little silly.
- Don't be judgmental or make fun of children's language. If you are overly critical of children's language or try to catch and correct all errors, they will stop talking to you.
- Allow enough time for children to respond.
- Treat children with courtesy by not interrupting when they are talking.
- Include children in family and classroom discussions. Encourage participation and listen to their ideas.
- Be accepting of children and of their language. Hugs and acceptance can go a long way.
- Provide opportunities for children to use language and to have that language work for them to accomplish their goals.

Source: Based on Owens, Robert E., Jr., Language Disorders: A Functional Approach to Assessment and Intervention, 5e. Published by Allyn and Bacon, Boston, MA. Copyright © 2010 by Pearson Education. Adapted by permission of the publisher.

Students with Emotional or Behavioral Difficulties

Students with **emotional and behavioral disorders** can be among the most difficult to teach in a general education class, and they are a source of concern for many prospective teachers (Avramidis, Bayliss, & Burden, 2000). The future is not bright for students with emotional and behavioral disorders who do not get appropriate help. About one third of these students are arrested during their school years, and half are unemployed 3 to 5 years after leaving school (Rosenberg et al., 2011), so early intervention is really important.

Professionals in education define behavioral disorders as behaviors that deviate so much from the norm that they interfere with the child's own growth and development and/or the lives of others. The language in IDEA describes emotional disturbances that involve inappropriate behaviors, unhappiness or depression, fears and anxieties, and trouble with relationships. Table 4.8 on the next page shows the IDEA definition.

However they are defined, what you will observe as a teacher are students who are aggressive, anxious, withdrawn, or depressed and who often have difficulty following rules, paying attention, or interacting with others. More than 400,000 students in the United States have emotional disturbances, making this the fifth-largest group receiving services. This number has increased about 20% since 1991–1992. As with learning disabilities and ADHD, more boys than girls are diagnosed with these disorders—at least three times as many boys as girls are identified. One troubling fact is that African American students are overrepresented in this category. They make up about 13% of the total population but about 26% of the students identified with emotional and behavioral disorders.

The range of possible emotional and behavioral disorders is wide. And students with other disabilities—learning disabilities, intellectual disabilities, or ADHD, for example—may also have emotional or behavioral problems as they struggle in school. Methods from applied behavior analysis (Chapter 7) and direct teaching of self-regulation skills (Chapter 11) are two useful approaches. Another possibility that has proved helpful for these students is to provide structure, organizational tools, and choices. Here are some ideas from Terri Swanson (2005):

- Structure the environment by minimizing visual and auditory stimulation, establishing clear visual boundaries between areas where different behaviors are expected, or organizing supplies in easy-to-use holders.
- Structure schedules by posting monthly and daily schedules, having clear starting and ending signals and clear procedures for turning in work.

Video 4.4
The general education teacher and special education teacher shown here work together effectively to provide structure, organizational tools, and support for students with emotional and behavioral disorders.

ENHANCEDetext *video example*

TABLE 4.8 • **IDEA Definition of Emotional Disturbance**

Emotional disturbance means a condition exhibiting one or more of the following characteristics over a long period of time and to a marked degree that adversely affects a child's educational performance:
a. An inability to learn that cannot be explained by intellectual, sensory, or health factors.
b. An inability to build or maintain satisfactory interpersonal relationships with peers and teachers.
c. Inappropriate types of behavior or feelings under normal circumstances.
d. A general pervasive mood of unhappiness or depression.
e. A tendency to develop physical symptoms or fears associated with personal or school problems.
f. Emotional disturbance includes schizophrenia. The term does not apply to children who are socially maladjusted, unless it is determined that they have an emotional disturbance.

Source: IDEA Regulations, Sec. 300.8 c 4, Child with a disability. Retrieved from http://idea.ed.gov/explore/home U.D. Department of Education.

- Structure activities by color-coding subject folders (blue for math, etc.), posting verbal instructions with visual prompts, or putting all materials needed for an activity in a "Science box."
- Structure rules and routines, for example, giving students a script to use in asking other students to play a game with them, writing rules in a positive way, or preparing students for changes in routines such as spring break by reviewing pictures of what will be happening over the break.
- Offer choices by providing a short list of alternatives for completing assignments or projects.

Because students with emotional and behavioral disorders frequently break rules and push the limits, teachers often find themselves disciplining them. Be aware that there have been court rulings on disciplining students with serious emotional problems (Yell, 1990). The *Guidelines: Disciplining Students with Emotional Problems* may help when you are faced with these situations.

Let's consider an area where teachers may be able to detect problems and make a difference—suicide.

SUICIDE. Of course, not every student with emotional or behavioral problems will consider suicide, but depression often is associated with suicide. Up to 10% of adolescents have attempted suicide at some point, but even more have considered it. The suicide rate today among American teens is four times higher than it was in the 1950s. Native Americans and students living in rural communities are more likely to commit suicide. There are several general risk factors, and they seem to apply to both male and female African American, Latino, and White adolescents: depression and substance abuse, history of suicide in the family, being under stress, tendency to be impulsive or perfectionistic, belief that a person goes to a better place after dying, and family rejection or conflict. Having more than one of these risk factors is especially dangerous (Arnett, 2013; Friend, 2014; Steinberg, 2005). In addition, some drugs prescribed for depression or ADHD may increase the risk of suicide in adolescents.

Suicide often comes as a response to life problems—problems that parents and teachers sometimes dismiss. There are many warning signs that trouble is brewing. Watch for changes in eating or sleeping habits, weight, grades, disposition, activity level, drug or alcohol use, or interest in friends or activities that were once fun. Students at risk sometimes suddenly give away prized possessions such as iPads, books, clothing, or pets. They may seem depressed or hyperactive and may say things like, "Nothing matters anymore," "I shouldn't be here," "If I died, people might love me more," "You won't have to worry about me anymore," or "I wonder what dying is like." They may start missing school or quit doing work. It is especially dangerous if the student not only talks about suicide but also has a plan for carrying it out. And sometimes the suicide risk increases as depression begins to improve because deeply depressed young people are immobilized and don't have the energy to plan or make a suicide attempt (Arnett, 2013).

If you suspect that there is a problem, talk to the student directly, and ask about his or her concerns. One feeling shared by many people who attempt suicide is that no one cared enough to ask.

GUIDELINES
Disciplining Students with Emotional Problems

Be careful not to violate the due process rights of students. Students and parents must know the behaviors expected and the consequences for misbehavior.

Examples

1. Communicate expectations clearly and in writing.
2. Ask parents and students to sign a copy of the classroom rules.
3. Post rules and consequences in class and on a class Web page.

Be very careful with severe punishments that remove students from class for a long time. These constitute a change in the child's IEP and require due process.

Examples

1. Always follow due process for suspensions of more than 10 days.
2. Be aware of possible due process requirements for prolonged periods of time-out (in-school suspension).

Punishments for students with severe emotional problems must serve a clear educational purpose.

Examples

1. Give a rationale for punishment or correction that ties an action to a student's learning or the learning of others in the class.
2. Use written behavior contracts that include a rationale.

Make sure the rule and the punishment are reasonable.

Examples

1. Consider the student's age and physical condition.
2. Does the punishment match the offense and the way others in the class are treated?

3. Do other teachers handle similar situations in the same way?
4. Try less-intrusive punishments first. Be patient. Move to more-severe actions only when less-severe procedures fail.

Keep good records, and work collaboratively so all involved are informed.

Examples

1. Document the punishment of all students in a journal or log. List what precipitated the punishment, what procedures were used, how long the punishment lasted, the results, modifications to the punishment, and new results.
2. Note meetings with families, special education teachers, and the principal.
3. Make any changes involving management plans with families and other teachers.

Always use positive consequences in conjunction with negative ones.

Examples

1. If students lose points for breaking rules, give them ways to regain points through positive behavior.
2. Recognize genuine accomplishment and small steps—DON'T say, "Well, it's about time you. . . ."

For more information on disciplining students with disabilities, see: nasponline.org/communications/spawareness/effdiscipfs.pdf

---

Ask about specifics, and take the student seriously. You may need to become an advocate for the student with administrators, parents, or other adults who dismiss the warning signs. Also, be aware that teenage suicides often occur in clusters. After one student acts or when stories about a suicide are reported in the media, other teens are more likely to copy the suicide (Lewinsohn, Rohde, & Seeley, 1994; F. P. Rice & Dolgin, 2002). Table 4.9 on the next page lists common myths and facts about suicide.

DRUG ABUSE. Although drug abuse is not always associated with emotional or behavioral problems and people without these challenges may abuse drugs, many adolescents with emotional problems also abuse drugs. Abusing drugs is especially dangerous for African American males. In one study that followed a sample of adolescents from ages 19 to 27, about 33% of the African American young men who abused drugs died by age 27, compared to 3% for White males. The death rate for both African American and White females who abused drugs was 1% (D. B. Clark, Martin, & Cornelius, 2008).

Modern society makes growing up a very confusing process. Notice the messages from films and billboards. "Beautiful," popular, happy people drink alcohol and smoke cigarettes, with little concern for their health. Males are encouraged to "drink like a man!" We have over-the-counter drugs for almost every common ailment, and constant ads from drug companies broadcast the benefits of new prescription medications. Coffee or an "energy drink" wakes us up, and a pill helps us sleep. And then we tell students to "say no!" to drugs.

TABLE 4.9 • **Myths and Facts about Suicide**

Myth	People who talk about suicide don't kill themselves, they are just trying to get attention.
Fact	People who die by suicide usually talk about it first. They are in pain and often reach out for help because they do not know what to do and have lost hope. Always take talk about suicide seriously. Always.
Myth	Only certain types of people commit suicide.
Fact	All types of people commit suicide—male and female, young and old, rich and poor, country people and city people. It happens in every racial, ethnic, and religious group.
Myth	You should never ask people who are suicidal if they are thinking about suicide or if they have thought about a method, because just talking about it will give them the idea.
Fact	Asking people if they are thinking about suicide does not give them the idea for suicide. And it is important to talk about suicide with people who are suicidal because you will learn more about their mindset and intentions, and allow them to diffuse some of the tension that is causing their suicidal feelings.
Myth	Most people who kill themselves really want to die.
Fact	The vast majority of people who are suicidal do not want to die. They are in pain, and they want to stop the pain. Suicide is often intended as a cry for help.
Myth	Young people never think about suicide, they have their entire life ahead of them.
Fact	Suicide is the third leading cause of death for young people ages 15 to 24. Sometimes children under 10 die by suicide.

Source: Based on Caruso, K., Suicide Myths. Retrieved from http://www.suicide.org/suicide-myths.html.

For many reasons, not just because of these contradictory messages, drug use has become a problem for students. Accurate statistics are hard to find, but estimates from the *Monitoring the Future* survey by researchers at the University of Michigan (Johnston, O'Malley, Bachman, & Schulenberg, 2013) indicate that 7.7% of 8th graders, 18.6% of 10th graders, and 25.2% of 12th graders reported using an illicit drug *in the past 30 days,* with marijuana being the most popular for younger students and alcohol for 12th graders (see Table 4.10). In fact, marijuana use increased among older teens from 2008 through 2012—the last data available when I wrote this chapter, with about 1% of 8th graders, 4% of 10th graders, and 7% of 12th graders reporting they use marijuana *daily.* Younger adolescents are more likely to use inhalants (glues, paint thinners, nail polish remover, aerosol sprays, etc.). They are inexpensive and available. And students don't realize that they are risking injury or death when they use inhalants.

Remarkably, about 15% of high school boys and 2% of girls have used some form of spit or other type of smokeless tobacco. The use of smokeless tobacco can cause cancers of the mouth, throat, larynx, esophagus, stomach, and pancreas; receding gums and gum disease (leading finally to tooth loss and precancerous spots in the mouth), nicotine addiction, and possibly to heart disease and stroke (American Cancer Society, 2010).

PREVENTION. We should distinguish between experimentation and abuse. Many students try something at a party but do not become regular users. Providing information or "scare" tactics such as the DARE drug prevention program seems to have little positive effect and may even encourage curiosity and experimentation (Dusenbury & Falco, 1995; Tobler & Stratton, 1997).

So what is more effective? Adam Fletcher and his colleagues analyzed research on school programs around the world. One overwhelmingly frequent finding was that after taking into account students' prior drug use and personal characteristics, "disengagement from school and poor

TABLE 4.10 • **Percentage of Students in the United States Grades 8 through 12 Who Reported Using these Drugs in the Past 30 Days**

DRUG	8TH GRADE	10TH GRADE	12TH GRADE
Any illicit drug	7.7	18.6	25.2
Marijuana	6.5	17.0	22.9
Inhalants	2.7	1.4	.9
Ecstasy	.5	1.0	.9
Cocaine	.5	.8	1.1
Heroin	0.2	.4	.3
Amphetamines	1.3	2.8	3.3
Been drunk	3.6	14.5	28.1
Cigarettes	4.9	10.8	17.1
Smokeless tobacco	2.8	7.4	7.9

teacher–student relations were associated with subsequent drug use and other risky health behaviors" (Fletcher, Bonell, & Hargreaves, 2008, p. 217). For example, the researchers describe one study that found that being disconnected with school predicted young adolescents' drug use 2 to 4 years later. One implication is that engaging adolescents in schools, forming positive relationships, and connecting the students to caring adults and peers are all critical in creating a protective environment.

Students with Intellectual Disabilities

A word about terms. Intellectual disability is a more current name for *mental retardation*. You may also have heard the terms *cognitive impairment, general learning disability, developmental disability,* or *cognitive disability.* Intellectual disability is the preferred name, because the term *mental retardation* is considered offensive and stigmatizing; however, mental retardation still is used in the IDEA definitions and in many schools. In 2007, the American Association on Mental Retardation changed its name to the American Association on Intellectual and Developmental Disabilities (AAIDD) to reflect this rejection of the term *mental retardation.* The AAIDD definition of *intellectual disability* is "a disability characterized by significant limitations in both intellectual functioning and adaptive behavior as expressed in conceptual, social, and practical adaptive skills. This disability originates before age 18" (AAIDD.org).

Intellectual function is usually measured by IQ tests, with a score below 70 being one of the indicators. But an IQ score below the 70 range is not enough to diagnose a child as having intellectual disabilities. There must also be problems with adaptive behavior, day-to-day independent living, and social functioning. This caution is especially important when interpreting the scores of students from different cultures. Defining disability based on test scores alone can create what some critics call "the 6-hour retarded child"—students who are seen as disabled only for the part of the day they attend school.

Only about 1% of the population fit the AAIDD's definition of disability in both intellectual functioning and adaptive behavior. For years, this group was further divided into mild (IQ 50–69), moderate (IQ 35–49), severe (IQ 20–34), and profound levels (IQ below 20). Many school districts still use this system, and so does the World Health Organization. However, the IQ ranges are not perfect predictors of individuals' abilities to function, so the AAIDD now recommends a classification scheme based on the amount of support that a person requires to function at his or her highest level. Support varies from intermittent (e.g., as needed during stressful times), to limited (consistent support, but time-limited, e.g., employment training), to extensive (daily care, e.g., living in a group home), to pervasive (constant, high-intensity care for all aspects of living) (R. L. Taylor, Richards, & Brady, 2005).

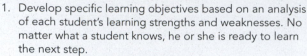

GUIDELINES
Teaching Students with Intellectual Disabilities

1. Develop specific learning objectives based on an analysis of each student's learning strengths and weaknesses. No matter what a student knows, he or she is ready to learn the next step.
2. Work on practical skills and concepts based on the demands of adult life.
3. Analyze the task the student will be learning: identify the specific steps involved in successful completion, and don't overlook any steps in your planning.
4. State and present objectives simply.
5. Present material in small, logical steps. Practice extensively before going on to the next step. Use resources such as computer drill-and-practice exercises in class, or have volunteers and family members continue guiding practice outside class.
6. Do not skip steps. Students with average intelligence can form conceptual bridges from one step to the next and make metacognitive judgments about how they are doing, but children with below-average intelligence need every step and bridge made explicit. Make connections for the student. Do not expect him or her to "see" the connections.
7. Be prepared to present the same idea in many different ways using different representations (verbal, visual, hands on, etc.).
8. Go back to a simpler level if you see the student is not following.
9. Be especially careful to motivate the student and maintain attention. Allow and encourage different ways of expressing understanding—written, drawings, oral responses, gestures, and so on.
10. Find materials that do not insult the student. A middle school boy may need the low vocabulary of "See Spot run," but will be insulted by the age of the characters and the content of the story.
11. Focus on a few target behaviors or skills so you and the student have a chance to experience success. Everyone needs positive reinforcement.
12. Be aware that students with below-average intelligence must overlearn, repeat, and practice more than children of average intelligence. They must be taught how to study, and they must frequently review and practice their newly acquired skills in different settings.
13. Pay close attention to social relations. Simply including students with below-average intelligence in a general education class will not guarantee that they will be accepted or that they will make and keep friends.
14. Establish peer-tutoring programs, and train all students in the class to serve as tutors and as tutees—see Chapter 10 for specifics.

For more information, see aaidd.org/

As a general education teacher, you may not have contact with children needing extensive or pervasive support unless your school is participating in a full-inclusion program, but you probably will work with children needing intermittent or limited support. In the early grades, these students may simply learn more slowly than their peers. They need more time and more practice to learn, and they may have difficulty transferring learning from one setting to another or putting small skills together to accomplish a more complex task. They often have difficulties with metacognitive skills and executive functioning required to plan, monitor, and redirect attention and learning strategies (T. Simon, 2010), so very structured and complete teaching and guidance make sense. The *Guidelines: Teaching Students with Intellectual Disabilities* list more suggestions.

Learning goals for many students with intellectual disabilities who are between the ages of 9 and 13 include basic reading, writing, and arithmetic; learning about the local environment; social behavior; and personal interests. In middle and senior high school, the emphasis is on vocational and domestic skills, literacy for living (reading signs, labels, and newspaper ads; completing a job application), job-related behaviors such as courtesy and punctuality; health self-care; and citizenship skills. Today, there is a growing emphasis on **transition programming**—preparing the student to live and work in the community. As you saw earlier in the chapter, the law requires that schools design an IEP for every child with disabilities. An ITP (individualized transition plan) may be part of the IEP for students with intellectual disabilities (Friend, 2014).

Students with Health and Sensory Impairments

Some health impairments you may encounter are cerebral palsy, seizure disorders, asthma, HIV/AIDS, diabetes, visual impairments, and hearing impairments.

CEREBRAL PALSY AND MULTIPLE DISABILITIES. Damage to the brain before or during birth or during infancy can cause a child to have difficulty coordinating his or her body movements.

The problem may be very mild, so the child simply appears a bit clumsy, or so severe that voluntary movement is practically impossible. The most common form of **cerebral palsy** is characterized by **spasticity** (overly tight or tense muscles). Many children with cerebral palsy also have secondary handicaps. In the classroom, these secondary handicaps are the greatest concern—and these are usually what the general education teacher can help with most. For example, many children with cerebral palsy also have visual impairments or speech problems, and about 50% to 60% have mild-to-severe intellectual disabilities. But many students with cerebral palsy are average to well above average in measured intelligence (Pellegrino, 2002).

SEIZURE DISORDERS (EPILEPSY). A seizure is a cluster of behaviors that occurs in response to abnormal neurochemical activities in the brain (Hardman et al., 2014). People with **epilepsy** have recurrent seizures, but not all seizures are the result of epilepsy; temporary conditions such as high fevers, infections, or withdrawal from drugs can also trigger seizures. Seizures take many forms and differ with regard to the length, frequency, and movements involved.

Most **generalized seizures** (once called *grand mal*) are accompanied by uncontrolled jerking movements that ordinarily last 2 to 5 minutes, possible loss of bowel or bladder control, and irregular breathing, followed by a deep sleep or coma. On regaining consciousness, the student may be very weary, confused, and in need of extra sleep. Most seizures can be controlled by medication. If a student has a seizure accompanied by convulsions in class, the teacher must take action so the student will not be injured. The major danger to a student having such a seizure is being injured from striking a hard surface during the violent jerking.

If a student has a seizure, stay calm and reassure the rest of the class. Do not try to restrain the child's movements; you can't stop the seizure once it starts. Lower the child gently to the floor, away from furniture or walls. Move hard objects away. Loosen scarves, ties, or anything that might make breathing difficult. Turn the child's head gently to the side, and put a soft coat or blanket under his or her head. Never put anything in the student's mouth; it is NOT true that people having seizures can swallow their tongues. Don't attempt artificial respiration unless the student does not start breathing again after the seizure stops. Find out from the student's parents how they deal with seizures. If one seizure follows another and the student does not regain consciousness in between, if the student is pregnant or has a medical ID that does not say "epilepsy, seizure disorder," if there are signs of injury, or if the seizure goes on for more than 5 minutes, get medical help right away (Friend, 2014).

Not all seizures are dramatic. Sometimes the student just loses contact briefly. The student may stare, fail to respond to questions, drop objects, and miss what has been happening for 1 to 30 seconds. These were once called *petit mal,* but they are now referred to as **absence seizures** and can easily go undetected. If a child in your class appears to daydream frequently, does not seem to know what is going on at times, or cannot remember what has just happened when you ask, you should consult the school psychologist or nurse. The major problem for students with absence seizures is that they miss the continuity of the class interaction, because these seizures can occur as often as 100 times a day. If their seizures are frequent, students will find the lessons confusing. Question these students to be sure they are understanding and following the lesson. Be prepared to repeat yourself periodically.

OTHER SERIOUS HEALTH CONCERNS: ASTHMA, HIV/AIDS, AND DIABETES. Many other health problems affect students' learning, in great part because the students miss school, leading to lost instructional time and missed opportunities for friendships. Asthma is a chronic lung condition affecting 5 to 6 million children in America; it is more common for students in poverty. You probably have heard quite a bit about HIV/AIDS, a chronic illness that often can be controlled with medication. Luckily, we are making great progress in preventing HIV infection in children in the United States.

Type 2 diabetes is a chronic disease that affects the way the body metabolizes sugar (glucose). Diabetes needs to be taken seriously because it can affect almost every major organ in the body, including the heart, blood vessels, nerves, eyes, and kidneys (Mayo Clinic, 2009). For most children, Type 2 diabetes can be managed, or prevented altogether, by eating healthy foods, being physically active, and maintaining a healthy body weight. When diet and exercise modifications are not enough, children will need medications, such as insulin, to manage their blood sugar (Rosenberg et al., 2011; Werts, Culatta, & Tompkins, 2007).

With all health conditions, teachers need to talk to parents to find out how the problems are handled, what the signs are that a dangerous situation might be developing, and what resources are available for the student. Keep records of any incidents. They may be useful in the student's medical diagnosis and treatment.

STUDENTS WITH VISION IMPAIRMENTS. In the United States, about 1 in every 2,000 children and adolescents ages 6 to 17 (.05%) have a visual disability so serious that special services are needed. Most members of this group needing special services are classified as having **low vision**. This means they can read with the aid of a magnifying glass, large-print books, or other aids. A small group of students, about 1 in every 2,500, must use hearing and touch as their predominant learning channels. There is a definition for **legally blind** that focuses on visual acuity (20/200 or less after correction) and field of vision. To qualify as legally blind, a student must see at 20 feet what a person with normal vision would see at 200 feet and/or have severely restricted peripheral vision (Erickson, Lee, & von Schrader, 2013; Hallahan et al., 2012).

Students who have difficulty seeing often hold books either very close to or very far from their eyes. They may squint, rub their eyes frequently, close one eye, blink often, or say that their eyes burn or itch. After close-up work, they may complain that they are dizzy, have a headache, or are sick to their stomach. The eyes may actually be swollen, red, or encrusted. Students with vision problems may misread material on the whiteboard or chalkboard, describe their vision as being blurred, be very sensitive to light, or hold their heads at an odd angle. They may become irritable when they have to do deskwork or lose interest if they have to follow an activity that is taking place across the room (Hallahan et al., 2012; N. Hunt & Marshall, 2002). Any of these signs should be reported to a qualified school professional.

Special materials and equipment that help these students to function in general education classrooms include large-print books; software that converts printed material to speech or to Braille; personal organizers that have talking appointment books or address books; special calculators; an abacus; three-dimensional maps, charts, and models; and special measuring devices. For students with visual problems, the quality of the print is often more important than the size, so watch out for hard-to-read handouts and blurry copies.

The arrangement of the room is also an issue. Students with visual problems need to know where things are, so consistency matters—a place for everything and everything in its place. Leave plenty of space for moving around the room, and make sure to monitor possible obstacles and safety hazards such as trash cans in aisles and open cabinet doors. If you rearrange the room, give students with visual problems a chance to learn the new layout. Also make sure these students have a buddy for fire drills or other emergencies (Friend & Bursuck, 2012).

STUDENTS WHO ARE DEAF. You will hear the term *hearing impaired* to describe these students, but the Deaf community and researchers object to this label, so I will use their preferred terms, *deaf* and *hard of hearing*. The number of deaf students has been declining over the past three decades (now about 1 in every 750 students ages 6 to 17), but when the problem does occur, the consequences for learning are serious. Signs of hearing problems are turning one ear toward the speaker, favoring one ear in conversation, or misunderstanding conversation when the speaker's face cannot be seen. Other indications include not following directions, seeming distracted or confused at times, frequently asking people to repeat what they have said, mispronouncing new words or names, and being reluctant to participate in class discussions. Take note particularly of students who have frequent earaches, sinus infections, or allergies.

In the past, educators have debated whether oral or manual approaches are better for children who are deaf or hard of hearing. Oral approaches involve speech reading (also called *lip reading*) and training students to use whatever limited hearing they may have. Manual approaches include sign language and finger spelling. Research indicates that children who learn some manual method of communicating perform better in academic subjects and are more socially mature than students who are exposed only to oral methods. Today, the trend is to combine both approaches (Hallahan et al., 2012).

By the way, the capital "D" in Deaf community in the first paragraph of this section refers to a group of people who want to be recognized as having their own culture and language, much like any other language-minority group (Hallahan et al., 2012). From this perspective, people who are deaf are part of a different culture with a different language, values, social institutions, and literature. N. Hunt and Marshall (2002) quote one deaf professional: "How would women like to be referred to as male-impaired, or whites like to be called black-impaired? I'm not impaired; I'm deaf!" (p. 348). From this perspective, a goal is to help deaf children become bilingual and bicultural, to enable them to function effectively in both cultures. Technological innovations and the many avenues of communication through e-mail and the Internet have expanded communication possibilities for all people.

Autism Spectrum Disorders and Asperger Syndrome

You may be familiar with the term *autism*. In 1990 autism was added to the IDEA list of disabilities qualifying for special services. It is defined as "a developmental disability significantly affecting verbal and nonverbal communication and social interaction, generally evident before age three, that adversely affect the child's educational performance" (34 *Federal Code of Regulations* § 300.7). I will use the term preferred by professionals in the field, autism spectrum disorders, to emphasize that autism includes a range of disorders from mild to major. You might also hear the term pervasive developmental disorder (PDD), especially if you are talking with medical professionals. Estimates of the number of children with autism vary greatly but are increasing dramatically. The Centers for Disease Control put the numbers at 1 in every 252 girls and 1 in every 54 boys (Centers for Disease Control, 2013).

The latest *Diagnostic and Statistical Manual of Mental Disorders* (*DSM-5*, 2013b) of the American Psychiatric Association describes children with autism spectrum disorders as having "communication deficits, such as responding inappropriately in conversations, misreading nonverbal interactions, or having difficulty building friendships appropriate to their age." Other possible characteristics include being "overly dependent on routines, highly sensitive to changes in their environment, or intensely focused on inappropriate items" (p. 2). To qualify on the autism spectrum, these characteristics must be apparent from early childhood. Children with autism spectrum disorders may have difficulties in social relations. They may not form connections with others, may avoid eye contact, or may not share feelings such as enjoyment or interest in others. Communication is impaired. About half of these students are nonverbal; they have no or very few language skills. Others make up their own language. They may obsessively insist on regularity and sameness in their environments; change is very disturbing. They may repeat behaviors or gestures and have restricted interests, watching the same DVD over and over, for example. They may be very sensitive to light, sound, touch, or other sensory information. Sounds may be painful, for example, or the slight flickering of fluorescent lights may seem like constant bursts, causing severe headaches. They may be able to memorize words or steps in problem solving, but not use them appropriately or become very confused when the situation changes or questions are asked in a different way (Franklin, 2007; Friend, 2014; Matson, Matson, & Rivet, 2007).

Asperger syndrome is one of the disabilities included in the autism spectrum. Children with Asperger syndrome have many of the characteristics just described, but they have the greatest trouble with social relations. Language is less affected. Their speech may be fluent but unusual, mixing up pronouns of "I" and "you," for example. Many students with autism also have moderate-to-severe intellectual disabilities, but those with Asperger syndrome usually have average-to-above-average intelligence (Friend, 2014).

INTERVENTIONS. Early and intense interventions that focus on communications and social relations are particularly important for children with autism spectrum disorders. Without interventions, behaviors such as poor eye contact and odd-seeming mannerisms tend to increase over time (Matson et al., 2007). As they move into elementary school, some of these students will be in inclusive settings, others will be in specialized classes, and many will be in some combination of these two. Collaboration among teachers and the family is particularly important.

Video 4.5
In this video, two teachers discuss their experiences teaching children with autism. As you watch, note how they focus on the unique and special characteristics of each individual child.

ENHANCEDetext *video example*

Strategies such as providing smaller classes, offering structured environments, finding a class "buddy" to give support, maintaining a safe "home base" for times of stress, ensuring consistency in instruction and transition routines, implementing assistive technologies, and using visuals may be part of a collaborative plan (Friend, 2014; Harrower & Dunlap, 2001). Through adolescence and the transition to adulthood, instruction and guidance in life, work, and social skills are important educational goals.

Response to Intervention

One of the problems for students with serious learning problems is that they have to struggle through the early grades, often falling farther and farther behind, until they are identified, assessed, qualified for an IDEA category, receive an IEP, and finally get appropriate help. This has been called the "wait to fail" model. The reauthorization of IDEA in 2004 gave educators a new option for assessing and educating students who might have serious learning problems. The process is called **response to intervention (RTI)**. The main goal of RTI is to make sure students get appropriate research-based instruction and support as soon as possible, in kindergarten if they need it, before they have fallen too far behind. A second goal is to make sure teachers are systematic in documenting the interventions they have tried with these students and describing how well each intervention worked. In addition, instead of using the discrepancy between IQ scores and student achievement to identify students with learning disabilities, educators can now use RTI criteria to determine who needs more intensive learning support (Klinger & Orosco, 2010). However, this last use of RTI has been criticized for not being a valid or reliable way of assessing students with learning disabilities because it does not provide a comprehensive and thorough picture of the student's strengths and weaknesses, including documenting other problems that might be present (Reynolds & Shaywitz, 2009).

One common way of reaching these RTI goals is to use a three-tiered system (see Figure 4.4). The first tier is to use a strong, well-researched way of teaching all students (we will look at these kinds of approaches in Chapter 14). Students who are struggling in the Tier 1 curriculum, as identified by ongoing quality classroom assessments, are moved to the second tier and receive extra support and additional small-group instruction. If some students still make limited progress, they move to the third tier for additional one-to-one intensive help and perhaps a special needs assessment (Buffum, Mattos, & Weber, 2010; Denton et al., 2013). The approach has at least two advantages—students get extra help right away, and the information gained based on their responses to the different interventions can be used for IEP planning, if the students reach the third stage of RTI. But to achieve these advantages, general education teachers, particularly in the early grades, must be able to teach and assess using high-quality, research-based approaches.

Even with intensive, high-quality Tier 3 interventions, some students may continue to struggle and will need extended support, instruction, and practice (Denton et al., 2013). For more information on RTI, go to the Web site for the National Center on Response to Intervention (rti4success.org/).

We end the chapter with another group of students who have special needs but are not covered by IDEA or Section 504—students who are highly intelligent or talented.

ENHANCEDetext *self-check*

STUDENTS WHO ARE GIFTED AND TALENTED

Consider this situation, a true story.

> Latoya was already an advanced reader when she entered 1st grade in a large urban school district. Her teacher noticed the challenging chapter books Latoya brought to school and read with little effort. After administering a reading assessment, the school's reading consultant confirmed that Latoya was reading at the 5th grade level. Latoya's parents reported with pride that she had started to read independently when she was 3 years old and "had read every book she could get her hands on." (Reis et al., 2002, p. 32)

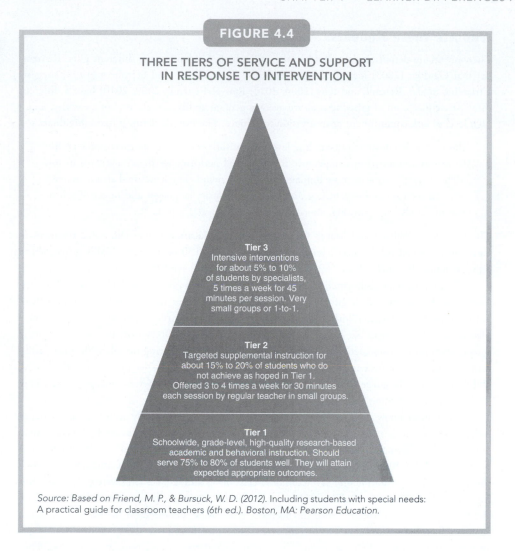

FIGURE 4.4

**THREE TIERS OF SERVICE AND SUPPORT
IN RESPONSE TO INTERVENTION**

Tier 3
Intensive interventions
for about 5% to 10%
of students by specialists,
5 times a week for 45
minutes per session. Very
small groups or 1-to-1.

Tier 2
Targeted supplemental instruction for
about 15% to 20% of students who do
not achieve as hoped in Tier 1.
Offered 3 to 4 times a week for 30 minutes
each session by regular teacher in small groups.

Tier 1
Schoolwide, grade-level, high-quality research-based
academic and behavioral instruction. Should
serve 75% to 80% of students well. They will attain
expected appropriate outcomes.

Source: Based on Friend, M. P., & Bursuck, W. D. (2012). Including students with special needs: A practical guide for classroom teachers (6th ed.). Boston, MA: Pearson Education.

In her struggling urban school, Latoya received no particular accommodations, and by 5th grade, she was still reading at just above the 5th grade level. Her 5th grade teacher had no idea that Latoya had ever been an advanced reader.

Here is another true story:

Alex Wade's field is linguistics. In his search for the perfect language—and "annoyed," he says, with Esperanto—he has created 10 languages and 30 or 40 alphabets, including one language without verbs, just for the challenge. He's taking courses at the University of Nevada, Reno, in Basque, linguistics, and microbiology (because he also has a talent for science). . . . Alex is 13. (Kronholz, 2011, p. 1)

Latoya and Alex are not alone. They are part of a group with special needs that is often overlooked by the schools: students who are **gifted and talented**. There is growing recognition that students who are gifted are being poorly served by most public schools. In 1990, a national study found that more than one half of all students who are gifted did not achieve in school at a level equal to their ability (Tomlinson-Keasey, 1990). Yet a survey of the states in 2008 by the National Association for Gifted Children (NAGC) found that at least a dozen states would not allow students to start kindergarten early, even if they were reading at a high level. At least 30 states allow only 11th and 12th graders to take college courses. What would that mean for students like Latoya and Alex (Kronholz, 2011)?

Who Are These Students?

There are many definitions of *gifted* because individuals can have many different gifts. Remember that Gardner (2003) identified eight separate "intelligences," and Sternberg (1997) suggests a triarchic model. Renzulli and Reis (2003, 2011; Reis & Renzulli, 2009, 2010) have a different three-part conception of giftedness: above-average general ability, a high level of creativity, and a high level of task commitment or motivation to achieve. The NAGC define gifted individuals as

> those who demonstrate outstanding levels of aptitude (defined as an exceptional ability to reason and learn) or competence (documented performance or achievement in top 10% or rarer) in one or more domains. Domains include any structured area of activity with its own symbol system (e.g., mathematics, music, language) and/or set of sensorimotor skills (e.g., painting, dance, sports). (NAGC, 2013, p. 1)

The College of William and Mary's Center for Gifted Education makes additional distinctions based on measured IQ: learners who are gifted score above 130 on IQ tests; highly gifted, above 145; exceptionally gifted, above 160; and profoundly gifted, above 175 (Kronholz, 2011).

Children who are truly gifted are not the students who simply learn quickly with little effort. The work of students who are gifted is original, extremely advanced for their age, and potentially of lasting importance. These children may read fluently with little instruction by age 3 or 4. They may play a musical instrument like a skillful adult, turn a visit to the grocery store into a mathematical puzzle, and become fascinated with algebra when their friends are having trouble with simple addition (Winner, 2000). Recent conceptions widen the view of giftedness to include attention to the children's culture, language, and special needs (NAGC, 2013). These newer conceptions are more likely to identify children like Latoya.

What do we know about these remarkable individuals? A classic study of the characteristics of individuals who are academically and intellectually gifted was started decades ago by Lewis Terman and colleagues (Terman, Baldwin, & Bronson, 1925; Terman & Oden, 1947, 1959; Holahan & Sears, 1995; Jolly, 2008). This huge project, the longest running longitudinal study ever, followed the lives of 1,528 predominantly White, middle-class males and females who were gifted, continuing until 2020. The subjects all had IQ scores in the top 1% of the population (140 or above on the Stanford-Binet individual test of intelligence). They were identified on the basis of these test scores and teacher recommendations. Terman and colleagues found that these children were larger, stronger, and healthier than the norm. They often walked sooner and were more athletic. They were more emotionally stable than their peers and became better-adjusted adults than the average individual. They had lower rates of delinquency, emotional difficulty, divorce, drug problems, and so on. Of course, the teachers in Terman's study who made the nominations may have selected students who were better adjusted initially. And remember, Terman's study included only students who were academically gifted. There are many other kinds of gifts.

WHAT IS THE ORIGIN OF THESE GIFTS? Studies of prodigies and geniuses in many fields document that deep and prolonged practice is necessary to achieve at the highest levels. For example, it took Newton 20 years to move from his first ideas to his ultimate contribution (Howe, Davidson, & Sloboda, 1998; Winner, 2000). I remember listening to the early reports of Bloom's study of world-class concert pianists, sculptors, Olympic swimmers, research neurologists, mathematicians, and tennis champions (B. S. Bloom, 1982). To study talent in tennis, Bloom's research team interviewed the top tennis players in the world, their coaches, parents, siblings, and friends. One coach said that he would make a suggestion, and a few days later the young athlete would have mastered the move. Then the parents told how the child had practiced that move for hours on end after getting the coach's tip. So, focused, intense practice plays a role. Also, the families of prodigies tend to be child-centered and to devote hours to supporting the development of their child's gifts. Bloom's research team described tremendous sacrifices made by families: rising before dawn to drive their child to a swimming coach or piano teacher in another city, working two jobs, or even moving the whole family to another part of the country to find the best teachers or coaches. The children responded to the family's sacrifices by working harder, and the families responded to the child's hard work by sacrificing more—an upward spiral of investment and achievement.

But hard work will never make me a world-class tennis player or a Newton. There is a role for nature as well. The children Bloom studied showed early and clear talent in the areas they later developed. As children, great sculptors were constantly drawing and great mathematicians were fascinated with dials, gears, and gauges. Parents' investments in their children came after the children showed early high-level achievement (Winner, 2000, 2003). Recent research suggests that children who are gifted, at least those with extraordinary abilities in mathematics, music, and visual arts, may have unusual brain organization—which can have both advantages and disadvantages. Giftedness in mathematics, music, and visual arts appears to be associated with superior visual-spatial abilities and enhanced development of the right side of the brain. Children with these gifts are also more likely not to have right-hand dominance and to have language related-problems. These brain differences are evidence that "gifted children, child prodigies, and savants are not made from scratch but are born with unusual brains that enable rapid learning in a particular domain" (Winner, 2000, p. 160).

WHAT PROBLEMS DO STUDENTS WHO ARE GIFTED FACE? In spite of Bloom's (B. S. Bloom, 1982) and Terman's (Terman, Baldwin, & Bronson, 1925; Terman & Oden, 1947, 1959) findings, it would be incorrect to say that every student who is gifted is superior in adjustment and emotional health. In fact, adolescents who are gifted, especially girls, are more likely to be depressed, and both girls and boys may be bored, frustrated, and isolated. Schoolmates may be consumed with baseball or worried about failing math, while the child with gifts and talents is fascinated with Mozart, focused on a social issue, or totally absorbed in computers, drama, or geology. Children who are gifted may be impatient with friends, parents, and even teachers who do not share their interests or abilities (Woolfolk & Perry, 2015). One researcher asked 13,000 students who are gifted in seven states to name one word for their experiences. The most commonly used word was "waiting." "Waiting for teachers to move ahead, waiting for classmates to catch up, waiting to learn something new—always waiting" (Kronholz, 2011, p. 3).

Because their language is well developed, students who are gifted may be seen as show-offs when they are simply expressing themselves. They are sensitive to the expectations and feelings of others, so these students may be very vulnerable to criticisms and taunts. Because they are goal directed and focused, they may seem stubborn and uncooperative. Their keen sense of humor can be used as a weapon against teachers and other students or as a defense to diffuse the pain of being bullied (Hardman et al., 2014; Peters & Bain, 2011). Adjustment problems seem to be greatest for the students among the most highly gifted, those in the highest range of academic ability (e.g., above 180 IQ). The chance of any teacher encountering a student in this highest IQ range is only about 1 in 80 over an entire 40-year career—but what if such a student walks into your class (Kronholz, 2011)?

Identifying Students Who Are Gifted and Talented

Identifying children who are gifted is not always easy, and teaching them well may be even more challenging. Many parents provide early educational experiences for their children. In middle and high school, some very able students deliberately earn lower grades, making their abilities even harder to recognize. Girls are especially likely to hide their abilities (Woolfolk & Perry, 2015).

RECOGNIZING GIFTS AND TALENTS. In general, teachers make reasonable, but not perfect predictions of students' academic achievement (Südkamp, Kaiser, & Möller, 2012). Table 4.11 on the next page lists the characteristics to notice to make better identifications.

Certainly, the students described at the beginning of this section—Latoya who read so early and Alex with his intense interests and creativity in inventing languages, had some of these characteristics. In addition, students who are gifted may prefer to work alone, have a keen sense of justice and fairness, be energetic and intense, form strong commitments to friends—often older students—and struggle with perfectionism.

TABLE 4.11 • **Characteristics to Observe in Identifying Students Who Are Gifted**

READING BEHAVIORS
• Has early knowledge of the alphabet • Often reads early or unlocks the reading process quickly and sometimes idiosyncratically • Reads with expression • Has a high interest in reading; reads voraciously
WRITING BEHAVIORS
• Displays early ability to make written sound–symbol correspondence • Exhibits fluency and elaboration in story writing • Uses advanced sentence structure and patterns • May show an interest in adult topics for writing, such as the state of the environment, death, war, and so on • Writes on a topic or story for an extended period of time • Generates many writing ideas, often of a divergent nature • Uses precise, descriptive language to evoke an image
SPEAKING BEHAVIORS
• Learns to speak early • Has a high-receptive vocabulary • Uses advanced sentence structure • Uses similes, metaphors, and analogies in daily conversation • Exhibits highly verbal behavior in speech (i.e., talks a lot, speaks rapidly, articulates well) • Enjoys acting out story events and situations
MATHEMATICAL BEHAVIORS
• Has early curiosity and understanding about the quantitative aspects of things • Is able to think logically and symbolically about quantitative and spatial relationships • Perceives and generalizes about mathematical patterns, structures, relations, and operations • Reasons analytically, deductively, and inductively • Abbreviates mathematical reasoning to find rational, economical solutions • Displays flexibility and reversibility of mental processes in mathematical activity • Remembers mathematical symbols, relationships, proofs, methods of solution, and so forth • Transfers learning to novel situations and solutions • Displays energy and persistence in solving mathematical problems • Has a mathematical perception of the world

Source: Friend, M. P. (2014). Special education: Contemporary perspectives for school professionals, 5th Edition, © 2014. Reprinted by permission of Pearson Education, Inc.

Group achievement and intelligence tests tend to underestimate the IQs of very bright children. Group tests may be appropriate for screening, but they are not appropriate for making placement decisions. Some evidence suggests that using individual IQ tests such as the Wechsler Intelligence Scale for Children IV (WISC-IV, Wechsler, 2004), which include evaluations of verbal comprehension and working memory, are the best predictors of achievement in reading and math for students who are gifted (E. W. Rowe, Kingsley, & Thompson, 2010). Many psychologists recommend a case study approach. This means gathering many kinds of information about the student in different contexts: test scores, grades, examples of work, projects and portfolios, letters or ratings from community or church members, self-ratings, nominations from teachers or peers, and so on (Renzulli & Reis, 2003). Especially for recognizing artistic talent, experts in the field can be called in to judge the merits of a child's creations. Science projects, exhibitions, performances, auditions, and interviews are all possibilities. Creativity tests and tests of self-regulation skills may identify some children not picked up by other measures, particularly minority students who may be at a disadvantage on the other types of tests (Grigorenko et al., 2009). Given the different definitions and wide-ranging procedures for identifying students who are gifted, between 1% and 25% of students in each state in the United States are served in programs for students who are gifted, or about 3 million total (Friend, 2014).

TABLE 4.12 • **Recognizing and Supporting All Students with Gifts and Talents—Especially Girls and Students Living in Poverty**

RECOGNIZING STUDENTS WHO ARE GIFTED AND HAVE LEARNING DISABILITIES
Here are some ideas for supporting students who are gifted with learning disabilities (McCoach, Kehle, Bray, & Siegle, 2001):   • Identify these students by looking longitudinally at achievement.   • Remediate skill deficits, but also identify and develop talents and strengths.   • Provide emotional support; it is important for all students, but especially for this group.   • Help students learn to compensate directly for their learning problems, and assist them in "tuning in" to their own strengths and difficulties.
RECOGNIZING GIFTS IN GIRLS
As young girls develop their identities in adolescence, they often reject being labeled as gifted—being accepted and popular and "fitting in" may become more important than achievement (Basow & Rubin, 1999; Stormont et al., 2001). How can teachers reach girls who are gifted?   • Notice when girls' test scores seem to decline in middle or high school.   • Encourage assertiveness, achievement, high goals, and demanding work from all students.   • Provide models of achievement through speakers, internships, or readings.   • Look for and support gifts in arenas other than academic achievement.
RECOGNIZING STUDENTS WHO ARE GIFTED WHO LIVE IN POVERTY
Health problems, lack of resources, homelessness, fears about safety and survival, frequent moves, and responsibilities for the care of other family members all make achievement in school more difficult. To identify students with gifts: • Use alternative assessment, teacher nomination, and creativity tests.   • Be sensitive to cultural differences in values about cooperative or solitary achievement (Ford, 2000).   • Use multicultural strategies to encourage both achievement and the development of racial identities.

Remember, students with remarkable abilities in one area may have much less impressive abilities in others. And up to 180,000 students in American schools may be gifted *and* learning disabled. In addition, two other groups are underrepresented in education programs for students who are gifted: girls and students living in poverty (Stormont, Stebbins, & Holliday, 2001). See Table 4.12 for ideas about identifying and supporting these students.

Teaching Students with Gifts and Talents

Some educators believe that students who are gifted should be *accelerated*—moved quickly through the grades or through particular subjects. Other educators prefer *enrichment*: giving the students additional, more sophisticated, and more thought-provoking work but keeping them with their age-mates in school. Both may be appropriate (Torrance, 1986). One way of doing this is through *curriculum compacting*—assessing students' knowledge of the material in the instructional unit, then teaching only for those goals not yet reached (Reis & Renzulli, 2004). Using curriculum compacting, teachers may be able to eliminate about half of the usual curriculum content for some students who are gifted without any loss of learning. The time saved can be used for learning goals that include enrichment, sophistication, and novelty (Werts et al., 2007).

ACCELERATION. Many people object to acceleration, but most careful studies indicate that students who are truly gifted who begin primary, elementary, middle, or high school, college, or even graduate school early do as well as, and usually better than, students who are not gifted who are progressing at the standard pace. You may remember from Chapter 1 that students who were mathematically talented and who skipped grades in elementary or secondary school were more likely to go on to earn advanced degrees and publish widely cited articles in scientific journals (Park, Lubinski, & Benbow, 2012). Social and emotional adjustment does not appear to be impaired either. Students who are gifted tend to prefer the company of older playmates (G. A. Davis, Rimm, & Siegle, 2011). Colangelo, Assouline, and Gross (2004) collected the research on the many benefits of acceleration and published two volumes called *A Nation Deceived: How Schools Hold Back America's Brightest Children.* These publications from the University of Iowa make a powerful case for acceleration.

An alternative to skipping grades is to accelerate students in one or two particular subjects or to allow concurrent enrollment in advanced placement or college courses, but keep them with peers for the rest of the time. For students who are extremely advanced intellectually (e.g., those scoring 160 or higher on an individual intelligence test), the only practical solution likely is to accelerate their education (G. A. Davis et al., 2011; Kronholz, 2011).

METHODS AND STRATEGIES. Teaching methods for students who are gifted should encourage abstract thinking (formal-operational thought), creativity, reading of high-level and original texts, and independence, not just the learning of greater quantities of facts. In 25-year longitudinal studies following students who were mathematically gifted, those students who had more advanced and enriched opportunities in science and math in middle and high school were more accomplished in STEM (science, technology, engineering, and mathematics) areas as adults (Wai, Lubinski, Benbow, & Steiger, 2010).

One approach that *does not* seem promising with students who are gifted is cooperative learning in mixed-ability groups. Students who are gifted tend to learn more when they work in groups with other high-ability peers (Fuchs, Fuchs, Hamlett, & Karns, 1998; A. Robinson & Clinkenbeard, 1998). Students in programs for gifted students appear to be less bored when they are ability grouped with others like themselves. An interesting tradeoff for students who are gifted is that their academic self-concepts tend to decrease when they are grouped with other high-ability students—an example of the "Little-Fish-in-a-Big-Pond" effect described in Chapter 3 (Preckel, Goetz, & Frenzel, 2010).

In working with students who are gifted and talented, a teacher must be imaginative, flexible, tolerant, and unthreatened by the capabilities of these students. The teacher must ask: What do these children need most? What are they ready to learn? Who can help me to challenge them? Challenge and support are critical for all students. But challenging students who know more than anyone else in the school about history or music or science or math can be a challenge! Answers might come from faculty members at nearby colleges, retired professionals, books, museums, the Internet, or older students. Strategies might be as simple as letting the child do math with the next grade. Other options are summer institutes; courses at nearby colleges; classes with local artists, musicians, or dancers; independent research projects; selected classes in high school for younger students; honors classes; and special-interest clubs (Rosenberg, Westling, & McLeskey, 2011).

In the midst of providing challenge, don't forget the support. We all have seen the ugly sights of parents, coaches, or teachers forcing the joy out of their talented students by demanding practice and perfection beyond the child's interest. Just as we should not force children to stop investing in their talent ("Oh, Michelangelo, quit fooling with those sketches and go outside and play"), we also should avoid destroying intrinsic motivation with heavy doses of pressure and external rewards.

This has been a brief, selective look at the needs of children. If you decide that students in your class might benefit from special services of any kind, the first step is making a referral. How would you begin? Table 4.13 guides you through the referral process. In Chapter 14, when we discuss differentiated teaching, we will look at more ways to reach all your students.

ENHANCEDetext *self-check*

TABLE 4.13 • Making a Referral

1. Contact the student's parents. It is very important that you discuss the student's problems with the parents *before* you refer.
2. Before making a referral, check *all* the student's school records. Has the student ever:
   - had a psychological evaluation?
   - qualified for special services?
   - been included in other special programs (e.g., for disadvantaged children; speech or language therapy)?
   - scored far below average on standardized tests?
   - been retained?

   Do the records indicate:
   - good progress in some areas, poor progress in others?
   - any physical or medical problem?
   - that the student is taking medication?
3. Talk to the student's other teachers and professional support personnel about your concern for the student. Have other teachers also had difficulty with the student? Have they found ways of dealing successfully with the student? Document the strategies that you have used in your class to meet the student's educational needs. Your documentation will be useful as evidence that will be helpful to or be required by the committee of professionals who will evaluate the student. Demonstrate your concern by keeping written records. Your notes should include items such as:
   - exactly what you are concerned about
   - why you are concerned about it
   - dates, places, and times you have observed the problem
   - precisely what you have done to try to resolve the problem
   - who, if anyone, helped you devise the plans or strategies you have used
   - evidence that the strategies have been successful or unsuccessful

   Remember that you should refer a student only if you can make a convincing case that the student probably cannot be served appropriately without special services. Referral begins a time-consuming, costly, and stressful process that is potentially damaging to the student and has many legal ramifications.

SUMMARY

- **Intelligence (pp. 120–131)**

   What are the advantages of and problems with labels? Labels and diagnostic classifications can easily become both stigmas and self-fulfilling prophecies, but they can also open doors to special programs and help teachers develop appropriate instructional strategies.

   What is person-first language? "Person-first" language ("students with intellectual disabilities," "students placed at risk," etc.) is an alternative to labels that describe a complex person with one or two words, implying that the condition labeled is the most important aspect of the person. With person-first language, the emphasis is on the students first, not on the special challenges they face.

   Distinguish between a disability and a handicap. A disability is an inability to do something specific such as see or walk. A handicap is a disadvantage in certain situations. Some disabilities lead to handicaps, but not in all contexts. Teachers must avoid imposing handicaps on learners with disabilities.

   What is *g*? Spearman suggested there is one mental attribute, which he called *g*, or general intelligence, that is used to perform any mental test, but that each test also requires some specific abilities in addition to *g*. A current version of the general plus specific abilities theory is Carroll's work identifying a few broad abilities (e.g., learning and memory, visual perception, verbal fluency) and at least 70 specific abilities. Fluid and crystallized intelligence are two of the broad abilities identified in most research.

   What is Gardner's view of intelligence and his position on *g*? Gardner contends that an intelligence is a biological and psychological potential to solve problems and create outcomes that are valued by a culture. These intelligences are realized or reached to a greater or lesser extent as a consequence of the experiential, cultural, and motivational factors in a person's environment. The intelligences are linguistic, musical, spatial, logical-mathematical, bodily-kinesthetic, interpersonal, intrapersonal, naturalist, and perhaps existential. Gardner does not deny the existence of *g*, but questions how useful *g* is as an explanation for human achievements.

What are the elements in Sternberg's theory of intelligence? Sternberg's triarchic theory of intelligence is a cognitive process approach to understanding intelligence: Analytic/componential intelligence involves mental processes that are defined in terms of components: metacomponents, performance components, and knowledge-acquisition components. Creative/experiential intelligence involves coping with new experiences through insight and automaticity. Practical/contextual intelligence involves choosing to live and work in a context where success is likely, adapting to that context, and reshaping it if necessary. Practical intelligence is made up mostly of action-oriented tacit knowledge learned during everyday life.

How is intelligence measured, and what does an IQ score mean? Intelligence is measured through individual tests (Stanford-Binet, Wechsler, etc.) and group tests (Otis-Lennon School Abilities Tests, Slosson Intelligence Test, Raven Progressive Matrices, Naglieri Nonverbal Ability Test—Multiform, Differential Abilities Scales, Wide Range Intelligence Test, etc.). Compared to an individual test, a group test is much less likely to yield an accurate picture of any one person's abilities. The average score is 100. About 68% of the general population will earn IQ scores between 85 and 115. Only about 16% of the population will receive scores below 85, and another 16% will have scores above 115. These figures hold true for White, native-born Americans whose first language is Standard English. Intelligence predicts success in school but is less predictive of success in life when level of education is taken into account.

What is the Flynn effect, and what are its implications? Since the early 1900s, IQ scores have been rising. To keep 100 as the average for IQ test scores, questions have to be made more difficult. This increasing difficulty has implications for any program that uses IQ scores as part of the entrance requirements. For example, students who were not identified as having learning problems a generation ago might be identified as having intellectual disabilities now because the test questions are harder.

Are there sex differences in cognitive abilities? Girls seem to be better on verbal tests, especially when writing is involved. Males seem to be superior on tasks that require mental rotation of objects. The scores of males tend to be more variable in general, so there are more males than females with very high and very low scores on tests. Research on the causes of these differences has been inconclusive, except to indicate that academic socialization and teachers' treatment of male and female students in mathematics classes may play a role.

- **Learning and Thinking Styles (pp. 131–134)**
  Distinguish between learning styles and learning preferences. Learning styles are the characteristic ways a person approaches learning and studying. Learning preferences are individual preferences for particular learning modes and environments. Even though learning styles and learning preferences are not related to intelligence or effort, they can affect school performance.

  Should teachers match instruction to individual learning styles? Results of some research indicate that students learn more when they study in their preferred setting and manner, but most research does not show a benefit. Many students would do better to develop new—and perhaps more effective—ways to learn.

  What learning style distinctions are the most well supported by research? One distinction that is repeatedly found in research is deep versus surface processing. Individuals who have a deep-processing approach see the learning activities as a means for understanding some underlying concepts or meanings. Students who take a surface-processing approach focus on memorizing the learning materials, not understanding them. A second is Mayer's visualizer–verbalizer dimension that has three facets: cognitive spatial ability (low or high), cognitive style (a visualizer vs. a verbalizer), and learning preference (a verbal learner vs. a visual learner).

- **Individual Differences and the Law (pp. 134–139)**
  Describe the main legal requirements that pertain to students with disabilities. Beginning with Public Law 94–142 (1975) and continuing with many reauthorizations including IDEA, the Individuals with Disabilities Education Act (2004), the requirements for teaching students with disabilities have been spelled out. Each learner or student with special needs (zero reject) should be educated in the LRE according to an IEP. The laws also protect the rights of students with special needs and their parents. In addition, Section 504 of the Vocational Rehabilitation Act of 1973 prevents discrimination against people with disabilities in any program that receives federal money, such as public schools. Through Section 504, all school-age children are ensured an equal opportunity to participate in school activities. The definition of disability is broad in Section 504 and in the Americans with Disabilities Act.

- **Students with Learning Challenges (pp. 139–156)**
  What does research in neuroscience tell us about learning problems? Studies of the brains of students with learning disabilities and with attention-deficit disorders show some differences in structure and activity compared to those of

students without problems. Students with learning disabilities have problems in using the system of working memory that holds verbal and auditory information while you work with it. Because children with learning disabilities have trouble holding on to words and sounds, it is difficult for them to put the words together to comprehend the meaning of a sentence or to figure out what a math story problem is really asking about. Students with learning disabilities also may have difficulties retrieving needed information from long-term memory while transforming new incoming information, such as the next numbers to add. Important bits of information keep getting lost.

What is a learning disability? Specific learning disabilities are disorders in one or more of the basic psychological processes involved in understanding or using spoken or written language. Listening, speaking, reading, writing, reasoning, or mathematical abilities might be affected. These disorders are intrinsic to the individual, presumed to be the result of central nervous system dysfunction, and may occur across the life span. Students with learning disabilities may become victims of learned helplessness when they come to believe that they cannot control or improve their own learning and therefore cannot succeed. A focus on learning strategies often helps students with learning disabilities.

What is ADHD, and how is it handled in school? ADHD is the term used to describe individuals of any age with hyperactivity and attention difficulties. Use of medication to address ADHD is controversial but currently on the rise. For many students the medication has negative side effects. In addition, little is known about the long-term effects of drug therapy. And no evidence indicates that the drugs lead to improvement in academic learning or peer relationships. Approaches that combine motivational training with instruction in learning and memory strategies and behavior modification seem effective.

What are the most common communication disorders? Common communication disorders include speech impairments (articulation disorders, stuttering, and voicing problems) and oral language disorders. If these problems are addressed early, great progress is possible.

What are the best approaches for students with emotional and behavioral disorders? Methods from applied behavior analysis and direct teaching of social skills are two useful approaches. Students also may respond to structure and organization in the environment, schedules, activities, and rules.

What are some warning signs of potential suicide? Students at risk of suicide may show changes in eating or sleeping habits, weight, grades, disposition, activity level, or interest in friends. They sometimes suddenly give away prized possessions such as iPods, CDs, clothing, or pets. They may seem depressed or hyperactive and may start missing school or quit doing work. It is especially dangerous if the student not only talks about suicide but also has a plan for carrying it out.

What defines intellectual disabilities? Before age 18, students must score below about 70 on a standard measure of intelligence and must have problems with adaptive behavior, day-to-day independent living, and social functioning. The AAIDD now recommends a classification scheme based on the amount of support that a person requires to function at his or her highest level. Support varies from intermittent (e.g., as needed during stressful times), to limited (consistent support, but time-limited, e.g., employment training), to extensive (daily care, e.g., living in a group home), to pervasive (constant, high-intensity care for all aspects of living).

How can schools accommodate the needs of students with physical disabilities? If the school has the necessary architectural features, such as ramps, elevators, and accessible rest rooms, and if teachers allow for the physical limitations of students, little needs to be done to alter the usual educational program. Identifying a peer to help with movements and transitions can be useful.

How would you handle a seizure in class? Do not restrain the child's movements. Lower the child gently to the floor, away from furniture or walls. Move hard objects away. Turn the child's head gently to the side, put a soft coat or blanket under the student's head, and loosen any tight clothing. Never put anything in the student's mouth. Find out from the student's family how they deal with seizures. If one seizure follows another and the student does not regain consciousness in between, if the student is pregnant, or if the seizure goes on for more than 5 minutes, get medical help right away.

What are some signs of visual and hearing impairments? Holding books very close or far away, squinting, rubbing eyes, misreading the chalkboard, and holding the head at an odd angle are possible signs of visual problems. Signs of hearing problems are turning one ear toward the speaker, favoring one ear in conversation, or misunderstanding conversation when the speaker's face cannot be seen. Other indications include not following directions, seeming distracted or confused at times, frequently asking people to repeat what they have said, mispronouncing new words or names, and being reluctant to participate in class discussions.

How does autism differ from Asperger syndrome? Asperger syndrome is one of the autism spectrum disorders.

Many students with autism also have moderate-to-severe intellectual disabilities, but those with Asperger syndrome usually have average-to-above-average intelligence and better language abilities than children with autism.

What Is Response to Intervention (RTI)? RTI is an approach to supporting students with learning problems as early as possible, not waiting for years to assess, identify, and plan a program. One RTI process is a three-tiered system. The first tier is to use a strong, well-researched way of teaching all students. Students who do not do well with these methods are moved to the second tier and receive extra support and additional small-group instruction. If some students still make limited progress, they move to the third tier for one-to-one intensive help and perhaps a special needs assessment.

- **Students Who Are Gifted and Talented (pp. 156–163)**

  What are the characteristics of students who are gifted? Students who are gifted learn easily and rapidly and retain what they have learned; use common sense and practical knowledge; know about many things that the other children don't; use a large number of words easily and accurately; recognize relations and comprehend meaning; are alert and keenly observant and respond quickly; are persistent and highly motivated on some tasks; and are creative or make interesting connections. Teachers should make special efforts to support underrepresented students who are gifted—girls, students who also have learning disabilities, and children living in poverty.

  Is acceleration a useful approach with students who are gifted? Many people object to acceleration, but most careful studies indicate that students who are truly gifted who are accelerated do as well as and usually better than students who are not gifted who are progressing at the normal pace. Students who are gifted tend to prefer the company of older playmates and may be bored if kept with children their own age. Skipping grades may not be the best solution for a particular student, but for students who are extremely advanced intellectually (with a score of 160 or higher on an individual intelligence test), the only practical solution may be to accelerate their education.

PRACTICE USING WHAT YOU HAVE LEARNED

To access and complete the exercises, click the link under the images below.

Supporting a Student with Special Needs

ENHANCEDetext *application exercise*

Multiple Intelligences

ENHANCEDetext *application exercise*

KEY TERMS

Absence seizure   153
Americans with Disabilities Act
    of 1990 (ADA)   136
Articulation disorders   146
Attention-deficit hyperactivity
    disorder (ADHD)   143
Autism/autism spectrum disorders   155
Automaticity   127
Cerebral palsy   153
Crystallized intelligence   123
Deviation IQ   128
Disability   120
Emotional and behavioral disorders   147
Epilepsy   153
Fluid intelligence   123
Flynn effect   128
Free, appropriate public education
    (FAPE)   134

General intelligence (*g*)   123
Generalized seizure   153
Gifted and talented   157
Handicap   120
Inclusion   135
Individualized Education Program
    (IEP)   135
Individuals with Disabilities Education
    Act (IDEA)   134
Insight   127
Integration   135
Intellectual disabilities/Mental
    retardation   151
Intelligence   122
Intelligence quotient (IQ)   128
Learned helplessness   142
Learning disability   140
Learning preferences   132

Learning styles   132
Least restrictive environment (LRE)   134
Legally blind   154
Low vision   154
Mainstreaming   135
Mental age   127
Pervasive developmental disorder
    (PDD)   155
Response to intervention (RTI)   156
Section 504   136
Spasticity   153
Speech disorder   146
Theory of multiple intelligences (MI)   123
Transition programming   152
Triarchic theory of successful
    intelligence   126
Voicing problems   146
Zero reject   134

CONNECT AND EXTEND TO LICENSURE

MULTIPLE-CHOICE QUESTIONS

1. African American students are more likely to be identified for special education services and placed outside of the general education system than White students. Which one of the following is not a likely explanation for this overrepresentation?
    A. High poverty rates, which lead to poor prenatal care, nutrition, and health care
    B. Teachers who are unprepared to work with ethnic minority students
    C. Biases in teachers' attitudes and in the curriculum
    D. The fact that African American students comprise 80% of the population of gifted and talented individuals

2. Developmental psychologist Howard Gardner's multiple intelligences theory continues to have an impact on classrooms in the United States today, based on its reflection of which current classroom strategy?
    A. Differentiated instruction
    B. Sternberg's triarchic theory of successful intelligence
    C. Mainstreaming
    D. Response to Intervention (RTI)

3. When a student has been identified as needing special education services, the Individuals with Disabilities Education Act mandates all but which one of the following?
    A. Accommodations must be made during state standardized testing of all students receiving special education services.
    B. The law requires states to provide a free, appropriate public education (FAPE) for every student with disabilities who participates in special education.
    C. States are required to develop procedures for educating children in the least restrictive environment.

    D. Students receiving special education services must each have an Individualized Education Program (IEP).

4. Several students in Mr. Collins's kindergarten class appear to have deficits in their abilities. The school is unable to assess the children and will not begin providing special education services until next year. Which one of the following solutions would be the best?
    A. Mr. Collins should contact the parents of the students who need services and encourage them to work with their children at home.
    B. The school should wait until next year to begin services.
    C. Mr. Collins should begin Response to Intervention (RTI).
    D. The students in question should be sent to a school that specializes in special education services.

CONSTRUCTED-RESPONSE QUESTIONS

Case

Many beginning teachers become overwhelmed when they discover they have numerous students in their class with special needs. First-year teacher Paige Morris was no exception. Of her 25 students, 7 were identified as needing special education services. Although Ms. Morris was certified in special education and elementary education, she felt ill-equipped to write and implement so many Individualized Education Plans (IEPs). To make matters more concerning, three of her students were identified as having ADHD. Ms. Morris began to imagine herself trying to control a chaotic classroom without the tools she needed to succeed.

5. List the parts of an IEP that must be in writing. Identify the aspect(s) of the IEP for which Ms. Morris is responsible.
6. Which parts of each child's program would assist Ms. Morris in better understanding her students before they begin the school year?

ENHANCEDetext *licensure exam*

TEACHERS' CASEBOOK

WHAT WOULD THEY DO? INCLUDING EVERY STUDENT

Here is how several expert teachers said they would work with students with a wide range of abilities.

BARBARA PRESLEY—Transition/Work Study Coordinator—High School Level
BESTT Program (Baldwinsville Exceptional Student Training and Transition Program), C. W. Baker High School, Baldwinsville, NY

As a transition coordinator, it is my responsibility to link the special education standards to transition. Therefore, connecting work and tasks assigned at work sites to classroom standards was done in conjunction with classroom teachers. All requisite work skills and behaviors were reinforced in the classroom. Classroom instructional topics were integrated at each work site and reinforced by Job Coaches while students were at their work site. Job Coaches, teachers, and the transition coordinator communicate daily through goal books. Success breeds confidence for adults and students. For special needs students, the importance of linking and aligning classroom education with community education cannot be overstated.

JENNIFER PINCOSKI—Learning Resource Teacher: K–12
Lee County School District, Fort Myers, FL

One of the most important considerations when setting up the classroom is how to group students to maximize learning. Students should be assessed early on to provide the teacher with information on individual learning styles, interests, strengths, and needs; teachers who are prepared with this knowledge will be better able to group students appropriately.

Learning groups should be fluid, meaning that they will change often, depending on objectives and circumstances. Students may be grouped in a variety of ways, including heterogeneously (a student with strengths in a skill area can assist a student who struggles), homogeneously by skill deficit (to provide interventions), by learning styles, and by areas of interest.

Part of the process of understanding students' needs also includes research. Numerous resources are available for teachers to educate themselves on support strategies for students with ADHD, autism spectrum disorders, learning disabilities, and health impairments. These resources can include staff members on campus (counselor, nurse, special education teacher, etc.), as well as community advocacy groups, scholarly journals and literature (accessible at the local library), and, of course, the Internet.

Ultimately, the best way to support students is to learn about their strengths and challenges and use this information to assist in the physical and educational organization of the classroom community.

JESSICA N. MAHTABAN—Eighth-Grade Math Teacher
Woodrow Wilson Middle School, Clifton, NJ

It is vital for me to become very familiar with all of the students' IEPs and to discuss the modifications that need to take place in the classroom with the special education teacher. Once everything has been reviewed, I can begin to construct the curriculum, which must accommodate all my students. Differentiated instruction will be integrated into the curriculum. Portfolios will be the major source of assessment for my students. Each student learns differently and at a different pace, which is why the portfolio would be the best assessment; portfolios show the individual growth of each student. Frequent contact with parents is the key component for helping each student succeed in the classroom and beyond.

LAUREN ROLLINS—First-Grade Teacher
Boulevard Elementary School, Shaker Heights, OH

Meeting the individual needs of all students is a challenging but essential part of teaching! In this situation, I would create differentiated learning centers, where students could work on curricular components in skill-based groups. The opportunity to work with smaller groups of students whose abilities are similar would allow me to differentiate the curriculum to best meet their academic needs. Groupings would need to be fluid and flexible to ensure that the students were continually being challenged by the curriculum. At each learning center, I would provide a variety of materials and literature related to the subject matter that are designed to meet the wide range of learning styles presented by the students. Additionally, I would allow the students working in the centers to choose which of the provided materials they would like to use to support their learning. Giving the students choices will help with student motivation. I would even consider enlisting their input as to which materials they would like in each center. Finally, I would enlist willing and able parent or community volunteers to assist me in managing the students at the learning centers. The combination of small, skill-based groups, engaging learning materials, and choice will allow students to tackle the curriculum to their fullest potential.

LINDA SPARKS—First Grade Teacher
John F. Kennedy School, Billerica, MA

Most of our classes are inclusion classes, with limited resources for additional help. At the beginning of the year, I go through all of the records, IEPs, and 504 plans and write down my questions, concerns, and specific information that will help the student. Next, we all meet as a team with the teachers from the previous year and specialists who work with the students. I have found this very helpful in setting up a plan for the students in my class. Then, I don't spend time re-evaluating students in areas where team members already know how students can be most successful. I am given the resources needed to start the year, and we continue to meet throughout the year as additional resources are needed. We are also fortunate to have a volunteer program through the senior center, parent community, and local businesses. These adult volunteers commit to a specific number of hours a week, are trained by school staff for specific skills the students will need help with, and begin to implement these skills with the students.

PAUL DRAGIN—ESL Teacher, Grades 9–12
Columbus East High School, Columbus OH

This situation has become the norm—at least in public schools in large urban areas. The students with special needs who have been identified should each have an IEP that addresses specifics pertaining to their own cognitive and/or behavioral issues. This would guide my instructional deviation to help ensure that I am providing the curriculum in a format that is more easily comprehended by those who may have challenges that are greater than mainstream students. The

medical issue concerning the student with asthma is something that requires a greater sensitivity to ensure that I am alert to any possible medical emergency that may occur in the classroom. Confidence in this trying situation comes from attempting various strategies with the students and discovering, through trial and error, which are most effective at meeting their diverse educational needs.

PAULA COLEMERE—Special Education Teacher— English, History
McClintock High School, Tempe, AZ

It is every teacher's dream to have a room full of eager learners who are all on grade level. In my experience, this never happens! In any classroom, there are students who are below, at, or above grade level in their abilities. First, teachers need to know that fair doesn't mean equal. If I assign a five-paragraph essay to the class, but a student with a learning disability in writing struggles to write that much, I could either extend the due date or modify it to a three-paragraph essay. If the student is really low ability, I may only require a solid paragraph. Likewise, I would challenge the brightest students to go deeper. I would make sure my students knew I believed in them and would build their confidence in their abilities. Proximity is huge in classroom management; by constantly moving around the classroom, I could prompt my students to stay on task or to remind them of appropriate classroom behavior. This would be done very quietly and privately. I would also give a great deal of positive reinforcement while walking around and pointing out all of the things students are doing right. The positive messages must outnumber negative messages.

5 | LANGUAGE DEVELOPMENT, LANGUAGE DIVERSITY, AND IMMIGRANT EDUCATION

TEACHERS' **CASEBOOK**

WHAT WOULD YOU DO? CULTURES CLASH IN THE CLASSROOM

Your high school classes this year are about equally divided among three groups—African Americans, Asians, and Latinos/as. Students from each of the three groups seem to stick together, rarely making friends with students from "outside." When you ask students to select partners for projects, the divisions are usually based on shared ethnicity or shared language. At times, insults are exchanged between the groups, and the atmosphere of the class is becoming tense. Often the Asian or Latino students communicate in their native languages—which you don't understand—and

you assume that the joke is on you because of the looks and laughs directed your way. You realize that you are having trouble establishing positive relationships with many of the students whose language, culture, and background are very different from yours, and many other students, picking up on your discomfort, shy away from them too.

CRITICAL THINKING

- What is the real problem here?
- How would you help the students (and yourself) to feel more comfortable with each other?
- What are your first goals in working on this problem?
- How will these issues affect the grade levels you will teach?

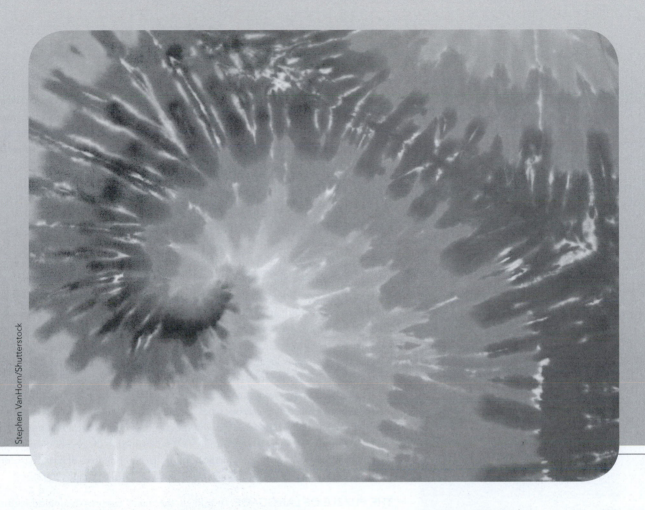

Stephen VanHorn/Shutterstock

OVERVIEW AND OBJECTIVES

Virtually all developed countries, and many developing ones, are becoming more diverse. Multiple languages fill many classrooms. For a range of reasons, including unrest across the globe, families are immigrating to find a better, safer life—and their children will likely be in your classrooms. In this chapter, we look at how the over 6,000 natural languages in the world developed, the role of culture, the stages in language development, and the emergence of literacy. Next we consider diversity in language development and dual-language development. But language diversity is more than bilingualism. Because all of us speak at least one dialect, we examine what teachers need to know about dialects and genderlects—a new term for me—along with the role of schools in second- (or third-) language learning. Finally, we turn to the critical issue for you—how to become a capable and confident teacher of immigrant students and second-language learners. What is the role of bilingual education and sheltered instruction? Do the emotions and concerns of these students affect their learning? How can you identify students

who are English language learners with special talents or special needs? By the time you have completed this chapter, you should be able to:

Objective 5.1   Understand how language develops and know how to support emergent literacy.

Objective 5.2   Discuss what happens when children develop two languages.

Objective 5.3   Address whether dialect differences affect learning and discuss what teachers can do.

Objective 5.4   Compare and contrast immigrant, refugees, and Generation 1.5 students, including their learning characteristics and needs.

Objective 5.5   Discuss teaching for English language learners including English immersion, bilingual instruction, and sheltered instruction.

Objective 5.6   Discuss how teachers can recognize special learning needs and talents when they do not speak their students' first language.

THE DEVELOPMENT OF LANGUAGE

All children in every culture master the complicated system of their native language, unless severe deprivation or physical problems interfere. This knowledge is remarkable. To have a conversation, children must coordinate sounds, meanings, words and sequences of words, volume, voice tone, inflection, and turn-taking rules. Yet, by about age 4, most children have a vocabulary of thousands of words and knowledge of the grammar rules for basic conversations (Colledge et al., 2002).

What Develops? Language and Cultural Differences

More than 6,000 natural languages are spoken worldwide (Tomasello, 2006). In general, cultures develop words for the concepts that are important to them. For example, how many different shades of green can you name? Mint, olive, emerald, teal, sea foam, chrome, turquoise, chartreuse, lime, apple . . . and visual artists can add cobalt titanate green, cinnabar green, phthalo yellow green, viridian green, and many others. English-speaking countries have more than 3,000 words for colors. In contrast, the Himba people of Namibia and a tribe of hunter-gatherer people in Papua New Guinea who speak Berinmo have five words for colors, even though they can recognize many color variations. But whether the terms for color are few or many, children gradually acquire the color categories appropriate for their culture (Roberson, Davidoff, Davies, & Shapiro, 2004).

Languages change over time to reflect changing cultural needs and values. The Shoshoni Native Americans have one word that means, "to make a crunching sound walking on the sand." This word was valuable in the past to communicate about hunting, but today new words describing technical tools have been added to the Shoshoni language, as the group's life moves away from nomadic hunting. To hear hundreds of new 21st-century tool words, listen to techies talk about computers (W. F. Price & Crapo, 2002).

THE PUZZLE OF LANGUAGE. It is likely that many factors—biological, cultural, and experiential—play a role in language development. To master a language, children must be able to (1) read the intentions of others so they can acquire the words, phrases, and concepts of their language and also (2) find patterns in the ways other people use these words and phrases to construct the grammar of their language (Tomasello, 2006). The important point is that children learn language as they develop other cognitive abilities by actively trying to make sense of what they hear and by looking for patterns and making up rules to put together the jigsaw puzzle of language.

In this process, humans may have built-in biases, rules, and constraints about language that restrict the number of possibilities considered. For example, young children seem to have a constraint specifying that a new label refers to a whole object, not just a part. Another built-in bias leads children to assume that the label refers to a class of similar objects. So the child learning about the rabbit is equipped naturally to assume that "rabbit" refers to the whole animal (not just its ears) and that other similar-looking animals are also rabbits (Jaswal & Markman, 2001; Markman, 1992). Reward and correction play a role in helping children learn correct language use, but the child's thinking in putting together the parts of this complicated system is very important (Waxman & Lidz, 2006).

When and How Does Language Develop?

Table 5.1 shows the milestones of language development, ages 2 to 6, in Western cultures, along with ideas for encouraging development.

SOUNDS AND PRONUNCIATION. By about age 5, most children have mastered the sounds of their native language, but a few sounds may remain unconquered. You saw in Chapter 4 that the sounds of the consonants *l, r, y, s, v,* and *z* and the consonant blends *sh, ch, ng, zh,* and *th* are the last to be mastered (Friend, 2014). Young children may understand and be able to use many words but prefer to use the words they can pronounce easily. As children learn to hear differences in the sounds of language, they enjoy rhymes, songs, and general sound silliness. They like stories by Dr. Seuss partly because of the sounds, as evident in the book titles—*All Aboard the Circus McGurkus* or *Wet Pet, Dry Pet, Your Pet, My Pet.* The young son of a friend of mine wanted to name his new baby sister Brontosaurus "just because it's fun to say."

VOCABULARY AND MEANING. As you can see in Table 5.1, children between ages 2 and 3 can use about 450 words (**expressive vocabulary**) even though they can understand many more (**receptive vocabulary**). By age 6, children's expressive vocabularies will grow to about 2,600 words, and their receptive vocabularies will be an impressive 20,000-plus words (Otto, 2010). Some researchers estimate that students in the early grades learn up to 20 words a day (P. Bloom, 2002). In the early elementary years, some children may have trouble with abstract words such as *justice* or *economy.* They also may not understand the subjunctive case ("If I were a butterfly") because they lack the cognitive ability to reason about things that are not true ("But you aren't a butterfly"). They may interpret all statements literally and thus misunderstand sarcasm or metaphor. For example, fables are understood concretely simply as stories instead of as moral lessons. Many children are in their preadolescent years before they are able to distinguish being kidded from being taunted, or before they know that a sarcastic remark is not meant to be taken literally. But by adolescence, students are able to use their developing cognitive abilities to learn abstract word meanings and to use poetic, figurative language (Owens, 2012).

TABLE 5.1 • Milestones in Early Childhood Language and Ways to Encourage Development

AGE RANGE	MILESTONE	STRATEGIES TO ENCOURAGE DEVELOPMENT
Between 2 and 3	Identifies body parts; calls self "me" instead of name; combines nouns and verbs; has a 450-word vocabulary; uses short sentences; matches 3–4 colors; knows *big* and *little;* likes to hear same story repeated; forms some plurals; answers "where" questions	• Help the child listen and follow instructions by playing simple games • Repeat new words over and over • Describe what you are doing, planning, thinking • Have the child deliver simple messages for you • Show the child you understand what he or she says by answering, smiling, and nodding your head • Expand what the child says. Child: "more juice." You say, "You want more juice?"
Between 3 and 4	Can tell a story; sentence length of 4–5 words; vocabulary about 1,000 words; knows last name, name of street, several nursery rhymes	• Talk about how objects are the same or different • Help the child to tell stories using books and pictures • Encourage play with other children • Talk about places you've been or will be going
Between 4 and 5	Sentence length of 4–5 words; uses past tense; vocabulary of about 1,500 words; identifies colors, shapes; asks many questions like "why?" and "who?"	• Help the child sort objects and things (e.g., things to eat, animals) • Teach the child how to use the telephone • Let the child help you plan activities • Continue talking about the child's interests • Let the child tell and make up stories for you
Between 5 and 6	Sentence length of 5–6 words; average 6-year-old has vocabulary of about 10,000 words; defines objects by their use; knows spatial relations (like "on top" and "far") and opposites; knows address; understands *same* and *different;* uses all types of sentences	• Praise children when they talk about feelings, thoughts, hopes, fears • Sing songs, rhymes • Talk with them as you would an adult
At Every Age		• Listen and show your pleasure when the child talks to you • Carry on conversations with the child • Ask questions to get the child to think and talk • Read books to the child every day, increasing in length as the child develops

Source: Reprinted from LDOnLine.org with thanks to the Learning Disabilities Association of America.

"WHEN I SAY 'RUNNED', YOU KNOW I MEAN 'RAN'. LET'S NOT QUIBBLE."

Young children begin to elaborate their simple language by adding plurals; endings for verbs such as *-ed* and *-ing;* small words like *and, but,* and *in;* articles (*a, the*); and possessives (*the girl's hair*). A classic study by Jean Berko (1958) demonstrated that children could even apply these rules to make words that they had never encountered plural, possessive, or past tense. For example, when shown a picture of a single "wug," the preschool children in the study could answer correctly "wugs" when the researcher said, "Now there is another one. There are two of them. There are two _____." In the process of figuring out the rules governing these aspects of language, children make some very interesting mistakes.

GRAMMAR AND SYNTAX. For a brief time, children may use irregular forms of particular words properly, as if they are saying what they have heard. Then, as they begin to learn rules, they **overregularize** words by applying the rules to everything. Children who once said, "Our car is broken" begin to insist, "Our car is broked." A child who once talked about her *feet* may discover the *-s* for plurals and refer to her *foots* or *feets,* then learn about *-es* for plurals (*horses, kisses*) and describe her *footses,* before she finally returns to talking about her *feet* (Flavell et al., 2002). Parents often wonder why their child seems to be "regressing." Actually, these "mistakes" show how logical and rational children can be as they try to assimilate new words into existing schemes. Apparently these overregularizations happen in all languages, including American Sign Language. Because most languages have many irregular words, accommodation is necessary in mastering language. According to Joshua Hartshore and Michael Ullman (2006), girls tend to overregularize verb tenses more than boys, so they are more likely to say *holded* instead of *held.* The researchers speculate that because girls may have better memory for words, they have better access to similar words (*folded, molded, scolded*) and generalize to *holded.*

Early on, children master the basics of **syntax** (word order) in their native language, but overregularizing plays a role in mastering syntax too. For example, because the usual order in English is subject–verb–object, preschoolers just mastering the rules of language have trouble with sentences in any other order. If 4-year-old Justin hears a statement in the passive voice, like "The truck was bumped by the car," he probably thinks the truck did the bumping to the car because "truck" came first in the sentence. Interestingly, however, in languages where the passive voice is more important, such as the South African language Sesotho, children use this construction much earlier, as young as 3 or 4 (Demuth, 1990). So in talking with young children, in English at least, it is generally better to use direct language. By early elementary school, many children can understand the meaning of passive sentences, but they do not use such constructions in their normal conversations, unless the passive construction is common in their culture.

PRAGMATICS: USING LANGUAGE IN SOCIAL SITUATIONS. **Pragmatics** involves the appropriate use of language to communicate in social situations—how to enter a conversation, tell a joke, interrupt, keep a conversation going, or adjust your language for the listener. Children show an understanding of pragmatics when they talk in simpler sentences to younger children or command their pets to "Come here!" in louder, deeper voices, or provide more detail when describing an event to a parent who was absent from the event (Flavell et al., 2002; M. L. Rice, 1989). So even young children seem quite able to fit their language to the situation, at least with familiar people.

Rules for the appropriate use of language vary across cultures. For example, Shirley Brice Heath (1989) spent many hours observing White middle-class families and African American families who were poor. She found that the adults asked different kinds of questions and encouraged different kinds of "talk." White middle-class adults asked test-like questions with right answers, such as "How many cars are there?" or "Which car is bigger?" These questions seemed odd to African American children whose families don't ask about what they already know. The African American child might wonder, "Why would my aunt ask me how many cars? She can see there are 3." Instead, African American families encouraged rich storytelling and also teasing that hones their children's quick wit and assertive responses.

METALINGUISTIC AWARENESS. Around the age of 5, students begin to develop **metalinguistic awareness**. This means their understanding about language and how it works becomes explicit. They have knowledge about language itself. They are ready to study and extend the rules that have been implicit—understood but not consciously expressed. This process continues throughout life, as we all become better able to use language. Learning to read and write, which begins with *emergent literacy*, encourages metalinguistic awareness.

Emergent Literacy

Today, in most languages, reading is a cornerstone of learning, and the foundation for reading is built in early childhood. Because young children vary greatly in their knowledge and skills related to reading, research has expanded to study what supports these emerging literacy skills (often called **emergent literacy**). Look at Figure 5.1, which shows a 6-year-old's emergent story and grocery list, to see some emerging literacy skills.

What are the most important skills that help literacy emerge? Here, the answers are not certain, but research has identified two broad categories of skills that are important for later reading: category 1 skills related to understanding sounds and codes such as knowing that letters have names, that sounds are associated with letters, and that words are made up of sounds; and category 2 oral language skills such as expressive and receptive vocabulary, knowledge of syntax, and the ability to understand and tell stories (Dickinson et al., 2003; Florit & Cain, 2011; Storch & Whitehurst, 2002).

FIGURE 5.1

A STORY AND A GROCERY LIST

This child knows quite a bit about reading and writing—letters make words that communicate meaning, writing goes from left to right and lists go down the page, and stories look different than shopping lists.
Emergent writing samples provided by Kalla Terpenning, who just turned 6.

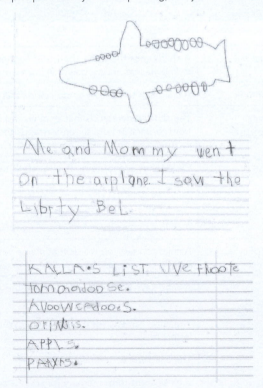

Source: Woolfolk, A., & Nancy, N.E. (2015). Child and Adolescent Development. *Reprinted by permission of Pearson Education, Inc.*

An example of category 1 skills is *letter naming*. The ability to name 10 letters is a common preschool/kindergarten benchmark goal in many U.S. states and programs. Is this a good indicator of reading readiness for English? Shayne Piasta and her colleagues (2012) addressed this question in a longitudinal study that followed 371 children from the end of preschool to the end of first grade. The researchers found that a better predictor of all reading outcomes was the ability to name 18 uppercase letters and 15 lowercase letters. Letter naming is not the most important skill, but it is easy to assess.

Some educators emphasize decoding skills (e.g., letter naming); others emphasize oral language. A study by the National Institute of Child Health and Human Development (NICHD) Early Childhood Research Network (2005b) that followed more than 1,000 children from age 3 through third grade concluded, "preschool oral language skills [for example, size of vocabulary, ability to use syntax, ability to understand and tell stories] play an important role along side code skills in predicting reading in the transition to school" (p. 439). The results of this study suggest that decoding such as letter naming and oral language skills such as vocabulary are likely an important part of the puzzle; these skills often support each other. *Beware of either/or choices* between emphasizing decoding *or* oral language—both are important. Some evidence, however, indicates that early in the learning-to-read process in English, decoding skills are more important because students need to become fast and automatic in processing letters and words so they have more mental resources available for comprehending what they read. Using all your mental capacity to identify letters and sounds leaves very little space for making meaning. As decoding becomes automatic, the emphasis can change to language comprehension skills (Florit & Cain, 2011).

INSIDE-OUT AND OUTSIDE-IN SKILLS. One way to think about emergent literacy that captures both code and oral language skills for emergent literacy is the notion of **inside-out skills** and **outside-in skills** and processes, described in Table 5.2.

TABLE 5.2 • Components of Emergent Literacy

COMPONENT	BRIEF DEFINITION	EXAMPLE
Outside-in Processes		
Language	Semantic, syntactic, and conceptual knowledge	A child reads the word "bat" and connects the meaning to knowledge of baseball or flying mammals.
Narrative	Understanding and producing narrative	A child can tell a story, understands that books have stories.
Conventions of print	Knowledge of standard print formats	The child understands that print is read from left-to-right and front-to-back in English; understands the difference between pictures and print or the cover and the inside of the book.
Emergent reading	Pretending to read	Child takes a favorite book and retells the "story," often by using pictures as cues.
Inside-out Processes		
Knowledge of graphemes	Letter-name knowledge	A child can recognize letters and name letters.
Phonological awareness	Detection of rhyme; manipulation of syllables; manipulation of individual phonemes	A child can tell you words that rhyme with "hat." A child can clap as she says sounds in a word *cat*: /k/ /ă/ /t/
Syntactic awareness	Repair grammatical errors	A child says, "No! you say I *went* to the zoo, not I *goed* to the zoo."
Phoneme–grapheme correspondence	Letter-sound knowledge	The child can answer the question, "What sounds do these letters make?"
Emergent writing	Phonetic spelling	The child writes "eenuf," or "hambrgr."
Other Factors	Emergent literacy also depends on other factors such as short-term memory for sounds and sequences, the ability to recognize and name lists of letters, motivation, and interest.	

Source: Woolfolk, A., & Nancy, N.E. (2015). Child and Adolescent Development. *Reprinted by permission of Pearson Education, Inc.*

This model, developed by Grover Whitehurst and Christopher Lonigan (1998), includes two inter-dependent sets of skills and processes:

> A reader must decode units of print into units of sound and units of sound into units of language. This is an inside-out process. However, being able to say a written word or series of written words is only a part of reading. The fluent reader must understand those auditory derivations, which involves placing them in the correct conceptual and contextual framework. This is an outside-in process. (p. 855)

For example, to understand even a simple sentence in print, such as, "She ordered an eBook from Amazon?" the reader must know about letters, sounds, grammar, and punctuation. The reader also has to remember the first words as he is reading the last ones. But these inside-out skills are not enough. To understand, the reader needs to have conceptual knowledge—what is an eBook? What does it mean to order? Is this the Amazon River or Amazon online? Why the question mark? Who is asking? How does this sentence fit in the context of the story? Answering these questions takes outside-in skills and knowledge.

BUILDING A FOUNDATION. What builds this foundation of emergent literacy skills? Two related activities are critical: (1) conversations with adults that develop knowledge about language and (2) joint reading, using books as supports for talk about sounds, words, pictures, and concepts (NICHD Early Childhood Research Network, 2005a). Especially in the early years, the children's home experiences are central in the development of language and literacy (Lonigan, Farver, Nakamoto, & Eppe, 2013; Sénéchal & LeFevre, 2002). In homes that promote literacy, parents and other adults value reading as a source of pleasure, and books and other printed materials are everywhere. Parents read to their children, take them to bookstores and libraries, limit the amount of television everyone watches, and encourage literacy-related play such as setting up a pretend school or writing "letters" (Pressley, 1996; C. E. Snow, 1993; Whitehurst, Epstein, Angell, Payne, Crone, & Fischel, 1994). Childcare workers and teachers can help. In a study that followed almost 300 low-income children from kindergarten to fifth grade, researchers found that the more families were involved with the school, the better their children's literacy development. School involvement was especially valuable when mothers had less education themselves (Dearing, Kreider, Simpkins, & Weiss, 2006).

WHEN THERE ARE PERSISTENT PROBLEMS. Not all children come to first grade with a firm foundation for literacy. Direct teaching of inside-out and outside-in skills in kindergarten and first grade can help many students "crack the code" and move forward. But for some students, reading problems persist (Wanzek et al., 2013). Benita Blachman and her colleagues (2014) reviewed research on outcomes for struggling readers, and their findings were not encouraging. About 70% to 80% of students who had reading disabilities in the early grades were still behind over a decade later. Intensive early intervention with direct teaching and practice in reading can make a difference, but there is an important additional consideration—*continued support is needed*. Even good interventions lasting many months are not magic bullets that change poor readers into good readers for the rest of their lives. For example, Blachman and her colleagues (2014) followed 58 students who participated in an intensive reading intervention program in second or third grade. The students had individual tutoring 50 minutes a day, 5 days a week, for 8 months. More than a decade later, when these students were 18 to 22 years old, the researchers found only small-to-moderate differences in reading and spelling skills for this group compared to similar students who had not participated in the intensive reading intervention. For students with persistent reading problems, we should think of reading intervention as being more like "insulin therapy, rather than as an inoculation against further reading failure" (Blachman et al., 2014, p. 10). Like people who need insulin on an ongoing basis to be healthy, struggling readers need ongoing teaching and support in reading—you can't "fix it and forget it."

Video 5.1
The preschool child in this video has very clear ideas about literacy already. What types of activities would you expect that she and her family engage in regularly?

ENHANCEDetext *video example*

Emergent Literacy and Language Diversity

Emergent literacy skills are critical for school readiness, regardless of the child's language or languages (Hammer, Farkas, & Maczuga, 2010). Research so far indicates that inside-out (letter-sound) skills and outside-in (language comprehension/meaning) skills are important in learning to read in all languages. But does emergent literacy "emerge" the same way in languages other than English, where much of the research has happened? There are differences—read on!

LANGUAGES AND EMERGENT LITERACY. English is not an easy language to learn. The same letter can have different pronunciations (how many ways can you pronounce "c"? Think "cook" and "city" for openers), the same sound can be written different ways, and irregular spellings are plentiful. It makes sense that children would have to become quick and automatic in decoding this complicated system in English before they could devote their mental resources to comprehension. But when languages have more transparent letter-sound systems (e.g., Spanish, German, Italian,

---

GUIDELINES
Supporting Language and Promoting Literacy

FOR FAMILIES

Read with your children.

Examples

1. Help children understand that books contain stories, that they can visit the stories as often as they like, that the pictures in the books go along with the story meaning, and that the words are always the same when they visit the story—that's reading! (Hulit & Howard, 2006)
2. Have a night-time reading ritual.

Choose appropriate books and stories.

Examples

1. Choose books with simple plots and clear illustrations.
2. Make sure illustrations precede the text related to the illustration. This helps children learn to predict what is coming next.
3. Ensure that language is repetitive, rhythmic, and natural.

FOR TEACHERS

Use stories as a springboard for conversations.

Examples

1. Retell stories you have read with your students.
2. Talk about the words, activities, and objects in the books. Do the students have anything like these in their home or classroom?

Identify and build on strengths the families already have (Delpit, 2003).

Examples

1. What are the histories, stories, and skills of family members? Students can draw or write about these.
2. Show respect for the student's language by celebrating poems or songs from the language.

Provide home activities to be shared with family members.

Examples

1. Encourage family members to work with children to read and follow simple recipes, play language games, keep diaries or journals for the family, and visit the library. Get feedback from families or students about the activities.
2. Give families feedback sheets, and ask them to help evaluate the child's schoolwork.

3. Provide lists of good children's literature available locally—work with libraries, clubs, and churches to identify sources.

FOR SCHOOL COUNSELORS AND ADMINISTRATORS

Communicate with families about the goals and activities of your program.

Examples

1. Have someone from the school district, the community, or even an older student translate into the language of the child's family any material you plan to send home.
2. At the beginning of school, send home a description of the goals to be achieved in your class—make sure it is in a clear and readable format.
3. As you start each unit, send home a newsletter describing what students will be studying—give suggestions for home activities that support the learning.

Involve families in decisions about curriculum.

Examples

1. Have planning workshops at times family members can attend—provide childcare for younger siblings, but let children and families work together on projects.
2. Invite parents to come to class to read to students, take dictation of stories, tell stories, record or bind books, and demonstrate skills.

Make it easier for families to come to school.

Examples

1. Provide babysitting for younger children while families meet with teachers.
2. Consider transportation needs of families—can they get to school?

For more information on Family Literacy Partnerships, see famlit.org/

Source: Hulit, Lloyd M.; Howard, Merle R., Born to Talk: An Introduction to Speech and Language Development, 4th edition, © 2006. Reprinted by permission of Pearson Education, Inc., Upper Saddle River, NJ.

and Finnish)—when the letters and the sounds have consistent, predictable connections and few exceptions or irregular spellings—then decoding skills develop more easily, so early schooling can place less emphasis on decoding and more on comprehension (Florit & Cain, 2011).

BILINGUAL EMERGENT LITERACY. Most school programs expect all children to learn to read in English. According to research by Carol Hammer and her colleagues, this emphasis on reading only in English may not be necessary. In fact, one key factor may facilitate literacy development—growth in receptive language. You probably remember that *receptive* language is made up of the words and language structures you understand, even if you do not use them in your *expressive* language, the words and structures you actually use when you talk.

In one study, Hammer followed 88 children for 2 years in a Head Start program (Hammer, Lawrence, & Miccio, 2007). The mothers of all the children spoke the Puerto Rican dialect of Spanish. There were two groups of students—those who had been expected to speak both English and Spanish from birth and those who were not expected to learn English until they began Head Start at age 3. The researchers found that it was not a particular score on any test but *growth in receptive language* in general during the program that predicted early reading outcomes. And it did not matter if the students spoke English and Spanish from birth or if they just started speaking English in school. Hammer and colleagues concluded "that growth in children's English receptive language abilities during Head Start, as opposed to the level of English they had achieved by the end of Head Start, positively predicted the children's emergent reading abilities in English and the children's ability to identify letters and words in English. This was the case regardless of the level of the children's prior exposure to English" (p. 243). In addition, growth in Spanish language abilities predicted reading performance in Spanish.

One implication is that teachers and parents should focus on continuing language development and not worry about rushing children into speaking English exclusively. As Hammer and her colleagues note, "If bilingual children's language growth is progressing well in either Spanish or English during the preschool years, positive early English and Spanish reading outcomes result in kindergarten" (2007, p. 244). These findings are consistent with the recommendations of the Society for Research in Child Development (SRCD): "Investing in dual-language instead of English-only programs and encouraging pre-kindergarten attendance can improve learning opportunities for Hispanic children and increase their chances of success" (SRCD, 2009, p. 1). The *Guidelines: Supporting Language and Promoting Literacy* give some ideas.

ENHANCEDetext *self-check*

DIVERSITY IN LANGUAGE DEVELOPMENT

Many children learn two languages simultaneously while they are growing up. What does this involve?

Dual-Language Development

If you mastered your own first language, then added a second or third language, you are an example of *additive bilingualism*—you kept your first language and added another. But if you lost your first language when you added a second one, you experienced *subtractive bilingualism* (Norbert, 2005). If family members and the community value a child's first language, he or she is more likely to keep that language when a second one is learned. But if a child experiences discrimination against the first language, he or she may leave the first language behind as proficiency is gained in a new language (Hamers & Blanc, 2000; Montrul, 2010). Immigrants are more likely to experience discrimination and therefore "subtract" their first language.

If they are exposed to two languages from birth, **bilingual** children (children who speak two languages) reach the language milestones in both languages on the same schedule as **monolingual** children (children learning only one language). Initially, bilingual children may have a larger vocabulary in the language that they are learning from the person with whom they spend the most

Connect and Extend to PRAXIS II®

Bilingual Issues (IV, B4)
Identify the major issues related to the debate over bilingual education. Explain the major approaches to bilingual education, and describe steps that a teacher can take to promote the learning and language acquisition of non–English-speaking students.

time or have the closest bond, so a child who stays home all day with a Chinese-speaking parent will likely use more Chinese words. But over time, these children can become fully and equally bilingual if the dual-language exposure (1) begins early in life (before age 5); (2) occurs across a wide and rich range of contexts; and (3) is systematic, consistent, and sustained in the home and community (Petitto, 2009; Rojas & Iglesias, 2013). Another requirement is that the second language must provide more than 25% of the child's language input; with less exposure, the child is unlikely to learn the second language (Pearson, Fernandez, Lewedeg, & Oller, 1997; Topping, Dekhinet, & Zeedyk, 2011). Bilingual children may mix vocabularies of the two languages when they speak, but this is not necessarily a sign that they are confused, because their bilingual parents often intentionally mix vocabularies as well, selecting the word that best expresses their intent (Creese, 2009). So, with consistent and sustained engagement in two languages, children can be fully bilingual.

Recent research on the brain and bilingualism shows that people who learn two languages before about age 5 process both languages in the same way as those who learn only one language and use the same parts of their brains (mostly in the left hemisphere). In contrast, people who learn a second language later have to use both hemispheres of their brain as well as the frontal lobe and working memory. They have to apply more cognitive effort. As Laura-Ann Petitto (2009) notes, "*Later* bilingual exposure does *change* the typical pattern of the brain's neural organization for language processing, but early bilingual exposure does not" (p. 191).

SECOND-LANGUAGE LEARNING. What if you didn't learn two languages as you were growing up? When and how should you learn a second language? To answer that question, you have to remember the distinction between **critical periods** for learning (if learning doesn't happen then, it never will) and **sensitive periods**, times when we are especially responsive to learning. There is no critical period that limits the possibility of language learning by adults (Marinova-Todd, Marshall, & Snow, 2000). In fact, older children go through the stages of language learning faster than young children. Adults have more learning strategies and greater knowledge of language in general to bring to bear in mastering a second language (Diaz-Rico & Weed, 2002). But recent research on the brain and bilingualism suggests "*there is most definitely a 'sensitive period' for optimal bilingual language and reading exposure and mastery.* Age of first bilingual exposure predicts how strong a reader a bilingual child can and will become in each of their two languages" (Petitto, 2009, p. 192).

Even though there is no *critical* period for learning a language, there appears to be a critical period for learning accurate language pronunciation. The earlier people learn a second language, the more their pronunciation is near native. This is because from birth to about 4 months, infants can discriminate all the basic sound building blocks from any of the world's 6,000 or so languages. But after about 14 months they lose this capability and hone in on the sounds of the language they are learning. For children learning two languages at once, however, this developmental window seems to stay open longer, so these children can continue to differentiate sounds past 14 months (Petitto, 2009).

After adolescence it is almost impossible to learn a new language without speaking with an accent (P. J. Anderson & Graham, 1994). Even if a child overhears a language, without actually learning it formally, this can improve later learning. After studying college students learning Spanish, Terry Au and colleagues concluded that "Although waiting until adulthood to learn a language almost guarantees a bad accent, having overheard the target language during childhood seems to lessen this predicament substantially" (T. K. Au, Knightly, Jun, & Oh, 2002, p. 242). So the best time to acquire two languages on your own through exposure (and to learn native pronunciation for both languages) is early childhood (T. K. Au, Oh, Knightly, Jun, & Romo, 2008).

BENEFITS OF BILINGUALISM. There is no cognitive penalty for children who learn and speak two languages. In fact, there are benefits. Higher degrees of bilingualism are correlated with increased cognitive abilities in such areas as concept formation, creativity, theory of mind, cognitive flexibility, attention and executive functioning, and understanding that printed words are symbols for language (Kempert, Saalbach, & Hardy, 2011). In addition, bilingual children have more advanced *metalinguistic* understanding of how language works; for example, they are more likely to notice grammar errors. Even more impressive, children from monolingual English-speaking families who attended bilingual schools and learned Spanish had better phoneme awareness and reading comprehension than their peers who were educated in an English-only program. Looking at all this research, Petitto (2009) concluded that "early bilingualism offers no disadvantages; on the contrary, young bilinguals may be afforded a linguistic and a reading advantage. . . . Moreover, learning to read in two languages may afford an advantage to children from monolingual homes in key phoneme awareness skills vital to reading success" (p. 193). In addition, speaking two languages is an asset when graduates enter the business world (Mears, 1998).

These conclusions hold as long as there is no stigma attached to being bilingual and as long as children are not expected to abandon their first language to learn the second (Bialystok, 2001; Bialystok, Majumder, & Martin, 2003; Galambos & Goldin-Meadow, 1990; Hamers & Blanc, 2000). Laura-Anne Petitto and Ioulia Kovelman (2003) suggest that perhaps humans evolved to speak multiple languages because this would have survival value, so perhaps the "contemporary pockets of civilization where one language is spoken are the aberrant deviation; in other words, perhaps our brains were neurologically set to be multilingual" (p. 14).

LANGUAGE LOSS. Even though the advantages of bilingualism seem clear, many children and adults are losing their heritage language (Montrul, 2010). Heritage language is the language spoken in a student's home or by older relatives when the larger society outside the home speaks a different language (English in the United States). Often students who lose their heritage language were born in a new country after their parents or grandparents immigrated, so the students never lived in the country where everyone spoke their heritage language. Years ago, in a large survey of eighth- and ninth-grade first- and second-generation children of immigrants in Miami and San Diego, Portes and Hao (1998) found that only 16% had retained the ability to speak their heritage language well. And 72% said they preferred to speak English. The languages of Native Americans are disappearing as well. Only about one third still exist, and 9 out of 10 of those are no longer spoken by the children (Krauss, 1992). Two Chinese American college students interviewed by K. F. Wong and Xiao (2010) expressed concerns this way:

> One of my biggest fears is that later on having kids and them not being able to speak Chinese, because my level of Chinese is not at the same level of my parents, and so I'm scared that it will get lost. (p. 161)
>
> My heritage language is definitely Toishan (Taishan), but even so, my parents don't always speak it fluently, so . . . I know somewhere down the line, I'm probably the last one to even speak it . . . and I feel like it is not my heritage anymore. (p. 165)

Rather than losing one language to gain another, the goal should be balanced bilingualism—being equally fluent in both languages (V. Gonzalez, 1999). Students' home language connects them to extended family and important cultural traditions, but outside their homes, English connects them to academic, social, and economic opportunities (Borrero & Yeh, 2010).

Many countries have schools that focus on retaining heritage languages and cultures. Students attend these schools afternoons, weekends, or summers in addition to their regular public school. In Great Britain, these institutions are called *supplementary* or *complementary* schools. In Australia they are called *community language* or *ethnic schools*. In the United States and Canada, the name often is *heritage language schools* (Creese, 2009). Look at Table 5.3 on the next page for a sampling of these schools and their missions.

Here are some ideas for learning about heritage schools in your area, suggested by Angela Creese (2009), a professor of educational linguistics at the University of Birmingham, United Kingdom:

- Find out which complementary/heritage schools are located in your area, and make contact with them.
- When your students attend complementary/heritage schools, attend their awards ceremonies and presentations. Show your commitment to their bilingual and multicultural projects.
- Find out if teachers work in both the complementary/heritage and mainstream school sectors. Ask them to undertake professional development workshops for other teachers in school.
- Ask a lead teacher of a complementary/heritage school to give an assembly.
- Encourage small-scale research and/or practical projects to harness the potential links between complementary and mainstream schooling (p. 272).

TABLE 5.3 • **Schools That Support Heritage Languages in the United States and Canada**

LANGUAGE	SCHOOL	DESCRIPTION
German	German Heritage Language School, Halifax Nova Scotia german-language-school.ca/	Offers classes for adults and children. Lessons once a week for 2 hours on Thursday afternoons. German language skills (reading, writing, speaking, listening).
Chinese	Reidmount Saturday School, Markam, Ontario rhls.ca/	A co-educational Saturday school that offers Chinese (Mandarin and Cantonese), Chinese History, English (grammar and writing), Mathematics, Science, Communications, and Drawing for students from junior kindergarten to Grade 11.
Chinese	Chinese Heritage School, Monmouth Junction, NJ chsnj2000.0rg/	In addition to the regular language class, they also emphasize verbal conversation, Chinese Culture, and family values. Their intention is to create a fun environment where children are motivated to study Chinese language and feel proud to be Chinese.
Many languages	The Alliance for the Advancement of Heritage Languages in America cal.org/heritage/index.html	The mission of the Alliance is to promote the maintenance and development of heritage languages for the benefit of individuals, communities, and society.
Spanish	Grupo Educa elgrupoeduca.org/	Grupo Educa's mission is to enhance the Spanish language opportunities for children with a pre-existing knowledge of Spanish. Founded in June 2003 by a group of Southern California parents looking to expose their preschool-aged children to a dual-English/Spanish education.
Arabic and Hindi	Arabic and Hindi Heritage Language Classes, UCLA, Los Angeles hslanguages.ucla.edu/	Intensive 5-week courses are for high school students who speak Hindi or Arabic at home and want to develop literacy and a deeper understanding of historical and contemporary South Asian culture. The project-based curriculum uses culturally relevant themes as a vehicle for listening, writing, speaking, and reading tasks.

Signed Languages

People who can communicate in both a spoken and a signed language or in two different signed languages are considered bilingual (Petitto, 2009). There are a number of other parallels between spoken languages and the many signed languages used around the world, such as American Sign Language (ASL), Signed English (United States, Ireland, New Zealand, Australia, Great Britain), Lingua de Signos Nicaraguense (Nicaraguan Sign Language), Warlpiri Sign Language (Australia Aboriginal), and Langue des Signes Quebecoise (LSQ), or Quebec Sign Language. Each of these languages is distinct and not simply a derived version of a spoken language. For example, people using Quebec Sign Language and French Sign Language cannot understand each other, even though the French spoken language is common to both countries.

Both spoken and signed languages have large vocabularies and complex grammars. Laura-Ann Petitto and Ioulia Kovelman (2003) suggest that the same mechanisms for language acquisition are used for both spoken and signed languages. In addition, the milestones for signed language are the same as for spoken language. For example, children "say" their first words at about the same time, around 12 months, with both spoken and signed languages (P. Bloom, 2002). In fact, research with children learning a signed and a spoken language from infancy demonstrates that "being exposed to two languages from birth—and, in particular, being exposed to a signed and a spoken language from birth—does not cause a child to be language delayed or confused" (Petitto & Kovelman, 2003, p. 16). As with two spoken languages, children can become balanced bilinguals in a spoken and a signed language.

In the 1970s, language researchers studied the birth of a new socially shared signed language when Nicaragua established its first school for the deaf. The students arrived at the school using their own unique invented sign languages. Over the years, a new language emerged that was based on the students' own sign languages. As the children developed the new Lingua de Signos Nicaraguense (Nicaraguan Sign Language), it became more systematic. The vocabulary expanded, and the grammar grew more complex. New students learned the developing Nicaraguan Sign Language as their native language (Hoff, 2006; Senghas & Coppola, 2001).

What Is Involved in Being Bilingual?

In the United States from 1995 to 2005, the number of students speaking Asian languages increased almost 100%, and the number of Spanish-speaking students increased 65%. The United States has the fifth-largest Spanish-speaking population in the world (Lessow-Hurley, 2005). The states with the largest number of English learners are Texas, California, Florida, New York, and Illinois, but numbers are surging in the Midwest, the South, Nevada, and Oregon (Peregoy & Boyle, 2009). With these increased numbers come many misconceptions about bilingualism, as you can see in Table 5.4.

What does it really mean to be bilingual? Some definitions of *bilingualism* focus exclusively on a language-based meaning: People who are bilingual speak two languages. Other definitions are more rigorous: "adults who had early, intensive, and maintained dual-language exposure and who use their two languages in their adult daily life" (Petitto, 2009, p. 186). But being bilingual and bicultural also means mastering the knowledge necessary to communicate in two cultures as well as dealing with potential discrimination (Borrero & Yeh, 2010). Consider these two students:

> A 9th-grade boy, who recently arrived in California from Mexico: "There is so much discrimination and hate. Even from other kids from Mexico who have been here longer. They don't treat us like brothers. They hate even more. It makes them feel more like natives. They want to be American. They don't want to speak Spanish to us; they already

TABLE 5.4 • Myths and Misconceptions About Being Bilingual
In this table, L1 means the original language and L2 means the second language.

MYTH	TRUTH
Learning a second language (L2) takes little time and effort.	Learning English as a second language takes 2–3 years for oral and 5–7 years for academic language use.
All language skills (listening, speaking, reading, writing) transfer from L1 to L2.	Reading is the skill that transfers most readily.
Code-switching is an indication of a language disorder.	Code-switching indicates high-level language skills in both L1 and L2.
All bilinguals easily maintain both languages.	It takes great effort and attention to maintain high-level skills in both languages.
Children do not lose their first language.	Loss of L1 and underdevelopment of L2 are problems for second language learners (semilingual in L1 and L2).
Exposure to English is sufficient for L2 learning.	To learn L2, students need to have a reason to communicate, access to English speakers, interaction, support, feedback, and time.
To learn English, students' parents need to speak only English at home.	Children need to use both languages in many contexts.
Reading in L1 is detrimental to learning English.	Literacy-rich environments in either L1 or L2 support development of necessary prereading skills.
Language disorders must be identified by tests in English.	Children must be tested in both L1 and L2 to determine language disorders.

Source: Brice, A. E. (2002). The Hispanic Child: Speech, Language, Culture, and Education. *Reprinted by permission of Pearson Education, Inc.*

know English and how to act. If they are with us, other people will treat them more like wetbacks, so they try to avoid us." (Olsen, 1988, p. 36)

Over 20 years later, a Chinese American college student is conflicted: "Because I was born here, my parents . . . think that English is the language of the world, (but) I tell my mom that Mandarin is important, and she doesn't think so. She's kind of stuck in the old ways . . . like America is the only way to make money . . . I feel that as a Chinese American . . . second generation, I'm the first one to actually not follow what was followed before." (K. F. Wong & Xiao, 2010, p. 168)

The experiences of these two students show that you must also be able to move back and forth between two cultures and two languages while still maintaining a sense of your own identity, so bilingualism requires biculturalism as well (S. J. Lee, Wong, & Alvarez, 2008). Being a successful bilingual student has one more requirement—learning *academic language*.

Contextualized and Academic Language

Proficiency in a second language has two separate aspects: face-to-face communication (*basic* or *contextualized language skills*) and academic uses of language such as reading and doing grammar exercises (*academic language*) (Fillmore & Snow, 2000; E. E. Garcia, 2002). Academic language is the entire range of language used in elementary and secondary schools and universities. In fact, academic language should be considered a *new language* that people must learn in order to succeed in school. So all students, but especially those who may not speak formal English at home, must become bilingual and bicultural; they must learn the new ways of speaking and cultural rules required for school. Academic language includes the general words and concepts used in many subjects such as *analyze, evaluate,* or *summarize,* as well as words and strategies specific to disciplines such as *factor the equation* or *derivative* in math, a *factor* in statistics, or a *derivative* in finance (you see how complicated this gets when the same word has two very different meanings in different fields). Academic language is associated with abstract, higher-order, complex concepts (Vogt, Echevarría, & Short, 2010).

It takes about 2 to 3 years in a good-quality program for children who are learning a new language to be able to use *basic* or contextualized language face-to-face in conversations. The stages for basic second-language learning are shown in Table 5.5.

Mastering *academic* language skills such as reading texts in the new language takes much longer than 3 years—more like 5 to 7 years, depending on how much academic knowledge the student already had in his or her native language. So children who seem to "know" a second language in conversation may still have great difficulty with complex schoolwork in that language (Bialystok, 2001; Verplaetse & Migliacci, 2008). Here is how one Spanish-speaking international student, who earned a doctoral degree and taught at a university, described her struggles with texts in college:

I could not understand why I was doing so poorly. After all, my grammar and spelling were excellent. It took me a long time to realize that the way text is organized in English is considerably different from the way text is organized in a romance language, Spanish. The process involved a different set of rhetorical rules which were grounded in cultural ways of being. I had never heard of the thesis statement, organizational rules, cohesion, coherence, or other features of discourse. (Sotillo, 2002, p. 280)

One 10th grader from Mexico described how her teacher helped her master academic language:

What I really love about my ESL teacher is that she explains how to organize our thoughts and how to write in school ways. She also teaches us what to do to be good, critical readers. That is so helpful in my other classes and I know it will be good for life. (Walqui, 2008, p. 111)

Cultural differences might interfere with developing academic English and content understanding in many ways. For example, many Asian students come from a culture that believes asking the teacher questions is rude and inappropriate because questioning implies that the teacher has done a poor job of instruction. In Asian classrooms this might cause the teacher to lose face in front of the

TABLE 5.5 • **Common Errors and Accomplishments as Students Learn a Second Language**

LANGUAGE STAGE	COMMON ERRORS AND LIMITATIONS	ACCOMPLISHMENTS
During the first year of learning the language	• No speech at all • Only understands one word at a time • Mispronounces words • Leaves out words • One- or two-word responses • Relies heavily on context	• Uses pantomiming, gestures, pointing to communicate • Can use "yes," "no," or single words
During the second year of learning the language	• Basic pronunciation and grammar mistakes • Limited vocabulary	• Uses whole sentences • Good comprehension (in context) • Uses language to function well socially
During the third year and beyond of learning the language	• Some errors with complex grammar	• Can tell whole stories • Good comprehension • Beginning to understand and use academic language • Larger vocabulary

Source: Based on Miranda, T. Z. (2008). Bilingual Education for All Students: Still Standing after All These Years. In L. S. Verplaetse & N. Migliacci (Eds.), Inclusive Pedagogy for English Language Learners: A Handbook of Research-Informed Practices (pp. 257–275). New York, NY: Erlbaum.

GUIDELINES
Promoting Language Learning

Provide structures, frameworks, scaffolds, and strategies.
Examples
1. "Think aloud" as you solve a problem by building on and clarifying the input of students.
2. Use visual organizers, story maps, or other aids to help students organize and relate information.

Teach relevant background knowledge and key vocabulary concepts.
Examples
1. Informally assess students' current background knowledge. Directly teach needed information, if missing.
2. Focus on key vocabulary words, and use those words consistently.

Give focused and useful feedback.
Examples
1. Focus feedback on meaning, not grammar, syntax, or pronunciation.
2. Give frequent, brief, clear feedback. Use words from the student's first language when you can.
3. Make sure to let students know when they are successful.
4. Break assignments and activities into smaller, "bite-sized pieces" with feedback after each "bite."

Keep students involved and engaged.
Examples
1. Use small-group and pairs work.
2. Create situations where students talk at length.
3. Challenge students with clear higher-order questions. Allow time to think and write out answers, maybe in pairs.

Show authentic respect for students' culture and language.
Examples
1. Learn about your students' personal and language background: What languages are spoken at home? When did the family arrive? How long have they lived in the United States? What schooling did they receive in other countries?
2. Learn about the students' religious background, food preferences and restrictions, and family customs; then incorporate students' experiences into writing and language arts activities.
3. Learn some key words in the students' languages.
4. View diversity as an asset; reject cultural deficit notions.

Sources: Based on Peregoy, S. F., & Boyle, O. F. (2009). Reading, Writing, and Learning in ESL: A Resource Book for Teaching K–12 English Learners (5th ed.). Boston, MA: Pearson; Echevarría, J., & Graves, A. (2011). Sheltered Content Instruction: Teaching English Learners with Diverse Abilities (4th ed.). Columbus, OH: Pearson; and Gersten, R. (1996b). Literacy Instruction for Language-Minority Students: The Transition Years. The Elementary School Journal, 96, 217–220.

students—an entirely unacceptable situation. Thus, teachers need to ask themselves why their English learners are not asking questions. And class discussion may be considered a waste of time in cultures in which the teacher is viewed as the source of authoritative knowledge. How would students learn from other students who are not authorities? So beliefs about learning shaped by culture and previous experiences in different kinds of classrooms may explain why English learners seem quiet and reluctant to speak in class. English language learners also may think that their teachers are not very good because they do not explain everything. They also may strongly prefer memorization as a learning strategy if memorization was emphasized in their previous schools (thanks to Dr. Alan Hirvela at Ohio State University for pointing out these possible cultural differences in beliefs about schools and teachers).

The *Guidelines: Promoting Language Learning* on the previous page give ideas for promoting language learning, but you should also keep cultural differences in mind as you teach.

DIALECT DIFFERENCES IN THE CLASSROOM

Communication is at the heart of teaching, but as we have seen in this chapter, culture affects communication. In this section, we examine two kinds of language differences—dialect differences and genderlects.

Dialects

- -

STOP & THINK When you want a soft drink, what do you call it? Do you think people in other parts of the United States use the same term? •

- -

Growing up in Texas, we always asked, "Do you want a *coke?*" If the answer was yes, the next question was, "What kind—Coca-Cola, root beer, 7-Up, orange?" When I moved to New Jersey, I had to ask for a *soda*. If I asked for a coke, then that is just what I got. Twenty years later, at our moving-to-Ohio party, my colleague who had grown up in Columbus, Ohio, said, "You are going to have to learn to speak Midwestern and ask for a '*bottlapop*.'" Different regions have different ways of speaking—both in their accents and in their word usage. For example, in New England, many people refer to a traffic circle as a "rotary," and ice cream sprinkles are "jimmies."

A **dialect** is any variety of a language spoken by a particular group. Eugene Garcia (2002) defines a dialect as "a regional variation of language characterized by distinct grammar, vocabulary, and pronunciation" (p. 218). The dialect is part of the group's collective identity. Actually, every person reading this book speaks at least one dialect, maybe more, because there is no one absolute standard English. The English language has several dialects; for example, Australian, Canadian, British, and American. Within each of these dialects are variations. A few examples of dialects of American English are Southern, Bostonian, Cajun, and African American Vernacular (E. E. Garcia, 2002).

Dialects differ in their rules about pronunciation, grammar, and vocabulary, but it is important to remember that these differences are not errors. Each dialect is logical, complex, and rule governed. An example of this is the use of the double negative (Brice & Brice, 2009). In many versions of American English, the double-negative construction, such as "I don't have no more," is incorrect. But in many dialects such as some varieties of African American Vernacular and in other languages (e.g., Russian, French, Spanish, and Hungarian), the double negative is part of the grammatical rules. To say "I don't want anything" in Spanish, you must literally say, "I don't want nothing," or, "No quiero nada." My husband, from Pennsylvania, drops "to be" in some sentences such as, "The lawn needs mowed" and "The car needs washed."

DIALECTS AND PRONUNCIATION. Dialects also differ in pronunciation, which can lead to spelling problems. In some varieties of African American Vernacular and in Southern dialects, for instance, less attention is paid to pronouncing the ends of words. A lack of attention to final consonants, such as *s,* can lead to failure to indicate possession, third-person singular verbs, and plurals in the standard way. So *John's book* might be *John book,* and the singular and plural will sound the same for words such as *thinks, wasps,* and *lists.* When endings are not pronounced, there are more *homonyms* (words that sound alike but have different meanings) in the student's speech than the unknowing teacher may expect; *spent* and *spend* might sound alike, for example. Even without the confusions caused by dialect differences, English has many homonyms. Usually, teachers give special attention to words such as these when they come up in spelling lessons. If teachers are aware of the special homonyms in student dialects, they can teach these differences directly.

DIALECTS AND TEACHING. How can teachers cope with linguistic diversity in the classroom? First, they can be sensitive to their own possible negative stereotypes about children who speak a different dialect. Second, teachers can ensure comprehension by repeating instructions using different words and by asking students to paraphrase instructions or give examples. The best teaching approach seems to be to focus on understanding the students and accepting their language as a valid and correct system, but to teach the alternative forms of English (or whatever the dominant language is in your country) that are used in more formal work settings and writing so that the students will have access to a range of opportunities. Jean Anyon (2012) described how she accomplished this naturally in her elementary classes:

> Indeed, I thought the language my students used was inventive and lovely. I had my students write poems and stories in their own language. We would appreciate the music of their voices. Then, we would talk about the differences between what they wrote and the way I spoke, as I was from a different culture—the white middle class. We would do some translations of their talk and mine, back and forth. In this way, language patterns were seen as different, not good or bad. Discussion of the need for them to learn standard English to function in a white world came naturally out of our activities, not as an imposition. (p. 2)

Moving between two speech forms is called code switching—something we all have learned to do. Sometimes, the code is formal speech for educational or professional communication. At other times, the code is informal for talk among friends and family. And occasionally, the codes are different dialects. Even young children recognize variations in codes. Delpit (1995) describes the reaction of one of her first-grade students to her very first reading lesson. After she carefully recited the memorized introduction from the teacher's manual, a student raised his hand and asked, "Teacher, how come you talkin' like a white person? You talkin' just like my momma talk when she get on the phone."

Learning the alternative versions of a language is easy for most children, as long as they have good models, clear instruction, and opportunities for authentic practice.

Video 5.2
In this video, Dr. Walt Wolfram differentiates between dialect and accent, and he reminds teachers of the need to be sensitive to the social functions of dialectical differences and code switching.

ENHANCEDetext *video example*

Genderlects

If you had to guess what genderlects are, based on what you know about dialects, you probably would figure out that genderlects are different ways of talking for males and females. Boys and girls have some small differences in their speech. Girls tend to be slightly more talkative and affiliative in their speech (affiliative speech is talk intended to establish and maintain relationships). But much of the research has been conducted with White, middle-class children, and the results do not necessarily hold for other groups and cultures. For example, some research reports that girls are more likely to cooperate and to talk about caring, whereas boys are more competitive and talk about rights and justice. But other studies have found that African American girls in one study were just as likely as boys to compete and talk about their rights in conversations (Leaper & Smith, 2004).

As with most aspects of language, cultural differences occur in genderlects. Interrupting is a good example. In America, boys interrupt more often than girls, but in Africa, the Caribbean, South America, and Eastern Europe, females interrupt males much more often than they do in America. And in Thailand, Hawaii, Japan, and Antigua, the style of speaking for boys and girls is overlapping; this overlapping talk is not interruption but cooperative turn taking (Owens, 2012).

ENHANCEDetext *self-check*

TEACHING IMMIGRANT STUDENTS

Felipe Vargas is a fifth grader who came with his family from Mexico to the United States more than 3 years ago so his father could take a job in a chicken-processing plant. Many Mexicans have come to work at the plant, and now there is a Spanish-speaking church, a Mexican grocery, and a Mexican bar and restaurant in the little northern Georgia town where they live. Felipe's mother, who takes care of the home and children, speaks no English, but his father and his older brother, Enrique, both speak a little. Enrique was 15 when the family came to this country. He left school after 1 year in a program for English for speakers of other languages (ESOL) and went to work in the chicken plant. He is proud to be contributing to the family but dreams of being a car mechanic; he spends all his free time fixing cars for neighbors and earns a little extra money that way. Felipe's oldest sister is 15 now, and, like him, spent 2 years in an ESOL program before transitioning to regular English-speaking classes. Her parents have chosen a husband for her from "back home," and she plans to leave school as soon as she turns 16, although she would rather not marry the man her parents have chosen. His two younger sisters are 8 and 4; the youngest is in a special Head Start class to learn English, and the other is repeating second grade because she is having a hard time learning to read.

Felipe gets mostly Cs in school. He still struggles a bit with reading his textbooks, but he has many Anglo friends in his class and has no trouble talking English with them; in fact, he translates for his parents when they come to school for parent conferences, which they do whenever his father can get off work. Math is his real talent; he consistently gets As on his tests, and he is in the highest "math group," so he goes to another teacher for math. That teacher calls him "Phillip" and tells him he could be an accountant or maybe an engineer when he grows up. Felipe likes this idea, but his father says that college would cost too much money and reminds him that the family plans to go back to Mexico someday, when they have saved enough to buy a small farm, which is his father's dream.

There are so many students like Felipe and his siblings in American schools today. For the remainder of this chapter, we explore ways of teaching these students so that their dreams of college and careers can come true wherever they finally live.

Immigrants and Refugees

In 2010, 12% of the people living in the United States were born in another country. Many of these children, like Felipe Vargas and his siblings, will be immigrants. **Immigrants** are people who voluntarily leave their country to become permanent residents in a new place. People from Mexico, like Felipe's family, are the largest U.S. immigrant group (Okagaki, 2006). **Refugees** are a special group of immigrants who also relocate voluntarily, but they are fleeing their home country because it is not safe. The United States requires that individuals seeking refugee status have "a well-founded fear of persecution on account of race, religion, nationality, membership in a particular social group, or political opinion" (U.S. Citizenship and Immigration Services, 2011). Since 1975, more than 3,000,000 refugees have permanently resettled in the United States, half of them children. The average number admitted annually is 98,000 (Refugee Council USA, 2013).

In earlier decades, these new immigrants were expected to assimilate—to enter the cultural **melting pot** and become like those who had arrived earlier. For years, the goal of American schools was to be the fire under the melting pot. Immigrant children who spoke different languages and had diverse religious and cultural heritages were expected to come to the schools, master English, and learn to become mainstream Americans. Of course, most schools were designed to serve European American middle-class children, so it was the immigrant children who were expected to do the adapting and changing—rather than the schools. *Involuntary immigrants,* descendants of the slaves forced to migrate to the United States, often were not welcome at all in the cultural melting pot.

In the 1960s and 1970s, some educators suggested that immigrants, students of color, and poor students had problems in school because they were "culturally disadvantaged" or "culturally handicapped." The assumption of this **cultural deficit model** was that the students' home culture was inferior because it had not prepared them to fit into the schools. Today, educational psychologists reject the idea of cultural deficits. They believe that no culture is deficient, but rather that incompatibilities may exist between the student's home culture and the expectations of the school (Gallimore & Goldenberg, 2001). Also, there is an increasing sense among many ethnic groups that they do not want to assimilate completely into mainstream American society. Rather, they want to maintain their culture and identity while still being a respected part of the larger society. Multiculturalism is the goal—more like a salad bowl filled with many ingredients instead of the prior melting pot idea (J. A. Banks, 1997, 2006; Stinson, 2006).

In past decades, most U.S. immigrants were concentrated in large urban areas and in California, Texas, Arizona, and New York. But today there are "New Ellis Islands" in many other cities and towns, particularly in the Midwestern states. Given the challenges of teaching students who have a range of English speaking abilities coupled with the demands of accountability testing, it is clear that teachers everywhere are under pressure (S. B. Garcia & Tyler, 2010). And there is not much help; less than 1% of elementary and secondary school teachers are prepared to teach English as a second language (Aud et al., 2010).

Classrooms Today

English language learners are the fastest growing segment of the U.S. population. From 1994 to 2004, there was a 125% increase in students with limited English proficiency in Ohio where I teach (Newman, Samimy, & Romstedt, 2010). In 2008, nearly 21% of school-age children in the United States spoke a language other than English at home—almost three times as many as in 1979 (Aud et al., 2010). Some researchers project that by 2030, about 40% of the students in pre-kindergarten through high school will speak limited English (Guglielmi, 2012). By some estimates, Latinos alone will comprise about one quarter of the U.S. population by 2050 (U.S. Census Bureau, 2011b). And U.S.-born children of immigrant families make up another group needing specialized language teaching. These students are about 6% of the school population and the fastest growing group in American schools, especially at the high school level. More than half of these U.S.-born students are still designated as students who are English language learners. Even at the beginning of high school, these students may still lack the skills in academic English—school language—needed to succeed in their often complex, abstract courses (Dixon et al., 2012; Slama, 2012).

These changes are not limited to the United States. By 2031, it is projected that one in three Canadians will belong to a visible minority and one in four will be foreign born, so it is likely that the number of people who speak languages other than the official English and French will increase in Canada as well (Freisen, 2010). In fact, all the developed countries have many immigrant students. For example, more than half of the students under age 12 in the Amsterdam schools are from immigrant families. In Great Britain from 2000 to 2010, the number of foreign-born students increased 50%, and in Australia one in four people were born overseas (Crul & Holdaway, 2009; Martin, Liem, Mok, & Xu, 2012).

Because immigrant families tend to live in particular neighborhoods, the schools in these communities generally have the largest number of immigrants and students who are **English language learner (ELLs)**. Some of these students may not even be able to read and write in their native language. Clearly, schools serving these students need extra resources to hire and train native-language-speaking teachers and aides, provide smaller classes, and purchase well-designed materials to teach complex academic subjects to students with limited English language skills (Crul & Holdaway, 2009). As you can guess, these extra resources are not always available.

FOUR STUDENT PROFILES. Following are four general profiles of students who are ELLs in today's classrooms (Echevarría & Graves, 2011).

- *Balanced bilinguals.* These students speak, read, and write well both in their first language and in English. They have the academic knowledge needed to continue learning in both languages and the skills and attitudes to do so. These students may not present difficult teaching challenges, but they do need to maintain their skills in both languages and cultures.

- *Monolingual/literate students.* These students are literate in their native language (at or above grade level when working in their native language), but speak limited English. The teaching challenge here is to help the students develop English and continue to learn academic subjects.

- *Monolingual/preliterate students.* These students are not literate. They may not read or write in their native language or they may have very limited literacy skills. Some have never attended school. In addition, they speak limited English. These students require the greatest support in learning both academic subjects and language.

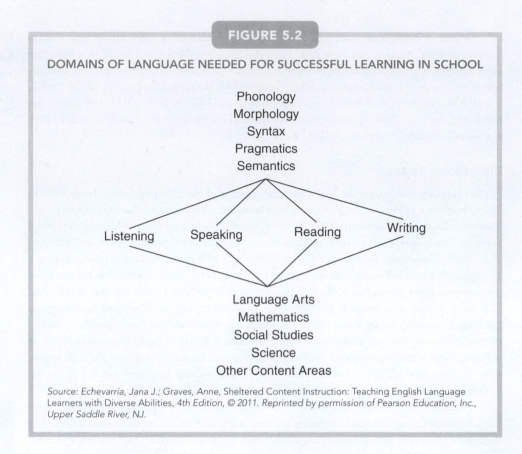

FIGURE 5.2

DOMAINS OF LANGUAGE NEEDED FOR SUCCESSFUL LEARNING IN SCHOOL

Phonology
Morphology
Syntax
Pragmatics
Semantics

Listening   Speaking   Reading   Writing

Language Arts
Mathematics
Social Studies
Science
Other Content Areas

Source: Echevarría, Jana J.; Graves, Anne, Sheltered Content Instruction: Teaching English Language Learners with Diverse Abilities, 4th Edition, © 2011. Reprinted by permission of Pearson Education, Inc., Upper Saddle River, NJ.

- *Limited bilingual.* These students can converse well in both languages, but for some reason they have trouble learning academically. They may have underlying challenges such as learning disabilities or emotional problems. Further testing often is helpful to diagnose problems.

These student profiles are related to the distinction we encountered earlier in the chapter between contextualized conversational language and academic language. You may remember that it takes from 2 to 3 years to develop good conversational language, but 5 to 7 (or even as many as 10) years to master academic language. *Conversational* skills include, for example, using appropriate vocabulary and sentences, asking and answering questions, starting and stopping conversations, listening, and understanding and using idioms.

Academic language includes reading and writing fluency; grammar and syntax; knowledge of specialized vocabulary; following written and oral directions; collaborating with other students on assignments; understanding different types of texts and forms of writing such as fiction, poetry, math problems, science charts and graphs, and timelines in history; and study skills such as outlining, summarizing, and reading comprehension (Echevarría & Graves, 2011). To succeed in learning content, students who are ELLs must put together an understanding of language with knowledge of terms, concepts, and conventions specific to a particular subject such as mathematics or biology. Figure 5.2 shows all the different domains of language that must come together for learning.

If you teach at a school with many students who are ELLs, school personnel will probably do formal assessments to provide appropriate placements for these students.

Generation 1.5: Students in Two Worlds

STOP & THINK Imagine you are this person:

You came to the United States at about the age of 1. Your family was undocumented. You have a younger brother and sister who were born in the United States and are legal citizens, but you are not. Your parents and older siblings worked hard, often two jobs, so that the younger children could get a good education. You attended kindergarten, elementary, and high school in your family's new community in the United States. You graduated from high school with good grades and hoped to attend college, but soon discovered you did not qualify for scholarship support and would have to pay international student tuition, which you cannot afford. Even as a hardworking and promising student, you cannot legally work, vote, or drive in many states, in spite of the fact that you have lived virtually all your life in the United States and speak fluent English. •

If you were this student, you would be a member of a large group, often called Generation 1.5 because their characteristics, educational experiences, and language fluencies are somewhere in between those of students born in the United States and students who are recent immigrants (A. L. Gonzalez, 2010). They were not born in the United States, but have lived here most of their lives because they came with their families when they were young. The language spoken in their homes may not be English, but they often speak fluent conversational English, even if their academic English is not as well developed. Several kinds of Generation 1.5 students have been described by Dubarry and Alves de Lima (2003).

- Students from U.S. territories such as Puerto Rico, sometimes called "in-migrants."
- U.S.-born children of immigrants who live in close-knit communities where the heritage language is maintained by the residents for family and business life.
- Children who are sent by their often-wealthy parents to live with older siblings in order to receive education in the United States, sometimes called "parachute children."
- Children of families who move back and forth between different countries.
- Immigrants who speak other "Englishes" such as English from Jamaica, East India, or Singapore.

These students may share several characteristics and challenges. They may not have developed strong literacy skills in the language used at home because their schooling was not in that language. They may have acquired much of their English through listening to and speaking with friends or older siblings, watching television, or listening to music. They have been called "ear learners" because they have built their knowledge of English on the language they have heard in their environment. But what they hear is often colloquial language or slang, so they may have trouble learning how to read and write accurately in English. Many of us know if the grammar is correct in what we hear or read because we have heard (mostly) accurate grammar all our lives—our ears have taught us well. But for many Generation 1.5 students, their ear learning has given them an imperfect, even inaccurate conception of English grammar. Because they are "ear learners," they may use incorrect verb or noun forms, mispronounce plurals, or mix up words that sound very similar; for example, *confident* and *confidence*. They rely on context, gestures, facial cues, and intonations to make sense of language, so reading is more difficult and proofreading is hard because they cannot "hear" mistakes. Complex academic reading and writing assignments are very challenging (Harklau, Losey, & Siegal, 1999; Reid & Byrd, 1998; Roberge, 2002). In contrast, many of my international graduate students who learned English mostly as "eye learners" through reading, writing, and vocabulary and grammar exercises can write well, but they have more difficulty with oral interactions. Knowing what kind of students you have and how they first learned English should help you understand the mistakes they make and the challenges they face.

ENHANCEDetext *self-check*

TEACHING STUDENTS WHO ARE ENGLISH LANGUAGE LEARNERS

Several terms are associated with bilingual education. In the United States, students who are just learning English are sometimes described as being limited English proficient (LEP). More often, as we have seen, these students are called ELLs, because their primary or heritage language is not English. English as a second language (ESL) is the name given to the *classes* devoted to teaching these students English. Many people prefer term ESOL because students learning English may be adding it as a third or fourth language. This was the name for Felipe Vargas's program (you met him earlier). Limited proficiency in English often means lower academic achievement and poorer job prospects. So one issue around diversity in language development is how we should teach these students.

Two Approaches to English Language Learning

Virtually everyone agrees that all citizens should learn the official language of their country. But when and how should instruction in that language begin? Is it better to teach students who are ELLs to read first in their native language, or should they begin reading instruction in English? Do these children need some oral lessons in English before reading instruction can be effective? Should other subjects, such as mathematics and social studies, be taught in the primary (home) language until the children are fluent in English? As you can see in the *Point/Counterpoint,* debates about this question have raged for quite a while.

RESEARCH ON BILINGUAL EDUCATION. There are strong advantages for simultaneous bilingual learning. Remember Petitto's (2009) finding that monolingual English speakers who participated in a bilingual program excelled in the skills needed for reading in both languages. When the National Literacy Panel on Language—Minority Children and Youth reviewed studies of English-only *immersion* versus native language *maintenance* programs, they found that the students in the native language maintenance programs performed better on many different measured outcomes (Francis, Lesaux, & August, 2006). In a study that directly compared immersion and maintenance programs in 128 classrooms in Texas and California, Lee Branum-Martin and his colleagues (Branum-Martin, Foorman, Francis, & Mehta, 2010) found that the amount of teaching conducted in English and Spanish could not be predicted by type of program—there were many local variations. Some English immersion teachers used quite a bit of Spanish, and some Spanish language maintenance programs taught quite a bit in English. Another finding was that Spanish language maintenance programs had a positive impact on English performance.

A study funded by the U.S. Department of Education (Gersten et al., 2007) identified five major recommendations for English learners, summarized here (Peregoy & Boyle, 2009).

1. Begin instruction with a formative assessment (see Chapter 15) of reading to determine exactly what the English learners know and what they are ready to learn, and to identify students who will need more help in reading.
2. Use small-group interventions to focus instruction on the areas of need identified in the assessments.
3. Target teaching essential vocabulary for the content in your curriculum as well as common words, phrases, and expressions used in class.
4. Directly teach academic English—develop the students' abilities to read texts, write academic assignments, and use formal language and argument.
5. Make wide use of peer-assisted learning, particularly work in pairs, to complete academic tasks.

BILINGUALISM FOR ALL: TWO-WAY IMMERSION. Students in the United States need to master both conversational and academic English to achieve at high levels, but they should not sacrifice their native language in the process. The goal of schools should be balanced bilingualism. One approach to reaching this goal is to create two-way immersion classes that mix students who are learning a second language with students who are native speakers. The objective is for both groups to become fluent in both languages (Peregoy & Boyle, 2009; Sheets, 2005). My daughter spent a summer in such a program in Quebec and was ahead in every French class after that.

For truly effective education for students who are ELLs, we will need many bilingual teachers. If you have a competence in another language, you might want to develop it fully for your teaching. Because there is only one qualified teacher for every 100 ELLs (Hawkins, 2004), promoting language learning is a responsibility for most teachers. Figure 5.3 on page 194 shows teaching strategies that will support language and literacy development across the grade levels.

POINT/COUNTERPOINT
What Is the Best Way to Teach Students Who Are ELLs?

There are two basic positions on this question, which have given rise to two contrasting teaching approaches: one that focuses on *immersion* in English-only teaching to make the transition to English as quickly as possible. The other approach attempts to *maintain or improve* the native language and use that language as the primary teaching language until English skills are more fully developed.

POINT Structured English immersion is the best approach for ELL students. Proponents of the *immersion/fast transition* approach believe that English ought to be introduced as early and as intensively as possible; they argue that valuable learning time is lost if students are taught in their native language. Advocates cite the successes of the Canadian Immersion program as evidence that language immersion works (Baker, 1998). In an article for educational administrators, Kevin Clark claims, "These programs have the potential to accelerate ELLs' English language development and linguistic preparation for grade-level academic content" (K. Clark, 2009, p. 42). Many schools today follow this line of thinking and offer **Structured English immersion (SEI)**. Perspectives on SEI differ, but usually it is defined as having two basic features: (1) teachers use English as much as possible in instruction, and (2) the level of the students' abilities in the class determines how teachers use and teach English: English use and teaching must be appropriate for student abilities (Ramirez, Yuen, & Ramey, 1991). There are at least three reasons why schools adopt this approach (K. Clark, 2009):

1. Some states have mandated this immersion by law and have limited the amount of teaching that can be done in the child's native language.
2. The accountability tests that all school districts in the United States must administer are in English. Schools where students don't score well on these tests face penalties, so getting the test takers to achieve English proficiency as fast as possible benefits the schools.
3. Schools are concerned that ELL students who do not get intensive and continuing English instruction may learn adequate conversational English but never develop the academic English needed for achievement in secondary schools and beyond.

Immersion in a language is the best way to learn a new language and is the basis for many language-learning programs around the world (K. Clark, 2009).

COUNTERPOINT Students' native language should be maintained. Teaching *in* English and hoping students will figure it out is not the same as *teaching* English. Proponents of *native-language maintenance instruction* raise four important issues (Gersten, 1996b; Goldenberg, 1996; Hakuta & Garcia, 1989).

1. Deep learning in the first language supports second-language learning. For example, research on a large national sample that followed eighth graders for 12 years found that for Latino students, proficiency in the first language of Spanish predicted reading ability in English and English reading ability predicted achievement in school and in careers (Guglielmi, 2008, 2012). The metacognitive strategies and knowledge developed when students learn to read in their first language are transferred to reading in a second language as well (van Gelderen, Schoonen, Stoel, de Glopper, & Hulstijn, 2007). So maintaining and increasing proficiency in the first language is important. The learning strategies and academic content (math, science, history, etc.) that students learn in their native language are not forgotten when they learn English. In addition, vocabulary learned in one language can support vocabulary learning in another language (Goodrich, Lonigan, & Farver, 2013).

2. Children who are forced to try to learn math or science in an unfamiliar language are bound to have trouble. What if you had been forced to learn fractions or biology in a second language that you had studied for only a semester? Some psychologists believe students taught by this approach may become **semilingual**; that is, they are not proficient in either language. Being semilingual may be one reason the dropout rate is so high for Latino students from low socioeconomic status backgrounds (Ovando & Collier, 1998).

3. If the first language is neglected and the entire emphasis is on English, students may get the message that their home languages (and therefore, their families and cultures) are second class.

4. Years ago, Kenji Hakuta cited a "paradoxical attitude of admiration and pride for school-attained bilingualism on the one hand and scorn and shame for home-brewed immigrant bilingualism on the other" (Hakuta, 1986, p. 229). Ironically, by the time students have mastered academic

English and let their home language deteriorate, they reach secondary school and are encouraged to learn a "second" language. Sometimes native speakers of Spanish are encouraged to learn French or German, so they risk becoming semilingual in three languages (Miranda, 2008).

BEWARE OF EITHER/OR

It is difficult to separate politics from practice in the debate about bilingual education. It is clear that high-quality bilingual education programs can have positive results. Students improve in the subjects that were taught in their native language, in their mastery of English, and in self-esteem as well (Crawford, 1997; Francis, Lesaux, & August, 2006). ESL programs seem to have positive effects on reading comprehension (Proctor, August, Carlo, & Snow, 2006). But attention today is shifting from debate about general approaches to a focus on effective teaching strategies. As you will see many times in this book, a combination of clarity of learning goals and direct instruction in needed skills seems to be effective and includes learning strategies and tactics, teacher- or peer-guided practice leading to independent practice, authentic and engaging tasks, opportunities for interaction and conversation that are academically focused, and warm encouragement from the teacher (Cheung & Slavin, 2012; Gersten, 1996b; Goldenberg, 1996).

FIGURE 5.3

TEACHING STRATEGIES FOR PROMOTING LEARNING AND LANGUAGE ACQUISITION

Effective teaching for students in bilingual and ESL classrooms combines many strategies—direct instruction, mediation, coaching, feedback, modeling, encouragement, challenge, and authentic activities—many opportunities to read, write, and talk.

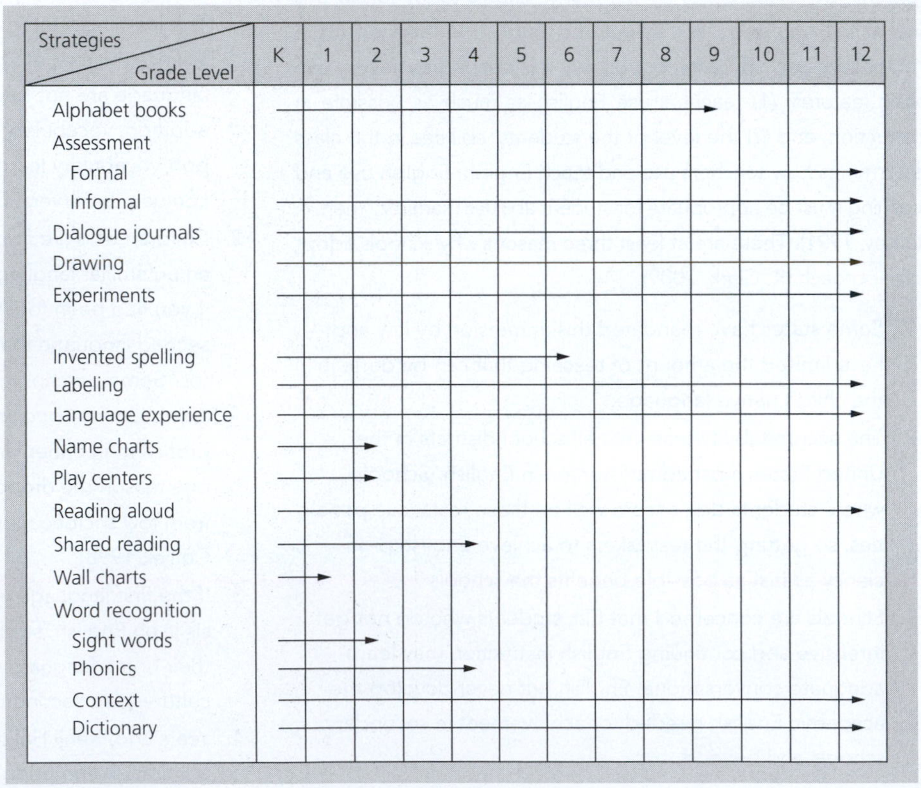

Strategies \ Grade Level	K	1	2	3	4	5	6	7	8	9	10	11	12
Alphabet books	───────────────────────────────→ (K–9)												
Assessment													
Formal			───────────────────────────────→ (3–12)										
Informal	───────────────────────────────→ (K–12)												
Dialogue journals	───────────────────────────────→ (K–12)												
Drawing	───────────────────────────────→ (K–12)												
Experiments	───────────────────────────────→ (K–12)												
Invented spelling	────────────────→ (K–5)												
Labeling	───────────────────────────────→ (K–12)												
Language experience	───────────────────────────────→ (K–12)												
Name charts	───→ (K–2)												
Play centers	───→ (K–2)												
Reading aloud	───────────────────────────────→ (K–12)												
Shared reading	──────────→ (K–4)												
Wall charts	──→ (K–1)												
Word recognition													
Sight words	───→ (K–2)												
Phonics	──────→ (K–3)												
Context	───────────────────────────────→ (K–12)												
Dictionary	───────────────────────────────→ (K–12)												

Source: Peregoy, Suzanne F.; Boyle, Owen F., *Reading, Writing and Learning in ESL: A Resource Book for Teaching K-12 English Learners*, 5th edition, © 2009. Reprinted by permission of Pearson Education, Inc., Upper Saddle River, NJ.

When students exit an immersion or a bilingual program with some English skills, they are not finished learning. The next phase for many students is sheltered instruction.

Sheltered Instruction

The challenge for most teachers working with immigrant and ELL students is to teach the subject matter and develop students' English language skills at the same time. Sheltered instruction is one approach that has proved successful in reaching both goals. Sheltered instruction teaches content to ELL students by putting the words and concepts of the content into context to make the content more understandable. Strategies include simplifying and controlling language, giving attention to the relevant grammar and forms of English—helping students "crack the code," using visuals and gestures, and including real-life supports and examples. In addition, there is an emphasis on student talk and discussion instead of the teacher doing all the talking. To be clearer about what good sheltered instruction looks like, Jana Echevarría and her colleagues (Echevarría, Vogt, & Short, 2014) identified eight key elements: preparation, building background, comprehensible input, strategies, interaction, practice and application, lesson delivery, and review and assessment. Then the researchers developed an observational system to check that each element was included in teaching. The system is called the Sheltered Instruction Observation Protocol (SIOP®). Figure 5.4 gives some examples of what each element of SIOP® might include.

What might a SIOP* lesson look like? There are many ways to design lessons that meet the standards in Figure 5.4. Table 5.6 on page 197 describes seven different lesson structures and activities to help students understand content and develop language skills.

Video 5.4
The challenge for most teachers working with immigrant and ELL students is to teach the subject matter and develop students' English language skills at the same time. **Sheltered instruction** is one approach that has proved successful in reaching both goals. In this video, Dr. Vogt explains why sheltered instruction is important for immigrant and ELL students.

ENHANCEDetext *video example*

FIGURE 5.4

SOME EXAMPLES OF THE SHELTERED INSTRUCTION OBSERVATION PROTOCOL (SIOP®)

The SIOP® has 30 characteristics or areas to assess during observation. Each characteristic is rated from 4 (Highly Evident) to 0 (Not Evident) or NA (Not Applicable). These ratings are converted into a score. (L1 means the original language, and L2 means the second language.)

Observer: _____   Teacher: _____

Date: _____   School: _____

Grade: _____   ESL level: _____

Class: _____   Lesson: Multi-day Single-day (circle one)

Total Points Possible: 120 (Subtract 4 points for each NA given)

Total Points Earned _____   *Percentage Score* _____

Directions: Circle the number that best reflects what you observe in a sheltered lesson. You may give a score from 0–4. Cite under "Comments" specific examples of the behaviors observed.

	Highly Evident	Somewhat Evident		Not Evident	NA
	4	3	2	1	0	
Preparation						
1. **Content objectives** clearly defined, displayed, and reviewed with students	☐	☐	☐	☐	☐	☐
2. **Language objectives** clearly defined, displayed, and reviewed with students	☐	☐	☐	☐	☐	☐
3. **Content concepts** appropriate for age and educational background level of students	☐	☐	☐	☐	☐	☐
4. **Supplementary materials** used to a high degree, making the lesson clear and meaningful (e.g., computer programs, graphs, models, visuals)	☐	☐	☐	☐	☐	☐
5. **Adaptation of content** (e.g., text, assignment) to all levels of student proficiency	☐	☐	☐	☐	☐	☐
6. **Meaningful activities** that integrate lesson concepts (e.g., interviews, letter writing, simulations, models) with language practice opportunities for reading, writing, listening, and/or speaking	☐	☐	☐	☐	☐	☐

Comments:

(*continued*)

FIGURE 5.4 (Continued)

	Highly Evident		Somewhat Evident		Not Evident	NA
	4	3	2	1	0	
Building Background						
7. **Concepts explicitly linked** to students' background experiences	☐	☐	☐	☐	☐	☐
8. **Links explicitly made** between past learning and new concepts	☐	☐	☐	☐	☐	☐
9. **Key vocabulary emphasized** (e.g., introduced, written, repeated, and highlighted for students to see) *Comments:*	☐	☐	☐	☐	☐	☐
Comprehensible						
10. **Speech** appropriate for students' proficiency level (e.g., slower rate, enunciation and simple sentence structure for beginners)	☐	☐	☐	☐	☐	☐
11. **Clear explanation** of academic tasks	☐	☐	☐	☐	☐	☐
12. A variety of techniques used to make **content concepts** clear (e.g., modeling, visuals, hands-on activities, demonstration, gestures, body language) *Comments:*	☐	☐	☐	☐	☐	☐
Strategies						
13. Ample opportunities for students to use **learning strategies**	☐	☐	☐	☐	☐	☐
14. **Scaffolding techniques** consistently used assisting and supporting student understanding (e.g., think-alouds)	☐	☐	☐	☐	☐	☐
15. A variety of questions or tasks that promote **higher-order thinking skills** (e.g., literal, analytical, and interpretive questions) *Comments:*	☐	☐	☐	☐	☐	☐
Interaction						
16. Frequent opportunities for **interaction** and discussion between teacher/student and among students, which encourage elaborated responses about lesson concepts	☐	☐	☐	☐	☐	☐
17. **Grouping configurations** support language and content objectives of the lesson	☐	☐	☐	☐	☐	☐
18. Sufficient **wait time for student response** consistently provided	☐	☐	☐	☐	☐	☐
19. Ample opportunities for students to **clarify key concepts in L1** as needed with aide, peer, or L1 text *Comments:*						
Practice/Application						
20. **Hands-on materials and/or manipulatives** provided for students to practice using new content knowledge	☐	☐	☐	☐	☐	☐
21. Activities provided for students to **apply content and language knowledge** in the classroom	☐	☐	☐	☐	☐	☐
22. Activities integrate all **language skills** (i.e., reading, listening, and speaking) *Comments:*	☐	☐	☐	☐	☐	☐
Lesson Delivery						
23. **Content objectives** clearly supported by lesson delivery	☐	☐	☐	☐	☐	☐
24. **Language objectives** clearly supported by lesson delivery	☐	☐	☐	☐	☐	☐
25. **Students engaged** approximately 90%–100% of the period	☐	☐	☐	☐	☐	☐
26. **Pacing** of the lesson appropriate to the students' ability level *Comments:*	☐	☐	☐	☐	☐	☐
Review/Assessment						
27. Comprehensive **review of key vocabulary**	☐	☐	☐	☐	☐	☐
28. Comprehensive **review of key content concepts**	☐	☐	☐	☐	☐	☐
29. Regular **feedback provided** to students on their output (e.g., language, content, work)	☐	☐	☐	☐	☐	☐
30. **Assessment of student comprehension** and learning of all lesson objectives (e.g., spot checking, group response) throughout the lesson *Comments:*	☐	☐	☐	☐	☐	☐

Source: Echevarría, J., Vogt, M., & Short, D. J. (2014). Making Content Comprehensible for Secondary English Learners: The SIOP® Model (2nd ed.). Reprinted with permission from Pearson Education, Inc.

TABLE 5.6 • Ideas for Lesson Structures in SIOP® That Encourage Understanding of Content and Build Language Skills

STRUCTURE	EXAMPLE/WHAT DOES IT LOOK LIKE?	RATIONALE/WHY DOES IT WORK?
Think-Pair-Share	Instead of asking questions of the whole class and calling on two or three students to respond, the teacher asks everyone to think of an answer or respond to a prompt and tell it to a partner. Then, the teacher calls on some students to share their responses with the whole class.	All students have a chance to think and speak about the topic. Allows teachers to monitor student understanding of the content and language objectives during a lesson.
Chunk and Chew	The teacher pauses after every 10 minutes and directs students to talk with a partner or in a small group about what they have just learned. In SIOP® lessons, the student talk is carefully structured by the teacher with specific prompts and/or sentence starters, such as "If I could interview any author we read this year, it would be. . . . because. . . ."	Makes new information easier to learn by "chunking" it into learnable, bite-size pieces (see Chapter 8 for why this is important). Gives students a chance to talk using concepts and content from the lesson.
Roam and Review	The teacher poses a reflection question (e.g., "What was the most important thing you learned today?" or "What surprised you in our studies today?") and students think silently, then stand and roam the classroom, discussing their ideas with classmates.	Students synthesize what they have learned and communicate it in a more conversational manner. They practice communicating.
Podcasts	Students prepare a 2- to 3-minute oral summary on a topic they have selected or the teacher has assigned. They rehearse and then record it on a podcast or an audio file for use on the class computer.	Provides practice in speaking and the chance to hear and improve language. Having an audience increases motivation and encourages careful preparation.
TV Talk Show	Small groups plan a talk show on a topic with multiple parameters that they have studied. One student is the host and interviewer; others are the guests. For example, after studying extreme weather phenomena, one guest might be an expert on hurricanes, another on blizzards, a third on earthquakes, and a fourth on tornadoes.	Video recording of the show allows the teacher or the students to assess how well the students spoke, used key vocabulary, responded to host questions, and so forth. Having an audience increases motivation and encourages careful preparation.
Writing Headlines	Students capture the essence of a day's lesson, section of a text read, video watched, or information presented orally by writing a headline, and then share their headline.	Encourages students to use descriptive language and focus on word choice to create compelling headlines.
E-Journals and Wiki Entries	Students write in an e-journal daily or once a week to reflect on what they have been learning. At the end of a unit, the teacher might ask students to write an online entry for a class wiki that presents key information on a topic being studied.	Encourages synthesizing information and writing longer pieces.

Source: Based on Echevarría, J., Vogt, M., & Short, D. J. (2014). Making Content Comprehensible for Secondary English Learners: The SIOP® Model (2nd ed.), pp. 198–199. Boston, MA: Pearson.

Affective and Emotional/Social Considerations

STOP & THINK You walk into one of your education classes. The instructor moves to the lectern and says:

Mina-san, ohayō gozaimasu. Kyō wa, kyō iku shinrigaku no jū gyō ja arimasen. Kyō wa, nihon no bangō, ichi kara jū made benkyō -oshimasu. Soshite, kono kyō shitsu wa Amerika no kyō shitsu ja arimasen. Ima wa Nihon no kyō shitsu desu. Nihon no kyō shitsu dewa, shinakerebanaranai koto wa mittsu mo arimasu. Tatsu, rei, suwaru. Mina-san, tatte kudasai. Doshite tatteimasen ka? Wakarimasen ka?

The class continues in the same way until you are handed the "test" and told to "Do your best—this is 20% of your grade." You can't believe it! What would you do? •

Does this seem impossible? Actually, one of my doctoral students (Yough, 2010) designed this lesson (without the test) so his educational psychology class would experience how it feels to have important content taught in a language you don't speak (assuming your Japanese is a bit rusty!). Research on ELL students shows that they may experience severe challenges and stress in school. They may feel that they don't belong and that others are making fun of them or just ignoring them. Everyone else seems to know the rules and the right words. It takes courage and persistence to keep trying to communicate; it is easier to say as little as possible. So the practice in communicating that these students desperately need just doesn't happen.

What can teachers do to support students' courage and persistence in communicating? The first step is to create a classroom community that is caring and respectful. We explore strategies for creating classroom community in Chapter 13. Echevarría and Graves (2011) suggest additional steps to provide emotional support and increase self-esteem for ELL students, as you can see in the *Guidelines: Providing Emotional Support and Increasing Self-Esteem for Students Who Are ELLs*.

Another problem is related to cultural differences. As we saw earlier, students who immigrate to the United States in their middle or high school years may have experienced very different educational systems and educational values "back home." They may have been very successful in those systems, perhaps by excelling in the memorizing required by the curriculum. When they encounter a different approach to education, suddenly they may struggle and feel as if they know little or nothing. As a teacher, you need to learn the strengths of these students and acknowledge their abilities—and build on their knowledge. We turn to that topic next.

GUIDELINES
Providing Emotional Support and Increasing Self-Esteem for Students Who Are ELLs

Create learning activities that promote success in reading and writing.

Examples

1. Have weekly individual conferences with younger students and record their retelling of a story. Let students edit and revise the dictation and read it to a partner.
2. Do interactive journals with older students—collect each week and write back.

Make sure students have plenty of time to practice and get careful, targeted corrections.

Examples

1. Point out privately what is correct, almost correct, and wrong in written work.
2. Be sensitive about public oral corrections, and build on what is correct, but do not accept clearly incorrect answers.

Connect teaching to relevant knowledge from students' lives.

Examples

1. Ask students to survey family members about favorite films. Use film characters to discuss elements of literature—plot, point of view, and so on.
2. Have students create construction firms and plan projects to learn math concepts.

Actively involve learners.

Examples

1. Use timelines in history compared to personal timelines based on family history.
2. Do projects in science based on animals or farming for rural students.

Use different grouping strategies.

Examples

1. Try pairs for writing stories and practicing oral presentations.
2. Create small teams to research recent immigrant groups' culture and language.

Provide native language support.

Examples

1. Learn and use as much of the students' language as possible—if they can learn, so can you.
2. Find Internet translation sources and local native-speaking volunteers.
3. Bring native-language magazines and books into the classroom.

Involve family and community members.

Examples

1. Bring in storytellers, local business owners, artists, craftspeople.
2. Create a Welcome Center for your class.

Hold high expectations for all students, and communicate these expectations clearly.

Examples

1. Keep scrapbooks of previous students who have gone on to careers or college.
2. Don't accept mediocre work.
3. Be a model of respect for diversity and an enemy of bigotry.

Source: Echevarría, Jana J.; Graves, Anne, Sheltered Content Instruction: Teaching English Language Learners with Diverse Abilities, 4th Edition, © 2011. Reprinted by permission of Pearson Education, Inc., Upper Saddle River, NJ.

Working with Families: Using the Tools of the Culture

As noted earlier in the chapter, when families are more involved in the schools, their children are more successful (Dearing et al., 2006). Here we consider several ways to engage families: building on funds of knowledge, Welcome Centers, and student-led conferences.

FUNDS OF KNOWLEDGE AND WELCOME CENTERS. Luis Moll and his colleagues wanted a better way to teach the children of working-class Mexican American families in the barrio schools of Tucson, Arizona (Moll et al., 1992). Rather than adopt a model of remediating the students' deficits, Moll decided to identify and build on the tools and cultural funds of knowledge of their families. By interviewing the families, the researchers identified their extensive knowledge about agriculture, economics, medicine, household management, mechanics, science, and religion. When teachers based their assignments on these funds of knowledge, students were more engaged and teachers were educated about their students' lives. For example, by participating in a funds of knowledge project, one teacher realized that she always had thought about her students in terms of deficits and problems—poor achievement, alienation, family troubles, and poverty. But then she got to know the families by focusing on their resources, not their limitations. She also learned that her students' actions often were misinterpreted:

> Strong family values and responsibility are characteristics of the families I visited. . . . My students were expected to participate in household chores such as cleaning house, car maintenance, food preparation, washing dishes, and caring for younger siblings. I learned what this insight meant when one of my students was unable to attend school drama and chorus rehearsals one day. In my journal entry detailing this project, I noted the following incident:
>
> Wednesday (11/25/92) The music teacher commented (to me), "You know, Leticia has missed two chorus rehearsals." Before I could answer, the school drama teacher stepped in to add, "Oh, she's very irresponsible." She had signed up to be in the Drama Club and had only been to two meetings. I said "Wait a minute. . . ." I then told her how Leticia's younger brother was being hospitalized for a series of operations, and when the mother had to leave, she left Leticia in charge of caring for her two younger siblings. In fact, her missing after-school rehearsals was an act of responsibility, obedience and loyalty to her family. (Gonzales et al., 1993)

By engaging with students' families, this teacher learned about the valuable cognitive resources in the community, and her respect for her students and their families increased. Moll's work also was the basis for the Welcome Center project in a pre-kindergarten through fifth-grade elementary school in the Southwest. Within 4 years the school had gone from 12% to 43% Latino/a, with most of these students recently arrived immigrants. The Welcome Center was a "social and instructional space where recent immigrant families in the school would come to trade a variety of expertise, meet each other, gather information about their children's education, and share general information on practical matters" (DaSilva Iddings, 2009, p. 207). The center was a bright, comfortable, informal space with a small kitchen, picnic tables, computer and printer, books and magazines in Spanish and English, math manipulatives, showcases for children's work, and other welcoming features. Fifth-graders offered homework assistance after school at the center. Spanish-speaking families taught classes in Spanish, cooking, and dancing for community members. English literacy activities were provided for adults and children learning together. The center produced many success stories— teachers who connected with students' families and came to appreciate the value of their students' language and culture, immigrant families who moved toward citizenship, and others who opened businesses and restaurants. Connections with families may be especially important for the success of immigrant students. The *Guidelines: Family and Community Partnerships* on the next page has more ideas.

STUDENT-LED CONFERENCES. Parent–teacher conferences have been around for as long as I can remember. These can be productive but also disappointing or confrontational too. One way to get students more invested in the conferences and maybe even in learning itself is to put the students in charge of leading the conference, presenting work to their parents, explaining what they

Video 5.5
In this brief video, Dr. Olmedo describes funds of knowledge that emphasize the importance of tapping into the cultural funds of knowledge children bring to the classroom.

ENHANCEDetext *video example*

GUIDELINES
Family and Community Partnerships

WELCOMING ALL FAMILIES

Make sure communication with families is understandable.

Examples

1. Use the families' home languages wherever possible.
2. Use oral forms of communication—phone calls or home visits—whenever possible.

Balance positive and negative messages.

Examples

1. Send home notes or descriptions about their child's accomplishments or acts of kindness.
2. Explain disciplinary actions as ways of helping children succeed.

Establish systems for welcoming new families.

Examples

1. Assign more experienced "buddy" parents to communicate with new families.
2. Connect with multilingual media in your community to make announcements about school.

Make sure messages get through.

Examples

1. Establish telephone trees or texting networks.
2. Set the expectation that you will send a weekly note home so parents can ask their children about it.
3. Establish a class newsletter or Web site, and incorporate multiple languages.

---

have learned and how they learned it. Students take more responsibility for why they succeeded, and perhaps why they failed. How could they improve? What are their goals for the next marking period? When students lead conferences, parents may be more likely to attend and more engaged. With careful planning and preparation, teachers can create a sense of a team working for the good of the student (Haley & Austin, 2014).

There are many ways to use and design student-led conferences. Most teachers work with students to set clear learning goals for specific projects and perhaps provide rubrics to guide self-assessment (see Chapter 15 for more idea rubrics). It is important to notify families well in advance and perhaps even gather information from them about their hopes and concerns for their child, their interests, and their funds of knowledge. Let them know that their child will be leading the conference and if necessary will be translating for them. Also assure families that there will be time at the end of the conference for them to meet with you privately, without their child, to share concerns and ask questions.

During the conference, the student leads the discussion, showing work and perhaps responding to prompts such as, "What I like about this paper is. . . ." "I learned. . . ." "If I did this again, I would improve. . . ." "My next goal is. . . ." To do a good job of leading the conference and explaining their work, students should practice with each other. With all this preparation, it is discouraging if family members do not show up, so you should have a back-up plan for another adult to sit in the parent's place and engage with the student. See Table 5.7 for a timeline planning guide.

SPECIAL CHALLENGES: STUDENTS WHO ARE ENGLISH LANGUAGE LEARNERS WITH DISABILITIES AND SPECIAL GIFTS

If you remember the four profiles of ELLs described earlier, you know that one type of student may have learning disabilities, but it is very difficult to tell because the student's language is limited. ELLs with disabilities are difficult to diagnose—expert assessment is necessary (S. B. Garcia & Tyler, 2010). Sometimes students are inappropriately placed in special education just because they have problems with English, but other times, students who would benefit from special services are denied placement because their problems are assumed to be simply language learning issues (U.S. Department of Education, 2004). In addition, students with special talents and gifts may be difficult to recognize.

TABLE 5.7 • **Timeline for Planning and Conducting Student-Led Conferences**

WHEN	WHAT
At the beginning of the grading period	Identify several pieces of student work: projects, essays, drawings, quizzes, reports, and so on, that will be the focus of the student-led conference at the end of the grading period. Establish clear assessment criteria and perhaps a rubric for each.
During the grading period	Have students practice self-assessment using the criteria or rubrics and share their assessments with others in the class.
A few weeks before the conferences	Send a notice to families explaining the student-led conferences and asking for information such as the child's interests, responsibilities at home, likes and dislikes about school, time spent watching TV or gaming, number and age of siblings, or hours spent on homework. You might also ask about family favorite activities, parents' interests and funds of knowledge, and their concerns and goals for their child.
A week before the conferences	Have students make final notes about how they will present their work to their families, and then role-play conferences with each other, taking the role of both parents and students.
In the week after the conference	Ask students to reflect about what they learned preparing for and leading the conference. How will they use the experience to guide their future learning?

Students Who Are English Language Learners with Disabilities

As a teacher, one of your decisions will be whether to refer a struggling ELL student for testing. Of course, the first step is to use the best teaching approaches, incorporating sheltered instruction to develop both subject matter learning and English language development. But if progress seems much slower than usual, you might ask the following questions, suggested by George De George (2008): What is the student's educational background, and what is the background of his or her family? When did the student come to the United States? Being born in the United States but speaking another language at home or immigrating when very young can make learning in the early grades more difficult. Students who immigrate after successfully learning in their home country schools have literacy skills to build on. They know some academic content, and they know they can learn in school. In contrast, the children who speak another language at home and have never been to school have no oral English to use as they learn the letters and sounds of written English. Bilingual instruction is the best strategy here.

Other questions to ask when considering a referral are: Were there any problems or complications during the mother's pregnancy? Has the child experienced any serious injuries or illnesses? Has the child moved around a great deal? Has the child had adequate opportunities to learn in a good bilingual or ESL program? Have the teachers who worked with the child been trained in teaching ESL? Is the student making progress, even if he or she is behind others the same age? Does the student have any talents or special skills to build on? These questions will help you determine if the student's difficulties are due to lack of learning opportunities, inadequate teaching, or a disability. No matter what the diagnosis—attention and appropriate teaching are needed. Students who have difficulties with English are much more likely to drop out of school (U.S. Department of Education, 2004).

Reaching Every Student: Recognizing Giftedness in Bilingual Students

Because they may be struggling with academic English, even though they are very knowledgeable, bilingual students may be overlooked for gifted and talented programs. A 10th-grade boy from Mexico, in the United States for 2 years, told an interviewer in Spanish:

> High school is hard for me because my English is so limited. . . . There are times when I feel a lot of pressure because I want to say something, but I don't know how to say it. There are many times when the teacher is asking questions, I know the answer, but I am afraid that people might laugh at me. (Walqui, 2008, p. 104)

TABLE 5.8 • **Identifying Bilingual Students with Gifts and Talents**
Here are some ideas for identifying bilingual students with gifts and talents.
Watch for students who.

_____ Learn English quickly
_____ Take risks in trying to communicate in English
_____ Practice English skills by themselves
_____ Initiate conversations with native English speakers
_____ Do not frustrate easily
_____ Are curious about new words or phrases and practice them
_____ Question word meanings; for example, "How can a bat be an animal and also something you use to hit a ball?"
_____ Look for similarities between words in their native language and English
_____ Are able to modify their language for less-capable English speakers
_____ Use English to demonstrate leadership skills; for example, use English to resolve disagreements and to facilitate cooperative learning groups
_____ Prefer to work independently or with students whose level of English proficiency is higher than theirs
_____ Are able to express abstract verbal concepts with a limited English vocabulary
_____ Are able to use English in a creative way; for example, can make puns, poems, jokes, or original stories in English
_____ Become easily bored with routine tasks or drill work
_____ Have a great deal of curiosity
_____ Are persistent; stick to a task
_____ Are independent and self-sufficient
_____ Have a long attention span
_____ Become absorbed with self-selected problems, topics, and issues
_____ Retain, easily recall, and use new information
_____ Demonstrate social maturity, especially in the home or community

Source: Castellano, Jaime A.; Diaz, Eva, Reaching New Horizons: Gifted and Talented Education for Culturally and Linguistically Diverse Students, © 2002. Reprinted by permission of Pearson Education, Inc., Upper Saddle River, NJ.

This student might well be gifted. To identify bilingual students who are gifted, you can use a case study or portfolio approach in order to collect a variety of evidence, including interviews with parents and peers, formal and informal assessments, samples of student work and performances, and student self-assessments. The checklist in Table 5.8, from Castellano and Diaz (2002), is a useful guide.

ENHANCEDetext *self-check*

SUMMARY

- **The Development of Language (pp. 172–179)**

  How are humans predisposed to develop language? What roles do culture and learning play? Cultures create words for the concepts that are important to them. Children develop language as they build on other cognitive abilities by actively trying to make sense of what they hear, looking for patterns, and making up rules. In this process, built-in biases and rules may limit the search and guide the pattern recognition. Reward and correction play a role in helping children learn correct language use, but the child's thought processes are very important.

  What are the elements of language? By age 5, most children have mastered almost all the sounds of their native language. In terms of vocabulary, we understand more words than we use. By age 6, children understand up to 20,000 words and use about 2,600 words. Understanding of words that express abstract ideas and hypothetical situations comes later as cognitive abilities develop. As children develop an understanding of grammar, they may apply new rules too widely, saying "broked" for "broken," for example. Understanding the passive voice in syntax develops after understanding active voice.

  What are pragmatics and metalinguistic awareness? Pragmatics is knowledge about how to use language—when, where, how, and to whom to speak. Metalinguistic awareness, knowledge about your own use of language and how language works, begins around age 5 or 6 and grows throughout life.

  What are the most important skills that help literacy emerge? Research has identified two broad categories of skills that are important for later reading: (1) understanding sounds and codes such as knowing that letters have names, that sounds are associated with letters, and that words are made up of sounds; and (2) oral language skills such as expressive and receptive vocabulary, knowledge of syntax, and the ability to understand and tell stories. One way to think about emergent literacy that captures both code and oral language skills for emergent literacy is the notion of inside-out skills (the ability to decode units of print into units of sound and units of sound into units of language) and outside-in skills and processes (the ability to understand those auditory derivations, which involves placing them in the correct conceptual and contextual framework). For bilingual Spanish-speaking students, growth in receptive language in Spanish or English predicts early reading outcomes. Parents and teachers can support emerging literacy by reading with children, retelling stories and talking about them, and limiting time spent watching television.

- **Diversity in Language Development (pp. 179–186)**

  What is involved in learning two languages? Children can learn two languages at once if they have adequate opportunities in both languages. There are cognitive advantages to learning more than one language, so it is valuable to retain your heritage language even as you learn another. The best time to learn accurate pronunciation is early childhood, but people of any age can learn a new language. Having overheard a language as a child can improve one's ability to learn that language as an adult. Even though the advantages of bilingualism seem clear, many children and adults are losing their heritage language. Rather than losing one language to gain another, the goal should be balanced bilingualism—being equally fluent in both languages. People who can communicate in both a spoken and a signed language or in two different signed languages are considered bilingual.

  What does it mean to be truly bilingual? Some definitions of bilingualism focus exclusively on a language-based meaning: Bilingual people, or bilinguals, speak two languages. Other definitions are more rigorous and define bilinguals as adults who use their two languages effectively in their adult daily life, which includes being bicultural as well—moving back and forth between two cultures and two languages while still maintaining a sense of identity. Proficiency in a second language has two separate aspects: face-to-face communication (*contextualized language skills*) that take about 2 to 3 years in a good program to develop, and academic uses of language such as reading and doing grammar exercises (known as *academic English*) that take about 5 to 10 years to develop. Bilingual students also often struggle with social adjustment problems relating to biculturalism.

  How do cultural differences affect bilingual students? Cultural differences might interfere with developing academic English and content understanding. For example, many Asian students come from a culture that believes asking the teacher questions is rude and inappropriate because questioning implies that the teacher has done a poor job of instruction. Teachers need to ask themselves why their students who are ELLs are not asking questions. Beliefs about learning shaped by culture and previous experiences in different kinds of classrooms may explain why students who are ELLs seem quiet and reluctant to speak in class. These students may also think that their teachers are not very good because the teachers do not explain everything. They also may strongly prefer memorization as a learning strategy if memorization was emphasized in their previous schools.

- **Dialect Differences in the Classroom (pp. 186–187)**

What is a dialect? A dialect is any variety of a language spoken by a particular group. The dialect is part of the group's collective identity. Every person reading this book speaks at least one dialect, maybe more, because there is no one absolute standard English. Dialects differ in their rules about pronunciation, grammar, and vocabulary, but it is important to remember that these differences are not errors. Each dialect is logical, complex, and rule governed. There are even some differences in how males and females talk, called genderlects.

How should teachers take dialects into account? Teachers can be sensitive to their own possible negative stereotypes about children who speak a different dialect. Teachers also can ensure comprehension by repeating instructions using different words and by asking students to paraphrase instructions or give examples. The best teaching approach seems to be to focus on understanding the students and to accept their language as a valid and correct system, but to teach the alternative forms of English (or whatever the dominant language is in your country) that are used in more formal work settings and writing so that the students will have access to a range of opportunities.

- **Teaching Immigrant Students (pp. 187–191)**

Distinguish between the terms *immigrant* and *refugee*. Immigrants are people who voluntarily leave their country to become permanent residents in a new place. Refugees are a special group of immigrants who also relocate voluntarily, but they are fleeing their home country because it is not safe.

Distinguish between the "melting pot" and multiculturalism. Statistics point to increasing cultural diversity in American society. Old views—that minority group members and immigrants should lose their cultural distinctiveness and assimilate completely in the American "melting pot" or be regarded as culturally deficient—are being replaced by new emphases on multiculturalism, equal educational opportunity, and the celebration of cultural diversity.

What is Gen 1.5? Generation 1.5 are students whose characteristics, educational experiences, and language fluencies are somewhere in between those of students born in the United States and students who are recent immigrants. They were not born in the United States but have lived here most of their lives because they came with their families when they were young. The language spoken in their homes may not be English, but they often speak fluent conversational English, even if their academic English is not as well developed. They may tend to be "ear learners" who have mastered language by listening to and interacting with the language models around them.

- **Teaching Students Who Are English Language Learners (pp. 191–200)**

What are the names related to English learners? English learners sometimes are called LEP. More often, these students are described as students who are ELLs, because their primary or heritage language is not English. The classes devoted to teaching these students English are called ESL classes. Limited proficiency in English often means lower academic achievement and poorer job prospects. So one issue around diversity in language development is how we should teach these students.

What are four general profiles of students who are ELLs? Students who are *balanced bilinguals* speak, read, and write well both in their first language and in English. *Monolingual/literate students* are literate in their native language (at or above grade level when working in their native language), but speak limited English. *Monolingual/preliterate students* are not literate. They may not read or write in their native language, or they may have very limited literacy skills. *Limited bilingual* students can converse well in both languages, but for some reason they have trouble learning academically. There may be underlying challenges such as learning disabilities or emotional problems.

What is bilingual education? Although there is much debate about the best way to help bilingual students master English, studies show it is best if they are not forced to abandon their first language. The more proficient students are in their first language, the faster they will master the second.

What is sheltered instruction? Sheltered instruction is one approach that has proved successful in teaching English and academic content. Sheltered instruction teaches content to students who are ELLs by putting the words and concepts of the content into context to make the content more understandable. Strategies include simplifying and controlling language, giving attention to the relevant grammar and forms of English—helping students "crack the code," using visuals and gestures, and including real life supports and examples. In addition, there is an emphasis on student talk and discussion instead of the teacher doing all the talking. There are affective and emotional considerations for students who are ELLs. They may experience severe challenges and stress in school. They may feel that they don't belong, that others are making fun of them, or just ignoring them. Building on students' funds of cultural knowledge and using student-led conferences are ways to make classrooms more supportive and teaching more effective.

- **Special Challenges: Students Who Are English Language Learners with Disabilities and Special Gifts (pp. 200–202)**

  How do teachers deal with the special needs of students who are English language learners? As a teacher, one of your decisions will be whether to refer a struggling student who is an ELL for testing. Of course, the first step is to use the best teaching approaches, incorporating sheltered instruction to develop both subject matter learning and English language development. But if progress seems much slower than usual, you might refer the student for observation or testing. No matter what the diagnosis—attention and appropriate teaching are needed. Students who have difficulties with English are much more likely to drop out of school. And because language differences can mask giftedness, teachers should make special efforts to identify bilingual students and students who are ELLs who have gifts and talents.

PRACTICE USING WHAT YOU HAVE LEARNED

To access and complete the exercises, click the link under the images below.

Sheltered Instruction

ENHANCEDetext *application exercise*

Emergent Literacy

ENHANCEDetext *application exercise*

KEY TERMS

Academic language   184
Balanced bilingualism   181
Bilingual   179
Code switching   187
Critical periods   180
Cultural deficit model   188
Dialect   186
Emergent literacy   175
English as a second language (ESL)   191
English language learners (ELLs)   189
Expressive vocabulary   173

Funds of knowledge   199
Genderlects   187
Generation 1.5   191
Heritage language   181
Immigrants   188
Inside-out skills   176
Limited English proficient (LEP)   191
Melting pot   188
Metalinguistic awareness   175
Monolingual   179
Outside-in skills   176

Overregularize   174
Pragmatics   174
Receptive vocabulary   173
Refugees   188
Semilingual   193
Sensitive periods   180
Sheltered instruction   195
Sheltered Instruction Observation
    Protocol (SIOP®)   195
Structured English immersion (SEI)   193
Syntax   174

CONNECT AND EXTEND TO LICENSURE

MULTIPLE-CHOICE QUESTIONS

1. During the 1960s and 1970s, some educators suggested that students of color and students living in poverty were culturally disadvantaged. The cultural deficit model implied students' home cultures were inferior because they failed to prepare students to fit into school. What is the current idea held by educational psychologists with respect to mismatches between students' home environments and school?

   A. Incompatibilities may exist between the students' home culture and the expectations of the school.

   B. Deficits between the home culture and the school can be compensated through special education services.

   C. Historically, the gap between the home environment and the school environment is inconsequential.

   D. There is an increasing sense that ethnic groups should want to assimilate completely into mainstream American society.

2. Ms. Carney decided to visit the Mexican families of her ELL students to gain a better understanding of their backgrounds and culture. Drawing upon the research of Luis Moll and current best practices, what do you think Ms. Carney decided to do with the new information she gained from her family visits?

   A. She shared it with her supervisors and continued to remediate the students' deficits.

   B. She made notations about the information she gathered in her students' cumulative files.

   C. She decided to identify and build on the tools and cultural funds of knowledge of her students' families.

   D. She decided to not share the information because her supervisors may not have approved of her family visits.

3. Once Mr. Heney learned that his Asian ELL students consider it rude to ask the teacher questions because questioning implies that the teacher has done a poor job of teaching, he could generalize to which one of the following assumptions?

   A. If his English language learners are not asking questions, he needs to ask them why.

   B. He should always quiz his Asian students because they may not be able to understand.

   C. Asian students are always very polite, but their silence can mean they do not respect him as a teacher.

   D. Mr. Heney cannot make any generalizations about culture and learning.

4. One important way in which a teacher can motivate students is to show an interest in their lives. All but which one of the following are appropriate motivational strategies that demonstrate an interest in the lives of students from diverse backgrounds?

   A. Incorporate students' traditions into writing and language arts activities.

   B. Show respect for students' diversity by learning some key words in their language.

   C. Ask students to write a three-page essay in English about their family.

   D. Inquire about students' past experiences in their native country.

CONSTRUCTED-RESPONSE QUESTIONS

Case

Nick Takis was delighted that his portfolio had helped him land his first teaching job in Texas. Although he had never been to that state, he was excited about the prospect of his own classroom. When he arrived for his 2-week induction period in August, his sunny mood began to wane. He learned that several of the students in his class were not fluent in English. To prepare for the challenge ahead, he drew upon what one of his favorite professors always suggested, "Break big projects down to bite size, and make sure you have all the information you need to make decisions."

5. What are the four general profiles of English learners in today's classroom with which Nick should familiarize himself?

6. What tips could you offer Nick Takis that would help him to promote language learning in his class?

ENHANCEDetext *licensure exam*

TEACHERS' CASEBOOK

WHAT WOULD THEY DO? CULTURES CLASH IN THE CLASSROOM

Here is how several expert teachers said they would establish positive relationships with the class described at the beginning of the chapter that included African American, Asian, and Latino/a students who did not get along.

JENNIFER PINCOSKI—Learning Resource Teacher: K–12
Lee County School District, Fort Myers, FL

The teacher has difficulty connecting with his/her students because the cultures are so different and the groups don't understand each other. The teacher's discomfort is evident, which is problematic because as the classroom leader, a teacher's attitude and behavior set the tone for everyone. Establishment of an inclusive and accepting learning environment starts at the top. It is important to model understanding and acceptance by respecting students as individuals, celebrating their differences, and showing a genuine interest in their lives.

This is a good opportunity to get to know students on a more personal level. After assigning a quiet, independent task, the teacher can use this time to have brief conferences with each student one on one. Conferences should focus on becoming acquainted with the students, learning about their interests, and discussing goals. Not only does this help develop positive relationships, it also provides important information that can be used to plan future lessons and activities.

Furthermore, in an effort to get students from different cultures to interact, the teacher may need to change the physical arrangement of the room and/or reassign seats. Rather than allowing students to choose their own groups, the teacher could either assign groups randomly or purposefully group students according to strengths, interests, learning styles, and so on. Groups should change frequently, and assignments should be thoughtfully designed to complement students' individual characteristics.

LAUREN ROLLINS—First-Grade Teacher
Boulevard Elementary School, Shaker Heights, OH

At the beginning of each school year, I set aside a significant amount of time to get to know my students, for them to get to know each other, and for them to get to know me. This is an integral part of building a classroom community. Familiarization with each group's culture is mandatory to achieve a successful outcome. It is also important that the groups of students learn to have mutual respect for each other. This is so important that it is worth suspending the curriculum until these goals are met. One activity would be to invite the students to share their backgrounds and cultures in a "show and tell" situation. Another activity would be to create "compliment charts" for each other. The students would write compliments, positive statements, and qualities that they like about each other on the charts. At the end of the activity, each student will walk away feeling respected and appreciated. It is a "feel good" activity and a big step toward respecting and appreciating the members of the classroom.

LINDA SPARKS—First Grade Teacher
John F. Kennedy School, Billerica, MA

Students are very quick to pick up on what a person thinks about them or how someone feels about them. I have not had this specific incident happen in my class, because I am in an elementary school. But I believe this can happen at any level, especially when the teacher feels uncomfortable in the setting. Students pick right up on how a teacher feels about them. They need to be respected in order to learn to be respectful, while building their trust and confidence. Once that trust is earned, the students are more willing to participate in activities in the classroom. I would have to do some flexible grouping as simple as, "If you have green sneakers on, move to the left corner." They are not moving because they are of a specific ethnic group. I always have a jar with these quirky questions to move kids around, especially when I am changing desks. This also will maximize instruction because now they want their group to beat out their friends' group. When this happens, students will begin to get along socially while academic needs are being met.

PAULA COLEMERE—Special Education Teacher— English, History
McClintock High School, Tempe, AZ

My first goal is always to create a safe learning environment for my students. With underlying issues based on racial divisions in a class, it would be difficult for students to come to class prepared to learn. The hostility needs to be erased in this class. To work toward this goal, I would have the class do a team-building activity. This activity would be built to show students that no matter how they look, they are much more alike than different. There is an activity I have done where students walk to the center line if they have ever experienced something. It starts simple, but gets deeper. For example, the facilitator might say, "Go to the center line if you know someone who has been murdered." Sadly, many students have experienced this, and they will see they are not alone. Following this activity, I would have a discussion with the students about leaving our differences at the door. This is a teachable moment, as we will come across people throughout our lives that we don't like or who are different from us, but we have to find a way to make the relationship work to hold a job.

6 | CULTURE AND DIVERSITY

TEACHERS' CASEBOOK

WHAT WOULD YOU DO? WHITE GIRLS CLUB

You teach in a fairly homogeneous primary school. In fact, most of your kindergarten and first-grade students are middle- or upper middle-class and White. In January, a new student came to your school—the daughter of an African American professor who recently arrived to teach at the nearby college. After a few weeks, you notice that the new student is not being included in many activities. She sits alone in the library and plays alone at recess. No one sits with her at lunch, and at recess she is the last to be chosen for any team. This is troubling enough, but then one day you overhear two of your higher-achieving girls talking about their "White Girls Club."

CRITICAL THINKING

- Would you investigate to learn more about this "Club"? How?
- If you found that your students had created a club that excluded non-White students, what would you do?
- If you teach older students, what can you do about student groups that define themselves by who *cannot* be members?

Clivewa/Shutterstock

OVERVIEW AND OBJECTIVES

The cultural composition of American classrooms is changing. The same can be said for classrooms in many countries today. In a talk to the American Educational Research Association, Frank Pajares, one of the wisest educational psychologists I know, said, "The critical questions in education involve matters that cannot be settled by universal prescription. They demand attention to the cultural forces that shape our lives" (Pajares, 2000, p. 5). I believe he is right. In this chapter, we examine the many cultures that form the fabric of our society. We begin by considering some statistics about diversity in schools and then meet four individuals whose stories bring the statistics to life—you met another one, Felipe, in Chapter 5. Next, we trace the schools' responses to different ethnic and cultural groups. With a broad conception of culture as a basis, we then examine three important dimensions of every student's identity: social class, race/ethnicity, and gender. Then, we turn to a consideration of multicultural education, a general process of school reform that incorporates and embraces diversity, and we look at approaches to creating culturally compatible and resilient classrooms. The last

section presents three general principles for teaching every student. By the time you have completed this chapter, you should be able to:

Objective 6.1 Describe the meaning of culture and how cultural diversity in American schools today impacts learning and teaching.

Objective 6.2 Discuss what defines social class and socioeconomic status, including how SES differences relate to school achievement.

Objective 6.3 Explain how race, ethnicity, prejudice, discrimination, and stereotype threat might affect student learning and achievement in schools.

Objective 6.4 Describe the development of gender identity, sexual orientation, and the role of gender in teaching.

Objective 6.5 Define multicultural education and apply research on diversity to the creation of culturally compatible classrooms.

Connect and Extend to PRAXIS II®

The Larger Community (IV, B1, 3)
Familiarize yourself with the predicted changes in the U.S. population over the next several decades. How are those changes likely to affect education? What can schools and teachers do to adjust positively to those changes?

TODAY'S DIVERSE CLASSROOMS

In this text we take a broad interpretation of cultural diversity, so we will examine social class, race, ethnicity, and gender as aspects of diversity. We begin with a look at the meaning of culture. Many people associate this concept with the "cultural events" section of the newspaper—art galleries, museums, Shakespeare festivals, classical music concerts, and so on. Culture has a much broader meaning; it embraces the whole way of life of a group of people.

STOP & THINK Take a quick break from reading, and turn on the television. (Don't do this if you won't come back to reading until next Tuesday!) Find a channel with commercials. (I know, it's harder to find one without.) Listen to about 15 commercials. For each one, is the voice or the character in the ad old or young? Economically privileged or poor? Male or a female? What is the character's ethnicity or race? Do a quick tally of how many instances you observe in each category. •

American Cultural Diversity

There are many definitions of **culture**. Most include some or all of the following: the knowledge, skills, rules, norms, practices, traditions, self-definitions, institutions (educational, legal, communal, religious, political, etc.), language, and values that shape and guide beliefs and behavior in a particular group of people as well as the art, literature, folklore, and artifacts produced and passed down to the next generation (A. B. Cohen, 2009, 2010; Pai & Adler, 2001). The group constructs a culture—a program for living—and communicates the program to members. Groups can be defined along regional, ethnic, religious, racial, gender, social class, or other lines. Each of us is a member of many groups, so we all are influenced by many different cultures. Sometimes, the influences are incompatible or even contradictory. For example, if you are a feminist but also a Roman Catholic, you may have trouble reconciling the two different cultures' beliefs about the ordination of women as priests. Your personal belief will be based, in part, on how strongly you identify with each group.

Many different cultures thrive within every modern country. In the United States, students growing up in a small rural town in the Great Plains are part of a cultural group that is very different from that of students in a large Northeastern urban center or students in a Texas suburb. Within those small towns in the Great Plains, the son or daughter of a convenience store clerk grows up in a different culture from the child of the town doctor or dentist. Individuals of African, Asian, Hispanic, Native American, or European descent have distinctive histories and traditions. Everyone living within a particular country shares many common experiences and values, especially because of the influence of the mass media. But other aspects of their lives are shaped by differing cultural backgrounds.

Culture has been compared to an iceberg. One third of the iceberg is visible; the rest is hidden and unknown. The visible signs of culture, such as costumes and marriage traditions, reflect only a small portion of the differences among cultures, as you can see in Figure 6.1.

Many cultural differences are "below the surface." They are implicit, unstated, even unconscious biases and beliefs (Sheets, 2005). Cultures differ in rules for conducting interpersonal relationships, for example. In some groups, listeners give a slight affirmative nod of the head and perhaps an occasional "uh huh" to indicate they are listening carefully. But members of other cultures listen without giving acknowledgment, or with eyes downcast, as a sign of respect. In some cultures, high-status individuals initiate conversations and ask the questions, and low-status individuals only respond. In other cultures, the pattern is reversed.

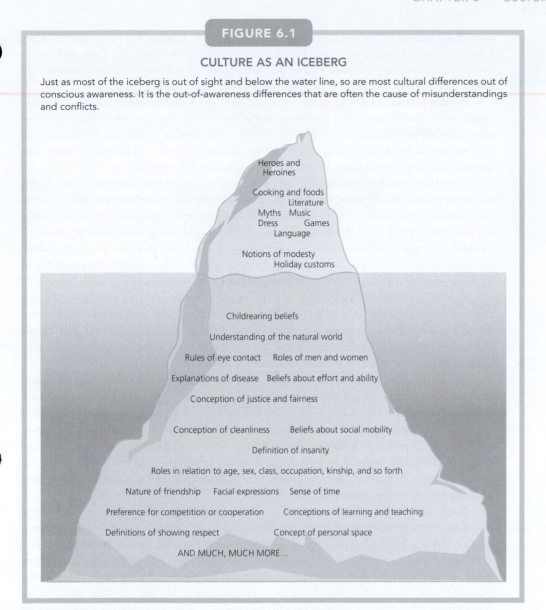

FIGURE 6.1

CULTURE AS AN ICEBERG

Just as most of the iceberg is out of sight and below the water line, so are most cultural differences out of conscious awareness. It is the out-of-awareness differences that are often the cause of misunderstandings and conflicts.

Heroes and Heroines

Cooking and foods
Literature
Myths   Music
Dress   Games
Language

Notions of modesty
Holiday customs

Childrearing beliefs

Understanding of the natural world

Rules of eye contact   Roles of men and women

Explanations of disease   Beliefs about effort and ability

Conception of justice and fairness

Conception of cleanliness   Beliefs about social mobility

Definition of insanity

Roles in relation to age, sex, class, occupation, kinship, and so forth

Nature of friendship   Facial expressions   Sense of time

Preference for competition or cooperation   Conceptions of learning and teaching

Definitions of showing respect   Concept of personal space

AND MUCH, MUCH MORE…

Cultural influences are widespread and pervasive. Some psychologists even suggest that culture defines intelligence. For example, physical grace is essential in Balinese social life, so the ability to master physical movements is a mark of intelligence in that culture. Manipulating words and numbers is important in Western societies, so in these cultures such skills are indicators of intelligence (Gardner, 2011). Even symptoms of psychological disorders are affected by culture. In industrialized cultures where cleanliness is emphasized, people with obsessive-compulsive disorders often become obsessed with cleaning their hands, whereas in Bali, where social networks are emphasized, people with obsessive-compulsive disorders often become obsessed with knowing all the details about the lives of their friends and family—their social network (Lemelson, 2003).

Let's get more specific about cultural diversity by meeting some students.

Meet Four More Students

In Chapter 1 you read some statistics about students in America. Look back at those statistics now to get a broad picture of American students today and tomorrow. As you can see, classrooms are becoming more diverse. But teachers do not work with statistics; they work with students—unique

PODCAST 6.1

In this podcast, textbook author Anita Woolfolk talks about how important it is for teachers to understand and accept cultural differences in their students. Listen to find out how cultural awareness can prevent conflicts between students, teachers, and parents.

ENHANCEDetext *podcast*

individuals, such as Felipe Vargas, the fifth-grader you met in Chapter 5. In this section, Nancy Knapp from the University of Georgia invites us to meet four more individuals. These students are not specific people; they are composites of the characteristics of real people Nancy has known and taught. The names and schools are fictional, but the lives are very real.

Ternice Mattox is a seventh-grader who lives with her mother and three younger siblings in a large city in the Northeast. Her mother works the 7:00 to 3:00 shift at a dry-cleaning plant and then cleans offices some nights and weekends to make ends meet, so Ternice gets her brothers and sister up and ready for school every day, feeds them dinner when they get home, and makes sure they do their homework at night; she has been doing this since she was 10.

School hasn't ever been very hard for Ternice; in elementary school she usually got Bs, even though a lot of the teachers said she talked too much. But she never really liked school until last year. Her sixth-grade English teacher seemed to want students to talk. She had them reading stories about real people, like you could meet any day downtown. In class, she got people talking about what the characters should do and why the authors wrote the stories the way they did. Best of all, she let you write about whatever you wanted, even your own life; and she didn't count off for every mistake right away, but let you work with her and with the other kids until you had a final copy you could be really proud of. In that class, Ternice found out that she really liked to write, and her teacher said she was good at it; one of her stories even got published in the school newspaper. Ternice talked and wrote so much in that class that Anthony Bailey got on her about why she was "actin' so White." She got mad and told him that acting foolish was worse than acting White, but it still bothered her. She and Anthony kind of go together, and she likes him a lot; she has "Ternice and 'Tone" written all over her notebooks.

Her English class this year is not nearly as good. Her teacher from last year wants her to take some tests, to see if she can get into the program for students with gifts and talents, but Ternice is not so sure about that. Even if she got in, she's afraid she wouldn't know anyone; almost all the kids in "gifted" are White, and the few Black kids are from another part of town. Besides, her friends might not like it, especially Anthony; at her school, "brains" don't go around with "regulars," and vice versa. Her mama wants her to try and says there's no telling where she can go from there, but Ternice doesn't want to go anywhere that's away from all her friends. Still, she wishes she could have more classes like her English class last year.

Ben Whittaker lives in a suburb of Colorado Springs with his father, the vice president at a local bank and member of the board of a local hospital. His mother and father are divorced, but Ben still sees his mom every 2 weeks for the weekend. His older sister is in her second year of college, taking a pre-veterinary course. Ben started high school this year; he's taking algebra, world history, French, English, and freshman chemistry. His course schedule was his father's idea, especially the freshman chemistry. Ben feels completely out of his league in that class, but his father insisted that if he was going to get into pre-med in college, he had to get a jump-start on science. Ben's mother says medicine is where the money is, and she knows Ben can do it, if he just gets focused.

Ben's not so sure. He has never been a star student like his sister, and he really struggled at the beginning of middle school. He just couldn't get the hang of taking notes; either he couldn't figure out what was most important, so he'd try to write down everything the teachers said, or he'd get distracted by something, and miss whole sections of the lecture. He also had a hard time keeping track of his assignments, and when he did remember to do them, his notebooks and backpack were such a mess that sometimes he'd lose them before he got them turned in. At the end of the first semester, his homeroom teacher suggested he be evaluated for attention-deficit hyperactivity disorder (ADHD), and his family doctor put him on a trial dose of Ritalin, which seemed to help. With some additional coaching on organizational skills, Ben gradually improved and finished eighth grade with a solid B average. He still takes Ritalin on school days, but not on the weekends, which is when he does most of his artwork.

Art is what Ben really loves; since he was a little boy he has been drawing people and animals and whole scenes out of his imagination. Sometimes when he's working on a drawing, he loses all track of time; his mom calls it being "zoned in," and teases him that he'd forget to eat if she didn't come up and get him. Lately, he's been experimenting with the graphics program on his computer, and he's even drawn a few panels of his own Web comic. He's only shown it to some friends, but they thought it was pretty funny. It's weird, he never has trouble focusing on his art, but even with the Ritalin, he's having more and more trouble focusing on his schoolwork this year. He's worried his grades won't be very good; he may even flunk chemistry. Ben knows he could do better if he took a lighter load, especially if he could move out of the advanced track and take some art courses; but his parents say art is nice for a hobby, but it's no way to make a living.

Davy Walker is a second-grader who is worried he will be held back this year, but he's afraid to ask his teacher about it. He doesn't really like asking questions, anyway, because everyone looks at you, and sometimes they laugh if you ask a dumb one. The problem is, he just can't seem to catch on to reading the way most of the other kids do. He can read some of the words if he has enough time, especially if no one is listening to him, but he hates it when the teacher has them take turns reading aloud. Everyone else seems to read so much better and faster that he just freezes up and makes stupid mistakes.

His teacher had a conference with his mom and dad last fall and told them he needed to read more at home. His parents own a family restaurant in the small town in Oregon where they live, and his mom and dad both work pretty long hours there; even his older sister helps out some on weekends. His mom tried for a while to get him to read to her when she put him to bed at night, but it didn't work out very well. He got sick of the baby books that were all he could read, and when she got him to try something harder, it went so slowly that she got impatient and quit. Davy was fine with that. When he grows up, he's going to run the restaurant for his dad. He can already clear tables and stack the dishes in the big dishwasher, and sometimes his dad lets him help run the cash register and make change. When he's older, he'll learn to take orders and work the grill. Davy doesn't see what reading has to do with running a good restaurant.

Jessie Kinkaid is a junior at Red Falls High School in Wisconsin. She lives with her mother, who works as a doctor's receptionist, in a small house in town. Her father owns the Ford car dealership and lives just outside of town with his second wife and Jessie's 3-year-old half-brother, so she sees him pretty often.

Jessie is in the vocational track at school and mostly makes Cs, with a few Ds. Once in a while, she fails a course, but she'll have enough credits to graduate by the end of next year, which is all she really cares about. Her home economics teacher says she has a real flair for cooking and wants Jessie to bring up her grades so she can apply to chef's school. Jessie likes to cook and knows she's good at it, but doesn't see any point in going to more school. She's only graduating to please her parents; she knows what she's going to do with her life. After graduation she's going to get a job in town somewhere for a couple years to save up some money, and then she'll marry Walter Aiken. She and Walt have been going together since she was a freshman and he was a junior. Walt started this year at UW-Platteville to get a degree in animal science, and they plan to wait until he is finished before they get married. Then they'll move into the small house on the Aiken's farm until Walt's dad is ready to retire, probably in another 3 or 4 years. Then Walt will take over the farm, and they'll move into the big house; Jessie hopes they'll have at least one child by then.

So Jessie doesn't see any point in worrying about her grades, as long as she graduates. Her father agrees it would be foolish to waste time and money on extra schooling she'll never use. Jessie's mother, who left school at 17 to marry, is the one urging Jessie to think about going on. She says she just wants Jessie to "keep all her options open."

Felipe, Ternice, Ben, Davy, and Jessie are just five students, and there are millions more—unique collections of abilities and experiences. They speak different languages, have different ethnic and racial backgrounds, and live in different kinds of communities. Some come from families in poverty, others from families with power and privilege—but all face challenges in their education. For the remainder of the chapter, we look at the dimensions of cultural differences in schools today.

Cautions: Interpreting Cultural Differences

Before we discuss cultural differences, two cautions are necessary. First, we will consider social class, ethnicity, race, and gender separately, because much of the available research focuses on only one

Connect and Extend to PRAXIS II®

Cultural and Gender Differences in the Classroom (III, B)
What are the sources of possible miscommunication between students and teachers in the classroom because of cultural or gender differences? Identify steps a teacher can take to minimize such problems.

of these variables. Of course, real children are not just African American, or middle class, or male; they are complex beings and members of many groups, just like the five students you met earlier.

The second caution is that group membership is not destiny. Just knowing a student is a member of a particular cultural group does not define what that student is like. People are individuals. For example, if a student in your class consistently arrives late, it may be that the student has a job before school, must walk a long distance, is responsible for getting younger siblings to school like Ternice, or even that he or she dreads school.

CULTURAL CONFLICTS AND COMPATIBILITIES. The differences between cultures may be very obvious, tip-of-the iceberg characteristics such as holiday customs and dress, or they may be very subtle, below-the-surface differences such as how to get your turn in conversations. When subtle cultural differences meet, misunderstandings and conflicts are common. These conflicts can happen when the values and competencies of the dominant, mainstream culture are used to determine what is considered "normal" or appropriate behavior in schools. In these cases, children who have been socialized in a different culture may be perceived as acting inappropriately, not following the rules, or being rude and disrespectful.

Rosa Hernandez Sheets (Sheets, 2005) describes a 5-year-old Mexican American girl who tried to bring a bread roll, part of her school cafeteria lunch, home to give to her little brother every day. Her parents were proud of her for sharing, but the school officials made her throw the roll away, because it was against school rules to take food from the cafeteria. The girl was conflicted about following school rules versus honoring her family's cultural values. The teacher in this case solved the problem by talking to the cafeteria cook, putting the roll in a plastic bag, and placing the bag in the girl's backpack to be taken home after school.

Not all cultural differences lead to clashes in school, however. For example, compared to other ethnic groups, Asian Americans have the highest graduation rates from high school, college, and graduate school—so sometimes they are labeled as "model minorities" (S. J. Lee, 2008). Is this fair?

Video 6.1
As this teacher learned from a student, respecting a student's culture is very different than expecting a student to have particular interests, skills, or behaviors simply because he or she has a particular cultural background.

ENHANCEDetext *video example*

DANGERS IN STEREOTYPING. There are dangers in stereotyping both Asians and Asian Americans as model students—quiet, hardworking, and passive. Acting on these stereotypes can reinforce conformity and stifle assertiveness. Stacey Lee (2008) describes another stereotype confronting Asian Americans. They are seen as perpetual foreigners. No matter how many decades their families have lived in America, even fourth- or fifth-generation Asian American students are not seen as "real" Americans. In fact, Lee's research shows that teachers tend to refer to these students as "Asian," not "Asian American" or "American." That would be like calling me a German student because my great-grandfather came to Wisconsin from Germany. I was born in Texas, and my knowledge of German culture is limited to my grandmother's recipe for pfeffernüsse—excellent, by the way. Too often, students take these stereotypes to heart and feel "foreign" even in the country of their birth—America. One high school student told Lee (2008), "Watching MTV affected the way I acted very much. I wanted to be more Americanized. I changed my hair color. I got colored contact lenses" (p. 78). Later in this chapter, we explore ways to make classrooms compatible with the home cultures of students. First, however, we need to examine some of the effects of cultural conflicts and discrimination on student achievement.

ENHANCEDetext *self-check*

ECONOMIC AND SOCIAL CLASS DIFFERENCES

Even though most researchers would agree that social class is one of the most meaningful cultural dimensions in people's lives, those same researchers have great difficulty defining *social class* (Liu et al., 2004; Macionis, 2013). Different terms are used—social class, socioeconomic status, economic background, wealth, poverty, or privilege. Some people consider only economic differences; others add considerations of power, influence, mobility, control over resources, and prestige.

Social Class and Socioeconomic Status

In modern societies, levels of wealth, power, and prestige are not always consistent. Some people—for instance, university professors—are members of professions that are reasonably high in terms of social status but provide little wealth or power (believe me). Other people have political power even though they are not wealthy, or they may be members of the elite social register in a town, even though their family money is long gone. Most people are generally aware of their social class: that is, they perceive that some groups are above them in social class and some are below. They may even show a kind of "*classism*" (like racism or sexism), believing that they are "better" than members of lower social classes and avoiding association with them. For example, in an ethnographic study (see Chapter 1 and the Glossary), Marissa, a member of the most popular and privileged clique in her high school, described the "grits"—the least popular group:

> Grits are poor. I think they mostly live in the country. We—[quickly correcting herself] some of my friends call them hicks or rednecks. I guess most live on the Hill—that's over on the west side of town. It's the slums. Grits smoke, do drugs, dress grungy. They have those hick accents. They usually get bad grades. They don't like school so I think they drop out a lot. They don't really fit in. They are troublemakers. I don't see them much; they aren't in any of my classes. (Brantlinger, 2004, pp. 109–110)

In addition to social class, there is another way of thinking about differences that is commonly used in research. Sociologists and psychologists combine variations in wealth, power, control over resources, and prestige into an index called **socioeconomic status (SES)**. In contrast to social class, most people are not conscious of their SES designation. SES is usually ascribed to people by researchers; different formulas for determining SES might lead to different assignments (Macionis, 2013; Sirin, 2005). No single variable, not even income, is an effective measure of SES. Most researchers identify four general levels of SES: upper, middle, working, and lower. The main characteristics of these four SES levels are summarized in Table 6.1 on the next page. As you watched the commercials in the *Stop & Think* activity at the beginning of this chapter, how many people did you see who appeared to be in the lower-class SES?

Extreme Poverty: Homeless and Highly Mobile Students

When families live in extreme poverty, they sometimes lack even a stable home. In the 2011–2012 school year, more than 1 million students were homeless, a 24% increase over the number in 2009 (National Center for Homeless Education, 2013). Students who are homeless or who move very often are at additional risk for a range of physical, social, and learning difficulties. For example, even after taking many other risk factors and income levels into account, students who moved three or more times in a school year were 60% more likely to repeat a grade (Cutuli et al., 2013). Homelessness and high mobility contribute to chronic risks and problems in school, problems that are difficult to overcome.

Even with these risks, many of these students are resilient in the face of problems. J. J. Cutuli and his colleagues (2013) analyzed the math and reading test scores of over 26,000 students from third through eighth grades and found that 45% of the homeless and highly mobile students achieved in the average or better range across time, in spite of their challenges. The researchers concluded that factors such as effective parenting, student self-regulation skills (see Chapter 11), academic motivation (see Chapter 12), and the quality of teaching and teachers' relationships with students (see this whole book) supported resiliency for these students. The early years in school are particularly important. Homeless students who develop reading and self-regulation skills in the early grades are more likely to be successful throughout school (Buckner, 2012). Because self-regulation is so important for everyone, we will spend quite a bit of time in Chapter 11 exploring how to help students develop these skills.

Poverty and School Achievement

You saw in Chapter 1 that almost 1 in 5 Americans under the age of 18 lives below the poverty level: $23,550 annual income for a family of four. That is 22% of all children in the United States.

Connect and Extend to PRAXIS II®

Economic Conditions/Socioeconomic Status (SES) (IV, B2)
Be aware of the possible effects of SES on student achievement. Consider what steps teachers can take to minimize those effects.

TABLE 6.1 • **Selected Characteristics of Different Social Classes**

	UPPER CLASS		MIDDLE CLASS	WORKING CLASS	LOWER CLASS
	UPPER-UPPER CLASS	UPPER CLASS			
Income	$500,000 to billions	$200,000+	$114,000–$200,000 (1/2) $48,000–$114,000 (1/2) (but in very expensive areas such as San Francisco, it may take at least $150,000 to be middle class)	$27,000–$48,000	Below $27,000
Occupation/ Source of Money	Family money, "old money," investments	Corporate, professional, income earned in some way	White-collar, skilled blue-collar	Blue-collar	Minimum wage, unskilled labor
Education	Home-schooled, tutors, Prestigious private schools and colleges	Prestigious colleges and graduate schools	High school, college, or professional school	High school	High school or less
Home Ownership	Several homes, private jets for transportation	At least one home	Usually own home	About half own a home	Uncommon
Health Coverage	Full	Full	Usually	Limited	Uncommon
Neighborhoods	The most exclusive	Exclusive or comfortable	Comfortable	Modest	Deteriorating
Afford Children's College	Easily	Easily	Usually	Seldom	Uncommon
Political Power	National (perhaps international), state, local	National, state, local	State or local	Limited	No

Source: Information from Macionis, J. J. (2013). Society: The basics (12th ed). Upper Saddle River, NJ: Pearson; and Macionis, personal communication, April 2, 2010.

In fact, about 10% of all children live in extreme poverty, existing on about $2 a day. For a while, there were improvements. In 2000, the number of families in poverty was the lowest in 21 years—about 6.2 million (Bishaw, 2013), but rates have been rising again since then to over 16 million. If we add children living in low-income families (under about $46,000 for a family of four), then 45% of all children in the United States live in low-income or poor families (Koppelman, 2011). In 2013 in the United States, 31 million students qualified for free or reduced lunches at school (U.S. Department of Agriculture, 2013a). To meet some of these students and get a glimpse of their lives, read *Fire in the Ashes: Twenty-Five Years Among the Poorest Children in America*. Jonathan Kozol (2012) tells the amazing stories, trials, and triumphs of children living amid extreme poverty. Every teacher should read this book.

The absolute number of children living in poverty is similar for non-Hispanic White children (5 million), Latina/o children (6 million), and African American children (5 million). But the rate of poverty is higher for African American, Latino, and Native American children—38% of African American, and 35% of Latino children lived in poverty in 2012, whereas 14% of Asian and 12% of non-Hispanic White children were poor (National Poverty Center, 2014). Contrary to many stereotypes, more poor children live in suburban and rural areas than in central cities. But poverty rates are high in urban schools.

The average correlation between SES and achievement tests is moderate, about .30 to .40 (Sackett, Kuncel, Arneson, Cooper, & Waters, 2009; Sirin, 2005). In general, students of all ethnic groups with high SES show higher average levels of achievement on test scores and stay in school longer than students with low SES, and this difference widens with the student's age from 7 to 15 (Berliner, 2005; Cutuli et al., 2013). And the longer the child is in poverty, the stronger the impact is on achievement. For example, even when we take into account parents' education, the chance that children will be retained in grades or placed in special education classes increases by 2% to 3% for every year the children live in poverty (Ackerman, Brown, & Izard, 2004; Bronfenbrenner, McClelland, Wethington, Moen, & Ceci, 1996). Figure 6.2 shows the trends in reading achievement from third through eighth grade for students in several income risk groups (homeless/highly mobile, free lunch, reduced cost lunch) compared to the national average for those grades and to students who were not ever a part of any of the these risk groups (labeled "general" in Figure 6.2). You can see that the growth rates are similar, but these groups begin at different levels in third grade. This is another reason early interventions (preschool and primary school) are important for students placed at risk.

One troubling trend is that the achievement gap is growing between children from privileged families (income at the 90th percentile) and children from poor families (income at the 10th percentile). This gap is *30% to 40% greater* for children born in 2001 compared to children born in 1976. These increasingly dramatic income differences between wealthy and poor have led to greater segregation of low-income children in lower-quality schools. The emphasis on standardized tests may have led wealthy parents to pay for extra tutoring and better preparation for their children—resources that poor families can't afford (Reardon, 2011).

FIGURE 6.2

TRENDS IN READING ACHIEVEMENT FROM THIRD THROUGH EIGHTH GRADE FOR STUDENTS IN SEVERAL INCOME RISK GROUPS

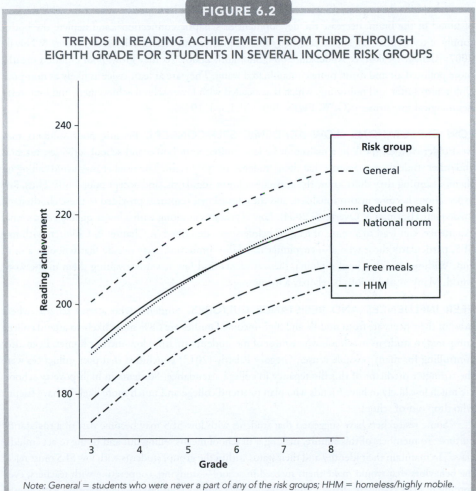

Note: General = students who were never a part of any of the risk groups; HHM = homeless/highly mobile.
Source: Reprinted with permission from Cutuli, J. J., Desjardins, C. D., Herbers, J. E., Long, J. D., Heistad, D., Chan, C-K, Hinz, E., & Masten, A. S. (2013). Academic achievement trajectories of homeless and highly mobile students: Resilience in the context of chronic and acute risk. Child Development, 84, p. 851.

What are the effects of low SES that might explain the lower school achievement of these students? No single cause is to blame (G. W. Evans, 2004). Poor health care for mother and child, dangerous or unhealthy home environments, limited resources, family stress, interruptions in schooling, exposure to violence, overcrowding, homelessness, discrimination, and other factors lead to school failures, low-paying jobs—and another generation born into poverty. G. W. Evans (2004), E. Jensen (2009), and McLoyd (1998) describe other possible explanations. Let's take a closer look at each of them.

HEALTH, ENVIRONMENT, AND STRESS. The negative effects of poverty begin even before a child is born. Families in poverty have less access to good prenatal and infant health care and nutrition. Over half of all adolescent mothers receive no prenatal care at all. Poor mothers and adolescent mothers are more likely to have premature babies, and prematurity is associated with many cognitive and learning problems. Children in poverty are more likely to be exposed to both legal drugs (nicotine, alcohol) and illegal drugs (cocaine, heroin) before birth. Children whose mothers take drugs during pregnancy can have problems with organization, attention, and language skills.

Poor children are four times as likely to experience stress due to evictions, lack of food, over-crowding, or utility disconnections. Increased stress is related to increased school absences, decreased attention and concentration, problems with memory and thinking, reduced motivation and effort, increased depression, and reduced neurogenesis (growth of new brain cells) (E. Jensen, 2009). In the early years, children in poverty experience higher levels of stress hormones than children in middle-class and wealthy families. High levels of these hormones can interfere with the flow of blood in the brain, decrease the development of synaptic connections, and deplete the body's supply of tryptophan, an amino acid that calms impulsive and violent behaviors (Hudley & Novak, 2007; Richell, Deakin, & Anderson, 2005; Shonkoff, 2006). As they grow, poor children breathe more polluted air and drink more contaminated water. They are at least twice as likely as non-poor children to suffer lead poisoning, which is associated with lower school achievement and long-term neurological impairment (G. W. Evans, 2004; McLoyd, 1998).

LOW EXPECTATIONS—LOW ACADEMIC SELF-CONCEPT. Because poor students may wear older clothes, speak in a dialect, or be less familiar with books and school activities, teachers and other students may assume that these students are not bright. The teacher may avoid calling on them, assuming they don't know the answer, set lower standards, and accept poor work. Thus, low expectations become institutionalized, and the educational resources provided to these children are inadequate (Borman & Overman, 2004). Low expectations, along with a lower-quality educational experience, can lead to a sense of learned helplessness, described in Chapter 4. Children with low SES, particularly those who also encounter racial discrimination, may decide that school is a dead end. Without a high school diploma, these students find few rewards awaiting them in the work world. Many available jobs barely pay a living wage.

PEER INFLUENCES AND RESISTANCE CULTURES. Students who attend schools where most of their peers are from middle and high-income families are 68% more likely to attend college compared to students in schools where most of the students are from low-income homes. Even after controlling for many possible causes, Gregory Palardy (2013) concluded that peer influences were the strongest predictor of this discrepancy in college attendance. Students in high-poverty schools are much less likely to have friends who plan to attend college and much more likely to have friends who drop out of school.

Some researchers have suggested that students with low SES may become part of a **resistance culture**. To members of this culture, making it in school means selling out and trying to act "middle class." To maintain their identity and their status within the group, students with low SES must reject the behaviors that would make them succeed in school—studying, cooperating with teachers, even coming to class (Bennett, 2011; Ogbu, 1987, 1997). John Ogbu linked identification with a resistance culture to poor Latino/a American, Native American, and African American groups, but similar reactions have been noted for poor White students both in the United States and in England and high school students in Papua New Guinea (Woolfolk Hoy, Demerath, & Pape, 2002). This is not to say that all students with low SES resist achievement. Adolescents whose parents value academic achievement tend to select friends who also share those values (Berndt & Keefe, 1995). Many young people are high achievers in spite of either their economic situation or negative peer influences (O'Connor, 1997). And we should not forget that some aspects of schooling—competitive grading, public reprimands, stressful testing and assignments, and repetitive work that is too hard or too easy—can encourage resistance in all students (Okagaki, 2001). To focus solely on students' resistance is a way of blaming students for their lower achievement; instead, educators should focus on making school an inclusive place that does not invite resistance for anyone (Stinson, 2006).

HOME ENVIRONMENT AND RESOURCES. Families in poverty seldom have access to high-quality preschool care for their young children, the kind of care that enhances cognitive and social development (G. J. Duncan & Brooks-Gunn, 2000; Vandell, 2004). Poor children read less and spend more time watching television; they have less access to books, computers, libraries, trips, and museums (J. S. Kim & Guryan, 2010). Again, not all low-income families lack resources. Many families provide rich learning environments for their children. When parents of any SES level support and encourage their children—by reading to them, providing books and educational toys, taking the children to the library, making time and space for learning—the children tend to become better, more enthusiastic readers (Peng & Lee, 1992). Home and neighborhood resources seem to have the greatest impact on children's achievement when school is not in session—during the summer or before students enter school.

SUMMER SETBACKS. Students in poverty begin school about 6 months behind in reading skills compared to students from wealthier homes, but the difference between the groups grows to almost 3 years by sixth grade. This gap in reading skills between students in poverty and middle-class students has been increasing since the early 1970s. One explanation for this growing gap is that the children from poorer homes, and especially those whose first language in not English, lose ground over the summer. Even though both groups make comparable achievement gains during the school year, every summer vacation creates about a 3-month reading achievement gap between poor and advantaged children (J. S. Kim & Guryan, 2010; J. S. Kim & Quinn, 2013). One study suggested that the four summer vacations between second and sixth grade accounted for 80% of the achievement differences between poor and advantaged students (Allington & McGill-Frazen, 2003, 2008). This truly is a case of the rich getting richer. Wealthier children have greater access to books all the time, but especially over the summer. They read more, and the more children read, the better readers they become—volume of reading matters. The good news is that quality summer reading programs for low-income families and their children can be effective in helping students improve their reading skills (J. S. Kim & Quinn, 2013).

TRACKING: POOR TEACHING. A final explanation for the lower achievement of many students with low SES is that these students experience tracking and therefore have a different academic socialization; that is, they are actually taught differently (Oakes, 1990). If they are tracked into "low-ability," "general," "practical," or "vocational" classes, they may be taught to memorize and be passive. Middle-class students are more likely to be encouraged to think and be creative in their classes. Is tracking a problem? Read the *Point/Counterpoint* on the next page for the arguments.

Even if they are not tracked, students from low-income families are more likely to attend schools with inadequate resources and less-effective teachers (G. W. Evans, 2004). For example, in high-poverty schools, over 50% of math teachers and over 60% of science teachers are inexperienced or teaching outside their subject expertise; they were not trained for the subjects they are teaching (E. Jensen, 2009). When students with low SES receive a substandard education, this gives them inferior academic skills and limits their life chances, beginning with not preparing them for higher education (Anyon, 1980; Knapp & Woolverton, 2003). See the *Guidelines: Teaching Students Who Live in Poverty* on page 221 for a few ideas about quality teaching for students who live in poverty.

ENHANCEDetext *self-check*

POINT/COUNTERPOINT
Is Tracking an Effective Strategy?

Tracking students into different classes or strands (college prep, vocational, remedial, gifted, etc.) has been standard procedure in many schools for a long time, but does it work? Critics say tracking is harmful, whereas supporters claim it is useful, even though it presents challenges.

POINT Tracking is harmful and should be eliminated. Braddock and Slavin (1993); Carnegie Council on Adolescent Development (1995); Oakes (1985); and Wheelock (1992) make the argument that tracking is harmful. What is the basis for these claims? Surprisingly, the evidence is not clear or direct. For example, a few early, well-done, and carefully designed studies found that tracking increases the gap between high and low achievers by depressing the achievement of low-track students and boosting the achievement of high-track students (Gamoran, 1987; Kerckhoff, 1986). And Gamoran also found that the achievement gap between low- and high-track students is greater than the gap between students who drop out of school and students who graduate. Low-achieving, students who are from ethnic and minority groups, as well as students living in poverty, are all more likely to be assigned to novice teachers, especially in middle and high school. On average, novice teachers are not as effective initially than more-experienced teachers, so sorting and tracking tends to put students with the greatest academic challenges with the least-experienced teachers (Kalogrides & Loeb, 2013). Because students from low-income families and students of color are overrepresented in the lower tracks, they suffer the greatest harm from tracking and should benefit the most from the elimination of tracking (Oakes, 1990; Oakes & Wells, 2002). Is this likely? In an interview with Marge Scherer (1993), Jonathan Kozol described the cruel predictive side of tracking:

> [T]racking is so utterly predictive. The little girl who gets shoved into the low reading group in 2nd grade is very likely to be the child who is urged to take cosmetology instead of algebra in the 8th grade, and most likely to be in vocational courses, not college courses, in the 10th grade, if she hasn't dropped out by then. (2012, p. 8)

COUNTERPOINT Eliminating tracking will hurt many students. Researchers who have looked closely at tracking believe that tracking may be harmful for some students some of the time, but not for all students and not all of the time. First, as most people agree, tracking seems to have positive effects for the high-track students. Programs for students with gifts and talents, honors classes, and Advanced Placement (AP) classes seem to work (Fuchs, Fuchs, Hamlett, & Karns, 1998; A. Robinson & Clinkenbeard, 1998). No one, especially parents, wants to eliminate the positive effects of these programs.

What would happen if schools were detracked? Loveless (1999) identifies some possible hidden costs. First, results of a large national study suggest that when low-track 10th-graders are assigned to heterogeneous classes rather than low tracks, they gain about 5 percentage points in achievement. So far, so good. But students who are average achievers lose 2 percentage points when put into heterogeneous classes, and students with high abilities lose about 5 points.

> The achievement gap is indeed narrowed, but apparently at the expense of students in regular and high tracks, representing about 70% of 10th-graders in the United States. (Loveless, 1999, p. 29)

Another consequence of detracking is bright flight—the withdrawal of the brightest students from the schools. Both African American and White parents distrust mixed-ability classes to meet the needs of their children (Public Agenda Foundation, 1994).

BEWARE OF EITHER/OR

In some classes, using a mixed-ability structure seems to hinder the achievement of all students. For example, students in heterogeneous algebra classes don't learn as much as students in tracked classes—whatever the ability level of the students (Epstein & MacIver, 1992). And a meta-analysis of student self-esteem found that students in low-track classes did *not* have lower self-esteem than students in heterogeneous classes (Kulik & Kulik, 1997).

So what is the answer? As usual, it is more complicated than simply detracking versus tracking. Careful attention to every student's achievement may mean different answers at different times.

GUIDELINES
Teaching Students Who Live in Poverty

Educate yourself about the effects of poverty on student learning.

Examples

1. Read articles from good journals.
2. Seek reliable sources such as Eric Jensen's (2009), *Teaching with Poverty in Mind: What Being Poor Does to Kids' Brains and What Schools Can Do about It.*

Set and maintain high expectations.

Examples

1. Guard against feeling sorry for students, excusing poor work, and expecting less. Replace pity with empathy based on solid knowledge of your students.
2. Communicate to students that they can succeed with good effort.
3. Provide constructive criticism because you believe your students can do quality work.
4. Add challenging subjects and AP classes.

Develop caring relationships with your students.

Examples

1. Use inclusive language—"our class," "our projects," "our school," "our efforts."
2. Talk to students outside class. Make a point to identify their interests and abilities.
3. Attend sports or other events where your students participate.
4. Create a class Welcome Center for families (see Chapter 5).

Build learning and self-regulation skills as part of the curriculum.

Examples

1. Teach students how to organize work, focus attention, or seek appropriate help.
2. Include conflict management and social problem-solving skills in lessons.

Notice health problems.

Examples

1. Notice who seems to be absent or tardy often.
2. Check to see whether some students struggle to hear the class discussions. Can they see from the back of the room?
3. Model healthy eating and physical activity.

Assess student knowledge, start where they are, but don't stay there (Milner, 2010).

Examples

1. Use short, ungraded assessments that target the learning objectives for each unit.
2. Differentiate instruction (Chapter 14) based on results.

Source: Based on Jensen, E. (2009). Teaching with Poverty in Mind: What Being Poor Does to Kids' Brains and What Schools Can Do About It. Alexandria, VA: Association for Supervision and Curriculum Development.

ETHNICITY AND RACE IN TEACHING AND LEARNING

The United States truly is a diverse society. By the year 2023, almost two thirds of the school-age population will be African American, Asian, Latino/a, or from other ethnic groups (Children's Defense Fund, 2010). Before we look at the research on ethnicity and race, let's clarify some terms.

Terms: Ethnicity and Race

Ethnicity usually refers to a group's shared common cultural characteristics such as history, homeland, language, traditions, or religion. We all have some ethnic heritage, whether our background is Italian, Ukrainian, Hmong, Chinese, Japanese, Navajo, Hawaiian, Puerto Rican, Cuban, Hungarian, German, African, or Irish—to name only a few.

Race, on the other hand, is defined as "a socially constructed category of people who share biologically transmitted traits that members of a society consider important," such as skin color or hair texture (Macionis, 2013, p. 274). In effect, race is a label people apply to themselves and to others based on appearances. There are no biologically pure races. For any two humans chosen at random, an average of only .012% (about one-hundredth of 1%) of the alphabetic sequence of their genetic codes is different due to race (Myers, 2005). Today many psychologists emphasize that ethnicity and race are socially constructed ideas. Still, race is a powerful construct. At the individual level, race is part of our identity—how we understand ourselves and interact with others. At the group level, race is involved with economic and political structures (Macionis, 2013).

Sociologists sometimes use the term **minority group** to label a group of people that receives unequal or discriminatory treatment. Strictly speaking, however, the term refers to a numerical minority compared to the total population. Referring to particular racial or ethnic groups as minorities is technically incorrect in some situations, because in certain places, such as Chicago or Mississippi, the "minority" group—African Americans—is actually the majority. This practice of referring to people as minorities because of their racial or ethnic heritage has been criticized because it is misleading and has negative historical connotations (Milner, 2010).

Ethnic and Racial Differences in School Achievement

A major concern in schools is that some ethnic groups consistently achieve below the average for all students (Matthews, Kizzie, Rowley, & Cortina, 2010; Uline & Johnson, 2005). This pattern of results tends to hold for all standardized achievement tests, but the gaps have been narrowing since about the 1980s and are less than the gaps seen between wealthy and poor students (Raudenbush, 2009; Reardon, 2011). For example, as you can see in Figure 6.3 on the National Assessment of Educational Progress in mathematics, the gap between scores of White and African American fourth-graders has narrowed from 34 points in 1996 to 26 points in 2013. The gap between White and Hispanic fourth-graders has narrowed from 25 in 1996 to 19 in 2013 (National Center for Education Statistics, 2013).

Proponents of this notion of an "achievement gap" have been criticized for taking a narrow view, assuming that the scores of White, middle-class students are the norm that all other students must be compared to and measured by (Anyon, 2012). Multicultural scholar H. Richard Milner (2010, 2013) reminds teachers that "people of color may experience a different type of 'normal' life and that excellence can and does emerge in multiple and varied forms: people of color from all walks of life are successful" (p. 9). He suggests that we think about other kinds of "gaps," such as teacher education and quality gaps, challenging curriculum gaps, affordable housing and health care gaps, school integration and funding gaps, and quality childcare gaps, digital divide gaps, wealth and income gaps, employment gaps—all culminating in *opportunity gaps* for many students of color. Gloria Ladson-Billings (2006) described the *educational debt* that we owe students of color and students living in poverty based on decades of underinvestment and discrimination.

Opportunity gaps and educational debts lead to education completion gaps. Across the United States in 2011, about 76% of the White students graduated from high school, compared to 60% of African American students, 58% of Hispanic students, and 79% of Asian/Pacific Islanders. But again, these are averages across all the states. If we look state by state, we see some interesting differences. Nevada had the lowest overall completion rate (62%), followed by New Mexico (63%), Georgia (67%), and Alaska and Oregon (68%). Iowa had the highest graduation rate, at 88%. Wisconsin, Vermont, Nebraska, Indiana, New Hampshire, North Dakota, Tennessee, and Texas all had rates above 86%. But completion rates vary widely by ethnicity. Rates for White students range from 70% in Oregon to 92% in Texas; for African American students, from 43% in Nevada to 81% in Montana and Texas; for Hispanic students, from 51% in Minnesota to more than 87% in Maine and 82% in Texas; and for Asian American students, from 45% in South Dakota to 95% in Texas (Nhan, 2012). These differences probably have multiple causes. Some states have many more students of all ethnicities than other states. Some states have more families in poverty, more urban schools, less support for education, and other challenges.

Although consistent differences still exist among ethnic groups on tests of cognitive abilities, most researchers agree that the reasons for these differences are mainly the legacy of discrimination, the product of cultural mismatches and language differences, or a result of growing up in poverty. Because many students from ethnic groups are also economically disadvantaged, it is important to separate the effects of these two sets of influences on school achievement (G. Roberts, Mohammed, & Vaughn, 2010). For example, one study found that learning and self-regulation skills (e.g., attentiveness, persistence, organization, learning independence) explained the literacy development of African

SCORES ON THE NATIONAL ASSESSMENT OF EDUCATIONAL PROGRESS IN FOURTH-GRADE MATHEMATICS

This figure compares the changes in the scores of White, African American, and Hispanic American fourth-graders between 1990 and 2013.

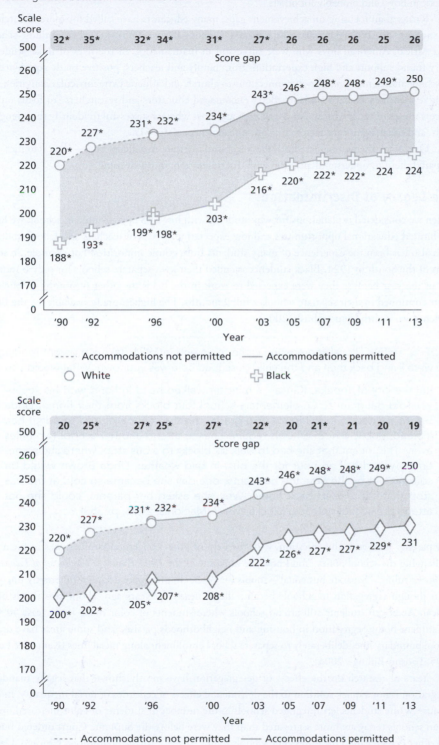

Note: Black includes African American, and Hispanic includes Latino. Race categories exclude Hispanic origin. Score gaps are calculated based on differences between unrounded average scores.
Source: National Assessment of Educational Progress. (2013). National Report Card. Retrieved from http://nationsreportcard.gov/reading_math_2013/#/achievement-gaps

American boys from kindergarten to fifth grade, even after taking into account the effects of the boys' SES, home environment, and problem behaviors (Matthews, Kizzie, Rowley, & Cortina, 2010). So, early development of these learning skills can help to close the opportunity gap, at least for African American boys, and probably for others.

Rather than focusing on achievement gaps, many educators have called for more research on the successes of African American and Latino/a students. Berry (2005) studied two middle-school-aged African American boys who were successful in mathematics. In the lives of those students, Berry found support and high expectations from family and teachers; positive math experiences in preschool and elementary school; connections to church and athletic extracurricular activities; and positive identities as math students. Berry encouraged educators and researchers "to focus on the success stories of those African American men and boys who are successful to identify the strengths, skills, and other significant factors it takes to foster success" (p. 61).

One final theme characterized the successful African American boys—their families had prepared them to understand and deal with discrimination, our next topic.

The Legacy of Discrimination

When we considered explanations for why students with low SES have trouble in school, we listed the limited educational opportunities and low expectations/biases of teachers and fellow students. This also has been the experience of many students from ethnic minorities. For example, in some areas of the South in 1924, Black students attended their own separate schools for only 6 months out of the year because they were expected to work in the fields the other 6 months. White students continued in their separate schools a full 9 months. The highest grade available for the Black students was eighth (Raudenbush, 2009).

STOP & THINK Legal segregation came to an end in 1954. Take a moment to imagine you were living back then and the child described here was your own. What would you do?

[In] the city of Topeka, Kansas, a minister walked hand in hand with his seven-year-old daughter to an elementary school four blocks from their home. Linda Brown wanted to enroll in the 2nd grade, but the school refused to admit her. Instead, public school officials required her to attend another school two miles away. This meant that she had to walk six blocks to a bus stop, where she sometimes waited half an hour for the bus. In bad weather, Linda Brown would be soaking wet by the time the bus came; one day she became so cold at the bus stop that she walked back home. Why, she asked her parents, could she not attend the school only four blocks away? (Macionis, 2003, p. 353) •

Her parents' answer to this question, with the help of other concerned families, was to file a suit challenging the school policy. You know the outcome of the 1954 *Brown* v. *the Board of Education of Topeka* ruling. "Separate but equal" schools for Black children were declared inherently unequal. Even though segregation in schools became illegal nearly 60 years ago, about two thirds of all African American students still attend schools where students of color make up at least 50% of the student body. Segregation in housing and neighborhoods persists, and some areas have drawn school boundary lines deliberately to separate school enrollment along racial lines (Kantor & Lowe, 1995; Ladson-Billings, 2004).

Years of research on the effects of desegregation have mostly shown that legally mandated integration is not a quick solution to the detrimental effects of centuries of racial inequality. In part because White students left integrated schools as the number of students of color increased, many urban schools today are more segregated than they were before the Supreme Court ordered busing and other desegregation measures. The schools in Los Angeles, Miami, Baltimore, Chicago, Dallas, Memphis, Houston, and Detroit have fewer than 11% non-Hispanic White students. In fact, two thirds of the schools that African American and Latino students attend are quite segregated with high concentrations of students living in poverty, so racial segregation becomes economic segregation as well (Ladson-Billings, 2004; Mickelson, Bottia, & Lambert, 2013; Raudenbush, 2009).

Video 6.2
This brief video documents several historical events surrounding desegregation and attempts by the federal government to end discrimination. Consider the achievement gaps that prevail in today's schools as a result of continued inequality.

ENHANCEDetext *video example*

Too often, even in integrated schools, students from minority groups are resegregated in low-ability tracks. Simply putting people in the same building does not mean that they will come to respect each other or even that they will experience the same quality of education (Ladson-Billings, 2004; Mickelson et al., 2013).

WHAT IS PREJUDICE? The word *prejudice* is closely related to the word *prejudge*. Prejudice is a rigid and unfair generalization—a prejudgment—about an entire category of people. Prejudice is made up of *beliefs, emotions,* and tendencies toward particular *actions*. For example, you are prejudiced against people who are overweight if you think they are lazy (belief), feel disgusted (emotion), and refuse to date them (action) (Aboud et al., 2012; Myers, 2010). Prejudice can be positive or negative; that is, you can have positive as well as negative irrational beliefs about a group, but the term usually refers to negative attitudes. Targets of prejudice can be based on race, ethnicity, religion, politics, geographic location, language, sexual orientation, gender, or appearance.

Racial prejudice (racism) is pervasive, and it is not confined to one group. Blatant racism has decreased. For example, in 1970, more than 50% of Americans agreed that it was all right to keep members of minority groups out of their neighborhoods. By 1995, the number had dropped to about 10% (Myers, 2005). But subtle, below-the-surface racism continues. In response to several police shootings of unarmed Black men, researchers created a videogame that showed a series of White or Black men holding either a gun or a non-weapon such as a flashlight or wallet. Participants in the research were told to "shoot" whenever the person in the videogame held a weapon. Race was not mentioned. Nevertheless, participants shot armed targets more quickly and more frequently when those targets were Black, rather than White, but decided not to shoot unarmed targets more quickly and more frequently when they were White (Greenwald, Oakes, & Hoffman, 2003). When the participants in another study were actual police officers, they were more likely to mistakenly shoot unarmed Black suspects compared with unarmed White suspects (Plant & Peruche, 2005). Research in psychology also shows that prejudice against individuals can undermine their mental and physical health, educational achievement, and success on the job (McKown, 2005).

THE DEVELOPMENT OF PREJUDICE. Prejudice starts early. Results from studies around the world in areas with multiethnic populations show that prejudice begins by age 4 or 5 (Aboud et al., 2012; Anzures et al., 2013). Two popular beliefs are that young children are innocently colorblind and that they will not develop biases unless their parents teach them to be prejudiced. Although these beliefs are appealing, they are not supported by research. Even without direct coaching from their parents, many young children develop racial prejudice. Current explanations of the development of prejudice combine personal, social, and societal factors (Aboud et al., 2012; P. A. Katz, 2003; McKown, 2005).

One source of prejudice is the human tendency to divide the social world into two categories: us and them, or the in-group and the out-group. These divisions may be made on the basis of race, religion, sex, age, ethnicity, or even athletic team membership. We tend to see members of the out-group as inferior to and different from us, but similar to each other—"they all look alike." In fact, infants as young as 3 months show a preference for faces of their own race if they have had no experience with other races. By 9 months, infants have better recognition of own-race faces (Anzures et al., 2013). Also, adults who have more (more money, more social status, more prestige) may justify their privilege by assuming that they deserve to "have" because they are superior to the "have-nots." This can lead to blaming the victims: People who live in poverty or women who are raped are seen as causing their problems by their behavior—"they got what they deserved." Emotions play a part as well. When things go wrong, we look for someone or some whole group to blame. For example, after the tragic events of 9/11, some people vented their anger by attacking innocent Arab Americans (Myers, 2010).

But prejudice is more than a tendency to form in-groups, a self-justification, or an emotional reaction—it is also a set of cultural values. Children learn about valued traits and characteristics from their families, friends, teachers, and the world around them. Think back to your analysis of commercials. Did you observe many women or people of color? For years, most of the models presented in books, films, television, and advertising were European Americans. People of

Connect and Extend to PRAXIS II®

Racial Bias (IV, B4)
Describe the possible effects of racial discrimination and bias on minority students. What can teachers and schools do to address the lingering effects of this discrimination?

different ethnic and racial backgrounds were seldom the "heroes" (Ward, 2004). This is changing. In 2002, the Oscar awards for best actress and best actor went to African Americans, but Denzel Washington won for his portrayal of a villain. In 2005, Jamie Foxx won an Oscar for his remarkable portrayal of Ray Charles—a hero. And of course, at the time I am writing, Barack Obama is president of the United States.

STOP & THINK List three traits most characteristic of:
College freshmen
Politicians
Athletes
Buddhists
Members of the National Rifle Association •

Prejudice is difficult to combat because it can be part of our thinking processes. You will see in Chapter 8 that children develop schemas—organized bodies of knowledge—about objects, events, and actions. We have schemas that organize our knowledge about people we know and all our daily activities. We can also form schemas about groups of people. For the *Stop & Think* asking you to list the traits most characteristic of college freshmen, politicians, athletes, Buddhists, and members of the National Rifle Association, you probably could generate a list. That list would show that you have a stereotype—a schema—about each group. **Stereotypes** are simplified descriptions that you apply to every member of a group. These stereotypes actually are schema that organize what you know, believe, and feel about the group. Stereotypes may incorporate prejudiced (rigid, unfair) beliefs about a group, but they don't have to (Macionis, 2013).

As with any schema, we use our stereotypes to make sense of the world. You will see in Chapter 8 that having a schema allows you to process information more quickly and efficiently, but it also allows you to distort information to make it fit your schema better, especially if your stereotypes include prejudiced beliefs about the group (Macrae, Milne, & Bodenhausen, 1994). We notice information that confirms or agrees with our stereotype—our schema—and miss or dismiss information that does not fit. For example, if a juror has a stereotype of Asian Americans that includes negative prejudices and the juror is listening to evidence in the trial of an Asian American, the juror may interpret the evidence more negatively. The juror may actually forget testimony in favor of the defendant and remember more-damaging testimony instead. Information that fits the stereotype is even processed more quickly (S. M. Anderson, Klatzky, & Murray, 1990; Baron, 1998).

CONTINUING DISCRIMINATION. Prejudice consists of rigid, irrational *beliefs* and *feelings* (usually negative) about an entire category of people. The third element of prejudice is a tendency to *act,* called discrimination. **Discrimination** is unequal treatment of particular categories of people. Clearly, many Americans face prejudice and discrimination in subtle or blatant ways every day. For example, Hispanic, African Americans, and Native Americans make up about 35% of the U.S. population, but in 2012, about 6% of the doctorates awarded went to Hispanic students, 5% to African Americans, and 0.2% to Native Americans. In contrast, 35% of the doctorates were awarded to nonresidents of the United States (National Science Foundation, 2014). Black and Hispanic students begin to lose out in science and math as early as elementary school. They are chosen less often for gifted classes and acceleration or enrichment programs. They are more likely to be tracked into "basic skills" classes. As they progress through middle school, high school, and college, their paths take them farther and farther out of the pipeline that produces our scientists. If they do persist and become scientists or engineers, they, along with women, will still be paid less than White employees for the same work (Mendoza & Johnson, 2000; National Science Foundation, 2011).

The families of racial and ethnic minority students often have to be vigilant about discrimination to protect their children. They may teach their children to notice and resist possible discrimination. Teachers may unintentionally offend these families if they are not sensitive to possible messages of discrimination. Carol Orange (2005) described a teacher who sent home a holiday worksheet that featured an alphabetical list of all the students in the class. Three students' names were not in the typed list, but were handwritten, out of order, and on the side of the sheet. Two of these students were Latino and one was African American. The mother of the African American student was very upset that her son was truly "marginalized" (written in the margins) on the list. These three students were added to the class (and hence, the list) later in the year, after the list was set up, but the teacher could have avoided this insult (unintended on her part) by redoing the list to give every student a place—a small but important symbol that she valued each one of them.

There is another problem caused by stereotypes and prejudice that can undermine academic achievement—stereotype threat.

Stereotype Threat

Stereotype threat is an "apprehensiveness about confirming a stereotype" (J. Aronson, 2002, p. 282). The basic idea is that when individuals are in situations in which a stereotype applies, they bear an extra emotional and cognitive burden—the possibility of confirming the stereotype, either in the eyes of others or in their own eyes. So, when girls are asked to solve complicated mathematics problems or African Americans take the SATs, for example, they are at risk of confirming widely held stereotypes that girls are inferior to boys in mathematics or African Americans score lower on SATs. It is not necessary that the individual believe the stereotype. All that matters is that the person is aware of the stereotype and cares about performing well enough to disprove its unflattering implications. The impact seems to be worse for adolescents who identify with the group threatened ("I am proud to be African American") and with the subject ("Science is really important to me!") (Appel & Kronberger, 2012; J. Aronson, Lustina, Good, Keough, Steele, & Brown, 1999; Huguet & Régner, 2007).

WHO IS AFFECTED BY STEREOTYPE THREAT. In a series of experiments, Joshua Aronson, Claude Steele, and their colleagues demonstrated that when African American or Latino college students are put in situations that induce stereotype threat, their performance suffers (Aronson, 2002; Aronson & Steele, 2005; Okagaki, 2006). For example, African American and White undergraduate subjects in an experiment at Stanford University were told that the test they were about to take would precisely measure their verbal ability. A similar group of subjects was told that the purpose of the test was to understand the psychology of verbal problem solving and not to assess individual ability. When the test was presented as diagnostic of verbal ability, the African American students solved about half as many problems as the White students. In the nonthreat situation, the two groups solved about the same number of problems.

Many people, not just women or students from minority groups, can be susceptible to stereotype threat. In other studies, stereotype threat depressed the performance of students from lower-SES backgrounds, elderly test takers, White male college students who were very strong in mathematics but were told that Asian students performed much better than White students on that particular test, and school-age children (J. Aronson, Lustina, et al., 1999; Hartley & Sutton, 2013). For example, Bonny Hartley and Robbie Sutton (2013) conducted three studies of stereotype threat in young students. In the first study they found that girls from age 4 and boys from age 7 believed that girls are better in school than boys and thought that adults believed that too. In the second study, a group of 7- to 8-year-old boys and girls took a test. The experimental group was told that girls do better on this test, but a control group was told that the researchers just wanted to "see how you do." Figure 6.4 on the next page shows the results. Boys in the stereotype condition did significantly worse, but girls' test performance was not affected. In a third study, when students in the experimental condition were told the researchers expected boys and girls to do the same on the test, the effects of stereotype threat disappeared.

Amazingly, students as young as 5 or 6 can be affected by stereotype threat. The individuals most vulnerable to stereotype threat are those who care the most and who are most deeply invested in high performance (Hartley & Sutton, 2013; K. E. Ryan & Ryan, 2005).

Why and how does stereotype threat affect learning? Recent research provides answers that should interest all teachers. There are three main links between stereotype threat and school achievement. Experiencing this threat: (1) prevents individuals from performing at their best on tests and

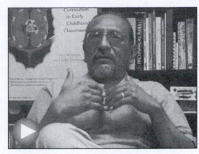

Video 6.3
A Native American who grew up on a reservation talks about the effect of being taught the majority culture's perspective. His ancestors occupied this land long before Columbus "discovered" America. Consider how the self-worth of Native Americans has been affected by discrimination. Consider comparable types of discrimination that affect other groups in our classrooms.

ENHANCEDetext *video example*

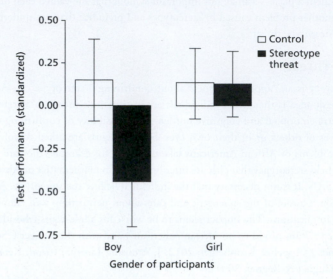

FIGURE 6.4

THE IMPACT OF STEREOTYPE THREAT ON STUDENT PERFORMANCE

When boys were told "girls do better than boys" on this test (stereotype threat), the boys' performance was depressed, but when there was no stereotype threat, the boys and girls performed the same.

Source: Reprinted with permission from Hartley, B. L., & Sutton, R. M. (2013). A stereotype threat account of boys' academic underachievement. Child Development, 84, p. 1724.

assignments, (2) interferes with attention and learning in the subject (e.g., math), and (3) decreases connections to and valuing of that subject (Appel & Kronberger, 2012; Huguet & Régner, 2007). Thus stereotype threat may be one cause, but not the sole cause, of the achievement gap between some ethnic groups (Nadler & Clark, 2011). Let's examine what the effects of stereotype threat look like in school.

SHORT-TERM EFFECTS: TEST PERFORMANCE. One review of the research on women, math, and stereotype threat concluded that very subtle clues that might activate anxiety, such as asking test takers to indicate their gender on an answer sheet before taking a math test, tend to lower math scores for women, especially when tests are difficult, the women are moderately identified with the math field, and being female is an important part of their identity. The differences are small on average—something like a female with average math ability scoring 450 instead of the expected average of 500 on an SAT- or GRE-type test. One study estimated that removing stereotype threat might mean an additional 6% of women getting a passing score on a high-stakes calculus test (Nguyen & Ryan, 2008; Wout, Dasco, Jackson, & Spencer, 2008). In other studies, girls in high school and college scored below boys on a math test when stereotype threats were present but scored the same as boys when these threats were not present (C. S. Smith & Hung, 2008). Just telling the girls that the math test they are about to take does not reveal gender differences is enough to eliminate any differences in scores.

Katherine Ryan and Allison Ryan (2005) developed a model to explain the links between stereotype threat and lower math performance for women and African Americans. When these students are in situations that evoke stereotype threats, such as high-pressure tests, they tend to adopt performance-avoidance goals. We will examine this kind of goal more deeply in Chapter 12. Setting performance-avoidance goals means the students want to avoid looking dumb. Students who set these kinds of self-protective goals don't persist or use effective strategies. They tend to adopt self-handicapping strategies such as not trying or procrastinating—they just want to survive without looking. But because they put off studying or didn't try, they are anxious and unprepared during the test. Ryan and Ryan sum up their model:

> Concerns about fulfilling a negative stereotype (females and Blacks do not do well in math) bring about a performance-avoid goal orientation towards the test-taking situation for students who are invested in doing well on the test. A performance-avoid goal will lead to an increase in the worry component of test anxiety, make self-efficacy vulnerable, and [lead] to cognitive disorganization or diminishment. (K. E. Ryan & Ryan, 2005, p. 60)

Two other related explanations are that stereotype threat reduces working memory capacity—so students can't hold as much in their minds (Okagaki, 2006)—and that it also decreases interest and engagement in the task. Why get absorbed in something that will make you look incompetent? (J. L. Smith, Sansone, & White, 2007; Thoman, Smith, Brown, Chase, & Lee, 2013).

LONG-TERM EFFECTS: DISIDENTIFICATION. Students who experience stereotype threat are less likely to feel a sense of belonging and connection in the context where the threat is "in the air." When they feel disconnected, motivation and engagement suffer (Thoman et al., 2013). If students continue to adopt performance-avoidance goals, develop self-defeating strategies to avoid looking stupid, lose interest, lack a sense of belonging, and feel anxious in testing situations, they may withdraw, claim to not care, exert little effort, or even drop out of school. They psychologically disengage from success and claim "math is for nerds" or "school is for losers." Once students define academics as "uncool," it is unlikely they will exert the effort needed for real learning. Some evidence indicates that Black male students are more likely than Black female students and White students to disidentify with academics—to separate their sense of self-esteem from their academic achievement (Cokley, 2002; Major & Schmader, 1998; C. Steele, 1992). Other studies have questioned this disidentification connection, however. Historically, education has been valued among African American communities (V. S. Walker, 1996). One study found that African American adolescents who had strong Afrocentric beliefs also had higher achievement goals and self-esteem than adolescents who identified with the larger White culture (Spencer, Noll, Stoltzfus, & Harpalani, 2001).

The message for teachers is to help all students see academic achievement as part of their ethnic, racial, and gender identity.

COMBATING STEREOTYPE THREAT. Joshua Aronson, Fried, and Good (2002) demonstrated the powerful effects of changing beliefs about intelligence. African American and White undergraduates were asked to write letters to middle school students who were "at risk," to encourage them to persist in school. Some of the undergraduates were given evidence that intelligence is improvable and encouraged to communicate this information to their pen pals. Others were given information about multiple intelligences but not told that these multiple abilities can be improved. The middle school students were not real, but the process of writing persuasive letters about improving intelligence proved powerful. The African American college students—and the White students to a lesser extent—who were encouraged to believe that intelligence can be improved had higher grade-point averages and reported greater enjoyment of and engagement in school when contacted at the end of the next school quarter. In another study, changing their beliefs about the improvability of intelligence led to higher year-end math achievement scores for middle school girls (C. Good, Aronson, & Inzlicht, 2003). So, believing that intelligence can be improved might inoculate students against stereotype threat. And another study demonstrated that reframing a threatening test as a "challenge" that "sharpens the mind" decreased the impact of stereotype threat for fourth- to sixth-grade African American students and for Princeton University students from high schools that rarely send students to Ivy League schools (Alter, Aaronson, Darley, Rodriguez, & Ruble, 2009).

A book by Carol Dweck (2006) called *Mindset: The New Psychology of Success* discusses how a positive mindset of growth and improvement can be learned and will be an asset throughout life. Other ideas include using role models and emphasizing that if a boy does better than a girl in math, he probably studied harder or persisted longer. The same is true for a girl who does better in writing—stress that she may have worked harder or revised more. Also, completing self-affirmation tasks in school such as writing about personal values seems to combat stereotype threat (Sherman et al., 2013).

In Chapter 12, we will discuss test anxiety and how to overcome the negative effects of anxiety. Many of these strategies are also appropriate for helping students resist stereotype threat.

ENHANCEDetext *self-check*

GENDER IN TEACHING AND LEARNING

In this section, we examine the development of two related identities—sexual identity and gender-role identity. We particularly focus on how men and women are socialized and the role of teachers in providing an equitable education for both sexes.

Sex and Gender

The word *gender* usually refers to traits and behaviors that a particular culture judges to be appropriate for men and for women. In contrast, *sex* refers to biological differences (Brannon, 2002; Deaux, 1993). An individual's identity in terms of gender and sex has three components: gender identity, sexual orientation, and gender-role behaviors (C. Patterson, 1995; Ruble, Martin, & Berenbaum, 2006). Gender identity is a person's self-identification as male or female. *Gender-role behaviors* are those behaviors and characteristics that the culture associates with each gender, and *sexual orientation* involves the person's choice of a sexual partner.

Relations among these three elements are complex. For example, a woman may identify herself as a female (gender identity) but behave in ways that are not consistent with the gender role (play football or wrestle) and may be heterosexual, bisexual, or homosexual in her sexual orientation. So sexual identity is a complicated construction of beliefs, attitudes, and behaviors. Erikson and many other earlier psychologists thought that identifying your gender identity was straightforward; you simply realized that you were male or female and acted accordingly. But today, we know that some people experience conflicts about their gender. For example, transsexuals often report feeling trapped in the wrong body; they experience themselves as female, but their biological sex is male, or vice versa (Ruble et al., 2006; Yarhouse, 2001).

SEXUAL ORIENTATION. Sexual orientation is about feelings of attraction—"an internal mechanism that directs a person's sexuality to females, males, or both, perhaps to varying degrees" (Savin-Williams & Vrangalova, 2013, p. 59). During adolescence, about 8% of boys and 6% of girls report engaging in some same-sex activity or feeling strong attractions to individuals of their own sex. Males are more likely than females to experiment with same-sex partners as adolescents, but females are more likely to experiment later, often in college. Fewer adolescents actually have a homosexual or bisexual orientation; about 4% of adolescents identify themselves as gay (males who choose male partners), lesbian (females who choose female partners), or bisexual (people who have partners of both sexes). This number increases to between 5% and 13% for adults (Savin-Williams, 2006). An acronym you may see is LGBTQ, which stands for lesbian, gay, bisexual, transgendered, and questioning. *Transgendered* individuals are those whose gender identity or self-identification as male or female does not match how others perceive their sex. Transgendered people may identify as heterosexual, homosexual, or bisexual, so being transgendered is not the same as sexual orientation. Finally, "questioning" indicates students who are not yet sure of their sexual orientation (J. P. Robinson & Espelage, 2012).

Scientists debate the origins of homosexuality. Most of the research has been with men, so less is known about women. Evidence so far suggests that both biological and social factors are involved. For example, sexual orientation is more similar for identical twins than for fraternal twins, but not all identical twins have the same sexual orientation (Ruble et al., 2006).

Quite a few models describe the development of sexual orientation as part of identity. Generally, the models include the following or similar stages (Yarhouse, 2001):

- *Feeling different*—Beginning around age 6, the child may be less interested in the activities of other children who are the same sex. Some children may find this difference troubling and fear being "found out." Others do not experience these anxieties.
- *Feeling confused*—In adolescence, as they feel attractions for peers of the same sex, students may be confused, upset, lonely, and unsure of what to do. They may lack role models and may try to change themselves by becoming involved in activities and dating patterns that fit heterosexual stereotypes.
- *Acceptance*—As young adults, many individuals sort through sexual orientation issues and identify themselves as gay, lesbian, or bisexual. They may or may not make their sexual orientation public but might share the information with a few friends.

The problem with phase models of identity development is that the identity achieved is assumed to be final. Actually, newer models emphasize that sexual orientation can be flexible, complex, and multifaceted; it can change over the lifetime. For example, people may have dated or married opposite-sex partners at one point in their lives but have same-sex attractions or partners later in their lives, or vice versa (Garnets, 2002).

LGBTQ students are more likely than their heterosexual peers to be bullied and are at greater risk for missing school and for attempting suicide (J. P. Robinson & Espelage, 2012). We talk about bullying and teachers' roles in handling all types of bullying in Chapter 13. For now, let's consider what you can do if students come to you with concerns about sexual identity or orientation. Even though parents and teachers are seldom the first people to hear about the adolescent's sexual identity concerns, you can be prepared. If a student does seek your counsel, Table 6.2 provides some ideas for reaching out.

TABLE 6.2 • Reaching Out to Help Students Struggling with Sexual Identity
These ideas come from the Attic Speakers Bureau, a program of The Attic Youth Center, where trained peer educators reach out to youth and youth-service providers in schools, organizations, and health care facilities.

REACHING OUT
If a lesbian, gay, bisexual, or transgender youth or a youth questioning his or her own sexual orientation should come to you directly for assistance, remember the following simple, 5-point plan:
LISTEN It seems obvious, but the best thing that you can do in the beginning is allow that individual to vent and express what is going on in his or her life.
AFFIRM Tell them, "You are not alone." This is crucial. A lot of LGBTQ youth feel isolated and lack peers with whom they can discuss issues around sexual orientation. Letting them know that there are others dealing with the same issues is invaluable. This statement is also important because it does not involve a judgment call on your part.
REFER You do not have to be the expert. A referral to someone who is trained to deal with these issues is a gift you are giving to that student, not a dismissal of responsibility.
ADDRESS Deal with harassers—do not overlook issues of verbal or physical harassment around sexual orientation. It is important to create and maintain an environment where all youth feel comfortable and welcome.
FOLLOW-UP Be sure to check in with the individual to see if the situation has improved and if there is anything further you may be able to do.
There are also some things that you as an individual can do to better serve l/g/b/t/q youth and youth dealing with issues around sexual orientation:
• Work on your own sense of comfort around issues of sexual orientation and sexuality. • Get training on how to present information on sexual orientation effectively. • Dispel myths around sexual orientation by knowing facts and sharing that information. • Work on setting aside your own personal biases to better serve students dealing with issues around sexual orientation and sexuality.

Source: From The Attic Speakers Bureau and Carrie E. Jacobs, Ph.D. Reprinted with permission.

Gender Roles

Gender roles are expectations about how males and females should behave—about what is masculine and what is feminine. Gender roles vary by culture, time, and place. What was expected of women in the United States in the 1700s definitely has changed, even though women generally still are the primary caregivers and in charge of the home.

When and how do children develop gender roles? As early as age 2, children are aware of gender differences. They know whether they are girls or boys and that mommies are girls and daddies are boys. By age 3 or so, they realize that their sex cannot be changed; they will always be male or female. Biology plays a part in gender-role development. Very early, hormones affect activity level and aggression, with boys tending to prefer active, rough, noisy play. Play styles lead young children to prefer same-sex play partners with similar styles, so by age 4, children spend three times as much play time with same-sex playmates as with opposite-sex playmates; by age 6, the ratio is 11 to 1 (Halim, Ruble, Tamis-LeMonda, & Shrout, 2013; M. Hines, 2004; Maccoby, 1998).

But biology is not the whole story; boys and girls may be treated differently, too. Researchers have found that boys are given more freedom to roam the neighborhood and are allowed to attempt potentially dangerous activities earlier, such as crossing the street alone. Thus, independence and initiative seem to be encouraged more in boys than in girls. In fact, parents, peers, and teachers may reward behaviors that seem gender appropriate—gentle kindness in girls and strong assertiveness in boys (Brannon, 2002).

And then there are the toys! Walk through any store's toy section, and see what is offered to girls and boys. Dolls and kitchen sets for girls and toy weapons for boys have been with us for decades. Now we have aisles of princess paraphernalia for girls and battle video games for boys. But we cannot blame the toy makers alone. Adults buying for children favor gender-typed toys; fathers also tend to discourage young sons from playing with "girls" toys (Brannon, 2002).

Through their interactions with family, peers, teachers, toys, and the environment in general, children begin to form **gender schemas**, or organized networks of knowledge about what it means to be male or female. Gender schemas help children make sense of the world and guide their behavior (see Figure 6.5). So a young girl whose schema for "girls" includes "girls play with dolls and not with trucks" or "girls can't be scientists" will pay attention to, remember, and interact more with dolls than trucks, and she may avoid science activities (Golombok et al., 2008; Leaper, 2002). Of course, these are averages, and individuals do not always fit the average. An individual girl might decide, for example, that the gender schema "trucks are for boys" doesn't matter to her. She plays with the truck if it interests her (Liben & Bigler, 2002).

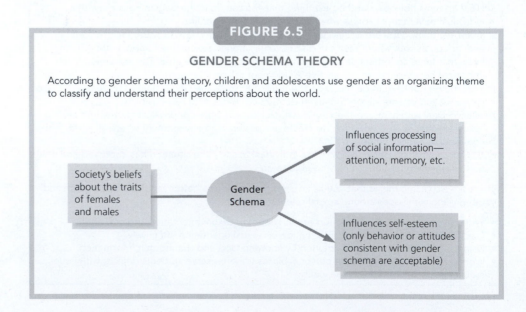

FIGURE 6.5

GENDER SCHEMA THEORY

According to gender schema theory, children and adolescents use gender as an organizing theme to classify and understand their perceptions about the world.

Society's beliefs about the traits of females and males → Gender Schema → Influences processing of social information—attention, memory, etc.

Influences self-esteem (only behavior or attitudes consistent with gender schema are acceptable)

By age 4, children have an initial sense of gender roles, and by 5 or so, they have developed a gender schema that describes what clothes, games, toys, behaviors, and careers are "right" for boys and girls—and these ideas can be quite rigid (Brannon, 2002; Halim et al., 2013). Even in this era of great progress toward equal opportunity, a preschool girl is more likely to tell you she wants to become a nurse than to say she wants to be an engineer. After she had given a lecture on the dangers of sex stereotyping in schools, a colleague of mine brought her young daughter to her college class. The students asked the little girl, "What do you want to be when you grow up?" The child immediately replied, "A doctor," and her professor/mother beamed with pride. Then the girl whispered to the students in the front row, "I really want to be a nurse, but my Mommy won't let me." Actually, this is a common reaction for young children. Preschoolers tend to have more stereotyped notions of sex roles than older children, and all ages seem to have more rigid and traditional ideas about male occupations than about what occupations females should pursue (Woolfolk & Perry, 2015). Later, as adolescents go through puberty, they may become even more focused on behaving in "masculine" or "feminine" ways, as defined by their peer culture. So many factors, from biology to cultural norms, play a role in gender-role development. Beware of either/or explanations.

While I was proofreading this very page for a previous edition, riding cross-country on a train, the conductor stopped beside my seat. He said, "I'm sorry, dear, for interrupting your *homework*, but do you have a ticket?" I had to smile at his (I'm sure unintended) sexism. I doubt that he made the same comment to the man across the aisle who was writing on his legal pad. Like racial discrimination, messages of sexism can be subtle, and they can appear in classrooms.

Gender Bias in Curriculum Materials

Unfortunately, schools often foster gender biases in a number of ways. Publishers have established guidelines to prevent gender bias in teaching materials, but it still makes sense to check them for stereotypes. For example, even though children's books now have an equal number of males and females as central characters, there still are more males in the titles and the illustrations, and the characters (especially the boys) continue to behave in stereotypic ways. Boys are more aggressive and argumentative, and girls are more expressive and affectionate. Girl characters sometimes cross gender roles to be more active, but boy characters seldom show "feminine" expressive traits (Brannon, 2002; L. Evans & Davies, 2000). Also, video learning packages, virtual worlds, social media sites, and sources such as YouTube have not been carefully screened for gender, racial, ethnic, economic, religious, or age stereotypes and biases, and they can be sources of stereotyped messages (Henry, 2011). Digital teaching and testing materials and computer programs often feature boys more than girls and include other biases. One look at the body builds of males and females in video combat games shows what unreal and unhealthy body images they promote.

Another "text" that students read long before they arrive in your classroom is television. A content analysis of television commercials found that White male characters were more prominent than any other group (did you find that when you took the "commercial break" in the *Stop & Think* activity earlier?). Even when only the actor's voice could be heard, men were 10 times more likely to narrate commercials. And the same pattern of men as the "voice of authority" on television occurred in the United Kingdom, Europe, Australia, and Asia. Women were more likely than men to be shown as dependent on men and often were depicted at home (Brannon, 2002). So, both before and after going to school, students are likely to encounter texts that overrepresent males.

Gender Bias in Teaching

Quite a bit of research has studied teachers' treatment of male and female students. You should know, however, that most of these studies have focused on White students, so the results reported in this section hold mostly for White male and female students.

Many studies describe what seem like biases favoring boys. One of the best-documented findings of the past 30 years is that teachers have more overall interactions with boys than with girls; however, this includes more negative interactions with boys but not more positive interactions (S. M. Jones & Dindia, 2004). This is true from preschool to college. Teachers ask more questions of males, give males more feedback (praise, criticism, and correction), and offer more specific and

Video 6.4
In this video, 7-year-old Callie answers questions about subjects she likes and dislikes in school and math games she likes to play. As you listen to her answer the questions, consider the extent to which her answers do or do not follow stereotypical gender patterns.

ENHANCEDetext *video example*

Connect and Extend to PRAXIS II®

Gender Bias (IV, B4)
There has been much debate in the news media over possible gender bias in schools. What can you as a teacher do to reduce or eliminate gender bias and its effects?

GUIDELINES
Avoiding Gender Bias in Teaching

Check to see if textbooks and other materials you are using present an honest view of the options open to both males and females.

Examples

1. Identify whether both males and females are portrayed in traditional and nontraditional roles at work, at leisure, and at home.
2. Discuss your analyses with students, and ask them to help you find sex-role biases in other materials—magazine advertising, TV programs, news reporting, for example.

Watch for any unintended biases in your own classroom practices.

Examples

1. Monitor whether you group students by sex for certain activities. Is the grouping appropriate?
2. Monitor whether you call on one sex or the other for certain answers—boys for math and girls for poetry, for example.
3. Monitor your metaphors. Don't ask students to "tackle the problem."

Look for ways in which your school may be limiting the options open to male or female students.

Examples

1. Find out what advice guidance counselors give to students in course and career decisions.
2. Look into whether there is a good sports program for both girls and boys.
3. See if girls are encouraged to take AP courses in science and mathematics and if boys are encouraged in English and foreign language classes.

Use gender-free language as much as possible.

Examples

1. Make sure you speak of "law-enforcement officer" and "mail carrier" instead of "policeman" and "mailman."
2. Be sure you name a committee "head" instead of a "chairman."

Provide role models.

Examples

1. Assign articles in professional journals written by female research scientists or mathematicians.
2. Have recent female graduates who are majoring in science, math, engineering, or other technical fields come to class to talk about college.
3. Create electronic mentoring programs for both male and female students to connect them with adults working in areas of interest to the students.

Make sure all students have a chance to do complex, technical work.

Examples

1. Experiment with same-sex lab groups so girls do not always end up as the secretaries, boys as the technicians.
2. Rotate jobs in groups or randomly assign responsibilities.

What if you witness gender bias as a student teacher? See this site for ideas: tolerance.org/teach/magazine/features .jsp?p=0&is=36&ar=563#

valuable comments to boys. The effect of these differences is that from preschool through college, girls, on the average, receive 1,800 fewer hours of attention and instruction than boys (Sadker, Sadker, & Klein, 1991). Of course, these differences are not evenly distributed. Some boys, generally high-achieving White students, receive more than their share, whereas high-achieving White girls receive the least teacher attention.

Not all biases in school favor boys. In the past 10 years in North America, Western Europe, Australia, and some Asian countries, educators have raised questions about whether schools are serving boys well. This concern is fueled by data from many countries that seem to show underachievement in boys. In fact, the underachievement of boys in school has been called "one of the most pressing educational equality challenges of current times" (Hartley & Sutton, 2013, p. 1716). More dramatic accusations include that schools are trying to destroy "boys' culture" and force "feminine, frilly content" on boys.

One explanation for why boys struggle in school is that the expectations of schooling do not fit the way boys learn (Gurian & Henley, 2001), particularly African American boys (Stinson, 2006). Another suggestion is that boys sabotage their own learning by resisting school expectations and rules to "display their masculinity and get respect" (Kleinfeld, 2005, p. B6). Critics of the schools suggest that boys need smaller classes, more discussions, better discipline, mentoring programs, and more men in their schools—90% of elementary teachers are female (Svoboda, 2001).

A current suggestion for making schools more effective for both boys and girls is single-sex classrooms. In 2008, the *New York Times Magazine* had a cover story about that topic (Weil, 2008), and some school districts are experimenting with single-sex classrooms in core subjects such as English, science, and mathematics (Herron, 2013). Some research has shown advantages, but often the students or their families have self-selected to attend a single-sex or a mixed-sex school. One study in Korea randomly assigned students to a type of school and found no differences in student achievement as measured by the Trends in International Science and Mathematics (TIMSS) for eighth-grade students (Pahlke, Shibley Hyde, & Mertz, 2013). So do single-sex schools or classrooms improve learning? The answer is, "It depends." Teaching boys and girls in separate classes can have positive effects on student learning, motivation, and engagement, but only if certain demanding conditions are met. Teachers must realize that there are no boy- or girl-specific teaching strategies—good teaching is good teaching. Regrouping students by sex does not make teaching easier; in fact, it can make class management more difficult. To succeed, both teachers and students must understand that the goal of their single-sex classrooms is better learning for everyone in an atmosphere that supports more open discussions with less concern about making impressions on peers (Younger & Warrington, 2006). The *Guidelines: Avoiding Gender Bias in Teaching* provides additional ideas about avoiding gender bias for all students in your classes.

We have dealt with a wide range of differences in this chapter. How can teachers provide an appropriate education for all of their students? One answer is multicultural education with culturally compatible classrooms.

ENHANCEDetext *self-check*

MULTICULTURAL EDUCATION: CREATING CULTURALLY COMPATIBLE CLASSROOMS

Multicultural education is

> [a] process of comprehensive school reform and basic education for all students. It challenges and rejects racism and other forms of discrimination in schools and society and accepts and affirms the pluralism (ethnic, racial, linguistic, religious, economic, and gender, among others) that students, their communities, and their teachers reflect. (Nieto & Bode, 2012, p. 42)

James Banks (2014) suggests that multicultural education has five dimensions: *content integration, the knowledge construction process, prejudice reduction, an empowering school culture and social structure,* and an *equity pedagogy,* as shown in Figure 6.6 on the next page. Many people are familiar only with the dimension of *content integration,* or using examples and content from a variety of cultures when teaching a subject. And because they believe that multicultural education is simply a change in content, some teachers assume that it is irrelevant for subjects such as science and mathematics. But if you consider the other four dimensions—helping students understand how knowledge is constructed, reducing prejudice, creating social structures in schools that support learning and development for all students, and using equity pedagogy or teaching methods that reach all students—then you will see that this view of multicultural education is relevant to all subjects and all students.

An examination of the alternative approaches to multicultural education is beyond the scope of an educational psychology text, but be aware that there is no general agreement about the "best" approach. Many educators have suggested that culturally relevant pedagogy should be an element in multicultural education reform.

Culturally Relevant Pedagogy

Several researchers have focused on teachers who are especially successful with students of color and students in poverty (Delpit, 1995; Ladson-Billings, 1994, 1995; Moll, Amanti,

Connect and Extend to PRAXIS II®

Multicultural Education (III, B)
Know the major dimensions of multicultural education. Describe how these dimensions influence each other.

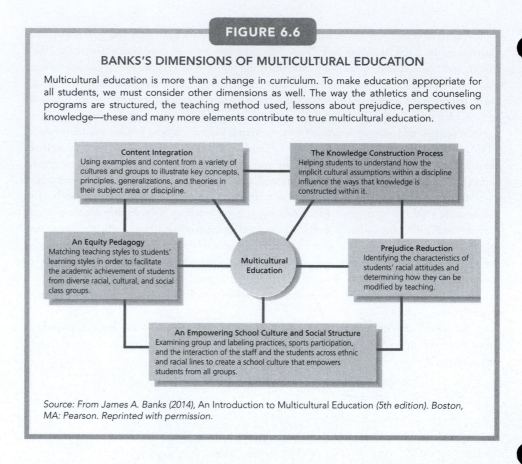

FIGURE 6.6

BANKS'S DIMENSIONS OF MULTICULTURAL EDUCATION

Multicultural education is more than a change in curriculum. To make education appropriate for all students, we must consider other dimensions as well. The way the athletics and counseling programs are structured, the teaching method used, lessons about prejudice, perspectives on knowledge—these and many more elements contribute to true multicultural education.

Content Integration
Using examples and content from a variety of cultures and groups to illustrate key concepts, principles, generalizations, and theories in their subject area or discipline.

The Knowledge Construction Process
Helping students to understand how the implicit cultural assumptions within a discipline influence the ways that knowledge is constructed within it.

An Equity Pedagogy
Matching teaching styles to students' learning styles in order to facilitate the academic achievement of students from diverse racial, cultural, and social class groups.

Multicultural Education

Prejudice Reduction
Identifying the characteristics of students' racial attitudes and determining how they can be modified by teaching.

An Empowering School Culture and Social Structure
Examining group and labeling practices, sports participation, and the interaction of the staff and the students across ethnic and racial lines to create a school culture that empowers students from all groups.

Source: From James A. Banks (2014), An Introduction to Multicultural Education (5th edition). Boston, MA: Pearson. Reprinted with permission.

Neff, & Gonzalez, 1992; Siddle Walker, 2001). The work of Gloria Ladson-Billings (1990, 1992, 1995) is a good example. For 3 years, she studied excellent teachers in a California school district that served an African American community. To select the teachers, she asked parents and principals for nominations. Parents nominated teachers who respected them, created enthusiasm for learning in their children, and understood their children's need to operate successfully in two different worlds— the home community and the White world beyond. Principals nominated teachers who had few discipline referrals, high attendance rates, and high standardized test scores. Ladson-Billings was able to examine in depth eight of the nine teachers who were nominated by *both* parents and principals.

Based on her research, Ladson-Billings developed a conception of teaching excellence. She uses the term **culturally relevant pedagogy** to describe teaching that rests on three propositions.

1. *Students must experience academic success.* "Despite the current social inequities and hostile classroom environments, students must develop their academic skills. The ways those skills are developed may vary, but all students need literacy, numeracy, technological, social, and political skills in order to be active participants in a democracy" (Ladson-Billings, 1995, p. 160).

2. *Students must develop/maintain their cultural competence.* As they become more academically skilled, students still retain their cultural competence. "Culturally relevant teachers utilize students' culture as a vehicle for learning" (Ladson-Billings, 1995, p. 161). For example, one teacher used rap music to teach about literal and figurative meaning, rhyme, alliteration, and onomatopoeia in poetry. Another brought in a community expert known for her sweet potato pies to work with students. Follow-up lessons included investigations of George Washington Carver's sweet potato research, numerical analyses of taste tests, marketing plans for selling pies, and research on the educational preparation needed to become a chef.

3. *Students must develop a critical consciousness to challenge the status quo.* In addition to developing academic skills while retaining cultural competence, excellent teachers help students "develop a broader sociopolitical consciousness that allows them to critique the social norms,

values, mores, and institutions that produce and maintain social inequities" (Ladson-Billings, 1995, p. 162). For example, in one school, students were upset that their textbooks were out of date. They mobilized to investigate the funding formulas that allowed middle-class students to have newer books, wrote letters to the newspaper editor to challenge these inequities, and updated their texts with current information from other sources.

Ladson-Billings (1995) noted that many people have said her three principles "are just good teaching." She agrees that she is describing good teaching, but questions "why so little of it seems to be occurring in classrooms populated by African American students" (p. 159). Geneva Gay (2000) uses the term *culturally responsive teaching* to describe a similar approach that uses the "cultural knowledge, prior experiences, frames of reference, and performance styles of ethnically diverse students to make learning encounters more relevant to and effective for them. It teaches to and through the strengths of these students. It is culturally validating and affirming" (p. 29).

Lisa Delpit (2003) describes three steps for teaching students of color that are consistent with culturally relevant pedagogy: (1) Teachers must be convinced of the inherent intellectual capability, humanity, and spiritual character of their students—they must believe in the children. There are many examples around the country of schools where African American students from low-income families are reading well above grade level and doing advanced math. When scores are low, the fault is not in the students but in their education. (2) Teachers must fight the foolishness that high test scores or scripted lessons are evidence of good learning and good teaching. Successful instruction is "constant, rigorous, integrated across disciplines, connected to students' lived cultures, connected to their intellectual legacies, engaging, and designed for critical thinking and problem solving that is useful beyond the classroom" (p. 18). (3) Teachers must learn who their students are and the legacies they bring. Then, students can explore their own intellectual legacies and understand the important reasons for academic, social, physical, and moral excellence—not just to "get a job" but also "for our community, for your ancestors, for your descendents" (p. 19).

Michael Pressley and his colleagues (2004) did a case study of a very successful K–12 school for African American students. The characteristics of effective teaching at the school are shown in Table 6.3 on the next page.

In the past, discussions of teaching low-income students from racial, ethnic, or language-minority groups have focused on remediating problems or overcoming perceived deficits. But thinking today emphasizes teaching to the strengths and the resilience of these students.

Fostering Resilience

In any given week, 12% to 15% of school-age children who have urgent needs for social and emotional support do not receive the help they need. Community and mental health services often don't reach the students who are at the highest risk. But many children at risk for academic failure not only survive—they thrive. They are resilient students. What can we learn from these students? What can teachers and schools do to encourage resilience?

RESILIENT STUDENTS. Students who seem able to thrive in spite of serious challenges are actively engaged in school. They have good interpersonal skills, confidence in their own ability to learn, positive attitudes toward school, pride in their ethnicity, and high expectations (Borman & Overman, 2004; R. M. Lee, 2005). Also, students who have high intelligence or valued talents are more protected from risks. Being easygoing and optimistic is associated with resilience as well. Factors outside the student—interpersonal relationships and social support—matter, too. It helps to have a warm relationship with a parent who has high expectations and supports learning by organizing space and time at home for study. But even without such a parent, a strong bond with someone competent—a grandparent, aunt, uncle, teacher, mentor, or other caring adult—can serve the same supportive function. Involvement in school, community, or religious activities can provide more connections to concerned adults and also teach lessons in social skills and leadership (Berk, 2005).

RESILIENT CLASSROOMS. You can't choose personalities or parents for your students. And if you could, stresses can build up for even the most resilient students. Beth Doll and her colleagues

TABLE 6.3 • **Research-Based Characteristics of Schools and Teachers Associated with Academic Achievement for African American Students**

CHARACTERISTICS OF SCHOOLS	CHARACTERISTICS OF EFFECTIVE TEACHING	OTHER CHARACTERISTICS
Strong administrative leadership	Dedicated teachers who are accountable to produce results	Much total academic time: A very long functional school day/week, including before-school-hours to after-school-hours interactions and tutoring, good use of almost every minute of every class hour, and summer school for students who need it
Frequent evaluation of student progress	Much teacher scaffolding, encouraging student self-regulation	Students who help one another with academics
Emphasis on academics	Curriculum and instruction emphasizing understanding	Strong family–school connections
Safe and orderly environment	Mentoring, especially with regard to college admissions	Donors and visibly supportive, successful alumni
High expectations for student achievement including selective recruitment/retention of students, with the school weeding out students who are not using the opportunity well in favor of students who will (i.e., weeding out misbehaving students, students not meeting academic standards)	Intentional, massive, and frequent attempts to motivate students, including use of the following mechanisms: Positive expectations Visible care by teachers and administrators Praise of specific accomplishments Generally positive atmosphere, encouragement of effort attributions Cooperative learning experiences Tangible rewards for achievements	Motivational mechanisms not often encountered in schools: Extreme community celebrations of academic achievements Encouragement of a possible self as college graduate and successful professional Discouragement of negative possible selves Development of informed pride in African American heritage and life
Excellent classroom management in most classrooms, resulting in a high proportion of academic time on task	Teachers who provide strong instructional supports for academic achievement (e.g., study guides, test expectations made apparent, informative, feedback on homework and before exams)	Many extracurricular and curricular-enrichment activities—almost all academically oriented or intended to increase commitment to academic pursuits
		An attractive school building loaded with resources to support academic pursuits

Source: Based on Pressley, M., Raphael, L., Gallagher, J. D., & DiBella, J. (2004). Providence St. Mel School: How a school that works for African American students works. Journal of Educational Psychology, 96(2), pp. 234–235.

(2005) suggest that we have to change classrooms instead of kids because "alternative strategies will be more enduring and most successful when they are integrated into naturally occurring systems of support [like schools] that surround children" (p. 3). In addition, some evidence shows that changes in classrooms—such as reducing class size, creating an orderly and safe environment, and forming supportive relationships with teachers—have a greater impact on the academic achievement of African American students compared to Latino/a and White students (Borman & Overman, 2004). So how can you create a classroom that supports resilience?

In formulating their suggestions for characteristics of resilient classrooms, Doll and her colleagues (2005) drew on research in education and psychology on best practices for children in poverty and children with disabilities. Two strands of elements bind students to their classroom community: self-agency and connected relationships.

SELF-AGENCY STRAND.
- *Academic self-efficacy,* a belief in your own ability to learn, is one of the most consistent predictors of academic achievement. As you will see in Chapter 11, self-efficacy emerges when students tackle challenging, meaningful tasks with the support needed to be successful and observe other students doing the same thing. Accurate and encouraging feedback from teachers also helps.
- *Behavioral self-control,* or student self-regulation, is essential for a safe and orderly learning environment. Chapters 7, 11, and 13 will give you ideas for helping students develop self-control.

- *Academic self-determination,* which includes making choices, setting goals, and following through, is the third element in the self-agency strand. As you will see in Chapter 12, students who are self-determined are more motivated and committed to learning.

RELATIONSHIP STRAND.

- *Caring teacher–student relationships* are consistently associated with better school performance, especially for students who face serious challenges. You saw the power of caring teachers in Chapters 1 and 3, and you will continue to see the value of these relationships throughout this text.
- *Effective peer relations,* as you saw in Chapter 3, also are critical in connecting students to school.
- *Effective home–school relationships* are the final element in building a caring, connected network for students. In the School Development program, James Comer has found that when parents stay involved, their children's grades and test scores improve (Comer, Haynes, & Joyner, 1996). The *Guidelines: Family and Community Partnerships* taken from Epstein (1995) gives some ideas for connecting with families.

GUIDELINES
Family and Community Partnerships

Building Learning Communities

Parenting partnerships: Help all families establish home environments to support children as students.

Examples

1. Offer workshops, videos, courses, family literacy fairs, and other informational programs to help parents cope with parenting situations that they identify as important.
2. Establish family support programs to assist with nutrition, health, and social services.
3. Find ways to help families share information with the school about the child's cultural background, talents, and needs—learn from the families.

Communication: Design effective forms for school-to-home and home-to-school communication.

Examples

1. Make sure communications fit the needs of families. Provide translations, visual support, large print—whatever is needed to make communication effective.
2. Visit families in their neighborhoods after gaining their permission. Don't expect family members to come to school until a trusting relationship is established.
3. Balance messages about problems with communications of accomplishments and positive information.

Volunteering: Recruit and organize parent help and support.

Examples

1. Do an annual postcard survey to identify family talents, interests, times available, and suggestions for improvements.
2. Establish a structure (telephone tree, etc.) to keep all families informed. Make sure families without telephones are included.
3. If possible, set aside a room for volunteer meetings and projects.

Learning at home: Provide information and ideas for families about how to help children with schoolwork and learning activities.

Examples

1. Provide assignment schedules, homework policies, and tips on how to help with schoolwork without doing the work.
2. Get family input into curriculum planning. Have idea and activity exchanges.
3. Send home learning packets and enjoyable learning activities, especially over holidays and summers.

Decision-making partnerships: Include families in school decisions, developing family and community leaders and representatives.

Examples

1. Create family advisory committees for the school with parent representatives.
2. Make sure all families are in a network with their representative.

Community partnerships: Identify and integrate resources and services from the community to strengthen school programs, family practices, and student learning and development.

Examples

1. Have students and parents research existing resources. Build a database.
2. Identify service projects for students. Explore service learning.
3. Identify community members who are school alumni, and get them involved in school programs.

Source: Excerpt from pp. 704–705, "School/Family/Community Partnerships: Caring for the Children We Share," by J. L. Epstein, Phi Delta Kappan, 76, pp. 701–712. Copyright © 1995 by Phi Delta Kappan. Reprinted with permission of Phi Delta Kappan and the author, Joyce L. Epstein.

Diversity in Learning

Years ago Roland Tharp (1989) outlined several dimensions of classrooms that reflect the diversity of the students and can be tailored to better fit their backgrounds: social organization, cultural values, learning preferences, and sociolinguistics. His advice is still relevant today.

SOCIAL ORGANIZATION. "A central task of educational design is to make the organization of teaching, learning, and performance compatible with the social structures in which students are most productive, engaged, and likely to learn" (Tharp, 1989, p. 350). Social structure or social organization in this context means the ways people interact to accomplish a particular goal. For example, the social organization of Hawaiian society depends heavily on collaboration and cooperation. Children play together in groups of friends and siblings, with older children often caring for the younger ones. When cooperative work groups of four or five boys and girls were established in Hawaiian classrooms, student learning and participation improved (Okagaki, 2001, 2006). The teacher worked intensively with one group while the children in the remaining groups helped each other. But when the same structure was tried in a Navajo classroom, students would not work together. These children are socialized to be more solitary and not to play with children of the opposite sex. By setting up same-sex working groups of only two or three Navajo students, teachers encouraged them to help each other. If you have students from several cultures, you may need to provide choices and variety in grouping structures.

CULTURAL VALUES AND LEARNING PREFERENCES. Results of some research suggest that Hispanic American students are more oriented toward family and group loyalty. This may mean that these students prefer cooperative activities and dislike being made to compete with fellow students (E. E. Garcia, 1992; Vasquez, 1990). Four values shared by many Latina/o students are:

Familismo: Tightly knit families. Discussing family problems or business may be seen as disloyal.
Simpatia: Value of interpersonal harmony. Assertively voicing personal opinions or arguing may be seen as inappropriate.
Respeto: Respect for people in authority, for example, teachers and government officials.
Personalismo: Valuing of close interpersonal relationships; discomfort with distant, cold, professional relationships. (Dingfelder, 2005)

The learning styles of African Americans may be inconsistent with teaching approaches in most schools. Some of the characteristics of this learning style are a visual/global approach rather than a verbal/analytic approach; a preference for reasoning by inference rather than by formal logic; a focus on people and relationships; a preference for energetic involvement in several activities simultaneously rather than routine, step-by-step learning; a tendency to approximate numbers, space, and time; and a greater dependence on nonverbal communication. Students of color who identify with their traditional cultures tend to respond better to open-ended questions with more than one answer, as opposed to single, right-answer questions. Questions that focus on meaning or the "big picture" may be more productive than questions that focus on details (Bennett, 2011; Gay, 2000; Sheets, 2005).

Native Americans also appear to have a more global, visual style of learning. For example, Navajo students prefer hearing a story all the way through to the end before discussing parts of the story. Teachers who stop reading to ask comprehension questions seem odd to these students and interrupt their learning process (Tharp, 1989). Also, these students sometimes show strong preferences for learning privately, through trial and error, rather than having their mistakes made public (Vasquez, 1990).

Little research on the learning styles of Asian Americans exists, perhaps because they are viewed as a "model minority," as you saw earlier. Some educators suggest that Asian American children tend to value teacher approval and to work well in structured, quiet learning environments with clear goals and social support (M. L. Manning & Baruth, 1996). Other research suggests clear and deep differences in Asian and Western styles of learning. Students from Asian cultures tend be more interdependent and to value learning with others, which might explain some of their success in school. Western values emphasize independence and individual learning, which might explain some of the United States' successes in science, technology, and innovation (Chang et al., 2011). But, as you saw earlier, there are dangers in stereotyping any group, especially in terms of cultural learning styles.

CAUTIONS (AGAIN) ABOUT LEARNING STYLES RESEARCH. In considering this research on learning styles, you should keep two points in mind. First, the validity of some of the learning styles research has been strongly questioned, as you saw in Chapter 4. Second, there is a heated debate today about whether identifying ethnic group differences in learning styles and preferences is a dangerous, racist, sexist exercise. In our society, we are quick to move from the notion of "difference" to the idea of "deficits" and stereotypes (E. W. Gordon, 1991; O'Neil, 1990). I have included the information about learning style differences because I believe that, used sensibly, this information can help you better understand your students. But it is dangerous and incorrect to assume that every individual in a group shares the same learning style (Sheets, 2005). The best advice for teachers is to be sensitive to individual differences in all your students and to make available alternative paths to learning. Never prejudge how a student will learn best based on assumptions about the student's ethnicity or race. Get to know the individual.

SOCIOLINGUISTICS. **Sociolinguistics** is the study of "the courtesies and conventions of conversation across cultures" (Tharp, 1989, p. 351). Knowledge of sociolinguistics will help you understand why communication sometimes breaks down in classrooms. The classroom is a special setting for communicating; it has its own set of rules for when, how, to whom, about what subject, and in what manner to use language. Sometimes, the sociolinguistic skills of students do not fit the expectations of teachers or counselors, as we saw earlier.

To be successful, students must know the communication rules; that is, they must understand the **pragmatics** of the classroom—when, where, and how to communicate. This is not such an easy task. As class activities change, rules change. Sometimes you have to raise your hand (during the teacher's presentation), but sometimes you don't (during story time on the rug). Sometimes it is good to ask a question (during discussion), but other times it isn't so good (when the teacher is reprimanding you). These differing activity rules are called **participation structures**, and they define appropriate participation for each class activity. Most classrooms have many different participation structures. To be competent communicators in the classroom, students sometimes have to read very subtle, nonverbal cues telling them which participation structures are currently in effect. For example, when the teacher moves to the white board, students should look up and be ready for instructions.

SOURCES OF MISUNDERSTANDINGS. Some children are simply better than others at reading the classroom situation because the participation structures of the school match the structures they have learned at home. The communication rules for most school situations are similar to those in middle-class homes, so children from these homes often appear to be more competent communicators. They know the unwritten rules. Students who are not White and middle class may not know the rules. For example, researchers found that Pueblo Indian students participated twice as much in classes where teachers waited longer to react. Waiting longer also helps girls to participate more freely in math and science classes (Grossman & Grossman, 1994). Students from different cultural backgrounds may have learned participation structures that conflict with the behaviors expected in school. For example, one study found that the home conversation style of Hawaiian children is to chime in with contributions to a story. In school, however, this overlapping style is viewed as "interrupting." When the teachers learned about these differences and made their reading groups more like their students' home conversation groups, the young Hawaiian children in their classes improved in reading (K. H. Au, 1980; Tharp, 1989).

It seems that even students who speak the same language as their teachers may still have trouble communicating and so have trouble learning school subjects. What can teachers do? Especially in the early grades, you should make communication rules for activities clear and explicit. Do not assume students know what to do. Use cues to signal students when changes occur. Explain and demonstrate appropriate behavior. I have seen teachers show young children how to use their "inside voice," "six-inch voice," or "whisper voice." One teacher said and then demonstrated, "If you have to interrupt me while I'm working with other children, stand quietly beside me until I can help you." Be consistent in responding to students. If students are supposed to raise their hands, don't call on those who break the rules. In these ways you will teach students how to learn in school.

Lessons for Teachers: Teaching Every Student

As explained at the outset, the goal of this chapter is to give you a sense of the diversity in today's and tomorrow's schools and to help you meet the challenges of teaching in a multicultural classroom. How will you understand and build on all the cultures of your students? How will you deal with many different languages? Here are three general teaching principles to guide you in finding answers to these questions.

KNOW YOUR STUDENTS. We must learn who our students are and understand the legacies they bring (Delpit, 2003). Nothing you read in a chapter on cultural differences will teach you enough to understand the lives of all your students. If you can take other courses in college or read about other cultures, I encourage you to do it. But reading and studying are not enough. You should get to know your students' families and communities. Elba Reyes, a successful bilingual teacher for children with special needs, describes her approach:

> Usually I find that if you really want to know a parent, you get to know them on their own turf. This is key to developing trust and understanding the parents' perspective. First, get to know the community. Learn where the local grocery store is and what the children do after school. Then schedule a home visit at a time that is convenient for the parents. The home environment is not usually as ladened with failure. I sometimes observed the child being successful in the home, for example, riding a bicycle or helping with dinner. (Bos & Reyes, 1996, p. 349)

Try to spend time with students and parents on projects outside school. Ask parents to help in class or to speak to your students about their jobs, their hobbies, or the history and heritage of their ethnic group. In the elementary grades, don't wait until a student is in trouble to have the first meeting with a family member. Watch for and listen to the ways that your students interact in large and small groups. Have students write to you, and write back to them. Eat lunch with one or two students. Spend some nonteaching time with them.

RESPECT YOUR STUDENTS. From knowledge should come respect for your students' learning strengths—for the struggles they face and the obstacles they have overcome. We must believe in our students (Delpit, 2003). For a child, genuine acceptance is a necessary condition for developing self-esteem. Sometimes the self-image and occupational aspirations of minority children actually decline in their early years in public school, probably because of the emphasis on majority culture values, accomplishments, and history. By presenting the accomplishments of particular members of an ethnic group or by bringing that group's culture into the classroom (in the form of literature, art, music, or any cultural knowledge), teachers can help students maintain a sense of pride in their cultural group. This integration of culture must be more than the "tokenism" of sampling ethnic foods or wearing costumes. Students should learn about the socially and intellectually important contributions of the various groups. Many excellent references provide background information, history, and teaching strategies for different groups of students (e.g., J. A. Banks, 2002; Gay, 2000; Irvine & Armento, 2001; Ladson-Billings, 1995).

TEACH YOUR STUDENTS. The most important thing you can do for your students is teach them to read, write, speak, compute, think, and create—through constant, rigorous, culturally connected

Video 6.5
The teacher in this video uses a community building writing activity with her students. Her teaching practices model teaching principles for teaching in a multicultural classroom: know your students, respect your students, teach your students.

ENHANCEDetext *video example*

instruction (Delpit, 2003). A strong emphasis on academics and high expectations combined with caring support for students is a key (Palardy, 2013). Sometimes, in an attempt to be compassionate or to relieve the stress on students placed at risk, teachers give these students more positive feedback than they would privileged students. This well-intended but overly positive feedback can contribute to lowering expectations and reducing the academic challenge for these students (Harber et al., 2012). Too often, goals for students with low SES or from minority groups have focused exclusively on basic skills. Students are taught words and sounds, but the meaning of the story is supposed to come later. Knapp, Turnbull, and Shields (1990, p. 5) make these suggestions:

- Focus on meaning and understanding from beginning to end—for example, by orienting instruction toward comprehending reading passages, communicating important ideas in written text, or understanding the concepts underlying number facts.
- Balance routine skill learning with novel and complex tasks from the earliest stages of learning.
- Provide context for skill learning that establishes clear reasons for needing to learn the skills.
- Influence attitudes and beliefs about the academic content areas as well as skills and knowledge.
- Eliminate unnecessary redundancy in the curriculum (e.g., repeating instruction in the same mathematics skills year after year).

And finally, teach students directly about how to be students. In the early grades, this could mean directly teaching the courtesies and conventions of the classroom: how to get a turn to speak, how and when to interrupt the teacher, how to whisper, how to get help in a small group,

---

GUIDELINES
Culturally Relevant Teaching

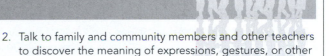

Experiment with different grouping arrangements to encourage social harmony and cooperation.

Examples

1. Try "study buddies" and pairs.
2. Organize heterogeneous groups of four or five.
3. Establish larger teams for older students.

Provide a range of ways to learn material to accommodate a range of learning styles.

Examples

1. Give students verbal materials at different reading levels.
2. Offer visual materials—charts, diagrams, and models.
3. Provide tapes for listening and viewing.
4. Set up activities and projects.

Teach classroom procedures directly, even ways of doing things that you thought everyone would know.

Examples

1. Tell students how to get the teacher's attention.
2. Explain when and how to interrupt the teacher if students need help.
3. Show which materials students can take and which require permission.
4. Demonstrate acceptable ways to disagree with or challenge another student.

Learn the meaning of different behaviors for your students.

Examples

1. Ask students how they feel when you correct or praise them. What gives them this message?

2. Talk to family and community members and other teachers to discover the meaning of expressions, gestures, or other responses that are unfamiliar to you.

Emphasize meaning in teaching.

Examples

1. Make sure students understand what they read.
2. Try storytelling and other modes that don't require written materials.
3. Use examples that relate abstract concepts to everyday experiences; for instance, relate negative numbers to being overdrawn in your checkbook.

Get to know the customs, traditions, and values of your students.

Examples

1. Use holidays as a chance to discuss the origins and meaning of traditions.
2. Analyze different traditions for common themes.
3. Attend community fairs and festivals.

Help students detect racist and sexist messages.

Examples

1. Analyze curriculum materials for biases.
2. Make students "bias detectives," reporting comments from the media.
3. Discuss the ways that students communicate biased messages about each other, and decide what should be done when this happens.
4. Discuss expressions of prejudice such as anti-Semitism.

how to give an explanation that is helpful. In the later grades, it may mean teaching the study skills that fit your subject. You can ask students to learn "how we do it in school" without violating the second principle—respect your students. Ways of asking questions around the kitchen table at home may be different from ways of asking questions in school, but students can learn both ways, without deciding that either way is superior. And you can expand ways of doing it in school to include more possibilities. The *Guidelines: Culturally Relevant Teaching* on the previous page gives more ideas.

ENHANCEDetext *self-check*

SUMMARY

- **Today's Diverse Classrooms (pp. 210–214)**

  What is culture, and how does cultural diversity affect learning and teaching? There are many conceptions of culture, but most include the knowledge, skills, rules, traditions, beliefs, and values that guide behavior in a particular group of people: Culture is a program for living. Everyone is a member of many cultural groups, defined in terms of geographic region, nationality, ethnicity, race, gender, social class, and religion. Membership in a particular group does not determine behavior or values, but makes certain values and kinds of behavior more likely. Wide variations exist within each group. You met four individuals, Ternice, Benjamin, Davy, and Jessie, who embody that diversity.

  The differences between cultures may be very obvious, tip-of-the iceberg characteristics, or they may be very subtle, below-the-surface differences. When subtle cultural differences meet, misunderstandings and conflicts are common. These conflicts can happen when the values and competencies of the dominant, mainstream culture are used to determine what is considered "normal" or appropriate behavior in schools. In these cases, children who have been socialized in a different culture may be perceived as acting inappropriately, not following the rules, or being rude and disrespectful.

- **Economic and Social Class Differences (pp. 214–221)**

  What is SES, and how does it differ from social class? Social class reflects a group's prestige and power in a society. Most people are aware of the social class that they share with similar peers. Sociologists use the term *SES* for variations in wealth, power, control over resources, and prestige. Socioeconomic status is determined by several factors—not just income—and often overpowers other

cultural differences. No single variable is an effective measure of SES, but most researchers identify four general levels of SES: upper, middle, working, and lower classes. The main characteristics of these four SES levels are summarized in Table 6.1.

What is the relationship between SES and school achievement? Socioeconomic status and academic achievement are moderately correlated. Students of all ethnic groups with high SES show higher average levels of achievement on test scores and stay in school longer than students with low SES. The longer the child is in poverty, the stronger the impact is on achievement. Why is there a correlation between SES and school achievement? Students with low SES may suffer from inadequate health care, teachers' lowered expectations of them, low self-esteem, learned helplessness, participation in resistance cultures, school tracking, understimulating home environments, and summer setbacks. This last striking finding is that children with low SES lose academic ground outside school over the summer, whereas children with higher SES continue to advance.

- **Ethnicity and Race in Teaching and Learning (pp. 221–230)**

  Distinguish between ethnicity and race. Ethnicity (culturally transmitted behavior) and race (biologically transmitted physical traits) are socially significant categories people use to describe themselves and others. Minority groups (either numerically or historically unempowered) are rapidly increasing in population.

  How can differences in ethnicity of teachers and students affect school performance? Conflicts can arise from differences between teachers and students in culture-based beliefs, values, and expectations. Cultural conflicts are usually about below-the-surface differences, because when subtle cultural differences meet, misunderstandings are common. Students in some cultures learn attitudes and behaviors that are more consistent with school expectations. Differences among ethnic groups in cognitive and academic abilities are largely the legacy of racial segregation and continuing prejudice and discrimination.

Distinguish among *prejudice, discrimination, and stereotype threat.* Prejudice is a rigid and unfair generalization—a prejudgment or attitude—about an entire category of people. Prejudice may target people in particular racial, ethnic, religious, political, geographic, or language groups, or it may be directed toward the gender or sexual orientation of the individual. Discrimination is unequal treatment of or actions toward particular categories of people. Stereotype threat is the extra emotional and cognitive burden that your performance in an academic situation might confirm a stereotype that others hold about you. It is not necessary that the individual even believe the stereotype. All that matters is that the person is aware of the stereotype and cares about performing well enough to disprove its unflattering implications. In the short run, the fear that you might confirm a negative stereotype can induce test anxiety and undermine performance. Over time, experiencing stereotype threat may lead to disidentification with schooling and academic achievement.

• **Gender in Teaching and Learning (pp. 230–235)**

What are the stages of achieving a sexual orientation for gay and lesbian youth? Stages of achieving a sexual orientation for gay and lesbian students can also follow a pattern from discomfort to confusion to acceptance. Some researchers contend that sexual identity is not always permanent and can change over the years.

What are gender roles, and how do they develop? Gender role is the image each individual has of himself or herself as masculine or feminine in characteristics—a part of self-concept. Biology (hormones) plays a role, as does the differential behavior of parents and teachers toward male and female children. Through their interactions with family, peers, teachers, and the environment in general, children begin to form gender schemas, or organized networks of knowledge about what it means to be male or female.

How are gender biases communicated? In children's books, there are more males in the titles and the illustrations, and the characters (especially the boys) continue to behave in stereotypic ways. Girl characters sometimes cross gender roles to be more active, but boy characters seldom show "feminine" expressive traits. Some overrepresentation of gender exists in television commercials, too. Teachers interact more with boys in both positive and negative ways. Lately some educators have claimed that schools are not supportive of boys, and same-sex classrooms have been suggested as an answer. The research on the value of these classrooms is mixed.

• **Multicultural Education: Creating Culturally Compatible Classrooms (pp. 235–244)**

What is multicultural education? Multicultural education is a field of study designed to increase educational equity for all students. According to the multicultural ideal, America should be transformed into a society that values diversity. James Banks suggests that multicultural education has five dimensions: integrating content, helping students understand how knowledge is influenced by beliefs, reducing prejudice, creating social structures in schools that support learning and development for all students, and using teaching methods that reach all students.

What is culturally relevant pedagogy? "Culturally relevant pedagogy is an approach to teaching that uses the cultural knowledge, prior experiences, frames of reference, and learning styles of ethnically diverse students to make learning encounters more relevant and effective for them. It teaches to and through the strengths of these students" (Gay, 2000). Gloria Ladson-Billings (1995, 2004) describes culturally relevant teaching that rests on three propositions: Students must experience academic success, develop/maintain their cultural competence, and develop a critical consciousness to challenge the status quo.

What are the elements of a resilient classroom? Two strands of elements bind students to their classroom community. One strand emphasizes the self-agency of students—their capacity to set and pursue goals. This includes academic self-efficacy, self-control, and self-determination. The second strand emphasizes caring and connected relationships with the teacher, peers, and the home.

PRACTICE USING WHAT YOU HAVE LEARNED

To access and complete the exercises, click the link under the images below.

Continuing Discrimination - Cinderella Stories

ENHANCEDetext *application exercise*

Multicultural Education

ENHANCEDetext *application exercise*

KEY TERMS

Culturally relevant pedagogy   236
Culture   210
Discrimination   226
Ethnicity   221
Gender biases   233
Gender identity   230
Gender schemas   232
LGBTQ (lesbian, gay, bisexual,
   transgender, and questioning)   230

Minority group   222
Multicultural education   235
Participation structures   241
Pragmatics   241
Prejudice   225
Race   221
Resilience   237
Resistance culture   218
Sexual identity   230

Socioeconomic status (SES)   215
Sociolinguistics   241
Stereotype   226
Stereotype threat   227
Tracking   219

CONNECT AND EXTEND TO LICENSURE

MULTIPLE-CHOICE QUESTIONS

1. Socioeconomic status and school achievement are often correlated. Which one of the following statements is not true regarding the relationship between SES and levels of achievement?

   A. The longer a child lives in poverty, the greater the impact on achievement.

   B. Children who are poor are no more likely to be kept back in school than children who are not.

   C. Students of all ethnic groups with high SES generally show higher levels of achievement on test scores and stay in school longer than students with low SES.

   D. Children who are poor are more likely to live in suburban and rural areas than to live in central cities.

2. Educators often assume students are not bright because they have inadequate resources at home. This inadequacy manifests itself as a lack of familiarity with school-related activities. When this occurs, what is the likely outcome?

   A. These students work harder to prove themselves to their teachers.

   B. Teachers may have low expectations that have a negative impact on future academic success.

   C. The students will perform poorly because they will never catch up with their peers.

   D. Teachers understand that not all students will be able to achieve academically.

3. Damon, an African American student in Diane Collins's math class, pushed his math test away after a few minutes and proclaimed, "This is stupid. I don't know why we even have to do this." What is Ms. Collins most likely to think?

    A. She should send Damon to the principal's office for insubordination.

    B. She might have made the test too difficult for her African American students, so she should make an easier test next time.

    C. Damon may be exhibiting performance-avoidance goals because he doesn't want to look dumb.

    D. Damon's high self-efficacy makes him think that testing is a waste of his time.

4. To avoid gender bias in his fourth-grade classroom, Mr. Bonner used gender-free language, provided positive role models, and ensured that all students had opportunities to engage in various activities by rotating classroom jobs and activities. His school was also experimenting with single-sex classrooms. Next year, Mr. Bonner thought he might opt to teach in one of those classrooms. Which of the following statements concerning single-sex classrooms is not true?

    A. Single-sex classrooms have positive effects on learning, motivation, and engagement if certain conditions are met.

    B. Teaching is not easier in a single-sex classroom than it is in a mixed-sex classroom.

    C. Teachers must use teaching strategies that are geared specifically for students of a particular sex.

    D. Students in single-sex classrooms are often less concerned about making impressions on peers.

CONSTRUCTED-RESPONSE QUESTIONS

Case

Paulo Nzambi moved from his home in Angola to the United States in the fifth grade. Although Paulo's English and schooling were adequate, his teacher Katie Wyant worried about his social adjustment. His quiet demeanor and soft voice were, in many ways, the opposite of his male peers. Paulo appeared hesitant when interacting with her, as if he was unsure about how to behave. As the year progressed, Katie noticed he had not made any progress in adjusting to the classroom. She decided she needed to be proactive in finding a solution.

5. To acquire a better understanding of Paulo and make school a more positive experience, what three types of relationships would assist Paulo as well as Miss Wyant?

6. What aspects of culturally relevant teaching might Katie Wyant employ to assist Paulo Nzambi in his transition to an American classroom?

ENHANCEDetext *licensure exam*

TEACHERS' CASEBOOK

WHAT WOULD THEY DO? WHITE GIRLS CLUB

Here is how some expert teachers responded to the situation described at the beginning of the chapter about the "White Girls Club."

JENNIFER PINCOSKI—Learning Resource Teacher: K–12
Lee County School District, Fort Myers, FL

All teachers feel the pressure of high-stakes testing and meeting academic standards, and unfortunately, this leaves little time to provide character education and team-building activities. Even kindergarten classrooms have sacrificed social skills/friendship lessons for additional academic instruction, even though many students come to school not knowing how to appropriately interact with peers.

In the face of No Child Left Behind and Race to the Top mandates, briefly suspending content instruction to teach kindness and build a respectful classroom community may sound like a waste of valuable academic time. However, teachers who establish a positive learning environment where students feel safe and valued ultimately spend less time redirecting and correcting misbehaviors. Students who feel accepted and appreciated will demonstrate longer time on task and greater interest in learning than those who don't.

In this case, the entire class could benefit from lessons on diversity, respect, and tolerance. School counselors are a great resource for these types of activities and are often available to teach or co-teach the lessons.

In the long run, a proactive approach is far more efficient than a reactive one. Taking the time to build rapport and establish a sense of community will preserve hours of instruction that would have been lost to peer conflict, off-task behaviors, and noncompliance.

LAUREN ROLLINS—First-Grade Teacher
Boulevard Elementary School, Shaker Heights, OH

Discrimination of any kind will not be tolerated in my classroom! I would attack this unfortunate situation through a variety of different approaches—whole-class instruction, private small-group discussions, and one-on-one meetings with my new student and her parents. I would start my whole-class lesson by passing out candy (or some other desired object—stickers, pencils, etc.) to one chosen group of people—only boys, students with brown eyes, etc. I would purposely choose a group that excluded the girls who have formed the "White Girls Club." This activity would spark a conversation with the class about how unfair it is that one group of students got to do something that another group did not. We would talk about how the excluded group felt by this slight and why it is important not to discriminate against people for any reason. I would also include a read-aloud of a children's book that supported this topic. I would stop throughout my reading to discuss the feelings of the different characters in the book. Next, I would meet privately with the girls who have formed the club. I would remind them that excluding people from a group is unacceptable and will not be tolerated by me. Either everyone gets to play, or no one does. Last, I would meet with my new student and her parents. I would ask her to give me the names of a few students in my class with whom she would be interested in building a relationship. I would encourage her parents to set up one-on-one play dates for their daughter outside of school with the hope of building relationships.

LINDA SPARKS—First-Grade Teacher
John F. Kennedy School, Billerica, MA

We begin each year setting up classroom rules and expectations. We write them down and all students sign the "contract." It is then posted in a visible place in the classroom. Throughout the year we will go over the rules. The first one always states that we treat others the way we want to be treated. We have had these "clubs" pop up, from "only boys can play a sport at recess" to "the way a child looks." When I notice a change in classroom climate, I always begin with a generalized scenario (e.g., out at recess, the principal noticed that only the boys were playing basketball but some of the girls were watching and wanting to play). We would then brainstorm a list of what the principal could do to help let the girls play. It is amazing the wonderful ideas that come up when the student is not being put on the spot, but rather the whole class is getting the chance to share their thoughts. I find that starting this way, students will start to think of specific times when this has happened to them and how it was resolved. It is amazing how quickly these "clubs" or "groups" disappear once the lesson has been presented. We have a few programs we use in our school for teaching tolerance. We have Second Step, in which scenarios are presented and students role-play the scene. This is one of their favorites. Another is a bucket filler, where students can be caught doing something good either by another student or by a staff member. The person who catches them fills out a bucket-filling slip and it gets put into a big silver bucket. No one wants to be a bucket dipper by making people feel sad or left out. No matter what the age, clubs can quickly

dissipate when the students are the ones who are given the chance to resolve the problem.

PAULA COLEMERE—Special Education Teacher—English, History
McClintock High School, Tempe, AZ

In one of my favorite lessons for the beginning of the year, I give each student five mixed beans and have students choose which is the "best" one. We then discuss why they chose the bean as the best and discuss the differences in beans before connecting to people. After the discussion, we role-play different scenarios that deal with diversity; this is a good lesson because it addresses self-esteem in addition to diversity. While all students can use a boost to self-esteem, it would hopefully help the new girl to feel better about the situation. This lesson can be tailored to younger or older students. Because these students are young, I would hope this would be a gentle way for the girls in the "club" to see that what they have been doing is wrong. My next step would be to conference with the girls and mediate if necessary.

PAUL DRAGIN—ESL Teacher Grades 9–12
Columbus East High School, Columbus, OH

Based on the observations, I would not hesitate to act quickly in this situation of exclusion. Based on the age group of the students, I would attack this problem two ways initially. I would spend classroom time talking about building community and present some scenarios and videos about how it feels to be excluded or left out. With children at this impressionable age, this troubling dilemma may leave an indelible mark on some if handled in such a way that they internalize the feelings that the excluded student is inevitably confronted with being the "other." I would contact the parents of the girls who made the "White girls club" comment and let them know what I overheard and witnessed regarding the new student. Hopefully, this could turn an unfortunate situation into a great learning opportunity that would stick with the students whenever they are confronted with someone racially, ethnically, or culturally different from them.

JESSICA N. MAHTABAN—Eighth-Grade Math
Woodrow Wilson Middle School, Clifton, NJ

My immediate response would be to investigate the "club." I could talk to each girl individually and ask why she started the club as well as why they felt it was important to exclude people from their club. Also, I must make sure the parents, administration, and counselors are aware of the situation as well.

It is my job to explain to my students as best I can that it's not polite to exclude anyone. I would give them different scenarios about exclusion and ask for them to reflect on their personal feelings for each scenario. We would discuss in groups as well as the whole class about the scenarios and their feelings. Problem solving together would be the best approach to finding various solutions to problems as well as figuring out who can help them in different situations. Hopefully, by the end of these lessons, each student will understand that our classroom is a family, and that, as a family, we celebrate differences—not segregate.

BARBARA PRESLEY—Transition/Work Study Coordinator—High School Level, BESTT Program (Baldwinsville Exceptional Student Training and Transition Program)
C.W. Baker High School, Baldwinsville, NY

Eliminating bias can be achieved only through exposure, knowledge, and experience. In my work with students who are severely disabled, I found that their peers without disabilities were less judgmental and exclusionary when they were given the opportunity to interact with our students. I would definitely find out about any "club" that has the potential to be destructive. We created situations where the skills and aptitudes of our students with special needs were spotlighted; they then invited peers without disabilities to join them. Almost everyone wants to share in a success, so our students' peers joined in, and the prejudice and malice diminished.

SARA VINCENT—Special Education Teacher
Langley High School, McLean, VA

Discrimination and racism often occur because of ignorance. The best solution to minimize discrimination is educating individuals about diverse cultures. The teacher can invite the new student's family into the classroom to talk about their backgrounds and experiences, or she can have the entire class complete a project on family history. Once the other students in the classroom learn more about the new student's culture, they will be more likely to accept her differences and understand that she is not much different from them. In addition, the teacher can have the new student be team leader at recess or in the classroom so that she will not be picked last. This will help her gain confidence in befriending her peers. While the teacher attempts to focus on positive aspects of educating her students, she should make the administration aware of the "White Girls Club" situation. Administrators should intervene and bring attention to the situation if the troubling behaviors of the other girls continue.

7 | BEHAVIORAL VIEWS OF LEARNING

WHAT WOULD YOU DO? SICK OF CLASS

One of your students asks for permission to see the school nurse at least twice a week. According to the nurse, most of his complaints have been groundless. True, once he was coming down with the flu, but 9 out of 10 times, nothing has been wrong at all. Recently you have noticed that he tends to "get sick" during oral assignments or when he has to speak before the class. What steps would you take to deal with this situation?

CRITICAL THINKING

- Could this be a case of a classically conditioned phobia? If so, what would you do?
- What functions might this behavior be serving?
- How would you support more positive behaviors and help the student find other ways to meet his needs?
- Would giving rewards or administering punishments be useful in this situation? Why or why not?

OVERVIEW AND **OBJECTIVES**

We begin this chapter with a general definition of learning that takes into account the opposing views of different theoretical groups. We will highlight one group, the behavioral theorists, in this chapter and another major group, the cognitive theorists, in Chapters 8 and 9; then, we will look at constructivism in Chapter 10 and social cognitive views in Chapter 11. As you can see, there are many ways to look at learning, and each has something to offer educators.

Our discussion in this chapter will focus on four behavioral learning processes: contiguity, classical conditioning, operant conditioning, and observational learning, with the greatest emphasis placed on the last two processes. After examining the implications of applied behavior analysis for teaching, we look at recent directions in behavioral approaches to learning—functional behavioral assessments, positive behavior support, and self-management. Finally, we investigate Bandura's challenge to behavioral views of learning as well as other criticisms, cautions, and ethical considerations for educators.

By the time you have completed this chapter, you should be able to:

Objective 7.1 Define learning from a behavioral perspective, including ties to neuroscience and the processes involved in learning through contiguity, classical conditioning, operant, and observational learning.

Objective 7.2 Explain early views of learning through contiguity and classical conditioning and describe their implications for teaching.

Objective 7.3 Explain operant conditioning, particularly the differences and similarities between positive and negative reinforcement and presentation and removal punishment and how reinforcement schedules affect learning.

Objective 7.4 Apply behavioral approaches to modifying behavior in and out of the classroom using applied behavioral analysis approaches to encourage and discourage behaviors, shaping, positive practice, contingency contracts, token reinforcement, group consequences, and the appropriate use of punishment.

Objective 7.5 Apply functional behavioral assessment, positive behavioral supports, and self-management techniques.

Objective 7.6 Evaluate contemporary challenges to behavioral theories of learning and address concerns about their application.

UNDERSTANDING LEARNING

When we hear the word *learning*, most of us think of studying and school. We think about subjects or skills we intend to master, such as algebra, Spanish, chemistry, or karate. But learning is not limited to school. We learn every day of our lives. Babies learn to kick their legs to make the mobile above their cribs move, young girls learn the lyrics to all their favorite Katy Perry songs, middle-aged people like me learn to change their diet and exercise patterns, and every few years we all learn to find a new style of dress attractive when the old styles (the ones we once loved) go out of fashion. This last example shows that learning is not always intentional. We don't try to like new styles and dislike old ones; it just seems to happen that way. We don't intend to become nervous when we hear a teacher call our name or when we step onto a stage, yet many of us do. So what is this powerful phenomenon called *learning*?

In the broadest sense, learning occurs when experience (including practice) causes a relatively permanent change in an individual's knowledge, behavior, or potential for behavior. The change may be deliberate or unintentional, for better or for worse, correct or incorrect, and conscious or unconscious (Mayer, 2011; Schunk, 2012). To qualify as learning, this change must be brought about by experience—by the interaction of a person with his or her environment. Changes simply caused by maturation, such as growing taller or turning gray, do not qualify as learning. Temporary changes resulting from illness, fatigue, drugs, or hunger are also excluded from a general definition of learning. A person who has gone without food for 2 days does not learn to be hungry, and a person who is ill does not learn to move more slowly. Of course, learning plays a part in how we respond to hunger or illness.

Our definition specifies that the changes resulting from learning take place in the individual's knowledge, behavior, or potential for behavior. Most psychologists would agree with this statement, but some tend to emphasize the change in knowledge, and others focus on the change in behavior. The potential for behavior means that learning can take place even if the individual does not always act on the change unless the situation or motivation is right. The potential is there, even if the behavior does not occur. Cognitive psychologists, who focus on changes in knowledge, believe learning is an internal mental activity that cannot be observed directly. As you will see in Chapter 8, cognitive psychologists studying learning are interested in unobservable mental activities such as thinking, remembering, and solving problems (S. B. Klein, 2015).

The psychologists discussed in this chapter favor **behavioral learning theories**. The behavioral view generally assumes that the outcome of learning is a change in behavior, and it emphasizes the effects of external events on the individual. Some early behaviorists such as J. B. Watson (1919) took the radical position that because thinking, intentions, and other internal mental events could not be seen or studied rigorously and scientifically, these "mentalisms," as he called them, should not even be included in an explanation of learning.

Neuroscience of Behavioral Learning

You saw in Chapter 2 that we are learning more and more about the brain. Researchers conducting animal and human studies have discovered quite a bit about the areas of the brain involved with learning new behaviors. For example, parts of the cerebellum are involved in simple reflex learning, like learning to blink following a particular tone, and other parts of the brain are involved in learning how to avoid painful stimulation such as shock (Schwartz, Wasserman, & Robbins, 2002). Other lines of research ask why animals and people will behave in certain ways to gain stimulation or reinforcers. Stimulation to certain parts of the brain will cause hungry rats to ignore food and keep doing whatever it takes to keep the stimulation coming. These same brain systems are associated with the pleasures people experience from many things, including food and music. It is likely that many parts of the brain and complex patterns of activity allow us to enjoy some experiences, "learn to want them, and learn how to get them" (Bernstein & Nash, 2008, p. 187).

Before we look in depth at behavioral explanations of learning, let's step into an actual classroom and note the possible results of learning.

Learning Is Not Always What It Seems

After weeks of working with her cooperating teacher in an eighth-grade social studies class, Elizabeth was ready to take over on her own. As she moved to the front of the room, she saw another adult approach the classroom door. It was Mr. Ross, her supervisor from college. Elizabeth's neck and facial muscles suddenly became very tense.

"I've stopped by for my first observation," Mr. Ross said. "I couldn't reach you last night to tell you."

Elizabeth tried to hide her reaction, but her hands trembled as she gathered the notes for the lesson. She turned to face her students and introduced the day's topic.

"Let's start today with a kind of game. I will say some words, then I want you to tell me the first words you can think of, and I will write them on the board. Don't all speak at once, though. Wait until someone else has finished to say your word. Okay, here is the first word: Slavery."

"Civil War." "Lincoln." "Freedom." "Emancipation Proclamation." The answers came quickly, and Elizabeth was relieved to see that the students understood the game.

"All right, very good," she said. "Now try another one: South."

"South Carolina." "South Dakota." "South Park," "No, the Confederacy, you dummy." "*Cold Mountain.*" "Jude Law." With this last answer, a ripple of laughter moved across the room.

"Jude Law!" Elizabeth sighed dreamily. "*Cold Mountain* was on television last week." Then she laughed too. Soon all the students were laughing. "Okay, settle down," Elizabeth said. "Here is another word: North."

"Bluebellies." The students continued to laugh. "Jelly Bellies." "Belly-dancers." More laughter and a few inappropriate gestures.

"Just a minute," Elizabeth pleaded. "These ideas are getting a little off base!"

"Off base? Baseball," shouted the boy who had first mentioned Jude Law. He stood up and started throwing balls of paper to a friend in the back of the room, simulating the style of Tim Lincecum.

"The San Francisco Giants." "No, the Red Sox." "Ball games." "Hot dogs." "Popcorn." "Movies." "Netflix." "*Cold Mountain.*" "Jude Law." The responses now came too fast for Elizabeth to stop them. For some reason, the Jude Law line got an even bigger laugh the second time around, and Elizabeth suddenly realized she had lost the class.

"Okay, because you know so much about the Civil War, close your books and take out a pen," Elizabeth said, obviously angry. She passed out the worksheet that she had planned as a cooperative, open-book project. "You have 20 minutes to finish this test!"

"You didn't tell us we were having a test!" "This isn't fair!" "We haven't even covered this stuff yet!" "I didn't do anything wrong!" There were moans and disgusted looks, even from the most mellow students. "I'm reporting you to the principal; it's a violation of students' rights!"

This last comment hit hard. The class had just finished discussing human rights as preparation for this unit on the Civil War. As she listened to the protests, Elizabeth felt terrible. How was she going to grade these "tests"? The first section of the worksheet involved facts about events during the Civil War, and the second section asked students to create a news-style program interviewing ordinary people touched by the war.

"All right, all right, it won't be a test. But you do have to complete this worksheet for a grade. I was going to let you work together, but your behavior this morning tells me that you are not ready for group work. If you can complete the first section of the sheet working quietly and seriously, you may work together on the second section." Elizabeth knew that her students would like to work together on writing the script for the news interview program.

Elizabeth was afraid to look back at her supervisor. What was he writing on his observation form?

It appears, on the surface at least, that very little learning of any sort was taking place in Elizabeth's classroom. Elizabeth had some good ideas, but she also made some mistakes in her application of learning principles. We will return to this episode several times in the chapter to analyze various aspects of what took place. To get us started, four events can be singled out, each possibly related to a different learning process.

First, the students were able to associate the words *Carolina, Dakota,* and *Park* with the word *South.* Second, Elizabeth's hands trembled when her college supervisor entered the room. Third, one student continued to disrupt the class with inappropriate responses. And fourth, after Elizabeth laughed at a student's comment, the class joined in her laughter. The four learning processes represented are contiguity, classical conditioning, operant conditioning, and observational learning. In the following pages we will examine these four kinds of learning, starting with contiguity.

EARLY EXPLANATIONS OF LEARNING: CONTIGUITY AND CLASSICAL CONDITIONING

One of the earliest explanations of learning came from Aristotle (384–322 BC). He said that we remember things together (1) when they are similar, (2) when they contrast, and (3) when they are contiguous. This last principle is the most important, because it is included in all explanations of learning by association. The principle of **contiguity** states that whenever two or more sensations occur together often enough, they will become associated. Later, when only one of these sensations (a **stimulus**) occurs, the other will be remembered too (a **response**) (S. B. Klein, 2015; Rachlin, 1991). For example, when Elizabeth said "South," students associated the words "Carolina" and "Dakota." They had heard these words together many times. Other processes may also be involved when students learn these phrases, but contiguity is a factor. Contiguity also plays a major role in another learning process best known as *classical conditioning.*

Video 7.1
A kindergarten teacher begins on the first day to teach her students the procedures for good listening. Observe this example of the principle of contiguity and identify the stimulus used by the teacher.

ENHANCEDetext *video example*

Connect and Extend to PRAXIS II®

Learning by Association (I, A1)
Quite a bit of classroom learning can be attributed to contiguity (i.e., learning by association). What are some things that you might have learned because your teacher paired certain stimuli (e.g., names of the letters of the alphabet)?

STOP & THINK Close your eyes and focus on a vivid image of the following: The smell of French fries cooking. A time you were really embarrassed in school. The taste of chocolate fudge. The sound of a dentist's drill. What did you notice as you formed these images? •

If you are like me, imagining the sound of the dentist's drill tightens your neck muscles. I can actually salivate when I imagine salty fries or smooth rich chocolate (especially because it is 6:00 p.m. and I haven't had dinner yet). The first embarrassing school incident I remembered was falling flat as I did a cartwheel in front of the whole high school. A small cringe still accompanies the memory. **Classical conditioning** focuses on the learning of involuntary emotional or physiological responses such as fear, increased muscle tension, salivation, or sweating. These sometimes are called **respondents** because they are automatic responses to stimuli. Through the process of classical conditioning, humans and animals can be trained to react involuntarily to a stimulus that previously had no effect—or a very different effect—on them. The stimulus comes to elicit, or bring forth, the response automatically.

Classical conditioning was discovered in the 1920s by Ivan Pavlov, a Russian physiologist who was trying to determine how long it took a dog to secrete digestive juices after it had been fed. But the intervals of time kept changing. At first, the dogs salivated as expected while they were being fed. Then the dogs began to salivate as soon as they saw the food, and finally they salivated as soon as they heard the scientists walking toward the lab. Pavlov decided to make a detour from his original experiments and examine these unexpected interferences or "psychic reflexes" as he called them at first.

In one of his first experiments, Pavlov began by sounding a tuning fork and recording a dog's response. As expected, there was no salivation. At this point, the sound of the tuning fork was a **neutral stimulus** because it brought forth no salivation. Then Pavlov fed the dog. The response was salivation. The food was an **unconditioned stimulus (US)** because no prior training or "conditioning" was needed to establish the natural connection between food and salivation. The salivation was an **unconditioned response (UR)**, again because it was elicited automatically—no conditioning required.

Using these three elements—the food, the salivation, and the tuning fork—Pavlov demonstrated that a dog could be *conditioned* to salivate after hearing the tuning fork. He did this by contiguous pairing of the sound with food. He sounded the fork and then quickly fed the dog. After Pavlov repeated this several times, the dog began to salivate after hearing the sound, but before receiving the food. Now the sound had become a **conditioned stimulus (CS)** that could bring forth salivation by itself. The response of salivating after the tone was now a **conditioned response (CR)**. One explanation for how this occurs focuses on expectations or predictability—the dog learns that the previously neutral stimulus (the sound of the tuning fork) now predicts the appearance of the US (the food), so the animal responds to the sound with an anticipatory response (salivating)—getting ready for or anticipating the food. The association or conditioning of the sound to salivating will occur as long as the sound is information that helps the dog expect that "food is on the way" (Gluck, Mercado, & Myers, 2014; Rescorla & Wagner, 1972).

If you think that Pavlovian conditioning is of historical interest only, consider this excerpt from *USA Today* describing an advertising campaign for products aimed at "Gen Y," those people born between 1977 and 1994:

> Mountain Dew executives have their own term for this [advertising strategy]: the Pavlovian connection. By handing out samples of the brand at surfing, skateboard and snowboard tournaments, "There's a Pavlovian connection between the brand and the exhilarating experience," says Dave Burwich, a top marketing executive at Pepsi, which makes Mountain Dew. (Horovitz, 2002, p. B2)

Maybe they could hand out math homework too! The *Guidelines: Applying Classical Conditioning* gives some additional ideas.

GUIDELINES
Applying Classical Conditioning

Associate positive, pleasant events with learning tasks.
Examples
1. Emphasize group competition and cooperation over individual competition. Many students have negative emotional responses to individual competition that may generalize to other learning.
2. Make division drills fun by having students decide how to divide refreshments equally, then letting them eat the results.
3. Make voluntary reading appealing by creating a comfortable reading corner with pillows, colorful displays of books, and reading props such as puppets (see Morrow & Weinstein, 1986, for more ideas).

Help students to risk anxiety-producing situations voluntarily and successfully.
Examples
1. Assign a shy student the responsibility of teaching two other students how to distribute materials for map study.
2. Devise small steps toward a larger goal. For example, give ungraded practice tests daily, and then weekly, to students who tend to "freeze" in test situations.

3. If a student is afraid of speaking in front of the class, let the student read a report to a small group while seated, then read it while standing, then give the report from notes instead of reading it verbatim. Next, move in stages toward having the student give a report to the whole class.

Help students recognize differences and similarities among situations so they can discriminate and generalize appropriately.
Examples
1. Explain that it is appropriate to avoid strangers who offer gifts or rides, but safe to accept favors from adults when parents are present.
2. Assure students who are anxious about taking college entrance exams that this test is like all the other achievement tests they have taken.

If you would like to learn more about classical conditioning, see
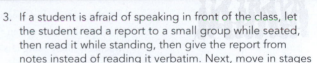
psychology.about.com/od/behavioralpsychology/a/classcond.htm

Connect and Extend to PRAXIS II®

Basics of Operant Conditioning (I, A1)
Be able to explain learning from the behavioral perspective. Incorporate concepts of classical and operant conditioning into your explanation. Have a firm grasp of the effects of reinforcement schedules on learning.

It is possible that many of our emotional reactions to various situations are learned in part through classical conditioning. Physicians have a term, *white coat syndrome*, that describes people whose blood pressure (an involuntary response) goes up when it is tested in the doctor's office, usually by someone in a white coat. Another example, Elizabeth's trembling hands when she saw her college supervisor, might be traced to previous unpleasant experiences during past evaluations of her performance. Now just the thought of being observed elicits a pounding heart and sweaty palms. Classical conditioning has implications for teachers as well as marketing managers. Remember that emotions and attitudes as well as facts and ideas are learned in classrooms. This emotional learning can sometimes interfere with academic learning. Procedures based on classical conditioning also can be used to help people learn more adaptive emotional responses, as the *Guidelines: Applying Classical Conditioning* on the previous page suggests.

ENHANCEDetext *self-check*

OPERANT CONDITIONING: TRYING NEW RESPONSES

So far, we have concentrated on the automatic conditioning of reflex-like responses such as salivation and fear. Clearly, not all human learning is so unintentional and not all behaviors are so automatic. People actively "operate" on their environment. These deliberate actions are called **operants**. The learning process involved in operant behavior is called **operant conditioning** because we learn to behave in certain ways as we operate on the environment.

The person generally thought to be responsible for developing the concept of operant conditioning is B. F. Skinner (1953). Skinner began with the belief that the principles of classical conditioning account for only a small portion of learned behaviors. Many human behaviors are operants, not respondents. Classical conditioning describes only how existing responses might be paired with new stimuli; it does not explain how new operant behaviors are acquired.

Behavior, like response or action, is simply a word for what a person does in a particular situation. Conceptually, we may think of a behavior as sandwiched between two sets of environmental influences: those that precede it (its **antecedents**) and those that follow it (its **consequences**) (Skinner, 1950). This relationship can be shown very simply as antecedent–behavior–consequence, or A–B–C (Kazdin, 2008). As behavior is ongoing, a given consequence becomes an antecedent for the next A–B–C sequence. Research in operant conditioning shows that operant behavior can be altered by changes in the antecedents, the consequences, or both. Early work focused on consequences, often using rats or pigeons as subjects.

Types of Consequences

- -

STOP & THINK Think back over teachers you have had who used rewards or punishments. *Try to remember different types of rewards:*
Concrete rewards (stickers, food, prizes, certificates)
Activity rewards (free time, puzzles, free reading)
"Exemption" rewards (no homework, no weekly test)
Social rewards (praise, recognition)
What about punishments?
Loss of privileges (cannot sit where you want, cannot work with friends)
Fines (lost points, grades, money)
Extra work (homework, laps, push-ups) •

- -

According to the behavioral view, consequences determine to a great extent whether a person will repeat the behavior that led to the consequences. The type and timing of consequences can strengthen or weaken behaviors. We will look first at consequences that strengthen behavior.

REINFORCEMENT. Although **reinforcement** is commonly understood to mean "reward," this term has a particular meaning in psychology. A **reinforcer** is any consequence that strengthens the behavior it follows. So, by definition, reinforced behaviors increase in frequency or duration. Whenever you see a behavior persisting or increasing over time, you can assume the consequences of that behavior are reinforcers for the individual involved (Alberto & Troutman, 2012; S. B. Klein, 2015; Landrum & Kauffman, 2006). The reinforcement process can be diagrammed as follows:

CONSEQUENCE EFFECT

Behavior ———> Reinforcer ———> Strengthened or repeated behavior

We can be fairly certain that food will be a reinforcer for a hungry animal, but what about people? It is not clear why an event acts as a reinforcer for an individual, but there are many theories about why reinforcement works. For example, some psychologists suggest that reinforcers are preferred activities or that they satisfy needs, whereas other psychologists believe that reinforcers reduce tension or stimulate a part of the brain (S. B. Klein, 2015; Rachlin, 1991). Whether the consequences of any action are reinforcing probably depends on the individual's perception of the event and the meaning it holds for her or him. For example, students who repeatedly get sent to the principal's office for misbehaving may be indicating that something about this consequence is reinforcing for them, even if it doesn't seem desirable to you. By the way, Skinner did not speculate about why reinforcers increase behavior. He believed that it was useless to talk about "imaginary constructs" such as meaning, expectations, needs, or tensions. Skinner simply described the tendency for a given operant behavior to increase after certain consequences (Skinner, 1953, 1989).

There are two types of reinforcement. The first, called **positive reinforcement**, occurs when the behavior or response produces a new stimulus, so positive reinforcement is the *contingent presentation of a stimulus following a response* (Alberto & Troutman, 2012). I use the words *behavior* and *response* to mean the same thing. Examples of positive reinforcement include the occurrence of food pellets when a pigeon pecks on the red key, compliments when you wear a new outfit, or cheers and laughter from classmates when a student falls out of his chair.

Notice that positive reinforcement can occur even when the response being reinforced (falling out of a chair) is not "positive" from the teacher's point of view. Positive reinforcement of inappropriate responses occurs unintentionally in many classrooms. Teachers help maintain problem behaviors by inadvertently reinforcing them. For example, Elizabeth may have unintentionally reinforced problem responses in her class by laughing the first time the boy answered, "Jude Law." The problem behavior may have persisted for other reasons, but the consequence of Elizabeth's laughter could have played a role.

When the consequence that strengthens a behavior is the *presentation* (addition) of a new stimulus, the situation is defined as *positive reinforcement*. In contrast, when the consequence that strengthens a behavior is the *removal* (subtraction) of a stimulus, the process is called **negative reinforcement**. So, negative reinforcement is the *contingent removal of an aversive (unpleasant) stimulus* right after a response that increases the future rate of the response (Alberto & Troutman, 2102). If a particular action leads to avoiding or escaping an aversive situation, the action is likely to be repeated in a similar situation. A common example is the car seatbelt buzzer. As soon as you put on your seatbelt, the irritating buzzer stops. You are likely to *repeat* this "buckling up" action in the future (so the process is *reinforcement*) because the response *removed* an aversive buzzing stimulus (so the kind of reinforcement is *negative*).

Consider our opening case student who continually "gets sick" right before a test or oral presentation and then is sent to the nurse's office. This behavior allows him to escape aversive situations—tests—so getting "sick" is being maintained, in part, through negative reinforcement. It is negative because getting sick *removed* the unpleasant stimulus (the test or report); it is reinforcement because the behavior that removed the stimulus (getting "sick") increases or repeats in the future. It is also possible that classical conditioning plays a role. The student may have been conditioned to experience unpleasant physiological reactions to tests.

It is important to remember that the "negative" in negative reinforcement does not imply that the behavior being reinforced is necessarily negative or bad. The meaning is closer to that of "negative" numbers—*something is subtracted*. Try to associate positive and negative reinforcement with the *consequence* of adding or subtracting something following a behavior that has the *effect* of strengthening (reinforcing) the behavior.

PUNISHMENT. Negative reinforcement is often confused with punishment. To avoid this mistake, remember that the process of reinforcement (positive or negative) always involves strengthening behavior. **Punishment**, on the other hand, involves *decreasing* or *suppressing* behavior. A behavior followed by a punisher is less likely to be repeated in similar situations in the future. Again, it is the effect that defines a consequence as punishment, and different people have different perceptions of what is punishing. One student may find suspension from school punishing, whereas another student wouldn't mind the break at all. The process of punishment is diagrammed as follows:

CONSEQUENCE   EFFECT

Behavior ——→ Punisher ——→ Weakened or decreased behavior

Like reinforcement, punishment may take one of two forms. The first type has been called Type I punishment, but this name isn't very informative, so I use the term **presentation punishment**. It occurs when presenting or adding a stimulus following the behavior suppresses or decreases the behavior. When teachers reprimand students, assign extra work, or make students run extra laps, and so on, they are using presentation punishment. I call the other type of punishment (Type II punishment) **removal punishment** because it involves removing a stimulus. When teachers or parents take away privileges after a young person has behaved inappropriately, they are applying removal punishment. With both types, the effect is to decrease the behavior that led to the punishment. Figure 7.1 summarizes the processes of reinforcement and punishment.

Reinforcement Schedules

When individuals are learning a new behavior, they will learn it faster if they are reinforced for every correct response. This is a **continuous reinforcement schedule**. Then, when they have mastered the new behavior, they will maintain it best if they are reinforced intermittently rather than every time. An **intermittent reinforcement schedule** helps students to maintain skills without expecting constant reinforcement.

There are two basic types of intermittent reinforcement schedules. One—called an **interval schedule**—is based on the amount of time that passes between reinforcers. The other—a **ratio schedule**—is based on the number of responses learners give between reinforcers. Interval and ratio schedules may be either fixed (predictable) or variable (unpredictable). Table 7.1 on page 260 summarizes the five possible reinforcement schedules (the continuous schedule and the four kinds of intermittent schedules).

What are the effects of different schedules? Speed of performance depends on control. If reinforcement is based on the number of responses you give, then you have more control over the reinforcement: The faster you accumulate the correct number of responses, the faster the

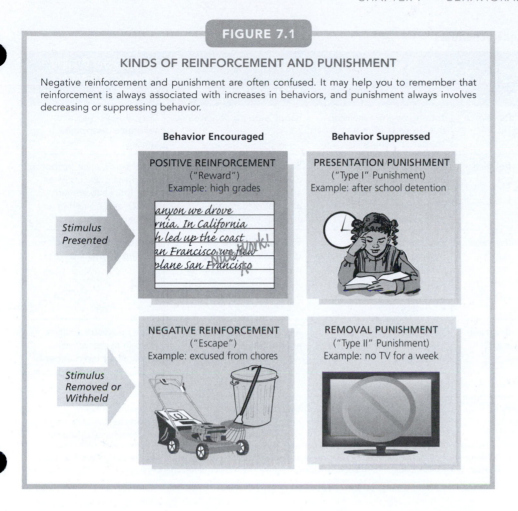

FIGURE 7.1

KINDS OF REINFORCEMENT AND PUNISHMENT

Negative reinforcement and punishment are often confused. It may help you to remember that reinforcement is always associated with increases in behaviors, and punishment always involves decreasing or suppressing behavior.

	Behavior Encouraged	Behavior Suppressed
Stimulus Presented	POSITIVE REINFORCEMENT ("Reward") Example: high grades	PRESENTATION PUNISHMENT ("Type I" Punishment) Example: after school detention
Stimulus Removed or Withheld	NEGATIVE REINFORCEMENT ("Escape") Example: excused from chores	REMOVAL PUNISHMENT ("Type II" Punishment) Example: no TV for a week

reinforcement will come. A teacher who says, "As soon as you complete these 10 problems correctly, you may listen to your iPods," can expect higher rates of performance than a teacher who says, "Work on these 10 problems for the next 20 minutes. Then I will check your papers and those with 10 correct may listen to their iPods."

Persistence in performance depends on unpredictability. Continuous reinforcement and both kinds of fixed reinforcement (ratio and interval) are quite predictable. We come to expect reinforcement at certain points and are generally quick to give up when the reinforcement does not meet our expectations. To encourage persistence of response, variable schedules are most appropriate. A great example of student persistence on a variable schedule was presented in an article about Valorie Lewis, a member of the *USA Today* All-USA teacher team. Describing Lewis's third-grade class, one of her colleagues said that the students are "afraid to be absent because they don't want to take the chance they will miss anything. Mrs. Lewis doesn't tell them when she is planning something special, so they have to be there every day just in case" (S. Johnson, 2008, p. 7D). If the reinforcement schedule is gradually changed until it becomes very "lean"—meaning that reinforcement occurs only after many responses or after a long time interval—then people can learn to work for extended periods without any reinforcement at all. Just watch gamblers playing slot machines to see how powerful a lean reinforcement schedule can be.

Reinforcement schedules influence how persistently we will respond when reinforcement is withheld. What happens when reinforcement is completely withdrawn?

TABLE 7.1 • **Five Reinforcement Schedules**

SCHEDULE	DEFINITION	EXAMPLE	RESPONSE PATTERN	REACTION WHEN REINFORCEMENT STOPS
Continuous	Reinforcement after every response	Turning on the television Buying soda from a vending machine	Rapid learning of response	Very little persistence; response disappears quickly
Fixed-interval	Reinforcement after a set period of time	Studying as weekly quiz approaches Dishwashing cycle (dishes are clean after a specific time period)	Response rate increases as time for reinforcement approaches, then drops after reinforcement	Little persistence; response disappears quickly when time for reinforcement passes and no reinforcer appears
Variable-interval	Reinforcement after varying lengths of time	Pop quizzes Texting (get an answer after variable time periods) Birding (variable times between spotting a new kind of bird)	Slow, steady rate of responding; very little pause after reinforcement	Greater persistence; slow decline in response rate
Fixed-ratio	Reinforcement after a set number of responses	Telemarketer gets a bonus after every 100 credit cards enrolled Bake sale	Rapid response rate; pause after reinforcement	Little persistence; rapid drop in response rate when expected number of responses are given and no reinforcer appears
Variable-ratio	Reinforcement after a varying number of responses	Slot machines	Vary high response rate; little pause after reinforcement	Greatest persistence; response rate stays high and gradually drops off

Source: Based on information in Alberto, P. A., & Troutman, A. C. (2012). Applied behavior analysis for teachers (9th ed.). Boston, MA: Pearson; Klein, S. B. (2015). Learning: Principles and applications (7th ed.). Thousand Oaks, CA: Sage; and http://en.wikipedia.org/wiki/Reinforcement#Schedules

EXTINCTION. In classical conditioning, the CR is extinguished (disappears) when the CS appears, but the US does not follow (sound, but no food). In operant conditioning, a person or an animal will not persist in a certain behavior if the usual reinforcer is withheld long enough. The behavior will eventually be extinguished (stop). For example, if you repeatedly e-mail a professor but never get a reply, you may give up. Removal of reinforcement altogether leads to **extinction**. The process may take a while, however, as you know if you have tried to extinguish a child's tantrums by withholding your attention. Often the child wins—because you give up ignoring her—and instead of extinction, intermittent reinforcement occurs. This, of course, may encourage even more persistent tantrums in the future.

Connect and Extend to PRAXIS II®

Antecedents (I, A1)
Understand how antecedents can affect learning. Be particularly familiar with the effective uses of prompting and cueing.

Antecedents and Behavior Change

In operant conditioning, antecedents—the events preceding behaviors—provide information about which behaviors will lead to positive consequences and which will lead to unpleasant ones. Skinner's pigeons learned to peck for food when a light was on, but not to bother when the light was off, because no food followed pecking when the light was off. In other words, they learned to use the antecedent light as a cue to discriminate the likely consequence of pecking. The pigeons' pecking was under **stimulus control**—controlled by the discriminative stimulus of the light. This happens in humans too. For example, I found myself (more than once) about to turn into my old office parking lot, even after my department had been relocated to a new building across town. As I drove, the old landmark cues kept me heading automatically to the old office. Another example is the supposedly true story of a getaway car driver in a bank robbery who sped through town, only to be caught by the police when she dutifully stopped at a red light. The stimulus of the red light had come to have automatic control.

We all learn to discriminate—to read situations. When should you ask to borrow your room-mate's car—after a major disagreement or after you both have had a great time at a party? The antecedent cue of a school principal standing in the hall helps students discriminate the probable consequences of running or attempting to break into a locker. We often respond to such anteced-ent cues without fully realizing that they are influencing our behavior. But teachers can use cues deliberately in the classroom.

EFFECTIVE INSTRUCTION DELIVERY. One important antecedent to increase positive student responses is the type of instructions you give. Research on **effective instruction delivery (EID)** has found instructions that are concise, clear, and specific, and that communicate an expected result are more effective than vague directions. Statements work better than questions. You should be within a few feet of the students; directions shouted from across the room are less likely to work. Ideally, you should make eye contact with the students first, and then give the directions (D. S. Roberts, Tingstrom, Olmi, & Bellipanni, 2008).

CUEING. By definition, cueing is the act of providing an antecedent stimulus just before a specific behavior is supposed to take place. Cueing is particularly useful in setting the stage for behaviors that must occur at a given time but are easily forgotten. In working with young people, teachers often find themselves correcting behaviors after the fact, asking students, "When are you going to start remembering to . . . ?" These reminders often lead to irritation. The mistake is already made, and the young person is left with only two choices: to promise to try harder or to think, "Why don't you leave me alone?" Neither response is very satisfying. Presenting a nonjudgmental cue can help prevent such negative confrontations. When a student performs the appropriate behavior after a cue, the teacher can reinforce the student's accomplishment instead of punishing failure.

PROMPTING. Sometimes students need help learning to respond to a cue in an appropriate way so the cue becomes a discriminative stimulus. One approach is to provide an additional cue, called a prompt, following the first cue. There are two principles for using a cue and a prompt to teach a new behavior. First, make sure the environmental stimulus that you want to become a cue occurs immediately before the prompt you are using, so students will learn to respond to the cue and not rely only on the prompt. Second, fade (gradually reduce or delay) the prompt as soon as possible so students do not become dependent on it (Alberto & Troutman, 2012).

One way to incorporate cueing and prompting is by providing students with a checklist or reminder sheet. Figure 7.2 on the next page is a checklist for the steps in peer tutoring. Working in pairs is the cue; the checklist is the prompt. As students learn the procedures, the teacher may stop using the checklist but may remind the students of the steps. When no written or oral prompts are necessary, the students have learned to respond appropriately to the environmental cue of working in pairs; they have learned how to behave in peer-tutoring situations. However, the teacher should continue to monitor the process, recognize good work, and correct mistakes. Before a peer-tutoring session, the teacher might ask students to close their eyes and "see" the checklist, focusing on each step. As students work, the teacher could listen to their interactions and continue to provide coaching as they improve their peer-tutoring skills.

What would these principles look like in action? We turn to that next.

ENHANCEDetext *self-check*

FIGURE 7.2

WRITTEN PROMPTS: A PEER-TUTORING CHECKLIST

By using this checklist, students are reminded how to be effective tutors. As they become more proficient, the checklist may be less necessary.

Remember to...

_____ 1. Have the lesson ready.

_____ 2. Talk clearly.

_____ 3. Be friendly.

_____ 4. Tell the student when the answer is right.

_____ 5. STOP! Correct mistakes.

_____ 6. Praise good work!

_____ 7. Make the lesson fun.

_____ 8. Do not give TOO MUCH help.

_____ 9. Fill out the daily sheet.

_____ 10. Can you add a suggestion?

Source: From Achieving Educational Excellence: Behavior Analysis for School Personnel (Figure, p. 89), by B. Sulzer-Azaroff and G. R. Mayer, 1994, San Marcos, CA: Western Image, P.O. Box 427. Copyright © 1994 by Beth Sulzer-Azaroff and G. Roy Mayer. Reprinted by permission of the authors. Originally published as Achieving Educational Excellence: Using Behavioral Strategies in 1986.

PUTTING IT ALL TOGETHER TO APPLY OPERANT CONDITIONING: APPLIED BEHAVIOR ANALYSIS

Connect and Extend to PRAXIS II®

Applied Behavior Analysis (I, C4)
When teachers need to change inappropriate or ineffective classroom behaviors that have not changed in response to standard behavioral techniques (e.g., response cost), they often employ applied behavior analysis. Familiarize yourself with the steps in developing and implementing an intervention based on that technique.

The behavioral approach to learning has inspired several important contributions to instruction, including systems for specifying learning objectives and direct instruction (we will look at these topics in Chapter 14 when we discuss teaching) and class management systems such as group consequences, contingency contracts, and token economies (Landrum & Kauffman, 2006). These approaches are useful when the goal is to learn explicit information or change behaviors and when the material is sequential and factual. Applied behavior analysis is the application of behavioral learning principles to change behavior in these kinds of situations. The method is sometimes called behavior modification, but this term has negative connotations for many people and is often misunderstood (Alberto & Troutman, 2012; Kazdin, 2001, 2008).

Ideally, applied behavior analysis requires clear specification of the behavior to be changed; careful measurement of the behavior; analysis of the antecedents and reinforcers that might be maintaining inappropriate or undesirable behavior; interventions based on behavioral principles to change the behavior; and careful measurement of changes. In research on applied behavior analysis, an ABAB design (described in Chapter 1) is common. That is, researchers take a baseline measurement of the behavior (A), then apply the intervention (B), then stop the intervention to see if the behavior goes back to the baseline level (A), and then reintroduce the intervention (B).

In classrooms, teachers usually cannot follow all the ABAB steps, but they can do the following:

1. Clearly specify the behavior to be changed and the goal. For example, if the student makes "careless" errors in computation, is your goal only one error for every 10 problems? 20 problems?
2. Carefully observe and note the current level of the behavior. How many errors per 10 or 20 problems now? What seems to be the reason or cause for the errors? Are there more errors on timed tests? Homework? In group work? Does time of day matter?
3. Plan a specific intervention using antecedents, consequences, or both. For example, offer the student one extra minute of computer time for every problem completed with no computation errors.
4. Keep track of the results, and modify the plan if necessary.

Let's consider some specific methods for accomplishing step 3—the intervention.

Methods for Encouraging Behaviors

As we discussed earlier, to encourage behavior is to reinforce it. There are several specific ways to encourage existing behaviors or teach new ones. These include teacher attention and praise, the Premack principle, shaping, and positive practice.

REINFORCING WITH TEACHER ATTENTION. Many psychologists advise teachers to "accentuate the positive"—praise students for good behavior, while ignoring misbehavior. Some researchers believe that "the systematic application of praise and attention may be the most powerful motivational and classroom management tool available to teachers" (Alber & Heward, 1997, p. 277; Alber & Heward, 2000). A related strategy is *differential reinforcement,* or ignoring inappropriate behaviors, while being sure to reinforce appropriate behaviors as soon as they occur. For example, if a student is prone to making irrelevant comments ("When is the game this Friday?"), you should ignore the off-task comment, but recognize a task-related contribution as soon as it occurs (Landrum & Kauffman, 2006).

This praise-and-ignore approach can be helpful, but don't expect it to solve all classroom management problems. Several studies have shown that disruptive behaviors persist when teachers use positive consequences (mostly praise) as their *only* classroom management strategy (McGoey & DuPaul, 2000; Pfiffner & O'Leary, 1987; Sullivan & O'Leary, 1990). Also, if attention from other students is reinforcing the problem behaviors, the teacher's ignoring them won't help much.

There is a second consideration in using praise. The positive results found in research occur when teachers carefully and systematically praise their students (Landrum & Kauffman, 2006). Merely "handing out compliments" will not improve behavior. To be effective, praise must (1) be contingent on the behavior to be reinforced, (2) specify clearly the behavior being reinforced, and (3) be believable (O'Leary & O'Leary, 1977). In other words, the praise should be sincere recognition of a well-defined behavior so students understand what they did to warrant the recognition. Teachers who have not received special training often violate these conditions (Brophy, 1981). Ideas for using praise effectively, based on Brophy's extensive review of the subject and Alan Kazdin's (2008) work with parents and teachers, are presented on the next page in the *Guidelines: Applying Operant Conditioning—Using Praise Appropriately on the next page.*

Some psychologists have suggested that teachers' use of praise tends to focus students on learning to win approval rather than on learning for its own sake. Perhaps the best advice is to be aware of the potential dangers of the overuse or misuse of praise and to navigate accordingly.

SELECTING REINFORCERS: THE PREMACK PRINCIPLE. In most classrooms, many reinforcers other than teacher attention are readily available, such as the chance to talk to other

GUIDELINES
Applying Operant Conditioning: Using Praise Appropriately

Be clear and systematic in giving praise.

Examples

1. Make sure praise is tied directly to appropriate behavior.
2. Make sure the student understands the specific action or accomplishment that is being praised. Say, "I am impressed that you made sure everyone in your group got a chance to speak," not, "Good job leading the group."

Make praise "appreciative" not "evaluative" (Ginott, 1972).

Examples

1. Praise and appreciate the student's efforts, accomplishments, and actions—especially when the actions help others.
2. Don't evaluate the student's character or personality—praise the action, not the person.

Set standards for praise based on individual abilities and limitations.

Examples

1. Praise progress or accomplishment in relation to the individual student's past efforts.
2. Focus the student's attention on his or her own progress, not on comparisons with others.

Attribute the student's success to effort and ability so the student will gain confidence that success is possible again.

Examples

1. Don't imply that the success may be based on luck, extra help, or easy material.

2. Ask students to describe the problems they encountered and how they solved them.

Make praise really reinforcing.

Examples

1. Don't attempt to influence the rest of the class by singling out some students for praise. This tactic frequently backfires, because students know what's really going on. In addition, you risk embarrassing the student you have chosen to praise.
2. Don't give undeserved praise to students simply to balance failures. It is seldom consoling and calls attention to the student's inability to earn genuine recognition.
3. Don't use "caboosing"—tacking a criticism on at the end, as in "Good job on completing your home-work this week. Why can't you do that every week?" (Kazdin, 2008).

Recognize genuine accomplishments.

Examples

1. Reward the attainment of specified goals, not just participation.
2. Do not reward uninvolved students just for being quiet and not disrupting the class.
3. Tie praise to students' improving competence or to the value of their accomplishment. Say, "I noticed that you double-checked all your problems. Your score reflects your careful work."

Source: For more information on teacher praise, see interventioncentral .org/home and search for "teacher praise."

Video 7.2
In this lesson, a second-grade teacher meets with one of her reading groups (the "Tigers") while other students work on individual assignments at their desks. As you watch, notice the methods of reinforcement used by this teacher.

ENHANCEDetext *video example*

students, work at computers, or feed the class animals. However, teachers tend to offer these opportunities in a rather haphazard way. Just as with praise, by making privileges and rewards directly contingent on learning and positive behavior, the teacher can greatly increase both learning and desired behavior.

A helpful guide for choosing the most effective reinforcers is the **Premack principle**, named for David Premack (1965). According to the Premack principle, a high-frequency behavior (a pre-ferred activity) can be an effective reinforcer for a low-frequency behavior (a less-preferred activity). This is sometimes referred to as "Grandma's rule": First, do what I want you to do, and then you may do what you want to do. Elizabeth used this principle in her class when she told them they could work together on their Civil War news program after they quietly completed the first section of the worksheet on their own.

If students didn't have to study, what would they do? The answers to this question may sug-gest many possible reinforcers. For most students, talking, moving around the room, sitting near a friend, being exempt from assignments or tests, editing the class Webpage, using the computer, making a video, or playing games are preferred activities. The best way to determine appropriate reinforcers for your students may be to watch what they do in their free time. (For more ideas, see http://www.interventioncentral.org/home and search for "rewards"or jimwrightonline.com/php/ jackpot/jackpot.php.)

For the Premack principle to be effective, the low-frequency (less-preferred) behavior must happen first. In the following dialogue, observe how the teacher loses a perfect opportunity to use the Premack principle:

> *Students:* Oh, no! Do we have to work on grammar again today? The other classes got to discuss the play we saw in the auditorium this morning.
>
> *Teacher:* But the other classes finished the lesson on sentences yesterday. We're almost finished too. If we don't finish the lesson, I'm afraid you'll forget the rules we reviewed yesterday.
>
> *Students:* Why don't we finish the sentences at the end of the period and talk about the play now?
>
> *Teacher:* Okay, if you promise to complete the sentences later.

Discussing the play could have served as a reinforcer for completing the lesson. As it is, the class may well spend the entire period discussing the play. Just as the discussion becomes fascinating, the teacher will have to end it and insist that the class return to the grammar lesson.

SHAPING. What happens when students continually fail to gain reinforcement because they simply cannot perform a skill in the first place? Consider these examples:

- A 4th-grade student looks at the results of the latest mathematics test. "No credit on almost half of the problems again because I made one dumb mistake in each problem. I hate math!"
- A 10th-grade student finds some excuse each day for avoiding the softball game in gym class. The student cannot catch a ball and now refuses to try.

In both situations, the students are receiving no reinforcement for their work because the end product of their efforts is not good enough. A safe prediction is that the students will soon learn to dislike the class, the subject, and perhaps the teacher and school in general. One way to prevent this problem is the strategy of shaping, also called **successive approximations**. Shaping involves reinforcing progress instead of waiting for perfection.

To use shaping, the teacher must take the final complex behavior the student is expected to master and break it down into a number of small, manageable steps. One approach that identifies the small steps is **task analysis**, originally developed by R. B. Miller (1962) to help the armed services train personnel. Miller's system begins with a definition of the final performance requirement—what the trainee (or student) must be able to do at the end of the program or unit. Then, the steps that will lead to the final goal are specified. The procedure simply breaks skills and processes down into subskills and subprocesses—small steps to success.

Consider an example of task analysis in which students must write a position paper based on research. If the teacher assigned the position paper without analyzing the task, what could happen? Some of the students might not know how to do systematic computer research. They might read one or two entries in Wikipedia and then write about their position based only on this brief reading. Another group of students might know how to use computers and search engines to do research online and how to find information from indexes in books but have difficulty integrating information to reach conclusions. They might hand in lengthy papers listing summaries of different ideas without any synthesis or conclusions. Another group of students might be able to draw conclusions, but their written presentations might be so confusing and grammatically incorrect that the teacher could not understand what they were trying to say. Each of the groups would have failed to fulfill the assignment, but for different reasons.

A task analysis gives a picture of the logical sequence of steps leading toward the final goal. An awareness of this sequence can help teachers make sure that students have the necessary skills before they move to the next step. In addition, when students have difficulty, the teacher can pinpoint problem areas. Many behaviors can be improved through shaping, especially the acquisition of skills that involve persistence, endurance, increased accuracy, greater speed, or extensive practice to master. Because shaping is a time-consuming process, however, it should not be used if success can be attained through simpler methods such as cueing.

Connect and Extend to PRAXIS II®

Encouraging/Discouraging Behaviors (I, B2)
Understand the appropriate uses of techniques to encourage or discourage various classroom behaviors. Know the limitations and problems associated with these types of interventions.

GUIDELINES
Applying Operant Conditioning: Encouraging Positive Behaviors

Make sure you recognize positive behavior in ways that students value.

Examples

1. When presenting class rules, set up positive consequences for following rules as well as negative consequences for breaking rules.
2. Recognize honest admissions of mistakes by giving a second chance: "Because you admitted that you copied your paper from a book, I'm giving you a chance to rewrite it."
3. Offer desired rewards for academic efforts, such as extra recess time, exemptions from homework or tests, or extra credit on major projects.

When students are tackling new material or trying new skills, give plenty of reinforcement.

Examples

1. *Find and comment on something right in every student's first life drawing.*
2. Reinforce students for encouraging each other. "French pronunciation is difficult and awkward at first. Let's help each other by eliminating all giggles when someone is brave enough to attempt a new word."

After new behaviors are established, give reinforcement on an unpredictable schedule to encourage persistence.

Examples

1. Offer surprise rewards for good participation in class.
2. Start classes with a short, written extra-credit question. Students don't have to answer, but a good answer will add points to their total for the semester.
3. Make sure the good students get compliments for their work from time to time. Don't take them for granted.

Use the Premack principle to identify effective reinforcers.

Examples

1. Watch what students do with their free time.
2. Notice which students like to work together. The chance to work with friends is often a good reinforcer.

Use cueing to help establish new behaviors.

Examples

1. Put up humorous signs in the classroom to remind students of rules.
2. At the beginning of the year, as students enter class, call their attention to a chart posted on the board listing all of the materials they should have with them when they come to class.

Make sure all students, even those who often cause problems, receive some praise, privileges, or other rewards when they do something well.

Examples

1. Review your class list occasionally to make sure all students are receiving some reinforcement.
2. Set standards for reinforcement so that all students will have a chance to be rewarded.
3. Check your biases. Are boys getting more opportunities for reinforcement than girls, or vice versa? How about students of different races?

Establish a variety of reinforcers.

Examples

1. Let students suggest their own reinforcers or choose from a "menu" of reinforcers with "weekly specials."
2. Talk to other teachers or parents about ideas for reinforcers.

POSITIVE PRACTICE. In positive practice, students replace one behavior with another. This approach is especially appropriate for dealing with academic errors. When students make a mistake, they must correct it as soon as possible and practice the correct response. The same principle can be applied when students break classroom rules. Instead of being punished, the student might be required to practice the correct alternative action; for example, entering the room and immediately putting backpacks in assigned places. This process sometimes is called *positive practice overcorrection* because the correct behavior is practiced until it becomes almost automatic (G. A. Cole, Montgomery, Wilson, & Milan, 2000; Marvin, Rapp, Stenske, Rojas, Swanson, & Bartlett, 2010). The *Guidelines: Applying Operant Conditioning—Encouraging Positive Behaviors* summarizes different ways of encouraging positive behaviors.

Remember, there is one element that is part of every behavioral learning program—specific practice of correct behaviors. Contrary to popular wisdom, practice does not make perfect. Instead, practice makes permanent the behaviors practiced, so practicing accurate behaviors is important.

Contingency Contracts, Token Reinforcement, and Group Consequences

You've just learned about ways to incorporate positive reinforcement, the Premack principle, shaping, and positive practice into your classroom management system. As other examples of

FIGURE 7.3

A CONTINGENCY CONTRACT FOR COMPLETING ASSIGNMENTS

The teacher and student agree on the due dates for each assignment, marking them in blue on the chart. Each time an assignment is turned in, the date of completion is marked in black on the chart. As long as the actual completion line is above the planned completion line, the student earns free time or other contracted rewards.

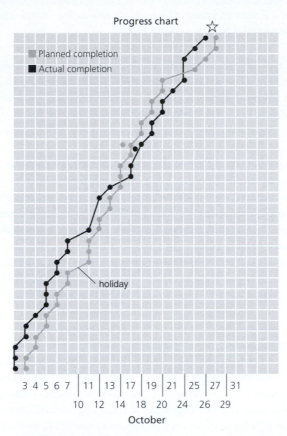

Source: From Achieving Educational Excellence: Behavior Analysis for School Personnel (Figure, p. 89), by B. Sulzer-Azaroff and G. R. Mayer, 1994, San Marcos, CA: Western Image, P.O. Box 427. Copyright © 1994 by Beth Sulzer-Azaroff and G. Roy Mayer. Reprinted by permission of the authors. Originally published as Achieving Educational Excellence: Using Behavioral Strategies in 1986.

effective classroom management, consider contingency contracts, token reinforcement, and group consequences.

CONTINGENCY CONTRACTS. In a contingency contract program, the teacher draws up an individual contract with each student, describing exactly what the student must do to earn a particular privilege or reward. In some programs, students suggest behaviors to be reinforced and the rewards that can be gained. The negotiating process itself can be an educational experience, as students learn to set reasonable goals and abide by the terms of a contract. And, if students participate in setting the goals, they often are more committed to reaching them (Locke & Latham, 2002; Schunk, 2012; Schunk, Meece, & Pintrich, 2014).

An example of a contract for completing assignments that is appropriate for intermediate and upper-grade students is presented in Figure 7.3. This chart serves as a contract, assignment sheet, and progress record. Information about progress can support student motivation. Something like this might even help you keep track of assignments and due dates in your college classes.

TOKEN REINFORCEMENT SYSTEMS.

STOP & THINK Have you ever participated in a program where you earned points or credits that you could exchange for a reward? Are you a member of a frequent flyer club, or do you get points on your credit card? Do you get one free coffee for every 10 coffee purchases or a free smoothie when you fill a punch card? Does being a part of such a program affect your buying habits? How? I know I pay for everything I can with my credit card to get the points and always try to fly on one airline for the same reason. I am participating in a token reinforcement system. •

Often, it is difficult to provide positive consequences for all the students who deserve them. A **token reinforcement system** can help solve this problem by allowing all students to earn tokens for both academic work and positive classroom behavior. The tokens may be points, checks, holes punched in a card, chips, play money, or anything else that is easily identified as the student's property. Periodically, the students exchange the tokens they have earned for some desired reward (Alberto & Troutman, 2012; Kazdin, 2001).

Depending on the age of the student, the rewards could be small toys, school supplies, free time, special class jobs, positive notes sent home, time to listen to music, or other privileges. When a "token economy," as this kind of system is called, is first established, the tokens should be given out on a fairly continuous schedule, with chances to exchange the tokens for rewards available early and often. Once the system is working well, however, tokens should be distributed on an intermittent schedule and saved for longer periods of time before they are exchanged for rewards.

Another variation is to allow students to earn tokens in the classroom and then exchange them for rewards at home. These plans are very successful when parents are willing to cooperate. Usually a note or report form is sent home daily or twice a week. The note indicates the number of points earned in the preceding time period. The points may be exchanged for minutes of television viewing, access to special toys, or private time with parents. Points can also be saved up for larger rewards such as trips. Do not use this procedure, however, if you suspect the child might be pressured for perfection or punished for poor reports (Jurbergs, Palcic, & Kelly, 2007).

Token reinforcement systems are complicated and time-consuming. Generally, they should be used in only three situations: (1) to motivate students who are completely uninterested in their work and have not responded to other approaches; (2) to encourage students who have consistently failed to make academic progress; and (3) to deal with a class that is out of control. Some groups of students seem to benefit from token economies more than others. Students with intellectual disabilities, children who have failed often, students with few academic skills, and students with behavior problems all seem to respond to the concrete, direct nature of token reinforcement.

Before you try a token system, you should be sure that your teaching methods and materials are right for the students. Sometimes, class disruptions or lack of motivation indicate that teaching practices need to be changed. Maybe the class rules are unclear or are enforced inconsistently. Perhaps your instructions are vague. Maybe the text is too easy or too hard or the pace is wrong. If these problems exist, a token system may improve the situation temporarily, but the students will still have trouble learning the academic material. Improve your teaching first. The few pages devoted here to token reinforcement and contingency contracts can offer only an introduction to these programs. If you want to set up a large-scale reward program in your classroom, you should probably seek professional advice. Often, the school psychologist, counselor, or principal can help.

GROUP CONSEQUENCES. A teacher can base reinforcement for the class on the behavior of selected target students (e.g., "If Jamarcus, Evan, and Mei stay on their mats until the end of nap time, then we will have a special snack"). Also, the class can earn rewards based on the collective behavior of everyone in the class, usually by adding each student's points to a class or a team total. The **good behavior game** is an example of this approach. Teachers and students discuss what

Video 7.3
In this class, students receive paper raindrops when they achieve a perfect score on an assignment. How is this system similar to and different from the token reinforcement systems described here?

ENHANCEDetext *video example*

would make the classroom a better place. Then, they identify behaviors that get in the way of learning. Based on this discussion, class rules are developed and the class is divided into two or three teams. Each time a student breaks one of the rules, that student's team is given a mark. The team with the fewest marks at the end of the period receives a special reward or privilege (longer recess, first to lunch, the team "spaceship" is moved closer to the "moon," and so on). If all teams earn fewer than a preestablished number of marks, all receive the reward. Sometimes a class needs a "no tattling" rule so the teams don't spend all their time pointing out each other's mistakes. Most studies indicate that even though the game generates only small improvements in academic achievement, it can produce definite improvements in the behaviors listed in the good behavior rules, and it can prevent many behavior problems (Embry, 2002; Tingstrom, Sterling-Turner, & Wilczynski, 2006).

What happens if we add interventions that target academic achievement to the proven power of the good behavior game? Catherine Bradshaw and her colleagues did just that (Bradshaw, Zmuda, Kellam, & Ialongo, 2009). They followed 678 mostly African American students from urban first-grade classes through their high school years. In first grade these students participated in either a control group or one of two specific programs: (a) a classroom-centered intervention that combined the good behavior game with an enhanced academic curriculum (read-alouds, journal writing, Reader's Theater, critical thinking skills, Mimosa math, small-group activities, etc.) or (b) a family-centered intervention that promoted parent involvement in home reading and math activities and helped parents develop better child management strategies. Students who participated in the classroom intervention that combined the good behavior game with an enhanced academic curriculum in first grade had higher scores on standardized achievement tests in grade 12, reduced referrals for special education services, higher rates of high school graduation, and higher rates of college attendance 12 years later! The parent involvement program had positive but not significant effects on all these measures and a small significant effect on reading test scores. So early investment in helping students learn positive behaviors and academic skills can make a difference for years to come.

You can also use **group consequences** without dividing the class into teams; that is, you can base reinforcement on the behavior of the whole class. However, caution is needed using group approaches—the whole group should not suffer for the misbehavior or mistakes of one individual if the group has no real influence over that person. I once saw an entire class break into cheers when the teacher announced that one boy was transferring to another school. The chant "No more points! No more points!" filled the room. The "points" referred to the teacher's system of giving one point to the whole class each time anyone broke a rule. Every point meant 5 minutes of recess lost. The boy who was transferring had been responsible for the loss of many recess periods. He was not very popular to begin with, and the point system, though quite effective in maintaining order, had made the boy an outcast in his own class.

Peer pressure in the form of support and encouragement, however, can be a positive influence. Group consequences are recommended when students care about the approval of their peers (Theodore, Bray, Kehle, & Jenson, 2001). If the misbehavior of several students seems to be encouraged by the attention and laughter of other students, then group consequences could be helpful. Teachers might show students how to give support and constructive feedback to classmates. If a few students seem to enjoy sabotaging the system, those students may need separate arrangements such as putting all the saboteurs together in their own group.

The next section describes two examples that successfully applied behavioral principles to improve behaviors of students with special needs.

Handling Undesirable Behavior

No matter how successful you are at accentuating the positive, there are times when you must cope with undesirable behavior, either because other methods fail or because the behavior itself is dangerous and calls for direct action. For this purpose, negative reinforcement, reprimands, response cost, and social isolation all offer possible solutions.

NEGATIVE REINFORCEMENT. Recall the basic principle of negative reinforcement: If an action stops or avoids something unpleasant, then that action is likely to occur again in similar situations. Negative reinforcement was operating in Elizabeth's classroom. When they moaned and complained, her students escaped the test, so negative reinforcement probably increased the frequency of complaining in the future.

Negative reinforcement can also be used to enhance learning. To do this, you place students in mildly unpleasant situations so they can "escape" when their behavior improves. Consider these examples:

Teacher to a third-grade class: "When the supplies are put back in the cabinet and each of you is sitting quietly, we will go outside. Until then, we will miss our recess."

High school teacher to a student who seldom finishes in-class assignments: "As soon as you complete the assignment, you may join the class in the auditorium. But until you finish, you must work in the study hall."

Antonio Banderas in the film Take the Lead: Working with a group of totally uncooperative high school students, Banderas blasts the students with music they hate, only turning it off when the entire class is lined up and ready to practice their ballroom dance moves.

Actually, a true behaviorist might object to identifying these situations as examples of negative reinforcement because too much student thinking and understanding are required to make the negative reinforcers work. Teachers cannot treat students like lab animals, subjecting them to loud noises or cold environments until they give a right answer. But teachers can make sure that unpleasant situations improve when student behavior improves.

You may wonder why these negative reinforcement examples are not considered punishment. Surely, staying in during recess, not accompanying the class to a special program, or being subjected to music you hate is punishing. But the focus in each case is on strengthening specific behaviors (putting away supplies, finishing in-class assignments, lining up and cooperating with the teacher). The teacher strengthens (reinforces) the behaviors by removing something aversive as soon as the desired behaviors occur. Because the consequence involves removing or "subtracting" a stimulus, the reinforcement is negative.

Negative reinforcement also gives students a chance to exercise control. Missing recess or hearing music you hate are unpleasant situations, but in each case, the students retain control. As soon as they perform the appropriate behavior, the unpleasant situation ends. In contrast, punishment occurs after the fact, and a student cannot so easily control or terminate it.

There are several rules for negative reinforcement: Describe the desired change in a positive way. Don't bluff. Make sure you can enforce your unpleasant situation. Follow through despite complaints. Insist on action, not promises. If the unpleasant situation terminates when students promise to be better next time, you have reinforced making promises, not making changes (Alberto & Troutman, 2012; O'Leary, 1995).

REPRIMANDS. In the *Junction Journal,* my daughter's elementary school newspaper, I read the following lines in a story called "Why I Like School," written by a fourth grader: "I also like my teacher. She helps me understand and learn. She is nice to everyone. I like it when she gets mad at somebody, but she doesn't yell at them in front of the class, but speaks to them privately."

Soft, calm, private reprimands are more effective than loud, public reprimands in decreasing disruptive behavior (Landrum & Kauffman, 2006). Research has shown that when reprimands are loud enough for the entire class to hear, disruptions increase or continue at a constant level. Some students enjoy public recognition for misbehavior, or they don't want classmates to see them "lose" to the teacher. If they are not used too often, and if the classroom is generally a positive, warm environment, then students usually respond quickly to private reprimands (J. S. Kaplan, 1991).

RESPONSE COST. The concept of response cost is familiar to anyone who has ever paid a fine. For certain infractions of the rules, people must lose some reinforcer—money, time, privileges (J. E. Walker, Shea, & Bauer, 2004). In a class, the concept of response cost can be applied in a number of ways. The first time a student breaks a class rule, the teacher gives a warning. The second time, the teacher makes a mark beside the student's name in the grade book. The student loses 2 minutes of recess for each mark accumulated. For older students, a certain number of marks might mean losing the privilege of working in a group or using the computers.

SOCIAL ISOLATION. One of the most controversial behavioral methods for decreasing undesirable behavior is the strategy of social isolation, often called time out from reinforcement. The process involves removing a highly disruptive student from the classroom for 5 to 10 minutes. The student is placed in an empty, uninteresting room alone—the punishment is brief isolation from other people. A trip to the principal's office or confinement to a chair in the corner of the general classroom does not have the same effect as sitting alone in an empty room. But beware. If a brief time out does not help improve the situation, don't try a longer time out. Alan Kazdin (2008), who has been helping teachers and parents work positively with children for decades, says, "If you are giving longer and longer time-outs, it means your strategy is failing. The answer is not to escalate—just the opposite in fact. If you are giving more and longer time-outs, this should tell you that you need to do more to positively reinforce good behaviors to replace the unwanted behaviors" (p. 10)—good advice for any form of punishment.

SOME CAUTIONS ABOUT PUNISHMENT. Remember the "no more points" chant I described under group consequences? The teacher actually was using a punishment-based system—*removal punishment* to be exact. For every rule-breaking point, the class had 5 minutes of recess removed. The system led to rejection of the main rule breaker. Unfortunately, punishment seems to be a very common part of parenting and schooling. I say *unfortunately* because study after study shows that punishment by itself, as usually practiced in homes and schools, just doesn't work. It tells children what to stop doing (often, they knew that already), but it does not teach them what to do instead (Kazdin, 2008). Whenever you consider the use of punishment, you should make it part of a two-pronged attack. The first goal is to carry out the punishment and suppress the undesirable behavior. The second goal is to make clear what the student should be doing instead and to provide reinforcement for those desirable actions. Thus, while the problem behaviors are being suppressed, positive alternative responses are being strengthened. As you will see in the next section, recent approaches really emphasize supporting positive behaviors. The *Guidelines: Applying Operant Conditioning—Using Punishment* on the next page gives ideas for using punishment for positive purposes.

I'll repeat: Punishment in and of itself does not lead to any positive behavior. Harsh punishment communicates to students that "might makes right" and may encourage retaliation. In addition, punishment works best when the potential punisher—the teacher—is around. Students learn to "be good" when the teacher is in the room, but when the teacher leaves or there is a substitute teacher, the system might fall apart. Punishment tends to focus students on the consequences of their actions for themselves instead of challenging them to think about the impact of their behavior on others; as a result punishment does not instill compassion or empathy for others. Finally, punishment can interfere with developing a caring relationship with your students (Alberto & Troutman, 2012; Hardin, 2008; Kohn, 1996a, 1996b, 2005; J. E. Walker et al., 2004).

Reaching Every Student: Severe Behavior Problems

Students with severe behavior problems provide some of the most difficult challenges for teachers. Three studies show how applied behavioral principles can be useful in helping these students.

Lea Theodore and her colleagues (2001) worked with the teacher of five adolescent males who were diagnosed as having severe emotional disorders. A short list of clear rules was established (e.g., use no obscene words, comply with the teacher's requests within 5 seconds, make no verbal putdowns). The rules were written on index cards taped to each student's desk. The teacher had a checklist on his desk with each student's name to note any rule breaking. This checklist was easily

Connect and Extend to PRAXIS II®

**Teaching and Management
(I, A1; II, A3; I, C4)**
Identify major approaches to teaching and classroom management that are based on behavioral principles. Understand the advantages and disadvantages of each.

GUIDELINES
Applying Operant Conditioning: Using Punishment

Try to structure the situation so you can use negative reinforcement rather than punishment.

Examples

1. Allow students to escape unpleasant situations (completing additional workbook assignments, weekly tests of math facts) when they reach a level of competence.
2. Insist on actions, not promises. Don't let students convince you to change the terms of the agreement.

If you do use punishment, keep it mild and brief—then pair it with doing the right thing.

Examples

1. Time out for young children—no more than 2 to 5 minutes; loss of points—no more than 1 sticker if the student can earn 5 in a day (Kazdin, 2008).
2. Pair the brief, mild punishment with reinforcement for doing the right thing or restitution. If a student writes graffiti in the restroom, use brief punishment plus cleaning off the graffiti.

Be consistent in your application of punishment.

Examples

1. Avoid inadvertently reinforcing the behavior you are trying to punish. Keep confrontations private, so that students don't become heroes for standing up to the teacher in a public showdown.
2. Let students know in advance the consequences of breaking the rules by posting major class rules for younger students or outlining rules and consequences in a course syllabus for older students.
3. Tell students they will receive only one warning before punishment is given. Give the warning in a calm way, and then follow through.
4. Make punishment as unavoidable and immediate as is reasonably possible.
5. Don't punish when you are angry—you may be too harsh, then need to take it back later—which shows a lack of consistency.

Focus on the students' actions, not on the students' personal qualities.

Examples

1. Reprimand in a calm but firm voice.
2. Avoid vindictive or sarcastic words or tones of voice. You might hear your own angry words later when students imitate your sarcasm.
3. Stress the need to end the problem behavior instead of expressing any dislike you might feel for the student.
4. Be aware that students of color are disproportionately punished, sent to detention, and expelled from school. Are your policies fair?

Adapt the punishment to the infraction.

Examples

1. Ignore minor misbehaviors that do not disrupt the class, or stop these misbehaviors with a disapproving glance or a move toward the student.
2. Make sure the punishment isn't worse than the crime—don't take away all the free time a student has earned for one infraction of the rules, for example (Landrum & Kauffman, 2006). Less punishment is more effective, as long as it is paired with reinforcement for doing the right thing.
3. Don't use homework as a punishment for misbehaviors such as talking in class.
4. When a student misbehaves to gain peer acceptance, removal from the group of friends can be effective, because this is really time out from a reinforcing situation.
5. If the problem behaviors continue, analyze the situation and try a new approach. Your punishment may not be very punishing, or you may be inadvertently reinforcing the misbehavior.

Source: For more information on punishment, see interventioncentral.orgl and search for "punishment."

observable, so students could monitor their own and each other's performance. At the end of the 45-minute period, a student chose a "criterion" from a jar. The possible criteria were performance of the whole group, student with the highest score, student with the lowest score, the average of all students, or a random single student. If the student or students selected to be the criterion had five checks or fewer for rule breaking, then the whole group got a reward, also chosen randomly from a jar. The possible rewards were things like a power drink, a bag of chips, a candy bar, or a late-to-class pass. An ABAB design was used—baseline, 2-week intervention, 2-week withdrawal of intervention, and 2-week return to group consequences. All students showed clear improvement in following the rules when the reward system was in place. Students liked the approach, and the teacher found it easy to implement.

In the second study, Kara McGoey and George DuPaul (2000) worked with teachers in three preschool classrooms to address problem behaviors of four students diagnosed as having attention-deficit hyperactive disorder. The teachers tried both a token reinforcement program (students earned small and large buttons on a chart for following class rules), and a response cost system (students began with five small buttons and one large button per activity each day and lost buttons for not following rules). Both procedures were effective in lowering rule breaking, but the teachers found the response cost system easier to implement.

Behavioral interventions are often used with children with autism (see S. M. Bartlett, Rapp, Krueger, & Henrickson, 2011; L. J. Hall, Grundon, Pope, & Romero, 2010; Soares, Vannest, & Harrison, 2009). For example, Sara Bartlett and her colleagues tested a *response cost* strategy to treat the problem of spitting by Evan, an 8-year-old boy with autism who had very limited verbal abilities. The researchers let the boy listen to a radio, identified as a favorite toy by his teachers, as he worked at a table in a therapy room in his school. When the boy spit, the radio was removed for 10 seconds, and then replaced. Evan's spitting went to near zero rates during these training sessions. Then the researchers stopped the response cost strategy and the radio was not removed when Evan spit. The rates of spitting went back up. Next the researchers reinstituted the response cost, removing the radio for 10 seconds, and Evan's spitting went back down again to near zero. (Notice this also is an example of an ABAB research design—baseline, treatment, return to baseline, reinstate treatment.) The researchers moved Evan back into the classroom and conducted his training sessions there. Finally they taught Evan's teachers to use the strategy and Evan's spitting stayed at near zero in his general education classroom through the entire 4-month follow-up period.

ENHANCEDetext *self-check*

CONTEMPORARY APPLICATIONS: FUNCTIONAL BEHAVIORAL ASSESSMENT, POSITIVE BEHAVIOR SUPPORTS, AND SELF-MANAGEMENT

Teachers in both general and special education classes have had success with a new approach that begins by asking, "What are students getting out of their problem behaviors—what functions do these behaviors serve?" The focus is on the *why* of the behavior, not on the *what* (Lane, Falk, & Wehby, 2006; Stage et al., 2008; Warren et al., 2006). The reasons for problem behaviors generally fall into four categories (Barnhill, 2005; Maag & Kemp, 2003). Students act out to:

1. Receive attention from others—teachers, parents, or peers.
2. Escape from some unpleasant situation—an academic or social demand.
3. Get a desired item or activity.
4. Meet sensory needs, such as stimulation from rocking or flapping arms for some children with autism.

If the reason for the behavior is known, then the teacher can devise ways of supporting positive behaviors that will serve the same "why" function. For example, I once worked with a middle school principal who was concerned about a boy who had lost his father a few years earlier and was having trouble in a number of subjects, especially math. The student disrupted math class at least twice a week and ended up in the principal's office. There, the boy enjoyed the principal's undivided attention. After a scolding, they talked about sports because the principal liked the student and was concerned that he had no male role models. It is easy to spot the function of the classroom disruptions—they always led to (1) escape from math class (negative reinforcement) and (2) one-on-one time with the principal (positive reinforcement after a little bit of reprimanding). The principal, teacher, and I developed a way to support the student's positive behaviors in math by getting him some extra tutoring and by giving him time with the principal when he completed math problems instead of when he acted up in class. The new positive behaviors served many of the same functions as the old problem behaviors.

Discovering the "Why": Functional Behavioral Assessments

The process of understanding the "why" of a problem behavior is known as **functional behavioral assessment (FBA)**. Using a wide range of procedures to map the A–B–Cs of the situation (antecedents–behaviors–consequences), teachers try to identify the reason for the behavior (Barnhill, 2005). Figure 7.4 summarizes the possible functions of many school behaviors.

Many different procedures might help you determine the functions of a specific behavior in your classes. You can begin by interviewing students about their behaviors. In one study, students were asked to describe what they did that got them in trouble in school, what happened just before they acted out, and what happened right after. Even though the students were not always sure why they acted out, they seemed to benefit from talking to a concerned adult who was trying to

---

FIGURE 7.4

THE POSSIBLE FUNCTIONS AND CONSEQUENCES THAT MAINTAIN SOME TROUBLING BEHAVIORS

Functions of Behavior	Maintaining Consequences
To gain attention: Social from adult (teacher, parent, paraeducator, customer, etc.) Social from peer	*Positive Reinforcement* Receiving attention increases the future rate or probability of the student engaging in the behavior again.
To gain a tangible: Assistance in getting: Object Activity Event	*Positive Reinforcement* Receiving the tangible increases the future rate or probability of the student engaging in the behavior again.
To gain sensory stimulations: Visual Gustatory Auditory Kinesthetic Olfactory Proprioceptive	*Positive Automatic Reinforcement* Provision of the sensory input by engaging in the behavior itself increases the future rate or probability of the student engaging in the behavior again.
To escape from attention: Attention from peer or adult Social interaction with peer	*Negative Reinforcement* Removing the student from the interaction that is aversive increases the future rate or probability of the behavior.
To escape from: Demanding or boring task Setting, activity, event	*Negative Reinforcement* Removing the stimulus the student finds aversive increases the future rate or probability of the behavior.
To escape from sensory stimulation: Internal stimulation that is painful or discomforting	*Negative Automatic Reinforcement* Attenuation of painful or discomforting internal stimulation by engaging in the behavior itself increases the future rate and/or probability of the student engaging in the behavior again.

Source: From Alberto, P. A., & Troutman, A. C., (2012). Applied Behavior Analysis for Teachers, 9th Edition. Reprinted by permission of Pearson, Education, Inc., Boston, MA.

understand their situation, not just reprimand them (S. G. Murdock, O'Neill, & Cunningham, 2005). But you will need to do more than just talk to students. You might also talk to parents or other teachers. You could conduct an A–B–C observation with these questions in mind: When and where does the problem behavior occur? What people or activities are involved? What happens right before—what do others do or say, and what did the target student do or say? What happens right after the behavior—what did you, other students, or the target student do or say? What does the target student gain or escape from by engaging in the behavior—what changes after the student acts out? A more structured approach is shown in Figure 7.5, an observation guide for FBA based on a simple A–B–C analysis. Using this information, the teacher found out that the student acted out whenever the class was transitioning to another activity. The sources of reinforcement for the student are clear too.

The same behaviors may serve different functions for different students. For example, an FBA of three preschool students found that two of the students were aggressive and uncooperative in order to gain the teacher's attention, but the third child actually was trying to escape or avoid teacher attention (Dufrene, Doggett, Henington, & Watson, 2007). With information from an FBA, teachers developed an intervention package, including positive behavior supports (PBS) for each child. Two students met specific standards to get the teacher attention they wanted, but the third child got to be "left alone" as long as he met certain standards.

Positive Behavior Supports

The Individuals with Disabilities Education Act (IDEA, 2004) discussed in Chapter 4 requires PBS for students with disabilities and those at risk for special education placement. Positive behavior supports are the actual interventions designed to replace problem behaviors with new actions that serve the same purpose for the student.

Positive behavior supports can help students with disabilities succeed in inclusion classrooms. For example, the disruptive behavior of a 5-year-old boy with an intellectual disability was nearly eliminated in a relatively short time through a PBS intervention that was based on an FBA conducted by the general education teaching staff and the special education teacher. The intervention included making sure the tasks assigned were at the right difficulty level, providing assistance with these tasks, teaching the student how to request assistance, and teaching the student how to request a break from assigned work (Soodak & McCarthy, 2006; Umbreit, 1995).

FIGURE 7.5

A SIMPLE STRUCTURED OBSERVATION GUIDE FOR FUNCTIONAL BEHAVIORAL ASSESSMENT USING THE A–B–C FRAME

Student Name: Denton R.
Location: Algebra II—Ms. B
Start time: 1:02

Date: 2/25/2015
Observer: Mr. D.
Stop time: 1:15

A: Antecedents	B: Behaviors	C: Consequences
1:03 Students get out books and open to begin class.	D. pulls out his cap and puts it on.	Students around D. start laughing and saying "Hey."
1:05 Teacher notices D. and tells him to remove his cap.	D. stands, slowly removes his cap, and bows.	Students applaud.
1:14 Teacher asks D. a question.	D. says, "Man, I don't know."	Another student says, "Yeah, you're stupid." Others laugh.

Source: Based on Friend, M. & Bursuck, W. D. (2012). Including Students with Special Needs: A Practical Guide for Classroom Teachers, 6th Ed. Adapted by permission of Pearson Education, Inc.

But PBS approaches are not only for students with special needs. Research shows that disciplinary referrals decrease when the whole school uses PBS approaches for all students (T. J. Lewis, Sugai, & Colvin, 1998). Because about 5% of students account for about 50% of the discipline referrals, it makes sense to develop interventions for those students. Positive behavior interventions based on FBAs can reduce these behavior problems by 80% (Crone & Horner, 2003). At the classroom level, teachers are encouraged to use such preventive strategies as precorrection, which involves identifying the context for a student's misbehavior, clearly specifying the alternative expected behavior, modifying the situation to make the problem behavior less likely (e.g., providing a cue or moving the student away from tempting distractions), then rehearsing the expected positive behaviors in the new context and providing powerful reinforcers when the positive behaviors occur. Using PBS, teachers attempt to keep students engaged, provide a positive focus, consistently enforce school/class rules, correct disruptive behavior proactively, and plan for smooth transitions (J. Freiberg, 2006).

Positive behavior supports also can be part of a schoolwide program. At the school level, the teachers and administrators can

- Agree on a common approach for supporting positive behaviors and correcting problems.
- Develop a few positively stated, specific behavioral expectations and procedures for teaching these expectations to all students.
- Identify a continuum of ways (from small and simple, to more complex and stronger) to acknowledge appropriate behaviors and correct behavioral errors.
- Integrate the positive behavior support procedures with the school's discipline policy.

Research on schoolwide PBS is limited, but results so far have been good. A study comparing middle school students in a behavior support program with students outside the program showed that program students reported more positive reinforcement for appropriate behavior. Disciplinary referrals as well as verbal and physical aggression significantly decreased. In addition, students' perceptions of school safety improved (Metzler, Biglan, Rusby, & Sprague, 2001). Studies of schoolwide PBS efforts also indicate decreases in disciplinary referrals (Lewis, Sugai, & Colvin, 1998; Soodak & McCarthy, 2006).

Even with new approaches such as PBS, in recent years, most behavioral psychologists have found that operant conditioning offers too limited an explanation of learning. As behavioral approaches to learning developed, some researchers added a new element—thinking about behavior.

Video 7.4
The school shown here employs a schoolwide positive behavior support system.

ENHANCEDetext *video example*

Self-Management

STOP & THINK What area of your life needs some self-management? Write down one behavior you would like to increase and one behavior you would like to eliminate. •

As you will see throughout this book, the role of students in managing their own learning is a major concern of psychologists and educators today. This concern is not restricted to any one group or theory. Different areas of research and theory all converge on one important idea: that the responsibility and the ability to learn rest within the student. Students must be active—no one can learn for someone else (Mace, Belfiore, & Hutchinson, 2001; B. H. Manning & Payne, 1996; Winne, 1995; Zimmerman & Schunk, 2004). From a behavioral perspective, students may be involved in any or all of the steps in a basic behavior change program. They may help set goals, observe their own work, keep records of it, and evaluate their own performance. Finally, they can select and deliver reinforcement.

GOAL SETTING. It appears that the goal-setting phase is very important in self-management (Reeve, 1996; Schunk, Meece, & Pintrich, 2014). Some research suggests that setting specific goals and making them public may be the critical elements of self-management programs. For example, S. C. Hayes and his colleagues identified college students who had serious problems with studying and taught them how to set specific study goals. Students who set goals and announced them to the experimenters performed significantly better on tests covering the material they were studying than students who set goals privately and never revealed them to anyone (Hayes, Rosenfarb, Wulfert, Munt, Korn, & Zettle, 1985). A review of 20 years of research on self-management found that adults most often set the goals for students (Briesch & Chafouleas, 2009).

Higher standards tend to lead to higher performance (Locke & Latham, 2002). Unfortunately, student-set goals have a tendency to reflect increasingly lower expectations. Teachers can help students maintain high standards by monitoring the goals set and reinforcing high standards.

MONITORING AND EVALUATING PROGRESS. Students may also participate in the monitoring and evaluation phases of a behavior change program. These are the elements of self-management that most often are handled by the students themselves (Briesch & Chafouleas, 2009; Mace, Belfiore, & Hutchinson, 2001). Some examples of behaviors that are appropriate for self-monitoring are the number of assignments completed, time spent practicing a skill, number of books read, number of problems correct, and time taken to run a mile. Tasks that must be accomplished without teacher supervision, such as homework or private study, are also good candidates for self-monitoring. Students keep a chart, diary, or checklist that records the frequency or duration of the behaviors in question. A progress record card can help older students break down assignments into small steps, determine the best sequence for completing the steps, and keep track of daily progress by setting goals for each day. The record card itself serves as a prompt that can be faded out.

Self-evaluation is somewhat more difficult than simple self-recording because it involves making a judgment about quality. Students can evaluate their behavior with reasonable accuracy, especially if they learn standards for judging a good performance or product. One key to accurate self-evaluation seems to be for the teacher to periodically check students' assessments and give reinforcement for accurate judgments. Older students may learn accurate self-evaluation more readily than younger students. Again, bonus points can be awarded when the teachers' and students' evaluations match (J. S. Kaplan, 1991). Self-correction can accompany self-evaluation. Students first evaluate, then alter and improve their work, and finally, compare the improvements to the standards again (Mace, Belfiore, & Hutchinson, 2001).

SELF-REINFORCEMENT. The last step in self-management is self-reinforcement. There is some disagreement, however, as to whether this step is actually necessary. Some psychologists believe that setting goals and monitoring progress alone are sufficient and that self-reinforcement adds nothing to the effects (Hayes et al., 1985). Others believe that rewarding yourself for a job well done can lead to higher levels of performance than simply setting goals and keeping track of progress (Bandura, 1986). If you are willing to be tough and really deny yourself something you want until your goals are reached, then perhaps the promise of the reward can provide extra incentive for work. With that in mind, you may want to think of some way to reinforce yourself when you finish reading this chapter. A similar approach helped me write the chapter in the first place.

Sometimes, teaching students self-management can solve a problem for teachers and provide fringe benefits as well. For example, the coaches of a competitive swim team with members ages 9 to 16 were having difficulty persuading swimmers to maintain high work rates. Then the coaches drew up four charts indicating the training program to be followed by each member and posted the charts near the pool. The swimmers were given the responsibility of recording both their numbers of laps and their completion of each training unit. Because the recording was public, swimmers could see their own and their teammates' progress and keep accurate track of the work units completed. Work output increased by 27%. The coaches also liked the system because swimmers could begin to work immediately without waiting for instructions (McKenzie & Rushall, 1974).

At times, families can be enlisted to help their children develop self-management abilities. Working together, teachers and parents can focus on a few goals and, at the same time, support the growing independence of the students. The *Guidelines: Family and Community Partnerships* gives some ideas.

GUIDELINES
Family and Community Partnerships

Applying Operant Conditioning: Student Self-Management

Introduce the system to parents and students in a positive way.

Examples

1. Invite family participation and stress possible benefits to all family members.
2. Consider starting the program just with volunteers.
3. Describe how you use self-management programs yourself.

Help families and students establish reachable goals.

Examples

1. Have examples of possible self-management goals for students such as starting homework early in the evening, or keeping track of books read.
2. Show families how to post goals and keep track of progress. Encourage everyone in the family to work on a goal.

Give families ways to record and evaluate their child's progress (or their own).

Examples

1. Divide the work into easily measured steps.
2. Provide models of good work where judgments are more difficult, such as in creative writing.

3. Give families a record form or checklist to keep track of progress.

Encourage families to check the accuracy of student records from time to time, and help their children to develop forms of self-reinforcement.

Examples

1. Have many checkups when students are first learning, and fewer later.
2. Have siblings check one another's records.
3. Where appropriate, test the skills that students are supposed to be developing at home and reward students whose self-evaluations match their test performances.
4. Have students brainstorm ideas with their families for rewarding themselves for jobs well done.

For more about self-management, see selfmanagementforkids.org

CHALLENGES, CAUTIONS, AND CRITICISMS

In this section we look at some of the challenges to earlier behavioral approaches to learning as well as some important criticisms and cautions.

Beyond Behaviorism: Bandura's Challenge and Observational Learning

Over 35 years ago, Albert Bandura (1977) noted that the traditional behavioral view of learning had many limitations. Sometimes Bandura has been characterized as a neo-behaviorist, but he has corrected that label:

> At the time of my graduate training, the entire field of psychology was behaviorally oriented with an almost exclusive focus on the phenomenon of learning. But I never really fit the behavioral orthodoxy. At the time virtually all of the theorizing and research centered on learning through the effects of reinforcing outcomes. In my first major program of research, I argued against the primacy of conditioning in favor of observational learning, in which people neither emit responses nor receive reinforcements during the process of learning. (quoted in Pajares, 2008, p. 1)

In his early work, called social learning theory, Bandura pointed out two key distinctions between enactive and observational learning and between learning and performance.

ENACTIVE AND OBSERVATIONAL LEARNING. Bandura distinguished between enactive and vicarious, or observational, learning. Enactive learning is learning by doing and experiencing the consequences of your actions. This may sound like operant conditioning all over again, but it is not, and the difference has to do with the role of consequences. Proponents of operant conditioning believe that consequences strengthen or weaken behavior. In enactive learning, however, consequences are seen as providing information. Bandura emphasized reinforcement does not "stamp in" responses, but instead instills expectations about outcomes—what will happen if I do that behavior? He explained this position in his early book, *Social Learning Theory* (1977). In other words, our interpretations of the consequences create expectations, influence motivation, and shape beliefs (Schunk, 2012).

Vicarious learning is learning by observing others, so it often is called **observational learning**. People and animals can learn merely by observing another person or animal learn, and this fact challenges the behaviorist idea that cognitive factors are unnecessary in an explanation of learning. If people can learn by watching, they must be focusing their attention, constructing images, remembering, analyzing, and making decisions that affect learning. Thus, much is going on mentally before performance and reinforcement can even take place. Cognitive apprenticeships, discussed in Chapter 10, are examples of vicarious learning—learning by observing others.

LEARNING AND PERFORMANCE. To explain some limitations of the behavioral model, Bandura also distinguished between the acquisition of knowledge (learning) and the observable performance based on that knowledge (behavior). In other words, Bandura suggested that we all may know more than we show. An example is found in one of Bandura's early studies (1965). Preschool children saw a film of a model kicking and punching an inflatable "Bobo" doll. One group saw the model rewarded for the aggression, another group saw the model punished, and a third group observed no consequences. When they were moved to a room with the Bobo doll, the children who had seen the punching and kicking reinforced on the film were the most aggressive toward the doll. Those who had seen the attacks punished were the least aggressive. But when the children were promised rewards for imitating the model's aggression, all of them demonstrated that they had learned the behavior.

Thus, incentives can affect performance. Even though learning may have occurred, it may not be demonstrated until the situation is appropriate or there are incentives to perform. This might explain why some students don't perform "bad behaviors" such as swearing or smoking that they all see modeled by adults, peers, and the media. Personal consequences may discourage them from performing the behaviors. In other examples, children may have learned how to write the alphabet, but perform badly because their fine motor coordination is limited, or they may have learned how to simplify fractions, but perform badly on a test because they are anxious. In these cases, their performance is not an indication of their learning.

Bandura provided an alternative to the behavioral theories of the time. His work continued as he developed *social cognitive theory*—one of the most influential theories of learning and motivation in educational psychology today. We will devote Chapter 11 to a closer look at social cognitive theory.

Criticisms of Behavioral Methods

This chapter gave you an overview of several strategies for changing classroom behavior. However, you should be aware that these strategies are tools that can be used either responsibly or irresponsibly. What, then, are some issues you should keep in mind? While you think about your answer to the *Stop & Think* question, look at the *Point/Counterpoint: Should Students Be Rewarded for Learning?* on the next page to see two different perspectives. Properly used, the strategies in this chapter can be effective tools to help students learn academically and grow in self-sufficiency. Effective tools, however, do not automatically produce excellent work, and behavioral strategies are often implemented haphazardly, inconsistently, incorrectly, or superficially (Landrum & Kauffman, 2006). The indiscriminate use of even the best tools can lead to difficulties.

STOP & THINK During your job interview, the principal asks, "A teacher last year got in trouble for bribing his students with homework exemptions to get them to behave in class. What do you think about using rewards and punishments in teaching?" What will you say? •

POINT/COUNTERPOINT
Should Students Be Rewarded for Learning?

For years, educators and psychologists have debated whether students should be rewarded for schoolwork and academic accomplishments. In the early 1990s, Paul Chance and Alfie Kohn exchanged opinions in several issues of *Phi Delta Kappan* (Chance, 1991, 1992, 1993; Kohn, 1993). Then, Judy Cameron and W. David Pierce (1996) published an article on reinforcement in the *Review of Educational Research* that precipitated extensive criticisms and rebuttals in the same journal from Mark Lepper, Mark Keavney, Michael Drake, Alfie Kohn, Richard Ryan, and Edward Deci (Kohn, 1996b; Lepper, Keavney, & Drake, 1996; R. M. Ryan & Deci, 1996). Many of the same people exchanged opinions in the November 1999 issue of *Psychological Bulletin* (Deci, Koestner, & Ryan, 1999; R. Eisenberg, Pierce, & Cameron, 1999). What are the arguments?

POINT Students are punished by rewards. Alfie Kohn (1993) argues, "Applied behaviorism, which amounts to saying, 'do this and you'll get that,' is essentially a technique for controlling people. In the classroom it is a way of doing things to children rather than working *with* them" (p. 784). He contends that rewards are ineffective because when the praise and prizes stop, the behaviors stop too. After analyzing 128 studies of extrinsic rewards, Edward Deci, Richard Koestner, and Richard Ryan (1999) concluded that "tangible rewards tend to have a substantial effect on intrinsic motivation, with the limiting conditions we have specified. Even when tangible rewards are offered as indicators of good performance, they typically decrease intrinsic motivation for interesting activities" (pp. 658–659).

The problem with rewards does not stop here. According to Kohn, rewarding students for learning actually makes them less interested in the material:

> All of this means that getting children to think about learning as a way to receive a sticker, a gold star, or a grade—or even worse, to get money or a toy for a grade, which amounts to an extrinsic motivator for an extrinsic motivator—is likely to turn learning from an end into a means. Learning becomes something that must be gotten through in order to receive the reward. Take the depressingly pervasive program by which children receive certificates for pizzas when they have read a certain number of books. John Nicholls of the University of Illinois

comments, only half in jest, that the likely consequence of this program is "a lot of fat kids who don't like to read." (1993, p. 785)

COUNTERPOINT Learning should be rewarding. According to Paul Chance (1993):

> Behavioral psychologists in particular emphasize that we learn by acting on our environment. As B. F. Skinner put it: "[People] act on the world, and change it, and are changed in turn by the consequences of their actions." Skinner, unlike Kohn, understood that people learn best in a responsive environment. Teachers who praise or otherwise reward student performance provide such an environment. . . . If it is immoral to let students know they have answered questions correctly, to pat students on the back for a good effort, to show joy at a student's understanding of a concept, or to recognize the achievement of a goal by providing a gold star or a certificate—if this is immoral, then count me a sinner. (p. 788)

Do rewards undermine interest? In their review of research, Cameron and Pierce (1994) concluded, "When tangible rewards (e.g., gold star, money) are offered contingent on performance on a task [not just on participation] or are delivered unexpectedly, intrinsic motivation is maintained" (p. 49). In a later review of research, R. Eisenberg and colleagues (1999) added "Reward procedures requiring specific high task performance convey a task's personal or social significance, increasing intrinsic motivation" (p. 677). Even psychologists such as Edward Deci and Mark Lepper who suggest that rewards might undermine intrinsic motivation agree that rewards can also be used positively. When rewards provide students with information about their growing mastery of a subject or when the rewards show appreciation for a job well done, then the rewards bolster confidence and make the task more interesting to the students, especially students who lacked ability or interest in the task initially. Nothing succeeds like success. As Chance points out, if students master reading or mathematics with the support of rewards, they will not forget what they have learned when the praise stops. Would they have learned without the rewards? Some would, but some might not. Would you continue working for a company that didn't pay you, even though you liked the work? Will freelance writer Alfie Kohn, for that matter, lose interest in writing because he gets paid fees and royalties?

BEWARE OF EITHER/OR

Ask any experienced teacher and you will find that rewards have a place in the classroom. In fact, life in classrooms ought to be "rewarding" experiences. Many of those rewards come naturally with learning and being a member of the classroom community. But when some students need extra structure or incentives to get going, persist, practice, or resist distractions, then rewards could help support their efforts.

Some psychologists fear that rewarding students for all learning will cause them to lose interest in learning for its own sake (Deci, 1975; Deci & Ryan, 1985; Kohn, 1993, 1996b; Lepper & Greene, 1978; Lepper, Keavney, & Drake, 1996; R. M. Ryan & Deci, 1996). Studies have suggested that using reward programs with students who are already interested in the subject matter may, in fact, cause students to be less interested in the subject when the reward program ends, as you saw in the *Point/Counterpoint*. In addition, some evidence indicates that praising students for being intelligent when they succeed can undermine their motivation if they do not perform as well the next time. After they fail, students who had been praised for being smart may be less persistent and enjoy the task less compared to students who had been praised earlier for working hard (Mueller & Dweck, 1998).

Just as you must take into account the effects of a reward system on the individual, you must also consider its impact on other students. Using a reward program or giving one student increased attention may have a detrimental effect on the other students in the classroom. Is it possible that other students will learn to be "bad" in order to be included in the reward program? Most of the evidence on this question suggests that using individual adaptations such as reward programs does not have any adverse effects on students who are not participating if the teacher believes in the program and explains the reasons for using it to the nonparticipating students. After interviewing 98 students in grades 1 through 6, Cindy Fulk and Paula Smith (1995) concluded, "Teachers may be more concerned about equal treatment of students than students are" (p. 416). If the conduct of some students does seem to deteriorate when their peers are involved in special programs, many of the same procedures discussed in this chapter should help them return to previous levels of appropriate behavior (Chance, 1992, 1993).

Ethical Issues

The ethical questions related to the use of the strategies described in this chapter are similar to those raised by any process that seeks to influence people. What are the goals? How do these goals fit with those of the school as a whole? What effect will a strategy have on the individuals involved? Is too much control being given to the teacher, or to a majority?

GOALS. The strategies described in this chapter could be applied exclusively to teaching students to sit still, raise their hands before speaking, and remain silent at all other times (Winett & Winkler, 1972). This certainly would be an unethical use of the techniques. It is true that a teacher may need to establish some organization and order, but stopping with improvements in conduct will not ensure academic learning. On the other hand, in some situations, reinforcing academic skills may lead to improvements in conduct. Whenever possible, teachers should emphasize applying the strategies to academic learning. Academic improvements generalize to other situations more successfully than do changes in classroom conduct.

STRATEGIES. Punishment can have negative side effects: It can serve as a model for aggressive responses, and it can encourage negative emotional reactions. Punishment is unnecessary and even unethical when positive approaches, which have fewer potential dangers, might work as well. When simpler, less-restrictive procedures fail, then more complicated procedures should be tried.

A second consideration in the selection of a strategy is the impact of the strategy on the individual student. For example, some teachers arrange for students to be rewarded at home with a gift or special activities based on good work in school. But if a student has a history of being severely punished at home for bad reports from school, a home-based reinforcement program might be very harmful to that student. Reports of unsatisfactory progress at school could lead to increased abuse at home.

Behavioral Approaches: Lessons for Teachers

There is great diversity in the learning histories of students. Every person in your class will come to you with different fears and anxieties. Some students may be terrified of speaking in public or of failing at competitive sports. Others will be anxious around various animals. Different activities or objects will serve as reinforcers for some students, but not others. Some students will work for the promise of good grades—others could care less. All of your students will have learned different behaviors in their homes, neighborhoods, churches, or communities.

The research and theories presented in this chapter should help you understand how the learning histories of your students might have taught them to respond automatically to tests with sweaty palms and racing hearts—possible classical conditioning at work. Their learning histories might have included being reinforced for persistence, or for whining—operant conditioning at work. The chance to work in a group may be a reinforcer for some students and a punisher for others. Remember, what works for one student may not be right for another. And students can get "too much of a good thing"; reinforcers can lose their potency if they are overused.

Even though your students will have many different learning histories, there are some convergences—principles that apply to all people:

1. No one eagerly repeats behaviors that have been punished or ignored. Without some sense of progress, it is difficult to persist.
2. When actions lead to consequences that are positive for the person involved, those actions are likely to be repeated.
3. Teachers often fail to use reinforcement to recognize appropriate behavior; they respond instead to inappropriate behaviors, sometimes providing reinforcing attention in the process.
4. To be effective, praise must be a sincere recognition of a real accomplishment.
5. Whatever their current level of functioning, students can learn to be more self-managing.

ENHANCEDetext *self-check*

SUMMARY

- **Understanding Learning (pp. 252–254)**

  What is learning? Although theorists disagree about the definition of learning, most would agree that learning occurs when experience causes a change in a person's knowledge or behavior. Changes simply caused by maturation, illness, fatigue, or hunger are excluded from a general definition of learning. Behavioral theorists emphasize the role of environmental stimuli in learning and focus on behavior—observable responses. Behavioral learning processes include contiguity learning, classical conditioning, operant conditioning, and observational learning.

- **Early Explanations of Learning: Contiguity and Classical Conditioning (pp. 254–256)**

  How does a neutral stimulus become a CS? In classical conditioning, which was discovered by Pavlov, a previously neutral stimulus is repeatedly paired with a stimulus that evokes an emotional or physiological response. Later, the previously neutral stimulus alone evokes the response—that is, the neutral stimulus is conditioned to bring forth a CR. The neutral stimulus has become a CS.

  What are some everyday examples of classical conditioning? Here are a few; add your own: Salivating when you smell your favorite foods, tension when you hear a dentist's drill, nervousness when you step on stage.

- **Operant Conditioning: Trying New Responses (pp. 256–262)**

What defines a consequence as a reinforcer? As a punisher? According to Skinner's concept of operant conditioning, people learn through the effects of their deliberate responses. For an individual, the effects of consequences following an action may serve as either reinforcers or punishers. A consequence is defined as a reinforcer if it strengthens or maintains the response that brought it about, but as a punishment if it decreases or suppresses the response that brought it about.

Negative reinforcement is often confused with punishment. How are they different? The process of reinforcement (positive or negative) always involves strengthening behavior. The teacher strengthens (reinforces) desired behaviors by removing something aversive as soon as the desired behaviors occur. Because the consequence involves removing or "subtracting" a stimulus, the reinforcement is negative. Punishment, on the other hand, involves decreasing or suppressing behavior. A behavior followed by a "punisher" is less likely to be repeated in similar situations in the future.

How can you encourage persistence in a behavior? Ratio schedules (based on the number of responses) encourage higher rates of response, and variable schedules (based on varying numbers of responses or varying time intervals) encourage persistence of responses.

What is the difference between a cue and a prompt? A cue is an antecedent stimulus just before a particular behavior is to take place. A prompt is an additional cue following the first cue. Make sure the environmental stimulus that you want to become a cue occurs immediately before the prompt you are using, so students will learn to respond to the cue and not rely only on the prompt. Then, fade the prompt as soon as possible so students do not become dependent on it.

- **Putting It All Together to Apply Operant Conditioning: Applied Behavior Analysis (pp. 262–273)**

What are the steps in applied behavior analysis? (1) Clearly specify the behavior to be changed and your goal. (2) Observe the current level of the behavior and possible causes. (2) Plan a specific intervention using antecedents, consequences, or both. (3) Keep track of the results, and modify the plan if necessary.

How can teachers use praise and reinforcers well? Teacher attention is a powerful reinforcer. Praise, if used appropriately, can support positive behaviors, but praise-and-ignore strategies all by themselves usually are not enough to change students' behaviors. The Premack principle states that a high-frequency behavior (a preferred activity) can be an effective reinforcer for a low-frequency behavior (a less-preferred activity). The best way to determine appropriate reinforcers for your students may be to watch what they do in their free time. For most students, talking, moving around the room, sitting near a friend, being exempt from assignments or tests, computer time, or playing games are preferred activities.

When is shaping an appropriate approach? Shaping helps students develop new responses a little at a time, so it is useful for building complex skills, working toward difficult goals, and increasing persistence, endurance, accuracy, or speed. Because shaping is a time-consuming process, however, it should not be used if success can be attained through simpler methods such as cueing.

Describe the managerial strategies of group consequences, contingency contracts, and token programs. Using group consequences involves basing reinforcement for the whole class on the behavior of the whole class. In a contingency contract program, the teacher draws up an individual contract with each student, describing exactly what the student must do to earn a particular privilege or reward. In token programs, students earn tokens (points, checks, holes punched in a card, chips, etc.) for both academic work and positive classroom behavior. Periodically, the students exchange the tokens they have earned for some desired reward. A teacher must use these programs with caution, emphasizing learning and not just "good" behavior.

What are some cautions in using punishment? Punishment in and of itself does not lead to any positive behavior or compassion for others, and it may interfere with developing caring relationships with students. Thus, whenever you consider the use of punishment, you should make it part of a two-pronged attack. First, carry out the punishment, and suppress the undesirable behavior. Second, make clear what the student should be doing instead, and provide reinforcement for those desirable actions. Thus, while the problem behaviors are being suppressed, positive alternative responses are being strengthened.

- **Contemporary Applications: Functional Behavioral Assessment, Positive Behavior Supports, and Self-Management (pp. 273–278)**

How can FBA and PBS be used to improve student behaviors? In doing an FBA, a teacher studies the antecedents and consequences of problem behaviors to determine the reason or function of the behavior. Then, PBSs are designed to replace problem behaviors with new actions that serve the same purpose for the student, but do not have the same problems.

What are the steps in self-management? Students can apply behavior analysis on their own to manage their own behavior. Teachers can encourage the development of self-management skills by allowing students to participate in setting goals, keeping track of progress, evaluating accomplishments, and selecting and giving their own reinforcers.

- **Challenges, Cautions, and Criticisms (pp. 278–282)**

  What was Bandura's challenge to behavioral learning? Bandura believed that the traditional behavioral view of learning had many limitations. Even though he was educated during a time when behavioral learning was dominant, his views never really fit the behavioral orthodoxy. He argued in favor of observational learning, in which people neither emit responses nor receive reinforcements during the process of learning.

  Distinguish between enactive and vicarious (observational) learning. Enactive learning is learning by doing and experiencing the consequences of your actions. Vicarious (observational) learning is learning by observing, which challenges the behaviorist idea that cognitive factors are unnecessary in an explanation of learning. Much is going on mentally before performance and reinforcement can even take place. In behavioral views, reinforcement and punishment directly affect behavior. In social learning theory, seeing another person, a model, reinforced or punished can have similar effects on the observer's behavior. Social cognitive theory expanded social learning theory to include cognitive factors such as beliefs, expectations, and perceptions of self.

  Distinguish between learning and performance. Social learning theory recognized the differences between learning and performance—in other words, we all may know more than we show. You can learn something, but not perform it until the situation and incentives are right. Even though learning may have occurred, it may not be demonstrated until the situation is appropriate or there are incentives to perform.

  What are the main criticisms of behavioral approaches? The misuse or abuse of behavioral learning methods is unethical. Critics of behavioral methods also point out the danger that reinforcement could decrease interest in learning by overemphasizing rewards and could have a negative impact on other students. Teachers can use behavioral learning principles appropriately and ethically.

PRACTICE USING WHAT YOU HAVE LEARNED

To access and complete the exercises, click the link under the images below.

Operant Conditioning

ENHANCEDetext *application exercise*

Self-Management

ENHANCEDetext *application exercise*

KEY TERMS

CONNECT AND EXTEND TO LICENSURE

MULTIPLE-CHOICE QUESTIONS

1. After a long spring time with many bee stings, several of the kindergartners at Teddy Bear Cave Kindergarten refused to go outside for activities on the playground. Once an exterminator found and removed the nest, Miss Cochran announced the bees were gone. Later that day when Miss Cochran lined up the children to go to the playground, several of the students burst into tears and begged to not go. Which of the following would be an explanation for this event?

   A. Operant conditioning

   B. Successive approximations

   C. Classical conditioning

   D. Response cost

2. Which one of the following behavioral principles does NOT apply to all people?

   A. No one eagerly repeats behaviors that have been punished or ignored. Without some sense of progress, it is difficult to persist.

   B. When actions lead to consequences that are positive for the person involved, those actions are likely to be repeated.

   C. To be effective, praise must be general in nature.

   D. Teachers often fail to use reinforcement to recognize appropriate behavior; they respond instead to inappropriate behaviors, sometimes providing reinforcing attention in the process.

3. Several of the students in Mr. Camp's class had difficulty behaving in line. He thought he had managed to get them under control with reinforcement. He had been giving them a token every time they lined up in an orderly fashion. While it initially worked like magic, now the students were falling back into their old patterns. What type of reinforcement schedule should Mr. Camp have used after his students had mastered lining up in an orderly fashion?

   A. Shaping

   B. Intermittent

   C. Continuous

   D. Applied behavior analysis

4. Applied behavior analysis requires several steps for a behavior to be changed. Which of the following steps is not one of the required?

   A. Clear specification of the behavior to be changed and careful measurement of the behavior

   B. Analysis of the antecedents and reinforcers that might be maintaining inappropriate or undesirable behavior

   C. Interventions based on behavioral principles to change the behavior

   D. Concrete reinforcement for good behavior

CONSTRUCTED-RESPONSE QUESTIONS

Case

Haley Williams sat in Dr. Karr's office, once again, having to explain why she could not get along with her teacher. "I don't know why she picks on me in front of the class. All I know is that when she starts to yell at me, I lose my temper. I'm not even sure what I am supposed to do! It seems like *everything* I do is wrong according to Miss Kemp. I know we have talked about getting along and how that would be better for everyone, but Dr. Karr, I just don't like her and she does not like me. Can't I be switched to another class?

5. Is Miss Kemp doing anything that actually contributes to Haley's poor behavior? Explain your answer.

6. What could one assume about Miss Kemp's reprimands if Haley's behavior has not decreased?

ENHANCEDetext *licensure exam*

TEACHERS' CASEBOOK

WHAT WOULD THEY DO? SICK OF CLASS

Here is how some expert teachers responded to the situation described at the beginning of the chapter about the disruptive student.

PAULA COLEMERE—Special Education Teacher— English, History
McClintock High School, Tempe, AZ

If this is a chronic issue, I would conduct a functional behavior assessment (FBA) and develop a behavior intervention plan (BIP) to address the student's needs. The real problem here is the student's avoiding a task that he does not want to participate in. I would work with this student to find a way to make the task less daunting and try to ease his fears. If the student is just nervous about speaking in front of class, as many students are, maybe he can present in front of a smaller group. This way, the student is still working on the skill. I have had students who are terrified to read in class practice a small part of a passage with me to build confidence, and then I call on them in class to read in front of peers. If just escaping class is the function of the behavior, I would look to find a replacement for seeing the nurse. This would be tied to completing the task first. For example, "After you answer your question, you can deliver this to the office." This offers the student the movement as a reward for completing the task.

LINDA SPARKS—First Grade Teacher
John F. Kennedy School, Billerica, MA

Every year, we always have a few "frequent flyers" to the nurse. Some just need to take a walk, while others try to remove themselves from an uncomfortable situation in the class where they think they may be made fun of, talked about, or put down. I always let them go in the beginning until the nurse or I have time to just observe and ask different questions. I find that when a child is away from the situation, he is more comfortable sharing what is going on. Sometimes it is as simple as he didn't complete an assignment, he is afraid he will make a mistake, or maybe something is happening at home. I had one student who tried to make himself sick daily. It was a new behavior, and we were trying to figure out what was going on. We called home and the parents assured us nothing had changed. We eventually found out that the parents were selling their home and the student overheard them talking on the phone about moving and looking at houses. After days of trying to put this together, he finally shared with me that he was afraid to be at school because he thought his mommy and daddy were going to move while he was at

school and no one would be home when he got there. This is another instance where time is needed, trust needs to be earned, and compassion needs to be present.

JENNIFER L. MATZ—Sixth Grade Teacher
Williams Valley Elementary, Tower City, PA

This type of behavior in students is usually attention seeking or avoidance of a situation. First, speak to the student privately. Tell him he seems to ask to see the nurse frequently. This causes him to miss valuable instruction time. Is there something about class that he doesn't like? When he opens up, explain that many adults say their biggest fear in life is public speaking. This shows him he is not alone. Explain to him that unfortunately in life, there will be times you will have to do it. Share with him from your experience. Explain that some students have worked out a "signal" that they can use when they know the answer and are ready to speak. Work this out between the two of you so no one else would know. It could be something as simple as tugging on your earlobe or touching the tip of your nose. The signal should be something that is not obvious to anyone but you and the student. Make a deal with him that at first he must volunteer once a day. As he progresses, gradually increase how many times a day he should be volunteering.

JENNIFER PINCOSKI—Learning Resource Teacher: K–12
Lee County School District, Fort Myers, FL

The student's apparent anxiety over public speaking needs to be acknowledged. Punishing him or forcing him to participate will only worsen the situation. Steps can be taken to help the student become more comfortable with oral presentations, but in the meantime, alternate activities should be provided for him to demonstrate his knowledge.

Several things can be done to ease the student's anxiety. The teacher can meet with him beforehand to go over the assignment and let him practice without an audience. Students can then be divided into pairs so they only have to present to one other person; the first time, he can even be permitted to select his own partner (discussed privately, so he does not feel embarrassed). The pairs can gradually be increased to groups of 3, 4, and so on. Pairs and groups can be rotated so the student presents to all of his classmates, a few at a time. Students can also be paired up to work on the assignment and present it together.

The process of increasing this student's confidence with oral presentations will take time; patience and positive reinforcement are critical. Ultimately, it is most important to make sure he has adequate means of demonstrating his learning and being assessed on content objectives.

JESSICA N. MAHTABAN—Eighth-Grade Math
Woodrow Wilson Middle School, Clifton, NJ

I would first speak to the student alone and discuss my concerns. Together we would try to find a way for him to come up with various solutions to facing his fear. Maybe the student could start by just presenting to me and gradually we could add more people to the group until he is comfortable with the whole class. Or the student could tape record his presentation and play it to the class as part of the group presentation. If it were a severe case of a phobia, I would involve the school counselor, administration, school psychiatrist, the student, and, of course, his parents. Together we could address the child's needs. I don't feel rewards or punishment would help this situation. Students need to learn how to handle their problems on their own without always having a reward once the task is accomplished. Nor is it fair to feel the pressure of being punished if the task is not completed. The goal is to have all students be intrinsically motivated; in turn, this will help them to be prepared for the real world.

LAUREN ROLLINS—First-Grade Teacher
Boulevard Elementary School, Shaker Heights, OH

This student is clearly uncomfortable speaking in class. Punishing him for this would be a huge mistake! Instead, I would have an individual conference with him. During our meeting, I would tell him that I have noticed his frequent trips to the nurse when public speaking situations occur, and I would like to help him to overcome his fear. I would start by assuring him that his thoughts are important to me and offering him the opportunity to respond by writing his answers down, rather than sharing them aloud. I would also offer him the opportunity to give his oral presentations to me privately. Then, I would slowly raise my expectations for his

class participation—asking him to contribute one response aloud each week, then twice, and so on. I would praise him and reward him for this in a way that would be motivating and meaningful to him. I would continue to add to my expectations until he felt comfortable being a participant in class discussions. As for oral presentations, as he became comfortable presenting to me one-on-one, I would ask him to invite one or two friends to his presentations and then a small group. My goal would be for him to slowly feel more and more comfortable presenting to a group of his choice. Eventually, my expectations for him would be the same as my expectations for the rest of his peers.

SARA VINCENT—Special Education Teacher
Langley High School, McLean, VA

The student is exhibiting task avoidance behavior. To extinguish the behavior of the student, modifications should first be made to the assignment. The student should have the choice to either perform the oral assignments in front of the teacher only or record his work in a location that is comfortable to him. Over time, the student can be introduced to a slightly larger group and given rewards when he completes the work. The rewards can slowly be faded until the student is comfortable with speaking in front of the class.

PAUL DRAGIN—ESL Teacher, Grades 9–12
Columbus East High School, Columbus OH

After speaking with the nurse and determining that there is no merit to the repeated trips, I would speak with the student and try to get him to open up about the possible fear that the classroom activity is provoking. Assuming that it is the fear of public speaking, I would propose some strategies to slowly integrate him into the oral activities by modifying the requirements and affirming his attempts. Fear of public speaking is common, and I would acknowledge this fact with all of the students and communicate why it is so important to practice this skill in the classroom setting.

8 | COGNITIVE VIEWS OF LEARNING

TEACHERS' CASEBOOK

WHAT WOULD YOU DO? REMEMBERING THE BASICS

You have just graded the first large unit test of the year. About two thirds of the students seem to have mastered the material and understood the key ideas. The other third, however, seems to be totally lost. Somehow they failed to remember the basic vocabulary and facts—the foundation they must know before they can move on to the more complicated work in the next unit. These students often have trouble remembering key information from one day or week to the next.

CRITICAL THINKING

- How could you help these students retain and retrieve the necessary information?
- What are your options besides a rote memory approach?
- How would you use what the students already know to help them learn in better, more meaningful ways?
- How will these issues affect the grade levels you will teach?

OVERVIEW AND OBJECTIVES

We turn from behavioral theories of learning to the cognitive perspective in this chapter. This means a shift from "viewing the learners and their behaviors as products of incoming environmental stimuli" to seeing the learners as "sources of plans, intentions, goals, ideas, memories, and emotions actively used to attend to, select, and construct meaning from stimuli and knowledge from experience" (Wittrock, 1982, pp. 1–2). We will begin with a discussion of the general cognitive approach to learning and memory and the importance of knowledge in learning. To understand memory, we will consider early information processing models of memory, along with the recent improvements on those models suggested by findings in the interdisciplinary fields of cognitive science. These new models point to key processes of working memory, cognitive load, and knowledge. Then, we turn to ideas about how teachers can help their students become more knowledgeable. By the time you have completed this chapter, you should be able to:

Objective 8.1   Differentiate between behavioral and cognitive views of learning, including the role of knowledge in the cognitive view.

Objective 8.2   Explain early information processing models of memory and recent cognitive science models, including working memory, cognitive load theory, and individual differences in working memory.

Objective 8.3   Describe current views of long-term memory, particularly the contents and types of long-term memory, individual differences, and the processes of retrieving information from long-term memory.

Objective 8.4   Describe strategies for supporting students' construction of long-lasting knowledge.

ELEMENTS OF THE COGNITIVE PERSPECTIVE

The cognitive perspective is both the oldest and one of the youngest members of the psychological community. It is old because discussions of the nature of knowledge, the value of reason, and the contents of the mind date back at least to the ancient Greek philosophers (Gluck, Mercado, & Myers, 2008). From the late 1800s until several decades ago, however, cognitive studies fell from favor and behaviorism thrived. Today, there is renewed interest in learning, thinking, and problem solving. The focus is the scientific study of memory and cognition—broadly defined as "the mental events and knowledge we use when we recognize an object, remember a name, have an idea, understand a sentence, or solve a problem" (Ashcraft & Radvansky, 2010, p. 2). The emphasis is on everyday thinking, even though the study of abnormal thinking (as in schizophrenia) can help us understand cognition better at times. The cognitive view of learning can be described as a generally agreed-upon philosophical orientation. Most importantly, cognitive psychologists assume that mental processes exist, that they can be studied scientifically, and that humans are active information processors.

In the past few years, the study of memory and cognition has become interdisciplinary and often is called cognitive science—the study of thinking, language, and, increasingly, the brain. Cognitive science views cognition as the operation of a very complex but coordinated system of multiple memory components interacting rapidly and simultaneously (Ashcraft & Radvansky, 2010). In Chapter 10 we will look more closely at cognitive science, or as it is sometimes called even more broadly, *the learning sciences.*

Comparing Cognitive and Behavioral Views

The cognitive and behavioral views differ in their assumptions about what is learned. According to the cognitive view, knowledge and strategies are learned, then changes in knowledge and strategies make changes in behavior possible. According to the behavioral view, the new behaviors themselves are learned. Both behavioral and cognitive theorists believe reinforcement is important in learning, but for different reasons. The strict behaviorist maintains that reinforcement strengthens responses; cognitive theorists perceive reinforcement as a source of information about what is likely to happen if behaviors are repeated or changed.

VIEWS OF LEARNING. In the cognitive view, learning is extending and transforming the understanding we already have, not simply writing associations on the blank slates of our brains (Greeno, Collins, & Resnick, 1996). Instead of being passively influenced by environmental events, people actively choose, practice, pay attention, ignore, reflect, and make many other decisions as they pursue goals. Older cognitive views emphasized the acquisition of knowledge, but newer approaches stress its construction (J. R. Anderson, Reder, & Simon, 1996; Mayer, 2011).

GOALS. The goal of behavioral researchers is to identify a few general laws of learning that apply to all higher organisms—including humans, regardless of age, intelligence, or other individual differences. Cognitive psychologists, on the other hand, study a wide range of learning situations. Because of their focus on individual and developmental differences in cognition, they have not been as concerned with general laws of learning. This is one of the reasons that no single cognitive model or theory of learning represents the entire field.

The Brain and Cognitive Learning

The brain continues to change throughout life, and learning affects those changes. One study found that part of the brain hippocampus is larger in taxi drivers than in other car drivers, and this increased size is related to the length of time the person has been driving a taxi. The explanation is that part of the brain grew larger because it was used more in navigating around the city (Maguire et al., 2000). In another study, when people learned to read musical notations, they developed an automatic response to just looking at a sheet of music—they read it without being told to, and their motor cortex prepared to play the notes (Stewart, Henson, Kampe, Walsh, Turner, & Frith, 2003). Observing and visualizing also support learning because the brain automatically responds. For example, when observing someone perform an action, the area of the observer's brain that would be involved in the action is activated just by watching—the brain rehearses the action it sees another person perform. These areas of the brain that fire both during perception of an action and when performing the action have been called *mirror neurons* in monkeys (where they were first discovered) and mirror systems in humans because the activated areas in humans contain millions of neurons (Ehrenfeld, 2011; Rizzolatti, Fadiga, Gallese, & Fogassi, 1996). When you actually look at an object, a certain area of the brain is activated. Just mentally visualizing the object activates at least two thirds of the same area of the brain (Ganis, Thompson, & Kosslyn, 2004).

Clearly, the brain is involved whenever learning takes place. As Blakemore and Frith (2005) note in their book on lessons for education from research in neuroscience: "We start with the idea that the brain has evolved to educate and be educated, often instinctively and effortlessly" (p. 459). The brain shapes and is shaped by cognitive processing activities. Even at the neural level, new synapses are formed a few minutes after a child is unsuccessful at processing information. So unsuccessful processing triggers development too (Siegler, 2004).

Because of the continuing development of the brain, particularly as the prefrontal cortex matures, children become more able to integrate past and present experiences. An infant or a toddler reacts impulsively, but the 8-year-old can remember and reflect. Analysis, control, abstraction, memory space, speed of processing, and interconnection of information make self-regulation and continuing cognitive development possible. Many of these developmental and brain changes involve knowledge—a key element in the cognitive perspective.

The Importance of Knowledge in Cognition

STOP & THINK Quickly, list 10 terms that pertain to educational psychology. Now list 10 terms that relate to ceramic engineering. •

When you read *Stop & Think,* unless you are studying ceramic engineering, it probably took you longer to list 10 terms from that field than from educational psychology. Some of you may still be asking, "What is ceramic engineering anyway?" Your answers depend on your knowledge. (Think fiber optics, ceramic teeth and bones, ceramic semi-conductors for computers, heat-shielding tiles for space shuttles.)

Knowledge and knowing are the outcomes of learning. When we learn the history of cognitive psychology, the products of ceramic engineering, or the rules of tennis, we know something new. However, knowing is more than the end product of previous learning; it also guides new learning. The cognitive approach suggests that one of the most important elements in the learning process is what the individual brings to new learning situations. What we already know is the foundation and frame for constructing all future learning. Knowledge determines to a great extent what we will pay attention to, perceive, learn, remember, and forget (Bransford, Brown, & Cocking, 2000; Sawyer, 2006). For example, compared to fourth-graders with little knowledge of soccer, fourth-graders who were soccer experts learned and remembered far more new soccer terms, even though the abilities of the two groups to learn and remember nonsoccer terms were the same. The difference was the soccer experts used their soccer knowledge to organize and cluster the soccer terms, which helped them remember (Schneider & Bjorklund, 1992).

GENERAL AND SPECIFIC KNOWLEDGE. Knowledge in the cognitive perspective includes both subject-specific understandings (math, history, soccer, etc.) and general cognitive abilities, such as planning, solving problems, and comprehending language (Greeno, Collins, & Resnick, 1996). So, there are different kinds of knowledge. Some is domain-specific knowledge that

PODCAST 8.1
In this podcast, textbook author Anita Woolfolk discusses not only the differences between behavioral, cognitive, and constructivist learning theories but also the importance of understanding and appreciating all three when thinking about learning.

ENHANCEDetext *podcast*

Video 8.1
The fourth-grade teacher in this video prompts students to connect prior knowledge with new learning. The cognitive approach suggests that one of the most important elements in the learning process is what the individual brings to new learning situations. What we already know is the foundation and frame for constructing all future learning.

ENHANCEDetext *video example*

pertains to a particular task or subject. For example, knowing that the shortstop plays between second and third base is specific to the domain of baseball. Some knowledge, on the other hand, is general—it applies to many different situations. For example, general knowledge about how to read or use a computer or focus attention is useful both in and out of school.

Of course, there is no absolute line between general and domain-specific knowledge. When you were first learning to read, you may have studied specific facts about the sounds of letters. At that time, knowledge about letter sounds was specific to the domain of reading. But now you can use both knowledge about letter sounds and the ability to read in more general ways (Bruning, Schraw, & Norby, 2011; Schunk, 2012). And learning in school generally requires both domain-specific and domain-general knowledge and skills. For example, Steven Hecht and Kevin Vagi (2010) followed students from fourth through fifth grade as the students were learning about fractions. Difficulty mastering fractions was associated both with lack of specific knowledge about fractions and lack of general knowledge about how to behave and pay attention in class.

To have knowledge of something is to remember it over time and to be able to find it when you need it. Cognitive psychologists have studied memory extensively and have learned more about knowledge in the process. Let's see what they have learned.

ENHANCEDetext *self-check*

COGNITIVE VIEWS OF MEMORY

There are a number of theories of memory, but the most common are the information processing explanations (Ashcraft & Radvansky, 2010; Bruning et al., 2011; Sternberg & Sternberg, 2012). We will use this well-researched framework for examining learning and memory.

Early information processing views of memory used the computer as a model. Like the computer, the human mind takes in information, performs operations on it to change its form and content, stores the information, retrieves it when needed, and generates responses to it. But for most cognitive psychologists, the computer model is only a metaphor for human mental activity. Figure 8.1 is a schematic representation of an early information processing model of memory (R. C. Atkinson & Shiffrin, 1968).

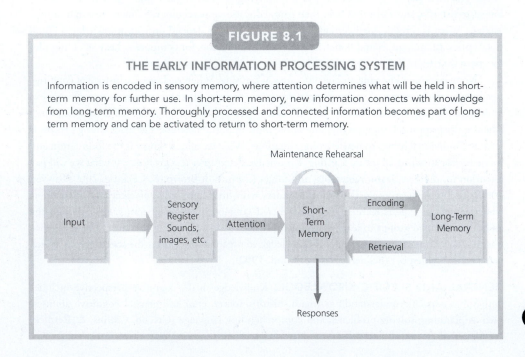

FIGURE 8.1

THE EARLY INFORMATION PROCESSING SYSTEM

Information is encoded in sensory memory, where attention determines what will be held in short-term memory for further use. In short-term memory, new information connects with knowledge from long-term memory. Thoroughly processed and connected information becomes part of long-term memory and can be activated to return to short-term memory.

According to this model, stimuli from the environment (input) flow into the sensory registers, one for each sensing modality (seeing, hearing, tasting, etc.). From there, some information is encoded and moves to short-term memory. Short-term memory holds information very briefly, combines it with information from long-term memory, and with enough effort, moves some information into long-term memory storage. Short-term memory is also responsible for generating responses or output.

This model proved helpful, but also incomplete. For example, in the model, information moved through the system mostly in one way, from sensory registers to long-term memory, but research indicated many more interactions and connections among the processes. The model could not explain how out-of-awareness memories or knowledge could influence learning or how several cognitive processes could happen simultaneously—like many small computers operating in parallel. A more recent cognitive science information processing model retains some of the features of the old approach, but emphasizes the role of working memory, attention, and the interactions among the elements of the system, as shown in Figure 8.2, which is based on several sources (Ashcraft & Radvansky, 2010; Bruning et al., 2011; Sternberg & Sternberg, 2012).

To understand this model, let's examine each element more carefully.

FIGURE 8.2

A RECENT VERSION OF THE INFORMATION PROCESSING SYSTEM

Information is encoded in sensory memory, where perception and attention determine what will be held in working memory for further use. In working memory, executive processes manage the flow of information and integrate new information with knowledge from long-term memory. Thoroughly processed and connected information becomes part of long-term memory, and when activated again, becomes part of working memory. Implicit memories are formed without conscious effort. All three elements of the system interact with each other to guide perception; represent, organize, and interpret information; apply and modify propositions, concepts, images, schemas, and strategies; construct knowledge; and solve problems. Attention has a role in all three memory processes and in the interactions among them.

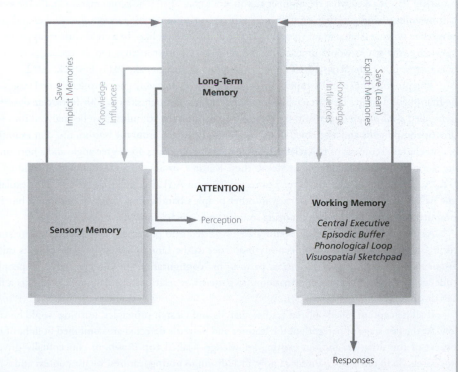

Sensory Memory

Stimuli from the environment (sights, sounds, smells, etc.) constantly bombard our body's mechanisms for seeing, hearing, tasting, smelling, and feeling. **Sensory memory** is the initial processing that transforms these incoming stimuli into information so we can make sense of them. Other names for the sensory memory are *sensory buffer, iconic memory* (for images), and *echoic memory* (for sounds).

Connect and Extend to PRAXIS II®

Attention (I, A1)
Attention has an important place in instructional activities. What steps can a teacher take to gain and maintain student attention during instruction?

CAPACITY, DURATION, AND CONTENTS OF SENSORY MEMORY. The capacity of sensory memory is very large, and it can take in more information than we can possibly handle at once. But this vast amount of sensory information is fragile in duration. It lasts less than 3 seconds.

STOP & THINK Wave a pencil (or your finger) back and forth before your eyes while you stare straight ahead. What exactly do you see? Pinch your arm and let go. What do you feel just after you let go? •

You just experienced this brief holding of sensory information in your own sensory memory. You could see a trace of the pencil after the actual stimulus had been removed and feel the pinch after you let go. The sensory memory held information about the stimuli very briefly after the actual stimulus had left (Lindsay & Norman, 1977).

The information content of sensory memory resembles the sensations from the original stimulus. Visual sensations are coded briefly as images, almost like photographs. Auditory sensations are coded as sound patterns, similar to echoes. It may be that the other senses also have their own codes. Thus, for a second or so, a wealth of data from sensory experience remains intact. In these moments, we have a chance to select and organize information for further processing. Perception and attention are critical at this stage.

PERCEPTION. The process of detecting a stimulus and assigning meaning to it is called **perception**. This meaning is constructed based on both physical representations from the world and our existing knowledge. For example, consider these marks: **13**. If asked what the letter is, you would say "B." If asked what the number is, you would say "13." The actual marks remain the same; their meaning changes in keeping with your expectation to recognize a letter or a number and your knowledge of what Arabic numbers and the Latin alphabet look like. To a child without appropriate knowledge, the marks would probably be meaningless. Context matters too. In the series **A 13 C**, 13 is a *letter,* but in the series **12 13 14**, it is a *number* (Bruning et al., 2011; Eysenck, 2012).

The process from sensory input to recognized objects probably goes through several stages. In the first phase, features are extracted, or analyzed, to give a rough sketch. This feature analysis has been called *data-driven* or **bottom-up processing** because the stimulus must be analyzed into features or components and assembled into a meaningful pattern "from the bottom up." For example, a capital letter A consists of two relatively straight lines joined at a 45-degree angle and a horizontal line through the middle. Whenever we see these features, or anything close enough, including A, *A,* **A**, A, *A*, and *A*, we are on the road to recognizing an A (J. R. Anderson, 2010). This explains how we are able to read words written in other people's handwriting, and why humans, but not computer bots, can fill in those annoying security codes such as *axqⓄℛ*.

As perception continues, the features are organized into patterns. These processes were studied in Germany early in the 20th century (and later in the United States) by psychologists called *Gestalt theorists.* **Gestalt**, which means "pattern" or "configuration" in German, refers to people's tendency to organize sensory information into patterns or relationships. Figure 8.3 presents a few Gestalt principles.

If all perception relied only on feature analysis and Gestalt principles, learning would be very slow. At the last stage of perception, the features and patterns detected are combined in light of the context of the situation and our existing knowledge—called **top-down**, or conceptually driven, processing. So to recognize patterns rapidly, in addition to noting features, we use context and what we already know about the situation—our knowledge about words or pictures or the way the world

---

FIGURE 8.3

EXAMPLES OF GESTALT PRINCIPLES

Gestalt principles of perception explain how we "see" patterns in the world around us.

a. Figure-ground
What do you see? Faces or a vase? Make one figure—the other ground.

b. Proximity
You see these lines as 3 groups because of the proximity of the lines.

c. Similarity
You see these lines as an alternating pattern because of the similarity in height of lines.

d. Closure
You perceive a circle instead of a series of curved lines.

Source: Schunk, D. H. (2012). Learning Theories: An Educational Perspective, 6th Ed. Reprinted by permission of Pearson Education, Inc.

---

generally operates. For example, you would not have seen the earlier marks as the letter A if you had no knowledge of the Latin alphabet. So, what you know also affects what you are able to perceive. In Figure 8.2, the role of knowledge in perception is represented by the arrows between long-term memory (stored knowledge), working memory, and sensory memory.

THE ROLE OF ATTENTION. If every variation in color, movement, sound, smell, temperature, and other features ended up in working memory, life would be impossible. But **attention** is selective. By paying attention to selected stimuli and ignoring others, we limit the possibilities of what we will perceive and process. What we pay attention to is guided to a certain extent by what we already know and what we need to know, so attention is involved in and influenced by all three memory processes shown in Figure 8.2. Attention is also affected by what else is happening at the time, by the type and complexity of the task, by the resources you bring to the situation, and by your ability to control or focus your attention. Some students with attention-deficit disorder have great difficulty focusing attention or ignoring competing stimuli.

But attention takes effort and is a limited resource. I imagine you have to work a bit to pay attention to these words about attention! We can pay attention to only one cognitively demanding task at a time (Sternberg & Sternberg, 2012). For example, when I was learning to drive, I couldn't listen to the radio and drive at the same time. After some practice, I could listen, but I had to turn the radio off when traffic was heavy. After years of practice, I can plan a class, listen to the radio, and carry on a conversation as I drive. This is possible because many processes that initially require attention and concentration become automatic with practice. Actually, **automaticity** probably is a matter of degree; we are not completely automatic, but rather more or less automatic in our performances depending on how much practice we have had, the situation, and whether we are intentionally focusing our attention and directing our own cognitive processing. For example, even experienced drivers might become very attentive and focused during a blinding blizzard—and no one should text or talk on a cell phone while driving. But the AAA Foundation for Traffic Safety found that over half of the adult drivers in the United States admit to using a phone while driving, even though research has shown that driving while chatting is equivalent to driving while drinking. Estimates are that about 2,600 deaths, 330,000 injuries, and 1.5 million instances of property damage in the United States result each year from driver cell phone use (M. R. Cohen & Graham, 2003). Other studies show that using a cell phone while driving increases your risk of having an accident by 400%, and hands free sets do not make any improvement in safety (Novotney, 2009).

ATTENTION AND MULTITASKING. Drivers who text or chat say they are *multitasking,* and often they think all is fine. Adolescents are multitasking more than ever, perhaps because they have access to so much technology. In one survey of 8- to 18-year-olds, about one third reported multitasking with multimedia while they do their homework and also using media about 6 to 7 hours each day on average (Azzam, 2006). You may be multitasking right now. For example, Moreno et al. (2012) conducted actual real-time samples of how older adolescents use the Internet. They describe how many college students do homework (is this familiar?):

> A student may pursue homework and have Facebook open in another window, send an email to a teaching assistant about a particularly challenging homework question, and intermittently browse the internet as a break from studying. Further, these clusters suggest that both at work and at play, college students' online activities typically involve multitasking. (p. 1101)

Multitaskers often see no problems, but is multitasking a good idea? Research by David Meyer and his colleagues at the Brain, Cognition, and Actions Laboratory at the University of Michigan says *it depends* (cited in Hamilton, 2009). Actually, there are two types of multitasking—*sequential multitasking*, in which you switch back and forth from one task to another, but focus on only one at a time, and *simultaneous multitasking*, in which there is overlapping focus on several tasks at time. Also, the content of the tasks makes a difference. Some tasks, such as walking and chewing gum, call on different cognitive and physical resources; and both walking and chewing are pretty automatic. But other complex tasks, such as driving and talking on the phone, require some of the same cognitive resources—paying attention to traffic and paying attention to what the caller is saying. The problem with multitasking comes with *simultaneous, complex* tasks.

For tasks that are at all complicated, no matter how good you have become at multitasking, your performance of the task will suffer (Hamilton, 2009). As soon as you turn your attention to something else, the brain starts to lose connections to what you were thinking about, like the answer to question 4 in your math assignment. To find that brain pathway again (to *spread activation* toward the needed information) means repeating what you did to find the path in the first place, so finding the answer to question 4 takes more time. In fact, it can take up to 400% longer to do a homework assignment if you are multitasking (Paulos, 2007). Terry Judd (2013) summarizes the effects of multitasking for most people: "While there is some evidence that multitasking efficiency—that is, the mechanics of multitasking—can be improved through practice (Dux et al., 2009) any advantage this confers would appear to be more than offset by a reduction in the encoding of information acquired during multitasking into both shorter and longer-term memory" (p. 366). In complicated situations, the brain prioritizes and focuses on one thing. You may be able to listen to quiet instrumental music in the background while you study, but favorite songs with words will steal your attention away and it will take time to get back to what you were doing.

ATTENTION AND TEACHING. The first step in learning is paying attention. Students cannot process information that they do not recognize or perceive (Lachter, Forster, & Ruthruff, 2004). But how successfully information is processed depends on several things, not just attention. Some tasks are *resource limited.* Performance on those tasks will improve if we allocate more resources, for example, turn off the iPod and give the complicated lecture your full attention. Other tasks are *data limited,* which means that successful processing depends on the amount and quality of the data available. If the quality of the information available is inadequate, then no matter how hard we focus attention, we will not be successful. For example, if you just can't hear the lecture or if you know very few of the terms being used, more focused attention will not help you understand. We have already discussed a third kind of task—*automated*—that happens without much attention because we have practiced it so thoroughly, for example, the way an expert musician moves her fingers on the strings of a guitar (Bruning et al., 2011).

Many factors in the classroom influence student attention. Bright colors, underlining, highlighting of written or spoken words, calling students by name, surprise events, intriguing questions, variety in tasks and teaching methods, and changes in voice level, lighting, or pacing can all be used to *gain* attention. But then students have to *maintain* attention; they have to stay focused on the important features of the learning situation. The *Guidelines: Gaining and Maintaining Attention* offers ideas for capturing and maintaining students' attention.

GUIDELINES
Gaining and Maintaining Attention

Use signals.

Examples

1. Develop a signal that tells students to stop what they are doing and focus on you. Some teachers move to a particular spot in the room, flick the lights, tap the table, or play a chord on the class piano. Mix visual and auditory signals.
2. Avoid distracting behaviors, such as tapping a pencil while talking, that interfere with both signals and attention to learning.
3. Give short, clear directions before, not during, transitions.
4. Be playful with younger children: Use a dramatic voice, sensational hat, or clapping game (S. A. Miller, 2005).

Reach out rather than call out (S. A. Miller, 2005).

Examples

1. Walk to the child, look into his or her eyes.
2. Speak in a firm but nonthreatening voice.
3. Use the child's name.

Make sure the purpose of the lesson or assignment is clear to students.

Examples

1. Write the goals or objectives on the board, and discuss them with students before starting. Ask students to summarize or restate the goals.
2. Explain the reasons for learning, and ask students for examples of how they will apply their understanding of the material.
3. Tie the new material to previous lessons—show an outline or map of how the new topic fits with previous and upcoming material.

Incorporate variety, curiosity, and surprise.

Examples

1. Arouse curiosity with questions such as "What would happen if?"
2. Create shock by staging an unexpected event such as a loud argument just before a lesson on communication.
3. Alter the physical environment by changing the arrangement of the room or moving to a different setting.
4. Shift sensory channels by giving a lesson that requires students to touch, smell, or taste.
5. Use movements, gestures, and voice inflection—walk around the room, point, and speak softly and then more emphatically. (My husband has been known to jump up on his desk to make an important point in his college classes!)

Ask questions and provide frames for answering.

Examples

1. Ask students why the material is important, how they intend to study, and what strategies they will use.
2. Give students self-checking or self-editing guides that focus on common mistakes or have them work in pairs to improve each other's work—sometimes it is difficult to pay attention to your own errors.

For more ideas about gaining student attention, see atozteacherstuff.com/Tips/Attention_Getters/

Working Memory

Working memory is the "workbench" of the memory system, the interface where new information is held temporarily and combined with knowledge from long-term memory to solve problems or comprehend a lecture, for example. This information held briefly in working memory points your thinking toward the knowledge you need to retrieve from long-term memory to understand and solve problems, so working memory "contains" what you are thinking about at the moment (Demetriou, Spanoudis, & Mouyi, 2011). Unlike sensory memory or long-term memory, working memory capacity is very limited—something many of your professors seem to forget as they race through a lecture while you work to hold on to and make sense of their words and PowerPoints.

In Figure 8.1 you saw **short-term memory**. Short-term memory is not exactly the same as working memory. Working memory includes both temporary storage and active processing—the workbench of memory—where active mental effort is applied to both new information and old information from your store of knowledge—your long-term memory. But short-term memory usually means just storage, the immediate memory for new information that can be held about 15 to 20 seconds (Baddeley, 2001). Early experiments suggested that the capacity of short-term memory was only about 5 to 9 (the "magic 7," + or -2) separate new bits of information at once (G. A. Miller, 1956). Later, we will see that this limitation can be overcome using strategies such as chunking or grouping, but the 5-to-9 limit generally holds true in everyday life. It is quite common to remember a new phone number after finding it on the Internet, as you make the call. But what if you have two phone calls to make in succession? Two new phone numbers (14 digits) probably cannot be stored simultaneously.

Alan Baddeley and his colleagues are responsible for the model of working memory that is central to our current understanding of human cognition (Baddeley, 2007; Eysenck, 2012; Jarrold, Tam, Baddeley, & Harvey, 2011). In this model, working memory is composed of at least four elements: *the central executive* that controls attention and other mental resources (the "worker" of working memory), the *phonological loop* that holds verbal and acoustical (sound) information, the *visuospatial sketchpad* for visual and spatial information, and the *episodic buffer* where information from the phonological loop, visuospatial sketchpad, and long-term memory is integrated together to create representations based on verbal, spatial, and visual information. Actually, the interaction among the components of working memory takes place in the long-term memory system where the visuospatial sketchpad activates visual meaning (semantics) in long-term memory, the phonological loop activates verbal meaning (language), and long-term memory for events and episodes integrates all this visual and verbal information to make sense of it all.

The phonological loop and visuospatial sketchpad are short-term memory storage for sounds and images, so they are like what was considered short-term memory in earlier information processing models. The phonological loop, visuospatial sketchpad, and episodic buffer do some lower-level work for the central executive—holding on to and combining information. Baddeley also said there may be other lower-level worker/storage systems for different information, but phonological loop, visuospatial sketchpad, and episodic buffer are the ones we know about Figure 8.4 shows the working memory system.

Let's experience the parts of the working memory system in action.

STOP & THINK Solve this problem from Ashcraft and Radvansky (2010, p. 161), and pay attention to how you go about the process:

$$\frac{(4 + 5) \times 2}{3 + (12/4)}$$

THE CENTRAL EXECUTIVE. As you solved the problem in *Stop & Think*, the central executive of your working memory focused your attention on the facts that you needed (what is 4 + 5? what is 12/4?), retrieved from your long-term memory the rules for which operations to do first, and recalled how to divide. The central executive supervises attention, makes plans, and decides what information to retrieve and how to allocate resources, as you can see in Figure 8.4.

THE PHONOLOGICAL LOOP. The phonological loop is a speech- and sound-related system for holding and rehearsing (refreshing) words and sounds in short-term memory. It briefly holds verbal information and keeps it active by keeping it "in the loop"—rehearsing and paying attention to the information. The short-term storage of the phonological loop is where you put the "18" (4 + 5 = 9; 9 × 2 = 18) from the top line of the problem while you calculated the 3 + (12/4) on the bottom of the problem. Baddeley (2001, 2007) suggests that we can hold as much in the phonological loop as we can rehearse (say to ourselves) in 1.5 to 2 seconds. The 7-digit telephone number fits this limitation. But what if you tried to hold these 7 words in mind: *disentangle appropriation gossamer anti-intellectual preventative foreclosure documentation* (Gray, 2011)? Besides being a mouthful, these words take longer than 2 seconds to rehearse and are more difficult to hold in working memory than 7 single digits or 7 short words. In addition, some of the words may be unfamiliar to you, so they are harder to rehearse.

Remember—put in your working memory—that we are discussing temporarily holding new information. In daily life we certainly can hold more than 5 to 9 bits or 1.5 seconds of information at once. While you are keying in that 7-digit phone number you just looked up, you are bound to have other things "on your mind"—in your memory—such as how to use a telephone, whom you are calling, and why. You don't have to pay attention to these things; they are not new knowledge.

Connect and Extend to PRAXIS II®

Memory and Instruction (II, A1)
To maximize the learning derived from instructional activities, a teacher should be aware of the characteristics of working memory. Consider the techniques or tactics a teacher can employ that complement those characteristics.

FIGURE 8.4

THREE PARTS OF WORKING MEMORY

The central executive system is the pool of mental resources for such cognitive activities as focusing attention, reasoning, and comprehension. The phonological loop holds verbal and sound information, and the visuospatial sketchpad holds visual and spatial information. The episodic buffer integrates information from the phonological loop, visuospatial sketchpad, and long-term memory. The system is limited and can be overwhelmed if there is too much information or it is too difficult. The interaction among the components of working memory actually takes place in the long-term memory where the visuospatial sketchpad activates visual meaning (semantics) in long-term memory, the phonological loop activates verbal meaning (language), and long-term memory for events and episodes integrates all this visual and verbal information.

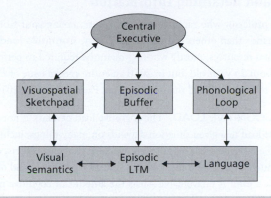

Some of the processes, such as using the keypad on the phone, are *automated* tasks. However, because of the working memory's limitations, if you were in a foreign country and were attempting to use an unfamiliar telephone system, you might very well have trouble remembering the phone number because your central executive was searching for strategies to use the phone system at the same time. Even a few bits of new information can be too much to remember if the new information is very complex or unfamiliar or if you have to integrate several elements to make sense of a situation (Sweller, van Merriënboer, & Paas, 1998).

THE VISUOSPATIAL SKETCHPAD. Now try the problem shown in the next *Stop & Think*.

- -

STOP & THINK If you rotate a *d* 180 degrees clockwise, do you get a *b* or a *p*? •

- -

Most people answer this question by creating a visual image of a *d* and rotating it. The **visuospatial sketchpad** is the place in your mind where you manipulated the image (after your central executive retrieved the meaning of "180 degrees," and "clockwise," of course). Working in the visuospatial sketchpad has some of the same aspects as actually looking at a picture or object. If you have to solve the "d" problem and also pay attention to an image on a screen, you will be slowed down just like you would be if you had to look back and forth between two different objects. But if you had to solve the "d" problem while repeating digits, there is little slow-down. You can use your phonological loop and your visuospatial sketchpad at the same time, but each is quickly filled and easily overburdened. Each kind of task—verbal and visual—appears to happen in different areas of the brain, and there are some individual differences in the capacities of these systems, too (Ashcraft & Radvansky, 2010; Gray, 2011).

THE EPISODIC BUFFER. If working memory is the workbench of memory, the episodic buffer is the workbench of working memory. The **episodic buffer** is the process that brings together and integrates information from the phonological loop, visuospatial sketchpad, and long-term memory under the supervision of the central executive, to create complex memories, such as storing the appearance, voice, words, and actions of an actor in a film to create a complete character.

THE DURATION AND CONTENTS OF WORKING MEMORY. It is clear that the duration of information in the working memory system is short, about 5 to 20 seconds, unless you keep rehearsing the information or process it in some other way. It may seem to you that a memory system with a 20-second time limit is not very useful, but, without this system, you would have already forgotten what you read in the first part of this sentence before you came to these last few words. This would clearly make understanding sentences difficult.

The contents of information in working memory may be in the form of sounds and images that resemble the representations in sensory memory, or the information may be structured more abstractly, based on meaning.

Cognitive Load and Retaining Information

Let's get back to that professor who raced through a lecture, taxing your working memory. Some tasks make more demands than others on working memory. **Cognitive load** is a term that refers to the amount of mental resources, mostly working memory, required to perform a particular task. The concept is only about 25 years old, but in 2010 an entire special issue of *Educational Psychology Review* was dedicated to cognitive load theory (van Gog, Paas, & Sweller, 2010).

THREE KINDS OF COGNITIVE LOAD. The cognitive load of a task is not an absolute "weight." The extent of cognitive load in a given situation depends on many things, including what the person already knows about the task and what supports are available (Kalyuga, Rikers, & Paas, 2012). There are three kinds of cognitive load. One is unavoidable, one gets in the way, and one is valuable.

Intrinsic cognitive load is unavoidable—it is the amount of cognitive processing required to figure out the material. That amount depends on how many elements you have to take into account, how complicated the interactions among the elements are, and your level of expertise in the problem area (Antonenko, Paas, Grabner, & van Gog, 2010). Even though working memory can hold 5 to 9 new bits of information, it can process only about 2 to 4 at a time, so if you have to understand how many separate elements interact in a complex system, such as grasping the structure and function of DNA, you will be in trouble unless you already understand some of the parts: vocabulary, concepts, procedures, and so on (van Merriënboer & Sweller, 2005). Intrinsic cognitive load is essential to the task—it cannot be eliminated. But good instruction can help manage intrinsic load.

Extraneous cognitive load is the cognitive capacity you use to deal with problems not related to the learning task, like trying to get your roommate (spouse, children, partner) to quit interrupting you or struggling with a disorganized lecture or a poorly written textbook (not this one of course!). Instruction can help manage extraneous load by providing supports, focusing attention on the main ideas, and generally supplying scaffolding (see Chapter 2).

The good cognitive load is called *germane* because it is directly related to (germane to) high-quality learning. **Germane cognitive load** comes from deep processing of relevant information—organizing and integrating the material with what you already know and forming new understandings. Instruction can support this process by asking students to explain the material to each other or to themselves, draw or chart their understandings, take useful notes, and use other strategies we will discuss in upcoming chapters (Berthold & Renkl, 2009; Mayer, 2011, van Gog et al., 2010). The goal of good instructional design and good teaching is to *manage* intrinsic load (keep it just right for the students' abilities—in their zone of proximal development), *reduce* extraneous load (clear away as much as possible), and ideally *promote* germane load (support deep processing). The three kinds of cognitive load are summarized in Table 8.1. Just a note: Some psychologists suggest that there is no practical distinction between intrinsic and germane load; a student must deal with both to learn (Kalyuga, 2011).

RETAINING INFORMATION IN WORKING MEMORY. Information in working memory must be kept activated in order for it to be retained. Activation is high as long as you are focusing on information, but activation decays or fades quickly when attention shifts away. Holding information in working memory is like a circus performer keeping a series of plates spinning on top of several poles. The performer gets one plate spinning, moves to the next plate, and the next, but

TABLE 8.1 • **Three Kinds of Cognitive Load**
There are three types of cognitive load that make demands during learning, with different causes and effects.

TYPE OF COGNITIVE LOAD	WHAT IS IT?	WHAT CAUSES IT?	WHAT'S AN EXAMPLE?	WHAT HAPPENS?
Intrinsic	*Unavoidable:* the essential processing needed to attend to and represent the material	Caused by the inherent complexity of the task: the more complex, the more basic processing needed	More intrinsic processing needed to recognize and organize a complicated task such as quadratic equations	Processing focuses attention and begins to organize learning, rote learning possible
Extraneous	*Avoidable or manageable:* unhelpful processing needed to deal with problems that are not related to the learning task itself	Caused by poor learning strategies, divided attention and distractibility, poor instruction, inadequate background knowledge	Students scan back and forth between the text and a graph, but don't know how to read the graph or integrate the visual and verbal information	Inappropriate processing, no learning, possible discouragement
Germane	*Desirable:* the deep processing (organizing, integrating, connecting to prior knowledge) required to generate understandings	Learner motivation to understand, make strong effort, try new strategies when first attempts fall short	Learner diagrams relationships in a problem, connects to key ideas in the text	Appropriate organizing, elaborating, and visualizing lead to deep learning

Source: Based on Bruning, R. H., Schraw, G. J., & Norby, M. M. (2011). Cognitive Psychology and Instruction (5th ed.). Boston, MA: Pearson, Mayer, R. E. (2011). Applying the Science of Learning. Boston, MA: Pearson.

has to return to the first plate before it slows down too much and falls off its pole. If we don't keep the information "spinning" in working memory—keep it activated—it will "fall off" (Anderson, 1995, 2010). When activation fades, forgetting follows.

To keep information activated, most people continue rehearsing the information mentally. There are two types of rehearsal. **Maintenance rehearsal** involves repeating the information in your phonological loop or refreshing information in your visuospatial sketchpad. As long as you revisit the information, it can be maintained in working memory indefinitely. Maintenance rehearsal is useful for retaining something you plan to use and then forget, such as a phone number or a location on a map.

Elaborative rehearsal involves connecting the information you are trying to remember with something you already know—with knowledge from long-term memory. For example, if you meet someone at a party whose name is the same as your brother's, you don't have to repeat the name to keep it in memory; you just have to make the connection. This kind of rehearsal not only retains information in working memory but also helps create long-term memories. Rehearsal is a process the central executive controls to manage the flow of information through the information processing system (Ashcraft & Radvansky, 2010).

LEVELS OF PROCESSING THEORY. Craik and Lockhart (1972) first proposed their **levels of processing theory** (sometimes called *depth of processing theory*) as an alternative to short-/long-term memory models, but levels of processing theory is particularly related to the notion of elaborative rehearsal. Craik and Lockhart suggested that the length of time that information is remembered is determined by the extent to which the information is analyzed and connected with other information. The more completely information is processed, the better are our chances of remembering it. For example, according to the levels of processing theory, if I ask you to sort pictures of dogs based on the color of their coats, you might not remember many of the pictures later. But if I ask you to rate each dog on how likely it is to chase you as you jog, you probably would remember more of the pictures. To rate the dogs, you must pay attention to details in the pictures, relate features of the dogs to characteristics associated with danger, and so on. This rating procedure requires elaborative rehearsal (associating the information with what you already know), so processing is deeper and more focused on the *meaning*, not the surface features, of the photos.

Video 8.2
The adolescent in this video describes methods she uses to remember what she learns at school. Note her strategies for holding information in her working memory.

ENHANCEDetext *video example*

The limited capacity of working memory can also be somewhat circumvented by the process of **chunking**. Because the number of bits of information, not the size of each bit, is a limitation for working memory, you can retain more information if you can group individual bits of information. You can experience this effect of chunking by trying to hold these letters in memory:

HBOUSACIALOLATM

Now try these:

HBO USA CIA LOL ATM

You just used chunking to group the string of letters into memorable (and meaningful) chunks, so you could hold more in memory. Also, you brought your knowledge of the world to bear on the memory task. Chunking helps you remember a password or social security number.

FORGETTING. Information may be lost from working memory through *interference* or *decay*. **Interference** is fairly straightforward: Processing new information interferes or gets confused with old information. As new thoughts accumulate, old information is lost from working memory. Information is also lost by time **decay**. If you don't continue to pay attention to information, the activation level decays (weakens) and finally drops so low that the information cannot be reactivated—it disappears altogether. Some cognitive psychologists argue that interference is the main factor in forgetting in working memory—your mind starts processing other information and the previous information is "written over" (Sternberg & Sternberg, 2012).

Actually, forgetting is very useful. Without forgetting, people would quickly overload their working memories and learning would cease. Also, it would be a problem if you remembered permanently every sentence you ever read, every sound you ever heard, every picture you ever saw . . . you get the idea. Finding a particular bit of information in all that sea of knowledge would be impossible. It is helpful to have a system that provides temporary storage and that "weeds out" some information from everything you experience.

Individual Differences in Working Memory

As you might expect, there are both developmental and individual differences in working memory. Let's examine a few.

DEVELOPMENTAL DIFFERENCES. All of the components of working memory are in place by about age 4. Performance on working memory tasks improves steadily over the elementary and secondary school years, but visual/spatial memory appears to develop earlier. Working memory is very important in the middle school years—it is related to academic achievement, math computation, and solving complex word problems in math (T. P. Alloway, Gathercole, & Pickering, 2006; Jarrold, Tam, Baddeley, & Harvey, 2011; H. L. Swanson, 2011) as well as second- and third-language learning (Engel de Abreu & Gathercole, 2012). In fact, working memory capacity is a good predictor of a range of cognitive skills including language understanding, reading and mathematics abilities, and fluid intelligence—discussed in the next section (Bayliss et al., 2005; H. L. Swanson, 2011).

Three basic aspects of memory improve over time: memory span or the amount of information that can be held in short-term/working memory, memory processing efficiency, and speed of processing. As they get older, children can process many different kinds of information (verbal, visual, mathematical, etc.) faster, so increased speed of processing seems to be a general factor. In addition, the increase in speed with age is the same for American and Korean children, so increasing processing speed with age may be universal (Kail, 2000; Kail & Park, 1994).

These three basic capacities act together and influence each other; more efficient processing allows greater amounts to be held in memory, for example (Demetriou, Christou, Spanoudis, & Platsidou, 2002). You experienced this effect of efficient processing when you remembered HBOUSACIALOLATM by chunking the letters into HBO USA CIA LOL ATM. Your more efficient and faster processing expanded your memory span. Young children have fewer strategies and less knowledge, so they have more trouble with memorizing a longer series. But as they grow older, children develop more effective strategies for remembering information. Most children spontaneously discover rehearsal around age 5 or 6 and continue to use it. Also around age 6, most children discover the value of using organizational strategies, and by 9 or 10, they use these strategies spontaneously. So, given the following words to learn:

couch, orange, rat, lamp, pear, sheep, banana, rug, pineapple, horse, table, dog

an older child or an adult might organize the words into three short lists of furniture, fruit, and animals. Also remember that expertise in an area helps you use categories to organize and remember, as we saw with the expert fourth-grade soccer players earlier. Younger children can be taught to use rehearsal or organization to improve memory, but they probably won't apply the strategies unless they are reminded. Children also become more able to use elaboration as they mature, but this strategy develops late in childhood. Creating images or stories to assist in remembering ideas is more likely for older elementary school students and adolescents (Siegler, 1998).

In terms of strategies, for young children, using a new strategy or operation—such as reaching for a toy, counting, or finding a word—takes up a large portion of their working memory. But once an operation is mastered and becomes more automatic, more working memory is available for short-term storage of new information (A. Johnson, 2003). So, through changes in the brain, faster processing of information, the development and automating of strategies, and added knowledge, working memory increases in capacity from ages 4 through adolescence (T. P. Alloway et al., 2006; Gathercole, Pickering, Ambridge, & Wearing, 2004). Children are 10 to 11 years old before they have adult-like memories (Bauer, 2006).

INDIVIDUAL DIFFERENCES. Besides developmental differences, there are other individual variations in working memory, and these differences have implications for learning. Try the *Stop & Think* exercise.

STOP & THINK Read the following sentences and words in caps out loud once:
For many years my family and friends have been working on the farm. SPOT
Because the room was stuffy, Bob went outside for some fresh air. TRAIL
We were fifty miles out to sea before we lost sight of the land. BAND
Now cover the sentences and answer these questions (be honest):
Name the words that were in all caps. Who was in the stuffy room? Who worked on the farm? •

You have just taken a few items from a test of working memory span (Engle, 2001). The test required you to both process and store—process the meaning of the sentences and store the words. How did you do?

The more educational psychologists study working memory, the more we realize how important it is in learning and development at every age (T. P. Alloway, Banner, & Smith, 2010; Welsh, Nix, Blair, Bierman, & Nelson, 2010). For adolescents and adults, the correlation between scores on a test of working memory span (like the one you just took in the *Stop & Think* exercise) and the verbal portion of the Scholastic Assessment Test (SAT) is about .59. But there is no correlation between the SAT and simple short-term memory span (repeating digits). For elementary school students, growth in working memory (but not simple short-term memory) is related to reading abilities and reading comprehension; problems with working memory are associated with reading disabilities. Working memory is related to academic achievement, math computation, and solving complex word problems in math in elementary school. For young children, growth in working memory and attention control during the preschool years predicts emergent literacy and number skills.

Working memory span is also related to scores on intelligence tests. If a task requires controlled attention or higher-level thinking, then working memory probably is a factor in performing that task (Ackerman, Beier, & Boyle, 2005; Hambrick, Kane, & Engle, 2005; Unsworth & Engle, 2005). Some people seem to have more efficient working memories than others (Cariglia-Bull & Pressley, 1990; DiVesta & Di Cintio, 1997; Jurden, 1995), and differences in working memory may be associated with giftedness in math and verbal areas.

We turn next to long-term memory. Because this is such an important topic for teachers, we will spend quite a bit of time on it.

ENHANCEDetext *self-check*

LONG-TERM MEMORY

Working memory holds the information that is currently activated, such as the name of the person you just met. **Long-term memory** holds the information that is well learned, such as the names of all the people you know.

Capacity, Duration, and Contents of Long-Term Memory

There are a number of differences between working and long-term memory. Information enters working memory very quickly, but it takes time and effort to store memories for the long term. The capacity of working memory is limited, but the capacity of long-term memory appears to be, for all practical purposes, unlimited. And once information is securely stored in long-term memory, it can remain there permanently. Our access to information in working memory is immediate because we are thinking about the information at that very moment. But gaining access to information in long-term memory requires time and effort.

Recently, some psychologists have suggested that there are not two separate memory stores (working and long-term). Rather, working memory is the part of long-term memory that works on (processes) currently activated information. The difference between working memory and long-term memory just may be in how activated or inactive a particular memory is (J. R. Anderson, 2010; Wilson, 2001). This model sees memory as a set of nested systems with very short-term storage (phonological loop, visuospatial sketchpad, other brief holding areas) nested in working memory, which is just the active part of long-term memory that does the integrating of old and new information (Sternberg & Sternberg, 2012).

CONTENTS: DECLARATIVE, PROCEDURAL, AND SELF-REGULATORY KNOWLEDGE. Earlier, we talked about general and specific knowledge. Another way to categorize knowledge is as *declarative, procedural,* or *self-regulatory* (Schraw, 2006).

Declarative knowledge is knowledge that can be declared, through words and symbol systems of all kinds—Braille, sign language, dance or musical notation, mathematical symbols, and so on. Declarative knowledge is "knowing that" something is the case. The range of declarative knowledge is tremendous. You can know very specific facts (the atomic weight of gold is 196.967), or generalities (leaves of some trees change color in autumn), or personal preferences (I don't like lima beans), or rules (to divide fractions, invert the divisor and multiply). Small units of declarative knowledge can be organized into larger units; for example, principles of reinforcement and punishment can be organized in your thinking into a theory of behavioral learning.

Procedural knowledge is "knowing how" to do something such as divide fractions or design a Web site; it is knowledge in action. Procedural knowledge must be demonstrated. Notice that repeating the rule "to divide fractions, invert the divisor and multiply" shows declarative knowledge. The student can state the rule. But to show procedural knowledge, the student must act. When faced with a fraction to divide, the student must divide correctly. Students demonstrate procedural knowledge when they translate a passage into Spanish, correctly categorize a geometric shape, or craft a coherent paragraph.

Self-regulatory knowledge is knowing how to manage your learning—knowing how and when to use your declarative and procedural knowledge (Schraw, 2006). It takes self-regulatory knowledge to know when to read every word in a text and when to skim or when to apply a strategy for overcoming procrastination. Self-regulatory knowledge has also been called *conditional knowledge* (Paris & Cunningham, 1996). For many students, this kind of knowledge is a stumbling block. They have the facts and can do the procedures, but they don't seem to understand how to apply what they know at the appropriate time. Self-regulatory knowledge can be specific to a subject

Video 8.3
The high-school students in this video are using domain-specific knowledge in their geometry lesson. Notice the use of declarative knowledge and procedural knowledge as students process new concepts.

ENHANCEDetext *video example*

TABLE 8.2 • **Kinds of Knowledge**

	GENERAL KNOWLEDGE	DOMAIN-SPECIFIC KNOWLEDGE
Declarative	Hours the library is open Rules of grammar	The definition of *hypotenuse* The lines of the poem "The Raven"
Procedural	How to use your cell phone How to drive	How to solve an oxidation-reduction equation How to throw a pot on a potter's wheel
Self-Regulatory/Conditional	When to give up and try another approach When to skim and when to read carefully	When to use the formula for calculating volume When to rush the net in tennis

area (when to use the formula for calculating area, not perimeter, in geometry) or more general (how to summarize key points or use diagrams to organize information). In fact, all three kinds of knowledge—declarative, procedural, and self-regulatory—can be either general or domain-specific, as you can see in Table 8.2 (Schraw, 2006).

Most cognitive psychologists distinguish between two categories of long-term memory, explicit and implicit, with subdivisions under each category, as shown in Figure 8.5. **Explicit memory** is knowledge from long-term memory that can be recalled and consciously considered. We are aware of these memories; we know we have remembered them. Declarative knowledge fits under this category. **Implicit memory**, on the other hand, is knowledge that we are not conscious of recalling, but that influences behavior or thought without our awareness. These different kinds of memory are associated with different parts of the brain (Ashcraft & Radvansky, 2010; Gray, 2011).

This view has been challenged recently. Lynne Reder and her colleagues claim that implicit and explicit are not different memory systems, but just different kinds of tasks that are accomplished with one memory system (Reder, Park, & Kieffaber, 2009). Stay tuned as new theories develop. For now, we will stick with the idea of explicit and implicit systems, and look at explicit memories first.

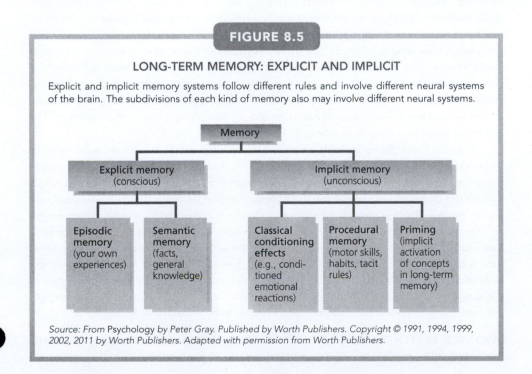

FIGURE 8.5

LONG-TERM MEMORY: EXPLICIT AND IMPLICIT

Explicit and implicit memory systems follow different rules and involve different neural systems of the brain. The subdivisions of each kind of memory also may involve different neural systems.

Source: From Psychology by Peter Gray. Published by Worth Publishers. Copyright © 1991, 1994, 1999, 2002, 2011 by Worth Publishers. Adapted with permission from Worth Publishers.

Explicit Memories: Semantic and Episodic

In Figure 8.5, you saw that explicit memories can be either semantic (based on meaning) or episodic (based on the sequence of events, such as memory for your own experiences).

Semantic memory, very important in schools, is memory for meaning, including words, facts, theories, and concepts—*declarative* knowledge, so sometimes the name *declarative memory* is used. These memories are not tied to particular experiences and are represented and stored as propositions, images, concepts, and schemas (J. R. Anderson, 2010; Schraw, 2006).

PROPOSITIONS AND PROPOSITIONAL NETWORKS.   How do we represent the meaning of sentences and pictures in our memories? One answer is with propositions connected in networks. A proposition is the smallest unit of knowledge that can be judged true or false. Anderson (2010, p. 123) gives this example of a statement with three propositions: "Lincoln, who was president of the United States during a bitter war, freed the slaves." The three basic propositions are:

1. Lincoln was president of the United States during a war.
2. The war was bitter.
3. Lincoln freed the slaves.

Propositions that share information are linked in what cognitive psychologists call propositional networks. It is the meaning, not the exact words or word order, that is stored in the network. The same propositional network would apply to the sentence: "The slaves were freed by Lincoln, who, during a bitter war, was president of the United States." The meaning is the same, and it is this meaning that is stored in memory as a set of relationships among propositions.

It is possible that most information is stored and represented in propositional networks. When we want to recall a bit of information, we can translate its meaning (as represented in the propositional network) into familiar phrases and sentences, or mental pictures. Also, because propositions are networked, recall of one bit of information can trigger or activate recall of another. We are not aware of these networks, because they are not part of our conscious memory (J. R. Anderson, 2010). In much the same way, we are not aware of underlying grammatical structure when we form a sentence in our own language; we don't have to diagram a sentence to say it.

IMAGES. Images are representations based on the structure or appearance of the information (J. R. Anderson, 2010). As we form images (like you did in the rotating *d* problem), we try to remember or recreate the physical attributes and spatial structure of information. For example, when asked what store is beside the Starbucks at a particular intersection in town, many people would look "in their mind's eye" to view the intersection and then "look" beside the Starbucks. However, researchers don't agree on exactly how images are stored in memory. Some psychologists believe that images are stored as pictures; others believe we store propositions in long-term memory (Radio Shack is beside Starbucks) and convert to pictures in working memory when necessary. The debate continues (Sternberg & Sternberg, 2012).

Features of each process probably are involved—some memory for images and some verbal or propositional descriptions of the image. Seeing images "in your mind's eye" is not exactly the same as seeing the actual image. It is more difficult to perform complicated transformations on mental images than on real images. For example, if you had a plastic *d* magnet on your refrigerator, you could very quickly rotate it. Rotating mentally takes more time for most people. And it is easier to form images for some words or concepts than others. It is probably easier for you to form an image of *Starbucks* than one of *justice,* for example. Nevertheless, images are useful in making many practical decisions such as how a sofa might look in your living room or how to line up a golf shot. Images may also be helpful in abstract reasoning. Physicists, such as Faraday and Einstein, report creating images to reason about complex new problems. Einstein claimed that he was visualizing chasing a beam of light and catching up to it when the concept of relativity came to him (Kosslyn & Koenig, 1992).

TWO ARE BETTER THAN ONE: WORDS AND IMAGES. Allan Paivio's (1986, 2006; J. M. Clark & Paivio, 1991) dual coding theory suggests that information is stored in long-term memory as either visual images or verbal units, or both. Psychologists who agree with this point of view believe that information coded both visually and verbally is easiest to learn (Butcher, 2006). This may be one reason why explaining an idea with words and then representing it visually in a figure, as we do in textbooks, has proved helpful to students.

- -

STOP & THINK What makes a cup a cup? List the characteristics of *cupness*. What is a fruit? Is a banana a fruit? Is a tomato a fruit? How about a squash? A watermelon? A sweet potato? An olive? A coconut? How did you learn what makes a fruit a fruit? •

- -

CONCEPTS. Most of what we know about cups and fruits and the world involves concepts and relations among concepts (Ashcraft & Radvansky, 2010; Eysenck, 2012). But what exactly is a concept? A concept is a mental representation used to group similar events, ideas, objects, or people into a category. When we talk about a particular concept such as *student,* we refer to our mental representation of a category of people who are similar to one another: they all study a subject. The people may be old or young, in school or not; they may be studying basketball or Bach, but they all can be categorized as students. Concepts are abstractions. They do not exist in the real world. Only individual examples of concepts exist. Concepts help us organize vast amounts of information into manageable units. For instance, there are about 7.5 million distinguishable differences in colors. By mentally categorizing these colors into some dozen or so groups, we manage to deal with this diversity quite well (Bruner, 1973).

In early research, psychologists assumed that people create concepts based on rules about defining attributes, or distinctive features. For example, books all contain pages that are bound together in some way (but what about "eBooks"?). Your concept of a cat might include defining attributes such as a round head on a small body, triangle-shaped ears, whiskers, four legs, and fur. This concept enables you to identify cats whether they are calico or Siamese without relearning "cat" each time you encounter a new cat. The defining attributes theory of concepts suggests that we recognize specific examples by noting key required features.

Since about 1970, however, these views about the nature of concepts have been challenged (Ashcraft & Radvansky, 2010). Although some concepts, such as equilateral triangle, have clear-cut defining attributes, most concepts do not. Take the concept of *party.* What are the defining attributes? You might have difficulty listing these attributes, but you probably recognize a party when you see or hear one (unless, of course we are talking about political parties, or the other party in a lawsuit, where the sound might not help you recognize the *party*). What about the concept of *bird?* Your first thought might be that birds are animals that fly. But is an ostrich a bird? What about a penguin? A bat?

PROTOTYPES, EXEMPLARS, AND THEORY-BASED CATEGORIES. One current view of concept learning suggests that we have in our minds a prototype of a party or a bird or the letter *A*—an image that captures the essence of each concept. A prototype is the best representative of its category—an example that has the most important "core" features of the category. For instance, the best representative of the "birds" category for many North Americans might be a robin (Rosch, 1973). Other members of the category may be very similar to the prototype (sparrow) or similar in some ways but different in others (chicken, ostrich). At the boundaries of a category, it may be difficult to determine if a particular instance really belongs. For example, is a television "furniture"? Is an elevator a "vehicle"? Is an olive a "fruit"? Whether something fits into a category is a matter of degree or graded membership. Thus, categories have fuzzy boundaries. Some events, objects, or ideas are simply better examples of a concept than others (Ashcraft & Radvansky, 2010; Eysenck, 2012).

Another explanation of concept learning suggests that we identify members of a category by referring to exemplars. Exemplars are our actual memories of specific birds, parties, furniture, and so on that we use to compare with an item in question to see if that item belongs in the same category as our exemplar. Prototypes probably are built from experiences with many exemplars. This happens naturally because memories of particular events (episodic memories) tend to blur together over time, creating an average or typical sofa prototype from all the sofa exemplars you have experienced (E. E. Smith & Kosslyn, 2007).

Connect and Extend to PRAXIS II®

Teaching Concepts (II, A2)
Teachers devote much effort to the development of concepts that are vital in learning subject matter and skills. Understand the major approaches to teaching concepts and be able to describe their strengths and limitations.

There are some drawbacks to prototype and exemplar theories. For example, how do you know which "bird experiences" to blur or average together to create a bird concept if you don't already have a bird concept? One answer is that our classifications are essentially **theory-based** ideas about the world that we create to make sense of things. So a *brick,* a *rock,* and a *shoe* are in the same category if the category is "things to pound a nail with if I don't have a hammer." Our theory of what might work creates the "things to pound with" category. Some of the knowledge used to create concepts based on theories may be implicit and out-of-awareness, for example, what makes for "good music"—I just know it when I hear it (Ashcraft & Radvansky, 2010; Sternberg & Sternberg, 2012).

Jacob Feldman (2003) suggests a final aspect of concept formation—the simplicity principle. Feldman says that when humans are confronted with examples, they induce the simplest category or rule that would cover all the examples. Sometimes it is easy to come up with a simple rule (triangles), and sometimes it is more difficult (fruit), but humans seek a simple hypothesis for collecting all the examples under one concept. Feldman suggests that this simplicity principle is one of the oldest ideas in cognitive psychology: "organisms seek to understand their environment by reducing incoming information to a simpler, more coherent, and more useful form" (p. 231). Does this remind you of the Gestalt principles of perception?

SCHEMAS. Propositions, concepts, and single images are fine for representing single ideas and simple relationships, but often our knowledge about a topic combines many concepts, images, and propositions. To explain this kind of complex knowledge, psychologists developed the idea of a schema. **Schemas** (sometimes called *schemata*) are abstract knowledge structures that organize vast amounts of information. A schema (the singular form) is a mental framework that guides our perception and helps us make sense of our experience based on what we already know and what we expect to happen (Sternberg & Sternberg, 2012). Figure 8.6 is a partial representation of a schema for knowledge about reinforcement.

The schema tells you what features are typical of a category, what to expect about an object or situation. The pattern has "slots" that are filled with specific information as we apply the schema in a particular situation. And schemas are personal. For example, my schema of *reinforcement* is less

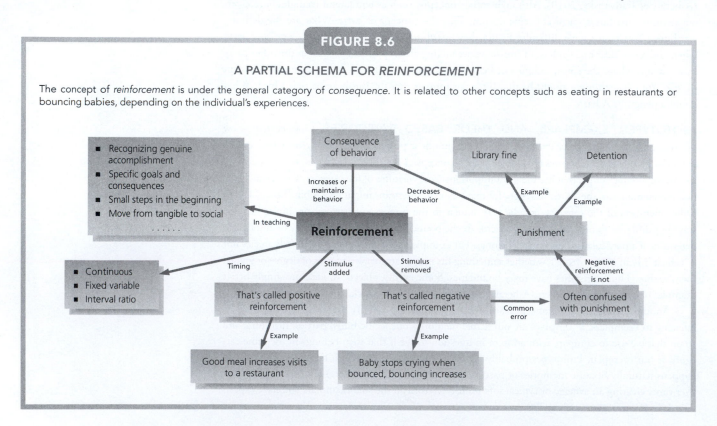

FIGURE 8.6

A PARTIAL SCHEMA FOR *REINFORCEMENT*

The concept of *reinforcement* is under the general category of *consequence*. It is related to other concepts such as eating in restaurants or bouncing babies, depending on the individual's experiences.

richly developed than Skinner's schema must have been. You encountered a very similar concept of *schemes* (organized systems of action and thought) in the discussion of Piaget's theory of cognitive development in Chapter 2.

When you hear the sentence, "Lincoln, who was president of the United States during a bitter war, freed the slaves," you know even more about it than the three propositions. You probably can infer that reuniting the country after the war was difficult based on your schema for a "bitter" conflict. Your schema for "slaves" gives you some sense of the kind of life they were freed from. None of this information was explicitly stated in the sentence.

Schematic knowledge helps us to form and understand concepts. How do we know that counterfeit money is not "real" money, even though it perfectly fits our "money" prototype and exemplars and looks like real money? We know because of its history. The "wrong" people printed the money. So our understanding of the concept of money is connected with concepts of crime, forgery, the federal treasury, and many others in a larger schema for "money."

Another type of schema, a **story grammar** (sometimes called a *schema for text* or *story structure*), helps students to understand and remember stories. A general story grammar is setting, initiating events, reactions, goals, actions, outcomes, and endings (van den Broek, Lorch, & Thurlow, 1996). A more specific story grammar could be something like this: murder discovered, search for clues, murderer's fatal mistake identified, trap set to trick suspect into confessing, murderer takes bait . . . mystery solved! To comprehend a story, we select a schema that seems appropriate. Then, we use this framework to decide which details are important, what information to seek, and what to remember. It is as though the schema is a theory about what should occur in the story. The schema guides us in "interrogating" the text, pointing to the specific information we expect to find so that the story makes sense. If we activate our "murder mystery schema," we may be alert for either clues or a murderer's fatal mistake. Without an appropriate schema, trying to understand a story, textbook, or classroom lesson is a very slow, difficult process, something like finding your way through a new town without a map or GPS.

Propositions, images, concepts, and schemas are all explicit *semantic* memories. The second kind of explicit memory is *episodic*.

EPISODIC MEMORY. Memory for information tied to a particular place and time, especially information about the events or episodes of your own life, is called **episodic memory**. Episodic memory is about events we have experienced, so we often can explain when the event happened. In contrast, we usually can't describe when we acquired a semantic memory. For example, you may have a difficult time remembering when you developed semantic memories for the meaning of the word *injustice,* but you can easily remember a time that you felt unjustly treated. Episodic memory also keeps track of the order of things, so it is a good place to store jokes, gossip, or plots from films.

Memories for dramatic or emotional moments in your life are called **flashbulb memories**. These memories are vivid and complete, as if your brain demanded that you "record this moment." Under stress, more glucose energy goes to fuel brain activity, while stress-induced hormones signal the brain that something important is happening (Myers, 2005; Sternberg & Sternberg, 2012). So when we have intense emotional reactions, memories are stronger and more lasting. Many people have vivid memories of very positive or very negative events in school such as winning a prize or being humiliated. You probably know just where you were and what you were doing on 9/11. People over 50 have vivid memories of the day John Kennedy was assassinated. My whole school had walked to the main street of our suburb of Fort Worth, Texas, to applaud as his motorcade drove by en route to the airport for the flight to Dallas. By the time I got back to geometry class, we heard the announcement that he had been shot in Dallas. My friend, who had been at a press breakfast with him that very morning, was devastated.

Implicit Memories

Look back at Figure 8.5. You will see that there are three kinds of implicit, or out-of-awareness, memories: *classical conditioning, procedural memory,* and *priming effects*. In classical conditioning, as we saw in Chapter 7, some out-of-awareness memories may cause you to feel anxious as you take a test or make your heart rate increase when you hear a dentist's drill or a siren.

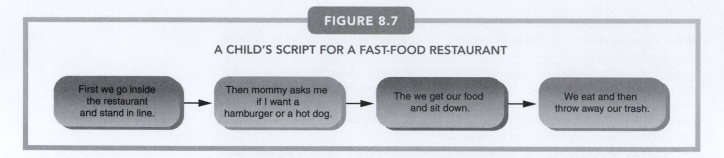

FIGURE 8.7

A CHILD'S SCRIPT FOR A FAST-FOOD RESTAURANT

First we go inside the restaurant and stand in line. → Then mommy asks me if I want a hamburger or a hot dog. → The we get our food and sit down. → We eat and then throw away our trash.

The second type of implicit memory is **procedural memory** for skills, habits, and how to perform tasks—in other words, memory for procedural knowledge. It may take a while to learn a procedure such as how to ski, factor an equation, or design a teaching portfolio, but once learned, this knowledge tends to be remembered for a long time. Procedural knowledge is represented as scripts and condition-action rules, sometimes called *productions*.

Scripts are action sequences or plans for actions stored in memory (Schraw, 2006). We all have scripts for events like ordering food in restaurants, and these scripts differ depending on whether the restaurant is a four-star bistro or a fast-food drive-through. Even young children have scripts for how to behave during snack time at preschool, or at a friend's birthday party, or in a restaurant, as you can see in Figure 8.7. In fact, for very young children, scripts seem to help them organize and remember the predictable aspects of their world. This frees up some working memory to learn new things and recognize when something is out of place in the situation. In terms of human survival, it probably is useful to remember what is likely to keep happening and to notice when something is out of place (K. Nelson & Fivush, 2004).

Productions specify what to do under certain conditions: If A occurs, then do B. A production might be something like, "If you want to snow ski faster, lean back slightly," or "If your goal is to increase student attention and a student has been paying attention a bit longer than usual, then praise the student." People can't necessarily state all their scripts and condition-action rules, and they don't even realize that they are following these rules, but they act on them nevertheless. The more practiced the procedure, the more automatic the action and the more implicit the memory (J. R. Anderson, 2010; Schraw, 2006).

STOP & THINK Fill in these blanks: MEM _ _ _ •

The final type of implicit memory involves **priming**, or activating information that already is in long-term memory through some out-of-awareness process. You might have seen an example of priming in the *Stop & Think* fill-in-the-blank question. If you wrote MEMORY instead of MEMOIR or MEMBER, or other MEM words, then priming may have played a role because the word *memory* has occurred many times in this chapter. Priming may be the fundamental process for retrieval as associations are activated and spread through the memory system (Ashcraft & Radvansky, 2010).

Retrieving Information in Long-Term Memory

The final section of this chapter will examine in depth what you have to do to "save" information permanently—to create explicit and implicit memories. Here we consider some general ideas about retrieving and forgetting information from long-term memory. When we need to use information from long-term memory, we search for it. Sometimes, the search is conscious, as when you see a friend approaching and search for her name. At other times, locating and using information from long-term memory is automatic, as when you enter a computer password or the word *memory* pops to mind when you see MEM _ _ _. Think of long-term memory as a huge cabinet full of tools (skills, procedures) and supplies (knowledge, concepts, schemas) ready to be brought to the workbench of working memory to accomplish a task. The cabinet (long-term memory) stores an incredible amount, but it may be hard to find what you are looking for quickly. The workbench (working memory) is small, but anything on it is immediately available. Because it is small, however, supplies (bits of information) sometimes are lost when the workbench is overloaded or when one bit of information covers (interferes with) another (E. Gagné, 1985). Of course you have to walk into the room through the door of attention to get to the workbench and the cabinet (Silverman, 2008).

SPREADING ACTIVATION. The size of the network in long-term memory is huge, but only small parts from it are activated at any one time—in fact, as you saw earlier, some psychologists say the smaller activated part of long-term memory *is* working memory. Information is retrieved in this network through spreading activation. When a particular proposition or image is active—when we are thinking about it—other closely associated knowledge can be primed or triggered as well, and activation can spread through the network (J. R. Anderson, 2010). Thus, as I focus on the propositions, "I'd like to go for a drive to see the fall leaves," related ideas such as, "I should rake leaves," and "The car needs an oil change," come to mind. As activation spreads from the "car trip" to the "oil change," the original thought, or active memory, disappears from working memory because of the limited space. Thus, retrieval from long-term memory occurs partly through the spreading of activation from one bit of knowledge to related ideas in the network.

RECONSTRUCTION. In long-term memory, the information is still available, even when it is not activated, even when you are not thinking about it at the moment. If spreading activation does not "find" the information we seek, then we might still come up with an answer through reconstruction, a cognitive tool or problem-solving process that makes use of logic, cues, and other knowledge to construct a reasonable answer by filling in any missing parts (Koriat, Goldsmith, & Pansky, 2000). Sometimes reconstructed recollections are incorrect. For example, in 1932, F. C. Bartlett conducted a series of famous studies on remembering stories. He read a complex, unfamiliar Native American tale to students at England's Cambridge University and, after various lengths of time, asked the students to recall the story. Stories the students recalled were generally shorter than the original and were translated into the concepts and language of the Cambridge student culture. The story told of a seal hunt, for instance, but many students remembered (reconstructed) a "fishing trip," an activity closer to their experiences and more consistent with their schemas.

FORGETTING AND LONG-TERM MEMORY. Over 100 years ago, Hermann Ebbinghaus (1885/1964), a pioneer in studying memory for verbal information, said simply, "All sorts of ideas, if left to themselves, are gradually forgotten. This fact is generally known" (p. 62). Information appears to be lost from long-term memory through time decay and interference. For example, memory for Spanish–English vocabulary decreases for about 3 years after a person's last course in Spanish, then stays level for about 25 years, then drops again for the next 25 years. One explanation for this decline is that neural connections, like muscles, grow weak without use. After 25 years, it may be that the memories are still somewhere in the brain, but they are too weak to be reactivated. Also, the physiological deterioration that comes with age could account for the later declines because some neurons simply die (J. R. Anderson, 2010). Finally, newer memories may interfere with or obscure older memories, and older memories may interfere with memory for new material.

Even with decay and interference, long-term memory is remarkable. Information in working memory can be lost and forgotten, but information stored in long-term memory may be available for a long time, given the right cues (Erdelyi, 2010). Teaching strategies that encourage student engagement, deeper processing of information, and higher levels of initial learning are associated with longer retention. Examples of such strategies are frequent reviews and tests, elaborated feedback, high standards, mastery learning, and active involvement in learning projects.

Individual Differences in Long-Term Memory

The major individual difference that affects long-term memory is knowledge. As we saw earlier with the fourth-grade soccer experts, when people have more domain-specific declarative and procedural knowledge, they are better at learning and remembering material in that domain (Alexander, 1997). Think about what it is like to read a very technical textbook in an area you know little about. Every line is difficult. You have to stop and look up words or turn back to earlier sections to read about concepts you don't understand. It is hard to remember what you are reading because you are trying to understand and remember at the same time. But with a good basis of knowledge, learning and remembering become easier; the more you know, the easier it is to know more. This may be why classes in your major seem easier than the required classes outside your major. Another factor could be interest. To develop expert understanding and recall in a domain requires the "continuous interplay of skill (i.e., knowledge) and thrill (i.e., interest)" (Alexander, Kulikowich, & Schulze, 1994, p. 334).

Now let's turn to the really important question: How can teachers support the development of long-lasting knowledge?

ENHANCEDetext *self-check*

TEACHING FOR DEEP, LONG-LASTING KNOWLEDGE: BASIC PRINCIPLES AND APPLICATIONS

How can we make the most effective use of our practically unlimited capacity to learn and remember? For decades, cognitive psychologists have focused on ways of constructing long-lasting declarative, procedural, and self-regulatory knowledge. We will discuss the development of *declarative* and *procedural* knowledge separately, but keep in mind that real learning is a combination and integration of these elements. We look at developing the third type, *self-regulatory* knowledge, in the next chapter when we discuss metacognition.

Constructing Declarative Knowledge: Making Meaningful Connections

We begin with some basic principles that apply across all situations. The way you learn information in the first place—the way you process it in working memory at the outset—strongly affects its recall later. One important requirement for building lasting knowledge is that you integrate new information with your prior knowledge—what you already know—as you construct an understanding. Here, *elaboration, organization, imagery,* and *context* play a role.

ELABORATION, ORGANIZATION, IMAGERY, AND CONTEXT. Elaboration is adding meaning to new information by connecting with already existing knowledge. In other words, we apply our schemas and draw on already existing knowledge to construct an understanding. Frequently, we change our existing knowledge in the process, as Piaget noted years ago. We often elaborate automatically. For example, a paragraph about an historic figure in ancient Rome tends to activate our existing knowledge about that period; we use the old knowledge to understand the new.

Material that is elaborated when first learned will be easier to recall later. First, as we saw earlier, elaboration is a form of rehearsal that leads to deeper levels of processing because the information is thoroughly analyzed and connected with existing information (Craik & Tulving, 1975). Elaboration keeps the information activated in working memory long enough to have a chance for the new information to be integrated with knowledge in long-term memory. Second, elaboration builds extra links to existing knowledge. The more one bit of information or knowledge is associated with other bits, the more routes there are to follow to get to the original bit. To put it another way, you have several "handles" or priming/retrieval cues to "pick up" or recognize the information you might be seeking (Bruning et al., 2011).

The more students elaborate new ideas, the more they "make them their own," the deeper their understanding and the better their memory for the knowledge will be. We help students to elaborate when we ask them to:

- translate information into their own words
- create examples
- explain to a peer
- create a metaphor
- draw a diagram of the situation
- act out the relations
- apply the information to new problems

GUIDELINES
Family and Community Partnerships

Organizing Learning

Give families specific strategies to help their children practice and remember.

Examples

1. Develop "super learner" homework assignments that include material to be learned and a "parent coaching card" with a description of a simple memory strategy—appropriate for the material—that parents can teach their child.
2. Provide a few comprehension check questions so a family member can review reading assignments and check the child's understanding.
3. Describe the value of distributed practice, and give family members ideas for how and when to work skills practice into home conversations and projects.

Ask family members to share their strategies for organizing and remembering.

Examples

1. Create a family calendar.
2. Encourage planning discussions in which family members help students break large tasks into smaller jobs, identify goals, and find resources.

Discuss the importance of attention in learning.

Examples

1. Encourage families to create study spaces that are away from distractions.
2. Make sure parents know the purpose of homework assignments.

For a website dedicated to high school study skills that might help parents, see mtsu.edu/~studskl/hsindex.html

Of course, if students elaborate new information by developing misguided explanations, these misconceptions will be remembered, too.

Organization is a second element of processing that improves learning. Material that is well organized is easier to learn and to remember than bits and pieces of information, especially if the material is complex or extensive. Chunking is one kind of organization—putting small bits of information into larger, more meaningful chunks. Placing a concept in a structure also will help you learn and remember both general definitions and specific examples. The structure serves as a guide back to the information when you need it. For example, Table 8.2 organizes information about types of knowledge and Figure 8.6 organizes my knowledge about reinforcement. The *Guidelines: Family and Community Partnerships* gives ideas for working with families to give all your students more support and practice in organizing learning.

IMAGERY. You may remember that the dual coding theory of memory suggests that information coded both visually and verbally is easiest to learn (Butcher, 2006; Paivio, 2006). Imagery can support memory if the information to be learned lends itself to images. It is easier to form an image for *car* than for *internal combustion,* for example—at least for me. Also the ability to form and use mental images appears to vary among individuals; some people are simply better at this task than others (Bruning et al., 2011). That said, is a picture worth 1,000 words in teaching? Richard Mayer (2001, 2005, 2011) has studied this question for several years and has found that the right combination of pictures and words can make a significant difference in students' learning, at least for older students. Mayer's cognitive theory of multimedia learning includes three ideas that should be familiar to you now:

- *Dual coding:* Visual and verbal materials are processed in different systems (Clark & Paivio, 1991).
- *Limited capacity:* Working memory for verbal and visual material is severely limited. Cognitive load has to be managed (Baddeley, 2001; van Merriënboer & Sweller, 2005).
- *Generative learning:* Meaningful learning happens when students focus on relevant information and generate or build connections (Mayer, 2008, 2011).

The problem: How to build complex understandings that integrate information from visual (pictures, diagrams, graphs, animations, films) and verbal (text, lecture) sources, given the limitations of working memory. *The solution:* Make sure the information is available at the same time

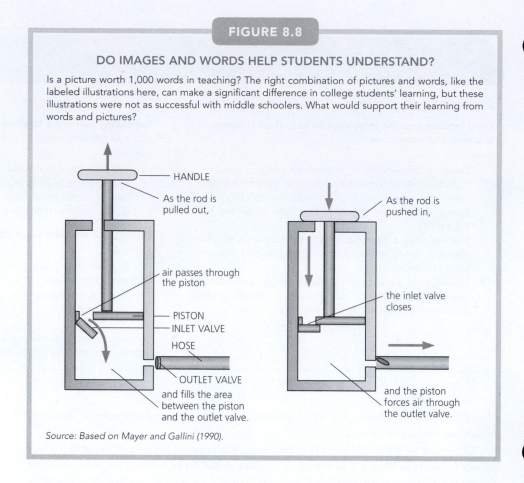

FIGURE 8.8

DO IMAGES AND WORDS HELP STUDENTS UNDERSTAND?

Is a picture worth 1,000 words in teaching? The right combination of pictures and words, like the labeled illustrations here, can make a significant difference in college students' learning, but these illustrations were not as successful with middle schoolers. What would support their learning from words and pictures?

HANDLE

As the rod is pulled out,

air passes through the piston

PISTON

INLET VALVE

HOSE

OUTLET VALVE

and fills the area between the piston and the outlet valve.

As the rod is pushed in,

the inlet valve closes

and the piston forces air through the outlet valve.

Source: Based on Mayer and Gallini (1990).

or in focused small bites. Mayer and Gallini (1990) provide an example. They used three kinds of texts to explain how a bicycle pump works. One text used only words, the second had pictures that just showed the parts of the pump system and the steps, and the third (this one improved student learning and recall) showed both the "on" and the "off" states of the pumps with labels right on the illustration for each step in the pumping process, as you can see in Figure 8.8.

There are several cautions about using multiple representations to teach, however. First, Vernon Hall and his colleagues (1997) found that students who drew their own illustrations of how a pump works did as well as students who were provided Mayer's illustrations. Second, the students in both Mayer's and Hall's studies were in college. When Erin McTigue (2009) tried to replicate these kinds of results with middle school students in life and physical sciences, the labeled pictures led to small improvements in students' understanding for life science texts, but not for physical science texts.

So research has shown that just using multiple representations (words, pictures, diagrams, charts, animations, etc.) does not necessarily lead to better learning. Students, especially younger ones, need supports such as color coding to draw attention to relevant relations in pictures and diagrams, or frequent checks for understanding with corrections if they are forming misconceptions (Berthold & Renkl, 2009). The moral of the story? Give students multiple ways to understand—pictures and explanations. But don't overload working memory—"package" the visual and verbal information together in bite-size (or memory-size) pieces, and teach students directly how to learn from illustrations or how to draw their own.

Context is a fourth element of processing that influences learning. Aspects of physical and emotional context—places, rooms, moods, who is with us—are learned along with other information. Later, if you try to remember the information, it will be easier if the current context is similar to the original one (Ashcraft & Radvansky, 2010). Context is a kind of priming that activates the information. For example, in a classic study, scuba divers who learned a list of words underwater and then were tested underwater remembered more than scuba divers who learned underwater but were tested on dry land (Godden & Baddeley, 1975). In another study, students who learned material in one type of room performed better on tests taken in a similar room than they did on comparable tests taken in a very different-looking room (S. M. Smith, Glenberg, & Bjork, 1978). So, studying for a test under "test-like" conditions (e.g., not at McDonald's) may result in improved performance. Of course, you can't always go back to the same place or a similar one to recall something. But if you can picture the setting, the time of day, and your companions, you may eventually reach the information you seek.

As you have seen, people learn best when they have a good base of knowledge in the area they are studying. With many well-elaborated schemas and scripts to guide them, new material makes more sense, and there are many possible spots in the long-term memory network for connecting new information with old. What are some possible strategies? Perhaps the best single method for helping students learn is to make each lesson as meaningful as possible.

Reaching Every Student: Make it Meaningful

Meaningful lessons are presented in vocabulary that makes sense to the students. New terms are clarified through ties with more familiar words and ideas. Meaningful lessons are well organized, with clear connections between the different elements of the lesson. Finally, meaningful lessons make natural use of old information to help students understand new information through examples or analogies.

The importance of meaningful lessons is emphasized in *Stop & Think*—an example presented years ago by F. Smith (1975).

STOP & THINK Look at the three lines below. Begin by covering all but the first line. Look at it for a second, close the book, and write down all the letters you remember. Then repeat this procedure with the second and third lines.
1. KBVODUWGPJMSQTXNOGMCTRSO
2. READ JUMP WHEAT POOR BUT SEEK
3. KNIGHTS RODE HORSES INTO WAR •

Each line has the same number of letters, but the chances are great that you remembered all the letters in the third line, a good number of letters in the second line, and very few in the first line. The first line makes no sense. There is no way to organize it in a brief glance. Working memory is simply not able to hold and process all those bits of information quickly. The second line is more meaningful. You do not have to see each letter because your long-term memory brings prior knowledge of spelling rules and vocabulary to the task. The third line is the most meaningful. Just a glance and you can probably remember all of it because you bring to this task prior knowledge not only of spelling and vocabulary but also of rules about syntax and probably some historical information about knights (they didn't ride in tanks). This sentence is meaningful because you have existing schemas for assimilating it (Sweller, van Merriënboer, & Paas, 1998).

The challenge for teachers is to make lessons less like learning the first line and more like learning the third line. Although this may seem obvious, think about the times when you have read a sentence in a text or heard an explanation from a professor that might just as well have been KBVODUWGPJMSQTXNOGMCTRSO. But beware, attempts to change the ways that students are used to learning—moving from memorizing to meaningful—are not always greeted with student enthusiasm. Students may be concerned about their grades; at least when memorization gains an A, they know what is expected. Meaningful learning can be riskier and more challenging. In Chapters 9, 10, and 11, we will examine a variety of ways in which teachers can support meaningful learning and understanding.

What can you do when students don't have a good base of knowledge? Mnemonics is a memory strategy for getting started.

Connect and Extend to PRAXIS II®

Prior Knowledge (I, A1)
Prior knowledge strongly influences how we build and reorganize new knowledge. Be familiar with the role of schemas and propositional networks in the construction of knowledge and how they affect learning.

Connect and Extend to PRAXIS II®

Memory Strategies (II, A1)
Medical students often use mnemonics to remember the vast amounts of information they encounter in their studies. Be familiar with the major mnemonic methods and the kinds of information that they are most suitable for.

MNEMONICS. Mnemonics are systematic procedures for improving memory (Rummel, Levin, & Woodward, 2003; Soemer & Schwan, 2012). When information has little inherent meaning, mnemonic strategies build in meaning by connecting what is to be learned with established words or images.

The loci method derives its name from the plural of the Latin word *locus,* meaning "place." To use loci, you must first imagine a very familiar place, such as your own house or apartment, and pick out particular locations to serve as "pegs" to "hang" memories. For instance, let's say you want to remember to buy milk, bread, butter, and cereal at the store. Imagine a giant jug of milk blocking the entry hall, a lazy loaf of bread sleeping on the living room couch, a stick of butter melting all over the dining room table, and cereal covering the kitchen floor. When you want to remember the items, all you have to do is take an imaginary walk through your house.

If you need to remember information for long periods of time, an acronym may be the answer. An acronym is a form of abbreviation—a word formed from the first letter of each word in a phrase, for example, HOMES to remember the Great Lakes (Huron, Ontario, Michigan, Erie, Superior). Another method forms phrases or sentences out of the first letter of each word or item in a list, for example, Every Good Boy Does Fine to remember the lines on the G clef—E, G, B, D, F. Because the words must make sense as a sentence, this approach also has some characteristics of chain mnemonics, methods that connect the first item to be memorized with the second, the second item with the third, and so on. In one type of chain method, each item on a list is linked to the next through some visual association or story. Another chain-method approach is to incorporate all the items to be memorized into a jingle such as "i before e except after c."

The mnemonic system that has been most extensively researched in teaching is the keyword method. Joel Levin and his colleagues use a mnemonic (the 3 Rs) to teach the keyword mnemonic method:

- *Recode* the to-be-learned vocabulary item as a more familiar, concrete keyword—this is the keyword.
- *Relate* the keyword clue to the vocabulary item's definition through a sentence.
- *Retrieve* the desired definition.

The keyword method has been used extensively in foreign language learning. For example, the Spanish word *carta* (meaning "letter") sounds like the English word *cart. Cart* becomes the keyword: You imagine a shopping cart filled with letters on its way to the post office, or you make up a sentence such as "The cart full of letters tipped over" (Pressley, Levin, & Delaney, 1982). A similar approach has been used to help students connect artists with particular aspects of their paintings. For example, students are told to imagine that the heavy dark lines of paintings by Rouault are made with a *ruler* (Rouault) dipped in black paint (Carney & Levin, 2000, 2002). Figure 8.9 is an example of using mnemonic pictures as aids in learning Japanese vocabulary (Soemer & Schwan, 2012).

Vocabulary learned with keywords can be easily forgotten if students are given keywords and images instead of being asked to supply words and images that are relevant to them. When the teacher provides the memory links, these associations may not fit the students' existing knowledge and may be forgotten or confused later; as a result, remembering suffers (Wang & Thomas, 1995; Wang, Thomas, & Ouellette, 1992). Younger students have some difficulty forming their own images. For them, memory aids that rely on auditory cues—rhymes such as "Thirty days hath September" seem to work better (Willoughby, Porter, Belsito, & Yearsley, 1999). Until learners have some knowledge to guide their learning, it may help to use some mnemonic approaches to build vocabulary and facts.

ROTE MEMORIZATION. Very few things need to be learned by rote. The greatest challenge teachers face is to help students think and understand, not just memorize. Unfortunately, many students view rote memorizing and learning as the same thing (Iran-Nejad, 1990).

On rare occasions we do have to memorize something word for word, such as lines in a song, poem, or play. How would you do it? If you have tried to memorize a list of items that are all similar to one another, you may have found that you tended to remember items at the beginning

---

FIGURE 8.9

USING MNEMONICS TO PROMOTE FOREIGN LANGUAGE LEARNING

Here is an example of a Sino-Japanese character and corresponding visual mnemonic (meaning: *mountain*).

Source: Reprinted with permission from Soemer, A., & Schwan, S. (2012). Visual mnemonics for language learning: static pictures versus animated morphs. Educational Psychology, 104, p. 566.

---

and at the end of the list, but forgot those in the middle. This is called the **serial-position effect**. **Part learning**, breaking the list into smaller segments, can help prevent this effect, because breaking a list into several shorter lists means there will be fewer middle items to forget.

Another strategy for memorizing a long selection or list is the use of **distributed practice**, something educational psychologists have known about since the late 1880s (Ebbinghaus, 1885/1964). A student who studies Hamlet's soliloquy intermittently throughout the weekend will probably do much better than a student who tries to memorize the entire speech on Sunday night. Studying for an extended period is called *massed practice*. **Massed practice** leads to cognitive overload, fatigue, and lagging motivation. Distributed practice gives time for deeper processing and strengthens the connections in the neural network of the brain. What is forgotten after one session can be relearned in the next with distributed practice (Agarwal, Bain, & Chamberlain, 2012; Karpicke & Grimaldi, 2012; Son & Simon, 2012). Be warned, however, research has consistently shown that even though *distributed practice* leads to better learning and remembering, students including adults prefer *massed practice*—another example that what we like best (I'm thinking nachos dripping with cheese and jalapeños for tomorrow's Super Bowl game) may not be best for us. To incorporate distributed practice into your classes, Shana Carpenter and her colleagues (2012) recommend:

- Review important information every several weeks—keep updating these reviews with recent information.
- Re-expose student to important information in homework assignments.
- Give exams and quizzes that are cumulative, so students will be motivated to review and space out their study sessions on their own.

Still, there is debate in education about how much memorization should be encouraged, as you can see in the *Point/Counterpoint* on the next page.

Development of Procedural Knowledge

One characteristic that distinguishes experts from novices in every arena, from reading to medical diagnosis, is that the experts' declarative knowledge has become "proceduralized," that is, incorporated into routines they can apply automatically without making many demands on working memory. Explicit memories have become implicit, and the expert is no longer aware of them. Skills that are applied without conscious thought are called **automated basic skills**. An example is shifting gears in a standard transmission car. At first, you have to think about every step, but as

Video 8.4
Students use many different study strategies and feel confident in their choices, but not all of these strategies have a solid research base to suggest that they are effective for long-term learning.

ENHANCEDetext *video example*

POINT/COUNTERPOINT
What's Wrong with Memorizing?

For years, students have relied on memorization to learn vocabulary, procedures, steps, names, and facts. Is this a bad idea?

POINT Rote memorization creates inert knowledge. More than 100 years ago, William James (1912) described the limitations of rote learning by telling a story about what can happen when students memorize but do not understand:

> A friend of mine, visiting a school, was asked to examine a young class in geography. Glancing at the book, she said: "Suppose you should dig a hole in the ground, hundreds of feet deep, how should you find it at the bottom—warmer or colder than on top?" None of the class replying, the teacher said: "I'm sure they know, but I think you don't ask the question quite rightly. Let me try." So, taking the book, she asked: "In what condition is the interior of the globe?" And received the immediate answer from half the class at once. "The interior of the globe is in a condition of igneous fusion." (p. 150)

The students had memorized the answer, but they had no idea what it meant. Perhaps they didn't understand the meaning of "interior," "globe," or "igneous fusion." At any rate, the knowledge was useful to them only when they were answering test questions, and only then when the questions were phrased exactly as they had been memorized. Students often resort to memorizing the exact words of definitions when they have no hope for actually understanding the terms or when teachers count off for definitions that are not exact.

Howard Gardner has been a vocal critic of rote memorization and a champion of "teaching for understanding." In an interview in *Phi Delta Kappan* (J. Siegel & Shaughnessy, 1994), Gardner says:

> My biggest concern about American education is that even our better students in our better schools are just going through the motions of education. In The Unschooled Mind, I review ample evidence that suggests an absence of understanding—the inability of students to take knowledge, skills, and other apparent attainments and apply them successfully in new situations. In the absence of such flexibility and adaptability, the education that the students receive is worth little. (pp. 563–564)

COUNTERPOINT Rote memorization can be effective. Memorization may not be such a bad way to learn new information that has little inherent meaning, such as foreign language vocabulary. Alvin Wang, Margaret Thomas, and Judith Ouellette (1992) compared learning Tagalog (the national language of the Philippines) using either rote memorization or the keyword approach for associating new words with existing words and images. In their study, even though the keyword method led to faster and better learning initially, long-term forgetting was *greater* for students who had used the keyword method than for students who had learned by rote memorization.

A study of preservice teachers found that they believed memorization is valuable for young children to build basic skills (Beghetto, 2008). There are times when students must memorize, and we do them a disservice if we don't teach them how. For example, "memorization in simple mathematics or word reading activities in the early grades may be desirable and promote future academic success; constructivist, problem-based learning by itself may not be as successful as a combination of both constructivist problem solving and memorization together." (Chang et al., 2011, p. 25)

BEWARE OF EITHER/OR

Every discipline has its own terms, names, facts, and rules. As adults, we want to work with physicians who have memorized the correct names for the bones and organs of the body or the drugs needed to combat particular infections. Of course, they can look up some information or research certain conditions, but they have to know where to start. We want to work with accountants who give us accurate information about the new tax codes, information they probably had to memorize because it changes from year to year in ways that are not necessarily rational or meaningful. We want to deal with computer salespeople who have memorized their stock and know exactly which printers will work with our computer. Just because something was learned through memorization does not mean it is inert knowledge. The real question, as Gardner points out, is whether you can *use* the information flexibly and effectively to solve new problems.

you become more expert (if you do), the procedure becomes automatic. But not all procedures can be automatic, even for experts in a particular domain. For example, no matter how expert you are in driving, you still have to consciously watch the traffic around you. This kind of conscious procedure is called a *domain-specific strategy.* Automated basic skills and domain-specific strategies are learned in different ways (Gagné, Yekovich, & Yekovich, 1993).

AUTOMATED BASIC SKILLS. Most psychologists identify three stages in the development of an automated skill: *cognitive, associative,* and *autonomous* (J. R. Anderson, 2010; Fitts & Posner, 1967). At the cognitive stage, when we are first learning, we rely on declarative knowledge and general problem-solving strategies to accomplish our goal. For example, to learn how to assemble a bookshelf, we might try to follow steps in the instruction manual, putting a check beside each step as we complete it to keep track of progress. At this stage, we have to "think about" every step and perhaps refer back to the pictures of parts to see what a "4-inch metal bolt with lock nut" looks like. The cognitive load on working memory is heavy. There can be quite a bit of trial-and-error learning at this stage when, for example, the bolt we chose doesn't fit.

At the *associative stage,* individual steps of a procedure are combined or "chunked" into larger units. We reach for the right bolt and put it into the right hole. One step smoothly cues the next. With practice, the associative stage moves to the *autonomous stage,* where the whole procedure can be accomplished without much attention. So if you assemble enough bookshelves, you can have a lively conversation as you do, paying little attention to the assembly task. This movement from the cognitive to the associative to the autonomous stage holds for the development of basic cognitive skills in any area, but science, medicine, chess, and mathematics have been most heavily researched. One thing is clear—it takes many hours of successful practice to make skills automatic.

What can teachers do to help their students pass through these three stages and become more expert learners? In general, it appears that two factors are critical: *prerequisite knowledge* and *practice with feedback.* First, if students don't have the essential prior knowledge (concepts, schemas, skills, etc.), the cognitive load on working memory will be too great. Second, practice with feedback allows you to form associations, recognize cues automatically, and combine small steps into larger condition-action rules, or productions. Even from the earliest stage, some of this practice should include a simplified version of the whole process in a real context. Practice in real contexts helps students learn not only *how* to do a skill but also *why and when* (A. Collins, Brown, & Newman, 1989; Gagné, Yekovich, & Yekovich, 1993). Of course, as every athletic coach knows, if a particular step, component, or process is causing trouble, that element might be practiced alone until it is more automatic, and then put back into the whole sequence, to lower the cognitive load on working memory (J. R. Anderson et al., 1996; A. Ericsson, 2011).

DOMAIN-SPECIFIC STRATEGIES. As we saw earlier, some procedural knowledge, such as monitoring the traffic while you drive, is not automatic because conditions are constantly changing. Once you decide to change lanes, the maneuver may be fairly automatic, but the decision to change lanes was conscious, based on the traffic conditions around you. Domain-specific strategies are consciously applied skills that organize thoughts and actions to reach a goal. To support this kind of learning, teachers need to provide opportunities for practice in many different situations—for example, practice reading with package labels, magazines, books, letters, operating manuals, web pages and so on. In the next chapter's discussion of problem-solving and study strategies, we will examine other ways to help students develop domain-specific strategies. For now, let's summarize these ideas for developing declarative and procedural knowledge in the *Guidelines: Helping Students Understand and Remember* on the next page. We will spend quite a bit of time in the next chapter on developing self-regulatory knowledge.

ENHANCEDetext *self-check*

Connect and Extend to PRAXIS II®

Developing Basic Skills (II, A3)
Efficient and effective performance as a learner requires the automatic use of basic skills. Describe what teachers can do to help students develop automatic basic skills.

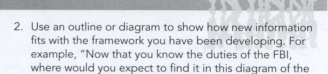

GUIDELINES
Helping Students Understand and Remember

Make sure you have the students' attention.

Examples

1. Develop a signal that tells students to stop what they are doing and focus on you. Make sure students respond to the signal—don't let them ignore it. Practice using the signal.
2. Move around the room, use gestures, and avoid speaking in a monotone.
3. Begin a lesson by asking a question that stimulates interest in the topic.
4. Regain the attention of individual students by walking closer to them, using their names, or asking them a question.

Help students separate essential from nonessential details and focus on the most important information.

Examples

1. Summarize instructional objectives to indicate what students should be learning. Relate the material you are presenting to the objectives as you teach: "Now I'm going to explain exactly how you can find the information you need to meet Objective One on the board—determining the tone of the story."
2. When you make an important point, pause, repeat, ask a student to paraphrase, note the information on the board in colored chalk, or tell students to highlight the point in their notes or readings.

Help students make connections between new information and what they already know.

Examples

1. Review prerequisites to help students bring to mind the information they will need to understand new material: "Who can tell us the definition of a quadrilateral? Now, what is a rhombus? Is a square a quadrilateral? Is a square a rhombus? What did we say yesterday about how you can tell? Today we are going to look at some other quadrilaterals."

2. Use an outline or diagram to show how new information fits with the framework you have been developing. For example, "Now that you know the duties of the FBI, where would you expect to find it in this diagram of the branches of the U.S. government?"
3. Give an assignment that specifically calls for the use of new information along with information already learned.

Provide for repetition and review of information.

Examples

1. Begin the class with a quick review of the homework assignment.
2. Give frequent, short tests.
3. Build practice and repetition into games, or have students work with partners to quiz each other.

Present material in a clear, organized way.

Examples

1. Make the purpose of the lesson very clear.
2. Give students a brief outline to follow. Put the same outline on an overhead transparency so you can keep yourself on track. When students ask questions or make comments, relate these to the appropriate section of the outline.
3. Use summaries in the middle and at the end of the lesson.

Focus on meaning, not memorization.

Examples

1. In teaching new words, help students associate the new word to a related word they already understand: "*Enmity* is from the same base as *enemy*."
2. In teaching about remainders, have students group 12 objects into sets of 2, 3, 4, 5, 6, and ask them to count the "leftovers" in each case.

Source: For more information on information processing, see edpsyinteractive.org/topics/cognition/infoproc.html

SUMMARY

- **Elements of the Cognitive Perspective (pp. 290–292)**

  Contrast cognitive and behavioral views of learning in terms of what is learned and the role of reinforcement. According to the cognitive view, knowledge is learned, and changes in knowledge make changes in behavior possible. According to the behavioral view, the new behaviors themselves are learned. Both behavioral and cognitive theorists believe reinforcement is important in learning, but

  for different reasons. The strict behaviorist maintains that reinforcement strengthens responses; cognitive theorists see reinforcement as a source of feedback about what is likely to happen if behaviors are repeated or changed—as a source of information.

  How does knowledge affect learning? The cognitive approach suggests that one of the most important elements in the learning process is knowledge the individual brings to the learning situation. What we already know determines to a great extent what we will pay attention to, perceive, learn, remember, and forget.

What is the brain's role in cognition? The human brain seems to both impact and be impacted by learning. For example, individuals who regularly complete tasks such as taxi driving develop certain regions of the brain more than others who do not engage in such activities. Research also suggests that learning changes communication among neurons. These changes enable children to engage in complex tasks such as integrating past and present experiences by approximately age 7.

- **Cognitive Views of Memory (pp. 292–304)**

Describe the path from sensory input to recognizing objects. The first phase in the process is feature analysis, or bottom-up processing, because the stimulus must be analyzed into features or components and assembled into a meaningful pattern. The Gestalt principles are one explanation for how features are organized into patterns. In addition to noting features and using these Gestalt principles, to recognize patterns rapidly, we use what we already know about the situation, information from the context, and our knowledge of prototypes or best examples.

What is working memory? Working memory is both short-term storage in the phonological loop and visuo-spatial sketchpad and processing in the episodic buffer, guided by the central executive—it is the workbench of conscious thought. To keep information activated in working memory for longer than 20 seconds, people use maintenance rehearsal (mentally repeating) and elaborative rehearsal (making connections with knowledge from long-term memory). Elaborative rehearsal also helps move new information to long-term memory. The limited capacity of working memory can also be somewhat circumvented by the control process of chunking. There are individual differences in working memory, and working memory span is related to performance on tasks that require higher-level thinking and controlled attention such as IQ tests and the SAT.

What is cognitive load, and how does it impact information processing? *Cognitive load* refers to the volume of cognitive resources, including perception, attention and memory, necessary to perform a task. These resources must be devoted not only to organizing and understanding the task, but also to analyzing the solution and ignoring irrelevant stimuli. If cognitive load is high, it can decrease or even inhibit one's ability to perform a task.

- **Long-Term Memory (pp. 304–312)**

Compare declarative, procedural, and self-regulatory knowledge and explicit and implicit memories. Declarative knowledge is knowledge that can be declared, usually in words or other symbols. Declarative knowledge is "knowing that" something is the case. Procedural knowledge is "knowing how" to do something; it must be demonstrated. Self-regulatory knowledge is "knowing when and why" to apply your declarative and procedural knowledge. Memories may be explicit (semantic/declarative or episodic) or implicit (procedural, classical conditioning, or priming).

How is information represented in explicit long-term memory, and what role do schemas play? In explicit (semantic) long-term memory, bits of information may be stored and interrelated in terms of propositional networks, images, concepts, and schemas. The dual coding theory suggests that information coded both verbally and visually (using images) is easier to remember. Much information is stored as concepts. A concept is a mental representation for a category of similar events, ideas, objects, or people that enables people to identify and recognize the members of a group such as books, students, or cats. Concepts provide a manner of organizing diversity among members of a group. Concepts are often represented by prototypes (an ideal example) and exemplars (a representative memory). Concepts also probably are theory-based, that is, based on our ideas about the world and how it works. To organize propositions, images, and concepts, we have schemas, which are data structures that allow us to represent large amounts of complex information, make inferences, and understand new information. In explicit episodic memory, information is stored as events, particularly events in your own life, and may include vivid flashbulb memories. Today some psychologists suggest that working memory is just the part of long-term memory that is currently activated—that you are thinking about at any given time.

What is implicit memory? Implicit memories are out-of-awareness memories that still can affect thinking and behavior. There are three kinds of implicit memories: *classical conditioning, procedural memory,* and *priming effects.* We discussed classical conditioning of automatic physiological and emotional responses in Chapter 7. Procedural memory includes skills, habits, and scripts—how to perform tasks—in other words, memory for procedural knowledge. Priming is activating information that already is in long-term memory through some out-of-awareness process. Priming may be the fundamental process for retrieval as associations are activated and spread through the memory system.

Why do we forget? Information lost from working memory truly disappears, but information in long-term memory may be available, given the right cues. Information appears to be lost from long-term memory through time decay (neural connections, like muscles, grow weak without use) and interference (newer memories may obscure older memories, and older memories may interfere with memory for new material).

- **Teaching for Deep, Long-Lasting Knowledge: Basic Principles and Applications (pp. 312–320)**

What supports the development of declarative knowledge? The way you learn information in the first place affects its recall later. One important requirement is to integrate new material with knowledge already stored in long-term memory using elaboration, organization, imagery, and context. The dual coding theory suggests that information coded both verbally and visually is easier to remember. Pictures and words help students learn as long as they are well organized and do not overload working memory. Another view of memory is the levels of processing theory, in which recall of information is determined by how completely it is processed.

Describe three ways to develop declarative knowledge. Declarative knowledge develops as we integrate new information with our existing understanding. The most useful and effective way to learn and remember is to understand and use new information. Making the information to be remembered meaningful is important and often is the greatest challenge for teachers. Mnemonics are memorization aids: They include approaches such as the loci method, acronyms, chain mnemonics, and the keyword method. A powerful but limiting way to accomplish this is rote memorization, which can best be supported by part learning and distributed practice.

Describe some methods for developing procedural knowledge. Automated basic skills and domain-specific strategies—two types of procedural knowledge—are learned in different ways. There are three stages in the development of an automated skill: cognitive (following steps or directions guided by declarative knowledge), associative (combining individual steps into larger units), and autonomous (where the whole procedure can be accomplished without much attention). Prerequisite knowledge and practice with feedback help students move through these stages. Domain-specific strategies are consciously applied skills of organizing thoughts and actions to reach a goal. To support this kind of learning, teachers need to provide opportunities for practice and application in many different situations.

PRACTICE USING WHAT YOU HAVE LEARNED

To access and complete the exercises, click the link under the images below.

Explicit Memories: Semantic and Episodic

Constructing Declarative Knowledge: Making Meaningful Connections

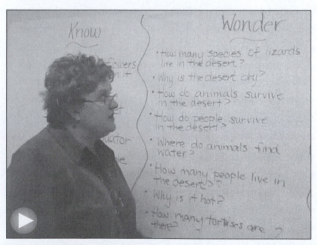

ENHANCEDetext *application exercise*

ENHANCEDetext *application exercise*

KEY TERMS

CONNECT AND EXTEND TO LICENSURE

MULTIPLE-CHOICE QUESTIONS

1. Rachel had been practicing her multiplication tables for weeks before her yearly standardized test. She knew all of her facts completely. This type of knowledge that Rachel now has attained does not require attention and concentration. This process is known as which one of the following?

   A. Declarative memory

   B. Flashbulb memory

   C. Automaticity

   D. Schema

2. Elaboration occurs when one adds meaning to new information by connecting with already existing knowledge. In other words, we apply our schemas and draw on already existing knowledge to construct an understanding. Which of the following is NOT true of elaboration?

   A. Elaboration can occur automatically.

   B. Material that is elaborated when first learned will be easier to recall later.

   C. Elaboration can limit the number of links to stored knowledge.

   D. The more students elaborate new ideas, the deeper their understanding and the better their memory for the knowledge will be.

3. Miss Campbell wanted to ensure that her driver's education students were safe under all circumstances. To ensure this, she had her students drive in the rain and snow. She also made sure they had adequate practice for driving in traffic and on the highway. Miss Campbell was encouraging the development of which of the following strategies?

   A. Domain-specific

   B. Mnemonic

   C. Declarative

   D. Elaborative

4. *Cognitive load* is a term that refers to the amount of mental resources, mostly working memory, required to perform a particular task. Of the three types of cognitive load, which can instruction support by asking students to explain the material to each other or to themselves, drawing or charting their understandings, or taking useful notes?

   A. Intrinsic cognitive load

   B. Extraneous cognitive load

   C. Germane cognitive load

   D. Working cognitive load

CONSTRUCTED-RESPONSE QUESTIONS
Case

Reflecting on his first year as a teacher, Mr. Beech was a little embarrassed at how little he understood the teaching and learning process when he began teaching. He remembered handing back a math test and admonishing his students with the following words. "Everybody in this room knew the test was today. I can't believe not one of you passed it. All I can say is, you had better master these concepts before we get into the testing season. Thirty percent of the standardized test is on algebra. I know we did several chapters quickly this time, more than you were used to, but we have to finish this book. And, no, I will not let you retake this test."

5. Explain the three types of knowledge Mr. Beech's students probably had to use while taking the algebra test.
6. In addition to not overloading his students with new information, how else can Mr. Beech assist his students in understanding and remembering in the future?

ENHANCEDetext *licensure exam*

TEACHERS' CASEBOOK

WHAT WOULD THEY DO? REMEMBERING THE BASICS

Here is how a number of expert teachers responded to the situation at the beginning of the chapter about students who often have trouble remembering key information from one day or week to the next.

PAULA COLEMERE—Special Education Teacher— English, History
McClintock High School, Tempe, AZ

I always evaluate my test results to see if student mistakes came from a poorly written question. If a number of students are missing the same test question, I review the answers to see what went wrong. This helps me to see if I need to alter my test or alter my instruction. As a teacher, I am constantly reflecting on my successes and defeats. Did I set a purpose for learning at the beginning of the unit? Did I make connections to prior knowledge? Before giving this unit test, was there sufficient formative assessment along the way? It makes more sense to pay attention during lessons to see what students understand and where they need more instruction. For students who are struggling along the way, I would spend a little more time on a concept and offer extra help during lunch or after school to help them gain a better understanding. I would teach them how to organize information and how to study. Chunking information is another good strategy to help students who struggle. I also teach test-taking skills to help students build confidence in their test-taking abilities.

LAUREN ROLLINS—First Grade Teacher
Boulevard Elementary School, Shaker Heights, OH

I promote different styles of teaching and learning in my classroom. However, I usually present some material, such as vocabulary words, math facts, and sight words, using a rote memory approach. In this situation, that method seemed to work well for the majority of the students, but not all of them. Therefore, it is my job as the teacher to create opportunities for those students to work with the material in a different way. In the example of the vocabulary, I would help the students create their own dictionaries where they would define each vocabulary word in a way that makes sense to them and provide examples that they would remember. Once the vocabulary becomes more meaningful to them, it will be easier for them to remember. In my classroom, I try to provide the students with a variety of methods to practice these types of concepts. Coloring pages, matching activities, word/number searches, secret codes, games, books, and so on are available to my students to help them practice sight words and math facts every day. I encourage my students to serve as peer tutors and enlist parents to work one on one with students as well. Every little bit helps!

SARA VINCENT—Special Education Teacher
Langley High School, McLean, VA

Every individual learns differently. The teacher in this scenario should first take time to identify how the students learn material effectively. Their inability to master the material may stem from a note-taking problem; students may benefit more from a cloze note-taking format rather than attempting to decipher what information is important. In addition, the teacher should administer smaller assessments more frequently before the final test in order to determine if all students are grasping the information. The teacher could then provide remediation to those students who are still struggling with the material. Every day, a teacher should evaluate her delivery of the information. She should also assess if the students are learning the material. In other words, no one can be a perfect teacher; effective teaching is always a work in progress.

JESSICA N. MAHTABAN—Eighth-Grade Math
Woodrow Wilson Middle School, Clifton, NJ

Mind mapping would be a great tool to help students retain and retrieve information. It is a fast and fun way to take visual notes, expand students' visual thinking skills, and make learning meaningful. Graphic organizers are another phenomenal instrument to use that steers the students away from just memorizing facts. A graphic organizer expands students' higher-level thinking skills and helps them make connections. A student's prior knowledge helps him or her build on lessons and make connections with new information. When a student can relate to the content and have meaningful connections, a whole new classroom emerges!

The next step would be to teach students how to comprehend the material rather than just retain the material. Teachers need to provide students with strategies they can use to comprehend all the subjects. Also, teachers need to provide students with plenty of modeling! Modeling all the strategies students can use to comprehend material will benefit the students the most!

JENNIFER L. MATZ—Sixth Grade Teacher
Williams Valley Elementary, Tower City, PA

I review vocabulary every day at the start of the lesson. This only takes a few minutes. My students make flip books. Flip books are better than flash cards because students can test themselves and flash cards can be lost. We write the definition, but then we write it in "kid" words too. I ask them to explain words or events in their own words.

Some review ideas are: Make up two sets of cards: one set with the words, the other set with the definition. Pass out both sets to the class, and ask "word people" to find their "matching definition." Another is to have a student come to the front and cover his eyes. Write the word on the board, and have the class give him clues. They may not say the word—he must guess it.

Make up songs to help students remember information. When I taught second grade, we had an array of grammar songs and rhymes to remember nouns, pronouns, and so on. My students made up movements. You can pair students who have mastered material with those who have not. Students often have better ways of remembering things than we can teach them.

9 | COMPLEX COGNITIVE PROCESSES

TEACHERS' **CASEBOOK**

WHAT WOULD YOU DO? UNCRITICAL THINKING

This year's class is worse than any you've ever had. You assigned a research paper, and you find more and more students are using the Web for their information. In itself, using the Web is not bad, but the students appear to be completely uncritical about what they find on the Internet. "If it is on the Web, it must be right" is the attitude of most students. Their first drafts are filled with quotes that seem very biased to you, but there are no sources cited or listed. It is not just that students don't know how to reference their work. You are more concerned that they cannot critically evaluate what they are reading. And all they are reading is the Net!

CRITICAL THINKING

- How would you help your students evaluate the information they are finding on the Web?
- Beyond this immediate issue, how will you help students think more critically about the subjects you are teaching?
- How will you take into account the cultural beliefs and values of your students as you support their critical thinking?

Thrashem/Shutterstock

OVERVIEW AND OBJECTIVES

In the previous chapter we focused on the development of knowledge—how people make sense of and remember information and ideas. In this chapter, we consider complex cognitive processes that lead to understanding. Understanding is more than memorizing. It is more than retelling in your own words. Understanding involves appropriately transforming and using knowledge, skills, and ideas. These understandings are considered "higher-level cognitive objectives" in a commonly used system of educational objectives (L. W. Anderson & Krathwohl, 2001; B. S. Bloom, Engelhart, Frost, Hill, & Krathwohl, 1956). We will focus on the implications of cognitive theories for the day-to-day practice of teaching.

Because the cognitive perspective is a philosophical orientation and not a unified theoretical model, teaching methods derived from it are varied. In this chapter, we will first examine the complex cognitive process of metacognition—using knowledge and skills about learning, motivation, and yourself to plan and regulate your own learning. Next we explore four important areas in which cognitive theorists have made suggestions for learning and teaching: learning strategies, problem solving, creativity,

and critical thinking, including argumentation. Finally, we will consider the question of how to encourage the transfer of learning from one situation to another to make learning more useful.

By the time you have completed this chapter, you should be able to:

Objective 9.1   Discuss the roles of metacognition in learning and remembering.

Objective 9.2   Describe several learning and study strategies that help students develop their metacognitive abilities.

Objective 9.3   Explain the processes involved in problem solving and the factors that can interfere with successful problem solving.

Objective 9.4   Explain how creativity is defined, assessed, and encouraged in the classroom.

Objective 9.5   Identify factors that influence students' abilities to think critically and to form and support arguments.

Objective 9.6   Discuss how, why, and when knowledge learned in one situation might be applied to new situations and problems.

The complex cognitive skills we will examine in this chapter take us beyond the more basic processes of perceiving, representing, and remembering (though after reading Chapter 8 you may believe that there is nothing "simple" about these). Much of what we consider in this chapter has been described as "higher-order" thinking, that is, thinking that moves beyond remembering or repeating facts and ideas to truly understanding, dissecting, and evaluating those facts or even creating new concepts and ideas of your own. Jerome Bruner (1973) once wrote a book about this kind of thinking entitled *Beyond the Information Given*—a good way to describe higher-level thinking. As Bruner (1996) later noted:

> Being able to "go beyond the information" given to "figure things out" is one of the few untarnishable joys of life. One of the great triumphs of learning (and of teaching) is to get things organized in your head in a way that permits you to know more than you "ought" to. And this takes reflection, brooding about what it is that you know. (p. 129)

In Chapter 14 you will encounter a way of thinking about higher-level thinking. We use Bloom's taxonomy to categorize levels of thinking in a hierarchy from the *lower levels* of remembering, understanding, and applying, to the *higher levels* of analyzing, evaluating, and creating. Of course, it is difficult to know exactly what kind of thinking any particular student is doing without also knowing what is the basis for that thinking. A child who invents a simple principle of balance by experimenting with a seesaw is thinking at a higher level than a student who parrots a principle of balance memorized from a textbook, even though the latter might sound "higher level." I am reminded of the great bar scene in the film *Good Will Hunting* when the pretentious graduate student tried to embarrass Matt Damon's friend with an impressive analysis of history, only to be devastated when Damon nailed him for basing his supposed creative analysis entirely on passages from textbooks—great stuff!

METACOGNITION

In Chapter 8 we discussed a number of **executive control processes**, including attention, rehearsal, organization, imagery, and elaboration. These executive control processes are sometimes called *metacognitive* skills, because they can be intentionally used to regulate cognition.

Metacognitive Knowledge and Regulation

Emily Fox and Michelle Riconscente define **metacognition** simply as "knowledge or awareness of self as knower" (2008, p. 373). Metacognition literally means cognition about cognition—or thinking about thinking—something William James wrote about over 100 years ago (although he did not give it that name). In the Bruner quote earlier, metacognition is involved in the "reflection, brooding about what it is that you know"—thinking about your own thinking. Metacognition is higher-order knowledge about your own thinking as well as your ability to use this knowledge to manage your own cognitive processes such as comprehension and problem solving (Bruning et al., 2011).

There are many metacognitive processes and skills, including judging if you have the right knowledge to solve a problem, deciding where to focus attention, determining if you understood what you just read, devising a plan, using strategies such as mnemonics, revising the plan as you proceed, determining if you have studied enough to pass a test, evaluating a problem solution, deciding to get help, and generally orchestrating your cognitive powers to reach a goal (Castel et al., 2011; Meadows, 2006; Schneider, 2004). In second-language learning, you have to focus on the important elements of the new language, ignore distracting information, and suppress what you know in the first language that interferes or confuses learning the second language (Engel de Abreu & Gathercole, 2012).

Metacognition involves all three kinds of knowledge we discussed earlier: (1) *declarative knowledge* about yourself as a learner, the factors that influence your learning and memory, and the skills, strategies, and resources needed to perform a task—*knowing what* to do; (2) *procedural knowledge* or *knowing how* to use the strategies; and (3) *self-regulatory knowledge* to ensure the completion of the task—*knowing the conditions,* when and why, to apply the procedures and strategies (Bruning et al., 2011). Metacognition is the strategic application of this declarative, procedural, and self-regulatory knowledge to accomplish goals and solve problems (Schunk, 2012). Metacognition also includes knowledge about the value of applying cognitive strategies in learning (Pressley & Harris, 2006).

Metacognition regulates thinking and learning (A. Brown, 1987; T. O. Nelson, 1996). There are three essential skills: *planning, monitoring,* and *evaluating. Planning* involves deciding how much time to give to a task, which strategies to use, how to start, which resources to gather, what order to follow, what to skim and what to give intense attention to, and so on. *Monitoring* is the real-time awareness of "how I'm doing." Monitoring is asking, "Is this making sense? Am I trying to go too fast? Have I studied enough?" *Evaluating* involves making judgments about the processes and outcomes of thinking and learning. "Should I change strategies? Get help? Give up for now? Is this paper (painting, model, poem, plan, etc.) finished?" The notion of *reflection* in teaching— thinking back on what happened in class and why, and thinking forward to what you might do next time—is really about metacognition in teaching (Sawyer, 2006).

Of course, we don't have to be metacognitive all the time. Some actions become routine or habits. Metacognition is most useful when tasks are challenging, but not too difficult. And even when we are planning, monitoring, and evaluating, these processes are not necessarily conscious, especially in adults. We may use them automatically without being aware of our efforts (Perner, 2000). Experts in a particular field plan, monitor, and evaluate as second nature; they have difficulty describing their metacognitive knowledge and skills (Pressley & Harris, 2006; Reder, 1996).

Individual Differences in Metacognition

People differ in how well and how easily they use metacognitive strategies. Some differences in meta-cognitive abilities are the result of development. Younger children, for example, may not be aware of the purpose of a lesson—they may think the point is simply to finish. They also may not be good at gauging the difficulty of a task—they may think that reading for fun and reading a science book are the same (Gredler, 2009b). As children grow older, they are more able to exercise executive control over strategies. For example, they are more able to determine if they have understood instructions or if they have studied enough to remember a set of items. Metacognitive abilities begin to develop around ages 5 to 7 and improve throughout school (Flavell, Green, & Flavell, 1995; Woolfolk & Perry, 2015). But as we will see many times in this book, knowing and doing are not the same. Students may know that it is better to study on a regular basis but still cram in the hopes of defying "just once" that long-established principle.

Not all differences in metacognitive abilities have to do with age or maturation (Lockl & Schneider, 2007; Vidal-Abarca, Mañá, & Gil, 2010). Some individual differences in metacognitive abilities are probably caused by differences in biology or learning experiences. Many students diagnosed as having learning disabilities have problems monitoring their attention (Hallahan, Kauffman, & Pullen, 2012), particularly with long tasks. Working to improve metacognitive skills can be especially important for students who often have trouble in school (Schunk, 2012; H. L. Swanson, 1990).

Lessons for Teachers: Developing Metacognition

Like any knowledge or skill, metacognitive knowledge and skills can be learned and improved.

METACOGNITIVE DEVELOPMENT FOR YOUNGER STUDENTS. In his second-grade classroom in Queens, New York, Daric Desautel (2009) worked with mostly Latino/a and Asian students. As part of teaching literacy, Desautel decided to focus on student metacognitive knowledge and skills such as setting goals, planning, evaluating achievements, and self-reflection to help students develop the habit of "looking in" at their own thinking. He also included self-reflections to help students evaluate their writing and gain insight into themselves as readers and writers. For example, one self-reflection included a checklist asking:

- Did you pick a topic that you know all about?
- Did you write a special beginning that makes the reader want more?
- Did you organize your thoughts and make a Table of Contents?
- Did you pick the right kind of paper and illustrate your book clearly?
- Did you re-read your work to check for SOUND, SENSE, ORDER, and GOOFS?

Desautel was successful in helping all his students, not just the most verbal and advanced, develop metacognitive knowledge. One student noted in his reflection, "I worked hard and did my best to make this book. I like nonfiction books better than stories. Next time, I would write about a different sport" (p. 2011).

In her work with first- and second-graders, Nancy Perry found that asking students two questions helped them become more metacognitive. The questions were "What did you learn about yourself as a reader/writer today?" and "What did you learn that you can do again and again and again?" When teachers asked these questions regularly during class, even young students demonstrated fairly sophisticated levels of metacognitive understanding and action (Perry et al., 2000).

Many of the cooperating teachers I work with use a strategy called KWL to guide reading and inquiry in general. This general frame can be used with most grade levels. The steps are:

K   What do I already know about this subject?
W   What do I want to know?
L   At the end of the reading or inquiry, what have I learned?

The KWL frame encourages students to "look within" and identify what they bring to each learning situation, where they want to go, and what they actually achieved—a very metacognitive approach to learning. Marilyn Friend and William Bursuck (2002, pp. 362–363) describe how one teacher used modeling and discussion to teach the KWL strategy. After reviewing the steps, the teacher models an example and a nonexample of using KWL to learn about "crayons."

Teacher: What do we do now that we have a passage assigned to read? First, I brainstorm, which means I try to think of anything I already know about the topic and write it down.

The teacher writes on the board or overhead known qualities of crayons, such as "made of wax," "come in many colors," "can be sharpened," and "several different brands."

Teacher: I then take this information I already know and put it into categories, like "what crayons are made of" and "crayon colors." Next, I write down any questions I would like to have answered during my reading, such as "Who invented crayons? When were they invented? How are crayons made? Where are they made?" At this point, I'm ready to read, so I read the passage on crayons. Now I must write down what I learned from this passage. I must include any information that answers the questions I wrote down before I read and any additional information. For example, I learned that colored crayons were first made in the United States in 1903 by Edwin Binney and E. Harold Smith. I also learned that the Crayola Company owns the company that made the original magic markers. Last, I must organize this information into a map so I can see the different main points and any supporting points.

At this point, the teacher draws a map on the chalkboard or overhead.

Teacher: Let's talk about the steps I used and what I did before and after I read the passage. A class discussion follows.
Teacher: Now I'm going to read the passage again, and I want you to evaluate my textbook reading skills based on the KWL Plus strategy we've learned.

Video 9.1
In this video, a young boy shows his metacognitive awareness as he talks about and shows his skills at remembering. What metacognitive skills does he show, and how might a teacher help to foster them?

ENHANCEDetext *video example*

The teacher then proceeds to demonstrate the strategy *incorrectly.*

> *Teacher:* The passage is about crayons. Well, how much can there really be to know about crayons besides there are hundreds of colors and they always seem to break in the middle? Crayons are for little kids, and I'm in junior high so I don't need to know that much about them. I'll just skim the passage and go ahead and answer the question. Okay, how well did I use the strategy steps?

The class discusses the teacher's inappropriate use of the strategy. Notice how the teacher provides both an *example* and a *nonexample*—good teaching.

METACOGNITIVE DEVELOPMENT FOR SECONDARY AND COLLEGE STUDENTS (LIKE YOU). For older students, teachers can incorporate metacognitive questions into their lessons, lectures, and assignments. For example, David Jonassen (2011, p. 165) suggests that instructional designers incorporate these questions into hypermedia learning environments to help students be more self-reflective:

What are my intellectual strengths and weaknesses?
How can I motivate myself to learn when I need to?
How good am I at judging how well I understand something?
How can I focus on the meaning and significance of new information?
How can I set specific goals before I begin a task?
What questions should I ask about the material before I begin?
How well have I accomplished my goals once I'm finished?
Have I learned as much as I could have once I finish a task?
Have I considered all options after I solve a problem?

Metacognition includes knowledge about using many strategies in learning—our next topic.

LEARNING STRATEGIES

Most teachers will tell you that they want their students to "learn how to learn." Years of research indicate that using good learning strategies helps students learn and that these strategies can be taught (Hamman, Berthelot, Saia, & Crowley, 2000; Pressley & Harris, 2006). But were you taught "how to learn"? Powerful and sophisticated learning strategies and study skills are seldom taught directly until high school or even college, so most students have little practice with them. In contrast, early on, students usually discover repetition and rote learning on their own, so they have extensive practice with these strategies. And, unfortunately, some teachers think that memorizing is learning (Beghetto, 2008; Woolfolk Hoy & Murphy, 2001). This may explain why many students cling to flash cards and memorizing—they don't know what else to do (Willoughby, Porter, Belsito, & Yearsley, 1999).

As you saw in Chapter 8, the way something is learned in the first place greatly influences how readily we remember the information and how appropriately we can apply the knowledge later. First, students must be *cognitively engaged* in order to learn; they have to *focus attention* on the relevant or important aspects of the material. Second, they have to *invest effort,* make connections, elaborate, translate, invent, organize, and reorganize to think and *process deeply*—the greater the practice and processing, the stronger the learning. Finally, students must *regulate and monitor* their own learning—keep track of what is making sense and notice when a new approach is needed; they must be *metacognitive.* The emphasis today is on helping students develop effective learning strategies that focus attention and effort, process information deeply, and monitor understanding.

Being Strategic About Learning

Learning strategies are a special kind of procedural knowledge—*knowing how* to do something. There are thousands of strategies. Some are general and taught in school, such as summarizing or outlining. Others are specific to a subject, such as using a mnemonic to remember the order of

Connect and Extend to PRAXIS II®

Learning Strategies (I, A1)
For suggestions about their effective use, take a look at the study skills site developed by the Virginia Polytechnic Institute (ucc.vt.edu/stdysk/stdyhlp. html), and also see studygs.net for more ideas.

the planets: "My Very Educated Mother Just Served Us Nachos" for Mercury, Venus, Earth, Mars, Jupiter, Saturn, Uranus, and Neptune. Other strategies may be unique, invented by an individual to learn Chinese characters, for example. Learning strategies can be cognitive (summarizing, identifying the main idea), metacognitive (monitoring comprehension—do I understand?), or behavioral (using an Internet dictionary, setting a timer to work until time's up) (Cantrell, Almasi, Carter, Rintamaa, & Madden, 2010). All are ways of accomplishing a learning task that are intentionally applied when usual methods have not worked and strategic effort is needed (K. R. Harris, Alexander, & Graham, 2008). Over time, as you become more expert at using the strategies, you need less intentional effort. Ultimately you may become more automatic in applying the strategies; in other words, the strategies will become your usual way of accomplishing that kind of task, until they don't work and you need new strategies.

Skilled learners have a wide range of learning strategies that they can apply fairly automatically. Using learning strategies and study skills is related to higher grade-point averages (GPAs) in high school and persistence in college (Robbins et al., 2004). Researchers have identified several important principles:

1. Students must be exposed to a number of different strategies, not only general learning strategies but also very specific strategies for particular subjects, such as the graphic strategies described later in this section.

2. Students should be taught self-regulatory (conditional) knowledge about when, where, and why to use various strategies. Although this may seem obvious, teachers often neglect this step. A strategy is more likely to be maintained and employed if students know when, where, and why to use it.

3. Students may know when and how to use a strategy, but unless they also develop the desire to employ these skills, general learning ability will not improve. Remember, left to their own, many students, adult students included, do not choose the most effective strategies, even if they know how to do the strategy (Son & Simon, 2012). Several learning strategy programs include a motivational training component.

4. Students need to believe that they can learn new strategies, that the effort will pay off, and that they can "get smarter" by applying these strategies.

5. Students need some background knowledge and useful schemas in the area being studied to make sense of learning materials. It will be difficult to find the main idea in a paragraph about *ichthyology*, for example, if you don't know much about fish. So students may need direct instruction in schematic (content) knowledge along with strategy training. Table 9.1 on the next page summarizes several learning strategies.

DECIDING WHAT IS IMPORTANT. You can see from the first entry in Table 9.1 that learning begins with focusing attention—deciding what is important. But distinguishing the main idea from less important information is not always easy. Often students focus on the "seductive details" or the concrete examples, perhaps because these are more interesting (Gardner, Brown, Sanders, & Menke, 1992). You may have had the experience of remembering a joke or an intriguing example from a lecture, but not being clear about the larger point the professor was trying to make. Finding the central idea is especially difficult if you lack prior knowledge in an area and if the amount of new information provided is extensive. Teachers can give students practice using signals in texts such as headings, bold words, outlines, or other indicators to identify key concepts and main ideas (Lorch, Lorch, Ritchey, McGovern, & Coleman, 2001).

SUMMARIES. Creating summaries can help students learn, but students have to be taught how to summarize (Byrnes, 1996; Palincsar & Brown, 1984). Jeanne Ormrod (2012) summarizes these suggestions for helping students create summaries. Ask students to:

• Find or create a topic sentence for each paragraph or section.
• Identify big ideas that cover several specific points.
• Find some supporting information for each big idea.
• Delete any redundant information or unnecessary details.

TABLE 9.1 • **Examples of Learning Strategies**

	EXAMPLES
Planning and Focusing Attention	Setting goals and timetables
	Underlining and highlighting
	Skimming, looking for headings and topic sentences
Organizing and Remembering	Making organizational charts
	Creating flowcharts, Venn diagrams
	Using mnemonics, imagery
Comprehension	Concept mapping, webs
	Summarizing, outlining, and note taking
	Creating examples
	Explaining to a peer
Cognitive Monitoring	Making predictions
	Self-questioning and self-testing
	Identifying what doesn't make sense
Practice	Using part practice
	Using whole practice

Begin by doing summaries of short, easy, well-organized readings. Introduce longer, less organized, and more difficult passages gradually. Initially it may be useful to provide a scaffold such as: This paragraph is about _____ and _____. They are the same in these ways: _____, but different in these ways: _____. Ask students to compare their summaries and discuss what ideas they thought were important and why—what's their evidence?

Two other study strategies that are based on identifying key ideas are underlining texts and taking notes.

STOP & THINK How do you make notes as you read? Look back over the past several pages of this chapter. Are my words highlighted yellow or pink? Are there marks or drawings in the margins, and if so, do the notes pertain to the chapter or are they grocery lists and doodles? •

UNDERLINING AND HIGHLIGHTING. Do you underline or highlight key phrases in textbooks? Underlining and note taking are probably two of the most frequent but ineffectively used strategies among college students. One common problem is that students underline or highlight too much. It is far better to be selective. In studies that limit how much students can underline—for example, only one sentence per paragraph—learning has improved (Snowman, 1984). In addition to being selective, you also should actively transform the information into your own words as you underline or take notes. Don't rely on the words of the book. Note connections between what you are reading and other things you already know. Draw diagrams to illustrate relationships. Finally, look for organizational patterns in the material, and use them to guide your underlining or note taking.

TAKING NOTES. Taking good lecture notes is not an easy task. You have to hold the lecture information in working memory; select, organize, and transform the important ideas and themes before the information "falls off" your working memory workbench; and write down the ideas and themes—all while you are still following the lecture (Bui, Myerson, & Hale, 2013; Kobayashi,

2005; Peverly et al., 2007). As you fill your notebook with words and try to keep up with a lecturer, you may wonder if taking notes makes a difference. It does, if the strategy is used well.

- Taking notes focuses attention during class. Of course, if taking notes distracts you from actually listening to and making sense of the lecture, then note taking may not be effective (Kiewra, 1989, 2002; Van Meter, Yokoi, & Pressley, 1994). Dung Bui and his colleagues (2013) found that taking organized notes worked well for students with good working memory, but using a laptop to transcribe lectures worked better for students with poor working memories, at least for short lectures.
- Taking organized notes makes you construct meaning from what you are hearing, seeing, or reading, so you elaborate, translate into your own words, and remember (Armbruster, 2000). Even if students don't review notes before a test, taking them in the first place appears to aid learning, especially for those who lack prior knowledge in an area.
- Notes provide extended external storage that allows you to return and review. Students who use their notes to study tend to perform better on tests, especially if they take many high-quality notes—more is better as long as you are capturing key ideas, concepts, and relationships, not just intriguing details (Kiewra, 1985, 1989; Peverly, Brobst, Graham, & Shaw, 2003).
- Expert students match notes to their anticipated use and modify strategies after tests or assignments; use personal codes to flag material that is unfamiliar or difficult; fill in holes by consulting relevant sources (including other students in the class); and record information verbatim only when a verbatim response will be required. In other words, they are *strategic* about taking and using notes (Van Meter, Yokoi, & Pressley, 1994).

Even with these advantages, remember the caveat mentioned earlier. It is possible that taking well-organized notes that capture the important ideas in lecture is easier for students with better working memory abilities. When students have more-limited working memories, they might need to focus on understanding the teacher and transcribing as much as possible, as long as they are fast typists.

Even though taking notes is valuable from middle school through graduate school, students with learning disabilities often have trouble (Boyle, 2010a, 2010b). Middle school and high school students with learning disabilities who used a strategic note-taking form recalled and understood significantly more key ideas from science lectures than students in control groups who used conventional note-taking methods (Boyle, 2010b; Boyle & Weishaar, 2001). For an example of this kind of form, see www.ldonline.org/article/6210/.

Figure 9.1 is a general form that can be used in many note-taking situations. Dividing up the page is an idea from Cornell notes, devised by Walter Pauk of Cornell University, who wrote the classic guide, *How to Study in College* in the 1950s. It is still available (Pauk & Owens, 2010). This form could be useful for any student who needs extra guidance in note taking.

Visual Tools for Organizing

To use underlining and note taking effectively, you must identify main ideas. In addition, you must understand the organization of the text or lecture—the connections and relationships among ideas. Some visual strategies have been developed to help students with this key organizational element (Van Meter, 2001). **Concept maps** are graphical tools for organizing and representing knowledge and relationships within a particular field or on a given topic (Hagemans, van der Meij, & de Jong, 2013; van der Meij, 2012). Figure 9.2 on page 336 is a concept map of a Web site for creating concept maps by the Institute for Human and Machine Cognition Cmap tools. You may have referred to these interconnected ideas as *webs*.

In a review of 55 studies with students from fourth grade to graduate school and subjects ranging from science to statistics to nursing, John Nesbit and Olusola Adesope (2006) concluded that, "in comparison with activities such as reading text passages, attending lectures, and participating in class discussions, concept mapping activities are more effective for attaining knowledge retention and transfer" (p. 434). Having students "map" relationships by noting causal connections, comparison/contrast connections, and examples improves recall. My students at Ohio State use **Cmaps**, the free downloadable tools from the Web site shown in Figure 9.2 on page 336, for creating concept

Connect and Extend to PRAXIS II®

Concept Mapping (II, A2)
For advice and additional information about the creation and use of concept maps, go to the Web site Graphic Organizers (graphic.org/concept.html).

FIGURE 9.1

A FORM FOR TAKING NOTES MORE STRATEGICALLY

Topic:	What do I already know about this topic?
Key Points/ Key Terms	Notes

Summaries: Write 3 to 5 sentences that capture the main ideas.

1.

2.

3.

4.

5.

Questions: What is still confusing or unclear?

Source: Based on ideas from Pauk, Walter; Owens, Ross J. Q. (2010), How to Study in College (10th ed.). (Original work published 1962) Florence, KY: Cengage Learning; and http://lsc.cornell.edu/ LSC_Resources/cornellsystem.pdf

maps—one even planned his dissertation and organized all the reading for his doctoral examinations with tools from the Web site. Computer Cmaps can be linked to the Internet, and students in different classrooms and schools all over the world can collaborate on them. Students should compare their filled-in "maps" and discuss the differences in their thinking with each other.

Instructor-provided maps can serve as guides for studying. Mieke Hagemans and her colleagues (2013) found that color-coded concept maps helped high school physics students master complex concepts. The concept maps were part of a computer program. The maps changed color as the students completed study in that section of the map, so students had a scaffold to guide them through the reading and assignments and even remind them, for example, that they had not spent enough time on the assignments on "acceleration" in their study of "velocity."

There are other ways to visualize organization, such as Venn diagrams, which show how ideas or concepts overlap, and tree diagrams, which show how ideas branch off each other. Time lines organize information in sequence and are useful in classes such as history or geology.

FIGURE 9.2

THE WEB SITE FOR THE INSTITUTE FOR HUMAN AND MACHINE COGNITION CMAP TOOLS

At this site, you can download concept mapping tools to construct, share, and criticize knowledge on any subject: cmap.imhc.us.

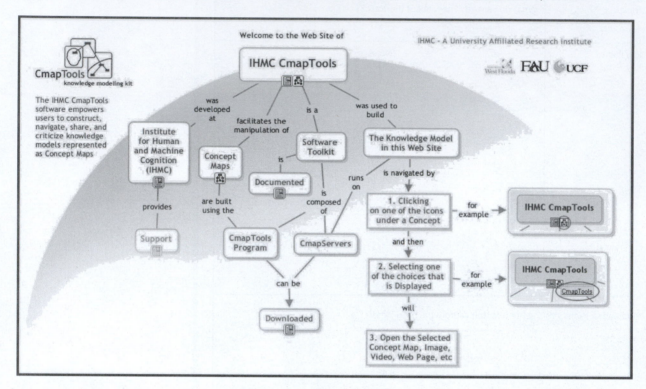

Source: Institute for Human and Machine Cognition Cmap Tools. *Retrieved from http://cmap.ihmc.us. Reprinted with permission from the IHMC.*

Reading Strategies

As we saw earlier, effective learning strategies should help students *focus attention, invest effort* (connect, elaborate, translate, organize, summarize) so they *process information deeply,* and *monitor* their understanding. A number of strategies support these processes in reading. Many strategies use mnemonics to help students remember the steps involved. For example, one strategy that can be used for any grade above later elementary is **READS**:

R   Review headings and subheadings.
E   Examine boldface words.
A   Ask, "What do I expect to learn?"
D   Do it—Read!
S   Summarize in your own words. (Friend & Bursuck, 2012)

A strategy that can be used in reading literature is **CAPS**:

C   Who are the characters?
A   What is the aim of the story?
P   What problem happens?
S   How is the problem solved?

These strategies are effective for several reasons. First, following the steps makes students more aware of the organization of a given chapter. How often have you skipped reading headings entirely and thus missed major clues about the way the information was organized? Next, these steps require students to study the chapter in sections instead of trying to learn all the information at once. This makes use of *distributed practice*. Answering questions about the material forces students to process the information more deeply and with greater elaboration.

No matter what strategies you use, students have to be taught how to use them. *Direct teaching, explanation, modeling,* and *practice with feedback* are necessary and are especially important for students with learning challenges and students whose first language is not English. For an example of direct teaching of strategies with explanations, modeling, and practice with feedback, see the KWL discussion on pages 330–331 of this chapter.

Applying Learning Strategies

One of the most common findings in research on learning strategies is what are known as **production deficiencies**. Students learn strategies, but do not apply them when they could or should (Pressley & Harris, 2006; Son & Simon, 2012). This is especially a problem for students with learning disabilities. For these students, executive control processes (metacognitive strategies) such as planning, organizing, monitoring progress, and making adaptations often are underdeveloped (Kirk, Gallagher, Anastasiow, & Coleman, 2006). It makes sense to teach these strategies directly. To ensure that students actually use the strategies they learn, several conditions must be met.

APPROPRIATE TASKS. First, of course, the learning task must be *appropriate*. Why would students use more complex learning strategies when the task set by the teacher is to "learn and return" the exact words of the text or lecture? With these tasks, teachers reward memorizing, and the best strategies involve distributed practice and perhaps mnemonics (described in Chapter 8). But hopefully, contemporary teachers use few of these kinds of tasks, so if the task is *understanding*, not memorizing, what else is necessary?

VALUING LEARNING. The second condition for using sophisticated strategies is that students must *care* about learning and understanding. They must have goals that can be reached using effective strategies (Zimmerman & Schunk, 2001). I was reminded of this in my educational psychology class one semester when I enthusiastically shared an article about study skills from the newspaper *USA Today*. The gist of the article was that students should continually revise and rewrite their notes from a course, so that by the end, all their understanding could be captured in one or two pages. Of course, the majority of the knowledge at that point would be reorganized and connected well with other knowledge. "See," I told the class, "these ideas are real—not just trapped in texts. They can help you study smarter in college." After a heated discussion, one of the best students said in exasperation, "I'm carrying 18 hours—I don't have time to *learn* this stuff!" She did not believe that her goal—to survive the 18 hours—could be reached by using time-consuming study strategies, and she might have been right.

EFFORT AND EFFICACY. My student also was concerned about effort. The third condition for applying learning strategies is that students must believe the effort and investment required to apply the strategies are reasonable, given the likely return (Winne, 2001). And of course, students must believe they are capable of using the strategies; they must have self-efficacy for using the strategies to learn the material in question (Schunk, 2012). This is related to another condition: Students must have a base of knowledge and/or experience in the area. No learning strategies will help students accomplish tasks that are completely beyond their current understandings.

The *Guidelines: Becoming an Expert Student* on the next page provides a summary of ideas for you and your students.

Reaching Every Student: Learning Strategies for Struggling Students

Reading is key in all learning. Strategy instruction can help many struggling readers. As you have seen, some approaches make use of mnemonics to help students remember the steps. For example, Susan Cantrell and her colleagues identified 862 students in sixth and ninth grade who were at least 2 years behind in reading (Cantrell, Almasi, Carter, Rintamaa, & Madden, 2010). The students were from 23 different schools. Students were randomly assigned to either a Learning Strategies Curriculum (Deshler & Schumaker, 2005) or the traditional curriculum. The Learning Strategies

GUIDELINES
Becoming an Expert Student

Be clear about your goals in studying.

Examples

1. Target a specific number of pages to read and outline.
2. Write the introduction section of a paper.

Make sure you have the necessary declarative knowledge (facts, concepts, ideas) to understand new information.

Examples

1. Keep definitions of key vocabulary available as you study.
2. Use your general knowledge. Ask yourself, "What do I already know about _____?"
3. Build your vocabulary by learning two or three new words a day using them in everyday conversation.

Find out what type of test the teacher will give (essay, short answer), and study the material with that in mind.

Examples

1. For a test with detailed questions, practice writing answers to possible questions.
2. For a multiple-choice test, use mnemonics to remember definitions of key terms.

Make sure you are familiar with the organization of the materials to be learned.

Examples

1. Preview the headings, introductions, topic sentences, and summaries of the text.
2. Be alert for words and phrases that signal relationships, such as *on the other hand, because, first, second, however, since*.

Know your own cognitive skills, and use them deliberately.

Examples

1. Use examples and analogies to relate new material to something you care about and understand well, such as sports, hobbies, or films.
2. If one study technique is not working, try another—the goal is to stay involved, not to use any particular strategy.
3. If you start to daydream, stand up from your desk and face away from your books, but don't leave. Then sit back down and study.

Study the right information in the right way.

Examples

1. Be sure you know exactly what topics and readings the test will cover.
2. Spend your time on the important, difficult, and unfamiliar material that will be required for the test or assignment. Resist the temptation to go over what you already know well, even if that feels good.
3. Keep a list of the parts of the text that give you trouble, and spend more time on those pages.
4. Process the important information thoroughly by using mnemonics, forming images, creating examples, answering questions, making notes in your own words, and elaborating on the text. Do not try to memorize the author's words—use your own.

Monitor your own comprehension.

Examples

1. Use questioning to check your understanding.
2. When reading speed slows down, decide if the information in the passage is important. If it is, note the problem so you can re-read or get help to understand. If it is not important, ignore it.
3. Check your understanding by working with a friend and quizzing one another.

Manage your time.

Examples

1. When is your best time for studying? Morning, late night? Study your most difficult subjects then.
2. Study in shorter rather than longer blocks, unless you are really engaged and making great progress.
3. Eliminate time wasters and distractions. Study in a room without a television or your roommate, then turn off your phone and maybe even the Internet.
4. Use bonus time—take your educational psychology notes to the doctor's office waiting room or laundromat. You will use time well and avoid reading old magazines.

Based on ideas from: ucc.vt.edu/stdysk/stdyhlp.html; d.umn.edu/student/loon/acad/strat/; Wong, L. (2015). Essential study skills (8th ed.) Stamford, CT: Cengage.

Curriculum focused on six strategies: word identification, visual imagery, self-questioning, LINCS vocabulary strategy, sentence writing, and paraphrasing. The **LINCS vocabulary strategy** uses stories and imagery to help students learn how to identify, organize, define, and remember words, which increases their ownership of their learning. The LINCS steps are:

L   "List the parts." Identify the vocabulary word and key information.

I   "Identify a reminding word." Pick a known word that reminds them of the vocabulary word.

N   "Note a LINCing story." Create a story that bridges the vocabulary word with the known word.

C   "Create a LINCing picture." Draw a picture that represents the story.

S   "Self-test." Check their learning of the vocabulary word by reciting all the parts of their LINCS.

TABLE 9.2 • Teaching Strategies for Improving Students' Metacognitive Knowledge and Skills

These eight guidelines taken from Pressley and Woloshyn (1995) should help you in teaching any metacognitive strategy.

- Teach a few strategies at a time, intensively and extensively as part of the ongoing curriculum.
- Model and explain new strategies.
- If parts of the strategy were not understood, model again and re-explain strategies in ways that are sensitive to those confusing or misunderstood aspects of strategy use.
- Explain to students where and when to use the strategy.
- Provide plenty of practice, using strategies for as many appropriate tasks as possible.
- Encourage students to monitor how they are doing when they are using strategies.
- Increase students' motivation to use strategies by heightening their awareness that they are acquiring valuable skills—skills that are at the heart of competent functioning.
- Emphasize reflective processing rather than speedy processing; do everything possible to eliminate high anxiety in students; encourage students to shield themselves from distractions so they can attend to academic tasks.

For a list of strategies and how to teach them see: unl.edu/csi/bank.html
Source: Based on *Pressley, M., & Woloshyn, V. (1995).* Cognitive Strategy Instruction That Really Improves Children's Academic Performance. *Cambridge, MA: Brookline Books.*

After a year, the sixth-graders who had participated in the Learning Strategies Curriculum performed significantly better on reading comprehension and strategy use, but there were no differences for ninth-graders. It is possible that reading strategy instruction is most effective in elementary and early middle school when students are learning how to learn through reading (Cantrell, Almasi, Carter, Rintamaa, & Madden, 2010).

Of course, you have to do more than just tell students about the strategy—you have to teach it. Michael Pressley and Vera Woloshyn (1995) developed the Cognitive Strategies Model as a guide for teaching students to improve their metacognitive strategies. Table 9.2 describes the steps in teaching these strategies.

ENHANCEDetext *self-check*

PROBLEM SOLVING

STOP & THINK You're interviewing with the district superintendent for a position as a school psychologist. The superintendent is known for his unorthodox interview questions. He hands you a pad of paper and a ruler and says, "Tell me, what is the exact thickness of a single sheet of paper?" •

The *Stop & Think* is a true story. I was asked the paper thickness question in an interview years ago. The answer was to measure the thickness of the entire pad and divide by the number of pages in the pad. I got the answer and the job, but what a tense moment that was. I suppose the superintendent was interested in my ability to solve problems—under pressure!

A **problem** has an initial state (the current situation), a goal (the desired outcome), and a path for reaching the goal (including operations or activities that move you toward the goal). Problem solvers often have to set and reach subgoals as they move toward the final solution. For example, if your goal is to drive to the beach, but at the first stop sign you skid through the intersection, you may have to reach a subgoal of fixing your brakes before you can continue toward the original goal (Schunk, 2012). Also, problems can range from *well structured* to *ill structured,* depending on how clear-cut the goals are and how much structure is provided for solving them. Most arithmetic problems are well structured, but finding the right college major or career is ill structured—many different solutions and paths to solutions are possible. Life presents many ill-structured problems (Belland, 2011).

Connect and Extend to PRAXIS II®

Problem Solving (II, A1)
Be prepared to identify the steps in the general problem-solving process. Describe the techniques that students can employ to build useful representations of problems.

Problem solving is usually defined as formulating new answers, going beyond the simple application of previously learned rules to achieve a goal. Problem solving is what happens when no solution is obvious—when, for example, you can't afford new brakes for the car that skidded on the way to the beach (Mayer & Wittrock, 2006). Some psychologists suggest that most human learning involves problem solving and that helping students become better problem solvers is one of education's greatest challenges (J. R. Anderson, 2010; Greiff et al., 2013). Solving complex, ill-structured problems is one key ability measured by the Programme for International Student Assessment (PISA), a comprehensive worldwide assessment of reading, mathematics and science for 15-year-olds. The United States ranked 36th out of 65 countries in total scores on this assessment in 2012 (Organisation for Economic Co-operation and Development, 2013), and 23rd out of 29 countries when you look at problem-solving performance alone (Belland, 2011), so U.S. students definitely could improve their problem-solving abilities.

There is a debate about problem solving. Some psychologists believe that effective problem-solving strategies are specific to the problem area. For example, the problem-solving strategies in mathematics are unique to math; the strategies in art are unique to art, and so on. The other side of the debate claims that there are some general problem-solving strategies that can be useful in many areas. General problem-solving strategies usually include the steps of *identifying* the problem, *setting goals, exploring* possible solutions and consequences, *acting,* and finally *evaluating* the outcome.

There is evidence for the value of both general and specific strategies. In their research with fourth- and fifth-graders, Steven Hecht and Kevin Vagi (2010) found that both domain-specific and general factors affected performance on problems involving fractions. The influences were specific conceptual knowledge about fractions and the general information processing skill of attentive classroom behavior. Other studies with elementary school students found that both specific arithmetic knowledge and general attention-focusing, working memory, and oral language skills were related to arithmetic problem solving (Fuchs et al., 2006, 2012, 2013).

People appear to move between general and specific approaches, depending on the situation and their level of expertise. Early on, when we know little about a problem area or domain, we can rely on general learning and problem-solving strategies to make sense of the situation. As we gain more domain-specific knowledge (particularly procedural knowledge about how to do things in the domain), we consciously apply the general strategies less and less; our problem solving becomes more automatic. But if we encounter a problem outside our current knowledge, we may return to relying on general strategies to attack the problem (Alexander, 1992, 1996).

A key first step in any problem solving—general or specific—is identifying that a problem exists (and perhaps treating the problem as an opportunity).

Identifying: Problem Finding

Problem identification is not always straightforward. I am reminded of a story about tenants who were angry because the elevators in their building were slow. Consultants hired to "fix the problem" reported that the elevators were no worse than average and improvements would be very expensive. One day, as the building supervisor watched people waiting impatiently for an elevator, he realized that the problem was not slow elevators, but the fact that people were bored; they had nothing to do while they waited. When the boredom problem was identified and seen as an opportunity to improve the "waiting experience," the simple solution of installing a mirror by the elevator on each floor eliminated complaints.

Even though problem identification is a critical first step, research indicates that people often "leap" to naming the first problem that comes to mind ("the elevators are too slow!"). Experts in a field are more likely to spend time carefully considering the nature of the problem (Bruning, Schraw, & Norby, 2011). Finding a solvable problem and turning it into an opportunity is the process behind many successful inventions, such as the ballpoint pen, garbage disposal, appliance timer, alarm clock, self-cleaning oven, and thousands of others.

Once a solvable problem is identified, what next?

Video 9.2
Problem solving is a skill these teachers address directly in their classes. In all disciplines, students may need scaffolding as they learn how to identify the problem and understand what is involved in finding a solution.

ENHANCEDetext *video example*

Defining Goals and Representing the Problem

Let's take a real problem: The machines designed to pick tomatoes are damaging the tomatoes. What should we do? If we represent the problem as a faulty machine design, then the goal is to improve the machine. But if we represent the problem as a faulty design of the tomatoes, then the goal is to develop a tougher tomato. The problem-solving process follows two entirely different paths, depending on which representation and goal are chosen (Nokes-Malach & Mestre, 2013). To represent the problem and set a goal, you have to *focus attention* on relevant information, *understand the words* of the problem, and *activate the right schema* to understand the whole problem.

STOP & THINK If you have black socks and white socks in your drawer, mixed in the ratio of four to five, how many socks will you have to take out to make sure you have a pair the same color? (Adapted from Sternberg & Davidson, 1982.) •

FOCUSING ATTENTION ON WHAT IS RELEVANT. Representing the problem often requires finding the relevant information and ignoring the irrelevant details. For example, what information was relevant in solving the sock problem in *Stop & Think*? Did you realize that the information about the four-to-five ratio of black socks to white socks is irrelevant? As long as you have only two different colors of socks in the drawer, you will have to remove only three socks before two of them match.

UNDERSTANDING THE WORDS. The second task in representing a problem is understanding the meaning of the words, sentences, and factual information in the problem. So problem solving requires comprehension of the language and relations in the problem. In math word problems, it also involves assigning mathematical operators (addition, division, etc.) to relations among numbers (Jitendra et al., 2009 K. Lee, Ng, & Ng, 2009). All this makes a demand on working memory. For example, the main stumbling block in representing many word problems and problems with fractions is the students' understanding of part–whole relations (Fuchs et al., 2013). Students have trouble figuring out what is part of what, as is evident in this dialogue between a teacher and a first-grader:

Teacher: Pete has three apples. Ann also has some apples. Pete and Ann have nine apples altogether. How many apples does Ann have?
Student: Nine.
Teacher: Why?
Student: Because you just said so.
Teacher: Can you retell the story?
Student: Pete had three apples. Ann also had some apples. Ann had nine apples. Pete also has nine apples. (Adapted from De Corte & Verschaffel, 1985, p. 19)

The student interprets "altogether" (the whole) as "each" (the parts).

A common difficulty for older students is understanding that ratio and proportion problems are based on multiplicative relations, not additive relations (Jitendra et al., 2009). So to solve

$$2:14 = ?:35$$

many students subtract to find the difference between 2 and 14 ($14 - 2 = 12$) and then subtract 12 from 35 to get 23, giving them the (wrong) answer

$$2:14 = 23:35$$

The real question is about the *proportional* relationship between 2 and 14. How many *times* larger than 2 is 14? The answer: 7 times larger. Then the real question is "35 is 7 times larger than what number?" The answer is 5 ($7 \times 5 = 35$). So

$$2:14 + 5:35$$

UNDERSTANDING THE WHOLE PROBLEM. The third task in representing a problem is to assemble all the relevant information and sentences into an accurate understanding or translation of the total problem. This means that students need to form a conceptual model of the problem—they have to understand what the problem is *really asking* (Jonassen, 2003). Consider the example of the trains in *Stop & Think.*

- -

STOP & THINK Two train stations are 50 miles apart. At 2 p.m. one Saturday afternoon, two trains start toward each other, one from each station. Just as the trains pull out of the stations, a bird springs into the air in front of the first train and flies ahead to the front of the second train. When the bird reaches the second train, it turns back and flies toward the first train. The bird continues to do this until the trains meet. If both trains travel at the rate of 25 miles per hour and the bird flies at 100 miles per hour, how many miles will the bird have flown before the trains meet? (Posner, 1973). •

- -

Your interpretation of the problem is called a *translation* because you translate the problem into a schema that you understand. If you translate this as a *distance* problem (activate a distance schema) and set a goal ("I have to figure out how far the bird travels before it meets the oncoming train and turns around, then how far it travels before it has to turn again, and finally add up all the trips back and forth"), then you have a very difficult task on your hands. But there is a better way to structure the problem. You can represent it as a question of *time* and focus on the time the bird is in the air. The solution could be stated like this:

> The trains are going the same speed so they will meet in the middle, 25 miles from each station. This will take one hour because they are traveling 25 mph. In an hour, the bird will cover 100 miles because it is flying at 100 miles per hour. Easy!

Research shows that students can be too quick to decide what a problem is asking. Once a problem is categorized—"Aha, it's a distance problem!"—a particular schema is activated. The schema directs attention to relevant information and sets up expectations for what the right answer should look like. For example, if you use a distance schema in the above problem, the right answer looks like adding up many small distance calculations (Kalyuga, Chandler, Tuovinen, & Sweller, 2001; Reimann & Chi, 1989).

When students lack the necessary schemas to represent problems, they often rely on surface features of the situation and represent the problem incorrectly, like the student who wrote "15 + 24 = 39" as the answer to, "Joan has 15 bonus points and Louise has 24. How many more does Louise have?" This student saw two numbers and the word *more,* so he applied the *add to get more* procedure. Focus on surface features often happens when students are taught to search for key words (*more, less, greater,* etc.), pick a strategy or formula based on the key words (*more* means "add"), and apply the formula. Actually, focusing on surface features gets in the way of forming a conceptual understanding of the whole problem and using the right schema (Van de Walle, Karp, & Bay-Williams, 2010).

When students use the wrong schema, they overlook critical information, use irrelevant information, and may even misread or misremember critical information so that it fits the schema. But when students use the proper schema to represent a problem, they are less likely to be confused by irrelevant information or tricky wording, such as the presence of the word *more* in a problem that really requires *subtraction* (Fenton, 2007; Resnick, 1981). Figure 9.3 gives examples of different ways students might represent a simple mathematics problem. Exposure to different ways of representing and solving problems helps develop mathematical understanding (Star & Rittle-Johnson, 2009).

How can students who lack a good base of knowledge improve their translation and schema selection? To answer this question, we usually have to move to area-specific problem-solving strategies because schemas are specific to content areas.

TRANSLATION AND SCHEMA TRAINING: DIRECT INSTRUCTION IN SCHEMAS. For students with little knowledge in an area, teachers can begin by directly teaching the necessary

FIGURE 9.3

FOUR DIFFERENT WAYS TO REPRESENT A PROBLEM

A teacher asks, "How many wildlife stamps will Jane need to fill her book if there are three pages and each page holds 30 stamps?" The teacher gives the students supplies such as a squared paper, number lines, and place-value frames and encourages them to think of as many ways as possible to solve the problem. Here are four different solutions, based on four different but correct representations.

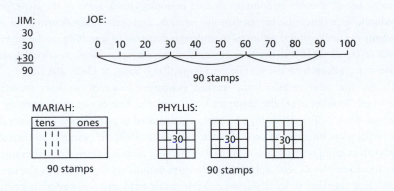

Source: Riedesel, C. A. & Schwartz, J. E. (1999). Essentials of Elementary Mathematics, *2nd Ed. Reprinted by permission of Pearson Education, Inc.*

schema using demonstration, modeling, and "think-alouds." As we just saw, ratio/proportion problems like the following are a big challenge for many students.

> Ernesto and Dawn worked separately on their social studies projects this weekend. The ratio of the number of hours Ernesto spent on the project to the number of hours Dawn spent on the project was 2:3. If Ernesto spent 16 hours on the project, how many hours did Dawn spend on the project? (Jitendra et al., 2009, p. 257)

The teacher used a "think-aloud" to focus students on the key schema for solving this problem, so she said, "*First,* I figure this is a ratio problem, because it compared the number of hours that Ernesto worked to the number of hours Dawn worked. This is a *part-part ratio* that tells about a multiplicative relationship (2 : 3) between the hours Ernesto and Dawn worked." The teacher went on to think aloud, "Next, I represented the information. . . ." *Finally,* I used the equivalent fractions strategy and. . . ." The think-aloud demonstration can be followed by providing students with many *worked examples*. In mathematics and physics it appears that in the *early stages* of learning, students benefit from seeing many different kinds of example problems worked out correctly for them (Moreno, Ozogul, & Reisslein, 2011). But before we explore worked examples in the next section, a caution is in order. Students with advanced knowledge improve when they solve new problems, not when they focus on already worked-out examples. Worked examples can actually interfere with the learning of more expert students. This has been called the *expert reversal effect* because what works for experts is the *reverse* of what works for beginners (Kalyuga & Renkl, 2010; Kalyuga, Rikers, & Paas, 2012).

TRANSLATION AND SCHEMA TRAINING: WORKED EXAMPLES. Worked examples reflect all the stages of problem solving—identifying the problem, setting goals, exploring solutions, solving the problem, and finally evaluating the outcome (Schworm & Renkl, 2007; van Gog, Paas, & Sweller, 2010). Worked examples are useful in many subject areas. Adrienne Lee and Laura Hutchinson (1998) found that undergraduate students learned more when they were provided with examples of chemistry problem solutions that were annotated to show an expert problem solver's thinking at critical steps. In Australia, Slava Kalyuga and colleagues (2001) found that worked-out examples helped apprentices to learn about electrical circuits when the apprentices had less experience in the area. Silke Schworm and Alexander Renkl (2007) used video examples to help student teachers learn how to make convincing arguments for or against a position.

Why are examples effective? Part of the answer is in *cognitive load theory*, discussed in the previous chapter. When students lack specific knowledge in domains—for example, fractions or proportions—they try to solve the problems using general strategies such as looking for key words or applying rote procedures. But these approaches put great strain on working memory—too much to "keep in mind" at once. In contrast, worked examples chunk some of the steps, provide cues and feedback, focus attention on relevant information, and make fewer demands on memory, so the students can use cognitive resources to understand instead of searching randomly for solutions (Wittwer & Renkl, 2010). It is especially useful if the examples focus on critical features of the problems that students have not yet mastered (Guo, Pang, Yang, & Ding, 2012).

To get the most benefit from worked examples, however, students have to actively engage—just "looking over" the examples is not enough. This is not too surprising when you think about what supports learning and memory. You need to pay attention, process deeply, and connect with what you already know. Students should explain the examples to themselves. This *self-explanation* component is a critical part of making learning from worked examples active, not passive. Examples of self-explanation strategies include trying to predict the next step in a solution, then checking to see if you are right or trying to identify an underlying principle that explains how to solve the problem. In their study with student teachers, Schworm and Renkl (2007) embedded prompts that required the student teachers to think about and explain elements of the arguments they saw on the tape, such as, "Which argumentative elements does this sequence contain? How is it related to Kirsten's statement?" (p. 289). Students have to be mentally engaged in making sense of the examples, and self-explanation is one key to engagement (R. K. Atkinson & Renkl, 2007; Wittwer & Renkl, 2010).

Another way to use worked examples is to have students compare examples that reach a right answer but are worked out in different ways. What is the same about each solution? What is different? Why? (Rittle-Johnson & Star, 2007). Also, worked-out examples should deal with one source of information at a time rather than having students move between text passages, graphs, tables, and so on. The cognitive load will be too heavy for beginners if they have to integrate many sources of information to make sense of the worked examples (Marcus, Cooper, & Sweller, 1996).

Worked examples can serve as analogies or models for solving new problems. But beware. Without explanations and coaching, novices may remember the surface features of a worked example or case instead of the deeper meaning or the structure. It is the meaning or structure, not the surface similarities, that helps in solving new, analogous problems (Gentner, Loewenstein, & Thompson, 2003; Goldstone & Day, 2012). I have heard students complain that the test preparation problems in their math classes were about boats and river currents, but the test asked about airplanes and wind speed. They protested, "There were no problems about boats on the test, and we never studied airplanes in class!" In fact, the problems on the test about wind were solved in exactly the same way as the "boat" problems, but the students were focusing only on the surface features. One way to overcome this tendency is to have students compare examples or cases so they can develop a problem-solving schema that captures the common structure, not the surface features, of the cases (Gentner et al., 2003).

How else might students develop the schemas they will need to represent problems in a particular subject area? Mayer (1983) has recommended giving students practice in the following: (1) recognizing and categorizing a variety of problem types; (2) representing problems, either concretely in pictures, symbols, or graphs, or in words; and (3) selecting relevant and irrelevant information in problems.

THE RESULTS OF PROBLEM REPRESENTATION. The problem representation stage of problem solving has two main outcomes, as shown in Figure 9.4. If your representation of the problem suggests an immediate solution, your task is done. In one sense, you haven't really solved a new problem; you have simply recognized the new problem as a "disguised" version of an old

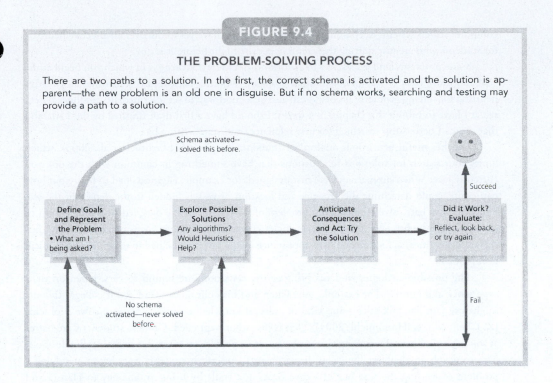

FIGURE 9.4

THE PROBLEM-SOLVING PROCESS

There are two paths to a solution. In the first, the correct schema is activated and the solution is apparent—the new problem is an old one in disguise. But if no schema works, searching and testing may provide a path to a solution.

problem that you already knew how to solve. This has been called schema-driven problem solving. In terms of Figure 9.4, you can use the schema-activated route and proceed directly to a solution.

But what if you have no existing way of solving the problem or your activated schema fails? Time to search for a solution!

Searching for Possible Solution Strategies

In conducting your search for a solution, you have available two general kinds of procedures: algorithmic and heuristic. Both of these are forms of procedural knowledge (Schraw, 2006).

ALGORITHMS. An algorithm is a step-by-step prescription for achieving a goal. It usually is domain specific; that is, it is tied to a particular subject area. In solving a problem, if you choose an appropriate algorithm (e.g., to find the mean, you add all the scores, then divide by the number of scores) and implement it properly, a right answer is guaranteed. Unfortunately, students often apply algorithms unsystematically, trying out one first, and then another. They may even happen on the right answer, but not understand how they got there, or they may forget the steps they used to find the answer. For some students, applying algorithms haphazardly could be an indication that formal operational thinking and the ability to work through a set of possibilities systematically (as described by Piaget) is not yet developed. But many problems cannot be solved by algorithms. What then?

HEURISTICS. A heuristic is a general strategy that might lead to the right answer (Schoenfeld, 2011). Because many of life's problems (careers, relationships, etc.) are not straightforward and have ill-defined problem statements and no apparent algorithms, the discovery or development of effective heuristics is important (Korf, 1999). Let's examine a few.

In means-ends analysis, the problem is divided into a number of intermediate goals or sub-goals, and then a means of solving each intermediate subgoal is figured out. For example, writing a 20-page term paper can loom as an insurmountable problem for some students. They would be better off breaking this task into several intermediate goals, such as selecting a topic, locating sources of information, reading and organizing the information, making an outline, and so on. As they attack a particular intermediate goal, they may find that other goals arise. For example, locating information may require that they find someone to refresh their memory about using the library computer search system. Keep in mind that psychologists have yet to discover an effective heuristic for students who are just starting their term paper the night before it is due.

Some problems lend themselves to a working-backward strategy, in which you begin at the goal and move back to the unsolved initial problem. Working backward is sometimes an effective heuristic for solving geometry proofs. It can also be a good way to set intermediate deadlines ("Let's see, if I have to submit this chapter in 4 weeks, I should have a first draft finished by the 11th, and that means I better stop searching for new references and start writing by . . . ").

Another useful heuristic is analogical thinking (Copi, 1961; Gentner et al., 2003), which limits your search for solutions to situations that have something in common with the one you currently face. When submarines were first designed, for example, engineers had to figure out how battleships could determine the presence and location of vessels hidden in the depths of the sea. Studying how bats solve an analogous problem of navigating in the dark led to the invention of sonar. Take note, however, that to use analogies effectively, you must focus on meaning and not surface similarities, so focusing on bats' appearance would not have helped to solve the communication problem.

The possible analogies students bring to the classroom are bound to vary, based on their experience and culture. For example, Zhe Chen and his colleagues wondered if college students might use familiar folk tales—one kind of cultural knowledge—as analogies to solve problems (Z. Chen, Mo, & Honomichl, 2004). That is just what happened. Chinese students were better at solving a problem of weighing a statue because the problem was similar to their folk tale about how to weigh an elephant (by water displacement). American students were better at solving a problem of finding the way out of a cave (leaving a trail) by using an analogy to Hansel and Gretel, a common European American folk tale.

Putting your problem-solving plan into words and giving reasons for selecting it can lead to successful problem solving (A. Y. Lee & Hutchinson, 1998). You may have discovered the effectiveness of this verbalization process accidentally, when a solution popped into your head as you were explaining a problem to someone else.

Anticipating, Acting, and Looking Back

After representing the problem and exploring possible solutions, the next step is to select a solution and anticipate the consequences. For example, if you decide to solve the damaged tomato problem by developing a tougher tomato, how will consumers react? If you take time to learn a new graphics program to enhance your term paper (and your grade), will you still have enough time to finish the paper?

After you choose a solution strategy and implement it, evaluate the results by checking for evidence that confirms or contradicts your solution. Many people tend to stop working before they reach the best solution and simply accept an answer that works in some cases. In mathematical problems, evaluating the answer might mean applying a checking routine, such as adding to check the result of a subtraction problem or, in a long addition problem, adding the column from bottom to top instead of top to bottom. Another possibility is estimating the answer. For example, if the computation was 11×21, the answer should be around 200, because 10×20 is 200. A student who reaches an answer of 2,311 or 32 or 562 should quickly realize these answers cannot be correct. Estimating an answer is particularly important when students rely on calculators or computers, because they cannot go back and spot an error in the figures.

Factors That Hinder Problem Solving

Sometimes problem solving requires looking at things in new ways. People may miss out on a good solution because they fixate on conventional uses for materials. This difficulty is called functional fixedness (Duncker, 1945). In your everyday life, you may often exhibit functional fixedness. Suppose a screw on a dresser-drawer handle is loose. Will you spend 10 minutes searching for a screwdriver, or will you fix it with a ruler edge or a dime?

Another kind of fixation that blocks effective problem solving is response set, getting stuck on one way of representing a problem. Try this:

In each of the four matchstick arrangements below, move only one stick to change the equation so that it represents a true equality such as V = V.

V = VII   VI = XI   XII = VII   VI = II

You probably figured out how to solve the first example quite quickly. You simply move one match-stick from the right side over to the left to make **VI** = **VI**. Examples two and three can also be solved without too much difficulty by moving one stick to change the **V** to an **X** or vice versa. But the fourth example (taken from Raudsepp & Haugh, 1977) probably has you stumped. To solve this problem, you must change your response set or switch schemas, because what has worked for the first three problems will not work this time. The answer here lies in changing from Roman numerals to Arabic numbers and using the concept of square root. By overcoming response set, you can move one matchstick from the right to the left to form the symbol for square root; the solution reads $\sqrt{1} = 1$, which is simply the symbolic way of saying that the square root of 1 equals 1. Recently, a creative reader of this text e-mailed some other solutions. Jamaal Allan, then a masters' student at Pacific University, pointed out that you could use any of the matchsticks to change the = sign to ≠. Then, the last example would be **V ≠ II** or 5 does not equal 2, an accurate statement. He suggested that you also might move one matchstick to change = to < or > and the statements would still be true (but not equalities as specified in the problem above). Bill Wetta, a student at Ashland University, offered another solution that used both Arabic and Roman numerals. You can move one matchstick to make the first V an X. Then VI = II becomes XI = II, or eleven (in Roman numerals) equals 11 (in Arabic numerals). Just this morning I received another creative approach from Ray Partlow, an educational psychology student in Newark, Ohio. He noted, "Simply remove a matchstick from the V from the left-hand side, and place it directly on top of the I, getting II = II." Covering one matchstick with another opens up a whole new set of possibilities! Can you come up with any other solutions? Be creative!

SOME PROBLEMS WITH HEURISTICS. We often apply heuristics automatically to make quick judgments; that saves us time in everyday problem solving. The mind can react automatically and instantaneously, but the price we often pay for this efficiency may be bad problem solving, which can be costly. Making judgments by invoking stereotypes leads even smart people to make dumb decisions. For example, we might use representativeness heuristics to make judgments about possibilities based on our prototypes—what we think is representative of a category. Consider this:

> If I ask you whether a slim, short stranger who enjoys poetry is more likely to be a truck driver or an Ivy League classics professor, what would you say?

You might be tempted to answer based on your prototypes of truck drivers or professors. But consider the odds. With about 10 Ivy League schools and 4 or so classics professors per school, we have 40 professors. Say 10 are both short and slim, and half of those like poetry—we are left with 5. But there are at least 400,000 truck drivers in the United States. If only 1 in every 800 of those truck drivers were short, slim poetry lovers, we have 500 truck drivers who fit the description. With 500 truck drivers versus 5 professors, it is 100 times more likely that our stranger is a truck driver (Myers, 2005).

Teachers and students are busy people, and they often base their decisions on what they have in their minds at the time. When judgments are based on the availability of information in our memories, we are using the availability heuristic. If instances of events come to mind easily, we think they are common occurrences, but that is not necessarily the case; in fact, it is often wrong. People remember vivid stories and quickly come to believe that such events are the norm, but again, they often are wrong. For example, you may be surprised to learn the average family in poverty has only 2.2 children (Children's Defense Fund, 2005a, 2005b) if you have vivid memories from viewing a powerful film about a large, poor family. Data may not support a judgment, but belief perseverance, or the tendency to hold on to our beliefs, even in the face of contradictory evidence, may make us resist change.

The confirmation bias is the tendency to search for information that confirms our ideas and beliefs: This arises from our eagerness to get a good solution. You have often heard the saying "Don't

GUIDELINES
Applying Problem Solving

Ask students if they are sure they understand the problem.

Examples

1. Can they separate relevant from irrelevant information?
2. Are they aware of the assumptions they are making?
3. Encourage them to visualize the problem by diagramming or drawing it.
4. Ask them to explain the problem to someone else. What would a good solution look like?

Encourage attempts to see the problem from different angles.

Examples

1. Suggest several different possibilities yourself, and then ask students to offer some.
2. Give students practice in taking and defending different points of view on an issue.

Let students do the thinking; don't just hand them solutions.

Examples

1. Offer individual problems as well as group problems, so that each student has the chance to practice.

2. Give partial credit if students have good reasons for "wrong" solutions to problems.
3. If students are stuck, resist the temptation to give too many clues. Let them think about the problem overnight.

Help students develop systematic ways of considering alternatives.

Examples

1. Think out loud as you solve problems.
2. Ask, "What would happen if?"
3. Keep a list of suggestions.

Teach heuristics.

Examples

1. Use analogies to solve the problem of limited parking in the downtown area. How are other "storage" problems solved?
2. Use the working-backward strategy to plan a party.

For more resources on problem solving, see hawaii.edu/suremath/home.html

confuse me with the facts." This aphorism captures the essence of the confirmation bias. Most people seek evidence that supports their ideas more readily than they search for facts that might refute them. For example, once you decide to buy a certain car, you are likely to notice reports about the good features of the car you chose, not the good news about the cars you rejected. Our automatic use of heuristics to make judgments, our eagerness to confirm what we like to believe, and our tendency to explain away failure combine to generate *overconfidence*. Students usually are overconfident about how fast they can get their papers written; it typically takes twice as long as they estimate (Buehler, Griffin, & Ross, 1994). In spite of their underestimation of their completion time, they remain overly confident of their next prediction.

The *Guidelines: Applying Problem Solving* gives some ideas for helping students become good problem solvers.

Expert Knowledge and Problem Solving

Most psychologists agree that effective problem solving is based on having an ample store of knowledge about the problem area (Belland, 2011; Schoenfeld, 2011). To solve the matchstick problem, for example, you had to understand Roman and Arabic numbers as well as the concept of square root. You also had to know that the square root of 1 is 1. Let's take a moment to examine this expert knowledge.

KNOWING WHAT IS IMPORTANT. Experts know where to focus their attention. For example, knowledgeable baseball fans (I am told) pay attention to the moves of the shortstop to learn if the pitcher will throw a fastball, curveball, or slider. But those with little knowledge about baseball may never see the movements of the shortstop, unless a hit is headed toward that part of the field (Bruning, Schraw, & Norby, 2011). In general, experts know what to pay attention to when judging a performance or product such as an Olympic high dive or a prize-winning chocolate cake. To nonexperts, most good dives or cakes look about the same, unless of course they "flop"!

MEMORY FOR PATTERNS AND ORGANIZATION. The modern study of expertise began with investigations of chess masters (D. P. Simon & Chase, 1973). Results indicated that masters can quickly recognize about 50,000 different arrangements of chess pieces. They can look at one of these patterns for a few seconds and remember where every piece on the board was placed. It is as though they have a "vocabulary" of 50,000 patterns. Michelene Chi (1978) demonstrated that third- through eighth-grade chess experts had a similar ability to remember chess piece arrangements. For all the masters, patterns of pieces are like words. If you were shown any word from your vocabulary store for just a few seconds, you would be able to remember every letter in the word in the right order (assuming you could spell the word). But a series of letters arranged randomly is hard to remember, as you saw in Chapter 8. An analogous situation holds for chess masters. When chess pieces are placed on a board randomly, masters are no better than average players at remembering the positions of the pieces. The master's memory is for patterns that make sense or could occur in a game.

A similar phenomenon occurs in other fields. There may be an intuition about how to solve a problem based on recognizing patterns and knowing the "right moves" for those patterns. Experts in physics, for example, organize their knowledge around central principles (e.g., Boyle's or Newton's laws), whereas beginners organize their smaller amounts of physics knowledge around the specific details stated in the problems (e.g., levers or pulleys) (K. A. Ericsson, 1999; Fenton, 2007).

PROCEDURAL KNOWLEDGE. In addition to representing a problem very quickly, experts know what to do next and can do it. They have a large store of *productions* or if–then schemas about what action to take in various situations. So, the steps of understanding the problem and choosing a solution happen simultaneously and fairly automatically (K. A. Ericsson & Charness, 1999). Of course, this means that experts must have many, many schemas available. A large part of becoming an expert is simply acquiring a great store of *domain knowledge* or knowledge that is particular to a field (Alexander, 1992). To do this, you must encounter many different kinds of problems in that field, observe others solving problems, and practice solving many yourself. Some estimates are that it takes 10 years or 10,000 hours of deliberate, focused, sustained practice to become an expert in most fields (A. Ericsson, 2011; K. A. Ericsson & Charness, 1994; H. A. Simon, 1995). Experts' rich store of knowledge is elaborated and well practiced, so that it is easy to retrieve from long-term memory when needed (J. R. Anderson, 1993).

PLANNING AND MONITORING. Experts spend more time analyzing problems, drawing diagrams, breaking large problems down into subproblems, and making plans. A novice might begin immediately—writing equations for a physics problem or drafting the first paragraph of a paper—but experts plan out the whole solution and often make the task simpler in the process. As they work, experts monitor progress, so time is not lost pursuing dead ends or weak ideas (Schunk, 2012).

So what can we conclude? Experts (1) know where to focus their attention; (2) perceive large, meaningful patterns in given information and are not confused by surface features and details; (3) hold more information in working and long-term memories, in part because they have organized the information into meaningful chunks and procedures; (4) take a great deal of time to analyze a given problem; (5) have automatic procedures for accomplishing pieces of the problem; and (6) are better at monitoring their performance. When the area of problem solving is fairly well defined, such as chess or physics or computer programming, then these skills of expert problem solvers hold fairly consistently. In these kinds of domains, even if students do not have the extensive background knowledge of experts, they can learn to approach the problem like an expert by taking time to analyze the problem, focusing on key features, using the right schema, and not trying to force old but inappropriate solutions on new problems (Belland, 2011). But when the problem-solving area is less well defined and has fewer clear underlying principles, such as problem solving in economics or psychology, then the differences between experts and novices are not as clear-cut (Alexander, 1992).

ENHANCEDetext *self-check*

CREATIVITY: WHAT IT IS AND WHY IT MATTERS

STOP & THINK Consider this student. He had severe dyslexia—a learning disability that made reading and writing exceedingly difficult. He described himself as an "underdog." In school, he knew that if the reading assignment would take others an hour, he had to allow 2 or 3 hours. He knew that he had to keep a list of all of his most frequently misspelled words to be able to write at all. He spent hours alone in his room. Would you expect his writing to be creative? Why or why not? •

The person described in this *Stop & Think* is John Irving, celebrated author of what one critic called "wildly inventive" novels such as *The World According to Garp, The Cider House Rules,* and *A Prayer for Owen Meany* (Amabile, 2001). How do we explain his amazing creativity? What is creativity?

Creativity is the ability to produce work that is original but still appropriate and useful (Plucker, Beghetto, & Dow, 2004). Most psychologists agree that there is no such thing as "all-purpose creativity"; people are creative in a particular area, as John Irving was in writing fiction. But to be creative, the "invention" must be intended. An accidental spilling of paint that produces a novel design is not creative unless the artist recognizes the potential of the "accident" or uses the spilling technique intentionally to create new works (Weisberg, 1993). Although we frequently associate the arts with creativity, any subject can be approached in a creative manner.

Assessing Creativity

STOP & THINK How many uses can you list for a brick? Take a moment and brainstorm—write down as many as you can. •

Like the author John Irving, Paul Torrance had a learning disability. He became interested in educational psychology when he was a high school English teacher (Neumeister & Cramond, 2004). Torrance was known as the "Father of Creativity." He developed two types of creativity tests: verbal and graphic (Torrance, 1972; Torrance & Hall, 1980). In the verbal test, you might be instructed to think up as many uses as possible for a brick (as you did above) or asked how a particular toy might be changed to make it more fun. On the graphic test, you might be given 30 circles and asked to create 30 different drawings, with each drawing including at least one circle. Figure 9.5 shows the creativity of an 8-year-old girl in completing this task.

These creativity tests require **divergent thinking**, an important component of many conceptions of creativity. Divergent thinking is the ability to propose many different ideas or answers. **Convergent thinking** is the more common ability to identify only one answer. Responses to all these creativity tasks are scored for originality, fluency, and flexibility—three aspects of divergent thinking. *Originality* is usually determined statistically. To be original, a response must be given by fewer than 5 or 10 people out of every 100 who take the test. *Fluency* is the number of different responses. *Flexibility* is generally measured by the number of different categories of responses. For instance, if you listed 20 uses of a brick, but each was to build something, your fluency score might be high, but your flexibility score would be low. Of the three measures, fluency—the number of responses—is the best predictor of divergent thinking, but there is more to real-life creativity than divergent thinking (Plucker et al., 2004).

A few possible indicators of creativity in your students are curiosity, concentration, adaptability, high energy, humor (sometimes bizarre), independence, playfulness, nonconformity, risk taking, attraction to the complex and mysterious, willingness to fantasize and daydream, intolerance for boredom, and inventiveness (Sattler & Hoge, 2006).

OK, But So What: Why Does Creativity Matter?

I cannot read any news these days without feeling a bit depressed about the problems facing the world. Economic problems, health problems, energy problems, political problems, violence, poverty, the list goes on. Certainly today's and tomorrow's complex problems will require creative

Video 9.3
The high-school reading teacher in this video provides six formats for book reports rather than requiring each student to present a traditional report. As you observe Ms. Walton's class, consider the divergent thinking involved in students' creative products.

ENHANCEDetext *video example*

FIGURE 9.5

A GRAPHIC ASSESSMENT OF THE CREATIVITY OF AN EIGHT-YEAR-OLD

The titles she gave her drawings, from left to right, are as follows: "Dracula," "one-eyed monster," "pumpkin," "Hula-Hoop," "poster," "wheelchair," "earth," "moon," "planet," "movie camera," "sad face," "picture," "stoplight," "beach ball," "the letter O," "car," "glasses."

Source: "A Graphic Assessment of the Creativity of an Eight-Year-Old," from The Torrance Test of Creative Thinking *by E. P. Torrance, 1986, 2000. Reprinted with permission of Scholastic Testing Service, Inc., Bensonville, IL 60106 USA.*

solutions. And creativity is important for an individual's psychological, physical, social, and career success. In addition, evidence shows that creativity and critical thinking are needed to prevent people or societies from being trapped by ideology and dogma (Ambrose & Sternberg, 2012; Plucker et al., 2004). Alene Starko (2014) described her recent visit to China, where educators all over that country kept asking her how to help their students become more creative, flexible thinkers. These Chinese students knock the top off of the international tests, but a focus on mastering academics comes at a cost to creativity and critical thinking. In fact, many teachers will tell you that the pressures of accountability and preparing their students for high-stakes tests have forced teaching for student creativity and creative teaching out of the classroom.

But we don't have to choose between understanding and creativity. Strategies that support creativity also support deep understanding in school subjects, because deep understanding comes from using the content in multiple ways and seeing different implications of the knowledge. Creativity also supports intrinsic motivation, engagement, and persistence in learning because creativity generates novelty and sparks interest (Starko, 2014).

What Are the Sources of Creativity?

Researchers have studied cognitive processes, personality factors, motivational patterns, and background experiences to explain creativity (Simonton, 2000). Teresa Amabile (1996, 2001) proposed a three-component model of creativity. Individuals or groups must have:

1. *Domain-relevant skills* including talents and competencies that are valuable for working in the domain, such as Michelangelo's skills in shaping stone, developed when he lived with a stonecutter's family as a child.

2. *Creativity-relevant processes* including work habits and personality traits such as John Irving's habit of working 10-hour days to write and rewrite and rewrite until he perfected his stories.
3. *Intrinsic task motivation* or a deep curiosity and fascination with the task. This aspect of creativity can be greatly influenced by teachers and parents who support autonomy, stimulate curiosity, encourage fantasy, and provide challenge.

CREATIVITY AND COGNITION. Having a rich store of knowledge in an area is the basis for creativity, but something more is needed. For many problems, that "something more" is the ability to see things in a new way—**restructuring** the problem, which leads to a sudden **insight**. Often this happens when a person has struggled with a problem or project and then sets it aside for a while. Some psychologists believe that time away allows for *incubation,* a kind of unconscious working through the problem. Actually, it is more complex than that. Incubation seems to help more on divergent thinking tasks than on verbal or visual tasks. Also incubation is more helpful when a longer preparation period precedes the individual's setting the problem aside (Sio & Ormerod, 2009). Leaving the problem for a time probably interrupts rigid ways of thinking so you can restructure your view of the situation and think more divergently (Gleitman, Fridlund, & Reisberg, 1999). Creativity requires extensive knowledge, flexibility, and the continual reorganizing of ideas. And we saw that motivation, persistence, and social support play important roles as well.

CREATIVITY AND DIVERSITY. As Dean Simonton said, even with years of research on creativity, "Psychologists still have a long way to go before they come anywhere close to understanding creativity in women and minorities" (2000, p. 156). Thus far, white males have been the focus of creativity research and writing over the years. However, patterns of creativity in other groups are complex—sometimes matching and sometimes diverging from patterns found in traditional research.

In another connection between creativity and culture, research suggests that being on the outside of mainstream society, being bilingual, or being exposed to other cultures might encourage creativity (Simonton, 2000). In fact, true innovators often break rules. "Creators have a desire to shake things up" (Winner, 2000, p. 167). And even for those who are not outside the mainstream, participation in multicultural experiences apparently fosters creativity. Angela Ka-Yee Leung and her colleagues (2008; Maddux, Leung, Chui, & Galinsky, 2009) reviewed theory and research, including experimental studies that exposed participants to information and images about other cultures. The researchers concluded that multicultural experiences support both creative processes, such as retrieving novel or unconventional ideas from memory, and creative performance, such as generating insightful solutions to problems. These effects are especially strong when people open themselves up to divergent ideas and when the situation does not emphasize finding quick, firm answers. Multicultural individuals are particularly willing to consider and build on unfamiliar ideas, entertain conflicting alternatives, and make unlikely connections between ideas (Leung & Chiu, 2010; Maddux & Galinsky, 2009). So even though your students may not be able to travel to Tibet or Turkey, they still could become more creative problem solvers if they learned about different cultures.

Creativity in the Classroom

STOP & THINK Consider these three students described by Alane Starko (2014, p. 3):

In first grade, Michelle was given an outline of a giant shark's mouth on a worksheet that asked, "What will our fishy friend eat next?" She dutifully colored several fish and boats, and then wrote the following explanation: "Once there was a shark named Peppy. One day he ate three fish, one jellyfish, and two boats. Before he ate the jellyfish, he made a peanut butter and jellyfish sandwich."

At 19, Juan was homeless and a senior in high school. One cold evening he thought that a warm space inside the school would be a more appealing sleeping place than any he could see. Getting into the building was no problem, but once he was inside a motion detector would make him immediately detectable to the guard on the floor below. Juan entered a storage room and carefully dislodged a pile of baseball bats. In the ensuing commotion, he located a comfortable sleeping place. The guard attributed the motion detector's outburst to the falling bats, and Juan slept until morning.

In 2003 Mark Zuckerberg hacked into Harvard's Web site and downloaded student ID photos into a Web site designed to compare student photos as "hot or not." The Web site lasted just a few days. Four months later he launched a new social networking Web site called "Thefacebook." The rest is history. •

Are these students creative? What might teachers do to foster or to inhibit this creative thinking? All too often, in the crush of day-to-day classroom life, teachers stifle creative ideas without realizing what they are doing. Teachers are in an excellent position to encourage or discourage creativity through their acceptance or rejection of the unusual and imaginative.

In addition to encouraging creativity through everyday interactions with students, teachers can try brainstorming. The basic tenet of **brainstorming** is to separate the process of creating ideas from the process of evaluating them because evaluation often inhibits creativity (Osborn, 1963). Evaluation, discussion, and criticism are postponed until all possible suggestions have been made. In this way, one idea inspires others; people do not withhold potentially creative solutions out of fear of criticism. Alene Starko (2014) gives these rules for brainstorming:

1. No criticism of any ideas until all the ideas are on the table. This includes both verbal and nonverbal criticism, so no eye-rolling or laughing.
2. Go for as many ideas as you can. Quantity may lead to quality as one idea inspires another.
3. Feel free to "hitchhike" on other ideas. This means that it's okay to borrow elements from ideas already on the table, or to make slight modifications of ideas already suggested.
4. Encourage wild ideas. Impossible, totally unworkable ideas may lead someone to think of other, more possible, more workable ideas. It's easier to take a wildly imaginative bad idea and tone it down to fit the constraints of reality than it is to take a boring bad idea and make it interesting enough to be worth thinking about.

Individuals as well as groups may benefit from brainstorming. In writing this book, for example, I have sometimes found it helpful to list all the different topics that could be covered in a chapter, then leave the list and return to it later to evaluate the ideas.

The Big C: Revolutionary Innovation

Ellen Winner (2000) describes the "big-C creativity" or innovation that establishes a new field or revolutionizes an old one. Even child prodigies do not necessarily become adult innovators. Prodigies have mastered well-established domains very early, but innovators change the entire domain. "Individuals who ultimately make creative breakthroughs tend from their earliest days to be explorers, innovators, and tinkerers. Often this adventurousness is interpreted as insubordination, though more fortunate tinkerers receive from teachers or peers some form of encouragement for their experimentation" (Gardner, 1993, pp. 32–33). What can parents and teachers do to encourage these tinkers and potential creators? Winner (2000) lists four dangers to avoid:

1. Avoid pushing so hard that the child's intrinsic passion to master a field becomes a craving for extrinsic rewards.
2. Avoid pushing so hard that the child later looks back on a missed childhood.
3. Avoid freezing the child into a safe, technically perfect way of performing that has led to lavish rewards.
4. Be aware of the psychological wounds that can follow when the child who can perform perfectly becomes the forgotten adult who can do nothing more than continue to perform perfectly—without ever creating something new.

Finally, teachers and parents can encourage students with outstanding abilities and creative talents to give back to the society; service learning, discussed in Chapter 10, is one opportunity.

The *Guidelines: Applying and Encouraging Creativity* on the next page, adapted from Fleith (2000) and Sattler and Hoge (2006), describes other possibilities for encouraging creativity.

GUIDELINES
Applying and Encouraging Creativity

Accept and encourage divergent thinking.

Examples

1. During class discussion, ask: "Can anyone suggest a different way of looking at this question?"
2. Reinforce attempts at unusual solutions to problems, even if the final product is not perfect.
3. Offer choices in topics for projects or modes of presentation (written, oral, visual or graphic, using technology).

Tolerate dissent.

Examples

1. Ask students to support dissenting opinions.
2. Make sure nonconforming students receive an equal share of classroom privileges and rewards.

Encourage students to trust their own judgment.

Examples

1. When students ask questions you think they can answer, rephrase or clarify the questions and direct them back to the students.
2. Give ungraded assignments from time to time.

Emphasize that everyone is capable of creativity in some form.

Examples

1. Avoid describing the feats of great artists or inventors as if they were superhuman accomplishments.
2. Recognize creative efforts in each student's work. Have a separate grade for originality on some assignments.

Provide time, space, and materials to support creative projects.

Examples

1. Collect "found" materials for collages and creations—buttons, stones, shells, paper, fabric, beads, seeds, drawing tools, clay—try flea markets and friends for donations. Have mirrors and pictures for drawing faces.
2. Make a well-lighted space available where children can work on projects, leave them, and come back to finish them.
3. Follow up on memorable occasions (field trips, news events, holidays) with opportunities to draw, write, or make music.

Be a stimulus for creative thinking.

Examples

1. Use class brainstorming sessions whenever possible.
2. Model creative problem solving by suggesting unusual solutions for class problems.
3. Encourage students to delay judging a particular suggestion for solving a problem until all the possibilities have been considered.

Capitalize on technology (Starko, 2014).

Examples

1. Have students use free apps such as Spider Scribe (spiderscribe.net) to create visual maps of ideas and share their ideas with others.
2. Spend the 5 minutes before lunch or at the end of class creatively by having students practice divergent thinking using Genius on the Go on their iPhone, iPod, or iPad.
3. Encourage students to create a Facebook page for a literary or historical figure using Fakebook from Classtools.net. Go to classtools.net/FB/home-page.
4. Use Wordle (wordle.net) or tagxedo (tagxedo.com) to create word clouds showing the frequency of words used in a particular text or the student's writing. See Figure 9.6 for a word cloud of this chapter made with Wordle.

For more ideas, see ecap.crc.illinois.edu and search for "creativity."

FIGURE 9.6

A WORD CLOUD OF THIS CHAPTER

In this word cloud, the frequency of the words in this chapter is indicated by the size of the word, so you can see that "students," "problem," and "strategies" appear most often.

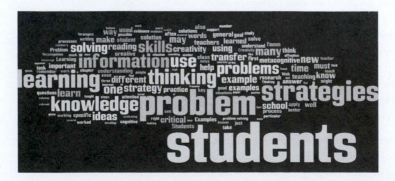

We may not all be revolutionary in our creativity, but we all can be experts in one area—critical thinking.

ENHANCEDetext *self-check*

CRITICAL THINKING AND ARGUMENTATION

Critical thinking skills are useful in almost every life situation—even in evaluating the media ads that constantly bombard us. When you see a group of gorgeous people extolling the virtues of a particular brand of orange juice as they frolic in skimpy bathing suits, you must decide if sex appeal is a relevant factor in choosing a fruit drink (remember Pavlovian advertising from Chapter 7). A formal definition of **critical thinking** is "the intellectually disciplined process of actively and skillfully conceptualizing, applying, analyzing, synthesizing, and/or evaluating information gathered from, or generated by, observation, experience, reflection, reasoning, or communication, as a guide to belief and action" (Scriven & Paul, 2013). Table 9.3 describes the characteristics of a critical thinker.

Many educational psychologists believe that good thinking can and should be developed in school. One way to develop students' thinking is to create a *culture of thinking* in your classrooms (Perkins, Jay, & Tishman, 1993). This means that there is a spirit of inquisitiveness and critical thinking, a respect for reasoning and creativity, and an expectation that students will learn to make and counter arguments based on evidence.

One Model of Critical Thinking: Paul and Elder

What is involved in critical thinking? Richard Paul and Linda Elder (2014; Elder & Paul, 2012) suggest the model in Figure 9.7 on the next page as a way of describing what critical thinkers do. As you can see, the center of critical thinking is reasoning, which is drawing conclusions based on reasons. When we reason, we have a purpose and a point of view. We reason based on certain assumptions that lead to implications for our conclusions. We use information (data, facts, experiences, etc.) to make inferences and judgments based on key concepts or ideas, all leading to answers to the main problem or question indicated in our original purpose. But to reason well—to think critically—we should apply standards such as clarity, accuracy, logic, and fairness, as indicated in Figure 9.7. With practice in clear, accurate, logical (etc.) reasoning, we develop intellectual traits such as humility, integrity, perseverance, and confidence.

So how would you develop critical thinking in your classes? No matter what approach you use to develop critical thinking, it is important to follow up with additional practice. One lesson is not enough. For example, if your class examined a particular historical document to determine if it reflected bias or propaganda, you should follow up by analyzing other written historical documents, contemporary advertisements, or news stories. Unless thinking skills become overlearned

Connect and Extend to PRAXIS II®

Thinking Skills (II, A1)
A nearly universal goal of educational programs across the country is the development of thinking skills. Describe what a teacher can do to cultivate these skills in the classroom. Search for *Teaching Thinking Skills* at edutopia.org for more ideas.

TABLE 9.3 • What Is a Critical Thinker?

Assuming that critical thinking is reasonable, reflective thinking focused on deciding what to believe or do, a critical thinker:

1. Is open minded and mindful of alternatives.
2. Tries to be well informed.
3. Judges well the credibility of sources.
4. Identifies conclusions, reasons, and assumptions.
5. Judges well the quality of an argument, including the acceptability of its reasons, assumptions, and evidence.
6. Can well develop and defend a reasonable position.
7. Asks appropriate clarifying questions.
8. Formulates plausible hypotheses; plans experiments well.
9. Defines terms in a way appropriate for the context.
10. Draws conclusions when warranted, but with caution.
11. Integrates all items in this list when deciding what to believe or do.

Source: Adapted from Robert H. Ennis: http://faculty.ed.uiuc.edu/rhennis/index.html

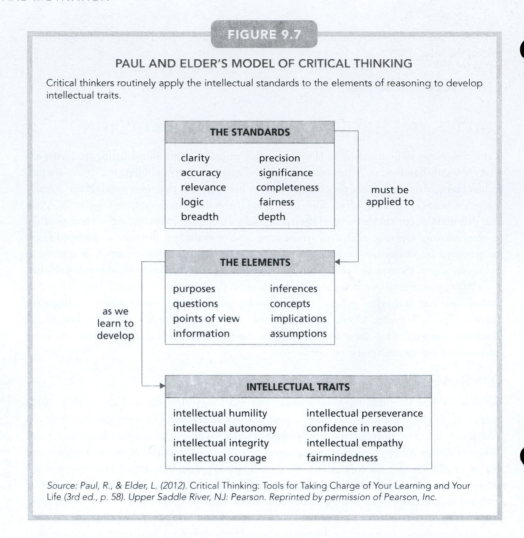

FIGURE 9.7

PAUL AND ELDER'S MODEL OF CRITICAL THINKING

Critical thinkers routinely apply the intellectual standards to the elements of reasoning to develop intellectual traits.

THE STANDARDS

clarity	precision
accuracy	significance
relevance	completeness
logic	fairness
breadth	depth

must be applied to

THE ELEMENTS

purposes	inferences
questions	concepts
points of view	implications
information	assumptions

as we learn to develop

INTELLECTUAL TRAITS

intellectual humility	intellectual perseverance
intellectual autonomy	confidence in reason
intellectual integrity	intellectual empathy
intellectual courage	fairmindedness

Source: Paul, R., & Elder, L. (2012). Critical Thinking: Tools for Taking Charge of Your Learning and Your Life (3rd ed., p. 58). Upper Saddle River, NJ: Pearson. Reprinted by permission of Pearson, Inc.

and relatively automatic, they are not likely to be transferred to new situations (Mayer & Wittrock, 2006). Instead, students will use these skills only to complete the lesson in social studies, not to evaluate the claims made by friends, politicians, car manufacturers, or diet plans.

Applying Critical Thinking in Specific Subjects

The characteristics of critical thinkers in Table 9.3 on the previous page would be useful in any subject. But some critical thinking skills are specific to a particular subject. For example, to teach history, Jeffrey Nokes and his colleagues investigated (1) using traditional texts versus multiple readings and (2) direct teaching of critical thinking skills versus no direct teaching of critical thinking skills (Nokes, Dole, & Hacker, 2007). The multiple texts included historical fiction, excerpts from speeches, government documents, photographs, charts and historical data, and short sections from texts. The history critical thinking skills taught were:

- **Sourcing:** Looking at the source of the document before reading and using that information to help interpret and make inferences about the reading. Is the source biased? Can I trust it?
- **Corroboration:** Making connections between the information in different texts and noting similarities and contradictions.
- **Contextualization:** Understanding the time, place, people, and culture that is the context for the event, with all the political and social forces that might be operating.

Students who learned with multiple texts instead of traditional textbooks actually learned more history content. Also, students were able to learn and apply two of the three critical thinking skills, *sourcing* and *corroboration,* when they were *directly taught* how to use the skills. Contextualization

Video 9.4
The students in this video are presenting various formulas for calculating the volume of a sphere. Notice the critical thinking skills involved as students analyze and evaluate formulas presented by classmates. Also notice the role of the teacher's questions.

ENHANCEDetext *video example*

proved more difficult, perhaps because the students lacked the background knowledge to fill in contextual information. So critical thinking for specific subjects can be taught along with the subject. But as you can see in the *Point/Counterpoint* on the next page, educators don't agree about the best way to foster critical thinking in schools.

Argumentation

The ability to construct and support a position is essential in science, politics, persuasive writing, and critical thinking, to name just a few areas. The heart of **argumentation** (the process of constructing and critiquing arguments, and debating claims) is supporting your position with evidence and understanding and then refuting your opponent's claims and evidence. Children are not good at argumentation, adolescents are a bit better, and adults are better still, but not perfect. Children don't pay very much attention to the claims and evidence of the other person in the debate. Adolescents understand that their opponent in a debate has a different position, but they tend to spend much more time presenting their own position than they do trying to understand and critique their opponent's claims. It is as if the adolescents believe "winning an argument" means making a better presentation, but they don't appreciate the need to understand and weaken the opponent's claims (Kuhn & Dean, 2004; Nussbaum, 2011).

Children and adolescents focus more on their own positions because it is too demanding to remember and process both their own and their opponent's claims and evidence at the same time—the *cognitive load* is just too much. In addition, argumentation skills are not natural. They take both time and instruction to learn (Kuhn, Goh, Iordanou, & Shaenfield, 2008; Udell, 2007).

But what has to be learned? To make a case while understanding and refuting the opponent's case, you must be aware of what you are saying, what your opponent is saying, and how to refute your opponent's claims. This takes planning, evaluating how the plan is going, reflecting on what the opponent has said, and changing strategies as needed—in other words, *metacognitive knowledge and skills for argumentation*. Deanna Kuhn and her colleagues (2008) designed a process for developing metacognitive argumentation skills. They presented a sixth-grade class with the following dilemma.

> The Costa family has moved to the edge of town from far away Greece with their 11-year-old son Nick. Nick was a good student and soccer player back home in Greece. Nick's parents have decided that in this new place, they want to keep Nick at home with them, and not have him be at the school with the other children. The family speaks only Greek, and they think Nick will do better if he sticks to his family's language and doesn't try to learn English. They say they can teach him everything he needs at home. What should happen? Is it okay for the Costa family to live in the town but keep Nick at home, or should they be required to send their son to the town school like all the other families do? (p. 1313)

Based on their initial position on the dilemma, the 28 students in the class were divided into two groups—"Nick should go to school" or "Nick should be taught at home." These two groups were divided again into same-gender pairs and all the "Nick should go to school" pairs moved to a room next door to their class. For about 25 minutes, each pair from one side "debated" a pair in the other room using instant messaging (IM). Later in the week the process was repeated, but with different pairs debating. In all, there were seven IM debates, so every "go to school" pair debated every "stay home" pair over several weeks. After four of the seven sessions, the pairs were given a transcript of the dialogue from their last debate, along with worksheets that scaffolded their *reflection* on their own arguments or the arguments of their opponents. The students evaluated their arguments and tried to improve them, with some adults coaching. These reflective sessions were repeated three times.

Next, there was a "showdown" debate—the entire "go to school" team debated the entire "stay home" team via one computer per team and a smart board. For this debate, half of each team prepared as experts on their position and half as experts *on the opponent's arguments*. After winter break and again after spring break, the whole process was repeated with new dilemmas.

You can see that the study employed three techniques, supported by technology, to help students become more metacognitive about argumentation. First, they had to work in pairs to collaborate and agree on each communication with the opposing pair. Second, the researchers provided the pairs with transcripts of parts of their dialogue with the opponents so the partners could reflect on

POINT/COUNTERPOINT
Should Schools Teach Critical Thinking and Problem Solving?

The question of whether schools should focus on process or content, problem-solving skills or core knowledge, higher-order thinking skills or academic information has been debated for years. Some educators suggest that students must be taught how to think and solve problems, while other educators assert that students cannot learn to "think" in the abstract. They must be thinking about something—some content. Should teachers focus on knowledge or thinking?

POINT **Problem solving and higher-order thinking can and should be taught.** An article in the April, 28, 1995, issue of the *Chronicle of Higher Education* makes this claim:

> Critical thinking is at the heart of effective reading, writing, speaking, and listening. It enables us to link together mastery of content with such diverse goals as self-esteem, self-discipline, multicultural education, effective cooperative learning, and problem solving. It enables all instructors and administrators to raise the level of their own teaching and thinking. (p. A-71)

Closer to home for you, Peter Facione (2011) claims that critical thinking is related to GPA in college and to reading comprehension. How can students learn to think critically? Some educators recommend teaching thinking skills directly with widely used techniques such as the Productive Thinking Program or CoRT (Cognitive Research Trust). Other researchers argue that learning computer programing languages will improve students' minds and teach them how to think logically. Finally, because expert readers automatically apply certain metacognitive strategies, many educators and psychologists recommend directly teaching novice or poor readers how to apply these strategies. Michael Pressley's Good Strategy User model (Pressley & Harris, 2006) and Palincsar and Brown's (1984) reciprocal teaching approach are successful examples of direct teaching of metacognitive skills. Research on these approaches generally shows improvements in achievement and comprehension for students of all ages who participate (Pressley & Harris, 2006; Rosenshine & Meister, 1994).

COUNTERPOINT **Thinking and problem-solving skills do not transfer.** According to E. D. Hirsch, a vocal critic of critical thinking programs:

> But whether such direct instruction of critical thinking or self-monitoring does in fact improve performance is a subject of debate in the research community. For instance, the research regarding critical thinking is not reassuring. Instruction in critical thinking has been going on in several countries for over a hundred years. Yet researchers found that students from nations as varied as Israel, Germany, Australia, the Philippines, and the United States, including those who have been taught critical thinking continue to fall into logical fallacies. (1996, p. 136)

The CoRT program has been used in over 5,000 classrooms in 10 nations. But Polson and Jeffries (1985) report that "after 10 years of widespread use we have no adequate evidence concerning the effectiveness of the program" (p. 445). In addition, Mayer and Wittrock (1996) note that field studies of problem solving in real situations show that people often fail to apply the mathematical problem-solving approaches they learn in school to actual problems encountered in the grocery store or home.

Even though educators have been more successful in teaching metacognitive skills, critics still caution that there are times when such teaching hinders rather than helps learning. Robert Siegler (1993) suggests that teaching self-monitoring strategies to low-achieving students can interfere with the students' development of adaptive strategies. Forcing students to use the strategies of experts may put too much burden on working memory as the students struggle to use an unfamiliar strategy and miss the meaning or content of the lesson. For example, rather than teach students strategies for figuring out words from context, it may be helpful for students to focus on learning more vocabulary words.

BEWARE OF EITHER/OR

One clear message from current research on learning is that both subject-specific knowledge and learning strategies are important. Students today need to be critical consumers of all kinds of knowledge, but critical thinking alone is not enough. Students need the knowledge, vocabulary, and concepts to understand what they are reading, seeing, and hearing. The best teachers can teach math content and how to learn math at the same time or can teach history and how to critically assess history sources.

the discussions. Third, the dialogues were conducted via IM, so the pairs had a permanent record of the discussion.

So what happened? The pairs, IM, and reflection strategies were successful for most students in helping them take into account the opponent's position and create strategies for rebutting the opponent's arguments. Working in pairs seemed to be especially helpful. When adolescents and even adults work alone, they often do not create effective counterarguments and rebuttals (Kuhn & Franklin, 2006).

ENHANCEDetext *self-check*

TEACHING FOR TRANSFER

STOP & THINK Think back for a moment to a class in one of your high school subjects that you have not studied in college. Imagine the teacher, the room, the textbook. Now remember what you actually learned in class. If it was a science class, what were some of the formulas you learned? Oxidation reduction? Boyle's law? •

If you are like most of us, you may remember *that* you learned these things, but you will not be quite sure exactly *what* you learned. Were those hours wasted? This question relates to the important topic of learning transfer. Let's begin with a definition of *transfer*.

Whenever something previously learned influences current learning or when solving an earlier problem affects how you solve a new problem, **transfer** has occurred. Erik De Corte (2003) calls transfer "the productive use of cognitive tools and motivations" (p. 142), and Chi and VanLehn (2012) describe transfer as the ability of students to treat a new situation, problem, concept, or challenge as similar to one they have experienced before. So *transfer* is doing something new (productive), not just reproducing a previous application of the tools. If students learn a mathematical principle in one class and use it to solve a physics problem days or weeks later in another class, then transfer has taken place. However, the effect of past learning on present learning is not always positive. Functional fixedness and response set (described earlier in this chapter) are examples of negative transfer because they are attempts to apply familiar but *inappropriate* strategies to a new situation.

Transfer has several dimensions (Barnett & Ceci, 2002). You can transfer learning across subjects (math skills used in science problems), across physical contexts (learned in school, used on the job), across social contexts (learned alone, used with your family or team), across time periods (learned in college, used months or years later), across functions (learned for academics, used for hobbies and recreation), and across modalities (learned from watching the Home and Garden cable channel, used to discuss ideas for a patio with a landscape architect). So transfer can refer to many different examples of applying knowledge and skills beyond where, when, and how you learned them.

The Many Views of Transfer

Transfer has been a focus of research in educational psychology for over 100 years. After all, the productive use of knowledge, skills, and motivations across a lifetime is a fundamental goal of education (Goldstone & Day, 2012; Shaffer, 2010). Early work focused on specific transfer of skills and the general transfer of *mental discipline* gained from studying rigorous subjects such as Greek or mathematics. But in 1924, E. L. Thorndike demonstrated that no mental discipline benefit is derived from learning Greek. Learning Greek just helps you learn more Greek. So, thanks to Thorndike, you were not required to take Greek in high school.

More recently, researchers have distinguished between the automatic, direct use of skills such as reading or writing in everyday applications and the thoughtful transfer of knowledge and strategies to arrive at creative solutions to problems (Bereiter, 1995; Bransford & Schwartz, 1999). Automatic transfer probably benefits from practice in different situations, but thoughtful transfer requires more than practice. Michelene Chi and Kurt VanLehn (2012) describe thoughtful transfer as involving two processes—*initial learning* and *reusing or applying* what was learned. For thoughtful transfer to succeed, students must first actually learn the underlying principle or concept, not

Connect and Extend to PRAXIS II®

Transfer of Learning
Successful transfer of learning from the school to other contexts is evidence of superior instruction. What can teachers do to optimize transfer of knowledge and skills to the broader world?

TABLE 9.4 • **Kinds of Transfer**

	DIRECT APPLICATION	PREPARATION FOR FUTURE LEARNING
Definition	Automatic transfer of highly practiced skill	Conscious application of abstract knowledge to a new situation
		Productive use of cognitive tools and motivations
Key Conditions	Extensive practice	Mindful focus on abstracting a principle, main idea, or procedure that can be used in many situations
	Variety of settings and conditions	Learning in powerful teaching–learning environments
	Overlearning to automaticity	
Examples	Driving many different cars	Applying KWL or READS strategies
	Finding your gate in an airport	Applying procedures from math in designing a page layout for the school newspaper

just the surface procedure or algorithm. So, essential to thoughtful transfer in the initial learning stage is *mindful abstraction,* which is the deliberate identification of a principle, main idea, strategy, or procedure that is not tied to one specific problem or situation but could apply to many. Such an abstraction becomes part of your metacognitive knowledge, available to guide future learning and problem solving. This may remind you of our discussion in Chapter 8 about how the way you learn something in the first place (through deeper processing) affects how well you remember it later. Bransford and Schwartz (1999) added another key—a resource-rich environment that supports productive, appropriate transfer. Table 9.4 summarizes the types of transfer.

Teaching for Positive Transfer

Here is a great perspective on transfer from David Perkins and Gavriel Salomon (2012):

> Schools are supposed to be stopovers in life, not ends in themselves. The information, skills, and understandings they offer are knowledge-to-go, not just to use on site. To be sure, often Monday's topics most conspicuously serve the Tuesday problem set, the Friday quiz, or the exam at the end of the year. However, in principle those topics are an investment toward thriving in family, civic, cultural, and professional lives. (p. 248)

Years of research and experience show that students will not always take advantage of knowledge-to-go. They may (seem to) learn new concepts, problem-solving procedures, and learning strategies Monday, but they may not use them for the year-end exam or even Friday unless prompted or guided. For example, studies of real-world mathematics show that people do not always apply math procedures learned in school to solve practical problems in their homes or at grocery stores (Lave, 1988; Lave & Wenger, 1991). This happens because learning is *situated*—tied to specific situations. Because knowledge is learned as a tool to solve particular problems, we may not realize that the knowledge is relevant when we encounter a problem that seems different, at least on the surface (Driscoll, 2005; Singley & Anderson, 1989). How can you make sure your students will use what they learn, even when situations change?

WHAT IS WORTH LEARNING? First, you must answer the question "What is worth learning?" The learning of basic skills such as reading, writing, computing, cooperating, and speaking will definitely transfer to other situations, because these skills are necessary for later work both in and out of school—writing job applications, reading novels, paying bills, working on a team, locating and evaluating health care services, among others. All later learning depends on positive transfer of these basic skills to new situations.

Teachers must also be aware of what the future is likely to hold for their students, both as a group and as individuals. What will society require of them as adults? As a child growing up in Texas in the 1950s and 1960s, I studied nothing about computers, even though my father was a computer systems analyst; yet now I spend hours at my Mac each day. Back then I learned to use a slide rule. Now, calculators and computers have made this skill obsolete. My mom encouraged me to take advanced math and physics instead of typing in high school. Those were great classes, but I struggle with typing every day at my computer—who knew? Undoubtedly, changes as extreme and unpredictable as these await the students you will teach. For this reason, the general transfer of principles, attitudes, learning strategies, self-motivation, time management skills, and problem solving will be just as important for your students as the specific transfer of basic skills.

HOW CAN TEACHERS HELP? For basic skills, greater transfer can also be ensured by overlearning, practicing a skill past the point of mastery. Many of the basic facts students learn in elementary school, such as the multiplication tables, are traditionally overlearned. Overlearning helps students develop automated basic skills as we saw in Chapter 8.

For higher-level transfer, students must first learn and understand. Students will be more likely to transfer knowledge to new situations if they have been actively involved in the learning process. Strategies include having students compare and contrast two examples, then identify the underlying principles; asking student to explain to themselves or each other the worked-out examples provided by the teacher; or identify for each step in a problem solution the underlying principle at work (Chi & VanLehn, 2012). Students should be encouraged to form abstractions that they will apply later, so they know transfer is an important goal. It also helps if students form deep connections between the new knowledge and their existing structures of knowledge as well as connections to their everyday experiences (Perkins & Salomon, 2012; Pugh & Phillips,, 2011). Erik De Corte (2003) believes that teachers support transfer, the productive use of cognitive tools and motivations, when they create powerful teaching–learning environments using these design principles:

- The environments should support constructive learning processes in all students.
- The environments should encourage the development of student self-regulation, so that teachers gradually give over more and more responsibilities to the students.
- Learning should involve interaction and collaboration.
- Learners should deal with problems that have personal meaning for them, that are similar to those they will face in the future.
- The classroom culture should encourage students to become aware of and develop their cognitive and motivational processes. To be productive users of these tools, students must know about and value them.

Chapters 10 to 13 delve in depth about how to support constructive learning, motivation, self-regulation, collaboration, and self-awareness in all students.

One last kind of transfer is especially important for students—the transfer of the *learning strategies* we encountered earlier. Learning strategies are meant to be applied across a wide range of situations.

STAGES OF TRANSFER FOR STRATEGIES. Gary Phye (1992, 2001; Phye & Sanders, 1994) describes three stages in developing strategic transfer. In the *acquisition phase,* students should not only receive instruction about a strategy and how to use it, but also rehearse the strategy and practice being aware of when and how they are using it. In the *retention phase,* more practice with feedback helps students hone their strategy use. In the *transfer phase,* students should be given new problems that they can solve with the same strategy, even though the problems appear different on the surface. To enhance motivation, teachers should point out to students how using the strategy will help them solve many problems and accomplish different tasks. These steps help build both procedural and self-regulatory knowledge—*how* to use the strategy as well as *when and why.*

For all students, there is a positive relationship between using learning strategies and academic gains such as high school GPA and retention in college (Robbins, Le, & Lauver, 2005). Some students will learn productive strategies on their own, but all students can benefit from direct teaching, modeling, and practice of learning strategies and study skills. This is one important way to prepare all of your students for the future. Newly mastered concepts, principles, and strategies must be

GUIDELINES
Family and Community Partnerships

Promoting Transfer

Keep families informed about their child's curriculum so they can support learning.

Examples

1. At the beginning of units or major projects, send a letter summarizing the key goals, a few of the major assignments, and some common problems students have in learning the material for that unit.
2. Ask parents for suggestions about how their child's interests could be connected to the curriculum topics.
3. Invite parents to school for an evening of "strategy learning." Have the students teach their family members one of the strategies they have learned in school.

Give families ideas for how they might encourage their children to practice, extend, or apply learning from school.

Examples

1. To extend writing, ask parents to encourage their children to write letters or e-mails to companies or civic organizations asking for information or free products. Provide a shell letter form for structure and ideas, and include addresses of companies that provide free samples or information.
2. Ask family members to include their children in some projects that require measurement, halving or doubling recipes, or estimating costs.

3. Suggest that students work with grandparents to do a family memory book. Combine historical research and writing.

Show connections between learning in school and life outside school.

Examples

1. Ask families to talk about and show how they use the skills their children are learning in their jobs, hobbies, or community involvement projects.
2. Ask family members to come to class to demonstrate how they use reading, writing, science, math, or other knowledge in their work.

Make families partners in practicing learning strategies.

Examples

1. Focus on one learning strategy at a time. Ask families to simply remind their children to use a particular strategy with homework that week.
2. Develop a lending library of books and videotapes to teach families about learning strategies.
3. Give parents a copy of the *Guidelines: Becoming an Expert Student* on page 338, rewritten for your grade level.

---

applied in a wide variety of situations and with many types of problems (Z. Chen & Mo, 2004). Positive transfer is encouraged when skills are practiced under authentic conditions, similar to those that will exist when the skills are needed later. Students can learn to write by corresponding with e-mail pen pals in other countries. They can learn historical research methods by studying their own family history. Some of these applications should involve complex, ill-defined, unstructured problems, because many of the problems to be faced in later life, both in school and out, will not come to students complete with instructions. The Guidelines: Family and Community Partnerships give ideas for enlisting the support of families in encouraging transfer.

ENHANCEDetext *self-check*

SUMMARY

• **Metacognition (pp. 328–331)**

What are the three metacognitive skills? The three metacognitive skills used to regulate thinking and learning are planning, monitoring, and evaluating. Planning involves deciding how much time to give to a task, which strategies to use, how to start, and so on. Monitoring is the real-time awareness of "how I'm doing." Evaluating involves making judgments about the processes and outcomes of thinking and learning and acting on those judgments.

What are some sources of individual differences in metacognition? Individual differences in metacognition may result from different paces of development (maturation) or biological differences among learners. For example, young students may not be able to understand a lesson's purpose as well as older students.

How can teachers help students develop metacognitive knowledge and skills? With younger students, teachers can help students "look inside" to identify what they do to read, write, or learn better. Systems such as KWL can help, if teachers demonstrate, explain, and model the strategy. For older students, teachers can build self-reflective questions into assignments and learning materials.

- **Learning Strategies (pp. 331–339)**

What are learning strategies? Learning strategies are a special kind of procedural knowledge—*knowing how* to do something. A strategy for learning might include mnemonics to remember key terms, skimming to identify the organization, and then writing answers to possible essay questions. Use of strategies and tactics reflects metacognitive knowledge.

What key functions do learning strategies play? Learning strategies help students become cognitively engaged—focus attention on the relevant, important aspects of the material. Second, they encourage students to invest effort, make connections, elaborate, translate, organize, and reorganize to think and process deeply; the greater the practice and processing, the stronger the learning. Finally, strategies help students regulate and monitor their own learning—keep track of what is making sense and notice when a new approach is needed.

Describe some procedures for developing learning strategies. Expose students to a number of different strategies, not only general learning strategies but also very specific tactics, such as the graphic strategies. Teach conditional knowledge about when, where, and why to use various strategies. Develop motivation to use the strategies and tactics by showing students how their learning and performance can be improved. Provide direct instruction in content knowledge needed to use the strategies.

When will students apply learning strategies? If they have appropriate strategies, students will apply them if they are faced with a task that requires good strategies, value doing well on that task, think the effort to apply the strategies will be worthwhile, and believe that they can succeed using the strategies. Also, to apply deep processing strategies, students must assume that knowledge is complex and takes time to learn and that learning requires their own active efforts.

- **Problem Solving (pp. 339–349)**

What is problem solving? Problem solving is both general and domain specific. Also, problems can range from *well structured* to *ill structured,* depending on how clear-cut the goal is and how much structure is provided for solving the problem. General problem-solving strategies usually include the steps of *identifying* the problem, *setting goals, exploring* possible solutions and consequences, *acting,* and finally *evaluating* the outcome. Both general and specific problem solving are valuable and necessary.

Why is the representation stage of problem solving so important? To represent the problem accurately, you must understand both the whole problem and its discrete elements. Schema training may improve this ability. The problem-solving process follows entirely different paths, depending on what representation and goal are chosen. If your representation of the problem suggests an immediate solution, the task is done; the new problem is recognized as a "disguised" version of an old problem with a clear solution. But if there is no existing way of solving the problem or if the activated schema fails, then students must search for a solution. The application of algorithms and heuristics—such as means-ends analysis, working-backward, analogical thinking, and verbalization—may help students solve problems.

Describe factors that can interfere with problem solving. Factors that hinder problem solving include functional fixedness or rigidity (response set). These disallow the flexibility needed to represent problems accurately and to have insight into solutions. Also, as we make decisions and judgments, we may overlook important information because we base judgments on what seems representative of a category (representativeness heuristic) or what is available in memory (availability heuristic), then pay attention only to information that confirms our choices (confirmation bias) so that we hold on to beliefs, even in the face of contradictory evidence (belief perseverance).

What are the differences between expert and novice knowledge in a given area? Expert problem solvers have a rich store of declarative, procedural, and conditional knowledge. They organize this knowledge around general principles or patterns that apply to large classes of problems. They work faster, remember relevant information, and monitor their progress better than novices.

- **Creativity: What It Is and Why It Matters (pp. 350–355)**

What is creativity, and how is it assessed? Creativity is a process that involves independently restructuring problems to see things in new, imaginative ways. Creativity is difficult to measure, but tests of divergent thinking can assess originality, fluency, and flexibility. Originality is usually determined statistically. To be original, a response must be given by fewer than 5 or 10 people out of every 100 who take the test. Fluency is the number of different responses. The number of different categories of responses measures flexibility.

What can teachers do to support creativity in the classroom? Multicultural experiences appear to help students think flexibly and creatively. Teachers can encourage creativity in their interactions with students by accepting unusual, imaginative answers; modeling divergent thinking; using brainstorming; and tolerating dissent.

- **Critical Thinking and Argumentation (pp. 355–359)**

What is critical thinking? Critical thinking skills include defining and clarifying the problem, making judgments about the consistency and adequacy of the information related to a problem, and drawing conclusions. No matter what approach you use to develop critical thinking, it is important to follow up activities with additional practice. One lesson is not enough—overlearning will help students use critical thinking in their own lives.

What is argumentation? The heart of argumentation (the process of debating a claim with someone else) is supporting your position with evidence and understanding, and then refuting your opponent's claims and evidence. Argumentation skills are not natural. They take both time and instruction to learn. It is especially difficult for children and adolescents to pay attention to, understand, and refute the opponent's position with evidence.

- **Teaching for Transfer (pp. 359–362)**

What is transfer? Transfer occurs when a rule, fact, or skill learned in one situation is applied in another situation; for example, applying rules of punctuation to write a job application letter. Transfer also involves applying to new problems the principles learned in other, often dissimilar situations.

What are some dimensions of transfer? Information can be transferred across a variety of contexts. Some examples include transfer from one subject to another, one physical location to another, or one function to another. These types of transfer make it possible to use skills developed in one area for many other tasks.

Distinguish between automatic and mindful, intentional transfer. Spontaneous application of well-learned knowledge and skills is automatic transfer. Mindful, intentional transfer involves reflection and conscious application of abstract knowledge to new situations. Learning environments should support active constructive learning, self-regulation, collaboration, and awareness of cognitive tools and motivational processes. In addition, students should deal with problems that have meaning in their lives. In addition, teachers can help students transfer learning strategies by teaching strategies directly, providing practice with feedback, and then expanding the application of the strategies to new and unfamiliar situations.

PRACTICE USING WHAT YOU HAVE LEARNED

To access and complete the exercises, click the link under the images below.

Metacognition

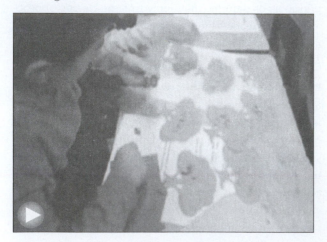

ENHANCEDetext *application exercise*

Problem Solving, Creativity, and Critical Thinking

ENHANCEDetext *application exercise*

KEY TERMS

CONNECT AND EXTEND TO LICENSURE

MULTIPLE-CHOICE QUESTIONS

1. What higher-order knowledge can make the difference between how well and quickly one's students learn material?
   A. Declarative
   B. Rote
   C. Metacognition
   D. Procedural

2. Knowing the importance of metacognition, Joanna Pappas decided she would try to focus her young students' attention on their own thinking skills. Joanna knew by having her students "think" about their thinking they would eventually increase their metacognitive skills. Which one of the following strategies should Joanna employ?
   A. Insight
   B. A KWL chart
   C. An algorithm
   D. Overlearning

3. Teachers often neglect to teach their students about when, where, and why they should use various strategies. A strategy is more apt to be retained and appropriately used when educators directly teach which type of knowledge?
   A. Declarative
   B. Procedural
   C. Self-regulatory
   D. Rote

4. Fourth-graders Richard and Bruce sat on the stoop outside of the school. They had missed their bus and now had to make the decision whether to walk taking a short-cut or just wait until their mothers notice they had not arrived home. "I think we should start walking on the path, and maybe we will get there before they notice we missed the bus."

"I think we should wait. If we walk on the path and our mothers come to get us, they won't see us, and they'll worry. Missing the bus is bad enough. If my mom can't find me, she'll be really mad!" In what type of problem solving are the two boys engaged?
   A. Heuristic
   B. Schema-driven
   C. Algorithm
   D. CAPS

CONSTRUCTED-RESPONSE QUESTIONS

Case

Karen Slagle walked away from her friends on the playground. She had just had an argument over who would win the spot as class president. "I know my brother will win. He has more friends and that equals more votes."

"Karen, you can't be serious. What about the issues such as school policies and procedures?"

"Those issues don't matter. Regina Hoyt won because she was popular last year. The only real issue is popularity."

"What about the year before last when the captain of the football team lost because his campaign didn't deal with anything but sports issues?"

"That was a fluke. Look at our freshman year. That popular basketball player won."

5. How is Karen Slagle's argument an example of confirmation bias?

6. In the current argument Karen Slagle is not practicing critical thinking. What types of strategies do critical thinkers employ?

ENHANCEDetext *licensure exam*

TEACHERS' **CASEBOOK**

WHAT WOULD THEY DO? UNCRITICAL THINKING

Here is how some practicing teachers would help students learn to critically evaluate the information they find on the Internet.

PAUL DRAGIN—ESL Teacher, Grades 9–12
Columbus East High School, Columbus, OH

This common problem does not have an easy fix. A few years ago, a student completed a research paper about 9/11, and the paper was filled with conspiracy theories that the student reported as fact. This dramatic example of undocumented, unsubstantiated research opened my eyes to the need to teach research methods far more explicitly to my students. Here is my general strategy to help ensure more quality research: After allowing the students to explore using Google and other common search engines to get some familiarity with their topic, I direct them to a reference database such as EBSCOhost or ProQuest, which, in our city, can be accessed with a library card via the public library Web site. Limiting the databases they can use reduces the likelihood that inaccurate and highly biased information makes its way into their reports. Demonstrating to them the difference between research-based, scholarly information and general information can go a long way in producing a product that demonstrates actual research.

SARA VINCENT—Special Education Teacher
Langley High School, McLean, VA

The Internet is a useful tool for students, but it is filled with a plethora of bad information. Luckily, the teacher in the described scenario can fix the problem before the students' submission of their final drafts. As an English teacher, I often encounter this problem but find that the majority of the students will comply if I set strict citation guidelines. After returning the first drafts to the students, I devote the next lesson to using credible sources rather than using less-reliable sources. I show examples of absurd claims from Internet Web sites. I also show the students how to find appropriate information. The students then exchange papers and complete a peer-editing lesson. In this lesson, students critique areas of their peers' drafts in which the sources were weak or nonexistent. To create strict citation guidelines, I tell my students that they are not allowed to use any Web site that ends in ".com." Instead, they only are allowed to use Web sites that end in ".edu" or ".gov," or they can use online databases such as JSTOR. Choosing to use an inappropriate site results in automatic failure on the assignment. If teachers use these strict guidelines, their students are highly likely to choose credible Web sites.

PAULA COLEMERE—Special Education Teacher— English, History
McClintock High School, Tempe, AZ

I usually teach my research unit after we have done persuasive reading and writing. Because I teach students how to evaluate information for bias during the persuasive unit, I know they have some prior knowledge before we tackle research. I show examples from scholarly journals, books, and general Web sites like Wikipedia. Then, as we discuss, I think aloud to model for students why I would or would not use a source. I typically do not allow my students to use any Web sources and keep them to the sites that are pre-approved in our library's database. If I were to allow a Web-based source, it would be limited to one. It is extremely helpful to students if you can show them sample research papers that are excellent, satisfactory, and poor. This way, they have an idea of what the finished product should look like. Another strategy would be to read a passage as a class and critically evaluate it together. Thinking critically is a skill that needs to be modeled and taught to kids. It is a mistake to assume they know how to do this on their own.

JESSICA N. MAHTABAN—Eighth-Grade Math Teacher
Woodrow Wilson Middle School, Clifton, NJ

The best way to show students how to evaluate information from Web sites is by modeling. I have a PowerPoint presentation that explains to students how to evaluate the authenticity of what they are reading on the Internet. Once the students become familiar with all the key points of how to evaluate Web sites, then I can show various Web sites on the Smart board, and as a class we can discuss and review the validity of the site.

We need to teach students how to articulate their thoughts by expanding on their ideas. Teachers can add "Why or why not?" or "explain" to the end of questions. If students are exposed to higher-level thinking questions and learn how to ask and answer these questions, then they can think more critically about school subjects.

JENNIFER PINCOSKI—Learning Resource Teacher: K–12
Lee County School District, Fort Myers, FL

Understanding that the Internet plays such a significant role in students' lives and that it does provide reliable information, the class needs to be taught how to appropriately use the Web for research. This involves teaching strategies on how to identify credible information, and providing ample opportunities for practice.

To understand that not all information on the Internet is accurate, students need to see real examples—examples that are relevant to them. This could be as simple as exposing them to several different sites that post conflicting information about the same topic and then asking them to define how they would decide which information to believe.

Once students recognize that they need to exercise discretion when retrieving information from the Internet, they can be taught HOW to do so. The teacher can provide a list of guiding questions that will help students critically evaluate their sources. The ultimate goal is for students to use the guiding questions independently and apply them across settings; however, in the beginning, students will require a much higher level of support. An "I do, we do, you do" approach is probably the best way to assist students in the development and practice of these skills.

LAUREN ROLLINS—First-Grade Teacher
Boulevard Elementary School, Shaker Heights, OH

The Internet is a fantastic resource when it is used properly. Unfortunately, because anyone can post information on the Internet, it is not always reliable or factual. With respect to evaluating information found on the Internet, I encourage my students to visit multiple sites with multiple viewpoints so they can weigh the relative merits of each. In this way, they practice their critical thinking skills. Using examples of "factual" information found on Web sites that contradict clearly accepted facts will teach the students that they must evaluate information in the context of what they know to be true. This will help them to understand that multiple sources, not just the Internet, should be used. In addition, I devote some time to teaching my students how to properly cite sources from the Internet and other sources. This is an important skill and also a necessary one so that they will not be suspected of plagiarism.

LINDA SPARKS—First Grade Teacher
John F. Kennedy School, Billerica, MA

Whenever I assign a new research project, I begin with a specific list of resource instructions. For example, I might state that I want two books, two magazine articles, and three Web sites. After the topic is picked, I have the students pull together their resources and come to me so that I can check them to make sure each student is headed in the right direction. It also gives me a better understanding of what they are researching and I can find out if they have any misconceptions about the project. I find I get better results this way, because the students know I am aware of what they are researching and have their lists of resources. (Even if they don't use all their sources, I want them to see what is available for them.) I also am more prepared to teach specific writing skills. The first skill I teach before I assign a project as they practice reading articles is how to take that information and transfer it into their own words. Limiting the number of quotes is a way to encourage higher-level thinking processes. Many times, when given the chance, students are more creative than the writers of the articles they read.

BARBARA PRESLEY—Transition/Work Study Coordinator—High School Level
BESTT Program (Baldwinsville Exceptional Student Training and Transition Program), C. W. Baker High School, Baldwinsville, NY

To me, discussion is key: whole-group discussion, small-group discussion, and one-to-one discussion, all the time being prepared to defend or criticize (with legitimate corroboration) topics raised. Students learn well from their mistakes as long as the correction is respectful and meaningful to them personally. They can't learn to think critically until someone questions their premises and they have to defend their position—as long as the discussions are conducted without malice. They are gaining experience in critical thinking through the process of criticism, both given and received.

10 | THE LEARNING SCIENCES AND CONSTRUCTIVISM

TEACHERS' CASEBOOK

WHAT WOULD YOU DO? LEARNING TO COOPERATE

You want to use cooperative learning with your middle school students. Many students have worked in groups, but few seem to have participated in true cooperative learning. When you surveyed the class members about their experiences, most rolled their eyes and groaned. You take it that their experiences have not been very positive. These students have a wide range of abilities, including some who are truly gifted and talented, several who are just learning English, and a few who are very shy; and then there are others who would take over and dominate every discussion if you let them. You believe that collaboration is a crucial 21st-century skill for all students and that learning together can deepen understanding as students question, explain, and build on each other's thinking. No matter what, you want the experience of learning together to build your students' confidence and your sense of efficacy as a teacher, so you want authentic successes.

CRITICAL THINKING

- How would you begin to introduce cooperative learning to your students?
- What tasks will you choose to start?
- How will you establish groups?
- What will you watch and listen for to be sure the students are making the most of the experience?

Stocklady/Fotolia

OVERVIEW AND **OBJECTIVES**

For the past three chapters, we have analyzed different aspects of learning. We considered behavioral, information processing, and cognitive science explanations of what and how people learn. We have examined complex cognitive processes such as metacognitive skills and problem solving. These explanations of learning focus on the individual and what is happening in his or her "head." In this chapter, we expand our investigation of learning to include insights from a relatively recent interdisciplinary approach called the *learning sciences*. This approach brings together work in many fields that study learning, including educational psychology, computer science, neuroscience, and anthropology. One of the foundations of the learning sciences is constructivism, a broad perspective that calls attention to two critical aspects of learning: social and cultural factors. In this chapter, we examine the role of other

people and the cultural context in learning. Sociocultural constructivist theories have roots in cognitive perspectives but have moved well beyond these early explanations. We will explore a number of teaching strategies and approaches that are consistent with constructivist perspectives—inquiry, problem-based learning, cooperative learning, cognitive apprenticeships, and service learning. Finally, we will examine learning in this digital age, including the considerations about learning in technology-rich environments.

By the time you have completed this chapter, you should be able to:

Objective 10.1   Describe the collaborative approach that led to the interdisciplinary field of learning sciences and the basic assumptions of this field.

Objective 10.2   Explain different perspectives on constructivism as a theory of learning and teaching.

Objective 10.3   Identify the common elements in most contemporary constructivist theories.

Objective 10.4   Apply constructivist principles to classroom practice, especially collaboration and cooperation.

Objective 10.5   Evaluate the use of community-based activities/service learning.

Objective 10.6   Describe positive and negative influences of technology on the learning and development of children and adolescents.

THE LEARNING SCIENCES

In the previous three chapters, psychologists were responsible for most of the theory and research we discussed. But many other people have also studied learning: Today, multiple perspectives are included in the learning sciences.

What Are the Learning Sciences?

The interdisciplinary field of the learning sciences encompasses research in psychology, education, computer science, philosophy, sociology, anthropology, neuroscience, and other fields that study learning. You already have explored some of the foundations of the learning sciences in Chapters 8 and 9, including the make-up of working memory and the role of cognitive load in learning; how information is represented in complex structures such as schemas; what experts know and how their knowledge differs from that of novices; metacognition; problem solving; thinking and reasoning; and how knowledge transfers (or doesn't transfer) from the classroom to the world beyond.

No matter what their focus, all knowledge workers in the learning sciences are interested in how deep knowledge in subjects like science, mathematics, and literacy is actually acquired and applied in the real world of scientists, mathematicians, and writers. In the *Cambridge Handbook of Learning Sciences,* R. Keith Sawyer (2006) contrasts what it takes for deep learning to occur with traditional classroom practices that have dominated schooling in many countries for decades. Look at Table 10.1 to see the differences.

Basic Assumptions of the Learning Sciences

Even though the different fields in the learning sciences approach their study from varying perspectives, there is growing agreement about some basic assumptions (Sawyer, 2006):

- *Experts have deep conceptual knowledge.* Experts know many facts and procedures, but just learning facts and procedures will not make you an expert. Experts have deep conceptual understanding that allows them to put their knowledge into action; they can apply and modify their knowledge to fit each situation. Experts' deep conceptual knowledge generates problem finding and problem solving.
- *Learning comes from the learner.* Better instruction alone will not transfer deep understandings from teachers to students. Learning is more than receiving and processing information transmitted by teachers or texts. Rather, students must actively participate in their own personal construction of knowledge. We are knowledge inventors, not copy machines (de Kock, Sleegers, & Voeten, 2004).
- *Schools must create effective learning environments.* It is the job of the school to create environments where students are active in constructing their own deep understandings so they can reason about real-world problems and transfer their learning from school to their lives beyond the school walls.
- *Prior knowledge and beliefs are key.* Students come into our classrooms filled with knowledge and beliefs about how the world works. Some of these preconceptions are right, some are part right, and some are wrong. If teaching does not begin with

TABLE 10.1 • **How Deep Learning Contrasts with Learning in Traditional Classrooms**

LEARNING IN TRADITIONAL CLASSROOMS	BUT FINDINGS FROM COGNITIVE SCIENCE SHOW OTHER REQUIREMENTS FOR DEEP LEARNING
Class material is not related to what students already know. Example: Teacher says, "Igneous rocks are. . . ."	Learners relate new understandings to what they already know and believe. Example: Teacher says, "Have any of you seen granite counter tops on TV home shows or maybe you have one in your house? What do they look like . . .?"
Class material presented and learned as disconnected bits of knowledge. "The definition of metamorphic rocks is. . . ."	Learners integrate and interconnect their knowledge in expanding conceptual systems. "We already have learned about two kinds of rocks. We also learned last week about how the earth has changed over the centuries, with some ocean floors becoming land areas. Today we will learn about how marble and diamonds. . . ."
Lessons involve memorizing facts and doing procedures without understanding how or why. "To divide fractions, invert and multiply. . . ."	Learners search for patterns and recognize or invent underlying principles. "Remind me what it means to divide. . . . Ok, so ¾ divided by ½ means how many sets of what are in . . .?"
Learners have trouble understanding ideas that are not straight from the textbook or explained in the same way. "What does your textbook say about . . .?"	Learners evaluate new ideas, even if not in the text, and integrate them into their thinking. "On TV yesterday there was a story about a new drug that is effective in curing one out of 8 cases of . . . What is the probability of a cure?"
Authorities and experts are the source of unchanging and accurate facts and procedures. "Scientists agree. . . ."	Learners understand that knowledge is socially constructed by people, so ideas require critical examination. "Here is an excerpt from the presidential debates last week. Let's think about how you would determine what statements are more supported by evidence . . .?"
Learners simply memorize everything instead of thinking about the purpose of learning and the best strategies for that purpose. "This will be on the test."	Learners think about why they are learning, monitor their understanding, and reflect on their own learning processes. "How could you use this concept in your own life? How can you tell if you are understanding it?"

Source: Based on Sawyer, R. K. (2006). The new science of learning. In R. K. Sawyer (Ed.), The Cambridge Handbook of the Learning Sciences (p. 4). New York: Cambridge University Press.

what the students "know," then the students will learn what it takes to pass the test, but their knowledge and beliefs about the world will not change (Hennessey, Higley, & Chesnut, 2012).

• *Reflection is necessary to develop deep conceptual knowledge.* Students need to express and perform the knowledge they are developing through writing, conversations, drawings, projects, skits, portfolios, reports, and so on. But the performance is not enough. To develop deep conceptual knowledge, students need to reflect—thoughtfully analyze their own work and progress.

Embodied Cognition

Recently a new theme has emerged in the cognitive and learning sciences—embodied cognition. This is awareness that "the way we think about and represent information reflects the fact that we need to interact with the world" (Ashcraft & Radvansky, 2010, p. 32). These interactions occur through our senses and bodies, and the way our bodies interact with the world to achieve our goals affects our thinking. In other words, our cognitive processes have deep roots in the interactions of our bodies with the real world—what develops cognitively depends on our sensorimotor engagement with the world. In this view of cognition, the body, not the mind, is primary, but the body needs the mind to successfully interact in the world. In some ways, this perspective is similar to Piaget's idea that thinking emerges early on from the infant's sensorimotor interaction in the world. Instead of being just simple conduits for outside world sounds and images, our senses and motor responses are central to how we think. So we have to understand how our physical body interacts with the world in order to understand our mind (Wilson, 2002). Observational learning is an example. Watching someone perform an action activates areas of the brain in observers that would be involved in performing that action themselves—almost as if the brain learns by doing the action. So using models, gestures and movement, simulations, drama, re-enactments, and other kinds of actions and movements can support learning (de Koning & Tabbers, 2011).

In educational psychology, these fundamental assumptions of the learning sciences and embodied cognition all lead to the conclusion that thinking is constructive. In the next section we look at both cognitive and social constructivism—topics you will hear about repeatedly in your preparation for teaching.

ENHANCEDetext *self-check*

COGNITIVE AND SOCIAL CONSTRUCTIVISM

Consider this situation:

> A young child who has never been to the hospital is in her bed in the pediatric wing. The nurse at the station down the hall calls over the intercom above the bed, "Hi Chelsea, how are you doing? Do you need anything?" The girl looks puzzled and does not answer. The nurse repeats the question with the same result. Finally, the nurse says emphatically, "Chelsea, are you there? Say something!" The little girl responds tentatively, "Hello, wall—I'm here."

Chelsea encountered a new situation—a talking wall. The wall is persistent. It sounds like a grown-up wall. She shouldn't talk to strangers, but she is not sure about walls. She uses what she knows and what the situation provides to construct meaning and to act.

Here is another example of constructing meaning. This time, Kate and her 9-year-old son Ethan co-construct understandings as they buy groceries:

Ethan: (running to get a shopping cart) Do we need the big one?
Kate: We might—better too big than not big enough. Here is our list—where do we go first?
Ethan: We need ice cream for the party! (Ethan heads toward frozen foods)
Kate: Whoa! What happened to the ice cream carton you left out on the kitchen counter?
Ethan: It melted and it wasn't out that long. I promise!
Kate: Right and we may be in this store a while, so let's start with things that won't melt while we are shopping—I usually buy produce first.
Ethan: What's "produce"?
Kate: Things that grow—fruits and vegetables "produced" by farmers.
Ethan: OK, the list says cucumbers. Here they are. Wait there are two kinds. Which do you want? The little ones say "local." What's local?
Kate: Local means from around here—close to us, close to our "location." Hmmm.—the big ones are 75 cents *each* and these smaller ones are $1.15 *a pound*. How would you decide which is a better deal?.
Ethan: I guess bigger is better, right? Or is local better?
Kate: Well, I wonder if they cost the same for the amount you get—per pound. How could you figure that out?
Ethan: I don't know—the price for a pound isn't on the big ones, just the price each.
Kate: When the doctor wants to know how many pounds you weigh, she puts you on a scale. What if you weighed a big cucumber over there on that food scale?

Ethan: OK—it weighs ½ a pound.

Kate: So half a pound costs 75 cents—what would a whole pound cost—that's two halves make a whole?

Ethan: 75 cents plus 75 cents—$1.50—Gee, the bigger ones are more expensive. So the smaller ones are better, and they are "local"—that's good too, right?

Kate: Maybe. I like to support our local farmers. Where are the small cucumbers from—look at the tiny print on the label.

Ethan: Virginia—is that close to us?

Kate: Not really—it is about a 6-hour drive from here. . . .

Look at the knowledge being co-constructed about planning ahead, vocabulary, math, problem solving, and even geography. Constructivist theories of learning focus on how people make meaning, both on their own like Chelsea and in interaction with others like Ethan.

Constructivist Views of Learning

Constructivism is a broad term used by philosophers, curriculum designers, psychologists, educators, and others. Ernst von Glasersfeld calls it "a vast and woolly area in contemporary psychology, epistemology, and education" (1997, p. 204). Constructivist perspectives are grounded in the research of Piaget; Vygotsky; the Gestalt psychologists; Bartlett, Bruner, and Rogoff; as well as the philosophy of John Dewey and the work in anthropology of Jean Lave, to mention just a few intellectual roots.

There is no one constructivist theory of learning, but most constructivist theories agree on two central ideas:

Central Idea 1: Learners are active in constructing their own knowledge.

Central Idea 2: Social interactions are important in this knowledge construction process (Bruning, Schraw, & Norby, 2011).

Constructivist approaches in science and mathematics education, in educational psychology and anthropology, and in computer-based education all embrace these two ideas. But even though many psychologists and educators use the term *constructivism,* they often mean very different things (J. Martin, 2006; McCaslin & Hickey, 2001; Phillips, 1997).

One way to organize constructivist views is to talk about two forms of constructivism: psychological and social construction (Palincsar, 1998; Phillips, 1997). We could oversimplify a bit and say that psychological constructivists focus on how individuals use information, resources, and even help from others to build and improve their mental models and problem-solving strategies—see Central Idea 1. In contrast, social constructivists view learning as increasing our abilities to participate with others in activities that are meaningful in the culture—see Central Idea 2 (Windschitl, 2002). Let's look a bit closer at each type of constructivism.

PSYCHOLOGICAL/INDIVIDUAL/COGNITIVE CONSTRUCTIVISM. Many psychological theories include some kind of constructivism because these theories embrace the idea that individuals construct their own cognitive structures as they interpret their experiences in particular situations (Palincsar, 1998). These psychological constructivists "are concerned with how individuals build up certain elements of their cognitive or emotional apparatus" (Phillips, 1997, p. 153). Because they study individual knowledge, beliefs, self-concept, or identity, they are sometimes called *individual constructivists* or *cognitive constructivists;* they all focus on the inner psychological life of people. When Chelsea talked to the wall in the previous section, she was making meaning using her own individual knowledge and beliefs about how to respond when someone (or something) talks to you. She was using what she knew to impose intellectual structure on her world (Piaget, 1971; Windschitl, 2002). When children observe that most plants need soil to grow and then conclude that plants "eat dirt," they are using what they know about how eating supports life to make sense of plant growth (M. C. Linn & Eylon, 2006).

Using these standards, the most recent information processing theories are constructivist because they are concerned with how individuals construct internal representations (propositions, images, concepts, schemas) that can be remembered and retrieved (Mayer, 1996). The outside

Video 10.1
The young students in this science class are investigating earthworms. In pairs, they are finding answers to their questions and constructing their own knowledge with the teacher's guidance. Notice the active role of the students in building understanding, and making sense of information about earthworms.

ENHANCEDetext *video example*

world is viewed as a source of input, but once the sensations are perceived and enter working memory, the important work is assumed to be happening "inside the head" of the individual (Schunk, 2012; Vera & Simon, 1993). Some psychologists, however, believe that information processing is "trivial" or "weak" constructivism because the individual's only constructive contribution is to build accurate internal representations of the outside world (Derry, 1992; Garrison, 1995; H. H. Marshall, 1996; Windschitl, 2002).

In contrast, Piaget's psychological (cognitive) constructivist perspective is less concerned with "correct" representations and more interested in meaning as it is constructed by the individual. As we saw in Chapter 2, Piaget proposed that as children develop, their thinking becomes more organized and adaptive and less tied to concrete events. Piaget's special concern was with logic and the construction of universal knowledge that cannot be learned directly from the environment— knowledge such as conservation or reversibility (P. H. Miller, 2011). Such knowledge comes from reflecting on and coordinating our own cognitions or thoughts, not from mapping external reality. Piaget saw the social environment as an important factor in development, but did not believe that social interaction was the main mechanism for changing thinking (Moshman, 1997). Some educational and developmental psychologists have referred to Piaget's kind of constructivism as **first-wave constructivism** or "solo" constructivism, with its emphasis on Central Idea 1, individual meaning making (De Corte, Greer, & Verschaffel, 1996; Paris, Byrnes, & Paris, 2001).

At the extreme end of individual constructivism is the notion of **radical constructivism**. This perspective holds that individuals can never know objective reality or truth; they can only know what they perceive and believe. Each of us constructs meaning (knowledge) from our own experiences as we try to explain to ourselves what we perceive, but we have no way of understanding or "knowing" the knowledge constructed by others or even whether our knowledge is "correct." Learning for radical constructivists consists of replacing one construction with another that better explains the person's current perceptions of reality (Hennessey et al., 2012). A difficulty with this position is that, when pushed to the extreme of relativism, all knowledge and all beliefs are equal because they are all valid individual perceptions. There are problems with this thinking for educators. First, teachers have a professional responsibility to emphasize some values, such as honesty or justice, over others, such as deception and bigotry. All perceptions and beliefs are not equal. Second, there are right answers in many fields such as mathematics, and students will have trouble learning if they hold on to the misconceptions of their construction. As teachers, we ask students to work hard to learn. If learning cannot advance understanding because all understandings are equally good, then, as David Moshman (1997) notes, "we might just as well let students continue to believe whatever they believe" (p. 230). Also, it appears that some knowledge, such as counting and one-to-one correspondence, is not constructed, but universal. Knowing one-to-one correspondence is part of being human (Geary, 1995; Schunk, 2012).

VYGOTSKY'S SOCIAL CONSTRUCTIVISM. As you also saw in Chapter 2, Vygotsky emphasized Central Idea 2, that social interaction, cultural tools, and activity shape individual development and learning, just as Ethan's interactions and activities in the grocery store with his mother shaped his learning about anticipating possible consequences (running out of space in the shopping cart and melted ice cream), the meaning of "produce" and "local," how to calculate price per pound, and geography (J. Martin, 2006). By participating in a broad range of activities with others, learners *appropriate* the outcomes produced by working together; these outcomes could include both new strategies and knowledge. **Appropriating** means being able to reason, act, and participate using cultural tools—for example, using conceptual tools such as "force" and "acceleration" to reason in physics (Mason, 2007). In psychological (cognitive) constructivism, learning means individually possessing knowledge, but in social constructivism, learning means belonging to a group and participating in the social construction of knowledge (Mason, 2007). Putting learning in social and cultural contexts is known as **second-wave constructivism** (Paris, Byrnes, & Paris, 2001).

Because his theory relies heavily on social interactions and the cultural context to explain learning, most psychologists classify Vygotsky as a social constructivist (Palincsar, 1998; Prawat, 1996). However, some theorists categorize him as a psychological constructivist because he was primarily interested in development within the individual (Moshman, 1997; Phillips, 1997). In a sense, Vygotsky was both. One advantage of Vygotsky's theory of learning is that it gives us a way to consider both the psychological and the social: He bridges both camps. For example, Vygotsky's concept of the *zone of proximal development*—the area in which a child can solve a problem with the help (scaffolding) of an adult or more able peer—has been called a place where culture and cognition create each other (M. Cole, 1985). Culture creates cognition when the adult uses tools and practices from the culture (language, maps, computers, looms, or music) to steer the child toward goals the culture values (reading, writing, weaving, dance). Cognition creates culture as the adult and child together generate new practices and problem solutions to add to the cultural group's repertoire (Serpell, 1993). So people are both products and producers of their societies and cultures (Bandura, 2001). One way of integrating individual and social constructivism is to think of knowledge as both *individually constructed* and *socially mediated* (Windschitl, 2002).

The term **constructionism** is sometimes used to describe how public knowledge is created. Although this is not our main concern in educational psychology, it is worth a quick look.

CONSTRUCTIONISM. Social constructionists do not focus on individual learning. Their concern is how public knowledge in disciplines such as science, math, economics, or history is constructed. Beyond this kind of academic knowledge, constructionists also are interested in how common-sense ideas, everyday beliefs, and commonly held understandings about people and the world are communicated to new members of a sociocultural group (Gergen, 1997; Phillips, 1997). Questions raised might include who determines what constitutes history, what is the proper way to behave in public, or how to get elected class president. Social constructionists believe all knowledge is socially constructed, and more important, some people have more power than others to define what constitutes such knowledge. Relationships between and among teachers, students, families, and the community are the central issues. Collaboration to understand diverse viewpoints is encouraged, and traditional bodies of knowledge often are challenged (Gergen, 1997). The philosophies of Jacques Dierrida and Michel Foucault are important sources for constructionists. Vygotsky's theory, with its attention to the way cognition creates culture, has some elements in common with constructionism.

These different perspectives on constructivism raise some general questions, and they disagree on the answers. These questions can never be fully resolved, but different theories tend to favor different positions. Let's consider the questions.

How Is Knowledge Constructed?

One tension among different approaches to constructivism is based on how knowledge is constructed. Moshman (1982) describes three explanations.

1. *The realities and truths of the external world direct knowledge construction.* Individuals reconstruct outside reality by building accurate mental representations such as propositional networks, concepts, cause-and-effect patterns, and condition–action production rules that reflect "the way things really are." The more the person learns, the deeper and broader his or her experience is, the closer that person's knowledge is to objective reality. Information processing holds this view of knowledge (Cobb & Bowers, 1999).
2. *Internal processes such as Piaget's organization, assimilation, and accommodation direct knowledge construction.* New knowledge is abstracted from old knowledge. Knowledge is not a mirror of reality, but rather an abstraction that grows and develops with cognitive activity. Knowledge is not true or false; it just grows more internally consistent and organized with development.
3. *Both external and internal factors direct knowledge construction.* Knowledge grows through the interactions of internal (cognitive) and external (environmental and social) factors. Vygotsky's description of cognitive development through the appropriation and use of cultural tools such as language is consistent with this view (Bruning, Schraw, & Norby, 2011). Another example is Bandura's theory of reciprocal interactions among people, behaviors, and environments described in Chapter 11 (Schunk, 2012). Table 10.2 on the next page summarizes the three general explanations about how knowledge is constructed.

TABLE 10.2 • **How Knowledge Is Constructed**

TYPE	ASSUMPTIONS ABOUT LEARNING AND KNOWLEDGE	EXAMPLE THEORIES
External Direction	Knowledge is acquired by constructing a representation of the outside world. Direct teaching, feedback, and explanation affect learning. Knowledge is accurate to the extent that it reflects the "way things really are" in the outside world.	Information processing
Internal Direction	Knowledge is constructed by transforming, organizing, and reorganizing previous knowledge. Knowledge is not a mirror of the external world, even though experience influences thinking and thinking influences knowledge. Exploration and discovery are more important than teaching.	Piaget
Both External and Internal Direction	Knowledge is constructed based on social interactions and experience. Knowledge reflects the outside world as filtered through and influenced by culture, language, beliefs, interactions with others, direct teaching, and modeling. Guided discovery, teaching, models, and coaching as well as the individual's prior knowledge, beliefs, and thinking affect learning.	Vygotsky

Knowledge: Situated or General?

A second question that cuts across many constructivist perspectives is whether knowledge is internal, general, and transferable, or bound to the time and place in which it is constructed. Psychologists who emphasize the social construction of knowledge and situated learning affirm Vygotsky's notion that learning is inherently social and embedded in a particular cultural setting (Cobb & Bowers, 1999). What is true in one time and place—such as the "fact" before Columbus's time that the earth was flat—becomes false in another time and place. Particular ideas may be useful within a specific community of practice, such as 15th-century navigation, but useless outside that community. What counts as new knowledge is determined in part by how well the new idea fits with current accepted practice. Over time, the current practice may be questioned and even overthrown, but until such major shifts occur, current practice will shape what is considered valuable.

Situated learning emphasizes that learning in the real world is not like studying in school. It is more like an apprenticeship where novices, with the support of an expert guide and model, take on more and more responsibility until they can function independently. Proponents of this view believe situated learning explains learning in factories, around the dinner table, in high school halls, in street gangs, in the business office, and on the playground.

Situated learning is often described as "enculturation," or adopting the norms, behaviors, skills, beliefs, language, and attitudes of a particular community. The community might be mathematicians or gang members or writers or students in your eighth-grade class or soccer players—any group that has particular ways of thinking and doing. Knowledge is viewed not as individual cognitive structures, but rather as a creation of the community over time. The practices of the community—the ways of interacting and getting things done, as well as the tools the community has created—constitute the knowledge of that community. Learning means becoming more able to participate in those practices and use the tools (Greeno, Collins, & Resnick, 1996; Mason, 2007; Rogoff, 1998).

At the most basic level, "situated learning emphasizes the idea that much of what is learned is specific to the situation in which it is learned" (J. R. Anderson, Reder, & Simon, 1996, p. 5). Thus, some would argue, learning to do calculations in school may help students do more school calculations, but it may not help them balance a checkbook, because the skills can be applied only in the context in which they were learned—namely, school (Lave, 1997; Lave & Wenger, 1991). But it also appears that knowledge and skills can be applied across contexts that were not part of the initial learning situation, as when you use your ability to read and calculate to do your income taxes, even though income tax forms were not part of your high school curriculum (J. R. Anderson et al., 1996).

Learning that is situated in school does not have to be doomed or irrelevant (Bereiter, 1997). As you saw in Chapter 9, a major question in educational psychology—and education in general—concerns the transfer of knowledge from one situation to another. How can you encourage this transfer from one situation to another? Help is on the way in the next section.

Common Elements of Constructivist Student-Centered Teaching

STOP & THINK What makes a lesson student centered? List the characteristics and features that put the student in the center of learning. •

We have looked at some areas of disagreement among the constructivist perspectives, but what about areas of agreement? All constructivist theories assume that knowing develops as learners, like Chelsea and Ethan, try to make sense of their experiences. "Learners, therefore, are not empty vessels waiting to be filled, but rather active organisms seeking meaning" (Driscoll, 2005, p. 487). Humans construct mental models or schemas and continue to revise them to make better sense of their experiences. Again, we are knowledge inventors, not filing cabinets. Our constructions do not necessarily resemble external reality; rather, they are our unique interpretations, like Chelsea's friendly, persistent wall. This doesn't mean that all constructions are equally useful or viable. Learners test their understandings against experience and the understandings of other people—they negotiate and co-construct meanings like Ethan did with his mother.

Constructivists share similar goals for learning. They emphasize knowledge *in use* rather than the *storing* of inert facts, concepts, and skills. Learning goals include developing abilities to find and solve ill-structured problems, critical thinking, inquiry, self-determination, and openness to multiple perspectives (Driscoll, 2005). Even though there is no single constructivist theory, many constructivist approaches recommend five conditions for learning:

1. Embed learning in complex, realistic, and relevant learning environments.
2. Provide for social negotiation and shared responsibility as a part of learning.
3. Support multiple perspectives, and use multiple representations of content.
4. Nurture self-awareness and an understanding that knowledge is constructed.
5. Encourage ownership in learning. (Driscoll, 2005; H. H. Marshall, 1992)

Before we discuss particular teaching approaches, let's look more closely at these dimensions of constructivist teaching.

COMPLEX LEARNING ENVIRONMENTS AND AUTHENTIC TASKS. Constructivists believe that students should not be given stripped-down, simplified problems and basic skills drills, but instead should encounter complex learning environments that deal with "fuzzy," ill-structured problems. The world beyond school presents few simple problems or step-by-step directions, so schools should be sure that every student has experience solving complex problems. Complex problems are not just difficult ones; rather, they have many parts. There are multiple, interacting elements in complex problems and multiple possible solutions. There is no one right way to reach a conclusion, and each solution may bring a new set of problems.

These complex problems should be embedded in authentic tasks and activities, the kinds of situations that students would face as they apply what they are learning to the real world. Students may need support (*scaffolding*) as they work on these complex problems, with teachers helping them find resources, keeping track of their progress, breaking larger problems down into smaller ones, and so on. This aspect of constructivist approaches is consistent with situated learning in emphasizing learning in situations where the knowledge will be applied.

Video 10.2
In Mr. Fireng's middle school science class, the students engage in peer teaching. Students work together in groups to develop expertise about one concept in their science unit, plan a lesson and activities around their concept, and teach that concept to their peers. Observe the student-centered focus of Mr. Fireng's approach.

ENHANCEDetext *video example*

Connect and Extend to PRAXIS II©

Student-Centered Learning (II, A3)
Many of the major initiatives to reform content-area curricula (e.g., science, mathematics) emphasize student-centered/constructivist approaches to learning. Describe the major principles of these approaches, and explain how they differ from teacher-centered approaches.

SOCIAL NEGOTIATION. Many constructivists share Vygotsky's belief that higher mental processes develop through social negotiation and interaction, so collaboration in learning is valued. A major goal of teaching is to develop students' abilities to establish and defend their own positions while respecting the positions of others and working together to negotiate or co-construct meaning. To accomplish this exchange, students must talk and listen to each other. It is a challenge for children in cultures that are individualistic and competitive, such as the United States, to adopt what has been called an intersubjective attitude—a commitment to build shared meaning by finding common ground and exchanging interpretations.

MULTIPLE PERSPECTIVES AND REPRESENTATIONS OF CONTENT. When students encounter only one model, one analogy, one way of understanding complex content, they often oversimplify as they try to apply that one approach to every situation. I saw this happen in my educational psychology class when six students were presenting an example of guided discovery learning. The students' presentation was a near copy of a guided discovery demonstration I had given earlier in the semester, but with some major misconceptions. My students knew only one way to represent discovery learning. Resources for the class should have provided multiple representations of content using different analogies, examples, and metaphors. This idea is consistent with Jerome Bruner's (1966) spiral curriculum, a structure for teaching that introduces the fundamental structure of all subjects—the "big ideas"—early in the school years, then revisits the subjects in more and more complex forms over time. Another example, the use of manipulatives in mathematics, allows students different ways to represent the quantities and processes in mathematics (Carbonneau, Marley, & Selig, 2012).

UNDERSTANDING THE KNOWLEDGE CONSTRUCTION PROCESS. Constructivist approaches emphasize making students aware of their own role in constructing knowledge. The assumptions we make, our beliefs, and our experiences shape what each of us comes to "know" about the world. Different assumptions and different experiences lead to different knowledge, as we saw in Chapter 6 when we explored the role of cultural differences in shaping knowledge. If students are aware of the influences that shape their thinking, they will be more able to choose, develop, and defend positions in a self-critical way while respecting the positions of others.

STUDENT OWNERSHIP OF LEARNING. "While there are several interpretations of what [constructivist] theory means, most agree that it involves a dramatic change in the focus of teaching, putting the students' own efforts to understand at the center of the educational enterprise" (Prawat, 1992, p. 357). Student ownership does not mean that the teacher abandons responsibility for instruction. Because the design of teaching is a central issue in this book, we will spend the rest of this chapter discussing examples of *ownership of learning* and *student-centered instruction*.

ENHANCEDetext *self-check*

APPLYING CONSTRUCTIVIST PERSPECTIVES

Even though there are many applications of constructivist views of learning, we can recognize constructivist approaches by the activities of the teacher and the students. Mark Windschitl (2002, p. 137) suggests that the following activities encourage meaningful learning:

- Teachers elicit students' ideas and experiences in relation to key topics, then fashion learning situations that help students elaborate on or restructure their current knowledge.
- Students are given frequent opportunities to engage in complex, meaningful, problem-based activities.
- Teachers provide students with a variety of information resources as well as the tools (technological and conceptual) necessary to mediate learning.
- Students work collaboratively and are given support to engage in task-oriented dialogue with one another.

- Teachers make their own thinking processes explicit to learners and encourage students to do the same through dialogue, writing, drawings, or other representations.
- Students are routinely asked to apply knowledge in diverse and authentic contexts, explain ideas, interpret texts, predict phenomena, and construct arguments based on evidence, rather than focus exclusively on the acquisition of predetermined "right answers."
- Teachers encourage students' reflective and autonomous thinking in conjunction with the conditions listed above.
- Teachers employ a variety of assessment strategies to understand how students' ideas are evolving and to give feedback on the processes as well as the products of their thinking. (p. 137)

In addition, constructivist approaches include scaffolding to support students' developing expertise. One implication of Vygotsky's theory of cognitive development is that deep understanding requires that students grapple with problems in their zone of proximal development; they need scaffolding in order to work in that zone. Here is a good definition of scaffolding that emphasizes its dynamic interactive nature as well as the knowledge that both teacher and student bring—both are experts on something: "Scaffolding is a powerful conception of teaching and learning in which teachers and students create meaningful connections between teachers' cultural knowledge and the everyday experience and knowledge of the student" (McCaslin & Hickey, 2001, p. 137). Look back at the grocery store conversation between Ethan and his mother at the beginning of the previous section. Notice how the mother used the melted ice cream on the kitchen counter and the scale in the doctor's office—connections to Ethan's experience and knowledge—to scaffold Ethan's understanding.

Even though educational psychologists have different views of scaffolding, most agree on three characteristics (Belland, 2011; van de Pol, Volman, & Beishuizen, 2010):

1. *Contingency Support:* The teacher is constantly adjusting, differentiating, and tailoring responses to the students.
2. *Fading:* The teacher gradually withdraws support as the students' understanding and skills deepen.
3. *Transferring Responsibility:* Students assume more and more responsibility for their own learning.

In addition, scaffolds that support students' growing expertise should be designed so the students make choices as they learn, consider the consequences of different options, make decisions about strategies, and select paths of action. If students are making choices, considering possible consequences, and then deciding on a path of action, they will be able to assume more and more responsibility for their own learning (Belland, 2011). In the next sections, we will examine three specific teaching approaches that put the student at the center and provide scaffolding: inquiry and learning, cognitive apprenticeships, and cooperative learning.

Inquiry and Problem-Based Learning

John Dewey described the basic inquiry learning format in 1910. Educators have developed many adaptations of this strategy, but the form usually includes the following elements (Echevarria, 2003; Lashley, Matczynski, & Rowley, 2002). The teacher presents a puzzling event, question, or problem. The students:

- formulate hypotheses to explain the event or solve the problem,
- collect data to test the hypotheses,
- draw conclusions, and
- reflect on the original problem and the thinking processes needed to solve it.

This is a general picture of inquiry learning, but what is actually going on? Erin Furtak and her colleagues (2012) categorized the actual activities and processes in inquiry as being either *procedural* (hands-on, posing scientific questions, doing science procedures, collecting data, graphing or charting data), *epistemic* (drawing conclusions based on evidence, generating and revising theories), *conceptual* (connecting to students' prior knowledge, eliciting students' mental models and ideas), or *social* (participating in class discussions, arguing and debating ideas, giving presentations,

Video 10.3
In Mr. Fireng's middle school science class, he provides scaffolding as needed. Observe how he prompts a student who needs a little help to answer the warm-up questions about ticks. Notice how he encourages the student from China when an English word becomes a barrier to her learning. What is the role of social interaction in the learning that is taking place in this classroom?

ENHANCEDetext *video example*

Connect and Extend to PRAXIS II®

Inquiry Learning (II, A2, 3)
Inquiry learning is a student-centered approach to learning that predates many "traditional" forms of instruction. Describe the basic structure of this approach to learning. What are its strengths and limitations? What roles does the teacher have?

working collaboratively). When the researchers analyzed 37 studies conducted from 1996 to 2006 that compared inquiry approaches with the traditional teaching of science, they found that the greatest impact on student learning came when the inquiry approach included epistemic activities or a combination of epistemic, procedural, and social activities. So having students collaborate to do hands-on scientific procedures, gather and represent data, draw conclusions, debate ideas, and make presentations was more effective than traditional teacher-centered approaches. But throughout these activities, teacher guidance and scaffolding were important. Just letting the students work completely on their own was not effective.

EXAMPLES OF INQUIRY. Shirley Magnusson and Annemarie Palincsar have developed a teachers' guide for planning, implementing, and assessing different phases of inquiry science units, called guided inquiry supporting multiple literacies (GisML) (Hapgood, Magnusson, & Palincsar, 2004; Palincsar, Magnusson, Collins, & Cutter, 2001; Palincsar, Magnusson, Marano, Ford, & Brown, 1998). The teacher first identifies a curriculum area and some general guiding questions, puzzles, or problems. For example, the teacher chooses *communication* as the area and asks this general question: "How and why do humans and animals communicate?" Next, the teacher poses several specific focus questions. "How do whales communicate?" "How do gorillas communicate?" The focus questions have to be carefully chosen to guide students toward important understandings. One key idea in understanding animal communication is the relationship among the animal's structures, survival functions, and habitat. Animals have specific *structures* such as large ears or echolocators, which function to find food, attract mates, or identify predators, and these structures and functions are related to the animals' *habitats—large ears for navigating in the dark, for example.* Thus, focus questions must ask about animals with different structures for communication, different functional needs for survival, and different habitats. Questions about animals with the same kinds of structures or the same habitats would not be good focus points for inquiry (Magnusson & Palincsar, 1995).

The next phase is to engage students in the inquiry, perhaps by playing different animal sounds, having students make guesses and claims about communication, and asking the students questions about their guesses and claims. Then, the students conduct both first-hand and second-hand investigations. First-hand investigations are direct experiences and experiments, for example, measuring the size of bats' eyes and ears in relation to their bodies (using pictures or videos—not real bats!). In second-hand investigations, students consult books, the Internet, interviews with experts, and other resources to find specific information or get new ideas. As part of their investigating, the students begin to identify patterns. The curved line in Figure 10.1 shows that cycles can be repeated. In fact, students might go through several cycles of investigating, identifying patterns, and reporting results before moving on to constructing explanations and making final reports. Another possible cycle is to evaluate explanations before reporting by making and then checking predictions, applying the explanation to new situations.

Inquiry teaching allows students to learn content and process at the same time. In the preceding examples, students learned about how animals communicate and how structures are related to habitats. In addition, they learned the inquiry process itself—how to solve problems, evaluate solutions, debate ideas, and think critically.

PROBLEM-BASED LEARNING. Whereas inquiry learning grew out of practices in science, problem-based learning grew out of research on expert knowledge in medicine (Belland, 2011). The goals of problem-based learning are to help students develop knowledge that is useful and flexible, not inert. Inert knowledge is information that is memorized but seldom applied (Cognition and Technology Group at Vanderbilt, 1996; Whitehead, 1929). Other goals of problem-based learning are to enhance intrinsic motivation and skills in problem solving, collaboration, evidence-based decision making, and self-directed lifelong learning.

In problem-based learning, students are confronted with a problem that launches their inquiry as they collaborate to find solutions. The students identify and analyze the problem based on the facts from the scenario; and then they begin to generate hypotheses about solutions. As they suggest

---

Connect and Extend to PRAXIS II®

Discovery Learning (I, A1)
Many teachers, especially in mathematics and science, believe that meaningful learning in their content areas is best supported by discovery learning. Be prepared to answer questions about the assumptions, techniques, strengths, and limitations of this instructional strategy.

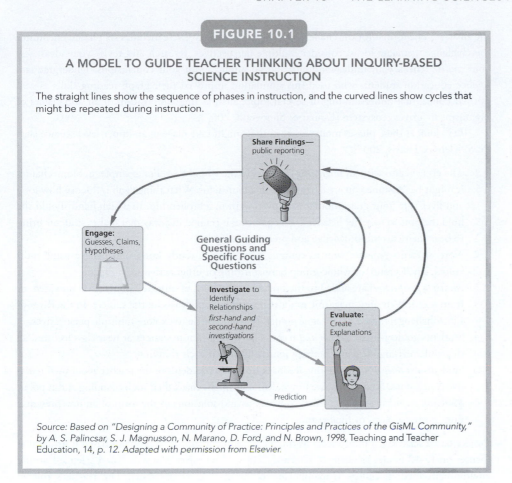

FIGURE 10.1

A MODEL TO GUIDE TEACHER THINKING ABOUT INQUIRY-BASED SCIENCE INSTRUCTION

The straight lines show the sequence of phases in instruction, and the curved lines show cycles that might be repeated during instruction.

Source: Based on "Designing a Community of Practice: Principles and Practices of the GisML Community," by A. S. Palincsar, S. J. Magnusson, N. Marano, D. Ford, and N. Brown, 1998, Teaching and Teacher Education, 14, p. 12. Adapted with permission from Elsevier.

hypotheses, they identify missing information—what do they need to know to test their solutions? This launches a phase of research. Then, students apply their new knowledge, evaluate their problem solutions, recycle to research again if necessary, and finally reflect on the knowledge and skills they have gained. Throughout the entire process, students are not alone or unguided. Their thinking and problem solving are scaffolded by the teacher, computer software supports, models, coaching, expert hints, guides and organizational aids, or other students in the collaborative groups—so working memory is not overloaded. For example, as students work, they may have to fill in a diagram that helps them distinguish between "claims" and "reasons" in a scientific argument (Derry, Hmelo-Silver, Nagarajan, Chernobilsky, & Beitzel, 2006; Hmelo-Silver, Ravit, & Chinn, 2007).

In true problem-based learning, the problem is real and the students' actions matter. For example, during the 2010 Deepwater oil spill, many teachers used the problem as a springboard for learning. Their students researched how this spill compared to others in size, location, costliness, causes, and attempted solutions. What could be done? How do currents and tides play a role? What locations, businesses, and wildlife are in the greatest danger? What will be the short-term and long-term financial and environmental impacts? What actions can students take to play a positive role? A number of teachers blogged about using the oil spill in problem-based learning and collected resources for other teachers (see edutopia.org/blog/oil-spill-project-based-learning-resources).

Some problems are not authentic because they do not directly affect the students' lives, but they are engaging. For example, in a computer simulation called the River of Life Challenge (Sherwood, 2002), students meet Billy and his lab partner, Suzie, who are analyzing the quality of water from a local river. Suzie is concerned that Billy's conclusions are careless and incomplete. Billy is challenged to research the issue in more depth by the Legacy League, a multiethnic group of characters who raise questions and direct Billy and Suzie to helpful resources so they can research the answers. The format for the challenge in the STAR Legacy Cycle includes six phases: encounter the challenge, generate ideas, consider multiple perspectives, research and revise your ideas, test your mettle (check your understanding), and go public about your conclusions. Undergraduate science education students who used this simulation improved their graph-reading skills as well as their conceptual understanding of several topics such as the composition of air and classes of organisms in a river ecosystem (Kumar & Sherwood, 2007).

Let's look at these phases more closely as they might take place in an upper-level science class (S. S. Klein & Harris, 2007).

1. The cycle begins with an *intriguing challenge* to the whole class. For example, in biomechanics it might be "Assume you are a living cell in a bioreactor. What things will influence how long you live?" or "Your grandmother is recovering from a broken hip. In which hand should she hold the cane to help her balance?" The question is framed in a way that makes students bring to bear their current knowledge and preconceptions.

2. Next, students *generate ideas* to compile what they currently know and believe using individual, small-group, or whole-group brainstorming or other activities.

3. *Multiple perspectives* are added to the process in the form of outside experts (live, on video, or from texts), Web sites, magazine or journal articles, or podcasts on the subject. In the River of Life Challenge, the Legacy League guided Billy and Suzie to explore multiple perspectives.

4. Students go deeper to *research and revise*. They consult more sources or hear class lectures, all the while revising ideas and perhaps journaling about their thinking.

5. Students *test their mettle* by getting feedback from other students or the teacher about their tentative conclusions. Some formative (ungraded) tests might check their understanding at this point.

6. Students *go public* with their final conclusions and solutions in the form of an oral presentation, poster/project, or final exam.

Project-based science is a multimedia learning environment similar to problem-based learning that focuses on K–12 grades (Krajcik & Czerniak, 2007). MyProject is a Web-based science-learning environment used in college (Papanikolaou & Boubouka, 2010–2011). The teacher's role in problem-based learning is to identify engaging problems and appropriate resources; orient students to the problem by describing objectives and rationales; organize the students by helping them set goals and define tasks; support, coach, and mentor students as they gather information, craft solutions, and prepare artifacts (models, reports, videos, PowerPoints, portfolios, etc.); and support student reflection on their own learning outcomes and processes (Arends & Kilcher, 2010).

RESEARCH ON INQUIRY AND PROBLEM-BASED LEARNING. Does using inquiry or problem-based learning activities lead to greater achievement? The debate has waged for years. Some research results say "yes" (Furtak et al., 2012). For example, using an open-ended and software-supported inquiry science approach called GenScope™ that explores genetics, students in high school science classrooms learned significantly more compared to students in traditional classrooms (Hickey et al., 1999, 2000). In a study of almost 20,000 middle school students in a large urban district who used inquiry-based materials, those who participated in inquiry learning had significantly higher passing rates on standardized tests. African American boys especially benefitted from these methods (Geier et al., 2008). Several other studies point to increases in student engagement and motivation with inquiry learning (Hmelo-Silver et al., 2007), as long as the learning is supported and students have adequate background knowledge. But not every educational psychologist agrees that problem-based learning is valuable, at least for all students, as you can see in the *Point/Counterpoint: Are Inquiry and Problem-Based Learning Effective Teaching Approaches?* on the next page.

Another constructivist approach that relies heavily on scaffolding is cognitive apprenticeships.

Cognitive Apprenticeships and Reciprocal Teaching

Over the centuries, apprenticeships have proved to be an effective form of education. By working alongside a master and perhaps other apprentices, young people have learned many skills, trades, and crafts. Knowledgeable guides provide models, demonstrations, and corrections, as well as a

POINT/COUNTERPOINT
Are Inquiry and Problem-Based Learning Effective Teaching Approaches?

Inquiry, discovery learning, and problem-based learning are very appealing, but are they effective? Specifically, does problem-based learning lead to deep understanding for most students?

POINT **Problem-based learning is overrated.** Paul Kirschner and his colleagues were clear and critical in their article in the *Educational Psychologist*. Even the title of the article was blunt: "Why minimal guidance during instruction does not work: An analysis of the failure of constructivist, discovery, problem-based, experiential, and inquiry-based teaching." They argued:

> Although unguided or minimally guided instructional approaches are very popular and intuitively appealing, the point is made that these approaches ignore both the structures that constitute human cognitive architecture and evidence from empirical studies over the past half-century that consistently indicate that minimally guided instruction is less effective and less efficient than instructional approaches that place a strong emphasis on guidance of the student learning process. (Kirschner, Sweller, & Clark, 2006, p. 75)

These respected researchers (and others more recently) cited decades of research demonstrating that unguided discovery/inquiry and problem-based learning are ineffective, especially for students with limited prior knowledge (Kalyuga, 2011; Klahr & Nigam, 2004; Tobias, 2010). Louis Alfieri and his colleagues (2011) examined the results from 108 studies going back over 50 years and found that explicit teaching was more beneficial than unassisted discovery, especially for studies published in the most well-rated journals. Their conclusion: "unassisted discovery generally does not benefit learning" (p. 12).

But what about problem-based learning in particular? Much of the research on problem-based learning has taken place in medical schools, and results have been mixed. In one study, students learning through problem-based instruction were better at clinical skills such as problem formation and reasoning, but they were worse in their basic knowledge of science and felt less prepared in science (Albanese & Mitchell, 1993). A review of problem-based learning curricula in medical schools concluded that this approach was not effective in promoting higher levels of student knowledge (Colliver, 2000).

COUNTERPOINT **Problem-based learning is a powerful teaching approach.** Problem-based learning has some advantages. In another study, medical students who learned with problem-based approaches created more accurate and coherent solutions to medical problems (Hmelo, 1998). In an extensive study of a problem-based medical program in the Netherlands, Schmidt and his colleagues (2009) concluded that, compared to graduates of conventional programs, graduates of the problem-based learning program performed better in practical medical and interpersonal skills, took less time to graduate, and had small positive differences in their medical knowledge and diagnostic reasoning. MBA students who learned a concept using problem-based methods were better at explaining the concept than students who had learned the concept from lecture and discussion (Capon & Kuhn, 2004). Students who are better at self-regulation may benefit more from problem-based methods (Evensen, Salisbury-Glennon, & Glenn, 2001), but using problem-based methods over time can help all students to develop self-directed learning skills.

Cindy Hmelo-Silver (2004; Hmelo-Silver et al., 2007) reviewed the research and found good evidence that problem-based learning supports the construction of flexible knowledge and the development of problem-solving and self-directed learning skills, but less evidence indicates that participating in problem-based learning is intrinsically motivating or that it teaches students to collaborate. In studies of high school economics and mathematics, recent research favors problem-based approaches for learning more complex concepts and solving multistep word problems.

BEWARE OF EITHER/OR

You don't have to choose between inquiry and content-focused methods. The best approach in elementary and secondary schools may be a balance of content-focused and inquiry or problem-based methods. For example, Eva Toth, David Klahr, and Zhe Chen (2000) tested a balanced approach for teaching fourth-graders how to use the controlled variable strategy in science to design good experiments. The method had three phases: (1) In small groups, students conducted exploratory experiments to identify variables that made a ball roll farther down a ramp; (2) the teacher led a discussion, explained the controlled variable strategy, and modeled good thinking about experiment design; and (3) the students designed and conducted application experiments to isolate which variables caused the ball to roll farther. The combination of inquiry, discussion, explanation, and modeling was successful in helping the students understand the concepts. Clearly, scaffolding supports are key factors in successful inquiry and problem-based learning. As Rich Mayer (2004) has observed, students need enough freedom and exploration to get mentally active and engaged, combined with the right amount of guidance to make the mental activity productive.

The difference seems to come down to completely unguided discovery versus guided, supported, and well-scaffolded inquiry. Alfieri and his colleagues (2011) concluded:

> Overall, the effects of unassisted-discovery tasks seem limited, whereas enhanced-discovery tasks requiring learners to be actively engaged and constructive seem optimal. On the basis of the current analyses, optimal approaches should include at least one of the following: (a) guided tasks that have scaffolding in place to assist learners, (b) tasks requiring learners to explain their own ideas and ensuring that these ideas are accurate by providing timely feedback, or (c) tasks that provide worked examples of how to succeed in the task. (p. 13)

But to make the matter a bit more complicated, evidence shows that the value of guidance and feedback depends on the student's prior knowledge or age. For example, in learning mathematics problem-solving strategies, students with little knowledge benefitted from feedback as they explored possible solutions, but students with some knowledge benefitted more from just exploring solutions independently without feedback and guidance (Fyfe, Rittle-Johnson, & DeCaro, 2012). Also, first-grade students learned some basic mathematics reasoning skills better from unguided discovery learning via computer than from direct instruction (Baroody et al., 2013).

personal bond that is motivating. The performances required of the learner are real and important and grow more complex as the learner becomes more competent (A. Collins, 2006; Hung, 1999; M. C. Linn & Eylon, 2006). With *guided participation* in real tasks comes *participatory appropriation*—students appropriate the knowledge, skills, and values involved in doing the tasks (Rogoff, 1995, 1998). In addition, both the newcomers to learning and the old-timers contribute to the community of practice by mastering and remastering skills—and sometimes improving these skills in the process (Lave & Wenger, 1991).

Allan Collins (2006) suggests that knowledge and skills learned in school have become too separated from their use in the world beyond school. To correct this imbalance, some educators recommend that schools adopt many of the features of apprenticeships. But rather than learning to sculpt or dance or build a cabinet, apprenticeships in school would focus on cognitive objectives such as reading comprehension, writing, or mathematical problem solving. There are many **cognitive apprenticeship** models, but most share six features:

- Students observe an expert (usually the teacher) *model* the performance.
- Students get external support through *coaching* or tutoring (including hints, tailored feedback, models, and reminders).
- Students receive conceptual *scaffolding*, which is then gradually faded as the student becomes more competent and proficient.
- Students continually *articulate* their knowledge—putting into words their understanding of the processes and content being learned.
- Students *reflect* on their progress, comparing their problem solving to an expert's performance and to their own earlier performances.
- Students are required to *explore* new ways to apply what they are learning—ways that they have not practiced at the master's side.

As students learn, they are challenged to master more complex concepts and skills and to perform them in many different settings.

How can teaching provide cognitive apprenticeships? Mentoring in teaching is one example. Another is cross-age grouping. In the Key School, an inner-city public elementary school in Indianapolis, Indiana, students of different ages work side by side for part of every day on a "pod" designed to have many of the qualities of an apprenticeship. The pods might focus on a craft or a discipline. Examples include gardening, architecture, and "making money." Many levels of expertise are evident in the students of different ages, so students can move at a comfortable pace but still have the model of a master available. Community volunteers, including many parents, visit to demonstrate a skill that is related to the pod topic.

Alan Schoenfeld's (1989, 1994) teaching of mathematical problem solving is another example of the cognitive apprenticeship instructional model.

COGNITIVE APPRENTICESHIPS IN READING: RECIPROCAL TEACHING. The goal of reciprocal teaching is to help students understand and think deeply about what they read (Palincsar, 1986; Palincsar & Brown, 1984, 1989). To accomplish this goal, students in small reading groups learn four strategies: *summarizing* the content of a passage, *asking a question* about the central point, *clarifying* the difficult parts of the material, and *predicting* what will come next. These are strategies skilled readers apply almost automatically but poor readers seldom do—or they don't know how. To use the strategies effectively, poorer readers need direct instruction, modeling, and practice in actual reading situations.

First, the teacher introduces these strategies, perhaps focusing on one strategy each day. As the expert, the teacher explains and models each strategy and encourages student apprentices to practice. Next, the teacher and the students read a short passage silently. Then, the teacher again provides a model by summarizing, questioning, clarifying, or predicting based on the reading. Everyone reads another passage, and the students gradually begin to assume the teacher's role. The teacher becomes a member of the group, and may finally leave, as the students take over the teaching. Often, the students' first attempts are halting and incorrect. But the teacher gives clues, guidance, encouragement, support doing parts of the task (e.g., providing question stems), modeling, and other forms of scaffolding to help the students master these strategies. The goal is for students to learn to apply these strategies independently as they read so they can make sense of text.

APPLYING RECIPROCAL TEACHING. Although reciprocal teaching seems to work with almost any age student, most of the research has been done with younger adolescents who can read aloud fairly accurately but who are far below average in reading comprehension. After 20 hours of practice with this approach, many students who were in the bottom quarter of their class moved up to the average level or above on tests of reading comprehension. Palincsar has identified three guidelines for effective reciprocal teaching:

1. *Shift gradually.* The shift from teacher to student responsibility must be gradual.
2. *Match demands to abilities.* The difficulty of the task and the responsibility must match the abilities of each student and grow as these abilities develop.
3. *Diagnose thinking.* Teachers should carefully observe the "teaching" of each student for clues about how the student is thinking and what kind of instruction he or she needs.

In contrast to some approaches that try to teach 40 or more strategies, an advantage of reciprocal teaching is that it focuses attention on four powerful strategies. But these strategies must be taught; not all students develop them on their own. One study of reciprocal teaching spanning over 3 years found that questioning was the strategy used most often but students had to be taught how to ask higher-level questions because most student questions were literal or superficial (Hacker & Tenent, 2002). Another advantage of reciprocal teaching is that it emphasizes practicing these four strategies in the context of actual reading—reading literature and reading texts. Finally, the idea of scaffolding and gradually moving the student toward independent and fluid reading comprehension is a critical component in reciprocal teaching and cognitive apprenticeships in general (Rosenshine & Meister, 1994).

Collaboration and Cooperation

Even with all the concern today about academic standards, performance on proficiency tests, and international comparisons of student achievement, schooling has always been about more than academic learning. Of course, academics are the prime directive, but the ability to participate productively in collaborative activities is a core 21st-century capability (Roschelle, 2013). An education today must prepare students to live and work cooperatively with all kinds of people:

Most corporations are looking for employees who are not only good at the mastery of a particular set of academic skills but who also have the ability to work harmoniously with a wide variety of coworkers as a cooperative team, to demonstrate initiative and responsibility, and to communicate effectively. (E. Aronson, 2000, p. 91)

Since the 1970s, researchers have examined collaboration and cooperation in schools. Despite some inconsistencies, the majority of the studies indicate that truly cooperative groups have positive effects—from preschool to college—on students' empathy, tolerance for differences, feelings of acceptance, friendships, self-confidence, awareness of the perspectives of others, higher-level reasoning, problem solving, and even school attendance (Galton, Hargreaves, & Pell, 2009; Gillies & Boyle, 2011; Solomon, Watson, & Battistich, 2001). It is even argued that cooperative learning experiences are crucial in preventing many of the social problems that plague children and adolescents (Gillies, 2003, 2004).

COLLABORATION, GROUP WORK, AND COOPERATIVE LEARNING. The terms *collaboration, group work,* and *cooperative learning* often are used as if they mean the same thing. Certainly there is some overlap, but there are differences as well. The distinctions between collaboration and cooperation are not always clear. Ted Panitz (1996) suggests collaboration is a philosophy about how to relate to others—how to learn and work. Collaboration is a way of dealing with people that respects differences, shares authority, and builds on the knowledge that is distributed among other people. Cooperation, on the other hand, is a way of working with others to attain a shared goal (Gillies, 2003). Collaborative learning has roots in the work of British teachers who wanted their students to respond to literature in more active ways as they learned. Cooperative learning has American roots in the work of psychologists John Dewey and Kurt Lewin. You could say that *cooperative* learning is one way to *collaborate* in schools.

Group work, on the other hand, is simply several students working together—they may or may not be cooperating. Many activities can be completed in groups. For example, students can work together to conduct a local survey. How do people feel about the plan to build a new mall that will bring more shopping and more traffic? Would the community support or oppose the building of a nuclear power plant? If students must learn 10 new definitions in a biology class, why not let them divide up the terms and definitions and teach one another? Be sure, however, that everyone in the group can handle the task. Sometimes, one or two students end up doing the work of the entire group.

Group work can be useful, but true cooperative learning requires much more than simply putting students in groups and dividing up the work. Angela O'Donnell and Jim O'Kelly, colleagues of mine from Rutgers University, describe a teacher who claimed to be using "cooperative learning" by asking students to work in pairs on a paper, each writing one part. Unfortunately, the teacher allowed no time to work together and provided no guidance or preparation in cooperative social skills. Students got a grade for their individual part and a group grade for the whole project. One student received an A for his part, but a C for the group project because his partner earned an F—he never turned in any work. So one student was punished with a C for a situation he could not control while the other was rewarded with a C for doing no work at all. This was not cooperative learning—it wasn't even group work (O'Donnell & O'Kelly, 1994).

BEYOND GROUPS TO COOPERATION. David and Roger Johnson (D. W. Johnson & Johnson, 2009a), two of the founders of cooperative learning in the United States, define formal cooperative learning as "students working together, for one class period to several weeks, to achieve shared learning goals and complete jointly specific tasks and assignments" (p. 373). Cooperative learning has a long history in American education, moving in and out of favor over the years. Today, evolving constructivist perspectives have fueled a growing commitment to learning situations that rely on elaboration, interpretation, explanation, and argumentation—cooperative learning (Webb & Palincsar, 1996, p. 844). David and Roger Johnson (D. W. Johnson & Johnson, 2009a) note:

> From being discounted and ignored, cooperative learning has steadily progressed to being one of the dominant instructional practices throughout the world. Cooperative learning is now utilized in schools and universities throughout most of the world in every subject area and from preschool through graduate school and adult training programs. (p. 365)

Different learning theory approaches favor cooperative learning for different reasons (O'Donnell, 2002, 2006). Information processing theorists point to the value of group discussion in helping participants rehearse, elaborate, and expand their knowledge. As group members question and

Connect and Extend to PRAXIS II®

Characteristics of Cooperative Learning (II, A2)
Many instructional strategies labeled as *cooperative learning* lack one or more qualities that are essential components of such techniques. List those essential qualities, and explain the role of each.

PODCAST 10.1
Textbook author Anita Woolfolk shares some ways that she has used cooperative learning in her college classes to take advantage of students as experts in technology.

ENHANCEDetext *podcast*

explain, they have to organize their knowledge, make connections, and review—all processes that support information processing and memory. Advocates of a Piagetian perspective suggest the interactions in groups can create the cognitive conflict and disequilibrium that lead an individual to question his or her understanding and try out new ideas—or, as Piaget (1985) said, "to go beyond his current state and strike out in new directions" (p. 10). Those who favor Vygotsky's theory suggest that social interaction is important for learning because higher mental functions such as reasoning, comprehension, and critical thinking originate in social interactions and are then appropriated and internalized by individuals. Students can accomplish mental tasks with social support before they can do them alone. Thus, cooperative learning provides the social support and scaffolding students need to move learning forward. To benefit from these dimensions of cooperative learning, groups must be cooperative—all members must participate. But, as any teacher or parent knows, cooperation is not automatic when students are put into groups.

WHAT CAN GO WRONG: MISUSES OF GROUP LEARNING. Without careful planning and monitoring by the teacher, group interactions can hinder learning and reduce rather than improve social relations in classes (Gillies & Boyle, 2011). For example, if there is pressure in a group for conformity—perhaps because rewards are being misused or one student dominates the others—interactions can be unproductive and unreflective. Misconceptions might be reinforced, or the worst, not the best, ideas may be combined to construct a superficial or even incorrect understanding (Battistich, Solomon, & Delucci, 1993). Students who work in groups but arrive at wrong answers may be more confident that they are right—a case of "two heads are worse than one" (Puncochar & Fox, 2004). Also, the ideas of low-status students may be ignored or even ridiculed while the contributions of high-status students are accepted and reinforced, regardless of the merit of either set of ideas (C. W. Anderson, Holland, & Palincsar, 1997; E. G. Cohen, 1986). Mary McCaslin and Tom Good (1996) list several other disadvantages of group learning:

- Students often value the process or procedures over the learning. Speed and finishing early take precedence over thoughtfulness and learning.
- Rather than challenging and correcting misconceptions, students support and reinforce misunderstandings.
- Socializing and interpersonal relationships may take precedence over learning.
- Students may simply shift dependency from the teacher to the "expert" in the group; learning is still passive, and what is learned can be wrong.
- Status differences may be increased rather than decreased. Some students learn to "loaf" because the group progresses with or without their contributions. Others become even more convinced that they are unable to understand without the support of the group.

The next sections examine how teachers can avoid these problems and encourage true cooperation.

Tasks for Cooperative Learning

Like so many other decisions in teaching, plans for using cooperative groups begin with a goal. What are students supposed to accomplish? Successful teachers interviewed in one study emphasized that group activities must be well planned, students need to be prepared to work in groups, and teachers' expectations for the task have to be explicitly stated (Gillies & Boyle, 2011). What is the task? Is it a true group task—one that builds on the knowledge and skills of several students—or is the task more appropriate for individuals (E. G. Cohen, 1994; O'Donnell, 2006)?

Tasks for cooperative groups may be more or less structured. Highly structured tasks include work that has specific answers—drill and practice, applying routines or procedures, answering questions from readings, computations in mathematics, and so on. Ill-structured complex tasks have multiple answers and unclear procedures, requiring problem finding and higher-order thinking. These ill-structured problems are true group tasks; that is, they are likely to require the resources (knowledge, skills, problem-solving strategies, creativity) of all the group members to accomplish, whereas individuals often can accomplish highly structured tasks just as effectively as groups. These distinctions are important because ill-structured, complex, true group tasks appear to require more and higher-quality interactions than routine tasks if learning and problem solving are to occur (E. G. Cohen, 1994; Gillies, 2004; Gillies & Boyle, 2011).

HIGHLY STRUCTURED, REVIEW, AND SKILL-BUILDING TASKS. A relatively structured task such as reviewing previously learned material for an exam might be well served by a structured technique such as student teams achievement divisions (STAD), in which teams of four students compete to determine which team's members can amass the greatest improvement over previous achievement levels (Slavin, 1995). Praise, recognition, or extrinsic rewards can enhance motivation, effort, and persistence under these conditions, and thus increase learning. Focusing the dialogue by assigning narrow roles also may help students stay engaged when the tasks involve practice or review.

ILL-STRUCTURED, CONCEPTUAL, AND PROBLEM-SOLVING TASKS. If the task is ill-structured and more cognitive in nature, then an open exchange and elaborated discussion will be more helpful (E. G. Cohen, 1994; Ross & Raphael, 1990). Thus, strategies that encourage extended and productive interactions are appropriate when the goal is to develop higher-order thinking and problem solving. In these situations, a tightly structured process, competition among groups for rewards, and rigid assignment of roles are likely to inhibit the richness of the students' interactions and to interfere with progress toward the goal. Open-ended techniques such as reciprocal questioning (King, 1994), reciprocal teaching (Palincsar & Brown, 1984; Rosenshine & Meister, 1994), pair–share (S. Kagan, 1994), or Jigsaw (E. Aronson, 2000) should be more productive because, when used appropriately, they encourage more extensive interaction and elaborative thought in situations where students are being exposed to complex materials. In these instances, the use of rewards may well divert the group away from the goal of in-depth cognitive processing. When rewards are offered, the goal often becomes achieving the reward as efficiently as possible, which could mean having the highest-achieving students do all the work (Webb & Palincsar, 1996).

SOCIAL SKILLS AND COMMUNICATION TASKS. When the goal of peer learning is enhanced social skills or increased intergroup understanding and appreciation of diversity, the assignment of specific roles and functions within the group might support communication (E. G. Cohen, 1994; S. Kagan, 1994). In these situations, it can be helpful to rotate leadership roles so that minority group students and females have the opportunity to demonstrate and develop leadership skills; in addition, all group members can experience the leadership capabilities of each individual (N. Miller & Harrington, 1993). Rewards probably are not necessary, and they may actually get in the way because the goal is to build community, a sense of respect, and responsibility for all team members.

Preparing Students for Cooperative Learning

David and Roger Johnson (D. W. Johnson & Johnson, 2009a) explain five elements that define true cooperative learning groups:

- Positive interdependence
- Promotive interaction
- Individual accountability
- Collaborative and social skills
- Group processing

Group members experience *positive interdependence*. The members believe they can attain their goals only if the others in the group attain their goals as well, so they need each other for support, explanations, and guidance. *Promotive interaction* means that group members encourage and facilitate each other's efforts. They usually interact face-to-face and close together, not across the room, but they also could interact via digital media around the world. Even though they feel a responsibility to the group to work together and help each other, students must ultimately demonstrate learning on their own; they are held *individually accountable* for learning, often through individual tests or other assessments. *Collaborative and social skills* are necessary for effective group functioning. Often, these skills, such as giving constructive feedback, reaching consensus, and involving every member, must be taught and practiced before the groups tackle a learning task. Finally, members monitor *group processes* and relationships to make sure the group is working effectively and to learn about the dynamics of groups. They take time to ask, "How are we doing as a group? Is everyone working together? What should we do more or less of next time?"

Research in grades 8 through 12 in Australia found that students in cooperative groups that were structured to require positive interdependence and mutual helping learned more in math, science, and English than students in unstructured learning groups (Gillies, 2003). In addition, compared to students in the unstructured groups, students in the structured groups also said learning was more fun.

SETTING UP COOPERATIVE GROUPS. How large should a cooperative group be? Again, the answer depends on your learning goals. If the purpose is for the group members to review, rehearse information, or practice, 4 to 5 or 6 students is about the right size. But if the goal is to encourage each student to participate in discussions, problem solving, or computer learning, then groups of 2 to 4 members work best. Also, when setting up cooperative groups, it often makes sense to balance the number of boys and girls. Some research indicates that when there are just a few girls in a group, they tend to be left out of the discussions unless they are the most able or assertive members. By contrast, when there are only one or two boys in the group, they tend to dominate and be "interviewed" by the girls unless these boys are less able than the girls or are very shy. In some, but not all, studies of mixed-gender groups, girls avoided conflict, and boys dominated discussion (O'Donnell & O'Kelly, 1994; Webb & Palincsar, 1996). Whatever the case, teachers must monitor groups to make sure everyone is contributing and learning.

If a group includes some students who are perceived as different or who are often rejected, then it makes sense to be sure that there are group members who are tolerant and kind. One successful teacher interviewed by Gillies and Boyle (2011) put it this way:

> I also try to make sure that there are one or two people in the group who have the ability to be tolerant. At least the kid in question will know that, while the other group members may not be his best friends, they won't give him a hard time. I try to put the least reactive kids in the group with the child in question. This year I've had a couple of girls who have been very good with difficult kids. They don't put up with nonsense but they don't over-react and are prepared to demonstrate some good social skills. (p. 72)

GIVING AND RECEIVING EXPLANATIONS. In practice, the effects of learning in a group vary, depending on what actually happens in the group and who is in it. If only a few people take responsibility for the work, these people will learn, but the nonparticipating members probably will not. Students who ask questions, get answers, and attempt explanations are more likely to learn than students whose questions go unasked or unanswered. In fact, evidence shows that the more a student provides elaborated, thoughtful explanations to other students in a group, the more the *explainer* learns. Giving good explanations appears to be even more important for learning than receiving explanations (O'Donnell, 2006; Webb, Farivar, & Mastergeorge, 2002). In order to explain, you have to organize the information, put it into your own words, think of examples and analogies (which connect the information to things you already know), and test your understanding by answering questions. These are excellent learning strategies (King, 1990, 2002; O'Donnell & O'Kelly, 1994).

Good explanations are relevant, timely, correct, and elaborated enough to help the listener correct misunderstandings; the best explanations tell why (Webb et al., 2002; Webb & Mastergeorge, 2003). For example, in a middle school mathematics class, students worked in groups on the following problem:

> Find the cost of a 20-minute telephone call to the prefix 239 where the first minute costs $0.25 and each additional minute costs $0.11.

The level of explanation and help students received was significantly related to learning; the higher the level, the more learning. At the highest level, the helper tells how to solve the problem and *why*. For example, a helper explaining the telephone call cost problem above might say, "OK, it is 25 cents for the first minute, then there are 19 minutes left and each of those minutes costs 11 cents, so you multiply 11 cents by 19. That equals $2.09—then add 25 cents for the first minute so it costs $2.34" A poor explanation might be just giving the solution, "11 times 19 plus 25" or even just provide the answer—"I got $2.34." If a helper says, "11 times 19," then the receiver should say, "Why is it 19?" or "Why do you multiply by 11?" Asking good questions and giving clear explanations are critical, and usually these skills must be taught.

ASSIGNING ROLES. Some teachers assign roles to students to encourage cooperation and full participation. Several roles are described in Table 10.3. If you use roles, be sure that they support learning. In groups that focus on social skills, roles should support listening, encouragement, and respect for differences. In groups that focus on practice, review, or mastery of basic skills, roles should support persistence, encouragement, and participation. In groups that focus on higher-order problem solving or complex learning, roles should encourage thoughtful discussion, sharing of explanations and insights, probing, brainstorming, and creativity. Make sure that you don't communicate to students that the major purpose of the groups is simply to do the procedures—the roles. Roles are supports for learning, not ends in themselves (Woolfolk Hoy & Tschannen-Moran, 1999).

Often, cooperative learning strategies include group reports to the entire class. If you have been on the receiving end of these class reports, you know that they can be deadly dull. To make the process more useful for the audience as well as the reporters, Annemarie Palincsar and Leslie Herrenkohl (2002) taught the class members to use *intellectual roles* as they listened to reports. These roles were based on the scientific strategies of predicting and theorizing, summarizing results, and relating predictions and theories to results. Some audience members were assigned the role of checking the reports for clear relationships between predictions and theories. Other students in the audience listened for clarity in the findings. And the rest of the students were responsible for evaluating how well the group reports linked prediction, theories, and findings. Research shows that using these roles promotes class dialogue, thinking and problem solving, and conceptual understanding (Palincsar & Herrenkohl, 2002).

TABLE 10.3 • Possible Student Roles in Cooperative Learning Groups

Depending on the purpose of the group and the age of the participants, having these assigned roles might help students cooperate and learn. Of course, students may have to be taught how to enact each role effectively, and roles should be rotated so students can participate in different aspects of group learning.

ROLE	DESCRIPTION
Encourager	Encourages reluctant or shy students to participate
Praiser/Cheerleader	Shows appreciation of others' contributions, and recognizes accomplishments
Gate Keeper	Equalizes participation, and makes sure no one dominates
Coach	Helps with the academic content, explains concepts
Question Commander	Makes sure all students' questions are asked and answered
Checker	Checks the group's understanding
Taskmaster	Keeps the group on task
Recorder	Writes down ideas, decisions, and plans
Reflector	Keeps group aware of progress (or lack of progress)
Quiet Captain	Monitors noise level
Materials Monitor	Picks up and returns materials

Source: Based on Cooperative Learning by S. Kagan. Published by Kagan Publishing, San Clemente, CA. Copyright © 1994 by Kagan Publishing.

Designs for Cooperation

Developing deep understandings in cooperative groups requires that all the group members *participate* in *high-quality discussions.* Discussions that support learning include talk that interprets, connects, explains, and uses evidence to support arguments. We now turn to different strategies that build in structures to support both participation and high-quality discussions.

RECIPROCAL QUESTIONING. Reciprocal questioning requires no special materials or testing procedures and can be used with a wide range of ages. After a lesson or presentation by the teacher, students work in pairs or triads to ask and answer questions about the material (King, 1990, 1994, 2002). The teacher provides question stems (see Figure 10.2), and then students are taught how to develop specific questions on the lesson material using the generic question stems. The students create questions and then take turns asking and answering. This process has proved more effective than traditional discussion groups because it seems to encourage deeper thinking about the material. Questions such as those in Figure 10.2, which encourage students to make connections between the lesson and previous knowledge or experience, seem to be the most helpful.

For example, using question stems like those in Figure 10.2, a small group in Mr. Garcia's ninth-grade world cultures class had the following discussion about the concept of culture:

Sally: In your own words, what does culture mean?

Jim: Well, Mr. Garcia said in the lesson that a culture is the knowledge and understandings shared by the members of a society. I guess it's all the things and beliefs and activities that people in a society have in common. It includes things like religion, laws, music, medical practices, stuff like that.

Sally: And dance, art, family roles.

Barry: Knowledge includes language. So, I guess cultures include language, too.

Jim: I guess so. Actually, I have a question about that: How does a culture influence the language of a society?

Barry: Well, for one thing, the language is made up of words that are important to the people of that culture. Like, the words name things that the people care about, or need, or use. And so, different cultures would have different vocabularies. Some cultures may not even have a word for *telephone,* because they don't have any. But, phones are important in our

---

FIGURE 10.2

QUESTION STEMS TO ENCOURAGE DIALOGUE IN RECIPROCAL QUESTIONING

After participating in a lesson or studying an assignment on their own, students use these stems to develop questions, create and compare answers, and collaborate to create the best response.

What is an everyday application of _____?
How would you define _____ in your own words?
What are the advantages and disadvantages of _____?
What do you already know about _____?
Explain why _____ applies to _____.
How does _____ influence _____?
What is the value of _____?
What are the reasons for _____?
What are some arguments for and against _____?
What is your first choice about _____? Your second choice? _____? Why?
What is the best _____ and why?
Compare _____ and _____ based only on _____.
How would _____ be different if _____?
Do you agree or disagree with this claim _____? What is your evidence?

culture, so we have lots of different words for phones, like *cell phone, digital phone, desk phone, cordless phone, phone machine,* and . . .

Jim (laughing): I'll bet desert cultures don't have any words for *snow* or *skiing.*

Sally (turning to Barry): What's your question?

Barry: I've got a great question! You'll never be able to answer it. What would happen if there were a group somewhere without any spoken language? Maybe they were all born not being able to speak, or something like that. How would that affect their culture, or could there even be a culture?

Sally: Well, it would mean they couldn't communicate with each other.

Jim: And they wouldn't have any music! Because they wouldn't be able to sing.

Barry: But wait! Why couldn't they communicate? Maybe they would develop a nonverbal language system, you know, the way people use hand signals, or the way deaf people use sign language. (King, 2002, pp. 34–35)

JIGSAW. Elliot Aronson and his graduate students invented the Jigsaw classroom when Aronson was a professor of social psychology (and I was a student) at the University of Texas at Austin. Some of my friends worked on his research team. Aronson developed the approach "as a matter of absolute necessity to help defuse a highly explosive situation" (E. Aronson, 2000, p. 137). The Austin schools had just been desegregated by court order. White, African American, and Hispanic students were together in classrooms for the first time. Hostility and turmoil ensued, with fistfights in corridors and classrooms. Aronson's answer was the Jigsaw Classroom.

In Jigsaw, each group member is given part of the material to be learned by the whole group. Students become "expert" on their piece. Because students have to learn and be tested on every piece of the larger "puzzle," everyone's contribution is important—the students truly are interdependent. A more recent version, Jigsaw II, adds expert groups in which the students who are responsible for the same material from each learning group confer to make sure they understand their assigned part and then plan ways to teach the information to their learning group members. Next, students return to their learning groups, bringing their expertise to the sessions. In the end, students take an individual test covering all the material and earn points for their learning team score. Teams can work for rewards or simply for recognition (E. Aronson, 2000; Slavin, 1995).

CONSTRUCTIVE/STRUCTURED CONTROVERSIES. Constructive conflict resolution is essential in classrooms because conflicts are inevitable and even necessary for learning. Piaget's theory tells us that developing knowledge requires cognitive conflict. David and Roger Johnson (D. W. Johnson & Johnson, 2009b) make a powerful case for constructive intellectual conflict:

> Conflict is to student learning what the internal combustion engine is to the automobile. The internal combustion engine ignites the fuel and the air with a spark to create the energy for movement and acceleration. Just as the fuel and the air are inert without the spark, so, ideas in the classroom are inert without the spark of intellectual conflict. (p. 37)

One study of 10th graders found that students who were wrong, but for different reasons, were sometimes able to correct their misunderstandings if they argued together about their conflicting wrong answers (Schwarz, Neuman, & Biezuner, 2000). Individuals trying to exist in groups will have interpersonal conflicts, too, which also can lead to learning. In fact, research over the last 40 years demonstrates that constructive controversy in classrooms can lead to greater learning, open-mindedness, seeing the perspectives of others, creativity, motivation, engagement, and self-esteem (D. W. Johnson & Johnson, 2009b; Roseth, Saltarelli, & Glass, 2011). Table 10.4 shows how academic and interpersonal conflicts can be positive forces in a learning community.

As you can see in Table 10.4, the structured part of *constructive/structured controversies* is that students work in pairs within their four-person cooperative groups to research a particular controversy, such as whether lumber companies should be allowed to cut down trees in national forests. Each pair of students researches the issue, develops a pro or con position, presents their position and evidence to the other pair, discusses the issue, and then reverses positions and argues for the other

Connect and Extend to PRAXIS II®

Forms of Cooperative Learning (II, A2)
STAD and Jigsaw are just two of many cooperative learning techniques, each designed for certain instructional purposes. Go to *Cooperative Learning* (edu/Teaching-Resource-Center/CoopLear.html), sponsored by the University of Tennessee at Chattanooga, to learn about techniques and uses for cooperative learning.

TABLE 10.4 • **Constructive/Structured Controversies: Learning from Academic and Interpersonal Conflicts**
Conflict, if handled well, can support learning. Academic conflicts can lead to critical thinking and conceptual change. Conflicts of interest are unavoidable but can be handled so no one is the loser.

CONSTRUCTIVE ACADEMIC CONTROVERSY	CONFLICTS OF INTEREST
One person's ideas, information, theories, conclusions, and opinions are incompatible with those of another, and the two seek to reach an agreement.	The actions of one person attempting to maximize his or her benefits prevents, blocks, or interferes with another person's maximizing her or his benefits.
Controversy Procedure	*Integrative (Problem-Solving) Negotiations*
Research and prepare positions.	Describe wants.
Present and advocate positions.	Describe feelings.
Refute opposing position and refute attacks on own position.	Describe reasons for wants and feelings.
Reverse perspectives.	Take other's perspective.
Synthesize and integrate best evidence and reasoning from all sides.	Invent three optional agreements that maximize joint outcomes. Choose one, and formalize agreement.

Source: From "The Three Cs of School and Classroom Management," by D. Johnson and R. Johnson. In H. J. Freiberg (Ed.), Beyond Behaviorism: Changing the Classroom Management Paradigm. Copyright © 1999. Adapted with permission from Pearson Education, Inc.

perspective. Then, the group develops a final report that summarizes the best arguments for each position and reaches a consensus (D. W. Johnson & Johnson, 2009b; O'Donnell, 2006).

The structured part of structured controversies is that students work in pairs within their four-person cooperative groups to research a particular controversy, such as whether lumber companies should be allowed to cut down trees in national forests. Each pair of students researches the issue, develops a pro or con position, presents their position and evidence to the other pair, discusses the issue, and then reverses positions and argues for the other perspective. Then, the group develops a final report that summarizes the best arguments for each position and reaches a consensus (D. W. Johnson & Johnson, 2009b; O'Donnell, 2006).

In addition to these approaches, Spencer Kagan (1994) has developed many cooperative learning structures designed to accomplish different kinds of academic and social tasks. The *Guidelines: Using Cooperative Learning* on the next page gives you ideas for incorporating cooperative learning in your classes.

Reaching Every Student: Using Cooperative Learning Wisely

Cooperative learning always benefits from careful planning, but sometimes including students with special needs requires extra attention to planning and preparation. For example, cooperative structures such as scripted questioning and peer tutoring depend on a balanced interaction between the person taking the role of questioner or explainer and the student who is answering or being taught. In these interactions, you want to see and hear explaining and teaching, not just telling or giving right answers. But many students with learning disabilities have difficulties understanding new concepts, so both the explainer and the student can get frustrated, and social rejection for the student with learning disabilities might follow. Because students with learning disabilities often have problems with social relations, it is not a good idea to put them in situations where more rejection is likely. So, when you are teaching new or difficult-to-grasp concepts, cooperative learning might not be the best choice for students with learning disabilities (Kirk et al., 2006). In fact, research has found that cooperative learning in general is not always effective for students with learning disabilities (D. D. Smith, 2006).

Gifted students also may not benefit from cooperative learning when groups are mixed in ability. The pace often is too slow, the tasks too simple, and there is just too much repetition. In addition, gifted students often fall into the role of teacher or end up just doing the work quickly for the whole group. If you use mixed-ability groups and include gifted students, the challenges are to use complex tasks that allow work at different levels and keep gifted students engaged without losing the rest of the class (D. D. Smith, 2006).

GUIDELINES
Using Cooperative Learning

Fit group size and composition to your learning goals.

Examples

1. For social skills and team-building goals, use groups of two to five, common interest groups, mixed groups, or random groups.
2. For structured fact- and skill-based, practice-and-review tasks, use groups of two to four, mixed-ability such as high-middle and middle-low or high-low and middle-middle group compositions.
3. For higher-level conceptual and thinking tasks, use groups of two to four; select members to encourage interaction.

Assign appropriate roles.

Examples

1. For social skills and team-building goals, assign roles to monitor participation and conflict; rotate leadership of the group.
2. For structured fact- and skill-based, practice-and-review tasks, assign roles to monitor engagement and ensure low-status students have resources to offer, as in Jigsaw.
3. For higher-level conceptual and thinking tasks, assign roles only to encourage interaction, divergent thinking, and extended, connected discourse, as in debate teams, or to assign a group facilitator. Don't let roles get in the way of learning.

Make sure you assume a supporting role as the teacher.

Examples

1. For social skills and team-building goals, be a model and encourager.
2. For structured fact- and skill-based, practice-and-review tasks, be a model, director, or coach.

3. For higher-level conceptual and thinking tasks, be a model and facilitator.

Move around the room, and monitor the groups.

Examples

1. For social skills and team-building goals, watch for listening, turn taking, encouraging, and managing conflict.
2. For structured fact- and skill-based, practice-and-review tasks, watch for questioning, giving multiple elaborated explanations, attention, and practice.
3. For higher-level conceptual and thinking tasks, watch for questioning, explaining, elaborating, probing, divergent thinking, providing rationales, synthesizing, and using and connecting knowledge sources.

Start small and simple until you and the students know how to use cooperative methods.

Examples

1. For social skills and team-building goals, try one or two skills, such as listening and paraphrasing.
2. For structured fact- and skill-based, practice-and-review tasks, try pairs of students quizzing each other.
3. For higher-level conceptual and thinking tasks, try reciprocal questioning using pairs and just a few question stems.

For more information on cooperative learning, see: co-operation .org/edtech.kennesaw.edu/intech/cooperativelearning.htm.

Source: Based on "Implications of Cognitive Approaches to Peer Learning for Teacher Education," by A. Woolfolk Hoy and M. Tschannen-Moran, 1999. In A. O'Donnell and A. King (Eds.), Cognitive Perspectives on Peer Learning. Mahwah, NJ: Lawrence Erlbaum.

Cooperative learning may be an excellent choice for students who are English language learners (ELLs), however. The Jigsaw cooperative structure is especially helpful because all students in the group, including the students who are ELLs, have information that the group needs, so they also must talk, explain, and interact. In fact, the Jigsaw approach was developed in response to the need to create high interdependence in diverse groups. In many classrooms today, four to six or more languages are represented. Teachers can't be expected to master every heritage language spoken by all of their students every year. In these classrooms, cooperative groups can help as students work together on academic tasks. Students who speak two languages can help translate and explain lessons to others in the group. Speaking in a smaller group may be less anxiety provoking for students who are learning another language; so the students who are ELLs may get more language practice with feedback in these groups (D. D. Smith, 2006).

Cooperative learning is only as good as its design and implementation. Cooperative methods probably are both misused and underused in schools, in part because using cooperative learning well requires time and investment in teaching students how to learn in groups (Blatchford, Baines, Rubie-Davis, Bassett, & Chowne, 2006).

Dilemmas of Constructivist Practice

Years ago, Larry Cremin (1961) observed that progressive, innovative pedagogies require infinitely skilled teachers. Today, the same could be said about constructivist teaching. We have already seen that many varieties of constructivism and many practices flow from these different conceptions.

TABLE 10.5 • **Teachers' Dilemmas of Constructivism in Practice**
Teachers face conceptual, pedagogical, cultural, and political dilemmas as they implement constructivist practices. Here are explanations of these dilemmas and some representative questions that teachers face as they confront them.

TEACHERS' DILEMMA CATEGORY	REPRESENTATIVE QUESTIONS OF CONCERN
I. *Conceptual dilemmas:* Grasping the underpinnings of cognitive and social constructivism; reconciling current beliefs about pedagogy with the beliefs necessary to support a constructivist learning environment.	Which version of constructivism is suitable as a basis for my teaching? Is my classroom supposed to be a collection of individuals working toward conceptual change or a community of learners whose development is measured by participation in authentic disciplinary practices? If certain ideas are considered correct by experts, should students internalize those ideas instead of constructing their own?
II. *Pedagogical dilemmas:* Honoring students' attempts to think for themselves while remaining faithful to accepted disciplinary ideas; developing deeper knowledge of subject matter; mastering the art of facilitation; managing new kinds of discourse and collaborative work in the classroom.	Do I base my teaching on students' existing ideas rather than on learning objectives? What skills and strategies are necessary for me to become a facilitator? How do I manage a classroom where students are talking to one another rather than to me? Should I place limits on students' construction of their own ideas? What types of assessments will capture the learning I want to foster?
III. *Cultural dilemmas:* Becoming conscious of the culture of your classroom; questioning assumptions about what kinds of activities should be valued; taking advantage of experiences, discourse patterns, and local knowledge of students with varied cultural backgrounds.	How can we contradict traditional, efficient classroom routines and generate new agreements with students about what is valued and rewarded? How do my own past images of what is proper and possible in a classroom prevent me from seeing the potential for a different kind of learning environment? How can I accommodate the worldviews of students from diverse backgrounds while at the same time transforming my own classroom culture? Can I trust students to accept responsibility for their own learning?
IV. *Political dilemmas:* Confronting issues of accountability with various stakeholders in the school community; negotiating with key others the authority and support to teach for understanding.	How can I gain the support of administrators and parents for teaching in such a radically different and unfamiliar way? Should I make use of approved curriculums that are not sensitive enough to my students' needs, or should I create my own? How can diverse problem-based experiences help students meet specific state and local standards? Will constructivist approaches adequately prepare my students for high-stakes testing for college admissions?

Source: M. Windschitl. (2002). Framing constructivism in practice as the negotiation of dilemmas: An analysis of the conceptual, pedagogical, cultural, and political challenges facing teachers. Review of Educational Research, 72, p. 133. Copyright © 2002 by the American Educational Research Association. Reproduced with permission of the publisher.

We also know that all teaching today happens in a context of high-stakes testing and accountability. In these situations, constructivist teachers face many challenges. Mark Windschitl (2002) identified four teacher dilemmas of constructivism in practice, summarized in Table 10.5. The first is conceptual: How do I make sense of cognitive versus social conceptions of constructivism and reconcile these different perspectives with my practice? The second dilemma is pedagogical: How do I teach in truly constructivist ways that both honor my students' attempts to think for themselves, but still ensure that they learn the academic material? Third are cultural dilemmas: What activities, cultural knowledge, and ways of talking will build a community in a diverse classroom? Finally, there are political dilemmas: How can I teach for deep understanding and critical thinking, but still satisfy the accountability demands of parents and the requirements of state achievement testing?

ENHANCEDetext *self-check*

SERVICE LEARNING

Service learning combines academic learning with personal and social development for secondary and college students (Woolfolk Hoy, Demerath, & Pape, 2002). A more formal definition of **service learning** is "a teaching and learning strategy that integrates meaningful community service with instruction and reflection to enrich the learning experience, teach civic responsibility, and strengthen communities" (National Service Learning Clearinghouse, n.d.). About half of

GUIDELINES
Family and Community Partnerships

Service Learning

The service should be ongoing, not just a brief project.
Examples

1. Instead of having a 2-week food drive with a party for the class that collected the most, encourage a longer commitment to cook or serve food at shelters for homeless families.
2. Contact local agencies to identify real needs that your students could address, or search online by zip code: volunteermatch.org.

Consider virtual volunteering. See serviceleader.org/virtual.
Examples

1. Translate a document into another language.
2. Provide multimedia expertise, such as preparing a PowerPoint™, QuickTime™, or other computer-based presentation.
3. Design an agency's newsletter or brochure, or copyedit an agency's publication or proposal.
4. Proofread drafts of papers and online publications.
5. Research and write articles for brochures, newsletters, Web sites.
6. Design a logo for an agency or program, or fill other illustration needs.

Be aware of service learning projects in school. Make sure learning is at the center.
Examples

1. Have clear learning objectives for the projects.
2. Examine grade-level standards in science, history, health, literature, and other areas to see how some might be met through service projects—for example, how might concepts in biology be learned through designing a nutrition education project for senior citizens or preschool students?
3. Do students reflect over time about their experiences, keep journals, write or draw what they have learned, and include these reflections in class discussions?

Make sure the service draws on your child's talents and skills so that it is actually valuable to the recipients and he or she gains a sense of accomplishment and usefulness from applying skills to help others.
Examples

1. Youth who have artistic talents might help redecorate a game room at a senior citizens' center.
2. Individuals who are good storytellers could work with children at a daycare center or in a children's clinic.
3. Students who are bilingual might help teachers translate school newsletters into the languages of fellow students' families or serve as translators at local clinics.

Design service learning opportunities so they are inclusive (Dymond, Renzaglia, & Chun, 2007).
Examples

1. Consider transportation needs for children with disabilities.
2. Link service learning projects to life skills such as social skills on the job, safety, and punctuality.
3. Encourage teachers to monitor interactions in groups for all students; be aware of how students with special needs are included.

For more ideas, see: service-learningpartnership.org/site/PageServer.

Video 10.4
Dr. Hudson's high school students are involved in a problem-based learning project that integrates learning goals with service to the community. Note the community needs being met and the learning skills being developed during the process.

ENHANCEDetext *video example*

American high schools have some form of service learning (Dymond, Renzaglia, & Chun, 2007). The Alliance for Service Learning in Education Reform (1993) lists several characteristics of service learning. The activities:

- Are organized and meet actual community needs.
- Are integrated into the student's curriculum.
- Provide time to reflect and write about the service experience.
- Provide opportunities to apply newly learned academic skills and knowledge.
- Enhance both academic learning and a sense of caring for others.

Service learning activities may involve direct service (tutoring, serving meals at homeless shelters), indirect service (collecting food for shelters, raising money), or advocacy (designing and distributing posters about a food drive, writing newspaper articles) (A. M. Johnson & Notah, 1999). Service learning also could be a form of problem-based learning.

Participation in service learning can promote political and moral development for adolescents. Through service learning projects, adolescents experience their own competence and agency by working with others in need. Students see themselves as political and moral agents, rather than as merely good citizens (Youniss & Yates, 1997). In addition, service learning can help adolescents think in new ways about their relationships with people who are unlike them, and thus can lead them to become more tolerant of differences (W. G. Tierney, 1993). Finally, service learning experiences foster an "ethic of care" that can result in a growing commitment to confront difficult social problems (Rhodes, 1997). In this sense, student involvement in service learning can motivate and empower adolescents to critically reflect on their role in society (Woolfolk Hoy, Demerath, & Pape, 2002). A number of schools now have participation in service learning as a graduation requirement, but some educators question if "required" service is fair or appropriate. At least three of the school requirements have been challenged in court, but so far, the requirements have been upheld (A. M. Johnson & Notah, 1999).

Studies of service learning have produced mixed results. Some studies have found modest gains on measures of social responsibility, tolerance for others, empathy, attitude toward adults, and self-esteem (Solomon et al., 2001). A case study at an urban parochial high school describes a successful service learning experience program that was required for juniors and was part of a yearlong course on social justice (Yates & Youniss, 1999). In the class, students examined the moral implications of current social issues such as homelessness, poverty, exploitation of immigrant laborers, and urban violence. Students also were required to serve four times (approximately 20 hours) at an inner-city soup kitchen. The researchers concluded that students emerged from the course with "a deeper awareness of social injustice, a greater sense of commitment to confront these injustices, and heightened confidence in their abilities overall" (Yates & Youniss, 1999, p. 64).

Your students may be involved in service learning both inside and outside the school. You might share the *Guidelines: Family and Community Partnership* on the previous page with families and use them yourself. Many are taken from Richard Sagor (2003) and M. J. Elias and Schwab (2006).

ENHANCEDetext *self-check*

LEARNING IN A DIGITAL WORLD

It seems that computers, smart phones, iPods, iPads, iTouches, tablets, digital readers, wikis, and interactive video games, along with iCloud, Facebook, Twitter, Google, WhatsApp, Snapchat, Instagram, Scratch, . . . and other digital tools and media have changed life for everyone. Homes and schools are filled with media. In 2012, 71% of the households with children ages 0 to 8 had smartphones, 42% had tablets such as iPads, and 35% had both. Over 35% of children *ages 6 months to 3 years* have a TV in their own bedroom, and 10% of children ages 4 to 8 have a computer. In almost 40% of homes surveyed in 2012, the TV was on half of the time, even if no one was watching (Rideout et al., 2003; Rosen, 2010; Wartella, Rideout, Lajricella, & Connell, 2013). In fact, many children spend more time watching TV than engaging in any other activity except sleep.

STOP & THINK How many digital devices are you using right now? How many do you own? •

For students, doing homework often involves exchanging messages with friends via e-mail, texting, or cell phones, searching the Web, and downloading resources—all the time listening to music via an iPod or watching TV (D. F. Roberts, Foehr, & Rideout, 2005). These students have never known a world without digital media, so they have been called digital natives, homo zappiens, the Net generation, iGenerations, or Google Generation (Kirschner & van Merriënboer, 2013).

Technology and Learning

Does technology use support academic learning? The answer is complex and even surprising. One review concluded that using computer tutorial programs appeared to improve achievement test scores for K–12 students, but simulations and enrichment programs had few effects—perhaps another example that when you teach and test specific skills, children learn the skills. Computers are more likely to increase achievement if they support the basic processes that lead to learning: active engagement, frequent interaction with feedback, authenticity and real-world connection, and productive group work (A. Jackson et al., 2006; Roschelle et al., 2000; Tamim, Bernard,

Video 10.5
In this video, high school students develop instruction for younger students to help them learn appropriate and safe behaviors for online exchanges. As you watch, consider how technology supports learning.

ENHANCEDetext *video example*

Borokhovski, Abrami, & Schmid, 2011). Computers can be useful to teach basic reading processes such as word decoding or phonological awareness or basic number sense because the computer programs can provide individual feedback, move at the right pace for each student, and increase motivation. Well-designed programs also can improve listening and reading comprehension (Baroody et al., 2013; Potocki, Ecalle, & Magnan, 2013; R. Savage et al., 2013). Like any teaching tool, computers can be effective if used well, but just being on a computer will not automatically increase academic achievement.

TECHNOLOGY-RICH ENVIRONMENTS. With all the technology available today, interest in technology-rich learning environments (TREs) is growing. These environments include virtual worlds, computer simulations that support problem-based learning such as the River of Life Challenge described earlier, intelligent tutoring systems, educational games, audio recordings, wikis, hand-held wireless devices, and multimedia environments—to name just a few.

There are three kinds of uses for technology in schools. First, teachers can design technology-based activities for their classrooms, for virtual learning environments, or for blended models using both in-class and virtual environments. Second, students can interact with technologies in a variety of ways, such as by using a computer or tablet to complete assignments or by collaborating in a virtual environment with other students or teachers using interactive cloud computing applications. Cloud computing allows computer users online access to applications such as Google documents or Microsoft Web Mail along with computing assets such as network-accessible data storage and processing. Finally, administrators use technology to track teacher, class, and student information in school, district, or state-wide systems. You could be involved with any or all three of these uses of technology in your teaching.

The primary goal for integrating technology into a classroom is to support student learning. Unfortunately, the story with technology and learning over the years has been great potential, but limited integration and use (Cuban, 2001). For example, creating and maintaining wikis allows teachers or students to collaborate, develop and edit content, and share resources and products—remarkable potential, but not always realized. There are a few exciting collaborations such as the Flat Classroom Project (flatclassroomproject.org), where students around the world produce wiki pages devoted to explaining the future of technology and society. To create multimedia wiki pages, students in Shanghai may film content and their collaborators in Vienna may edit and post the material. But such innovative wiki applications are not common. About 40% of the wikis produced in schools are one-time use or teacher-sharing sites, 34% deliver teacher content, 25% present individual student work, and only 1% are collaborative work spaces for students (Reich, Murnane, & Willett, 2012).

The process of integrating digital tools to support learning may seem difficult and troublesome at first, especially for teachers with few technological skills. Starting points include researching your school or district technology policies and procedures, identifying internal resources such as technology integration teams, seeking out training resources, and working with teachers who already use technology in their classes. Becoming familiar with available technological resources will help you to identify and include new technologies that will enhance your teaching. A golden rule for technology integration in any classroom is that you do not need to reinvent the wheel. Focus on identifying centers of expertise where existing resources are available to adapt and build on.

VIRTUAL LEARNING ENVIRONMENTS. Virtual learning environments (VLEs) is a broad term that describes many ways of learning in virtual systems. The most traditional VLE is referred to as a learning management system (LMS). LMSs deliver e-learning using applications such as Moodle, BlackBoard, RCampus, and Desire2Learn. LMSs are large, complex, and costly—my university uses a system we call "Carmen" to support every course on campus. My Carmen sites have readings, discussion groups, class-built wikis, PowerPoints, Weblinks, a calendar, and many other resources. We taught classes without these assets for decades, but the LMS has expanded our teaching and learning options. To deal with costs, some institutions use free *open-source software* to construct VLEs. Tools that support open-source software include Moodle, Google Apps, Microsoft SharePoint, and PBWorks.

Betty's Brain is a fascinating example of a VLE developed by Vanderbilt and Stanford Universities (teachableagents.org/research/bettysbrain.php). Using this computer-based system, students are challenged to "teach" a topic in science to a computer agent known as Betty. The system provides hypertext

FIGURE 10.3

BETTY'S BRAIN: A VIRTUAL LEARNING ENVIRONMENT

Betty's Brain is a computer-based learning environment that uses learning-by-teaching to engage students in learning about science topics.

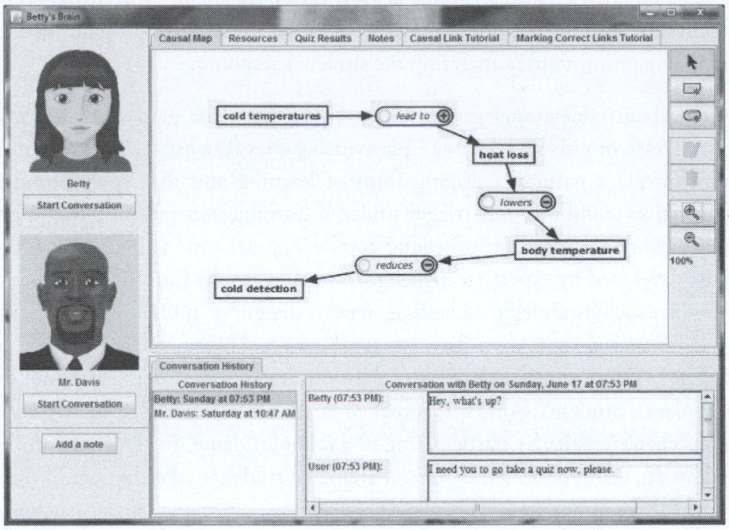

Source: Based on teachableagents.org/research/bettysbrain.php

resources for the students to use in planning their instruction (and learning the concepts and processes under study). As I have discovered so many times in my life, the best way to learn something is to teach it. Remember, the research on cooperative learning shows that the *explainer* learns more than the listener (O'Donnell, 2006). Like all good teachers, the students who are working with Betty must keep track of how well she is learning—by asking Betty to answer questions and take quizzes. The computer system also incudes an expert on the topic, Mr. Davis, who grades Betty's work and mentors the student "teachers." See Figure 10.3 for an example screen from Betty's Brain.

PERSONAL LEARNING ENVIRONMENTS. There are different kinds of VLEs. A **personal learning environment (PLE)** framework provides tools that support individualized learning in a variety of contexts and situations; the learners assume control of how and when their learning occurs. Students working in PLEs can download an assignment at Panera, read the material on the bus, and then post an analysis on the discussion board at 4:00 a.m. from their room. Learning in PLEs can be asynchronous—taking place any time and anywhere. Complex PLEs include tools that assess learners' knowledge and then adapt the next content to fit their needs. Tools that support PLEs include computer-based training modules, e-books, cognitive tutors, quizzes, and self-assessment tools.

A **personal learning network (PLN)** is a framework in which knowledge is constructed through online peer interactions. PLNs consist of both synchronous (real-time) and asynchronous technologies using interactive Web conferencing, hybrid classes, or online discussions. A PLN can be used for K–12 instructional purposes and also as a resource for professional development. Social networking tools such as Facebook, Twitter, Edutopia, and EdWeb allow the instruction to move outside the school, city, and even country to include learners with similar interests around the globe. Tools that support PLNs include Web conferencing tools, such as Adobe Connect and Elluminate, instant messaging, interactive video and audio messaging, social networking, discussion boards, and blogs.

IMMERSIVE VIRTUAL LEARNING ENVIRONMENTS. The most complex VLE is an **immersive virtual learning environment (IVLE)**. The IVLE is a simulation of a real-world environment. The purpose is to learn through enculturation, for example, by being eco explorers in the rainforest or reporters covering a story about an outbreak of food poisoning in a local school (Gee, 2008; Gibson, Aldrich, & Prensky, 2006; Shaffer et al., 2009). IVLEs are designed to be domain specific using realistic scenarios (Bagley & Shaffer, 2009; Shaffer et al., 2009). IVLE experiences mimic tasks required in a professional practicum, such as interviewing sources for a news story about food poisoning, following leads to identify the source of a problem, and crafting an accurate engaging article, thus blending real-world engagement in a virtual scenario. These immersive environments often include *cognitive tutors*; the technology is programmed to interact as a tutor by providing prompts after analyzing the student's response.

GAMES. What about educational games? Certainly students use games outside school. About 99% of boys and 94% of girls ages 12 to 17 play video games (Ownston, 2012). Many researchers suggest games provide a natural, engaging form of learning and that "combining games with educational objectives could not only trigger students' learning motivation, but also provide them with interactive learning opportunities" (Sung & Hwang, 2013, p. 44). Games might include a knowledge base developed by experts, a challenge to students in the form of a problem or role-play, and a final product such as creating a database, report, design, or problem solution. For example, in Taiwan, Han-Yu Sung and Gwo-Jen Hwang (Sung & Hwang, 2013) used a collaborative educational game to create an immersive learning environment for elementary school students who were studying plants. Students worked together to complete a knowledge matrix about different plants and their characteristics by participating in a role-play game. In the game, the people in an ancient kingdom are being poisoned by river water. The students take the role of the king trying to identify plants that might cure his people. The king must overcome barriers such as a maze and a misty forest, gather and organize detailed information about various plants, and then be tested by fairies to be sure he has the knowledge needed to use the plants to cure his people. When the students gather the right information and pass all the fairies' tests, they can move to the next level of the game. Participating in the collaborative game was successful in improving achievement as well as motivation and self-efficacy for learning.

But even with this promise, there is no guarantee that students will learn from all educational games or transfer their learning to situations outside the game (Ownston, 2012; Roschelle, 2013). Pieter Wouters and his colleagues in the Netherlands (2013) analyzed 38 studies of serious educational computer games conducted from 1990 to 2012. They concluded that games were more effective than traditional instruction in terms of learning and retention, but not in terms of motivation, the one thing you might think would be an asset for games. In addition, students participating in games learned more when the games were not the only method but were supplemented with other forms of instruction, when there were multiple sessions, and when the students worked in groups.

Massive multi-player online games (MMOGs) are interactive gaming environments constructed in virtual worlds in which the learner assumes a character role of avatar. Virtual world simulations incorporating MMOGs have been used for experiential and didactic learning in the medical field for several years and quickly are gaining attention in pre-K–12 classrooms. The pedagogic value in good gaming design is the ability to create complex scenarios by developing lessons using modeling and problem-based learning scenarios as alternative methods of instruction (Gee, 2008). For example, Project Evoke is a game developed by the World Bank (urgentevoke.com). As they play the game, adolescents from around the world work collectively to solve major world problems such as hunger. Stay tuned for more exciting learning worlds.

Developmentally Appropriate Computer Activities for Young Children

Digital media are appealing, but are they appropriate for preschool children? This is a hotly debated issue. Computers should not be used to do solitary drill-and-practice activities. Developmentally appropriate ways to use computers with 3- and 4-year-olds differ from the ways we use computers in kindergarten and the primary grades (kidsource.com/education/computers.children.html). With developmentally appropriate computer activities, young children can benefit cognitively without sustaining losses in creativity (Haugland & Wright, 1997). Software for children should include simple spoken directions; the activities should be open-ended and encourage discovery, exploration, problem solving, and understanding of cause and effect. Children should be able to remain in control of the activities through a variety of responses. Finally, the content should be appropriate for and respectful of diverse cultures, ages, and abilities (M. A. Fischer & Gillespie, 2003; Frost, Wortham, & Reifel, 2012). Linda Tsantis and her colleagues suggest that you ask this question about any program you are considering: "Does this software program help create learning opportunities that did not exist without it?" (Tsantis, Bewick, & Thouvenelle, 2003).

There is another important consideration: Does the program's multimedia features (e.g., embedded videos, zoom-ins, music, added sounds, images) add to learning or take away from it? One danger is that programs will include attractive visuals or sound effects that actually interrupt and interfere with the development of important concepts. For example, do the sounds of a buzz saw and the thud of a falling tree in a Peter Rabbit storytelling program foster distractibility and interfere with understanding the story, plot, and characters? Maybe (Tsantis et al., 2003).

Dealing with all of this stimulation might make children better at multitasking but also worse at deeper thought processes such as developing perspective-taking skills and understanding the plot, theme, and sequence of the story. So children learn to do several things at once but have a superficial understanding of what they are doing (Carpenter, 2000).

Research in the Netherlands, however, demonstrated that multimedia storybooks can provide support for understanding stories and remembering linguistic information for kindergarten students from families with low educational levels who are behind in language and literacy skills (Verhallen, Bus, & de Jong, 2006). The difference in this study seemed to be that the multimedia features of the story supported understanding and memory by providing multiple pathways to meaning, giving visual and verbal representations of key story elements, focusing attention on important information, and reinforcing key ideas. This extra scaffolding may be especially important for students with limited language and literacy skills. So the bottom line is that multimedia elements should focus on meaning and not just provide attractive "bells and whistles."

Computers and Older Students

A study that used real-time event sampling to assess Internet usage found that older adolescents spend about 60 minutes a day on the Internet, but the time varied by ethnicity. Adolescents of color used the Internet about 50% more (around 100 minutes per day on average) compared to White adolescents. The most common activities were visiting social networking sites, working on school assignments, browsing, e-mail, and streaming video. Surprisingly, participants in this study self-reported between *3 and 4 hours a day* of Internet use, so their self-reports exaggerated the time spent (Moreno et al., 2012). But just because adolescents' lives are filled with media does not mean that these students make the best use of technology for learning, unless they get guidance and instruction. For example, students may be skilled at clicking through a Google search, but suffer from the *butterfly defect*—they flutter from one enticing link to the next, often forgetting what they are researching. At best the knowledge they construct is fragile and easily forgotten (Kirschner & van Merriënboer, 2013). Even so, using some forms of technology can be engaging. In a study comparing learning from a desktop computer versus learning the same material on a mobile device (iPad), students using the mobile device were more involved and willing to continue learning (Sung & Mayer, 2013). See the *Guidelines: Using Computers* on the next page for more ideas.

COMPUTATIONAL THINKING AND CODING. Using technology for learning and for life has become so pervasive for all ages that some educators argue students should learn computational thinking, defined as the thought processes involved in formulating problems so "their solutions can be represented as computational [computing] steps and algorithms" (Aho, 2012, p. 832), in other words, thinking like a computer scientist.

Computational thinking includes, but is not limited to, programming and coding. Since the 1980s and 1990s when Seymore Papert (1980, 1991) introduced LOGO programming and turtle graphics for children, interest has grown in teaching students to code. Some educators claimed that programming taught students to think logically in all areas, but others said programming just helped students learn to program. Even so, there is ongoing interest in and advocacy for the value of coding as a way to foster computational thinking. See the Exploring Computer Science Web site for ideas about curriculum (exploringcs.org). Simple programing languages available today include Scratch, Alice, Game Maker, Kodu, and Greenfoot. There is even a version of Scratch (developed by MIT) called

GUIDELINES
Using Computers

IF YOU HAVE ONLY ONE COMPUTER IN YOUR CLASSROOM

Provide convenient access.

Examples

1. Find a central location if the computer is used to display material for the class.
2. Find a spot on the side of the room that allows seating and view of the screen, but does not crowd or disturb other students if the computer is used as a workstation for individuals or small groups.

Be prepared.

Examples

1. Check to be sure software needed for a lesson or assignment is installed and working.
2. Make sure instructions for using the software or doing the assignment are in an obvious place and clear.
3. Provide a checklist for completing assignments.

Create "trained experts" to help with computers.

Examples

1. Train student experts, and rotate experts.
2. Use adult volunteers—parents, grandparents, aunts and uncles, older siblings—anyone who cares about the students.

Develop systems for using the computer.

Examples

1. Make up a schedule to ensure that all students have access to the computer and no students monopolize the time.
2. Create standard ways of saving student work.

IF YOU HAVE MORE THAN ONE COMPUTER IN YOUR CLASSROOM

Plan the arrangement of the computers to fit your instructional goals.

Examples

1. For cooperative groups, arrange so students can cluster around their group's computer.
2. For different projects at different computer stations, allow for easy rotation from station to station.

Experiment with other models for using computers.

Examples

1. Navigator Model—four students per computer: One student is the (mouse and keyboard) driver, another is the "navigator." "Back-seat driver 1" manages the group's progress and "back-seat driver 2" serves as the timekeeper. The navigator attends a 10- to 20-minute training session in which the facilitator provides an overview of the basics of particular software. Navigators cannot touch the mouse. Driver roles are rotated.
2. Facilitator Model—six students per computer: the facilitator has more experience, expertise, or training and serves as the guide or teacher.
3. Collaborative Group Model—seven students per computer: Each small group is responsible for creating some component of the whole group's final product. For example, one part of the group writes a report, another creates a map, and a third uses the computer to gather and graph census data.

NO MATTER HOW MANY COMPUTERS YOU HAVE IN YOUR CLASSROOM

Select developmentally appropriate programs that encourage learning, creativity, and social interaction.

Examples

1. Encourage two children to work together rather than having children work alone.
2. Check the implicit messages in programs. For example, some drawing programs allow children to "blow up" their projects if they don't like them, so instead of solving a problem, they just destroy it. Tsantis et al. (2003) recommend a recycle metaphor instead of a "blow it up" option.
3. Look for programs that encourage discovery, exploration, problem solving, and multiple responses.

Monitor children as they work at computers.

Examples

1. Make sure computers are in areas where adults can observe them.
2. Discuss with children why some programs or Web sites are off limits.
3. Balance computer time with active play such as hands-on projects, blocks, sand, water, and art.

Keep children safe as they work at computers.

Examples

1. Teach children to shield their identity on the Internet and monitor any "friends" they may be communicating with.
2. Install filtering software to protect children from inappropriate content.

Sources: Suggestions from Frost, J. L., Wortham, S. C., & Reifel, S. (2005). Play and Child Development (2nd ed.). Upper Saddle River, NJ: Prentice-Hall, pp. 76–80, and Tsantis, L. A., Bewick, C. J., & Thouvenelle, S. (2003, November). Examining some common myths about computer use in the early years. Beyond the Journal: Young Children on the Web (pp. 1–9).

FIGURE 10.4

SCRATCH: CODING BY SNAPPING TOGETHER BLOCKS ON SCREEN

Scratch and Scratch Jr. are systems that allow children to "snap together" blocks like those shown here to control the actions of a character and design complete animations.

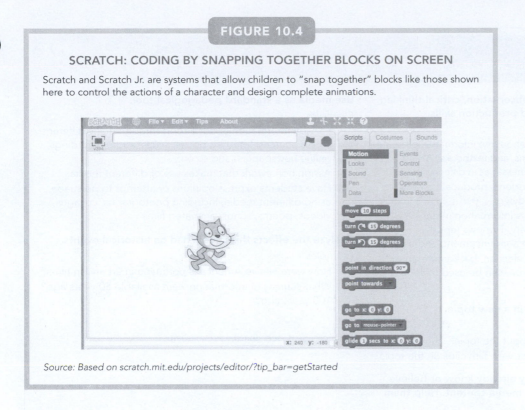

Source: Based on scratch.mit.edu/projects/editor/?tip_bar=getStarted

Scratch Jr. that will allow children from kindergarten through second grade to program (Guernsey, 2013)! Many of these languages allow even very young students to build programs by snapping together images of blocks on the computer screen. Figure 10.4 is a partial screen shot from Scratch. The way the blocks snap together controls actions of different characters on the computer screen (Grover & Pea, 2013). Costumes, sounds, colors, and other effects can be added. Other possibilities such as Lilypad Arduino are designed to engage more girls in programming activities.

MEDIA/DIGITAL LITERACY. With the advent of digital media comes a new concern with literacy—media or digital literacy. Today, to be literate—to be able to read, write, and communicate—children have to read and write in many media, not just printed words. Films, videos, DVDs, computers, photographs, artwork, magazines, music, TV, billboards, and more communicate through images and sounds. How do children read these messages? This is a new area of research and application in educational and developmental psychology (Hobbs, 2004).

As an example of practice, consider Project Look Sharp at Ithaca College, directed by Cynthia Scheibe, a developmental psychologist (ithaca.edu/looksharp). The goal of the project is to provide materials, training, and support as teachers integrate media literacy and critical thinking about media into their class lessons. Teachers participating in the project help their students become critical readers of media. For example, the goal of one project for elementary schools called "Introduction Africa" is to uncover stereotypes about Africa and teach about diversity. "In the first lesson, students challenge their own stereotypes about Africa through a series of photographs. After discussing the photographs, students examine how media constructions of Africa helped inform their responses. The second lesson uses currency as the medium to explore individual African countries' constructions of the continent" (Sperry, 2008).

Project Look Sharp suggests questions such as the following to guide discussion of media:

1. Who made—and who sponsored—this message, and why was it made? Who paid for it?
2. Who is the target audience, and how do you know?
3. What are the different techniques used, and why are they used?
4. What messages are communicated (and/or implied)? What is your interpretation, and why?
5. How current, accurate, and credible is the information in this message?
6. What is left out of the message that might be good to know?

GUIDELINES
Supporting the Development of Media Literacy

Use media to practice general observation, critical thinking, analysis, perspective taking, and production skills.

Examples

1. Ask students to think critically about the information presented in advertising, "news" programs, and textbooks. Would different people interpret the messages in differing ways?
2. Foster creativity by having students produce their own media on a topic you are studying.
3. Ask students to compare ways information might be presented in a documentary, TV news report, advertisement, public service announcement, and so on.
4. Give examples of how word selection, background music, camera angles, color, and so on, can be used to set a mood or bias a message.

Use media to stimulate interest in a new topic.

Examples

1. Analyze a magazine article about the topic.
2. Read sections from a novel, or view film clips on the topic.

Help students identify what they already know or believe about a topic based on popular media content. Help them identify erroneous beliefs.

Examples

1. What do students "know" about space travel?
2. What have they learned about biology from advertisements?

Use media as a standard pedagogical tool.

Examples

1. Provide information about a topic through many different media sources: Internet, books, DVDs, audio recordings, online newspapers, and so on.
2. Assign homework that makes use of different media.
3. Have students express opinions or attempt to persuade using different media, including photographs, collages, videos, poems, songs, animated films.

Analyze the effects that media had on historical events.

Examples

1. How were Native Americans portrayed in art and in films?
2. What sources of information were available 50 years ago? 100 years ago?

For more ideas, see: ithaca.edu/looksharp

The *Guidelines: Supporting the Development of Media Literacy* gives more ideas from Scheibe and Rogow (2004) for supporting the development of media literacy in your students.

ENHANCEDetext *self-check*

SUMMARY

- **The Learning Sciences (pp. 370–372)**

  What are some basic assumptions of the learning sciences? Key assumptions in the learning sciences are that experts develop deep conceptual knowledge, learning comes from the learner, creating learning environments is the responsibility of the school, students' prior knowledge is key, and reflection is a critical component of learning. These common assumptions enable researchers from a variety of disciplines to address the same issues of learning from a variety of perspectives.

- **Cognitive and Social Constructivism (pp. 372–378)**

  Describe two kinds of constructivism, and distinguish these from constructionism. *Psychological* constructivists such as Piaget are concerned with how individuals make sense of their world, based on individual knowledge, beliefs, self-concept, or identity—also called *first-wave constructivism*. *Social* constructivists such as Vygotsky believe that social interaction, cultural tools, and activity shape individual development and learning—also called *second-wave constructivism*. By participating in a broad range of activities with others, learners appropriate the outcomes produced by working together; they acquire new strategies and knowledge of their world. Finally, constructionists are interested in how public knowledge in academic disciplines is constructed as well as how everyday beliefs about the world are communicated to new members of a sociocultural group.

In what ways do constructivist views differ about knowledge sources, accuracy, and generality? Constructivists debate whether knowledge is constructed by mapping external reality, by adapting and changing internal understandings, or by an interaction of external forces and internal understandings. Most psychologists believe there is a role for both internal and external factors, but differ in how much they emphasize one or the other. Also, there is discussion about whether knowledge can be constructed in one situation and applied to another or whether knowledge is situated—specific and tied to the context in which it was learned. **What is meant by thinking as enculturation?** Enculturation is a broad and complex process of acquiring knowledge and understanding consistent with Vygotsky's theory of mediated learning. Just as our home culture taught us lessons about the use of language, the culture of a classroom can teach lessons about thinking by giving us models of good thinking; providing direct instruction in thinking processes; and encouraging practice of those thinking processes through interactions with others.

What are some common elements in most constructivist views of learning? Even though there is no single constructivist theory, many constructivist approaches recommend complex, challenging learning environments and authentic tasks; social negotiation and co-construction; multiple representations of content; understanding that knowledge is constructed; and student ownership of learning.

- **Applying Constructivist Perspectives (pp. 378–395)**

Distinguish between inquiry methods and problem-based learning. The inquiry strategy begins when the teacher presents a puzzling event, question, or problem. The students ask questions (only yes–no questions in some kinds of inquiry) and then formulate hypotheses to explain the event or solve the problem; collect data to test the hypotheses about casual relationships; form conclusions and generalizations; and reflect on the original problem and the thinking processes needed to solve it. Problem-based learning may follow a similar path, but the learning begins with an authentic problem—one that matters to the students. The goal is to learn math or science or history or some other important subject while seeking a real solution to a real problem.

Describe six features that most cognitive apprenticeship approaches share. Students observe an expert (usually the teacher) model the performance; get external support through coaching or tutoring; and receive conceptual scaffolding, which is then gradually faded as the students become more competent and proficient. Students continually articulate their knowledge—putting into words their understanding of the processes and content being learned. They reflect on their progress, comparing their problem solving to an expert's performance and to their own earlier performances. Finally, students explore new ways to apply what they are learning—ways that they have not practiced at the master's side.

Describe the use of dialogue in reciprocal teaching. The goal of reciprocal teaching is to help students understand and think deeply about what they read. To accomplish this goal, students in small reading groups learn four strategies: summarizing the content of a passage, asking a question about the central point, clarifying the difficult parts of the material, and predicting what will come next. These strategies are practiced in a classroom dialogue about the readings. Teachers first take a central role, but as the discussion progresses, the students take more and more control.

What are the differences between collaboration and cooperation? One view is that collaboration is a philosophy about how to relate to others—how to learn and work. Collaboration is a way of dealing with people that respects differences, shares authority, and builds on the knowledge that is distributed among other people. Cooperation, on the other hand, is a way of working together with others to attain a shared goal.

What are the learning theory underpinnings of cooperative learning? Learning can be enhanced in cooperative groups through rehearsal and elaboration (information processing theories), creation and resolution of disequilibrium (Piaget's theory), or scaffolding of higher mental processes (Vygotsky's theory).

Describe five elements that define true cooperative learning. Students interact face-to-face and close together, not across the room. Group members experience positive interdependence; they need each other for support, explanations, and guidance. Even though they work together and help each other, members of the group must ultimately demonstrate learning on their own. They are held individually accountable for learning, often through individual tests or other assessments. If necessary, the collaborative skills important for effective group functioning, such as giving constructive feedback, reaching consensus, and involving every member, are taught and practiced before the groups tackle a learning task. Finally, members monitor group processes and relationships to make sure the group is working effectively and to learn about the dynamics of groups.

How should tasks match design in cooperative learning? A relatively structured task works well with a structured technique; extrinsic rewards can enhance motivation, effort, and persistence under these conditions; roles, especially those that focus attention on the work to be accomplished, also may be productive. On the other hand, strategies that encourage extended and productive interactions are appropriate when the goal is to develop higher-order thinking and problem solving. The use of rewards may well divert the group away from the goal of in-depth cognitive processing. When the goal of peer learning is enhanced social skills or increased intergroup understanding and appreciation of diversity, the assignment of specific roles and functions within the group might support communication. Rewards probably are not necessary and may actually get in the way because the goal is to build community, a sense of respect, and responsibility for team members.

What are some possible strategies for cooperative learning? Strategies include reciprocal questioning, Jigsaw, structured controversy, and many cooperative structures described by Spencer Kagan.

- **Service Learning (pp. 395–397)**

What are some key characteristics of service learning? Service learning activities should be organized around and designed to meet actual community needs, as well as integrated into the student's curriculum. Teachers should provide time for students to reflect on and write about their service experience, offer opportunities to apply newly learned academic skills and knowledge, and strive to enhance both academic learning and a sense of caring for others. Service learning activities should not be supplementary to students' regular activities, but instead should be an integral part of their learning.

- **Learning in a Digital World (pp. 397–404)**

What are some possible uses of technology in education? Technology such as computers, iPods, smart phones, digital readers, and interactive gaming systems are extremely popular among young people. In fact, the many ways of communicating and interacting with others through technology may even shape the way students think about what it means to socialize. These technologies can be useful teaching tools, but they do have limitations. First, technology cannot necessarily replace the teacher when it comes to direct instruction (and not all programs are able to bring about learning). Classrooms of the future may take greater advantage of learning environments that immerse students in virtual worlds where they work alone or with others to solve problems, create projects, simulate the skills of experts, visit historical sites, tour world-class museums, or play games that teach and apply academic skills. The results of research on technology-enhanced learning emphasize that technology by itself will not guarantee improvement in academic achievement; like any tool, technology must be used well by confident, competent teachers. Some educators are suggesting that all students should learn computational thinking—thinking like a computer scientist—to formulate and solve problems that can be solved using the computational processes like those applied by computers. Many systems allow even very young students to create computer programs. Also, every student should learn to critically evaluate all the digital media that bombards us today.

PRACTICE USING WHAT YOU HAVE LEARNED

To access and complete the exercises, click the link under the images below.

Applying Constructivist Perspectives

ENHANCEDetext *application exercise*

Learning in a Digital World

ENHANCEDetext *application exercise*

KEY TERMS

CONNECT AND EXTEND TO LICENSURE

MULTIPLE-CHOICE QUESTIONS

1. Which one of the following activities would NOT be consistent with a constructivist environment?
   A. Students are given frequent opportunities to engage in complex, meaningful, problem-based activities.
   B. Students work collaboratively and are given support to engage in task-oriented dialogue with one another.
   C. Teachers elicit students' ideas and experiences in relationship to key topics, then fashion learning situations that assist students in elaborating on or restructuring their current knowledge.
   D. Teachers employ limited assessment strategies and give feedback on products rather than processes.

2. In Mr. Lawrence's classroom, students are engaged in learning the art of driving. They watch Mr. Lawrence model techniques, receive hints and feedback from him on their performance, and are encouraged to put into words the new skills they are practicing. This type of learning is best referred to as which one of the following?
   A. Reciprocal teaching
   B. Cognitive apprenticeship
   C. Cooperative learning
   D. Schema building

3. Group activities must be well planned. Students need to be prepared to work in groups, and teachers have to be explicit in stating their expectations. Which one of the following strategies is NOT an element that defines true cooperative learning?
   A. Positive interdependence and individual accountability
   B. Group processing
   C. Competition
   D. Collaborative and social skills

4. Research demonstrates that constructive controversy can lead to greater learning, open-mindedness, seeing the perspectives of others, creativity, motivation, and engagement. Which one of the following is a set-up for activities that engage students in constructive/structured controversies?
   A. Students work in pairs within their four-person cooperative groups to research a particular argument.
   B. Each student is part of a group, and each group member is given part of the material to be learned by the whole group. Students become experts on their piece and then teach it to the others in their group.
   C. Students intuitively understand the design that helps them think deeply about what they read.
   D. A combination of academic learning with personal and social development for secondary and college students is created.

CONSTRUCTED-RESPONSE QUESTIONS

Case

To infuse her class with constructivist strategies, Brenda Rhodes planned several problem-based learning scenarios. One of the scenarios required students to find a solution for their city's homeless population. Over the past few years, the number of homeless individuals and families had grown alarmingly quickly. Social service agencies, shelters, and businesses in the central city were struggling to deal with the challenge. Brenda believed her students would find the topic interesting and that it met the criteria for problem-based learning.

5. Does Brenda Rhodes's activity of finding a solution for the city's homeless population as a topic meet the requirements for problem-based learning? Explain your answer.

6. Identify several types of scaffolding the students might use to help them solve their problem.

ENHANCEDetext *licensure exam*

TEACHERS' **CASEBOOK**

WHAT WOULD THEY DO? LEARNING TO COOPERATE

Here is how some practicing teachers responded to the situation described at the beginning of the chapter about the class that hated cooperative learning.

PAULA COLEMERE—Special Education Teacher— English, History
McClintock High School, Tempe, AZ

First, cooperative learning should be introduced early in the year and used in a variety of ways. Simple activities such as "think-pair-share" or "tell partner two things you learned" are basic ways of having students learn cooperatively. In addition, Socratic seminars are a great way to get students to dialogue together and gain deeper understanding of a concept. A Socratic seminar begins with the facilitator posing an open-ended question to the group. Participants are encouraged to learn through a meaningful discussion rather than memorizing bits of information. This takes practice, but if introduced early and practiced throughout the year, students will gain higher-level thinking skills. Finally, when having students do a team activity in class, groups need to be placed together thoughtfully and deliberately by the teacher. Team members need to be taught skills necessary for successful group work such as active listening and how to give and receive constructive criticism. Groups should have a variety of abilities, and students should be assigned specific tasks within the group so everyone has a role and purpose.

PAUL DRAGIN—ESL Teacher, Grades 9–12
Columbus East High School, Columbus, OH

To introduce cooperative learning, I will begin with some exercises that require no talking, such as puzzles that can only be completed by group cooperation and sharing without any verbal communication. Each group member receives pieces that make up a puzzle; the catch is that some of the pieces belong to another group member's puzzle. By trading pieces strategically and rapidly, the goal is to be the first group to complete all puzzles. This sets the stage for a discussion about the need to work together, because each person in the group needs something that another team member has in order to complete his or her puzzle. All effective cooperative learning requires the input of each member, and without that input, the activity has no chance of reaching its full potential. The establishment of groups is open to myriad options, and this is a good thing. Randomly assigning students as well as strategically assigning students to

work together is an important learning opportunity for each student and better mimics real-world situations where we don't get to choose our coworkers.

JENNIFER PINCOSKI—Learning Resource Teacher, K–12
Lee County School District, Fort Myers, FL

To have effective groups, students need to respect each other and feel accepted by their peers. Therefore, it is important to incorporate some class-building and team-building exercises before the groups jump into academic content. The purpose of these activities is to acquaint students with one another and create a sense of community.

It will be easier to establish groups if the teacher collects information about the students first. This information can include anything from preferred learning style to favorite subject to career aspirations. It is also important to understand the students' levels of academic proficiency. Groups should be fluid, because different types of groups will accomplish different outcomes.

Teachers need to identify the objectives of an activity before creating the groups for that activity. In some situations, it might be appropriate to group students who are strong in a skill with students who have deficits in that skill. In other cases, it might be more effective to group together students with similar interests or career goals. It is up to the teacher to determine which type of group will result in the most worthwhile outcome for students.

LAUREN ROLLINS—First Grade Teacher
Boulevard Elementary School, Shaker Heights, OH

Group work is an important part of the curriculum and a teaching/learning method that I use with my students on a daily basis starting from the beginning of the school year. As I am getting to know my students and they are getting to know each other, cooperative learning activities are very simple and structured. These experiences allow them to build cooperative skills. Groups and the tasks for which each member is responsible are both assigned by me. As the school year progresses, I use cooperative learning to focus on specific skills, to facilitate peer tutoring, to accomplish a task, to play a game, and so on. Depending on what I want the students to gain from the learning activity, groups are chosen at random, picked by the students, or selected by me. My students enjoy the opportunity to learn in these different types of groupings. As groups are working, I rotate through the classroom, making sure that the groups are on task and that each member is contributing to the learning activity.

I spend a few minutes with each group to get a sense of how successfully the students are working together to accomplish the given task. I help facilitate when needed.

BARBARA PRESLEY—Transition/Work Study Coordinator—High School Level
BESTT Program (Baldwinsville Exceptional Student Training and Transition Program), C. W. Baker High School, Baldwinsville, NY

Throughout their high school experience, as students prepare for their life post high school, I send the youngest and newest students to "intern" with an older student who is secure and successful at the job site. The younger student is more comfortable going into a new situation with the company and support of one of his or her older peers. The older student gains confidence and takes pride in, and ownership of, the task of sharing knowledge and skills with his/her trainee. Entry-level job skills are practically universal, so each student gains from the experience.

LINDA SPARKS—First Grade Teacher
John F. Kennedy School, Billerica, MA

I have used cooperative learning groups a lot through the years. There are so many things that can be learned and shared from working together. There is always frustration with some students, but overall it seems to work. I also try to set it up in a variety of ways, from letting them select their own groups, picking names out of a hat, and passing out different topics and forming groups based on the topics. I will use assessments to organize a group as well as make sure that each student has a specific task. (Project editor, information manager, organizer, reporter, researcher, etc.) There always seems to be one student ready to take a back seat and let the others in the group do all of the work. We go over the social skills needed to work in a group. We often will post a list in the classroom of simple rules: using appropriate language, speaking quietly and respectfully while working, listening and encouraging team members, and asking for help

when needed. While they work in their groups, I will walk around the class and take notes on what is being worked on. I want to make sure there are no misconceptions about the project. After the project is completed, I grade them in a variety of ways. I give a grade to each participant for his/her contribution to the project, a group grade for the project and/or presentation, and a grade for group participation for the project. Students learn more when they are directly involved in what is being taught. This is yet another style of learning.

JESSICA N. MAHTABAN—Eighth-Grade Math Teacher,
Woodrow Wilson Middle School, Clifton, NJ

The lesson begins with a definition of cooperative learning as well as a real-world example. The first activity is simple; it is called Numbered Heads Together (taken from Kagan in a cooperative learning class). Students number off in their teams so each teammate has a different number; then the teacher asks a question and provides think time. Students put their "heads together" to discuss the question. The teacher calls a number and the student with that number from each group shares with the class the group's answer. The activities get more difficult as students get comfortable with cooperative learning.

To group students in the classroom, ideally four students per group face each other. On one side is a high student (based on grades); next is a medium-high student; across from this student is a low student; and next to the low student is a medium-low student. The high student rarely interacts with the low student because when paired off for activities they only work with medium-high and medium-low students. Based on my 10 years of teaching experience, the high student rarely has the patience to work with a low student, but the medium-high and medium-low students work very well with the low student. Another method of grouping students is according to personality as well as heterogeneously.

SOCIAL COGNITIVE VIEWS OF LEARNING AND MOTIVATION

TEACHERS' **CASEBOOK**

WHAT WOULD YOU DO?
FAILURE TO SELF-REGULATE

You know that your students need to be organized and self-regulating to do well in both their current and their future classes. But many of the students just don't seem to know how to take charge of their own learning. They have trouble completing larger projects—many wait until the last minute. They can't organize their work or decide what is most important. Some can't even keep up with assignments. Their book bags are disaster areas—filled with long overdue assignment sheets and class handouts from last semester crumbled in with school newsletters and permission slips

for field trips. You are concerned because they will need to be much more organized and on top of their work as they progress through their education. You have so much material to cover to meet district guidelines, but many of your students are drowning in the amount of work they already have.

CRITICAL THINKING

- What organizational skills do students need to be successful in your subject or class?
- What could you do to teach these skills, while still covering the material that will be on the proficiency or achievement tests the students will have to take in the spring?
- How would you help students develop an authentic sense of efficacy for guiding their own learning?

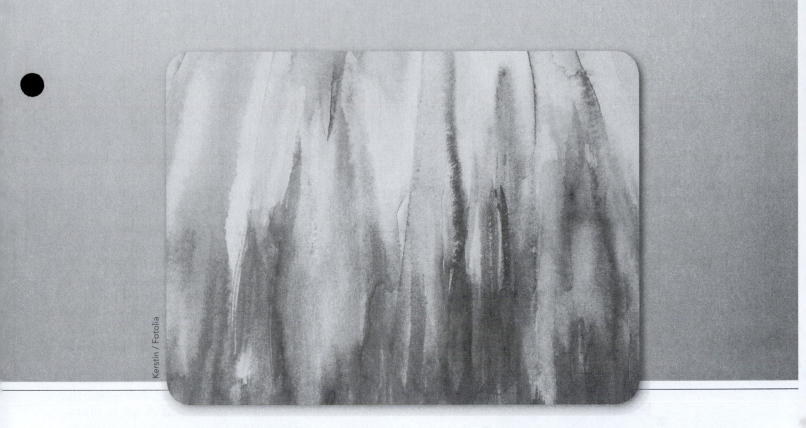

Kerstin / Fotolia

OVERVIEW AND OBJECTIVES

In the past four chapters, we analyzed different aspects of learning. We considered behavioral and information processing explanations of what and how people learn. We examined cognitive science and complex cognitive processes such as concept learning and problem solving. These explanations of learning focus on the individual and what is happening in his or her "head." Recent perspectives have called attention to two other aspects of learning that are critical: social and cultural factors. In the previous chapter, we examined social constructivism and the interdisciplinary learning sciences. In this chapter, we look at social cognitive theory—a current view of learning and motivation that discusses dynamic interactions among many of the behavioral, personal, and cultural factors involved in learning and motivation.

Social cognitive theory has its roots in Bandura's (1977, 1986) early criticisms of behavioral views of learning, as you read in Chapter 7. Social cognitive theory moved beyond behaviorism to focus on humans as self-directed agents who make choices and marshal resources to reach goals. Concepts such as self-efficacy, agency, and self-regulated learning are key in social cognitive theories. These concepts are important in understanding motivation as well, so this chapter provides a good path from learning to the discussion of motivation in the next chapter. We end the chapter with a look back at our tour through different models of instruction. Rather than debating

the merits of each approach, we will consider the contributions of these different models of instruction, grounded in different theories of learning. Don't feel that you must choose the "best" approach—there is no such thing. Even though theorists argue about which model is best, excellent teachers don't debate. They apply all the approaches, using each one when appropriate.

By the time you have completed this chapter, you should be able to:

Objective 11.1   Define the basic principles of social cognitive theories of learning and motivation including triarchic reciprocal causality, modeling/observational learning, self-efficacy, and agency.

Objective 11.2   Discuss the roles of observation and modeling in learning, including factors that support learning by observation.

Objective 11.3   Define self-efficacy and agency, distinguish these concepts from self-concept and self-esteem, explain the sources of self-efficacy, and discuss self-efficacy for teaching.

Objective 11.4   Describe important components of self-regulated learning.

Objective 11.5   Apply your knowledge to teach for self-efficacy and self-regulated learning.

Objective 11.6   Explain the meaning and different applications of four basic theories of learning.

SOCIAL COGNITIVE THEORY

As we saw in Chapter 7, in the early 1960s, Albert Bandura demonstrated that people can learn by observing both the actions of others and the consequences of those actions. Most of what is known today as *social cognitive theory* is based on the work begun by Albert Bandura in the 1950s at Stanford University. Before we talk about the theory, let's meet the man.

A Self-Directed Life: Albert Bandura

Albert Bandura's life story should be a movie. You could say he lived the American dream, except that he is from Canada. His parents were immigrants from Central Europe; they chose the rugged land of northern Alberta for their family farm. Bandura's parents never went to school, but they valued education. His father taught himself to read in three languages, giving young Albert a great model of self-regulated learning—a concept that figures prominently in social cognitive theory today. On the way to finishing high school, Bandura worked many jobs, including a stint as a carpenter at a furniture factory and one as a road worker on the Alaska Highway in the Yukon. He finished his undergraduate degree at the University of British Columbia in 3 years, even though he had to cram all his classes into the morning to have time for his afternoon jobs. Because he needed a morning class to fill one time slot, he enrolled in introductory psychology and found his future profession (Bandura, 2007, p. 46). His next stop was graduate school at the epicenter of psychological research in 1950—the University of Iowa. After earning his PhD (in 3 years again), Bandura joined the faculty at Stanford in 1953—he was 28 years old. More than 60 years later, he is the David Starr Jordan Professor of Social Science in Psychology/Emeritus at Stanford and has taught some of the children of his former students.

When I read Bandura's autobiography (see p20motivationlab.org for a summary with pictures), I was struck by how much his theories reflected his life as a self-directed, self-regulating learner growing up in a challenging environment. Describing his experiences in his two-teacher high school, Bandura said:

> We had to take charge of our own learning. Self-directed learning was an essential means of academic self-development, not a theoretical abstraction. The paucity of educational resources turned out to be an enabling factor that has served me well rather than an insurmountable handicapping one. The content of courses is perishable, but self-regulatory skills have lasting functional value whatever the pursuit might be. (p. 45)

In the next section we will look at the key features of Albert Bandura's work and social cognitive theory by considering four topics: moving beyond behaviorism, the concept of triarchic reciprocal causality, the power of observational learning, and the key beliefs of agency and self-efficacy.

Beyond Behaviorism

As you know from Chapter 7, Bandura found basic behavioral principles to be correct and useful as far as they went, but also too limited to explain complex human thinking and learning. His early social learning theory included *enactive learning* (learning through reinforcement and punishment of your *own behaviors*) and added learning through modeling and *observing others* being reinforced or punished for particular behaviors. In his autobiography, Bandura (2007) describes the shortcomings of behaviorism and the need to put people in social context:

> I found this behavioristic theorizing discordant with the obvious social reality that much of what we learn is through the power of social modeling. I could not imagine a culture in which its language; mores; familial

customs and practices; occupational competencies; and educational, religious, and political practices were gradually shaped in each new member by rewarding and punishing consequences of their trial-and-error performances. (p. 55)

Over time, Bandura's explanations of learning included more attention to cognitive factors such as *expectations* and *beliefs* in addition to the social influences of models (Bandura, 1986, 1997, 2001). His current perspective, **social cognitive theory**, retains an emphasis on the role of other people serving as models and teachers (the *social* part of social cognitive theory), but includes thinking, believing, expecting, anticipating, self-regulating, and making comparisons and judgments (the *cognitive* part). Social cognitive theory is a *dynamic system* that explains human adaptation, learning, and motivation. The theory addresses how people develop social, emotional, cognitive, and behavioral capabilities; how people regulate their own lives; and what motivates them (Bandura, 2007; Bandura & Locke, 2003). Many of the concepts from this chapter will help you understand motivation in the upcoming chapter.

Triarchic Reciprocal Causality

I claimed that social cognitive theory describes a system. This system, called **triarchic reciprocal causality**, is the dynamic interplay among three kinds of influences: personal, environmental, and behavioral, as shown in Figure 11.1. Personal factors (beliefs, expectations, cognitive abilities, motivation, attitudes, and knowledge), the physical and social environment (resources, consequences of actions, other people, models and teachers, and physical settings), and behavior (individual actions, choices, and verbal statements) all influence and are influenced by each other.

Figure 11.1 shows the interaction of person, environment, and behavior in learning settings (Schunk, Meece, & Pintrich, 2014). External factors such as models, instructional strategies, classroom environments, or teacher feedback (elements of the environment for students) can affect student personal factors such as goals, sense of efficacy for the task (described in the next section), attributions (beliefs about causes for success and failure), and processes of self-regulation such as planning, monitoring, and controlling distractions. For example, teacher feedback can lead

Video 11.1
In this video, students begin the school day with their usual classroom routine. The teacher sees one student working diligently on her assignment right after she arrives, and he reinforces her behavior with a slip of paper and a compliment. Consider how this type of reward might influence other students to model her behavior.

ENHANCEDetext *video example*

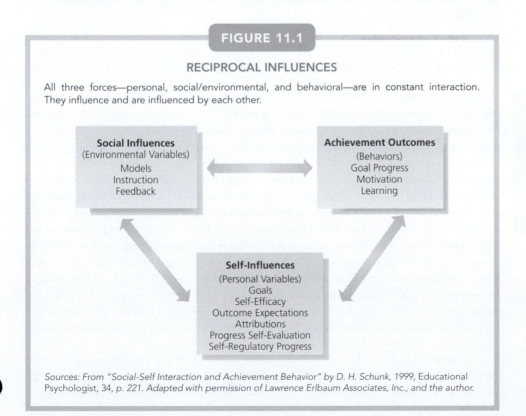

FIGURE 11.1

RECIPROCAL INFLUENCES

All three forces—personal, social/environmental, and behavioral—are in constant interaction. They influence and are influenced by each other.

Social Influences
(Environmental Variables)
Models
Instruction
Feedback

Achievement Outcomes
(Behaviors)
Goal Progress
Motivation
Learning

Self-Influences
(Personal Variables)
Goals
Self-Efficacy
Outcome Expectations
Attributions
Progress Self-Evaluation
Self-Regulatory Progress

Sources: From "Social-Self Interaction and Achievement Behavior" by D. H. Schunk, 1999, Educational Psychologist, 34, p. 221. Adapted with permission of Lawrence Erlbaum Associates, Inc., and the author.

students to feel either more confident or more discouraged, and then the students adjust their goals accordingly. Environmental factors such as rewards for turning in homework and personal factors such as challenging goals encourage behaviors including effort and persistence that lead to successful learning. But these behaviors also reciprocally impact personal factors. For example, as students achieve through increased effort (behavior), their self-efficacy and interest (personal factors) increase. Finally, student behaviors also affect the environment through choices made or actions taken. For example, if students do not persist or if they seem to misunderstand, teachers may change instructional strategies or learning group assignments, thus changing the learning environment for the students.

Think for a minute about the power of reciprocal causality in classrooms. If personal factors, behaviors, and the environment are in constant interaction, then cycles of events are progressive and self-perpetuating. Suppose a student had difficulties in his previous school. The first day at his new school he is late to class because he got lost in the unfamiliar building. The student has a tattoo and several visible pierced body parts. He is anxious about his first day and hopes to do better at this new school, but the teacher's initial reaction to his late entry and dramatic appearance is a bit hostile. The student feels insulted and responds in kind, so the teacher begins to form expectations about him and acts more vigilant, less trusting. The student senses the distrust. He decides that this school will be just as worthless as his previous one—and wonders why he should bother to try. The teacher sees the student's disengagement, invests less effort in teaching him, and the cycle continues. These reciprocal effects are more than hypothetical. When Trevor and Kitty Williams (2010) examined data on high school students' confidence in mathematics and achievement in mathematics in 30 different countries, they found evidence that math confidence and math achievement reciprocally influenced each other in 26 of the countries, just as Bandura would predict. You can see that if teachers' expectations are communicated to students (see Chapter 12), and these expectations affect student's confidence, then achievement can be impacted as well.

Two key elements of social cognitive theory are observational learning and self-efficacy. We will examine each of these more closely, with special emphasis on their implications for teaching.

MODELING: LEARNING BY OBSERVING OTHERS

Video 11.2
This teacher models "how to think" as she demonstrates a think-aloud strategy for her students. By modeling, she hopes her students will be able to perform the same skill and use think-aloud to make predictions as they read.

ENHANCEDetext *video example*

Learning by observing others is a key element of social cognitive theory. What causes an individual to learn and perform modeled behaviors and skills? Several factors play a role. First, the developmental level of the observer makes a difference in learning. As children grow older, they can focus attention for longer periods of time, more effectively identify the important elements of a model's behavior to observe, use memory strategies to retain information, and motivate themselves to practice, as you can see in Table 11.1 on the next page. A second influence is the status of the model. Children are motivated to imitate the actions of others who seem competent, powerful, prestigious, and enthusiastic, so parents, teachers, older siblings, athletes, action heroes, rock stars, or film personalities may serve as models, depending on the age and interests of the child. Third, by watching others, we learn about what behaviors are appropriate for people like ourselves as well as identify the range of behaviors we probably could execute; therefore, models who are seen as similar are more readily imitated (Schunk et al., 2014). All students need to see successful, capable models who look and sound like them, no matter what their ethnicity, socioeconomic status, or gender. Bandura (2006) describes television novellas (like soap operas) that provide models who deal effectively with social problems such as HIV prevention, women's rights, and overpopulation in India, Africa, Mexico, and China.

Look at Table 11.1. The last three influences involve goals and expectations. If observers expect that certain actions of models will lead to particular outcomes (e.g., specific practice regimens leading to improved athletic performance) and the observers value those outcomes or goals, then the observers will pay attention to the models and try to reproduce their behaviors. Finally,

TABLE 11.1 • **Factors that Affect Observational Learning**

CHARACTERISTIC	EFFECTS ON MODELING PROCESS
Developmental Status	Improvements with development include longer attention and increased capacity to process information, use strategies, compare performances with memorial representations, and adopt intrinsic motivators.
Model Prestige and Competence	Observers pay greater attention to competent, high-status models. Consequences of modeled behaviors convey information about functional value. Observers attempt to learn actions they believe they will need to perform.
Vicarious Consequences	Consequences to models convey information about behavioral appropriateness and likely outcomes of actions. Valued consequences motivate observers. Similarity in attributes or competence signals appropriateness and heightens motivation.
Outcome Expectations	Observers are more likely to perform modeled actions they believe are appropriate, attainable, and will result in rewarding outcomes.
Goal Setting	Observers are likely to attend to models who demonstrate behaviors that help observers attain goals.
Self-efficacy	Observers attend to models when they believe they are capable of learning or performing the modeled behavior. Observation of similar models affects self-efficacy ("If they can do it, I can too").

Source: From Schunk, D. H. (2012). Learning Theories: An Educational Perspective, 6th Ed. Reprinted by permission of Pearson Education, Inc.

observers are more likely to learn from models if the observers have a high level of self-efficacy—if they believe they are capable of doing the actions needed to reach the goals, or at least of learning how to do so (Bandura, 1997; Schunk et al., 2014).

Elements of Observational Learning

STOP & THINK Your interview for a position in the middle school is going well. Now you are asked, "Who are your models as teachers? Do you hear yourself saying or see yourself doing things that other teachers have done? Are there teachers from films or books that you would like to emulate?" •

Through observational learning, we discover not only *how* to perform a behavior but also what will happen to us in specific situations if we perform it. Observation can be a very efficient learning process. The first time children hold hairbrushes, cups, or tennis rackets, they usually brush, drink, or swing as well as they can, given their current muscle development and coordination. Through observation we also can compare our performance with the models and identify adjustments that may produce better outcomes. To learn new behaviors or refine current abilities, Bandura (1986) proposed that four elements of observational learning are essential: paying attention, retaining information or impressions, producing behaviors, and being motivated to repeat the behaviors.

ATTENTION. To learn through observation, we have to pay attention. This includes both selective attention (paying attention to the correct cues and information) as well as sustained attention (maintaining focus). In teaching, you will have to ensure students' attention to the critical features of the lesson by making clear presentations and highlighting important points. In demonstrating a skill (for example, threading a sewing machine, performing a dissection, or operating a lathe), you may need to have students look over your shoulder as you work. Seeing your hands from the same perspective as they see their own directs their attention to the right features of the situation and makes observational learning easier.

RETENTION. To imitate the behavior of a model, you have to remember each step. This involves mentally representing the model's actions in some way, probably as verbal steps ("Hwa-Rang, the eighth form in Tae Kwan Do karate, is a palm-heel block, then a middle riding stance punch, then . . ."), or as visual images, or both. Retention can be improved by mental rehearsal (imagining imitating the behavior) or by actual practice. In the retention phase of observational learning, practice helps us remember the elements of the desired behavior, such as the sequence of steps.

PRODUCTION. Once we "know" how a behavior should look and remember the elements or steps, we still may not perform it smoothly. Sometimes, we need a great deal of practice, feedback, and coaching about subtle points before we can reproduce the behavior of the model. In the production phase, practice makes the behavior smoother and more expert. Of course, if a child does not have the physical or developmental skills needed to produce the behavior, even extensive practice and feedback may not be enough. The ideal conditions for practice toward expert production will typically involve some form of feedback that compares the learner's performance to the model (e.g., specific teacher feedback, explicit coaching, reviewing video of the performance).

MOTIVATION AND REINFORCEMENT. As you saw in Chapter 7, social learning theory distinguishes between acquisition and performance. We may acquire a new skill or behavior through observation, but we may not perform that behavior until we have some motivation or incentive to do so. Reinforcement can play several roles in observational learning. If we anticipate being reinforced for imitating the actions of a model, we may be more motivated to pay attention, remember, and reproduce the behaviors. In addition, reinforcement is important in maintaining learning through persistence. A person who tries a new behavior is unlikely to persist without reinforcement (Schunk, 2012). For example, if an unpopular student adopted the dress of the "in" group, but was ignored or ridiculed, it is unlikely that the imitation would continue. Similarly, learning new academic tasks is usually accompanied by some failure—reinforcement for progressive gains helps learners maintain focus on their growth rather than their current struggles.

Bandura identifies three forms of reinforcement that can encourage observational learning. First, of course, the observer may reproduce the behaviors of the model and receive direct reinforcement, as when a gymnast successfully executes a front flip/round-off combination and the coach/model says, "Excellent!"

But the reinforcement need not be direct—it may be **vicarious reinforcement**. The observer may simply see others reinforced for a particular behavior and then increase his or her production of that behavior. For example, if you compliment two students on the attractive illustrations in their lab reports, several other students who observe your compliments may turn in illustrated lab reports next time. Most TV ads hope for this kind of effect. People in commercials become deliriously happy when they drive a particular car or drink a specific energy drink, and the viewer is supposed to do the same; the viewer's behavior is reinforced vicariously by the actors' obvious pleasure. Punishment can also be vicarious: You may slow down on a stretch of highway after seeing several people get speeding tickets there.

The final form of reinforcement is **self-reinforcement**, or controlling your own reinforcers—one aspect of *self-regulation* described later in this chapter. Self-reinforcers may be intrinsic (e.g., feelings of satisfaction at a job well-done) or extrinsic (e.g., rewarding yourself with a special treat after accomplishing a goal). This sort of reinforcement is important for both students and teachers. In fact, if one goal of education is to produce people who are capable of educating themselves, then students must learn to manage their own lives, set their own goals, and provide their own reinforcement. In adult life, rewards are sometimes vague and goals often take a long time to reach. Think about how many small steps are required to complete an education and find your first job. As a teacher, sometimes self-reinforcement is all that keeps you going in the face of difficult students and demanding parents. Life is filled with tasks that call for this sort of self-regulation (Rachlin, 2004).

Social cognitive theory has some powerful implications for teaching. In this section, we will look more closely at using observational learning in teaching.

Observational Learning in Teaching

STOP & THINK How would you incorporate observational learning into your teaching? What are the skills, attitudes, and strategies that can be modeled in teaching your subject? •

There are five possible outcomes of observational learning: directing attention, encouraging existing behaviors, changing inhibitions, teaching new behaviors and attitudes, and arousing emotions (Schunk, 2012). Let's look at each of these as they occur in classrooms.

DIRECTING ATTENTION. By observing others, we not only learn about actions but also notice the objects involved in the actions. For example, in a preschool class, when one child plays enthusiastically with a toy that has been ignored for days, many other children may want to have the toy, even if they play with it in different ways or simply carry it around. This happens, in part, because the children's attention has been drawn to that particular toy.

FINE TUNING ALREADY-LEARNED BEHAVIORS. All of us have had the experience of looking for cues from other people when we find ourselves in unfamiliar situations. Observing the behavior of others tells us which of our already-learned behaviors to use: the proper fork for eating the salad, when to leave a gathering, what kind of language is appropriate, and so on. Adopting the dress and grooming styles of TV or music idols is another example of this kind of effect.

STRENGTHENING OR WEAKENING INHIBITIONS. If class members witness one student breaking a class rule and getting away with it, they may learn that undesirable consequences do not always follow rule breaking. If the rule breaker is a well-liked, high-status class leader, the effect of the modeling may be even more pronounced. This **ripple effect** (Kounin, 1970) can work for the teacher's benefit. When the teacher deals effectively with a rule breaker, especially a class leader, the idea of breaking this rule may be inhibited for the other students viewing the interaction. This does not mean that teachers must reprimand each student who breaks a rule, but once a teacher has called for a particular action, following through is an important part of capitalizing on the ripple effect.

TEACHING NEW BEHAVIORS. Modeling has long been used, of course, to teach dance, sports, and crafts, as well as skills in subjects such as food science, chemistry, and welding. Cognitive modeling can also be applied deliberately in the classroom to teach mental skills and to broaden horizons—to teach new ways of thinking, such as thinking through the steps in a complex math problem. Teachers serve as models for a vast range of behaviors, from pronouncing vocabulary words, to reacting to the seizure of a student with epilepsy, to being enthusiastic about learning. For example, a teacher might model critical thinking skills by thinking "out loud" about a student's question. Or a high school teacher concerned about girls who seem to have stereotyped ideas about careers might invite women with nontraditional jobs to speak to the class or expose the girls to exemplary models in science, technology, engineering and mathematics (STEM), for example (see engineergirl.org). Teachers can share their love of reading or music or art or history by sharing their favorite books, films, artists, and so on. Studies indicate that modeling can be most effective when the teacher makes use of all the elements of observational learning—attention, retention, production, and especially reinforcement and practice. (Schunk, 2012). For students who doubt their own abilities, a good model is a low-achieving peer who keeps trying and finally masters the material (Schunk, 2012).

AROUSING EMOTION. Finally, through observational learning, people may develop emotional reactions to situations they have never experienced personally, and hearing or reading about a situation are forms of observation. News reports of shark attacks have many of us anxious about swimming in the ocean. A child who watches a friend fall from a swing and break an arm may

Connect and Extend to PRAXIS II®

Observational Learning (II, B2)
Identify situations in which observational learning may be a wise approach, and describe the essential elements of effective observational learning.

GUIDELINES
Using Observational Learning

Model behaviors and attitudes you want your students to learn.

Examples

1. Show enthusiasm for the subject you teach.
2. Be willing to demonstrate both the mental and the physical tasks you expect the students to perform. I once saw a teacher sit down in the sandbox while her 4-year-old students watched her demonstrate the difference between "playing with sand" and "throwing sand."
3. When reading to students, model good problem solving. Stop and say, "Now let me see if I remember what happened so far," or "That was a hard sentence. I'm going to read it again."
4. Model good problem solving—think out loud as you work through a difficult problem.
5. Model persistence and effort, sticking with a difficult problem even if you seem to reach a dead end.

Use peers, especially class leaders, as models.

Examples

1. In group work, pair students who do well with those who are having difficulties.
2. Ask students to demonstrate the difference between "whispering" and "silence—no talking."

Make sure students see that positive behaviors lead to reinforcement for others.

Examples

1. Point out the connections between positive behavior and positive consequences in stories.
2. Be fair in giving reinforcement. The same rules for rewards should apply to both the students with problems and the students who do not cause trouble.

Enlist the help of class leaders in modeling behaviors for the entire class.

Examples

1. Ask a well-liked student to be friendly to an isolated, fearful student.
2. Let high-status students lead an activity when you need class cooperation or when students are likely to be reluctant at first. Popular students can model dialogues in foreign-language classes or be the first to tackle dissection procedures in biology.

For more information on observational learning, see readwritethink.org/lessons/lesson_view.asp?id=275

become fearful of swings. The tragedies of school shootings reported on television prompt parents, teachers, and students alike to develop new concerns over safety in schools. Some terrible examples of modeling occur with "copy-cat killings" or suicide clusters in schools. When frightening things happen to people who are similar in age or circumstances to your students, they may need to be given an opportunity to talk about their emotions. But not all observations lead to negative emotions. Seeing media portrayals of acts of kindness or heroism can also arouse emotion that may prompt imitative behaviors or "faith" in humanity.

The *Guidelines: Using Observational Learning* will give you some ideas about using observational learning in the classroom.

Self-efficacy is a key element of social cognitive theory that is especially important in learning and teaching.

ENHANCEDetext *self-check*

SELF-EFFICACY AND AGENCY

Bandura (1986, 1994, 1997) suggests that predictions about possible outcomes of behavior are critical for learning because they affect goals, effort, persistence, strategies, and resilience. "Will I succeed or fail? Will I be liked or laughed at?" "Will I be more accepted by teachers in this new school?" These predictions are affected by **self-efficacy**—our beliefs about our personal competence or effectiveness in a given area. Bandura (1994) defines self-efficacy as "people's beliefs about their capabilities to produce designated levels of performance that exercise influence over events that affect their lives" (p. 71). Self-efficacy is essential for positive student outcomes across grade levels and content domains. Research has demonstrated that students with high self-efficacy exert greater levels of effort, persistence, and resilience when engaged in challenging tasks—as well as experience lower levels of stress and anxiety for the task (Pajares, 1997; Pajares & Valiante, 1997). In a study of students going from middle through high school, students with a higher level of self-efficacy for having control over their academic outcomes (i.e., self-regulation efficacy) had higher levels of confidence in their academic abilities, earned higher grades, and were more likely to graduate (Caprara, Pastorelli, Regalia, Scabini, & Bandura, 2005).

Bandura's more recent efforts (2006) and the work of many other researchers have focused on the role of self-efficacy in human agency—the *exercising influence over life events* in Bandura's definition of self-efficacy. Agency involves the ability to make intentional choices and plans, design appropriate courses of action, and then motivate and regulate the execution of these plans and actions. This is the major difference between social cognitive theory and behaviorism: In social cognitive theory we can change our environments, control our own behavior, support the actions of others, and take charge of our lives. When we discuss self-regulation later in the chapter, you will see how students and teachers can become more *agentic*—more self-directing and in charge of their own learning and motivation.

Self-Efficacy, Self-Concept, and Self-Esteem

Most people assume self-efficacy is the same as self-concept or self-esteem, but it isn't. *Self-efficacy* is future-oriented, a "context-specific assessment of competence to perform a specific task" (Pajares, 1997, p. 15). *Self-concept* is a more global construct that contains many perceptions about the self, including self-efficacy. Self-concept is developed as a result of external and internal comparisons, using other people or other aspects of the self as frames of reference. But self-efficacy focuses on your ability to successfully accomplish a particular task with no need for comparisons—the question is whether *you* can do it, not whether others would be successful. Also, self-efficacy beliefs are strong predictors of behavior, but self-concept has weaker predictive power (Anderman & Anderman, 2014; Bandura, 1997).

Self-efficacy is "context specific," which means it varies, depending on the subject or task. For example, my sense of efficacy for singing is really low, but I feel confident in my ability to read a map and navigate (except in certain cities that are hopeless). Even young students have different efficacy beliefs for different tasks. One study found that by the first grade, students already differentiated among their sense of efficacy for reading, for writing, and for spelling (Wilson & Trainin, 2007).

Self-efficacy is concerned with judgments of personal competence; self-esteem is concerned with judgments of self-worth. Self-esteem is determined in large part by the value we place on our performance in a domain (math, appearance, singing, soccer, etc.) and our concern over what others think about our competence (Harter & Whitesell, 2003). Self-esteem is not affected if we feel incompetent in areas we don't really value. There is no direct relationship between self-esteem and self-efficacy. It is possible to feel highly efficacious in one area and still not have a high level of self-esteem, or vice versa (Valentine, DuBois, & Cooper, 2004). For example, as I confessed earlier, I have very low self-efficacy for singing, but my self-esteem is not affected, probably because my life does not require singing. But if my self-efficacy for teaching a particular class (my teaching efficacy) started dropping after several bad experiences, I know my self-esteem would suffer because I value teaching.

Sources of Self-Efficacy

Bandura identified four sources of self-efficacy expectations: mastery experiences, physiological and emotional arousal, vicarious experiences, and social persuasion. Mastery experiences are our own direct experiences—usually the most powerful source of efficacy information. Successes raise efficacy beliefs, while failures lower efficacy. Level of arousal affects self-efficacy, depending on how the arousal is interpreted. As you face the task, are you anxious and worried (lowers efficacy) or excited and "psyched" (raises efficacy) (Bandura, 1997; Schunk et al., 2014; Usher & Pajares, 2009)?

In vicarious experiences, someone else models accomplishments. The more closely the student identifies with the model, the greater the impact on self-efficacy (Schunk et al., 2014). When the model performs well, the student's efficacy is enhanced, but when the model performs poorly, efficacy expectations decrease. The popularity of skill-based television shows that model how to cook, redesign your kitchen, improve your golf swing, or do yoga demonstrates the influence of

Connect and Extend to PRAXIS II®

Modeling (II, B2)
Teachers often use modeling to teach students new behaviors. Identify the characteristics that tend to make models effective in instructional contexts.

TABLE 11.2 • **Sources of Self-Efficacy**

SOURCE	EXAMPLE
Mastery Experiences	Past successes and failures in similar situations, as perceived by the individual. To increase efficacy, the success must be attributed to the ability, effort, choices, and strategies of the individual—not to luck or extensive help from others.
Physiological Arousal	Positive or negative arousal—excitement and a feeling of being "psyched" and ready (increases efficacy) or a sense of anxiety and foreboding (decreases efficacy).
Vicarious Experiences	Seeing other people like you succeed on a task or reach a goal that is similar to the one you face.
Social Persuasion	Encouragement, informational feedback, useful guidance from a trusted source.

PODCAST 11.1

Textbook author Anita Woolfolk explains the sources of self-efficacy and how teachers might use this information to invent ways of supporting their students' sense of efficacy for learning. Why is the belief about yourself so important, and where does it come from?

ENHANCEDetext *podcast*

vicarious experiences. These are particularly effective when you can identify with the subject in the show, and you think "if that person can do this, so can I." Although mastery experiences generally are acknowledged as the most influential source of efficacy beliefs in adults, Keyser and Barling (1981) found that children (sixth-graders in their study) rely more on **modeling** as a source of self-efficacy information.

Social persuasion can be a "pep talk" or specific performance feedback. Social persuasion alone can't create enduring increases in self-efficacy, but a persuasive boost in self-efficacy can lead a student to make an effort, attempt new strategies, or try hard enough to succeed (Bandura, 1982). Social persuasion from peers or trusted experts such as teachers can counter occasional setbacks that might have instilled self-doubt and interrupted persistence. The potency of persuasion depends on the credibility, trustworthiness, and expertise of the persuader. Social persuasion that highlights prior successes in similar tasks, identifies short-term goals and accomplishments, or focuses on the importance of effort are more likely to promote success in boosting self-efficacy and initiating successful performance (Bandura, 1997; Schunk et al., 2014). Table 11.2 summarizes the sources of self-efficacy. These same four sources were identified as supporting self-efficacy development for third-grade students in France (Joët, Usher, & Bressoux, 2011).

Self-Efficacy in Learning and Teaching

STOP & THINK On a scale from 1 to 100, how confident are you that you will finish reading this chapter today? •

Let's assume your sense of efficacy is around 90 for completing this chapter. Greater efficacy leads to greater effort and persistence in the face of setbacks, so even if you are interrupted in your reading, you are likely to return to the task. I believe I can finish writing this section today, so I have resumed work on it after my computer crashed and I had to start over on several pages. Of course, that could make for a late night, because I am going to a San Francisco Giants baseball game at 7:00 tonight and may have to finish the section after the game.

Self-efficacy also influences motivation and performance through goal setting. If we have a high sense of efficacy in a given area, we will set higher goals, be less afraid of failure, and find new strategies when old ones fail. If your sense of efficacy for reading this chapter is high, you are likely to set high goals for completing the chapter—maybe you will take some notes, too. If your sense of efficacy is low, however, you may avoid the reading altogether or give up easily when problems arise or you are interrupted with a better offer (Bandura, 1993, 1997; Pajares & Schunk, 2001).

Research indicates that performance in school is improved and self-efficacy is increased when students (a) adopt short-term goals so it is easier to judge progress; (b) are taught to use specific learning strategies such as outlining or summarizing that help them focus attention; and (c) receive

Video 11.3
The high school teacher in this video challenges students, but also provides supports. She gives her English learners opportunities to work collaboratively and learn from peer models. Observe the ways her teaching might help students develop a sense of self-efficacy about math skills.

ENHANCEDetext *video example*

GUIDELINES
Encouraging Self-Efficacy

Emphasize students' progress in a particular area.

Examples

1. Return to earlier material in reviews, and show how "easy" it is now.
2. Encourage students to improve projects when they have learned more.
3. Keep examples of particularly good work in portfolios as well as work that shows growth and improvement over time, and periodically have students review and reflect on their improvements.

Set learning goals for your students, and model a mastery orientation for them.

Examples

1. Guide students to set goals that focus on gaining skill, competency, or understanding.
2. Recognize progress and improvement.
3. Share examples of how you have developed your abilities in a given area, and provide other models of achievement who are similar to your students—no supermen or superwomen whose accomplishments seem unattainable.
4. Read stories about students who overcame physical, mental, or economic challenges.

5. Don't excuse failure because a student has problems outside school. Help the student succeed inside school.

Make specific suggestions for improvement, and revise grades when improvements are made.

Examples

1. Return work with specific comments noting what the students did right, what they did wrong, and why they might have made the mistakes.
2. Experiment with peer editing.
3. Show students how their revised, higher grade reflects greater competence and raises their class average.

Stress connections between past efforts and past accomplishments.

Examples

1. Have individual goal-setting and goal-review conferences with students, in which you ask students to reflect on how they solved difficult problems.
2. Confront self-defeating, failure-avoiding strategies directly.

For more information on self-efficacy, see p20motivationlab.org

---

rewards based on achievement, not just engagement, because achievement rewards signal increasing competence (S. Graham & Weiner, 1996). See the *Guidelines: Encouraging Self-Efficacy* for ideas about encouraging self-efficacy.

What is the most motivating level of efficacy? Should students be accurate, optimistic, or pessimistic in their predictions? Evidence indicates that a higher sense of self-efficacy supports motivation, even when the efficacy is an overestimation. Children and adults who are optimistic about the future are more mentally and physically healthy, less depressed, and more motivated to achieve (Flammer, 1995; Seligman, 2006). After examining almost 140 studies of motivation, Sandra Graham concluded that these qualities characterize many African Americans. She found that the African Americans studied had strong self-concepts, resilience, and high expectations, even in the face of difficulties (S. Graham, 1996; S. Graham & Taylor, 2002). Students who show academic resilience are more likely to succeed because they can effectively manage the stressors and barriers in their academic life (Martin & Marsh, 2009).

As you might expect, there are dangers in underestimating abilities because then students are more likely to put out a weak effort and give up easily. But there are dangers in continually overestimating performance as well. Students who think that they are better readers than they actually are may not be motivated to go back and repair misunderstandings as they read. They don't discover that they didn't really understand the material until it is too late (Pintrich & Zusho, 2002).

In schools, we are particularly interested in self-efficacy for learning mathematics, writing, history, science, sports, and other subjects, as well as self-efficacy for using learning strategies and for the many other challenges that classrooms present. For example, in research with students, self-efficacy is related to writing and math performance for students from third grade through high school (Fast et al., 2010; Kenney-Benson, Pomerantz, Ryan, & Patrick, 2006; Pajares, 2002), life satisfaction for adolescents (Vecchio, Gerbino, Pastorelli, Del Bove, & Caprara, 2007), use of deep processing learning strategies for college students (Prat-Sala & Redford, 2010), choice of college major (Pajares, 2002), and performance in college for older students (Elias & MacDonald, 2007).

PODCAST 11.2

There are three kinds of efficacy judgments at work in schools: student, teacher, and collective. All three kinds are related to student achievement, even after considering the powerful effects of SES. Textbook author Anita Woolfolk describes them and gives ideas for increasing each kind of efficacy.

ENHANCEDetext *podcast*

The value of self-efficacy seems to be cross-cultural. For example, self-efficacy is related to math/science goals and interests for Mexican American youth (Navarro, Flores, & Worthington, 2007), staying in school for Italian secondary students (Caprara et al., 2008), academic achievement in math for both male and female middle school students (Kenney-Benson et al., 2006), and mathematics achievement for both Anglo and South Asian Canadian middle school students (Klassen, 2004).

So, maybe you are thinking, sure, higher self-efficacy is related to higher achievement because students who have more ability have higher self-efficacy. But these relationships between self-efficacy and achievement hold even when we take ability into account. For example, when students with the same ability in math are compared, the ones with higher self-efficacy for math perform better in math (Wigfield & Wentzel, 2007). Self-efficacy encourages higher goals, persistence, and effort so we can take charge of our own lives—we *enact agency*.

Teachers' Sense of Efficacy

You saw in Chapter 1 that much of my own research has focused on **teachers' sense of efficacy**, defined as a teacher's belief that he or she can reach even difficult students to help them learn. This confident belief appears to be one of the few personal characteristics of teachers that predict student achievement (Tschannen-Moran & Woolfolk Hoy, 2001; Tschannen-Moran, Woolfolk Hoy, & Hoy, 1998; Woolfolk Hoy & Burke-Spero, 2005; Woolfolk Hoy, Hoy, & Davis, 2009). When teachers take responsibility for student success or failure (rather than assigning that responsibility to student ability or to external barriers), then the teachers are more "intentional" in their approaches to reaching their students and more successful in meeting their learning needs (Putman, Smith, & Cassady, 2009). Of course, teacher efficacy and student achievement probably are reciprocal—they affect each other. When teachers have a higher sense of efficacy, their students learn more, and when students learn more, teacher efficacy grows (Holzberger, Philipp, & Kunter, 2013).

As with any kind of efficacy, there may be both benefits and dangers in overestimating abilities. Optimistic teachers probably set higher goals, work harder, reteach when necessary, and persist in the face of problems. But some benefits might follow from having doubts about your efficacy. The *Point/Counterpoint* looks at both sides of teachers' efficacy judgments.

It takes self-efficacy to be self-regulated. We turn to this issue next to explore how you can help your students lead a self-directed life.

ENHANCEDetext *self-check*

SELF-REGULATED LEARNING

As you may remember from the beginning of this chapter, Albert Bandura said his early education in a tiny school in Canada had given him self-regulation skills that lasted a lifetime. He also noted:

> A major goal of formal education is to equip students with the intellectual tools, self-beliefs, and self-regulatory capabilities to educate themselves throughout their lifetime. The rapid pace of technological change and accelerated growth of knowledge are placing a premium on capability for self-directed learning. (Bandura, 2007, p. 10)

Today, people change jobs an average of seven times before they retire. Many of these career changes require new learning that must be self-initiated and self-directed (Martinez-Pons, 2002). Thus, one goal of teaching, as Bandura noted, should be to free students from the need for teachers, so the students can continue to learn independently throughout their lives. To continue learning independently throughout life, you must be self-regulated—what we refer to in conversations as a *self-starter*. Self-regulation may be even more important today as knowledge about virtually anything is available instantly on the Internet. How do you persist and stay focused on your goal as you browse all that information and are distracted by texts, tweets, and fascinating pictures of cute kittens . . . ?

POINT/COUNTERPOINT
Are High Levels of Teacher Efficacy Beneficial?

Based on Bandura's research on self-efficacy, we probably would assume that high sense of efficacy for teachers is a good thing. But not everyone agrees. Here is the debate.

POINT **Higher efficacy is better than lower.** The research on teachers' sense of efficacy points to many positive outcomes related to higher efficacy. With my husband and a colleague, I summarized this research (Woolfolk Hoy, Hoy, & Davis, 2009). Here are a few of the findings we identified. Teachers with a strong sense of efficacy tend to be more enthusiastic and spend more time teaching in subject areas where their sense of efficacy is higher, and they tend to avoid subjects when efficacy is lower. Teachers with higher efficacy judgments tend to be more open to new ideas; more willing to experiment with new methods to better meet the needs of their students; more likely to use powerful but potentially difficult-to-manage methods such as inquiry and small-group work; and less likely to use easy-to-adopt but weaker methods such as lectures. Higher-efficacy teachers are less likely to criticize students and more persistent in following up on incorrect student answers. Teachers with a higher sense of efficacy tend to select strategies that support student learning rather than those that simply cover the curriculum. Compared to low-efficacy teachers, those who report a higher sense of efficacy tend to be more active in monitoring seatwork and maintaining academic focus, and they respond quickly to student misbehavior by redirecting attention without showing anger or becoming threatened. What about the students? In addition to being related to student achievement, teachers' sense of efficacy has been associated with other student outcomes such as motivation and students' own sense of efficacy.

COUNTERPOINT **There are problems with high efficacy.** In spite of the large body of literature describing positive outcomes associated with higher self-efficacy, several researchers have questioned whether higher is always better. For example, Karl Wheatley (2002, 2005) suggested that several forms of teacher self-efficacy might be problematic. One is the excessive optimism of beginning teachers that interferes with their ability to accurately judge their own effectiveness. In an analysis of students who were about to begin their student teaching, Carol Weinstein (1988) found a strong sense of "unrealistic optimism"—the tendency to believe that problems experienced by others would not happen to them. Interestingly, the unrealistic optimism was greatest for activities having to do with controlling students (e.g., maintaining discipline, and establishing and enforcing class rules). When beginning teachers overrate their abilities, they don't take the needed steps to improve their skills—until they are confronted with serious problems. These findings are consistent with Emmer and Hickman's (1991) observations that student teachers who had trouble managing their classes still reported high levels of classroom management efficacy. Another problematic consequence of higher efficacy is resistance to acquiring new knowledge and skills and a tendency to "stick with what works"—with the ways of teaching that have provided the sense of mastery in the past. Overconfident efficacy may quickly be followed by giving up if the task proves more difficult than first thought. Wheatley (2002) believes "lower efficacy beliefs are essential for teacher learning; doubt motivates change" (p. 18).

BEWARE OF EITHER/OR

It is true that persistent high-efficacy perceptions in the face of poor performance (unrealistic optimism) can produce avoidance rather than action and interfere with teacher learning, but I believe that a sense of *efficacy for learning to teach* would be necessary to respond in these positive ways to the doubts described here. The challenge is to develop an authentic sense of self-efficacy—one that is accurate or just a bit optimistic.

STOP & THINK Think about the class you are taking where you are using this textbook. On a 7-point scale—from 1 = *not at all true of me*, to 7 = *very true of me*—answer the following questions:

1. When I study for a test, I try to put together the information from class and from the book.
2. When I do homework, I try to remember what the teacher said in class so I can answer the questions correctly.
3. I know I will be able to learn the material for this class.
4. I expect to do well in this class.
5. I ask myself questions to make sure I know the material I have been studying.
6. Even when study materials are dull and uninteresting, I keep working until I finish. •

By answering the questions in the *Stop & Think*, you have just responded to six items from the Motivated Strategies for Learning Questionnaire (MSLQ) (Midgley et al., 1998; Pintrich & De Groot, 1990). This questionnaire has been used in hundreds of studies to assess students' self-regulated learning and motivation. How did you do? The first two questions assess your use of *cognitive strategies*, like those we discussed in Chapter 9. The second two questions assess your *sense of efficacy* for this class. But the last two questions (5 and 6) specifically assess **self-regulation**, defined by Barry Zimmerman and Dale Schunk (2011) as the process we use to activate and sustain our thoughts, behaviors, and emotions in order to reach our goals. Bandura (2007) summarizes self-regulation as setting goals and mobilizing the efforts and resources needed to reach those goals. When the goals involve learning, we talk about *self-regulated learning* (Dinsmore, Alexander, & Loughlin, 2008).

Self-regulated learners are "metacognitive, motived to learn, and strategic" (Perry & Rahim, 2011, p. 122). This means they have a combination of academic learning skills, self-awareness, self-control, and motivation for learning; in other words, they have the skill and the will to learn (Murphy & Alexander, 2000; Schunk, 2005). Self-regulated learners transform their mental abilities, whatever they are, into academic skills and strategies (Zimmerman & Schunk, 2011). Many studies link self-regulated strategy use to measures of academic achievement, especially for middle school and high school students (Caprara et al., 2008; Fredricks et al., 2004). For younger students, self-regulation of attention and emotion are particularly important for learning and achieving in school (Valiente, Lemery-Chalfant, & Swanson, 2010). In fact, one study found that when the first-grade students in a class had better self-regulated learning skills, individual students in that class improved in vocabulary learning and reading comprehension. So, being in a class where the students' peers had self-regulation skills supported literacy development in individual students (Skibbe, Phillips, Day, Brophy-Herb, & Connor, 2012).

What Influences Self-Regulation?

The concept of self-regulated learning integrates much of what is known about effective learning and motivation. As you can see from the processes just described, three factors influence skill and will: knowledge, motivation, and self-discipline or volition. In addition, there are developmental differences among students.

KNOWLEDGE. To be self-regulated learners, students need knowledge about themselves, the subject, the task, strategies for learning, and the contexts in which they will apply their learning. "Expert" students know about themselves and how they learn best. This "metacognitive knowledge" includes knowing their preferred learning approaches; what is easy and what is hard for them; strategies that will help them cope with difficult material; their interests and talents; and how to use their strengths (Efklides, 2011). Experts also know quite a bit about the subject being studied, and they can adapt their knowledge to meet new demands; the more they know, the easier it is to learn more (Alexander, Schallert, & Reynolds, 2009). They probably understand that different learning tasks require different approaches on their part. A simple memory task, for example, might require a mnemonic strategy (see Chapter 8), whereas a complex comprehension task might be approached by means of concept maps of the key ideas (see Chapter 9). Also, these self-regulated learners know that learning is often difficult and knowledge is seldom absolute; there usually are different ways of looking at problems as well as different solutions (Greene, Muis, & Pieschl, 2010; Winne, 1995).

These expert students not only know what each task requires but also can apply the strategy needed. They can skim or read carefully. They can use memory strategies or reorganize the material. As they become more knowledgeable in a field, they apply many of these strategies automatically. In short, they have mastered a large, flexible repertoire of learning and help-seeking strategies (see Chapter 9). Finally, self-regulated learners think about the contexts in which they will apply their knowledge—when and where they will use their learning—so they can set motivating goals and connect present work to future accomplishments (Winne, 1995).

MOTIVATION. Self-regulated learners are motivated to learn (see Chapter 12). They find many tasks in school interesting because they value learning, not just performing well in the eyes of others. They believe their own intelligence and abilities are improvable. Even if they are not intrinsically motivated by a particular task, they are serious about getting the intended benefit from it. They focus their attention

Video 11.4
The teen in this video answers questions about school—what he likes and dislikes. As you listen, think about comments that indicate his level of self-regulation. Do you think he is a self-regulated learner?

ENHANCEDetext *video example*

and other cognitive and emotional resources on the task at hand. They know why they are studying, so their actions and choices are self-determined and not controlled by others (Zimmerman, 2011). But knowledge and motivation are not always enough. Self-regulated learners need volition or self-discipline. "Where motivation denotes commitment, volition denotes follow-through" (Corno, 1992, p. 72).

VOLITION. I am 1 month behind in this project. I have been up writing at 5:00 a.m. every day since I got back from Taiwan (great place!) where I gave a series of talks. I am still jet lagged, barely awake, but I want to keep writing because the deadline for this chapter is very near (well, passed actually). I have knowledge and motivation, but to keep going I need a good dose of volition. **Volition** is an old-fashioned word for will-power. The more technical definition for volition is *protecting opportunities to reach goals.*

Volition is influenced by the individual's level of perceived control for the given task (Efklides, 2011). People are more likely to exercise volitional control when they have experience in sticking with tasks to reach their goals, becoming active agents in achieving success (Metcalfe & Greene, 2007). I can stick with this writing because I have done it before and held the finished book. Self-regulated learners know how to protect themselves from distractions—where to study, for example, so they are not interrupted. They know how to cope when they feel anxious, drowsy, or lazy (Corno, 2011; R. E. Snow, Corno, & Jackson, 1996). And they know what to do when they are tempted to stop working and have (another) cup of coffee—the temptation I'm facing now—that, and a beautiful Florida day that beckons me to sweep out the garage (sweeping my garage always looks appealing when I face a tough writing job—cleaning closets is a close second).

Volition is deliberate and effortful, but with practice it can become more automatic—a habit or a "work ethic" (Corno, 2011). William James knew this over 100 years ago. One of my favorite James quotes is about making volition a habit. He said: "do every day or two something for no other reason than that you would rather not do it, so that when the hour of dire need draws nigh, it may find you not unnerved and untrained to stand the test" (James, 1890, IV, p. 126).

DEVELOPMENT OF SELF-REGULATION. There are developmental differences in self-regulation. Self-regulation generally improves over time. In the early grades, girls may be better than boys in self-regulation (Greene, Muis, & Pieschl, 2010; Matthews, Ponitz, & Morrison, 2009).

How do students develop knowledge, motivation, and volition? Two social processes support the development of self-regulation: co-regulation and shared regulation. **Co-regulation** is a transitional phase during which students gradually appropriate and internalize self-regulated learning and skills through modeling, direct teaching, feedback, and coaching from teachers, parents, or peers. **Shared regulation** happens when students work together to regulate each other through reminders, prompts, and other guidance.

Dale Schunk (1999) proposed a model of gradual self-regulation development. Control is gradually transferred from the exemplary models (e.g., teachers) to the individual learner. At the earliest phases of gaining these self-regulation competencies, the learners observe and emulate self-regulation skills. As they develop success in applying the skills, they begin to demonstrate self-control over the individual skills and eventually engage in independent adaptive self-regulation in novel situations (also implementing self-reinforcement strategies and enhancing their efficacy for self-regulation). In Chapter 14 you will read about Lyn Corno's model of adaptive teaching that intentionally builds student self-regulation development into teaching plans.

What does self-regulation look like when it has developed? Let's examine some models.

Models of Self-Regulated Learning and Agency

Albert Bandura may have gone from high school graduate to professor at Stanford in 6 years using his self-regulated learning knowledge and skills, but not all of your students will be Banduras with established *habits of volition*. In fact, some psychologists suggest that you think of this capacity as one of many characteristics that distinguish individuals (R. E. Snow et al., 1996). Some students are much better at it than others. How can you help more students become self-regulated learners in school? What is involved in being self-regulated?

Theoretical models of **self-regulated learning** describe how learners—like you!—set goals and mobilize the efforts and resources needed to reach those goals. There are several models of self-regulated

FIGURE 11.2

THE CYCLE OF SELF-REGULATED LEARNING

Analyzing the Task

Task Features
What is the task about?
What resources are available?
What are standards for success?

Personal Features
What knowledge can I apply?
What is the task's interest/value?
What is my self-efficacy?

Setting Goals

What is my learning goal orientation?
What consequences accompany various outcomes?
What effort is required?

Devising Plans

Have I participated in similar tasks before?
What are steps to complete the task?
What learning skills will be useful?
How will I monitor progress?
Is feedback available as work proceeds?

Regulating Learning

Metacognitive monitoring
Metacognitive control

Enacting Tactics and Strategies

Retrieve prior knowledge
Examine given information
Apply cognitive operations
Monitor products
Manage cognitive load

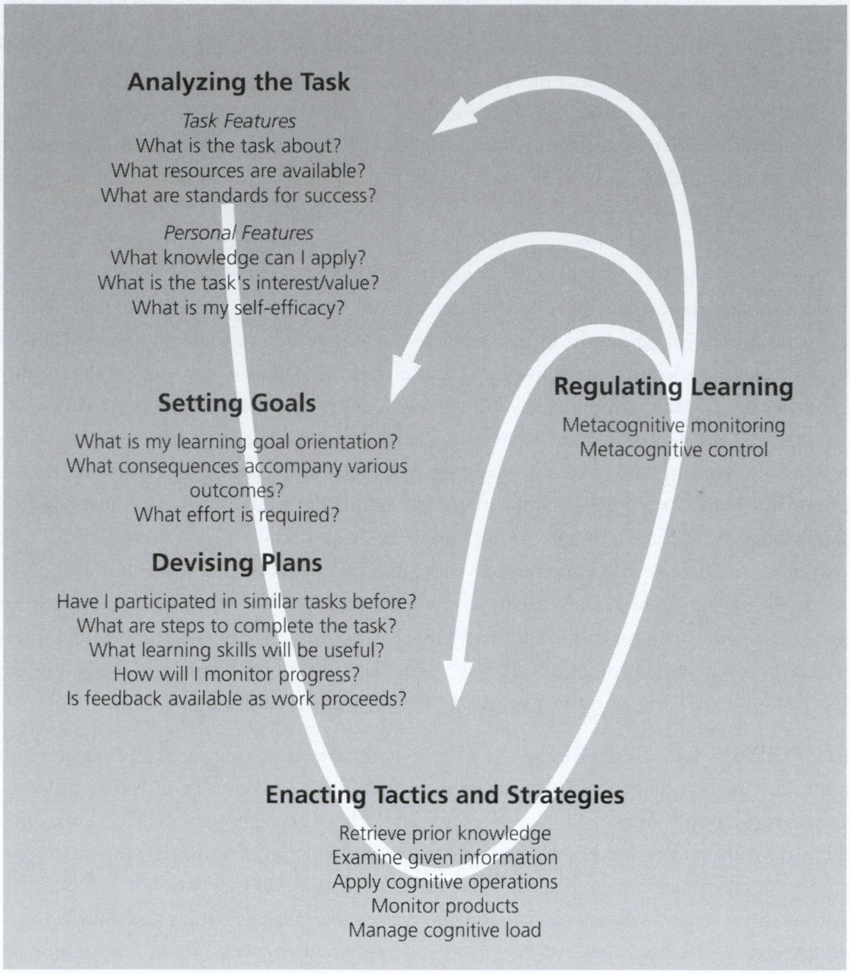

Source: From Educational Psychology (3rd Canadian ed.), by A. E. Woolfolk, P. H. Winne, and N. E. Perry. Adapted with permission of Pearson Education Canada and Philip Winne.

learning, but all agree that the cognitive processes needed for self-regulated learning require effort (Greene, Muis, & Pieschl, 2010; Puustinen & Pulkkinen, 2001; Winne, 2011). Let's look at one developed by Phil Winne and Allyson Hadwin (1998), shown in Figure 11.2. This depiction of self-regulated learning has many facets, as it should when the topic at hand is how you manage your academic life.

The model of self-regulated learning in Figure 11.2 is based on the belief that learners are *agents*. As we saw earlier, agency is the capacity to coordinate learning skills, motivation, and emotions to reach your goals (Bandura, 2006). Agents are not puppets on strings held by teachers, textbook authors, or Web page designers. Instead, agents control many factors that influence how they learn. Self-regulating learners exercise agency as they engage in a cycle with four main stages: analyze the task, set goals and devise plans, enact strategies, and regulate learning by making needed adjustments.

1. *Analyze the learning task.* You are familiar with this stage of self-regulated learning. What do you do when a professor announces there will be a test? You ask about conditions you believe will influence how you'll study. Is it essay or multiple-choice? Is your best friend up to date on the material to be tested and available to study with you? In general, learners examine whatever information they think is relevant to construct a sense of what the task is about, what

resources to bring to bear, and how they feel about the work to be done: Are they interested? confident? anxious? knowledgeable? clueless?

2. *Set goals and devise plans.* Knowing conditions that influence work on tasks provides information that learners use to create goals for learning. Then, plans can be developed about how to reach those goals. What goals for studying might you set for a quiz covering only one chapter that counts just 3% toward your course grade? Would your goals change if the test covered the last six chapters and counted 30% toward your course grade? What targets are identified in these goals—repeating definitions, being able to discuss how a teacher could apply findings from key research studies described in the textbook, or critiquing theoretical positions? Choosing goals affects the shape of a learner's plans for how to study. Is practicing definitions the best approach? Is a better plan to create examples and applications of key concepts?

3. *Enact strategies to accomplish the task.* In this phase, self-regulated learners consider what they know or need to know that will help them succeed with these strategies. They are especially alert as they enact their plan to monitor how well the plan is working. They ask themselves these questions: Is the cognitive load too great? Am I getting overwhelmed? What can I do to manage all this complex information? Is the approach I'm taking too effortful for the results I'm achieving? Am I reaching my goals? Is my progress rate fast enough to be prepared for the test?

4. *Regulate learning.* This is metacognitive monitoring and control (see Chapter 9). In this phase, learners come to decisions about whether changes are needed in any of the three preceding phases. For example, if learning is slow, they ask these questions: Should I study with my best friend? Do I need to review some prior material that provides the foundation for the content I am now studying? Do I need to start over—identifying what the task really is and then setting new (higher, lower, different) goals?

An Individual Example of Self-Regulated Learning

Students today are faced with constant distractions. Barry Zimmerman (2002, p. 64) describes Tracy, a high school student who is devoted to Facebook and Twitter:

> An important mid-term math exam is two weeks away, and she had begun to study while listening to popular music "to relax her." Tracy has not set any study goals for herself—instead she simply tells herself to do as well as she can on the test. She uses no specific learning strategies for condensing and memorizing important material and does not plan out her study time, so she ends up cramming for a few hours before the test. She has only vague self-evaluative standards and cannot gauge her academic preparation accurately. Tracy attributes her learning difficulties to an inherent lack of mathematical ability and is very defensive about her poor study methods. However, she does not ask for help from others because she is afraid of "looking stupid," or seek out supplementary materials from the library because she "already has too much to learn." She finds studying to be anxiety-provoking, has little self-confidence in achieving success, and sees little intrinsic value in acquiring mathematical skill.

Clearly, Tracy is unlikely to do well on the test. What would help? For an answer, let's consider Zimmerman's cycle of self-regulated learning. His cycle has three phases—*forethought, performance, reflection*—and is consistent with the Winne and Hadwin model just described. In Zimmerman's phase 1, the *forethought phase* (like Winne and Hadwin's steps 1 and 2 of analyzing the task and setting goals), Tracy needs to set clear, reasonable goals and plan a few strategies for accomplishing those goals. And Tracy's beliefs about motivation make a difference at this point, too. If Tracy had a sense of self-efficacy for applying the strategies that she planned, if she believed that using those strategies would lead to math learning and success on the test, if she saw some connections between her own interests and the math learning, and if she were trying to master the material—not just look good or avoid looking bad—then she would be on the road to self-regulated learning.

Moving from forethought to Zimmerman's *performance phase* (similar to Winne and Hadwin's step 3 of enacting the strategies) brings new challenges. Now Tracy must have a repertoire of self-control (volitional) and learning strategies, including using imagery, mnemonics, attention focusing, and other techniques such as those described in Chapters 8 and 9 (Kiewra, 2002). She also will need to self-observe—monitor how things are going—so she can change strategies if needed. Actual recording of time spent, problems solved, or pages written may provide clues about when or how to make the best use of study time. Turning off the music would help, too.

Finally, Tracy needs to move to Zimmerman's phase 3 of *reflection* (similar to Winne and Hadwin's step 4 of regulating learning) by looking back on her performance and reflecting on what happened. It will help her develop a sense of efficacy if she attributes successes to effort and good strategy use and avoids self-defeating actions and beliefs such as making weak efforts, pretending not to care, or assuming she is "no good at math."

Both Zimmerman's and Winne and Hadwin's models emphasize the cyclical nature of self-regulated learning: Each phase flows into the next, and the cycle continues as students encounter new learning challenges. Both models begin with being informed about the task so you can set good goals. Having a repertoire of learning strategies and tactics also is necessary in both models. And self-monitoring of progress followed by modifying plans if needed are critical to both. Notice also that the way students think about the task and their ability to do it—their *sense of efficacy for self-regulation*—is key as well (Zimmerman, 2011).

Two Classrooms

Students differ in their self-regulation knowledge and skills. But teachers must work with an entire classroom, and still "reach every student." Here are two examples of real situations where teachers did just that. The first involves writing, the second math problem solving—both complex tasks.

WRITING.   Carol is a second-grade student described by Nancy Perry and Lynn Drummond (2002). Ms. Lynn was Carol's teacher; she characterizes Carol as "a very weak writer." Carol has difficulty finding facts and then transforming those facts into meaningful prose for a research report. Also, she has difficulty with the mechanics of writing, which, according to Ms. Lynn, "holds her back."

Over the course of the year, Ms. Lynn involved her grade 2 and 3 students in three projects about animals. Through this writing, she wanted students to learn how to (a) do research, (b) write expository text, (c) edit and revise their writing, and (d) use the computer as a tool for researching and writing. For the first report, the class worked on one topic together (Chipmunks). They did the fact-finding and writing together, because Ms. Lynn needed to show them how to do research and write a report. Also, the class developed frameworks for working collaboratively as a community of learners. When they wrote the second report (on Penguins), Ms. Lynn offered students many more choices and encouraged them to depend more on themselves and one another. Finally, for the third report, students chose an animal, conducted a self-regulated research project, and wrote a report. Now that they knew how to do research and write a report, they could work alone or together and succeed at this complex task.

Carol worked with a third-grade boy who was doing research on a related topic. He showed Carol how to use a table of contents and offered advice about how to phrase ideas in her report. Also, Carol underlined words she thought were misspelled so she could check them later when she met with Ms. Lynn to edit her report. Unlike many low-achieving students who have not learned strategies for self-regulating learning, Carol was not afraid to attempt challenging tasks, and she was confident about her ability to develop as a writer. Reflecting on her progress across the school year, Carol said, "I learned a lot from when I was in grade 1 because I had a lot of trouble then."

MATH PROBLEM SOLVING.   Lynn Fuchs and her colleagues (2003) assessed the value of incorporating self-regulated learning strategies into math problem-solving lessons in real classrooms. The researchers worked with 24 teachers. All of the teachers taught the same content in their third-grade classes. The teachers were randomly assigned to one of three groups. The first taught in their usual way. The second incorporated strategies to encourage problem-solving transfer—using skills and knowledge learned in the lessons to solve problems in other situations and classes. The third group added transfer and self-regulated learning strategies to their units on math problem solving. Here are a few of the transfer and self-regulated learning strategies that were taught:

- Using a key, students scored their homework and gave it to a homework collector (a peer).
- Students graphed their completion of homework on a class report.
- Students used individual thermometer graphs that were kept in folders to chart their daily scores on individual problems.

- At the beginning of each session, students inspected their previous charts and set goals to beat their previous scores.
- Students discussed with partners how they might apply problem-solving strategies outside class.
- Before some lessons, students reported to the group about how they had applied problem-solving skills outside class.

Both transfer and self-regulated learning strategies helped students learn mathematical problem solving and apply this knowledge to new problems. The addition of self-regulated learning strategies was especially effective when students were asked to solve problems that were very different from those they encountered in the lessons. Students at every achievement level as well as students with learning disabilities benefited from learning the strategies.

Technology and Self-Regulation

In the previous chapter, we saw some examples of using technology-rich environments to explore complex concepts. But to learn in these rich environments, students need metacognitive and self-regulatory skills so they won't get lost in a sea of information. They need to actively evaluate the credibility and trustworthiness of information they find online. If the concepts they are learning are challenging and complicated, then they need some scaffolding to support their developing understandings (Azevedo, 2005; Azevedo, Johnson, Chauncey, & Graesser, 2011; Kingsley & Tancock, 2014). For example, Roger Azevedo and his colleagues (2004) studied undergraduate students who were learning about the circulatory system using a hypermedia encyclopedia. The materials available included texts, diagrams, photographs, video clips, and animated examples of how the circulatory system works. There were three different learning conditions. One group of students was told just to learn all they could about the circulatory system. A second group got the same instructions, but, in addition, they had a list of 10 subgoals to guide their learning. The third group had the list of subgoals plus a self-regulation "coach," who helped them plan their learning, monitor their developing understanding, try different strategies, and handle problems when they arose. Students in all three conditions were asked to "think out loud" as they used the hypermedia materials—describing what they were thinking as they went through the materials. Students who had the support of a self-regulation coach who focused on task analysis, goal setting, using strategies, and monitoring progress developed more complete and complex mental models of the circulatory system.

How could you provide this kind of self-regulation teaching and coaching for your students? Maybe peer coaches would be one way, or enlisting the help of families.

Reaching Every Student: Families and Self-Regulation

Children begin to learn self-regulation in their homes. Families can teach and support self-regulated learning through modeling, encouragement, facilitation, rewarding of goal setting, good strategy use, and other processes described in the next section (Martinez-Pons, 2002). The *Guidelines: Family and Community Partnerships* on the next page gives some ideas for helping students become more self-regulating.

Another Approach to Self-Regulation: Cognitive Behavior Modification

When some psychologists were studying a behavior modification approach called *self-management*—using reinforcement and punishment to manage your own behavior—Donald Meichenbaum (1977) was having success teaching impulsive students to "talk themselves through" tasks. Meichenbaum called his method *cognitive behavior modification* (B. H. Manning & Payne, 1996). Cognitive behavior modification focuses on self-talk to regulate behavior.

You may remember from Chapter 2 that there is a stage in cognitive development when young children seem to guide themselves through a task using private speech (Vygotsky, 1987a). They talk to themselves, often repeating the words of a parent or teacher. In cognitive behavior modification, students are taught directly how to use this self-instruction. Meichenbaum (1977) outlined the steps:

1. An adult model performs a task while talking to him- or herself out loud (cognitive modeling).
2. The child performs the same task under the direction of the model's instructions (overt, external guidance).

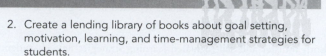

GUIDELINES
Family and Community Partnerships

SUPPORTING SELF-REGULATION AT HOME AND IN SCHOOL

Emphasize the value of encouragement.

Examples

1. Teach students to encourage each other.
2. Tell families about the areas that are most challenging for their child—those that will be the most in need of encouragement.

Model self-regulation.

Examples

1. Target small steps for improving an academic skill. Tailor goals to the student's current achievement level.
2. Discuss with your students how you set goals and monitor progress.
3. Ask parents and caregivers to show their children how they set goals for the day or week, write to-do lists, or keep appointment books.

Make families a source of good strategy ideas.

Examples

1. Have short, simple materials describing a "strategy of the month" that students can practice at home.

2. Create a lending library of books about goal setting, motivation, learning, and time-management strategies for students.
3. Encourage families to help their children focus on problem-solving processes and not turn immediately to the answers at the back of the book when doing homework. Teach checking routines.

Provide self-evaluation guidelines.

Examples

1. Develop rubrics for self-evaluation with students (see Chapter 15). Model how to use them.
2. Provide record-keeping sheets for assignments early in the year; then gradually have students develop their own.
3. Encourage parents and caregivers to model self-evaluation as they focus on areas they want to improve.
4. For family conferences, have examples of materials other families have successfully used to keep track of progress.

For more ideas to share with parents and caregivers, see pbs.org/ wholechild/parents/building.html

---

3. The child performs the task while instructing him- or herself aloud (overt, self-guidance).
4. The child whispers the instructions to him- or herself as he/she goes through the task (faded, overt self-guidance).
5. The child performs the task while guiding his/her performance via private speech (covert self-instruction). (p. 32)

Brenda Manning and Beverly Payne (1996) list four skills that can increase student learning: listening, planning, working, and checking. How might cognitive self-instruction help students develop these skills? One possibility is to use personal booklets or class posters that prompt students to "talk to themselves" about these skills. For example, one fifth-grade class designed a set of prompts for each of the four skills and posted the prompts around the classroom. The prompts for listening included "Does this make sense?" "Am I getting this?" "I need to ask a question now before I forget." "Pay attention!" "Can I do what he's saying to do?" Planning prompts were "Do I have everything together?" "Do I have my friends tuned out for right now?" "Let me get organized first." "What order will I do this in?" "I know this stuff!" Posters for these and the other two skills, working and checking, are shown in Figure 11.3. Part of the power of this process is in getting students involved in thinking about and creating their own guides and prompts. Many active reading programs encourage students to ask, "What do good readers do?" then use their answers as prompts. Having the discussion and posting the ideas makes students more self-aware and in control of their own learning.

Cognitive behavior modification as it is practiced by Meichenbaum and others has many more components than just teaching students to use self-instruction. Meichenbaum's methods also include dialogue and interaction between teacher and student, modeling, guided discovery, motivational strategies, feedback, careful matching of the task with the student's developmental level, and other principles of good teaching. The student is even involved in designing the program (Harris, 1990; Harris & Pressley, 1991). Given all this, it is no surprise that students seem to be able to generalize the skills developed with cognitive behavior modification to new learning situations (Harris, Graham, & Pressley, 1992).

FIGURE 11.3

POSTERS TO REMIND STUDENTS TO "TALK THEMSELVES THROUGH" LISTENING, PLANNING, WORKING, AND CHECKING IN SCHOOL

These four posters were designed by a fifth-grade class to help them remember to use self-instruction. Some of the reminders reflect the special world of these preadolescents.

Poster 1

While Listening:
1. Does this make sense?
2. Am I getting this?
3. I need to ask a question now before I forget.
4. Pay attention.
5. Can I do what he's saying to do?

Poster 3

While Working:
1. Am I working fast enough?
2. Stop staring at my girlfriend and get back to work.
3. How much time is left?
4. Do I need to stop and start over?
5. This is hard for me, but I can manage.

Poster 2

While Planning:
1. Do I have everything together?
2. Do I have my friends tuned out for right now?
3. Let me get organized first.
4. What order will I do this in?
5. I know this stuff!

Poster 4

While Checking:
1. Did I finish everything?
2. What do I need to recheck?
3. Am I proud of this work?
4. Did I write all the words? Count them.
5. I think I finished. I organized myself. Did I daydream too much?

Source: Manning, B.H. & Payne, B.D. Self-Talk for Teachers and Students: Metacognitive Strategies for Personal and Classroom Use, © 1996. Reprinted by permission of Pearson Education, Inc.

Today, entire school intervention programs are based on cognitive behavior modification. For example, the Coping Power Program includes training for both parents and their children, beginning in the last half of one academic year and continuing through the entire next school year. The training for students often focuses on anger and aggression. Different training sessions emphasize personal goal setting, awareness of feelings (especially anger), learning to relax and change the focus away from the angry feelings, making coping self-statements, developing organizational and study skills, seeing the perspectives of others, developing social problem-solving skills, and dealing with peer pressure by practicing how to say no (Lochman & Wells, 2003). Another similar approach is Tools for Getting Along (Daunic, Smith, Brank, & Penfield, 2006). Both programs have been effective in helping aggressive middle school students to "get along" with their classmates and teachers. In addition, in psychotherapy, tools based on cognitive behavior modification have proved to be some of the most effective ways of dealing with psychological problems such as depression.

Both the Coping Power Program and Tools for Getting Along programs include emotional self-regulation skills. We turn to this area of self-regulation next.

Emotional Self-Regulation

Social and emotional competencies and self-regulation are critical for both academic and personal development. Individuals who effectively interpret emotions in themselves and others (e.g., anxiety, anger, frustration, excitement), identify effective goals that incorporate those emotional signals, and eventually regulate emotion and behavior in ways that maximize successful engagement in social

Connect and Extend to PRAXIS II®

Self-Regulation (II, A1)
Take a look at *The Merton Ethel Harris Research and Training Centre* (mehritcentre.com) for tips to help students develop the goals, metacognitive skills, and self-regulatory practices that can support a lifelong devotion to learning.

situations are characterized as having high *emotional intelligence* (Cassady & Boseck, 2008). The most common focus for supporting success in emotionally laden situations is developing effective coping strategies that can be enacted to ensure that the emotional aspects of a social or learning situation do not become barriers to successfully achieving those goals. These coping strategies include a broad range of skills including emotional self-regulation (Matthews, Zeidner, & Roberts, 2002). To illustrate these important strategies, the Collaborative for Academic, Social, and Emotional Learning (CASEL) lists five core social and emotional skills and competencies:

- *Self-awareness*—accurately assessing your feelings, interests, values, and strengths; maintaining a well-grounded sense of self-confidence
- *Self-management*—regulating your emotions to handle stress, control impulses, and persevere in overcoming obstacles; setting and monitoring progress toward personal and academic goals; expressing emotions appropriately
- *Social awareness*—taking the perspective of and empathizing with others; recognizing and appreciating individual and group similarities and differences; recognizing and using family, school, and community resources
- *Relationship skills*—establishing and maintaining healthy and rewarding relationships based on cooperation; resisting inappropriate social pressure; preventing, managing, and resolving interpersonal conflict; seeking help when needed
- *Responsible decision making*—making decisions based on consideration of ethical standards, safety concerns, appropriate social norms, respect for others, and likely consequences of various actions; applying decision-making skills to academic and social situations; contributing to the well-being of one's school and community (casel.org/why-it-matters/what-is-sel/skills-competencies/)

A number of studies that followed students over several years in the United States and in Italy have found that prosocial behaviors and social competence in the early grades are related to academic achievement and popularity with peers as many as 5 years later (M. J. Elias & Schwab, 2006). Developing emotional

GUIDELINES
Encouraging Emotional Self-Regulation

Create a climate of trust in your classroom.
Examples
1. Avoid listening to "tattle tale" stories about students.
2. Follow through with fair consequences.
3. Avoid unnecessary comparisons, and give students opportunities to improve their work.

Help students recognize and express their feelings.
Examples
1. Provide a vocabulary of emotions, and note descriptions of emotions in characters or stories.
2. Be clear and descriptive about your own emotions.
3. Encourage students to write in journals about their own feelings. Protect the privacy of these writings (see trust above).

Help students recognize emotions in others and develop empathy.
Examples
1. For young children, "Look at Chandra's face. How do you think she feels when you say those things?"
2. For older students, use readings, analysis of characters in literature, films, or role reversals to help them identify the emotions of others.

Provide strategies for coping with emotions.
Examples
1. Discuss or practice alternatives such as stopping to think how the other person feels, seeking help, and using anger management strategies such as self-talk or leaving the scene.
2. Model strategies for students. Talk about how you handle anger, disappointment, or anxiety.

Help students recognize cultural differences in emotional expression.
Examples
1. Have students write about or discuss how they show emotions in their family.
2. Teach students to "check it out." Ask the other people how they are feeling.

For ideas about promoting emotional competence, see casel.org

self-regulation is especially important in the early years when students are learning how to learn in schools. For example, Carlos Valiente and his colleagues (2010) followed almost 300 students through kindergarten to assess the relations between effortful self-control, emotionality, and academic achievement. They found that students' anger, sadness, and shyness were negatively related to achievement and that self-control was positively related to achievement, particularly for students who showed lower levels of negative emotions. So helping students develop emotional self-regulation can set them on a good path for learning in school, increase their resilience, and probably can help them in social relations with their peers as well. How can teachers help students develop these skills? The *Guidelines: Encouraging Emotional Self-Regulation* gives some ideas.

ENHANCEDetext *self-check*

TEACHING TOWARD SELF-EFFICACY AND SELF-REGULATED LEARNING

Teacher stress is an area of considerable concern for teachers, school leaders, and researchers. In the first years of teaching, high levels of stress leads to "burnout" for teachers who are not able to develop effective coping strategies to handle the many pressures that face them (Chang, 2009). Those teachers who are most effective at handling stressors in the classroom demonstrate both the high levels of teaching self-efficacy discussed earlier as well as a positive level of emotional self-regulation (Montgomery & Rupp, 2005). The most commonly reported sources of teacher stress are student misbehaviors, interpersonal challenges, and work-related pressure—such as meeting standards (Cano-Garcia, Padilla-Munoz, & Carrasco-Ortiz, 2005; Griffith, Steptoe, & Cropley, 1999). Teachers are more likely to maintain a healthy professional life if they can manage professional stressors such as student disruptions and pressures from parents without becoming emotionally charged, keep things in perspective, and seek support from their peers (Collie, Shapka, & Perry, 2012; Kyraciou, 1987; Wilkinson, 1988; Woolfolk Hoy, 2013).

Applying these emotion-regulation strategies promotes more appropriate teacher behaviors, which often then limit the impact of the external stressors (Ramon, Roache, & Romi, 2011), reduce professional burnout (Van Dick & Wagner, 2001), or serve to buffer the negative views teachers develop even when the stressor is beyond their control (Chan, 1998). One promising practice that has received recent support in research is providing teachers "mindfulness training," which helps teachers focus attention and emotional resources on the present situation without judgment, recognizing and releasing unnecessary expectations and biases, and developing greater compassion for self and others (Roeser et al., 2013).

STOP & THINK How are you studying right now? What goals have you set for your reading today? What is your plan for learning, and what strategies are you using right now to learn? How did you learn those strategies? •

Most teachers agree that students need to develop skills and attitudes for independent, lifelong learning (*self-regulated learning* and a *sense of efficacy for learning*). Fortunately, a growing body of research offers guidance about how to design tasks and structure classroom interactions to support students' development of and engagement in self-regulated learning (Neuman & Roskos, 1997; Perry, 1998; Sinatra & Taasoobshirazi, 2011; Stoeger & Ziegler, 2011; Zimmerman & Schunk, 2011). This research indicates that students develop academically effective forms of self-regulated learning and a sense of efficacy for learning when teachers involve them in *complex, meaningful tasks* that extend over *long periods of time*, much like the constructivist activities described in Chapter 10. Also, to develop self-regulated learning and self-efficacy for learning, students need to have some *control over their learning processes and products*; they need to make choices about what to work on, where, and with whom. They also need to have *control over the difficulty* of the task—how much to read or write, at what pace, and with what level of support. And because self-monitoring and self-evaluation are key to effective self-regulated learning and a sense of efficacy, teachers can help students develop self-regulated learning by involving them in *setting criteria* for evaluating their learning processes and products, and then giving them opportunities to *reflect* on and make judgments about their progress using those standards. It helps to work in *collaboration* with peers and seek feedback from them. As you saw earlier, this has been called *shared regulation.* Throughout the entire process, teachers must *co-regulate* the task by "providing just enough and just in time information and support to facilitate students' acquisition and application of" self-regulated learning (Perry & Rahim, 2011, p. 130). Let's examine each of these research-based ways to support self-regulation development more closely.

Complex Tasks

Teachers don't want to assign students tasks that are too difficult and that lead to frustration. This is especially true when students have learning struggles or disabilities. In fact, research indicates that the most motivating and academically beneficial tasks for students are those that challenge but don't overwhelm them (Rohrkemper & Corno, 1988; Turner, 1997); complex tasks need not be overly difficult for students.

The term *complex* refers to the design of tasks, not their level of difficulty. From a design point of view, tasks are complex when they address multiple goals and involve large chunks of meaning—for example, projects and thematic units. Furthermore, complex tasks extend over long periods of time, engage students in a variety of cognitive and metacognitive processes, and allow for the production of a wide range of products (Perry, VandeKamp, Mercer, & Nordby, 2002). For example, a study of Egyptian pyramids might result in the production of written reports, maps, diagrams, skits, and models.

Even more important, complex tasks provide students with information about their learning progress. These tasks require them to engage in deep, elaborative thinking and problem solving. In the process, students develop and refine their cognitive and metacognitive strategies. Furthermore, succeeding at such tasks increases students' self-efficacy and intrinsic motivation (McCaslin & Good, 1996; Turner, 1997). Rohrkemper and Corno (1988) advised teachers to design complex tasks that provide opportunities for students to modify the learning conditions in order to cope with challenging problems. Learning to cope with stressful situations, regulate emotions, and make adaptations is an important educational goal (Matthews, Zeidner, & Roberts, 2002). Remember from Chapter 4 that, according to Sternberg (1997, 2000), one aspect of intelligence is choosing or adapting environments so that you can succeed.

Control

Teachers can share control with students by giving them choices. When students have choices (e.g., about what to produce, how to produce it, where to work, whom to work with), they are more likely to anticipate a successful outcome (increased self-efficacy) and consequently increase effort and persist when difficulty arises (Turner & Paris, 1995). Also, by involving students in making decisions, teachers invite them to take responsibility for learning by planning, setting goals, monitoring progress, and evaluating outcomes (Turner, 1997). Finally, when students perceive they have control over their learning activities, they maintain higher levels of motivation to complete the task, as predicted by theories of motivation presented in Chapter 12 (e.g., R. M. Ryan & Deci, 2000). These are qualities of highly effective, self-regulating learners.

Giving students choices creates opportunities for them to adjust the level of challenge that particular tasks present (e.g., they can choose easy or more challenging reading materials, determine the nature and amount of writing in a report, supplement writing with other expressions of learning). But what if students make poor academic choices? Highly effective teachers who are high in self-regulated learning carefully consider the choices they give to students. They make sure students have the knowledge and skills they need to operate independently and make good decisions (Perry & Rahim, 2011). For example, when students are learning new skills or routines, teachers can offer choices with constraints (e.g., students must write a minimum of four sentences/paragraphs/pages, but they can choose to write more; they must demonstrate their understanding of an animal's habitat, food, and babies, but they can write, draw, or speak their knowledge).

Highly effective teachers also teach and model good decision making. For example, when students are choosing partners, teachers can ask them to consider what they need from their partner (e.g., shared interest and commitment, perhaps knowledge or skills that they need to develop). When students are making choices about how best to use their time, these teachers ask, "What can you do when you're finished? What can you do if you are waiting for my help?" Often, lists are generated and posted, so students can refer to them while they work. Finally, highly effective teachers give students feedback about the choices they make and tailor the choices they give to suit the unique characteristics of particular learners. For example, they might encourage some students to select research topics for which resources are readily available and written at a level that is accessible to the learner. Alternatively, they might encourage some students to work collaboratively versus independently to ensure they have the support and shared regulation they need to be successful.

Self-Evaluation

Evaluation practices that support self-regulated learning are nonthreatening. They are embedded in ongoing activities, emphasize process as well as products, focus on personal progress, and help students to interpret errors as opportunities for learning to occur. In these contexts, students enjoy and actually seek challenging tasks because the risk of participation—or perceived risk—is low (Paris & Ayres, 1994). Involving students in generating evaluation criteria and evaluating their own work also reduces the anxiety that often accompanies assessment by giving students a sense of control over the outcome. Students can judge their work in relation to a set of qualities both they and their teachers identify as "good" work. They can consider the effectiveness of their approaches to learning and alter their behaviors in ways that enhance it (Winne, 2011; Winne & Perry, 2000).

Classrooms that are high in self-regulated learning have both formal and informal opportunities for students to evaluate their learning. For example, one student teacher asked fourth- and fifth-grade students to submit reflection journals describing the games they designed with a partner or a small group of collaborators for a probability and statistics unit (Perry, Phillips, & Dowler, 2004). Their journals explained their contribution to the group's process and product and also described what they learned from participating. The student teacher took these reflections into account when she evaluated the games. More informally, teachers ask students, "What have you learned about yourself as a writer today?" "What do good researchers and writers do?" "What can we do that we couldn't do before?" Questions like these, posed to individuals or embedded in class discussions, prompt students' metacognition, motivation, and strategic action—the components of self-regulated learning.

Collaboration

The Committee on Increasing High School Students' Engagement and Motivation to Learn (2004) concluded that when students can put their heads together, they are more receptive to challenging assignments—the very kind of complex task that develops self-regulation. The Committee added:

> Collaborative work also can help students develop skills in cooperation. Furthermore, it helps create a community of learners who have responsibility for each other's learning, rather than a competitive environment, which is alienating to many students, particularly those who do not perform as well as their classmates. (p. 51)

The most effective uses of cooperative/collaborative relationships to support self-regulated learning are those that reflect a climate of community and shared problem solving (Perry & Drummond, 2002; Perry, VandeKamp, Mercer, & Nordby, 2002). In these contexts, teachers and students actually co-regulate one another's learning (McCaslin & Good, 1996), offering support, whether working alone, in pairs, or in small groups. This support is instrumental to individuals' development and use of metacognition, intrinsic motivation, and strategic action (e.g., sharing ideas, comparing strategies for solving problems, identifying everyone's area of expertise). Teachers who are high in self-regulated learning spend time at the start of each school year teaching routines and establishing norms of participation (e.g., how to give constructive feedback and how to interpret and respond to peers' suggestions). As you will see in Chapter 13, developing useful management and learning

Video 11.5
In this class, students choose work to include in their portfolios by identifying their best work and explicitly stating how each sample reflects improvement. They are involved in self-evaluation and see evidence of their growth.

ENHANCEDetext *video example*

procedures and routines takes time at the beginning of the year, but it is time well spent. Once routines and patterns of interaction are established, students can focus on learning and teachers can attend to teaching academic skills and the curriculum.

BRINGING IT ALL TOGETHER: THEORIES OF LEARNING

How can we make sense of the diversity in perspectives on learning we have explored for the last four chapters? We have considered behavioral, cognitive, constructivist (individual and social), and social cognitive explanations of what people learn and how they learn it. Table 11.3 presents a summary of these perspectives on learning.

TABLE 11.3 • Four Views of Learning

There are variations within each of these views of learning and overlaps as well, especially in constructivist views.

	BEHAVIORAL	COGNITIVE	CONSTRUCTIVIST		SOCIAL COGNITIVE
	APPLIED BEHAVIORAL ANALYSIS *B. F. SKINNER*	INFORMATION PROCESSING *J. ANDERSON*	INDIVIDUAL *JEAN PIAGET*	SOCIAL/SITUATED *LEV VYGOTSKY*	SOCIAL COGNITIVE THEORY *ALBERT BANDURA*
Knowledge	Fixed body of knowledge to acquire Stimulated from outside	Fixed body of knowledge to acquire Stimulated from outside Prior knowledge influences how information is processed	Changing body of knowledge, individually constructed in social world Built on what learner brings	Socially constructed knowledge Built on what participants contribute, construct together	Changing body of knowledge, constructed in interaction with others and the environment
Learning	Acquisition of facts, skills, concepts Occurs through drill, guided practice	Acquisition of facts, skills, concepts, and strategies Occurs through the effective application of strategies	Active construction, restructuring prior knowledge Occurs through multiple opportunities and diverse processes to connect to what is already known	Collaborative construction of socially defined knowledge and values Occurs through socially constructed opportunities	Active construction of knowledge based on observation, interacting in the physical and social world, and developing agency—becoming more self-regulating
Teaching	Transmission presentation (Telling)	Transmission Guide students toward more "accurate" and complete knowledge	Challenge, guide thinking toward more complete understanding	Co-construct knowledge with students	Presenting models, demonstrating, supporting self-efficacy and self-regulation
Role of Teacher	Manager, supervisor Correct wrong answers	Teach and model effective strategies Correct misconceptions	Facilitator, guide Listen for student's current conceptions, ideas, thinking	Facilitator, guide Co-participant Co-construct different interpretation of knowledge; listen to socially constructed conceptions	Model, facilitator, motivator Model of self-regulated learning
Role of Peers	Not usually considered	Not necessary but can influence information processing	Not necessary but can stimulate thinking, raise questions	Ordinary and necessary part of process of knowledge construction	Serve as models Ordinary and necessary part of process of knowledge construction
Role of Student	Passive recipient of information Active listener, direction-follower	Active processor of information, strategy user Organizer and reorganizer of information Rememberer	Active construction (within mind) Active thinker, explainer, interpreter, questioner	Active co-construction with others and self Active thinker, explainer, interpreter, questioner Active social participator	Active co-construction with others and self Active thinker, explainer, interpreter, questioner Active social participator

Rather than debating the merits of each approach in Table 11.3, consider their contributions to understanding learning and improving teaching. Don't feel that you must choose the "best" approach—there is no such thing. Chemists, biologists, and nutritionists rely on different theories to explain and improve health. Different views of learning can be used together to create productive learning environments for the diverse students you will teach. Behavioral theory helps us understand the role of cues in setting the stage for behaviors and the role of consequences and practice in encouraging or discouraging particular behaviors. But much of humans' lives and learning is more than behaviors. Language and higher-order thinking require complex information processing and memory—something the cognitive models help us understand. And what about the person as a creator and constructor of knowledge, not just a processor of information? Here, constructivist perspectives have much to offer. Social cognitive theory illustrates the powerful learning opportunities afforded through modeling and observational learning and highlights the important role of agency and self-direction. Finally, life requires self-regulated learning, and promoting effective self-regulation skills promotes greater success in learning regardless of the operational process of learning.

I like to think of the four main learning theories in Table 11.3 as four pillars for teaching. Students must first understand and make sense of the material (constructivist); then, they must remember what they have understood (cognitive—information processing); then, they must practice and apply (behavioral) their new skills and understanding to make them more fluid and automatic—a permanent part of their repertoire. Finally, they must take charge of their own learning (social cognitive). Failure to attend to any part of the process results in lower-quality learning.

ENHANCEDetext *self-check*

SUMMARY

- **Social Cognitive Theory (pp. 412–414)**

Distinguish between social learning and social cognitive theories. Social learning theory expanded behavioral views of reinforcement and punishment. In behavioral views, reinforcement and punishment directly affect behavior. In social learning theory, observing another person, a model, and being reinforced or punished can have similar effects on the observer's behavior. Social cognitive theory expands social learning theory to include cognitive factors such as beliefs, expectations, and perceptions of self. Current social cognitive theory is a dynamic system that explains human adaptation, learning, and motivation. The theory addresses how people develop social, emotional, cognitive, and behavioral capabilities; how people regulate their own lives; and what motivates them.

What is triarchic reciprocal causality? Triarchic reciprocal causality is the dynamic interplay between three kinds of influences: personal, environmental, and behavioral. Personal factors (beliefs, expectations, attitudes, and knowledge), the physical and social environment (resources, consequences of actions, other people, models and teachers, and physical settings), and behavior (individual actions, choices, and verbal statements) all influence and are influenced by each other.

- **Modeling: Learning by Observing Others (pp. 414–418)**

What is modeling? Learning by observing others is a key element of social cognitive theory. Modeling is influenced by the developmental characteristics of the observer, the status and prestige of the model, the consequences of the model's actions as seen by the observer, the observer's expectations about performing the observed behaviors (will I be rewarded?), the links that the observers perceive between their goals and the models' behaviors (will doing what the model does get me what I want?), and the observer's self-efficacy (can I do it?).

What kinds of outcomes can observational learning encourage? Observational learning can lead to five possible outcomes: directing attention, encouraging existing behaviors, changing inhibitions, teaching new behaviors and attitudes, and arousing emotions. By directing attention, we gain insight into how others do things and what objects are involved in their actions. Encouraging or fine tuning existing behaviors can lead to the development of good habits or can make work more efficient. Observing others also has the capacity to cue us in to others' attention, which can cause us to become more or less "self-conscious" about our behavior; when others are doing something, it's easier for us to do the same. Young children in particular learn by watching and emulating others, but everyone can gain insight into how something is done well (or poorly) by observing someone else do it. Finally, observing can lead to the association of emotions with certain activities. If others are observed enjoying an activity, the observer may learn to enjoy the activity as well.

- **Self-Efficacy and Agency (pp. 418–422)**

What is self-efficacy, and how is it different from other self-schemas? Self-efficacy is distinct from other self-schemas in that it involves judgments of capabilities specific to a particular task. Self-concept is a more global construct that contains many perceptions about the self, including self-efficacy. Compared to self-esteem, self-efficacy is concerned with judgments of personal capabilities; self-esteem is concerned with judgments of self-worth.

What are the sources of self-efficacy? Four sources are mastery experiences (direct experiences), level of arousal as you face the task, vicarious experiences (accomplishments are modeled by someone else), and social persuasion (a "pep talk" or specific performance feedback).

How does self-efficacy affect motivation? Greater efficacy leads to greater effort, persistence in the face of setbacks, higher goals, and finding new strategies when old ones fail. If sense of efficacy is low, however, people may avoid a task altogether or give up easily when problems arise.

What is teachers' sense of efficacy? One of the few personal characteristics of teachers related to student achievement is a teacher's sense of self-efficacy—the belief that he or she can reach even difficult students to help them learn. Teachers with a high sense of efficacy work harder, persist longer, and are less likely to experience burnout. Teachers' sense of efficacy is higher in schools where the other teachers and administrators have high expectations for students and where teachers receive help from their principals in solving instructional and management problems. Self-efficacy grows from real success with students, so any experience or training that helps you succeed in the day-to-day tasks of teaching will give you a foundation for developing a sense of efficacy in your career. There may be some benefits to lower sense of efficacy, if this encourages teachers to pursue professional development and improvement.

- **Self-Regulated Learning (pp. 422–433)**

What factors are involved in self-regulated learning? One important goal of teaching is to prepare students for lifelong learning. To reach this goal, students must be self-regulated learners; they must have a combination of the knowledge, motivation to learn, and volition that provides the skill and will to learn independently and effectively. Knowledge includes an understanding of self, subject, task, learning strategy, and contexts for application. Motivation to learn provides the commitment, and volition is the follow-through that combats distraction and protects persistence.

What is the self-regulated learning cycle? There are several models of self-regulated learning. Winne and Hadwin describe a four-phase model: analyzing the task, setting goals and designing plans, enacting strategies to accomplish the task, and regulating learning. Zimmerman notes three similar phases: forethought (which includes setting goals, making plans, self-efficacy, and motivation); performance (which involves self-control and self-monitoring); and reflection (which includes self-evaluation and adaptations, leading to the forethought/planning phase again).

What are some examples of teaching students to be more self-regulating? Self-regulating learners engage in four types of activities: analyzing the task, setting goals and designing plans, engaging in learning, and adjusting their approach to learning. Teaching students to be more self-regulating might take the form of providing opportunities to identify and analyze the task at hand. Students should ask themselves: What is the task? What is an ideal outcome of the task? Students may also benefit from goal-setting practice; they may ask: What are my short-term goals? What are my long-term goals? Learning strategies such as identifying important details and developing a big picture of material is the next step in the process. Finally, students need to reflect on whether they were successful and devise strategies for overcoming shortcomings in their self-regulation process. They may ask themselves: Where was I successful? Where do I need to improve in order to meet my goals in the future?

What is cognitive behavior modification? Cognitive behavior modification is a process in which self-talk is used to regulate behavior. Cognitive behavior modification may take many forms, including helping to keep students engaged in their learning or helping them deal effectively with anger and aggression. Some research has identified four skills that are particularly helpful self-talk strategies: listening, planning, working, and checking. Cognitive behavior modification can be used with students of all ages, but helping students engage in self-talk may require more adult assistance and guidance for younger children, or those who have not had opportunities to practice good self-regulation strategies.

What are the skills involved in emotional self-regulation? Emotionally self-regulating individuals are aware of their own emotions and the feelings of others—realizing that inner emotions can differ from outward expressions. They can talk about and express emotions in ways that are appropriate for their cultural group. They can feel empathy for others in distress and also cope with their own distressing emotions—they can handle stress. Emotional self-regulators can also employ a variety of problem-solving and coping strategies to help them manage the personal and social emotional stimuli to promote optimal performance. These individuals know that relationships are defined in part by how emotions are communicated within the relationship. All these skills come together to produce a capacity for emotional self-regulation.

- **Teaching Toward Self-Efficacy and Self-Regulated Learning (pp. 433–436)**

How can teachers support the development of self-efficacy and self-regulated learning? Teachers should involve students in complex meaningful tasks that extend over long periods of time. Teachers should provide students control over their learning processes and products, allowing them to make choices. They should involve students in setting criteria for evaluating their learning processes and products, and then give them opportunities to make judgments about their progress using those standards. Finally, teachers should encourage students to work collaboratively with and seek feedback from peers.

- **Bringing It All Together: Theories of Learning (pp. 436–437)**

What is the value of the four different perspectives on learning? The behavioral, cognitive, constructivist, and social cognitive learning theories are four pillars for teaching. Students must first understand and make sense of the material (constructivist); then, they must remember what they have understood (cognitive—information processing); then, they must practice and apply (behavioral) their new skills and understanding to make them more fluid and automatic—a permanent part of their repertoire. Finally, they must take charge of their own learning (social cognitive). Failure to attend to any part of the process results in lower-quality learning.

PRACTICE USING WHAT YOU HAVE LEARNED

To access and complete the exercises, click the link under the images below.

Modeling: Learning by Observing Others

ENHANCEDetext *application exercise*

Self-Regulated Learning

ENHANCEDetext *application exercise*

KEY TERMS

CONNECT AND EXTEND TO LICENSURE

MULTIPLE-CHOICE QUESTIONS

1. "I believe I will do well in this class," Chris declared to her brother. "I received a perfect score on the verbal part of the SAT, and I have always excelled in my literature classes." Chris is demonstrating which of the following?

    A. High self-esteem
    B. High levels of empathy
    C. High self-efficacy in English
    D. Low self-efficacy in English

2. Modeling is defined as changes in behavior, thinking, or emotions that happen through observing another person. Which theory and theorist are associated with learning through observation?

    A. Behaviorist theory, Skinner
    B. Constructivist theory, Piaget
    C. Social cognitive theory, Bandura
    D. Sociocultural theory, Vygotsky

3. Miss Hutton turned around with a scowl on her face and addressed her second graders. "What do you think you're doing, Johnny? Did I tell you to get out of your seat? Don't you ever let me catch you up without permission." The class sat silently with their eyes wide. When the lunch bell rang an hour later, not one of the children dared to move from their seats. This is an example of which one of the following?

    A. Self-regulation
    B. Self-efficacy
    C. Reciprocal causality
    D. Vicarious learning

4. Through observational learning, one learns how to perform a behavior and also what will happen in specific situations if one performs it. Observation can be a very efficient learning process. What four elements must be met in order to learn from observation?

    A. Attention, retention, production, and motivation/reinforcement
    B. Attention, cognition, belief, and value
    C. Observation, desire, developmental capability, and suitability
    D. Observation, motivation, abstraction, and reinforcement

CONSTRUCTED-RESPONSE QUESTIONS

Case

"Marcus! Look how well you did on your spelling test!" Mr. Bonner smiled at Marcus, who beamed in response. "I knew when we started to chart your progress you would really do well. You have had three perfect scores on the last three tests. It just goes to show, you studied every night for a few minutes, and your grade has gone up, up, up! I'm looking at the chart we made at the beginning of the year, and I think it really helped."

"Mr. Bonner, I would like to do the same thing in math. I think if I practice every night and chart my progress, I'll get perfect grades in math, too! I'll make a chart and pick out some math games I can play at home to improve."

5. How is Mr. Bonner encouraging Marcus's self-efficacy?
6. How is Marcus's response to Mr. Bonner an example of self-regulated learning?

ENHANCEDetext *licensure exam*

TEACHERS' CASEBOOK

WHAT WOULD THEY DO? FAILURE TO SELF-REGULATE

Here is how several expert teachers responded to the situation at the beginning of the chapter of the teacher with a class of disorganized students.

JANE W. CAMPBELL—Second-Grade Teacher
John P. Faber Elementary School, Dunellen, NJ

To begin the year, I teach several routines that help students to become more independent and successful. First they are introduced to a homework folder labeled with the classroom number and school name. Ownership is important, so they write their own names on the label, too. There are also designated sections for parent signatures, homework to be returned to school, and homework to be kept at home. Each day students put their things into the proper section. I check the students' success by walking through the room and looking at their folders. As different students become proficient, they become student helpers to help spot check other students as well. Organizing the students takes time, but once the routine is established, most students can successfully complete the task. As the routine is practiced and established, the students become successful and more self-reliant. Everyone is happy: the students, the parents, and the teacher.

CARLA S. HIGGINS—K–5 Literacy Coordinator
Legend Elementary School, Newark, OH

I don't make assumptions about my students' organizational skills. Instead, I explicitly teach them skills that work for our class and support future organization such as using a structured folder for class paperwork, frequent checkpoints, and an assignment calendar or agenda. I include students in planning due dates by considering what it would take to complete each assignment. For longer assignments, I ask students to help create a reasonable timeline for completing steps of the project and offer frequent checks for completion of the steps. Finally, since we live in a culture where technology drives much of our communication, I set up a Web site or e-mail reminder system to provide additional support for students and to communicate with parents to keep them involved.

MARIE HOFFMAN HURT—Eighth-Grade Foreign-Language Teacher (German and French)
Pickerington Local Schools, Pickerington, OH

Part of being a good teacher is learning how to teach the "process" of learning alongside the required content material. In the grand scheme of teaching, content-specific learning is only a small percentage of what I teach—something I didn't expect when I started my career in education. A large part of succeeding in life (and on achievement tests!), rather than just knowing how to conjugate a French verb, is knowing the habits, routines, and learning skills that students master *while* learning those French verbs. With this in mind, it is much easier to keep the task at hand in perspective. If a teacher focuses on fundamental strategies such as organization and planning, and inextricably links these strategies to the operation of the classroom, these concepts become second

nature to the students. Students are better able to absorb and learn the content-specific material because they have the tools necessary to do so.

KELLY L. HOY—Fifth Grade Teacher
The Phillips Brooks School, Menlo Park, CA

In an elementary school classroom, organizational skills are central to alleviating stress for students, teachers, and even parents. From the desk to the binder to the backpack, somehow students' paperwork mysteriously disappears. There are ways to battle the infamous "black hole" book bag or desk. Teachers should take time at the end of each period to clearly state where the assignment should be placed, and each child can give a signal that his or her paper is in the correct place. For time-sensitive projects, having different dates in which notes, drafts, and final projects are due will help students learn time management. Students can check off that they have the correct materials in assignment logs and get a teacher's initials. Periodic "book bag checks" can help students organize their book bags for homework.

PATRICIA A. SMITH—High School Math Teacher
Earl Warren High School, San Antonio, TX

In my high school mathematics classes, I spend the first 2 months of the school year training my students in organizational skills. All of my students are given a schedule that outlines topics of discussion, assignment due dates, and quiz and test dates. I also give each of them a "scorecard" where they keep track of their own grades. This serves as a double check for me as the teacher and also provides a sense of ownership of earned grades to the students.

All my students have a three-ring binder with a plastic cover–; their schedule fits inside the plastic cover. Early in the year, I start every class with a look at the schedule and question students on assignment due dates. In addition, I collect all assignments and tests in colored folders unique to each class section. When the students walk into my classroom and see their designated color of folder on my desk, they know that something is due. Most of my quizzes are the take-home variety. I place them on a table in the back of the room, and students are responsible for locating, completing, and returning them. In fact, I put them out several days in advance and do not accept late quizzes, thereby increasing student responsibility and organization. Graded papers are also processed in the same manner, thereby perpetuating the new and orderly system and disabling the old unorganized ways.

12 | MOTIVATION IN LEARNING AND TEACHING

TEACHERS' CASEBOOK

WHAT WOULD YOU DO? MOTIVATING STUDENTS WHEN RESOURCES ARE THIN

It is July, and you finally have a teaching position. The district wasn't your first choice, but job openings are really tight, so you're pleased to have a job in your field. You are discovering that the teaching resources in your school are slim to none; the only materials available are some aging texts and the workbooks that go with them. Every idea you have suggested for software, simulation games, DVDs, science project supplies, field trips, or other more active teaching materials has been met with the same response, "There's no money in the budget for that." As you look over the texts and workbooks, you wonder how the students could be anything but bored by them.

To make matters worse, the texts look pretty high level for your students. But the objectives in the workbooks are important. Besides, the district curriculum requires these units. Students will be tested on them in district-wide assessments next spring.

CRITICAL THINKING

- How would you arouse student curiosity and interest about the topics and tasks in the workbooks?
- How would you establish the value of learning this material?
- How would you handle the difficulty level of the texts?
- What do you need to know about motivation to solve these problems?
- What do you need to know about your students to motivate them?

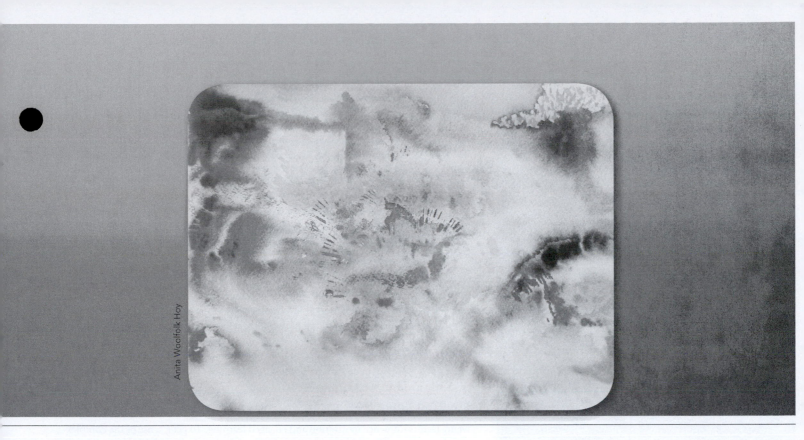

Anita Woolfolk Hoy

OVERVIEW AND OBJECTIVES

Most educators agree that motivating students is one of the critical tasks of teaching. To learn, students must be cognitively, emotionally, and behaviorally engaged in productive class activities. We begin with the question "What is motivation?" and examine many of the answers that have been proposed, including a discussion of intrinsic and extrinsic motivation and five general theories of motivation: behavioral, humanistic, cognitive, social cognitive, and sociocultural. As you review these theories of motivation, recall that just as different explanations for learning fit different types of behaviors or situations, so different explanations of motivation can promote engagement for specific learners in different contexts. Having a good understanding of theories of motivation will give you a broader set of tools for promoting positive motivation in your classroom.

Next, we consider more closely several personal factors that frequently appear in discussions of motivation: needs, goal orientations, beliefs and self-perceptions, interests and curiosity, emotions, and anxiety. How do we put all this information together in teaching? How do we create environments, situations, and relationships that encourage motivation and engagement in learning? First, we consider how the personal influences on motivation come together to support motivation to learn. Then, we examine how motivation is influenced by the academic work of the class, the value of the work, and the setting in which the work must be done. Finally, we discuss a number of strategies

for developing motivation as a constant state in your classroom and as a permanent trait in your students.

By the time you have completed this chapter, you should be able to:

Objective 12.1   Define motivation, contrast intrinsic and extrinsic motivation, and differentiate among five theoretical explanations for learner motivation.

Objective 12.2   Explain how learners' needs influence their motivation to learn.

Objective 12.3   Describe the different kinds of goal orientations and their influences on motivation.

Objective 12.4   Discuss how students' beliefs and attributions can influence motivation.

Objective 12.5   Describe the roles of interests, curiosity, emotions, and anxiety in motivation.

Objective 12.6   Explain how teachers can influence and encourage students' motivation to learn.

We began examining motivation in the previous chapter when we explored students' beliefs about their capabilities—their self-efficacy. I include another chapter on motivation because students' motivation has a direct and powerful impact on their social interactions and academic achievement in your classroom. Students with the same abilities and prior knowledge may perform quite differently, based on their motivation (Wigfield & Wentzel, 2007). So how does that work? Let's start with a basic question. What is motivation?

WHAT IS MOTIVATION?

Motivation is usually defined as an internal state that arouses, directs, and maintains behavior. Psychologists studying motivation have focused on five basic questions:

1. What choices do people make about their behavior? Why do some students, for example, focus on their homework and others play video games?
2. How long does it take to get started? Why do some students start their homework right away, while others procrastinate?
3. What is the intensity or level of involvement in the chosen activity? Once the backpack is opened, is the student engrossed and focused or is he just going through the motions?
4. What causes someone to persist or to give up? Will a student read the entire Shakespeare assignment or just a few pages?
5. What is the person thinking and feeling while engaged in the activity? Is the student enjoying Shakespeare, feeling competent, or worrying about an upcoming test (Anderman & Anderman, 2014; S. Graham & Weiner, 1996; Pintrich, Marx, & Boyle, 1993)?

Meeting Some Students

Many factors influence motivation and engaged learning. To get a sense of the complexity of motivation, let's step into a high school science classroom just after the teacher has given directions for a lab activity. The student profiles are adapted from Stipek (2002).

Hopeless Geraldo won't even start the assignment—as usual. He just keeps saying, "I don't understand," or "This is too hard." When he answers your questions correctly, he "guessed" and he "doesn't really know." Geraldo spends most of his time staring into space; he is falling farther and farther behind.

Safe Sumey checks with you about every step—she wants to be perfect. You once gave her bonus points for doing an excellent color drawing of the apparatus, and now she produces a work of art for lab every time. But Sumey won't risk getting a B. If it isn't required or on the test, Sumey isn't interested in doing the work.

Satisfied Spenser, on the other hand, is interested in this project. In fact, he knows more than you do about it. Evidently he spends hours reading about chemistry and performing experiments. But his overall grade in your class is between B- and C because he never turns in homework. Spenser is satisfied with the C he can get on tests without even trying.

Defensive Daleesha doesn't have her lab manual—again, so she has to share with another student. Then she pretends to be working, but spends most of her time making fun of the assignment or trying to get answers from other students when your back is turned. She is afraid to try because if she makes an effort and fails, she fears that everyone will know she is "dumb."

Anxious Aimee is a good student in most subjects, but she freezes on science tests and "forgets" everything she knows when she has to answer questions in class. Her parents are scientists and expect her to become one too, but her prospects for this future look dim.

- -

STOP & THINK Each of these students has problems with at least one of the five areas of motivation: (1) choices, (2) getting started, (3) intensity, (4) persistence, or (5) thoughts and feelings. Can you diagnose the problems? The answers are on bottom of page 445. •

- -

Each student presents a different motivational challenge, yet you have to figure out how to motivate and teach the entire class. In the next few pages, we will look more closely at the meaning of motivation so we can better understand these students.

Intrinsic and Extrinsic Motivation

We all know how it feels to be motivated, to move energetically toward a goal or to work hard, even if we are bored by the task. What energizes and directs our behavior? The explanation could be drives, basic desires, needs, incentives, fears, goals, social pressure, self-confidence, interests, curiosity, beliefs, values, expectations, and more. Some psychologists have explained motivation in terms of personal *traits* or individual characteristics. Certain people, so the theory goes, have a strong need to achieve, a fear of tests, a curiosity about mechanical objects, or an enduring interest in art, so they work hard to achieve, avoid tests, tinker endlessly in their garages, or spend hours in art galleries. Other psychologists see motivation more as a *state,* a temporary situation. If, for example, you are reading this paragraph because you have a test tomorrow, you are motivated (at least for now) by the situation. Of course, the motivation we experience at any given time usually is a combination of trait and state. You may be studying because you value learning *and* because you are preparing for a test. In addition, your motivational traits may set your general level or range of motivation, but certain situations (or states) may engage you more or less within that general range.

A classic distinction is made about amotivation, intrinsic motivation, and extrinsic motivation. **Amotivation** is a complete lack of any intent to act—no engagement at all. **Intrinsic motivation** is the natural human tendency to seek out and conquer challenges as we pursue personal interests and exercise our capabilities. When we are intrinsically motivated, we do not need incentives or punishments, because the activity itself is satisfying and rewarding (Anderman & Anderman, 2014; Deci & Ryan, 2002; Reiss, 2004). Satisfied Spenser studies chemistry outside school simply because he loves learning about chemistry; no one makes him do it. Intrinsic motivation is associated with many positive outcomes in school such as academic achievement, creativity, reading comprehension and enjoyment, and using deep learning strategies (Corpus, McClintic-Gilbert, & Hayenga, 2009).

In contrast, when we do something to earn a grade, avoid punishment, please the teacher, or for some other reason that has very little to do with the task itself, we experience **extrinsic motivation**. We are not really interested in the activity for its own sake; we care only about what it will gain us. Safe Sumey works for the grade; she has little interest in the subject itself. Extrinsic motivation has been associated with negative emotions, poor academic achievement, and maladaptive learning strategies (Corpus et al., 2009). However, extrinsic motivation also has benefits if it provides incentives as students try new things, gives them an extra push to get started, or helps them persist to complete a mundane task. Beware of either/or!

According to psychologists who adopt the intrinsic/extrinsic concept of motivation, it is impossible to tell just by looking if a behavior is intrinsically or extrinsically motivated. The essential difference between the two types of motivation is the student's *reason* for acting—whether the **locus of causality** for the action (the location of the cause) is internal or external—inside or outside the person. Students who read or practice their backstroke or paint may be reading, swimming, or painting because they freely chose the activity based on personal interests (*internal locus of causality/intrinsic motivation*), or because someone or something else outside is influencing them (*external locus of causality/extrinsic motivation*) (Reeve, 2002; Reeve & Jang, 2006a, 2006b).

As you think about your own motivation, you probably realize that the dichotomy between intrinsic and extrinsic motivation is too either/or—too all-or-nothing. Two explanations of motivation

Video 12.1
Students in this classroom are taking turns reading their creative writing to the class and receiving feedback to become better writers. Observe the use of extrinsic motivators as one child reads and receives feedback.

ENHANCEDetext *video example*

STOP & THINK ANSWERS Hopeless Geraldo has trouble with getting started (2) and with a sense of despair (5); during the activity he feels defeated and helpless. Safe Sumey makes good choices (1), gets started right away (2), and persists (4). But she is not really engaged and takes little pleasure in the work (4 and 5). As long as he is following his own choices (1), Satisfied Spenser is prompt in getting started (2), engaged (3), persistent (4), and enjoys the task (5). Defensive Daleesha makes poor choices (1), procrastinates (2), avoids engagement (3), and gives up easily (4) because she is so concerned about how others will judge her (5). Anxious Aimee's problems have to do with what she thinks and how she feels as she works (5). Her worry and anxiety may lead her to make poor choices (1) and procrastinate (2), which only makes her more anxious at test time. •

avoid either/or thinking. One is that our activities fall along a continuum from fully self-determined (intrinsic motivation) to fully determined by others (extrinsic motivation). Four types of extrinsic motivation are based on level of internal drive to engage in the activity. Starting with the *most extrinsic*, these four types are *external regulation* (completely controlled by outside consequences), *introjected regulation* (engaging in the task to avoid guilt or negative self-perceptions), *identification* (participating despite lack of interest because it serves a larger goal that is personally motivating), and *integrated regulation* (participating in a task because it is both interesting and has extrinsic reward value). As an example of integrated regulation, students may freely choose to work hard on activities that they don't find particularly enjoyable because they know the activities are important in reaching a valued goal—such as spending hours studying educational psychology to become a good teacher. Those students are freely choosing to accept outside causes such as licensure requirements and then trying to get the most benefit from the requirements (Vansteenkiste, Lens, & Deci, 2006).

A second explanation is that intrinsic and extrinsic motivations are not two ends of a continuum. Instead, intrinsic and extrinsic tendencies are two independent possibilities, and at any given time, we can be motivated by some aspects of each (Covington & Mueller, 2001). Teaching can create intrinsic motivation by connecting to students' interests and supporting growing competence. But you know this won't work all the time. Did you find fractions inherently interesting? Was your curiosity piqued by irregular verbs? If teachers count on intrinsic motivation to energize all their students all of the time, they will be disappointed. There are situations where incentives and external supports are necessary. Teachers must encourage and nurture intrinsic motivation, while making sure that extrinsic motivation supports learning (Anderman & Anderman, 2014; Brophy, 2003). To do this, they need to know about the factors that influence motivation.

Five General Approaches to Motivation

- -

STOP & THINK Why are you reading this chapter? Are you curious about motivation and interested in the topic? Or is there a test in your near future? Do you need this course to earn a teaching license or to graduate? Maybe you believe that you will do well in this class, and that belief keeps you working. Maybe you just got caught up in the ideas and can't put the book down 🙂. Perhaps it is some combination of these reasons. What motivates you to study motivation? •

- -

Motivation is a vast and complicated subject encompassing many theories. Some theories were developed through work with animals in laboratories. Others are based on research with humans in situations that used games or puzzles. The work done in clinical or industrial psychology inspired additional theories as well. Our examination of the field will be selective; otherwise we would never finish. To get the big picture, we consider five families of explanations.

BEHAVIORAL APPROACHES TO MOTIVATION. According to the behavioral view, an understanding of student motivation begins with a careful analysis of the incentives and rewards present in the classroom. A **reward** is an attractive object or event supplied as a consequence of a particular behavior. For example, Safe Sumey was *rewarded* with bonus points when she drew an excellent diagram. An **incentive** is an object or event that encourages or discourages behavior. The promise of an A+ was an *incentive* to Sumey. Actually receiving the grade was a *reward*. Providing grades, stars, stickers, and other reinforcers for learning—or demerits for misbehavior—is an attempt to motivate students by extrinsic means of incentives, rewards, and punishments.

HUMANISTIC APPROACHES TO MOTIVATION. In the 1940s, proponents of humanistic psychology such as Carl Rogers argued that neither of the dominant schools of psychology, behavioral or Freudian, adequately explained why people act as they do. **Humanistic interpretations** of motivation emphasize such intrinsic sources of motivation as a person's needs for "self-actualization" (Maslow, 1968, 1970), the inborn "actualizing tendency" (Rogers & Freiberg, 1994), or the need for "self-determination" (Deci, Vallerand, Pelletier, & Ryan, 1991). So, from the humanistic perspective, to motivate means to encourage people's inner resources—their sense of competence,

Connect and Extend to PRAXIS II®

Promoting Intrinsic Motivation to Learn (I, C2, 3)
For a set of practical tips, guidelines, and suggestions for boosting and maintaining motivation to learn, go to *Promoting Academic Engagement Through 21st Century Community Learning Centers: The Oregon Experience* (educationnorthwest.org/events/promoting-academic-engagement-through-21st-century-community-learning-centers-oregon).

self-esteem, autonomy, and self-actualization. Maslow's hierarchy of needs and Deci and Ryan's self-determination theory, discussed later, are influential humanistic explanations of motivation. Giving students choices in projects, goals, books, or topics is an example of applying humanistic approaches.

COGNITIVE APPROACHES TO MOTIVATION. In cognitive theories, people are viewed as active and curious, searching for information to solve personally relevant problems. Thus, cognitive theorists emphasize intrinsic motivation. In many ways, cognitive theories of motivation also developed as a reaction to the behavioral views. Cognitive theorists believe that behavior is determined by our thinking, not simply by whether we have been rewarded or punished for the behavior in the past. Behavior is initiated and regulated by plans (G. A. Miller, Galanter, & Pribram, 1960), goals (Locke & Latham, 2002), schemas (Ortony, Clore, & Collins, 1988), expectations (Vroom, 1964), and attributions (Weiner, 2010). We will look at goals, expectations, and attributions later in this chapter.

SOCIAL COGNITIVE THEORIES. Many influential social cognitive explanations of motivation can be characterized as expectancy × value theories. This means that motivation is seen as the product of two main forces: the individual's *expectation* of reaching a goal and the individual's *value* of that goal. In other words, the important questions are, "If I try hard, can I succeed?" and "If I succeed, will the outcome be valuable or rewarding to me?" Motivation is a product of these two forces, because if either factor is zero, then there is no motivation to work toward the goal. For example, if I believe I have a good chance of making the basketball team (high expectation), and if making the team is very important to me (high value), then my motivation should be strong. But if either factor is zero (I believe I haven't a prayer of making the team, or I couldn't care less about playing basketball), then my motivation will be zero, too (Tollefson, 2000).

Jacqueline Eccles and Allan Wigfield add the element of *cost* to the expectancy × value equation. Values have to be considered in relation to the cost of pursuing them. How much energy will be required? What could I be doing instead? What are the risks if I fail? Will I look stupid? Is the cost worth the possible benefit (Eccles, 2009; Eccles & Wigfield, 2002)?

SOCIOCULTURAL CONCEPTIONS OF MOTIVATION. Finish this sentence: I am a/an _____. What is your identity? With what groups do you identify most strongly? Sociocultural views of motivation emphasize participation in communities of practice. People engage in activities to maintain their identities and their interpersonal relations within the community. Thus, students are motivated to learn if they are members of a classroom or school community that values learning. Just as we learn through socialization to speak or dress or order food in restaurants—by watching and learning from more capable members of the culture—we also learn to be students by watching and learning from members of our school community. In other words, we learn by the company we keep (Eccles, 2009; Hickey, 2003; Rogoff, Turkanis, & Bartlett, 2001).

When we see ourselves as soccer players, or sculptors, or engineers, or teachers, or psychologists, we are claiming an identity within a group. In building an identity in the group, we move from legitimate peripheral participation to central participation. Legitimate peripheral participation means that beginners are genuinely involved in the work of the group, even if their abilities are undeveloped and their contributions are small. The novice weaver learns to dye wool before spinning and weaving, and the novice teacher learns to tutor one child before working with the whole group. Each task is a piece of the real work of the expert. The identities of both the novice and the expert are bound up in their participation in the community, which motivates them to learn the values and practices of the community (Lave & Wenger, 1991; Wenger, 1998). Another key issue in sociocultural models of student motivation and engagement in school is *cultural correspondence*—whether school tasks and activities connect with students' funds of knowledge and prior experiences (Lawson & Lawson, 2013).

The behavioral, humanistic, cognitive, social cognitive, and sociocultural approaches to motivation are summarized in Table 12.1 on the next page. These theories differ in their answers to the question, "What is motivation?" but each contributes in its own way toward a comprehensive understanding.

TABLE 12.1 • **Five Views of Motivation**

	BEHAVIORAL	HUMANISTIC	COGNITIVE	SOCIAL COGNITIVE	SOCIOCULTURAL
Source of Motivation	Extrinsic	Intrinsic	Intrinsic	Intrinsic and Extrinsic	Intrinsic
Important Influences	Reinforcers, rewards, incentives, and punishers	Need for self-esteem, self-fulfillment, and self-determination	Beliefs, attributions for success and failure, expectations	Goals, expectations, intentions, self-efficacy	Engaged participation in learning communities; maintaining identity through participation in activities of group
Key Theorists	Skinner	Maslow, Deci	Weiner, Graham	Locke & Latham, Bandura	Lave, Wenger

To organize the many ideas about motivation in a way that is useful for teaching, let's examine four broad areas. Most contemporary explanations of motivation include a discussion of needs, goals, beliefs, and finally, the emotional "hot" side of motivation–interests, curiosity, emotions, and anxiety (Murphy & Alexander, 2000).

NEEDS

Early research in psychology conceived of motivation in terms of trait-like needs or consistent personal characteristics. Three of the main needs studied extensively in this earlier work were the needs for *achievement, power,* and *affiliation* (Pintrich, 2003). Abraham Maslow's influential theory emphasized a hierarchy that included all these needs and more.

Maslow's Hierarchy of Needs

Maslow (1970) suggested that humans have a **hierarchy of needs** ranging from lower-level needs for survival and safety to higher-level needs for knowledge and understanding and finally self-actualization (see Figure 12.1). **Self-actualization** is Maslow's term for self-fulfillment, the realization of personal potential—"being all that you can be." Each of the lower needs must be met before the next higher need can be addressed.

Maslow (1968) called the four lower-level needs—for survival, then safety, followed by belonging, and then self-esteem—**deficiency needs**. When these needs are satisfied, the motivation for fulfilling them decreases. He labeled the three higher-level needs—cognitive needs, then aesthetic needs, and finally self-actualization—**being needs**. When they are met, a person's motivation does not cease; instead, it increases to seek further fulfillment. Unlike the deficiency needs, these being needs can never be completely filled. For example, the more successful you are in your efforts to develop as a teacher, the harder you are likely to strive for even greater improvement.

Maslow's theory has been criticized for the very obvious reason that people do not always appear to behave as the theory would predict. Most of us move back and forth among different types of needs and may even be motivated by many needs at the same time. Some people deny themselves safety or friendship to achieve knowledge, understanding, or greater self-esteem.

Criticisms aside, Maslow's theory does give us a way of looking at the whole student, whose physical, emotional, and intellectual needs are all interrelated. When children are hungry, they will have trouble focusing on academic learning. A child whose feelings of safety and sense of belonging are threatened by divorce may have little interest in learning how to divide fractions. If school is a fearful, unpredictable place where neither teachers nor students know where they stand, they are likely to be more concerned with security and less with learning or teaching. Belonging to a social group and maintaining self-esteem within that group, for example, are important to students. If doing what the teacher says conflicts with group rules, students may choose to ignore the teacher's wishes or even defy the teacher.

Self-determination theory is a more recent approach to motivation that focuses on human needs (Deci & Ryan, 2002; Reeve, 2009).

Video 12.2
Compare the notions of significance, competence, and power described in this video to the ideas of relatedness, competence, and autonomy in self-determination theory or to the concept of self-efficacy. Where are the overlaps and similarities in all these explanations of motivation?

ENHANCEDetext *video example*

Connect and Extend to PRAXIS II®

Maslow (I, C1)
Consider how problems with satisfying Maslow's hierarchy of needs can affect student learning. Link these ideas to direct or vicarious experiences you might have had in school.

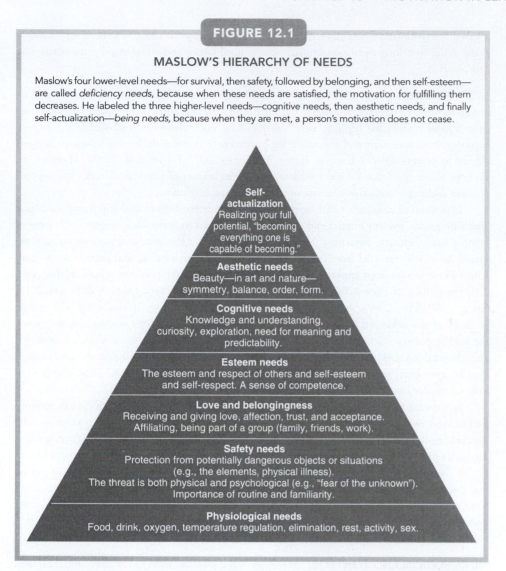

FIGURE 12.1

MASLOW'S HIERARCHY OF NEEDS

Maslow's four lower-level needs—for survival, then safety, followed by belonging, and then self-esteem—are called *deficiency needs*, because when these needs are satisfied, the motivation for fulfilling them decreases. He labeled the three higher-level needs—cognitive needs, then aesthetic needs, and finally self-actualization—*being needs*, because when they are met, a person's motivation does not cease.

Self-actualization
Realizing your full potential, "becoming everything one is capable of becoming."

Aesthetic needs
Beauty—in art and nature—symmetry, balance, order, form.

Cognitive needs
Knowledge and understanding, curiosity, exploration, need for meaning and predictability.

Esteem needs
The esteem and respect of others and self-esteem and self-respect. A sense of competence.

Love and belongingness
Receiving and giving love, affection, trust, and acceptance. Affiliating, being part of a group (family, friends, work).

Safety needs
Protection from potentially dangerous objects or situations (e.g., the elements, physical illness). The threat is both physical and psychological (e.g., "fear of the unknown"). Importance of routine and familiarity.

Physiological needs
Food, drink, oxygen, temperature regulation, elimination, rest, activity, sex.

Self-Determination: Need for Competence, Autonomy, and Relatedness

Self-determination theory suggests that we all need to feel competent and capable in our interactions in the world, to have some choices and a sense of control over our lives, and to be connected to others—to belong to a social group. Notice that these are similar to early conceptions of basic needs for achievement (*competence*), power (*autonomy and control*), and affiliation (*belonging and relatedness*). Because different cultures have divergent conceptions of self, some psychologists have asked whether the needs for competence, autonomy, and relatedness are universal. In a series of studies, Hyungshim Jang and her colleagues (2009) found that experiences of competence, autonomy, and relatedness were associated with satisfying learning experiences for Korean high school students, so even in a collectivistic culture, these needs may be important.

Need for competence is the individual's need to demonstrate ability or mastery over the tasks at hand. Satisfying this need results in a sense of accomplishment, promotes self-efficacy, and helps learners establish better learning goals for future tasks (J. Kim, Schallert, & Kim, 2010). **Need for autonomy** is central to self-determination because autonomy is the desire to have our own wishes, rather than external rewards or pressures, determine our actions (Deci & Ryan, 2002; Reeve, 2009; Reeve, Deci, & Ryan, 2004). People strive to have authority in their lives, to be in charge of their own behavior. They constantly struggle against pressure from external controls such as the rules, schedules, deadlines, orders, and limits imposed by others. Sometimes, even help is

Connect and Extend to PRAXIS II®

Self-Determination (I, C3)
Understand how self-determination can boost or diminish motivation and describe practical steps that teachers can take to establish a sense of self-determination in students.

rejected so that the individual can remain in command (deCharms, 1983). The need for *relatedness* is the desire to belong and to establish close emotional bonds and attachments with others who care about us.

SELF-DETERMINATION IN THE CLASSROOM. Student self-determination is influenced by several factors. For instance, research in both U.S. and Korean schools demonstrated that students' motivational profiles for learning were influenced by both classroom goal structure (teachers' messages about autonomy and demonstrating competence) as well as the level of autonomy support offered by parents (Friedel, Cortina, Turner, & Midgley, 2007; J. Kim et al., 2010). However, the findings also suggest that for older students, the direct impact of parental attitudes and support tends to decline, whereas the influence of teachers' messages remained.

Classroom environments that support student self-determination and autonomy are associated with greater student interest and curiosity (even interest in homework assignments), sense of competence, creativity, conceptual learning, grades, school attendance and satisfaction, engagement, use of self-regulated learning strategies, psychological well-being, and preference for challenge. These relationships appear to hold from first grade through graduate school (Hafen et al., 2012; Jang, Kim, & Reeve, 2012; Moller, Deci, & Ryan, 2006; Pulfrey, Darnon, & Butera, 2013; Reeve, 2009; Shih, 2008). Autonomy may also interact with interest. In one study with college students, choice enhanced interest, sense of competence, and valuing of a reading task only when the reading passage was boring (Patall, 2013), so choice may be less important when the reading is engaging and interesting already. But in general, when students have the authority to make choices, they are more likely to believe that the work is important, even if it is not "fun." Thus, they tend to internalize educational goals and take them as their own.

In contrast to autonomy-supporting classrooms, controlling environments tend to improve performance only on rote recall tasks. When students are pressured to perform, they often seek the quickest, easiest solution. But even though controlling styles of teaching are less effective, teachers are under pressure from administrators, accountability requirements, and cultural expectations to be "in charge," and parents expect good class "discipline." In addition, students often are passive and unengaged or even defiant. Finally, some teachers equate control with useful structure or feel more comfortable with a controlling style (Reeve, 2009). Assuming you are willing to resist those pressures, how can you support student autonomy? One answer is to focus on information, not control, in your interactions with students.

INFORMATION AND CONTROL. **Cognitive evaluation theory** (Deci & Ryan, 2002) explains how students' experiences such as being praised or criticized, reminded of deadlines, assigned grades, given choices, or lectured about rules can influence their intrinsic motivation by affecting their sense of self-determination and competence. According to this theory, all events have two aspects: *controlling* and *informational*. If an event is highly controlling—if it pressures students to act or feel a certain way—then students will experience less control, and their intrinsic motivation will be diminished. If, on the other hand, the event provides information that increases the students' sense of competence, then intrinsic motivation will increase. Of course, if the information provided makes students feel less competent, it is likely that motivation will decrease (Pintrich, 2003). Here is an example of a more *controlling* communication:

> Your paper is due on Monday. Today, we are going to the school library. In the library, you will find information from books and Internet sites to use for your paper. Don't waste your time; don't goof off; make sure to get your work done. In the library, you may work by yourself or with a partner. (Reeve, 2009, p. 169)

This teacher may believe that he is supporting autonomy because he offered a *choice*. Contrast his message with the following statement that gives *information* about why the library visit is valuable:

> Your paper is due on Monday. As a way of helping you write a well-researched paper, we are going to where the information is—the school library. The reason we are going to the library is to find the information you need from books and Internet sites. While

GUIDELINES
Supporting Self-Determination and Autonomy

Allow and encourage students to make choices.

Examples

1. Design several different ways to meet a learning objective (e.g., a paper, a compilation of interviews, a test, a news broadcast), and let students choose one. Encourage them to explain the reasons for their choice.
2. Appoint student committees to make suggestions about streamlining procedures such as caring for class pets or distributing equipment.
3. Provide time for independent and extended projects.
4. Allow students to choose work partners as long as they focus on the task.

Help students plan actions to accomplish self-selected goals.

Examples

1. Experiment with goal cards. Students list their short- and long-term goals and then record three or four specific actions that will move them toward the goals. Goal cards are personal—like credit cards.
2. Encourage middle and high school students to set goals in each subject area, record them in a goal book or on a thumb drive, and check progress toward the goals on a regular basis.

Hold students accountable for the consequences of their choices.

Examples

1. If students choose to work with friends and do not finish a project because too much time was spent socializing, grade the project as it deserves, and help the students see the connection between lost time and poor performance.
2. When students choose a topic that captures their imagination, discuss the connections between their investment in the work and the quality of the products that follow.

Provide rationales for limits, rules, and constraints.

Examples

1. Explain reasons for rules.
2. Respect rules and constraints in your own behavior.

Acknowledge that negative emotions are valid reactions to teacher control.

Examples

1. Communicate that it is okay (and normal) to feel bored waiting for a turn, for example.
2. Communicate that sometimes important learning involves frustration, confusion, weariness.
3. Acknowledge students' perspective: "Yes, this problem is difficult." Or "I can understand why you might feel that way."

Use noncontrolling, positive feedback.

Examples

1. See poor performance or behavior as a problem to be solved, not a target of criticism.
2. Avoid controlling language, "should," "must," "have to."
3. Provide unexpected, spontaneous, and genuine praise.

For more information on self-determination theory, see selfdeterminationtheory.org

Source: From 150 Ways to Increase Intrinsic Motivation in the Classroom, *by James P. Raffini. Copyright © 1996, by Pearson Education, and from* Motivating Others: Nurturing Inner Motivational Resources, *by Johnmarshall Reeve. Copyright © 1996 by Pearson Education. Adapted by permission of the publisher.*

there, you may be tempted to goof off, but students in the past have found that a trip to the library was a crucial part of writing an excellent paper. To help you write your best possible paper, you may work in the way you wish—by yourself or with a partner. (Reeve, 2009, p. 169)

As a teacher, what can you do to support student needs for autonomy and competence? An obvious first step is to limit your controlling messages to students because controlling language (*must, ought, have to, should* …) can undermine student motivation (Vansteenkiste, Simons, Lens, Sheldon, & Deci, 2004). Make sure the information you provide highlights students' growing competence by emphasizing gains made through persistence and practice and by encouraging student reflection, for example, on portfolio entries or work samples. The *Guidelines: Supporting Self-Determination and Autonomy* gives some more ideas.

THE NEED FOR RELATEDNESS. Think about your best teachers over the years. What were the qualities that made them great? I bet you remember teachers who cared and forged emotional connections with you. When teachers and parents are responsive and demonstrate that they care about the children's interests and well-being, the children show high intrinsic motivation. Students who feel a sense of connection and relatedness to teachers, parents, and peers are more emotionally engaged in school (Furrer & Skinner, 2003; Lawson & Lawson, 2013). All students need caring teachers, but students placed at risk have an even greater need for this kind of teacher. Positive relationships with teachers increase the likelihood that students will succeed in high school and go on to college (G. Thompson, 2008; Woolfolk Hoy & Weinstein, 2006). In addition, emotional and physical problems—ranging from eating disorders to suicide—are more common among individuals who lack social relationships (Baumeister & Leary, 1995). Relatedness is similar to a sense of belonging, discussed in Chapter 3 (Osterman, 2000) as well as to Maslow's basic need for belonging described earlier in this chapter.

Needs: Lessons for Teachers

From infancy to old age, people want to be competent, connected, and in control. Students are more likely to participate in activities that help them grow more competent and less likely to engage in activities that hold the possibility of failure. This means that your students need appropriately challenging tasks—not too easy, but not impossible either. They also benefit from watching their competence grow, perhaps through self-monitoring systems or portfolios. To be connected, students need to feel that people in school care about them and can be trusted to help them learn.

What else matters in motivation? Many theories include goals as key elements.

ENHANCEDetext *self-check*

GOAL ORIENTATIONS

A **goal** is an outcome or attainment an individual is striving to accomplish (Locke & Latham, 2002). When students strive to read a chapter or make a 4.0 GPA, they are involved in goal-directed behavior. In pursuing goals, students are generally aware of some current condition (I haven't even opened my book), some ideal condition (I have understood every page), and the discrepancy between the two. Goals motivate people to act in order to reduce the discrepancy between "where they are" and "where they want to be." Goal setting is usually effective for me. In addition to the routine tasks, such as eating lunch, which will happen without much attention, I often set goals for each day. For example, today I intend to finish this section, walk to the grocery store, order a medicine cabinet from Amazon, and wash another load of clothes (I know—not too exciting). Having decided to do these things, I will feel uncomfortable if I don't complete the list.

According to Locke and Latham (2002), there are four main reasons why goal setting improves performance. Goals:

1. Direct attention to the task at hand and away from distractions. Every time my mind wanders from this chapter, my goal of finishing the section helps direct my attention back to the writing.
2. Energize effort. The more challenging the goal, to a point, the greater the effort.
3. Increase persistence. When we have a clear goal, we are less likely to give up until we reach the goal: Hard goals demand effort, and tight deadlines lead to faster work.
4. Promote the development of new knowledge and strategies when old strategies fall short. For example, if your goal is making an A and you don't reach that goal on your first quiz, you might try a new study approach for the next quiz, such as explaining the key points to a friend.

Types of Goals and Goal Orientations

The types of goals we set influence the amount of motivation we have to reach them. Goals that are *specific, elaborated, moderately difficult,* and *proximal* (likely to be reached in the near future) tend to enhance motivation and persistence (Anderman & Anderman, 2014; Schunk, Meece, & Pintrich, 2014).

Video 12.3
In this video, high school students work in groups to solve problems and win points in algebra class. Consider the various goal orientations that play a part in motivating students to participate and learn.

ENHANCEDetext *video example*

Specific, elaborated goals provide clear standards for judging performance. If performance falls short, we keep going. For example, Ralph Ferretti and his colleagues (2009) gave fourth- and sixth-grade students either a general goal for writing a persuasive essay ("write a letter to a teacher about whether or not students should be given more out-of-class assignments . . .") or the general goal elaborated with specific subgoals such as:

- You need to say very clearly what your opinion or viewpoint is.
- You need to think of two or more reasons to back up your opinion.
- You need to explain why those reasons are good reasons for your opinion. (p. 580)

Students both with and without learning disabilities wrote more persuasive essays when they were given *specific subgoals.*

Moderate difficulty provides a challenge, but not an unreasonable one. Finally, goals that can be reached *fairly soon* are not likely to be pushed aside by more immediate concerns. Groups such as Alcoholics Anonymous show they are aware of the motivating value of short-term goals when they encourage their members to stop drinking "one day at a time." Also, breaking a long-term assignment into short-term steps is a way to take advantage of the motivating power of proximal goals.

STOP & THINK On a scale from 1 (Strongly Agree) to 5 (Strongly Disagree), how would you answer these questions:

I feel really pleased in school when

_____ I solve problems by working hard   _____ All the work is easy

_____ I know more than the others   _____ I learn something new

_____ I don't have to work hard   _____ I am the only one who gets an A

_____ I keep busy   _____ I am with my friends •

_____ I finish first

FOUR ACHIEVEMENT GOAL ORIENTATIONS IN SCHOOL. Goals are specific targets. **Goal orientations** are patterns of beliefs about goals related to achievement in school. Goal orientations include the *reasons* we pursue goals and the *standards* we use to evaluate progress toward those goals. For example, your target might be to make an A in this course. Are you doing so in order to *master* educational psychology—to learn all about it—or to *perform*—to look good in the eyes of your friends and family? There are four main goal orientations—mastery (learning), performance (looking good), work-avoidance, and social (Schunk et al., 2014; Senko, Hulleman, & Harackiewicz, 2011). In the *Stop & Think* exercise you just completed, can you tell which goal orientations are reflected in the different answers? Most of the questions were adapted from a study on students' theories about learning mathematics (Nicholls, Cobb, Wood, Yackel, & Patashnick, 1990).

The most common distinction in research on students' goals is between mastery goals (also called *task goals* or *learning goals*) and performance goals (also called *ability goals* or *ego goals*). The point of a **mastery goal** is to improve, to learn, no matter how awkward you appear. When students set mastery goals, the quality of their engagement in the task is higher—they are more invested, especially if they feel that they have choices and a sense of autonomy (Benita, Roth, & Deci, 2014). Students with mastery goals tend to seek challenges, persist when they encounter difficulties, and feel better about their work (Rolland, 2012). They focus on the task at hand and are not worried about how their performance "measures up" in comparison to others in the class. We often say that these people "get lost in their work." In addition, they are more likely to seek appropriate help, use deeper cognitive processing strategies, apply better study strategies, and generally approach academic tasks with confidence (Anderman & Patrick, 2012; Senko et al., 2011).

The second kind of goal is a performance goal. Students with **performance goals** care about demonstrating their ability to others. They may be focused on getting good test scores and grades, or they may be more concerned with winning and beating other students. Students whose goal is outperforming others may do things to look smart, such as reading easy books in order to "read the most books." The evaluation of their performance by others, not what they learn, is what matters. Students with performance goals may act in ways that actually interfere with learning. For example, they may cheat or use short-cuts to get finished, work hard only on graded assignments, be upset and hide papers with low grades, choose tasks that are easy, avoid collaborating with other students, and be very uncomfortable with assignments that have unclear evaluation criteria (Anderman & Anderman, 2014; Senko et al., 2011).

WAIT—ARE PERFORMANCE GOALS ALWAYS BAD? Performance goals sound pretty dysfunctional, don't they? Earlier research indicated that performance goals generally were detrimental to learning, but like extrinsic motivation, a performance goal orientation may not be all bad, all of the time. In fact, some research indicates that both mastery and performance goals are associated with using active learning strategies and high self-efficacy (Midgley, Kaplan, & Middleton, 2001). For college students, pursuing performance goals has been related to higher achievement. And, as is the case with intrinsic and extrinsic motivation, students can, and often do pursue mastery and performance goals at the same time (Anderman & Patrick, 2012).

To account for these recent findings, educational psychologists have added the distinction of approach/avoidance to the mastery/performance distinction. In other words, students may be motivated to either approach mastery or avoid misunderstanding. They may approach performance or avoid looking dumb. Table 12.2 shows examples and the effects of each kind of goal orientation. Where do you see the most problems? Do you agree that the real problems are with avoidance? Students who fear misunderstanding (mastery avoid) may be perfectionists—focused on getting it exactly right. Students who avoid looking dumb (performance avoid) may adopt defensive, failure-avoiding strategies like Defensive Daleesha, described earlier—they cheat, pretend not to care, or make a show of "not really trying," so they have an excuse for failure (Harackiewicz & Linnenbrink, 2005). Research in both Eastern and Western cultures has demonstrated that failure-avoiding strategies are associated with student helplessness, truancy, disengagement from school, and lower academic achievement (De Castella, Byrne, & Covington, 2013; Huang, 2012).

Two final cautions—performance-approach goals can turn into performance-avoidance goals if students are not successful in looking smart or winning. The path might lead from performance approach (trying to win), to performance avoidance (saving face and trying not to look dumb), to learned helplessness (I give up!). So teachers are wise to avoid trying to motivate using competition and social comparisons (Brophy, 2005). In addition, performance-approach and performance-avoidance goals tend to be moderately correlated, so students may pursue both types of performance goals at once (Linnenbrink-Garcia et al., 2012).

TABLE 12.2 • Goal Orientations

Students may have either an approach or an avoidance focus for mastery and performance goal orientations.

GOAL ORIENTATION	APPROACH FOCUS	AVOIDANCE FOCUS
Mastery	*Focus:* Mastering the task, learning, understanding	*Focus:* Avoiding misunderstanding or not mastering the task
	Standards Used: Self-improvement, progress, deep understanding (task-involved)	*Standards Used:* Just don't be wrong; perfectionists don't make mistakes
Performance	*Focus:* Being superior, winning, being the best	*Focus:* Avoiding looking stupid, avoiding losing
	Standards Used: Normative—getting the highest grade, winning the competition (ego-involved goal)	*Standards Used:* Normative—don't be the worst, get the lowest grade, or be the slowest (ego-involved goal)

Source: Based on Schunk, D. H., Meece, J., & Pintrich, P. R. (2014). Motivation in Education: Theory, Research, and Applications, 4th Ed. Pearson Education, Inc. Adapted by permission of the publisher.

BEYOND MASTERY AND PERFORMANCE. Some students don't want to learn, look smart, or avoid looking dumb; they just want to finish fast or avoid work altogether. These students try to complete assignments and activities as quickly as possible without exerting much effort (Schunk, Meece, & Pintrich, 2014). John Nicholls called these students **work-avoidant learners**—they feel successful when they don't have to try hard, when the work is easy, or when they can "goof off" (Nicholls & Miller, 1984).

A final category of goals becomes more important as students get older—**social goals**. As students move into adolescence, their social networks change to include more peers. Nonacademic activities such as athletics, dating, and "hanging out" compete with schoolwork. Social goals include a wide variety of needs and motives that have different relationships to learning; some help, but others hinder learning. For example, adolescents' goal of maintaining friendly relations can get in the way of learning when cooperative learning group members don't challenge wrong answers or misconceptions because they are afraid to hurt each other's feelings (Tschannen-Moran & Woolfolk Hoy, 2000). Certainly, pursuing social goals such as having fun with friends or avoiding being labeled a "nerd" can get in the way of learning. But the goal of bringing honor to your family or team by working hard or being part of a peer group that values academics certainly can support learning (Pintrich, 2003; A. Ryan, 2001; Urdan & Maehr, 1995; Zusho & Clayton, 2011). Social goals also are associated with students' emotional well-being and self-esteem. In one study, students who sought out social relationships were more likely to report positive emotional conditions such as joy, whereas students who avoided relationships reported higher levels of fear, shame, and sadness (Shim, Wang, & Cassady, 2013).

We talk about goals in separate categories, but students can and do pursue several goals at once (Bong, 2009; Darnon, Dompnier, Gillieron, & Butera, 2010). They have to coordinate their goals so they can make decisions about what to do and how to act. What if social and academic goals are incompatible? For example, if students do not see a connection between achievement in school and success in life, particularly because discrimination prevents them from succeeding, then they are not likely to set academic achievement as a goal. Such anti-academic peer groups probably exist in every high school (Committee on Increasing High School Students' Engagement and Motivation to Learn, 2004; Lawson & Lawson, 2013). Sometimes, succeeding in the peer group means not achieving in school—and succeeding in the peer group is important. The need for social relationships is basic and strong for most people.

GOALS IN SOCIAL CONTEXT. You have seen in other chapters that current thinking in educational psychology puts people in context. Goal orientation theory is no exception. The people in the situation socially construct the meaning of an activity, such as an assignment in a biology class; goals set for the activity will reflect the participants' understanding of "what they are doing." So, in a highly competitive classroom climate, students might be more likely to adopt performance goals. In contrast, in a supportive, learner-centered classroom, even a student with a lower sense of self-efficacy might be encouraged to aim for higher mastery goals. Goals are constructed as part of the triadic reciprocal interaction of person, environment, and behavior described by social cognitive theory—"interlocking perceptions of 'meaning,' 'purpose,' and 'self' in guiding and framing action, thought and emotion" (A. Kaplan & Maehr, 2007; Zusho & Clayton, 2011).

The way students perceive their class defines the *classroom goal structure*—the goals that students think are emphasized in the class (Murayama & Elliot, 2009). In one study, teachers who adopted a mastery goal orientation toward their teaching practice (e.g., become an excellent teacher) were more likely to report beliefs that all students could be successful in their classroom and to foster positive mastery goal structure. In contrast, teachers with performance-oriented goals (e.g., demonstrate they were good for the purpose of meeting state standards or job review criteria) promoted performance-oriented classroom goal structures and tended to see student ability as a fixed trait that was often outside their direct control (Shim, Cho, & Cassady, 2012). Mastery-oriented classroom goal structures matter for students. Lisa Fast and her colleagues (2010) found that fourth-through sixth-grade students had significantly higher levels of self-efficacy and mathematics achievement when they perceived their math classes as caring, challenging, and mastery oriented. So challenge, support, and a focus on learning, not looking good, seem to create a positive classroom environment.

Feedback, Goal Framing, and Goal Acceptance

In addition to having specific goals and creating supportive social relationships, three factors make goal setting in the classroom effective. The first is *feedback*. To be motivated by a discrepancy between "where you are" and "where you want to be," you must have an accurate sense of both your current status and how far you have to go. Evidence indicates that feedback emphasizing progress is the most effective. In one study, feedback to adults emphasized either that they had accomplished 75% of the standards set or that they had fallen short of the standards by 25%. When the feedback highlighted accomplishment, the subjects' self-confidence, analytic thinking, and performance were all enhanced (Bandura, 1997).

The second factor affecting motivation to pursue a goal is *goal framing*. Activities or assignments can be explained or framed as helping students' intrinsic goals, such as growing competence, self-determination, positive relationships with friends or teachers, or well-being. The alternative is portraying activities as helping students reach extrinsic goals such as working for a grade, meeting requirements, getting ready for classes next year, and so on. When activities are linked to students' intrinsic goals of becoming more competent, self-directed, and connected with others, then the students process information more deeply and persist longer to gain a conceptual (not superficial) understanding. Linking activities to the extrinsic goals of meeting someone else's standards promotes rote learning but not deep understanding or persistence (Vansteenkiste, Lens, & Deci, 2006).

The third factor is *goal acceptance*. Commitment matters: The relationship between higher goals and better performance is strongest when people are committed to the goals (Locke & Latham, 2002). If students reject goals set by others or refuse to set their own goals, then their motivation will suffer. Generally, students are more willing to commit to the goals of others if the goals seem realistic, reasonably difficult, and meaningful—and if the goals are validated by connecting activities to students' intrinsic interests (Grolnick, Gurland, Jacob, & Decourcey, 2002). So, rather than establishing the goals for the students directly, teachers can promote higher goal acceptance if the students are involved in setting goals and make an active commitment to the goal—for instance, by writing goals down and checking them off as they reach them.

Goals: Lessons for Teachers

Students are more likely to work toward goals that are clear, specific, reasonable, moderately challenging, and attainable within a relatively short period of time. If teachers focus on student performance, high grades, and competition, they may encourage students to set performance goals. This could undermine the students' ability to learn and become task-involved and set them on a path toward alienation from learning in school and learned helplessness (Anderman & Anderman, 2014; Brophy, 2005). Students may not yet be expert at setting their own goals or keeping these goals in mind, so encouragement and accurate feedback are necessary. If you use any reward or incentive systems, be sure the goal you set is to learn and improve in some area, not just to perform well or look smart. And be sure the goal is not too difficult. Students, like adults, are unlikely to stick with tasks or respond well to teachers who make them feel insecure or incompetent, which leads us to our next topic—the power of beliefs in motivation.

ENHANCEDetext *self-check*

BELIEFS AND SELF-PERCEPTIONS

Thus far, we have talked about needs and goals, but there is another factor that must be considered in explaining motivation. What do students believe about learning and about themselves—their competence and the causes for success or failure? Let's start with a basic question, What do students believe about knowing?

Beliefs About Knowing: Epistemological Beliefs

What students believe about knowledge and learning (their **epistemological beliefs**) will influence their motivation and the kinds of strategies that they use.

STOP & THINK How would you answer these questions taken from C. K. Chan and Sachs (2001)?

1. Which of the following is the most important thing in learning math? (a) remember what the teacher has taught you, (b) practice lots of problems, (c) understand the problems you work on.
2. Which of the following is the most important thing to do in learning science? (a) faithfully do the work the teacher tells you, (b) try to see how the explanation makes sense, (c) try to remember everything you are supposed to know.
3. If you wanted to know everything there is to know about something, say, animals, how long would you have to study it? (a) less than a year if you study hard, (b) about 1 or 2 years, (c) forever.
4. What happens when you learn more and more about something? (a) the questions get more and more complex, (b) the questions get easier and easier, (c) the questions all get answered. •

Using questions like those in *Stop & Think,* researchers have identified several dimensions of epistemological beliefs (C. K. Chan & Sachs, 2001; Schommer, 1997; Schommer-Aikins, 2002; Schraw & Olafson, 2002). For example:

- *Structure of Knowledge:* Is knowledge in a field a simple set of facts or a complex structure of concepts and relationships?
- *Stability/Certainty of Knowledge:* Is knowledge fixed, or does it evolve over time?
- *Ability to Learn:* Is the ability to learn fixed (based on innate ability) or changeable?
- *Speed of Learning:* Can we gain knowledge quickly, or does it take time to develop knowledge?
- *Nature of Learning:* Does learning mean memorizing facts passed down from authorities and keeping the facts isolated, or does it mean developing your own integrated understandings?

Students' beliefs about knowing and learning affect the goals they set and the learning strategies they apply. For example, if you believe that knowledge should be gained quickly, you are likely to try one or two quick strategies (read the text once, spend 2 minutes trying to solve the word problem) and then stop. If you believe that learning means developing integrated understandings, you will process the material more deeply, connect to existing knowledge, create your own examples, or draw diagrams, and generally elaborate on the information to make it your own (Kardash & Howell, 2000; Muis & Duffy, 2013; Muis & Franco, 2009). In one study, elementary school students (grades 4 and 6) who believed that learning is understanding processed science texts more deeply than others who believed that learning is reproducing facts (C. K. Chan & Sachs, 2001). The *Stop & Think* questions you just answered were used in that study to assess the students' beliefs. The answers associated with a belief in complex, evolving knowledge that takes time to understand and grows from active learning are 1c, 2b, 3c, and 4a. What are your beliefs? There is some evidence that teachers can help students move toward beliefs that support deep extended learning if the teachers model critical thinking, tie new information to students' prior knowledge, and demonstrate multiple solutions to problems (Muis & Duffy, 2013).

Beliefs about one dimension discussed here—ability to learn—are particularly powerful. Read on.

Beliefs About Ability

STOP & THINK Rate these statements taken from Dweck (2000) on a scale from 1 (Strongly Agree) to 6 (Strongly Disagree).

_____ You have a certain amount of intelligence, and you really can't do much to change it.
_____ You can learn new things, but you can't really change your basic intelligence.
_____ No matter who you are, you can change your intelligence a lot.
_____ No matter how much intelligence you have, you can always change it quite a bit. •

Some of the most powerful beliefs affecting motivation in school are about ability. Adults use two basic concepts of ability (Dweck, 2002, 2006; Gunderson et al., 2013). An entity view of ability assumes that ability is a stable, uncontrollable trait—a characteristic of the individual that cannot be changed. According to this view, some people have more ability than others, but the amount each person has is set. An incremental view of ability, on the other hand, suggests that ability is unstable and controllable—"an ever-expanding repertoire of skills and knowledge" (Dweck & Bempechat, 1983, p. 144). By hard work, study, or practice, knowledge can be increased and thus ability can be improved. What is your view of ability? Look back at your answers to the *Stop & Think* questions.

Young children tend to hold an exclusively incremental view of ability. Through the early elementary grades, most students believe that effort is the same as intelligence. Smart people try hard, and trying hard makes you smart. If you fail, you aren't smart and you didn't try hard (Dweck, 2000; Stipek, 2002). At around age 11 or 12, children can differentiate among effort, ability, and performance. At about this time, they come to believe that someone who succeeds without working at all must be really smart. This is when beliefs about ability begin to influence motivation (Anderman & Anderman, 2014).

Students who hold an *entity* (unchangeable) view of intelligence tend to set performance-avoidance goals to avoid looking bad in the eyes of others. They seek situations where they can look smart and protect their self-esteem. Like Safe Sumey, they keep doing those things they can do well without expending too much effort or risking failure, because either one—working hard or failing—indicates (to them) low ability. To work hard but still fail would be devastating. Students with learning disabilities are more likely to hold an entity view.

In contrast, holding an *incremental* view of ability is associated with greater motivation and learning. Believing that you can improve your ability helps you focus on the *processes* of problem solving and applying good strategies, instead of on the *products* of test scores and grades (Chen & Pajares, 2010).

Teachers who hold *entity* views are quicker to form judgments about students and slower to modify their opinions when confronted with contradictory evidence (Stipek, 2002). Teachers who hold *incremental* views, in contrast, tend to set mastery goals and seek situations in which students can improve their skills, because improvement means getting smarter. Failure is not devastating; it simply indicates more work is needed. Ability is not threatened. Incremental theorists tend to set moderately difficult goals, the kind we have seen are the most motivating. One intriguing study found that when parents praised their 2- to 3-year-old children for effort, those children had more incremental views of ability at ages 7 to 8 (Gunderson et al., 2013). So praising students for effort and persistence may be a good plan in teaching as well because beliefs about ability are related to other beliefs about what you can and cannot control in learning.

Beliefs About Causes and Control: Attribution Theory

One well-known explanation of motivation begins with the assumption that we try to make sense of our own behavior and the behavior of others by searching for explanations and causes. To understand our own successes and failures, particularly unexpected ones, we all ask, "Why?" Students ask themselves, "Why did I flunk my midterm?" or "Why did I do so well this grading period?" They may attribute their successes and failures to ability, effort, mood, knowledge, luck, help, interest, clarity of instructions, the interference of others, unfair policies, and so on. To understand the successes and failures of others, we also make attributions—that the others are smart or lucky or work hard, for example. Attribution theories of motivation describe how the individual's explanations, justifications, and excuses influence motivation (Anderman & Anderman, 2014).

Bernard Weiner is one of the main educational psychologists responsible for relating attribution theory to school learning (Weiner, 2000, 2010). According to Weiner, most of the attributed causes for successes or failures can be characterized in terms of three dimensions:

1. *Locus* (location of the cause—internal or external to the person). For example, attributing a great piano performance to your musical talent or hard work are internal attributions. Explaining that the performance is based on coaching from a great teacher is an external attribution.

Connect and Extend to PRAXIS II®

Attribution Theory (I, C1)
Go to the *Encyclopedia of Psychology* (psychology.org/links/Environment_Behavior_Relationships/Motivation/), and follow its link for attribution theory to learn more about using principles derived from this theory to boost intrinsic motivation to learn.

2. *Stability* (whether the cause of the event is the same across time and in different situations). For example, talent is stable, but effort can change.
3. *Controllability* (whether the person can control the cause). For example, effort and finding a great teacher are controllable, but innate musical talent is not.

Every cause for success or failure can be categorized on these three dimensions. For instance, luck is external (locus), unstable (stability), and uncontrollable (controllability). In attribution theory, ability is usually considered stable and uncontrollable, but incremental theorists (described earlier) would argue that ability is unstable and controllable. Weiner's locus and controllability dimensions are closely related to Deci's concept of locus of causality.

Weiner believes that these three dimensions have important implications for motivation because they affect expectancy and value. The *stability* dimension, for example, seems to be closely related to expectations about the future. If students attribute their failure to stable factors such as the difficulty of the subject or an unfair teacher, they will expect to keep failing in that subject or with that teacher. But if they attribute the outcome to unstable factors such as mood or luck, they can hope for better outcomes next time. The *internal/external locus* seems to be closely related to feelings of self-esteem. If success or failure is attributed to internal factors, success will lead to pride and increased motivation, whereas failure will diminish self-esteem. The *controllability* dimension is related to emotions such as anger, pity, gratitude, or shame. If we feel responsible for our failures, we may feel guilt; if we feel responsible for successes, we may feel proud. Failing at a task we cannot control can lead to shame or anger (Weiner, 2010).

Feeling in control of your own learning seems to be related to choosing more difficult academic tasks, putting out more effort, using better strategies, and persisting longer in school work (Anderman & Anderman, 2014; Weiner, 1994a, 1994b). Factors such as continuing discrimination against women, people of color, and individuals with special needs can affect these individuals' perceptions of their ability to control their lives (van Laar, 2000).

ATTRIBUTIONS IN THE CLASSROOM. People with a strong sense of self-efficacy (see Chapter 11) for a given task ("I'm good at math") tend to attribute their failures to lack of effort ("I should have double-checked my work"), misunderstanding directions, or just not studying enough. These are internal, controllable attributions. As a consequence, they usually focus on strategies for succeeding next time. This response often leads to achievement, pride, and a greater feeling of control. But people with a low sense of self-efficacy ("I'm terrible at math") tend to attribute their failures to lack of ability ("I'm just dumb"). These tendencies are apparent across age levels, cultural groups, and academic topics (Hsieh & Kang, 2010).

The greatest motivational problems arise when students attribute failures to stable, uncontrollable causes. Such students may seem resigned to failure, depressed, helpless—what we generally call "unmotivated" (Weiner, 2000, 2010). These students respond to failure by focusing even more on their own inadequacy; their attitudes toward schoolwork may deteriorate even further. Apathy is a logical reaction to failure if students believe the causes are stable, unlikely to change, and beyond their control anyway. In addition, students who view their failures in this light are less likely to seek help; they believe nothing and no one can help, so they conceal their needs for help. This creates a downward spiral of failure and concealment—"the motivationally 'poor' children, by concealing their difficulties, become 'poorer'" (Marchland & Skinner, 2007). You can see that if a student held an entity view (ability cannot be changed) and a low sense of self-efficacy, motivation would be destroyed when failures were attributed to lack of ability ("I just can't do this, and I'll never be able to learn"). Students with high levels of test anxiety and poor performance on tests report a higher degree of helplessness as well. After taking a test, these students are dissatisfied with their test performance, but they blame the poor performance test anxiety that "got in the way" of doing their best (Cassady, 2004). This leads to a spiral of reduced effort in future studying because they believe improved performance is outside their control—and naturally, their performance continues to suffer (Schunk, Meece, & Pintrich, 2014).

TEACHER ACTIONS AND STUDENT ATTRIBUTIONS. We also make attributions about the causes of other people's successes and failures. When a teacher assumes that student failure is

Video 12.4
In this video, observe the teacher's interactions with students who struggle. Consider the ways he helps students deal with difficulties during learning activities in the classroom. He does not attribute their struggles to inability. How might his encouragement affect their attributions about success or failure? How might it affect their beliefs about their self-worth?

ENHANCEDetext *video example*

attributable to forces beyond the student's control, the teacher tends to respond with sympathy and avoid giving punishments. If, however, the failures are attributed to a controllable factor such as lack of effort, the teacher's response is more likely to be irritation or anger, and reprimands may follow. These tendencies seem to be consistent across time and cultures (Weiner, 1986, 2000).

What do students make of these reactions from their teachers? Sandra Graham (1991, 1996) gives some surprising answers. Evidence indicates that when teachers respond to students' mistakes with pity, praise for a "good try," or unsolicited help, the students are more likely to attribute their failure to an uncontrollable cause—usually lack of ability. Does this mean that teachers should be critical and withhold help? Of course not! But it is a reminder that over-solicitous help can give unintended messages. Graham (1991) suggests that many minority group students could be the victims of well-meaning pity from teachers. Seeing the very real problems that the students face, teachers may "ease up" on requirements so the students will "experience success." But a subtle communication may accompany the pity, praise, and extra help: "You don't have the ability to do this, so I will overlook your failure." Graham says, "The pertinent question for blacks is whether their own history of academic failure makes them more likely to be the targets of sympathetic feedback from teachers and thus the recipients of low-ability cues" (1991, p. 28). This kind of benevolent feedback, even if well intended, can be a subtle form of racism.

Teachers can also positively impact student's attributions, with benefits to both achievement and motivation. In work with gifted girls in a physics class, when teachers encouraged the girls to attribute improved performance to personal effort and abilities, the girls were more engaged, and their achievement improved abilities (Ziegler & Heller, 2000). In addition, Dale Schunk (1983) found that when young students received attributional feedback during a learning activity that was either ability focused ("You're good at this") or effort focused ("You've been working hard"), their problem-solving effort and skills were increased. Interestingly, the ability-focused attributional feedback also promoted higher levels of perceived self-efficacy at the end of the session. So, merely telling the students they were good at the task boosted their feelings of confidence for the skill domain.

Beliefs About Self-Worth

Whatever the label, most theorists agree that a sense of efficacy, control, or self-determination is critical if people are to feel intrinsically motivated.

LEARNED HELPLESSNESS. When people come to believe that the events and outcomes in their lives are mostly uncontrollable, they have developed learned helplessness (Seligman, 1975). To understand the power of learned helplessness, consider this classic experiment (Hiroto & Seligman, 1975): Subjects received either solvable or unsolvable puzzles. In the next phase of the experiment, all subjects were given a series of solvable puzzles. The subjects who struggled with unsolvable puzzles in the first phase of the experiment usually solved significantly fewer puzzles in the second phase. They had learned that they could not control the outcome, so why even try?

Learned helplessness appears to cause three types of deficits: *motivational, cognitive,* and *affective.* Students who feel hopeless, like Hopeless Geraldo described earlier, expect to fail, so why should they even try? So *motivation* suffers. Because they are pessimistic about learning, these students miss opportunities to practice and improve skills and abilities, so they develop *cognitive* deficits. Finally, they often suffer from *affective* problems such as depression, anxiety, and listlessness (Alloy & Seligman, 1979). Once established, it is very difficult to reverse the effects of learned helplessness.

SELF-WORTH. What are the connections between attributions and beliefs about ability, self-efficacy, and self-worth? Covington and his colleagues suggest that these factors come together in three kinds of motivational sets: *mastery oriented, failure avoiding,* and *failure accepting,* as shown in Table 12.3 (Covington, 1992; Covington & Mueller, 2001).

Mastery-oriented students tend to value achievement and see ability as improvable (an incremental view), so they focus on mastery goals to increase their skills and abilities. They are not fearful of failure, because failing does not threaten their sense of competence and self-worth. This allows them to set moderately difficult goals, take risks, and cope with failure constructively.

TABLE 12.3 • **Mastery-Oriented, Failure-Avoiding, and Failure-Accepting Students**

	ATTITUDE TOWARD FAILURE	GOALS SET	ATTRIBUTIONS	VIEW OF ABILITY	STRATEGIES
Mastery Oriented	Low fear of failure	Learning goals: moderately difficult and challenging	Effort, use of right strategy, sufficient knowledge is cause of success	Incremental; improvable	Adaptive strategies (e.g., try another way, seek help, practice/ study more)
Failure Avoiding	High fear of failure	Performance goals; very hard or very easy	Lack of ability is cause of failure	Entity; set	Self-defeating strategies (e.g., make a feeble effort, pretend not to care)
Failure Accepting	Expectation of failure; depression	Performance goals or no goals	Lack of ability is cause of failure	Entity; set	Learned helplessness; likely to give up

They generally attribute success to their own effort, and thus they assume responsibility for learning and have a strong sense of self-efficacy. They learn fast, have more self-confidence and energy, are more aroused, welcome concrete feedback (it does not threaten them), and are eager to learn "the rules of the game" so that they can succeed. All of these factors make for persistent, successful learning (Covington & Mueller, 2001; McClelland, 1985).

Failure-avoiding students tend to hold an entity (fixed) view of ability, so they set performance goals. They lack a strong sense of their own competence and self-worth separate from their performance. In other words, they feel only as smart as their last test grade, so they never develop a solid sense of self-efficacy. To feel competent, they must protect themselves (and their self-worth) from failure. If they have been generally successful, they may seek to avoid failure like Safe Sumey, simply by taking few risks and "sticking with what they know." If, on the other hand, they have experienced a good bit of failure, then they, like Defensive Daleesha, may adopt self-defeating strategies such as feeble efforts, setting very low or ridiculously high goals, or claiming not to care. Just before a test, a student might say, "I didn't study at all!" or "All I want to do is pass." Then, any grade above passing is a success. Procrastination is another example. Low grades do not imply low ability if the student can claim, "I did okay considering I didn't start the term paper until last night." All these are **self-handicapping** strategies because the students are imposing handicaps on their own achievement. Very little learning is going on.

Unfortunately, failure-avoiding strategies generally lead to the very failure the students were trying to avoid. If failures continue and excuses wear thin, the students may finally decide that they are incompetent. Their sense of self-worth and self-efficacy deteriorate. They give up and thus become **failure-accepting students**. They are convinced that their problems are due to low ability. As we saw earlier, those students who attribute failure to low ability and believe ability is fixed are likely to become depressed, apathetic, and helpless. Like Hopeless Geraldo, they have little hope for change.

Teachers may be able to prevent some failure-avoiding students from becoming failure accepting by using multiple assessments and setting a number of goals. In this way all students have a realistic chance of succeeding on some assessments and reaching at least a few goals (L. H. Chen, Wu, Kee, Lin, & Shui, 2009). This is particularly important in contexts where sexual or ethnic stereotypes assert that certain groups of people "should not" be able to do well. These *stereotype threats* (see Chapter 6), which Claude Steele (1997) referred to as the "threat in the air," are common experiences in educational settings and can lead to beliefs about inequities—"Girls are no good at math." When learners adopt these stereotypic views, their performance subsequently suffers because they attribute their ability in the domain to stable personal traits that are beyond their control. Teachers can overcome the impact of these stereotype threats (which are common in math, science, and technology disciplines) by illustrating that the learner is in control and the stereotype is not accurate, minimizing stress, and promoting active coping strategies to succeed (Osborne, Tillman, & Holland, 2010). This kind of support could make all the difference. Instead of perpetuating outdated views of individual differences and pitying or excusing these students, teachers

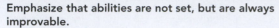

GUIDELINES
Encouraging Self-Worth

Emphasize that abilities are not set, but are always improvable.

Examples

1. Share examples of how you have improved your knowledge and skills, for example in writing, at a sport, or doing a craft.
2. Tell about your own failures that became successes when you tried new strategies or got the right help.
3. Save first drafts and finished products from students in previous classes to show how much the students improved with effort and support.

Teach directly about the difference between learning goals and performance goals.

Examples

1. Encourage students to set a small-step goal for one subject.
2. Recognize improvements often, with private authentic praise.
3. Use personal best goals, not between-student competition.

Make the classroom a place where failure is just diagnostic—failure tells what needs to be improved.

Examples

1. If a student gives a wrong answer in class, say, "I bet others would give that answer too. Let's examine why that is not the best answer. This gives us a chance to dig deeper—excellent!"
2. Encourage revising, improving, polishing, and redoing with an emphasis on improvement.
3. Show students connections between their revised work and a higher grade, but emphasize their growing competence.

Encourage help seeking and help giving.

Examples

1. Teach students how to ask explicit questions about what they do not understand.
2. Recognize students who are helpful.
3. Train class experts for some ongoing needs such as technology guides or progress checkers.

can teach them how to learn and then hold them accountable for their learning. This will help the students develop a sense of self-efficacy for learning and avoid learned helplessness. The *Guidelines: Encouraging Self-Worth* discusses more ways to encourage self-worth.

Beliefs and Attributions: Lessons for Teachers

If students believe they lack the ability to understand higher mathematics, they will probably act on this belief even if their actual abilities are well above average. These students are likely to have little motivation to tackle trigonometry or calculus, because they expect to do poorly in these areas. If students believe that failing means they are stupid, they are likely to adopt many self-handicapping, self-defeating strategies. And teachers who stress performance, grades, and competition can encourage self-handicapping without realizing they are doing so (Anderman & Anderman, 2014). Just telling students to "try harder" is not particularly effective. Students need real evidence that effort will pay off, that setting a higher goal will not lead to failure, that they can improve, and that abilities can be changed. They need authentic mastery experiences.

What else do we know about motivation? Feelings matter.

ENHANCEDetext *self-check*

INTERESTS, CURIOSITY, EMOTIONS, AND ANXIETY

Do you remember starting school? Were you curious about what might be in store, excited about your new world, interested and challenged? Many children are. But a common concern of parents and teachers is that curiosity and excitement about learning are replaced by a sense of drudgery and disinterest. School becomes a job you have to do—a workplace where the work is not that interesting (Wigfield & Wentzel, 2007). In fact, interest in school decreases over time from elementary to high school, with boys showing greater declines than girls. The transition to middle school is particularly linked to a decline in interest. These declines are troubling because results of research on learning in school show that interest is related to students' attention, goals, grades, and depth of learning (Dotterer, McHale, & Crouter, 2009; Renninger & Hidi, 2011).

Tapping Interests

STOP & THINK As part of your interview for a job in a large high school, the principal asks, "How would you get students interested in learning? Could you tap their interests in your teaching?" •

There are two kinds of interests—*personal* (individual) and *situational*—the trait and state distinction again. Personal or individual interests are more long-lasting aspects of the person, such as an enduring tendency to be attracted to or to enjoy subjects such as languages, history, or mathematics, or activities such as sports, music, or films. Students with individual interests in learning in general seek new information and have more positive attitudes toward schooling. Situational interests are more short-lived aspects of the activity, text, or materials that catch and keep the student's attention. Both personal and situational interests are related to learning from texts—greater interest leads to more positive emotional responses to the material, then to greater persistence in learning, deeper processing, better remembering of the material, and higher achievement (Ainley, Hidi, & Berndorf, 2002; Hofer, 2010; Pintrich, 2003). And interests increase when students feel competent, so even if students are not initially attracted to a subject or activity, they may develop interests as they experience success.

Ann Renninger and Suzanne Hidi (2011) describe a four-phase model of interest development.

situational interest triggered → situational interest maintained →
→ emerging individual interest → well-developed individual interest

For example, consider Julia, a graduating senior in college descried by Hidi and Renninger (2006). As she waits nervously in the dentist's office, flipping through a magazine, her attention is drawn (*situational interest trigger*) to an article about a man who left his engineering job to become a facilitator in legal conflict resolution. When she is called to the dentist's chair, she is still reading the article, so she marks her place and returns to finish reading after her appointment (*situational interest maintained*). She takes notes, and, over the next weeks, searches the Internet, visits the library, and meets with her advisor to get more information about this career option (*emerging individual interest*). Four years later, Julia is enjoying her job as a facilitator as she handles more and more arbitration cases for a law firm (*well-developed, enduring individual interest*).

In the early stages of this four-phase model, emotions play a big role—feelings of excitement, pleasure, fun, and curiosity. Situational interest may be triggered by positive feelings, as when Julia started reading. Curiosity followed and helped Julia stay engaged as she learned more about becoming a facilitator. As Julia added knowledge to her curiosity and positive feelings, her personal interest emerged, and the *cycle of positive feelings, curiosity, and knowledge* continued to build enduring interest.

CATCHING AND HOLDING INTERESTS. Whenever possible, it helps to connect academic content to students' enduring individual interests. But given that the content you will teach is determined by standards in most classrooms today, it will be difficult to tailor lessons to each student's interests. You will have to rely more on triggering and maintaining situational interest. Here, the challenge is to not only *catch* but also *hold* students' interest (Pintrich, 2003). For example, Mathew Mitchell (1993) found that using computers, groups, and puzzles caught students' interest in secondary mathematics classes, but the interests did not hold. Lessons that held the students' interest over time included math activities that were related to real-life problems and active participation in laboratory activities and projects. Another source of interest is fantasy. Cordova and Lepper (1996) found that students learned more math facts during a computer exercise in which they were challenged, as captains of star ships, to navigate through space by solving math problems. The students got to name their ships, stock the (imaginary) galley with their favorite snacks, and name all the crew members after their friends. Challenge, novelty, working with others, assuming the role of an expert, and participating in a group project also can support interest (Renninger & Hidi, 2011). In a study of math learning with older adolescents, Durik and Harackiewicz (2007) concluded that catching interest by using colorful learning materials with pictures was helpful for students with low initial interest in mathematics, but not for students who were already interested.

Video 12.5
The teacher in this preschool classroom used her students' curiosity about the teacher's injuries and their dissatisfaction with a play area in the classroom to develop a curriculum about hospitals that was both challenging and exciting for the children.

ENHANCEDetext *video example*

POINT/COUNTERPOINT
Does Making Learning Fun Make for Good Learning?

When many beginning teachers are asked about how to motivate students, they often mention making learning fun. But is it necessary for learning to be fun?

POINT **Teachers should make learning fun.** When I searched "making learning fun" on Google.com, I found 10 pages of resources and references. Clearly, there is interest in making learning fun. Research shows that passages in texts that are more interesting are remembered better (Schunk, Meece, & Pintrich, 2014). For example, students who read books that interested them spent more time reading, read more words in the books, and felt more positively about reading (Guthrie & Alao, 1997).

Games and simulations can make learning more fun, too. For example, when my daughter was in the eighth grade, all the students in her grade spent 3 days playing a game her teachers had designed called ULTRA. Students were divided into groups and formed their own "countries." Each country had to choose a name, symbol, national flower, and bird. They wrote and sang a national anthem and elected government officials. The teachers allocated different resources to the countries. To get all the materials needed for the completion of assigned projects, the countries had to establish trade with one another. There was a monetary system and a stock market. Students had to work with their fellow citizens to complete cooperative learning assignments. Some countries "cheated" in their trades with other nations, and this allowed debate about international relations, trust, and war. Liz says she had fun—but she also learned how to work in a group without the teacher's supervision and gained a deeper understanding of world economics and international conflicts.

A highly motivating third-grade teacher in a study had her class set up a post office for the whole school. Each classroom in the school had an address and zip code. Students had jobs in the post office, and everyone in the school used the post office to deliver letters to students and teachers. Students designed their own stamps and set postal rates. The teacher said that the system "improves their creative writing without them knowing it" (Dolezal, Welsh, Pressley, & Vincent, 2003, p. 254).

COUNTERPOINT **Fun can get in the way of learning.** As far back as the early 1900s, educators warned about the dangers of focusing on fun in learning. None other than John Dewey, who wrote extensively about the role of interest in learning, cautioned that you can't make boring lessons interesting by mixing in fun like you can make bad chili good by adding some spicy hot sauce. Dewey wrote, "When things have to be made interesting, it is because interest itself is wanting. Moreover, the phrase itself is a misnomer. The thing, the object, is no more interesting than it was before" (Dewey, 1913, pp. 11–12).

There is a good deal of research now indicating that adding interest by incorporating fascinating but irrelevant details actually gets in the way of learning the important information. These "seductive details," as they have been called, divert the readers' attention from the less-interesting main ideas (Harp & Mayer, 1998). For example, students who read biographies of historical figures remembered more very interesting—but unimportant—information compared to interesting main ideas (Wade, Schraw, Buxton, & Hayes, 1993).

Shannon Harp and Richard Mayer (1998) found similar results with high school science texts. These texts added emotional interest and seductive details about swimmers and golfers who are injured by lightning to a lesson on the process of lightning. They concluded that, "in the case of emotional interest versus cognitive interest, the verdict is clear. Adjuncts aimed at increasing emotional interest failed to improve understanding of scientific explanations" (p. 100). The seductive details may have disrupted students' attempts to follow the logic of the explanations and thus interfered with their comprehending the text. Harp and Mayer conclude that "the best way to help students enjoy a passage is to help them understand it" (p. 100).

BEWARE OF EITHER/OR

Of course we want our classes to be engaging, interesting, even fun—but the focus through it all should be on learning. Even if the work is tough and at times repetitious, students need to learn to persevere. Working hard is a part of life. Working hard together can be fun.

For the interested students, holding interest by showing how math could be personally useful was more effective. In addition complex materials can be more interesting, as long as students believe they can effectively cope with the complexity (Sylvia, Henson, & Templin, 2009).

There are other cautions in responding to students' interests, as you can see in the *Point/Counterpoint*.

Curiosity: Novelty and Complexity

In the 1960s, psychologists suggested that individuals are naturally motivated to seek novelty, surprise, and complexity (Berlyne, 1966). Exploration probably is innate; infants must explore the world to learn about it (Bowlby, 1969). More recently, Reiss (2004) listed curiosity as one of the 16 basic human motivations, and Flum and Kaplan (2006) made the case that schools should target developing an exploratory orientation in students as a major goal.

Interest and curiosity are related. Curiosity can be defined as a tendency to be interested in a wide range of areas (Pintrich, 2003). According to Renninger's (2009) four-phase model of interest described in the previous section, our individual interests begin to emerge as we raise and answer "curiosity questions" that help us organize our knowledge about a topic. For situational interests to develop into long-term individual interests, curiosity and the desire for exploration are necessary.

George Lowenstein (1994) suggests that adult curiosity arises when attention is focused on a gap in knowledge. These information gaps cause a sense of deprivation—a need to know that we call "curiosity." But what about children? Jamie Jirout and David Klahr (2012) reached a similar conclusion about scientific curiosity in young children. They defined curiosity as "the threshold of desired uncertainty in the environment that leads to exploratory behavior" (p. 150), or more simply, as the level of uncertainty that a child prefers. So the greater the child's preference of uncertainty, the more curious and the more likely the child is to explore to resolve uncertainty. This idea is similar to Piaget's concept of disequilibrium, discussed in Chapter 2, and has a number of implications for teaching. First, students need some base of knowledge before they can experience gaps in that knowledge leading to curiosity. Second, students must be aware of the gaps in order for curiosity to result. In other words, they need a metacognitive awareness of what they know and don't know (Hidi, Renninger, & Krapp, 2004). Asking students to make guesses and then providing feedback can be helpful. Also, proper handling of mistakes can stimulate curiosity by pointing to missing knowledge. Finally, the more we learn about a topic, the more curious we may become about that subject. As Maslow (1970) predicted, fulfilling the need to know increases, not decreases, the need to know more. See the *Guidelines: Building on Students' Interests and Curiosity* on the next page for more about building interest and curiosity in the classroom.

Flow

Have you ever been "in the zone" or "lost in thought"? You may have been experiencing **flow**—a mental state in which you are fully immersed in a challenging task that is accompanied by high levels of concentration and involvement (Csikszentmihalyi, 2000). Individuals in flow experience greater enjoyment in the task, continue working without prompting, and tend to generate higher quality, more creative products. A state of flow is most likely to occur when the learner is sufficiently prepared to understand the task, has high self-efficacy for performance, is intrinsically motivated by the activity, and has sufficient control or autonomy in the situation to direct and drive the learning experience; it is a delicate balance of environmental, personal, and task-related factors (Schweinle, Turner, & Meyer, 2008). Research on this concept has demonstrated that the enjoyment of being in flow is largely explained by the individual's focused attention while engaged in the task (Abuhamdeh & Csikszentmihalyi, 2012). To create flow in the classroom, teachers can provide students with moderately challenging tasks that are intrinsically interesting and capture their attention.

Emotions and Anxiety

How do you feel about learning? Excited, bored, curious, fearful? Today, researchers emphasize that learning is not just about the *cold cognition* of reasoning and problem solving. Learning and information processing also are influenced by emotion and mood, so *hot cognition* plays a role in learning as well (Bohn-Gettler & Rapp, 2011; Pintrich, 2003). Research on emotions, learning, and motivation is expanding, in part because we know more about the brain and emotion.

NEUROSCIENCE AND EMOTION. In mammals, including humans, stimulation to a small area of the brain called the *amygdala* seems to trigger emotional reactions such as the "fight or

GUIDELINES
Building on Students' Interests and Curiosity

Relate content objectives to student experiences.

Examples

1. With a teacher in another school, establish pen pals across the classes. Through writing letters, students exchange personal experiences, photos, drawings, written work, and ask and answer questions ("Have you learned cursive writing yet?" "What are you doing in math now?" "What are you reading?"). Letters can be mailed in one large mailer to save stamps or sent via e-mail.
2. Identify classroom experts for different assignments or tasks. Who knows how to use the computer for graphics? How to search the Net? How to cook? How to use an index?
3. Have a "Switch Day" when students exchange roles with a school staff or support person. Students must research the role by interviewing their staff member, prepare for the job, dress the part for the day they take over, and then evaluate their success after the switch.

Identify student interests, hobbies, and extracurricular activities that can be incorporated into class lessons and discussions.

Examples

1. Have students design and conduct interviews and surveys to learn about each other's interests.
2. Keep the class library stocked with books that connect to students' interests and hobbies.
3. Allow choices (stories in language arts or projects in science) based on students' interests.

Support instruction with humor, personal experiences, and anecdotes that show the human side of the content.

Examples

1. Share your own hobbies, interests, and favorites.

2. Tell students there will be a surprise visitor; then dress up as the author of a story and tell about "yourself" and your writing.

Use original source material with interesting content or details.

Examples

1. Letters and diaries in history.
2. Darwin's notes in biology.

Create surprise and curiosity.

Examples

1. Have students predict what will happen in an experiment, then show them whether they were right or wrong.
2. Provide quotes from history, and ask students to guess who said it.
3. Use high-novelty reading materials with elements such as active/emotional verbs (clinging vs. walking), unfamiliar characters (orangutan vs. fox), unusual adjectives (hairy vs. brown), and surprising endings (Beike & Zentall, 2012).

For more information on students' interests and motivation, see mathforum.org/~sarah/Discussion.Sessions/biblio.motivation.html

Source: From 150 Ways to Increase Intrinsic Motivation in the Classroom, by James P. Raffini. Copyright © 1996 by Pearson Education, Inc. Adapted by permission of the publisher. Also Motivation in Education (2nd ed.), by P. Pintrich and D. Schunk, © 2002 by Pearson Education, Inc.

---

flight" response. The responses in nonhuman animals can be strong. But human emotions are the outcome of physiological responses triggered by the brain, combined with interpretations of the situation and other information. So, hearing startling sounds during an action movie might cause a brief emotional reaction, but hearing the same sounds in the middle of the night as you are walking through a dark alley could lead to stronger and more lasting emotional reactions. Even though the amygdala plays a key role in emotions, many other brain regions are also involved. Emotions are a "constant interplay between cognitive assessments, conscious feelings, and bodily responses, with each able to influence the other" (Gluck, Mercado, & Myers, 2008, p. 418). Humans are more likely to pay attention to, learn about, and remember events, images, and readings that provoke emotional responses (Cowley & Underwood, 1998; Murphy & Alexander, 2000; Reisberg & Heuer, 1992). Emotions can affect learning by changing brain dopamine levels that influence long-term memory and by directing attention toward one aspect of the situation (Pekrun, Elliot, & Maier, 2006). Sometimes, emotions interfere with learning by taking up attention or working memory space that could be used for learning (Pekrun, Goetz, Titz, & Perry, 2002).

In teaching, we are concerned about a particular kind of emotions—those related to achievement in school. Experiences of success or failure can provoke achievement emotions such as pride, hope, boredom, anger, or shame (Pekrun, Elliot, & Maier, 2006). How can we use these findings to support learning in school?

ACHIEVEMENT EMOTIONS. In the past, with the exception of anxiety, emotions generally were overlooked in research on learning and motivation (Linnenbrink-Garcia & Pekrun, 2011). But as you just read, research in the neurosciences has shown that emotions are both causes and consequences of learning processes. Reinhard Pekrun and his colleagues (2006, 2010) have tested a model that relates different goal orientations to boredom and other emotions in older adolescents from the United States and Germany. The goal orientations are those we discussed earlier: mastery, performance approach, and performance avoidance.

With a *mastery goal,* students focused on an activity. They valued the activity as a way to get smarter, and they felt in control. They were not afraid of failing, so they could focus on the task at hand. The researchers found that having mastery goals predicted enjoyment in learning, hope, and pride. Students with mastery goals were less likely to feel angry or bored about learning. Boredom is a big problem in classrooms because it is associated with difficulties in paying attention, lack of intrinsic motivation, weak effort, shallow processing of information, and poor self-regulated learning (Pekrun et al., 2010).

With a *performance-approach goal,* students wanted to look good or be the best, and they focused their attention on positive outcomes. Performance-approach goals were related mostly to pride. Students with *performance-avoidance goals* focused on the fear of failing and the possibility of looking stupid. Performance-avoidance goals predicted feelings of anxiety, hopelessness, and shame. These findings are summarized in Table 12.4.

How can you increase positive achievement emotions and decrease boredom in the subject you teach? Students are more likely to feel bored if they believe they have little control over the learning activities and they don't value the activities. Matching challenge to the students' skill levels and giving choices can increase the students' sense of control. In addition, efforts to build student interest and show the value of the activities also help to fight boredom. And remember, achievement emotions are domain specific. The fact that students enjoy and feel proud of their work in math does not mean they will enjoy English or history (Goetz, Frenzel, Hall, & Pekrun, 2008; Pekrun et al., 2010). In addition, teachers who enjoy their subjects tend to be more enthusiastic and encourage student enjoyment, so make sure, as much **as** possible, that you are teaching from your own interests and passions (Brophy, 2008; Frenzel, Goetz, Lüdtke, Pekrun, & Sutton, 2009).

AROUSAL AND ANXIETY. Just as we all know how it feels to be motivated, we all know what it is like to be aroused. Arousal involves both psychological and physical reactions—changes in brain wave patterns, blood pressure, heart rate, and breathing rate. We feel alert, wide awake, even excited.

TABLE 12.4 • How Different Achievement Goals Influence Achievement Emotions

Different goals are associated with different emotions that can impact motivation.

GOAL ORIENTATION	STUDENT EMOTIONS
Mastery	
Focus on activity, controllability, positive value of activity	Increases: enjoyment of activity, pride, hope Decreases: boredom, anger
Performance approach	
Focus on outcome, controllability, positive outcome value	Increases: pride, hope
Performance avoidance	
Focus on outcome, lack of controllability, negative outcome value	Increases: anxiety, hopelessness, shame

Source: Based on Pekrun, R., Elliot, A. J., & Maier, M. A. (2006). Achievement goals and discrete achievement emotions: A theoretical model and prospective test. Journal of Educational Psychology, 98, 583–597.

To understand the effects of arousal on motivation, think of two extremes. The first is late at night. You are trying for the third time to understand a required reading, but you are so sleepy. Your attention drifts as your eyelids droop. You decide to go to bed and get up early to study (a plan that you know seldom works). At the other extreme, imagine that you have a critical test tomorrow—one that determines whether you will get into the school you want. You feel tremendous pressure from everyone to do well. You know that you need a good night's sleep, but you are wide awake. In the first case, arousal is too low and in the second, too high. Psychologists have known for years that there is an optimum level of arousal for most activities (Yerkes & Dodson, 1908). For each specific task, when arousal levels are too low, you won't be spurred to action. As arousal increases, it has a facilitative effect on the motivation to perform—to a point. Once the pressure to perform reaches a critical level, high anxiety begins to impede performance. Generally speaking, higher levels of arousal are helpful on simple tasks such as sorting laundry, but lower levels of arousal are better for complex tasks such as taking the SAT or GRE.

Connect and Extend to PRAXIS II®

Test Anxiety (I, C3)
Test Taking and Anxiety (ulrc.psu.edu/
studyskills/test_taking.html) provides
tips and insights into addressing the
problems associated with test anxiety.
(And the tips might be useful for doing
well on the PRAXIS II® exam!)

ANXIETY IN THE CLASSROOM. At one time or another, everyone has experienced anxiety, or a general uneasiness, a feeling of self-doubt, and sense of tension. Recent work on "academic anxieties," which is a broad term that encompasses anxiety experiences in educational settings, has demonstrated that many forms of anxiety—test anxiety, math anxiety, science anxiety, public speaking anxiety—can lead to patterns of beliefs and behaviors that hamper performance and promote disengagement in learning (Cassady, 2010). Anxiety can be both a cause and an effect of school failure—students do poorly because they are anxious, and their poor performance increases their anxiety, creating a vicious cycle for the learner. Academic anxiety has both *trait* and *state* components. That is, the level of trait anxiety tends to be constant across most situations for students, but each specific situation carries a degree of state anxiety as well that may increase the feelings of stress (Covington, 1992; Zeidner, 1998). The additive model of anxiety suggests that to accurately account for the impact of anxiety on learning outcomes we must recognize both trait and state components (Zohar, 1998), with the perception of threat imposed by specific conditions (state) dictating the degree of elevated anxiety above a person's standard trait level (Spielberger & Vagg, 1995).

Anxiety seems to have both cognitive and affective components. The cognitive side includes worry and negative thoughts—thinking about how bad it would be to fail and worrying that you will, for example. The affective side involves physiological and emotional reactions such as sweaty palms, upset stomach, racing heartbeat, or fear (Jain & Dowson, 2009; Schunk, Meece, & Pintrich, 2014). Whenever there are pressures to perform, severe consequences for failure, and competitive comparisons among students, anxiety may be encouraged (Wigfield & Eccles, 1989). Research with school-age children shows a relationship between the quality of sleep (how quickly and how well you sleep) and anxiety. Better-quality sleep is associated with positive arousal or an "eagerness" to learn. Poor-quality sleep, on the other hand, is related to debilitating anxiety and decreased school performance. You may have discovered these relationships for yourself in your own school career (Meijer & van den Wittenboer, 2004).

HOW DOES ANXIETY INTERFERE WITH ACHIEVEMENT? There are two broad models that explain the impact of academic anxieties on achievement, but most of the research on these models focuses on test anxiety. The first model rests on the classic notion that anxiety interferes with performance by drawing necessary cognitive resources away during the testing phase. This *cognitive interference model* presumes that the learner has effectively learned the material, but anxiety "blocks" adequate retrieval (Sarason, 1986; Zeidner & Matthews, 2005). The second model is based on basic research that demonstrates that students with high levels of anxiety are less effective at organizing information, engaging in effective study strategies, and performing on tests even in the absence of evaluative pressure (Cassady, 2004; Naveh-Benjamin, 1991).

Taking these two broad views together, contemporary orientations to academic anxiety suggest that anxiety affects the beliefs and behaviors of learners in three phases of the learning–testing cycle: preparation, performance, and reflection. During the *preparation* phase (classroom instruction, studying, test preparation), learners with anxiety tend to have difficulty effectively focusing attention on the relevant material, employing quality study tactics, and maintaining a positive self-worth orientation toward the learning event. Instead of concentrating, they keep noticing the tight feelings in their chest, thinking, "I'm so tense, I'll never understand this stuff!" From the beginning, anxious students may miss much of the information they are supposed to learn because their thoughts are focused on their own worries: whether the learner is unskilled at studying, avoiding the content due to uneasiness caused by the anxiety, or merely distracted by thoughts of the consequences of failing, the material to be learned is clearly compromised (Cassady & Johnson, 2002; Jain & Dowson, 2009; Zeidner & Matthews, 2005). But the problems do not end here. In the *performance* phase, anxiety blocks retrieval of what was (often poorly) learned (Schwarzer & Jerusalem, 1992). Finally, in the *reflection* phase learners with anxiety build attributions for failure that further impede their future performance by developing beliefs that they are simply incapable of succeeding at the task, determining that they have no control over the situation, and setting ineffective goals for future situations.

Reaching Every Student: Coping with Anxiety

Some students, particularly those with learning disabilities or emotional disorders, may be especially anxious in school. When students face stressful situations such as tests, they can use three kinds of coping strategies: problem-focused self-regulating learning strategies; emotional management; and avoidance. *Problem-focused, self-regulating strategies* might include planning a study schedule, borrowing good notes, or finding a protected place to study. *Emotion-focused strategies* are attempts to reduce the anxious feelings, for example, by using relaxation exercises or describing the feelings to a friend. Of course, the latter might become an *avoidance strategy,* along with going out for pizza or suddenly launching an all-out desk-cleaning attack (can't study until you get organized!). Different strategies are helpful at different points—for example, self-regulated learning before and emotion management during an exam. Different strategies fit different people and situations (Zeidner, 1995, 1998).

To help students cope with academic anxiety in classrooms, teachers can employ several motivational strategies discussed in this chapter. At the center of this support is helping students to develop effective coping and self-regulation strategies that will reduce the negative effect of anxiety. Because anxiety is an emotional construct, but the anxiety occurs in a performance context, both emotional and cognitive support strategies are necessary (K. L. Fletcher & Cassady, 2010; also see the discussion of self-regulation in Chapter 11).

First, teachers can help anxious learners become more effective at recognizing the source of their anxious feelings and accurately interpreting them. Connected to this, teachers can help students adopt attributional styles that recognize that they have control over their learning and performance. So, rather than developing a failure-accepting view, students can learn to identify situations where they have been successful and recognize that with support and effort, they can achieve better outcomes.

Second, teachers should help highly anxious students to set realistic goals, because these individuals often have difficulty making wise choices. They tend to select either extremely difficult or extremely easy tasks. In the first case, they are likely to fail, which will increase their sense of hopelessness and anxiety about school. In the second case, they will probably succeed on the easy tasks, but they will miss the sense of satisfaction that could encourage greater effort and ease their fears about schoolwork. Goal cards, progress charts, or goal-planning journals may help here. In addition, directly teaching students self-regulated learning strategies and supporting their self-efficacy can help them be more in control of their learning and their anxiety (Jain & Dowson, 2009).

Third, teachers can support improved performance by teaching students more effective methods for learning and studying. Research on anxious learners indicates that they tend to spend more time studying, but the methods they adopt tend to be repetitive and low quality (Cassady, 2004; Wittmaier, 1972). As teachers help students to build both the cognitive and emotional skills necessary to overcome anxiety, the students should begin to observe the steady gains in performance and ideally internalize the strategies that have helped them be more successful.

Finally, teachers can limit the environmental triggers for anxiety in their classrooms by examining their underlying biases (to reduce the presence of stereotype threat messages in their classrooms), promoting mastery-oriented classroom goal structures, and providing a positive

GUIDELINES
Coping with Anxiety

Use competition carefully.

Examples

1. Monitor activities to make sure no students are being put under undue pressure.
2. During competitive games, make sure all students involved have a reasonable chance of succeeding.
3. Experiment with cooperative learning activities.

Avoid situations in which highly anxious students will have to perform in front of large groups.

Examples

1. Ask anxious students questions that can be answered with a simple yes or no, or some other brief reply.
2. Give anxious students practice in speaking before smaller groups.

Make sure all instructions are clear. Uncertainty can lead to anxiety.

Examples

1. Write test instructions on the board or on the test itself instead of giving them orally.
2. Check with students to make sure they understand. Ask several students how they would do the first question, exercise, or sample question on a test. Correct any misconceptions.
3. If you are using a new format or starting a new type of task, give students examples or models to show how it is done.

Avoid unnecessary time pressures.

Examples

1. Give occasional take-home tests.
2. Make sure all students can complete classroom tests within the period given.

Remove some of the pressures from major tests and exams.

Examples

1. Teach test-taking skills; give practice tests; provide study guides.
2. Avoid basing most of a report-card grade on one test.
3. Make extra-credit work available to add points to course grades.
4. Use different types of items in testing because some students have difficulty with particular formats.

Develop alternatives to written tests.

Examples

1. Try oral, open-book, or group tests.
2. Have students do projects, organize portfolios of their work, make oral presentations, or create a finished product.

Teach students self-regulation strategies (Schutz & Davis, 2000).

Examples

1. Before the test: Encourage students to see the test as an important and challenging task that they have the capabilities to prepare for. Help students stay focused on the task of getting as much information as possible about the test.
2. During the test: Remind students that the test is important (but not overly important). Encourage task focus—pick out the main idea in the question, slow down, stay relaxed.
3. After the test: Think back on what went well and what could be improved. Focus on controllable attributions—study strategies, effort, careful reading of questions, relaxation strategies.

For more information about test anxiety, see counselingcenter.uiuc.edu/?page_id=193

---

role model for appropriate interest and excitement for the content (rather than starting off with statements such as, "This is REALLY hard stuff"). Also, when teachers are "stressed out" about accountability and statewide testing, they can transmit this anxiety to their students. The more teachers are visibly distressed or continually emphasize "how important this test is," the more students have the opportunity to recognize the tests as a state of "threat," prompting negative emotions and activating test anxiety.

Curiosity, Interests, and Emotions: Lessons for Teachers

Make efforts to keep the level of arousal right for the task at hand. If students are going to sleep, energize them by introducing variety, piquing their curiosity, surprising them, or giving them a brief chance to be physically active. Learn about their interests, and incorporate these interests into lessons and assignments. If arousal is too great, follow the *Guidelines: Coping with Anxiety*.

How can we put together all this information about motivation? How can teachers create environments, situations, and relationships that encourage motivation? We address these questions next.

ENHANCEDetext *self-check*

MOTIVATION TO LEARN IN SCHOOL: ON TARGET

Teachers are concerned about developing a particular kind of motivation in their students—the **motivation to learn**, defined as "a student tendency to find academic activities meaningful and worthwhile and to try to derive the intended academic benefits from them" (Brophy, 1988, pp. 205–206). Motivation to learn involves more than wanting or intending to learn. It includes the quality of the student's mental efforts. For example, reading the text 11 times may indicate persistence, but motivation to learn implies more thoughtful, active study strategies, such as summarizing, elaborating the basic ideas, outlining in your own words, drawing graphs of the key relationships, and so on (Brophy, 1988).

It would be wonderful if all our students came to us filled with the motivation to learn, but they don't. As teachers, we have three major goals. The first is to get students productively involved with the work of the class; in other words, to *catch* their interest and create a *state* of motivation to learn. The second and longer-term goal is to develop in our students enduring individual interests and the *trait* of being motivated to learn so they will be able to educate themselves for the rest of their lives. And finally, we want our students to be *cognitively engaged*—to think deeply about what they study. In other words, we want them to be thoughtful (Blumenfeld, Puro, & Mergendoller, 1992).

Earlier in this chapter we examined the roles of intrinsic and extrinsic motivation, attributions, goals, beliefs, self-perceptions, interests, curiosity, and emotions in motivation. Table 12.5 shows how each of these factors contributes to motivation to learn.

The central question for the remainder of the chapter is: How can teachers use their knowledge about attributions, goals, beliefs, self-perceptions, interests, and emotions to increase motivation to learn? To organize our discussion, we will use the TARGET model (Ames, 1992; Epstein, 1989), identifying six areas where teachers make decisions that can influence student motivation to learn.

T   task that students are asked to do
A   autonomy or authority students are allowed in working
R   recognition for accomplishments
G   grouping practices
E   evaluation procedures
T   time in the classroom

Video 12.6
The high school students in this video are engaged in authentic tasks. Notice the strategies the teacher uses to give the task value to the students and allow the students autonomy in creating their experimental design. She uses cooperative groups and incorporates accountability with the peer assessment structure. Consider the power of these elements to increase students' motivation to learn.

ENHANCEDetext *video example*

Connect and Extend to PRAXIS II®

Target (I, C1, 2, 3)
Describe the major features of the TARGET model, and identify related strategies that are likely to boost motivation.

TABLE 12.5 • Building a Concept of Motivation to Learn
Motivation to learn is encouraged when the following five elements come together.

SOURCE OF MOTIVATION	OPTIMUM CHARACTERISTICS OF MOTIVATION TO LEARN	CHARACTERISTICS THAT DIMINISH MOTIVATION TO LEARN
Type of Goal Set	INTRINSIC: Personal factors such as needs, interests, curiosity, enjoyment	EXTRINSIC: Environmental factors such as rewards, social pressure, punishment
Type of Involvement	LEARNING GOAL: Personal satisfaction in meeting challenges and improving; tendency to choose moderately difficult and challenging goals	PERFORMANCE GOAL: Desire for approval for performance in others' eyes; tendency to choose very easy or very difficult goals
	TASK-INVOLVED: Concerned with mastering the task	EGO-INVOLVED: Concerned with self in others' eyes
Achievement Motivation	Motivation to ACHIEVE: Mastery orientation	Motivation to AVOID FAILURE: Prone to anxiety
Likely Attributions	Successes and failures attributed to CONTROLLABLE effort and ability	Successes and failures attributed to UNCONTROLLABLE causes
Beliefs about Ability	INCREMENTAL VIEW: Belief that ability can be improved through hard work and added knowledge and skills	ENTITY VIEW: Belief that ability is a stable, uncontrollable trait

Tasks for Learning

To understand how an **academic task** can affect students' motivation, we need to analyze the task. Tasks have different values for students.

TASK VALUE. As you probably recall, many theories suggest that the strength of our motivation in a particular situation is determined by both our *expectation* that we can succeed and the *value* of that success to us. Perceptions of task value predict the choices students make, such as whether to enroll in advanced science classes or join the track team. Efficacy expectations predict achievement in actually doing the task—how well the students will perform in the science class or on the track team (Wigfield & Eccles, 2002).

We can think of task value as having four components: importance, interest, utility, and cost (Eccles & Wigfield, 2002; Hulleman, Godes, Hendricks, & Harackiewicz, 2010). **Importance or attainment value** is the significance of doing well on the task; this is closely tied to the needs of the individual (the need to be well liked, athletic, etc.). For instance, if someone has a strong need to appear smart and believes that a high grade on a test proves you are smart, then the test has high attainment value for that person. A second component is **interest or intrinsic value**. This is simply the enjoyment one gets from the activity itself. Some people like the experience of learning. Others enjoy the feeling of hard physical effort or the challenge of solving puzzles. Tasks also can have **utility value**; that is, they help us achieve a short-term or long-term goal such as earning a degree. Finally, tasks have costs—negative consequences that might follow from doing the task such as not having time to do other things or looking awkward as you perform the task.

You can see from our discussion of task value that personal and environmental influences on motivation interact constantly. The task we ask students to accomplish is an aspect of the environment; it is external to the student. But the value of accomplishing the task is bound up with the internal needs, beliefs, and goals of the individual. Because task value has to do with choices, positive values toward academic tasks can be life-changing because choices about courses in high school and education after high school affect career and life opportunities (Durik, Vida, & Eccles, 2006).

BEYOND TASK VALUE TO GENUINE APPRECIATION. Jere Brophy (2008, p. 140) reminds teachers that there is more to value than interest or utility; there is the power of knowing: "Powerful ideas expand and enrich the quality of students' subjective lives." These ideas give us lenses for viewing the world, tools for making decisions, and frames for appreciating the beauty in words and images. An entire issue of *Theory Into Practice,* the journal I once edited, is devoted to Jere's ideas about engaging students in the value and appreciation of learning (Turner, Patrick, & Meyer, 2011). One way to build appreciation is with authentic tasks.

AUTHENTIC TASKS. Recently, a great deal has been written about the use of authentic tasks in teaching. An **authentic task** has some connection to the real-life problems and situations that students will face outside the classroom, both now and in the future. If you ask students to memorize definitions they will never use, to learn the material only because it is on the test, or to repeat work they already understand, then there can be little motivation to learn. But if the tasks are authentic, students are more likely to see the genuine utility value of the work and are also more likely to find the tasks meaningful and interesting (Pugh & Phillips, 2011). **Problem-based learning** and service learning (Chapter 10) are two examples of the use of authentic tasks in teaching. For example, a physics teacher might use skateboarding as a basis for problems and examples, knowing that skateboarding is an authentic task for many of her students (Anderman & Anderman, 2014). For younger students, compare these two teachers described by Anderman and Anderman (2014, p. 11):

> Mrs. Rodriguez gives her class an initial lesson on halves and quarters, divides students into groups of three, and gives each group two Twinkies and a plastic knife. She asks the students to cut one Twinkie into two equally sized pieces, and the other Twinkie into four equally sized pieces. Next comes the challenge–use the Twinkie pieces to determine which fraction

is bigger, one half (1/2) or three fourths (3/4). Mrs. Rodriguez then visits each group; the members must explain their work to her. When they are correct, they get to eat the Twinkies.

Mr. Jackson gives the same initial lesson on halves and quarters. He then provides each student with a worksheet with a few simple questions that are designed to help the students to learn about fractions. For these questions, the students are supposed to imagine that they have several pieces of paper, and that they cut the paper with scissors into various quantities (e.g., they cut one paper into four equal-size pieces, they cut another paper into two equal-size pieces). The students are then asked to demonstrate whether one half (1/2) or three fourths (3/4) is the bigger fraction. They then have to write down their answer, along with a brief explanation.

The students in Mrs. Rodriguez's class were involved in a more authentic (and tasty) task involving cutting and dividing food, cooperating with others, and enjoying the fruits (or Twinkies) of their labor. They also had to figure out how to share two halves and four quarters equally among three people—advanced cooperation.

Supporting Autonomy and Recognizing Accomplishment

The second area in the TARGET model involves how much choice and autonomy students are allowed. Choice and control in schools are not the norm. Children and adolescents spend literally thousands of hours in schools where other people decide what will happen. Yet we know that self-determination and a sense of internal locus of causality are critical to maintaining intrinsic motivation and student engagement (Jang, Reeve, & Deci, 2010; Reeve, Nix, & Hamm, 2003). What can teachers do to support choice without creating chaos?

SUPPORTING CHOICES. Choices should provide a range of selections that allow students to follow their interests and pick an option that is important and relevant to them (I. Katz & Assor, 2007). But beware of giving too many choices. Like totally unguided discovery or aimless discussions, unstructured or unguided choices can be counterproductive for learning (R. Garner, 1998). I know that graduate students in my classes find it disconcerting if I ask them to design a final project that will determine their grade, just as I panic when I am asked to give a talk on "whatever you want."

The alternative is *bounded choice*—giving students a range of options that set valuable tasks for them but also allow them to follow personal interests. The balance must be just right: "too much autonomy is bewildering and too little is boring" (Guthrie et al., 1998, p. 185). Students can have input about work partners, seating arrangements, how to display work, or suggestions for class rules. But the most important kind of autonomy support teachers can provide probably is cognitive autonomy support—giving students opportunities to discuss different cognitive strategies for learning, approaches to solving problems, or positions on an issue (Stefanou, Perencevich, DiCintio, & Turner, 2004). Students also can exercise autonomy about how they receive feedback from the teacher or from classmates. Figure 12.2 on the next page describes a strategy called "Check It Out," in which students specify the skills that they want to have evaluated in a particular assignment. Over the course of a unit, all the skills have to be "checked out," but students choose when each one is evaluated.

RECOGNIZING ACCOMPLISHMENT. The third TARGET area is recognition for accomplishments. Students should be recognized for improving on their own personal best, for tackling difficult tasks, for persistence, and for creativity—not just for performing better than others. In Chapter 7 we noted that giving students rewards for activities that they already enjoy can undermine intrinsic motivation. What sort of recognition leads to engagement? One answer comes from a study by Ruth Butler (1987). Students in the fifth and sixth grades were given interesting divergent thinking tasks that were followed up by one of the following teacher responses: individual personalized comments, standardized praise ("very good"), grades, or no feedback. Interest, performance, attributions to effort, and task involvement were higher after personalized comments. Ego-involved motivation (the desire to look good or do better than others) was greater after grades and standard praise.

FIGURE 12.2

STUDENT AUTONOMY: CHECK IT OUT

Using this technique to support student autonomy, the teacher decides on a set of skills that will be developed over a unit, but the student decides which skill(s) will be evaluated on any given assignment. Over the course of the unit, all the skills have to be "checked out." This student has indicated that she wants the teacher to "check out" her creativity and verb tense.

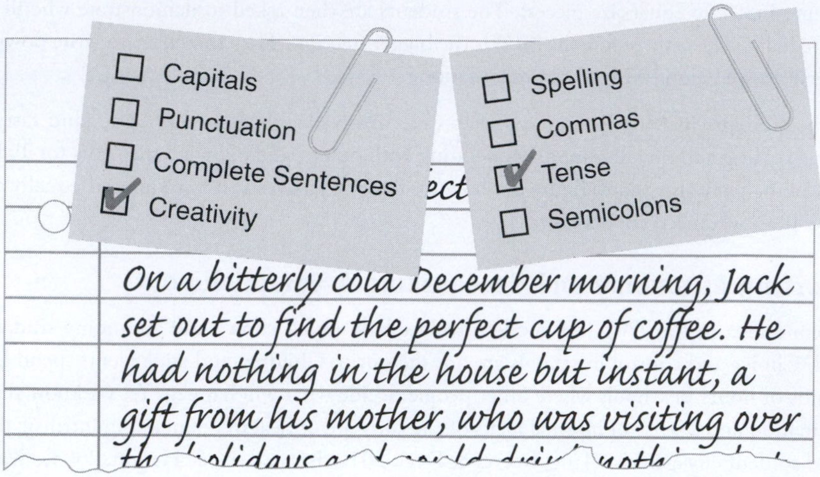

☐ Capitals
☐ Punctuation
☐ Complete Sentences
☑ Creativity

☐ Spelling
☐ Commas
☑ Tense
☐ Semicolons

On a bitterly cold December morning, Jack set out to find the perfect cup of coffee. He had nothing in the house but instant, a gift from his mother, who was visiting over

Source: From Raffini, J. P. (1996). 150 Ways to Increase Intrinsic Motivation to the Classroom. Pearson Education, Inc. Adapted by permission of the publisher.

Grouping, Evaluation, and Time

You may remember a teacher who made you want to work hard—someone who made a subject come alive. Or you may remember how many hours you spent practicing as a member of a team, orchestra, choir, or theater troupe. If you do, then you know the motivational power of relationships with other people.

GROUPING AND GOAL STRUCTURES. Motivation can be greatly influenced by the ways we relate to the other people who are also involved in accomplishing a particular goal. D. W. Johnson and Johnson (2009a) have labeled this interpersonal factor the goal structure of the task. There are three goal structures: cooperative, competitive, and individualistic, as shown in Table 12.6.

When the task involves complex learning and problem-solving skills, cooperation leads to higher achievement than competition, especially for students with lower abilities. Students learn to set attainable goals and negotiate. They become more altruistic. The interaction with peers that students enjoy so much becomes a part of the learning process. The result? The need for belonging described by Maslow is more likely to be met, and motivation is increased (Stipek, 2002; Webb & Palincsar, 1996). There are many approaches to peer learning or group learning, as you saw in Chapter 10. For example, to encourage motivation with a cooperative goal structure, form reading groups based on student interests instead of abilities and change the groups every month (Anderman & Anderman, 2014).

EVALUATION. The greater the emphasis on competitive evaluation and grading, the more students will focus on performance goals rather than mastery. And low-achieving students who have little hope of either performing well or mastering the task may simply want to get it over with (Brophy, 2005). How can teachers prevent students from simply focusing on the grade or doing the work "just to get finished"? The most obvious answer is to de-emphasize grades and to emphasize learning in the class. Students need to understand the value of the work. Instead

TABLE 12.6 • **Different Goal Structures**
Each goal structure is associated with a different relationship between the individual and the group. This relationship influences motivation to reach the goal.

	COOPERATIVE	COMPETITIVE	INDIVIDUALISTIC
Definition	Students believe their goal is attainable only if other students will also reach the goal.	Students believe they will reach their goal if and only if other students do not reach the goal.	Students believe that their own attempt to reach a goal is not related to other students' attempts to reach the goal.
Examples	Team victories—each player wins only if all the team members win: a relay race, a quilting bee, a barn raising, a symphony, a play.	Golf tournament, singles tennis match, a 100-yard dash, valedictorian, Miss America pageant.	Lowering your handicap in golf, jogging, learning a new language, enjoying a museum, losing or gaining weight, stopping smoking.

Source: Based on Learning Together and Alone: Cooperation, Competition, and Individualization *(5th ed.), by D. W. Johnson & R. Johnson. Copyright © 1999a by Pearson Education, Inc.*

of saying, "You will need to know this for the test," tell students how the information will be useful in solving problems they want to solve. Suggest that the lesson will answer some interesting questions. Communicate that understanding is more important than finishing. Unfortunately, many teachers do not follow this advice.

TIME. Most experienced teachers know that there is too much work and not enough time in the school day. Even if they become engrossed in a project, students must stop and turn their attention to another class when the bell rings or when the teacher's schedule indicates it's time to move on to a new subject. Furthermore, students must progress as a group. If particular individuals can move faster or if they need more time, they may still have to follow the pace of the whole group. So scheduling often interferes with motivation by making students move faster or slower than would be appropriate or by interrupting their involvement. It is difficult to develop persistence and a sense of self-efficacy when students are not allowed to stick with a challenging activity. As a teacher, will you be able to make time for engaged and persistent learning? Some elementary classrooms have *DEAR* time—Drop Everything And Read—to give extended periods when everyone, even the teacher, reads. Some middle and high schools have *block scheduling* in which teachers work in teams to plan larger blocks of class time.

PUTTING IT ALL TOGETHER. We can see how these motivational elements come together in real classrooms. Sara Dolezal and her colleagues observed and interviewed third-grade teachers in eight Catholic schools and determined if their students were low, moderate, or high in their level of motivation (Dolezal, Welsh, Pressley, & Vincent, 2003). Table 12.7 on the next page summarizes the dramatic differences in these classrooms between the use of strategies that support motivation and those that undermine it. Students in the *low-engagement* classes were restless and chatty as they faced their easy, undemanding seatwork. The classrooms were bare, unattractive, and filled with management problems. Instruction was disorganized. The class atmosphere was generally negative. The *moderately engaged* classrooms were organized to be "student friendly," with reading areas, group work areas, posters, and student artwork. The teachers were warm and caring, and they connected lessons to students' background knowledge. Management routines were smooth and organized, and the class atmosphere was positive. The teachers were good at catching student attention, but they had trouble *holding* attention, probably because the tasks were too easy. *Highly engaging* teachers had all the positive qualities of student-friendly classrooms—but they added more challenging tasks along with the support the students needed to succeed. These excellent motivators did not rely on one or two approaches to motivate their students; they applied a large repertoire of strategies from Table 12.7.

TABLE 12.7 • Strategies That Support and Undermine Motivation in the Classroom

A FEW STRATEGIES THAT SUPPORT MOTIVATION

STRATEGY	EXAMPLE
Messages of accountability	The teacher asks students to have parents review and sign some assignments.
Teacher communicates importance of work	"We need to check it for at least 1 minute, which means looking over it carefully."
Clear goals/directions	The teacher explains exactly how the students are to separate into groups and complete their nominations for their favorite book.
Connections across the curriculum	The teacher relates the concept of ratios in math to compare/contrast skills in reading.
Opportunities to learn about and practice dramatic arts	After studying about historical figures, students write and produce their own plays.
Attributions to effort	During a word game, the teacher says to a student, "Did you study last night?" The student nods. "See how it helps?"
Encouraging risk taking	"I need a new shining face. Someone I haven't called on yet. I need a risk taker."
Uses games and play to reinforce concept or review material	During a math lesson using balance, students spend 5 minutes weighing the favorite toy they were asked to bring in that day.
Home–school connections	As part of a math science unit, families keep a chart of everything they recycle in a week.
Multiple representations of a task	The teacher uses four ways to teach multiplication: "magic multipliers," sing-along multiplication facts, whole-class flash card review, "Around-the-World" game.
Positive classroom management, praise	"Thumbs up when you are ready to work. I like the way Table 7 is waiting patiently."
Stimulating creative thought	"We are going to use our imaginations today. We are going to take a trip to an imaginary theater in our heads."
Opportunities for choice	Students can choose to use prompts for their journal writing or pick their own topic.
Teacher communicates to students that they can handle challenging tasks	"This is hard stuff, and you are doing great. I know adults who have trouble with this."
Value students—communicate caring	The teacher allows a new student to sit with a buddy for the day.

A FEW STRATEGIES THAT DO NOT SUPPORT MOTIVATION TO LEARN

STRATEGY	EXAMPLE
Attributions to intellect rather than effort	When students remark during a lesson, "I'm stupid" or "I'm a dork," the teacher says nothing, then replies, "Let's have someone who is smart."
Teacher emphasizes competition rather than working together	The teacher conducts a poetry contest where students read poems to the class and the class members hold up cards with scores rating how well each student performed.
No scaffolding for learning a new skill	The teacher is loud and critical when students have trouble: "Just look back in the glossary, and don't miss it because you are too lazy to look it up."
Ineffective/negative feedback	"Does everyone understand?" A few students say yes, and the teacher moves on.
Lack of connections	On Martin Luther King Day, the teacher leads a brief discussion of King, then the remainder of the activities are about Columbus.
Easy tasks	The teacher provides easy work and "fun" activities that teach little.
Negative class atmosphere	"Excuse me, I said page number. If you follow and listen, you would know."
Punitive classroom management	The teacher threatens bad grades if students do not look up words in the glossary.
Work that is much too difficult	The teacher assigns independent math work that only one or two students can do.
Slow pacing	The pace is set for the slowest students—others finish and have nothing to do.
Emphasis on finishing, not learning	The teacher communicates the purpose is to finish, not learn or use the vocabulary.
Sparse, unattractive classroom	There are no decorated bulletin boards, maps, charts, or displays of student work.
Poor planning	Missing handouts force the teacher to have large instead of smaller work groups.
Public punishment	All students stand, and the teacher reads a list of those who finished the assignment and they sit down. The teacher gives public lecture on responsibility to those left standing.

Source: Based on "How do nine third-grade teachers motivate their students?" by S. E. Dolezal, L. M. Welsh, M. Pressley, & M. Vincent. Elementary School Journal, 2003, 103, pp. 247–248. Adapted with permission.

Diversity in Motivation

Because students differ in terms of language, culture, economic privilege, personality, knowledge, and experience, they will also differ in their needs, goals, interests, emotions, and beliefs. Teachers encourage motivation to learn by taking this diversity into account using TARGET—designing tasks, supporting autonomy, recognizing accomplishments, grouping, making evaluations, and managing time. Take interest, for example. Embedding student writing tasks in cultural contexts is one way to catch and hold situational interest (Alderman, 2004; Bergin, 1999). When Latina/o immigrant students in middle school classes moved from writing using worksheets and standard assignments to writing about such topics as immigration, bilingualism, and gang life—issues that were important to them and to their families—their papers were longer and the writing quality improved (Rueda & Moll, 1994).

Language is a central factor in students' connections with the school. When bilingual students are encouraged to draw on both English and their heritage language, motivation and participation can increase. Robert Jimenez (2000) found in his study of bilingual Latino/a students that successful readers viewed reading as a process of making sense; they used both of their languages to understand the material. For instance, they might look for Spanish word parts in English words to help them translate. Less-successful students had a different goal. They believed that reading just meant saying the words correctly in English. It is likely their interest and sense of efficacy for reading in English would be less, too.

Lessons for Teachers: Strategies to Encourage Motivation

Until four basic conditions are met for every student and in every classroom, no motivational strategies will succeed. First, the classroom must be relatively organized and free from constant interruptions and disruptions. (Chapter 13 will give you the information you need to make sure this requirement is met.) Second, the teacher must be a patient, supportive person who never embarrasses the students because they made mistakes. Everyone in the class should view mistakes as opportunities for learning (Clifford, 1990, 1991). Third, the work must be challenging, but reasonable. If work is too easy or too difficult, students will have little motivation to learn. They will focus on finishing, not on learning. Finally, the learning tasks must be authentic. And as we have seen, what makes a task authentic is influenced by the students' culture (Bergin, 1999; Brophy & Kher, 1986; Stipek, 2002).

Once these four basic conditions are met, the influences on students' motivation to learn in a particular situation can be summarized in four questions: Can I succeed at this task? Do I want to succeed? What do I need to do to succeed? Do I belong? (Committee on Increasing High School Students' Engagement and Motivation to Learn, 2004; Eccles & Wigfield, 1985). We want students to have confidence in their ability so they will approach learning with energy and enthusiasm. We want them to see the value of the tasks involved and work to learn, not just try to get the grade or get finished. We want students to believe that success will come when they apply good learning strategies instead of believing that their only option is to use self-defeating, failure-avoiding, face-saving strategies. When things get difficult, we want students to stay focused on the task and not get so worried about failure that they "freeze." And we want students to feel as though they belong in school—that their teachers and classmates care about them and can be trusted.

CAN I DO IT? BUILDING CONFIDENCE AND POSITIVE EXPECTATIONS. No amount of encouragement or "cheerleading" will substitute for real accomplishment. To ensure genuine progress:

1. *Begin work at the students' level, and move in small steps.* One possibility is to have very easy and very difficult questions on every test and assignment, so all students are both successful and challenged. When grades are required, make sure all the students in class have a chance to make at least a C if they work hard.

2. *Make sure learning goals are clear, specific, and possible to reach in the near future.* Break long-term projects into subgoals. If possible, give students a range of goals at different levels of difficulty, and let them choose.

3. *Stress self-comparison, not comparison with others.* Give specific feedback and corrections. Tell students what they are doing right as well as what is wrong and why it is wrong. Periodically, give students a question or problem that was once hard for them but now seems easy. Point out how much they have improved.

4. *Communicate to students that academic ability is improvable and specific to the task at hand.* In other words, the fact that a student has trouble in algebra doesn't necessarily mean that geometry will be difficult. Don't undermine your efforts to stress improvement by displaying only the 100% papers on the bulletin board.

5. *Model good problem solving, especially when you have to try several approaches.* Students need to see that learning is not smooth and error free, even for the teacher.

DO I WANT TO DO IT? SEEING THE VALUE OF LEARNING. Teachers can use intrinsic and extrinsic motivation strategies to help students see the value of the learning task.

Attainment and Intrinsic Value. To establish attainment value, we must connect the learning task with the needs of the students. It must be possible for students to meet their needs for safety, belonging, and achievement in our classes. Many students are quietly wounded by their teachers' words or by school practices that embarrass, label, or demean (K. Olson, 2008). We must make it clear that both women and men can be high achievers in all subjects: no subjects are the territory of only one sex. It is not "unfeminine" to be strong in mathematics, car mechanics, or sports. It is not "unmasculine" to be good in literature, art, or French.

There are many strategies for encouraging intrinsic (interest) motivation. Several of the following are taken from Brophy (1988).

1. *Tie class activities to student interests* in sports, music, current events, pets, common problems or conflicts with family and friends, fads, television, and movie personalities, or other significant features of their lives (Schiefele, 1991).

2. *Arouse curiosity.* Point out puzzling discrepancies between students' beliefs and the facts. For example, Stipek (1993) describes a teacher who asked her fifth-grade class if there were "people" on some of the other planets. When the students said yes, the teacher asked if people needed oxygen to breathe. Because the students had just learned this fact, they responded yes. Then the teacher told them that there is no oxygen in the atmosphere of the other planets. This surprising discrepancy between what the children knew about oxygen and what they believed about life on other planets led to a rousing discussion of the atmospheres of other planets.

3. *Make the learning task fun.* Many lessons can be taught through simulations or games (see the *Point/Counterpoint*). Used appropriately so that the activity connects with learning, these experiences can be very worthwhile and fun, too.

4. *Make use of novelty and familiarity.* Don't overuse a few teaching approaches or motivational strategies. We all need some variety. Varying the goal structures of tasks (cooperative, competitive, individualistic) can help. When the material being covered in class is abstract or unfamiliar to students, try to connect it to something they know and understand. For example, talk about the size of a large area, such as the Acropolis in Athens, in terms of football fields.

Instrumental Value. Sometimes it is difficult to encourage intrinsic motivation, and so teachers must rely on the utility or "instrumental" value of tasks. It is important to learn many skills because they will be needed in more advanced classes or for life outside school.

1. When these connections are not obvious, you should *explain the connections* to your students or ask them to explain how the material will be important in their lives (Hulleman, Godes, Hendricks, & Harackiewicz, 2010).

2. In some situations, teachers can *provide incentives and rewards* for learning (see Chapter 7). Remember, though, that giving rewards when students are already interested in the activity may undermine intrinsic motivation.

3. *Use ill-structured problems and authentic tasks* in teaching. Connect problems in school to real problems outside, such as buying your first car, making decisions about mobile phone plans, or writing a persuasive letter to a potential employer.

WHAT DO I NEED TO DO TO SUCCEED? STAYING FOCUSED ON THE TASK. When students encounter difficulties, as they must if they are working at a challenging level, they need to keep their attention on the task. If the focus shifts to worries about performance, fear of failure, or concern with looking smart, then motivation to learn is lost.

1. *Give students frequent opportunities to respond* through questions and answers, short assignments, or demonstrations of skills and correct problems quickly. You don't want students to practice errors too long.

2. When possible, *have students create a finished product.* They will be more persistent and focused on the task when the end is in sight. For example, I often begin a house-painting project thinking I will work for just an hour and then find myself still painting hours later because I want to see the finished product.

3. *Avoid heavy emphasis on grades and competition.* An emphasis on grades forces students to focus on performance, not learning. Anxious students are especially hard hit by highly competitive evaluation.

4. *Reduce the task risk without oversimplifying it.* When tasks are risky (failure is likely and the consequences of failing are grave), student motivation suffers. For difficult, complex, or ambiguous tasks, provide students with plenty of time, support, resources, help, and the chance to revise or improve work.

5. *Model motivation to learn* for your students. Talk about your interest in the subject and how you deal with difficult learning tasks (Xu, Coats, & Davidson, 2012).

6. *Teach the particular learning strategies* that students will need to master the material being studied. Show students how to learn and remember so they won't be forced to fall back on self-defeating strategies or rote memory.

DO I BELONG IN THIS CLASSROOM? This last question will take more than a page or two to address, so I have devoted a large part of Chapter 13 to the notion of creating learning environments. The support of families can be helpful as you design strategies for your students. The *Guidelines: Motivation to Learn—Family and Community Partnerships* on the next page gives ideas for working with families.

ENHANCEDetext *self-check*

GUIDELINES
Motivation to Learn: Family and Community Partnerships

Understand family goals for children.

Examples

1. In an informal setting, around coffee or snacks, meet with families individually or in small groups to listen to their goals for their children.
2. Mail out questionnaires or send response cards home with students, asking what skills the families believe their children most need to work on. Pick one goal for each child, and develop a plan for working toward the goal both inside and outside school. Share the plan with the families, and ask for feedback.

Identify student and family interests that can be related to goals.

Examples

1. Ask a member of the family to share a skill or hobby.
2. Identify "family favorites"—favorite foods, music, vacations, sports, activities, hymns, movies, games, snacks, recipes, memories. Tie class lessons to interests.

Give families a way to track progress toward goals.

Examples

1. Provide simple "progress charts" or goal cards that can be posted on the refrigerator.
2. Ask for parents' or caregivers' feedback (and mean it) about your effectiveness in helping their children.

Work with families to build confidence and positive expectations.

Examples

1. Avoid comparing one child in a family to another during conferences and discussions with family members.

2. Ask family members to highlight strong points of homework assignments. They might attach a note to assignments describing the three best aspects of the work and one element that could be improved.

Make families partners in showing the value of learning.

Examples

1. Invite family members to the class to demonstrate how they use mathematics or writing in their work.
2. Involve parents or caregivers in identifying skills and knowledge that could be applied at home and prove helpful to the family right now, for example, keeping records on service agencies, writing letters of complaint to department stores or landlords, or researching vacation destinations.

Provide resources that build skill and will for families.

Examples

1. Give family members simple strategies for helping their children improve study skills.
2. Involve older students in a "homework hotline" telephone network for helping younger students.

Have frequent celebrations of learning.

Examples

1. Invite families to a "museum" at the end of a unit on dinosaurs. Students create the museum in the auditorium, library, or cafeteria. After visiting the museum, families go to the classroom to examine their child's portfolio for the unit.
2. Place mini-exhibits of student work at local grocery stores, libraries, or community centers.

SUMMARY

- **What Is Motivation? (pp. 444–448)**

Define motivation. Motivation is an internal state that arouses, directs, and maintains behavior. The study of motivation focuses on how and why people initiate actions directed toward specific goals, how long it takes them to get started in the activity, how intensively they are involved in the activity, how persistent they are in their attempts to reach these goals, and what they are thinking and feeling along the way.

What is the difference between intrinsic and extrinsic motivation? Intrinsic motivation is the natural tendency to seek out and conquer challenges as we pursue personal interests and exercise capabilities—it is motivation to do something when we don't have to. Extrinsic motivation is based on factors not related to the activity itself. We are not really interested in the activity for its own sake; we care only about what it will gain us.

How does locus of causality apply to motivation? The essential difference between intrinsic and extrinsic motivation is the person's reason for acting, that is, whether the locus of causality for the action is inside or outside the person. If the locus is internal, the motivation is intrinsic; if the locus is external, the motivation is extrinsic. Most motivation has elements of both. In fact, intrinsic and extrinsic motivation may be two separate tendencies—both can operate at the same time in a given situation.

What are the key factors in motivation according to a behavioral viewpoint? A humanistic viewpoint? A cognitive viewpoint? A social cognitive viewpoint? A sociocultural viewpoint? Behaviorists tend to emphasize extrinsic motivation caused by incentives, rewards, and punishment. Humanistic views stress the intrinsic motivation created by the need for personal growth, fulfillment, and self-determination. Cognitive views stress a person's active search for meaning, understanding, and competence, and the power of the individual's attributions and interpretations. Social cognitive theories take into account both the behaviorists' concern with the consequences of behavior and the cognitivists' interest in the impact of individual beliefs and expectations. Many influential social cognitive explanations of motivation can be characterized as expectancy × value theories. Sociocultural views emphasize legitimate engaged participation and identity within a community.

What are expectancy × value theories? Expectancy × value theories suggest that motivation to reach a goal is the product of our expectations for success and the value of the goal to us. If either is zero, our motivation is zero also.

What is legitimate peripheral participation? Legitimate peripheral participation means that beginners are genuinely involved in the work of the group, even if their abilities are undeveloped and their contributions are small. The identities of the novice and the expert are bound up in their participation in the community. They are motivated to learn the values and practices of the community to keep their identity as community members.

- **Needs (pp. 448–452)**

Distinguish between deficiency needs and being needs in Maslow's theory. Maslow called four lower-level needs *deficiency needs*: survival, safety, belonging, and self-esteem. When these needs are satisfied, the motivation for fulfilling them decreases. He labeled the three higher-level needs *being needs*: cognitive needs, aesthetic needs, and self-actualization. When they are met, a person's motivation increases to seek further fulfillment.

What are the basic needs that affect motivation, and how does self-determination affect motivation? Self-determination theory suggests that motivation is affected by the need for competence, autonomy and control, and relatedness. When students experience self-determination, they are intrinsically motivated; they are more interested in their work, have a greater sense of self-esteem, and learn more. Students' experiencing self-determination depends in part on the teacher's communications with students providing information rather than seeking to control them. In addition, teachers must acknowledge the students' perspective, offer choices, provide rationales for limits, and treat poor performance as a problem to be solved rather than a target for criticism.

- **Goal Orientations (pp. 452–456)**

What kinds of goals are the most motivating? Goals increase motivation if they are specific, moderately difficult, and attainable in the near future.

Describe mastery, performance, work-avoidant, and social goals. A mastery goal is the intention to gain knowledge and master skills, leading students to seek challenges and persist when they encounter difficulties. A performance goal is the intention to get good grades or to appear smarter or more capable than others, leading students to be preoccupied with themselves and how they appear (ego-involved learners). Students can approach or avoid these two kinds of goals—the problems are greatest with avoidance. Another kind of avoidance is evident with work-avoidant learners, who simply want to find the easiest way to handle the situation. Students with social goals can be supported or hindered in their learning, depending on the specific goal (i.e., have fun with friends or bring honor to the family).

What makes goal setting effective in the classroom? For goal setting to be effective in the classroom, students need accurate feedback about their progress toward goals and they must accept the goals set. Generally, students are more willing to adopt goals that seem realistic, reasonably difficult, meaningful, and validated by activities connecting them to their intrinsic interests.

- **Beliefs and Self-Perceptions (pp. 456–462)**

What are epistemological beliefs, and how do they affect motivation? Epistemological beliefs are ways of understanding how you think and learn. Individuals' epistemological beliefs can impact their approach to learning, their expectations of themselves and the work they do, and the extent to which they engage in academic tasks. Specifically, epistemological beliefs include your understanding of the structure, stability, and certainty of knowledge. A belief that knowledge can be organized into a grand scheme in which all things are related, for example, may lead students to try to connect all new knowledge with previous knowledge in a meaningful way. If the task proves excessively challenging, these students may believe the new information is not relevant to them or worth understanding.

How do beliefs about ability affect motivation? When people hold an entity theory of ability—that is, they believe that ability is fixed—they tend to set performance goals and strive to protect themselves from failure. When they believe ability is improvable (an incremental theory), however, they tend to set mastery goals and handle failure constructively.

What are the three dimensions of attributions in Weiner's theory? According to Weiner, most of the attributed causes for successes or failures can be characterized in terms of three dimensions: locus (location of the cause internal or external to the person), stability (whether the cause stays the same or can change), and responsibility (whether the person can control the cause). The greatest motivational problems arise when students attribute failures to stable, uncontrollable causes. These students may seem resigned to failure, depressed, helpless—what we generally call "unmotivated."

What is learned helplessness, and what deficits does it cause? When people come to believe that the events and outcomes in their lives are mostly uncontrollable, they have developed learned helplessness, which is associated with three types of deficits: motivational, cognitive, and affective. Students who feel hopeless will be unmotivated and reluctant to attempt work. They miss opportunities to practice and improve skills and abilities, so they develop cognitive deficits and they often suffer from affective problems such as depression, anxiety, and listlessness.

How does self-worth influence motivation? Mastery-oriented students tend to value achievement and see ability as improvable, so they focus on mastery goals, take risks, and cope with failure constructively. A low sense of self-worth seems to be linked with the failure-avoiding and failure-accepting strategies intended to protect the individual from the consequences of failure. These strategies may seem to help in the short term but are damaging to motivation and self-esteem in the long run.

- **Interests, Curiosity, Emotions, and Anxiety (pp. 462–470)**

How do interests and emotions affect learning? Learning and information processing are influenced by emotion. Students are more likely to pay attention to, learn from, and remember events, images, and readings that provoke emotional responses or that are related to their personal interests. However, there are cautions in responding to students' interests. "Seductive details," interesting bits of information that are not central to the learning, can hinder learning.

How does curiosity affect learning, and what can teachers do to stimulate curiosity in their subject area? Curiosity is the tendency toward interest in a variety of things. Students' curiosity is guided by their interests, and

thus provides them with a self-driven motivation to explore new ideas and concepts. As a result, curiosity can be a powerful motivational tool that captures and maintains students' attention in school. Teachers can foster curiosity by tapping into students' interests, illustrating connections between course material and applications that may be interesting to students, and allowing students to find these connections for themselves. An example might include asking students to identify the simple machines at work in a skateboard or rollercoaster.

What is the role of arousal in learning? There appears to be an optimum level of arousal for most activities. Generally speaking, a higher level of arousal is helpful on simple tasks, but lower levels of arousal are better for complex tasks. When arousal is too low, teachers can stimulate curiosity by pointing out gaps in knowledge or using variety in activities. Severe anxiety is an example of arousal that is too high for optimal learning.

How does anxiety interfere with learning? Anxiety can be the cause or the result of poor performance; it can interfere with attention to, learning of, and retrieval of information. Many anxious students need help in developing effective test-taking and study skills.

- **Motivation to Learn in School: On TARGET (pp. 471–480)**

Define motivation to learn. Teachers are interested in a particular kind of motivation—student motivation to learn. Student motivation to learn is both a trait and a state. It involves taking academic work seriously, trying to get the most from it, and applying appropriate learning strategies in the process.

What does TARGET stand for? TARGET is an acronym for the six areas in which teachers make decisions that can influence student motivation to learn: the nature of the *task* that students are asked to do, the *autonomy* students are allowed in working, how students are *recognized* for their accomplishments, *grouping* practices, *evaluation* procedures, and the scheduling of *time* in the classroom.

How do tasks affect motivation? The tasks that teachers set affect motivation. When students encounter tasks that are related to their interests, stimulate their curiosity, or are connected to real-life situations, they are more likely to be motivated to learn. Tasks can have attainment, intrinsic, or utility value for students. Attainment value is the importance to the student of succeeding. Intrinsic value is the enjoyment the student gets from the task. Utility value is determined by how much the task contributes to reaching short-term or long-term goals.

Distinguish between bounded and unbounded choices. Like totally unguided discovery or aimless discussions, unstructured or unbounded choices can be counterproductive for learning. The alternative is bounded choice—giving students a range of options that set out valuable tasks for them but also allow them to follow personal interests. The balance must be just right so that students are not bewildered by too much choice or bored by too little room to explore.

How can recognition undermine motivation and a sense of self-efficacy? Recognition and reward in the classroom will support motivation to learn if the recognition is for personal progress rather than competitive victories. Praise and rewards should focus on students' growing competence. At times, praise can have paradoxical effects when students use the teacher's praise or criticism as cues about capabilities.

List three goal structures, and distinguish among them. How students relate to their peers in the classroom is influenced by the goal structure of the activities. Goal structures can be competitive, individualistic, or cooperative. Cooperative goal structures can encourage motivation and increase learning, especially for low-achieving students.

How does the evaluative climate affect goal setting? The more competitive the grading, the more students set performance goals and focus on "looking competent," that is, they are more ego-involved. When the focus is on performing rather than learning, students often see the goal of classroom tasks as simply finishing, especially if the work is difficult.

What are some effects of time on motivation? To foster motivation to learn, teachers should be flexible in their use of time in the classroom. Students who are forced to move faster or slower than they should or who are interrupted as they become involved in a project are not likely to develop persistence for learning.

PRACTICE USING WHAT YOU HAVE LEARNED

To access and complete the exercises, click the links under the images below.

Motivation and Needs

Interests, Curiosity, Emotions, and Anxiety

ENHANCEDetext *application exercise*

ENHANCEDetext *application exercise*

KEY TERMS

CONNECT AND EXTEND TO LICENSURE

MULTIPLE-CHOICE QUESTIONS

1. Miss Johnson would like her students to be motivated to do their work without bribing them with treats or promises of extra recess time. Which one of the following is the type of motivation she should encourage in her students?
   A. Extrinsic
   B. Intrinsic
   C. Locus of control
   D. Relatedness

2. Why should educators concern themselves with Abraham Maslow's hierarchy of needs?
   A. The stages in students' development might determine their ability to be successful in certain subjects.
   B. Social and emotional growth can impact students in their ability to cooperate with their peers.
   C. Deficiencies in students' lives can impact their ability to succeed academically.
   D. Parenting styles determine whether students succeed academically or not.

3. Teachers who select all content for their students and insist on students accomplishing their assignments on their own neglect which of the following aspects of self-determination?
   A. Autonomy and competence
   B. Autonomy and relatedness
   C. Relatedness and competence
   D. Autonomy, relatedness, and competence

4. Which of the following is true regarding extrinsic motivation?
   A. Extrinsic motivation should be avoided at all costs because it undermines a student's intrinsic desire.

   B. Extrinsic motivation is not associated with grades and incentives.
   C. Extrinsic motivation may be necessary to initially encourage students to engage in certain activities.
   D. Extrinsic motivation is more desirable than intrinsic motivation in the classroom because educators have increased control.

CONSTRUCTED-RESPONSE QUESTIONS

Case

Stephanie Wilson had been educated in "old school methods." Her teachers insisted on straight rows of seated students who did not talk during lectures or complain about assignments. While Stephanie had been successful in this model, not all of her past classmates flourished in such a rigid environment. As a new teacher she wanted a more student-friendly environment. She envisioned a classroom where students were stimulated by the activities and worked collaboratively. "I want my students to look forward to coming to school. I want them to be agents in the learning process, not just passive recipients of my curriculum." She imagined designing learning situations in which her students could all achieve. Step by step, they could all learn! As her students would progress, she would see when they got off the track and manage to remediate before they started to do poorly. In this way, Stephanie thought, none of her students would be failures.

5. Explain why Stephanie's plan to provide early remediation when students are struggling is a good idea.
6. How can Stephanie Wilson support self-determination and autonomy in her classroom?

ENHANCEDetext *licensure exam*

TEACHERS' CASEBOOK

WHAT WOULD THEY DO? MOTIVATING STUDENTS WHEN RESOURCES ARE THIN

Here is how some practicing teachers responded to motivate students when resources are slim.

AIMEE FREDETTE —Second Grade Teacher
Fisher Elementary School, Walpole, MA

A very effective way that I use to get the children curious and interested is to pose a question to the class before the start of a lesson. This gives the children a focus for the lesson. As the year progresses, the children begin coming up with questions of their own. Another very successful way to spark interest and curiosity is the use of three-column activators, a brainstorming activity that the teacher and students do together. The students brainstorm WHAT WE THINK WE KNOW about the topic. The teacher records all responses, writing them on chart paper. Then the children brainstorm WHAT WE WANT TO KNOW about the topic. Again the teacher records their responses. The third column, titled WHAT WE HAVE LEARNED, is added as the theme progresses. The first two columns are referred to as the children learn about the theme.

DANIELLE HARTMAN —Second Grade Teacher
Claymont Elementary School, Ballwin, MO

First of all, don't get discouraged. You don't need a textbook to be a successful teacher. Look over the district's curriculum guides, and see what the objectives are for each unit you will be teaching. Once you know the objectives, get creative. Keeping the students motivated and interested in learning is essential. By giving them choice and using a variety of teaching methods, you will allow them to stay actively engaged in their learning. You will be amazed at what the students will come up with when they are given choices.

MICHAEL YASIS—Fifth Grade Teacher
L. H. Tanglen Elementary School, Minnetonka, MN

Most learning is acquired through active learning and participation. Therefore, the workbooks that focus on drill and practice, if given as the primary source of learning, most likely would bore the students. I would approach this situation by first engaging the students in a discussion to assess their prior knowledge. I would then challenge and extend their understanding of the concepts through guided discovery, building on similar examples from the "boring" workbooks. While they work on the concepts independently in their workbooks, their confidence and self-esteem will increase.

KELLY MCELROY BONIN —High School Counselor
Klein Oak High School, Spring, TX

Simply being excited to be working with the third graders and showing interest and enthusiasm for the subject matter should arouse the students' interest and encourage them to learn. How many times have you heard it said, "Mrs. Energy was the best teacher I ever had. She took the most boring, difficult subject and made it fun and interesting." I have heard this so many times both as a student and as a teacher, and it proves my point. Just the fact that the teacher is excited about the material shows the students that this is important information that they need, plus they are curious about the material when they respect and like their teacher. If I felt like the difficulty level of the textbooks was too great, I would have to break the lessons down into smaller increments and use different techniques—discussion, re-teaching, group projects, and so on—to enrich the students and adapt to their level of learning. When your students are motivated, they can accomplish anything—it doesn't matter what materials are available to them, what the difficulty level of the textbook is. Kids will be motivated when their teacher truly cares about them, is passionate about the material, and makes school interesting.

PAM GASKILL —Second Grade Teacher
Riverside Elementary School, Dublin, OH

Teaching is inherently creative. Use your time and creativity this summer to acquaint yourself with the required objectives, and think about ways in which you can make them meaningful and relevant to your students. Explore other available resources in the community, such as libraries, speakers' bureaus, and resource centers. Plan to incorporate a variety of activities such as videos, group work, field trips, projects, and speakers so that your students will remain interested and involved. Use materials that your students have access to from home—books, videos, artifacts, Internet printouts. It is amazing how cooperative parents can be when asked to help in specified ways. You might even make use of the old workbook pages, not in the traditional way, but for cooperative work. You can facilitate student success by pairing weaker readers with more competent readers to discuss and complete the worksheets. Stress that everyone needs to work together to learn the material. Active participation and engagement with the materials will help your students to construct their own meanings more effectively.

13 | CREATING LEARNING ENVIRONMENTS

TEACHERS' CASEBOOK

WHAT WOULD YOU DO? BULLIES AND VICTIMS

Two boys are terrorizing one of your students. These boys are larger, stronger, and older than the boy in your class, who is small for his age and shy. Unfortunately, the bullies are fairly popular, in part because they are successful athletes. There are incidents on the bus before and after school, in the gym, in the hallways, and at lunch—including intimidation, extortion of lunch money, tripping, shoving, and verbal taunts—"fag" is a favorite chant. You do not have the two bullies in any of your classes. Your student has started to miss school routinely, and when he is in class, the quality of his work is declining.

CRITICAL THINKING

- How would you handle this situation?
- Who should be involved?
- What would you do about the verbal homophobic insults?
- What would you do if the bullies were in your classes?
- What would you do if the bullies and victim were girls?

Abigail210986/Fotolia

OVERVIEW AND OBJECTIVES

This chapter looks at the ways that teachers create social and physical environments for learning by examining classroom management—one of the main concerns of teachers, particularly beginning teachers. The very nature of classes, teaching, and students makes good management a critical ingredient of success, and we will investigate why this is true. Successful managers create more time for learning, involve more students, and help students to become self-managing.

A positive learning environment must be established and maintained throughout the year. One of the best ways to accomplish this is by working to prevent problems from occurring at all. But when problems arise—as they always do—an appropriate response is important. What will you do when students challenge you openly in class, when one student asks your advice on a difficult personal problem, or when another withdraws from all participation? We will examine the ways that teachers can communicate effectively with their students in these and many other situations.

By the time you have completed this chapter, you should be able to:

Objective 13.1   Relate academic learning time and student cooperation to creating and maintaining a classroom climate conducive to academic achievement and socio-emotional well-being.

Objective 13.2   Summarize the research on the roles of rules, procedures, consequences, and the design of the physical space in classroom management, with special attention to establishing your management system during the first weeks of class.

Objective 13.3   Discuss how to maintain a positive learning environment by encouraging student engagement, preventing problems, and developing caring, respectful relationships with your students.

Objective 13.4   Identify strategies for preventing and addressing student misbehaviors, including bullying.

Objective 13.5   Characterize successful teacher–student and student–student communication through such approaches as active listening, conflict resolution, peer mediation, and restorative justice.

Objective 13.6   Explain the need for and approaches to culturally-relevant classroom management.

THE WHAT AND WHY OF CLASSROOM MANAGEMENT

STOP & THINK What do you believe about classroom management? On a 5-point scale from *strongly disagree* (1) to *strongly agree* (5), how would you respond to these items?
1. Pupils can be trusted to work together without supervision.
2. Being friendly with pupils often leads them to become too familiar.
3. Teachers should consider revision of their teaching methods if these are criticized by their pupils.
4. Pupils often misbehave in order to make the teacher look bad.
5. It is often necessary to remind pupils that their status in school differs from that of teachers. •

Items 2, 4, and 5 in the *Stop & Think* challenge are *custodial* items. If you tended to agree with these items, you probably are more teacher centered in your philosophy of management and interested in maintaining order, rules, and structure in your classes. If you tended to agree more with items 1 and 3, you may tend to be more *humanistic* in your philosophy and are more optimistic about students' abilities to become responsible and self-regulated learners. You just took 5 items from the PCI (Pupil Control Ideology). It was developed by my husband, Wayne Hoy, and his colleagues (Willower, Eidell, & Hoy, 1967) almost 50 years ago and is still used widely today. If you want to take the full survey, go to waynekhoy.com/pupil_control.html.

Another survey that assesses your philosophy of discipline is the Beliefs About Discipline Inventory (Wolfgang, 2009), shown in Figure 13.1. When you answer these questions, you will see if your values about classroom management tend to focus on Relationship-Listening, Confronting-Contracting, Rules and Consequences, or some combination. There are successful teachers using all these strategies appropriately as the situation merits. What is your position? Let's dive into this important world of classroom management.

In study after study of the factors related to student achievement, classroom management stands out as the variable with the largest impact (Marzano & Marzano, 2003). Knowledge of and skill in classroom management are marks of expertise in teaching; and stress and exhaustion from managerial difficulties are precursors of burnout in teaching (Emmer & Stough, 2001). What is it about classrooms that makes management so critical?

Classes are particular kinds of environments. They have distinctive features that influence their inhabitants no matter how the students or the desks are organized or what the teacher believes about education (Doyle, 2006). Classrooms are *multidimensional*. They are crowded with people, tasks, and time pressures. Many individuals—all with differing goals, preferences, and abilities—must share resources, use and reuse materials without losing them, move in and out of the room, and so on. In addition, actions can have multiple effects. Calling on low-ability students may encourage their participation and thinking, but may also lead to management problems if the students are unable to answer your questions. And events occur *simultaneously*—everything happens at once, and the pace is fast. Teachers have literally hundreds of exchanges with students during a single day.

In this rapid-fire existence, events are *unpredictable*. Even when plans are carefully made, a lesson can still be interrupted by a technology glitch or a loud, angry discussion right outside the classroom. Because classrooms are *public*, the way the

FIGURE 13.1

BELIEFS ABOUT DISCIPLINE INVENTORY

This 12-question inventory will give you insights about yourself and where your personality and the discipline techniques you use would fall under the three philosophies of discipline. In each question, you are asked to choose between two competing value statements. For some questions, you will definitely agree with one statement and disagree with the second, making it easy for you to choose; for others, however, you will agree or disagree with both, and you must select the one you more closely identify with. There is no "right" or "wrong" answer—but merely indicators of your own personal views.

Forced Choices. Instructions: Circle a or b to indicate the statement with which you identify the most. You must choose between the two statements for each item.

1. a. Because students' thinking is limited, rules need to be established for them by mature adults.
    b. Each student's emotional needs must be taken into consideration, rather than having some preestablished rule imposed on all.
2. a. During the first class session of the new school year, the teacher needs to assign each student his or her own desk or table space, and the student should be taught routinely to take that space after transitions.
    b. Groups of students can decide through a class meeting what rules they need to govern themselves.
3. a. Students should be given a choice as to which topics for projects they wish to select. Once they choose, they must keep to that decision for most of that grading period.
    b. The material students must learn and the tasks to be performed must be determined by the teacher, and a specific sequence of instruction to accomplish these goals must be followed.
4. The books and similar classroom equipment are being misused, soiled, and at times destroyed. I will most likely:
    a. Hold a class meeting, show the damaged books to the class, and ask them how we may solve this problem, including what action should be taken toward a student found to be misusing books.
    b. Physically remove or limit the number of books available and observe closely to see who is misusing the books. I would then tell that student how such action was affecting other students and how I felt about the loss of such books.
5. Two students of equal power and abilities are in a rather loud verbal conflict over a classroom material. I would:
    a. Attempt to see that this does not get out of control by approaching the students, telling them of the classroom rule, and demanding that they desist in their actions, promising a sanction if they fail to comply.
    b. Avoid interfering in something that the students need to resolve themselves.
6. a. A student strongly requests not to work with the group today. I would permit this, feeling that this student has some emotional concerns related to the group experience.
    b. One student is being refused entry into group activities. I would raise this as an issue in a class meeting and ask for a discussion of the reasons and possible solutions from the student and the group.
7. The noise level in the classroom is at such a high level that it is bothering me. I would:
    a. Flick the classroom lights to get everyone's attention, ask the students to become quiet, and later praise those who are talking quietly.
    b. Select the two or three students really making most of the noise, take them aside to ask them to reflect (think) about their behavior and how it might affect others, and get an agreement from them to work quietly.
8. During the first few days of class, I would:
    a. Permit the students to test their ability to get along as a new group and make no predetermined rules until the students feel that rules are needed.
    b. Immediately establish the class rules and the fair sanction I will apply if these rules are broken.
9. My response to swearing by a student is:
    a. The student is frustrated by a classmate and has responded by swearing, so I do not reprimand the student but encourage him to talk out what is bothering him.
    b. I bring the two students together in a "knee-to-knee" confronting relationship and attempt to get them to work out this conflict while I ask questions and keep the focus on the negotiation.
10. If a student disrupts class while I am trying to lecture, I would:
    a. Ignore the disruption if possible and/or move the student to the back of the room as a consequence of his misbehavior.
    b. Express my feeling of discomfort to the student about being disrupted from my task.
11. a. Each student must realize that there are some school rules that need to be obeyed, and any student who breaks them will be punished in the same fair manner.
    b. Rules are never written in stone and can be renegotiated by the class, and sanctions will vary with each student.
12. A student refuses to put away her work or materials after using them. I would most likely:
    a. Express to the student how not putting her things away will affect future activities in this space, and how frustrating this will be for everyone. I would then leave the materials where they are for the remainder of the day.
    b. Confront the student to reflect on her behavior, think about how her noncompliance affects others, and tell her that if she cannot follow the rules, she will lose the use of the materials in the future.

(continued)

FIGURE 13.1 (Continued)

Scoring Key and Interpretation

Take your responses and circle them on the tables provided:

Table 1	Table 2	Table 3
4b 1b	2b 4a	2a 1a
6a 5b	3a 6b	3b 5a
9a 8a	7b 9b	7a 8b
12a 10b	11b 12b	11a 10a

Total number of responses in Table 1 _____

Total number of responses in Table 2 _____

Total number of responses in Table 3 _____

The table for which the total number of responses was the highest indicates the school of thought where your values tend to be clustered. Table 1 is *Relationship-Listening,* Table 2 is *Confronting-Contracting,* and Table 3 is *Rules and Consequences.* The table with the next highest score would be your second choice, and the table with the least number may be the philosophy that you associate with the least.

If your responses are equally distributed across all three tables, you may be an eclectic teacher who picks and chooses from all philosophies or your philosophy may not have consolidated at this time in your training.

Source: From Wolfgang, C. H. (2009). Solving discipline and classroom management problems (7th ed. pp. 6–7). Hoboken, NJ: Wiley & Sons. Reprinted with permission.

teacher handles these unexpected intrusions is seen and judged by all. Students are always noticing if the teacher is being "fair." Is there favoritism? What happens when a rule is broken? Finally, classrooms have *histories*. The meaning of a particular teacher's or student's actions depends in part on what has happened before. The fifteenth time a student arrives late requires a different teacher response compared to the first late arrival. In addition, the history of the first few weeks of school affects life in the class for the rest of the year.

The Basic Task: Gain Their Cooperation

The basic management task for teachers is to achieve order and harmony by gaining and maintaining student cooperation in class activities (Doyle, 2006). Given the multidimensional, simultaneous, fast-paced, unpredictable, public, and historical nature of classrooms, this is quite a challenge. Gaining student cooperation means planning activities, having materials ready, making appropriate behavioral and academic demands on students, giving clear signals, accomplishing transitions smoothly, foreseeing problems and stopping them before they start, selecting and sequencing activities so that flow and interest are maintained—and much more. Also, different activities require different managerial skills. For example, a new or complicated activity may be a greater threat to classroom management than a familiar or simple activity.

Obviously, gaining the cooperation of kindergartners is not the same task as gaining the cooperation of high school seniors. During kindergarten and the first few years of elementary school, direct teaching of classroom rules and procedures is important. For children in the middle elementary years, many classroom routines have become relatively automatic, but new procedures for a particular activity may have to be taught directly, and the entire system still needs monitoring and maintenance. Toward the end of elementary school, some students begin to test and defy authority. The management challenges at this stage are to deal productively with these disruptions and to motivate students who are becoming less concerned about teachers' opinions and more interested in their social lives. By the end of high school, the challenges are to manage the curriculum, fit academic material to students' interests and abilities, and help students become more self-managing (Emmer & Evertson, 2013; Evertson & Emmer, 2013).

The Goals of Classroom Management

STOP & THINK You are interviewing for a job in a great district—it is known for innovation. The assistant principal looks at you for a moment and then asks, "What is classroom management?" How would you answer? •

The aim of **classroom management** is to maintain a positive, productive learning environment. But order for its own sake is an empty goal. As we discussed in Chapter 7, it is unethical to use classroom management techniques just to keep students docile and quiet. What, then, is the point of working so hard to manage classrooms? There are at least three reasons, discussed next.

ACCESS TO LEARNING. Each classroom activity has its own rules for participation. Sometimes these rules are clearly stated by the teacher, but often they are implicit and unstated. Teacher and students may not even be aware that they are following different rules for different activities (Berliner, 1983). For example, in a reading group, students may have to raise their hands to make a comment, but in a show-and-tell circle in the same class, they may simply have to catch the teacher's eye.

As we saw in Chapter 6, the rules defining who can talk, what they can talk about, when and to whom they can talk, and how long they can talk are often called **participation structures**. To participate successfully in a given activity, students must understand the participation structure. Some students, however, seem to come to school less able to participate than others. The participation structures they learn at home in interactions with siblings, parents, and other adults do not match the participation structures of school activities (Cazden, 2001). What can we conclude? To reach the first goal of good classroom management—giving all students access to learning—you must make sure everyone knows how to participate in class activities. The key is awareness. What are your rules and expectations? Are they understandable, given your students' cultural backgrounds and home experiences? What unspoken rules or values may be operating? Are you clearly signaling appropriate ways to participate? Some students, particularly those with behavioral and emotional challenges, may require direct teaching and practicing of important behaviors (Emmer & Stough, 2001).

MORE TIME FOR LEARNING. I once used a stopwatch to time the commercials during a TV quiz show. I was amazed to find that half of the program was devoted to commercials. Actually, very little quizzing took place. If you used a similar approach in classrooms, timing all the different activities throughout the day, you might be surprised by how little actual teaching takes place. Many minutes each day are lost through interruptions, disruptions, late starts, and rough transitions. Obviously, students can only learn what they encounter. Almost every study examining time and learning has found a significant relationship between time spent on content and student learning (C. S. Weinstein & Novodvorsky, 2015). A school year seems like a long time, right? Let's say a typical high school class is mandated by the state to meet 126 hours per school year (180 days times 42 minutes a day). When we consider student absences and school interruptions such as assembly programs, those 126 hours are more like 119 hours available for learning. Thus, one important goal of classroom management is to expand the sheer number of minutes *available* for learning.

But in every class, elementary or secondary, there are interruptions, clerical tasks, collecting and distributing materials, taking roll, and dealing with behavior problems, so the actual time devoted to instruction is typically decreased by about 20%. Now we are left with 96 hours. Good classroom management can take back some of those hours for teaching, so that more *instructional time* can be captured.

Simply making more time for instruction will not automatically lead to achievement. To be valuable, time must be used effectively. As you saw in the chapters on cognitive learning, the way students process information is a central factor in what they learn and remember. Basically, students will learn what they practice and think about. Time spent actively involved in specific learning tasks often is called **engaged time**, or sometimes **time on task**—we can estimate this to be about 80% of the instructional time.

Video 13.1
In this video, sixth-grade teacher Robert Wimberly talks about his strategies for beginning every school day. The classroom is ready for students before they arrive, and they have a planned activity to work on the moment they enter the classroom.

ENHANCEDetext *video example*

PODCAST 13.1
With her colleague and friend, Carol Weinstein, textbook author Anita Woolfolk wrote a chapter for researchers and teachers about how beliefs affect classroom management. Here she talks about how teachers and students may have beliefs that get in the way of good classroom relationships.

ENHANCEDetext *podcast*

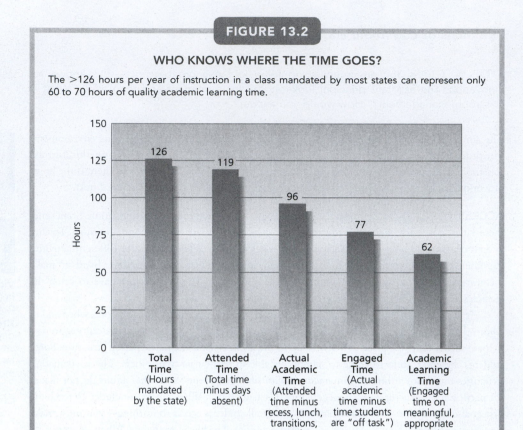

FIGURE 13.2

WHO KNOWS WHERE THE TIME GOES?

The >126 hours per year of instruction in a class mandated by most states can represent only 60 to 70 hours of quality academic learning time.

Bar	Value
Total Time (Hours mandated by the state)	126
Attended Time (Total time minus days absent)	119
Actual Academic Time (Attended time minus recess, lunch, transitions, etc.)	96
Engaged Time (Actual academic time minus time students are "off task")	77
Academic Learning Time (Engaged time on meaningful, appropriate tasks)	62

Source: From Middle and Secondary Classroom Management *(5th ed.), by C. S. Weinstein and I. Novodvorsky, New York: McGraw-Hill. Copyright © 2015 by The McGraw-Hill Companies, p. 182. Adapted with permission of The McGraw-Hill Companies, Inc.*

Again, however, engaged time doesn't guarantee learning. Students may be struggling with material that is too difficult, or they may be using the wrong learning strategies. When students are working with a high rate of success—really learning and understanding—we call the time spent **academic learning time**; again, we can estimate this to be about 80% of the time they are engaged. Now we are down to 62 hours. Figure 13.2 shows how the 126+ hours of time mandated for a high school class in most states can become only about 62 hours of quality academic learning time for a typical student. So the third goal of class management is to increase academic learning time by keeping students *actively engaged in worthwhile, appropriate learning activities*.

Getting students engaged in learning early in their school careers can make a big difference. Several studies have shown that teachers' rating of students' on-task, persistent engagement in first grade predicts achievement test score gains and grades through fourth grade, as well as the decision to drop out of high school (Fredricks, Blumenfeld, & Paris, 2004).

MANAGEMENT FOR SELF-MANAGEMENT. The third goal of any management system is to help students become better able to manage themselves. If teachers focus on student compliance, they will spend much of the teaching/learning time monitoring and correcting. Students come to perceive the purpose of school as just following rules, not constructing deep understanding of academic knowledge. And complex learning structures such as cooperative or problem-based learning require student *self-management*. Compliance with rules is not enough to make these learning structures work (McCaslin & Good, 1998).

The movement from demanding obedience to teaching self-regulation and self-control is a fundamental shift in discussions of classroom management today (Evertson & Weinstein, 2006).

Tom Savage (1999) says simply, "the most fundamental purpose of discipline is the development of self-control. Academic knowledge and technological skill will be of little consequence if those who possess them lack self-control" (p. 11). Through self-control, students demonstrate responsibility—the ability to fulfill their own needs without interfering with the rights and needs of others (Glasser, 1990). Students learn self-control by making choices and dealing with the consequences, setting goals and priorities, managing time, collaborating to learn, mediating disputes and making peace, and developing trusting relations with trustworthy teachers and classmates (Bear, 2005; Rogers & Freiberg, 1994).

Encouraging **self-management** requires extra time, but teaching students how to take responsibility is an investment well worth the effort. There is good evidence for this claim. Nancy Perry and Rebecca Collie (2011) compared a preservice preparation program that instructed student teachers about how to coach their students to be self-regulated learners with other programs that did not emphasize self-regulation. The student teachers who developed self-regulation knowledge and skills were more confident, less stressed, and more engaged during their student teaching compared to other prospective teachers who did not learn how to help their students to become self-regulated. This makes sense—if you teach your students to manage their own behavior and learning, you should have fewer management problems, less stress, and more time to teach, which would support your growing sense of teacher efficacy. When elementary and secondary teachers have very effective class management systems but neglect to set student self-management as a goal, their students often find that they have trouble working independently after they graduate from these "well-managed" classes.

CREATING A POSITIVE LEARNING ENVIRONMENT

When making plans for your class, much of what you have already learned in this book should prove helpful. You know, for example, that problems are prevented when individual variations such as those discussed in Chapters 2 through 6 are taken into account in instructional planning. Sometimes students become disruptive because the work assigned is too difficult. And students who are bored by lessons well below their ability levels may find more exciting activities to fill their time.

In one sense, teachers prevent discipline problems whenever they make an effort to motivate students. A student engaged in learning is usually not involved in a clash with the teacher or other students at the same time. All plans for motivating students are steps toward preventing problems.

Some Research Results

What else can teachers do? For several years, educational psychologists at the University of Texas at Austin studied classroom management quite thoroughly (Emmer, Evertson, & Anderson, 1980; Emmer & Gerwels, 2006; Emmer & Stough, 2001). Their general approach was to study a large number of classrooms, making frequent observations during the first weeks of school and less frequent visits later in the year. After several months, the researchers noted dramatic differences among the classes. Some classes had very few management problems, whereas others had many. The most- and least-effective teachers were identified on the basis of the quality of classroom management and student achievement later in the year.

Next, the researchers looked at their observation records of the first weeks of class to see how the effective teachers *got started,* and they made other comparisons between the teachers who ultimately had harmonious, high-achieving classes and those whose classes were fraught with problems. On the basis of these comparisons, the researchers developed management principles. They then taught these principles to a new group of teachers, and the results were quite positive. Teachers who applied the principles had fewer problems; their students spent more time learning and less time disrupting; and achievement was higher. The findings of these studies formed the basis for two books on classroom management (Emmer & Evertson, 2009, 2013; Evertson & Emmer, 2013). Many of the ideas in the following pages are from these books.

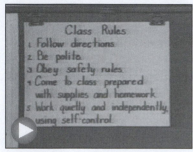

Video 13.2
In this video, a first-grade teacher introduces the classroom rules to her students. Observe the discussion about the purpose of rules, and notice that the rules are stated positively. What is the value of revisiting the rules after the first week of school?

ENHANCEDetext *video example*

Routines and Rules Required

STOP & THINK What are the three or four most important rules you will have for your classroom? •

At the elementary school level, teachers must lead 20 to 30 students of varying abilities through many different activities each day. Without efficient rules and procedures, a great deal of time is wasted dealing with the same questions and issues over and over. "My pencil broke. How can I do my math?" "I'm finished with my experiment. What should I do now?" "Carlos tripped me!" "I left my homework in my locker."

At the secondary school level, teachers must meet daily with more than 100 students who use dozens of materials and often change rooms. Secondary school students are also more likely to challenge teachers' authority. The effective managers studied by Emmer, Evertson, and their colleagues had planned *procedures* and *rules* for coping with these situations.

ROUTINES AND PROCEDURES. How will materials and assignments be distributed and collected? Under what conditions can students leave the room? How will grades be determined? What are the special routines for handling equipment and supplies in science, art, or vocational classes? **Procedures and routines** describe how activities are accomplished in classrooms, but they are seldom written down; they are simply the ways of getting things done in class. Carol Weinstein and her colleagues (Weinstein & Novodvorsky, 2015; Weinstein & Romano, 2015) suggest that teachers establish routines to cover the following areas:

1. *Administrative routines,* such as taking attendance
2. *Student movement,* such as entering and leaving or going to the bathroom
3. *Housekeeping,* such as watering plants or storing personal items
4. *Lesson-running routines,* such as how to collect assignments or return homework
5. *Interactions between teacher and student,* such as how to get the teacher's attention when help is needed
6. *Talk among students,* such as giving help or socializing

You might use these six areas as a framework for planning your class routines. The *Guidelines: Establishing Class Routines* should help you as you plan.

RULES. Unlike routines, rules are often written down and posted, because **rules** specify expected and forbidden actions in the class. They are the dos and don'ts of classroom life. In establishing rules, you should consider what kind of atmosphere you want to create. What student behaviors will help you teach effectively? What limits do the students need to guide their behavior? The rules you set should be consistent with school rules and also in keeping with principles of learning. For example, we know from the research on small-group learning that students benefit when they explain work to peers. They learn as they teach. A rule that forbids students to help each other may be inconsistent with good learning principles. Or a rule that says, "No erasures when writing" may make students focus more on preventing mistakes than on communicating clearly in their writing (Burden, 1995; Emmer & Stough, 2001; C. S. Weinstein & Romano, 2015).

Rules should be positive and observable (raise your hand to be recognized). Having a few general rules that cover many specifics is better than listing all the dos and don'ts. But, if specific actions are forbidden, such as leaving the campus or smoking in the bathrooms, then a rule should make this clear (Emmer & Gerwels, 2006).

RULES FOR ELEMENTARY SCHOOL. Evertson and Emmer (2013) give four examples of general rules for elementary school classes:

1. *Respect and be polite to all people.* Give clear explanations of what you mean by "polite," including not hitting, fighting, or teasing. Examples of polite behavior include waiting your

GUIDELINES
Establishing Class Routines

Determine procedures for student upkeep of desks, classroom equipment, and other facilities.

Examples

1. Set aside a cleanup time each day or once a week in self-contained classes.
2. Demonstrate and have students practice how to push chairs under the desk, take and return materials stored on shelves, sharpen pencils, use the sink or water fountain, assemble lab equipment, and so on.
3. Put a rotating monitor in charge of equipment or materials.

Decide how students will be expected to enter and leave the room.

Examples

1. Have a procedure for students to follow as soon as they enter the room. Some teachers have a standard assignment ("Have your homework out and be checking it over").
2. Inform students under what conditions they can leave the room, and make sure they understand when they need to ask for permission to do so.
3. Tell students how they should gain admission to the room if they are late.
4. Set up a policy about class dismissal. Many teachers require students to be in their seats and quiet before they can leave at the end of class. The teacher, not the bell, dismisses class.

Establish signals for getting students' attention, and teach them to your students.

Examples

1. In the classroom, flick the lights on and off, sound a chord on a piano or recorder, sound a bell like the "ring bell for service" at a sales counter, move to the podium and stare silently at the class, use a phrase like "Eyes, please," take out your grade book, or move to the front of the class.

2. In the halls, raise a hand, clap once, or use some other signal to indicate "Stop."
3. On the playground, raise a hand or whistle to indicate "Line up."

Set routines for student participation in class.

Examples

1. Decide whether you will have students raise their hands for permission to speak or simply require that they wait until the speaker has finished.
2. Determine a signal to indicate that you want everyone to respond at once. Some teachers raise a cupped hand to their ear. Others preface the question with "Everyone."
3. Make sure you are clear about differences in procedures for different activities: reading group, learning center, discussion, teacher presentation, seatwork, video watching, peer learning group, library, and so forth.
4. Establish how many students at a time can be at the pencil sharpener, teacher's desk, learning center, sink, bookshelves, reading corner, or bathroom.

Determine how you will communicate, collect, and return assignments.

Examples

1. Establish a place for listing assignments. Some teachers reserve a particular corner of the board for listing assignments. Others write assignments in colored chalk. For younger students, it may be better to prepare assignment sheets or folders, color-coding them for the math workbook, reading packet, and science kit.
2. Be clear about how and where assignments should be collected. Some teachers collect assignments in a box or bin; others have a student collect work while they introduce the next activity.

For ideas about involving students in developing rules and procedures, see educationworld.com/a_lesson/lesson/lesson274.shtml

---

turn, saying "please" and "thank you," and not calling names. This applies to behavior toward adults (including substitute teachers) and peers.

2. *Be prompt and prepared.* This rule highlights the importance of the academic work in the class. Being prompt includes the beginning of the day as well as transitions between activities.
3. *Listen quietly while others are speaking.* This applies to the teacher and other students, in both large-class lessons and small-group discussions.
4. *Obey all school rules.* This reminds students that all school rules apply in your classroom. Then students cannot claim, for example, that they thought it was okay to chew gum or listen to an iPod in your class, even though these are against school rules, "because you never made a rule against it for us."

Whatever the rule, students need to be taught the behaviors that the rule includes and excludes. Examples, practice, and discussion will be needed before learning is complete.

As you've seen, different activities often require different rules. This can be confusing for elementary students until they have thoroughly learned all the rules. To prevent confusion, you might consider making signs that list the rules for each activity. Then, before the activity, you can post the appropriate sign as a reminder. This provides clear and consistent cues about participation structures, so all students, not just the "well behaved," know what is expected. Of course, you'll need to explain and discuss these rules before the signs can have their full effect.

RULES FOR SECONDARY SCHOOL. Emmer and Evertson (2009) suggest six examples of rules for secondary students:

1. *Bring all needed materials to class.* The teacher must specify the type of pen, pencil, paper, notebook, texts, and so on.
2. *Be in your seat and ready to work when the bell rings.* Many teachers combine this rule with a standard beginning procedure for the class, such as a warm-up exercise on the board or a requirement that students have paper with a proper heading ready when the bell rings.
3. *Respect and be polite to all people.* This covers fighting, verbal abuse, and general trouble-making. All people includes the teacher.
4. *Listen and stay seated while someone else is speaking.* This applies when the teacher or other students are talking.
5. *Respect other people's property.* This means property belonging to the school, the teacher, or other students.
6. *Obey all school rules.* As with the elementary class rules, this covers many behaviors and situations, so you do not have to repeat every school rule for your class. It also reminds the students that you will be monitoring them inside and outside your class. Make sure you know all the school rules. Some secondary students are very adept at convincing teachers that their misbehavior "really isn't against the rules."

These rules are more than ways to maintain order. In their study of 34 middle school classrooms, Lindsay Matsumura and her colleagues (2008) found that having explicit rules about respecting others in the classroom predicted the number of students who participated in class discussion, so it seems clear that respect is a gateway to student engagement with the academic material and class dialogue that supports learning.

CONSEQUENCES. As soon as you decide on your rules and procedures, you must consider what you will do when a student breaks a rule or does not follow a procedure. It is too late to make this decision after the rule has been broken. For many infractions, the logical consequence is going back to "do it right." Students who run in the hall may have to return to where they started and walk properly. Incomplete papers can be redone. Materials left out should be put back. You can use natural or logical consequences to support social/emotional development by doing the following (M. J. Elias & Schwab, 2006):

- Separate the deed from the doer in your response. The problem is the behavior, not the student.
- Emphasize to students that they have the power to choose their actions and so avoid losing control.
- Encourage student reflection, self-evaluation, and problem solving. Avoid teacher lecturing.
- Help students identify and give a rationale for what they could do differently next time in a similar situation.

The main point here is that decisions about penalties (and rewards) must be made early on, so students know before they break a rule or use the wrong procedure what this will mean for them. I encourage my student teachers to get a copy of the school rules and their cooperating teacher's rules, and then plan their own. Sometimes, consequences are more complicated. In their case studies of four expert elementary school teachers, C. S. Weinstein and Romano (2015) found that the teachers' negative consequences fell into seven categories, as shown in Table 13.1.

WHO SETS THE RULES AND CONSEQUENCES? In the first chapter, I described Ken, an expert teacher who worked with his students to establish a students' "Bill of Rights" instead of defining rules. These "rights" cover most situations that might require a "rule" and help the students

TABLE 13.1 • Seven Categories of Penalties for Students

1. *Expressions of disappointment.* If students like and respect their teacher, then a serious, sorrowful expression of disappointment may cause students to stop and think about their behavior.
2. *Loss of privileges.* Students can lose free time. If they have not completed homework, for example, they can be required to do it during a free period or recess.
3. *Time-Out: Exclusion from the group.* Students who distract their peers or fail to cooperate can be separated from the group until they are ready to cooperate. Some teachers give a student a pass for 10 to 15 minutes. The student must go to another class or study hall, where the other students and teachers ignore the offending student for that time.
4. *Written reflections on the problem.* Students can write in journals, write essays about what they did and how it affected others, or write letters of apology—if this is appropriate. Another possibility is to ask students to describe objectively what they did; then the teacher and the student can sign and date this statement. These records are available if parents or administrators need evidence of the students' behavior.
5. *Visits to the principal's office.* Expert teachers tend to use this penalty rarely, but they do use it when the situation warrants. Some schools require students to be sent to the office for certain offenses, such as fighting. If you tell a student to go to the office and the student refuses, you might call the office saying the student has been sent. Then the student has the choice of either going to the office or facing the principal's penalty for "disappearing" on the way.
6. *Detentions.* Detentions can be very brief meetings after school, during a free period, or at lunch. The main purpose is to talk about what has happened. (In high school, detentions are often used as punishments; suspensions and expulsions are available as more extreme measures.)
7. *Contacting parents.* If problems become a repeated pattern, most teachers contact the student's family. This is done to seek support for helping the student, not to blame the parents or punish the student.

Source: From Elementary Classroom Management (6th ed.), pp. 298–301, by C. S. Weinstein and M. E. Romano, New York: McGraw-Hill. Copyright © 2015 by The McGraw-Hill Companies. Adapted with permission of The McGraw-Hill Companies, Inc.

move toward the goal of becoming self-managing. In a recent class, the Bill of Rights included the rights to whisper when the teacher is not talking, be treated politely, have a 2-minute break between working periods, make choices about the day's schedule, have privacy and not have people take your things, and chew gum without blowing bubbles, among several others. If you are going to involve students in setting rules or creating a constitution, you may need to wait until you have established a sense of community in your classroom. Before students can contribute meaningfully to the class rules, they need to trust the teacher and the situation (M. J. Elias & Schwab, 2006).

Developing rights and responsibilities rather than rules makes an important point to students. "Teaching children that something is wrong because there is a rule against it is not the same as teaching them that there is a rule against it because it is wrong, and helping them to understand why this is so" (C. S. Weinstein, 1999, p. 154). Students should understand that the rules are developed so that everyone can work and learn together. I might add that when Ken has had some very difficult classes, he and his students have had to establish some "laws" that protect students' rights, as you can see in Table 13.2 on the next page.

Another kind of planning that affects the learning environment is designing the physical arrangement of the class furniture, materials, and learning tools.

Planning Spaces for Learning

STOP & THINK Think back over all the rooms in all the schools you have attended. Which ones stand out as inviting or exciting? Which ones were cold and empty? Did one teacher have a design that let students do different things in various parts of the room? •

Spaces for learning should invite and support the activities you plan for your classes, and they should respect the inhabitants of the space. This respect begins at the door for young children by helping them identify their classroom. One school that has won awards for its architecture paints each classroom door a different bright color, so young children can find their "home" (Herbert, 1998).

TABLE 13.2 • **Laws to Protect Our Rights**

1. Follow directions the first time.
2. Speak nicely, be courteous, and respect other people, their feelings, and their things. Follow the Bill of Rights.
3. Laugh at the right time for the right time.
4. Respect others' right to learn. Do not distract others. Don't be nosy. Don't yell. Remember to get quiet at countdown.
5. Talk at the right times with the right tone of voice and volume.
6. Transitions and movements are calm, quiet, careful, and elegant.
7. Follow all classroom and school procedures, like: bathroom; pencil; lunch and recess; morning; dismissal; and . . .

Source: From Elementary Classroom Management (6th ed.), p. 103, by C. S. Weinstein and M. E. Romano, New York: McGraw-Hill. Copyright © 2015 by The McGraw-Hill Companies. Adapted with permission of The McGraw-Hill Companies, Inc.

Connect and Extend to PRAXIS II®

Classroom Space (I, C4)
The physical organization of a class has an effect on student behavior and learning. Describe how the physical layout of classrooms can affect the learning environment. Apply principles of classroom organization to enhance learning and minimize disruption.

Once inside, spaces can be created that invite quiet reading, group collaboration, or independent research. If students are to use materials, they should be able to reach them. In an interview with Marge Scherer (1999), Herb Kohl describes how he creates a positive environment in his classes.

> What I do is put up the most beautiful things I know—posters, games, puzzles, challenges—and let the children know these are provocations. These are ways of provoking them into using their minds. You have to create an environment that makes kids walk in and say, "I really want to see what's here. I would really like to look at this." (p. 9)

In terms of classroom arrangement, there are two basic ways of organizing space: personal territories and interest areas.

PERSONAL TERRITORIES. Can the physical setting influence teaching and learning in classrooms organized by territories? A front seat location does seem to increase participation for students who are predisposed to speak in class, but a seat in the back will make it more difficult to participate and easier to sit back and daydream (Woolfolk & Brooks, 1983). The **action zone** where participation is greatest may be in other areas such as on one side or near a particular learning center (T. L. Good, 1983a; Lambert, 1994). To "spread the action around," C. S. Weinstein and Romano (2015) suggest that teachers move around the room when possible, establish eye contact with and direct questions to students seated far away, and vary the seating so the same students are not always consigned to the back.

Horizontal rows share many of the advantages of the traditional row and column arrangements. Both are useful for independent seatwork and teacher, student, or media presentations; they encourage students to focus on the presenter and simplify housekeeping. Horizontal rows also permit students to work more easily in pairs. However, this is a poor arrangement for large-group discussion.

Clusters of four or circle arrangements are best for student interaction. Circles are especially useful for discussions but still allow for independent seatwork. Clusters permit students to talk, help one another, share materials, and work on group tasks. Both arrangements, however, are poor for whole-group presentations and may make class management more difficult.

The *fishbowl or stack* special formation, where students sit close together near the focus of attention (the back row may even be standing), should be used only for short periods of time, because it is not comfortable and can lead to discipline problems. On the other hand, the fishbowl can create a feeling of group cohesion and is helpful when the teacher wants students to watch a demonstration, brainstorm on a class problem, or see a small visual aid.

INTEREST AREAS. The design of interest areas can influence the way the areas are used by students. For example, working with a classroom teacher, Carol Weinstein (1977) made changes in interest areas that helped the teacher meet her objectives of having more girls involved in the science center and having all students experiment more with a variety of manipulative materials. In a second study, changes in a library corner led to more involvement in literature activities throughout the class (Morrow & Weinstein, 1986). If you design interest areas for your class, keep the *Guidelines: Designing Learning Spaces* in mind.

GUIDELINES
Designing Learning Spaces

Note the fixed features, and plan accordingly.

Examples

1. Remember that the audiovisual center and computers need electrical outlets.
2. Keep art supplies near the sink, small-group work by a blackboard.

Create easy access to materials and a well-organized place to store them.

Examples

1. Make sure materials are easy to reach and visible to students.
2. Have enough shelves so that materials need not be stacked.

Provide students with clean, convenient surfaces for studying.

Examples

1. Put bookshelves next to the reading area, games by the game table.
2. Prevent fights by avoiding crowded work spaces.

Avoid dead spaces and "racetracks."

Examples

1. Don't have all the interest areas around the outside of the room, leaving a large dead space in the middle.
2. Avoid placing a few items of furniture right in the middle of this large space, creating a "racetrack" around the furniture.

Arrange things so you can see your students and they can see all instructional presentations.

Examples

1. Make sure you can see over partitions.
2. Design seating so that students can see instruction without moving their chairs or desks.

Make sure work areas are private and quiet.

Examples

1. Make sure there are no tables or work areas in the middle of traffic lanes; a person should not have to pass through one area to get to another.
2. Keep noisy activities as far as possible from quiet ones. Increase the feeling of privacy by placing partitions, such as bookcases or pegboards, between areas or within large areas.

Provide choices and flexibility.

Examples

1. Establish private cubicles for individual work, open tables for group work, and cushions on the floor for whole-class meetings.
2. Give students a place to keep their personal belongings. This is especially important if students don't have personal desks.

Try new arrangements; then evaluate and improve.

Examples

1. Have a "2-week arrangement"; then evaluate.
2. Enlist the aid of your students. They have to live in the room, too, and designing a classroom can be a very challenging educational experience.

For more ideas on classroom design, see edfacilities.org/rl/ classroom_design.cfm

---

Personal territories and interest areas are not mutually exclusive; many teachers use a design that combines these types of organization. Individual students' desks—their territories—are placed in the center, with interest areas in the back or around the periphery of the room. This allows the flexibility needed for both large- and small-group activities. Figure 13.3 on the next page shows a secondary classroom that has individual desks (personal territories), but still works well for teacher presentations and demonstrations, small-group work, computer interactions, and lab activities.

Getting Started: The First Weeks of Class

Determining a room design, rules, and procedures are the first steps toward having a well-managed class, but how do effective teachers gain students' cooperation in those early critical days and weeks? One study carefully analyzed the first weeks' activities of effective and ineffective elementary teachers, and found striking differences. Let's spend some time in the next pages examining these important differences (Emmer, Evertson, & Anderson, 1980).

EFFECTIVE MANAGERS FOR ELEMENTARY STUDENTS. In the *effective teachers' classrooms*, the very first day was well organized. Nametags were ready. There was something interesting for each child to do right away. Materials were set up. The teachers had planned carefully to avoid any last-minute tasks that might take them away from their students. These teachers dealt with the

FIGURE 13.3

A SECONDARY CLASSROOM ARRANGEMENT

This chemistry teacher has designed a space that allows teacher presentations and demonstrations, small-group work, computer interactions, and lab activities without requiring constant rearrangements.

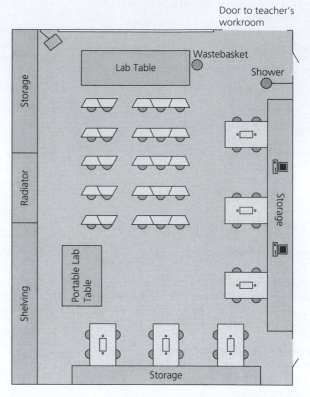

Source: Reprinted with permission from Middle and Secondary Classroom Management: Lessons from Research and Practice (5th ed.), by C. S. Weinstein & I. Novodvorsky. Published by McGraw-Hill, p. 35. Copyright © 2015 by McGraw-Hill. Reprinted with permission of the McGraw-Hill Companies, Inc.

children's pressing concerns first. "Where do I put my things?" "How do I pronounce my teacher's name?" "Can I whisper to my neighbor?" "Where is the bathroom?" The effective teachers were explicit about their expectations. They had a workable, easily understood set of rules and taught the students the most important rules right away. They taught the rules like any other subject—with lots of explanation, examples, and practice.

Throughout the first weeks, the effective managers continued to spend quite a bit of time teaching rules and procedures. Some used guided practice to teach procedures; others used rewards to shape behavior. Most taught students to respond to a bell or some other signal to gain their attention. These teachers worked with the class as a whole on enjoyable academic activities. They did not rush to get students into small groups or to start them in readers. This whole-class work gave the teachers a better opportunity to continue monitoring all students' learning of the rules and procedures. Misbehavior was stopped quickly and firmly, but not harshly.

In the *poorly managed classrooms,* the first weeks were quite different. Rules were not workable; they were either too vague or very complicated. For example, one teacher made a rule that students should "be in the right place at the right time." Students were not told what this meant, so their behavior could not be guided by the rule. Neither positive nor negative behaviors had clear, consistent consequences. After students broke a rule, ineffective managers might give a vague criticism, such as "Some of my children are too noisy," or issue a warning, but not follow through with the threatened consequence.

In the poorly managed classes, procedures for accomplishing routine tasks varied from day to day and were never taught or practiced. Instead of dealing with these obvious needs, ineffective managers spent time on procedures that could have waited. For example, one teacher had the class practice for a fire drill the first day, but left unexplained other procedures that would be needed every day. Students wandered around the classroom aimlessly and had to ask each other what they should be doing. Often the students talked to one another because they had nothing productive to do. Ineffective teachers frequently left the room. Many became absorbed in paperwork or in helping just one student. They had not made plans for how to deal with late-arriving students or interruptions. One ineffective manager tried to teach students to respond to a bell as a signal for attention, but later let the students ignore it. All in all, the first weeks in these classrooms were disorganized and filled with surprises for teachers and students alike.

EFFECTIVE MANAGERS FOR SECONDARY STUDENTS. What about getting started in a secondary school class? It appears that many of the differences between effective and ineffective elementary school teachers are the same at the secondary level. Again, *effective managers* focus on establishing rules, procedures, and expectations on the first day of class. These standards for academic work and class behavior are clearly communicated to students and consistently enforced during the first weeks of class. Student behavior is closely monitored, and infractions of the rules are dealt with quickly. In classes with lower-ability students, work cycles are shorter; students are not required to spend long, unbroken periods on one type of activity. Instead, during each period, they are moved smoothly through several different tasks. In general, effective teachers carefully follow each student's progress, so students cannot avoid work without facing consequences (Emmer & Evertson, 1982).

With all this close monitoring and consistent enforcement of the rules, you may wonder if effective secondary teachers have to be grim and humorless. Not necessarily. The effective managers in one classic study also smiled and joked more with their students (Moskowitz & Hayman, 1976). As any experienced teacher can tell you, there is much more to smile about when the class is cooperative. For more ideas about getting started on the first day of class, see the helpful book by Harry and Rosemary Wong, *The First Days of School: How To Be an Effective Teacher* (H. Wong & Wong, 2009).

ENHANCEDetext *self-check*

MAINTAINING A GOOD ENVIRONMENT FOR LEARNING

A good start is just that—a beginning. Effective teachers build on this beginning. They maintain their management system by preventing problems and keeping students engaged in productive learning activities. We have discussed several ways to keep students engaged. In Chapter 12, on motivation, for example, we considered stimulating curiosity, relating lessons to student interests, establishing learning goals instead of performance goals, and having positive expectations. What else can teachers do?

Encouraging Engagement

STOP & THINK What activities keep you completely engaged—the time just seems to disappear? What is it about those activities that keeps you focused? •

In general, as teacher supervision increases, students' engaged time also increases. One study found that elementary students working directly with a teacher were on task 97% of the time, but students working on their own were on task only 57% of the time (Frick, 1990). This does not mean that

Connect and Extend to PRAXIS II®

Promoting Student Engagement (I, C4)
A principle of educational psychology is that the more students are cognitively engaged in an activity, the more they are likely to learn. What tactics can teachers employ to maximize their students' cognitive engagement during learning tasks?

GUIDELINES
Keeping Students Engaged

Make basic work requirements clear.

Examples

1. Specify and post the routine work requirements for headings, paper size, pen or pencil use, and neatness.
2. Establish and explain rules about late or incomplete work and absences. If a pattern of incomplete work begins to develop, deal with it early; speak with parents if necessary.
3. Make due dates reasonable, and stick to them unless the student has a very good excuse for lateness.

Communicate the specifics of assignments.

Examples

1. With younger students, have a routine procedure for giving assignments, such as writing them on the board in the same place each day. With older students, assignments may be dictated, posted, or given in a syllabus.
2. Remind students of upcoming assignments.
3. With complicated assignments, give students a sheet describing what to do, what resources are available, due dates, and so on. Older students should also be told your grading criteria.
4. Demonstrate how to do the assignment, do the first few questions together, or provide a sample worksheet.

Monitor work in progress.

Examples

1. When you give an assignment in class, make sure each student gets started correctly. If you check only students who raise their hands for help, you will miss those who think they know what to do but don't really understand, those who are too shy to ask for help, and those who don't plan to do the work at all.
2. Check progress periodically. In discussions, make sure everyone has a chance to respond.

Give frequent academic feedback.

Examples

1. Elementary students should get papers back the day after they are handed in.
2. Good work can be displayed in the classroom, and graded papers sent home to parents each week.
3. Students of all ages can keep records of grades, projects completed, and extra credits earned.
4. For older students, break up long-term assignments into several phases, giving feedback at each point.

For more ideas, see pages.shanti.virginia.edu/engagedlearning/ and trc.virginia.edu/resources/engaging-students-from-beginning-to-end-2/

Video 13.3
A mathematics lesson about graphing comes alive for the students in this video. They find it easy to stay on task as they taste jellybeans and record their preferences. They determine the class's most popular flavor by creating a class graph of favorite flavors.

ENHANCEDetext *video example*

teachers should eliminate independent work for students. It simply means that this type of activity usually requires careful planning and monitoring.

When the task provides continuous cues for the student about what to do next, involvement will be greater. Activities with clear steps are likely to be more absorbing, because one step leads naturally to the next. When students have all the materials they need to complete a task, they tend to stay involved. If their curiosity is piqued, students will be motivated to continue seeking an answer. And, as you now know, students will be more engaged if they are involved in authentic tasks—activities that have connections to real life. Also, activities are more engaging when the level of challenge is higher and when students' interests are incorporated into the tasks (Emmer & Gerwels, 2006).

Of course, teachers can't supervise every student all the time or rely on curiosity to keep students motivated. Something else must keep students working on their own. In their study of elementary and secondary teachers, Evertson, Emmer, and their colleagues found that effective class managers at both levels had well-planned systems for encouraging students to manage their own work (Emmer & Evertson, 2009, 2013; Evertson & Emmer, 2013). The *Guidelines: Keeping Students Engaged* are based on their findings.

Prevention Is the Best Medicine

The ideal way to manage problems, of course, is to prevent them in the first place. In a classic study, Jacob Kounin (1970) examined classroom management by comparing effective teachers, whose classes were relatively free of problems, with ineffective teachers, whose classes were continually plagued by chaos and disruption. Observing both groups in action, Kounin found that the teachers were not very different in the way they handled discipline *once problems arose*. The difference was that the successful managers were much better at preventing problems. Kounin concluded that effective classroom managers were especially skilled in four areas: "withitness," overlapping activities, group focusing, and movement management. More recent research confirms the importance of these factors (Emmer & Stough, 2001).

WITHITNESS. Withitness means communicating to students that you are aware of everything that is happening in the classroom—that you aren't missing anything. "With-it" teachers seem to have eyes in the back of their heads. They avoid becoming absorbed by distractions or interacting with only a few students, because this encourages the rest of the class to wander. These teachers are always scanning the room, making eye contact with individual students, so the students know they are being monitored (Charles, 2011; C. S. Weinstein & Romano, 2015).

These teachers prevent minor disruptions from becoming major. They also know who instigated the problem, and they make sure they deal with the right people. In other words, they do not make what Kounin called *timing errors* (waiting too long before intervening) or *target errors* (blaming the wrong student and letting the real perpetrators escape responsibility for their behavior).

If two problems occur at the same time, effective managers deal with the more serious one first. For example, a teacher who tells two students to stop whispering but ignores even a brief shoving match at the pencil sharpener communicates a lack of awareness. Students begin to believe they can get away with almost anything if they are clever.

OVERLAPPING AND GROUP FOCUS. Overlapping means keeping track of and supervising several activities at the same time. For example, a teacher may have to check the work of an individual and at the same time keep a small group working by saying, "Right, go on," and stop an incident in another group with a quick "look" or reminder (Burden, 1995; Charles, 2011).

Maintaining a group focus means keeping as many students as possible involved in appropriate class activities and avoiding narrowing in on just one or two students. All students should have something to do during a lesson. For example, the teacher might ask everyone to write the answer to a question, and then call on individuals to respond while the other students compare their answers. Choral responses might be required while the teacher moves around the room to make sure everyone is participating. During a grammar lesson, the teacher might say, "Everyone who thinks the answer is *have run,* hold up the red side of your card. If you think the answer is *has run,* hold up the green side" (Hunter, 1982). This is one way teachers can ensure that all students are involved and that everyone understands the material.

MOVEMENT MANAGEMENT. Movement management means keeping lessons and the group moving at an appropriate (and flexible) pace, with smooth transitions and variety. The effective teacher avoids abrupt transitions, such as announcing a new activity before gaining the students' attention or starting a new activity in the middle of something else. When transitions are abrupt, one third of the class will be doing the new activity, many will be working on the old lesson, several will be asking other students what to do, some will be taking the opportunity to have a little fun, and most will be confused. Another transition problem Kounin noted is the slowdown, or taking too much time to start a new activity. Sometimes teachers give too many directions. Problems also arise when teachers have students work one at a time while the rest of the class waits and watches.

STUDENT SOCIAL SKILLS AS PREVENTION. But what about the students? What can they do? When students lack social and emotional skills such as being able to share materials, read the intentions of others, or handle frustration, classroom management problems often follow. So all efforts to teach social and emotional self-regulation are steps toward preventing management problems. Over the short term, educators can teach and model these skills, and then give students feedback and practice using them in a variety of settings. Over the long term, teachers can help to change attitudes that value aggression over cooperation and compromise (M. J. Elias & Schwab, 2006).

Debra Stipek and her colleagues (1999) describe many ways teachers embed social skills lessons into school subjects and informal discussions. For example, class rules emphasize respect ("there are no stupid questions"); students learn to give "put ups" not "put downs"; the lives of historical figures provide opportunities to discuss choices and how to deal with stresses; and student conflicts become life lessons in relationships. In addition, students are given a Toolbox of Coping Skills that contains concrete objects to be used to address problems. The toolbox includes sticky notes to record student concerns and troubling situations so the incidents can be dealt with at an appropriate time. Exit and U-turn signs remind students that the best strategy may be to "exit" the situation. "Exiting to a safe place, without explanation, is taught as one appropriate face-saving, and possibly life-saving, response" (Stipek et al., 1999, p. 443). Indicators are that students do learn to use these skills.

Caring Relationships: Connections with School

All efforts directed toward building positive relationships with students and creating a classroom community are steps toward preventing management problems. Students respect teachers who maintain their authority without being rigid or harsh, who are fair and honest with them, who make sure they understand the material, who ask if something is wrong when they seem upset, and who use creative instructional practices to "make learning fun." Students also value teachers who show academic and personal caring by acting like real people (not just as teachers), sharing responsibility, minimizing the use of external controls, including everyone, searching for students' strengths, communicating effectively, and showing an interest in their students' lives and pursuits (M. J. Elias & Schwab, 2006; Wentzel, 2002; Woolfolk Hoy & Weinstein, 2006).

Video 13.4
Mr. Wimberly develops positive teacher-student relationships with his sixth graders. Notice his routine of greeting students when the morning bell rings. Observe his command of the classroom and the students' respect for him. How does he encourage students to use their time effectively and develop their own abilities?

ENHANCEDetext *video example*

SCHOOL CONNECTIONS. Students who feel connected with school are happier, more engaged in school work, more self-disciplined, and less likely to be involved in dangerous behaviors such as substance abuse, violence, and early sexual activity (J. Freiberg, 2006; McNeely, Nonnemaker, & Blum, 2002; Ponitz, Rimm-Kaufman, Grimm, & Curby, 2009). In fact, in a synthesis of 119 studies published in either English or German conducted from 1948 to 2004, Jeffrey Cornelius-White (2007) concluded that positive, warm, encouraging relationships with teachers are related to many valuable student outcomes, including higher participation in class, greater critical thinking skills, lower dropout rates, higher self-esteem, increased motivation, less disruptive behavior, and better attendance. When Barbara Bartholomew (2008) asked a veteran special education teacher what keeps students engaged and motivated, the teacher replied without hesitation, "Students need to know that no matter what, you will never give up on them" (p. 58).

An example of respect for students and their lives comes from first-year teacher Esme Codell. "Madame Esme" (the name she preferred) had a morning ritual:

> In the morning, three things happen religiously. I say good morning, real chipper, to every single child and make sure they say good morning back. Then I collect "troubles" in a "Trouble Basket," a big green basket into which the children pantomime unburdening their home worries so they can concentrate on school. Sometimes a kid has no troubles. Sometimes a kid piles it in, and I in turn pantomime bearing the burden. This way, too, I can see what disposition the child is in when he or she enters. Finally, before they can come in, they must give me a word, which I print on a piece of tag board and keep in an envelope. It can be any word, but preferably one that they heard and don't really know or one that is personally meaningful. We go over the words when we do our private reading conferences. (Codell, 2001, p. 30)

If students perceive their schools are competitive places where they are treated differently based on race, gender, or ethnicity, then they are more likely to act out or withdraw altogether. But when they feel that they have choices, that the emphasis is on personal improvement and not comparisons, and that they are respected and supported by teachers, students are more likely to bond with schools (Osterman, 2000). One way of expressing respect and caring is by connecting with students' families and home lives. For example, students in China describe their teachers as high on caring. This may be because Chinese teachers spend quite a bit of time in students' homes, learning about their home life, and offering help outside school. These teachers show respect for the families and cultures of their students by their willingness to visit and to help (Jia et al., 2009; Suldo et al., 2009).

CREATING COMMUNITIES OF CARE FOR ADOLESCENTS. The transition to high school is a particularly important time to maintain caring teacher–student relationships. Students have more teachers and fewer close relationships, just at a time when emotional, social, and academic stresses are increasing. One diverse urban school with more than 2,000 students confronted this problem by creating small communities of care. These were interdisciplinary teams of students and teachers who shared common interests and participated in a Freshman Focus class during the first 9 weeks of school. The class helped students adjust to high school, get oriented to the building, and

GUIDELINES
Creating Caring Relationships

Get to know students as individuals.

Examples

1. Eat lunch with a different group of student every day.
2. Work with a club, extracurricular activity, or sports group and attend student activities.
3. Show your interest in your students as individuals.
4. Schedule individual conferences with students.

Communicate your respect for students' abilities.

Examples

1. "Model respect for diversity—by expressing admiration for a student's bilingual ability, by commenting enthusiastically about the number of different languages that are represented in the class, and by including examples and content from a variety of cultures" (C. S. Weinstein, Curran, & Tomlinson-Clarke, 2003, p. 272).
2. Comment to students privately about your observations of their performances in extracurricular activities.
3. Encourage students to use personal interests a subject for their writing.
4. Greet students at the door to the class every day.

Keep communications authentic but professional.

Examples

1. Send brief personal notes to students acknowledging a good job on assignments, hard work and persistence, a birthday, or concern about absences. Include a get-well card along with homework sent to a student who is ill.

2. Share some stories from your own life as examples of excitement about a subject, making mistakes (and learning from them), and persistence and overcoming difficulties.
3. Do not friend students on social media, and be very careful about your language and picture postings on all electronic communications—many things can be misinterpreted. Create school-related e-mail accounts that are different from personal accounts.
4. Check with your school policy about sharing personal information such as religion, sexual orientation, or political views.
5. If you are meeting alone with a student, do so in an area visible to others—sadly, teachers today must protect against having their positive relationships with students misinterpreted by others or by the student.

Seek student input and respect it, but don't take it too personally.

Examples

1. Consider a suggestion box or community meetings for younger students.
2. Listen to student concerns and complaints without getting defensive. Ask for suggestions, but also share your rationales for assignments and grades.
3. Ask students directly for anonymous feedback about whether they feel respected and cared for in your class. Use simple questionnaires that don't reveal the identity of the student through handwriting.

develop school skills like taking notes, social skills, and even skills for getting along with parents. The programs led to the development of positive teacher beliefs about students, supportive teacher–student relationships, and the promotion of academic and life skills (Ellerbrock & Kiefer, 2010).

Feeling a sense of belonging in high school is important for all students, but particularly for students who may, because of language or poverty, feel disconnected from the basically middle class culture of most schools (R. I. Chapman et al., 2013). In one study that followed 572 students from ninth grade through high school, Cari Gillen-O'Neel and Andrew Fuligni (2013) found that girls' sense of belonging in school was higher than boys' in ninth grade, but over the high school years, this connection declined for girls but not for boys. One possible reason is that boys participate more often than girls in extracurricular activities such as sports; these activities connect them to the school. So encouraging girls to participate in school activities, including sports, may build a sense of belonging for them. Also, caring teacher–student relationships build belonging, especially for Latino/a girls. In addition, having positive relationships with students appears to support teachers' sense of well-being. When we remember the basic human need for relatedness—the feeling that others care about you described in Chapter 12—we can understand why caring relationships in school would support both students' sense of belonging and teachers' well-being (Spilt, Koomen, & Thijs, 2011).

Students who have a greater sense of belonging feel that school is more enjoyable and useful, no matter what their level of achievement (Gillen-O'Neel & Fuligni, 2013). Teachers can encourage a sense of belonging by emphasizing empathy and social skills, cooperation, responsibility, and kindness, and by applying proactive, positive, preventative classroom management strategies. See the *Guidelines: Creating Caring Relationships* for more ideas, many taken from V. Jones (2015) and M. Marshall (2013).

DEALING WITH DISCIPLINE PROBLEMS

Before we even discuss dealing with discipline problems, remember that every school has policies and procedures for handling behavior problems, especially more serious issues. Make sure you know all these procedures and requirements before you develop your behavior management plan. Also keep in mind that being an effective manager does not mean publicly correcting every minor infraction of the rules. This kind of public attention may actually reinforce the misbehavior, as we saw in Chapter 7. The key is being aware of what is happening and knowing what is important so you can prevent problems.

Stopping Problems Quickly

Most students comply quickly when the teacher gives a *desist* (a "stop doing that") or redirects behavior. But some students are the targets of more than their share of desists. One study found that these disruptive students seldom complied with the first teacher request to stop. Often, the disruptive students responded negatively, leading to an average of four to five cycles of teacher desists and student responses before the student complied (J. R. Nelson & Roberts, 2000). Emmer and Evertson (2009) and Levin and Nolan (2000) suggest seven simple ways to stop misbehavior quickly, moving from least to most intrusive:

- *Make eye contact* with, or move closer to, the offender. Other nonverbal signals, such as pointing to the work students are supposed to be doing, might be helpful. Make sure the student actually stops the inappropriate behavior and gets back to work. If you do not, students will learn to ignore your signals.
- *Try verbal hints* such as "name-dropping" (simply insert the student's name into the lecture), asking the student a question, or making a humorous (not sarcastic) comment such as, "I must be hallucinating. I swear I heard someone shout out an answer, but that can't be because I haven't called on anyone yet!"
- *Ask students* if they are aware of the negative effects of their actions, or send an "I" message, described later in the chapter.
- If they are not performing a class procedure correctly, *remind the students* of the procedure, and have them follow it correctly. You may need to quietly collect a toy, comb, cell phone, or note that is competing with the learning activities, while privately informing the students that their possessions will be returned after class.
- In a calm, unhostile way, ask the student to *state the correct rule or procedure* and then to follow it. Glasser (1969) proposes three questions: "What are you doing? Is it against the rules? What should you be doing?"
- *Tell the student* in a clear, assertive, and unhostile way to stop the misbehavior. (Later in the chapter, we will discuss assertive messages to students in more detail.) If students "talk back," simply repeat your statement.
- *Offer a choice.* For example, when a student continued to call out answers no matter what the teacher tried, the teacher said, "John, you have a choice. Stop calling out answers immediately and begin raising your hand to answer or move your seat to the back of the room and you and I will have a private discussion later. You decide" (Levin & Nolan, 2000, p. 177).

Many teachers prefer the use of *logical consequences,* described earlier, as opposed to penalties. For example, if one student has harmed another, you can require the offending student to make an "apology of action," which includes a verbal apology plus somehow repairing the damage done. This helps offenders develop empathy and social perspective taking as they think about what would be an appropriate "repair" (M. J. Elias & Schwab, 2006).

There is a caution about penalties. Never use lower achievement status (moving to a lower reading group, giving a lower grade, giving excess homework) as a punishment for breaking class rules. These actions should be done only if the benefit of the action outweighs the possible risk of harm. As Carolyn Orange (2000) notes, "Effective, caring teachers would not use low achievement status, grades, or the like as a means of discipline. This strategy is unfair and ineffective. It only serves to alienate the student" (p. 76).

GUIDELINES
Imposing Penalties

Delay the discussion of the situation until you and the students involved are calmer and more objective.

Examples

1. Say calmly to a student, "Sit there and think about what happened. I'll talk to you in a few minutes," or, "I don't like what I just saw. Talk to me during your free period today."
2. Say, "I'm really angry about what just happened. Everybody take out journals; we are going to write about this." After a few minutes of writing, the class can discuss the incident.

Impose penalties privately.

Examples

1. Make arrangements with students privately. Stand firm in enforcing arrangements.
2. Resist the temptation to "remind" students in public that they are not keeping their side of the bargain.
3. Move close to a student who must be disciplined and speak so that only the student can hear.

After imposing a penalty, re-establish a positive relationship with the student immediately.

Examples

1. Send the student on an errand, or ask him or her for help.
2. Compliment the student's work, or give a symbolic "pat on the back" when the student's behavior warrants. Look hard for such an opportunity.

3. For 2 minutes each day for 10 days in a row, have a personal conversation with the student about something of interest to him or her—sports, games, films—make an effort to know what those interests are. This investment in time can pay off by regaining learning time for the student and the entire class.

Set up a graded list of penalties that will fit many occasions.

Example

1. For not turning in homework: (1) receive reminder; (2) receive warning; (3) hand homework in before close of school day; (4) stay after school to finish work; (5) participate in a teacher–student–parent conference to develop an action plan.

Always teach problem-solving strategies along with penalties to help students learn what to do next time (M. J. Elias & Schwab, 2006).

Examples

1. Use Problem Diaries, where students record what they were feeling, identify the problem and their goal, then think of other possible ways to solve the problem and achieve the goal.
2. Try Keep Calm 5–2–5: At the first physical signs of anger, students say to themselves: "Stop. Keep Calm," then take several slow breaths, counting to 5 breathing in, 2 holding breath, and 5 breathing out.

If you must impose penalties, the *Guidelines: Imposing Penalties* give ideas about how to do it. Some of these examples are based on ideas from expert teachers described by C. S. Weinstein and Novodvorsky (2015) and Weinstein and Romano (2015).

Marvin Marshall (2013) has a very interesting perspective on consequences and penalties. His focus is on promoting student responsibility. He suggests that a focus on obedience and teacher-imposed consequences often results in resistance, resentment, cheating, and even defiance, but a focus on responsibility creates classroom community and a culture of learning. He also believes that even though classroom management is the responsibility of the teacher, discipline is really the responsibility of the student. Classroom management is about how things are done in the classroom and involves procedures, routines, and structures—the teachers' responsibility. Discipline is about how people behave and involves self-control and emotional self-regulation—the student's responsibility. Students must discipline themselves to be self-regulated learners and ultimately productive, successful, happy adults.

Of course, anyone who has worked with children or adolescents knows that self-discipline is not automatic—it must be taught and practiced like any other skill. Marshall describes strategies for achieving these goals that focus on (1) communicating in positive terms and using "when–then" contingencies ("When you finish your work, you can listen to your iPod"); (2) offering choices and eliciting consequences from students ("What shall we do about. . . . ?"); and (3) encouraging reflection and self-evaluation. One approach that incorporates these three principles is to teach students a hierarchy of behaviors using explanations and examples. The hierarchy is:

- Level **A**: **A**narchy—Aimless, chaotic.
- Level **B**: **B**ossing/**B**ullying—Breaking laws and making your own standards; obeying only when the enforcer has more power or authority.

- Level **C**: **C**ooperation/**C**onformity—Complies with expectations, conforms to peer influence.
- Level **D**: **D**emocracy—Self-disciplined, initiative, responsibility of your own actions.

The behaviors at level C and D may look the same on the outside, but the difference is the motivation. For example, if a student picks up a piece of trash on the floor because the teacher asks (external motivation), the level is C (cooperation), but if the student picks up the trash without being asked (internal motivation), the level is D (democracy and self-discipline). When students do not act at least at level C or D, the teacher asks the student, "What level was that behavior?" For example:

> *Teacher:* On what level is that behavior?
> *Student:* I don't know!
> *Teacher:* What was the class doing?
> *Student:* Working the problem on the board.
> *Teacher:* So you were making up your own standards. What level is that?
> *Student:* B
> *Teacher:* Thank you.

If the student does not move to at least level C and cooperate, the teacher might ask the student to self-reflect and write an essay that addresses three questions: What did I do? What can I do to prevent it from happening again? What will I do now?

Figure 13.4 summarizes Marshall's model. His book *Discipline Without Stress* *Punishments or Rewards: How Teachers and Parents Promote Responsibility & Learning* (M. Marshall, 2013) has many other strategies to encourage student self-discipline.

Bullying and Cyberbullying

Video 13.5
In this video, a girl describes her experience with bullying in an elementary classroom. Children who are bullies, as well as those who are victims of bullying, are often rejected by their peers.

ENHANCEDetext *video example*

Bullying is a type of aggression characterized by systematic and repeated abuse of power intended to harm the victim (Bradshaw, Waasdorp, & O'Brennan, 2013). The line between good-natured exchanges and hostile teasing may seem thin, but a rule of thumb is that teasing someone who is less powerful or less popular or using any racial, ethnic, or religious slur should *not* be tolerated. Between 10% and 30% of children and youth are involved in bullying, and this seems to be the case around the world (C. R. Cook, Williams, Guerra, Kim, & Sadek, 2010; Guerra, Williams, & Sadek, 2011). Both bullies and victims are at risk for long-term academic, psychological, and behavioral problems (Patton et al., 2013; Swearer, Espelage, Vaillancourt, & Hymel, 2010). There are many ways to be a bully, as you can see in Table 13.3 on page 510.

VICTIMS. Studies from both Europe and the United States indicate that about 10% of children are chronic victims—the constant targets of physical or verbal attacks. One kind of victim tends to have low self-esteem and to feel anxious, lonely, insecure, and unhappy. These students often are prone to crying and withdrawal; in general, when attacked, they won't defend themselves. These victims may believe that they are rejected because they have flaws that they cannot change or control—no wonder they are depressed and helpless! There is a second kind of victim—highly emotional and hot-tempered students who seem to provoke aggressive reactions from their peers. Members of this group have few friends (Pellegrini, Bartini, & Brooks, 1999). Some groups are more likely to be bullied: students who are obese, unpopular, have disabilities, or are lesbian, gay, bisexual, transgender, and questioning (LGBTQ) (J. S. Hong & Garbarino, 2012; Swearer et al., 2010). Why do student intentionally harm others? What are their reasons for bullying?

About 160,000 children avoid school every day, and thousands more drop out of school altogether because they are always afraid. The risk for being a victim of bullying increases in late elementary school, peaks in middle school, and declines in high school. Children who have been chronic victims through elementary and middle school are more depressed and more likely to attempt suicide as young adults (Bradshaw et al., 2013; Garbarino & deLara, 2002). And students who kill or injure others in schools are more often victims than bullies (Reinke & Herman, 2002a,

FIGURE 13.4

THE DISCIPLINE WITHOUT STRESS® TEACHING MODEL

Here are the key concepts in Marshall's (2013) model.

I CLASSROOM MANAGEMENT vs. DISCIPLINE

The key to effective classroom management is teaching and practicing procedures. This is the teacher's responsibility. Discipline, on the other hand, has to do with behavior and is the student's responsibility.

II THREE PRINCIPLES TO PRACTICE

POSITIVITY	CHOICE	REFLECTION
Teachers practice changing negatives into positives. "No running" becomes "We walk in the hallways." "Stop talking" becomes "This is quiet time."	Choice response thinking is taught—as well as impulse control—so students are not victims of their own impulses.	Since a person can only control another person temporarily and because no one can actually change another person, asking REFLECTIVE questions is the most effective approach to actuate change in others.

III THE RAISE RESPONSIBILITY SYSTEM (RRSystem)

TEACHING THE HIERARCHY (Teaching)	CHECKING FOR UNDERSTANDING (Asking)	GUIDED CHOICES (Eliciting)
The hierarchy engenders a desire to behave responsibly and a desire to put forth effort to learn. Students differentiate between internal and external motivation—and learn to rise above inappropriate peer influence.	Students reflect on the LEVEL of chosen behavior. This approach SEPARATES THE PERSON FROM THE BEHAVIOR, thereby negating the usual tendency to defend one's actions. It is this natural tendency towards self-defense that leads to confrontations.	If disruptions continue, a consequence or procedure is ELICITED to redirect the inappropriate behavior. This approach is in contrast to the usual coercive approach of having a consequence IMPOSED.

IV USING THE SYSTEM TO INCREASE MOTIVATION & LEARNING

Using the hierarchy BEFORE a lesson or activity and AFTER a lesson or activity increases motivation, improves learning, and raises academic achievement.

Source: Reprinted with permission from Marshall, M. (2013). Discipline Without Stress® Punishments or Rewards: How Teachers and Parents Promote Responsibility & Learning (2nd ed.). Los Alamos, CA: Piper Press.

TABLE 13.3 • **What Does Bullying Look and Sound Like?**

TYPE OF BULLYING	DESCRIPTION	BEHAVIORS THAT COUNT AS BULLYING
Physical	Any unwanted physical contact in which one participant exerts power or force over another	Hitting, pinching, punching, kicking, shoving Withholding/stealing/destroying property
Verbal	Any comment considered offensive or threatening to the victim	Hurtful teasing, name-calling, criticizing, humiliating, threatening, making derogatory comments about others' religion, race, sex, abilities or disabilities
Social/Relational	Intentional manipulation of people's social lives, friendships, or reputation	Leaving people out on purpose, spreading rumors, convincing others not to be friends with someone, damaging friendships or reputations, setting someone up to look foolish
Cyber Bullying	Using an electronic platform to bully (e.g., FaceBook, cell phones, the Internet)	Spreading rumors through FaceBook, texting embarrassing/compromising pictures

Source: Based on National Children's Study. (2012). What is bullying? 4 Types of bullying. Retrieved from childrensstudymaine.org/health/what-is-bullying-4-types-of-bullying/. PREVNet. (2013), Types of bullying: Bullying evolves throughout childhood. Retrieved from prevnet.ca/bullying/types.

2002b). In the past years, we have seen tragic consequences when bullied students turned guns on their tormentors in schools in the United States and in Europe.

WHY DO STUDENTS BULLY? Ken Rigby (2012) examined the research and concluded that students bully for four main reasons. Rigby suggests that to effectively combat bullying, schools and teachers need to address the underlying motivation, not just the bullying behavior. See Table 13.4 on page 510 for the reasons and possible actions.

TABLE 13.4 • **Reasons for Bullying and Possible School Responses**

REASONS FOR BULLYING	POSSIBLE SCHOOL AND TEACHER ACTIONS
Bullies feel annoyed, insulted, or have some grievance against the victim, so they feel justified in lashing out. There may or may not be a reasonable basis for the grievance felt.	Help students read the intentions of others more accurately. Use role-plays, readings, and drama to develop the capacity to "walk in someone else's shoes." Try conflict resolution or peer mediation.
They simply enjoy putting the victim under pressure, especially if bystanders seem to find the whole situation "fun." The bullies claim it is innocent—"no big deal."	Stress with students that it is *not* fun unless the target of the aggression is genuinely laughing too. Develop empathy through literature activities and class community building such as circle time and shared concerns.
The bully believes the aggression against the victim will gain or maintain acceptance for the bully in a valued group.	In lessons and in relations with students, emphasize making moral judgment, thinking for yourself, and resisting conformity to group pressures. Also, sensitive discussion of prejudice and homophobia can help students resist pressures from groups to harm others based on their race, ethnicity, sexual identity, or language.
The bully wants something from the victim and is willing to inflict harm to get it, and/or the bully is basically sadistic—hurting other people feels good.	Restorative justice practices and community conferences may help the bullies feel genuine remorse. For older students, if the acts are criminal, there are legal sanctions.

BULLYING AND TEASING. A longitudinal study that followed a representative sample of first- through sixth-grade students for 2 years found that aggressive children whose teachers taught them conflict management strategies were moved away from a life path of aggression and violence (Aber, Brown, & Jones, 2003). But when teachers are silent about aggression and teasing, students may "hear" the teacher's agreement with the insult (C. S. Weinstein & Novodvorsky, 2015). Table 13.5 is a list of suggestions for educating students about teasing in schools.

TABLE 13.5 • Dos and Don'ts about Teasing

Teasing has led to some tragic situations. Talk about what to do in your class.

DO	DON'T
1. Be careful of others' feelings.	1. Tease someone you don't know well.
2. Use humor gently and carefully.	2. [If you are a boy] tease girls about sex.
3. Ask whether teasing about a certain topic hurts someone's feelings.	3. Tease about a person's body.
4. Accept teasing from others if you tease.	4. Tease about a person's family members.
5. Tell others if teasing about a certain topic hurts your feelings.	5. Tease about a topic when a student has asked you not to.
6. Know the difference between friendly gentle teasing and hurtful ridicule or harassment.	6. Tease someone who seems agitated or whom you know is having a bad day.
7. Try to read others' "body language" to see if their feelings are hurt—even when they don't tell you.	7. Be thin-skinned about teasing that is meant in a friendly way.
8. Help a weaker student when he or she is being ridiculed.	8. Swallow your feelings about teasing—tell someone in a direct and clear way what is bothering you.

Source: Based on information in: Middle and Secondary Classroom Management: Lessons from Research and Practice (5th ed.), by C. S. Weinstein & I. Novodvorsky. Published by McGraw-Hill. Copyright © 2015.

Besides following the guidelines in Table 13.5, research has shown that having a strong sense of community in your classroom is associated with more student empathy for the victims of bullying and less "blaming the victim" for being attacked (Gini, 2008). So anything you do to develop class community based on fairness and trust will be a step toward dealing with bullying. In a study of over 2,500 students in 59 schools, Nancy Guerra and her colleagues (2011) found that providing opportunities for success, promoting achievement and self-esteem, and improving teacher–student relationships also help to prevent bullying.

Unfortunately, the results are mixed on the effectiveness of many school-wide bullying prevention programs. And another discouraging finding is that administrators prefer to adopt anti-bullying programs that they heard about from colleagues rather than determine if there was any scientific evidence that the programs worked—and many don't (Swearer et al., 2010).

CHANGING ATTRIBUTIONS. Cynthia Hudley and her colleagues (2007) at the University of California at Los Angeles have developed a program to reduce physical aggression in elementary schools. The program, which is called BrainPower, is grounded in attribution theory, discussed in Chapter 12. The central goal of BrainPower is to teach aggressive students "to start from a presumption of accidental causes. When a social encounter with a peer results in a negative outcome (a spilled lunch tray, a bump in the lunch line, missing homework, etc.), the child will begin with the assumption that the outcome was due to accidental causes rather than intentional hostility from peers" (brainpowerprogram.com/index-1.html). The program also teaches accurate reading of social cues, so that students recognize when aggression against them is intentional. After students become more skillful at judging social cues, they learn and practice appropriate responses such as asking questions, being assertive—not aggressive—or seeking adult help. Two decades of research on this program show it has been successful in changing many students' attributions and behaviors (Hudley, Graham, & Taylor, 2007).

CYBERBULLYING. With all the possibilities of technology come problems, too. Now bullies have new ways to torment victims using e-mail, text messaging, SnapChat, Instagram, Twitter, Facebook, cell phones, YouTube, Web blogs, online voting booths, and more (C. S. Weinstein & Novodvorsky, 2015). For example, when 16-year-old Denise broke up with her boyfriend, he sought revenge by posting her e-mail address and cell phone number on Web sites and blogs devoted to sex. For months, she got embarrassing and frightening phone calls and messages

TABLE 13.6 • Ideas for Dealing with Cyberbullying

- Develop an explicit policy for acceptable in-school use of the Internet, and include it in the school handbook (or your class rules). The policy should spell out what constitutes cyberbullying and list consequences.
- Make sure that children and young people are aware that bullying will be dealt with seriously.
- Ensure that parents/guardians who express cyberbullying concerns are taken seriously.
- Explain to students that they
  - Should never share or give out personal information, PIN numbers, passwords, phone numbers, and so on.
  - Should not delete messages; they do not have to read them, but they should show them to an adult they trust. Messages can be used to take action against cyberbullies.
  - Should not open a message from someone they don't know.
  - Should *never* reply to the message.
  - Probably can block the sender's message if they are being bullied through cell phones, e-mail, Facebook, Twiter, Snapchat, WhatsApp, instant messaging, and so on.
  - Can forward the messages to their Internet service provider.
  - Should tell an adult.
  - Should show the message to the police if it contains physical threats.
  - Should speak out against cyberbullying.
  - Should never send messages when they are angry.
  - Should never send messages they wouldn't want others to see.
- Focus some class projects on cyberbullying. For example, students in one school posted on a "Wall of Shame" cruel comments that others in the school had posted on Facebook (without identifying information). The same could be done for Twitter or other social network sites.
- Make parents aware of the fact that all of the major Internet service providers offer some form of parental controls. For example, AOL has developed "AOL Guardian," which reports with whom youngsters exchange messages and what Web sites they visit and monitors chat rooms for children 13 and under.
- Encourage parents to keep computers in a public room in the house.
- Invite members of the local police department to come to school to speak with parents and students about proper Internet use.
- Make sure ethics are included in any computer instruction given at your school.

Source: From Middle and Secondary Classroom Management *(5th ed.), by C. S. Weinstein and Novodvorsky, New York: McGraw-Hill. Copyright © 2015 by The McGraw-Hill Companies, p. 182. Adapted with permission of the McGraw-Hill Companies, Inc.*

(Strom & Strom, 2005). This kind of bullying is difficult to combat because the perpetrators can hide, but the damage can be long term. Table 13.6 has some ideas for dealing with cyberbullying.

Special Problems with High School Students

Many secondary students never complete their schoolwork. Because students at this age have many assignments and teachers have many students, both teachers and students may lose track of what has and has not been turned in. It often helps to teach students how to use a daily planner—paper or electronic. In addition, teachers must keep accurate records. The most important thing is to enforce the established consequences for incomplete work. Do not pass a student because you know he or she is "bright enough" to pass. Make it clear to these students that the choice is theirs: They can do the work and pass, or they can refuse to do the work and face the consequences. You might also ask, in a private moment, if there is anything interfering with the student's ability to get the work done.

There is also the problem of students who continually break the same rules, always forgetting materials, for example, or getting into fights. What should you do? Seat these students away from others who might be influenced by them. Try to catch them before they break the rules, but if rules are broken, be consistent in applying established consequences. Do not accept promises to do better next time (Levin & Nolan, 2000). Teach the students how to monitor their own behavior; some of the self-regulation techniques described in Chapter 11 should be helpful. Finally, remain friendly with the students. Try to catch them in a good moment so you can talk to them about something other than their rule breaking.

A defiant, hostile student can pose serious problems. If there is an outburst, try to get out of the situation as soon as possible; everyone loses in a public power struggle. One possibility is

Connect and Extend to PRAXIS II®

Student Misbehavior (I, C4)
Even the most well-managed classroom will have instances of student misbehavior. Explain the principles for dealing with common student misbehaviors. What strategies can teachers employ to deal fairly and effectively with those problems?

to give the student a chance to save face and cool down by saying, "It's your choice to cooperate or not. You can take a minute to think about it." If the student complies, the two of you can talk later about controlling the outbursts. If the student refuses to cooperate, you can tell him or her to wait in the hall until you get the class started on work, then step outside for a private talk. If the student refuses to leave, send another class member for the assistant principal. Again, follow through. If the student complies before help arrives, do not let him or her off the hook. If outbursts occur frequently, you might have a conference with the counselor, family members, or other teachers. If the problem is an irreconcilable clash of personalities, the student should be transferred to another teacher.

It sometimes is useful to keep records of these incidents by logging the student's name, words and actions, date, time, place, and teacher's response. These records may help identify patterns and can prove useful in meetings with administrators, families, or special services personnel (Burden, 1995). Some teachers have students sign each entry to verify the incidents.

Fighting or destruction of property is a difficult and potentially dangerous problem. The first step is to send for help and get the names of participants and witnesses. Then, remove any students who may have gathered to watch; an audience will only make things worse. Do not try to break up a fight without help. Make sure the school office is aware of the incident; usually the school has a policy for dealing with these situations. What else can you do? The *Guidelines: Handling Potentially Explosive Situations* are based on C. S. Weinstein and Novodvorsky (2015). There is quite a bit of discussion today about zero tolerance for rule breaking in the schools. Is this a good idea? The *Point/Counterpoint: Is Zero Tolerance a Good Idea?* on the next page looks at both sides.

ENHANCEDetext *self-check*

GUIDELINES
Handling Potentially Explosive Situations

Move slowly and deliberately toward the problem situation.
Examples
1. Walk slowly; then be as still as possible.
2. Establish eye-level position.

Be respectful.
Examples
1. Keep a reasonable distance.
2. Do not crowd the student. Do not get "in the student's face."
3. Speak respectfully. Use the student's name.
4. Avoid pointing or gesturing.

Be brief.
Examples
1. Avoid long-winded statements or nagging.
2. Stay with the agenda. Stay focused on the problem at hand. Do not get sidetracked.
3. Deal with less-severe problems later.

Avoid power struggles.
Examples
1. Speak privately if possible; don't threaten.
2. Do not get drawn into "I won't, you will" arguments.
3. Don't make threats or raise your voice.

Inform the student of the expected behavior and the negative consequence as a choice or decision for the student to make. Then withdraw from the student and allow some time for the student to decide.
Examples
1. "Michael, you need to return to your desk, or I will have to send for the principal. You have a few seconds to decide." The teacher then moves away, perhaps attending to other students.
2. If Michael does not choose the appropriate behavior, deliver the negative consequences. ("You are choosing to have me call the principal.") Follow through with the consequence.

For more ideas, see njcap.org/templated/Programs.html

Source: Based on material in: Middle and Secondary Classroom Management: Lessons from Research and Practice (5th ed.), by C. S. Weinstein & I. Novodvorsky. Published by McGraw-Hill. Copyright © 2015 by McGraw-Hill. Adapted with permission from the McGraw-Hill Companies, Inc.

POINT/COUNTERPOINT
Is Zero Tolerance a Good Idea?

With the very visible violence in schools today, some districts have instituted "zero-tolerance" policies for rule breaking. One result? Two 8-year-old boys in New Jersey were suspended for making "terrorist threats." They had pointed paper guns at their classmates while playing. Do zero-tolerance policies make sense?

POINT **Zero tolerance means zero common sense.** An Internet search using the keywords ["zero-tolerance" and schools] will locate a wealth of information about the policy—much of it against. For example, Oren Dorrell reported this incident in the November 2, 2009 edition of *USA Today*:

> The most recent high-profile case [of zero tolerance] involved Zachary Christie, a 6-year-old who was suspended for five days on Sept. 29 after he brought a camping utensil that was part knife, fork and spoon to Downes Elementary in Newark, Del. School officials considered it a dangerous instrument and suspended the boy, adding that he couldn't return to Downes until he completed at least 45 days at an alternative school.

Research shows that punishment and zero-tolerance policies have not been very successful in preventing bullying, even though about 70% of teachers and counselors use punishment even in cases of mild bullying (Rigby, 2012). What else does the research say? In 2006, the American Psychological Association set up a Zero Tolerance Task force to answer that question (American Psychological Association Zero Tolerance Task Force, 2008). Analyzing a decade of research, they reached the following conclusions:

- Schools are not any safer or more effective in disciplining students now than before they instituted zero tolerance.
- The higher rates of suspension caused by zero tolerance have not led to less racial bias in disciplining students.
- Zero-tolerance policies can actually lead to increases in bad behavior that then lead to higher dropout rates.

In addition, zero-tolerance policies can discourage students from informing teachers when the students learn that a classmate is "planning to do something dangerous." The zero-tolerance rules get in the way of trusting relationships between teachers and students (Syvertsen, Flanagan, & Stout, 2009). Adolescents need both structure and support, but zero-tolerance policies can create a highly structured, rigid environment that ignores the need for support. Finally, many of the popular zero-tolerance interventions such as increased security guards, hallway monitors, and the introduction of metal detectors have no apparent effect on the incidence of school bullying (Hyman et al., 2006; National Center for Education Statistics, 2003).

COUNTERPOINT **Zero tolerance is necessary for now.** The arguments for zero tolerance focus on school safety and the responsibilities of schools and teachers to protect the students and themselves. Of course, many of the incidents reported in the news seem like overreactions to childhood pranks or, worse, to innocent mistakes or lapses of memory. But how do school officials separate the innocent from the dangerous? For example, it has been widely reported that Andy Williams (the boy who killed two classmates in Santee, California) assured his friends before the shootings that he was only joking about "pulling a Columbine."

On January 13, 2003, I read a story in *USA Today* by Gregg Toppo entitled "School Violence Hits Lower Grades: Experts Who See Violent Behavior in Younger Kids Blame Parents, Prenatal Medical Problems and an Angry Society; Educators Search for Ways to Cope." The story opened with these examples: a second-grader in Indiana takes off his shoe and attacks his teacher with it, a Philadelphia kindergartner hits a pregnant teacher in the stomach, and an 8-year-old in Maryland threatens to use gasoline (he knew exactly where he would pour it) to burn down his suburban elementary school. Toppo noted, "Elementary school principals and safety experts say they're seeing more violence and aggression than ever among their youngest students, pointing to what they see as an alarming rise in assaults and threats to classmates and teachers" (p. A2). Toppo cited statistics indicating that, although the incidence of school violence has decreased overall, attacks on elementary school teachers have actually increased.

BEWARE OF EITHER/OR

Surely we can ask adults to use good judgment in applying rules in dangerous situations but to not feel trapped by the rules when student actions are not intended to harm and are not dangerous.

THE NEED FOR COMMUNICATION

STOP & THINK A student says to you, "That book you assigned is really stupid—I'm not reading it!" What do you say? •

Communication between teacher and students is essential when problems arise. Communication is more than "teacher talks—student listens." It is more than the words exchanged between individuals. We communicate in many ways. Our actions, movements, voice tone, facial expressions, and many other nonverbal behaviors send messages to our students. Many times, the messages we intend to send are not the messages our students receive.

Message Sent—Message Received

> *Teacher:* Carl, where is your homework?
> *Carl:* I left it in my Dad's car this morning.
> *Teacher:* Again? You will have to bring me a note tomorrow from your father saying that you actually did the homework. No grade without the note.
> *Message Carl receives:* I can't trust you. I need proof you did the work.

★★★

> *Teacher:* Sit at every other desk. Put all your things under your desk. Jane and Laurel, you are sitting too close together. One of you move!
> *Message Jane and Laurel receive:* I expect you two to cheat on this test.

★★★

A new student comes to Ms. Lincoln's kindergarten. The child is messy and unwashed. Ms. Lincoln puts her hand lightly on the girl's shoulder and speaks:

> *Ms. Lincoln:* I'm glad you are here.
> (Her muscles tense, and she leans away from the child.)

> *Message student receives:* I don't like you. I think you are bad.

In all interactions, a message is sent and a message is received. Sometimes teachers believe they are sending one message, but their voices, body positions, choices of words, and gestures may communicate a different message.

Students may hear the hidden message and respond to it. For example, a student may respond with hostility if she or he feels insulted by the teacher (or by another student) but may not be able to say exactly where the feeling of being insulted came from. Perhaps it was in the teacher's tone of voice, not the words actually spoken. But the teacher feels attacked for no reason. The first principle of communication is that people respond to what they think was said or meant, not necessarily to the speaker's intended message or actual words.

Students in my classes have told me about one instructor who encourages accurate communication by using the paraphrase rule. Before any participant, including the teacher, is allowed to respond to any other participant in a class discussion, he or she must summarize what the previous speaker said. If the summary is wrong, indicating the speaker was misunderstood, the speaker must explain again. The respondent then tries again to paraphrase. The process continues until the speaker agrees that the listener has heard the intended message.

Paraphrasing is more than a classroom exercise. It can be the first step in communicating with students. Before teachers can deal appropriately with any student problem, they must know what the real problem is. A student who says, "This book is really dumb! Why did we have to read it?" may really be saying, "The book was too difficult for me. I couldn't read it, and I feel dumb."

Connect and Extend to PRAXIS II®

Teacher–Student Communication (III, A)
A well-managed classroom requires a bidirectional line of communication between the teacher and students. Describe the various communication styles that teachers employ when interacting with students, and explain how those styles affect student behavior.

Diagnosis: Whose Problem Is It?

As a teacher, you may find many student behaviors unacceptable, unpleasant, or troubling. It is often difficult to stand back from these problems, take an objective look, and decide on an appropriate response. According to Thomas Gordon (1981), the key to good teacher–student relationships is determining why you are troubled by a particular behavior and who "owns" the problem. The answer to these questions is critical. If it is really the student's problem, the teacher must become a counselor and supporter, helping the student find his or her own solution. But if the teacher "owns" the problem, it is the teacher's responsibility to find a solution through problem solving with the student.

Diagnosing who owns the problem is not always straightforward. Let's look at three troubling situations to get some practice in this skill:

1. A student writes obscene words and draws sexually explicit illustrations in a school encyclopedia.
2. A student tells you that his parents had a bad fight and he hates his father.
3. A student quietly reads a newspaper in the back of the room.

Why are these behaviors troubling? If you cannot accept the student's behavior because it has a serious effect on you as a teacher—if you are blocked from reaching your goals by the student's action—then you own the problem. It is your responsibility to confront the student and seek a solution. A teacher-owned problem appears to be present in the first situation described here—the young pornographer—because teaching materials are damaged.

If you feel annoyed by the behavior because it is getting in the student's own way or because you are embarrassed for the child, but the behavior does not directly interfere with your teaching, then it is probably the student's problem. The student who hates his father would not prevent you from teaching, even though you might wish the student felt differently. The problem is really the student's, and he must find his own solution.

The third situation is more difficult to diagnose. One argument is that the teacher is not interfered with in any way, so it is the student's problem. But teachers might find the student reading the paper distracting during a lecture, so it is their problem, and they must find a solution. In a gray area such as this, the answer probably depends on how the teacher actually experiences the student's behavior.

Having decided who owns the problem, it is time to act.

Counseling: The Student's Problem

Let's pick up the situation in which the student found the reading assignment "dumb." How might a teacher handle this positively?

Student: This book is really dumb! Why did we have to read it?
Teacher: You're pretty upset. This seemed like a worthless assignment to you. [Teacher paraphrases the student's statement, trying to hear the emotions as well as the words.]
Student: Yeah! Well, I guess it was worthless. I mean, I don't know if it was. I couldn't exactly read it.
Teacher: It was just too hard to read, and that bothers you.
Student: Sure, I felt really dumb. I know I can write a good report, but not with a book this tough.
Teacher: I think I can give you some hints that will make the book easier to understand. Can you see me after school today?
Student: Okay.

Here the teacher used empathetic listening to allow the student to find a solution. (As you can see, this approach relies heavily on paraphrasing.) By trying to hear the student and by avoiding the tendency to jump in too quickly with advice, solutions, criticisms, reprimands, or interrogations, the teacher keeps the communication lines open. Here are a few *unhelpful* responses the teacher might have made:

• I chose the book because it is the best example of the author's style in our library. You will need to have read it before your English II class next year. (The teacher justifies the choice; this prevents the student from admitting that this "important" assignment is too difficult.)

- Did you really read it? I bet you didn't do the work, and now you want out of the assignment. (The teacher accuses; the student hears, "The teacher doesn't trust me!" and must either defend herself or himself or accept the teacher's view.)
- Your job is to read the book, not ask me why. I know what's best. (The teacher pulls rank, and the student hears, "You can't possibly decide what is good for you!" The student can rebel or passively accept the teacher's judgment.)

Empathetic, active listening is more than a parroting of the student's words; it should capture the emotions, intent, and meaning behind them. Sokolove, Garrett, Sadker, and Sadker (1986, p. 241) have summarized the components of active listening: (1) blocking out external stimuli; (2) attending carefully to both the verbal and nonverbal messages; (3) differentiating between the intellectual and the emotional content of the message; and (4) making inferences regarding the speaker's feelings.

When students realize they really have been heard and not evaluated negatively for what they have said or felt, they begin to trust the teacher and to talk more openly. Sometimes the true problem surfaces later in the conversation.

Confrontation and Assertive Discipline

Now let's assume a student is doing something that actively interferes with teaching. The teacher decides the student must stop. The problem is the teacher's. Confrontation, not counseling, is required.

"I" MESSAGES. T. Gordon (1981) recommends sending an **"I" message** to intervene and change a student's behavior. Basically, this means telling a student in a straightforward, assertive, and nonjudgmental way what she or he is doing, how it affects you as a teacher, and how you feel about it. The student is then free to change voluntarily, and often does so. Here are two "I" messages:

If you leave your book bags in the aisles, I might trip and hurt myself.
When you all call out, I can't concentrate on each answer, and I'm frustrated.

ASSERTIVE DISCIPLINE. Lee and Marlene Canter (1992; Canter, 1996) suggest other approaches for dealing with a teacher-owned problem. They call their method **assertive discipline**. Many teachers are ineffective with students because they are either wishy-washy and passive or hostile and aggressive (Charles, 2011).

Instead of telling the student directly what to do, *passive* teachers tell, or often ask, the student to *try* or to *think about* the appropriate action. The passive teacher might comment on the problem behavior without actually telling the child what to do differently: "Why are you doing that? Don't you know the rules?" or "Sam, are you disturbing the class?" Or teachers may clearly state what should happen but never follow through with the established consequences, giving the students "one more chance" every time. Finally, teachers may ignore behavior that should receive a response, or they may wait too long before responding.

A *hostile response style* involves different mistakes. Teachers may make "you" statements that condemn the student without stating clearly what the student should be doing: "You should be ashamed of the way you're behaving!" or "You never listen!" or "You are acting like a baby!" Teachers may also threaten students angrily, but follow through too seldom, perhaps because the threats are too vague—"You'll be very sorry you did that when I get through with you!"—or too severe. For example, a teacher tells a student in a physical education class that he will have to "sit on the bench for 3 weeks." A few days later, the team is short one member, and the teacher lets the student play, never returning him to the bench to complete the 3-week sentence. Often a teacher who has been passive becomes hostile and explodes when students persist in misbehaving.

In contrast with both the passive and hostile styles, an *assertive response* communicates to the students that you care too much about them and the process of learning to allow inappropriate behavior to persist. Assertive teachers clearly state what they expect. To be most effective, the teachers often look into a student's eyes when speaking and address the student by name. Assertive teachers' voices are calm, firm, and confident. They are not sidetracked by accusations such as "You just don't understand!" or "You don't like me!" Assertive teachers do not get into a debate about the fairness of the rules. They expect changes, not promises or apologies.

Not all educators believe that assertive discipline is useful. Earlier critics questioned the penalty-focused approach and emphasized that assertive discipline undermined student self-management (Render, Padilla, & Krank, 1989). John Covaleskie (1992) observed, "What helps children become moral is not knowledge of the rules, or even obedience to the rules, but discussions about the reasons for acting in certain ways" (p. 56). These critics have had an impact. More recent versions of assertive discipline focus on teaching students how to behave responsibly and working to establish mutual respect and trust (Charles, 2011).

CONFRONTATIONS AND NEGOTIATIONS. If "I" messages or assertive responses fail and a student persists in misbehaving, teacher and student are in a conflict. Several pitfalls now loom. The two individuals become less able to perceive each other's behavior accurately. Research has shown that the more angry you get with another person, the more you see the other as the villain and yourself as an innocent victim. Because you feel the other person is in the wrong, and he or she feels just as strongly that the conflict is all your fault, very little mutual trust is possible. A cooperative solution to the problem is almost impossible. In fact, by the time the discussion has gone on a few minutes, the original problem is lost in a sea of charges, countercharges, and self-defense (Baron & Byrne, 2003).

There are three methods of resolving a conflict between a teacher and a student. One is for the teacher to impose a solution. This may be necessary during an emergency, as when a defiant student refuses to go to the hall to discuss a public outburst, but it is not a good solution for most conflicts. The second method is for the teacher to give in to the student's demands. You might be convinced by a particularly compelling student argument, but again, this should be used sparingly. It is generally a bad idea to be talked out of a position, unless the position was wrong in the first place. Problems arise when either the teacher or the student gives in completely.

Gordon recommends a third approach, which he calls the "no-lose method." Here, the needs of both the teacher and the student are taken into account in the solution. No one person is expected to give in completely; all participants retain respect for themselves and each other. The no-lose method is a six-step, problem-solving strategy:

1. *Define the problem.* What exactly are the behaviors involved? What does each person want? (Use active listening to help students pinpoint the real problem.)
2. *Generate many possible solutions.* Brainstorm, but remember, don't allow any evaluations of ideas yet.
3. *Evaluate each solution.* Any participant may veto any idea. If no solutions are found to be acceptable, brainstorm again.
4. *Make a decision.* Choose one solution through consensus—no voting. In the end, everyone must be satisfied with the solution.
5. *Determine how to implement the solution.* What will be needed? Who will be responsible for each task? What is the timetable?
6. *Evaluate the success of the solution.* After trying the solution for a while, ask, "Are we satisfied with our decision? How well is it working? Should we make some changes?"

Many of the conflicts in classrooms can be important learning experiences for all concerned.

Reaching Every Student: Peer Mediation and Restorative Justice

Handling conflict is difficult for most of us—and for young people it can be even harder. Years ago, a large study of more than 8,000 junior and senior high students and 500 faculty from three major cities concluded that 90% of the conflicts among students are resolved in destructive ways or are never resolved at all (DeCecco & Richards, 1974). The few studies conducted since that time have reached similar conclusions. Avoidance, force, and threats seem to be the major strategies for dealing with conflict (D. W. Johnson et al., 1995). But there are better ways—like peer mediation and negotiation strategies and restorative justice that teach lifelong lessons.

Video 13.6
Two students trained as conflict managers help two other students settle a dispute. The procedures and skills demonstrated by the conflict managers help the other students recognize ways to prevent conflicts in the future or resolve them without intervention.

ENHANCEDetext *video example*

PEER MEDIATION. David Johnson and his colleagues (1995) provided conflict resolution training to 227 students in second through fifth grade. Students learned a five-step negotiating strategy:

1. *Jointly define the conflict.* Separate the person from the problem and the actions involved, avoid win–lose thinking, and get both parties' goals clear.
2. *Exchange positions and interests.* Present a tentative proposal, and make a case for it; listen to the other person's proposal and feelings; and stay flexible and cooperative.
3. *Reverse perspectives.* See the situation from the other person's point of view, and reverse roles and argue for that perspective.
4. *Invent at least three agreements that allow mutual gain.* Brainstorm, focus on goals, think creatively, and make sure everyone has power to invent solutions.
5. *Reach an integrative agreement.* Make sure both sets of goals are met. If all else fails, flip a coin, take turns, or call in a third party—a mediator.

In addition to learning conflict resolution, all students in D. W. Johnson and Johnson's study were trained in mediation strategies. The role of the mediator was rotated—every day the teacher chose two students to be the class mediators and to wear the mediators' T-shirts. Johnson and his colleagues found that students learned the conflict resolution and mediation strategies and used them successfully to handle conflicts in a more productive way, both in school and at home.

Even if you do not have formal peer mediation training in your school, you can help your students handle conflict more productively. For example, Esme Codell, the excellent first-year teacher you met earlier in this chapter, taught her fifth-graders a simple four-step process and posted the steps on a bulletin board: "1. Tell person what you didn't like. 2. Tell person how it made you feel. 3. Tell person what you want in the future. 4. Person responds with what they can do. Congratulations! You are a Confident Conflict Conqueror!" (Codell, 2001, p. 23).

RESTORATIVE JUSTICE. Restorative justice focuses on righting the wrongs suffered when conflicts go badly (D. W. Johnson & Johnson, 2013). Probably the most famous example of restorative justice was the National Truth and Reconciliation Commission in South Africa, where injured parties described the injustices they had experienced and sometimes faced those who had harmed them. In classrooms, the goals of restorative justice look to the past and the future: re-establish cooperation in the classroom community by resolving *past* conflicts and create conditions for long-term *future* cooperation. The process must be voluntary. The participants in the conflict meet with a facilitator (often the teacher) and sometimes members of their family. The victim and the offender express their views and describe their experiences, with monitoring by the facilitator to keep discussions productive. When the process works well, the participants express remorse for hurting each other, forgive the perceived transgressions, and reconcile their conflict. David and Roger Johnson (2013) note that:

> Reconciliation usually includes an apology, communicates that justice has prevailed, recognizes the negativity of the acts perpetuated, restores respect for the social identity of those formerly demeaned, validates and recognizes the suffering undergone by the victim and relevant community members, establishes trust between victim and offender, and removes the reasons for either party to "right" the wrongs of the past. (p. 408).

The outcome of restorative justice usually is an agreement that includes how to re-establish cooperation and participation in the classroom community—perhaps an apology of action, restitution, and a plan for dealing positively with possible future conflicts.

THE 4 Rs. The 4Rs (Fusaro, 2011) is another approach to conflict resolution developed by the Morningside Center for Teaching Social Responsibility. The 4 Rs are reading, writing, respect, and resolution. In this curriculum, direct teaching of conflict resolution strategies is embedded in literacy lessons. Teachers use reading high-quality children's books as a launching pad for interactive activities such as discussion and role-plays. The activities focus on seven areas: building community, feelings, listening, assertiveness, problem solving, diversity, and cooperation. Results of research show improvements in students' social skills and self-regulation, and also improvements in academic achievement for the most aggressive students at the greatest risk of failing. For more information, see gse.harvard.edu/ and search for "fostering social responsibility."

We have looked at quite a few perspectives on classroom management. Clearly, there is no one-size-fits-all strategy for creating social and physical spaces for learning. What does the research tell us? Are some strategies better than others?

Research on Management Approaches

Research provides some guidance. Emmer and Aussiker (1990) conducted a meta-analysis of three general perspectives on management: *influencing* students through listening and problem solving, as described by T. Gordon (1981); *group management* through class meetings and student discussion, as advocated by Glasser (1969, 1990); and *control* through rewards and punishments, as exemplified by Canter and Canter (1992). No clear conclusions could be drawn about the impact of these approaches on student behaviors. However, some evaluations have found positive effects for H. J. Freiberg's (2013; H. J. Freiberg & Lamb, 2009) Consistency Management program and for programs that use rewards and punishments (R. Lewis, 2001).

INTEGRATING IDEAS. In a study conducted in Australia, Ramon Lewis (2001) found that recognizing and rewarding appropriate student behaviors, talking with students about how their behavior affects others, involving students in class discipline decisions, and providing nondirective hints and descriptions about unacceptable behaviors were associated with students' taking greater responsibility for their own learning. It is interesting that these interventions represent all three of the general approaches reviewed by Emmer and Aussiker: *influence, group management,* and *control.* In a study of over 3,000 ninth-grade students in Singapore, Youyan Nie and Shun Lau (2009) found that both caring and control were positively related to student engagement; so, blending control, influence, caring, and group management strategies may be necessary to create positive

---

GUIDELINES
Family and Community Partnerships

Classroom Management

Make sure families know the expectations and rules of your class and school.

Examples

1. At a Family Fun Night, have your students do skits showing the rules—how to follow them and what breaking them "looks like" and "sounds like."
2. Make a poster for the refrigerator at home that describes, in a light way, the most important rules and expectations.
3. For older students, give families a list of due dates for the major assignments, along with tips about how to encourage quality work by pacing the effort—avoiding last-minute panic. Some schools require family members to sign a paper indicating they are aware of the due dates.
4. Communicate in appropriate ways—use the family's first language when possible. Tailor messages to the reading level of the home.

Make families partners in recognizing good citizenship.

Examples

1. Send positive notes home when students, especially students who have had trouble with classroom management, work well in the classroom.

2. Give ideas for ways any family, even those with few economic resources, can celebrate accomplishment— a favorite food; the chance to choose a game to play; a comment to a special person such as an aunt, grandparent, or minister; the chance to read to a younger sibling.

Identify talents in the community to help build a learning environment in your class.

Examples

1. Have students write letters to carpet and furniture stores asking for donations of remnants to carpet a reading corner.
2. Find family members who can build shelves or room dividers, paint, sew, laminate manipulatives, write stories, repot plants, or network computers.
3. Contact businesses for donations of computers, printers, or other equipment.

Seek cooperation from families when behavior problems arise.

Examples

1. Talk to families over the phone or in their home. Keep good records about the problem behavior.
2. Listen to family members, and solve problems with them.

learning environments. This is not always easy. Lewis also concluded that teachers sometimes find using caring, influence, and group management difficult when students are aggressive—and most in need of these positive approaches. When teachers feel threatened, it can be difficult for them to do what students need, but that may be the most important time to act positively and combine caring with control.

CONNECTING WITH FAMILIES ABOUT CLASSROOM MANAGEMENT. As we have seen throughout this book, families are important partners in education. This statement applies to classroom management as well. When parents and teachers share the same expectations and support each other, they can create a more positive classroom environment and more time for learning. The *Guidelines: Family and Community Partnerships—Classroom Management* on the previous page provide ideas for working with families and the community. You can find more ideas through the Harvard Family Research Project (hfrp.org/family-involvement).

ENHANCEDetext *self-check*

DIVERSITY: CULTURALLY RESPONSIVE MANAGEMENT

Research on discipline shows that African Americans and Latino/a Americans, especially males, are punished more often and more harshly than other students. These students lose time from learning as they spend more hours in detention or suspension (Gay, 2006; Monroe & Obidah, 2002; Skiba, Michael, Nardo, & Peterson, 2000). Why?

The notion that African Americans and Latino/a students are punished more because they commit more serious offenses is NOT supported by the data. Instead, these students are punished more severely for minor offenses such as rudeness or defiance—words and actions that are interpreted by teachers as meriting severe punishment. One explanation is a lack of cultural synchronization between teachers and students. "The language, style of walking, glances, and dress of black children, particularly males, have engendered fear, apprehension, and overreaction among many teachers and school administrators" (Irvine, 1990, p. 27). African American students may be disciplined for behaviors that were never intended to be disruptive or disrespectful. Teachers do their students and themselves a service if they work at becoming bicultural—helping their students to learn how to function in both mainstream and home cultures, but also learning the meaning of their students' words and actions—so they do not misinterpret and then punish their students' unintended insults (Gay, 2006).

Culturally responsive management is simply a part of the larger concept of culturally relevant teaching. Geneva Gay (2006) sums it up:

> If the classroom is a comfortable, caring, embracing, affirming, engaging, and facilitative place for students then discipline is not likely to be much of an issue. It follows then that both classroom management and school achievement can be improved for students from different ethnic, racial, social, and linguistic backgrounds by ensuring that curriculum and instruction are culturally relevant and personally meaningful for them.

I once asked a gifted educator in an urban New Jersey high school which teachers were most effective with the really tough students. He said there are two kinds: teachers who can't be intimidated or fooled and expect their students to learn, and teachers who really care about the students. When I asked, "Which kind are you?" he answered "Both!" He is an example of a "warm demander," a teacher who seems to be most effective with students placed at risk (Irvine & Armento, 2001; Irvine & Fraser, 1998). Sometimes these warm demanders appear harsh to outside observers (Burke-Spero, 1999; Burke-Spero & Woolfolk Hoy, 2002). Carla Monroe and Jennifer Obidah (2002) studied Ms. Simpson, an African American teacher working with her eighth-grade science class. She describes herself as having high expectations for academics and behavior in her classes—so much so that she believed her students perceived her as "mean." Yet she often used humor and dialect to communicate her expectations, as in the following exchange:

> *Ms. Simpson [addressing the class]:* If you know you're going to act the fool just come to me and say, "I'm going to act the fool at the pep rally," so I can go ahead and send you to wherever you need to go. [Class laughs.]
>
> *Ms. Simpson:* I'm real serious. If you know you're having a bad day, you don't want anybody touching you, you don't want nobody saying nothing to you, somebody bump into you you're going to snap—you need to come up to me and say, "I'm going to snap and I can't go to the pep rally." [The students start to call out various comments.]
>
> *Ms. Simpson:* Now, I just want to say I expect you to have the best behavior because you're the most mature students in the building . . . don't make me stop the pep rally and ask the eighth-graders to leave.
>
> *Edward:* We'll have silent lunch won't we? [Class laughs.]
>
> *Ms. Simpson:* You don't want to dream about what you're going to have. [Class laughs.] Ok, 15 minutes for warm ups. [The students begin their warm-up assignment.]

Many African American students may be more accustomed to a directive kind of management and discipline outside of school. Their families might say, "Put down that candy" or "Go to bed," whereas White parents might ask, "Can we eat candy before dinner?" or "Isn't it time for bed?" As H. Richard Milner (2006, p. 498) says, "The question should not be which approach is right or wrong but which approach works with and connects with the students' prior knowledge and ways of knowing."

ENHANCEDetext *self-check*

SUMMARY

- **The What and Why of Classroom Management (pp. 488–493)**

  What are the challenges of classroom management? As you learn to teach, you should be aware of your philosophy of classroom management. Are you more teacher centered and structured or more student centered and humanistic? Do you tend to focus on *Relationship-Listening, Confronting-Contracting, Rules and Consequences,* or some combination? Classrooms are challenging because they are multidimensional, full of simultaneous activities, fast-paced and immediate, unpredictable, public, and affected by the history of students' and teachers' actions. A teacher must juggle all these elements every day. Productive classroom activity requires students' cooperation. Maintaining cooperation is different for each age group. Young students are learning how to "go to school" and need to learn the general procedures of school. Older students need to learn the specifics required for working in different subjects. Working with adolescents requires teachers to understand the power of the adolescent peer group.

  What are the goals of effective classroom management? The goals of effective classroom management are to make ample time for learning; improve the quality of time use by keeping students actively engaged; make sure participation structures are clear, straightforward, and consistently signaled; and encourage student self-management, self-control, and responsibility.

- **Creating a Positive Learning Environment (pp. 493–501)**

  Distinguish between rules and procedures. Rules are the specific dos and don'ts of classroom life. They usually are written and posted. Procedures cover administrative tasks, student movement, housekeeping, and routines for accomplishing lessons, interactions between students and teachers, and interactions among students. Rules can be written in terms of rights, and students may benefit from participating in establishing these rules. Consequences should be established for following and breaking the rules and procedures so that the teacher and the students know what will happen.

Distinguish between personal territories and interest area spatial arrangements. There are two basic kinds of spatial organization, territorial (the traditional classroom arrangement) and functional (dividing space into interest or work areas). Flexibility is often the key. Access to materials, convenience, privacy when needed, ease of supervision, and a willingness to reevaluate plans are important considerations in the teacher's choice of physical arrangements.

Contrast the first school week of effective and ineffective classroom managers. Effective classroom managers spent the first days of class teaching a workable, easily understood set of rules and procedures by using lots of explanation, examples, and practice. Students were occupied with organized, enjoyable activities, and they learned to function cooperatively in the group. Quick, firm, clear, and consistent responses to infractions of the rules characterized effective teachers. The teachers had planned carefully to avoid any last-minute tasks that might have taken them away from their students. These teachers dealt with the children's pressing concerns first. In contrast, for ineffective managers, procedures for accomplishing routine tasks varied from day to day and were never taught or practiced. Students talked to one another because they had nothing productive to do. Ineffective teachers frequently left the room. Many became absorbed in paperwork or in helping just one student. They had not made plans for how to deal with typical problems such as late-arriving students or interruptions.

- **Maintaining a Good Environment for Learning (pp. 501–505)**

How can teachers encourage engagement? In general, as teacher supervision increases, students' engaged time also increases. When the task provides continuous cues for the student about what to do next, involvement will be greater. Activities with clear steps are likely to be more absorbing, because one step leads naturally to the next. Making work requirements clear and specific, providing needed materials, and monitoring activities all add to engagement.

Explain the factors identified by Kounin that prevent management problems in the classroom. To create a positive environment and prevent problems, teachers must take individual differences into account, maintain student motivation, and reinforce positive behavior. Successful problem preventers are skilled in four areas described by Kounin: "withitness," overlapping, group focusing, and movement management. When penalties have to be imposed,

teachers should impose them calmly and privately. In addition to applying Kounin's ideas, teachers can prevent problems by establishing a caring classroom community and teaching students to use social skills and emotional self-regulation skills.

How do teachers help students form connections with schools? To get started on building connections, teachers should make expectations for both academic work and student behaviors clear. Respect for students' needs and rights should be at the center of class procedures. Students know that their teachers care about them when teachers try to make classes interesting, are fair and honest with them, make sure they understand the materials, and have ways to cope with students' concerns and troubles.

- **Dealing with Discipline Problems (pp. 506–514)**

Describe seven levels of intervention in misbehavior. Teachers can first make eye contact with the student or use other nonverbal signals, then try verbal hints such as simply inserting the student's name into the lecture. Next, the teacher asks if the offender is aware of the negative effects of the actions, then reminds the student of the procedure and has her or him follow it correctly. If this does not work, the teacher can ask the student to state the correct rule or procedure and then to follow it, and then tell the student in a clear, assertive, and nonhostile way to stop the misbehavior. If this fails too, the teacher can offer a choice—stop the behavior or meet privately to work out the consequences.

What can teachers do about bullying, teasing, and cyberbullying? Teachers often underestimate the amount of peer conflict and bullying that happens in schools. Bullying involves both an imbalance of power between students and repeated attempts at harm and may take place in a variety of settings—including those in which students are not face-to-face with one another at school. Teachers can think of bullying as a form of violence and approach strategies for overcoming bullying as they would strategies to overcoming other violent acts. For example, prevention of bullying can take the form of developing a respectful classroom community and discussing conflict.

What are some challenges in secondary classrooms? Teachers working in secondary schools should be prepared to handle students who don't complete schoolwork, repeatedly break the same rule, or openly defy teachers. These students may also be experiencing new and powerful stressors. As a result, secondary students may benefit if teachers provide opportunities or point out resources for these students to seek out help and support. Teachers might also find consultation with guidance counselors and parents or caregivers helpful.

- **The Need for Communication (pp. 515–521)**

What is meant by "empathetic listening"? Communication between teacher and student is essential when problems arise. All interactions between people, even silence or neglect, communicate some meaning. Empathetic, active listening can be a helpful response when students bring problems to teachers. Teachers must reflect back to the students what they hear them saying. This reflection is more than a parroting of words; it should capture the emotions, intent, and meaning behind them.

Distinguish among passive, hostile, and assertive response styles. The passive response style can take several forms. Instead of telling the student directly what to do, the teacher simply comments on the behavior, asks the student to think about the appropriate action, or threatens but never follows through. In a hostile response style, teachers may make "you" statements that condemn the student without stating clearly what the student should

be doing. An assertive response communicates to the students that the teacher cares too much about them and the process of learning to allow inappropriate behavior to persist. Assertive teachers clearly state what they expect.

What is peer mediation? Peer mediation is one good possibility for preventing violence in schools. The steps for peer mediation are: (1) Jointly define the conflict. (2) Exchange positions and interests. (3) Reverse perspectives. (4) Invent at least three agreements that allow mutual gain. (5) Reach an integrative agreement.

- **Diversity: Culturally Responsive Management (pp. 521–522)**

What is culturally responsive management, and why is it needed? African Americans and Latino/a Americans, especially males, are punished more often and more harshly than other students, but they do not commit more serious offenses. Instead, these students are punished more severely for minor offenses such as rudeness or defiance—words and actions that are interpreted by teachers as meriting severe punishment. One explanation is a lack of cultural synchronization between teachers and students. Culturally responsive management combines high expectations for students' appropriate behavior with warmth and caring for the students as individuals.

PRACTICE USING WHAT YOU HAVE LEARNED

To access and complete the exercises, click the link under the images below.

Routines and Procedures

Stopping Problems Quickly

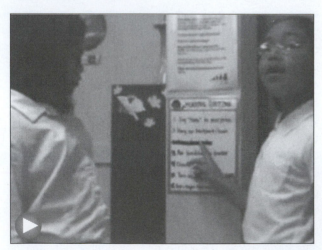

ENHANCEDetext *application exercise*

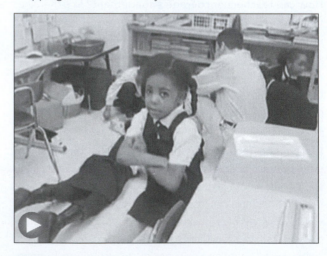

ENHANCEDetext *application exercise*

KEY TERMS

Academic learning time   492
Action zone   498
Assertive discipline   517
Classroom management   491
Culturally responsive management   521
Empathetic listening   516
Engaged time   491

Group focus   503
"I" message   517
Movement management   503
Natural/logical consequences   496
Overlapping   503
Paraphrase rule   515
Participation structures   491

Procedures/routines   494
Rules   494
Self-management   493
Time on task   491
Warm demanders   521
Withitness   503

CONNECT AND EXTEND TO LICENSURE

MULTIPLE-CHOICE QUESTIONS

1. What is the aim of classroom management?
   A. To keep an orderly classroom
   B. To establish the primacy of the teacher
   C. To sustain a quiet and disciplined environment
   D. To maintain a positive productive learning environment

2. Which of the following is NOT a benefit of teaching students to be self-regulated?
   A. Students demonstrate the ability to fulfill their own needs without interfering with the rights and needs of others.
   B. Teachers have fewer management problems, less stress, and more time to teach.
   C. Students require increased teacher attention; therefore, they learn more.
   D. Although it requires extra time initially, it leads to greater teacher self-efficacy.

3. Mr. Ruiz was constantly plagued by students disrupting his English class. Determined to finally gain control, he resorted to afterschool detention, dropping letter grades, and belittling his students. When his evaluation by the principal occurred at the end of the term, he received low scores on his classroom management skills. His principal, Dr. Simon, provided feedback based on research. Which one of the following would NOT be consistent with ideal ways to deal with Mr. Ruiz's problems?
   A. Teachers should begin the school year with severe consequences so students understand the teacher controls the classroom.
   B. Teachers should aim to prevent classroom problems before they occur.

   C. Teachers should exhibit withitness and overlapping in their activities.
   D. Teachers must understand and practice movement management.

4. Which of the following techniques is recommended for approaching and disciplining a student who may be prone to explosive behavior?
   A. Move swiftly and get as close to the misbehaving student as possible.
   B. Ensure that there are several witnesses to the confrontation.
   C. Be respectful and brief.
   D. Use a loud voice to establish power.

CONSTRUCTED-RESPONSE QUESTIONS

Case

It happened every day. Ginny Harding had to reprimand two boys in her class continually. Instead of feeling like a coach and mentor, Ginny started to feel like a nag. It wore on both boys and also on her. The boys were not malicious, they were just third-graders being third-graders. She remembered hearing an adage, one should not continue to do the same thing and expect different results. Over the next weekend Ginny decided to develop a more effective manner of handling this latest challenge.

5. List several simple ways in which Ginny Harding can quickly stop the boys from misbehaving.
6. Routines and procedures can also reduce the incidents of misbehavior by assisting students in smooth transitions from one activity to another. List several classroom operations and activities that should have an established routine or procedure.

ENHANCEDetext *licensure exam*

TEACHERS' CASEBOOK

WHAT WOULD THEY DO? BULLIES AND VICTIMS

Here is how some practicing teachers responded to the problems with bullies at school.

JOLITA HARPER—Third Grade Teacher
Preparing Academic Leaders Academy, Maple Heights, OH

I believe that the entire learning community has a clear role in preventing acts of intimidation between students, and that this is best accomplished with clear communication between all parties. Care should be taken to spread awareness between colleagues as to the nature of the situation. Classroom teachers who are alert to these instances of bullying are then able to provide an additional presence in situations, such as in hallways and the lunchroom, where this is likely to take place. Further, communication between individual classroom teachers and the victim of this bullying is essential. I would make certain to provide a sensitive ear to this student's plight as we work together to formulate alternatives toward improving the situation. Finally, in the event that the two bullying students were in my classes, I would communicate with them in such a way as to make clear the effect of their actions on others in an effort to promote empathy for their victim and, hopefully, initiate a change in their behaviors.

KEITH J. BOYLE—English Teacher, Grades 9–12
Dunellen High School, Dunellen, NJ

Errant behavior throughout the middle school may be indicative of future behavioral problems and, as many things in life, the more this misbehavior is allowed to exist, the longer it will have a chance to thrive. In this case of a child being continually bullied by two other children (gender having no bearing in this situation), the knowledge of this wrongdoing must not be ignored or isolated. I would interview both the victim and the bullies, separately, to glean as much information as possible. If this were a singular incident, I would attempt to handle it myself via contact with the pertinent parents. However, if this were a recurring problem, the administration must be made aware. Any administrator will acknowledge that to be left in the dark about a serious situation within the environs of his or her responsibility is

precarious. The appropriate guidance counselor should also be involved. The gravity of abusive behavior toward fellow students must be emphasized to the offenders. Significant punitive action is integral to send a message to the entire community that their school is indeed a haven in which one can feel the uninhibited freedom to learn.

DAN DOYLE—History Teacher, Grade 11
St. Joseph's Academy, Hoffman, IL

As a high school teacher I'd be especially concerned about the existence of bullying among older students. While such behavior in elementary school is hurtful and damaging, it can become downright dangerous as students get older (and bigger!). I'd also be frustrated to think that, perhaps, early warning signs among these children may have been ignored or under-addressed at the elementary level, when teachers and/or parents are better positioned to get a grip on them. My first step would be to alert school personnel, particularly those who monitor hallways, the cafeteria, and other common areas, to be on the lookout for any type of bullying behavior. I'd put those responsible in communication with the guidance counselor's office; the counselor would determine whether the parents needed to be involved from there. Events in our society in recent years preclude the option of taking this sort of behavior lightly, or assuming it will take care of itself.

KELLEY CROCKETT—Professor and Former Elementary School Teacher
San Diego State University, San Diego, CA, and Fort Worth, TX

Bullying cannot be tolerated. No school, no teacher, no administrator can afford a climate in which abusive behavior is allowed to germinate. Any incident of victimization must be immediately documented and submitted to the principal. As well, I would schedule a conference that same day with the school counselor for my student to both allow another avenue of documentation and reinforce support that the problem is being aggressively addressed.

How I handle the next step depends on the administration in place, but the important issue to remember is that there is a next step. The teacher must follow up with the student. Within 48 hours I would privately ask my student if there have been any further incidents. If he hesitates or acknowledges continued harassment I would direct him to write it down, and I would document any questions I had asked him and his responses. I would then include his statement and my own in another report for both the principal and the counselor.

As teachers, we hold the front line. To the children in our care, we represent one of the first relationships with authority and civilized society. We can do no less than lend our voice and action to the betterment of our world.

14 | TEACHING EVERY STUDENT

TEACHERS' CASEBOOK

WHAT WOULD YOU DO? REACHING AND TEACHING EVERY STUDENT

You have started a new job in a high school in your hometown. When you were in school, the students were fairly homogeneous—White, working to middle class, and English speaking. There was a "special education" class for students who had serious learning or developmental problems. But in the clases you are teaching, you find a wide range of reading levels, family incomes, and learning problems. Two of your students are virtually ready for college, but several others can barely read the texts, and their writing is impossible to decipher. Reading English texts is a challenge for some of your students who are English language learners, although they seem to speak English with little trouble.

CRITICAL THINKING

- How would you differentiate instruction for these very dissimilar students?
- Do different philosophies of teaching provide different answers to this question?
- How will you grade work if you have successfully differenti-ated instruction?

Celisfoto/Fotolia

OVERVIEW AND **OBJECTIVES**

Much of this text has been about learning and learners. In this chapter, we focus on teaching and teachers. Are there particular characteristics that distinguish effective from ineffective teachers? Research on whole-class teaching points to the importance of several factors that we will explore.

What else do we know about teaching? Teachers are designers—they create learning environments (Wiggins & McTighe, 2006). In the process they set goals for their students, develop teaching strategies and activities, and assess to see if goals have been met. We look at how teachers plan, including how to use taxonomies of learning objectives or themes as a basis for planning. With this foundation of knowing how to set goals and make plans, as well as an understanding of the characteristics of effective teachers, we move to a consideration of some general teacher-centered strategies: lecturing, seatwork, homework, questioning, recitation, and group discussion. We then pull goals and strategies together by exploring the Understanding by Design model.

In the final section of this chapter, we will focus on how to match teaching to the needs and abilities of students through differentiated instruction, flexible grouping, and adaptive teaching. Finally we explore how teachers' beliefs about their students' abilities—teacher expectations—might influence student learning and teacher–student relationships.

By the time you have completed this chapter, you should be able to:

Objective 14.1 Identify the methods used to study teaching as well as the characteristics of effective teachers and effective classroom climates.

Objective 14.2 Develop learning objectives using Bloom's taxonomy.

Objective 14.3 Discuss the appropriate uses of direct instruction, homework, questioning, and group discussion and how to use Understanding by Design to integrate objectives, evidence for reaching objectives, and teaching strategies.

Objective 14.4 Define differentiated instruction and adaptive teaching, and apply these approaches to teaching a diverse group of students.

Objective 14.5 Explain the possible effects of teacher expectations, and know how to avoid the negative implications.

RESEARCH ON TEACHING

This chapter is about teaching, so we will start with findings from several decades of research.

How would you go about identifying the keys to successful teaching? You might ask students, principals, college professors of education, or experienced teachers to list the characteristics of good teachers. Or you could do intensive case studies of a few classrooms over a long period. You might observe classes, rate different teachers on certain characteristics, and then see which characteristics were associated with teachers whose students either achieved the most or were the most motivated to learn. (To do this, of course, you would have to decide how to assess achievement and motivation.) You could identify teachers whose students, year after year, learned more than students working with other teachers; then you could observe the more successful teachers and note what they do. You might also train teachers to apply several different strategies to teach the same lesson and then determine which strategy led to the greatest student learning. You could videotape teachers, and then ask them to view the tapes and report what they were thinking about as they taught and what influenced their decisions while teaching, called *stimulated recall*. You might study transcripts of classroom dialogue to learn what helped students understand the material. You might use the relationships identified between teaching and learning as the basis for developing teaching approaches and testing these approaches in *design experiments*.

All of these approaches and more have been used to investigate teaching (Floden, 2001; Greeno, Collins, & Resnick, 1996; Gröschner, Seidel, & Shavelson, 2013). Let's examine some of the specific knowledge about teaching gained from these projects.

Characteristics of Effective Teachers

STOP & THINK Think about the most effective teacher you ever had—the one that you learned the most from. What were the characteristics of that person? What made that teacher so effective? •

Some of the earliest research on effective teaching focused on the personal qualities of the teachers themselves. Results revealed some lessons about three teacher characteristics: clarity, warmth, and knowledge. Recent research has focused on knowledge, so we will spend some extra time on that characteristic.

CLARITY AND ORGANIZATION. When Barak Rosenshine and Norma Furst (1973) reviewed about 50 studies of teaching, they concluded that *clarity* was the most promising teacher behavior for future research on effective teaching. Teachers who provide clear presentations and explanations tend to have students who learn more and who rate their teachers more positively (Comadena, Hunt, & Simonds, 2007; C. V. Hines, Cruickshank, & Kennedy, 1985). The clearer and less vague the teacher's explanations and instructions are, the more the students learn (Evertson & Emmer, 2013).

WARMTH AND ENTHUSIASM. As you are well aware, some teachers are much more enthusiastic than others. Some studies have found that ratings of teachers' enthusiasm for their subject are correlated with student achievement gains (M. Keller, Neumann, & Fischer, 2013), whereas warmth, friendliness, and understanding seem to be the teacher traits most strongly associated with students' liking the teacher and the class in general (Hamann, Baker, McAllister, & Bauer, 2000; K. Madsen, 2003). In studies of the emotional climate of the classroom, researchers consistently find that students learn more in classes where teacher–student relationships are warm, caring, nurturing, and congenial; the teacher takes student needs and perspectives into account; and teachers are not harsh or sarcastic. It is likely that the link between the positive emotional climate and student learning is student engagement (Reyes, Brackett, Rivers, White, & Salovey, 2012). Two possible connections with enthusiasm are that when teachers are enthusiastic, they capture and hold student attention, and that enthusiastic teachers model engagement and interest in learning. Student attention, interest, and engagement lead to learning. Of course, it is easier to be an enthusiastic teacher when your students are learning (M. Keller et al., 2013).

What about another important teacher characteristic—knowledge?

Knowledge for Teaching

As you saw in Chapters 8 and 9, knowledge is the defining characteristic of expertise. **Expert teachers** have elaborate systems of knowledge for understanding problems in teaching. For example, when a beginning teacher is faced with students' wrong answers on math or history tests, all of these answers may seem about the same—wrong. But for an expert teacher, wrong answers are part of a rich system of knowledge that could include how to recognize several types of wrong answers, the misunderstanding or lack of information behind each kind of mistake, the best way to reteach and correct the misunderstanding, materials and activities that have worked in the past, and several ways to test whether the reteaching was successful. This unique kind of teacher knowledge that combines mastery of *academic content* with knowing *how to teach* the content and how to match instruction to *student differences* is called **pedagogical content knowledge (PCK)**. This knowledge is very complex and specific to the *situation,* (e.g., first-period physics), *topic* (e.g., the concept of "force"), *students* (advanced? struggling? learning English as a second language?), and even the individual *teacher.* Within the particular situation and topic, expert teachers have clear goals and take individual differences into account when planning for their students (Gess-Newsome, 2013; van Driel & Berry, 2012). These teachers are **reflective** practitioners, constantly trying to understand and improve their work with students (Hogan, Rabinowitz, & Craven, 2003).

Do teachers who know more about their subject have a more positive impact on their students? It depends on the subject. When H. C. Hill, Rowan, and Ball (2005) tested U.S. first- and third-grade teachers' specific knowledge of the math concepts that they actually teach and their understanding of how to teach those concepts, they found that teachers with greater *content* and *pedagogical content knowledge* had students who learned more mathematics. High school students appear to learn more mathematics from teachers with degrees or significant coursework in mathematics (Wayne & Youngs, 2003). Studies in German high schools have found that math teachers with more pedagogical content knowledge have students who are more cognitively engaged and more supported in learning, and this higher-quality instruction predicts higher student math achievement (Baumert et al., 2010).

When we look at teachers' knowledge of facts and concepts in other subjects besides math, as measured by test scores and college grades, the relationship to student learning is unclear and may be indirect. The indirect effects are that teachers who know more may make clearer presentations and recognize student difficulties more easily. They are ready for any student questions and do not have to be evasive or vague in their answers. Thus, knowledge is necessary for effective teaching because being more knowledgeable helps teachers be *clearer,* more *organized,* and more *responsive* to student questions (Aloe & Becker, 2009). We know that the quality of teachers—as measured by whether the teachers are fully certified and have a major in their teaching field—is related to student performance. When we look at scores on teacher certification tests, there is a modest positive relationship between teachers' scores and students' achievement; the strongest evidence for this relationship is again in mathematics (Boyd, Goldhaber, Lankford, & Wyckoff, 2008; Darling-Hammond & Youngs, 2002).

Recent Research on Teaching

In Chapter 1 you learned about Charlotte Danielson's Framework for Teaching (2013), TeachingWorks, and the Measures of Effective Teaching (MET) project sponsored by the Bill and Melinda Gates Foundation. The developers of these models looked to research on teaching and student learning as a foundation for their conceptions of good teaching. In this chapter we look

Video 14.1
According to research on effective teaching, personal qualities of the teachers themselves include clarity, warmth, and knowledge. The first-grade teacher in this video demonstrates these qualities in her teaching.

ENHANCEDetext *video example*

TABLE 14.1 • **Dimensions of Classroom Climate**

AREA OF TEACHING	CLASSROOM CLIMATE DIMENSION	COMPONENTS	DEFINITIONS AND EXAMPLES
Affective	**Emotional Support**	*Positive Climate*	Warmth, mutual respect, positive emotional connections between teacher and students
		Negative Climate (negative predictor of learning)	Disrespect, anger, hostility
		Teacher Sensitivity	Consistency and effectiveness in responding to students' academic and emotional needs
		Regard for Students' Perspectives	Activities encourage student autonomy and emphasize students' interests, motivations, and points of view
Cognitive	**Instructional Support**	*Concept Development*	Activities and discussion promote higher-order thinking skills and cognition
		Quality of Feedback	Consistency in providing specific, process-oriented feedback and back-and-forth exchanges to extend students' learning
Behavioral	**Classroom Organization**	*Behavior Management*	Teachers' effectiveness in monitoring, preventing, and redirecting misbehavior
		Productivity	How consistently learning is maximized with clear activities and routines, teacher preparation, efficient transitions, and minimal disruptions
		Instructional Learning Formats	How well materials, modalities, and activities are used to engage students in learning

Source: Based on Brown, J. L., Jones, S. M., LaRusso, M. D., & Aber, J. L. (2010). *Improving classroom quality: Teacher influences and experimental impacts of the 4Rs Program.* Journal of Educational Psychology, 102, 153–167.

more closely at a program of large-scale, longitudinal research by Robert Pianta and his colleagues (Allen, Gregory, Mikami, Lun, Hamre, & Pianta, 2013; Crosnoe et al., 2010; Hafen, Allen, Mikami, Gregory, Hamre, & Pianta, 2012; Jerome, Hamre, & Pianta, 2009; Luckner & Pianta, 2011; Pianta, Belsky, et al., 2008; Pianta, LaParo, et al., 2008). This research program is one of the foundations for the models and frameworks described in Chapter 1.

Pianta's work has identified three aspects of classroom climate that are related to the development and learning of preschool and elementary school students; the relations probably hold in secondary school too. These three dimensions are consistent with the characteristics of teachers identified in earlier research on teaching, and they cover affective, behavioral, and cognitive dimensions, as you can see in Table 14.1. The *affective* dimension in Pianta's model is teacher *emotional support,* similar to teacher warmth and enthusiasm identified in early research. The *cognitive* dimension is instructional support, which includes concept development (activities and discussions that promote student higher-order thinking) and quality feedback that is specific and focused on the learning process. Concept development and quality feedback may be easier for teachers with greater knowledge for teaching. Pianta's third dimension is classroom organization, which includes *behavioral* concerns such as classroom and lesson management, with clear activities and routines that make more time for student learning and are really engaging—similar to the teacher characteristics of clarity and organization.

Now let's get to the specifics of teaching—the first step is planning.

ENHANCEDetext *self-check*

THE FIRST STEP: PLANNING

STOP & THINK Greta Morine-Dershimer (2006) asks which of the following are true about teacher planning:

Time is of the essence.

Plans are made to be broken.

Don't look back.

A little planning goes a long way.

You can do it yourself.

One size fits all. •

Research on Planning

When you thought about the "What Would You Do?" challenge at the beginning of this chapter, you were planning. In the past few years, educational researchers have become very interested in teachers' planning. They have interviewed teachers about how they plan, asked teachers to "think out loud" while planning or to keep journals describing their plans, and even studied teachers intensively for months at a time. What do you think they have found?

First, planning influences what students will learn, because planning transforms the available time and curriculum materials into activities, assignments, and tasks for students—*time is of the essence in planning*. When a teacher decides to devote 7 hours to language arts and 15 minutes to science in a given week, the students in that class will learn more language than science. Planning done at the beginning of the year is particularly important, because many routines and patterns, such as time allocations, are established early. So, *a little planning does go a long way* in terms of what will be taught and what will be learned.

Second, teachers engage in several levels of planning—by the year, term, unit, week, and day. All the levels must be coordinated. Accomplishing the year's plan requires breaking the work into terms, the terms into units, and the units into weeks and days. For experienced teachers, unit planning seems to be the most important level, followed by weekly and then daily planning. As you gain experience in teaching, it will be easier to coordinate these levels of planning and incorporate the state and district curriculum standards as well (Morine-Dershimer, 2006).

Third, plans reduce—but do not eliminate—uncertainty in teaching. Planning must allow flexibility. Some evidence shows that when teachers "overplan"—fill every minute and stick to the plan no matter what—their students do not learn as much as students whose teachers are flexible (Shavelson, 1987). So *plans are not made to be broken—but sometimes they need to be bent a bit*.

To plan creatively and flexibly, teachers need to have wide-ranging knowledge about students, their interests, and their abilities; the subjects being taught; alternative ways to teach and assess understanding; how to apply and adapt materials and texts; and how to pull all this knowledge together into meaningful activities. The plans of beginning teachers sometimes don't work because they lack knowledge about the students or the subject—they can't estimate how long it will take students to complete an activity, for example, or they stumble when asked for an explanation or a different example (Calderhead, 1996).

In planning, *you can do it yourself—but collaboration is better*. Working with other teachers and sharing ideas is one of the best experiences in teaching. Some educators think that a collaborative approach to planning used in Japan called *kenshu* or "mastery through study" is one reason why Japanese students do so well on international tests. A basic part of the kenshu process involves a small group of teachers developing a lesson and then videotaping one of the group members teaching the lesson. Next, all members review the tape, analyze student responses, and improve the lesson further. Other teachers try the revised lesson and more improvements follow. At the end of

Video 14.2
When a school has more than one class at each grade, planning conferences that include all the teachers for that grade, like this one, can be particularly effective.

ENHANCEDetext *video example*

© Randy Glasbergen
glasbergen.com

"On Mondays, I get ready to plan my week. On Tuesdays, I plan my week. On Wednesdays, I revise my plan for the week. On Thursdays, I put my plan for the week into my computer. On Fridays, I think about starting my plan for next week."

Reprinted with permission from Randy Glasbergen.

the school year, all the study groups may publish the results of their work. In the United States, this process is called **lesson study** (Morine-Dershimer, 2006). To learn about this approach, search the Internet using the keywords "lesson study." Then, explore some of the lesson plans available using the keywords "lesson plans," or search by subject or grade—for example, "math lesson plans" or "fourth-grade lesson plans."

But even great lesson plans taken from a terrific Web site on science must be adapted to your situation. Some of the adaptation comes before you teach and some comes after. In fact, much of what experienced teachers know about planning comes from looking back—reflecting—on what worked and what didn't, so *DO look back* on your plans and grow professionally in the process. Collaborative reflection and revising lessons are major components of the lesson study approach to planning.

Finally, there is no one model for effective planning. *One size does NOT fit all* in planning. Planning is a creative problem-solving process for experienced teachers; they know how to complete many lessons and can teach segments of lessons effectively. They know what to expect and how to proceed, so they don't necessarily continue to follow the detailed lesson-planning models they learned during their teacher preparation programs. Planning is more informal—"in their heads." However, many experienced teachers think it was helpful to learn this detailed system as a foundation (C. M. Clark & Peterson, 1986).

No matter how you plan, you must have a learning goal in mind. In the next section, we consider the range of goals that you might have for your students.

Objectives for Learning

It is difficult to get somewhere if you don't know where you are going. Similarly, it is difficult to plan a unit or lesson if you don't have a clear goal for learning. We hear quite a bit today about visions, goals, outcomes, and standards. At a very general, abstract level are the grand goals society may have for graduates of public schools such as preparing them "to succeed in college and the workplace and to compete in the global economy" (U.S. Department of Education, *Race to the Top,* 2009, p. 2). But very general goals are meaningless as potential guidelines for instruction. States may turn these grand goals into *standards* and *indicators,* such as the Colorado standard that students will "Use comprehension skills such as previewing, predicting, inferring, comparing and contrasting, rereading and self-monitoring, summarizing, etc." At this level, the indicators are close to being instructional objectives (Airasian, 2005). You can find your state's standards at education-world.com/standards/state/index.shtml.

AN EXAMPLE OF STANDARDS: THE COMMON CORE. The United States has a long history of local control of education, leading to many good things but also to vast differences in what students learn in each grade and school district across the nation. It is no secret that students in the United States have not performed well on international tests like the Program for International Student Assessment (PISA), a comprehensive worldwide assessment of reading, mathematics and science for 15-year-olds. For example, the United States ranked 36th out of 65 countries in total scores on this assessment in 2012 (Organisation for Economic Co-operation and Development, 2013), and 23 out of 29 countries when you look at problem-solving performance alone (Belland, 2011). In response to these concerns about vastly different grade-level standards and disappointing test results, in 2009 the Council of Chief State School Officers (CCSSO) and the National Governors Association Center for Best Practices (NGA Center) led an effort to define consistent national standards for each grade, K–12, in two broad areas: (1) English language arts and literacy in history/social studies, science, and technical subjects, and (2) mathematics. Table 14.2 gives a few examples of Common Core Standards in these areas.

If you watch the brief video at corestandards.org/about-the-standards/, you will learn that the purposes of the Common Core Standards are "clear goals" and "confident well-prepared students." To reach these targets, the standards are designed to be:

- Research- and evidence-based
- Clear, understandable, and consistent
- Aligned with college and career expectations

TABLE 14.2 • **A Few Examples of the Core Standards for Grades 6 and 11–12 in Literature, Writing, and Mathematics**

SUBJECT AND SKILL	GRADE 6	GRADES 11 AND 12
Reading Literature: Key Ideas and Details	Cite textual evidence to support analysis of what the text says explicitly as well as inferences drawn from the text.	Cite strong and thorough textual evidence to support analysis of what the text says explicitly as well as inferences drawn from the text, including determining where the text leaves matters uncertain.
Writing: Research to Build and Present Knowledge	Conduct short research projects to answer a question, drawing on several sources and refocusing the inquiry when appropriate.	Conduct short as well as more sustained research projects to answer a question (including a self-generated question) or solve a problem; narrow or broaden the inquiry when appropriate; synthesize multiple sources on the subject, demonstrating understanding of the subject under investigation.
Mathematics: Expressions and Equations	Understand that rewriting an expression in different forms in a problem context can shed light on the problem and how the quantities in it are related. For example, a + 0.05a = 1.05a means that "increase by 5%" is the same as "multiply by 1.05."	Explain each step in solving a simple equation as following from the equality of numbers asserted at the previous step, starting from the assumption that the original equation has a solution. Construct a viable argument to justify a solution method.

- Based on rigorous content and application of knowledge through higher-order thinking skills
- Built on the strengths and lessons of current state standards
- Informed by other top-performing countries in order to prepare all students for success in our global economy and society (corestandards.org/about-the-standards/)

When I wrote this paragraph, 45 states, the District of Columbia, and four territories had adopted the standards and were moving toward implementing them. To see what your state is doing, go to corestandards.org/standards-in-your-state/.

There is continuing debate about the Common Core Standards. As you read Table 14.2, you may have noticed that the expectations are high and the standards are rigorous. One other example of raised expectations is that the texts third- and fourth-graders are expected to read and comprehend are more complex than current texts for those grades. This could lead to less fluency and automaticity in recognizing words, decreased engagement in reading, and higher failure rates (Hiebert & Mesmer, 2013). As a teacher you should follow this discussion because the Common Core Standards probably will impact what is taught (curriculum materials, textbooks, course planning) and what is assessed in every grade.

AN EXAMPLE OF STANDARDS FOR TEACHERS: TECHNOLOGY. Here is an example of standards that relate to you—the teacher—and what you should know about technology. One widely adopted technology standard is from the ISTE, the International Society for Technology in Education (ISTE, at iste.org/docs/pdfs/20–14_ISTE_Standards-T_PDF.pdf). Teachers should:

1. *Facilitate and inspire student learning and creativity.* Teachers use their knowledge of subject matter, teaching and learning, and technology to facilitate experiences that advance student learning, creativity, and innovation in both face-to-face and virtual environments.
2. *Design and develop digital-age learning experiences and assessments.* Teachers design, develop, and evaluate authentic learning experiences and assessment incorporating contemporary tools and resources to maximize content learning in context and to develop the knowledge, skills, and attitudes identified in the ISTE standards for students.
3. *Model digital-age work and learning.* Teachers exhibit knowledge, skills, and work processes representative of an innovative professional in a global and digital society.
4. *Promote and model digital citizenship and responsibility.* Teachers understand local and global societal issues and responsibilities in an evolving digital culture and exhibit legal and ethical behavior in their professional practices.

5. *Engage in professional growth and leadership.* Teachers continuously improve their professional practice, model lifelong learning, and exhibit leadership in their school and professional community by promoting and demonstrating the effective use of digital tools and resources.

But what about your teaching? Let's move into the classroom and talk about clear rigorous goals for your students.

CLASSROOMS: INSTRUCTIONAL OBJECTIVES. Norman Gronlund and Susan Brookhart (2009) define instructional objectives as intended learning outcomes. Objectives are the performances expected of students after instruction in order to demonstrate their learning. Having a clear objective helps teachers avoid what Grant Wiggins and Jay McTighe (2006) call the "twin sins" of instructional design—*activity-focused teaching* (lots of hands-on, interesting activities—but no goal) and *coverage-focused teaching* (a forced march through the textbook—but no goal). In either case, learning can be lost if the teacher is not clear about why students are doing activities or the reading—what is the big idea guiding the teaching—the *objective*.

Objectives written by people with behavioral views focus on observable and measurable changes in the learner. Behavioral objectives use terms such as *list, define, add,* or *calculate.* Cognitive objectives, on the other hand, emphasize thinking and comprehension, so they are more likely to include words such as *understand, recognize, create,* or *apply.* Let's look at one well-developed method of writing specific behavioral objectives.

MAGER: START WITH THE SPECIFIC. According to Robert Mager (1975, 1997), a good behavioral objective has three parts. First, it describes the intended *student behavior.* What must the student do? Second, it lists the *conditions* under which the behavior will occur: How will this behavior be recognized or tested? Third, it gives the *criteria* for acceptable performance on the test. For example, an objective in social studies might be: "Given a recent article from an online political blog [*conditions*], the student will mark each statement with an F for fact or an O for opinion [*observable student behavior*], with 75% of the statements correctly marked [*criteria*]." With this emphasis on final behavior, Mager's system requires a very explicit statement. Mager contends that often students can teach themselves if they are given well-stated objectives.

GRONLUND: START WITH THE GENERAL. Gronlund and Brookhart (2009) offer a different approach, which is often used for writing cognitive objectives. They believe an objective should be stated first in general terms (*understand, solve, appreciate,* etc.). Then, the teacher should clarify by listing a few sample behaviors that provide evidence that the student has attained the objective. Look at the example in Table 14.3. The goal here is understanding a scientific concept. A teacher could never list all the behaviors that might be involved in "understanding," but stating an initial, general objective along with specific examples makes the purpose clear.

Connect and Extend to PRAXIS II®

Instructional Objectives (II, B1)
Describe the key elements of behavioral and instructional objectives. Be able to write each type of objective for a content area that you expect to teach.

TABLE 14.3 • **A Combined Method for Creating Objectives**

GENERAL OBJECTIVE
Understands scientific principles.

SPECIFIC EXAMPLES
1. Describes the principle in own words.
2. Identifies examples of the principle.
3. States tentative hypotheses based on the principle.
4. Uses the principle in solving novel problems.
5. Distinguishes between two given principles.
6. Explains the relationship between two given principles.

Source: Miller, M. D., Linn, R., & Gronlund, N. E. (2013). Measurement and Assessment in Teaching, 11th Ed. Upper Saddle River, NJ: Pearson Education, Inc. Adapted with permission.

Flexible and Creative Plans—Using Taxonomies

Connect and Extend to PRAXIS II®
Taxonomies of Educational Objectives (II, B1)
Taxonomies influence every aspect of instruction from textbook design to lesson planning. List the major objectives of each of the taxonomies, and describe the focus of each objective. Be able to incorporate these objectives into instructional objectives that you design.

STOP & THINK Think about your assignments for one of your classes. What kind of thinking is involved in doing the assignments?

Remembering facts and terms?

Understanding key ideas?

Applying information to solve problems?

Analyzing a situation, task, or problem?

Making evaluations or giving opinions?

Creating or designing something new? •

In the 1950s, a group of experts in educational evaluation led by Benjamin Bloom set out to improve college and university examinations. The impact of their work has touched education at all levels around the world (L. W. Anderson & Sosniak, 1994). Bloom and his colleagues developed a taxonomy, or classification system, of educational objectives. Objectives were divided into three domains: *cognitive, affective,* and *psychomotor.* A handbook describing the objectives in each area was eventually published. In real life, of course, behaviors from these three domains occur simultaneously. While students are writing (psychomotor), they are also remembering or reasoning (cognitive), and they are likely to have some emotional response to the task as well (affective).

THE COGNITIVE DOMAIN. Bloom's taxonomy of the thinking domain, or cognitive domain, is considered one of the most significant educational writings of the 20th century (L. W. Anderson & Sosniak, 1994). The six basic objectives in Bloom's taxonomy are *knowledge, comprehension, application, analysis, synthesis,* and *evaluation* (B. S. Bloom, Engelhart, Frost, Hill, & Krathwohl, 1956).

It is common in education to consider these objectives as a hierarchy, each skill building on those below, but this is not entirely accurate. Some subjects, such as mathematics, do not fit this structure very well (Kreitzer & Madaus, 1994). Still, you will hear many references to *lower-level* and *higher-level* objectives, with knowledge, comprehension, and application considered lower level and the other categories considered higher level. As a rough way of thinking about objectives, this can be helpful (Gronlund & Brookhart, 2009). The taxonomy of objectives can also be helpful in planning assessments because different procedures are appropriate for objectives at the various levels, as you will see in Chapter 15.

In 2001, a group of educational researchers published the first major revision of the cognitive taxonomy, and this is the one we use today (L. W. Anderson & Krathwohl, 2001).

1. *Remembering:* Remembering or recognizing something without necessarily understanding, using, or changing it.
2. *Understanding:* Understanding the material being communicated without necessarily relating it to anything else.
3. *Applying:* Using a general concept to solve a particular problem.
4. *Analyzing:* Breaking something down into its parts.
5. *Evaluating:* Judging the value of materials or methods as they might be applied in a particular situation.
6. *Creating:* Creating something new by combining different ideas.

The 2001 revision of Bloom's taxonomy added a new dimension—to recognize that cognitive processes must process *something*—you have to remember or understand or apply some form of knowledge. If you look at Table 14.4 on the next page, you will see the result. We now have the six processes of *remembering, understanding, applying, analyzing, evaluating,* and *creating* acting on four kinds of knowledge—*factual, conceptual, procedural,* and *metacognitive.*

Consider how this revised taxonomy might suggest objectives for a social studies/language arts class. Here's an example of an objective that targets analyzing conceptual knowledge:

After reading an historical account of the battle of the Alamo, students will be able to explain the author's point of view or bias.

TABLE 14.4 • **A Revised Taxonomy in the Cognitive Domain**
The revised taxonomy includes cognitive processes operating on different kinds of knowledge. The verbs in the chart are examples of what might be used to create objectives.

	THE COGNITIVE PROCESS DIMENSION					
THE KNOWLEDGE DIMENSION	**1. REMEMBER**	**2. UNDERSTAND**	**3. APPLY**	**4. ANALYZE**	**5. EVALUATE**	**6. CREATE**
A. Factual Knowledge	list	summarize	classify	order	rank	combine
B. Conceptual Knowledge	describe	interpret	experiment	explain	assess	plan
C. Procedural Knowledge	tabulate	predict	calculate	differentiate	conclude	compose
D. Metacognitive Knowledge	appropriate use	execute	select strategy	change strategy	reflect	invent

Source: From Anderson, L. W. & Krathwohl, D. R. (Eds.), (2001). A Taxonomy for Learning, Teaching, and Assessing. Boston, MA: Pearson Education, Inc. Reprinted by permission.

And here's an objective for evaluating metacognitive knowledge:

> Students will reflect on and describe their strategies for identifying the biases of the author.

See projects.coe.uga.edu/epltt/index.php?title=Bloom%27s_Taxonomy for more explanations and examples.

THE AFFECTIVE DOMAIN. The objectives in the taxonomy of the **affective domain**, or domain of emotional response, have not yet been revised from the original version. These objectives run from least to most committed (Krathwohl, Bloom, & Masia, 1964). At the lowest level, a student simply pays attention to a certain idea. At the highest level, the student adopts an idea or a value and acts consistently with that idea. The affective domain has five basic objectives:

1. *Receiving:* Being aware of or attending to something in the environment.
2. *Responding:* Showing some new behavior as a result of experience.
3. *Valuing:* Showing some definite involvement or commitment.
4. *Organization:* Integrating a new value into your general set of values, giving it some ranking among your general priorities.
5. *Characterization by value:* Acting consistently with the new value.

Like the basic objectives in the cognitive domain, these five objectives are very general. To write specific learning objectives, you must state what students will actually be doing when they are receiving, responding, valuing, and so on. For example, an objective for a nutrition class at the valuing level (showing involvement or commitment) might be stated: "After completing the unit on food contents and labeling, at least 50% of the class will commit to the junk-food boycott project by giving up fast food for a month."

THE PSYCHOMOTOR DOMAIN. James Cangelosi (1990) provided a useful way to think about objectives in the **psychomotor domain**, or realm of physical ability objectives, as either (1) voluntary muscle capabilities that require endurance, strength, flexibility, agility, or speed, or (2) the ability to perform a specific skill.

Here are two psychomotor objectives:

> Four minutes after completing a 1-mile run in 8 minutes or under, your heart rate will be below 120.
> Use a computer mouse effectively to "drag and drop" files.

CHAPTER 14 • TEACHING EVERY STUDENT   539

GUIDELINES
Using Instructional Objectives

Avoid "word magic"—phrases that sound noble and important, but say very little, such as, "Students will become deep thinkers."

Examples

1. Keep the focus on specific changes that will take place in the students' knowledge and skills.
2. Ask students to explain the meaning of the objectives. If they can't give specific examples of what you mean, the objectives are not communicating your intentions to your students.

Suit the activities to the objectives.

Examples

1. If the goal is the memorization of vocabulary, give the students memory aids and practice exercises.
2. If the goal is the ability to develop well-thought-out positions, consider position papers, debates, projects, or mock trials.

3. If you want students to become better writers, give many opportunities for writing and rewriting.

Make sure your tests are related to your objectives.

Examples

1. Write objectives and rough drafts for tests at the same time. Revise these drafts of tests as the units unfold and objectives change.
2. Weight the tests according to the importance of the various objectives and the time spent on each.

For additional ideas, see assessment.uconn.edu

The *Guidelines: Using Instructional Objectives* should help you if you use objectives for every lesson or even for just a few assignments.

Planning from a Constructivist Perspective

STOP & THINK Think about the same course assignments you analyzed in the previous *Stop & Think*. What are the big ideas that run through all those assignments? What other ways could you learn about those ideas besides the assignments? •

Connect and Extend to PRAXIS II®

Planning Thematic Units (II, A2)
Thematic learning units that integrate two or more content areas have become common in modern classrooms. Describe the principles involved in designing these activities, and explain how student learning can be assessed.

Traditionally, it has been the teacher's responsibility to do most of the planning for instruction, but new ways of planning are emerging. In **constructivist approaches**, planning is shared and negotiated. The teacher and students together make decisions about content, activities, and approaches. Rather than having specific student behaviors and skills as objectives, the teacher has overarching goals—"big ideas" or themes—that guide planning (Borich, 2011). These goals are understandings or abilities that the teacher returns to again and again. Since the 1990s, teaching with themes and integrated content has been a major element in planning and designing lessons and units from kindergarten (Roskos & Neuman, 1998) through high school (Clarke & Agne, 1997). For example, Elaine Homestead and Karen McGinnis (middle school teachers) and Elizabeth Pate (a college professor) designed a unit on "Human Interactions" that included studying racism, world hunger, pollution, and air and water quality. Students researched issues by reading textbooks and outside sources, learning to use databases, interviewing local officials, and inviting guest speakers into class. Students had to develop knowledge in science, mathematics, and social studies. They learned to write and speak persuasively, and, in the process, raised money for hunger relief in Africa (Pate, McGinnis, & Homestead, 1995).

Elementary-age students can benefit from integrated planning, too. There is no reason to work on spelling skills, then listening skills, then writing skills, and then social studies or science. All these abilities can be developed together if students work to solve authentic problems. Some topics for integrating themes with younger children are people, friendship, communications, habitats, communities, and patterns. Possibilities for older students are given in Table 14.5 on the next page.

Let's assume you have an idea of what you want students to understand, but how do you teach to encourage understanding? You still need to decide what's happening on Monday. You need to design teaching that is appropriate for your objectives.

ENHANCEDetext *self-check*

TABLE 14.5 • **Some Themes for Integrated Planning for Middle and High School Students**

Courage	Time and Space
Mystery	Groups and Institutions
Survival	Work
Human Interaction	Motion
Communities of the Future	Cause and Effect
Communication/Language	Probability and Prediction
Human Rights and Responsibilities	Change and Conservation
Identity/Coming of Age	Diversity and Variation
Interdependence	Autobiography

Source: Based on Clarke, J. H. & Agne, R. M. (1997). Curriculum Development: Interdisciplinary High School Teaching. Boston, MA: Pearson, and Thompson, G. (1991). Teaching through Themes. New York, NY: Scholastic.

TEACHING APPROACHES

In this section you will learn some basic formats for putting plans into action. The first challenge is to match your teaching methods to your objectives. We begin with strategies for teaching explicit facts and concepts.

Direct Instruction

For many people, "teaching" means an instructor explaining material to students; lecture is a classic form. An explosion of research in the 1970s and 1980s focused on these more traditional forms of teaching. The results of all this work identified a model of teaching that was related to improved student learning. Barak Rosenshine and Robert Stevens (1986) call this approach **direct instruction** or **explicit teaching**. Tom Good (1983a) uses the term **active teaching** to describe a similar approach.

The direct instruction model fits a specific set of circumstances because it was derived from a particular approach to research. Researchers identified the elements of direct instruction by comparing teachers whose students learned more than expected (based on entering knowledge) with teachers whose students performed at an expected or average level. The researchers focused on existing practices in American classrooms. Because the focus was on traditional forms of teaching, the research could not identify successful innovations. Effectiveness was usually defined as average improvement in standardized test scores for a whole class or school. So the results hold for large groups, but not necessarily for every student in the group. Even when the average achievement of a group improves, the achievement of some individuals may decline (T. L. Good, 1996; Shuell, 1996).

Given these conditions, you can see that direct instruction applies best to the teaching of **basic skills**—clearly structured knowledge and essential skills, such as science facts, mathematics computations, reading vocabulary, and grammar rules (Rosenshine & Stevens, 1986). These skills involve tasks that are relatively unambiguous, so they can be taught step by step and evaluated by standardized tests. Franz Weinert and Andreas Helmke (1995) describe direct instruction as having the following features:

> (a the teacher's classroom management is especially effective and the rate of student interruptive behaviors is very low (b the teacher maintains a strong academic focus and uses available instructional time intensively to initiate and facilitate students' learning activities (c the teacher insures that as many students as possible achieve good learning progress by carefully choosing appropriate tasks, clearly presenting subject-matter

Connect and Extend to PRAXIS II®

Teacher-Centered Instruction (II, A3)
Teacher-centered instruction is often thought of as the "traditional" approach to instruction. In what situations is this instructional format most effective? What are the basic steps involved in carrying out this form of instruction?

information and solution strategies, continuously diagnosing each student's learning progress and learning difficulties, and providing effective help through remedial instruction. (p. 138)

To this list, Xin Ma (2013) adds moving at a brisk pace and having a warm and accepting classroom climate.

How would a teacher turn these themes into actions?

ROSENSHINE'S SIX TEACHING FUNCTIONS. Rosenshine and his colleagues (Rosenshine, 1988; Rosenshine & Stevens, 1986) have identified six teaching functions based on the research on effective instruction. These could serve as a checklist or framework for teaching basic skills.

1. *Review and check the previous day's work.* Reteach if students misunderstood or made errors.
2. *Present new material.* Make the purpose clear, teach in small steps, and provide many examples and nonexamples of the ideas and concepts you are teaching.
3. *Provide guided practice.* Question students, give practice problems, and listen for misconceptions and misunderstandings. Reteach if necessary. Continue guided practice until students answer about 80% of the questions correctly.
4. *Give feedback and correctives based on student answers.* Reteach if necessary. (Remember, Pianta, LaParo, & Hamre's 2008 class climate component of instructional support included quality feedback.)
5. *Provide independent practice.* Let students apply the new learning on their own, in seatwork, cooperative groups, or homework. The success rate during independent practice should be about 95%. This means that students must be well prepared for the work by the presentation and guided practice and that assignments must not be too difficult. The point is for the students to practice until the skills become overlearned and automatic—until the students are confident. Hold students accountable for the work they do—check it.
6. *Review weekly and monthly to consolidate learning.* Include some review items as homework. Test often, and reteach material missed on the tests.

These six functions are not steps to be followed in a particular order, but all of them are elements of effective instruction. For example, feedback, review, or reteaching should occur whenever necessary and should match the abilities of the students. Also, keep in mind the age and prior knowledge of your students. The younger or the less-prepared your students are, the briefer your explanations should be. Use more and shorter cycles of presentation, guided practice, feedback, and correctives.

ADVANCE ORGANIZERS. Teachers using direct instruction often begin with an **advance organizer**. This is an introductory statement broad enough to encompass all the information that will follow. The organizers can serve three purposes: They direct your attention to what is important in the coming material, they highlight relationships among ideas that will be presented, and they remind you of relevant information you already have.

Advance organizers fall into one of two categories, comparative and expository (Mayer, 1984). *Comparative organizers* activate (bring into working memory) already existing schemas. They remind you of what you already know but may not realize is relevant. A comparative advance organizer for a history lesson on revolutions might be a statement that contrasts military uprisings with the physical and social changes involved in the Industrial Revolution; you could also compare the common aspects of the French, English, Mexican, Russian, Iranian, Egyptian, and American revolutions (Salomon & Perkins, 1989).

In contrast, *expository organizers* provide new knowledge that students will need in order to understand the upcoming information. In an English class, you might begin a large thematic unit on rites of passage in literature with a very broad statement of the theme and why it has been so central in literature—something like, "A central character coming of age must learn to know himself or herself, often makes some kind of journey of self-discovery, and must decide what in the society is to be accepted and what should be rejected." Such an organizer might precede reading novels such as *The Adventures of Huckleberry Finn.*

Connect and Extend to PRAXIS II®

Advance Organizers (II, A3)
The advance organizer is an important element in many teacher-centered/expository approaches to instruction. Be able to explain the role of the advance organizer in these approaches, and identify the basic types of organizers.

The general conclusion of research on advance organizers is that they do help students learn, especially when the material to be learned is quite unfamiliar, complex, or difficult—as long as two conditions are met (Langan-Fox, Waycott, & Albert, 2000; Morin & Miller, 1998). First, to be effective, the students must understand the organizer. This was demonstrated dramatically in a classic study by Dinnel and Glover (1985). They found that instructing students to paraphrase an advance organizer—which, of course, requires them to understand its meaning—increased the effectiveness of the organizer. Second, the organizer must really be an organizer: It must indicate relations among the basic concepts and terms that will be used. Concrete models, diagrams, or analogies seem to be especially good organizers (D. H. Robinson, 1998; D. H. Robinson & Kiewra, 1995).

WHY DOES DIRECT INSTRUCTION WORK? Well-organized presentations with clear explanations, the use of advance organizers, and reviews can all help students perceive connections among ideas. If done well, therefore, a direct instruction lesson could be a resource that students use to construct understanding. For example, reviews and advance organizers activate prior knowledge, so the student is ready to understand. Brief, clear presentations and guided practice avoid overloading the students' information processing systems and taxing their working memories. Numerous examples and nonexamples that highlight similarities and differences give many pathways and associations for building networks of concepts. Guided practice can also give the teacher a snapshot of the students' thinking as well as their misconceptions, so these can be addressed directly as misconceptions rather than simply as "wrong answers."

Every subject, even college English or chemistry, requires some direct instruction. Noddings (1990) reminds teachers that students may need some direct instruction in how to use various manipulative materials so they can actually learn from (not just play with) the materials. Students working in cooperative groups may need guidance, modeling, and practice in how to ask questions and give explanations. And to solve difficult problems, students may need some direct instruction in possible problem-solving strategies.

Some studies have found that teachers' presentations take up one sixth to one fourth of all classroom time. Teacher explanation is appropriate for communicating a large amount of material to many students in a short period of time, introducing a new topic, giving background information, or motivating students to learn more on their own. Teacher presentations are therefore most appropriate for cognitive and affective objectives at the lower levels of the taxonomies described earlier: for remembering, understanding, applying, receiving, responding, and valuing (Arends, 2001; Kindsvatter, Wilen, & Ishler, 1992).

EVALUATING DIRECT INSTRUCTION. Direct instruction, particularly when it involves extended teacher presentations or lectures, has some disadvantages. You may find that some students have trouble listening for more than a few minutes at a time and that they simply tune you out. Teacher presentations can put the students in a passive position by doing much of the cognitive work for them; this may prevent students from asking or even thinking of questions (H. J. Freiberg & Driscoll, 2005). Scripted cooperation is one way of incorporating active learning into lectures. Several times during the presentation, the teacher asks students to work in pairs. One person is the summarizer and the other critiques the summary, then they switch roles for the next summary/critique. This gives students a chance to check their understanding, organize their thinking, and translate ideas into their own words. Other possibilities are described in Table 14.6.

Critics also claim that direct instruction is based on the wrong theory of learning. Teachers break material into small segments, present each segment clearly, and reinforce or correct, thus transmitting accurate understandings from teacher to student. The student is viewed as an "empty vessel" waiting to be filled with knowledge, rather than an active constructor of knowledge (Berg & Clough, 1991; Driscoll, 2005). These criticisms of direct instruction echo the criticisms of behavioral learning theories.

Ample evidence, however, indicates that direct instruction and explanation can help students learn actively, not passively (Leinhardt, 2001). For younger and less-prepared learners, student-controlled learning without teacher direction and instruction can lead to systematic deficits in the students' knowledge. Without guidance, the understandings that students construct can be incomplete

TABLE 14.6 • **Active Learning and Teacher Presentations**
Here are some ideas for keeping students cognitively engaged in lessons.
They can be adapted for many ages.

Write an Answer: Pose a question, ask everyone to write a brief answer, then call on students to share what they wrote.	**Voting:** Pose two alternative explanations; ask how many agree with each (may be a good idea to ask the students to close their eyes and vote so they won't be swayed by the votes of others).
I used to think_____, but now I know_____: After a lesson, ask students to fill in the blanks then share their results with the person beside them.	**Choral Response:** Have the whole class restate in unison important facts and ideas, such as "In a right triangle, $a^2 + b^2 = c^2$."
Think-Pair-Share: Pose a question, students think of an answer on their own, then consult with a neighbor to improve the answer, then volunteers share their ideas.	**One-Minute-Write:** After a section of the lesson, students write for 1 minute to summarize the key points or raise a question about what is not clear to them.

and misleading (Sweller, Kirschner, & Clark, 2007). For example, Harris and Graham (1996) describe the experiences of their daughter Leah in a whole-language/progressive education school, where the teachers successfully developed their daughter's creativity, thinking, and understanding.

> Skills, on the other hand, have been a problem for our daughter and for other children. At the end of kindergarten, when she had not made much progress in reading, her teacher said she believed Leah had a perceptual problem or a learning disability. Leah began asking what was wrong with her, because other kids were reading and she wasn't. Finally, an assessment was done. (p. 26)

The testing indicated no learning disability, strong comprehension abilities, and poor word-attack skills. Luckily, Leah's parents knew how to teach word-attack skills. Direct teaching of these skills helped Leah become an avid and able reader in about 6 weeks. Deep understanding and fluid performance—whether in reading or dance or mathematical problem solving or reading—require models of expert performance and extensive practice with feedback (J. R. Anderson, Reder, & Simon, 1995). Guided and independent practice with feedback are at the heart of the direct instruction model. Deanna Kuhn (2007) said it well:

> As for direct instruction, of course it has a place. Each young student does not need to re-invent knowledge from the ground up. The challenge is to formulate what we want direct instruction to be. In doing so, it is well to keep in mind that it is students who construct meaning from such instruction and decide what it is that they will learn. (p. 112)

See the *Guidelines: Effective Direct Instruction* on the next page. for more ideas about teaching effectively.

Seatwork and Homework

SEATWORK. The conclusions of the limited research on seatwork (independent classroom-desk work) are clear; this technique is often overused. For example, a summary of research from 1975 to 2000 found that students with learning disabilities, who often have trouble improving without teacher guidance, were spending about 40% of their time on individual seatwork (Vaughn, Levy, Coleman, & Bos, 2002).

Seatwork should follow up a lesson and give students supervised practice. It should not be the main mode of instruction. Unfortunately, many workbook pages and worksheets do little to support the learning of important objectives. Before you assign work, ask yourself, "Does doing this work help students learn anything that matters?" Students should see the connection between the seatwork and the lesson. Tell them why they are doing the work. The objectives should be clear, all the materials that might be needed should be provided, and the work should be easy enough that students can succeed on their own. Success rates should be high—near 100%. When seatwork is too difficult, students often resort to guessing or copying just to finish.

GUIDELINES
Effective Direct Instruction

Use advance organizers.

Examples

1. English: Shakespeare used the social ideas of his time as a framework for his plays; *Julius Caesar, Hamlet,* and *Macbeth* deal with concepts such as natural order and a nation as the human body.
2. Social studies: Geography dictates economy in preindustrialized regions or nations.
3. History: Important concepts during the Renaissance were symmetry, admiration of the classical world, the centrality of the human mind.

Use a number of examples.

Examples

1. In mathematics class, ask students to point out all the examples of right angles that they can find in the room.
2. In teaching about islands and peninsulas, use maps, slides, models, postcards.

Organize your lessons carefully.

Examples

1. Provide objectives that help students focus on the purpose of the lesson.
2. Begin lessons by writing a brief outline on the board, or work on an outline with the class as part of the lesson.
3. If possible, break the presentation into clear steps or stages.
4. Review periodically.

Anticipate and plan for difficult parts in the lesson.

Examples

1. Plan a clear introduction to the lesson that tells students what they are going to learn and how they will learn it.
2. Do the exercises and anticipate student problems—consult the teachers' manual for ideas.
3. Have definitions ready for new terms, and prepare several relevant examples for concepts.
4. Think of analogies that will make ideas easier to understand.
5. Organize the lesson in a logical sequence; include checkpoints that incorporate oral or written questions or problems to make sure the students are following the explanations.

Strive for clear explanations.

Examples

1. Avoid vague words and ambiguous phrases: Steer clear of "the *somes*"—something, someone, sometime, somehow; "the *not verys*"—not very much, not very well, not very hard, not very often; and other unspecific fillers, such as *most, not all, sort of, and so on, of course, as you know, I guess, in fact, or whatever,* and *more or less.*
2. Use specific (and, if possible, colorful) names instead of *it, them,* and *thing.*
3. Refrain from using pet phrases such as *you know, like,* and *Okay?*
4. Record one of your lessons to check yourself for clarity.
5. Give explanations at several levels so all students, not just the brightest, will understand.
6. Focus on one idea at a time, and avoid digressions.

Make clear connections by using explanatory links such as *because, if–then,* or *therefore.*

Examples

1. "The North had an advantage in the Civil War because its economy was based on manufacturing."
2. Explanatory links are also helpful in labeling visual material such as graphs, concept maps, or illustrations.

Signal transitions from one major topic to another with phrases.

Examples

1. "The next area," "Now we will turn to," or "The second step is."
2. Outline topics, listing key points, drawing concept maps on the board, or using an overhead projector.

Communicate an enthusiasm for your subject and the day's lesson.

Examples

1. Tell students why the lesson is important. Have a better reason than "This will be on the test" or "You will need to know it next year." Emphasize the value of the learning itself.
2. Be sure to make eye contact with the students.
3. Vary your pace and volume in speaking. Use silence for emphasis.

There are several alternatives to workbooks and worksheets, such as reading silently and reading aloud to a partner; writing for a "real" audience; writing letters or journals; transcribing conversations and punctuating them properly; making up problems; working on long-term projects and reports; solving brainteasers and puzzles; and computer activities (Weinstein & Romano, 2015). One of my favorites is creating a group story. Two students begin a story on the computer. Then two more add a paragraph. The story grows with each new pair's addition. The students are reading and writing, editing and improving. With so many different authors, each writer may spark the creative thinking of other contributors.

Any independent work requires careful monitoring. Being available to students doing seat-work is more effective than offering students help before they ask for it. Short, frequent contacts are best (Brophy & Good, 1986). Sometimes you may be working with a small group while other students do seatwork. In these situations, it is especially important for students to know what to do if they need help. One expert teacher described by Weinstein and Romano (2015) taught students a rule, "Ask three, then me." Students have to consult three classmates before seeking help from the teacher. This teacher also spends time early in the year showing students how to help each other—how to ask questions and how to explain.

STOP & THINK Think back to your elementary and high school days. Do you remember any homework assignments? What sticks in your mind about those assignments? •

HOMEWORK. In contrast to the limited research on seatwork, educators have been studying the effects of homework for over 75 years (H. M. Cooper, 2004; H. M. Cooper, Robinson, & Patall, 2006; Corno, 2000; Trautwein, 2007).

To benefit from homework, students must understand the assignment. It may help to do the first few questions as a class, to clear up any misconceptions. This is especially important for students who may have no one at home to consult if they have problems with the assignment. A second way to keep students involved is to hold them accountable for completing the work correctly, not just for filling in the page. This means the work should be checked, the students given a chance to correct the errors or revise work, and the results counted toward the class grade. Expert teachers often have ways of correcting homework quickly during the first minutes of class by having students check each other's or their own work. There are other concerns about making homework effective, as you can see on the next page in the *Point/Counterpoint: Is Homework a Valuable Use of Time?*

If students get stuck on homework, they need help at home, someone who can scaffold their work without just "giving the answer" (Pressley, 1995). But many families don't know how to help (Hoover-Dempsey et al., 2001). The *Guidelines: Family and Community Partnerships—Homework* on page 547 provides ideas for helping families deal with homework.

Questioning, Discussion, and Dialogue

Teachers pose questions, students answer. This form of teaching, sometimes called *recitation,* has been with us for many years (C. S. Weinstein & Romano, 2015). The teacher's questions develop a framework for the subject matter involved. The pattern from the teacher's point of view consists of IRE: *Initiation* (teacher asks questions), *Response* (student answers), and *Evaluation/reaction* (praising, correcting, probing, or expanding) (Burbules & Bruce, 2001). These steps are repeated over and over. Let's consider the heart of recitation—the soliciting, or questioning, phase. Effective questioning techniques may be among the most powerful tools that teachers employ during lessons. An essential element of contemporary learning techniques is keeping students cognitively engaged—and that is where skillful questioning strategies are especially effective. Questions play several roles in cognition. They can help students rehearse information for effective recall. They can work to identify gaps in students' knowledge base, and provoke curiosity and long-term interest. They can initiate cognitive conflict and promote the disequilibrium that results in a changed knowledge structure. They can serve as cues, tips, or reminders as an expert guides a novice in a learning experience. And students as well as teachers should learn to question effectively. I tell my students that the first step in doing a good research project is asking a good question.

For now, we will focus on teachers' questions. Many of the beginning teachers I work with are surprised to discover how valuable good questions can be and how difficult they are to create.

STOP & THINK Think back to your most recent class. What kinds of questions does your professor ask? What sort of thinking is required to answer the questions? Remembering, understanding, applying, analyzing, evaluating, or creating? How long does the professor wait for an answer? •

Video 14.3
The teacher in this video supervises seatwork by circulating, posing questions to struggling students, and providing prompts that remind them of key elements of the lesson they have not yet transferred successfully.

ENHANCEDetext *video example*

Connect and Extend to PRAXIS II®

Questioning (III, C)
Effective questioning skills are among the most valuable skills that a teacher can possess—and among the more difficult to develop. For guidance on asking effective questions in the classroom, read *Question Types* (unl.edu/teaching/teachquestions.html).

POINT/COUNTERPOINT
Is Homework a Valuable Use of Time?

Like so many methods in education, homework has moved in and out of favor. In the early 1900s, homework was seen as an important path to mental discipline, but by the 1940s, homework was criticized as too much drill and low-level learning. Then, in the 1950s, homework was rediscovered as a way to catch up with the Soviet Union in science and mathematics, only to be seen as putting too much pressure on students during the more laid-back 1960s. By the 1980s, homework was in again as a way to improve the standing of American children compared to students around the world (H. M. Cooper & Valentine, 2001). Today, homework is increasing in early elementary schools (Hofferth & Sandberg, 2000). Everyone has done homework— were those hours well spent?

POINT Homework does not help students learn David Berliner and Gene Glass (2014) said it bluntly: "Let the dog eat it. Homework does not boost achievement" (p. 113). No matter how interesting an activity is, students will eventually get bored with it—so why give them work both in and out of school? They will simply grow weary of learning. And important opportunities are lost for community involvement or leisure activities that would create well-rounded citizens. When parents help with homework, they can do more harm than good—sometimes confusing their children or teaching them incorrectly. And students from poorer families often must work, so they miss doing the homework; then the learning discrepancy between the rich and poor grows even greater. Besides, the research is inconsistent about the effects of homework. For example, one study found that in-class work was better than homework in helping elementary students learn (H. M. Cooper & Valentine, 2001). In his book, *The Homework Myth: Why Our Kids Get Too Much of a Bad Thing*, Alfie Kohn (2006) suggests the schools adopt no homework as the default policy. "Changing the default to no homework would likely have two practical consequences: The number of assignments would decline and the quality of those assignments would rise. Both of these, I believe, represent significant improvements in our children's education" (p. 168).

Harris Cooper and his colleagues reviewed many studies of homework and concluded that there is little relationship between homework and learning for young students, but the relationship between homework and achievement grows progressively stronger for older students. Most of the studies involved math and reading or English homework, however, not social studies, science, or other subjects.

COUNTERPOINT Well-planned homework can work for many students Recent evidence indicates that students in high school who do more homework (and watch less television after school) have higher grades, even when other factors such as gender, grade level, ethnicity, socioeconomic status (SES), and amount of adult supervision are taken into consideration (H. M. Cooper, Robinson, & Patall, 2006; H. M. Cooper & Valentine, 2001; H. M. Cooper, Valentine, Nye, & Kindsay, 1999). Consistent with all these findings, the National PTA makes these recommendations:

> [F]or children in grades K–2, homework is most effective when it does not exceed 10–20 minutes each day; older students, in grades 3–6, can handle 30–60 minutes a day; in junior and senior high school, the amount of homework will vary by subject. (Henderson, 1996, p. 1)

Most research examines the relationship between amount of time spent on homework (as reported by students or parents) and achievement in terms of grades or achievement tests. Another approach is to focus on effort instead of time. Students' self-reported effort on homework is consistently and positively related to student achievement (Trautwein, Schnyder, Niggli, Neuman, & Lüdtke, 2009). "High homework effort means that a student does his or her best to solve the tasks assigned. There need not be a close relationship between effort and time on homework: A student putting as much effort as possible into a homework assignment might finish in 5 min or still be working after an hour" (Trautwein & Lüdtke, 2007, p. 432).

BEWARE OF EITHER/OR
The question probably is not assigning homework versus not assigning homework, but rather assigning the right kind of homework. Students are more likely to put in effort if they see the homework as interesting, valuable, reasonably challenging, and not anxiety provoking—this could require some differentiated homework assignments (Dettmers, Trautwein, Lüdtke, Kunter, & Baumert, 2010). So the challenge is to get students to put their best efforts into appropriate homework and not assign homework that is low quality.

GUIDELINES
Family and Community Partnerships

Homework

Make sure families know what students are expected to learn.

Examples

1. At the beginning of a unit, send home a list of the main objectives, examples of major assignments, key due dates, a homework "calendar," and a list of free resources available at libraries or on the Internet.
2. Provide a clear, concise description of your homework policy, including how homework is counted toward class grades; consequences for late, forgotten, or missing homework.

Help families find a comfortable and helpful role in their child's homework.

Examples

1. Remind families that "helping with homework" means encouraging, listening, monitoring, praising, discussing, brainstorming—not necessarily teaching and never doing the work for their child.
2. Encourage families to set aside a quiet time and place for everyone in the family to study. Make this time a regular part of the daily routine.
3. Have some homework assignments that are fun and involve the whole family—puzzles, family albums, watching a television program together and doing a "review."
4. In conferences, ask families how you could help them to support their child in completing and learning from homework. Check lists? Background reading? Web sites? Explanations of study skills?

Solicit and use suggestions from families about homework.

Examples

1. Find out what responsibilities the child has at home—how much time is available for homework.

2. Periodically, have a "homework hotline" for call-in questions and suggestions.

If no one is at home to help with homework, set up other support systems.

Examples

1. Assign study buddies who can be available over the phone.
2. If students have computers, provide lists of Internet help lines.
3. Locate free help in public libraries, and make these resources known.

Take advantage of family and community "funds of knowledge" to connect homework with life in the community and life in the community with lessons in school (Moll et al., 1992).

Examples

1. Create a class lesson about how family members use math and reading in sewing and in housing construction (Epstein & Van Voorhis, 2001).
2. Design interactive homework projects that families do together to evaluate needed products for their home, for example, deciding on the best buy on shampoo or paper towels.

For more ideas, see slideshare.net/stanfreeda/unit-7-homework-strategies-parental-involvement-notes

KINDS OF QUESTIONS. Some educators have estimated the typical teacher asks between 30 and 120 questions an hour, or about 1,500,000 questions over a teaching career (Sadker & Sadker, 2006). What are these questions like? Many can be categorized in terms of Bloom's taxonomy of objectives in the cognitive domain. Table 14.7 on the next page offers examples of questions at the different taxonomic levels.

Another way to categorize questioning is in terms of **convergent questions** (only one right answer) or **divergent questions** (many possible answers). Questions about concrete facts are convergent: "Who ruled England in 1540?" "Who wrote the original Peter Pan?" Questions dealing with opinions or hypotheses are divergent: "In this story, which character is most like you and why?" "In 100 years, which of the past five presidents will be most admired?"

FITTING THE QUESTIONS TO THE STUDENTS. All kinds of questions can be effective (Barden, 1995). Different patterns seem to be better for certain types of students, however. The best pattern for younger students and for lower-ability students of all ages is simple questions that allow a high percentage of correct answers, ample encouragement, help when the student does not have the correct answer, and praise. For high-ability students, the successful pattern includes harder questions at both higher and lower levels and more critical feedback (Berliner, 1987; T. L. Good, 1988).

TABLE 14.7 • **Classroom Questions for Objectives in the Cognitive Domain**
Questions can be posed that encourage thinking at every level of Bloom's taxonomy in the cognitive domain. Of course, the thinking required depends on what has gone before in the discussion.

CATEGORY	TYPE OF THINKING EXPECTED	EXAMPLES
Remembering	Recalling or recognizing information as learned without really using or changing it	List the capitals of. . . . What are the six parts . . . ? Which strategy does the text say you should use here . . . ?
Understanding	Demonstrating understanding of the materials without necessarily relating it to anything else	Summarize in your own words . . . What does _____ mean in this sentence? Predict the next step . . .
Applying	Using information to solve a problem with a single correct answer	Classify these plants. . . . Calculate the area of. . . . Select the best strategy for. . . .
Analyzing	Breaking something down into parts; identifying reasons and motives;- making inferences based on specific data; analyzing conclusions to see if supported by evidence	What was the first breakthrough in . . . ? The second? Explain why Washington, D.C., was chosen. . . . Which of the following are facts, and which are opinions . . .? Based on your experiment, what is the chemical . . . ?
Evaluating	Judging the merits of materials or methods as they might be applied in a particular situation, offering opinions, applying standards	Rank the top 10 U.S. senators in terms of effectiveness in. . . . Which painting do you believe to be better? Why? Which study strategy is the best for you in . . . ?
Creating	Creating something new; original thinking; original plan, proposal, design, or story	What's a good name for . . . ? How could we combine those two ideas? How could we raise money for . . . ? What would the United States be like if the South had won . . . ?

Whatever their age or ability, all students should have some experience with thought-provoking questions and, if necessary, help in learning how to answer them. As we saw in Chapter 9, to master critical thinking and problem-solving skills, students must have a chance to practice those skills. They also need time to think about their answers. But classic research shows that teachers wait an average of only 1 second for students to answer (M. B. Rowe, 1974). When teachers learn to pose a question, then wait at least 3 to 5 seconds before calling on a student to answer, students tend to give longer answers; more students are likely to participate, ask questions, and volunteer appropriate answers; student comments involving analysis, synthesis, inference, and speculation tend to increase; and the students generally appear more confident in their answers (Berliner, 1987; Sadker & Sadker, 2006).

This seems like a simple improvement in teaching, but 5 seconds of silence is not that easy to handle. It takes practice. You might try asking students to jot down ideas or even discuss the question with another student and formulate an answer together. This makes the wait more comfortable and gives students a chance to think. Of course, if it is clear that students are lost or don't understand the question, waiting longer will not help. When your question is met with blank stares, rephrase the question or ask if anyone can clarify it. However, some evidence shows that extending wait times does not affect learning in university classes (Duell, 1994), so with advanced high school students, you might conduct your own evaluation of wait time.

A word about selecting students to answer questions. If you call only on volunteers, then you may get the wrong idea about how well students understand the material. Also, the same people volunteer over and over again. Many expert teachers have some systematic way of making sure that they call on everyone: They pull names from a jar or check names off a list as each student speaks (C. S. Weinstein & Novodvorsky, 2015; C. S. Weinstein, & Romano, 2015). Another possibility is to put each student's name on an index card, then shuffle the cards and go through the deck as you call on people. You can use the card to make notes about the quality of students' answers or any extra help they seem to need.

RESPONDING TO STUDENT ANSWERS. What do you do after the student answers? The most common response, occurring about 50% of the time in most classrooms, is simple acceptance— "OK" or "Uh-huh" (Sadker & Sadker, 2006). But there are better reactions, depending on whether the student's answer is correct, partially correct, or wrong. If the answer is quick, firm, and correct, simply accept the answer or ask another question. If the answer is correct but hesitant, give the student feedback about why the answer is correct: "That's right, Chris, the Senate is part of the legislative branch of government because the Senate. . . ." This allows you to explain the material **again**. If this student is unsure, others may be confused as well. If the answer is partially or completely wrong but the student has made an honest attempt, you should probe for more information, give clues, simplify the question, review the previous steps, or reteach the material. If the student's wrong answer is silly or careless, however, it is better simply to correct the answer and go on (T. L. Good, 1988; Rosenshine & Stevens, 1986).

John Hattie and Helen Timperley (2007) reviewed several decades of research on feedback and constructed a model to guide teachers. The model proposes three feedback questions: "Where am I going?" "How am I going?" and "Where to next?" The first question is about goals and goal clarity. The second is about progress—movement toward goals. The third question is about moving forward to improve understandings when goals are not met yet or to build on attained goals. The Hattie and Timperley model also considers the focus of the feedback on four levels: task, process, self-regulation, and self-feedback. Here are some examples (p. 90):

Task Feedback: "You need to include more about the Treaty of Versailles."
Process Feedback: "This page may make more sense if you use the strategies we talked about earlier."
Self-Regulation Feedback: "You already know the key features of the opening of an argument. Check to see whether you have incorporated them in your first paragraph."
Self-Feedback: "You are a great student." "That's an intelligent response, well done."

Hattie and Timperley argue that feedback about *process* and *self-regulation* is the most powerful because it helps students move toward deep understanding, mastery, and self-direction in learning. Feedback about self (usually praise) is common in classes but is not effective unless the praise provides information about how effort, persistence, or self-regulation moved the student forward, as in, "You are terrific—you stuck with this, revised again, and now this essay makes a powerful argument."

GROUP DISCUSSION. **Group discussion** is in some ways similar to the recitation strategy. A teacher may pose questions, listen to student answers, react, and probe for more information, but in a true group dialogue, the teacher does not have a dominant role. Students ask questions, answer each other's questions, and respond to each other's answers. The hope is that through this dialogue and discussion, students will collectively construct meaning and complex understandings (Burbules & Bruce, 2001; Parker & Hess, 2001; Reznitskaya & Gregory, 2013). These kinds of student-centered dialogues are relatively rare, however. One study of 64 middle schools found that only 1.6 minutes per 60-minute class were devoted to these discussions (Applebee et al., 2003).

Group discussions have many advantages. The students are directly involved and have the chance to participate. Motivation and engagement can be higher. They learn to express themselves clearly, to justify opinions, and to tolerate different views. Group discussion also gives students a chance to ask for clarification, examine their own thinking, follow personal interests, and assume responsibility by taking leadership roles in the group. So group discussions help students evaluate ideas and synthesize personal viewpoints. Discussions are also useful when students are trying to understand difficult concepts that go against common sense. By thinking together, challenging each other, and suggesting and evaluating possible explanations, students are more likely to reach a genuine understanding (Wu, Anderson, Nguyen-Jahiel, & Miller, 2013).

Of course, there are disadvantages. Class discussions are quite unpredictable and may easily digress into exchanges of ignorance. You may have to do a good deal of preparation to ensure that participants have enough background knowledge for the discussion. Some members of the group may have great difficulty participating and may become anxious if forced to speak. And large groups are often unwieldy. In many cases, a few students will dominate the discussion while the others daydream (Arends, 2004; H. J. Freiberg & Driscoll, 2005).

Are discussions effective learning tools? In a major review of research conducted from 1964 to 2003 on the value of discussing texts for improving student comprehension, Karen Murphy and her colleagues (2009) reached some surprising conclusions. They examined a wide range of discussion formats including Instructional Conversations, Junior Great Books Shared Inquiry, Questioning the Author, Literature Circles, Book Club, and Grand Conversation—to name just a few. They found many of these approaches were very successful in increasing student talk, limiting teacher talk, and promoting students' literal interpretations of the texts they discussed. But getting students to talk more did not necessarily promote their critical thinking, reasoning, or argumentation skills. Also, discussion was more effective for students whose comprehension abilities are below average, perhaps because average and higher-ability students already have the skills to comprehend texts. A few discussion structures, such as Junior Great Books Shared Inquiry, used over a longer period of time seemed to support both comprehension of text and critical thinking. The researchers concluded, "Simply putting students into groups and encouraging them to talk is not enough to enhance comprehension and learning; it is but a step in the process" (p. 760). The *Guidelines: Productive Group Discussions* gives some ideas for facilitating a productive group discussion.

Fitting Teaching to Your Goals

In the midst of all our discussions about methods, we have to keep in mind that the first questions should be: What should students learn? and What is worth knowing today? Then, we can match methods to goals.

There is no one best way to teach. Different goals and student needs require different teaching methods. Direct instruction often leads to better performance on achievement tests, whereas the open, informal methods such as discovery learning or inquiry approaches are associated with better performance on tests of creativity, abstract thinking, and problem solving. In addition, the open methods are better for improving attitudes toward school and for stimulating curiosity, cooperation among students, and lower absence rates (Borich, 2011; Walberg, 1990). According to these conclusions, when the goals of teaching involve problem solving, creativity, understanding, and mastering processes, many approaches besides direct instruction should be effective. Every student may require direct, explicit teaching for some learning goals some of the time, but all students also need to experience more open, constructivist, student-centered teaching as well.

Putting It All Together: Understanding by Design

We have covered quite a bit of territory here, from objectives to teaching strategies. Grant Wiggins and Jay McTighe's (2006) Understanding by Design (UbD) pulls it all together—expectations for high-level critical thinking, objectives, evidence for learning, and teaching approaches. The focus is on deep understanding, which is characterized by the ability to (1) explain, (2) interpret, (3) apply, (4) have perspective, (5) empathize, and (6) have self-knowledge about a topic. The big idea behind UbD is *backward design*. Teachers first identify the important end results for students—the key understandings and big ideas that are the goals of instruction. To focus on understanding (not just fun activities or covering the text), teachers write essential questions—questions that go to the heart of the ideas and push thinking deeper: "What is the greatest problem of the democratic system?"

GUIDELINES
Productive Group Discussions

Invite shy children to participate.

Examples

1. "What's your opinion, Joel?" or "Does anyone have another opinion?"
2. Don't wait until there is a deadly silence to ask shy students to reply. Most people, even those who are confident, hate to break a silence.

Direct student comments and questions back to another student.

Examples

1. "That's an unusual idea, Steve. Kim, what do you think of Steve's idea?"
2. "That's an important question, John. Maura, do you have any thoughts about how you'd answer that?"
3. Encourage students to look at and talk to one another rather than wait for your opinion.

Make sure that you understand what a student has said. If you are unsure, other students may be unsure as well.

Examples

1. Ask a second student to summarize what the first student said; then, the first student can try again to explain if the summary is incorrect.
2. "Karen, I think you're saying. . . . Is that right, or have I misunderstood?"

Probe for more information, and ask students to elaborate and defend their positions.

Examples

1. "That's a strong statement. Do you have any evidence to back it up?"

2. "Did you consider any other alternatives?"
3. "Tell us how you reached that conclusion. What steps did you go through?"

Bring the discussion back to the subject.

Examples

1. "Let's see, we were discussing, . . . and Sarah made one suggestion. Does anyone have a different idea?"
2. "Before we continue, let me try to summarize what has happened thus far."

Give time for thought before asking for responses.

Example

1. "How would your life be different if television had never been invented? Jot down your ideas on paper, and we will share reactions in a minute." After a minute: "Hiromi, will you tell us what you wrote?"

When a student finishes speaking, look around the room to judge reactions.

Examples

1. If other students look puzzled, ask them to describe why they are confused.
2. If students are nodding assent, ask them to give an example of what was just said.

"Who is entitled to own the airways?" "What makes a mathematical argument convincing?" Next the teacher identifies what evidence would demonstrate deep understanding (performance tasks, quizzes, informal assessments?). Then and only then do the teachers design the learning plan—the instruction—they design backward *from* the end results *to* the teaching plan. This idea of going from clear objectives to teaching plans is at the heart of every approach to using standards and specific objectives in teaching.

Wiggins and McTighe provide a template to guide backward design planning. You can see many examples of these templates online. Go to www.jaymctighe.com/resources/downloads/ or do a Web search for "Understanding by Design template." The process for completing a plan using backward design for a unit is shown in Figure 14.1 on the next page. The teacher/designer moved backwards from a core mathematics standard by identifying key understandings and essential questions based on the standard, then planning assessments including traditional tests as well as textbook assignments and performance tasks that include real-life applications, and finally to creating learning experiences that will support understanding. Can you see how many levels of Bloom's taxonomy are represented here?

So far, we have talked about approaches to teaching—objectives, strategies, and learning plans. But in today's diverse classrooms, one size does not fit all. Within the general approach, teachers have to fit their instruction to the needs and abilities of their students—they have to differentiate instruction.

FIGURE 14.1

PLANNING BY DESIGN

The planning process for a lesson on the Pythagorean Theorem. The teacher/designer planned backwards from the core standards.

Step 1—Designing the Goal

Apply the Pythagorean Theorem to determine unknown side lengths in right triangles in real-world and mathematical problems in two and three dimensions.
Common Core www.corestandards.org/Math/Content/8/G/B/

Key Understandings	**Essential Questions**
1. The area formed by the square on top of the hypotenuse of a right triangle is equal to the total area of the two squares formed on the tops of the other two sides. 2. There are multiple ways to prove the Pythagorean Theorem. 3.....	1. What makes a mathematical argument of the Pythagorean Theorem convincing? 2. Are there any real world uses of the Pythagorean Theorem? 3....

What Will the Student Know?

1. What is a hypotenuse of a right triangle?
2. What is the length of any side of a right triangle, given the two other sides?
3. .....

What Will the Student Be Able to Do?

1. Draw a graphic illustration that demonstrates the validity of the Pythagorean Theorem.
2. ......

Step 2—Designing the Assessment

Authentic/Real-World Assessments
1. Can you calculate the height of a flagpole based on its shadow—how?
2. You have an old media cabinet with an opening that is 34" by 34". You want a new flat screen TV that is at least a 42" diagonal. Assume the ratio of a new TV height to width is 3/5. Will it fit? Why?
3. Given that the distance between successive bases in baseball is 90 feet, what is the distance a throw has to travel from third base and first base?
4.....

Traditional Assessments
1. Questions on homework
2. Self-questions developed based on chapter, along with answers and justifications.
3. Unit test
4.....

Step 3—Designing the Learning

1. In groups, investigate the area of squares, triangles, and rectangles around the classroom—compare your group's areas with the areas calculated by other groups for the same objects.
2. Using cardboard pieces, scissors, a ruler, and pencil, prove the Pythagorean Theorem.
3. Modules 6 & 7 in text
   (For more ideas, see http://questgarden.com/ and search for "Pythagorean Theorem.")

DIFFERENTIATED INSTRUCTION AND ADAPTIVE TEACHING

The idea of differentiated instruction—adapting teaching to the abilities and needs of each learner—is an ancient one. To prove it, Lyn Corno (2008, p. 161) quotes these words of Quintilian from the 5th century BC:

> Some students are slack and need to be encouraged; others work better when given a freer rein. Some respond best when there is some threat or fear; others are paralyzed by it. Some apply themselves to the task over time, and learn best; others learn best by concentration and focus in a single burst of energy.

Obviously Quintilian appreciated the need for fitting instruction to the student. One way to do this when teachers have many students is to use appropriate groupings.

Within-Class and Flexible Grouping

It is not unusual to have 3- to 5-year ability differences in any given classroom (Castle, Deniz, & Tortora, 2005). But even if you decided to simply forge ahead (against Quintilian's advice) and teach the same material in the same way to your entire class, you would not be alone. Differences in students' prior knowledge are a major challenge for teachers, especially in subjects that build on previous knowledge and skills such as math and science (Loveless, 1998). One answer has been ability grouping, but that also poses a number of problems.

Connect and Extend to PRAXIS II®

The Teacher's Role in Student-Centered Instruction (II, A3)
The teacher's role in student-centered instruction is significantly different from that in teacher-centered instruction.

THE PROBLEMS WITH ABILITY GROUPING. Students in many classes and schools are grouped by ability, even though there is no clear evidence that this within-class ability grouping is superior to other approaches. In a random sample of primary grade teachers in the United States, 63% reported using within-class ability groups for reading. Students in lower-ability groups were less likely to be asked critical comprehension questions and were given fewer opportunities to make choices about what to read (Chorzempa & Graham, 2006). For schools with students from lower SES families, grouping often means that these students are segregated into lower-ability tracks. According to Paul George (2005):

> In my 3 decades of experience with this issue, when homogenous grouping is the primary strategy for organizing students in schools with significant racial and ethnic diversity in the population, the result is almost always deep, and often starkly obvious, division of students on the basis of race, ethnicity, and social class. (p. 187)

Thoughtfully constructed and well-taught ability groups in math and reading can be effective, but the point of any grouping strategy should be to provide appropriate challenge and support—that is, to reach children within their zone of proximal development, that area where students can learn and develop, given the appropriate support (Vygotsky, 1997). Flexible grouping is one possible answer.

FLEXIBLE GROUPING. In flexible grouping, students are grouped and regrouped based on their learning needs. Assessment is continuous so that students are always working within their zone of proximal development. Arrangements might include small groups, partners, individuals, and even the whole class—depending on which grouping best supports each student's learning of the particular academic content. Flexible grouping approaches include high-level instruction and high expectations for all students, regardless of their group placement (Corno, 2008). One 5-year longitudinal study of flexible grouping in a high-needs urban elementary school found 10% to 57% increases in students who reached mastery level, depending on the subject area and grade level. Teachers received training and support in the assessment, grouping, and teaching strategies needed, and by the end of the study, 95% of the teachers were using flexible grouping. The teachers in the study believed that some of the gains came because students were more focused on learning and more confident (Castle et al., 2005).

Another way to use flexible grouping is in a nongraded elementary school. Students of several ages (e.g., 6, 7, and 8) are together in one class, but they are flexibly grouped within the class for instruction based on achievement, motivation, or interest in different subjects. This cross-grade grouping seems to be effective for students of all abilities as long as the grouping allows teachers to

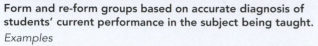

GUIDELINES
Using Flexible Grouping

Form and re-form groups based on accurate diagnosis of students' current performance in the subject being taught.

Examples

1. Use scores on the most recent reading assessments to establish reading groups and rely on current math performance to form math groups.
2. Assess continuously. Change group placement frequently when students' achievement changes.

Make sure different groups get appropriately different instruction, not just the same material. Make sure teachers, methods, and pace are adjusted to fit the needs of the group.

Examples

1. Vary more than pace; fit teaching to students' interests and knowledge.
2. Assign all groups research reports, but make some written, and others oral or PowerPoint® presentations.
3. Organize and teach groups so that low-achieving students get appropriate extra instruction—not just the same material again. Make lower-achieving groups smaller so students get extra attention.
4. Make sure all work is meaningful and respectful—no worksheets for lower-ability groups while the higher-ability groups do experiments and projects.
5. Try alternatives. For example, DeWayne Mason and Tom Good (1993) found that supplementing whole-class

instruction in math with remediation and enrichment for students when they needed it worked better than dividing the class into two ability groups and teaching these groups separately.

Discourage comparisons between groups, and encourage students to develop a whole-class spirit.

Examples

1. Don't seat groups together outside the context of their reading or math group.
2. Avoid naming ability groups—save the names for mixed-ability or whole-class teams.

Group by ability for one, or, at the most, two subjects.

Examples

1. Make sure that many lessons and projects mix members from the groups.
2. Experiment with learning strategies that stress cooperation (described in Chapter 10).
3. Keep the number of groups small (two or three at most) so that you can provide as much direct teaching as possible. Leaving students alone for too long leads to less learning.

For more information about classroom grouping, see this site:
eduplace.com/science/profdev/articles/valentino.html

give more direct instruction to the groups. But be sensible about cross-age grouping. Mixing third-, fourth-, and fifth-graders for math or reading class based on what they are ready to learn makes sense. However, sending a large fourth-grader to the second grade, where he is the only older student and stands out like a sore thumb, isn't likely to work well. Also, when cross-age classes are created just because there are too few students for one grade—and not in order to better meet the students' learning needs—the results are not positive (Veenman, 1997). As we have seen repeatedly throughout this text, working at a challenging level, but one you can master with effort and support, is more likely to encourage learning and motivation.

If you ever decide to use flexible grouping in your class, the *Guidelines: Using Flexible Grouping* should make the approach more effective (Arends, 2007; T. L. Good & Brophy, 2008).

Adaptive Teaching

Lyn Corno (2008) has developed a model of adaptive teaching that also addresses learner differences. In this approach, teachers see "learner variation as an opportunity for learning from teaching rather than as obstacles to be overcome" (p. 171). Adaptive teaching provides all students with challenging instruction and uses supports when needed, but removes those supports as students become able to handle more on their own. Figure 14.2 shows the continuum of support and type of instruction that matches students' needs. As shown on the far left of the figure, when students are novices in an area or have little prior knowledge and skills, the teaching is more direct and includes well-designed motivational strategies to keep them engaged. At the same time, students are taught how to apply appropriate cognitive strategies, to give them the "skills" to learn. There are short cycles of teaching, checking for understanding, and reteaching. As students develop aptitudes in the subject, teaching moves to modeling, guided practice, and coaching. By this time, students should have improved their cognitive "skills" strategies, so teaching can also focus on motivational and volitional strategies—the "will" to learn. Finally, as students gain more knowledge and skills,

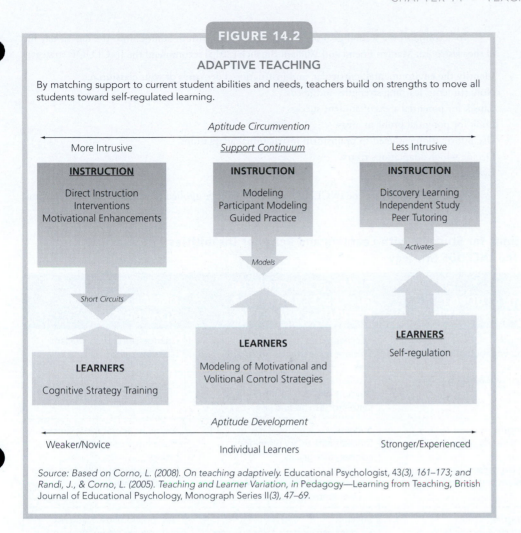

FIGURE 14.2

ADAPTIVE TEACHING

By matching support to current student abilities and needs, teachers build on strengths to move all students toward self-regulated learning.

Aptitude Circumvention

More Intrusive   *Support Continuum*   Less Intrusive

INSTRUCTION	**INSTRUCTION**	**INSTRUCTION**
Direct Instruction	Modeling	Discovery Learning
Interventions	Participant Modeling	Independent Study
Motivational Enhancements	Guided Practice	Peer Tutoring

Activates

Models

Short Circuits

LEARNERS	**LEARNERS**	**LEARNERS**
	Modeling of Motivational and	Self-regulation
Cognitive Strategy Training	Volitional Control Strategies	

Aptitude Development

Weaker/Novice   Individual Learners   Stronger/Experienced

Source: Based on Corno, L. (2008). On teaching adaptively. Educational Psychologist, 43(3), 161–173; and Randi, J., & Corno, L. (2005). Teaching and Learner Variation, in Pedagogy—Learning from Teaching, British Journal of Educational Psychology, Monograph Series II(3), 47–69.

teaching can move to guided discovery, independent study, and peer tutoring, with an emphasis on self-regulated learning—the kind of learning the students will need for the rest of their lives.

Adaptive teaching makes sure that everyone is challenged. For example, one teacher at a magnet school described how he "iced" his curriculum with some content "just beyond the reach" of even his most advanced students. He wanted to be sure all his students found some assignments difficult. He believed "everyone needs to stretch in my class" (Corno, 2008, p. 165).

Reaching Every Student: Differentiated Instruction in Inclusive Classrooms

STOP & THINK When you think about teaching in an inclusive classroom, what are your concerns? Do you have enough training? Will you get the support you need from school administrators or specialists? Will working with the students with disabilities take time away from your other responsibilities? •

These questions are common ones, and sometimes such concerns are justified. But effective teaching for students with disabilities does not require a unique set of skills. It is a combination of good teaching practices and sensitivity to all your students. Students with disabilities need to learn the academic material, and they need to be full participants in the day-to-day life of the classroom.

To accomplish the first goal of academic learning, students with learning disabilities appear to benefit from using extended practice distributed over days and weeks and from advanced organizers such as focusing students on what they already know or stating clear objectives (H. L. Swanson, 2001).

Video 14.4
In this video, Mrs. Casey differentiates instruction by grouping students for reading. She focuses on vocabulary in both reading groups in the video, but the content is different. Listen to her description of the diversity in her classroom, and consider the importance of differentiation in order to reach every student.

ENHANCEDetext *video example*

To accomplish the second goal of integrating students with disabilities into the day-to-day life of the classroom, Marilyn Friend and William Bursuck (2015) recommend the INCLUDE strategy:

Identify the environmental, curricular, and instructional demands of your classroom.
Note students' learning strengths and needs.
Check for potential areas of student success.
Look for potential problem areas.
Use information gathered to brainstorm instructional adaptations.
Decide which adaptations to try.
Evaluate student progress.

Table 14.8 shows how the INCLUDE strategy might be applied to students with learning and behavioral disabilities.

TABLE 14.8 • Making Adaptations for Students with Learning and Behavior Disabilities Using Steps in the INCLUDE Strategy

IDENTIFY CLASSROOM DEMANDS	NOTE STUDENT STRENGTHS AND NEEDS	CHECK FOR POTENTIAL SUCCESSES/LOOK FOR POTENTIAL PROBLEMS	DECIDE ON ADAPTATIONS
Student desks in clusters of four	*Strengths* Good vocabulary skills *Needs* Difficulty attending to task	*Success* Student understands instruction if on task *Problem* Student off task—does not face instructor as she teaches	Change seating so student faces instructor
Small-group work with peers	*Strengths* Good handwriting *Needs* Oral expressive language—problem with word finding	*Success* Student acts as secretary for cooperative group *Problem* Student has difficulty expressing self in peer learning groups	Assign as secretary of group Place into compatible small group Develop social skills instruction for all students
Expect students to attend class and be on time	*Strengths* Good drawing skills *Needs* Poor time management	*Success* Student uses artistic talent in class *Problem* Student is late for class and frequently does not attend at all	Use individualized student contract for attendance and punctuality—if goals met, give student artistic responsibility in class
Textbook difficult to read	*Strengths* Good oral communication skills *Needs* Poor reading accuracy Lacks systematic strategy for reading text	*Success* Student participates well in class Good candidate for class dramatizations *Problem* Student is unable to read text for information	Provide taped textbooks Highlight student text
Lecture on women's suffrage movement to whole class	*Strengths* Very motivated and interested in class *Needs* Lack of background knowledge	*Success* Student earns points for class attendance and effort *Problem* Student lacks background knowledge to understand important information in lecture	Give student video to view before lecture Build points for attendance and working hard into grading system
Whole-class instruction on telling time to the quarter hour	*Strengths* Good coloring skills *Needs* Cannot identify numbers 7–12 Cannot count by fives	*Success* Student is able to color clock faces used in instruction *Problem* Student is unable to acquire telling time skills	Provide extra instruction on number identification and counting by fives

Source: From Friend, M. & Bursuck, W. D. (2013). Including Students with Special Needs: A Practical Guide for Classroom Teachers, 6th Ed. Boston, MA: Pearson Education, Inc. Adapted with permission.

FIGURE 14.3

AN EXCERPT FROM AN IEP—INDIVIDUALIZED EDUCATION PROGRAM

This IEP was developed for a 15-year-old boy to help him manage anger and comply with teacher requests.

Student: __Curt__   Age: __15__   Grade: __9__   Date: __10/12/94__

Unique Characteristics/ Needs	Special Education, Related Services, Modifications	(begin duration)	Present Levels, Objectives, Annual Goals (Objectives to include procedure, criteria, schedule)
Social Needs: To learn anger management skills, especially regarding swearing To learn to comply with requests Present Level: Lashes out violently when not able to complete work, uses profane language, and refuses to follow further directions from adults	1. Teacher and/or counselor consult with behavior specialists regarding techniques and programs for teaching social skills, especially anger management. 2. Provide anger management training for Curt. 3. Establish a peer group which involves role playing, etc. so Curt can see positive role models and practice newly learned anger management skills. 4. Develop a behavior plan for Curt which gives him responsibility for charting his own behavior. 5. Provide a teacher or some other adult mentor to spend time with Curt (could be talking; game play, physical activity). 6. Provide training for the mentor regarding Curt's needs/goals.	30 min., 3 x week 30 min., 2 x week 30 min., 2 x week	Goal: During the last quarter of the academic year, Curt will have 2 or fewer detentions for any reason. Objective 1: At the end of the 1st quarter, Curt will have had 10 or fewer detentions. Objective 2: At the end of 2nd quarter, Curt will have had 7 or fewer detentions. Objective 3: At the end of 3rd quarter, Curt will have had 4 or fewer detentions. Goal: Curt will manage his behavior and language in a reasonably acceptable manner as reported by faculty/peers. Objective 1: At 2 weeks, asked at end of class if Curt's behavior language was acceptable or not, 3 out of 5 teachers will say "acceptable." Objective 2: At 6 weeks, asked same question, 4 out of 6 teachers will say "acceptable." Objective 3: At 12 weeks. 6 out of 6 will say "acceptable."

Adaptations to regular program:

In all classes, Curt should be near front of class.
Curt should be called on often to keep him involved and on task.
All teachers should help Curt with study skills as trained by spelling/language specialist and resource room teacher.
Teachers should monitor Curt's work closely in the beginning weeks/months of his program.

Source: From Better IEPs, 4th ed. (p. 127), by Barbara D. Bateman. Copyright 1996, 2006 by Barbara D. Bateman. Reprinted by permission of the author and Attainment Company, Inc.

When students have special needs, they may be referred for evaluation to child study teams, school psychologists, or teachers of students with special needs. (See Table 4.13 on page 163 for guidelines about referring students for evaluation.) The outcome of this process sometimes includes the preparation of an individualized education program (IEP), as described in Chapter 4. Figure 14.3 is an excerpt from the IEP of a boy who had difficulty managing anger and complying with teacher requests. You may help to develop these programs for students in your classes. Well-designed programs should provide guidance for you in your planning and teaching.

Technology and Differentiation

The Individuals with Disabilities Education Act (IDEA) requires that all students eligible for special education services must be considered for assistive technology. **Assistive technology** is any product, piece of equipment, or system that is used to increase, maintain, or improve the functional capabilities of individuals with disabilities (Goldman, Lawless, Pellegrino, & Plants, 2006). For students who require small steps and many repetitions to learn a new concept, computers are the perfect patient tutors, repeating steps and lessons as many times as necessary. A well-designed computer instructional program is engaging and interactive—two important qualities for students who have problems paying attention or a history of failure that has eroded motivation. For example, a math or spelling program might use images, sounds, and gamelike features to maintain the attention of a student with an attention-deficit disorder. Interactive digital media programs teach hearing people how to use sign language. Many programs do not involve sound, so students with hearing impairments can get the full benefit from the lessons. Students who have trouble reading can use programs that will "speak" a word for them if they touch the unknown word. With this immediate access to help, the students are much more likely to get the reading practice they need to prevent falling farther and farther behind. Other devices actually convert printed pages and typed texts to spoken words for students who are blind or others who benefit from hearing information. For the student with a learning disability whose writing can't be read, word processors produce perfect penmanship so the ideas can finally get on paper. Once the ideas are recorded, the student can reorganize and improve his or her writing without the agony of rewriting by hand (Hallahan, Kauffman, & Pullen, 2009).

With these tremendous advances in technology have come new barriers, however. Many computers have graphic interfaces. Manipulating the programs requires precise "mouse movements," as you may remember when you first learned to point and click. These maneuvers are often difficult for students with motor problems or visual impairments. And the information available on the Internet often is unusable for students with visual problems. Researchers are working on the problem—trying to devise ways for people to access the information nonvisually (Hallahan et al., 2009). For example, in 2010 the learning management system called Canvas was awarded the National Federation of the Blind—Nonvisual Accessibility Gold Level Certification because the system is equally accessible to blind and sighted users (National Federation of the Blind, 2010).

GUIDELINES
Teachers as Mentors

Beware of stereotypes in your thinking and teaching.
Examples
1. See every student as an individual, and communicate that clearly to the student.
2. Analyze curriculum materials for biases, and teach students to become bias detectors.

Take advantage of technology.
Examples
1. Use a Web program like Eyes to the Future, which link middle school girls with high school girls in their districts who have sustained their interest in math and science as well as women who use science, math, and technology in their careers. The purpose is to help middle school girls see how their work at school relates to "real life" (etf.terc.edu/).
2. Establish "e-mail pals" for students, with retired adults or successful former students as their mentors.
3. Download resources from the Northwest Regional Educational Laboratory's National Mentoring Center, especially their school-based mentoring and tutoring materials (nwrel.org/mentoring/topic_pubs.php#5).

Let students know you believe in them.
Examples
1. Set standards high, and give critical feedback, but also provide support and encouragement.
2. Showcase accomplishments of former students.

Take the time to establish and maintain relationships.
Examples
1. Don't expect trust right away; you may have to earn it.
2. Stay in touch with students, and keep the door open to provide guidance in the future.
3. Spend some time with students outside academics— before or after school, as part of clubs or extracurricular activities. Have some fun together. Find common interests.

If you set up a more formal mentoring system, be sure participants are trained and monitored.
Examples
1. Use materials from national mentor groups for training, for example, Elements of Effective Practice from MENTOR/ National Mentoring Partnership (mentoring.org/ start_a_program/planning_and_design/).
2. Have regular times to provide ongoing training and to deal with problems that may arise.

One current trend is universal design—considering the needs of all users in the design of new tools, learning programs, or Web sites (Pisha & Coyne, 2001).

For gifted students, computers can be a connection with databases and computers in universities, museums, and research labs. Computer networks allow students to work on projects and share information with others across the country. And students who are gifted could write programs for students and teachers. Quite a few principals around the country rely on their students to keep the technology networks in their schools working smoothly. These are just a few examples of what technology can do. Check with the resource teachers in your district to find out what is available in your school.

Mentoring Students as a Way of Differentiating Teaching

One way to make all instruction more appropriate and effective is to know your students and develop trusting relationships with them. The knowledge you gain about the students should help in adapting your teaching, and the positive relationship you establish will help students stay engaged in learning. See the *Guidelines: Teachers as Mentors* on the previous page for ideas.

No matter how you differentiate instruction, there is one part of your teaching that should be the same for all your students—*appropriate high expectations*.

ENHANCEDetext *self-check*

TEACHER EXPECTATIONS

Marvin Marshall (2013) tells the story of a teacher who was delighted when she saw the listing for her new class. "Wow, have I got a bright class this year! Look at these amazing IQs—116, 118, 122, 124. . . ." The teacher designed a host of challenging activities, set high expectations for her students, and communicated her confidence in them to excel. They did. Only much later did the teacher discover that the numbers beside the students' names were their locker numbers!

Can expectations make a difference? Over 40 years ago, a study by Robert Rosenthal and Lenore Jacobson (1968) captured the attention of the national media in a way that few studies by psychologists have since then. Debate about the meaning of the results continues (De Boer, Bosker, & van der Werf, 2010; Jussim, 2012; Jussim, Robustelli, & Cain, 2009; Rosenthal, 1995; R. E. Snow, 1995).

What did Rosenthal and Jacobson say that has caused such a stir? They randomly chose several students in a number of elementary school classrooms, and then told the teachers that these students probably would make significant intellectual gains during the year. The students did indeed make larger gains than normal that year. The researchers presented data suggesting the existence of a Pygmalion effect or self-fulfilling prophecy in the classroom. A self-fulfilling prophecy is a groundless expectation that leads to behaviors that then make the original expectation come true (Merton, 1948). An example is a false belief that a bank is failing; this leads to a rush of patrons withdrawing money, which then causes the bank to fail as expected.

- -

STOP & THINK When you thought about the most effective teacher you ever had, was one of the characteristics that the teacher believed in you or demanded the best from you? How did the teacher communicate that belief? •

- -

Two Kinds of Expectation Effects

Two kinds of expectation effects can occur in classrooms. In the self-fulfilling prophecy just described, the teacher's beliefs about the students' abilities have no basis in fact, but student behavior comes to match the initially inaccurate expectation. The second kind of expectation effect occurs when teachers are fairly accurate in their initial reading of students' abilities and respond to students appropriately. The problems arise when students show some improvement, but teachers do not alter their expectations to take account of the improvement. This is called a sustaining expectation effect, because the teacher's unchanging expectation sustains the student's achievement at the expected level. The chance to raise expectations, provide more appropriate teaching, and thus encourage greater student achievement is lost. In practice, self-fulfilling prophecy effects seem to be stronger in the early grades, and sustaining effects are more likely in the later grades (Kuklinski & Weinstein, 2001).

Sources of Expectations

There are many possible sources of teachers' expectations, including intelligence test scores (especially if they are not interpreted appropriately); gender (more behavior problems for boys and higher academic achievement for girls); notes from previous teachers; the medical or psychological reports in students' permanent files; prior knowledge about older brothers and sisters; appearance (higher expectations for attractive students); previous achievement; SES; race and ethnicity; and the actual behaviors of the student (Van Matre, Valentine, & Cooper, 2000). Young students at the greatest risk of low expectations are those with lower cognitive abilities who exhibit more behavior problems and come from families who face greater adversities such as poverty (Gut, Reiman, & Grob, 2013). Even the student's after-school activities can be a source of expectations. Teachers tend to hold higher expectations for students who participate in extracurricular activities than for students who do nothing after school. And recent research shows that some teachers may even hold expectations at the level of each of their individual classes; that is, they have higher or lower expectations for all the students in a particular class (Rubie-Davies, 2010).

Some students are more likely than others to be the recipients of sustaining expectations. For example, withdrawn children provide little information about themselves, so teachers may sustain their expectations about these children for lack of new input (M. G. Jones & Gerig, 1994). Also, self-fulfilling prophecy effects tend to be stronger for students from lower-SES families and for African American students (De Boer, Bosker, & van der Werf, 2010). In a synthesis of over 50 studies, Harriet Tenenbaum and Martin Ruck (2007) found that teachers held higher expectation for and directed more positive questions and encouragement toward European American compared to African American and Latino/a students. The highest expectations were reserved for Asian American students. It appears that early childhood teachers may hold higher expectations for students who are more socially competent (Hinnant, O'Brien, & Ghazarian, 2009). For example, in another study of 110 students whose development was followed from age 4 to age 18, Jennifer Alvidrez and Rhona Weinstein (1999) found that teachers tended to overestimate the abilities of preschool children they rated as independent and interesting and to underestimate the abilities of children perceived as immature and anxious.

Expectations and beliefs focus attention and organize memory, so teachers may pay attention to and remember the information that fits their initial expectations (Fiske, 1993; Hewstone, 1989). Even when student performance does not fit expectations, the teacher may rationalize and attribute the performance to external causes beyond the student's control. For example, a teacher may assume that the low-ability student who did well on a test must have cheated and that the high-ability student who failed must have been upset that day. In both cases, behavior that seems out of character is dismissed. It may take many instances of supposedly uncharacteristic behavior to change the teacher's beliefs about a particular student's abilities. Thus, expectations often remain in the face of contradictory evidence (Brophy, 1998).

Do Teachers' Expectations Really Affect Students' Achievement?

The answer to the question, "Do teachers expectations really affect students' achievement?" is more complicated than it might seem. There are two ways to investigate the issue. One is to give teachers unfounded expectations about their students and note if these baseless expectations have any effects. The other approach is to identify the naturally occurring expectations of teachers and study the effects of these expectations. The answer to the question of whether teacher expectations affect student learning depends in part on which approach is taken to study the question.

The original Rosenthal and Jacobson experiment used the first approach—giving teachers groundless expectations and noting the effects. A careful analysis of the results revealed that even though first-through sixth-grade students participated in the study, the self-fulfilling prophecy effects could be traced to dramatic changes in just five students in grades 1 and 2. After reviewing the research on teacher expectations, Raudenbush (1984) concluded that these expectations have only a small effect on student IQ scores (the outcome measure used by Rosenthal and Jacobson) and only in the early years of a new school setting—in the first years of elementary school and then again in the first years of middle school.

But what about the second approach—naturally occurring expectations? Research shows that teachers do indeed form beliefs about students' capabilities. Many of these beliefs are accurate

PODCAST 14.1

Listen as textbook author Anita Woolfolk describes academic optimism, a new concept that Anita developed along with her husband, Wayne Hoy, a professor of educational administration who works with principals and superintendents. How might academic optimism affect your teaching practice?

ENHANCEDetext *podcast*

assessments based on the best available data and are corrected as new information is collected (Jussim & Harber, 2005). But inaccuracies can make a difference. In a longitudinal study by Nicole Sorhagen (2013), teachers' over- and underestimations of students' math and language abilities in first grade predicted the students' math, reading comprehension, vocabulary knowledge, and verbal reasoning standardized test scores at age 15, and the impact was greater for students for lower-income families. Perhaps the underestimation of the abilities of children in poverty is one factor contributing to the achievement gap for those students. If teachers decide that some students are less able, and if the teachers lack effective strategies for working with lower-achieving students, then students may experience a double threat—low expectations and inadequate teaching (T. L. Good & Brophy, 2008).

Even though it is clear that teacher expectations can affect student achievement, the effects are modest on average and tend to dissipate somewhat over the years (Jussim, 2012). The power of the expectation effect depends on the age of the students (generally speaking, younger students are more susceptible) and on how differently a teacher treats high- versus low-expectation students, an issue we turn to next (Kuklinski & Weinstein, 2001). Teachers may use different instructional strategies and also have different relationships with students based on expectations.

INSTRUCTIONAL STRATEGIES. Different grouping processes may well have a marked effect on students because different groups get different instruction (De Boer et al., 2010). And some teachers leave little to the imagination; they make their expectations all too clear. For example, N. Alloway (1984) recorded comments such as these directed to low-achieving groups:

"I'll be over to help you slow ones in a minute." "The blue group will find this hard."

In these remarks, the teacher not only tells the students that they lack ability, but also communicates that finishing the work, not understanding, is the goal.

Once teachers divide students into ability groups, they usually differentiate by assigning different learning activities. To the extent that teachers choose activities that challenge students and increase achievement, these differences are probably necessary. Activities become inappropriate, however, when students who are ready for more challenging work are not given the opportunity to try it because teachers believe they cannot handle it. This is an example of a *sustaining expectation effect*.

TEACHER–STUDENT INTERACTIONS. However the class is grouped and whatever the assignments are, the quantity and the quality of teacher–student interactions are likely to affect the students. Students who are expected to achieve tend to be asked more and harder questions, to be given more chances and a longer time to respond, and to be interrupted less often than students who are expected to do poorly. Teachers also give these high-expectation students cues and prompts, communicating their belief that the students can answer the question (T. L. Good & Brophy, 2008; Rosenthal, 1995). They tend to smile at these students more often and to show greater warmth through such nonverbal responses as leaning toward the students and nodding their heads as the students speak (Woolfolk & Brooks, 1983, 1985).

In contrast, with low-expectation students, teachers ask easier questions, allow less time for answering, and are less likely to give prompts. They are more likely to respond with sympathetic acceptance or even praise for inadequate answers from low-achieving students, but to criticize these same students for wrong answers. Even more disturbing, low-achieving students receive less praise than high-achieving students for similar correct answers. This inconsistent feedback can be very confusing for low-ability students. Imagine how hard it would be to learn if your wrong answers were sometimes praised, sometimes ignored, and sometimes criticized, and your right answers received little recognition (T. L. Good 1983a, 1983b; Hattie & Timperley, 2007). Even though the effects of these communications may be small each day, the effects can be huge, as the expectation differences build year after year with many teachers (Trouilloud, Sarrazin, Bressoux, & Bois, 2006).

Lessons for Teachers: Communicating Appropriate Expectations

Of course, not all teachers form inappropriate expectations or act on their expectations in unconstructive ways (Babad, Inbar, & Rosenthal, 1982). The *Guidelines: Avoiding the Negative Effects of Teacher Expectations* on the next page may help you avoid some of these problems. But avoiding the problem

Video 14.5
Mrs. Casey communicates clear expectations as she prepares students to work in groups at various centers. She uses ability grouping for guided reading, but her instructions to the class do not show distinctions in levels of expectation. Notice how she expresses trust in her students and encourages them to support one another. In the reading group, notice her unbiased expectations and praise.

ENHANCEDetext *video example*

GUIDELINES
Avoiding the Negative Effects of Teacher Expectations

Use information about students from tests, cumulative folders, and other teachers very carefully.

Examples

1. Avoid reading cumulative folders early in the year.
2. Be critical and objective about the reports you hear from other teachers.
3. Be flexible in your expectations—a student's label or your judgment might be wrong.

Be flexible in your use of grouping strategies.

Examples

1. Review work of students often, and experiment with new groupings.
2. Use different groups for different subjects.
3. Use mixed-ability groups in cooperative exercises.

Provide both challenge and support.

Examples

1. Don't say, "This is easy, I know you can do it."
2. Offer a wide range of problems, and encourage all students to try a few of the harder ones for extra credit. Find something positive about these attempts.
3. Make sure your high expectations come with academic and emotional support for students' struggles. "Holding high standards without providing a warm environment is merely harsh. A warm environment without high standards lacks backbone" (Jussim, 2012).

Be especially careful about how you respond to low-achieving students during class discussions.

Examples

1. Give them prompts, cues, and time to answer.
2. Give ample praise for good answers.
3. Call on low achievers as often as high achievers.

Use materials that show a wide range of ethnic groups.

Examples

1. Check readers and library books. Is there ethnic diversity?
2. Ask students to research and create their own materials, based on community or family sources.

Make sure that your teaching does not reflect racial, ethnic, or sexual stereotypes or prejudice.

Examples

1. Use a checking system to be sure you call on and include all students.
2. Monitor the content of the tasks you assign. Do boys get the "hard" math problems to work at the board? Do you avoid having students with limited English give oral presentations?

Be fair in evaluation and disciplinary procedures.

Examples

1. Make sure equal offenses receive equal punishment. Find out from students in an anonymous questionnaire whether you seem to be favoring certain individuals.
2. Try to grade student work without knowing the identity of the student. Ask another teacher to give you a "second opinion" from time to time.

Communicate to all students that you believe they can learn—and mean it.

Examples

1. Return papers that do not meet standards with specific suggestions for improvements.
2. If students do not have the answers immediately, wait, probe, and then help them think through an answer.

Involve all students in learning tasks and in privileges.

Examples

1. Use some system to make sure you give each student practice in reading, speaking, and answering questions.
2. Keep track of who gets to do what job. Are some students always on the list, whereas others seldom make it?

Monitor your nonverbal behavior.

Examples

1. Do you lean away or stand farther away from some students? Do some students get smiles when they approach your desk, whereas others get only frowns?
2. Does your tone of voice vary with different students?

For more information see chiron.valdosta.edu/whuitt/files/teacherexpect.html

may be more difficult than it seems. In general, low-expectation students also tend to be the most disruptive students. (Of course, low expectations can reinforce their desire to disrupt or misbehave.) Teachers may call on these students less, wait a shorter time for their answers, and give them less praise for right answers, partly to avoid the wrong, careless, or silly answers that can cause disruptions, delays, and digressions. The challenge is to deal with these very real threats to classroom management without communicating low expectations to some students or fostering their own low expectations of themselves. And sometimes, low expectations become part of the culture of the school—beliefs shared by teachers and administrators alike (R. S. Weinstein, Madison, & Kuklinski, 1995).

ENHANCEDetext *self-check*

SUMMARY

- **Research on Teaching (pp. 530–532)**

  What methods have been used to study teaching? For years, researchers have tried to unravel the mystery of effective teaching using classroom observation, case studies, interviews, experimentation with different methods, stimulated recall (teachers view videotapes and explain their teaching), analysis of lesson transcripts, and other approaches to study teaching in real classrooms.

  What are the general characteristics of good teaching? A variety of teacher qualities are related to good teaching. Research suggests teachers who receive proper training and certification have more successful students. Although it is important, teacher knowledge of a subject is not sufficient for effective teaching. Thorough knowledge does lead to greater clarity and better organization, which are both tied to good teaching. Teachers who provide clear presentations and explanations tend to have students who learn more and who rate their teachers more positively. Teacher warmth, friendliness, and understanding seem to be the traits most strongly related to positive student attitudes about the teacher and the course in general.

  What do expert teachers know? It takes time and experience to become an expert teacher. These teachers have a rich store of well-organized knowledge about the many specific situations of teaching. This knowledge is very complex and specific to the *situation, topic, students,* and even the individual *teacher.* Within the particular situation and topic, expert teachers have clear goals and take individual differences into account when planning for their students. Expert teachers also know how to be reflective practitioners—how to use their experience as a way to grow and improve in their teaching.

  What does the new latest research on teaching show? A program of large-scale, longitudinal research has identified three aspects of classroom climate that are related to the development and learning of preschool and elementary school students. These three dimensions are consistent with the characteristics of teachers identified in earlier research on teaching and cover affective, behavioral, and cognitive dimensions. The *affective* dimension is teacher *emotional support,* similar to teacher warmth and enthusiasm identified in early research. The *cognitive* dimension is instructional support, which includes concept development (activities and discussions that promote student higher-order thinking) and quality feedback that is specific and focused on the learning process. The third dimension is classroom organization, which includes *behavioral* concerns such as classroom and lesson

  management with clear activities and routines that make more time for learning and really engage students—similar to the teacher characteristics of clarity and organization.

- **The First Step: Planning (PP. 533–540)**

  What are the levels of planning, and how do they affect teaching? Teachers engage in several levels of planning—by the year, term, unit, week, and day. All the levels must be coordinated. The plan determines how time and materials will be turned into activities for students. There is no single model of planning, but all plans should allow for flexibility. Planning is a creative problem-solving process for experienced teachers. It is more informal—"in their heads."

  What is an instructional objective? An instructional objective is a clear and unambiguous description of your educational intentions for your students. Mager's influential system for writing behavioral objectives states that a good objective has three parts—the intended student behavior, the conditions under which the behavior will occur, and the criteria for acceptable performance. Gronlund's alternative approach suggests that an objective should be stated first in general terms, and then the teacher should clarify by listing sample behaviors that would provide evidence that the student has attained the objective. The most recent research on instructional objectives tends to favor approaches similar to Gronlund's.

  Describe the three taxonomies of educational objectives. Bloom and others have developed taxonomies categorizing basic objectives in the cognitive, affective, and psychomotor domains. In real life, of course, behaviors from these three domains occur simultaneously. A taxonomy encourages systematic thinking about relevant objectives and ways to evaluate them. Six basic objectives are listed in the cognitive domain: remembering, understanding, applying, analyzing, evaluating, and creating, acting on four kinds of knowledge: factual, conceptual, procedural, and metacognitive. Objectives in the affective domain run from least committed to most committed. Objectives in the psychomotor domain generally move from basic perceptions and reflex actions to skilled, creative movements.

  Describe constructivist planning. Planning is shared and negotiated in student-centered, or constructivist, approaches. Rather than having specific student behaviors as objectives, the teacher has overarching goals or "big ideas" that guide planning. Integrated content and teaching with themes are often part of the planning. Assessment of learning is ongoing and mutually shared by teacher and students.

- ### Teaching Approaches (pp. 540–552)

What is direct instruction? Direct instruction is appropriate for teaching basic skills and explicit knowledge. It includes the teaching functions of review/overview, presentation, guided practice, feedback and correctives (with reteaching if necessary), independent practice, and periodic reviews. The younger or less able the students, the shorter the presentation should be, with more cycles of practice and feedback.

Distinguish between convergent and divergent and high-level versus low-level questions. Convergent questions have only one right answer. Divergent questions have many possible answers. Higher-level questions require analyzing, evaluating, and creating—students have to think for themselves. The best pattern for younger students and for lower-ability students of all ages is simple questions that allow a high percentage of correct answers, ample encouragement, help when the student does not have the correct answer, and praise. For high-ability students, the successful pattern includes harder questions at both higher and lower levels and more critical feedback. Whatever their age or ability, all students should have some experience with thought-provoking questions and, if necessary, help in learning how to answer them.

How can wait time affect student learning? When teachers pose a question and then learn to wait at least 3 to 5 seconds before calling on a student to answer, students tend to give longer answers; more students are likely to participate, ask questions, and volunteer appropriate answers; student comments involving analysis, synthesis, inference, and speculation tend to increase; and the students generally appear more confident in their answers.

What are the uses and disadvantages of group discussion? Group discussion helps students participate directly, express themselves clearly, justify opinions, and tolerate different views. Group discussion also gives students a chance to ask for clarification, examine their own thinking, follow personal interests, and assume responsibility by taking leadership roles in the group. So group discussions help students evaluate ideas and synthesize personal viewpoints. However, discussions are quite unpredictable and may easily digress into exchanges of ignorance.

How can you match teaching to your goals? Different goals and student needs require different teaching methods. Direct instruction often leads to better performance on achievement tests, but the open, informal methods such as discovery learning or inquiry approaches are associated with better performance on tests of creativity, abstract thinking, and problem solving. In addition, the open methods are better for improving attitudes toward school and for stimulating curiosity, cooperation among students, and lower absence rates.

How can you use Understanding by Design to plan quality instruction? The focus of UbD is on deep understanding, which is characterized by the ability to (1) explain, (2) interpret, (3) apply, (4) have perspective, (5) empathize, and (6) have self-knowledge about a topic. The big idea behind UbD is backward design. Teachers first identify the important end results for students—the key understandings and big ideas that are the goals of instruction. To focus on understanding (not just fun activities or covering the text), teachers write essential questions—questions that go to the heart of the ideas and push thinking deeper. The UbD template guides planning based on these considerations.

- ### Differentiated Instruction and Adaptive Teaching (pp. 553–559)

What are the problems with ability grouping? Academic ability groupings can have disadvantages and advantages for students and teachers. Students in higher-ability groups may benefit, but students in lower-ability groups are less likely to be asked critical comprehension questions and are given fewer opportunities to make choices about readings and assignments. For schools with students with lower SES, grouping often means that these students are segregated even in their own classes, so ability grouping can create segregation within diverse schools.

What are the alternatives available for grouping in classes, including flexible grouping? Cross-age grouping by subject can be an effective way to deal with ability differences in a school. Within-class ability grouping, if handled sensitively and flexibly, can have positive effects, but alternatives such as cooperative learning may be better.

What is adaptive teaching? Adaptive teaching provides all students with challenging instruction and uses supports when needed, but removes those supports as students are able to handle more on their own.

What characterizes effective teaching for students with disabilities? Effective teaching for students with disabilities does not require a unique set of skills. It is a combination of good teaching practices and sensitivity to all students. Students with disabilities need to learn the academic material, and they need to be full participants in the day-to-day life of the classroom.

What resources do teachers have to work effectively with students with disabilities? When students have special needs, they may be referred for evaluation to specialists such as child study teams, school psychologists, or teachers of students with special needs. The outcome of this process sometimes includes the preparation of an IEP, as described in Chapter 4, which will have teaching ideas and guidelines. In addition, differentiated instruction can improve learning for all students, and developing mentoring relationships with students can help teachers connect with student abilities and needs.

- **Teacher Expectations (pp. 559–562)**

What are some sources of teacher expectations? Sources include intelligence test scores, gender, notes from previous teachers, medical or psychological reports found in cumulative folders, ethnic background, prior knowledge about older brothers and sisters, physical characteristics, previous achievement, SES, and the actual behaviors of the student.

What are the two kinds of expectation effects, and how do they happen? The first is the self-fulfilling prophecy, in which the teacher's beliefs about the students' abilities have no basis in fact, but student behavior comes to match the initially inaccurate expectation. The second is a sustaining expectation effect, in which teachers are fairly accurate in their initial reading of students' abilities and respond to students appropriately, but they do not alter their expectations to take account of any improvement. When this happens, the teacher's unchanging expectation can sustain the student's achievement at the expected level. In practice, sustaining effects are more common than self-fulfilling prophecy effects.

What are the different avenues for communicating teacher expectations? Some teachers tend to treat students differently, depending on their own views of how well the students are likely to do. Differences in treatment toward low-expectation students may include setting less-challenging tasks, focusing on lower-level learning, giving fewer choices, providing inconsistent feedback, and communicating less respect and trust. Students may behave accordingly, fulfilling teachers' predictions or staying at an expected level of achievement.

PRACTICE USING WHAT YOU HAVE LEARNED

To access and complete the exercises, click the link under the images below.

The First Step: Planning

ENHANCEDetext *application exercise*

Differentiated Instruction and Adaptive Teaching

ENHANCEDetext *application exercise*

KEY TERMS

Active teaching 540
Adaptive teaching 554
Advance organizer 541
Affective domain 538
Assistive technology 557
Basic skills 540
Behavioral objectives 536

Cognitive domain 537
Cognitive objectives 536
Constructivist approach 539
Convergent questions 547
Differentiated instruction 553
Direct instruction/explicit teaching 540
Divergent questions 547

Expert teachers 531
Flexible grouping 553
Group discussion 549
Instructional objectives 536
Lesson study 534
Pedagogical content knowledge 531
Psychomotor domain 538

CONNECT AND EXTEND TO LICENSURE

MULTIPLE-CHOICE QUESTIONS

1. Direct instruction is best used when teachers do which one of the following?
   A. Teach basic skills
   B. Have their students explore numerous pathways to solve a mathematics problem
   C. Encourage their students to refine their creativity in art
   D. Assign critical thinking exercises

2. Homework has long been a staple of education. For students to gain the most from their homework experience, ALL BUT which one of the following suggestions should be followed?
   A. Establish that students understand the assignment
   B. Hold students accountable for completing the work correctly
   C. Check students' work and allow for corrections and revisions
   D. Require a parent signature to ensure collaboration with home

3. Ellen Baker knew that her new job in a middle school would require that she understand differentiated instruction. Using this strategy, her students would be more apt to progress and master the concepts they needed to succeed throughout their school years. One of the techniques she decided to use involved grouping students by their learning needs. She would group students who had scored poorly on their fractions tests with similar students to remediate and develop that skill. She likened this type of differentiated instruction to having students continually work in their zone of proximal development. The type of strategy Ellen Baker wants to use is referred to as which one of the following?
   A. Flexible grouping
   B. Jigsaw
   C. Collaborative group work
   D. Peer tutoring

4. Teachers sometimes make determinations about their students' abilities based on little evidence. When teachers expect their students will not do well, their words and actions can make that expectation come true regardless of the validity. This effect is referred to as which one of the following?
   A. Self-fulfilling prophecy
   B. The zone of proximal development
   C. Professional license
   D. Supportive withdrawal

CONSTRUCTED-RESPONSE QUESTIONS

Case

Although Casey Yost had done well in her college classes, she was having a difficult time with her student teaching. Her mentor teacher continually scolded her for not correctly writing her objectives and rushing through lessons. Casey did not understand how she could both make her lessons clear and manage to cover the material necessary for the students' upcoming standardized tests. "Casey, if your students don't understand the material, it won't make a difference if you cover the material or not. Let's review one of your objectives for the upcoming lesson. 'Students will understand fractions.' This objective is too general. How can you measure if your students 'understand'? You need to select words that correspond to specific actions that you can observe or measure. Let's try to develop a few objectives that are more specific."

5. In what ways can Casey Yost avoid writing objectives that are too general?

6. List several strategies that Casey can employ during instruction to teach her students more effectively.

ENHANCEDetext *licensure exam*

TEACHERS' CASEBOOK

WHAT WOULD THEY DO? REACHING AND TEACHING EVERY STUDENT

Here is how some practicing teachers would differentiate instruction for the class described at the beginning of the chapter.

LOU DE LAURO—Fifth-Grade Language Arts
John P. Faber School, Dunellen, NJ

In your hometown you probably know a lot of people. To be successful you are going to have to use the town to help you. If you plan properly, you should be able to secure one guest a week for the entire school year. The kids will love meeting new people each week and reading with them. But you need more than a guest a week to visit your classroom. So ask the businesses in town. Maybe a business can run a fundraiser so you can purchase alternative texts for your students. Maybe the local library can introduce you to their biggest donor who might donate texts to you. Maybe you can apply for a grant with the local educational foundation to get new materials.

But you need more help. You are a teacher; you were probably a strong student who connected with your former teachers. Visit any teachers that are still teaching, and get their advice on what to do. What has worked in the past may work well now, too.

Devote many hours after school to your students. Small-group instruction will help these kids. Get the two students who are practically ready for college small stipends donated by a local business so they stay after school and help you with your challenging students. I think that if you fully take advantage of your home court, this is one situation in which you can easily prevail.

MARIE HOFFMAN HURT—Eighth-Grade Foreign Language Teacher (German and French)
Pickerington Local Schools, Pickerington, OH

To start, I would encourage a teacher to look beyond the general classifications of "white, working, middle class, and English speaking." Even in a class full of students who fit this demographic, there is an array of individuals. Each student learns differently and has different interests. A good teacher will recognize this and challenge students as people, not as groups. Do your best to layer as much as you can throughout your lessons. Give students choices. Use what resources you have—in this case particularly resources for students who are learning English as a second language. Even praising students' individual characteristics and accomplishments outside the classroom sets the tone. Finally, keep in mind that you are only one person and can only give your best. Don't overwork yourself and burn out—you are no good to your students or your family if you are wiped out.

M. DENISE LUTZ—Technology Coordinator
Grandview Heights High School, Columbus, OH

Studies have shown that student success is directly related to teacher effectiveness. In today's diverse classrooms a teacher must develop effective classroom pedagogy that incorporates effective instructional strategies, uses effective classroom management strategies, and designs effective classroom curriculum to meet the needs of all learners. It is necessary to communicate learning goals for all students, track individual progress, and celebrate successes. Under the guidance of the teacher, students should learn to work collaboratively in small groups and as a cohesive class encouraging and helping one another to be successful. A teacher who establishes and maintains classroom rules and procedures while acknowledging students who do and do not follow these rules and procedures fosters this kind of environment. Consistency, trust, and authenticity will help to advance the development of effective relationships between the teacher, the home, and among class members. Effective classroom curriculum always begins with the end in mind. The teacher should have a clear picture of what mastery of content would look like for each of his or her students. Understanding the big idea and defining essential questions will guide the collection of activities and lessons that will move each student in the direction of success. The direction of success will remain the same for all students, but lessons and activities may present different paths for individuals to traverse. Today's teacher must work from day one to get to know each individual and to establish a culture of collaboration among the group.

PATRICIA A. SMITH—High School Math
Earl Warren High School, San Antonio, TX

Because this new teacher is a product of the same school system, it will be imperative to begin classroom instruction with absolutely no preconceived opinions toward any particular student. Likewise, a diverse population requires the teacher to resolve student situations discreetly and judiciously, and not publicly. The initial goals of the teacher would be to facilitate student work in a cooperative manner and engender teacher trust. Planning and organizing icebreaker exercises the first few days of the school year could prove extremely profitable.

With a wide range of reading levels, small groups would work to the teacher's advantage. I would not suggest grouping students according to reading level at all times, but would opt to appoint a recognized student leader to orchestrate daily oral recitations. Moreover, I would select reading materials suited to all students and keep the assignments brief to avoid overwhelming struggling readers. The student leader could also design questions to gauge comprehension and give the group a follow-up spelling test. Initially, the spelling test would be composed of 5 to 10 simple words that students could either print or write. Subsequently, as the students gain confidence and experience success, the readings could be assigned as homework and the students would be required to write a short paragraph answering a reading comprehension question.

If the teacher remains well organized, the instructional time allotted for small-group interaction should not extend over 15 minutes in a single class period. Thus, the teacher would not forfeit traditional grammar lessons for the entire class but would still provide limited individualized instruction. I would also supplement SAT reading and English practice for all college-bound students.

15 | CLASSROOM ASSESSMENT, GRADING, AND STANDARDIZED TESTING

TEACHERS' CASEBOOK

WHAT WOULD YOU DO? GIVING MEANINGFUL GRADES

Your school requires that you give letter grades to your class. You can use any method you want, as long as an A, B, C, D, or F appears for each of the subject areas on every student's report card, every grading period. Some teachers are using worksheets, quizzes, homework, and tests. Others are assigning group work and portfolios. A few teachers are individualizing standards by grading on progress and effort more than final achievement. Some are trying contract approaches and experimenting with longer-term projects, while others are relying almost completely on daily class work. Two teachers who use group work are considering giving credit toward grades for being a "good group member" or competitive bonus points for the top-scoring group. Others are planning to use improvement points for class rewards, but not for grades. Your only experience with grading was using written comments and a mastery approach that rated the students as making satisfactory or unsatisfactory progress toward particular objectives. You want a system that is reliable, fair, and manageable, but also encourages learning, not just performance. And you want a system that gives the students feedback they can use to prepare for the state proficiency tests.

CRITICAL THINKING

- What would you choose as your major graded assignments and projects?
- Would you include credit for behaviors such as group participation or effort?
- How would you put all the elements together to determine a grade for every student for every marking period?
- How would you justify your system to the principal and to the students' families, especially when the teachers in your school are using so many different criteria?
- What do you think of the wide range of criteria being used by different teachers—is this fair to students?
- How will these issues affect the grade levels you will teach?

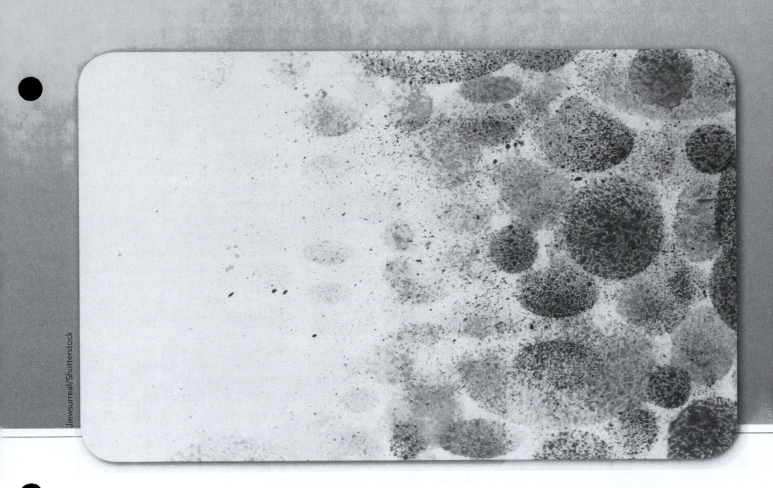

OVERVIEW AND OBJECTIVES

As you read this chapter, you will examine assessment, testing, and grading, focusing not only on the effects they are likely to have on students, but also on practical ways to develop better methods for testing and grading.

We begin with a consideration of the basic concepts in assessment including validity and reliability. Next we examine the many types of tests teachers prepare each year and approaches to assessment that don't rely on traditional testing. Then, we explore the effects grades are likely to have on students and the very important topic of communication with students and families. How will you justify the grades you give? Finally, because standardized tests are so important today, we spend some time looking at testing, the meaning of test scores, and alternatives to traditional testing.

By the time you have completed this chapter, you should be able to:

Objective 15.1   Describe the basics of assessment including similarities and differences among evaluation, measurement, and assessment, norm-referenced and criterion-referenced assessments, and how reliability, validity, and absence of bias are used to understand and judge assessments.

Objective 15.2   Describe two kinds of traditional classroom testing: how to use objective and essay testing appropriately in teaching, and the advantages as well as criticisms of traditional testing.

Objective 15.3   Explain how to design and evaluate authentic assessments, including portfolios, exhibitions, performances, informal assessments, journals, and the development of rubrics.

Objective 15.4   Describe the effects of grading on students and the types of strategies teachers can use to communicate to parents about grades.

Objective 15.5   Explain how to interpret common standardized test scores (percentile rank, stanine, grade-equivalent, scale score) as well as current issues and criticisms concerning accountability, high-stakes assessment, and standardized tests.

Connect and Extend to PRAXIS II®

Types of Assessment (II, C1, 4)
Understand the purposes of formative and summative assessment. Explain how teachers and students can make effective use of the information generated by each type of test.

BASICS OF ASSESSMENT

Would it surprise you to learn that published tests, such as college entrance exams and IQ tests, are creations of the 20th century? In the early to mid-1900s, college entrance was generally based on grades, essays, and interviews. From your own experience, you know that testing has come a long way since then—too far, say some critics. Published tests today are called standardized tests because they are administered, scored, and interpreted in a standard manner—same directions, time limits, and scoring for all (Popham, 2014). Standard methods of developing items, administering the test, scoring it, and reporting the scores are all implied by the term *standardized test*. The schools where you teach probably will use standardized tests, especially to meet the growing demands for accountability. In most schools, however, teachers do not have much say in selecting these tests.

Classroom assessments, on the other hand, are created and selected by teachers. Classroom assessments can take many different forms—unit tests, essays, portfolios, group projects, performances, oral presentations—the list is long. Assessments are critical because teaching involves making many kinds of judgments—decisions based on values: "Is this software appropriate for my students?" "Will Jacob do better if he repeats the first grade?" "Should Emily get a B− or a C+ on the project?" This chapter is about judgments that involve measurement, testing, and grading, and all forms of assessment. We look at both classroom assessment and standardized testing, with an emphasis on the former, because teachers are responsible for classroom assessments. Before we look at either classroom or standardized assessments, let's examine some key distinctions that apply to both, beginning with the difference between measurement and assessment.

Measurement and Assessment

Measurement is quantitative—the description of an event or characteristic using numbers. Measurement tells how much, how often, or how well by providing scores, ranks, or ratings. Instead of saying, "Sarah doesn't seem to understand addition," a teacher might say, "Sarah answered only 2 of the 15 problems correctly in her addition homework." Measurement also allows a teacher to compare one student's performance on a particular task with either a specific standard or the performances of other students on the same task.

Not all the decisions made by teachers involve measurement. Some decisions are based on information that is difficult to express numerically: student preferences, discussions with families, previous experiences, even intuition. But measurement does play a large role in many classroom decisions, and, when properly done, it can provide unbiased data for decision making.

Increasingly, measurement specialists are using the term *assessment* to describe the process of gathering information about students' learning. Assessment is broader than testing and measurement because it includes all kinds of ways to sample and observe students' skills, knowledge, and abilities (R. L. Linn & Miller, 2005). Assessments can be formal, such as unit tests, or informal, such as observing who emerges as a leader in group work. Assessments can be designed by classroom teachers or by local, state, or national agencies such as school districts or the Educational Testing Service. And today, assessments can go well beyond paper-and-pencil exercises to judgments based on students' performances, portfolios, projects, or products (Popham, 2014).

FORMATIVE AND SUMMATIVE ASSESSMENT. There are two general uses or functions for assessment: formative and summative. Formative assessment occurs before or during instruction. The purposes of formative assessment are to guide the teacher in planning and improving instruction and to help students improve learning. In other words, formative assessment helps *form* instruction and provides feedback that is "nonevaluative, supportive, timely, and specific" (Shute, 2008, p. 153). Students often take a formative test before instruction, a pretest that helps the teacher determine what students already know. Teachers sometimes give a test during instruction to see what areas of weakness remain, so they can direct teaching toward the problem areas. These formative tests are not graded, so students who tend to be very anxious about "real" tests may find this low-pressure practice in test taking especially helpful. Also, the feedback from formative tests can help students become more self-regulated in their learning (I. Clark, 2012).

Summative assessment occurs at the end of instruction. Its purpose is to let the teacher and the students know the level of accomplishment attained. Summative assessment, therefore, provides a summary of accomplishment. The final exam is a classic example.

The distinction between formative and summative assessment is based on how the results are used. And any kind of assessment—traditional, performance, project, oral, portfolio, and so on—can be used for either formative or summative purposes. If the purpose of the assessment is to improve your teaching and help students guide their own learning, then the evaluation is *formative.* But if the purpose is to evaluate final achievement (and help determine a course grade), the assessment is *summative* (Nitko & Brookhart, 2011). In fact, the same assessment could be used as a formative evaluation at the beginning of the unit and as a summative evaluation at the end. Table 15.1 gives some examples of different uses of assessment.

The formative uses of assessment are really the most important in teaching. In fact, Popham believes "any teacher who uses tests dominantly to determine whether students get high or low grades should receive a solid F in classroom assessment" (2008, p. 256). Tests and all assessments should be used to help teachers make better instructional decisions.

The answers given on any type of test have no meaning by themselves; we must make some kind of comparison in order to interpret test results. There are two basic types of comparisons: In the first, a test score is compared to the scores obtained by other people who have taken the same test. This is called a *norm-referenced comparison.* The second type is *criterion-referenced.* Here, the score is compared to a fixed standard or minimum passing score. The same test can be interpreted either in a norm-referenced or criterion-referenced way.

NORM-REFERENCED TEST INTERPRETATIONS. In norm-referenced testing and grading, the people who have taken the test provide the norms for determining the meaning of a given individual's score. You can think of a *norm* as being the typical level of performance for a particular group. By comparing the individual's raw score (the actual number correct) to the norm, we can determine if the score is above, below, or around the average for that group.

Connect and Extend to PRAXIS II®

Criterion-/Norm-Referenced Tests (II, C5) The ERIC Digest *Norm- and Criterion-Referenced Testing* (ericdigests .org/1998–1/norm.htm) describes the purposes, content, and issues related to criterion- and norm-referenced tests.

Giving accurate feedback to parents is part of a teacher's job. When talking with a parent about a child's abilities, do you think the use of norm-referenced or criterion-referenced test results is more desirable?

TABLE 15.1 • Using Tests to Make Instructional Decisions

The best use of assessment is to plan, guide, and target instruction. Here are some decisions that can benefit from assessment results.

DECISION CATEGORY	TYPICAL ASSESSMENT STRATEGY	DECISION OPTIONS
What to teach in the first place?	Preassessment before instruction	Whether to provide instruction for specific objectives?
How long to keep teaching toward a particular instructional objective?	En route assessments of students' progress	Whether to continue or cease instruction for an objective either for an individual or for the whole class?
How effective was an instructional sequence?	Comparing students' posttest to pretest performances	Whether to retain, discard, or modify a given instructional sequence the next time it's used?

Source: From Popham, W. J. (2014). Classroom Assessment: What Teachers Need to Know, 7th Ed. Boston, MA: Pearson Education, Inc. Adapted with permission.

There are at least four types of norm groups (comparison groups) in education—the class or school itself, the school district, national samples, and international samples. Students in national norm groups used for large-scale assessment programs are tested one year, and then the scores for that group serve as comparisons or norms every year for several years until the test is revised, or *re-normed*. The norm groups are selected so that all socioeconomic status (SES) groups are included in the sample. Because students from high-SES backgrounds tend to do better on many standardized tests, a high-SES school district will almost always have higher scores compared to the national norm group.

Norm-referenced tests cover a wide range of general objectives. They are especially appropriate when only the top few candidates can be admitted to a program. However, norm-referenced measurement has its limitations. The results of a norm-referenced test do not tell you whether students are ready to move on to more advanced material. For instance, knowing that two students are in the top 3% of the class on a test of algebraic concepts will not tell you if they are ready to move on to advanced math; everyone else in the class may have a limited understanding of the algebraic concepts.

Nor are norm-referenced tests particularly appropriate for measuring affective and psychomotor objectives. To measure individuals' psychomotor learning, you need a clear description of standards. (Even the best gymnast in school performs certain exercises better than others and needs specific guidance about how to improve.) In the affective area, attitudes and values are personal; comparisons among individuals are not really appropriate. For example, how could we measure an "average" level of political values or opinions? Finally, norm-referenced tests tend to encourage competition and comparison of scores. Some students compete to be the best. Others, realizing that being the best is impossible, may compete to be the worst. Both goals have their casualties.

CRITERION-REFERENCED TEST INTERPRETATIONS. When test scores are compared, not to the scores of others, but to a given criterion or standard of performance, this is criterion-referenced testing or grading. To decide who should be allowed to drive a car, it is important to determine just what standard of performance works for selecting safe drivers. It does not matter how your test results compare to the results of others. If your performance on the test was in the top 10%, but you consistently ran through red lights, you would not be a good candidate for receiving a license, even though your score was high.

Criterion-referenced tests measure the mastery of very specific objectives. The results of a criterion-referenced test should tell the teacher exactly what the students can and cannot do, at least under certain conditions. For example, a criterion-referenced test would be useful in measuring the students' ability to add three-digit numbers. A test could be designed with 20 different problems, and the standard for mastery could be set at 17 correct out of 20. (The standard is often somewhat arbitrary and may be based on such things as the teacher's experience.) If two students receive scores of 7 and 11, it does not matter that one student did better than the other because neither met the standard of 17. Both need more help with addition.

When teaching basic skills, comparison to a preset standard is often more important than comparison to the performance of others. It is not very comforting to know, as a parent, that your child is better in reading than most of the students in her class if none of the students is reading at grade level. Sometimes standards for meeting the criterion must be set at 100% correct. You would not like to have your appendix removed by a surgeon who left surgical instruments inside the body *only* 10% of the time.

Criterion-referenced tests are not appropriate for every situation. Many subjects cannot be broken down into a set of specific objectives. And, although standards are important in criterion-referenced testing, they can often be arbitrary, as you have already seen. When deciding whether a student has mastered the addition of three-digit numbers comes down to the difference between 16 or 17 correct answers, it seems difficult to justify one particular standard over another. Finally, at times, it is valuable to know how the students in your class compare to other students at their grade level both locally and nationally. You can see that each type of test is well suited for certain situations, but each also has its limitations.

Assessing the Assessments: Reliability and Validity

One of the most common problems with the use of assessments, especially tests, is misinterpretation of results. This often happens when people believe tests are precise measurements of a student's ability. No test provides a perfect picture of a person's abilities; a test is only one small sample of behavior. Three factors are important in developing good tests and interpreting results: *reliability*, *validity*, and *absence of bias*.

RELIABILITY OF TEST SCORES. Scores are reliable if a test gives a consistent and stable "reading" of a person's ability from one occasion to the next, assuming the person's ability remains the same. A reliable thermometer works in a similar manner, giving you a reading of 100°C each time you measure the temperature of boiling water. Measuring **reliability** this way, by giving the test on two different occasions, indicates *stability*, or *test–retest reliability*. If a group of people take two equivalent versions of a test and the scores on both tests are comparable, this indicates *alternate-form reliability*. Reliability can also refer to the *internal consistency* or the precision of a test. This type of reliability, known as *split-half reliability*, is calculated by comparing performance on half of the test questions with performance on the other half. If, for example, someone did quite well on all the odd-numbered items and not at all well on the even-numbered items, we could assume that the items were not very consistent or precise in measuring what they were intended to measure.

There are several ways to compute reliability, but all the possibilities give numbers between 0.0 and 1.0, like a correlation coefficient. Above .90 is considered very reliable; .80 to .90 is good, and below .80 is not very good reliability for commercially produced standardized tests such as the SAT or ACT (Haladyna, 2002). Generally speaking, longer tests are more reliable than shorter ones.

ERROR IN SCORES. All tests are imperfect estimators of the qualities or skills they are trying to measure. There are errors in every testing situation. There are sources of error related to the student such as mood, motivation, test-taking skills, or even cheating. Sometimes the errors are in your favor, and you score higher than your ability might warrant; sometimes the errors go against you. There are also sources of error related to the test itself: the directions are unclear, the reading level is too high, the items are ambiguous, or the time limits are wrong.

The score each student receives always includes some amount of error. How can error be reduced? As you might guess, this returns us to the question of reliability. The more reliable the test scores are, the less error there will be in the score actually obtained. On standardized tests, test developers take this into consideration and make estimations of how much the students' scores would probably vary if they were tested repeatedly. This estimation is called the **standard error of measurement**. Thus, a reliable test can also be defined as one with a small standard error of measurement.

CONFIDENCE INTERVAL. Never base an opinion of a student's ability or achievement on the exact score the student obtains. For standardized tests, many test companies now report scores using a **confidence interval**, or "standard error band," that encloses the student's actual score. This makes use of the standard error of measurement and allows a teacher to consider the range of scores that might include a student's **true score**—the score the student would get if the measurement were completely accurate and error-free.

Assume, for example, that two students in your class take a standardized achievement test in Spanish. The standard error of measurement for this test is 5. One student receives a score of 79 and the other, a score of 85. At first glance, these scores seem quite different. But when you consider the standard error bands around the scores, not just the scores alone, you see that the bands overlap. The first student's true score might be anywhere between 74 and 84 (that is, the actual score of 79 plus and minus the standard error of 5). The second student's true score might be anywhere between 80 and 90. Both students could have the same true score of 80, 81, 82, 83, or 84, because the score bands overlap at those numbers. It is crucial to keep in mind the idea of standard error bands when selecting students for special programs. No child should be rejected simply because the score obtained missed the cutoff by 1 or 2 points. The student's true score might well be above the cutoff point. See Figure 15.5 later in this chapter for a report with these score bands.

VALIDITY. If test scores are sufficiently reliable, the next question is whether the scores are valid, or more accurately, whether the judgments and decisions based on the test scores are valid. To have validity, the decisions and inferences based on the test must be supported by evidence. This means that validity is judged in relation to a particular use or purpose—that is, in relation to the actual decision being made and the evidence for that decision. A particular test might be valid for one purpose, but not for another (Oosterhof, 2009; Popham, 2014).

Different kinds of evidence support a particular judgment. If the purpose of a test is to measure the skills covered in a course or unit, then we would hope to see test questions on all the important topics and not on extraneous information. If this condition is met, we would have *content-related evidence of validity.* Have you ever taken a test that dealt only with a few ideas from one lecture or just a few pages of the textbook? Then decisions based on that test (like your grade) certainly lacked content-related evidence of validity.

Some tests are designed to predict outcomes. The SATs, for example, are intended to predict performance in college. If SAT scores correlate with academic performance in college as measured by the criterion of, say, grade-point average in the first year, then we have *criterion-related evidence of validity* for the use of the SAT in admissions decisions.

Most standardized tests are designed to measure some psychological characteristic or "construct" such as reasoning ability, reading comprehension, achievement motivation, intelligence, creativity, and so on. It is a bit more difficult to gather *construct-related evidence of validity,* yet this is a very important requirement—probably the most important. Construct-related evidence of validity is gathered over many years. It is indicated by a pattern of scores. For example, older children can answer more questions on intelligence tests than younger children can. This fits with our *construct* of intelligence. If the average 5-year-old answered as many questions correctly on a test as the average 13-year-old, we would doubt that the test really measured intelligence. Construct-related evidence for validity can also be demonstrated when the results of a test correlate with the results of other well-established, valid measures of the same construct.

Today, many psychologists suggest that construct validity is the broadest category and that gathering content- and criterion-related evidence is another way of determining if the test actually measures the construct it was designed to measure. Nearly 40 years ago, Sam Messick (1975) raised two important questions to consider in making any decisions about using a test: *Is the test a good measure of the characteristic it is assumed to assess? Should the test be used for the proposed purpose?* The first question is about construct validity; the second is about ethics and values.

A test must be reliable in order to be valid. For example, if an intelligence test yields different results each time it is given to the same child over the course of a few months, then, by definition, it is not reliable. Certainly, it couldn't be a valid measure of intelligence because intelligence is assumed to be fairly stable, at least over a short period of time. However, reliability will not guarantee validity. If that intelligence test gave the same score every time for a particular child, but didn't predict school achievement, speed of learning, or other characteristics associated with intelligence, then performance on the test would not be a true indicator of intelligence. The test would be reliable—but invalid. Reliability and validity are issues with all assessments, not just standardized tests. Classroom tests should yield scores that are *reliable,* that are as free from error as possible, and *valid*—accurately measure what they are supposed to.

ABSENCE OF BIAS. The third important criterion for judging assessments is absence of bias. Assessment bias "refers to qualities of an assessment instrument that offend or unfairly penalize a group of students because of the students' gender, race, ethnicity, socioeconomic status, religion, or other such group-defining characteristic" (Popham, 2014, p. 127). Biases are aspects of the test such as content, language, or examples that might distort the performance of a group—either for better or for worse. For example, if a reading test used passages that described boxing or football scenarios, we might expect males on average to do better than females.

Two forms of assessment bias are *unfair penalization* and *offensiveness.* The reading assessment with heavy sports content is an example of unfair penalization—girls may be penalized for their lack of boxing or football knowledge. Offensiveness occurs when a particular group might be insulted by the content of the assessment. Offended, angry students may not perform at their best.

What about biases based on ethnicity or social class? Research on test bias shows that most standardized tests predict school achievement equally well across all groups of students (Sattler, 2008). But even so, many people believe that the tests still can be unfair to some groups. Tests may not have *procedural fairness;* that is, some groups may not have an equal opportunity to show what they know on the test. Here are a few examples:

1. The language of the test and the tester is often different from the languages of the students.
2. Answers that support middle-class values are often rewarded with more points.
3. On individually administered intelligence tests, being very verbal and talking a lot is rewarded. This favors students who feel comfortable in that particular situation.

Also, tests may not be fair because different groups have had different opportunities to learn the material tested. The questions asked tend to center on experiences and facts more familiar to students from the dominant culture than to students from minority groups. Consider this test item for fourth-graders described by Popham (2014, p. 391):

> My uncle's field is computer programming.

Look at the sentences below. In which sentence does the word *field* mean the same as it does in the boxed sentence above?
A. The softball pitcher knew how to *field* her position.
B. They prepared the *field* by spraying and plowing it.
C. I know the *field* I plan to enter when I finish college.
D. The doctor used a wall chart to examine my *field* of vision.

Items like this are included on most standardized and textbook tests. But not all families describe their work as a *field* of employment. If your parents work in professional fields such as computers, medicine, law, or education, the item would make sense, but what if your parents worked at a grocery store or a car repair shop? Are these fields? Life outside class has prepared some students, but not others, for this item.

Concern about cultural bias in testing has led some psychologists to try to develop **culture-fair,** or **culture-free, tests.** These efforts have not been very successful. On many of the so-called culture-fair tests, the performance of students from lower-SES backgrounds and ethnic groups has been the same as or worse than their performance on the standard Wechsler and Binet Intelligence scales (Sattler, 2008). And when you think about it, how can you separate culture from cognition? Every student's learning is embedded in his or her culture, and every test question emerges from some kind of cultural knowledge.

Today, most standardized tests are checked carefully for assessment bias, but teacher-made tests may have biased content as well. It makes sense to have colleagues check your tests for bias, especially when you are getting started in teaching (Popham, 2014).

With this background in the basic concepts of formative and summative assessments; norm-referenced and criterion-referenced interpretations; and attention to reliability, validity, and absence of bias, we are ready to enter the classroom, where *learning is supported by frequent assessments using cumulative questions that ask students to apply and integrate knowledge* (Rawson & Dunlosky, 2012).

ENHANCEDetext *self-check*

CLASSROOM ASSESSMENT: TESTING

- -

STOP & THINK Think back to your most recent test. What was the format? Did you feel that the test results were an accurate reflection of your knowledge or skills? Have you ever had to design a test? What makes a good, fair test? •

- -

Connect and Extend to PRAXIS II®

Traditional Assessment (II C1, 2, 4)
Objective and essay tests continue to have important roles in effective assessment and evaluation programs. Describe the appropriate uses of these types of tests. Identify the advantages and limitations of each.

PODCAST 15.1
Some people are just better at taking tests than others. What do they know, and how do they do it? Hear textbook author Anita Woolfolk discuss some ideas for improving your own test taking and also how to help your students improve.

ENHANCEDetext *podcast*

When most people think of assessments in a classroom, they usually think of testing. As you will see shortly, teachers today have many other options, but testing is still a significant activity in most classrooms. In this section, we will examine how to evaluate the tests that accompany standard curriculum materials and show you how to write your own test questions.

Using the Tests from Textbooks

Most elementary and secondary school texts today come complete with supplemental materials such as teaching manuals and ready-made tests. Using these tests can save time, but is this good teaching practice? The answer depends on your objectives for your students, the way you teach the material, and the quality of the tests provided. If the textbook test is of high quality, matches your testing plan, and fits the instruction you actually provided for your students, then it may be the right test to use. Check the reading level of the items provided and be prepared to revise and improve them (McMillan, 2004; Russell & Airasian, 2012). Table 15.2 gives key points to consider in evaluating textbook tests.

What if no tests are available for the material you want to cover, or the tests provided in your teachers' manuals are not appropriate for your students? Then it's time for you to create your own tests. We will consider the two major kinds of traditional tests—objective and essay.

Objective Testing

Multiple-choice questions, matching exercises, true/false statements, and short-answer or fill-in items are all types of **objective testing**. The word *objective* in relation to testing means "not open to many interpretations," or "not subjective." The scoring of these types of items is relatively straightforward compared to the scoring of essay questions because the answers are more clear-cut than essay answers.

How should you decide which item format is best for a particular test? Use the one that provides the most direct measure of the learning outcome you intended for your students (Waugh & Gronlund, 2013). In other words, if you want to see how well students can write a letter, have them write a letter, don't ask multiple-choice questions about letters. But if many different item formats will work equally well, then use multiple-choice questions because they are easier to score fairly and can cover many topics. Switch to other formats if writing good multiple-choice items for the material is not possible or appropriate. For example, if related concepts such as terms and definitions need to be linked, then a matching item is a better format than multiple-choice. If it is difficult to come up with several wrong answers for a multiple-choice item, try a true/false question instead. Alternatively, ask the student to supply a short answer that completes a statement (fill in the blank). Variety in objective testing can lower students' anxiety because the entire grade does not depend on one type of question that a particular student may find difficult. We will look closely at the multiple-choice format because it is the most versatile—and the most difficult to use well.

TABLE 15.2 • Key Points to Consider in Judging Textbook Tests

1. The decision to use a textbook test or pre-made standard achievement test must come *after* a teacher identifies the objective that he or she has taught and now wants to assess.
2. Textbook and standard tests are designed for the typical classroom, but because few classrooms are typical, most teachers deviate somewhat from the text to accommodate their pupils' needs.
3. The more classroom instruction deviates from the textbook, the less valid the textbook tests are likely to be.
4. The main consideration in judging the adequacy of a textbook or standard achievement test is the match between its test questions and what pupils were taught in their classes:
   a. Are questions similar to the teacher's objectives and instructional emphases?
   b. Do questions require pupils to perform the behaviors they were taught?
   c. Do questions cover all or most of the important objectives taught?
   d. Is the language level and terminology appropriate for pupils?
   e. Does the number of items for each objective provide a sufficient sample of pupil performance?

Source: From Classroom Assessment: Concepts and Applications (7th ed.), by M. K. Russell & P. W. Airasian (2012), p. 134. New York: McGraw-Hill, p. 161. With permission from The McGraw-Hill Companies.

USING MULTIPLE-CHOICE TESTS. Even though about three fourths of education professors reject the use of multiple-choice tests in determining students' grades, about half of public school teachers endorse these tests (S. R. Banks, 2012), so you should know how to use these tests well. In fact, many schools require teachers to give students experience answering multiple-choice tests to prepare them for state achievement testing (McMillan, 2004). Of course, multiple-choice items can test facts, but these items can assess more than recall and recognition if they require the student to deal with new material by applying or analyzing the concept or principle being tested (McMillan, 2004; Waugh & Gronlund, 2013). For example, the following multiple-choice item is designed to assess students' ability to recognize unstated assumptions, one of the skills involved in analyzing an idea:

An educational psychology professor states, "A z score of $+1$ on a test is equivalent to a percentile rank of approximately 84." Which of the following assumptions is the professor making?

1. The scores on the test range from 0 to 100.
2. The standard deviation of the test scores is equal to 3.4.
3. The distribution of scores on the test is normal. (Correct answer)
4. The test is valid and reliable.

If you did not know the correct answer above, don't worry. We will get to z scores later in this chapter, and it will all make sense.

WRITING MULTIPLE-CHOICE QUESTIONS. All test items require skillful construction, but good multiple-choice items are a real challenge. Some students jokingly refer to multiple-choice tests as "multiple-guess" tests—a sign that these tests are often poorly designed. Your goal in writing test items is to design them so that they measure student achievement, not test-taking and guessing skills.

The **stem** of a multiple-choice item is the part that asks the question or poses the problem. The choices that follow are called *alternatives*. The wrong answers are called distractors because their purpose is to distract students who have only a partial understanding of the material. If there were no good distractors, students with only a vague understanding would have no difficulty in finding the right answer. The *Guidelines: Writing Objective Test Items* on the next page should help you write good stems and alternatives.

Essay Testing

The best way to measure some learning objectives is to ask students to create answers on their own; essay questions are one way to accomplish this. The most difficult part of essay testing is judging the quality of the answers, but writing good, clear questions is not particularly easy, either. We will look at writing, administering, and grading essay tests. We will also consider factors that can bias the scoring of essay questions and ways you can overcome these problems.

CONSTRUCTING ESSAY TESTS. Because answering takes time, true essay tests cover less material than objective tests. Thus, for efficiency, essay tests should be limited to the assessment of important, complex learning outcomes. A good essay question gives students a clear and precise task and indicates the elements to be covered in the answer. The students should know how extensive their answer needs to be and about how much time they should spend on each question. Evaluate these two essay questions from Popham (2014, pp. 201):

1. (High school level) You have just viewed a videotape containing three widely seen television commercials. What is the one classic propaganda technique present in all three commercials?
2. (Middle school level) Thinking back over the mathematics lesson and homework assignments you had during the past 12 weeks, what conclusions can you draw? Take no more than one page for your response.

Question 1 is pretty clear (do you agree?), but some indication of desired length would be helpful. Question 2 gives a page limit, but would you know what is being asked? What is the specific question here?

GUIDELINES
Writing Objective Test Items

Make the stem clear and simple, and present only a single problem. Unessential details should be left out.

Example

Poor	*Better*
There are several different kinds of standard or derived scores. An IQ score is especially useful because	An advantage of an IQ score is

State the problem in the stem in positive terms. Negative language is confusing. If you must use words such as *not*, *no*, *all but*, or *except*, underline them or type them in all capitals.

Example

Poor	*Better*
Which of the following is not a standard score?	Which of the following is **NOT** a standard score?

Do not expect students to make extremely fine discriminations among answer choices.

Example

The percentage of area in a normal curve falling between +1 and −1 standard deviations is about:

Poor		*Better*	
a. 66%	c. 68%	a. 14%	c. 68%
b. 67%	d. 69%.	b. 34%	d. 95%.

Make sure each alternative answer fits the grammatical form of the stem, so that no answers are obviously wrong.

Example

Poor	*Better*
The Stanford-Binet test yields an	The Stanford-Binet is a test of
a. IQ score.	a. intelligence.
b. reading level.	b. reading level.
c. vocational preference.	c. vocational preference.
d. mechanical aptitude.	d. mechanical aptitude.

Avoid including two distractors that have the same meaning.
If only one answer can be right and if two answers are the same, then these two must both be wrong. This narrows down the choices considerably.

Avoid using categorical words such as *always, all, only*, or *never* unless they can appear consistently in all the alternatives.
Most smart test takers know that categorical answers are usually wrong.

Avoid using the exact wording found in the textbook.
Poor students may recognize the answers without knowing what they mean.

Avoid overuse of *all of the above* and *none of the above*.
Such choices may be helpful to students who are simply guessing. In addition, using *all of the above* may trick a quick student who sees that the first alternative is correct and does not read on to discover that the others are correct, too.

Avoid obvious patterns on a test. They aid students who are guessing.
The position of the correct answer should be varied, as should its length.

Students need ample time for answering. If more than one essay is assigned in the same class period, you may want to suggest time limits for each question. Remember, however, that time pressure increases anxiety and may prevent accurate assessment of some students. Whatever your approach, do not try to make up for the limited amount of material an essay test can cover by including a large number of questions. It would be better to plan on more frequent testing than to include more than two or three essay questions in a single class period. Combining an essay question with a number of objective items is one way to avoid the problem of limited sampling of course material (Waugh & Gronlund, 2013).

EVALUATING ESSAYS. When possible, a good first step in grading essays is to construct a set of scoring criteria or a rubric (more on this later) and share it with students. Then, decide what type of information should be in every answer. Here is an example from TenBrink (2003, p. 326).

Question: Defend or refute the following statement: Civil wars are necessary to the growth of a developing country. Cite reasons for your argument, and use examples from history to help substantiate your claim.

Scoring Rubric: All answers, regardless of the position taken, should include (1) a clear statement of the position, (2) at least five logical reasons, (3) at least four examples from history that clearly substantiate the reasons given.

Once you have set your expectations for answers, you can assign points to the various parts of the essay. You might also give points for the organization of the answer and the internal consistency of the essay. You can then assign grades such as 1 to 5 or A, B, C, D, and F, and sort the papers into piles by grade. As a final step, skim the papers in each pile to see if they are comparable in quality. These techniques will help ensure fairness and accuracy in grading.

When grading essay tests that contain several questions, it makes sense to grade all responses to one question before moving on to the next. This helps prevent the quality of a student's answer to one question from influencing your reaction to the student's other answers. After you finish reading and scoring the first question, shuffle the papers so that no students end up having all their questions graded first (e.g., when you may be taking more time to give feedback or are applying stricter standards) or last (when you may be tired of writing feedback or more lax in your standards). You may achieve greater objectivity if you ask students to put their names on the back of the paper, so that grading is anonymous. A final check on your fairness as a grader is to have another teacher who is equally familiar with your goals and subject matter look over a few of your tests without knowing what grades you have assigned. This can give you valuable insights into areas of bias in your grading practices.

THE VALUE OF TRADITIONAL TESTING. Right answers are important. Even though schooling is about learning to think and solve problems, it is also about knowledge. Students must have something to think about—facts, ideas, concepts, principles, theories, explanations, arguments, images, opinions. Well-designed traditional tests can evaluate students' knowledge effectively and efficiently (Russell & Airasian, 2012). Some educators believe that traditional testing should play an even greater role than it currently does. Educational policy analysts suggest that American students, compared to students in many other developed countries, lack essential knowledge because American schools emphasize process—critical thinking, self-esteem, problem solving— more than content. To teach more about content, teachers will need to determine how well their students are learning the content, and traditional testing provides useful information about content learning. Tests are also valuable in motivating and guiding students' learning. Research evidence indicates that frequent testing encourages learning and retention. In fact, taking more frequent tests improves learning, even if there is no feedback from the test—bad teaching, but a powerful result (Roediger & Karpicke, 2006).

CRITICISMS OF TRADITIONAL TESTS. Traditional testing has been under fire since at least the 1990s. As Grant Wiggins (1991) noted then:

> We do not judge Xerox, the Boston Symphony, the Cincinnati Reds, or Dom Perignon vineyards on the basis of indirect, easy to test, and common indicators. Nor would the workers in those places likely produce quality if some generic, secure test served as the only measure of their success in meeting a standard. Demanding and getting quality, whether from students or adult workers, means framing standards in terms of the work that we undertake and value. (p. 22)

Wiggins continues to argue for assessment that makes sense, that tests knowledge as it is applied in real-world situations. Understanding cannot be measured by tests that ask students to use skills and knowledge out of context.

Your stand on traditional testing is part of your philosophy of teaching. Let's look at a few alternative approaches to classroom assessment.

AUTHENTIC CLASSROOM ASSESSMENTS

Authentic assessments ask students to apply skills and abilities as they would in real life. For example, they might use fractions to enlarge or reduce recipes. Grant Wiggins (1989) made this argument in the 1980s, and it is still good today:

> If tests determine what teachers actually teach and what students will study for—and they do—then the road to reform is a straight but steep one: test those capabilities and habits we think are essential, and test them in context. Make [tests] replicate, within reason, the challenges at the heart of each academic discipline. Let them be—authentic. (p. 41)

Wiggins goes on to say that if our instructional goals for students include the abilities to write, speak, listen, create, think critically, do research, solve problems, or apply knowledge, then our tests should ask students to write, speak, listen, create, think, research, solve, and apply. How can this happen?

Many educators suggest we look to the arts and sports for analogies to solve this problem. If we think of the "test" as being the recital, exhibition, game, mock court trial, or other performance, then teaching to the test is just fine. All coaches, artists, and musicians gladly "teach" to these "tests" because performing well on these tests is the whole point of instruction. Authentic assessment asks students to perform. The performances may be thinking performances, physical performances, creative performances, or other forms. So **performance assessment** is any form of assessment that requires students to carry out an activity or produce a product to demonstrate learning (Russell & Airasian, 2012).

It may seem odd to talk about thinking as a performance, but there are many parallels. Serious thinking is risky, because real-life problems are not well defined. Often, the outcomes of our thinking are public; others evaluate our ideas. Like a dancer auditioning for a Broadway show, we must cope with the consequences of being evaluated. Like a potter looking at a lump of clay, a student facing a difficult problem must experiment, observe, redo, imagine, and test solutions; apply both basic skills and inventive techniques; make interpretations; decide how to communicate results to the intended audience; and often accept criticism and improve the initial solution (Clark, 2012; Eisner, 1999).

Portfolios and Exhibitions

The concern with authentic assessment has led to the development of several approaches based on the goal of performance in context. Instead of circling answers to "factual" questions about nonexistent situations, students are required to solve real problems. Facts are used in a context where they apply. For example, instead of asking students, "If you bought a toy for 69 cents and gave the clerk a dollar, how much change would you get back?" have students work in pairs with real money to role-play making different purchases, or set up a mock class store and have students make purchases and give change (Waugh & Gronlund, 2013).

The Center for Technology in Learning of SRI International, a nonprofit science research institute, also provides an online resource bank of performance-based assessments linked to the National Science Education Standards. The resource is called PALS (Performance Assessment Links in Science). Go to pals.sri.com; see the performance tasks for kindergarten through 12th grade. You can select tasks by standard and grade level. Here is the beginning of the properties of matter Rubber Band task for eighth-graders. To see the entire task, instructions for administering, a rubric for scoring, and examples of student work, go to pals.sri.com/tasks/5–8/RubberBand/:

Description:
Students investigate what would happen to the length of a rubber band as more and more rings were hung on it.

Materials:
At each station students should have:
- A clipboard with a rubber band
- A large paper clip attached to one end of the rubber band
- Metal rings to hang on the large paper clip

Connect and Extend to PRAXIS II®

Authentic Tests (II, C1, 2, 4)
The emphasis on student-centered learning has been accompanied by an emphasis on authentic tests. Understand the purpose, value, and advantages of these forms of assessment. Describe their characteristics and the potential problems with their use.

- 30 cm ruler
- Some sheets of plain paper
- 2 sheets of graph or squared paper

Portfolios and exhibitions are two approaches to assessment that require performance in context. With these approaches, it is difficult to tell where instruction stops and assessment starts because the two processes are interwoven (Oosterhof, 2009; Popham, 2014).

PORTFOLIOS. For years, photographers, artists, models, and architects have had portfolios to display their skills and show to prospective employers. A **portfolio** is a systematic collection of work, often including work in progress, revisions, student self-analyses, and reflections on what the student has learned. Written work or artistic pieces are common contents of portfolios, but student portfolios might also include letters to the portfolio readers describing each entry and its importance, graphs, diagrams, pictures or digital slideshows, PowerPoint presentations, recordings of the students reading their work, unedited and final drafts of persuasive essays or poems, lists of books read, annotated Web site addresses, peer comments, video recordings, laboratory reports, and computer programs—anything that demonstrates learning in the area being taught and assessed (Popham, 2014). There is a distinction between process portfolios and final, or "best-work," portfolios. The distinction is similar to the difference between formative and summative evaluation. Process portfolios document learning and show progress. Best-work portfolios showcase final accomplishments (D. W. Johnson & Johnson, 2002). Table 15.3 shows some examples of portfolios for both individuals and groups.

EXHIBITIONS. An **exhibition** is a performance test that has two additional features. First, it is public, so students preparing exhibitions must take the audience into account; communication

Connect and Extend to PRAXIS II®

Portfolio Assessment (II, C1, 2)
For a discussion of the advantages, limitations, design, and implementation of portfolio programs, go to nea.org/assets/docs/June2011AdvOnline.pdf.

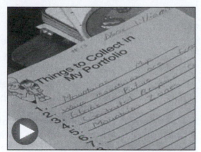

Video 15.1
In this video, elementary students collect items for portfolios in social studies, and high school art students collect 12 pieces of their original art centered around a central idea. Notice how these two types of portfolios demonstrate students' achievement and growth.

ENHANCEDetext *video example*

TABLE 15.3 • **Process and Best-Works Portfolios for Individuals and Groups**
Here are a few examples of how to use portfolios in different subjects.

THE PROCESS PORTFOLIO		
SUBJECT AREA	**INDIVIDUAL STUDENT**	**COOPERATIVE GROUP**
Science	Documentation (running records or logs) of using the scientific method to solve a series of laboratory problems	Documentation (observation checklists) of using the scientific method to solve a series of laboratory problems
Mathematics	Documentation of mathematical reasoning through double-column mathematical problem solving (computations on the left side and running commentary explaining thought processes on the right side)	Documentation of complex problem solving and use of higher-level strategies
Language Arts	Evolution of compositions from early notes through outlines, research notes, response to others' editing, and final draft	Rubrics and procedures developed to ensure high-quality peer editing
THE BEST-WORKS PORTFOLIO		
SUBJECT AREA	**INDIVIDUAL STUDENT**	**COOPERATIVE GROUP**
Language Arts	The best compositions in a variety of styles—expository, humor/satire, creative (poetry, drama, short story), journalistic (reporting, editorial columnist, reviewer), and advertising copy	The best dramatic production, video project, TV broadcast, newspaper, advertising display
Social Studies	The best historical research paper, opinion essay on historical issue, commentary on current event, original historical theory, review of a historical biography, account of participation in academic controversy	The best community survey, paper resulting from academic controversy, oral history compilation, multidimensional analysis of historical event, press corps interview with historical figure
Fine Arts	The best creative products such as drawings, paintings, sculptures, pottery, poems, thespian performance	The best creative products such as murals, plays written and performed, inventions thought of and built

Source: Based on D. W. Johnson and R. T. Johnson (2002), Meaningful Assessment: A Manageble and Cooperative Process. Boston, MA: Pearson Education, Inc.

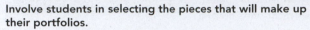

GUIDELINES
Creating Portfolios

Involve students in selecting the pieces that will make up their portfolios.

Examples

1. During the unit or semester, ask each student to select work that fits certain criteria, such as "my most difficult problem," "my best work," "my most improved work," or "three approaches to."
2. For their final submissions, ask students to select pieces that best show how much they have learned.

Make sure the portfolios include information that shows student self-reflection and self-criticism.

Examples

1. Ask students to include a rationale for their selections.
2. Have each student write a "guide" to his or her portfolio, explaining how strengths and weaknesses are reflected in the work included.
3. Include self- and peer critiques, indicating specifically what is good and what might be improved.
4. Model self-criticism of your own productions.

Make sure the portfolios reflect the students' activities in learning.

Examples

1. Include a representative selection of projects, writings, drawings, and so forth.
2. Ask students to relate the goals of learning to the contents of their portfolios.

Be aware that portfolios can serve different functions at different times of the year.

Examples

1. Early in the year, it might hold unfinished work or "problem pieces."
2. At the end of the year, it should contain only what the student is willing to make public.

Be certain portfolios demonstrate students' growth.

Examples

1. Ask students to make a "history" of their progress along certain dimensions and to illustrate points in their growth with specific works.
2. Ask students to include descriptions of activities outside class that reflect the growth illustrated in the portfolio.

Teach students how to create and use portfolios.

Examples

1. Keep models of very well-done portfolios as examples, but stress that each portfolio is an individual statement.
2. Examine your students' portfolios frequently, especially early in the year when they are just getting used to the idea. Give constructive feedback.

For more ideas about using portfolios, see teachervision.fen.com/assessment/teaching-methods/20153.html

Video 15.2
A science fair is a public exhibition of student achievement.

ENHANCEDetext *video example*

and understanding are essential. Second, an exhibition often requires many hours of preparation, because it is the culminating experience of a whole program of study. Thomas Guskey and Jane Bailey (2001) suggest that exhibits help students understand the qualities of good work and recognize those qualities in their own productions and performances. Students also benefit when they select examples of their work to exhibit and articulate their reasons for making the selections. Being able to judge quality can encourage student motivation by setting clear goals. The *Guidelines: Creating Portfolios* gives some ideas for using portfolios in your teaching.

Evaluating Portfolios and Performances

Checklists, rating scales, and scoring rubrics are helpful when you assess performances, because assessments of performances, portfolios, and exhibitions are criterion-referenced, not norm-referenced. In other words, the students' products and performances are compared to established public standards, not ranked in relation to other students' work (Wiggins, 1991).

SCORING RUBRICS. A checklist or rating scale gives specific feedback about elements of a performance. **Scoring rubrics** are rules that are used to determine the quality of a student performance, often on a 4-point scale from "excellent" (4) to "inadequate" (1) or on a scale that assigns points to each category—10 points for excellent, 6 for good, and so on (Mabry, 1999). For example, a rubric describing excellent *delegation of responsibility* in a group research project might be:

Each student in the group can clearly explain what information is needed
by the group, what information s/he is responsible for locating,
and when the information is needed.

GUIDELINES
Developing a Rubric

1. *Make sure the skill to be assessed is important.* It takes time to develop good rubrics, so make sure the skill being assessed is worth everyone's time and that the skill can be taught.
2. *Look at models.* Show students examples of good and not-so-good work based on composites of work not linked to individual students. Identify the characteristics that make the good ones good and the bad ones bad.
3. *List criteria.* Use the discussion of models to begin a list of what counts in quality work.
4. *Articulate gradations of quality.* Describe the best and worst levels of quality; then fill in the middle levels based on your knowledge of common problems and the discussion of not-so-good work.
5. *Practice on models.* Have students use the rubrics to evaluate the models you gave them in Step 1.
6. *Use self- and peer assessment.* Give students their task. As they work, stop them occasionally for self- and peer assessment.
7. *Revise.* Always give students time to revise their work based on the feedback they get in Step 5.
8. *Use teacher assessment.* In your grading, be sure to use the same rubric students used to assess their work.

Note: Step 2 may be necessary only when you are asking students to engage in a task with which they are unfamiliar. Steps 4 and 5 are useful but time-consuming; you can do these on your own, especially when you've been using rubrics for a while. A class experienced in rubric-based assessment can streamline the process so that it begins with listing criteria, after which the teacher writes out the gradations of quality, checks them with the students, makes revisions, then uses the rubric for self-, peer, and teacher assessment.

For a great explanation of using rubrics, see pareonline.net/getvn .asp?v=7&n=25. The article includes several links that allow you to create and customize rubrics for your class, including teach-nology .com/web_tools/rubrics/ and rubistar.4teachers.org/

This rubric was generated using Rubistar (rubistar.4teachers.org/index.php), an online service for educators that allows you to select a subject area and category, then create a rubric. To get this rubric, I chose the subject of writing—"group planning and research project"—and the category of "delegation of responsibility."

James Popham (2014) emphasizes that rubrics should be neither too specific nor too general. A very specific rubric might apply only to one task, such as writing a two-paragraph poem about trees using four adjectives and two adverbs, but not to the more general skill of writing poems. A rubric that is too general (such as "poems will be judged poor, fair, good, or excellent") provides no more information than grading poems as "D, C, B, or A." Rubrics should be focused on worthwhile skills that can be taught and assessed. Here is a skill-focused rubric for judging the organization of students' narrative essays:

> Two aspects of organization will be employed in the appraisal of students' narrative essays—namely, overall structure and sequence. To earn maximum credit, an essay must embody an overall structure containing an introduction, a body, and a conclusion. The content of the body of the essay must be sequenced in a reasonable manner—for instance, in a chronological, logical, or order-of-importance sequence. (Popham, 2014, p. 219)

This type of skill-focused rubric gives teachers guidance in teaching and students guidance in writing. In addition, the rubric focuses on skills that can be applied in many forms of narrative writing. The *Guidelines: Developing a Rubric* gives more ideas; some are taken from Goodrich (1997), D. W. Johnson and Johnson (2002), and Popham (2014).

Performance assessment requires careful judgment on the part of teachers and clear communication to students about what is good and what needs improving. In some ways, the approach is similar to the clinical method first introduced by Binet to assess intelligence: It is based on observing the student perform a variety of tasks and comparing his or her performance to a standard. Just as Binet never wanted to assign a single number to represent the child's intelligence, teachers who use authentic assessments do not try to assign one score to the student's performance. Even if rankings, ratings, and grades have to be given, these judgments are not the ultimate goals—improvement of learning is.

It is often helpful to have students join in the development of rating scales and scoring rubrics. When students participate, they are challenged to decide what quality work looks or sounds like

Connect and Extend to PRAXIS II®

Scoring Rubrics (II, C3)
Kathy Schrock's Guide for Educators (schrockguide.net/assessment-and-rubrics.html) provides information about every aspect of the use of scoring rubrics in the classroom as well as an extensive collection of rubrics that can be used or adapted by teachers.

FIGURE 15.1

THREE WAYS OF RATING AN ORAL PRESENTATION

Numerical Rating Scale

Directions:

Indicate how often the pupil performs each of these behaviors while giving an oral presentation. For each behavior circle **1** if the pupil **always** performs the behavior, **2** if the pupil **usually** performs the behavior, **3** if the pupil **seldom** performs the behavior, and **4** if the pupil **never** performs the behavior.

Physical Expression

A. Stands straight and faces audience.

    1 2 3 4

B. Changes facial expression with change in the tone of the presentation.

    1 2 3 4

Graphic Rating Scale

Directions:

Place an **X** on the line that shows how often the pupil did each of the behaviors listed while giving an oral presentation.

Physical Expression

A. Stands straight and faces audience.

    always   **usually**   **seldom**   **never**

B. Changes facial expression with change in the tone of the presentation.

    always   **usually**   **seldom**   **never**

Descriptive Rating Scale

Directions:

Place an **X** on the line at the place that best describes the pupil's performance of each behavior.

Physical Expression

A. Stands straight and faces audience.

stands straight, always looks at audience	**weaves, fidgets, eyes roam from audience to ceiling**	**constant, distracting movements, no eye contact with audience**

B. Changes facial expression with change in the tone of the presentation.

matches facial expressions to content and emphasis	**facial expressions usually appropriate, occasional lack of expression**	**no match between tone and facial expression; expression distracts**

Source: Reprinted from Classroom Assessment: Concepts and Applications (7th ed.), by M. K. Russell & P. W. Airasian (2012), p. 221. New York: McGraw-Hill, p. 161. With permission from The McGraw-Hill Companies.

in a particular area. They know in advance what is expected. As students gain practice in designing and applying scoring rubrics, their work and their learning often improve. Figure 15.1 gives three alternatives—numerical, graphic, and descriptive—for rating an oral presentation.

RELIABILITY, VALIDITY, GENERALIZABILITY. Because the teacher's personal judgment plays such a central role in evaluating performances, issues of reliability, validity, and generalizability are critical considerations. One teacher's "excellent" could be another teacher's "adequate." Research shows that when raters are experienced and scoring rubrics are well developed and refined, reliability may improve (Herman & Winters, 1994; LeMahieu, Gitomer, & Eresh, 1993). Some of this improvement in reliability occurs because a rubric focuses the raters' attention on a few dimensions of the work and gives limited scoring levels to choose from. If scorers can give only a rating of 1, 2, 3, or 4, they are more likely to agree than if they could score based on a 100-point scale. So the rubrics may achieve reliability not because they capture underlying agreement among raters, but because the rubrics limit options and thus limit variability in scoring (Mabry, 1999).

In terms of validity, some evidence shows that students who are classified as "master" writers on the basis of portfolio assessment are judged less capable using standard writing assessments. Which form of assessment is the best reflection of enduring qualities? It is hard to say. In addition, when rubrics are developed to assess specific tasks, the results of applying them may not predict performance on anything except very similar tasks, so we do not know whether a student's performance on a specific task will generalize to the larger area of study (Haertel, 1999; Herman & Winters, 1994; McMillan, 2004).

DIVERSITY AND BIAS IN PERFORMANCE ASSESSMENT. Equity is an issue in all assessment and no less so with performances and portfolios. With a public performance, there could be bias effects based on a student's appearance and speech or the student's access to expensive audio, video, or graphic tools. Performance assessments have the same potential as other tests to discriminate unfairly against students who are not wealthy or who are culturally different. And the extensive group work, peer editing, and out-of-class time devoted to portfolios means that some students may have access to greater networks of support and outright help. Many students in your classes will come from families that have sophisticated computer graphics and desktop publishing capabilities. Others may have little support from home. These differences can be sources of bias and inequity, especially in portfolios and exhibitions.

Informal Assessments

Informal assessments are ungraded (formative) assessments that gather information from multiple sources to help teachers make decisions (S. R. Banks, 2012). Early on in the unit, assessments should be formative (provide feedback, but not count toward a grade), saving the actual graded assessments for later in the unit when all students have had the chance to learn the material (Tomlinson, 2005a). Some examples of informal assessment are journals, student observations and checklists, questioning, and student self-assessment.

JOURNALS. Journals are very flexible and widely used informal assessments. Students usually have personal or group journals and write in them on a regular basis. In their study, Michael Pressley and his colleagues (2007) found that excellent first-grade literacy teachers used journaling for three purposes:

- As communication tools that allowed students to express their own thoughts and ideas
- As an opportunity to apply what they have learned
- As an outlet to encourage fluency and creative expression in language usage

Teachers may use journals to learn about their students in order to better connect their teaching to the students' concerns and interests. But often journals focus on academic learning, usually through responses to prompts. S. R. Banks (2012, p. 113) describes one high school physics teacher who asked his students to respond to these three questions in their journals:

1. How can you determine the coefficient of friction if you know only the angle of the inclined plane?
2. Compare and contrast magnetic, electronic, and gravitational fields.
3. If you were to describe the physical concept of sound to your best friend, what music would you use to demonstrate this concept?

When he read the students' journals, the teacher realized that many of the students' basic assumptions about friction, acceleration, and velocity came from personal experiences and not from scientific reasoning. His approach to teaching had to change to reach the students. The teacher never would have known to make the changes in his instruction without reading the journals.

TABLE 15.4 • **Aligning Different Assessment Tools with Their Targets**

Different learning outcomes require different assessment methods.

TARGET TO BE ASSESSED	ASSESSMENT METHOD			
	SELECTED RESPONSE	ESSAY	PERFORMANCE ASSESSMENT	PERSONAL COMMUNICATION
Knowledge Mastery	Multiple-choice, true/false, matching, and fill-in can sample mastery of elements of knowledge	Essay exercises can tap understanding of relationships among elements of knowledge	Not a good choice for this target—three other options preferred	Can ask questions, evaluate answers, and infer mastery—but a time-consuming option
Reasoning Proficiency	Can assess understanding of basic patterns of reasoning	Written descriptions of complex problem solutions can provide a window into reasoning proficiency	Can watch students solve some problems and infer about reasoning proficiency	Can ask student to "think aloud" or can ask follow-up questions to probe reasoning
Skills	Can assess mastery of the prerequisites of skillful performance—but cannot tap the skill itself	Can assess mastery of the prerequisites of skillful performance—but cannot tap the skill itself	Can observe and evaluate skills as they are being performed	Strong match when skill is oral communication proficiency; also can assess mastery of knowledge prerequisite to skillful performance
Ability to Create Products	Can assess mastery of knowledge prerequisite to the ability to create quality products—but cannot assess the quality of products themselves	Can assess mastery of knowledge prerequisite to the ability to create quality products—but cannot assess the quality of products themselves	A strong match can assess: (a) proficiency in carrying out steps in product development and (b) attributes of the product itself	Can probe procedural knowledge and knowledge of attributes of quality products—but not product quality

Source: From "Where Is Our Assessment Future and How Can We Get There?" by R. J. Stiggins. In R. W. Lissitz, W. D. Schafer (Eds.), Meaningful Assessment: A Manageable and Cooperative Process. Published by Allyn & Bacon, Boston, MA. Copyright © 2002 by Pearson Education. Adapted by permission of the publisher.

There are many other kinds of informal assessments—keeping notes and observations about student performance, rating scales, and checklists. Every time teachers ask questions or watch students perform skills, the teachers are conducting informal assessments. Look at Table 15.4, which summarizes the possibilities and limitations of aligning different assessment tools with their targets. One major message in this chapter is the importance of correctly matching the type of assessment tools used to the target—to what is being assessed.

INVOLVING STUDENTS IN ASSESSMENTS. One way to connect teaching and assessment while developing students' sense of efficacy for learning is to involve the students in the assessment process. Students can keep track of their own progress and assess their improvement. Here are other ideas, some taken from Stiggins and Chappuis (2005). Students might:

- Learn about the criteria for judging work by examining and discussing with a peer examples of good, average, and poor products or performances. Then pick a poor example, and revise to improve it.
- Describe to the teacher or a peer (orally or in writing) the way they approached an assignment, the problems they encountered, the options they considered, and the final result.
- Analyze their strengths and weaknesses before starting a project, then discuss with the teacher or peers how they will use their strengths and overcome their weaknesses as they work on the project.
- In pairs, make up questions that might be on the test, explain why those are good questions, and then answer them together.
- Look back at earlier work and analyze how they have grown by describing "I used to think . . . but now I know. . . ." After doing a few of these analyses, summarize using a frame such as: What did I know before I started? What did I learn? What do I want to learn next?
- Before a major test, do a free write on these prompts "What exactly will be on the test?" "What kinds of questions will be asked (multiple-choice, essay, etc.)?" "How well will I do?" "What do I need to study to make sure I am ready?"

One last idea—the teacher arranges items on a test according to specific learning targets, and prepares a "test analysis" chart for students, with three boxes: "My strengths," "Quick review," and "Further study." After handing back the corrected test, students identify learning targets they have mastered and write them in the "My strengths" box. Next, students categorize their wrong answers as either "simple mistake" or "further study." Then, students list the simple mistakes in the "Quick review" box. Last, students write the rest of the learning targets represented by wrong answers in the "Further study" box.

No matter how you assess students, ultimately you will assign grades. We turn to that job next.

ENHANCEDetext *self-check*

GRADING

Video 15.3
A portfolio conference is a good way to involve students in the assessment process and help them learn to regulate their own learning.

ENHANCEDetext *video example*

- -
STOP & THINK Think back on your report cards and grades over the years. Did you ever receive a grade that was lower than you expected? How did you feel about yourself, the teacher, the subject, and school in general as a result of the lower grade? What could the teacher have done to help you understand and profit from the experience? •
- -

In determining a final grade, the teacher must make a major decision. Should a student's grade reflect the student's status in comparison with the rest of the class, or should the grade reflect the amount of material learned and how well it has been learned? In other words, should grading be *norm referenced* or *criterion referenced?*

Norm-Referenced versus Criterion-Referenced Grading

In norm-referenced grading, the major influence on a grade is the student's standing in comparison with others who also took the course. If a student studies very hard and almost everyone else does too, the student may receive a disappointing grade, perhaps a C or D. One common type of norm-referenced grading is called grading on the curve. How you feel about this approach probably depends on where your grades generally fall along that "curve." There is good evidence that this type of grading damages the relationships among students and between teachers and students and also diminishes motivation for most students (Krumboltz & Yeh, 1996). When you think about it, if the curve arbitrarily limits the number of good grades that can be given, then, in the game of grading, most students will be losers (Guskey & Bailey, 2001; Haladyna, 2002; Kohn, 1996b). Over 30 years ago, Benjamin Bloom (of Bloom's taxonomy) and his colleagues (1981) pointed out the fallacy of grading on the curve:

> There is nothing sacred about the normal curve. It is the distribution most appropriate to chance and random activity. Education is a purposeful activity, and we seek to have students learn what we have to teach. If we are effective in our instruction, the distribution of achievement should be very different from the normal curve. In fact, we may even insist that our educational efforts have been unsuccessful to the extent that the distribution of achievement approximates the normal distribution. (pp. 52–53)

In criterion-referenced grading, the grade represents a list of accomplishments. If clear objectives have been set for the course, the grade may represent a certain number of objectives met satisfactorily. When a criterion-referenced system is used, criteria for each grade generally are spelled out in advance. It is then up to the student to earn the grade she or he wants to receive. Theoretically, in this system, all students can achieve an A if they reach the criteria. Criterion-referenced grading has the advantage of relating judgments about a student to the achievement of clearly defined instructional goals. Some school districts have developed reporting systems where report cards list objectives along with judgments about the student's attainment of each. Reporting is done at the end of each unit of instruction. The elementary school report card shown in Figure 15.2 on the next page demonstrates the relationship between assessment and the goals of the unit.

Most schools have a specified grading system, so we won't spend time here on the many possible systems. Let's consider a different question—one with research behind it. What is the effect of grades on students?

FIGURE 15.2

A CRITERION-REFERENCED REPORT CARD

This is one example of a criterion-referenced report card. Other forms are possible, but all criterion-referenced reports indicate student progress toward specific goals.

LINCOLN ELEMENTARY SCHOOL
GRADE 5

Student _____ Teacher _____ Principal _Muriel Simms_ Quarter 2 3 4

E = Excellent   S = Satisfactory   P = Making progress   N = Needs improvement

READING PROGRAM

Materials Used: _____
_____

____ Reads with understanding
____ Is able to write about what is read
____ Completes reading group work accurately and on time
____ Shows interest in reading

Reading Skills
____ Decodes new words
____ Understands new words

Independent Reading Level
Below/At Grade Level/Above

LANGUAGE ARTS

____ Uses oral language effectively
____ Listens carefully
____ Masters weekly spelling

Writing Skills
____ Understands writing as process
____ Creates a rough draft
____ Makes meaningful revisions
____ Creates edited, legible final draft

Editing Skills
____ Capitalizes
____ Punctuates
____ Uses complete sentences
____ Uses paragraphs
____ Demonstrates dictionary skills

Writing Skill Level:
Below/At Grade Level/Above

MATHEMATICS

Problem Solving
____ Solves teacher-generated problems
____ Solves self-/student-generated problems
____ Can create story problems

Interpreting Problems
____ Uses appropriate strategies
____ Can use more than one strategy
____ Can explain strategies in written form
____ Can explain strategies orally

Math Concepts
　Understands Base Ten
Beginning/Developing/Sophisticated
　Multiplication, Basic Facts
Beginning/Developing/Sophisticated
　2-Digit Multiplications
Beginning/Developing/Sophisticated
　Division
Beginning/Developing/Sophisticated
　Geometry
Beginning/Developing/Sophisticated

Overall Math Skill Level:
Beginning/Developing/Sophisticated

Attitude/Work Skills
____ Welcomes a challenge
____ Persistent
____ Takes advantage of learning from others
____ Listens to others
____ Participates in discussion

It Figures
Is working on: _____

Goals: _____
Is working on achieving goal:
_____

SOCIAL STUDIES

____ Understands subject matter
____ Shows curiosity and enthusiasm
____ Contributes to class discussions
____ Uses map skills
____ Demonstrates control of reading skills by interpreting text
Topics covered: individual cultures, Columbus–first English colonies

SCIENCE

____ Shows curiosity about scientific subject matter
____ Asks good scientific questions
____ Shows knowledge of scientific method
____ Uses knowledge of scientific method to help set up and run experiment(s)
____ Makes good scientific observations
____ Has researched scientific topic(s)
　　Topic(s) _____

I Wonder
Is currently working on _____

WORKING SKILLS

____ Listens carefully
____ Follows directions
____ Works neatly and carefully
____ Checks work
____ Completes work on time
____ Uses time wisely
____ Works well independently
____ Works well in a group
____ Takes risks in learning
____ Welcomes a challenge

HOMEWORK

____ Self-selects homework
____ Completes work accurately
____ Completes work on time

PRESENTATIONS/PROJECTS
_____
_____

HUMAN RELATIONS

____ Shows courtesy
____ Respects rights of others
____ Shows self-control
____ Interacts well with peers
____ Shows a cooperative and positive attitude in class
____ Shows a cooperative attitude when asked to work with other students
____ Is willing to help other students
____ Works well with other adults (subs, student teacher, parents, etc.)

Attendance

	1st	2nd	3rd	4th
Present				
Absent				
Tardy				

Placement for next year:

Source: From Lincoln Elementary School, Grade 5, Madison, WI. Used with permission.

Effects of Grading on Students

When we think of grades, we often think of competition. Highly competitive classes may be particularly hard on anxious students, students who lack self-confidence, and students who are less prepared. So, although high standards and competition do tend to be generally related to increased academic learning, it is clear that a balance must be struck between high standards and a reasonable chance to succeed. Rick Stiggins and Jan Chappuis (2005) observe:

> From their very earliest school experiences, our students draw life-shaping conclusions about themselves as learners on the basis of the information we provide to them as a

result of their teachers' classroom assessments. As the evidence accumulates over time, they decide if they are capable of succeeding or not. They decide whether the learning is worth the commitment it will take to attain it. They decide . . . whether to risk investing in the schooling experience. These decisions are crucial to their academic well-being. (p. 11)

It may sound as though low grades and failure should be avoided in school. But the situation is not that simple.

THE VALUE OF FAILING? After reviewing many years of research on the effects of failure from several perspectives, Margaret Clifford (1990, 1991) concluded:

> It is time for educators to replace easy success with challenge. We must encourage students to reach beyond their intellectual grasp and allow them the privilege of learning from mistakes. There must be a tolerance for error-making in every classroom, and gradual success rather than continual success must become the yardstick by which learning is judged. (1990, p. 23)

Some level of failure may be helpful for most students, especially if teachers help the students see connections between hard work and improvement. Efforts to protect students from failure and to guarantee success may be counterproductive. Carol Tomlinson, an expert on differentiated instruction, puts it this way: "Students whose learning histories have caused them to believe that excellence can be achieved with minimal effort do not learn to expend effort, and yet perceive that high grades are an entitlement for them" (2005b, p. 266). So maybe not failure, but accurate and critical feedback can be especially important for students who are used to easy As (Shute, 2008).

RETENTION IN GRADE. So far, we have been talking about the effects of failing a test or perhaps a course. But what about the effect of failing an entire grade—that is, of being "held back"? One study in North Carolina found that kindergarten retention had more than doubled from 1992 to 2002, with over 6% of students retained in 2002. About 10% of U.S. students ages 16 to 19 have been retained at least once (Wu, West, & Hughes, 2010). Retained children are more likely to be male, members of minority groups, living in poverty, and younger, and less likely to have participated in early childhood programs (Beebe-Frankenberger, Bocian, Macmillan, & Gresham, 2004; G. Hong & Raudenbush, 2005). Is retention a good policy? See the *Point/Counterpoint* on the next page to examine the issue.

Grades and Motivation

If you are relying on grades to motivate students, you had better think again (J. K. Smith, Smith, & De Lisi, 2001). The assessments you give should support students' motivation to learn—not their motivation to work for a good grade. But is there really a difference between working for a grade and working to learn? The answer depends in part on how a grade is determined. If you test only at a simple but detailed level of knowledge, you may force students to choose between complex learning and a good grade. But when a grade reflects meaningful learning, working for a grade and working to learn become the same thing. As a teacher, you can use grades to motivate the kind of learning you intend students to achieve in your course. Finally, low grades generally do not encourage greater efforts. Students receiving low grades are more likely to withdraw, blame others, decide that the work is "dumb," or feel responsible for the low grade but helpless to make improvements. They give up on themselves or on school (Tomlinson, 2005b). Rather than assigning a failing grade, you might consider the work incomplete and give students support in revising or improving. Maintain high standards, and give students a chance to reach them (Guskey, 2011; Guskey & Bailey, 2001).

Another effect on motivation that occurs in high schools is the race for valedictorian. Sometimes, students and families find clever ways to move ahead of the competition—but the strategies have little to do with learning. As Tom Guskey and Jane Bailey (2001) note, when a valedictorian

POINT/COUNTERPOINT
Should Children Be Held Back?

Nearly 450,000 first- through eighth-graders are retained each year (Warren & Salimba, 2012). For the last 100 years, parents and educators have debated about the value of retention versus *social promotion* (passing students on to the next grade with their peers). What does the evidence say? What are the arguments?

POINT **Yes, it just makes sense.** Retention in kindergarten for children considered "not ready" for first grade is a common practice. Compared to students who are relatively younger (January to August birthdays), students who are relatively older (born September to November) have higher achievement in school on average (Cobley, McKenna, Baker, & Wattie, 2009). In fact, some parents hold their son or daughter back to give the child an edge over peers in each grade thereafter or because the child was born late in the year—a practice sometimes called "academic red-shirting." In the mid-1960s, 96% of 6-year-olds were enrolled in first grade in the United States. By 2008, the number was 84% (Barnard-Brak, 2008). The results on academic red-shirting are mixed. Some studies have found benefits for students who have been held back by their parents, but other studies have found no benefits.

With the increased emphasis on high standards and accountability, the idea of social promotion has come under fire, and retention is seen as the better way. Guanglei Hong and Stephen Raudenbush (2005) summarize this and other arguments that have been made in favor of retention:

> A widely endorsed argument is that, when low-achieving students are retained in a grade, the academic status of children in a classroom will become more homogeneous, easing the teacher's task of managing instructional activities (Byrnes, 1989; also see Shepard & Smith, 1988, for a review). In particular, retaining some children in kindergarten may allow the first-grade teacher to teach at a higher level, benefiting those who would be promoted under the policy. Meanwhile, children who view grade retention as a punishment may study harder to avoid being retained in the future. Some have argued that, in comparison with the social promotion policy, repeating a grade is perhaps developmentally more appropriate and may make learning more meaningful for children who are struggling (Plummer & Graziano, 1987; Shepard &

Smith, 1988). If these arguments are correct, adopting a policy of grade retention will benefit those promoted and those retained, thus boosting achievement overall. (p. 206)

COUNTERPOINT **No, retention is not effective.**
After summarizing the arguments in favor of kindergarten retention, G. Hong and Raudenbush (2005) review the findings of almost a century of research. They note that even though a small number of studies support the value of retention, the weight of the evidence indicates that it is not helpful and may even be harmful. Most research finds that grade retention is associated with poor long-term outcomes such as dropping out of school, higher arrest rates, fewer job opportunities, lower self-esteem (Jimerson, 1999; Jimerson, Anderson, & Whipple, 2002; Jimerson & Ferguson, 2007; Shepard & Smith, 1989). Lucy Barnard-Brak (2008) studied a national sample of 986 children who had been identified as having learning disabilities and concluded, "delayed kindergarten entrance was not associated with better academic achievement for children with learning disabilities across time" (p. 50).

The study by G. Hong and Raudenbush (2005) examined data on 11,843 kindergarten students who participated in a longitudinal study that followed them to the end of first grade. The researchers compared retained and promoted students from schools that practice retention as well as promoted students from schools that practice social promotion. They found no evidence that retention improved either reading or mathematics achievement. In addition, retention did not seem to improve instruction in the first grade by making the class more similar in academic ability. After 1 year, the retained students were an average of 1 year behind, and evidence indicated that these children would have done better if promoted. The researchers concluded that retention "seemed to have constrained the learning potential for all but the highest-risk children" (p. 220). Another study that followed retained and promoted students for 4 years found some short-term advantages for retained students in social and behavioral skills, followed by long-term problems and vulnerabilities. The authors suggest that the "struggle-succeed-struggle" pattern may undermine academic motivation for retained students and interfere with peer relations (Wu, West, & Hughes, 2010).

BEWARE OF EITHER/OR: USING RESEARCH FOR CHILDREN

No matter what, children who are having trouble should get help, whether they are promoted or retained. However, just covering the same material again in the same way won't solve the children's academic or social problems. As Jeannie Oakes (1999) has said, "No sensible person advocates social promotion as it is currently framed—simply passing incompetent children on to the next grade" (p. 8). The best approach may be to promote the children along with their peers, but to give them special remediation during the summer or over the next year (Mantzicopoulos & Morrison, 1992). In addition, because the inability to focus attention and self-regulate is an important aspect of readiness to learn (Blair, 2002), help should also focus on improving these skills as well. An even better approach would be to prevent the problems before they occur by providing extra resources in the early years (McCoy & Reynolds, 1999).

wins by a 1/1,000 of a decimal point, how meaningful is the learning behind the difference? Some high schools now name multiple valedictorians—as many as meet the highest standards of the school—because they believe that the educators' job is "not to select talent, but, rather, to develop talent" (Guskey & Bailey, 2001, p. 39).

The *Guidelines: Using Any Grading System* on the next page gives ideas for fair and reasonable use of any grading system.

Beyond Grading: Communicating with Families

No number or letter grade conveys the totality of a student's experience in a class or course. Students, families, and teachers sometimes become too focused on the end point—the grade. But communicating with families should involve more than just sending home grades. There are a number of ways to communicate with and report to families. Many teachers I know have a beginning-of-the-year newsletter or student handbook that communicates homework, behavior, and grading policies to families. Other options described by Guskey and Bailey (2001) are:

- Notes attached to report cards
- Phone calls, especially "Good News" calls
- School open houses
- Student-led conferences
- Portfolios or exhibits of student work
- Homework hotlines
- School or class Web pages
- Home visits

Video 15.4
The teacher in this video holds a conference to discuss Cody's progress with his mother. The teacher is concerned about reporting more than just a grade. She and Cody's mother discuss how to improve his understanding of math concepts.

ENHANCEDetext *video example*

Conferences with parents or caregivers are often expected of teachers in elementary school and can be equally important in middle and high school. Clearly, the more skilled teachers are at communicating, the more effective they will be at conducting these conferences. Listening and problem-solving skills such as those discussed in Chapter 13 can be particularly important. When you are dealing with families or students who are angry or upset, make sure you really hear their concerns, not just their words. The atmosphere should be friendly and unrushed. Any observations about the student should be as factual as possible, based on observation or information from assignments. Information gained from a student or a parent/caregiver should be kept confidential.

One kind of information that will interest parents is their child's standardized test scores. In the next section we look at these tests.

ENHANCEDetext *self-check*

GUIDELINES
Using Any Grading System

Explain your grading policies to students early in the course, and remind them of the policies regularly.

Examples

1. Give older students a handout describing the assignments, tests, grading criteria, and schedule.
2. Explain to younger students in a low-pressure manner how their work will be evaluated.

Base grades on clearly specified, reasonable standards.

Examples

1. Specify standards by developing a rubric with students. Show anonymous examples of poor, good, and excellent work from previous classes.
2. Discuss workload and grading standards with more experienced teachers.
3. Give a few formative tests to get a sense of your students' abilities before you give a graded test.
4. Take tests yourself first to gauge the difficulty of the test and to estimate the time your students will need.

Base your grades on as much objective evidence as possible.

Examples

1. Plan in advance how and when you will test.
2. Keep a portfolio of student work. This may be useful in student or parent conferences.

Be sure students understand test directions.

Examples

1. Outline the directions on the board.
2. Ask several students to explain the directions.
3. Go over a sample question first.

Correct, return, and discuss test questions as soon as possible.

Examples

1. Have students who wrote good answers read their responses for the class; make sure they are not the same students each time.
2. Discuss why wrong answers, especially popular wrong choices, are incorrect.
3. As soon as students finish a test, give them the answers to questions and the page numbers where answers are discussed in the text.

As a rule, do not change a grade.

Examples

1. Make sure you can defend the grade in the first place.
2. DO change any clerical or calculation errors.

Guard against bias in grading.

Examples

1. Ask students to put their names on the backs of their papers.
2. Use an objective point system or model papers when grading essays.

Keep pupils informed of their standing in the class.

Examples

1. Write the distribution of scores on the board after tests.
2. Schedule periodic conferences to go over work from previous weeks.

Give students the benefit of the doubt. All measurement techniques involve error.

Examples

1. Unless there is a very good reason not to, give the higher grade in borderline cases.
2. If a large number of students miss the same question in the same way, revise the question for the future and consider throwing it out for that test.

Avoid reserving high grades and high praise for answers that conform to your ideas or to those in the textbook.

Examples

1. Give extra points for correct and creative answers.
2. Withhold your opinions until all sides of an issue have been explored.
3. Reinforce students for disagreeing in a rational, productive manner.
4. Give partial credit for partially correct answers.

Make sure each student has a reasonable chance to succeed, especially at the beginning of a new task.

Examples

1. Pretest students to make sure they have prerequisite abilities.
2. When appropriate, provide opportunities for students to retest to raise their grades, but make sure the retest is as difficult as the original.
3. Consider failing efforts as "incomplete," and encourage students to revise and improve.
4. Base grades more on work at the end of the unit; give ungraded work in the beginning of the unit.

Balance written and oral feedback.

Examples

1. Consider giving short, lively written comments with younger students and more extensive written comments with older students.
2. When the grade on a paper is lower than the student might have expected, be sure the reason for the lower grade is clear.
3. Tailor comments to the individual student's performance; avoid writing the same phrases over and over.
4. Note specific errors, possible reasons for errors, ideas for improvement, and work done well.

Make grades as meaningful as possible.

Examples

1. Tie grades to the mastery of important objectives.
2. Give ungraded assignments to encourage exploration.
3. Experiment with performances and portfolios.

Base grades on more than just one criterion.

Examples

1. Use essay questions as well as multiple-choice items on a test.
2. Grade oral reports and class participation.

For more thoughts about grading, see teaching.berkeley.edu/bgd/grading.html

Source: General conferencing guidelines adapted from Problems in Middle and High School Teaching: A Handbook for Student Teachers and Beginning Teachers *(pp. 182–187), by A. M. Drayer, 1979, Boston: Allyn & Bacon. Copyright © 1979 by Allyn & Bacon. Adapted by permission of the author and publisher.*

STANDARDIZED TESTING

For as long as I can remember, educators and policy makers have been concerned about the test performance of American students. In 1983, the National Commission on Excellence in Education published *A Nation at Risk: The Imperative for Educational Reform.* According to this report, standardized test scores were at a 25-year low. More recently, politicians point to the Trends in International Mathematics and Science Study (TIMSS) data collected in 1995, 1999, 2003, 2007, and 2011 showing that the United States is behind many other developed countries in math and science test scores (timss.bc.edu/timss2011/index.html). There is great variability across groups, however. For example, in the latest TIMSS testing, if Massachusetts were a country, it would be second in the world in science, right behind Singapore (K. Chang, 2013).

Part of the response to these test results has been more testing. In 2002, President Bush signed the No Child Left Behind Act, which requires each state to create content standards in reading, mathematics, and science, as well as assessments to measure student achievement linked to those standards (R. L. Linn, Baker, & Betebenner, 2002). Even though the Obama administration allowed exemptions and extensions to the strict requirements, the increase in testing and assessments will continue, especially as states move toward implementing the Common Core Standards in mathematics and English language arts described in Chapter 14. All these initiatives probably mean more standardized testing, so the changes will affect you, no matter what grade you teach. Teachers must be knowledgeable about testing. Understanding what standardized test scores really mean and how they can be used (or misused) is a good start. Let's look first at the results you will see from testing—the scores.

Types of Scores

Connect and Extend to PRAXIS II®

STOP & THINK At your first parent conference, a mother and father are concerned about their child's percentile rank of 86. They say that they expect their child to "get close to 100 percent. We know she should be able to do that because her grade-equivalent score is half a year above her grade!" What would you say? Do they understand the meaning of these scores? •

Concepts of Standardized Testing (II, C5) Be able to define norm groups, measures of central tendency, standard deviation, normal distribution, reliability, and validity, and to explain their roles in standardized tests.

To understand the scores from tests, you need to know some basics about different types of scores and what they tell you, but first you need to know some (easy) statistics.

MEASUREMENTS OF CENTRAL TENDENCY AND STANDARD DEVIATION. You have probably had a great deal of experience with means. A **mean** is simply the arithmetical average of a group of scores. To calculate the mean, you add the scores and divide the total by the number of scores in the distribution. The mean offers one way of measuring **central tendency**, the score that is typical or representative of the whole distribution of scores. Very high or very low scores affect the mean. Two other measures of central tendency are the median and the mode. The **median** is the middle score in a ranked list of scores, the point at which half the scores are larger and half are smaller. When there are a few very high or low scores, the median may be a better representative of the central tendency of a group than the mean. The **mode** is the score that occurs most often.

The measure of central tendency gives a score that is representative of the group of scores, but it does not tell you anything about how the scores are distributed. Two groups of scores may both have a mean of 50, but be alike in no other way. One group might contain the scores 50, 45, 55, 55, 45, 50, 50; the other group might contain the scores 100, 0, 50, 90, 10, 50, 50. In both cases, the mean, median, and mode are all 50, but the distributions are quite different.

The **standard deviation** is a measure of how widely the scores vary from the mean. The larger the standard deviation, the more spread out the scores are in the distribution. The smaller the standard deviation, the more the scores are clustered around the mean. For example, in the distribution 50, 45, 55, 55, 45, 50, 50, the standard deviation is much smaller than in the distribution 100, 0, 50, 90, 10, 50, 50. Another way of saying this is that distributions with very small standard deviations have less **variability** in the scores.

Knowing the mean and the standard deviation of a group of scores gives you a better picture of the meaning of an individual score. For example, suppose you received a score of 78 on a test. You would be very pleased with the score if the mean of the test were 70 and the standard deviation were 4. In this case, your score would be 2 standard deviations above the mean, a score well above average.

Consider the difference if the mean of the test had remained at 70, but the standard deviation had been 20. In the second case, your score of 78 would be less than 1 standard deviation from the mean. You would be much closer to the middle of the group, with a score above average, but not high. Knowing the standard deviation tells you much more than simply knowing the range of scores. No matter how the majority scored on the tests, one or two students may do very well or very poorly and thus make the range very large.

THE NORMAL DISTRIBUTION. Standard deviations are very useful in understanding test results. They are especially helpful if the results of the tests form a normal distribution. You may have encountered the normal distribution before. It is the bell-shaped curve, the most famous frequency distribution because it describes many naturally occurring physical and social phenomena. Many scores fall in the middle, giving the curve its bell appearance. You find fewer and fewer scores as you look out toward the end points, or *tails,* of the distribution. The normal distribution has been thoroughly analyzed by statisticians. The mean of a normal distribution is also its midpoint. Half the scores are above the mean, and half are below it. In a normal distribution, the mean, median, and mode are all the same point.

Another convenient property of the normal distribution is that the percentage of scores falling within each area of the curve is known, as you can see in Figure 15.3. A person scoring within 1 standard deviation of the mean obviously has company. Many scores pile up here. In fact, 68% of all scores are located in the area from 1 standard deviation below to 1 standard deviation above the mean. About 16% of the scores are higher than 1 standard deviation above the mean. Of this higher group, only 2% are higher than 2 standard deviations above the mean. Similarly, only about 16% of the scores are less than 1 standard deviation below the mean, and of that group only about 2% are lower than 2 standard deviations below the mean. At 2 standard deviations from the mean in either direction, the scorer has left the pack.

The SAT college entrance exam is one example of a normal distribution. The mean of the SAT Mathematics and the SAT Critical Reading tests is about 500 and the standard deviation is about 100. If you know people who made scores of 700 on one of these tests, you know they did very well. Only about 2% of the people who take the test do that well, because only 2% of the

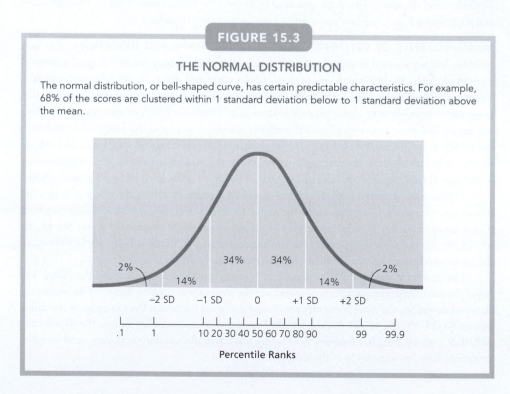

FIGURE 15.3

THE NORMAL DISTRIBUTION

The normal distribution, or bell-shaped curve, has certain predictable characteristics. For example, 68% of the scores are clustered within 1 standard deviation below to 1 standard deviation above the mean.

scores are better than 2 standard deviations above the mean in a normal distribution. Your score of 78 would be in the top 2% on a test with a mean of 70 and a standard deviation of 4.

Now we are ready to look at different kinds of test scores.

PERCENTILE RANK SCORES. Ranking is the basis for one very useful kind of score reported on standardized tests, a percentile rank score. In percentile ranking, each student's *raw score* (actual number correct) is compared with the raw scores of the students in the *norm group* (comparison group). The percentile rank shows the percentage of students in the norm group that scored at or below a particular raw score. If a student's score were the same as or better than three quarters of the students in the norm group, the student would score in the *75th percentile* or have a percentile rank of 75. You can see that this does not mean that the student had a raw score of 75 correct answers or even that the student answered 75% of the questions correctly. Rather, the 75 refers to the percentage of people in the norm group whose scores on the test were equal to or below this student's score. A percentile rank of 50 means that a student has scored as well as or better than 50% of the norm group and has achieved an average score.

There is one caution in interpreting percentile scores. Differences in percentile ranks do not mean the same thing in terms of raw score points in the middle of the scale as they do at the fringes. For example, the difference between the 50th and 60th percentile might be just 2 raw points, whereas the difference on the same test between the 90th and 99th percentile could be about 10 points. So a few answers right or wrong can make a bigger difference in percentile scores if you are near the middle.

GRADE-EQUIVALENT SCORES. Grade-equivalent scores are generally obtained from separate norm groups for each grade level. The average of the scores of all the 10th-graders in the norm group defines the 10th-grade–equivalent score. Suppose the raw-score average of the 10th-grade norm group is 38. Any student who attains a raw score of 38 on that test will be assigned a grade-equivalent score of 10th grade. Grade-equivalent scores are generally listed in numbers such as 8.3, 4.5, 7.6, 11.5, and so on. The whole number gives the grade. The decimals stand for tenths of a year, but they are usually interpreted as months.

Suppose a student with the grade-equivalent score of 10 is a seventh-grader. Should this student be promoted immediately? Probably not. Different forms of tests are used at different grade levels, so the seventh-grader may not have had to answer items that would be given to 10th-graders. The high score may represent superior mastery of material at the seventh-grade level rather than a capacity for doing advanced work. Even though an average 10th-grader could do as well as our seventh-grader on this particular test, the 10th-grader would certainly know much more than this seventh-grade test covered. Also, grade-equivalent score units do not mean the same thing at every grade level. For example, a second-grader reading at the first-grade level would have more trouble in school than an 11th-grader who reads at the 10th-grade level.

Because grade-equivalent scores are misleading and are often misinterpreted, especially by parents, most educators and psychologists strongly believe *they should not be used at all.* Several other forms of reporting are more appropriate.

STANDARD SCORES. As you may remember, one problem with percentile ranks is the difficulty in making comparisons among ranks. A discrepancy of a certain number of raw-score points has a different meaning at different places on the scale. With standard scores, on the other hand, a difference of 10 points is the same everywhere on the scale.

Standard scores are based on the standard deviation. A very common standard score is called the z score. A z score tells how many standard deviations above or below the average a raw score is. In the example described earlier, in which you were fortunate enough to get a 78 on a test where the mean was 70 and the standard deviation was 4, your z score would be $+2$, or 2 standard deviations above the mean. If a person were to score 64 on this test, the score would be 1.5 standard deviation units below the mean, and the z score would be -1.5. A z score of 0 would be no standard deviations above the mean—in other words, right on the mean. Measurements similar to z scores are used when you take a bone density test. Your score will compare your bone density to that of a healthy 30-year-old. If your score is below -1, you are moving toward osteoporosis. Below -2, you are there.

To calculate the *z* score for a given raw score, subtract the mean from the raw score and divide the difference by the standard deviation. The formula is

$$z = \frac{\text{Raw Score } - \text{ Mean}}{\text{Standard Deviation}}$$

Because it is often inconvenient to use negative numbers, other standard scores have been devised to eliminate this difficulty. The **T score** has a mean of 50 and uses a standard deviation of 10. Thus, a *T* score of 50 indicates average performance. If you multiply the *z* score by 10 (which eliminates the decimal) and add 50 (which gets rid of the negative number), you get the equivalent *T* score as the answer. The person whose *z* score was −1.5 would have a *T* score of 35.

First multiply the *z* score by 10: −1.5 × 10 = −15
Then add 50:   −15 + 50 = 35

As you saw, the scoring of the SAT test is based on a similar procedure, with a mean score set at 500, and a standard deviation of 100. Most IQ tests have a mean score of 100 and a standard deviation of 15. Different states have different ways of determining standards-based scores. For example, scale scores for each grade and subject on the California Standards Tests (CSTs) range from 150 to 600 (star.cde.ca.gov/star2013/help_scoreexplanations.aspx).

Before we leave this discussion of types of scores, we should look at one other widely used method. **Stanine scores** (the name comes from "standard nine") are standard scores. There are only nine possible scores on the stanine scale, the whole numbers 1 through 9. The mean is 5, and the standard deviation is 2. Each unit from 2 to 8 is equal to half a standard deviation.

Stanine scores provide a method of considering a student's rank, because each of the nine scores includes a specific range of percentile scores in the normal distribution. For example, a stanine score of 1 is assigned to the bottom 4% of scores in a distribution. A stanine of 2 is assigned to the next 7%. Of course, some raw scores in this 7% range are better than others, but they all get a stanine score of 2.

Each stanine score represents a wide range of raw scores. This has the advantage of encouraging teachers and parents to view a student's score in more general terms instead of making fine distinctions based on a few points. Figure 15.4 compares the four types of standard scores we have considered, showing how each would fall on a normal distribution curve.

FIGURE 15.4

FOUR TYPES OF STANDARD SCORES ON A NORMAL DISTRIBUTION CURVE

Using this figure, you can translate one type of standard into another.

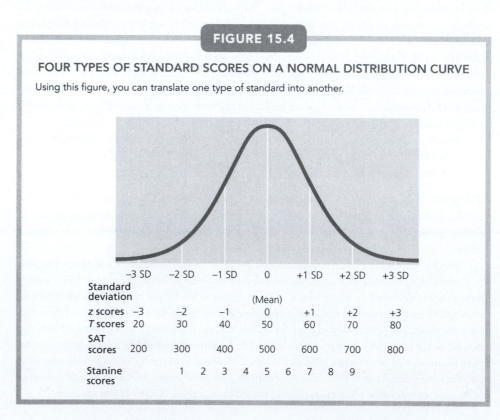

Standard deviation	−3 SD	−2 SD	−1 SD	0 (Mean)	+1 SD	+2 SD	+3 SD
z scores	−3	−2	−1	0	+1	+2	+3
T scores	20	30	40	50	60	70	80
SAT scores	200	300	400	500	600	700	800
Stanine scores		1 2	3	4 5 6	7	8 9	

Interpreting Standardized Test Reports

STOP & THINK Look at the test printout in Figure 15.5. What are this student's strengths and weaknesses? How do you know? •

What specific information can teachers expect from achievement test results? Test publishers usually provide individual profiles for each student, showing scores on each subtest. Figure 15.5 is an example of a Student Report for a fourth-grader, Sally Valenzuela, on the *Stanford Achievement Test, 10th Edition*. Note that the Student Report has three sections. The first (About This Student's Performance), is a brief narrative explanation that may include a Lexile Measure™, which is computed from the Reading Comprehension score and helps teachers identify Sally's reading level in order to select appropriate texts.

The second section (Subtests and Totals) attempts to paint a picture of the student's achievement in *Reading, Mathematics, Language, Spelling, Science, Social Science, Listening,* and *Thinking*

Connect and Extend to PRAXIS II®

Interpreting Achievement Tests (II, C4) Accurate information from the teacher is essential for students' academic progress. See Chapter 6 for a discussion of how to use praise effectively. These guidelines apply to written feedback as well.

FIGURE 15.5

A TYPICAL SCORE REPORT

A sample test score report, with no actual test data used.

Student Report | SALLY VALENZUELA   National Comparison

TEACHER: TILTON
SCHOOL: NEWTOWN ELEMENTARY - 215648
DISTRICT: NEWTOWN
GRADE: 04
TEST DATE: 04/03
AGE: 09 Yrs 08 Mos
STUDENT NO.: 8

About This Student's Performance:

Sally recently took the *Stanford Achievement Test*, Tenth Edition (Stanford 10). This test is one measure of this child's achievement. This report compares this child's performance to students in the same grade across the nation. Percentile Bands show ranges within which this child's true scores likely fall. For example, a student whose Percentile Band spans the 70th percentile performed as well as or better than 70% of students nationally in that subject - but not as well as 30% of students.

The chart below shows this child's performance in each subject area tested.

Lexile measure = 730L
Information on the use of Lexiles can be found at www.lexile.com. Lexiles used with permission.

Subtests and Totals	Number Possible	Number Correct	Scaled Score	National PR-S	National NCE	Grade Equivalent	AAC Range
Total Reading	114	82	639	59-5	54.8	5.4	MIDDLE
Word Study Skills	30	25	664	76-6	64.9	7.6	HIGH
Reading Vocabulary	30	22	627	46-5	47.9	4.5	MIDDLE
Reading Comprehension	54	35	634	53-5	51.6	5.0	MIDDLE
Total Mathematics	80	56	633	64-6	57.5	5.0	MIDDLE
Mathematics Problem Solving	48	30	623	54-5	52.1	5.0	MIDDLE
Mathematics Procedures	32	26	650	74-6	63.5	6.3	HIGH
Language	48	28	610	39-4	44.1	3.5	MIDDLE
Language Mechanics	24	15	617	46-5	47.9	4.3	MIDDLE
Language Expression	24	13	603	36-4	42.5	3.5	MIDDLE
Spelling	40	30	647	73-6	62.9	6.4	HIGH
Science	40	30	643	69-6	60.4	6.3	MIDDLE
Social Science	40	22	607	40-5	44.7	3.5	MIDDLE
Listening	40	22	608	35-4	41.9	3.4	MIDDLE
Thinking Skills	190	122	623	56-5	53.2	5.1	MIDDLE
Basic Battery	322	218	NA	57-5	53.6	5.0	MIDDLE
Complete Battery	402	270	NA	56-5	53.4	5.0	MIDDLE

Otis-Lennon School Ability Test®	Number Possible	Number Correct	SAI	Age PR-S	Scaled Score	Natl Grade PR-S
Total	72	38	106	65-6	605	55-5
Verbal	36	21	112	77-7	613	63-6
Nonverbal	36	17	102	55-5	597	46-5

Clusters	NP	NA	NC	Below Avg	Avg	Above Avg
Word Study Skills	30	30	25		✓	
C Structural Analysis	12	12	10		✓	
C Phonetic Analysis-Consonants	9	9	8			✓
C Phonetic Analysis-Vowels	9	9	7		✓	
Reading Vocabulary	30	30	22		✓	
C Synonyms	12	12	9		✓	
C Multiple Meaning Words	9	9	5	✓		
C Context Clues	9	9	8		✓	
P Thinking Skills	18	18	13		✓	
Reading Comprehension	54	54	35		✓	
C Literary	18	18	12		✓	
C Informational	18	18	10		✓	
C Functional	18	18	13		✓	
P Initial Understanding	12	12	11		✓	
P Interpretation	20	20	12		✓	
P Critical Analysis	12	12	8		✓	
P Strategies	10	10	4		✓	
P Thinking Skills	42	42	24		✓	
Mathematics Problem Solving	48	48	30		✓	
C Number Sense & Operations	24	24	16		✓	
C Patterns/Relationships/Algebra	6	6	6			✓
C Data, Statistics & Probability	8	8	4		✓	
C Geometry & Measurement	8	8	4		✓	
P Communication & Representation	6	6	2	✓		
P Estimation	8	8	5		✓	
P Mathematical Connections	21	21	13		✓	
P Reasoning & Problem Solving	13	13	10		✓	
P Thinking Skills	40	40	26		✓	

Clusters	NP	NA	NC	Below Avg	Avg	Above Avg
Mathematics Procedures	32	32	26		✓	
C Computation w/Whole Numbers	18	18	14		✓	
C Computation with Decimals	8	8	6		✓	
C Computation with Fractions	6	6	6			✓
C Computation in Context	16	16	13		✓	
C Computation/Symbolic Notation	16	16	13		✓	
P Thinking Skills	16	16	13		✓	
Language Mechanics	24	24	15		✓	
C Capitalization	8	8	7		✓	
C Usage	8	8	3	✓		
C Punctuation	8	8	5		✓	
Language Expression	24	24	13		✓	
C Sentence Structure	8	8	4		✓	
C Prewriting	5	5	3		✓	
C Content and Organization	11	11	6		✓	
P Thinking Skills	12	12	6		✓	
Spelling	40	40	30		✓	
C Phonetic Principles	18	18	14		✓	
C Structural Principles	10	10	7			✓
C No Mistake	7	7	7			✓
C Homophones	5	5	2		✓	
Science	40	40	30		✓	
C Life	11	11	9		✓	
C Physical	11	11	6		✓	
C Earth	11	11	10		✓	
C Nature of Science	7	7	5		✓	
P Models	14	14	11		✓	
P Constancy	13	13	10		✓	

Clusters	NP	NA	NC	Below Avg	Avg	Above Avg
Science (cont.)						
P Form & Function	13	13	9		✓	✓
P Thinking Skills	20	20	16		✓	
Social Science	40	40	22		✓	
C History	10	10	6		✓	
C Geography	10	10	8		✓	✓
C Political Science	10	10	6		✓	
C Economics	10	10	2	✓		
P App. of Knowledge/Comp.	14	14	7		✓	
P Org., Summ. & Interp. of Info.	15	15	7		✓	
P Determination of Cause/Effect	11	11	8		✓	
P Thinking Skills	20	20	11		✓	
Listening	40	40	22		✓	
C Vocabulary	10	10	3	✓		
C Comprehension	30	30	19		✓	
P Initial Understanding	8	8	6		✓	
P Interpretation	12	12	7		✓	
P Analysis	7	7	4		✓	
P Strategies	3	3	2		✓	
C Literary	10	10	7		✓	
C Informational	10	10	7		✓	
C Functional	10	10	5		✓	
P Thinking Skills	22	22	13		✓	
Thinking Skills	190	190	122		✓	

STANFORD LEVEL/FORM: INTERMEDIATE 1/A
2002 NORMS: Spring   National

OLSAT LEVEL/FORM: E/5
2002 NORMS: Spring   National

C = Content Cluster   P = Process Cluster

Scores based on normative data copyright © 2003 by Harcourt, Inc. All rights reserved.

COPY 01
PROCESS NO. 103000255-1531251-M109-00058-1

Source: Sample Stanford Student Report in Score Report Sampler: Guide-Teaching and Learning Toward High Academic Standards for the Stanford Achievement Test Series, 10th Edition (Stanford 10). Copyright © 2003 by NCS Pearson, Inc. Reproduced with permission. All rights reserved.

Skills. That section also includes total scores on the battery of tests and scores on the Otis-Lennon School Ability test—a kind of group IQ or scholastic aptitude test. Some of the subtests are further divided into more specific assessments. For example, *Reading* is broken down into "word study skills," "reading vocabulary," and "reading comprehension." Next to each subtest are several different ways of reporting Sally's score. The school decides which scores are reported, based on a list of possible reporting formats. This school chose the following types of scores:

Number Correct: Under the second column is the number of items that Sally answered correctly for that subtest (the total number of items on the subtest is in the first column).

Scaled Score: This is the basic score used to derive all the other scores, sometimes called a *growth score* because it describes growth in achievement that typically occurs as students move through the grades. For example, the average score for third-graders might be 585, whereas the average score for 10th-graders might be 714 on tests with possible scores that range from 0 to 1,000 across the entire K–12 grades. Often, the difficulty of items is included in calculating scale scores. Schools are increasingly using this score because they can compare across years, classes, or schools in the district (Popham, 2005).

National PR-S (National Percentile Rank and Stanine): This score tells us where Sally stands in relation to students at her grade level across the country in terms of percentile rank (percent with the same score or lower) and stanine.

National NCE (Normal Curve Equivalent): This is a standard score derived from the percentile rank, with a range of 1 to 99, a mean of 50, and a standard deviation of 21.

Grade Equivalent: This indicates that Sally's scaled score is the same as an average student in the indicated grade and month of school. Beware of the problems with grade-equivalent scores described earlier.

AAC (Achievement/Ability Comparison) Range: The ACC score compares Sally's achievement on each subtest to a norm group of other students who have her same ability as measured by the Otis-Lennon School Ability test. The ACC range categorizes Sally's ACC score as HIGH, MIDDLE, or LOW. You can see that Sally is in the middle on most of the subtests, so her achievement is in the middle compared to students with abilities similar to hers.

National Grade Percentile Bands: The range of national percentile scores in which Sally's true score is likely to fall. You may remember from our discussion of true scores that this range, or confidence interval, is determined by adding and subtracting the standard error of the test from Sally's actual score. Chances are high that Sally's true score is within this range. Bands that do not overlap indicate likely differences in achievement.

The bottom of Figure 15.5 (Clusters) breaks Sally's subtests down into even more specific skills. For each skill we see the number of questions possible to answer (NP), the number Sally attempted (NA), and the number she got correct (NC). The check marks beside the skills indicate if she is average, above average, or below average in each. Notice that some skills are assessed with only a few (3 to 8) questions. Remember that fewer items means less reliability.

DISCUSSING TEST RESULTS WITH FAMILIES. Teachers often have formal conferences and informal talks with parents or caregivers. Often the topic is testing results. At times, you will be expected to explain or describe test results to your students' families. The *Guidelines: Family and Community Partnerships* on the next page gives some ideas.

Accountability and High-Stakes Testing

STOP & THINK   How has standardized testing affected your life so far? What opportunities have been opened or closed to you based on test scores? Was the process fair? •

Every day, many decisions about individuals are based on the results of tests. Should Russell be issued a driver's license? How many and which students from the eighth grade would benefit from an accelerated program in science? Who needs extra tutoring? Who will be admitted to college or

GUIDELINES
Family and Community Partnerships

Conferences and Explaining Test Results

GENERAL CONFERENCING GUIDELINES
Decide on a few clear goals for the conference.

Examples

1. Gather information about the student to help in your instruction
2. Explain grades or test results
3. Let parents know what is coming during the next unit or marking period
4. Solicit help from parents
5. Make suggestions for use at home

Begin and end with a positive statement.

Examples

1. "Jacob is a natural leader."
2. "Eve really enjoys the science center."
3. "Yesim is really supportive when other students are upset."
4. "Ashanti's sense of humor keeps the class positive."

Listen actively.

Examples

1. Accept the emotions of parents or caregivers. Don't try to talk them out of what they feel.
2. "You seem to feel frustrated when Lee doesn't do his homework."

Respect family members' time and their concern about their child—Establish a partnership.

Examples

1. Speak plainly, briefly, and avoid jargon.
2. Be tactful, but don't avoid talking about tough issues.
3. Ask families to follow through on class goals at home: "Ask Leona for her homework checklist, and help her keep it up to date. I will do the same at school."

Learn from the family members.

Examples

1. What are the students' strengths as revealed in hobbies or extracurricular activities?
2. What are the students' interests?

Follow-up and follow through.

Examples

1. Send a brief note thanking the family members for attending.
2. Share student successes through notes or e-mail messages.
3. Keep families informed before problems develop.

EXPLAINING AND USING TEST RESULTS
In nontechnical terms, explain the meaning of each type of score on the test report and explain why tests are not "perfect."

Examples

1. If the test is norm referenced, know what the comparison group was (national? state? local district?). Explain that the child's score shows how he or she performed in relation to the other students in the comparison group.
2. If the test is criterion referenced, explain that the scores show how well their child performs specific tasks such as word problems or reading comprehension.
3. Encourage parents to think of the score not as a single point, but as a range or band that includes the score.
4. Ignore small differences between scores.

For norm-referenced tests, use percentile scores. They are the easiest to understand.

Examples

1. Percentile scores tell what percentage of students in the comparison group made the same score or lower. Higher percentiles are better, and 99 is as high as you can get; 50 is average.
2. Percentile scores do not tell the "percent correct," so scores that would be bad on a classroom test (say 65% to 75% or so) often are above average—even good—as percentile scores.

Avoid using grade-equivalent scores.

Examples

1. If parents want to focus on the "grade level" of their child, tell them that high grade-equivalent scores reflect a thorough understanding of the current grade level and NOT the capacity to do higher grade-level work.
2. Tell parents that the same grade-equivalent score has different meanings in different subjects—reading versus mathematics, for example.

Source: Based on ideas from The Successful Classroom: Management Strategies for Regular and Special Education Teachers, *by D. P. Fromberg & M. Driscoll. Published by Teachers College, Columbia University; Scholastic. (2011). Planning for parent conferences, retrieved from* http://www2.scholastic.com/browse/article.jsp?id=4194; *and T. E. Eissenberg & Lawrence M. Rudner (1988). Explaining test results to parents. Retrieved from* http://pareonline.net/getvn.asp?v=1&n=1

professional school? Test scores may affect "admission" to first grade, promotion from one grade to the next, high school graduation, access to special programs, placement in special education classes, teacher licensure and tenure, and school funding.

MAKING DECISIONS. When making decisions about individuals based on test results, it is important to distinguish between the *quality* of the test itself and the way the test is *used*. Even

Connect and Extend to PRAXIS II®

Standardized Testing: Major Issues (II, C5)
Since their inception, there have been controversies regarding the use of standardized tests in the schools. Familiarize yourself with the major issues that underlie these controversies. Explain the positions of the different camps in these controversies.

the best assessments can be, and have been, misused. Years ago, for example, using otherwise valid and reliable individual intelligence tests, many students were inappropriately identified as having mental retardation, the term used at that time (Snapp & Woolfolk, 1973). The problem was not with the tests, but with the fact that the test score was the only information used to classify students. Much more information is always needed to make this type of placement decision.

Behind all the statistics and terminology are issues related to values and ethics. Who will be tested? What are the consequences of choosing one test over another for a particular purpose with a given group? What is the effect of the testing on the students? How will the test scores of minority-group students be interpreted? What do we really mean by *intelligence, competence,* and *scholastic aptitude?* Do our views agree with those implied by the tests we use to measure these constructs? How will test results be integrated with other information about the individual to make judgments? Answering these questions requires choices based on values, as well as accurate information about what tests can and cannot tell us. Keep these values issues in mind as we examine testing uses and decisions.

Because the decisions affected by test scores are so critical, many educators call this process **high-stakes testing.** One of the high-stakes uses for test results is to hold teachers, schools, and administrators **accountable** for student performance. For example, teacher bonuses might be tied to their students' achievement or schools' funding may be affected by testing results.

WHAT DO TEACHERS THINK? The teachers I work with are frustrated that test results often come too late in the year to help them plan instruction or remediation for their current students. They also are troubled by the amount of time that testing takes—to prepare for the tests and to give them. They complain that the tests cover material that their curriculum does not include. Teachers around the country echo these concerns. In 2012, The New Teacher Project (tntp.org) surveyed 117 of the nation's top teachers, called the *Irreplaceables.* These teachers represented 36 states and all the 10 largest school districts; many were teaching award winners. What did this select group say about standardized testing? Most of the teachers (81%) felt successful when their students did well on standardized tests, but 50% felt that on balance, these tests do more harm than good. The perspectives of these teachers were complex; they viewed tests as useful in providing an objective measure of student achievement that allowed comparisons across groups. One teacher said, "I think they are a helpful way to determine if our students are making progress, but they are not the 'end-all, be-all' of student growth and achievement" and another said, "I believe that our students are over-tested and many schools feel pressure to teach to the test, which is actually a very low bar" (The New Teacher Project, 2013, p. 9). Are these teachers right? What are the problems with high-stakes testing?

DOCUMENTED PROBLEMS WITH HIGH-STAKES TESTING. When so much rides on the results of a test, you would assume that the test actually measured what had been taught. In the past, this match has been a problem. Recently, the overlap between what is taught and what is tested has been improving, but it still makes sense to be aware of possible mismatches. The Common Core Standards are meant to help eliminate great variability in what is taught and what is tested.

What about time? Studies have found that in some states, 80% of the elementary schools spend about 20% of their instructional time preparing for the end-of-grade tests (Abrams & Madaus, 2003). Studies of the actual high-stakes tests in action show other troubling consequences. Testing narrows the curriculum. In fact, after examining the results of years of testing, Lisa Abrams and George Madaus (2003) concluded, "In every setting where a high-stakes test operates, the exam content eventually defines the curriculum" (p. 32). For example, using the Texas Assessment of Academic Skills has led to curriculum changes that overemphasize what is tested and neglect other areas. In addition, it seems that the test of mathematics is also a test of reading. Students with poor reading ability have trouble with the math test, especially if their first language is not English.

Another unintended consequence of the early-warning testing in elementary school is to "push out" students who believe they are going to fail the high school graduation test. If they won't graduate anyway, they see no point in continuing to attend school (McNeil & Valenzuela, 2000).

TABLE 15.5 • **Inappropriate Uses for High-Stakes Test Results**
Beware of some uses for standardized test results. Tests were not designed for these purposes.

Pass/Fail Decisions	To deny students graduation from any grade, there must be strong evidence that the test used is valid, reliable, and free of bias. Some tests, for example, the Texas Assessment of Academic Skills (TAAS), have been challenged in the courts and found to meet these standards, but not all tests are good enough to make pass/fail decisions.
State-to-State Comparisons	You cannot really compare states using standardized test scores. States do not have the same curriculum, tests, resources, or challenges. If comparisons are made, they usually tell us what we already know—some states have more funding for schools and families with higher incomes or education levels.
Evaluation of Teachers or Schools	Many influences on test scores—family and community resources—are outside the control of teachers and schools. Often students move from school to school, so many students taking a test in spring may have been in the school only for a few weeks.
Identifying Where to Buy a House	Generally speaking, the schools with the highest test scores are in the neighborhoods where families have the highest levels of education and income. They may not be the "best schools" in terms of teaching, programs, or leadership, but they are the schools lucky enough to have the "right" students.

Source: From Haladyna, T. H. (2012). Essentials of Standardized Achievement Testing: Validity & Accountability. Boston, MA: Pearson Education, Inc. Adapted by permission.

For example, in the 2000–2001 school year, about one third of the English language learners dropped out of high school in New York. The main reason given was their inability to pass the required Regents Exam (Medina, 2002). No matter how good the test, some uses of high-stakes tests are not appropriate. Table 15.5 describes some of them.

USING HIGH-STAKES TESTING WELL. To be valuable, testing programs must have a number of characteristics. Of course, the tests used must be reliable, valid for the purposes used, and free of bias. In addition, the testing program must:

1. Match the content standards of the district—this is a vital part of validity.
2. Be part of the larger assessment plan. No individual test provides all the necessary information about student achievement. It is critical that schools avoid making pass/fail decisions based on a single test.
3. Test complex thinking, not just skills and factual knowledge.
4. Provide alternate assessment strategies for students with identifiable disabilities.
5. Provide opportunities for retesting when the stakes are high.
6. Include all students in the testing, but also provide informative reports of the results that make the students' situations clear if they have special challenges or circumstances such as disabilities.
7. Provide appropriate remediation when students fail.
8. Make sure all students taking the test have adequate opportunities to learn the material being tested.
9. Take into account the student's language. Students who have difficulty reading or writing in English will not perform well on tests that require English proficiency.
10. Use test results for children, not against them (Haladyna, 2002).

This is important, so I will repeat it: High-stakes standardized **achievement tests** must be chosen so that the items on the test actually measure knowledge gained in the classes. Also, students must have the necessary skills to take the test. If students score low on a science test not because they lack knowledge about science, but because they have difficulty reading the questions, don't speak English fluently, or have too little time to finish, then the test is not a valid measure of science achievement for those students.

Connect and Extend to PRAXIS II®

Alternatives to Standardized Testing (II, C1)
For an overview of the major forms of authentic testing, go to Teachervision. com (teachervision.com/lesson-plans/lesson-6385.html).

Video 15.5
In this video, a principal and assistant principal discuss their school's approach to using state test data. Note the overall goals of state tests and the constructive use of test data to improve teaching and learning to help every student achieve.

ENHANCEDetext *video example*

GUIDELINES
Preparing Yourself and Your Students for Testing

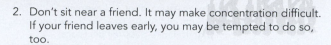

ADVICE FOR TEACHERS

Make sure the test actually covers the content of the unit of study.

Examples

1. Compare test questions to course objectives. Make sure that there is good overlap.
2. Check to see if the test is long enough to cover all important topics.
3. Find out if there are any difficulties your students experience with the test, such as not enough time, too difficult a level of reading, and so on. If there are, discuss these problems with appropriate school personnel.

Make sure students know how to use all the test materials.

Examples

1. Several days before the testing, do a few practice questions with a similar format.
2. Demonstrate the use of the answer sheets, especially computer-scored answer sheets.
3. Check with new students, shy students, slower students, and students who have difficulty reading to make sure they understand the questions.
4. Make sure students know if and when guessing is appropriate.

Follow instructions for administering the test exactly.

Examples

1. Practice giving the test before you actually use it.
2. Follow the time limits exactly.

Make students as comfortable as possible during testing.

Examples

1. Do not create anxiety by making the test seem like the most important event of the year.
2. Help the class relax before beginning the test, perhaps by telling a joke or having everyone take a few deep breaths. Don't be tense yourself!
3. Make sure the room is quiet.
4. Discourage cheating by monitoring the room. Don't become absorbed in your own paperwork.

ADVICE FOR STUDENTS

Use the night before the test effectively.

Examples

1. Study the night before the exam, ending with a final look at a summary of the key points, concepts, and relationships.
2. Get a good night's sleep. If you know you generally have trouble sleeping the night before an exam, try getting extra sleep on several previous nights.

Set the situation so you can concentrate on the test.

Examples

1. Give yourself plenty of time to eat and get to the exam room.

2. Don't sit near a friend. It may make concentration difficult. If your friend leaves early, you may be tempted to do so, too.

Make sure you know what the test is asking.

Examples

1. Read the directions carefully. If you are unsure, ask the instructor or proctor for clarification.
2. Read each question carefully to spot tricky words, such as *not, except, all of the following but one.*
3. On an essay test, read every question first, so you know the size of the job ahead of you and can make informed decisions about how much time to spend on each question.
4. On a multiple-choice test, read every alternative, even if an early one seems right.

Use time effectively.

Examples

1. Begin working right away and move as rapidly as possible while your energy is high.
2. Do the easy questions first.
3. Don't get stuck on one question. If you are stumped, mark the question so you can return to it easily later, and go on to questions you can answer more quickly.
4. On a multiple-choice test, if you know you will not have time to finish, fill in all the remaining questions with the same letter if there is no penalty for guessing.
5. If you are running out of time on an essay test, do not leave any questions blank. Briefly outline a few key points to show the instructor you knew the answer but needed more time.

Know when to guess on multiple-choice or true/false tests.

Examples

1. Always guess when only right answers are scored.
2. Always guess when you can eliminate some of the alternatives.
3. Don't guess if there is a penalty for guessing, unless you can confidently eliminate at least one alternative.
4. Are correct answers always longer? shorter? in the middle? more likely to be one letter? more often true than false?
5. Does the grammar give the right answer away or eliminate any alternatives?

Check your work.

Examples

1. Even if you can't stand to look at the test another minute, reread each question to make sure you answered the way you intended.
2. If you are using a machine-scored answer sheet, check occasionally to be sure the number of the question you are answering corresponds to the number of the answer on the sheet.

(continued)

On essay tests, answer as directly as possible.

Examples

1. Avoid flowery introductions. Answer the question in the first sentence and then elaborate.
2. Don't save your best ideas till last. Give them early in the answer.
3. Unless the instructor requires complete sentences, consider listing points, arguments, and so on by number in your answer. It will help you organize your thoughts and concentrate on the important aspects of the answer.

Learn from the testing experience.

Examples

1. Pay attention when the teacher reviews the answers. You can learn from your mistakes, and the same question may reappear in a later test.
2. Notice if you are having trouble with a particular kind of item; adjust your study approach next time to handle this type of item better.

For more test-taking strategies, see eop.mu.edu/study/ *or* testtakingtips.com

Reaching Every Student: Helping Students with Disabilities Prepare for High-Stakes Tests

Erik Carter and his colleagues (2005) tested a procedure for preparing students with learning disabilities, mild intellectual disabilities, and language impairments for a high-stakes state test. The students were ages 15 to 19; over half were African American males, and all had individualized education programs (IEPs—see Chapter 4) to guide their education. None had passed the state-required achievement tests. Over six class periods, an instructor taught the students strategies such as filling in bubbles on answer sheets completely, sorting problems by difficulty and doing the easy ones first, using rounding to estimate answers in math, identifying exactly what the question is asking by underlining key words and phrases, and strategies for eliminating alternatives that have redundant information or extreme qualifiers.

The good news is that after completing the preparation program, students improved their scores significantly on the tests. But the bad news is that the increases were not large enough to bring most of the students to the passing level. The authors recommend that preparation for testing should occur much earlier for students with disabilities. At an average age of 16, the students in this study already were discouraged. The strategies taught should be closely aligned with the specific types of problems that the students will encounter on the test and should be embedded in good content instruction. Finally, these students often are anxious about the negative consequences of failing—not receiving a regular diploma, or no access to college or trade school. The best way to deal with this anxiety is to better equip the students with the academic skills they will need to succeed (Carter et al., 2005). The *Guidelines: Preparing Yourself and Your Students for Testing* should help you and all your students prepare for high-stakes testing.

Current Directions: Value-Added and PARCC

Concerns about the problems with high-stakes tests, the unfairness in evaluating teachers based on test scores for students who began the year far below grade level, and the variability in curriculum in different school districts and states have led to new ideas about test scores and testing.

VALUE-ADDED MEASURES. What would you say about a teacher whose students began the year reading at the third-grade level and ended the year reading at the fifth-grade level? Sounds like a great year of growth in reading, right? But what if the students were sixth-graders? If we judge that teacher only by her students' achievement at the end of the year, we might think the teacher failed—students ending the sixth-grade and still reading at the fifth-grade level! No teaching awards for her. But actually the teacher was very effective (assuming she had the students all year). She added value to their learning—2 years' worth, in fact. The idea of value-added measures is to assess actual growth compared to some baseline of expected average growth. If students can be expected to grow one grade level, but they grow two, that is above expected growth. Value-added measures use statistical procedures to determine what students could be expected to learn based on student data from previous years in the subject and maybe other relevant information. If the actual student achievement is greater than predicted, then the estimate of the teacher's or school's effect is positive (value is added). If students score as predicted, the effect is zero, and if they score lower than predicted, then the effect is negative. So a simple definition of a teachers' value-added is "the average test-score gain for his or her students, adjusted for differences across classrooms in student characteristics such as prior scores" (Chetty, Friedman, & Rockoff, 2011, p. 1).

You can imagine that, to make good judgments with a value-added approach, the tests used must be valid and reliable, the tests must be aligned with the curriculum, and there must be room at the top and the bottom of the test to capture a full range of achievement. Teachers should have the students for most of the year. Also, the smaller the focus (on just one class instead of a whole school), the more uncertain is the estimate of effects, so the same teacher might seem to have larger effects some years and smaller effects in other years. These measures are not perfect, so they should be used to identify strengths and weaknesses in the school or the curriculum and guide professional development, but not to evaluate individual teachers (Battelle for Kids, 2011). Still, you may be in a school that uses value-added measures, so it makes sense to learn about them. One useful guide is available from Battelle for Kids (battelleforkids.org/how-we-help/strategic-measures/student-growth-measures).

PARCC TESTS. One goal of the Common Core Standards is to ensure that all U.S. students are prepared for success in college, careers, and life at the end of high school (corestandards.org/read-the-standards/). How do we know if students are moving toward meeting these standards? This is where high-quality assessment is needed. The Partnership for Assessment of Readiness for College and Careers (PARCC) is developing "a common set of K–12 assessments in English and math anchored in what it takes to be ready for college and careers" (parcconline.org/about-parcc). PARCC is a consortium of 17 states plus the District of Columbia and the U.S. Virgin Islands working together on this project. So far the PARCC states include Arizona, Arkansas, Colorado, District of Columbia, Florida, Illinois, Indiana, Louisiana, Maryland, Massachusetts, Mississippi, New Jersey, New Mexico, New York, Ohio, Pennsylvania, Rhode Island, and Tennessee. The goal of the tests is to be engaging and authentic. The assessments will be online—no more paper-and-pencil tests—so feedback can be faster and can help inform instruction. The tests are meant to replace current state achievement tests in English Language Arts/Literacy and Mathematics, the areas of the Common Core Standards. Stay tuned for changes in your state.

Lessons for Teachers: Quality Assessment

Quality teaching and quality assessment share the same basic principles, and these principles hold for all students. Carol Tomlinson (2005b, pp. 265–266) suggests that good instruction and good grading both depend on a teacher who:

- Is aware of and responds to student differences.
- Specifies clear learning outcomes.
- Uses pretests and formative assessments to monitor student progress toward learning goals.
- Adapts instruction in a variety of ways to ensure, as much as possible, that each student continues to progress.
- Makes sure students know the criteria for success on summative assessments that are tightly aligned to the stated learning goals.
- Provides varied forms of assessment to ensure that students have an unobstructed opportunity to express what they have learned.

ENHANCEDetext *self-check*

SUMMARY

- **Basics of Assessment (pp. 570–575)**

Distinguish between measurement and assessment. Measurement is the description of an event or characteristic using numbers. Assessment includes measurement but is broader because it includes all kinds of ways to sample and observe students' skills, knowledge, and abilities.

Distinguish between formative and summative assessment. In the classroom, assessment may be formative (ungraded, diagnostic) or summative (graded). Formative assessment helps form instruction, and summative assessment summarizes students' accomplishments.

Distinguish between norm-referenced and criterion-referenced tests. In norm-referenced tests, a student's performance is compared to the average performance of others. In criterion-referenced tests, scores are compared to a pre-established standard. Norm-referenced tests cover a wide range of general objectives. However, results of norm-referenced tests do not tell whether students are ready for advanced material, and they are not appropriate for affective and psychomotor objectives. Criterion-referenced tests measure the mastery of very specific objectives.

What is test reliability? Some tests are more reliable than others; that is, they yield more stable and consistent estimates. Care must be taken in the interpretation of test results. Each test is only a sample of a student's performance on a given day. The score is only an estimate of a student's hypothetical true score. The standard error of measurement takes into account the possibility for error and is one index of test reliability.

What is test validity? The most important consideration about a test is the validity of the decisions and judgments that are based on the test results. Evidence of validity can be related to content, criterion, or construct. Construct-related evidence for validity is the broadest category and encompasses the other two categories of content and criterion. Tests must be reliable to be valid, but reliability does not guarantee validity.

What is absence of bias? Tests must be free of assessment bias. Bias occurs when tests include material that offends or unfairly penalizes a group of students because of the students' gender, SES, race, religion, or ethnicity. Culture-fair tests have not proved to solve the problem of assessment bias.

- **Classroom Assessment: Testing (pp. 575–579)**

How can testing support learning? Learning is supported by frequent testing using cumulative questions that ask students to apply and integrate knowledge. With the goals of assessment in mind, teachers are in a better position to design their own tests or evaluate the tests provided by textbook publishers.

Describe two kinds of traditional testing. Two traditional formats for testing are the objective test and the essay test. Objective tests, which can include multiple-choice, true/false, fill-in, and matching items, should be written with specific guidelines in mind. Writing and scoring essay questions require careful planning, in addition to criteria to discourage bias in scoring.

- **Authentic Classroom Assessments (pp. 580–587)**

What is authentic assessment? Critics of traditional testing believe that teachers should use authentic tests and other authentic assessment procedures. Authentic assessment requires students to perform tasks and solve problems that are similar to the real-life performances that will be expected of them outside of school.

Describe portfolios and exhibitions. Portfolios and exhibitions are two examples of authentic assessment. A portfolio is a collection of the student's work, sometimes chosen to represent growth or improvement or sometimes featuring "best work." Exhibitions are public performances of the student's understandings. Portfolios and exhibitions emphasize performing real-life tasks in meaningful contexts.

What are the issues of reliability, validity, and equity with portfolios and performance assessment? Using authentic assessments does not guarantee reliability, validity, and equity (absence of bias). Using rubrics is one way to make assessment more reliable and valid. But the results from assessment based on rubrics may not predict performance on related tasks. Also, rater bias based on the appearance, speech, or behavior of students or a lack of resources may place students from minority groups at a disadvantage in performance assessments or projects.

How can teachers use informal assessments? Informal assessments are ungraded (formative) assessments that gather information from multiple sources to help teachers make decisions. Some examples of informal assessment are student observations and checklists, questioning, and student self-assessment. Journals are very flexible and widely used informal assessments. Students usually have personal or group journals and write in them on a regular basis.

- **Grading (pp. 587–592)**

Describe two kinds of grading. Grading can be either norm referenced or criterion referenced. One popular norm-referenced system is grading on the curve, based on a ranking of students in relation to the average performance level. This is not recommended. Criterion-referenced report cards usually indicate how well the individual student has met each of several objectives.

How can failure support learning? Students need experience in coping with failure, so standards must be high enough to encourage effort. Occasional failure can be positive if appropriate feedback is provided. Students who never learn how to cope with failure may give up quickly when their first efforts are unsuccessful.

Which is better, "social promotion" or being "held back"? Simply retaining or promoting a student who is having difficulty will not guarantee that the student will learn. Unless the student is very young or emotionally immature compared to others in the class, the best approach may be to promote, but provide extra support such as tutoring or summer school sessions. Differentiated instruction could prevent problems.

Can grades promote learning and motivation? Written or oral feedback that includes specific comments on errors or faulty strategies, but that balances this criticism with suggestions about how to improve along with comments on the positive aspects of the work, increases learning. Grades can encourage students' motivation to learn if they are tied to meaningful learning.

How can communications with families support learning? Not every communication from the teacher needs to be tied to a grade. Communication with students and families can be important in helping a teacher understand students and present effective instruction by creating a consistent learning environment. Students and families have a legal right to see all the information in the students' records, so the contents of files must be appropriate, accurate, and supported by evidence.

- **Standardized Testing (pp. 593–604)**

What are mean, median, mode, and standard deviation? The mean (arithmetical average), median (middle score), and mode (most common score) are all measures of central tendency. The standard deviation reveals how scores spread out around the mean. A normal distribution is a frequency distribution represented as a bell-shaped curve. Many scores cluster in the middle; the farther from the midpoint, the fewer the scores.

Describe different kinds of scores. There are several basic types of standardized test scores: percentile rankings, which indicate the percentage of others who scored at or below an individual's score; grade-equivalent scores, which indicate how closely a student's performance matches average scores for a given grade; and standard scores, which are based on the standard deviation. *T* and *z* scores are both common standard scores. A stanine score is a standard score that incorporates elements of percentile rankings.

What are some current issues in testing? Controversy over standardized testing has focused on the role and interpretation of tests, the widespread use of tests to evaluate schools, the problems with accountability based on test scores, and the testing of teachers. If the test matches important objectives of the curriculum, is given to students who actually studied the curriculum for a reasonable period of time, is free of bias, fits the students' language capabilities, and was administered properly, then test results provide some information about the effectiveness of the school. But studies of the actual tests in action show troubling consequences such as narrowing the curriculum and pushing some students out of school early. Expert teachers see both advantages and problems with standardized testing, but about 50% believe such tests do more harm than good. Teachers should use results to improve instruction, not to stereotype students or justify lowered expectations.

Can students become better test takers? How? Performance on standardized tests can be improved if students gain experience with this type of testing and are given training in study skills and problem solving. Many students can profit from direct instruction about how to prepare for and take tests. Involving students in designing these test preparation programs can be helpful. Students with learning challenges may benefit from intensive and ongoing preparation for taking tests, particularly if the test-taking strategies are tied to specific problems and content learned and tested.

What are some current directions in testing? Concerns about the problems with high-stakes tests, the unfairness in evaluating teachers based on test scores for students who began the year far below grade level, and the variability in curriculum in different school districts and states have led to new ideas about test scores and testing.

Value-added measures indicate the average test score gain for students, adjusted for their characteristics such as prior level of achievement (where they started the year). PARCC, a consortium of 17 states and the District of Columbia, is developing a new set of K–12 assessments in English and math anchored in what it takes to be ready for college and careers and consistent with the Common Core Standards.

PRACTICE USING WHAT YOU HAVE LEARNED

To access and complete the exercises, click the link under the images below.

Authentic Classroom Assessments

Grading

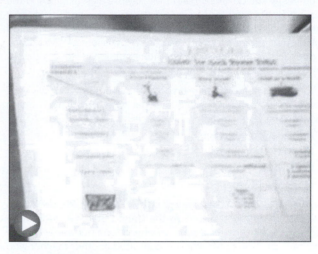

ENHANCEDetext *application exercise*

ENHANCEDetext *application exercise*

KEY TERMS

CONNECT AND EXTEND TO LICENSURE

MULTIPLE-CHOICE QUESTIONS

1. Which of the following assessment methods provides feedback that is nonevaluative, occurs before or during instruction, and guides teachers in planning and improving instruction?
   - A. Summative
   - B. Criterion referenced
   - C. Formative
   - D. Norm referenced

2. The yearly standardized test in Mr. Taylor's class is given in the spring. By the summer, Mr. Taylor's students received their scores in the mail. Many of the parents were upset and contacted Mr. Taylor regarding their children's "low scores." "Mr. Taylor, I don't understand how my daughter could be in Honors classes and have scores on her standardized test in the 70s?"

   "Your daughter's scores are above the average nationally. The average score would be a 50." What type of scoring is being used in the yearly tests Mr. Taylor's class must take?
   - A. Criterion referenced
   - B. Norm referenced
   - C. Raw scores
   - D. Authentic scoring

3. Maria had proven to be a very good student in Mr. Rhodes's class despite having just moved to the United States from another country. So, it came as a surprise when Maria performed poorly on her tests. When Mr. Rhodes consulted another teacher who also had Maria as a student, he learned that his test questions may have had something to do with it. His colleague explained that Maria comes from a relatively primitive area that does not have television. Her exposure to concepts that draw on a wide variety of cultural experiences was limited. This indicated to Mr. Rhodes that his tests unfairly penalized Maria. This type of assessment that unfairly penalizes a student for his or her lack of resources or culture demonstrates which of the following?
   - A. Attribution bias
   - B. Assessment bias
   - C. Reliability bias
   - D. Validity bias

4. Which one of the following types of assessments would be most beneficial for assessing a student's ability to debate?
   - A. Formative assessment
   - B. Portfolio assessment
   - C. Summative assessment
   - D. Performance assessment

CONSTRUCTED-RESPONSE QUESTIONS

Case

"How will you grade our oral book reports, Miss Wren?"

"I am going to grade them *with* each of you! We will develop what is called a *rubric*. It is a list of items on which you should focus while preparing and presenting your book report."

"How will we be involved?"

"You will help me make the rubric. What are some of the things you think should be included in your oral report?"

"I think we should have to have audience participation, or else it gets too boring!"

"Good idea, Terry. What else?" The class continued to add to the rubric until there were six aspects on which to focus. "Class, you will also assist me in grading your performance by using the rubric. By making the rubric and using it to grade yourself, you should do very well."

"There are no surprises that way!" Lisa shouted.

5. In addition to listing the criteria for what constitutes quality work and having students self-assess, list some additional guidelines for Miss Wren to remember when developing a rubric.

6. Grades, a form of extrinsic reinforcement, can be a source of celebration for Miss Wren's students or a punishment. To make the most of grades and increase her students' chances for success, what should Miss Wren keep in mind when grading her students?

ENHANCEDetext *licensure exam*

TEACHERS' CASEBOOK

WHAT WOULD THEY DO? GIVING MEANINGFUL GRADES

Here is how some practicing teachers responded to the grading challenge at the beginning of the chapter.

KATIE CHURCHILL—Third-Grade Teacher
Oriole Parke Elementary School, Chicago, IL

I use a combination of assessment tools to evaluate my students. Using a rubric that students and parents alike are familiar with provides an easy-to-follow-and-understand grading system. The rubric needs to remain in a focal area in the classroom as a constant reminder to the students of what their expectations are.

By differentiating instruction consistently to cover all learning styles and modalities, the students hopefully become more involved and invested in their own learning and, as a result, produce better quality work and exceed expectations.

Several factors play a part in obtaining a particular letter grade. The letter grade is earned through a combination of group work, completing objectives, and following the rubric guidelines for quality work.

MADYA AYALA—High School Teacher of Preperatoria
Eugenio Garza Lagüera, Campus Garza Sada, Monterrey, N. L. Mexico

I think it is important to assess a cross-section of student work. First, portfolios can be a useful way to gather various types of work throughout the year. Using a portfolio, a teacher can then attach a letter grade to student progress and achievement. It is important to grade children not only on progress, but also on their understanding of material. I use meaningful, written assessments to test for retention and understanding of my students' knowledge. Finally, I grade various projects and experiments so that the students who are better project-based learners will be graded fairly. I also like the idea of using a rubric system to grade students on writing or projects. Under a rubric system, a teacher allocates a certain number of points to each content area. It is then easy to attach a letter grade based on the number of points received.

KATIE PIEL—K-6 Teacher
West Park School, Moscow, ID

Students should be given the latitude to express achievement in different ways like group projects, daily class work, tests, and individual projects. All students are held accountable for demonstrating their own learning. With each teacher grading on a different standard, the teachers must also take on the responsibility of collaborating with their peers. Communicating to other teachers the skills a student can be expected to bring with him or her to the next level is crucial.

AIMEE FREDETTE—Second-Grade Teacher
Fisher Elementary School, Walpole, MA

I believe that students are not all smart in the same ways. I give the students a variety of ways to demonstrate their knowledge. I also focus on the students' ability to take their knowledge and integrate it into other subject areas across the curriculum.

I use a student portfolio for each child, compiled throughout the year to show growth and development. Each time I correct papers, I choose a couple of pieces of work that each child has done. I put these papers in the portfolio folder. I try to choose a variety of work, not necessarily their "prize work." At the end of the year, the children receive the entire folder to keep.

ALLAN OSBORNE—Assistant Principal
Snug Harbor Community School, Quincy, MA

Any grading system should consider a student's progress and effort. Grading systems also should be individualized to account for a student's unique strengths and weaknesses. Thus, a student with a learning disability should not be held to the same expectations as a gifted student.

The most critical aspect of any successful grading system is that it is fair. Fairness dictates that students and their parents be given information in advance about class requirements and expectations, along with a description of grading criteria. A system that is fair can be easily justified. It is also important to keep accurate and detailed records of student progress. In addition to recording grades on tests, quizzes, and projects, anecdotal records describing a student's typical performance should be kept. These records can be valuable if a report card grade is questioned.

Although group assignments can be an important learning experience, I would be reluctant to place too much emphasis on a group project grade. As we all know, each member of the group does not participate equally, and thus, a group grade does not reflect the contribution of each individual member.

Licensure Appendix

PART 1
Licensure Examination Study Guide

You probably will have to take a licensure examination in order to become a teacher in your state. In over 40 states and jurisdictions, the Praxis II* test is the required licensure examination. This section highlights the concepts from each chapter that may be on your licensure test.

CHAPTER 1

Developing relationships with professionals: Until you become a teacher, it will be difficult to establish a working relationship with other practitioners. However, you might find this site beneficial: K–12 Practitioners' Circle (nces.ed.gov/practitioners/teachers.asp).

    Keeping current with educational issues: Education Week (edweek.org) will keep you up-to-date about innovations in teaching, policy initiatives, and changes in public laws related to education. These issues are often highly complex. The use of critical thinking skills is essential when making judgments about the information you will encounter in this type of publication.

CHAPTER 2

For Piagetian and Vygotskian theories of development, you should understand:

- Basic assumptions of each
- How students build their unique knowledge bases
- How students acquire skills
- Important terms and concepts related to each theory
- The key steps, mechanisms, or milestones related to each theory
- The limitations of each theory

CHAPTER 3

Understand the major concepts and progressions related to:

- Bronfenbrenner and the social context for development
- Erikson's theory of psychosocial development
- Piaget's and Kohlberg's perspectives on moral development
- Gilligan's theory of caring

Design or choose strategies that:

- Support optimal social and emotional development of students
- Help students cope with major life transitions and challenges to safety, as well as physical and mental health
- Help students build a sense of self-concept, self-esteem, and self-identity (including racial identity)

Recognize signs or behaviors that indicate sexual abuse or child abuse.

CHAPTER 4

Explain the effects of legislation on public education:

- Americans with Disabilities Act
- Individuals with Disabilities Education Improvement Act
- Section 504
- Individualized education programs
- Inclusion and least restrictive environment

Understand views of intelligence and describe its measurement:

- Types of intelligence tests and their uses
- Multiple intelligences
- Interpreting intelligence scores
- Modifications to testing

Accommodate the needs of students with exceptionalities:

- Attention-deficit hyperactivity disorder
- Visual, speech, and physical difficulties
- Learning disabilities
- Intellectual disabilities/mental retardation

CHAPTER 5

For the development of language, you should understand:

- Basic assumptions of major theories
- The major accomplishments of language development of school-age children
- The relationship between language and literacy
- Basic steps that teachers can take to enhance literacy among their students
- Strategies that support English acquisition in non-English–speaking students

CHAPTER 6

Recognize the influences that ethnicity, socioeconomic status, and community values may have on:

- Student–teacher relationships and parent–teacher relationships
- Student learning styles
- Academic achievement
- Attitudes, self-esteem, and expectations for success
- Opportunities for quality educational experiences

Understand the influences that gender may have on:

- Teachers' attention to students
- Differences in mental abilities

Devise strategies that:

- Eliminate sexist teaching practices
- Promote positive school–home relationships
- Reduce or eliminate racial and ethnic stereotypes and biases

CHAPTER 7

Understand the basic assumptions and contributions of these behaviorists:

- Pavlov
- Skinner

Determine appropriate behavioral techniques to:

- Foster appropriate classroom conduct
- Help students monitor and regulate learning

Understand basic processes of operant conditioning and their roles in learning, including:

- Antecedents and consequences
- Types of reinforcement and reinforcement schedules
- Punishment
- Shaping

CHAPTER 8

Understand how memory and recall are affected by:

- The limitations, capacities, and capabilities of the various structures of human memory (e.g., memory stores)
- The manner in which humans process information
- Prior knowledge of a topic
- Executive control processes

Explain how students and teachers can enhance learning through the use of:

- Elaboration and mnemonic devices
- Organized presentations
- Meaningful learning and instructional activities

CHAPTER 9

Focus on each of these major topics:

- Metacognitive knowledge and learning
- Learning strategies
  - Basic principles of teaching these strategies
  - Cognitive processes involved in various strategies
  - Appropriate uses of different strategies
- Problem solving
  - General problem-solving strategies/heuristics and algorithms
  - The value of problem representation
  - Factors that impede problem solving
- Creativity
  - Meaning of creativity
  - Encouraging student creativity
- Critical thinking
- Transfer of learning
  - Types of transfer and promoting transfer

CHAPTER 10

Explain the advantages and appropriate uses of major student-centered approaches to learning and instruction:

- Inquiry method
- Problem-based learning
- Cognitive apprenticeships
- Cooperative learning
- Service learning

Understand important concepts related to student-centered models of instruction:

- Situated learning
- Complex learning environments
- Authentic tasks
- Multiple representations of content
- Piaget and Vygotsky: theories of constructivism

CHAPTER 11

Focus on these major topics:

- Bandura
- Modeling and observational learning
- Social cognitive theory
- Self-regulated learning
- Self-efficacy
- Teachers' sense of efficacy

CHAPTER 12

Describe the theoretical foundations of the major approaches to motivation.

- Identify and define important terms related to motivation including goals, attributions, intrinsic and extrinsic motivation, and self-determination.
- Use your knowledge of motivation to:
  — Identify situations and conditions that can enhance or diminish student motivation to learn
  — Design strategies to support individual and group work in the classroom
  — Implement practices that help students become self-motivated

CHAPTER 13

Understand principles of classroom management that promote positive relationships by:

- Establishing daily procedures and routines
- Responding effectively to minor student misbehavior
- Implementing reasonable rules, penalties, and rewards
- Keeping students actively engaged in purposeful learning

Diagnose problems and prevent or reduce inappropriate behaviors by:

- Communicating with students and parents
- Addressing misbehaviors in the least intrusive way possible
- Confronting disruptive behaviors in an effective, efficient manner

CHAPTER 14

Develop plans for instruction and consider:

- The role of objectives in instruction
- Writing behavioral and cognitive objectives
- The use of educational taxonomies to design effective objectives
- The role of independent practice (i.e., seatwork and homework)
- Direct instruction and expository teaching
  — Basic assumptions
  — Appropriate uses/principles of implementation

Understand the basic principles of teacher-centered and student-centered forms of instruction, including:

- Appropriate uses and limitations
- The role of the teacher
- Effective questioning techniques
- Whole-group discussions
- Recitation
- Thematic/interdisciplinary instruction
- Differentiated instruction and adaptive teaching

CHAPTER 15

Describe the characteristics and purposes of major types of tests:

- Criterion-referenced and norm-referenced tests
- Achievement, aptitude, and diagnostic tests

Explain the major issues related to concerns about standardized testing, including:

- High-stakes testing
- Bias in testing
- Test-taking programs

Understand major concepts related to classroom assessment and grading:

- Formative and summative assessment
- Reliability and validity
- Criterion-referenced and norm-referenced grading

Describe the characteristics, uses, and limitations of major assessment techniques, including:

- Multiple-choice items
- Essays
- Portfolios
- Exhibitions

Design a scoring rubric for an authentic learning task that possesses:

- Validity
- Reliability
- Generalizability
- Equity

PART 2
Correlating Text Content to the PRAXIS II®
Principles of Learning and Teaching Tests
and InTASC Standards

Each state in the country has its own set of licensure requirements that new teachers must meet in order to work in the classroom. An increasing number of states are basing their requirements on standards developed by InTASC (Interstate Teacher Assessment and Support Consortium). These standards are based on 10 principles of effective teaching that InTASC has identified as essential for optimal student learning. Many states assess new teachers' knowledge of those principles through the use of tests from the Praxis II* series published by the Educational Testing Service. Within the Praxis II series are three Principles of Learning and Teaching (PLT) tests, one each for grades K–6, 5–9, and 7–12. Each PLT test assesses students' knowledge of educational psychology and its application in the classroom.

The following table is designed to help you study for your PLT test and meet the Knowledge standards for each of InTASC's 10 principles of effective teaching. The left-hand column of the table lists the topics assessed in a PLT test. The right-hand column contains InTASC's Knowledge standards. In the center column, you will find the chapters, sections, and page numbers in this textbook that correspond to the PLT tests and InTASC standards.

PRAXIS II® Topics	Woolfolk Text Connections	InTASC Principles
I. Students as Learners		
A. Student Development and the Learning Process		
1. Theoretical foundations about how learning occurs: how students construct knowledge, acquire skills, and develop habits of mind	*Chapters 2, 7–12* (entire chapters)	1(d) The teacher understands how learning occurs—how learners construct knowledge, acquire skills, and develop disciplined thinking processes—and knows how to use instructional strategies that promote student learning.
■ Examples of important theorists:		
• Jean Piaget	*Chapter 2*/Piaget's Theory of Cognitive Development (pp. 44–56)	
• Lev Vygotsky	*Chapter 2*/Vygotsky's Sociocultural Perspective (pp. 56–62)	
• Howard Gardner	*Chapter 4*/Multiple Intelligences (pp. 123–126)	
• Robert Sternberg	*Chapter 4*/Intelligence as a Process (pp. 126–127)	
• Albert Bandura	*Chapter 7*/Beyond Behaviorism: Bandura's Challenge and Observational Learning (pp. 278–279) *Chapter 11*/Social Cognitive Theory (pp. 412–414)	
• Urie Bronfenbrenner	*Chapter 3*/Bronfenbrenner: The Social Context for Development (pp. 80–82)	

PRAXIS II® Topics	Woolfolk Text Connections	InTASC Principles
■ Important terms that relate to learning theory:		
• Adaptation	*Chapter 2*/Basic Tendencies in Thinking (pp. 45–46)	
• Conservation	*Chapter 2*/Four Stages of Cognitive Development (pp. 46–53)	
• Constructivism	*Chapter 2*/The Role of Learning and Development (p. 61); Implications of Piaget's and Vygotsky's Theories for Teachers (pp. 62–66) *Chapter 10*/The Learning Sciences and Constructivism (entire chapter)	
• Equilibration	*Chapter 2*/Basic Tendencies in Thinking (pp. 45–46)	
• Co-constructed process	*Chapter 2*/The Social Sources of Individual Thinking (pp. 57–58)	
• Private speech	*Chapter 2*/The Role of Language and Private Speech (pp. 59–61)	
• Scaffolding	*Chapter 2*/Private Speech and the Zone (p. 61); Vygotsky: What Can We Learn? (pp. 63–64); *Guidelines:* Applying Vygotsky's Ideas in Teaching (p. 66) *Chapter 10*/Cognitive Apprenticeships and Reciprocal Teaching (pp. 382–385)	
• Zone of proximal development	*Chapter 2*/The Zone of Proximal Development (p. 61); Reaching Every Student: Teaching in the "Magic Middle" (p. 65)	
• Learning	*Chapter 2*/Cognitive Development (entire chapter) *Chapter 7*/Understanding Learning (pp. 252–254) *Chapter 8*/Comparing Cognitive and Behavioral Views (p. 290) *Chapter 10*/Cognitive Apprenticeships and Reciprocal Teaching (pp. 382–385) *Chapter 12*/Motivation in Learning and Teaching (entire chapter)	
• Knowledge	*Chapter 2*/The Social Sources of Individual Thinking (pp. 57–58); Activity and Constructing Knowledge (p. 63) *Chapter 8*/The Importance of Knowledge in Cognition (pp. 291–292); Teaching for Deep, Long-Lasting Knowledge: Basic Principles and Applications (pp. 312–319) *Chapter 10*/How Is Knowledge Constructed? (pp. 375–376); Knowledge: Situated or General? (pp. 376–377)	
• Memory	*Chapter 8*/Cognitive Views of Memory (pp. 292–304); Long-Term Memory (pp. 304–312)	
• Schemas	*Chapter 8*/Schemas (pp. 308–309)	
• Transfer	*Chapter 9*/Teaching for Transfer (pp. 359–362)	

PRAXIS II® Topics	Woolfolk Text Connections	InTASC Principles
2. Human development in the physical, social, emotional, moral, and cognitive domains		1(e) The teacher understands that each learner's cognitive, linguistic, social, emotional, and physical development influence learning and knows how to make instructional decisions that build on learners' strengths and needs
■ Contributions of important theorists:		
• Jean Piaget	*Chapter 2*/Piaget's Theory of Cognitive Development (pp. 44–56)	
• Lev Vygotsky	*Chapter 2*/Vygotsky's Sociocultural Perspective (pp. 56–62)	
• Erik Erikson	*Chapter 3*/Erikson: Stages of Psychosocial Development (pp. 93–99)	
• Lawrence Kohlberg	*Chapter 3*/Kohlberg's Theories of Moral Development (pp. 105–107)	
• Carol Gilligan	*Chapter 3*/Criticisms of Kohlberg's Theory (pp. 106–107)	
■ Major progressions in each developmental domain and the ranges of individual variation within each domain	*Chapter 2*/Four Stages of Cognitive Development (pp. 46–53); Information Processing, Neo-Piagetian, and Neuroscience Views of Cognitive Development (pp. 53–54); Some Limitations of Piaget's Theory (pp. 54–56); The Social Sources of Individual Thinking (pp. 57–58) *Chapter 3*/Physical Development (pp. 74–80); Young Children (p. 74); Elementary School (p. 74); Adolescent Years (p. 75); Understanding Others and Moral Development (pp. 105–112) *Chapter 5*/The Development of Language (pp. 172–179)	
■ Impact of students' physical, social, emotional, moral, and cognitive development on their learning and ways to address these factors when making decisions	*Chapter 2*/Four Stages of Cognitive Development (pp. 46–53); Some Limitations of Piaget's Theory (pp. 54–56); *Guidelines:* Family and Community Partnerships (p. 49); *Guidelines:* Teaching the Concrete-Operational Child (p. 51); *Guidelines:* Helping Students to Use Formal Operations (p. 53); The Social Sources of Individual Thinking (pp. 57–58); Assisted Learning (p. 64); The Zone of Proximal Development (p. 61) *Chapter 3*/Physical Development (pp. 74–80); The Preschool Years: Trust, Autonomy, and Initiative (pp. 94–95); The Elementary and Middle School Years: Industry versus Inferiority (p. 95); Adolescence: The Search for Identity (pp. 95–97); Kohlberg's Theories of Moral Development (pp. 105–106); Self-Concept (pp. 100–102); Self-Esteem (pp. 103–105); Sex Differences in Self-Concept of Academic Competence (pp. 102–103); Theory of Mind and Intention (p. 105); Moral Judgments, Social Conventions, and Personal Choices (pp. 107–109) *Chapter 5*/The Development of Language (pp. 172–179) *Chapter 13*/Maintaining a Good Environment for Learning (pp. 501–505)	
■ How development in one domain, such as physical, may affect performance in another domain, such as social	*Chapter 2*/General Principles of Development (p. 34); The Brain and Cognitive Development (pp. 34–44); Influences on Development (p. 45) *Chapter 3*/Physical Development (pp. 74–80)	

PRAXIS II® Topics	Woolfolk Text Connections	InTASC Principles
B. Students as Diverse Learners		
1. Differences in the ways students learn and perform	Chapter 4/Learner Differences and Learning Needs (entire chapter) Chapter 6/Culture and Diversity (entire chapter)	2(g) The teacher understands and identifies differences in approaches to learning and performance and knows how to design instruction that uses each learner's strengths to promote growth.
• Learning styles	Chapter 4/Learning Styles/Preferences (pp. 132–133) Chapter 6/Diversity in Learning (pp. 239–242)	
• Multiple intelligences	Chapter 4/Multiple Intelligences (pp. 123–126)	
• Performance modes — Concrete operational thinking — Visual and aural learners	Chapter 2/Later Elementary to the Middle School Years: The Concrete-Operational Stage (pp. 49–51); Guidelines: Teaching the Concrete-Operational Child (p. 51) Chapter 4/Learning and Thinking Styles (pp. 131–134); Students with Learning Challenges (pp. 139–156)	
• Gender differences	Chapter 3/Sex Differences in Self-Concept of Academic Competence (pp. 102–103) Chapter 4/Gender Differences in Intelligence (pp. 130–131) Chapter 6/Gender in Teaching and Learning (pp. 230–235); Guidelines: Avoiding Gender Bias in Teaching (p. 234)	
• Cultural expectations and styles	Chapter 6/Today's Diverse Classrooms (pp. 210–214); Ethnicity and Race in Teaching and Learning (pp. 221–230); Guidelines: Culturally Relevant Teaching (p. 243) Chapter 14/Teacher Expectations (pp. 559–562)	
2. Areas of exceptionality in students' learning	Chapter 4/Learner Differences and Learning Needs (entire chapter)	2(h) The teacher understands students with exceptional needs, including those associated with disabilities and giftedness, and knows how to use strategies and resources to address these needs.
• Special physical or sensory challenges	Chapter 4/Students with Communication Disorders (pp. 145–147); Students with Health and Sensory Impairments (pp. 152–155)	
• Learning disabilities	Chapter 4/Students with Learning Disabilities (pp. 140–142); Individualized Education Program (pp. 135–136); Section 504 Protections (pp. 136–139)	
• Attention-deficit hyperactivity disorder (ADHD)	Chapter 4/Students with Hyperactivity and Attention Disorders (pp. 142–145)	
• Functional and mental retardation	Chapter 4/Students with Intellectual Disabilities (pp. 151–152); Guidelines: Teaching Students with Intellectual Disabilities (p. 152)	

PRAXIS II® Topics	Woolfolk Text Connections	InTASC Principles
3. Legislation and institutional responsibilities relating to exceptional students	*Chapter 4*/Individual Differences and the Law (pp. 134–139); Section 504 Protections (pp. 136–139)	9(j) The teacher understands laws related to learners' rights and teacher responsibilities (e.g., for educational equity, appropriate education for learners with disabilities, confidentiality, privacy, appropriate treatment of learners, reporting in situations related to possible child abuse).
• Americans with Disabilities Act (ADA), Individuals with Disabilities Education Act (IDEA); Section 504 Protections for Students	*Chapter 4*/IDEA (pp. 134–136); Section 504 Protections (pp. 136–139)	
• Inclusion, mainstreaming, and least restrictive environment	*Chapter 4*/Individual Differences and the Law (pp. 134–139); Least Restrictive Environment (pp. 134–135) *Chapter 14*/Reaching Every Student: Differentiated Instruction in Inclusive Classrooms (pp. 555–557)	
4. Approaches for accommodating various learning styles and intelligences	*Chapter 4*/Learner Differences and Learning Needs (entire chapter)—Focus on: Multiple Intelligences Go to School (pp. 125–126); Learning Styles/Preferences (pp. 132–134); Individual Differences and the Law (pp. 134–139); Teaching Students with Gifts and Talents (pp. 161–162)	2(g) The teacher understands and identifies differences in approaches to learning and performance and knows how to design instruction that uses each learner's strengths to promote growth.
• Differentiated instruction	*Chapter 14*/Differentiated Instruction and Adaptive Teaching (pp. 553–557); Technology and Differentiation (pp. 557–559)	
• Alternative assessment	*Chapter 15*/Authentic Classroom Assessments (pp. 580–587)	
• Testing modifications	*Chapter 15*/Reaching Every Student: Helping Students with Disabilities Prepare for High-Stakes Tests (p. 603)	
5. Process of second language acquisition and strategies to support the learning of students	*Chapter 5*/Contextualized and Academic Language (pp. 184–186); Dialect Differences in the Classroom (pp. 186–187); Teaching Students Who Are English Language Learners (pp. 191–200)	2(i) The teacher knows about second language acquisition processes and knows how to incorporate instructional strategies and resources to support language acquisition.
6. Understanding of influences of individual experiences, talents, and prior learning, as well as language, culture, family, and community values on students' learning		
• Multicultural backgrounds	*Chapter 6*/American Cultural Diversity (pp. 210–211); Ethnic and Racial Differences in School Achievement (pp. 222–224)	2(j) The teacher understands that learners bring assets for learning based on their individual experiences, abilities, talents, prior learning, and peer and social group interactions, as well as language, culture, family and community values.
		2(k) The teacher knows how to access information about the values of diverse cultures and communities and how to incorporate learners' experiences, cultures, and community resources into instruction.

PRAXIS II® Topics	Woolfolk Text Connections	InTASC Principles
• Age-appropriate knowledge and behaviors	*Chapter 2*/Four Stages of Cognitive Development (pp. 46–53); Vygotsky's Sociocultural Perspective (pp. 56–62); Implications of Piaget's and Vygotsky's Theories for Teachers (pp. 62–66) *Chapter 3*/The Self, Social, and Moral Development (entire chapter)—Focus on: The Preschool Years: Trust, Autonomy, and Initiative (pp. 94–95); The Elementary and Middle School Years: Industry versus Inferiority (p. 95); Adolescence: The Search for Identity (pp. 95–97); Understanding Others and Moral Development (pp. 105–112)	
• The student culture at the school	*Chapter 3*/Bronfenbrenner: The Social Context for Development (pp. 80–82); Peers (pp. 85–89) *Chapter 12*/Learned Helplessness (p. 460)	
• Family backgrounds	*Chapter 3*/Families (pp. 81–85) *Chapter 6*/Poverty and School Achievement (pp. 215–219) *Family and Community Partnership Guidelines* (all chapters)	
• Linguistic patterns and differences	*Chapter 4*/Students with Communication Disorders (pp. 145–147) *Chapter 5*/The Development of Language (pp. 172–175); Dialects (pp. 186–187); What Is Involved in Being Bilingual? (pp. 183–184)	1(g) The teacher understands the role of language and culture in learning and knows how to modify instruction to make language comprehensible and instruction relevant, accessible, and challenging.
• Cognitive patterns and differences	*Chapter 4*/Learning and Thinking Styles (pp. 131–134) *Chapter 8*/Individual Differences in Working Memory (pp. 302–304); Long-Term Memory (pp. 304–312)	
• Social and emotional issues	*Chapter 3*/Moral Development (pp. 105–107) *Chapter 4*/Students with Emotional or Behavioral Difficulties (pp. 147–151)	
C. Student Motivation and the Learning Environment		
1. Theoretical foundations about human motivation and behavior	*Chapter 12*/What Is Motivation? (pp. 444–446); Five General Approaches to Motivation (pp. 446–448)	3(i) The teacher understands the relationship between motivation and engagement and knows how to design learning experiences using strategies that build learner self-direction and ownership of learning.
• Important terms that relate to motivation and behavior	*Chapter 7*/Operant Conditioning: Trying New Responses (pp. 256–262); Reinforcement Schedules (pp. 258–260) *Chapter 11*/Social Cognitive Views of Learning and Motivation (entire chapter) *Chapter 12*/Motivation in Learning and Teaching (entire chapter) *Chapter 14*/Teacher Expectations (pp. 559–562)	
2. How knowledge of human emotion and behavior should influence strategies for organizing and supporting individual and group work in the classroom	*Chapter 12*/Emotions and Anxiety (pp. 465–470); *Guidelines:* Coping with Anxiety (p. 470); *Guidelines:* Supporting Self-Determination and Autonomy (p. 451) *Chapter 14*/Teacher Expectations (pp. 559–562)	3(j) The teacher knows how to help learners work productively and cooperatively with each other to achieve learning goals.

PRAXIS II® Topics	Woolfolk Text Connections	InTASC Principles
3. Factors and situations that are likely to promote or diminish students' motivation to learning, and how to help students to become self-motivated	*Chapter 12*/Needs: Lessons for Teachers (p. 452); Goals: Lessons for Teachers (p. 456); Curiosity, Interests, and Emotions: Lessons for Teachers (p. 470); Supporting Autonomy and Recognizing Accomplishment (pp. 473–474)	3(i) The teacher understands the relationship between motivation and engagement and knows how to design learning experiences using strategies that build learner self-direction and ownership of learning.
4. Principles of effective management and strategies to promote positive relationships, cooperation, and purposeful learning	*Chapter 7*/Methods for Encouraging Behaviors (pp. 263–266); *Guidelines:* Applying Operant Conditioning: Encouraging Positive Behaviors (p. 266); Handling Undesirable Behavior (pp. 269–271); Reaching Every Student: Severe Behavior Problems (pp. 271–273); Contemporary Applications: Functional Behavioral Assessment, Positive Behavior Supports, and Self-Management (pp. 273–278)	3(k) The teacher knows how to collaborate with learners to establish and monitor elements of a safe and productive learning environment including norms, expectations, routines, and organizational structures.
• Establishing daily procedures and routines	*Chapter 13*/Routines and Rules Required (pp. 494–497); *Guidelines:* Establishing Class Routines (p. 495);	
• Establishing classroom rules, punishments, and rewards	Prevention Is the Best Medicine (pp. 502–504); Reaching Every Student: Peer Mediation and Restorative Justice (pp. 518–520) *Chapter 14*/Teacher Expectations (pp. 559–562)	
• Giving timely feedback	*Chapter 7*/*Guidelines:* Applying Operant Conditioning: Using Praise Appropriately (p. 264) *Chapter 13*/The Need for Communication (pp. 515–521) *Chapter 14*/Responding to Student Answers (p. 549) *Chapter 15*/Effects of Grading on Students (pp. 588–589)	
• Maintaining accurate records	*Chapter 15*/Portfolios and Exhibitions (pp. 580–582); *Guidelines:* Creating Portfolios (p. 582); Evaluating Portfolios and Performances (pp. 582–585)	
• Communicating with parents and caregivers	*Chapters 2–15*/Family and Community Partnerships (one in each chapter)	
• Using objective behavior descriptions	*Chapter 7*/Putting It All Together to Apply Operant Conditioning: Applied Behavior Analysis (pp. 262–273)	
• Responding to student misbehavior	*Chapter 7*/Group Consequences (pp. 268–269); Handling Undesirable Behavior (pp. 269–271); *Guidelines:* Applying Operant Conditioning: Using Punishment (p. 272) *Chapter 13*/Dealing with Discipline Problems (pp. 506–508); Special Problems with High School Students (pp. 512–514); *Guidelines:* Imposing Penalties (p. 507); Counseling: The Student's Problem (pp. 516–517); Confrontation and Assertive Discipline (pp. 517–518); *Guidelines:* Handling Potentially Explosive Situations (p. 513)	
• Arranging classroom space	*Chapter 13*/Planning Spaces for Learning (pp. 497–499); *Guidelines:* Designing Learning Spaces (p. 499)	
• Pacing and the structure of the lesson	*Chapter 13*/Encouraging Engagement (pp. 501–502); *Guidelines:* Keeping Students Engaged (p. 502); Withitness (p. 503); Overlapping and Group Focus (p. 503); Movement Management (p. 503) *Chapter 14*/Clarity and Organization (p. 530); *Guidelines:* Effective Direct Instruction (p. 544)	

PRAXIS II® Topics	Woolfolk Text Connections	InTASC Principles
II. Instruction and Assessment		
A. Instructional Strategies		
1. Major cognitive processes associated with student learning		
• Critical thinking • Creative thinking	*Chapter 9*/Creativity: What It Is and Why It Matters (pp. 350–355); *Guidelines:* Applying and Encouraging Creativity (p. 354); Critical Thinking and Argumentation (pp. 355–359)	8(j) The teacher understands the cognitive processes associated with various kinds of learning (e.g., critical and creative thinking, problem framing and problem solving, invention, memorization and recall) and how these processes can be stimulated.
• Inductive and deductive thinking	*Chapter 2*/Formal Thinking (pp. 51–52)	
• Problem structuring and problem solving	*Chapter 9*/Problem Solving (pp. 339–349); *Guidelines:* Applying Problem Solving (p. 348)	
• Invention	*Chapter 9*/Creativity in the Classroom (pp. 352–353); The Big C: Revolutionary Innovation (p. 353–355)	
• Memorization and recall	*Chapter 8*/Cognitive Views of Learning (focus on sections related to memory)	
2. Major categories, advantages, and appropriate uses of instructional strategies		8(k) The teacher knows how to apply a range of developmentally, culturally, and linguistically appropriate instructional strategies to achieve learning goals.
• Cooperative learning	*Chapter 10*/Collaboration and Cooperation (pp. 385–387); *Guidelines:* Using Cooperative Learning (p. 394)	
• Direct instruction (often referred to as *teacher-centered instruction*)	*Chapter 14*/Direct Instruction (pp. 540–543)	
• Discovery learning	*Chapter 10*/Inquiry and Problem-Based Learning (pp. 379–382)	
• Whole-group discussion	*Chapter 14*/Group Discussion (pp. 549–550); *Guidelines:* Productive Group Discussions (p. 551)	
• Independent study	*Chapter 9*/Learning Strategies (pp. 331–339); *Guidelines:* Becoming an Expert Student (p. 338) *Chapter 11*/Models of Self-Regulated Learning and Agency (pp. 425–427)	
• Interdisciplinary instruction (sometimes referred to as *thematic instruction*)	*Chapter 10*/Inquiry and Problem-Based Learning (pp. 379–382) *Chapter 14*/Planning from a Constructionist Perspective (pp. 539–540)	5(j) The teacher understands how current interdisciplinary themes (e.g., civic literacy, health literacy, global awareness) connect to the core subjects and knows how to weave those themes into meaningful learning experiences.
• Questioning	*Chapter 14*/Questioning, Discussion, and Dialogue (pp. 545–550)	

PRAXIS II® Topics	Woolfolk Text Connections	InTASC Principles
3. Principles, techniques, and methods associated with major instructional strategies		8(k) The teacher knows how to apply a range of developmentally, culturally, and linguistically appropriate instructional strategies to achieve learning goals.
• Direct instruction (*often referred to as teacher-centered instruction*)	*Chapter 14*/Direct Instruction (pp. 540–543); Questioning, Discussion, and Dialogue (pp. 545–550); Rosenshine's Six Teaching Functions (p. 541)	
• Student-centered models	*Chapter 10*/Cognitive and Social Constructivism (pp. 372–378); Applying Constructivist Perspectives (pp. 378–395)	
4. Methods for enhancing student learning through the use of a variety of resources and materials	*Chapter 10*/Service Learning (pp. 395–397) *Chapter 14*/Technology and Differentiation (pp. 557–559)	8(n) The teacher knows how to use a wide variety of resources, including human and technological, to engage students in learning.

B. Planning Instruction

PRAXIS II® Topics	Woolfolk Text Connections	InTASC Principles
1. Techniques for planning instruction to meet curriculum goals, including the incorporation of learning theory, subject matter, curriculum development, and student development		7(i) The teacher understands learning theory, human development, cultural diversity, and individual differences and how these impact ongoing planning.
• National and state learning standards • State and local curriculum frameworks • State and local curriculum guides	*Chapter 15*/Accountability and High-Stakes Testing (pp. 598–601)	7(g) The teacher understands content and content standards and how these are organized in the curriculum.
• Scope and sequence in specific disciplines • Units and lessons	*Chapter 14*/The First Step: Planning (pp. 533–539); Planning from a Constructivist Perspective (pp. 539–540)	
• Behavioral objectives: affective, cognitive, and psychomotor • Learner objectives and outcomes	*Chapter 14*/Objectives for Learning (pp. 534–536); The Cognitive Domain (pp. 537–538); The Affective Domain (p. 538); The Psychomotor Domain (pp. 538–539); *Guidelines:* Using Instructional Objectives (p. 539)	
2. Techniques for creating effective bridges between curriculum goals and students' experiences • Modeling	*Chapter 7*/Beyond Behaviorism: Bandura's Challenge and Observational learning (pp. 278–279)	7(j) The teacher understands the strengths and needs of individual learners and how to plan instruction that is responsive to these strengths and needs.
• Guided practice	*Chapter 2*/Assisted Learning (p. 64) *Chapter 10*/Cognitive Apprenticeships and Reciprocal Teaching (pp. 382–385) *Chapter 14*/Rosenshine's Six Teaching Functions (p. 541)	
• Independent practice, including homework	*Chapter 11*/Models of Self-Regulated Learning and Agency (pp. 425–427); *Family and Community Partnerships:* Supporting Self-Regulation at Home and in School (p. 430) *Chapter 14*/Seatwork and Homework (pp. 543–545)	

PRAXIS II® Topics	Woolfolk Text Connections	InTASC Principles
• Transitions	Chapter 13/Overlapping and Group Focus (p. 503); Movement Management (p. 503); Guidelines: Keeping Students Engaged (p. 502)	
• Activating students' prior knowledge	Chapter 8/The Importance of Knowledge in Cognition (pp. 291–292); Capacity, Duration, and Contents of Long-Term Memory (pp. 304–305) Chapter 9/Defining Goals and Representing the Problem (pp. 341–345)	
• Anticipating preconceptions	Chapter 9/Factors That Hinder Problem Solving (pp. 346–348)	
• Encouraging exploration and problem solving	Chapter 2/Implications of Piaget's and Vygotsky's Theories for Teachers (pp. 62–66) Chapter 9/Problem Solving (pp. 339–349); Creativity and Cognition (p. 352); Creativity in the Classroom (pp. 352–353) Chapter 11/Models of Self-Regulated Learning and Agency (pp. 425–427)	
• Building new skills on those previously acquired	Chapter 2/Basic Tendencies in Thinking (pp. 45–46) Chapter 4/Students with Intellectual Disabilities (pp. 151–152); Guidelines: Teaching Students with Intellectual Disabilities (p. 152) Chapter 8/Capacity, Duration, and Contents of Long-Term Memory (pp. 304–305); Constructing Declarative Knowledge: Making Meaningful Connections (pp. 312–315); Development of Procedural Knowledge (pp. 317–319) Chapter 11/Observational Learning in Teaching (pp. 417–418)	
C. Assessment Strategies		
1. Types of assessments	Chapter 15/Norm-Referenced versus Criterion-Referenced Grading (pp. 587–589); Authentic Classroom Assessments (pp. 580–587); Formative and Summative Assessment (pp. 570–571); Objective Testing (pp. 576–577); Essay Testing (pp. 577–579); Portfolios and Exhibitions (pp. 580–582); Informal Assessments (pp. 585–587)	6(j) The teacher understands the differences between formative and summative applications of assessment and knows how and when to use each.
2. Characteristics of assessments	Chapter 15/Reliability of Test Scores (p. 573); Validity (p. 574); Writing Multiple-Choice Questions (p. 577); Constructing Essay Tests (pp. 577–578); Reliability, Variability, Generalizability (pp. 584–585); Guidelines: Developing a Rubric (p. 583)	6(k) The teacher understands the range of types and multiple purposes of assessment and how to design, adapt, or select appropriate assessments to address specific learning goals and individual differences, and to minimize sources of bias.
3. Scoring assessments	Chapter 15/Using Multiple-Choice Tests (p. 577); Evaluating Essays (pp. 578–579); Evaluating Portfolios and Performances (pp. 582–585); Guidelines: Developing a Rubric (p. 583)	
4. Uses of assessments	Chapter 15/Norm-Referenced versus Criterion-Referenced Grading (pp. 587–589); Accountability and High-Stakes Testing (pp. 598–601); Formative and Summative Assessment (pp. 570–571); Authentic Classroom Assessments (pp. 580–587)	6(1) The teacher knows how to analyze assessment data to understand patterns and gaps in learning, to guide planning and instruction, and to provide meaningful feedback to all learners.

PRAXIS II® Topics	Woolfolk Text Connections	InTASC Principles
5. Understanding of measurement theory and assessment-related issues	*Chapter 15*/Norm-Referenced versus Criterion-Referenced Grading (pp. 587–589)	
III. Communication Techniques		
A. **Basic, effective verbal and nonverbal communication techniques**	*Chapter 13*/The Need for Communication (pp. 515–521); Prevention Is the Best Medicine (pp. 502–504)	8(m) The teacher understands how multiple forms of communication (oral, written, nonverbal, digital, visual) convey ideas, foster self expression, and build relationships.
B. **Effect of cultural and gender differences on communications in the classroom**	*Chapter 5*/Dialect Differences in the Classroom (pp. 186–187) *Chapter 6*/Sociolinguistics (p. 241); Gender in Teaching and Learning (pp. 230–235); Multicultural Education: Creating Culturally Compatible Classrooms (pp. 235–244)	3(l) The teacher understands how learner diversity can affect communication and knows how to communicate effectively in differing environments.
C. **Types of questions that can stimulate discussion in different ways for different purposes**	*Chapter 14*/Questioning, Discussion, and Dialogue (pp. 545–550)	
1. Probing for learner understanding	*Chapter 14*/Questioning, Discussion, and Dialogue (pp. 545–550)	
2. Helping students articulate their ideas and thinking processes	*Chapter 9/Guidelines:* Applying Problem Solving (p. 348) *Chapter 14*/Group Discussion (pp. 549–550); *Guidelines:* Productive Group Discussions (p. 551)	5(n) The teacher understands communication modes and skills as vehicles for learning (e.g., information gathering and processing) across disciplines as well as vehicles for expressing learning.
3. Promoting risk taking and problem solving	*Chapter 9*/Problem Solving (pp. 339–348)	8(j) The teacher understands the cognitive processes associated with various kinds of learning (e.g., critical and creative thinking, problem framing and problem solving, invention, memorization and recall) and how these processes can be stimulated.
4. Facilitating factual recall	*Chapter 14*/Questioning, Discussion, and Dialogue (pp. 545–550)	
5. Encouraging convergent and divergent thinking	*Chapter 9*/Assessing Creativity (p. 350) *Chapter 14*/Kinds of Questions (p. 547)	
6. Stimulating curiosity	*Chapter 12*/Tapping Interests (p. 463–464); *Guidelines:* Building on Students' Interests and Curiosity (p. 466); Curiosity: Novelty and Complexity (p. 465)	
7. Helping students to question	*Chapter 14*/Fitting the Questions to the Students (pp. 547–549)	

PRAXIS II® Topics	Woolfolk Text Connections	InTASC Principles
IV. Profession and Community		
A. The Reflective Practitioner		
1. Types of resources available for professional development and learning • Professional literature • Colleagues	*Chapters 2–15/Teachers' Casebook* (opening and closing sections of each chapter)	
2. Ability to read and understand articles about current views, ideas, and debates regarding best teaching practices	*Chapter 1/Using Research to Understand and Improve Learning* (pp. 16–21) *Chapters 2–15/Point/Counterpoint* (one in each chapter)	
3. Why personal reflection on teaching practices is critical, and approaches that can be used to achieve this	*Chapters 2–15/Point/Counterpoint* (one in each chapter)	9(g) The teacher understands and knows how to use a variety of self-assessment and problem-solving strategies to analyze and reflect on his/her practice and to plan for adaptations/adjustments.
B. The Larger Community		
1. Role of the school as a resource to the larger community	*Chapter 6/Culture and Diversity* (entire chapter) *Chapter 13/Caring Relationships: Connections with School* (pp. 504–505)	10(1) The teacher understands schools as organizations within a historical, cultural, political, and social context and knows how to work with others across the system to support learners.
2. Factors in the students' environment outside of school (family circumstances, community environments, health, and economic conditions) that may influence students' life and learning	*Chapter 3/Families* (pp. 81–85); *Peers* (pp. 85–89) *Chapter 4/Students with Learning Challenges* (pp. 139–156)	10(m) The teacher understands that alignment of family, school, and community spheres of influence enhances student learning and that discontinuity in these spheres of influence interferes with learning.
3. Basic strategies for involving parents/guardians and leaders in the community in the educational process	*Chapter 6/Culture and Diversity* (entire chapter) *Chapter 10/Service Learning* (pp. 395–397) *Chapters 2–14/Family and Community Partnerships* (one in each chapter)	10(n) The teacher knows how to work with other adults and has developed skills in collaborative interaction appropriate for both face-to-face and virtual contexts.
4. Major laws related to students' rights and teacher responsibilities • Equal education • Appropriate education for handicapped children • Confidentiality and privacy • Appropriate treatment of students Reporting situations related to possible child abuse	*Chapter 4/Individual Differences and the Law* (pp. 134–139); *The Rights of Students and Families* (p. 136) *Chapter 13/The Need for Communication* (pp. 515–521) *Chapter 3/Teachers and Child Abuse* (pp. 91–92)	9(j) The teacher understands laws related to learners' rights and teacher responsibilities (e.g., for educational equity, appropriate education for learners with disabilities, confidentiality, privacy, appropriate treatment of learners, reporting in situations related to possible child abuse).

Note: The InTASC (Interstate Teacher Assessment and Support Consortium) standards were developed by the Council of Chief State School Officers and member states. Copies may be downloaded from the council's Web site at http://www.ccsso.org.

Source: Council of Chief State School Officers. (2011, April). Interstate Teacher Assessment and Support Consortium (InTASC) model core teaching standards: A resource for state dialogue. Washington, DC: Author. Available from http://www.ccsso.org/Documents/2011/InTASC_Model_Core_Teaching_Standards_2011.pdf

Glossary

Absence seizure: A seizure involving only a small part of the brain that causes a child to lose contact briefly with ongoing events—short lapses of consciousness.

Academic language: The entire range of language used in elementary, secondary, and university-level schools including words, concepts, strategies, and processes from academic subjects.

Academic learning time: Time when students are actually succeeding at the learning task.

Academic tasks: The work the student must accomplish, including the product expected, resources available, and the mental operations required.

Accommodation: Altering existing schemes or creating new ones in response to new information.

Accountable: Making teachers and schools responsible for student learning, usually by monitoring learning with high-stakes tests.

Achievement tests: Standardized tests measuring how much students have learned in a given content area.

Acronym: Technique for remembering by using the first letter of each word in a phrase to form a new, memorable word.

Action research: Systematic observations or tests of methods conducted by teachers or schools to improve teaching and learning for their students.

Action zone: Area of a classroom where the greatest amount of interaction takes place.

Active teaching: Teaching characterized by high levels of teacher explanation, demonstration, and interaction with students.

Adaptation: Adjustment to the environment.

Adaptive teaching: Provides all students with challenging instruction and uses supports when needed, but removes these supports as students become able to handle more on their own.

Adolescent egocentrism: Assumption that everyone else shares one's thoughts, feelings, and concerns.

Advance organizer: Statement of inclusive concepts to introduce and sum up material that follows.

Affective domain: Objectives focusing on attitudes and feelings.

Algorithm: Step-by-step procedure for solving a problem; prescription for solutions.

Americans with Disabilities Act of 1990 (ADA): Federal legislation prohibiting discrimination against persons with disabilities in employment, transportation, public access, local government, and telecommunications.

Amotivation: A complete lack of any intent to act—no engagement at all.

Analogical thinking: Heuristic in which one limits the search for solutions to situations that are similar to the one at hand.

Anorexia nervosa: Eating disorder characterized by very limited food intake.

Antecedents: Events that precede an action.

Anxiety: General uneasiness, a feeling of tension.

Applied behavior analysis: The application of behavioral learning principles to understand and change behavior.

Appropriating: Being able to internalize or take for yourself knowledge and skills developed in interaction with others or with cultural tools.

Argumentation: The process of debating a claim with someone else.

Arousal: Physical and psychological reactions causing a person to feel alert, attentive, wide awake, excited, or tense.

Articulation disorders: Any of a variety of pronunciation difficulties, such as the substitution, distortion, or omission of sounds.

Assertive discipline: Clear, firm, nonhostile response style.

Assessment: Procedures used to obtain information about student performance.

Assessment bias: Qualities of an assessment instrument that offend or unfairly penalize a group of students because of the students' gender, socioeconomic status, race, ethnicity, and so on.

Assimilation: Fitting new information into existing schemes.

Assisted learning: Providing strategic help in the initial stages of learning, gradually diminishing as students gain independence.

Assistive technology: Devices, systems, and services that support and improve the capabilities of individuals with disabilities.

Attachment: Forming an emotional bond with another person, initially a parent or family member.

Attention: Focus on a stimulus.

Attention-deficit hyperactivity disorder (ADHD): Current term for disruptive behavior disorders marked by overactivity, excessive difficulty sustaining attention, or impulsiveness.

Attribution theories: Descriptions of how individuals' explanations, justifications, and excuses influence their motivation and behavior.

Authentic assessments: Assessment procedures that test skills and abilities as they would be applied in real-life situations.

Authentic task: Tasks that have some connection to real-life problems the students will face outside the classroom.

Autism/Autism spectrum disorders: Developmental disability significantly affecting verbal and nonverbal communication and social interaction, generally evident before age 3 and ranging from mild to major.

Automated basic skills: Skills that are applied without conscious thought.

Automaticity: The ability to perform thoroughly learned tasks without much mental effort. The result of learning to perform a behavior or thinking process so thoroughly that the performance is automatic and does not require effort.

Autonomy: Independence.

Availability heuristic: Judging the likelihood of an event based on what is available in your memory, assuming those easily remembered events are common.

Aversive: Irritating or unpleasant.

Balanced bilingualism: Adding a second language capability without losing your heritage language.

Basic skills: Clearly structured knowledge that is needed for later learning and that can be taught step by step.

Behavior modification: Systematic application of antecedents and consequences to change behavior.

Behavioral learning theories: Explanations of learning that focus on external events as the cause of changes in observable behaviors.

Behavioral objectives: Instructional objectives stated in terms of observable behaviors.

Being needs: Maslow's three higher-level needs, sometimes called *growth needs*.

Belief perseverance: The tendency to hold on to beliefs, even in the face of contradictory evidence.

Bilingual: Speaking two languages and dealing appropriately with the two different cultures.

Bioecological model: Bronfenbrenner's theory describing the nested social and cultural contexts that shape development. Every person develops within a *microsystem*, inside a *mesosystem*, embedded in an *exosystem*, all of which are a part of the *macrosystem* of the culture. All development occurs in and is influenced by the time period—the *chronosystem*.

Blended families: Parents, children, and stepchildren merged into families through remarriages.

Body mass index (BMI): A measure of body fat that evaluates weight in relation to height.

Bottom-up processing: Perceiving based on noticing separate defining features and assembling them into a recognizable pattern.

Brainstorming: Generating ideas without stopping to evaluate them.

Bulimia: Eating disorder characterized by overeating, then getting rid of the food by self-induced vomiting or laxatives.

CAPS: A strategy that can be used in reading literature: *Characters*, *Aim* of story, *Problem*, *Solution*.

Case study: Intensive study of one person or one situation.

Central executive: The part of working memory that is responsible for monitoring and directing attention and other mental resources.

Central tendency: Typical score for a group of scores.

Cerebral palsy: Condition involving a range of motor or coordination difficulties due to brain damage.

Chain mnemonics: Memory strategies that associate one element in a series with the next element.

Chunking: Grouping individual bits of data into meaningful larger units.

Classical conditioning: Association of automatic responses with new stimuli.

Classification: Grouping objects into categories.

Classroom assessments: Classroom assessments are selected and created by teachers and can take many different forms—unit tests, essays, portfolios, projects, performances, oral presentations, and so on.

Classroom management: Techniques used to maintain a healthy learning environment, relatively free of behavior problems.

Cloud computing: Allows computer users to access applications, such as Google documents or Microsoft Web Mail, as well as computing assets such as network-accessible data storage and processing to use online applications.

Cmaps: Tools for concept mapping developed by the Institute for Human and Machine Cognition that are connected to many knowledge maps and other resources on the Internet.

Coactions: Joint actions of individual biology and the environment—each shapes and influences the other.

Co-constructed process: A social process in which people interact and negotiate (usually verbally) to create an understanding or to solve a problem. The final product is shaped by all participants.

Code switching: Moving between two speech forms.

Cognitive apprenticeship: A relationship in which a less-experienced learner acquires knowledge and skills under the guidance of an expert.

Cognitive behavior modification: Procedures based on both behavioral and cognitive learning principles for changing your own behavior by using self-talk and self-instruction.

Cognitive development: Gradual orderly changes by which mental processes become more complex and sophisticated.

Cognitive domain: In Bloom's taxonomy, memory and reasoning objectives.

Cognitive evaluation theory: Suggests that events affect motivation through the individual's perception of the events as controlling behavior or providing information.

Cognitive load: The volume of resources necessary to complete a task.

Cognitive objectives: Instructional objectives stated in terms of higher-level thinking operations.

Cognitive science: The interdisciplinary study of thinking, language, intelligence, knowledge creation, and the brain.

Cognitive view of learning: A general approach that views learning as an active mental process of acquiring, remembering, and using knowledge.

Collaboration: A philosophy about how to relate to others—how to learn and work.

Collective monologue: Form of speech in which children in a group talk but do not really interact or communicate.

Commitment: In Marcia's theory of identity statuses, individuals' choices concerning political and religious beliefs, for example, usually as a consequence of exploring the options.

Community of practice: Social situation or context in which ideas are judged useful or true.

Compensation: The principle that changes in one dimension can be offset by changes in another.

Complex learning environments: Problems and learning situations that mimic the ill-structured nature of real life.

Computational thinking: The thought processes involved in formulating problems so you can represent their solution steps and algorithms for computing.

Concept: A category used to group similar events, ideas, objects, or people.

Concept map: A drawing that charts the relationships among ideas.

Concrete operations: Mental tasks tied to concrete objects and situations.

Conditioned response (CR): Learned response to a previously neutral stimulus.

Conditioned stimulus (CS): Stimulus that evokes an emotional or physiological response after conditioning.

Confidence interval: Range of scores within which an individual's true score is likely to fall.

Confirmation bias: Seeking information that confirms our choices and beliefs, while ignoring disconfirming evidence.

Consequences: Events that follow an action.

Conservation: Principle that some characteristics of an object remain the same despite changes in appearance.

Constructionism: How public knowledge in disciplines such as science, math, economics, or history is constructed.

Constructivism/constructivist approach: View that emphasizes the active role of the learner in building understanding and making sense of information.

Constructivist approach: See *constructivism*.

Context: Internal and external circumstances and situations that interact with the individual's thoughts, feelings, and actions to shape development and learning. The physical or emotional backdrop associated with an event.

Contiguity: Association of two events because of repeated pairing.

Contingency contract: A contract between the teacher and a student specifying what the student must do to earn a particular reward or privilege.

Continuous reinforcement schedule: Presenting a reinforcer after every appropriate response.

Convergent questions: Questions with only one right answer—usually factual questions or rote knowledge questions.

Convergent Thinking: Narrowing possibilities to a single answer.

Cooperation: Way of working with others to attain a shared goal.

Cooperative learning: Situations in which elaboration, interpretation, explanation, and argumentation are integral to the activity of the group and where learning is supported by other individuals.

Co-regulation: A transitional phase during which students gradually appropriate self-regulated learning and skills through modeling, direct teaching, feedback, and coaching from teachers, parents, or peers.

Correlations: Statistical descriptions of how closely two variables are related.

Creativity: Imaginative, original thinking or problem solving.

Criterion-referenced grading: Assessment of each student's mastery of course objectives.

Criterion-referenced testing: Testing in which scores are compared to a set performance standard.

Critical periods: If learning doesn't happen during these periods, it never will.

Critical thinking: Evaluating conclusions by logically and systematically examining the problem, the evidence, and the solution.

Crystallized intelligence: Ability to apply culturally approved problem-solving methods.

Cueing: Providing a stimulus that "sets up" a desired behavior.

Cultural deficit model: A model that explains the school achievement problems of ethnic minority students by assuming that their culture is inadequate and does not prepare them to succeed in school.

Cultural tools: The real tools (computers, scales, etc.) and symbol systems (numbers, language, graphs) that allow people in a society to communicate, think, solve problems, and create knowledge.

Culturally relevant pedagogy: Excellent teaching for students of color that includes academic success, developing/maintaining cultural competence, and developing a critical consciousness to challenge the status quo.

Culturally responsive management: Taking cultural meanings and styles into account when developing management plans and responding to students.

Culture: The knowledge, values, attitudes, and traditions that guide the behavior of a group of people and allow them to solve the problems of living in their environment.

Culture-fair/culture-free test: A test without cultural bias.

Cyber aggression: Using e-mail, Twitter, Facebook, or other social media to spread rumors, make threats, or otherwise terrorize peers.

Decay: The weakening and fading of memories with the passage of time.

Decentering: Focusing on more than one aspect at a time.

Declarative knowledge: Verbal information; facts; "knowing that" something is the case.

Deficiency needs: Maslow's four lower-level needs, which must be satisfied first before higher-level needs can be addressed.

Defining attribute: Qualities that connect members of a group to a specific concept.

Descriptive studies: Studies that collect detailed information about specific situations, often using observation, surveys, interviews, recordings, or a combination of these methods.

Development: Orderly, adaptive changes we go through between conception and death; these developmental changes remain for a reasonably long period of time.

Developmental crisis: A specific conflict whose resolution prepares the way for the next stage.

Deviation IQ: Score based on a statistical comparison of an individual's performance with the average performance of others in that age group.

Dialect: Any variety of a language spoken by a particular group.

Differentiated instruction: A flexible approach to teaching that matches content, process, and product based on student differences in readiness, interests, and learning needs. Takes into account students' abilities, prior knowledge, and challenges so that instruction matches not only the subject being taught but also students' needs.

Direct instruction/explicit teaching: Systematic instruction for mastery of basic skills, facts, and information.

Disability: The inability to do something specific such as walk or hear.

Discrimination: Treating or acting unfairly toward particular categories of people.

Disequilibrium: In Piaget's theory, the "out-of-balance" state that occurs when a person realizes that his or her current ways of thinking are not working to solve a problem or understand a situation.

Distractors: Wrong answers offered as choices in a multiple-choice item.

Distributed practice: Practice in brief periods with rest intervals.

Distributive justice: Beliefs about how to divide materials or privileges fairly among members of a group; follows a sequence of development from equality to merit to benevolence.

Divergent questions: Questions that have no single correct answer.

Divergent thinking: Coming up with many possible solutions.

Domain-specific knowledge: Information that is useful in a particular situation or that applies mainly to one specific topic.

Domain-specific strategies: Consciously applied skills to reach goals in a particular subject or problem.

Dual coding theory: Suggests that information is stored in long-term memory as either visual images or verbal units, or both.

Educational psychology: The discipline concerned with teaching and learning processes; applies the methods and theories of psychology and has its own as well.

Effective instruction delivery (EID): Instructions that are concise, clear, and specific, and that communicate an expected result. Statements work better than questions.

Egocentric: Assuming that others experience the world the way you do.

Elaboration: Adding and extending meaning by connecting new information to existing knowledge.

Elaborative rehearsal: Keeping information in working memory by associating it with something else you already know.

Embodied cognition: Theory stating that cognitive processes develop from real-time, goal-directed interactions between humans and their environment.

Emergent literacy: The skills and knowledge, usually developed in the preschool years, that are the foundation for the development of reading and writing.

Emotional and behavioral disorders: Behaviors or emotions that deviate so much from the norm that they interfere with the child's own growth and development and/or the lives of others—inappropriate behaviors, unhappiness or depression, fears and anxieties, and trouble with relationships.

Empathetic listening: Hearing the intent and emotions behind what another says and reflecting them back by paraphrasing.

Empirical: Based on systematically collected data.

Enactive learning: Learning by doing and experiencing the consequences of your actions.

Engaged time: Time spent actively engaged in the learning task at hand. Also referred to as *time on task.*

English as a second language (ESL): The classes devoted to teaching English to students who are English language learners.

English language learners (ELLs): Students who are learning English and whose primary or heritage language is not English.

Entity view of ability: Belief that ability is a fixed characteristic that cannot be changed.

Epilepsy: Disorder marked by seizures and caused by abnormal electrical discharges in the brain.

Episodic buffer: The process that brings together and integrates information from the phonological loop, visuospatial sketchpad, and long-term memory under the supervision of the central executive.

Episodic memory: Long-term memory for information tied to a particular time and place, especially memory of the events in a person's life.

Epistemological beliefs: Beliefs about the structure, stability, and certainty of knowledge, and how knowledge is best learned.

Equilibration: Search for mental balance between cognitive schemes and information from the environment.

Ethnicity: A cultural heritage shared by a group of people.

Ethnography: A descriptive approach to research that focuses on life within a group and tries to understand the meaning of events to the people involved.

Event-related potential (ERP): Measurements that assess electrical activity of the brain through the skull or scalp.

Evidence-based practice in psychology (EBPP): Practices that integrate the best available research with the insights of expert practitioners and knowledge of the characteristics, culture, and preferences of the client.

Executive control processes: Processes such as selective attention, rehearsal, elaboration, and organization that influence encoding, storage, and retrieval of information in memory.

Executive functioning: All those processes that we use to organize, coordinate, and perform goal-directed, intentional actions, including focusing attention, inhibiting impulsive responses, making and changing plans, and using memory to hold and manipulate information.

Exemplar: An actual memory of a specific object.

Exhibition: A performance test or demonstration of learning that is public and usually takes an extended time to prepare.

Expectancy × value theories: Explanations of motivation that emphasize individuals' expectations for success combined with their valuing of the goal.

Experimentation: Research method in which variables are manipulated and the effects recorded.

Expert teachers: Experienced, effective teachers who have developed solutions for classroom problems. Their knowledge of teaching process and content is extensive and well organized.

Explicit memory: Long-term memories that involve deliberate or conscious recall.

Exploration: In Marcia's theory of identity statuses, the process by which adolescents consider and try out alternative beliefs, values, and behaviors in an effort to determine which will give them the most satisfaction.

Expressive vocabulary: All the different words a person uses in speaking or writing.

Extended families: Different family members—grandparents, aunts, uncles, cousins, and so on—living in the same household or at least in daily contact with the children in the family.

Extinction: The disappearance of a learned response.

Extraneous cognitive load: The resources required to process stimuli irrelevant to the task.

Extrinsic motivation: Motivation created by external factors such as rewards and punishments.

Failure-accepting students: Students who believe their failures are due to low ability and there is little they can do about it.

Failure-avoiding students: Students who avoid failure by sticking to what they know, by not taking risks, or by claiming not to care about their performance.

First-wave constructivism: A focus on the individual and psychological sources of knowing, as in Piaget's theory.

Flashbulb memories: Clear, vivid memories of emotionally important events in your life.

Flexible grouping: Grouping and regrouping students based on learning needs.

Flow: A mental state in which you are fully immersed in a challenging task that is accompanied by high levels of concentration and involvement.

Fluid intelligence: Mental efficiency, nonverbal abilities grounded in brain development.

Flynn effect: Because of better health, smaller families, increased complexity in the environment, and more and better schooling, IQ test scores are steadily rising.

Formal operations: Mental tasks involving abstract thinking and coordination of a number of variables.

Formative assessment: Ungraded testing used before or during instruction to aid in planning and diagnosis.

Free, appropriate public education (FAPE): Public funding to support appropriate educational programs for all students, no matter what their needs.

Functional behavioral assessment (FBA): Procedures used to obtain information about antecedents, behaviors, and consequences to determine the reason or function of the behavior.

Functional fixedness: Inability to use objects or tools in a new way.

Functional magnetic resonance imaging (fMRI): An MRI is an imaging technique that uses a magnetic field along with radio waves and a computer to create detailed pictures of the inside of the body. A functional MRI uses the MRI to measure the tiny changes that take place in the brain during brain activity.

Funds of knowledge: Knowledge that families and community members have acquired in many areas of work, home, and religious life that can become the basis for teaching.

Gender biases: Different views of males and females, often favoring one gender over the other.

Gender identity: The sense of self as male or female as well as the beliefs one has about gender roles and attributes.

Gender schemas: Organized cognitive structures that include gender-related information that influences how children think and behave.

Genderlects: Different ways of talking for males and females.

General intelligence (g): A general factor in cognitive ability that is related in varying degrees to performance on all mental tests.

General knowledge: Information that is useful in many different kinds of tasks; information that applies to many situations.

Generalized seizure: A seizure involving a large portion of the brain.

Generation 1.5: Students whose characteristics, educational experiences, and language fluencies are somewhere in between those of students born in the United States and students who are recent immigrants.

Generativity: Sense of concern for future generations.

Germane cognitive load: Deep processing of information related to the task, including the application of prior knowledge to a new task or problem.

Gestalt: German for *pattern* or *whole*. Gestalt theorists hold that people organize their perceptions into coherent wholes.

Gifted and talented: Students who demonstrate outstanding aptitudes and competences in one or more of many domains.

Glial cells: The *white matter* of the brain. These cells greatly outnumber neurons and appear to have many functions such as fighting infections, controlling blood flow and communication among neurons, and providing the *myelin* coating around axon fibers.

Goal: What an individual strives to accomplish.

Goal orientations: Patterns of beliefs about goals related to achievement in school.

Goal structure: The way students relate to others who are also working toward a particular goal.

Goal-directed actions: Deliberate actions toward a goal.

Good behavior game: Arrangement where a class is divided into teams and each team receives demerit points for breaking agreed-upon rules of good behavior.

Grade-equivalent score: Measure of grade level based on comparison with norming samples from each grade.

Grading on the curve: Norm-referenced grading that compares students' performance to an average level.

Group consequences: Rewards or punishments given to a class as a whole for adhering to or violating rules of conduct.

Group discussion: Conversation in which the teacher does not have the dominant role; students pose and answer their own questions.

Group focus: The ability to keep as many students as possible involved in activities.

Handicap: A disadvantage in a particular situation, sometimes caused by a disability.

Heritage language: The language spoken in the student's home or by members of the family.

Heuristic: General strategy used in attempting to solve problems.

Hierarchy of needs: Maslow's model of seven levels of human needs, from basic physiological requirements to the need for self-actualization.

High-stakes testing: Standardized tests whose results have powerful influences when used by school administrators, other officials, or employers to make decisions.

Hostile aggression: Bold, direct action that is intended to hurt someone else; unprovoked attack.

Human agency: The capacity to coordinate learning skills, motivation, and emotions to reach your goals.

Humanistic interpretation: Approach to motivation that emphasizes personal freedom, choice, self-determination, and striving for personal growth.

Hypothesis/hypotheses: A prediction of what will happen in a research study based on theory and previous research.

Hypothetico-deductive reasoning: A formal-operations problem-solving strategy in which an individual begins by identifying all the factors that might affect a problem and then deduces and systematically evaluates specific solutions.

"I" message: Clear, nonaccusatory statement of how something is affecting you.

Identity: Principle that a person or object remains the same over time. (Piaget) The complex answer to the question: "Who am I?" (Erikson).

Identity achievement: Strong sense of commitment to life choices after free consideration of alternatives.

Identity diffusion: Uncenteredness; confusion about who one is and what one wants.

Identity foreclosure: Acceptance of parental life choices without consideration of options.

Images: Representations based on the physical attributes—the appearance—of information.

Immersive virtual learning environment (IVLE): A simulation of a real-world environment that immerses students in tasks like those required in a professional practicum.

Immigrants: People who voluntarily leave their country to become permanent residents in a new place.

Implicit memory: Knowledge that we are not conscious of recalling but that influences our behavior or thought without our awareness.

Importance/attainment value: The importance of doing well on a task; how success on the task meets personal needs.

Incentive: An object or event that encourages or discourages behavior.

Inclusion: The integration of all students, including those with severe disabilities, into regular classes.

Incremental view of ability: Belief that ability is a set of skills that can be changed.

Individualized education program (IEP): Annually revised program for an exceptional student, detailing present achievement level, goals, and strategies, drawn up by teachers, parents, specialists, and (if possible) the student.

Individuals with Disabilities Education Act (IDEA): Latest amendment of PL 94–142; guarantees a free public education to all children regardless of disability.

Industry: Eagerness to engage in productive work.

Informal assessments: Ungraded (formative) assessments that gather information from multiple sources to help teachers make decisions.

Information processing: The human mind's activity of taking in, storing, and using information.

Initiative: Willingness to begin new activities and explore new directions.

Inquiry learning: Approach in which the teacher presents a puzzling situation and students solve the problem by gathering data and testing their conclusions.

Inside-out skills: The emergent literacy skills of knowledge of graphemes, phonological awareness, syntactic awareness, phoneme–grapheme correspondence, and emergent writing.

Insight: In problem solving, the sudden realization of a solution. In the triarchic theory of intelligence, the ability to deal effectively with novel situations.

Instructional objectives: Clear statement of what students are intended to learn through instruction.

Instrumental aggression: Strong actions aimed at claiming an object, place, or privilege—not intended to harm, but may lead to harm.

Integration: Fitting the child with special needs into existing class structures.

Integrity: Sense of self-acceptance and fulfillment.

Intellectual disabilities/mental retardation: Significantly below-average intellectual and adaptive social behavior, evident before age 18.

Intelligence: Ability or abilities to acquire and use knowledge for solving problems and adapting to the world.

Intelligence quotient (IQ): Score comparing mental and chronological ages.

Interest or intrinsic value: The enjoyment a person gets from a task.

Interference: The process that occurs when remembering certain information is hampered by the presence of other information.

Intermittent reinforcement schedule: Presenting a reinforcer after some but not all responses.

Internalize: Process whereby children adopt external standards as their own.

Intersubjective attitude: A commitment to build shared meaning with others by finding common ground and exchanging interpretations.

Interval schedule: Length of time between reinforcers.

Intimacy: Forming close, enduring relationships with others.

Intrinsic cognitive load: The resources required by the task itself, regardless of other stimuli.

Intrinsic motivation: Motivation associated with activities that are their own reward.

Jigsaw classroom: A learning process in which each student is part of a group and each group member is given part of the material to be learned by the whole group. Students become "expert" on their piece and then teach it to the others in their group.

Keyword method: System of associating new words or concepts with similar-sounding cue words and images.

KWL: A strategy to guide reading and inquiry: Before—What do I already *know*? What do I *want* to know? After—What have I *learned*?

Lateralization: The specialization of the two hemispheres (sides) of the brain cortex.

Learned helplessness: The expectation, based on previous experiences with a lack of control, that all of one's efforts will lead to failure.

Learning: Process through which experience causes permanent change in knowledge or behavior.

Learning disability: Problem with acquisition and use of language; may show up as difficulty with reading, writing, reasoning, or math.

Learning management system (LMS): Systems that deliver e-learning, provide tools and learning materials, keep records, administer assessments, and manage learning.

Learning preferences: Preferred ways of studying and learning, such as using pictures instead of text, working with other people versus alone, learning in structured or in unstructured situations, and so on.

Learning sciences: An interdisciplinary science of learning, based on research in psychology, education, computer science, philosophy, sociology, anthropology, neuroscience, and other fields that study learning.

Learning strategies: A special kind of procedural knowledge—*knowing how* to approach learning tasks.

Learning styles: Characteristic approaches to learning and studying.

Least restrictive environment (LRE): Educating each child with peers in the general education classroom to the greatest extent possible.

Legally blind: Seeing at 20 feet what a person with normal vision would see at 200 feet and/or having severely restricted peripheral vision.

Legitimate peripheral participation: Genuine involvement in the work of the group, even if your abilities are undeveloped and contributions are small.

Lesson study: As a group, teachers develop, test, improve, and retest lessons until they are satisfied with the final version.

Levels of processing theory: Theory that recall of information is based on how deeply it is processed.

LGBTQ: Individuals whose sexual orientation is lesbian, gay, bisexual, or transgendered, or who are currently questioning their sexual orientation.

Limited English proficient (LEP): A term also used for students who are learning English when their primary or heritage language is not English—not the preferred term (English language learner; ELL) because of the negative connotations.

LINCS vocabulary strategy: A strategy that uses stories and imagery to help students learn how to identify, organize, define, and remember words and their meanings.

Loci method: Technique of associating items with specific places.

Locus of causality: The location—internal or external—of the cause of behavior.

Long-term memory: Permanent store of knowledge.

Low vision: Vision limited to close objects.

Mainstreaming: Teaching children with disabilities in regular classes for part or all of their school day.

Maintenance rehearsal: Keeping information in working memory by repeating it to yourself.

Massed practice: Practice for a single extended period.

Massive multi-player online games (MMOG): Interactive gaming environments constructed in virtual worlds where the learner assumes a character role, or avatar.

Mastery experiences: Our own direct experiences—the most powerful source of efficacy information.

Mastery goal: A personal intention to improve abilities and learn, no matter how performance suffers.

Mastery-oriented students: Students who focus on learning goals because they value achievement and see ability as improvable.

Maturation: Genetically programmed, naturally occurring changes over time.

Mean: Arithmetical average.

Means-ends analysis: Heuristic in which a goal is divided into subgoals.

Measurement: An evaluation expressed in quantitative (number) terms.

Median: Middle score in a group of scores.

Melting pot: A metaphor for the absorption and assimilation of immigrants into the mainstream of society so that ethnic differences vanish.

Menarche: The first menstrual period in girls.

Mental age: In intelligence testing, a performance that represents average abilities for that age group.

Metacognition: Knowledge about our own thinking processes.

Metalinguistic awareness: Understanding about one's own use of language.

Microgenetic studies: Detailed observation and analysis of changes in a cognitive process as the process unfolds over a several-day or several-week period of time.

Minority group: A group of people who have been socially disadvantaged—not always a minority in actual numbers.

Mirror systems: Areas of the brain that fire both during perception of an action by someone else and when performing the action.

Mnemonics: Techniques for remembering; the art of memory.

Mode: Most frequently occurring score.

Modeling: Changes in behavior, thinking, or emotions that happen through observing another person—a model.

Monolingual: Speaking only one language.

Moral dilemma: Situations in which no choice is clearly and indisputably right.

Moral realism: Stage of development wherein children see rules as absolute.

Moral reasoning: The thinking process involved in judgments about questions of right and wrong.

Morality of cooperation: Stage of development wherein children realize that people make rules and people can change them.

Moratorium: Identity crisis; suspension of choices because of struggle.

Motivation: An internal state that arouses, directs, and maintains behavior.

Motivation to learn: The tendency to find academic activities meaningful and worthwhile and to try to benefit from them.

Movement management: Keeping lessons and the group moving at an appropriate (and flexible) pace, with smooth transitions and variety.

Multicultural education: Education that promotes equity in the schooling of all students.

Multiple representations of content: Considering problems using various analogies, examples, and metaphors.

Myelination: The process by which neural fibers are coated with a fatty sheath called *myelin* that makes message transfer more efficient.

Natural/logical consequences: Instead of punishing, have students redo, repair, or in some way face the consequences that naturally flow from their actions.

Need for autonomy: The desire to have our own wishes, rather than external rewards or pressures, determine our actions.

Need for competence: The individual's need to demonstrate ability or mastery over the tasks at hand.

Negative correlation: A relationship between two variables in which a high value on one is associated with a low value on the other. Example: height and distance from top of head to the ceiling.

Negative reinforcement: Strengthening behavior by removing an aversive stimulus when the behavior occurs.

Neo-Piagetian theories: More recent theories that integrate findings about attention, memory, and strategy use with Piaget's insights about children's thinking and the construction of knowledge.

Neurogenesis: The production of new neurons.

Neurons: Nerve cells that store and transfer information.

Neutral stimulus: Stimulus not connected to a response.

Nigrescence: The process of developing a Black identity.

Norm group: Large sample of students serving as a comparison group for scoring tests.

Norm-referenced grading: Assessment of students' achievement in relation to one another.

Norm-referenced testing: Testing in which scores are compared with the average performance of others.

Normal distribution: The most commonly occurring distribution, in which scores are distributed evenly around the mean.

Object permanence: The understanding that objects have a separate, permanent existence.

Objective testing: Multiple-choice, matching, true/false, short-answer, and fill-in tests; scoring answers does not require interpretation.

Observational learning: Learning by observation and imitation of others—vicarious learning.

Operant conditioning: Learning in which voluntary behavior is strengthened or weakened by consequences or antecedents.

Operants: Voluntary (and generally goal-directed) behaviors emitted by a person or an animal.

Operations: Actions a person carries out by thinking them through instead of literally performing the actions.

Organization: Ongoing process of arranging information and experiences into mental systems or categories. Ordered and logical network of relations.

Outside–in skills: The emergent literacy skills of language, narrative, conventions of print, and emergent reading.

Overlapping: Supervising several activities at once.

Overlearning: Practicing a skill past the point of mastery.

Overregularize: To apply a rule of syntax or grammar in situations where the rule does not apply, for example, "the bike was broked."

Overt aggression: A form of hostile aggression that involves physical attack.

Paraphrase rule: Policy whereby listeners must accurately summarize what a speaker has said before being allowed to respond.

Parenting styles: The ways of interacting with and disciplining children.

Part learning: Breaking a list of items into shorter lists.

Participant observation: A method for conducting descriptive research in which the researcher becomes a participant in the situation in order to better understand life in that group.

Participants/subjects: People or animals studied.

Participation structures: The formal and informal rules for how to take part in a given activity.

Pedagogical content knowledge: Teacher knowledge that combines mastery of *academic content* with knowing *how to teach* the content and how to match instruction to *student differences*.

Peer cultures: Groups of children or adolescents with their own rules and norms, particularly about such things as dress, appearance, music, language, social values, and behavior.

Percentile rank: Percentage of those in the norming sample who scored at or below an individual's score.

Perception: Interpretation of sensory information.

Performance assessments: Any form of assessment that requires students to carry out an activity or produce a product in order to demonstrate learning.

Performance goal: A personal intention to seem competent or perform well in the eyes of others.

Personal development: Changes in personality that take place as one grows.

Personal learning environment (PLE): Provides tools that support individualized learning in a variety of contexts and situations.

Personal learning network (PLN): Framework in which knowledge is constructed through online peer interactions.

Perspective-taking ability: Understanding that others have different feelings and experiences.

Pervasive developmental disorder (PDD): A term favored by the medical community to describe autism spectrum disorders.

Phonological loop: Part of working memory. A speech- and sound-related system for holding and rehearsing (refreshing) words and sounds in short-term memory for about 1.5 to 2 seconds.

Physical development: Changes in body structure and function over time.

Plasticity: The brain's tendency to remain somewhat adaptable or flexible.

Portfolio: A collection of the student's work in an area, showing growth, self-reflection, and achievement.

Positive behavior supports (PBS): Interventions designed to replace problem behaviors with new actions that serve the same purpose for the student.

Positive correlation: A relationship between two variables in which the two increase or decrease together. Example: calorie intake and weight gain.

Positive practice: Practicing correct responses immediately after errors.

Positive reinforcement: Strengthening behavior by presenting a desired stimulus after the behavior.

Positron emission tomography (PET): A method of localizing and measuring brain activity using computer-assisted motion pictures of the brain.

Pragmatics: The rules for when and how to use language to be an effective communicator in a particular culture.

Precorrection: A tool for positive behavior support that involves identifying the context for a student's misbehavior, clearly specifying the alternative expected behavior, modifying the situation to make the problem behavior less likely, then rehearsing the expected positive behaviors in the new context and providing powerful reinforcers.

Prejudice: Prejudgment or irrational generalization about an entire category of people.

Premack principle: Principle stating that a more-preferred activity can serve as a reinforcer for a less-preferred activity.

Preoperational: The stage before a child masters logical mental operations.

Presentation punishment: Decreasing the chances that a behavior will occur again by presenting an aversive stimulus following the behavior; also called *Type I punishment*.

Pretest: Formative test for assessing students' knowledge, readiness, and abilities.

Priming: Activating a concept in memory or the spread of activation from one concept to another.

Principle: Established relationship between factors.

Private speech: Children's self-talk, which guides their thinking and action. Eventually, these verbalizations are internalized as silent inner speech.

Problem: Any situation in which you are trying to reach some goal and must find a means to do so.

Problem solving: Creating new solutions for problems.

Problem-based learning: Students are confronted with a problem that launches their inquiry as they collaborate to find solutions and learn valuable information and skills in the process.

Procedural knowledge: Knowledge that is demonstrated when we perform a task; "knowing how."

Procedural memory: Long-term memory for how to do things.

Procedures/routines: Prescribed steps for an activity.

Production deficiency: Students learn problem-solving strategies, but do not apply them when they could or should.

Productions: The contents of procedural memory; rules about what actions to take, given certain conditions. Units of knowledge that combine conditions with actions in "if this happens, do that" relationships that often are automatic.

Prompt: A reminder that follows a cue to make sure the person reacts to the cue.

Propositional network: Set of interconnected concepts and relationships in which long-term knowledge is held.

Prototype: A best example or best representative of a category.

Psychomotor domain: Physical ability and coordination objectives.

Psychosocial: Describing the relation of the individual's emotional needs to the social environment.

Puberty: The physiological changes during adolescence that lead to the ability to reproduce.

Punishment: Process that weakens or suppresses behavior.

Pygmalion effect: Exceptional progress by a student as a result of high teacher expectations for that student; named for mythological king, Pygmalion, who made a statue, then caused it to be brought to life.

Qualitative research: Exploratory research that attempts to understand the meaning of events to the participants involved using such methods as case studies, interviews, ethnography, participant observation, and other approaches that focus on a few people in depth.

Quantitative research: Research that studies many participants in a more formal and controlled way using objective measures such as experimentation, statistical analyses, tests, and structured observations.

Quasi-experimental studies: Studies that fit most of the criteria for true experiments, with the important exception that the participants are not assigned to groups at random. Instead, existing groups such as classes or schools participate in the experiments.

Race: A socially constructed category based on appearances and ancestry.

Racial and ethnic pride: A positive self-concept about one's racial or ethnic heritage.

Radical constructivism: Knowledge is assumed to be the individual's construction; it cannot be judged right or wrong.

Random: Without any definite pattern; following no rule.

Range: Distance between the highest and the lowest scores in a group.

Ratio schedule: Reinforcement based on the number of responses between reinforcers.

READS: A five-step reading strategy: *Review* headings; *Examine* boldface words; *Ask*, "What do I expect to learn?"; *Do it*—Read; *Summarize* in your own words.

Receptive vocabulary: The words a person can understand in spoken or written words.

Reciprocal questioning: Students work in pairs or triads to ask and answer questions about lesson material.

Reciprocal teaching: Learning to apply the strategies of questioning, summarizing, predicting, and clarifying; designed to help students understand and think deeply about what they read.

Reconstruction: Recreating information by using memories, expectations, logic, and existing knowledge.

Reflective: Thoughtful and inventive. Reflective teachers think back over situations to analyze what they did and why, and to consider how they might improve learning for their students.

Refugees: A special group of immigrants who also relocate voluntarily, but who are fleeing their home country because it is not safe.

Reinforcement: Use of consequences to strengthen behavior.

Reinforcer: Any event that follows a behavior and increases the chances that the behavior will occur again.

Relational aggression: A form of hostile aggression that involves verbal attacks and other actions meant to harm social relationships.

Reliability: Consistency of test results.

Removal punishment: Decreasing the chances that a behavior will occur again by removing a pleasant stimulus following the behavior; also called *Type II punishment*.

Representativeness heuristic: Judging the likelihood of an event based on how well the events match your prototypes—what you think is representative of the category.

Reprimands: Criticisms for misbehavior; rebukes.

Resilience: The ability to adapt successfully in spite of difficult circumstances and threats to development.

Resistance culture: Group values and beliefs about refusing to adopt the behaviors and attitudes of the majority culture.

Respondents: Responses (generally automatic or involuntary) elicited by specific stimuli.

Response: Observable reaction to a stimulus.

Response cost: Punishment by loss of reinforcers.

Response set: Rigidity; the tendency to respond in the most familiar way.

Response to intervention (RTI): A process to make sure students get appropriate research-based instruction and support as soon as possible and that teachers are systematic in documenting the interventions they have tried with these students so they can use this information in planning instruction.

Restructuring: Conceiving of a problem in a new or different way.

Retrieval: Process of searching for and finding information in long-term memory.

Reversibility: A characteristic of Piagetian logical operations—the ability to think through a series of steps, then mentally reverse the steps and return to the starting point; also called reversible thinking.

Reversible thinking: Thinking backward, from the end to the beginning.

Reward: An attractive object or event supplied as a consequence of a behavior.

Ripple effect: "Contagious" spreading of behaviors through imitation.

Rote memorization: Remembering information by repetition without necessarily understanding the meaning of the information.

Rules: Statements specifying expected and forbidden behaviors; dos and don'ts.

Scaffolding: Support for learning and problem solving. The support could be clues, reminders, encouragement, breaking the problem down into steps, providing an example, or anything else that allows the student to grow in independence as a learner. Teachers and students make meaningful connections between what the teacher knows and what the students know and need in order to help the students learn more.

Schema-driven problem solving: Recognizing a problem as a "disguised" version of an old problem for which one already has a solution.

Schemas (singular, *schema*): In cognitive theory, basic structures for organizing information; concepts.

Schemes: In Piagetian theory, mental systems or categories of perception and experience.

Scoring rubrics: Rules that are used to determine the quality of a student's performance.

Script: Schema, or expected plan, for the sequence of steps in a common event such as buying groceries or ordering pizza.

Scripted cooperation: Learning strategy in which two students take turns summarizing material and criticizing the summaries.

Seatwork: Independent classroom work.

Second-wave constructivism: A focus on the social and cultural sources of knowing, as in Vygotsky's theory.

Section 504: A part of civil rights law that prevents discrimination against people with disabilities in programs that receive federal funds, such as public schools.

Self-actualization: Fulfilling one's potential.

Self-concept: Individuals' knowledge and beliefs about themselves—their ideas, feelings, attitudes, and expectations.

Self-efficacy: A person's sense of being able to deal effectively with a particular task. Beliefs about personal competence in a particular situation.

Self-esteem: The value each of us places on our own characteristics, abilities, and behaviors.

Self-fulfilling prophecy: A groundless expectation that is confirmed because it has been expected.

Self-handicapping: Students may engage in behavior that blocks their own success in order to avoid testing their true ability.

Self-instruction: Talking oneself through the steps of a task.

Self-management: Management of your own behavior and acceptance of responsibility for your own actions. Also the use of behavioral learning principles to change your own behavior.

Self-regulated learning: A view of learning as skills and will applied to analyzing learning tasks, setting goals and planning how to do the task, applying skills, and especially making adjustments about how learning is carried out.

Self-regulation: Process of activating and sustaining thoughts, behaviors, and emotions in order to reach goals.

Self-regulatory knowledge: Knowing how to manage your learning, or knowing how and when to use your declarative and procedural knowledge.

Self-reinforcement: Controlling (selecting and administering) your own reinforcers.

Semantic memory: Memory for meaning.

Semilingual: A lack of proficiency in any language; speaking one or more languages inadequately.

Semiotic function: The ability to use symbols—language, pictures, signs, or gestures—to represent actions or objects mentally.

Sensitive periods: Times when a person is especially ready to learn certain things or responsive to certain experiences.

Sensorimotor: Involving the senses and motor activity.

Sensory memory: System that holds sensory information very briefly.

Serial-position effect: The tendency to remember the beginning and the end, but not the middle of a list.

Seriation: Arranging objects in sequential order according to one aspect, such as size, weight, or volume.

Service learning: A teaching strategy that invites students to identify, research, and address real community challenges, using knowledge and skills learned in the classroom.

Sexual identity: A complex combination of beliefs about gender roles and sexual orientation.

Shaping: Reinforcing each small step of progress toward a desired goal or behavior.

Shared regulation: Students working together to regulate each other through reminders, prompts, and other guidance.

Sheltered instruction: Approach to teaching that improves English language skills while teaching content to students who are English language learners by putting the words and concepts of the content into context to make the content more understandable.

Sheltered Instruction Observation Protocol (SIOP®): An observational system to check that each element of sheltered instruction is present for a teacher.

Short-term memory: Component of memory system that holds information for about 20 seconds.

Single-subject experimental studies: Systematic interventions to study effects with one person, often by applying and then withdrawing a treatment.

Situated learning: The idea that skills and knowledge are tied to the situation in which they were learned and that they are difficult to apply in new settings.

Social cognitive theory: Theory that adds concern with cognitive factors such as beliefs, self-perceptions, and expectations to social learning theory.

Social conventions: Agreed-upon rules and ways of doing things in a particular situation.

Social development: Changes over time in the ways we relate to others.

Social goals: A wide variety of needs and motives to be connected to others or part of a group.

Social isolation: Removal of a disruptive student for 5 to 10 minutes.

Social learning theory: Theory that emphasizes learning through observation of others.

Social negotiation: Aspect of learning process that relies on collaboration with others and respect for different perspectives.

Social persuasion: A "pep talk" or specific performance feedback—one source of self-efficacy.

Sociocultural theory: Emphasizes role in development of cooperative dialogues between children and more knowledgeable members of society. Children learn the culture of their community (ways of thinking and behaving) through these interactions.

Sociocultural views of motivation: Perspectives that emphasize participation, identities, and interpersonal relations within communities of practice.

Socioeconomic status (SES): Relative standing in the society based on income, power, background, and prestige.

Sociolinguistics: The study of the formal and informal rules for how, when, about what, to whom, and how long to speak in conversations within cultural groups.

Spasticity: Overly tight or tense muscles, characteristic of some forms of cerebral palsy.

Speech disorder: Inability to produce sounds effectively for speaking.

Spermarche: The first sperm ejaculation for boys.

Spiral curriculum: Bruner's design for teaching that introduces the fundamental structure of all subjects early in the school years, then revisits the subjects in more and more complex forms over time.

Spreading activation: Retrieval of pieces of information based on their relatedness to one another. Remembering one bit of information activates (stimulates) recall of associated information.

Standard deviation: Measure of how widely scores vary from the mean.

Standard error of measurement: Hypothetical estimate of variation in scores if testing were repeated.

Standard scores: Scores based on the standard deviation.

Standardized tests: Tests given, usually nationwide, under uniform conditions and scored according to uniform procedures.

Stanine scores: Whole-number scores from 1 to 9, each representing a wide range of raw scores.

Statistically significant: Not likely to be a chance occurrence.

Stem: The question part of a multiple-choice item.

Stereotype: Schema that organizes knowledge or perceptions about a category.

Stereotype threat: The extra emotional and cognitive burden that your performance in an academic situation might confirm a stereotype that others hold about you.

Stimulus: Event that activates behavior.

Stimulus control: Capacity for the presence or absence of antecedents to cause behaviors.

Story grammar: Typical structure or organization for a category of stories.

Structured controversy: Students work in pairs within their four-person cooperative groups to research a particular controversy.

Structured English immersion (SEI): An environment that teaches English rapidly by maximizing instruction in English and using English at a level appropriate to the abilities of the students in the class who are English language learners.

Successive approximations: Reinforcing small steps to reach a goal; the small component steps that make up a complex behavior.

Summative assessment: Testing that follows instruction and assesses achievement.

Sustaining expectation effect: Student performance is maintained at a certain level because teachers don't recognize improvements.

Synapses: The tiny space between neurons—chemical messages are sent across these gaps.

Synaptic plasticity: See *plasticity*.

Syntax: The order of words in phrases or sentences.

_T_ score: Standard score with a mean of 50 and a standard deviation of 10.

Task analysis: System for breaking down a task hierarchically into basic skills and subskills.

Taxonomy: Classification system.

Teachers' sense of efficacy: A teacher's belief that he or she can reach even the most difficult students and help them learn.

Theory: Integrated statement of principles that attempts to explain a phenomenon and make predictions.

Theory of mind: An understanding that other people are people too, with their own minds, thoughts, feelings, beliefs, desires, and perceptions.

Theory of multiple intelligences (MI): In Gardner's theory of intelligence, a person's eight separate abilities: logical-mathematical, linguistic, musical, spatial, bodily-kinesthetic, interpersonal, intrapersonal, and naturalist.

Theory-based: An explanation for concept formation that suggests our classifications are based on ideas about the world that we create to make sense of things.

Time on task: Time spent actively engaged in the learning task at hand. Also referred to as *engaged time*.

Time out: Technically, the removal of all reinforcement. In practice, isolation of a student from the rest of the class for a brief time.

Token reinforcement system: System in which tokens earned for academic work and positive classroom behavior can be exchanged for some desired reward.

Top-down: Making sense of information by using context and what we already know about the situation; sometimes called *conceptually driven perception*.

Tracking: Assignment to different classes and academic experiences based on achievement.

Transfer: Influence of previously learned material on new material; the productive (not reproductive) uses of cognitive tools and motivations.

Transition programming: Gradual preparation of students with special needs to move from high school into further education or training, employment, or community involvement.

Triarchic reciprocal causality: An explanation of behavior that emphasizes the mutual effects of the individual and the environment on each other.

Triarchic theory of successful intelligence: A three-part description of the mental abilities (thinking processes, coping with new experiences, and adapting to context) that lead to more or less intelligent behavior.

True score: The score the student would get if the measurement were completely accurate and error free.

Unconditioned response (UR): Naturally occurring emotional or physiological response.

Unconditioned stimulus (US): Stimulus that automatically produces an emotional or physiological response.

Understanding by Design (UbD): A system of lesson and unit planning that starts with key objectives for understandings and then moves backwards to design assessments and learning activities.

Universal design: Considering the needs of all users in the design of new tools, learning programs, or Web sites.

Utility value: The contribution of a task to meeting one's goals.

Validity: Degree to which a test measures what it is intended to measure.

Value-added measures: Measures that use statistical analyses to indicate the average test score gain for students, adjusted for their student characteristics such as prior level of achievement.

Variability: Degree of difference or deviation from mean.

Verbalization: Putting your problem-solving plan and its logic into words.

Vicarious experiences: Accomplishments that are modeled by someone else.

Vicarious reinforcement: Increasing the chances that we will repeat a behavior by observing another person being reinforced for that behavior.

Virtual learning environments (VLE): A broad term that describes many ways of learning in virtual or online systems.

Visuospatial sketchpad: Part of working memory. A holding system for visual and spatial information.

Voicing problems: Inappropriate pitch, quality, loudness, or intonation.

Volition: Will power; self-discipline; work styles that protect opportunities to reach goals by applying self-regulated learning.

Warm demanders: Teachers who are especially effective with African American students; they show both high expectations and great caring for their students.

Within-class ability grouping: System of grouping in which students in a class are divided into two or three groups based on ability in an attempt to accommodate student differences.

Withitness: According to Kounin, awareness of everything happening in a classroom.

Work-avoidant learners: Students who don't want to learn or to look smart, but just want to avoid work.

Working memory: The brain system that provides temporary holding and processing of information to accomplish complex cognitive tasks such as language comprehension, learning, and reasoning; the information that you are focusing on at a given moment.

Working-backward strategy: Heuristic in which you start with the goal and move backward to solve the problem.

_z_ score: Standard score indicating the number of standard deviations above or below the mean that a particular score falls.

Zero reject: A basic principle of the Individuals with Disabilities Education Act specifying that no student with a disability, no matter what kind or how severe, can be denied a free public education.

Zone of proximal development (ZPD): In Vygotsky's theory, the phase at which a child can master a task if given appropriate help and support.

References

Aamodt, S., & Wang, S. (2008). *Welcome to your brain: Why you lose your car keys but never forget how to drive and other puzzles of everyday life.* New York, NY: Bloomsbury.

Aber, J. L., Brown, J. L., & Jones, S. M. (2003). Developmental trajectories toward violence in middle childhood: Course, demographic differences, and response to school-based intervention. *Developmental Psychology, 39,* 324–348.

Aboud, F. E., Tredoux, C., Tropp, L. R., Brown, C. S., Niens, U., Noor, N. M., & the Una Global Evaluation Group. (2012). Interventions to reduce prejudice and enhance inclusion and respect for ethnic differences in early childhood: A systematic review. *Developmental Review, 32,* 307–336.

About.com Elementary Education. (2014). *Scaffolding instruction strategies.* Retrieved from http://k6educators.about.com/od/helpfornewteachers/a/scaffoldingtech.htm

Abrams, L. M., & Madaus, G. F. (2003). The lessons of high stakes testing. *Educational Leadership, 61*(32), 31–35.

Abuhamdeh, S., & Csikzentmihalyi, M. (2012). Attentional involvement and intrinsic motivation. *Motivation & Emotion, 36*(3), 257–267.

Ackerman, B. P., Brown, E. D., & Izard, C. E. (2004). The relations between contextual risk, earned income, and the school adjustment of children from economically disadvantaged families. *Developmental Psychology, 40,* 204–216.

Ackerman, P. L., Beier, M. E., & Boyle, M. O. (2005). Working memory and intelligence: The same or different constructs? *Psychological Bulletin, 131,* 30–60.

Adams, G. R., Berzonsky, M. D., & Keating, L. (2006). Psychosocial resources in first-year university students: The role of identity processes and social relationships. *Journal of Youth and Adolescence, 35*(1), 78–88.

Agarwal, P. K., Bain, P. M., & Chamberlain, R. W. (2012). The value of applied research: Retrieval practice improves classroom learning and recommendations from a teacher, a principal, and a scientist. *Educational Psychology Review, 24,* 437–448.

Aho, A. V. (2012). Computation and computational thinking. *Computer Journal, 55,* 832–835.

Ainley, M., Hidi, S., & Berndorf, D. (2002). Interest, learning, and the psychological processes that mediate their relationship. *Journal of Educational Psychology, 94,* 545–561.

Airasian, P. W. (2005). *Classroom assessment: Concepts and applications* (5th ed.). New York, NY: McGraw-Hill.

Alarcon, G. M., & Edwards, J. M. (2013). Ability and motivation: Assessing individual factors that contribute to university retention. *Journal of Educational Psychology, 105,* 129–137.

Albanese, M. A., & Mitchell, S. A. (1993). Problem-based learning: A review of literature on its outcomes and implementation issues. *Academic Medicine, 68,* 52–81.

Alber, S. R., & Heward, W. L. (1997). Recruit it or lose it! Training students to recruit positive teacher attention. *Intervention in School and Clinic, 32,* 275–282.

Alber, S. R., & Heward, W. L. (2000). Teaching students to recruit positive attention: A review and recommendations. *Journal of Behavioral Education, 10,* 177–204.

Alberto, P. A., & Troutman, A. C. (2012). *Applied behavior analysis for teachers* (9th ed.). Boston, MA: Pearson.

Alderman, M. K. (2004). *Motivation for achievement: Possibilities for teaching and learning.* Mahwah, NJ: Erlbaum.

Alexander, P. A. (1992). Domain knowledge: Evolving themes and emerging concerns. *Educational Psychologist, 27,* 33–51.

Alexander, P. A. (1996). The past, present, and future of knowledge research: A reexamination of the role of knowledge in learning and instruction. *Educational Psychologist, 31,* 89–92.

Alexander, P. A. (1997). Mapping the multidimensional nature of domain learning: The interplay of cognitive, motivational, and strategic forces. *Advances in Motivation and Achievement, 10,* 213–250.

Alexander, P. A., Kulikowich, J. M., & Schulze, S. K. (1994). How subject-matter knowledge affects recall and interest. *American Educational Research Journal, 31,* 313–337.

Alexander, P. A., Schallert, D. L., & Reynolds, R. E. (2009). What is learning anyway? A topographical perspective considered. *Educational Psychologist, 44,* 176–192.

Alexander, P. A., & Winne, P. H. (2006). *Handbook of educational psychology* (2nd ed.). Mahwah, NJ: Erlbaum.

Alferink, L. A., & Farmer-Dougan, V. (2010). Brain-(not) based education: Dangers of misunderstanding and misapplication of neuroscience research. *Exceptionality, 18,* 42–52.

Alfieri, L., Brooks, P. J., Aldrich, N. J., & Tenenbaum, H. R. (2011). Does discovery-based instruction enhance learning? *Journal of Educational Psychology, 103,* 1–18.

Allen, J., Gregory, A., Mikami, A., Lun, J., Hamre, B., & Pianta, R. (2013). Observations of effective teacher-student interactions in secondary school classrooms: Predicting student achievement with the Classroom Assessment Scoring System—Secondary. *School Psychology Review, 42,* 76–98.

Alliance for Service Learning in Education Reform. (1993). Standards of quality for school based service learning. *Equity and Excellence in Education, 26*(2), 71–77.

Allington, R. L., & McGill-Frazen, A. (2003). The impact of summer setback on the reading achievement gap. *Phi Delta Kappan, 85*(1), 68–75.

Allington, R. L., & McGill-Frazen, A. (2008). Got books? *Educational Leadership, 65*(7), 20–23.

Alloway, N. (1984). *Teacher expectations.* Paper presented at the meetings of the Australian Association for Research in Education, Perth, Australia.

Alloway, T. P., Banner, G. E., & Smith, P. (2010). Working memory and cognitive styles in adolescents' attainment. *British Journal of Educational Psychology, 80,* 567–581.

Alloway, T. P., Gathercole, S. E., & Pickering, S. J. (2006). Verbal and visuo-spatial short-term and working memory in children: Are they separable? *Child Development, 77,* 1698–1716.

Alloy, L. B., & Seligman, M. E. P. (1979). On the cognitive component of learned helplessness and depression. *The Journal of Learning and Motivation, 13,* 219–276.

Aloe, A. M., & Becker, B. J. (2009). Teacher verbal ability and school outcomes: Where is the evidence? *Educational Researcher, 38,* 612–624.

Alter, A. L., Aaronson, J., Darley, J. M., Rodriguez, C., & Ruble, D. N. (2009). Rising to the threat: Reducing stereotype threat by reframing the threat as a challenge. *Journal of Experimental Social Psychology, 46,* 166–171.

Altermatt, E. R., Pomerantz, E. M., Ruble, D. N., Frey, K. S., & Greulich, F. K. (2002). Predicting changes in children's self-perceptions of academic competence: A naturalistic examination of evaluative discourse among classmates. *Developmental Psychology, 38,* 903–917.

Alvidrez, J., & Weinstein, R. S. (1999). Early teacher perceptions and later student academic achievement. *Journal of Educational Psychology, 91,* 731–746.

Amabile, T. M. (1996). *Creativity in context.* Boulder, CO: Westview Press.

Amabile, T. M. (2001). Beyond talent: John Irving and the passionate craft of creativity. *American Psychologist, 56,* 333–336.

Amato, L. F., Loomis, L. S., & Booth, A. (1995). Parental divorce, marital conflict, and offspring well-being during early adulthood. *Social Forces, 73,* 895–915.

Amato, P. R. (2001). Children of divorce in the 1990s: An update of the Amato and Keith (1991) meta-analysis. *Journal of Family Psychology, 15,* 355–370.

Amato, P. R. (2006). Marital discord, divorce, and children's well-being. In A. Clarke-Stewart & J. Dunn (Eds.), *Families count: Effects on child and adolescent development* (pp. 179–202). New York, NY: Cambridge University Press.

Ambrose, D., & Sternberg, R. (Eds.). (2012). *How dogmatic beliefs harm creativity and higher-level thinking.* New York, NY: Taylor and Francis.

American Association on Intellectual and Developmental Disabilities. (AAIDD). (2010). Definition of intellectual disability. Retrieved from http://www.aamr.org/content_100.cfm?navID_21

American Cancer Society. (2010). Child and teen tobacco use: Understanding the problem. Atlanta, GA: Author. Retrieved from http://www.cancer.org/cancer/cancercauses/tobaccocancer/childandteentobaccouse/child-and-teen-tobacco-use

American Psychiatric Association. (2013a). *Autism spectrum disorders.* Washington, DC: American Psychiatric Publishing fact sheet. Retrieved from http://www.dsm5.0rg/Documents/Autism%20Spectrum%20Disorder%20Fact%20Sheet.pdf

American Psychiatric Association. (2013b). *Diagnostic and statistical manual of mental disorders* (5th ed.) *DSM-V.* Washington, DC: Author.

American Psychological Association. (2004). An overview of the psychological literature on the effects of divorce on children. Retrieved from http://www.apa.org/about/gr/issues/cyf/divorce.aspx

American Psychological Association Zero Tolerance Task Force. (2008). Are Zero Tolerance policies effective in the schools? An evidentiary review and recommendations. *American Psychologist, 63*, 852–862. doi: 10.1037/0003–066X.63.9.852

Ames, C. (1992). Classrooms: Goals, structures, and student motivation. *Journal of Educational Psychology, 84*, 261–271.

Anderman, E. (2011). Educational psychology in the twenty-first century: Challenges for our community. *Educational Psychologist, 46*, 185–196. doi: 10.1080/00461520.2011.587724

Anderman, E. M., & Anderman, L. H. (2014). *Motivating children and adolescents in schools.* Columbus, OH: Pearson.

Anderman, E. M., Cupp, P. K., & Lane, D. (2009). Impulsivity and academic cheating. *Journal of Experimental Education, 78*, 135–150.

Anderman, E. M., & Midgley, C. (2004). Changes in self-reported academic cheating across the transition from middle school to high school. *Contemporary Educational Psychology, 29*, 499–517.

Anderman, E. M., & Patrick, H. (2012). Achievement goal theory, conceptualization of ability/intelligence, and classroom climate. In S. L. Christenson, A. L. Reschly, & C. Wylie (Eds.), *The handbook of research on student engagement.* New York, NY: Springer Science.

Anderson, C. A., Berkowitz, L., Donnerstein, E., Huesmann, L. R., Johnson, J. D., Linz, D., & Wartella, E. (2003). The influence of media violence on youth. *Psychological Science in the Public Interest, 4*, 81–110.

Anderson, C. A., Shibuya, Al, Ihori, N., Swing, E. L., Bushman, B. J., Sakamoto, A., . . . Saleem, M. (2010). Violent video game effects on aggression, empathy, and prosocial behavior in eastern and western countries: A meta-analytic review. *Psychological Bulletin, 136*, 151–173.

Anderson, C. W., Holland, J. D., & Palincsar, A. S. (1997). Canonical and sociocultural approaches to research and reform in science education: The story of Juan and his group. *The Elementary School Journal, 97*, 359–384.

Anderson, J. R. (1993). Problem solving and learning. *American Psychologist, 48*, 35–44.

Anderson, J. R. (1995). *Cognitive psychology and its implications* (4th ed.). New York, NY: Freeman.

Anderson, J. R. (2010). *Cognitive psychology and its implications* (7th ed.). New York, NY: Worth.

Anderson, J. R., Reder, L. M., & Simon, H. A. (1995). *Applications and misapplication of cognitive psychology to mathematics education.* Unpublished manuscript. Retrieved from http://www.psy.cmu.edu/~mm4b/misapplied.html

Anderson, J. R., Reder, L. M., & Simon, H. A. (1996). Situated learning and education. *Educational Researcher, 25*, 5–11.

Anderson, L. W., & Krathwohl, D. R. (Eds.). (2001). *A taxonomy for learning, teaching, and assessing: A revision of Bloom's taxonomy of educational objectives.* New York, NY: Longman.

Anderson, L. W., & Sosniak, L. A. (Eds.). (1994). *Bloom's taxonomy: A forty-year retrospective.* Ninety-third yearbook for the National Society for the Study of Education: Part II. Chicago, IL: University of Chicago Press.

Anderson, P. J., & Graham, S. M. (1994). Issues in second-language phonological acquisition among children and adults. *Topics in Language Disorders, 14*, 84–100.

Anderson, R. C., Nguyen-Jahiel, K., McNurlen, B., Archodidou, A., Kim, S-Y., Reznitskaya, A., et al. (2001). The snowball phenomenon: Spread of ways of talking and ways of thinking across groups of children. *Cognition and Instruction, 19*, 1–46.

Anderson, S. M., Klatzky, R. L., & Murray, J. (1990). Traits and social stereotypes: Efficiency differences in social information processing. *Journal of Personality and Social Psychology, 59*, 192–201.

Angier, N., & Chang, K. (2005, January 24). Gray matter and the sexes: Still a scientific gray area. *The New York Times*, p. A11.

Antonenko, P., Paas, F., Grabner, R., & van Gog, T. (2010). Using electroencephalography to measure cognitive load. *Educational Psychology Review, 22*, 425–438.

Anyon, J. (1980). Social class and the hidden curriculum of work. *Journal of Education, 162*, 67–92.

Anyon, J. (2012). Schools and poverty, *Teachers College Record, 114*, 1–3. ID Number: 16696. Retrieved from www.tcrecord.org

Anzures, G., Kelly, D. J., Pascalis, O., Quinn, P. C., Slater, A. M., Viviés, X. D., & Lee, K. (2013). Own- and other-race face identity recognition in children: The effects of pose and feature composition. *Developmental Psychology*. doi: 10.1037/a0033166

Appel, M., & Kronberger, N. (2012). Stereotypes and the achievement gap: Stereotype threat prior to test taking. *Educational Psychology Review, 24*, 609–635. doi: 10.1007/s10648–012–9200–4

Applebee, A. N., Langer, J. A., Nystrand, M., & Gamoran, A. (2003). Discussion-based approaches to developing understanding: Classroom instruction and student performance in middle and high school English. *American Educational Research Journal, 40*, 685–730. doi:10.3102/00028312040003685

Archer, S. L., & Waterman, A. S. (1990). Varieties of identity diffusions and foreclosures: An exploration of the subcategories of the identity statuses. *Journal of Adolescent Research, 5*, 96–111.

Arends, R. I. (2001). *Learning to teach* (5th ed.). New York, NY: McGraw-Hill.

Arends, R. I. (2004). *Learning to teach* (6th ed.). New York, NY: McGraw-Hill.

Arends, R. I. (2007). *Learning to teach* (7th ed.). New York, NY: McGraw-Hill.

Arends, R. I., & Kilcher, A. (2010). *Teaching for student learning: Becoming an accomplished teacher.* New York, NY: Routledge.

Arens, A. K., Yeung, A. S., Craven, R. G., & Hasselhorn, M. (2011, August 22). The twofold multidimensionality of academic self-concept: Domain specificity and separation between competence and affect components. *Journal of Educational Psychology, 103*, 970–981. doi: 10.1037/a0025047

Armbruster, B. B. (2000). Taking notes from lectures. In R. F. Flippo & D. C. Caverly (Eds.), *Handbook of college reading and study strategy research* (pp. 175–200). Mahwah, NJ: Erlbaum.

Arnett, J. J. (2013). *Adolescence and emerging adulthood: A cultural approach* (5th ed.). Boston, MA: Pearson.

Arnold, M. L. (2000). Stage, sequence, and sequels: Changing conceptions of morality, post-Kohlberg. *Educational Psychology Review, 12*, 365–383.

Aronson, E. (2000). *Nobody left to hate: Teaching compassion after Columbine.* New York, NY: Worth.

Aronson, J. (2002). Stereotype threat: Contending and coping with unnerving expectations. In J. Aronson & D. Cordova (Eds.), *Improving education: Classic and contemporary lessons from psychology* (pp. 279–301). New York, NY: Academic Press.

Aronson, J., Fried, C. B., & Good, C. (2002). Reducing the effects of stereotype threat on African American college students: The role of theories of intelligence. *Journal of Experimental Social Psychology, 33*, 113–125.

Aronson, J., Lustina, M. J., Good, C., Keough, K., Steele, C. M., & Brown, J. (1999). When White men can't do math: Necessary and sufficient factors in stereotype threat. *Journal of Experimental Social Psychology, 35*, 29–46.

Aronson, J., & Steele, C. M. (2005). Stereotypes and the fragility of human competence, motivation, and self-concept. In C. Dweck & E. Elliot (Eds.), *Handbook of competence and motivation.* New York, NY: Guilford.

Ashcraft, M. H., & Radvansky, G. A. (2010). *Cognition* (5th ed.). Upper Saddle River, NJ: Prentice-Hall/Pearson.

Astington, J. W., & Dack, L. A. (2008). Theory of mind. In M. M. Haith & J. B. Benson (Eds.), *Encyclopedia of infant and early childhood development* (Vol. 3, pp. 343–356). San Diego, CA: Academic Press.

Atkinson, R. C., & Shiffrin, R. M. (1968). Human memory: A proposed system and its control processes. In K. Spence & J. Spence (Eds.), *The psychology of learning and motivation* (Vol. 2, pp. 89–195). New York, NY: Academic Press.

Atkinson, R. K., & Renkl, A. (2007). Interactive example-based learning environments: Using interactive elements to encourage effective processing of worked examples. *Educational Psychology Review, 19*, 375–386.

Au, K. H. (1980). Participation structures in a reading lesson with Hawaiian children: Analysis of a culturally appropriate instructional event. *Anthropology and Education Quarterly, 11*, 91–115.

Au, T. K., Knightly, L. M., Jun, S., & Oh, J. S. (2002). Overhearing a language during childhood. *Psychological Science, 13*, 238–243.

Au, T. K., Oh, J. S., Knightly, L. M., Jun, S-A., & Romo, L. F. (2008). Salvaging a child language. *Journal of Memory and Language, 58*, 998–1011.

Aud, S., Hussar, W., Planty, M., Snyder, T., Bianco, K., Fox, M., Frohlich, L., Kemp, J., & Drake, L. (2010). *The condition of education 2010* (NCES 2010–028). National Center for Education Statistics, U.S. Department of Education. Washington, DC: U.S. Government Printing Office.

Avramidis, E., Bayliss, P., & Burden, R. (2000). Student teachers' attitudes toward the inclusion of children with special education needs in the ordinary school. *Teaching and Teacher Education, 16*, 277–293.

Azevedo, R. (2005). Using hypermedia as a metacognitive tool for enhancing student learning? The role of self-regulated learning. *Educational Psychologist, 40*, 199–209.

Azevedo, R., Cromley, J. G., & Seibert, D. (2004). Does adaptive scaffolding facilitate students' ability to regulate their learning with hypermedia? *Contemporary Educational Psychology, 29*, 344–370.

Azevedo, R., Johnson, A., Chauncey, A., & Graesser, A. (2011). Use of hypermedia to assess and convey self-regulated learning. In B. Zimmerman & D. Schunk (Eds.), *Handbook of self-regulation of learning and performance* (pp. 102–121). New York, NY: Routledge.

Azzam, A. M. (2006, April). A generation immersed in media. *Educational Leadership*, 92–93.

Babad, E. Y., Inbar, J., & Rosenthal, R. (1982). Pygmalion, Galatea, and the Golem: Investigations of biased and unbiased teachers. *Journal of Educational Psychology, 74*, 459–474.

Baddeley, A. D. (2001). Is working memory still working? *American Psychologist, 56*, 851–864.

Baddeley, A. D. (2007). *Working memory, thought, and action.* New York, NY: Oxford University Press.

Bagley, E., & Shaffer, D. W. (2009). When people get in the way: Promoting civic thinking through epistemic gameplay. *International Journal of Gaming and Computer-mediated Simulations, 1*, 36–52.

Bailey, U. L., Lorch, E. P., Milich, R., & Charnigo, R. (2009). Developmental changes in attention and comprehension among children with attention deficit hyperactivity disorder. *Child Development, 80*, 1842–1855.

Baillargeon, R. (1999). Young infants' expectations about hidden objects: A reply to three challenges. *Developmental Psychology, 2*, 115–132.

Baker, K. (1998). Structured English immersion breakthrough in teaching limited-English-proficient students. *Phi Delta Kappan, 80*(3), 199–204. Retrieved from http://pdkintl.org/kappan/kbak9811.htm

Balass, M., Nelson, J. R., & Perfetti, C. A. (2010). Word learning: An ERP investigation of word experience effects on recognition and word processing. *Contemporary Educational Psychology, 35*, 126–140.

Baldwin, J. M. (1895). *Mental development in the child and the race: Methods and processes*. New York, NY: Macmillan.

Ball, D. L., Thames, M. H., & Phelps, G. (2008). Content knowledge for teaching: What makes it special. *Journal of Teacher Education, 59*, 389–497.

Bandura, A. (1965). Influence of models' reinforcement contingencies on the acquisition of imitative responses. *Journal of Personality and Social Psychology, 1*, 589–595.

Bandura, A. (1977). *Social learning theory*. Englewood Cliffs, NJ: Prentice-Hall.

Bandura, A. (1982). Self-efficacy mechanisms in human agency. *American Psychologist, 37*, 122–147.

Bandura, A. (1986). *Social foundations of thought and action*. Englewood Cliffs, NJ: Prentice-Hall.

Bandura, A. (1993). Perceived self-efficacy in cognitive development and functioning. *Educational Psychologist, 28*, 117–148.

Bandura, A. (1994). Self-efficacy. In V. S. Ramachaudran (Ed.), *Encyclopedia of human behavior* (Vol. 4, pp. 71–81). New York, NY: Academic Press.

Bandura, A. (1997). *Self-efficacy: The exercise of control*. New York, NY: Freeman.

Bandura, A. (2001). Social cognitive theory: An agentic perspective. *Annual Review of Psychology* (Vol. 52, pp. 1–26). Palo Alto, CA: Annual Reviews, Inc.

Bandura, A. (2006). Adolescent development from an agentic perspective. In F. Pajares & T. Urdan (Eds.), *Self-efficacy beliefs of adolescents* (pp. 1–43). Greenwich, CT: Information Age.

Bandura, A. (2007). Albert Bandura. In L. Gardner & W. M. Runyan (Eds.), *A history of psychology in autobiography* (Vol. IX, pp. 43–75). Washington, DC: American Psychological Association.

Bandura, A., & Locke, E. (2003). Negative self-efficacy and goal effects revisited. *Journal of Applied Psychology, 88*, 87–99.

Bandura, A., Ross, D., & Ross, S. A. (1963). Vicarious reinforcement and imitative learning. *Journal of Abnormal and Social Psychology, 67*, 601–607.

Banks, J. A. (1997). *Teaching strategies for ethnic studies* (6th ed.). Boston, MA: Allyn & Bacon.

Banks, J. A. (2002). *An introduction to multicultural education* (3rd ed.). Boston, MA: Allyn & Bacon.

Banks, J. A. (2006). *Cultural diversity and education: Foundations, curriculum, and teaching* (5th ed.). Boston, MA: Allyn & Bacon.

Banks, J. A. (2014). *An introduction to multicultural education* (5th ed.). Boston, MA: Pearson.

Banks, S. R. (2012). *Classroom assessment: Issues and practice* (2nd ed.). Boston, MA: Pearson.

Barden, L. M. (1995). Effective questioning and the ever-elusive higher-order question. *American Biology Teacher, 57*, 423–426.

Barkley, R. A. (Ed.). (2006). *Attention-deficit/hyperactivity disorder: A handbook for diagnosis and treatment* (3rd ed., pp. 547–588). New York, NY: Guilford.

Barnard-Brak, L. (2008). Academic red-shirting among children with learning disabilities. *Learning Disabilities: A Contemporary Journal, 6*, 43–54.

Barnett, M. S., & Ceci, S. J. (2002). When and where do we apply what we learn? A taxonomy for far transfer. *Psychological Bulletin, 128*, 612–637.

Barnhill, G. P. (2005). Functional behavioral assessment in schools. *Intervention in School and Clinic, 40*, 131–143.

Baron, R. A. (1998). *Psychology* (4th ed.). Boston, MA: Allyn & Bacon.

Baron, R. A., & Byrne, D. (2003). *Social psychology* (10th ed.). Boston, MA: Allyn & Bacon.

Baroody, A. J., Eiland, M. D., Purpura, D. J., & Reid, E. E. (2013). Can computer-assisted discovery learning foster first graders' fluency with the most basic addition combinations? *American Educational Research Journal, 50*, 533–573. doi: 10.3102/0002831212473349

Barros, E., Silver, J., & Stein, R. E. K. (2009). School recess and group classroom behavior. *Pediatrics, 123*, 431–436.

Bartholomew, B. (2008). Sustaining the fire. *Educational Leadership, 65*(6), 55–60.

Bartlett, F. C. (1932). *Remembering: A study in experimental and social psychology*. New York, NY: Macmillan.

Bartlett, S. M., Rapp, J. T., Krueger, T. K., & Henrickson, M. L. (2011). The use of response cost to treat spitting by a child with autism. *Behavioral Interventions, 26*, 76–83.

Basow, S. A., & Rubin, L. R. (1999). Gender influences on adolescent development. In N. G. Johnson, M. C. Roberts & J. Worell (Eds.), *Beyond appearance: A new look at adolescent girls* (pp. 25–52). Washington, DC: American Psychological Association.

Bateman, B. D. (2006). *Better IEPs* (4th ed., p. 127). Verona, WI: Attainment Company.

Battelle for Kids. (2011). Retrieved from http://www.battelleforkids.org/how-we-help/strategic-measures/student-growth-measures

Battistich, V., Solomon, D., & Delucci, K. (1993). Interaction processes and student outcomes in cooperative groups. *Elementary School Journal, 94*, 19–32.

Bauer, P. J. (2006). Event memory. In D. Kuhn & R. S. Siegler (Eds.), *Cognition, perception, and language* (6th ed., Vol. 2, pp. 373–425). New York, NY: Wiley.

Baumeister, R. F., Campbell, J. D., Krueger, J. L., & Vohs, K. D. (2003). Does high self-esteem cause better performance, interpersonal success, happiness, or healthier lifestyles? *Psychological Science in the Public Interest, 4*, 1–44.

Baumeister, R. F., & Leary, M. R. (1995). The need to belong: Desire for interpersonal attachments as a fundamental human motivation. *Psychological Bulletin, 117*, 497–529.

Baumert, J., Kunter, M., Blum, W., Brunner, M., Voss, T., Jordan, A., Klusmann, U., Krauss, S., Neubrand, M., & Tsai, Y.-M. (2010). Teachers' mathematical knowledge, cognitive activation in the classroom, and student progress. *American Educational Research Journal, 47*(1), 133–180.

Baumrind, D. (1991). Effective parenting during early adolescent transitions. In P. A. Cowan & M. Hetherington (Eds.), *Family transitions* (pp. 111–165). Mahwah, NJ: Erlbaum.

Baumrind, D. (1996). The discipline controversy revisited. *Family Relations, 45*, 405–414.

Baumrind, D. (2005). Patterns of parental authority and adolescent authority. *New Directions for Child and Adolescent Development, 108*, 61–69. doi:10.1002/cd.128

Bayliss, D. M., Jarrold, C., Baddeley, A. D., Gunn, D., & Leigh, E. (2005). Mapping the developmental

constraints on working memory span performance. *Developmental Psychology, 41*, 579–597.

Beane, J. A. (1991). Sorting out the self-esteem controversy. *Educational Leadership, 49*(1), 25–30.

Bear, G. G. (2005). *Developing self-discipline and preventing and correcting misbehavior* (with Cavalier, A. R., & Manning, M. A.). Boston, MA: Allyn & Bacon.

Beauchamp, C., & Beauchamp, M. H. (2013). Boundary as bridge: An analysis of the educational neuroscience literature from a boundary perspective. *Educational Psychology Review, 25*, 47–67.

Becker, M., Lüdtke, O., Trautwein, U., Köller, O., & Baumert, J. (2012). The differential effects of school tracking on psychometric intelligence: Do academic-track schools make students smarter?. *Journal of Educational Psychology, 104*, 682–699.

Beebe-Frankenberger, M., Bocian, K. L., MacMillan, D. L., & Gresham, F. M. (2004). Sorting second grade students with academic deficiencies: Characteristics differentiating those retained in grade from those promoted to third grade. *Journal of Educational Psychology, 96*, 204–215.

Beghetto, R. A. (2008). Prospective teachers' beliefs about imaginative thinking in K–12 schooling. *Thinking Skills and Creativity, 3*, 134–142.

Begley, S. (2007, October). The case for chutes and ladders. *Newsweek*. Retrieved from http://www.newsweek.com/2007/10/13/the-case-for-chutes-and-ladders.html

Beike, S. M., & Zentall, S. S. (2012). "The snake raised its head": Content novelty alters the reading performance of students at risk for reading disabilities and ADHD. *Journal of Educational Psychology, 104*, 529–540. doi: 10.1037/a0027216

Belland, B. R. (2011). Distributed cognition as a lens to understand the effects of scaffolds: The role of transfer of responsibility. *Educational Psychology Review, 23*, 577–600.

Benita, M., Roth, G., & Deci, E. L. (2014). When are mastery goals more adaptive? It depends on experiences of autonomy support and autonomy. *Journal of Educational Psychology, 106*, 258–267.

Bennett, C. I. (2011). *Comprehensive multicultural education: Theory and practice* (7th ed.). Boston, MA: Allyn & Bacon.

Bereiter, C. (1995). A dispositional view of transfer. In A. McKeough, J. Lupart, & A. Marini (Eds.), *Teaching for mastery: Fostering generalization in learning* (pp. 21–34). Mahwah, NJ: Erlbaum.

Bereiter, C. (1997). Situated cognition and how I overcome it. In D. Kirshner & J. A. Whitson (Eds.), *Situated cognition: Social, semiotic, and psychological perspectives* (pp. 281–300). Mahwah, NJ: Erlbaum.

Berg, C. A., & Clough, M. (1991). Hunter lesson design: The wrong one for science teaching. *Educational Leadership, 48*(4), 73–78.

Berger, K. S. (2006). *The developing person through childhood and adolescence* (7th ed.). New York, NY: Worth.

Berger, K. S. (2012). *The developing person through the life span* (8th ed.). New York, NY: Worth.

Bergin, D. (1999). Influences on classroom interest. *Educational Psychologist, 34*, 87–98.

Berk, L. E. (2005). *Infants, children, and adolescents* (5th ed.). Boston, MA: Allyn & Bacon.

Berk, L. E., & Garvin, R. A. (1984). Development of private speech among low-income Appalachian children. *Developmental Psychology, 20*, p. 272.

Berk, L. E., & Spuhl, S. T. (1995). Maternal interaction, private speech, and task performance in preschool children. *Early Childhood Research Quarterly, 10*, 145–169.

Berko, J. (1958). The child's learning of English morphology. *Word, 14*, 150–177.

Berliner, D. C. (1983). Developing concepts of classroom environments: Some light on the T in studies of ATI. *Educational Psychologist, 18*, 1–13.

Berliner, D. C. (1987). But do they understand? In V. Richardson-Koehler (Ed.), *Educators' handbook: A research perspective* (pp. 259–293). New York, NY: Longman.

Berliner, D. C. (2002). Educational research: The hardest science of all. *Educational Researcher, 31*(8), 18–20.

Berliner, D. C. (2005). Our impoverished view of educational reform. *The Teachers College Record, 108*, 949–995.

Berliner, D. C. (2006). Educational psychology: Searching for essence throughout a century of influence. In P. A. Alexander & P. H. Winne (Eds.), *Handbook of educational psychology* (2nd ed., pp. 3–27). Mahwah, NJ: Erlbaum.

Berliner, D. C., & Glass, G. V. (2014). *Myths and lies that threaten America's public schools: The real crisis in education*. New York: Teachers College Press.

Berlyne, D. (1966). Curiosity and exploration. *Science, 153*, 25–33.

Berndt, T. J., & Keefe, K. (1995). Friends' influence on adolescents' adjustment to school. *Child Development, 66*, 1312–1329.

Bernstein, D. A., & Nash, P. W. (2008). *Essentials of psychology* (4th ed.). Boston, MA: Houghton-Mifflin.

Berry, R. Q., III. (2005). Voices of success: Descriptive portraits of two successful African American male middle school mathematics students. *Journal of African American Studies, 8*(4), 46–62.

Berthold, K., & Renkl, A. (2009). Instructional aids to support a conceptual understanding of multiple representations. *Journal of Educational Psychology, 101*, 70–87.

Best, J. R., & Miller, P. H. (2010). A developmental perspective on executive functioning. *Child Development, 81*, 1641–1660.

Bialystok, E. (2001). *Bilingualism in development: Language, literacy, and cognition*. New York, NY: Cambridge University Press.

Bialystok, E., Majumder, S., & Martin, M. M. (2003). Developing phonological awareness: Is there a bilingual advantage? *Applied Linguistics, 24*, 27–44.

Biggs, J. (2001). Enhancing learning: A matter of style of approach. In R. Sternberg & L. Zhang (Eds.), *Perspectives on cognitive, learning, and thinking styles* (pp. 73–102). Mahwah, NJ: Erlbaum.

Bishaw, A. (2013). *Poverty: 2000–2012: American community survey briefs*. Washington, DC: U.S. Census Bureau. Retrieved from http://www.census.gov/prod/2013pubs/acsbr12-01/pdf

Blachman, B. A., Schatschneider, C., Fletcher, J. M., Murray, M. S., Munger, K. A., & Vaughn, M. G. (2014). Intensive reading remediation in grade 2 or 3: Are there effects a decade later? *Journal of Educational Psychology, 106*, 46–57. doi: 10.1037/a0033663

Blair, C. (2002). School readiness: Integrating cognition and emotion in a neurobiological conceptualization of children's functioning at school entry. *American Psychologist, 57*, 111–127.

Blair, C. (2006). How similar are fluid cognition and general intelligence? A developmental neuroscience perspective on fluid cognition as an aspect of human cognition. Main article with commentaries. *Behavioral and Brain Sciences, 29*, 109–160.

Blakemore, S. K., & Frith, U. (2005). The learning brain: Lessons for education: A precis. *Developmental Science, 8*, 459–461.

Blatchford, P., Baines, E., Rubie-Davis, C., Bassett, P., & Chowne, A. (2006). The effect of a new approach to group work on pupil–pupil and teacher–interactions. *Journal of Educational Psychology, 98*, 750–765.

Bloom, B. S. (1981). *All our children learning: A primer for parents, teachers, and other educators*. New York, NY: McGraw-Hill.

Bloom, B. S. (1982). The role of gifts and markers in the development of talent. *Exceptional Children, 48*, 510–522.

Bloom, B. S., Engelhart, M. D., Frost, E. J., Hill, W. H., & Krathwohl, D. R. (1956). *Taxonomy of educational objectives. Handbook I: Cognitive domain*. New York, NY: David McKay.

Bloom, B. S., Madaus, G. F., & Hastings, J. T. (1981). *Evaluation to improve learning*. New York, NY: McGraw-Hill.

Bloom, B. S., Sosniak, L. A., Sloane, K. D., Kalinowski, A. G., Gustin, W. C., & Monsaas, J. A. (1985). *Developing talent in young people*. New York, NY: Ballantine Books.

Bloom, P. (2002). *How children learn the meanings of words*. Cambridge, MA: MIT Press.

Blumenfeld, P. C., Puro, P., & Mergendoller, J. R. (1992). Translating motivation into thoughtfulness. In H. Marshall (Ed.), *Redefining student learning: Roots of educational change* (pp. 207–240). Norwood, NJ: Ablex.

Bodrova, E., & Leong, D. J. (2012). Tools of the mind: Vygotskian approach to early childhood education. In J. L. Rooparine & J. Jones, *Approaches to early childhood education* (6th ed., pp. 241–260). Columbus, OH: Pearson.

Bohn-Gettler, C. M., & Rapp, D. N. (2011). Depending on my mood: Mood-driven influences on text comprehension. *Journal of Educational Psychology, 103*, 562–577. doi: 10.1037/a0023458

Boivin, M., Brendgen, M., Viraro, F., Dionne, G., Girard, A., Perusse, D., & Tremblay, R. E. (2013). Strong genetic contribution to peer relationship difficulties at school entry: Findings from a longitudinal twin study. *Child Development, 84*, 1098–1114.

Bong, M. (2009). Age-related differences in achievement goal differentiation. *Journal of Educational Psychology, 101*, 879–896.

Borich, G. D. (2011). *Effective teaching methods: Research-based practice* (7th ed.). Columbus, OH: Pearson.

Borko, H., & Putnam, R. (1996). Learning to teach. In D. Berliner & R. Calfee (Eds.), *Handbook of educational psychology* (pp. 673–708). New York, NY: Macmillan.

Borman, G. D., & Overman, L. T. (2004). Academic resilience in mathematics among poor and minority students. *The Elementary School Journal, 104*, 177–195.

Bornstein, M. H., Hahn, C-S, & Wolke, D. (2013). Systems and cascades in cognitive development and academic achievement. *Child Development, 84*, 154–162.

Borrero, N. E., & Yeh, C. J. (2010). Ecological English language learning among ethnic minority youth. *Educational Researcher, 39*, 571–581.

Borst, G., Poirel, N., Pineau, A., Cassotti, M., & Houdé, O. (2013). Inhibitory control efficiency in a Piaget-like class-inclusion task in school-age children and adults: A developmental negative priming study. *Developmental Psychology, 49*, 1366–1374.

Bos, C. S., & Reyes, E. I. (1996). Conversations with a Latina teacher about education for language-minority students with special needs. *The Elementary School Journal, 96*, 344–351.

Bowlby, J. (1969). *Attachment and loss: Attachment*. New York, NY: Basic Books.

Boyd, D., Goldhaber, D., Lankford, H., & Wyckoff, J., (2008). The effect of certification and preparation on teacher quality. *The Future of Children, 17*(1), 45.

Boyle, J. R. (2010a). Note-taking skills of middle school students with and without learning disabilities. *Journal of Learning Disabilities, 43*, 530–540.

Boyle, J. R. (2010b). Strategic note-taking for middle school students with learning disabilities in science classes. *Learning Disabilities Quarterly, 33*, 93–109.

Boyle, J. R., & Weishaar, M. (2001). The effects of a strategic note-taking technique on the comprehension and long term recall of lecture information for high school students with LD. *Learning Disabilities Research and Practice, 16*, 125–133.

Braddock, J., II, & Slavin, R. E. (1993). Why ability grouping must end: Achieving excellence and equity in American education. *Journal of Intergroup Relations, 20*(2), 51–64.

Bradshaw, C. P., Waasdorp, T. E., & O'Brennan, L. M. (2013). A latent class approach to examining forms of peer victimization. *Journal of Educational Psychology, 105*, 839–849. doi: 10.1037/a0032091

Bradshaw, C. P., Zmuda, J. H., Kellam, S. G., & Ialongo, N. S. (2009). Longitudinal impact of two universal preventive interventions in first grade on educational outcomes in high school. *Journal of Educational Psychology, 101*, 926–937.

Brainerd, C. J. (2003). Jean Piaget, learning research, and American education. In B. J. Zimmerman & D. H. Schunk (Eds.), *Educational psychology: A century of contributions* (pp. 251–287). Mahwah, NJ: Erlbaum.

Brannon, L. (2002). *Gender: Psychological perspectives* (3rd ed.). Boston, MA: Allyn & Bacon.

Bransford, J. D., Brown, A. L., & Cocking, R. R. (2000). *How people learn: Brain, mind, experience, and school*. Washington, DC: National Academy Press.

Bransford, J. D., & Schwartz, D. (1999). Rethinking transfer: A simple proposal with multiple implications. In A. Iran-Nejad & P. D. Pearson (Eds.), *Review of research in education* (Vol. 24, pp. 61–100). Washington, DC: American Educational Research Association.

Brantlinger, E. (2004). Who wins and who loses? Social class and students' identities. In M. Sadowski (Ed.), *Adolescents at school: Perspectives on youth, identity, and education* (pp. 107–126). Cambridge, MA: Harvard University Press.

Branum-Martin, L., Foorman, B. R., Francis, D. J., & Mehta, P. D. (2010). Contextual effects of bilingual programs on beginning reading. *Journal of Educational Psychology, 102*, 341–355.

Bredekamp, S. (2011). *Effective practices in early childhood education: Building a foundation*. Columbus, OH: Merrill.

Bredekamp, S., & Copple, C. (1997). *Developmentally appropriate practice in early childhood programs*. Washington, DC: National Association for the Education of Young Children.

Brice, A. E. (2002). *The Hispanic child: Speech, language, culture and education* (1st ed.). Upper Saddle River, NJ: Pearson Education.

Brice, A. E., & Brice, R. G. (2009). Language development: Monolingual and bilingual acquisitions. Boston, MA: Allyn & Bacon.

Briesch, A. M., & Chafouleas, S. M. (2009). Review and analysis of literature on self-management interventions to promote appropriate classroom behaviors (1988–2008). *School Psychology Quarterly, 24*, 106–118.

Broidy, L. M., Nagin, D. S., Tremblay, R. E., Bates, J. E., Brame, B., Dodge, K., . . . Vitaro, F. (2003). Developmental trajectories of childhood disruptive behaviors and adolescent delinquency: A six site, cross-national study. *Developmental Psychology, 39*, 222–245.

Bronfenbrenner, U. (1989). Ecological systems theory. In R. Vasta (Ed.), *Annals of child development* (Vol. 6, pp. 187–249). Boston, MA: JAI Press.

Bronfenbrenner, U., McClelland, P., Wethington, E., Moen, P., & Ceci, S. (1996). *The state of Americans: This generation and the next.* New York, NY: Free Press.

Bronfenbrenner, U., & Morris, P. A. (2006). The bioecological model of human development. In W. Damon & R. M. Lerner (Eds.), *Handbook of child psychology: Theoretical models of human development* (6th ed., Vol. 1, pp. 793–827). Hoboken, NJ: Wiley.

Brooks-Gunn, J. (1988). Antecedents and consequences of variations in girls' maturational timing. In M. D. Levin & E. R. McAnarney (Eds.), *Early adolescent transitions* (pp. 101–121). Lexington, MA: Lexington Books.

Brophy, J. E. (1981). Teacher praise: A functional analysis. *Review of Educational Research, 51,* 5–21.

Brophy, J. E. (1988). On motivating students. In D. Berliner & B. Rosenshine (Eds.), *Talks to teachers* (pp. 201–245). New York, NY: Random House.

Brophy, J. E. (1998). *Motivating students to learn.* New York, NY: McGraw-Hill.

Brophy, J. E. (2003). An interview with Jere Brophy by B. Gaedke & M. Shaughnessy. *Educational Psychology Review, 15,* 199–211.

Brophy, J. E. (2005). Goal theorists should move on from performance goals. *Educational Psychologist, 40,* 167–176.

Brophy, J. E. (2008). Developing students' appreciation for what is taught in school, *Educational Psychologist, 43,* 132–141.

Brophy, J. E., & Good, T. (1986). Teacher behavior and student achievement. In M. Wittrock (Ed.), *Handbook of research on teaching* (3rd ed.) (pp. 328–375). New York, NY: Macmillan.

Brophy, J. E., & Kher, N. (1986). Teacher socialization as a mechanism for developing student motivation to learn. In R. Feldman (Ed.), *Social psychology applied to education* (pp. 256–288). New York, NY: Cambridge University Press.

Brown, A. (1987). Metacognition, executive control, self-regulation, and other more mysterious mechanisms. In F. Weinert & R. Kluwe (Eds.), *Metacognition, motivation, and understanding* (pp. 65–116). Mahwah, NJ: Erlbaum.

Brown, B. B. (2004). Adolescents' relationships with peers. In R. M. Lerner & L. Steinberg (Eds.), *Handbook of adolescent psychology* (2nd ed., pp. 363–394). Hoboken, NJ: Wiley.

Brown, J. L., Jones, S. M., LaRusso, M. D., & Aber, J. L. (2010). Improving classroom quality: Teacher influences and experimental impacts of the 4Rs Program. *Journal of Educational Psychology, 102,* 153–167.

Bruer, J. T. (1999). In search of . . . brain-based education. *Phi Delta Kappan, 80,* 648–657.

Bruer, J. T. (2002). Avoiding the pediatrician's error: How neuroscientists can help educators (and themselves). *Nature Neuroscience, 5,* 1031–1033.

Bruner, J. S. (1966). *Toward a theory of instruction.* New York, NY: Norton.

Bruner, J. S. (1973). *Beyond the information given: Studies in the psychology of knowing.* New York, NY: Norton.

Bruner, J. (1996). *The culture of education.* London, Harvard University Press.

Bruning, R. H., Schraw, G. J., & Norby, M. M. (2011). *Cognitive psychology and instruction* (5th ed.). Boston, MA: Pearson.

Brunner, M., Keller, U., Dierendinck, C., Reichert, M., Ugen, S., Fischbach, A., & Martin, R. (2010). The structure of academic self-concepts revisited: The nested Marsh/Shavelson model. *Journal of Educational Psychology, 102,* 964–981.

Buckner, J. C. (2012). Education research on homeless and housed children living in poverty:

Comments on Masten, Fantuzzo, Herbers, and Voight. *Educational Researcher, 41,* 403–407. doi: 10.3102/0013189X12466588

Buehler, R., Griffin, D., & Ross, M. (1994). Exploring the "planning fallacy": Why people underestimate their task completion times. *Journal of Personality and Social Psychology, 67,* 366–381.

Buffum, A., Mattos, M., & Weber, C. (2010). The why behind RTI. *Educational Leadership, 68*(2), 10–16.

Buhs, E. S., Ladd, G. W., & Herald, S. L. (2006). Peer exclusion and victimization: Processes that mediate the relation between peer group rejection and children's classroom engagement. *Journal of Educational Psychology, 98,* 1–13.

Bui, D. C., Myerson, J., & Hale, S. (2013). Note-taking with computers: Exploring alternative strategies for improved recall. *Journal of Educational Psychology, 105,* 299–309. doi: 10.1037/a0030367

Burbules, N. C., & Bruce, B. C. (2001). Theory and research on teaching as dialogue. In V. Richardson (Ed.), *Handbook of research on teaching* (4th ed., pp. 1102–1121). Washington, DC: American Educational Research Association.

Burden, P. R. (1995). *Classroom management and discipline: Methods to facilitate cooperation and instruction.* White Plains, NY: Longman.

Burke-Spero, R. (1999). Toward a model of "civitas" through an ethic of care: A qualitative study of preservice teachers' perceptions about learning to teach diverse populations (Doctoral dissertation, The Ohio State University, 1999). *Dissertation Abstracts International, 60,* 11A, 3967.

Burke-Spero, R., & Woolfolk Hoy, A. (2002). *The need for thick description: A qualitative investigation of developing teacher efficacy.* Unpublished manuscript, University of Miami.

Buss, D. M. (1995). Psychological sex differences: Origin through sexual selection. *American Psychologist, 50,* 164–168.

Butcher, K. R. (2006). Learning from text with diagrams: Promoting mental model development and inference generation. *Journal of Educational Psychology, 98,* 182–197.

Butler, R. (1987). Task-involving and ego-involving properties of evaluation: Effects of different feedback conditions on motivational perceptions, interest, and performance. *Journal of Educational Psychology, 79,* 474–482.

Byrne, B. M. (2002). Validating the measurement and structure of self-concept: Snapshots of past, present, and future research. *American Psychologist, 57,* 897–909.

Byrnes, D. A. (1989). Attitudes of students, parents, and educators toward repeating a grade. In L. A. Shepard & M. L. Smith (Eds.), *Flunking grades: Research and policies on retention* (pp. 108–131). Philadelphia, PA: Falmer.

Byrnes, J. P. (1996). *Cognitive development and learning in instructional contexts.* Boston, MA: Allyn & Bacon.

Byrnes, J. P., & Fox, N. A. (1998). The educational relevance of research in cognitive neuroscience. *Educational Psychology Review, 10,* 297–342.

Cairns, R. B., & Cairns, B. D. (2006). The making of developmental psychology. In R. M. Lerner (Ed.), *Handbook of child psychology* (6th ed.), *Vol. 1: Theoretical models of human development* (pp. 89–165). New York, NY: Wiley.

Çakıroğlu, J., Aydın, Y. C, & Woolfolk Hoy, A. (2012). Science teaching efficacy beliefs. In B. Frazer, K. Tobin, & C McRobbie (Eds.), *Second international handbook of science education* (pp. 449–462). New York, NY: Springer.

Calderhead, J. (1996). Teacher: Beliefs and knowledge. In D. Berliner & R. Calfee (Eds.), *Handbook of*

educational psychology (pp. 709–725). New York, NY: Macmillan.

Callaghan, T., Moll, H., Rakoczy, H., Warneken, F., Liszkowski, U., Behne, T., & Tomasello, M. (2011). Early social cognition in three cultural contexts. *Monographs of the Society for Research in Child Development, 76*(2), 1–142.

Callahan, C. M., Tomlinson, C. A., & Plucker, J. (1997). *Project STATR using a multiple intelligences model in identifying and promoting talent in high-risk students.* Storrs, CT: National Research Center for Gifted and Talented. University of Connecticut Technical Report.

Cameron, J., & Pierce, W. D. (1994). Reinforcement, reward, and intrinsic motivation: A meta-analysis. *Review of Educational Research, 64,* 363–423.

Cameron, J., & Pierce, W. D. (1996). The debate about rewards and intrinsic motivation: Protests and accusations do not alter the results. *Review of Educational Research, 66,* 39–52.

Cangelosi, J. S. (1990). *Designing tests for evaluating student achievement.* New York, NY: Longman.

Cano-Garcia, F. J., Padilla-Munoz, E. M., & Carrasco-Ortiz, M. A. (2005). Personality and contextual variables in teacher burnout. *Personality and Individual Differences, 38,* 929–940.

Canter, L. (1996). First the rapport—then the rules. *Learning, 24*(5), 121.

Canter, L., & Canter, M. (1992). *Lee Canter's Assertive Discipline: Positive behavior management for today's classroom.* Santa Monica, CA: Lee Canter and Associates.

Cantrell, S. C., Almasi, J. F., Carter, J. S., Rintamaa, M., & Madden, A. (2010). The impact of a strategy-based intervention on the comprehension and strategy use of struggling adolescent readers. *Journal of Educational Psychology, 102,* 257–280.

Capa, Y. (2005). *Novice teachers' sense of efficacy.* (Unpublished doctoral dissertation). The Ohio State University, Columbus, OH.

Capon, N., & Kuhn, D. (2004). What's so good about problem-based learning? *Cognition and Instruction, 22,* 61–79.

Caprara, G. V., Fida, R., Vecchione, M., Del Bove, G., Vecchio, G. M., Barbaranelli, C., & Bandura, A. (2008). Longitudinal analysis of the role of perceived self-efficacy for self-regulated learning in academic continuance and achievement. *Journal of Educational Psychology, 100,* 525–534.

Caprara, G., Pastorelli, C., Regalia, C., Scabini, E., & Bandura, A. (2005). Impact of adolescents' filial self-efficacy on quality of family functioning and satisfaction. *Journal of Research on Adolescence, 15,* 71–97. doi:10.1111/j.1532–7795 2005 00087

Carbonneau, K. J., Marley, S. C., & Selig, J. P. (2012). A meta-analysis of the efficacy of teaching mathematics with concrete manipulatives. *Journal of Educational Psychology, 105,* 380–400.

Cariglia-Bull, T., & Pressley, M. (1990). Short-term memory differences between children predict imagery effects when sentences are read. *Journal of Experimental Child Psychology, 49,* 384–398.

Carnegie Council on Adolescent Development. (1995). *Great transitions: Preparing adolescents for a new century.* New York, NY: Carnegie Corporation of New York.

Carney, R. N., & Levin, J. R. (2000). Mnemonic instruction, with a focus on transfer. *Journal of Educational Psychology, 92,* 783–790.

Carney, R. N., & Levin, J. R. (2002). Pictorial illustrations *still* improve students' learning from text. *Educational Psychology Review, 14,* 5–26.

Carpenter, S. (2000). In the digital age experts pause to examine the effects on kids. *Monitor on Psychology, 31*(11), 48–49.

Carpenter, S., Cepeda, N. J., Rohrer, D., Kang, S. H. K., & Pashler, H. (2012). Using spacing to enhance diverse forms of learning: Review of recent research and implications for instruction. *Educational Psychology Review, 24*, 369–378.

Carroll, J. B. (1997). The three-stratum theory of cognitive abilities. In D. P. Flanagan, J. L. Genshaft, & P. L. Harrison (Eds.), *Contemporary intellectual assessment: Theories, tests, and issues* (pp. 122–130). New York, NY: Guilford.

Carter, E. W., Wehby, J., Hughes, C., Johnson, S. M., Plank, D. R., Barton-Arwood, S. M., & Lunsford, L. B. (2005). Preparing adolescents with high-incidence disabilities for high-stakes testing with strategy instruction. *Preventing School Failure, 49*(2), 55–62.

Case, R. (1985). A developmentally-based approach to the problem of instructional design. In R. Glaser, S. Chipman, & J. Segal (Eds.), *Teaching thinking skills* (Vol. 2, pp. 545–562). Mahwah, NJ: Erlbaum.

Case, R. (1992). *The mind's staircase: Exploring the conceptual underpinnings of children's thought and knowledge.* Mahwah, NJ: Erlbaum.

Case, R. (1998). The development of conceptual structures. In D. Kuhn & R. S. Siegler (Eds.), *Handbook of child psychology: Vol. 2. Cognition, perception, and language* (pp. 745–800). New York, NY: Wiley.

Casey, B. J., Getz, S., & Galvan, A. (2008). The adolescent brain. *Developmental Review, 28,* 62–77.

Casilli, A. A., Pailler, F., & Tubaro, P. (2013). Online networks of eating-disorder websites: Why censoring pro-ana might be a bad idea. *Perspectives in Public Health, 133,* 94–95.

Casilli, A. A., Tubaro, P., & Araya, P. (2012). Ten years of Ana. Lessons from a transdisciplinary body of literature on online pro-eating disorder websites. *Social Science Information, 51,* 121–139.

Cassady, J. C. (2004). The influence of cognitive test anxiety across the learning-testing cycle. *Learning and Instruction, 14*(6), 569–592.

Cassady, J. C. (2010). *Anxiety in schools: The causes, consequences, and solutions for academic anxieties.* New York: Peter Lang.

Cassady, J. C., & Boseck, J. J. (2008). Educational psychology and emotional intelligence: Toward a functional model for emotional information processing. In J. C. Cassady & M. A. Eissa (Eds.), *Emotional intelligence: Perspectives on educational and positive psychology* (pp. 3–24). New York, NY: Peter Lang.

Cassady, J. C., & Johnson, R. E. (2002). Cognitive anxiety and academic performance. *Contemporary Educational Psychology, 27,* 270–295.

Castel, A. D., Humphreys, K. L., Balota, D. A., Lee, S. S., Galvan, A., & McCabe, D. P. (2011). The development of memory efficiency and value directed remembering across the life span: A cross-sectional study of memory and selectivity. *Developmental Psychology, 47,* 1553–1564.

Castellano, J. A., & Diaz, E. I. (Eds.). (2002). *Reaching new horizons. Gifted and talented education for culturally and linguistically diverse students.* Boston, MA: Allyn & Bacon.

Castle, S., Deniz, C. B., & Tortora, M. (2005). Flexible grouping and student learning in a high-needs school. *Education and Urban Society, 37,* 139–150.

Cattell, R. B. (1963). Theory of fluid and crystallized intelligence: A critical experiment. *Journal of Educational Psychology, 54,* 1–22.

Caughy, M. O., O'Campo, P. J., Randolph, S. M., & Nickerson, K. (2002). The influence of racial socialization practices on the cognitive and behavioral competence of African American preschoolers. *Child Development, 73,* 1611–1625.

Cazden, C. (2001). *Classroom discourse: The language of teaching and learning* (2nd ed.). Portsmouth, NH: Heinemann.

Centers for Disease Control. (2009). *Defining childhood overweight and obesity.* Retrieved from http://www.cdc.gov/obesity/childhood/defining .html

Centers for Disease Control. (2011). *Attention deficit hyperactivity disorder (ADHD).* Retrieved from http://www.cdc.gov/nchs/fastats/adhd.htm

Centers for Disease Control. (2013). *Autism spectrum disorders (ASDs).* Retrieved from http://www.cdc .gov/ncbddd/autism/data.html

Chan, C. K., & Sachs, J. (2001). Beliefs about learning in children's understanding of science texts. *Contemporary Educational Psychology, 26,* 192–210.

Chan, D. W. (1998). Stress, coping strategies, and psychological distress among secondary school teachers in Hong Kong. *American Educational Research Journal, 35,* 145–163.

Chance, P. (1991). Backtalk: A gross injustice. *Phi Delta Kappan, 72,* 803.

Chance, P. (1992). The rewards of learning. *Phi Delta Kappan, 73,* 200–207.

Chance, P. (1993). Sticking up for rewards. *Phi Delta Kappan, 74,* 787–790.

Chang, K. (2013). Expecting the best yields results in Massachusetts. *New York Times Education Issue,* September 2, 2013. Retrieved from http://www.nytimes.com/2013/09/03/science/ expecting-the-best-yields-results-in-massachusetts. html?pagewanted=all

Chang, L., Mak, M. C. K., Li, T., Wu, B. P., Chen, B. B., & Lu, H. J. (2011). Cultural adaptations to environmental variability: An evolutionary account of East–West differences. *Educational Psychology Review, 23,* 99–129.

Chang, M.-L. (2009). An appraisal perspective of teacher burnout: Examining the emotional work of teachers, *Educational Psychology Review, 21,* 193–218.

Chao, R. (2001). Extending research on the consequences of parenting style for Chinese Americans and European Americans. *Child Development, 72,* 1832–1843.

Chao, R., & Tseng, V. (2002). Parenting of Asians. In M. H. Bornstein (Ed.), *Handbook of parenting: Social conditions and applied parenting* (2nd ed., Vol. 4, pp. 59–93). Mahwah, NJ: Erlbaum.

Chapman, J. W., Tunmer, W. E., & Prochnow, J. E. (2000). Early reading-related skills and performance, reading self-concept, and the development of academic self-concept: A longitudinal study. *Journal of Educational Psychology, 92,* 703–708.

Chapman, R. I., Buckley, L., Sheehan, M., & Shochet, I. (2013). School-based programs for increasing connectedness and reducing risk behavior: A systematic review. *Educational Psychology Review, 25,* 95–114.

Charles, C. M. (2011). *Building classroom discipline* (10th ed.). Boston, MA: Allyn & Bacon.

Charmaraman, L., & Grossman, J. M. (2010). Importance of race and ethnicity: An exploration of Asian, Black, Latino, and multiracial adolescent identity. *Cultural Diversity and Ethnic Minority Psychology, 16,* 144–151.

Cheeseman Day, J., & Newburger, E. C. (2002). The big payoff: Educational attainment and synthetic estimates of work-life earnings. Washington DC: U.S. Census Bureau. Retrieved from http:// usgovinfo.about.com/od/moneymatters/a/ edandearnings.htm

Chen, J. A., & Pajares, F. (2010). Implicit theories of ability of Grade 6 science students: Relation to epistemological beliefs and academic motivation and achievement in science. *Contemporary Educational Psychology, 35,* 75–87.

Chen, J.-Q. (2004). Theory of multiple intelligences: Is it a scientific theory? *Teachers College Record, 106,* 17–23.

Chen, L. H., Wu, C.-H., Kee, Y. H., Lin, M.-S., & Shui, S.-H. (2009). Fear of failure, 2 × 2 achievement goal and self-handicapping: An examination of the hierarchical model of achievement motivation in physical education. *Contemporary Educational Psychology, 34,* 298–305.

Chen, Z., & Mo, L. (2004). Schema induction in problem solving: A multidimensional analysis. *Journal of Experimental Psychology: Learning, Memory, and Cognition, 30,* 583–600.

Chen, Z., Mo, L., & Honomichl, R. (2004). Having the memory of an elephant: Long-term retrieval and the use of analogues in problem solving. *Journal of Experimental Psychology: General, 133,* 415–433.

Chetty, R., Friedman, J. N., & Rockoff, J. (2011). *The long-term impacts of teachers: Teacher value-added and student outcomes in adulthood* (NBER Working Paper No. 17699). Cambridge, MA: National Bureau of Economic Research.

Cheung, A. C. K., & Slavin, R. E. (2012). Effective reading programs for Spanish—dominant English language learners (ELLs) in the elementary grades: A synthesis of research. *Review of Educational Research, 82,* 351–395.

Chi, M. T. H. (1978). Knowledge structures and memory development. In R. Siegler (Ed.), *Children's thinking: What develops?* (pp. 73–96). Mahwah, NJ: Erlbaum.

Chi, M. T. H., & VanLehn, K. A. (2012). Seeing deep structure from the interactions of surface features. *Educational Psychologist, 47,* 177–188.

Child Trends. (2013). *What do we know about the high school class of 2013?* Retrieved from http:// www.childtrends.org/news/news-releases/ whatdo-we-know-about-the-high-school-class-of- 2013/#sthash.3dH00FCZ.dpuf

Children's Defense Fund. (2005a). *Child poverty.* Washington, DC: Author.

Children's Defense Fund. (2005b, January). *The minimum wage will not support a family of four.* Washington, DC: Author.

Children's Defense Fund. (2010). *The state of America's children: 2010.* Washington, DC: Author. Retrieved from http://www.childrensdefense.org/child-research-data-publications/data/state-of-americas-children-2010-report.html

Children's Defense Fund. (2012). *The state of America's children: Handbook 2012.* Washington, DC: Author.

Children's Defense Fund. (2013a). *Each day in America.* Washington, DC: Author. Retrieved from http:// www.childrensdefense.org/child-research-data-publications/each-day-in-america.html

Children's Defense Fund. (2013b). *Moments in America for children.* Washington, DC: Author. Retrieved from http://www.childrensdefense.org/child-research-data-publications/moments-in-america-for-children.html

Chorzempa, B. F., & Graham, S. (2006). Primary-grade teachers' use of within-class ability grouping in reading. *Journal of Educational Psychology, 98,* 529–541.

Clark, C. M., & Peterson, P. L. (1986). Teachers' thought processes. In M. Wittrock (Ed.), *Handbook of research on teaching* (3rd ed., pp. 255–296). New York, NY: Macmillan.

Clark, D. B., Martin, C. S., & Cornelius, J. R. (2008). Adolescent-onset substance use disorders predict young adult mortality. *Journal of Adolescent Health, 42,* 637–639.

Clark, I. (2012). Formative assessment: Assessment is for self-regulated learning. *Educational Psychology Review, 24,* 205–249.

Clark, J. M., & Paivio, A. (1991). Dual coding theory and education. *Educational Psychology Review, 3,* 149–210.

Clark, K. (2009). The case for Structured English Immersion. *Educational Leadership, 66*(7), 42–46.

Clarke, J. H., & Agne, R. M. (1997). *Curriculum development; Interdisciplinary high school teaching.* Boston, MA: Allyn & Bacon.

Clifford, M. M. (1990). Students need challenge, not easy success. *Educational Leadership, 48*(1), 22–26.

Clifford, M. M. (1991). Risk taking: Empirical and educational considerations. *Educational Psychologist, 26,* 263–298.

Cobb, P., & Bowers, J. (1999). Cognitive and situated learning: Perspectives in theory and practice. *Educational Researcher, 28*(2), 4–15.

Cobley, S., McKenna, J., Baker, J., & Wattie, N. (2009). How pervasive are relative age effects in secondary school education? *Journal of Educational Psychology, 101,* 520–528.

Codell, E. R. (2001). *Educating Esme: Diary of a teacher's first year.* Chapel Hill, NC: Algonquin Books.

Coffield, F. J., Moseley, D. V., Hall, E., & Ecclestone, K. (2004). *Learning styles and pedagogy in post–16 learning: A systematic and critical review.* London, England: Learning and Skills Research Centre/University of Newcastle upon Tyne.

Cognition and Technology Group at Vanderbilt. (1996). Looking at technology in context: A framework for understanding technology and educational research. In D. Berliner & R. Calfee (Eds.), *Handbook of educational psychology* (pp. 807–840). New York, NY: Macmillan.

Cohen, A. B. (2009). Many forms of culture. *American Psychologist, 64,* 194–204.

Cohen, A. B. (2010). Just how many different forms of culture are there? *American Psychologist, 65,* 59–61.

Cohen, E. G. (1986). *Designing group work: Strategies for the heterogeneous classroom.* New York, NY: Teachers College Press.

Cohen, E. G. (1994). *Designing group work* (2nd ed.). New York, NY: Teachers College Press.

Cohen, M. R., & Graham, J. D. (2003). A revised economic analysis of restrictions on the use of cell phones while driving. *Risk Analysis, 23,* 5–17.

Coie, J. D., & Dodge, K. A. (1998). Aggression and antisocial behavior. In N. Eisenberg (Ed.), *Handbook of child psychology: Vol. 3. Social, emotional, and personality development* (5th ed., pp. 779–862). New York, NY: Wiley.

Cokley, K. O. (2002). Ethnicity, gender, and academic self-concept: A preliminary examination of academic disidentification and implications for psychologists. *Cultural Diversity and Ethnic Minority Psychology, 8,* 378–388.

Colangelo, N., Assouline, S. G., & Gross, M. U. M. (2004). *A nation deceived: How schools hold back America's brightest children: Vols. 1 & 2.* The Connie Belin & Jacqueline N. Blank International Center for Gifted Education and Talent Development, College of Education, The University of Iowa, Ames, IA. Retrieved from http://www.accelerationinstitute.org/Nation_Deceived/Get_Report.aspx

Cole, G. A., Montgomery, R. W., Wilson, K. M., & Milan, M. A. (2000). Parametric analysis of overcorrection duration effects: Is longer really better than shorter? *Behavior Modification, 24,* 359–378.

Cole, M. (1985). The zone of proximal development: Where culture and cognition create each other.

In J. V. Wertsch (Ed.), *Culture, communication, and cognition: Vygotskian perspectives* (pp. 146–161). New York, NY: Cambridge University Press.

Coleman, J. S. (1966). *Equality of educational opportunity.* Washington, DC: U.S. Government Printing Office.

Colledge, E., Bishop, D. V. M., Koeppen-Schomerus, G., Price, T. S., Happe, F., Eley, T., . . . Plomin, R. (2002). The structure of language abilities at 4 years: A twin study. *Developmental Psychology, 38,* 749–757.

Collie, R. J., Shapka, J. D., & Perry, N. E. (2012). School climate and social–emotional learning: Predicting teacher stress, job satisfaction, and teaching efficacy. *Journal of Educational Psychology, 104,* 1189–1204. doi: 10.1037/a0029356

Collins, A. (2006). Cognitive apprenticeship. In R. K. Sawyer (Ed.), *The Cambridge handbook of the learning sciences* (pp. 47–77). New York, NY: The Cambridge University Press.

Collins, A., Brown, J. S., & Newman, S. E. (1989). Cognitive apprenticeship: Teaching the crafts of reading, writing, and mathematics. In L. B. Resnick (Ed.), *Knowing, learning, and instruction: Essays in honor of Robert Galser* (pp. 453–494). Mahwah, NJ: Erlbaum.

Collins, W. A., & Steinberg, L. (2006). Adolescent development in interpersonal context. In W. Damon & R. Lerner (Series Eds.) & N. Eisenberg (Vol. Ed.), *Handbook of child psychology: Vol. 3. Social, emotional, and personality development* (5th ed., pp. 1003–1067). New York, NY: Wiley.

Colliver, J. A. (2000). Effectiveness of problem-based learning curricula: Research and theory. *Academic Medicine, 75,* 259–266.

Comadena, M. E., Hunt, S. K., & Simonds, C. J. (2007). The effects of teacher clarity, nonverbal immediacy, and caring on student motivation, affective and cognitive learning. *Communication Research Reports, 24,* 241–248.

Comer, J. P., Haynes, N. M., & Joyner, E. T. (1996). The School Development Program. In J. P. Comer, N. M. Haynes, E. T. Joyner, & M. Ben-Avie (Eds.), *Rallying the whole village: The Comer process for reforming education* (pp. 1–26). New York, NY: Teachers College Press.

Committee on Increasing High School Students' Engagement and Motivation to Learn. (2004). *Engaging schools: Fostering high school students' motivation to learn.* Washington, DC: The National Academies Press.

Common Sense Media. (2012). *Social media, social life: How teens view their digital lives.* San Francisco: Author.

Common Sense Media. (2013). *Zero to eight: Children's media use in America 2013.* San Francisco: Author.

Confrey, J. (1990). A review of the research on students' conceptions in mathematics, science, and programming. *Review of Research in Education, 16,* 3–56.

Conway, P. F., & Clark, C. M. (2003). The journey inward and outward: A re-examination of Fuller's concerns-based model of teacher development. *Teaching and Teacher Education, 19,* 465–482.

Cook, C. R., Williams, K. R., Guerra, N. G., Kim, T. E., & Sadek, S. (2010). Predictors of bullying and victimization in childhood: A meta-analytic investigation. *School Psychology Quarterly, 25,* 65–83.

Cook, J. L., & Cook, G. (2014). *The world of children* (3rd ed.). Boston, MA: Allyn & Bacon.

Cooke, B. L., & Pang, K. C. (1991). Recent research on beginning teachers: Studies of trained and untrained novices. *Teaching and Teacher Education, 7,* 93–110.

Cooper, C. R. (1998). *The weaving of maturity: Cultural perspectives on adolescent development.* New York, NY: Oxford University Press.

Cooper, H. M. (2004). Special issue: Homework. *Theory Into Practice, 43*(3).

Cooper, H. M., Robinson, J. C., & Patall, E. A. (2006). Does homework improve academic achievement? A synthesis of research, 1987–2003. *Review of Educational Research, 76,* 1–62.

Cooper, H. M., & Valentine, J. C. (Eds.). (2001). Special issue: Homework. *Educational Psychologist, 36*(3), Summer.

Cooper, H. M., Valentine, J. C., Nye, B., & Kindsay, J. J. (1999). Relationships between five after-school activities and academic achievement. *Journal of Educational Psychology, 91,* 369–378.

Copi, I. M. (1961). *Introduction to logic.* New York, NY: Macmillan.

Coplan, R. J., Prakash, K., O'Neil, K., & Armer, M. (2004). Do you "want" to play? Distinguishing between conflicted shyness and social disinterest in early childhood. *Developmental Psychology, 40,* 244–258.

Cordova, D. I., & Lepper, M. R. (1996). Intrinsic motivation and the process of learning: Beneficial effects of contextualization, personalization, and choice. *Journal of Educational Psychology, 88,* 715–730.

Cornelius-White, J. (2007). Learner-centered teacher–student relationships are effective: A meta-analysis. *Review of Educational Research, 77,* 113–143.

Corno, L. (1992). Encouraging students to take responsibility for learning and performance. *Elementary School Journal, 93,* 69–85.

Corno, L. (2000). Looking at homework differently. *Elementary School Journal, 100,* 529–548.

Corno, L. (2008). On teaching adaptively. *Educational Psychologist, 43,* 161–173.

Corno, L. (2011). Studying self-regulation habits. In B. Zimmerman & D. Schunk (Eds.), *Handbook of self-regulation of learning and performance* (pp. 361–375). New York, NY: Routledge.

Corpus, J. H., McClintic-Gilbert, M. S., & Hayenga, A. O. (2009). Within-year changes in children's intrinsic and extrinsic motivational orientations: Contextual predictors and academic outcomes. *Contemporary Educational Psychology, 34,* 154–166.

Cota-Robles, S., Neiss, M., & Rowe, D. C. (2002). The role of puberty in violent and nonviolent delinquency among Anglo American, Mexican American and African American boys. *Journal of Adolescent Research, 17,* 364–376.

Cothran, D. J., & Ennis, C. D. (2000). Building bridges to student engagement: Communicating respect and care for students in urban high school. *Journal of Research and Development in Education, 33*(2), 106–117.

Covaleskie, J. F. (1992). Discipline and morality: Beyond rules and consequences. *The Educational Forum, 56*(2), 56–60.

Covington, M. V. (1992). *Making the grade: A self-worth perspective on motivation and school reform.* New York, NY: Holt, Rinehart & Winston.

Covington, M. V., & Mueller, K. J. (2001). Intrinsic versus extrinsic motivation: An approach/avoidance reformulation. *Educational Psychology Review, 13,* 157–176.

Cowley, G., & Underwood, A. (1998, June 15). Memory. *Newsweek, 131*(24), 48–54.

Craik, F. I. M., & Lockhart, R. S. (1972). Levels of processing: A framework for memory research. *Journal of Verbal Learning and Verbal Behavior, 11,* 671–684.

Craik, F. I. M., & Tulving, E. (1975). Depth of processing and the retention of words in episodic memory. *Journal of Experimental Psychology: General, 104,* 268–294.

Crawford, J. (1997). *Best evidence: Research foundations of the Bilingual Education Act.*

Washington, DC: National Clearinghouse for Bilingual Education.

Creese, A. (2009). Building on young people's linguistic and cultural continuity: Complementary schools in the United Kingdom. *Theory Into Practice, 48,* 267–273.

Cremin, L. (1961). *The transformation of the school: Progressivism in American education, 1876–1957.* New York, NY: Vintage.

Crick, N. R., Casas, J. F., & Mosher M. (1997). Relational and overt aggression in preschool. *Developmental Psychology, 33,* 579–588.

Crocker, J., & Park, L. E. (2004). Reaping the benefits of pursuing self-esteem without the costs. *Psychological Bulletin, 130,* 392–414.

Croker, S. (2012). *The development of cognition.* Independence, KY: Cengage Learning.

Crone, D. A., & Horner, R. H. (2003). *Building positive behavior support systems in schools: Functional behavioral assessment.* New York, NY: Guilford Press.

Crosnoe, R., Morrison, F., Burchinal, M., Pianta, R., Keating, D., Friedman, S. L., & Clarke-Stewart, K. A. (2010). Instruction, teacher–student relations, and math achievement trajectories in elementary school. *Journal of Educational Psychology, 102,* 407–417.

Cross, W. E. (1991). *Shades of black: Diversity in African-American identity.* Philadelphia, PA: Temple University Press.

Cross, W. E., Jr., & Cross, T. B. (2007). Theory, research, and models. In S. M. Quintana & C. McKown (Eds.), *Race, racism and developing child* (pp. 154–181). New York, NY: Wiley.

Crow, S. J., Peterson, C. B., Swanson, S. A., Raymond, N. C., Specker, S., Eckert, E. D., & Mitchell, J. E. (2009). Increased mortality in bulimia nervosa and other eating disorders. *American Journal of Psychiatry, 166,* 1342–1346.

Crul, M., & Holdaway, J. (2009). Children of immigrants in schools in New York and Amsterdam: The factors shaping attainment. *Teachers College Record, 111(6),* 1476–1507.

Csikszentmihalyi, M. (2000). *Beyond boredom and anxiety. Experiencing flow in work and play.* San Francisco: Jossey-Bass.

Cuban, L. (2001). *Oversold and underused: Computers in the classroom.* Cambridge, MA: Harvard University Press.

Cutuli, J. J., Desjardins, C. D., Herbers, J. E., Long, J. D., Heistad, D., Chan, C-K, Hinz, E., & Masten, A. S. (2013). Academic achievement trajectories of homeless and highly mobile students: Resilience in the context of chronic and acute risk. *Child Development, 84,* 841–857.

D'Amico, A., & Guarnera, M. (2005). Exploring working memory in children with low arithmetical achievement. *Learning and Individual Differences, 15,* 189–202.

Daley, T. C., Whaley, S. E., Sigman, M. D., Espinosa, M. P., & Neumann, C. (2003). IQ on the rise: The Flynn Effect in rural Kenyan children. *Psychological Science, 14(3),* 215–219.

Damon, W. (1994). Fair distribution and sharing: The development of positive justice. In B. Puka (Ed.), *Fundamental research in moral development* (pp. 189–254). *Moral development: A compendium, Vol. 2.* New York, NY: Garland.

Danielson, C. (2013). *The Framework for Teaching evaluation instrument: 2013 edition.* Princeton, NJ: The Danielson Group.

Darcey, J. S., & Travers, J. F. (2006). *Human development across the lifespan* (6th ed.). New York, NY: McGraw-Hill.

Darling-Hammond, L., & Youngs, P. (2002). Defining "Highly Qualified Teachers": What does

"Scientifically-Based Research" actually tell us? *Educational Researcher,* pp. 13–25.

Darnon, C., Dompnier, B., Gillieron, O., & Butera, F. (2010). The interplay of mastery and performance goals in social comparison: A multiple-goal perspective. *Journal of Educational Psychology, 102,* 212–222.

Das, J. P. (1995). Some thoughts on two aspects of Vygotsky's work. *Educational Psychologist, 30,* 93–97.

DaSilva Iddings, A. C. (2009). Bridging home and school literacy practices: Empowering families of recent immigrant children. *Theory Into Practice, 48,* 304–311.

Daunic, A. P., Smith, S. W., Brank, E. M., & Penfield, R. D. (2006). Classroom based cognitive-behavioral intervention to prevent aggression: Efficacy and social validity. *Journal of School Psychology, 44,* 123–139.

Davis, G. A., Rimm, S. B., & Siegle, D. (2011). *Education of the gifted and talented* (6th ed.). Boston, MA: Pearson.

Davis, H. A. (2003). Conceptualizing the role and influence of student–teacher relationships on children's social and cognitive development, *Educational Psychologist, 38,* 207–234.

Dawson-Tunik, T., Fischer, K. W., & Stein, Z. (2004). Do stages belong at the center of developmental theory? *New Ideas in Psychology, 22,* 255–263.

De Boer, H., Bosker, R. J., & van der Werf, M. P. C. (2010). Sustainability of teacher expectation bias effects on long-term student performance. *Journal of Educational Psychology, 102,* 168–179.

De Castella, K., Byrne, D., & Covington, M. (2013). Unmotivated or motivated to fail? A cross-cultural study of achievement motivation, fear of failure, and student disengagement. *Journal of Educational Psychology, 105(3),* 861–880.

De Corte, E. (2003). Transfer as the productive use of acquired knowledge, skills, and motivations. *Current Directions in Psychological Research, 12,* 142–146.

De Corte, E., Greer, B., & Verschaffel, L. (1996). Mathematics learning and teaching. In D. Berliner & R. Calfee (Eds.), *Handbook of educational psychology* (pp. 491–549). New York, NY: Macmillan.

De Corte, E., & Verschaffel, L. (1985). Beginning first graders' initial representation of arithmetic word problems. *Journal of Mathematical Behavior, 4,* 3021.

De George, G. (2008). Is it language or is it special needs? Appropriately diagnosing English language learners having achievement difficulties. In L. S. Verplaetse & N. Migliacci (Eds.), *Inclusive pedagogy for English language learners: A handbook of research-informed practices* (pp. 277–303). New York, NY: Erlbaum.

de Kock, A., Sleegers, P., & Voeten, M. J. M. (2004). New learning and the classification of learning environments in secondary education. *Review of Educational Research, 74(2),* 141–170.

de Koning, B. B., & Tabbers, H. K. (2011). Facilitating understanding of movements in dynamic visualizations: An embodied perspective. *Educational Psychology Review, 23,* 501–521.

Dearing, E., Kreider, H., Simpkins, S., & Weiss, H. B. (2006). Family involvement in school and low-income children's literacy: Longitudinal associations between and within families. *Journal of Educational Psychology, 98,* 653–664.

Deaux, K. (1993). Commentary: Sorry, wrong number: A reply to Gentile's call. *Psychological Science, 4,* 125–126.

DeCecco, J., & Richards, A. (1974). *Growing pains: Uses of school conflicts.* New York, NY: Aberdeen.

deCharms, R. (1983). Intrinsic motivation, peer tutoring, and cooperative learning: Practical

maxims. In J. Levine & M. Wang (Eds.), *Teacher and student perceptions: Implications for learning* (pp. 391–398). Mahwah, NJ: Erlbaum.

Deci, E. L. (1975). *Intrinsic motivation.* New York, NY: Plenum.

Deci, E. L., Koestner, R., & Ryan, R. M. (1999). A meta-analytic review of experiments examining the effects of extrinsic rewards on intrinsic motivation. *Psychological Bulletin, 125,* 627–668.

Deci, E. L., & Ryan, R. M. (1985). *Intrinsic motivation and self-determination in human behavior.* New York, NY: Plenum.

Deci, E. L., & Ryan, R. M. (Eds.). (2002). *Handbook of self-determination research.* Rochester, NY: University of Rochester Press.

Deci, E. L., Vallerand, R. J., Pelletier, L. G., & Ryan, R. M. (1991). Motivation and education: The self-determination perspective. *Educational Psychologist, 26,* 325–346.

DeCuir-Gunby, J. T. (2009). A review of the racial identity development of African American adolescents: The role of education. *Review of Educational Research, 79,* 103–124.

Delazer, M., Ischebeck, A., Domahs, F., Zamarian, L., Koppelstaetter, F., Siednetoph, C. M., . . . Benke, T. (2005). Learning by strategies and learning by drill: Evidence from an fMRI study. *NeuroImage, 25,* 838–849.

Delpit, L. (1995). *Other people's children: Cultural conflict in the classroom.* New York, NY: New York Press.

Delpit, L. (2003). Educators as "Seed People": Growing a new future. *Educational Researcher, 7(32),* 14–21.

Demetriou, A., Christou, C., Spanoudis, G., & Platsidou, M. (2002). The development of mental processing: Efficiency, working memory and thinking. *Monographs of the Society for Research in Child Development, 67(1).*

Demetriou, A., Spanoudis, G., & Mouyi, A. (2011). Educating the developing mind: Towards an overarching paradigm. *Educational Psychology Review, 23,* 601–663.

Demuth, K. (1990). Subject, topic, and Sesotho passive. *Journal of Child Language, 17,* 67–84.

Denton, C. A., Tolar, T. D., Fletcher, J. M., Barth, A. E., Vaughn, S., & Francis, D. J. (2013). Effects of tier 3 intervention for students with persistent reading difficulties and characteristics of inadequate responders. *Journal of Educational Psychology, 105,* 633–648. doi: 10.1037/a0032581

DeRose, L. M., Shiyko, M. P., Foster, H., & Brooks-Gunn, J. (2011). Associations between menarcheal timing and behavioral developmental trajectories for girls from age 6 to age 15. *Journal of Youth and Adolescence, 40,* 1329–1342.

Derry, S. J. (1992). Beyond symbolic processing: Expanding horizons for educational psychology. *Journal of Educational Psychology, 84,* 413–419.

Derry, S. J., Hmelo-Silver, C. E., Nagarajan, A., Chernobilsky, E., & Beitzel, B. (2006). Cognitive transfer revisited: Can we exploit new media to solve old problems on a large scale? *Journal of Educational Computing Research, 35,* 145–162.

Desautel, D. (2009). Becoming a thinking thinker: Metacognition, self-reflection, and classroom practice. *Teachers College Record, 111,* 1997–2020. ID Number: 15504. Retrieved from http://www.tcrecord.org

Deshler, D., & Schumaker, J. (2005). *Teaching adolescents to be strategic learners.* Thousand Oaks, CA: Corwin Press.

Dettmers, S., Trautwein, U., Lüdtke, O., Kunter, M., & Baumert, J. (2010). Homework works if homework quality is high: Using multilevel modeling to predict the development of achievement in mathematics. *Journal of Educational Psychology, 102*, 467–482.

Dewan, S. (2010, January 10). Southern schools mark two minorities. *New York Times*, p. A19+.

Dewey, J. (1896). The university school. *University Record (University of Chicago), 1*, 417–419.

Dewey, J. (1913). *Interest and effort in education.* Boston, MA: Houghton-Mifflin.

Diaz-Rico, L. T., & Weed, K. Z. (2002). *The crosscultural, language, and academic development handbook* (2nd ed.). Boston, MA: Allyn & Bacon.

Dickinson, D., McCabe, A., Anastopoulos, L., Peisner-Feinberg, E., & Poe, M. (2003). The comprehensive language approach to early literacy: The interrelationships among vocabulary, phonological sensitivity, and print knowledge among preschool-aged children. *Journal of Educational Psychology, 95*, 465–481.

Dillon, S. (2011, August 8). Overriding a key education law: Waivers offered to sidestep a 100 percent proficiency rule. *New York Times*, p. A11.

Dingfelder, S. F. (2005). Closing the gap for Latino patients. *Monitor on Psychology, 36*(1), 58–61.

Dinnel, D., & Glover, J. A. (1985). Advance organizers: Encoding manipulations. *Journal of Educational Psychology, 77*, 514–522.

Dinsmore, D. L., Alexander, P. A., & Loughlin, S. M. (2008). Focusing the conceptual lens on metacognition, self-regulation, and self-regulated learning. *Educational Psychology Review, 20*, 391–409.

DiVesta, F. J., & Di Cintio, M. J. (1997). Interactive effects of working memory span and text comprehension on reading comprehension and retrieval. *Learning and Individual Differences, 9*, 215–231.

Dixon, L. Q., Zhao, J., Shin, J-Y, Wu, S., Su, J-H, Burgess-Brigham, R., Gezer, M. U., & Snow, C. (2012). What we know about second language: Acquisition: A synthesis from four perspectives. *Review of Educational Research, 82*, 5–60.

Dodge, K. A. (2011). Context matters in child and family policy. *Child Development, 82*, 433–442.

Dodge, K. A., & Pettit, G. S. (2003). A biopsychosocial model of the development of chronic conduct problems in adolescence. *Developmental Psychology, 39*, 349–371.

Doggett, A. M. (2004). ADHD and drug therapy: Is it still a valid treatment? *Child Health Care, 8*, 69–81.

Dolezal, S. E., Welsh, L. M., Pressley, M., & Vincent, M. (2003). How do nine third-grade teachers motivate their students? *Elementary School Journal, 103*, 239–267.

Doll, B., Zucker, S., & Brehm, K. (2005). *Resilient classrooms: Creating healthy environments for learning.* New York, NY: Guilford.

Domenech Rodriguez, M. M., Donovick, M. R., & Crowley, S. L. (2009). Parenting styles in a cultural context: Observations of protective parenting in first-generation Latinos. *Family Process, 48*(2), 195–210.

Dotterer, A. M., McHale, S. M., & Crouter, A. C. (2009). The development and correlates of academic interests from childhood through adolescence. *Journal of Educational Psychology, 101*, 509–519.

Downs, K. J., & Blow, A. J. (2013). A substantive and methodological review of family-based treatment for eating disorders: The last 25 years of research. *Journal of Family Therapy, 35*, 3–28.

Doyle, W. (2006). Ecological approaches to classroom management. In C. Evertson & C. S. Weinstein (Eds.), *Handbook for classroom management: Research, practice, and contemporary issues.* Mahwah, NJ: Erlbaum.

Driscoll, M. P. (2005). *Psychology of learning for instruction* (3rd ed.). Boston, MA: Allyn & Bacon.

Dubarry, M., & Alves de Lima, D. (2003). *Notes on Generation 1.5.* De Anza College, Cupertino, CA. Retrieved from http://faculty.deanza.edu/alvesdelimadiana/stories/storyReader$438

Dubinsky, J. M., Roehrig, G., & Varma, S. (2013). Infusing neuroscience into teacher professional development. *Educational Researcher, 42*, 317–329.

DuBois, D. L., Burk-Braxton, C., Swenson, L. P., Tevendale, H. D., & Hardesty, J. L. (2002). Race and gender influences on adjustment in early adolescence: Investigation of an integrative model. *Child Development, 73*, 1573–1592.

Du Bois, W. E. B. (1903). *The souls of black folk.* New York, NY: Bantam Classic.

Duckworth, A. L., Quinn, P. D., & Tsukayama, E. (2012). What *No Child Left Behind* leaves behind: The roles of IQ and self-control in predicting standardized achievement test scores and report card grades. *Journal of Educational Psychology, 104*, 439–451.

Duell, O. K. (1994). Extended wait time and university student achievement. *American Educational Research Journal, 31*, 397–414.

Dufrene, B. A., Doggett, R. A., Henington, C., & Watson, T. S. (2007). Functional assessment and intervention for disruptive classroom behaviors in preschool and Head Start classrooms. *Journal of Behavioral Education, 16*, 368–388.

Duncan, A. (2013, January 25). We must provide equal opportunity in sports to students with disabilities. *Homeroom: The official blog of the Department of Education.* Retrieved from http://www.ed.gov/blog/2013/01/we-must-provide-equal-opportunityin-sports-to-students-with-disabilities

Duncan, G. J., & Brooks-Gunn, J. (2000). Family poverty, welfare reform, and child development. *Child Development, 71*, 188–196.

Duncan, R. M., & Cheyne, J. A. (1999). Incidence and functions of self-reported private speech in young adults: A self-verbalization questionnaire. *Canadian Journal of Behavioural Sciences, 31*, 133–136.

Duncker, K. (1945). On solving problems. *Psychological Monographs, 58*(5, Whole No. 270).

Dunn, K., & Dunn, R. (1978). *Teaching students through their individual learning styles.* Reston, VA: National Council of Principals.

Dunn, K., & Dunn, R. (1987). Dispelling outmoded beliefs about student learning. *Educational Leadership, 44*(6), 55–63.

Dunn, R., Dunn, K., & Price, G. E. (1989). *Learning Styles Inventory (LSI): An inventory for identification of how individuals in grades 3 through 12 prefer to learn.* Lawrence, KS: Price Systems.

Dunn, R., & Griggs, S. (2003). *Synthesis of the Dunn and Dunn Learning-Style Model Research: Who, what, when, where, and so what?* New York, NY: St. John's University.

Durik, A. M., & Harackiewicz, J. M. (2007). Different strokes for different folks: How individual interest moderates the effects of situational factors on task interest. *Journal of Educational Psychology, 99*, 597–610.

Durik, A. M., Vida, M., & Eccles, J. S. (2006). Task values and ability beliefs as predictors of high school literacy choices: A developmental analysis. *Journal of Educational Psychology, 98*(2), 382–393.

Durlak, J. A., Weissberg, R. P., Dymnicki, A. B., Taylor, R. D., & Schellinger, K. B. (2011). The impact of enhanced students' social emotional learning: A metaanalysis of school-based universal interventions. *Child Development, 82*, 405–432.

Dusenbury, L., & Falco, M. (1995). Eleven components of effective drug abuse prevention curricula. *Journal of School Health, 65*, 420–425.

Dux, P. E., Tombu, M. N., Harrison, S., Rogers, B. P., Tong, F., & Marois, R. (2009). Training improves multitasking performance by increasing the speed of information processing in human prefrontal cortex. *Neuron, 16*, 127–138.

Dweck, C. S. (2000). *Self-theories: Their role in motivation, personality, and development.* Philadelphia, PA: Routledge Press.

Dweck, C. S. (2002). The development of ability conceptions. In A. Wigfield & J. Eccles (Eds.), *The development of achievement motivation.* San Diego, CA: Academic Press.

Dweck, C. S. (2006). *Mindset: The new psychology of success.* New York, NY: Random House.

Dweck, C. S., & Bempechat, J. (1983). Children's theories on intelligence: Consequences for learning. In S. Paris, G. Olson, & W. Stevenson (Eds.), *Learning and motivation in the classroom* (pp. 239–256). Mahwah, NJ: Erlbaum.

Dymond, S. K., Renzaglia, A., & Chun, E. (2007). Elements of effective high school service learning programs that include students with and without disabilities. *Remedial and Special Education, 28*, 227–243.

Ebbinghaus, H. (1964). *Memory* (H. A. Ruger & C. E. Bussenius, Trans.). New York, NY: Dover. (Original work published 1885)

Ebersbach, M. (2009). Achieving a new dimension: Children integrate three stimulus dimensions in volume estimations. *Developmental Psychology, 45*, 877–883.

Eccles, J. (2009). Who am I and what am I going to do with my life? Personal and collective identities as motivators of action. *Educational Psychologist, 44*, 78–89.

Eccles, J., & Wigfield, A. (1985). Teacher expectations and student motivation. In J. Dusek (Ed.), *Teacher expectancies* (pp. 185–226). Mahwah, NJ: Erlbaum.

Eccles, J., & Wigfield, A. (2002). Motivational beliefs, values, goals. *Annual Review of Psychology, 53*, 109–132.

Eccles, J., Wigfield, A., & Schiefele, U. (1998). Motivation to succeed. In W. Damon (Series Ed.) & N. Eisenberg (Vol. Ed.), *Handbook of child psychology: Vol. 3. Social, emotional, and personality development* (5th ed., pp. 1017–1095). New York, NY: Wiley.

Echevarría, J., & Graves, A. (2011). *Sheltered content instruction: Teaching English learners with diverse abilities* (4th ed.). Columbus, OH: Pearson.

Echevarría, J., Vogt, M., & Short, D. J. (2014). *Making content comprehensible for elementary English learners: The SIOP® Model* (2nd ed.). Boston, MA: Pearson.

Echevarría, M. (2003). Anomalies as a catalyst for middle school students' knowledge construction and scientific reasoning during science inquiry. *Journal of Educational Psychology, 95*, 357–374.

Efklides, A. (2011). Interactions of metacognition with motivation and affect in self-regulated learning: The MASRL model. *Educational Psychologist, 46*, 6–25.

Egan, S. K., Monson, T. C., & Perry, D. G. (1998). Social-cognitive influences on change in aggression over time. *Developmental Psychology, 34*, 996–1006.

Ehrenfeld, T. (2011). Reflections on mirror neurons. *Observer: Association for Psychological Science, 24*(3), 11–13.

Eisenberg, N., & Fabes, R. A. (1998). Prosocial development. In W. Damon (Series Ed.) & N. Eisenberg (Vol. Ed.), *Handbook of child psychology: Vol. 3. Social, emotional, and personality development* (5th ed., pp. 701–778). New York, NY: Wiley.

Eisenberg, R., Pierce, W. D., & Cameron, J. (1999). Effects of rewards on intrinsic motivation—Negative, neutral, and positive: Comment on Deci,

Koestner, and Ryan (1999). *Psychological Bulletin, 125*, 677–691.

Eisner, E. W. (1999). The uses and limits of performance assessments. *Phi Delta Kappan, 80*, 658–660.

Eissenberg, T. E., & Rudner, L. M. (1988). *Explaining test results to parents.* Retrieved from http://pareonline.net/getvn.asp?v=1&n=1

Elder, L., & Paul, R. (2012). *Critical thinking: Tools for taking charge of your learning and your life* (3rd ed.). Upper Saddle River, NJ: Prentice-Hall.

Elias, M. J., & Schwab, Y. (2006). From compliance to responsibility: Social and emotional learning and classroom management. In C. Evertson & C. S. Weinstein (Eds.), *Handbook for classroom management: Research, practice, and contemporary issues.* Mahwah, NJ: Erlbaum.

Elias, S. M., & MacDonald, S. (2007). Using past performance, proxy efficacy, and academic self-efficacy to predict college performance. *Journal of Applied Social Psychology, 37*, 2518–2531.

Elkind, D. (1981). Obituary—Jean Piaget (1896–1980). *American Psychologist, 36*, 911–913.

Elkind, D. (1985). Egocentrism redux. *Developmental Review, 5*, 127–134.

Ellerbrock, C. R., & Kiefer, S. M. (2010). Creating a ninth-grade community of care. *The Journal of Educational Research, 103*, 393–406.

Ellington, A. J. (2003). A meta-analysis of the effects of calculators on students' achievement and attitude levels in precollege mathematics classes. *Journal for Research in Mathematics Education, 34*, 433–463.

Ellington, A. J. (2013). The impact of calculators on student achievement in the K-12 mathematics classroom. In J. Hattie & E. M. Anderman (Eds.), *International guide to student achievement* (pp. 303–306). New York, NY: Routledge.

Else-Quest, N. M., Hyde, J. S., & Linn, M. C. (2010). Cross-national patterns of gender differences in mathematics: A meta-analysis. *Psychological Bulletin, 136*, 103–127.

Embry, D. D. (2002). The Good Behavior Game: A best practice candidate as a universal behavior vaccine. *Clinical Child and Family Psychology Review, 5*, 273–297.

Emerson, M. J., & Miyake, A. (2003). The role of inner speech in task switching: A dual-task investigation. *Journal of Memory and Language, 48*, 148–168.

Emmer, E. T., & Aussiker, A. (1990). School and classroom discipline problems: How well do they work? In O. Moles (Ed.), *Student discipline strategies: Research and practice.* Albany, NY: SUNY Press.

Emmer, E. T., & Evertson, C. M. (1982). Effective classroom management at the beginning of the school year in junior high school classes. *Journal of Educational Psychology, 74*, 485–498.

Emmer, E. T., & Evertson, C. M. (2009). *Classroom management for middle and high school teachers* (8th ed.). Boston, MA: Allyn & Bacon.

Emmer, E. T., & Evertson, C. M. (2013). *Classroom management for middle and high school teachers* (9th ed.). Boston, MA: Allyn & Bacon.

Emmer, E. T., & Gerwels, M. C. (2006). Classroom management in middle school and high school classrooms. In C. Evertson & C. S. Weinstein (Eds.), *Handbook for classroom management: Research, practice, and contemporary issues.* Mahwah, NJ: Erlbaum.

Emmer, E., & Hickman, J. (1991). Teacher efficacy in classroom management. *Educational and Psychological Measurement, 51*, 755–765.

Emmer, E. T., & Stough, L. M. (2001). Classroom management: A critical part of educational psychology with implications for teacher education. *Educational Psychologist, 36*, 103–112.

Emmer, E. T., Evertson, C. M., & Anderson, L. M. (1980). Effective classroom management at the beginning of the school year. *Elementary School Journal, 80*, 219–231.

Engel de Abreu, P. M. J., & Gathercole, S. (2012). Executive and phonological processes in second language acquisition. *Journal of Educational Psychology, 104*, 974–986.

Engle, R. W. (2001). What is working memory capacity? In H. Roediger, J. Nairne, I. Neath, & A. Suprenant (Eds.), *The nature of remembering: Essays in honor of Robert G. Crowder* (pp. 297–314). Washington, DC: American Psychological Association.

Epstein, J. L. (1989). Family structure and student motivation. In R. E. Ames & C. Ames (Eds.), *Research on motivation in education: Vol. 3. Goals and cognitions* (pp. 259–295). New York, NY: Academic Press.

Epstein, J. L. (1995). School/Family/Community partnerships: Caring for the children we share. *Phi Delta Kappan, 76*, 701–712.

Epstein, J. L., & MacIver, D. J. (1992). *Opportunities to learn: Effects on eighth graders of curriculum offerings and instructional approaches.* (Report No. 34). Baltimore, MD: Center for Research on Elementary and Middle Schools, Johns Hopkins University.

Epstein, J. L., & Van Voorhis, F. L. (2001). More than minutes: Teachers' roles in designing homework. *Educational Psychologist, 36*, 181–193.

Erdelyi, M. H. (2010). The ups and downs of memory. *American Psychologist, 65*, 623–633.

Erickson, W., Lee, C., & von Schrader, S. (2013). *Disability statistics from the 2011 American Community Survey (ACS).* Ithaca, NY: Cornell University Employment and Disability Institute (EDI). Retrieved from ID Number: www.disabilitystatistics.org

Ericsson, A. (2011, August). *Deliberate practice and the future of education and professional training.* Keynote address at the European Association for Research on Learning and Instruction, University of Exeter, UK.

Ericsson, K. A. (1999). Expertise. In R. Wilson & F. Keil (Eds.), *The MIT encyclopedia of the cognitive sciences* (pp. 298–300). Cambridge, MA: MIT Press.

Ericsson, K. A., & Charness, N. (1994). Expert performance: Its structure and acquisition. *American Psychologist, 49*(8), 725–747.

Ericsson, K. A., & Charness, N. (1999). Expert performance: Its structure and acquisition. In S. Ceci & W. Williams (Eds.), The nature-nurture debate: The essential readings. *Essential readings in developmental psychology.* Malden, MA: Blackwell.

Erikson, E. H. (1963). *Childhood and society* (2nd ed.). New York, NY: Norton.

Erikson, E. H. (1980). *Identity and the life cycle* (2nd ed.). New York, NY: Norton.

Evans, G. W. (2004). The environment of childhood poverty. *American Psychologist, 59*, 77–92.

Evans, L., & Davies, K. (2000). No sissy boys here: A content analysis of the representation of masculinity in elementary school reading texts. *Sex Roles, 42*, 255–270.

Evensen, D. H., Salisbury-Glennon, J. D., & Glenn, J. (2001). A qualitative study of six medical students in a problem-based curriculum: Toward a situated model of self-regulation. *Journal of Educational Psychology, 93*, 659–676.

Evertson, C. M., & Emmer, E. T. (2009). *Classroom management for elementary school teachers* (8th ed.). Boston, MA: Allyn & Bacon.

Evertson, C. M., & Emmer, E. T. (2013). *Classroom management for elementary school teachers* (9th ed.). Boston, MA: Allyn & Bacon.

Evertson, C. M., & Weinstein, C. S. (Eds.). (2006). *Handbook of classroom management: Research, practice, and contemporary issues.* Mahwah, NJ: Erlbaum.

Eysenck, M. W. (2012). *Fundamentals of cognition* (2nd ed.). New York: Taylor and Francis.

Fabiano, G. A., Pelham, W. E., Coles, E. K., Gnagy, E. M., Chronis-Tuscano, A., & O'Connor, B. C. (2009). A meta-analysis of behavioral treatments for attention-deficit/hyperactivity disorder. *Clinical Psychology Review, 29*, 129–140.

Facione, P. A. (2011). *Think critically.* Boston, MA: Pearson.

Fantuzzo, J., Davis, G., & Ginsburg, M. (1995). Effects of parent involvement in isolation or in combination with peer tutoring on student self-concept and mathematics achievement. *Journal of Educational Psychology, 87*, 272–281.

Fast, L. A., Lewis, J. L., Bryant, M. J., Bocian, K. A., Cardullo, R. A., Rettig, M., & Hammond, K. A. (2010). Does math self-efficacy mediate the effect of the perceived classroom environment on standardized math test performance? *Journal of Educational Psychology, 102*, 729–740.

Feldman, J. (2003). The simplicity principle in human concept learning. *Current Directions in Psychological Science, 12*, 227–232.

Feldman, R. S. (2004). *Child development* (3rd ed.). Upper Saddle River, NJ: Prentice-Hall.

Fenton, D. F. (2007). The implications of research on expertise for curriculum and pedagogy. *Educational Psychology Review, 19*, 91–110.

Ferguson, C. J., & Donnellan, M. B. (2013). Is the association between children's baby video viewing and poor language development robust? A reanalysis of Zimmerman, Christakis, and Meltzoff (2007). *Developmental Psychology, 50*, 129–137. doi: 10.1037/a0033628

Ferguson, R. F. (2008). *The TRIPOD Project framework.* Cambridge, MA: Harvard University.

Fernet, C., Guay, F., Senécal, C., & Austin, S. (2012). Predicting intraindividual changes in teacher burnout: The role of perceived school environment and motivational factors. *Teaching and Teacher Education, 28*, 514–525.

Ferrer, E., & McArdle, J. J. (2004). An experimental analysis of dynamic hypotheses about cognitive abilities and achievement from childhood to early adulthood. *Developmental Psychology, 40*, 935–952.

Ferretti, R. P., Lewis, W. E., & Andrews-Weckerly, S. (2009). Do goals affect the structure of students' argumentative writing strategies? *Journal of Educational Psychology, 101*, 577–589.

Fillmore, L. W., & Snow, C. (2000). What teachers need to know about language. Retrieved from http://citeseerx.ist.psu.edu/viewdoc/download?doi=10.1.1.92.9117&rep=rep1&type=pdf

Finkel, D., Reynolds, C. A., McArdle, J. J., Gatz, M., & Pedersen, N. L. (2003). Latent growth curve analyses of accelerating decline in cognitive abilities in adulthood. *Developmental Psychology, 39*, 535–550.

Fischer, K. W. (2009). Mind, brain, and education: Building a scientific groundwork for learning and teaching. *Mind, Brain, and Education, 3*, 2–16.

Fischer, M. A., & Gillespie, C. S. (2003). Computers and young children's development. *Young Children, 58*(4), 85–91.

Fiske, S. T. (1993). Social cognition and social perception. *Annual Review of Psychology, 44*, 155–194.

Fitts, P. M., & Posner, M. I. (1967). *Human performance.* Belmont, CA: Brooks Cole.

Fives, H. R., Hamman, D., & Olivarez, A. (2005, April). *Does burnout begin with student teaching? Analyzing efficacy, burnout, and support during the student-teaching semester.* Paper presented at the Annual Meeting of the American Educational Research Association, Montreal, CA.

Flammer, A. (1995). Developmental analysis of control beliefs. In A. Bandura (Ed.), *Self-efficacy in changing societies* (pp. 69–113). New York, NY: Cambridge University Press.

Flavell, J. H., Green, F. L., & Flavell, E. R. (1995). Young children's knowledge about thinking. *Monographs of the Society for Research in Child Development, 60*(1) (Serial No. 243).

Flavell, J. H., Miller, P. H., & Miller, S. A. (2002). *Cognitive development* (4th ed.). Upper Saddle River, NJ: Prentice-Hall.

Fleith, D. (2000). Teacher and student perceptions of creativity in the classroom environment. *Roeper Review, 22,* 148–153.

Fletcher, A., Bonell, C., & Hargreaves, J. (2008). School effects on young people's drug use: A systematic review of intervention and observational studies. *Journal of Adolescent Health, 42,* 209–220.

Fletcher, K. L., & Cassady, J. C. (2010). Overcoming academic anxieties: Promoting effective coping and self-regulation strategies. In J. C. Cassady (Ed.), *Anxiety in schools: The causes, consequences, and solutions for academic anxieties* (pp. 177–200). New York: Peter Lang.

Floden, R. E. (2001). Research on effects of teaching: A continuing model for research on teaching. In V. Richardson (Ed.), *Handbook of research on teaching* (4th ed., pp. 3–16). Washington, DC: American Educational Research Association.

Florit, E., & Cain, K. (2011). The simple view of reading: Is it valid for different types of alphabetic orthographies? *Educational Psychology Review, 23,* 553–576.

Flum, H., & Kaplan, A. (2006). Exploratory orientation as an educational goal. *Educational Psychologist, 41,* 99–110.

Flynn, J. R. (2012). *Are we getting smarter?: Rising IQ in the twenty-first century.* Cambridge, UK: Cambridge University Press.

Folger, T. (2012). Can we keep getting smarter? *Scientific American, 307*(3), 44–47.

Ford, D. Y. (2000). *Infusing multicultural content into the curriculum for gifted students.* (ERIC EC Digest #E601). Arlington, VA: The ERIC Clearinghouse on Disabilities and Gifted Education.

Fox, E., & Riconscente, M. (2008). Metacognition and Self-Regulation in James, Piaget, and Vygotsky. *Educational Psychology Review, 20,* 373–389.

Francis, D. J., Lesaux, N., & August, D. (2006). Language of instruction. In D. August & T. Shanahan (Eds.), *Developing literacy in second language learners: Report of the National Literacy Panel on Language Minority Children and Youth* (pp. 365–413). Mahwah, NJ: Erlbaum.

Frank, S. J., Pirsch, L. A., & Wright, V. C. (1990). Late adolescents' perceptions of their parents: Relationships among deidealization, autonomy, relatedness, and insecurity and implications for adolescent adjustment and ego identity status. *Journal of Youth and Adolescence, 19,* 571–588.

Franklin, J. (2007). Achieving with autism: Dispelling common misconceptions is essential for success. *Education Update, 49*(7), 1–9.

Fredricks, J. A., Blumenfeld, P. C., & Paris, A. H. (2004). School engagement: Potential of the concept, state of the evidence. *Review of Educational Research, 74,* 59–109.

Freeman, S. (2011). *Top 10 myths about the brain, How Stuff Works.* Retrieved from http://health.howstuffworks.com/human-body/systems/nervous-system/10-brain-myths.htm

Freiberg, H. J. (2013). Classroom management and student achievement. In J. Hattie and E. Anderman (Eds.). *International guide to student achievement* (pp. 228–231). New York, NY: Routledge.

Freiberg, H. J., & Driscoll, A. (2005). *Universal teaching strategies* (4th ed.). Boston, MA: Allyn & Bacon.

Freiberg, H. J., & Lamb, S. M. (2009). Dimensions of person-centered classroom management. *Theory Into Practice, 48,* 99–105.

Freiberg, J. (2006). Research-based programs for preventing and solving discipline problems. In C. Evertson & C. S. Weinstein (Eds.), *Handbook for classroom management: Research, practice, and contemporary issues.* Mahwah, NJ: Erlbaum.

Freisen, J. (2010, March 10). The hanging face of Canada: Booming minority populations by 2031. *The Globe and Mail: National.*

French, D. C., Chen, X., Chung, J., Li, M., Chen, H., & Li, D. (2011). Four children and one toy: Chinese and Canadian children faced with potential conflict over a limited resource. *Child Development, 82,* 830–841.

Frenzel, A. C., Goetz, T., Lüdtke, O., Pekrun, R., & Sutton, R. E. (2009). Emotional transmission in the classroom: Exploring the relationship between teacher and student enjoyment. *Journal of Educational Psychology, 101,* 705–716.

Frey, N., & Fisher, D. (2010). Reading and the brain: What early childhood educators need to know. *Early Childhood Education Journal, 38,* 103–110.

Frick, T. W. (1990). Analysis of patterns in time: A method of recording and quantifying temporal relations in education. *American Educational Research Journal, 27,* 180–204.

Friedel, J. M., Cortina, K. S., Turner, J. C., & Midgley, C. (2007). Achievement goals, efficacy beliefs and coping strategies in mathematics: The roles of perceived parent and teacher goal structures. *Contemporary Educational Psychology, 32,* 434–458.

Friedman-Weieneth, J. L., Harvey, E. A., Youngswirth, S. D., & Goldstein, L. H. (2007). The relation between 3-year-old-children's skills and their hyperactivity, inattention, and aggression. *Journal of Educational Psychology, 99,* 671–681.

Friend, M., & Bursuck, W. D. (2002). *Including students with special needs* (3rd ed.). Boston, MA: Allyn & Bacon.

Friend, M., & Bursuck, W. D. (2012). *Including students with special needs: A practical guide for classroom teachers* (6th ed.). Boston, MA: Allyn & Bacon/ Pearson.

Friend, M., & Bursuck, W. D. (2015). *Including students with special needs: A practical guide for classroom teachers* (7th ed.). Boston, MA: Allyn & Bacon/ Pearson.

Friend, M. P. (2014). *Special education: Contemporary perspectives for school professionals* (4th ed.). Boston, MA: Pearson Education.

Frost, J. L., Wortham, S. C., & Reifel, S. (2005). *Play and child development* (2nd ed.). Upper Saddle River, NJ: Prentice-Hall.

Frost, J. L. Wortham, S. C., & Reifel, S. C. (2012). *Play and child development* (5th ed.). Boston, MA: Pearson.

Fuchs, L. S., Compton, D. L., Fuchs, D., Powell, S. R., Schumacher, R. F., Hamlett, C. L., Vernier, E., Namkung, J. M., & Vukovic, R. K. (2012). Contributions of domain-general cognitive resources and different forms of arithmetic development to pre-algebraic knowledge. *Developmental Psychology, 48,* 1315–1326 doi: 10.1037/a0027475

Fuchs, L. S., Fuchs, D., Compton, D. L., Rowell, S. R., Seethaler, P. M., Capizzi, A. M, . . . Fletcher, J. M. (2006). The cognitive correlates of third-grade skill in arithmetic, algorithmic, computation, and arithmetic work problems. *Journal of Educational Psychology, 98,* 29–43.

Fuchs, L. S., Fuchs, D., Hamlett, C. L., & Karns, K. (1998). High-achieving students' interactions and performance on complex mathematical tasks as a function of homogeneous and heterogeneous pairings. *American Educational Research Journal, 35,* 227–268.

Fuchs, L. S., Fuchs, D., Prentice, K., Burch, M., Hamlett, C. L., Owen, R., Hosp, M., & Jancek, D. (2003). Explicitly teaching for transfer: Effects on third-grade students mathematical problem solving. *Journal of Educational Psychology, 95,* 239–305.

Fuchs, L. S., Schumacher, R. F., Long, J., Namkung, J., Hamlett, C. L., Cirino, P. T., Jordan, N. C., Siegler, R., Gersten, R., & Changas, P. (2013). Improving at-risk learners' understanding of fractions. *Journal of Educational Psychology, 105,* 683–700. doi: 10.1037/a0032446

Fulk, C. L., & Smith, P. J. (1995). Students' perceptions of teachers' instructional and management adaptations for students with learning or behavior problems. *The Elementary School Journal, 95*(5), 409–419.

Fuller, F. G. (1969). Concerns of teachers: A developmental conceptualization. *American Educational Research Journal, 6,* 207–226.

Fuller-Thomson, E., & Dalton, A. (2011, January 5) Suicidal ideation among individuals whose parents have divorced: Findings from a representative Canadian community survey. *Psychiatry Research.* Retrieved from http://www.ncbi.nlm.nih.gov/pubmed/21251718

Furrer, C., & Skinner, E. (2003). Sense of relatedness as a factor in children's academic engagement and performance. *Journal of Educational Psychology, 95*(11), 148–161.

Furtak, E. M., Seidel, T., Iverson, H., & Briggs, D. C. (2012). Experimental and quasi-experimental studies of inquiry-based science teaching: A meta-analysis. *Review of Educational Research, 82,* 300–329. doi: 10.3102/0034654312457206

Fusaro, M. (2011). *An evidence-based approach for fostering positive social behaviors in schools.* Retrieved from http://www.gse.harvard.edu/news-impact/2010/07/an-evidence-based-approach-for-fostering-positive-social-behaviors-in-schools/#ixzz2ujdIRDZB

Fyfe, E. R., Rittle-Johnson, B., & DeCaro, M. S. (2012). The effects of feedback during exploratory mathematics problem solving: Prior knowledge matters. *Journal of Educational Psychology, 104,* 1094–1108. doi: 10.1037/a0028389

Gage, N. L. (1991). The obviousness of social and educational research results. *Educational Researcher, 20*(A), 10–16.

Gagné, E. D. (1985). *The cognitive psychology of school learning.* Boston, MA: Little, Brown.

Gagné, E. D., Yekovich, C. W., & Yekovich, F. R. (1993). *The cognitive psychology of school learning* (2nd ed.). New York, NY: Harper-Collins.

Galambos, S. J., & Goldin-Meadow, S. (1990). The effects of learning two languages on metalinguistic development. *Cognition, 34,* 1–56.

Gallimore, R., & Goldenberg, C. (2001). Analyzing cultural models and settings to connect minority achievement and school improvement research. *Educational Psychologist, 36,* 45–56.

Galton, M., Hargreaves, L., & Pell, T. (2009). Group work and whole-class teaching with 11–14-year-olds compared. *Cambridge Journal of Education, 39,* 119–140.

Gamoran, A. (1987). The stratification of high school learning opportunities. *Sociology of Education, 60,* 135–155.

Ganis, G., Thompson, W. L., & Kosslyn, S. M. (2004). Brain areas underlying visual mental imagery and visual perception: An fMRI study. *Cognitive Brain Research, 20,* 226–241.

Garbarino, J., & deLara, E. (2002). *And words can hurt forever: How to protect adolescents from bullying, harassment, and emotional violence.* New York, NY: Free Press.

Garcia, E. E. (1992). "Hispanic" children: Theoretical, empirical, and related policy issues. *Educational Psychology Review, 4,* 69–94.

Garcia, E. E. (2002). *Student cultural diversity: Understanding the meaning and meeting the challenge.* Boston, MA: Houghton Mifflin.

Garcia, S. B., & Tyler, B.-J. (2010). Meeting the needs of English language learners with learning disabilities in the general curriculum. *Theory Into Practice, 49,* 113–120.

Gardner, H. (1983). *Frames of mind: The theory of multiple intelligences.* New York, NY: Basic Books.

Gardner, H. (1993). *Creating minds: An anatomy of creativity seen through the lives of Freud, Einstein, Picasso, Stravinsky, Elliot, Graham, and Gandhi.* New York, NY: Basic Books.

Gardner, H. (1998). Reflections on multiple intelligences: Myths and messages. In A. Woolfolk (Ed.), *Readings in educational psychology* (2nd ed., pp. 61–67). Boston, MA: Allyn & Bacon.

Gardner, H. (1999). Are there additional intelligences? The case for the naturalist, spiritual, and existential intelligences. In J. Kane (Ed.), *Educational information and transformation* (pp. 25–40). Upper Saddle River, NJ: Prentice-Hall.

Gardner, H. (2003, April 21). *Multiple intelligence after twenty years.* Paper presented at the American Educational Research Association, Chicago, IL.

Gardner, H. (2006). *Multiple intelligences: New horizons in theory and practice.* Cambridge, MA: Perseus Books.

Gardner, H. (2009). Birth and the spreading of a meme. In J.-Q. Chen, S. Moran, & H. Gardner (Eds.), *Multiple intelligences around the world* (pp. 3–16). San Francisco, CA: Wiley.

Gardner, H. (2011). *Frames of mind: The theory of multiple intelligences* (4th ed.). New York: Basic Books.

Gardner, H., & Hatch, T. (1989). Multiple intelligences go to school. *Educational Researcher, 18*(8), 4–9.

Gardner, H., & Moran, S. (2006). The science of multiple intelligences theory: A response to Lynn Waterhouse. *Educational Psychologist, 41,* 227–232.

Gardner, R., Brown, R., Sanders, S., & Menke, D. J. (1992). "Seductive details" in learning from text. In K. A. Renninger, S. Hidi, & A. Krapp (Eds.), *The role of interest in learning and development* (pp. 239–254). Mahwah, NJ: Erlbaum.

Garmon, L. C., Basinger, K. S., Gregg, V. R., & Gibbs, J. C. (1996). Gender differences in stage and expression of moral judgment. *Merrill-Palmer Quarterly, 42,* 418–437.

Garner, P. W., & Spears, F. M. (2000). Emotion regulation in low-income preschool children. *Social Development, 9,* 246–264.

Garner, R. (1998). Choosing to learn and not-learn in school. *Educational Psychology Review, 10,* 227–238.

Garnets, L. (2002). Sexual orientations in perspective. *Cultural Diversity and Ethnic Minority Psychology, 8,* 115–129.

Garrison, J. (1995). Deweyan pragmatism and the epistemology of contemporary social constructivism. *American Educational Research Journal, 32,* 716–741.

Gaskill, P. (Ed.). (2013). Special issue: Fifty years of *Theory Into Practice:* Learning from the past, looking to the future. *Theory Into Practice, 52,* 1–150.

Gathercole, S. E., Pickering, S. J., Ambridge, B., & Wearing, H. (2004). The structure of working memory from 4 to 15 years of age. *Developmental Psychology, 40,* 177–190.

Gay, G. (2000). *Culturally responsive teaching: Theory, research, and practice.* New York, NY: Teachers College Press.

Gay, G. (2006). Connections between classroom management and culturally responsive teaching. In C. Evertson & C. S. Weinstein (Eds.), *Handbook for classroom management: Research, practice, and contemporary issues.* Mahwah, NJ: Erlbaum.

Geary, D. C. (1995). Sexual selection and sex differences in spatial cognition. *Learning and Individual Differences, 7,* 289–303.

Geary, D. C. (1999). Evolution and developmental sex differences. *Current Directions in Psychological Science, 8,* 115–120.

Geary, D. C., & Bjorklund, D. F. (2000). Evolutionary developmental psychology. *Child Development, 7,* 57–65.

Gee, J. P. (2008). Learning and games. In K. Salen (Ed.), *The ecology of games: Connecting youth, games, and learning* (pp. 21–40). Cambridge, MA: The MIT Press, The John D. and Catherine T. MacArthur Foundation Series on Digital Media and Learning. doi:10.1162/dma1.9780262693646.021

Gehlbach, H. (2004). A new perspective on perspective taking: A multidimensional approach to conceptualizing an aptitude. *Educational Psychology Review, 16,* 207–234.

Geier, R., Blumenfeld, P., Marx, R., Krajcik, J., Fishman, B., Soloway, E., & Clay-Chambers, J. (2008). Standardized test outcomes for students engaged in inquiry based science curriculum in the context of urban reform. *Journal of Research in Science Teaching, 45,* 922–939.

Gelman, R. (2000). The epigenesis of mathematical thinking. *Journal of Applied Developmental Psychology, 21,* 27–37.

Gelman, R., & Cordes, S. A. (2001). Counting in animals and humans. In E. Dupoux (Ed.), *Essay in honor of Jacques Mehler.* Cambridge, MA: MIT Press.

Gentner, D., Loewenstein, J., & Thompson, L. (2003). Learning and transfer: A general role for analogical encoding. *Journal of Educational Psychology, 95,* 393–408.

George, P. S. (2005). A rationale for differentiated instruction in the regular classroom. *Theory Into Practice, 44,* 185–193.

Gergen, K. J. (1997). Constructing constructivism: Pedagogical potentials. *Issues in Education: Contributions from Educational Psychology, 3,* 195–202.

Gersten, R. (1996a). The language-minority students in transition: Contemporary instructional research. *The Elementary School Journal, 96,* 217–220.

Gersten, R. (1996b). Literacy instruction for language-minority students: The transition years. *The Elementary School Journal, 96,* 217–220.

Gersten, R., Baker, S. K., Shanahan, T., Linan-Thompson, S., Collins, P., & Scarcella, R. (2007). *Effective literacy and English language instruction for English learners in the elementary grades.* IES Practice Guide. Princeton, NJ: What Works Clearinghouse.

Gerwe, M., Stollhoff, K., Mossakowski, J., Kuehle, H-J., Goertz, U., Schaefer, C., . . . Heger, S. (2009). Tolerability and effects of OROS® MPH (Concerta®) on functioning, severity of disease and quality of life in children and adolescents with ADHD: Results from a prospective, non-interventional trial. *Attention Deficit Hyperactive Disorder, 1,* 175–186.

Gess-Newsome, J. (2013). Pedagogical content knowledge. In J. Hattie & E. Anderman (Eds.), *International guide to student achievement* (pp. 257–259). New York, NY: Routledge.

Gibson, D., Aldrich, C., & Prensky, M. (Eds.). (2006). *Games and simulations in online learning: Research and development frameworks.* Hershey, PA: Information Science Publishing.

Gillen-O'Neel, C., & Fuligni, A. (2013). A longitudinal study of school belonging and academic motivation across high school. *Child Development, 84,* 678–692.

Gillies, R. (2003). The behaviors, interactions, and perceptions of junior high school students during small-group learning. *Journal of Educational Psychology, 96,* 15–22.

Gillies, R. (2004). The effects of cooperative learning on junior high school students during small group learning. *Learning and Instruction, 14,* 197–213.

Gillies, R., & Boyle, M. (2011). Teachers' reflections of cooperative learning (CL): A two-year follow-up. *Teaching Education, 22,* 63–78.

Gilligan, C. (1982). *In a different voice: Psychological theory and women's development.* Cambridge, MA: Harvard University Press.

Gilligan, C., & Attanucci, J. (1988). Two moral orientations: Gender differences and similarities. *Merrill-Palmer Quarterly, 34,* 223–237.

Gini, G. (2008). Italian elementary and middle school students' blaming the victim of bullying and perception of school moral atmosphere. *The Elementary School Journal, 108,* 335–354.

Ginott, H. G. (1972). *Teacher and child: A book for parents and teachers.* New York, NY: Collier Books.

Ginsburg, K. R. (2007). The importance of play in promoting healthy child development and maintaining strong parent-child bonds. *Pediatrics, 119,* 182–191.

Glasser, W. (1969). *Schools without failure.* New York, NY: Harper & Row.

Glasser, W. (1990). *The quality school: Managing students without coercion.* New York, NY: Harper & Row.

Gleitman, H., Fridlund, A. J., & Reisberg, D. (1999). *Psychology* (5th ed.). New York, NY: Norton.

Gluck, M. A., Mercado, E., & Myers, C. E. (2008). *Learning and memory: From brain to behavior.* New York, NY: Worth.

Gluck, M. A., Mercado, E., & Myers, C. E. (2014). *Learning and memory: From brain to behavior* (2nd ed.). New York, NY: Worth.

Godden, D. R., & Baddeley, A. D. (1975). Context-dependent memory in two natural environments: On land and underwater. *British Journal of Psychology, 66,* 325–331.

Goe, L. (2013). Quality of teaching. In J. Hattie & E. Anderman (Eds.), *International guide to student achievement* (pp. 237–239), New York, NY: Routledge.

Goetz, T., Cronjaeger, H., Frenzel, A. C., Ludtke, O., & Hall, N. (2010). Academic self-concept and emotion relations: Domain specificity and age effects. *Contemporary Educational Psychology, 35,* 44–58.

Goetz, T., Frenzel, A. C., Hall, N. C., & Pekrun, R. (2008). Antecedents of academic emotions: Testing the internal/external frame of reference model for academic enjoyment. *Contemporary Educational Psychology, 33,* 9–33.

Goldenberg, C. (1996). The education of language-minority students: Where are we, and where do we need to go? *The Elementary School Journal, 96,* 353–361.

Goldman, S. R., Lawless, K., Pellegrino, J. W., & Plants, R. (2006). Technology for teaching and learning with understanding. In J. Cooper (Ed.), *Classroom teaching skills* (8th ed., pp. 104–150). Boston, MA: Houghton-Mifflin.

Goldstone, R. L., & Day, S. B. (2012). Introduction to "New Conceptualizations of Transfer of Learning." *Educational Psychologist, 47,* 149–152, doi: 10.1080/00461520.2012.695710

Goleman, D. (1995). *Emotional intelligence*. New York, NY: Bantam.

Golombok, S., Rust, J., Zervoulis, K., Croudace, T., Golding, J., & Hines, M. (2008). Developmental trajectories of sex-typed behavior in boys and girls: A longitudinal general population study of children aged 2.5–8 years. *Child Development, 79*, 1583–1593.

Gonzales, N., Moll, L. C., Floyd-Tenery, M., Rivera, A., Rendon, P., Gonzales, R., & Amanti, C. (1993). *Teacher research on funds of knowledge: Learning from households*. Washington, DC: The Georgetown University National Center for Research on Cultural Diversity and Second Language Learning. Retrieved from http://www.ncela.gwu.edu/pubs/ncrcdsll/epr6.htm

Gonzalez, A. L. (2010, June). *Hispanics in the US: A new generation*. BBC News: US and Canada. Retrieved from http://www.bbc.co.uk/news/10209099

Gonzalez, N., Moll, L. C., & Amanti, C. (2005). *Funds of knowledge: Theorizing practices in households and classrooms*. Mahwah, NJ: Erlbaum.

Gonzalez, V. (1999). *Language and cognitive development in second language learning: Educational implications for children and adults*. Boston, MA: Allyn & Bacon.

Gonzalez, V., Brusca-Vega, R., & Yawkey, T. (1997). *Assessment and instruction of culturally diverse students with or at-risk of learning problems: From research to practice*. Boston, MA: Allyn & Bacon.

Good, C., Aronson, J., & Inzlicht, M. (2003). Improving adolescents' standardized test performance: An intervention to reduce the effects of stereotype threat. *Journal of Applied Developmental Psychology, 24*, 645–662.

Good, T. L. (1983a). Classroom research: A decade of progress. *Educational Psychologist, 18*, 127–144.

Good, T. L. (1983b). Research on classroom teaching. In L. Shulman & G. Sykes (Eds.), *Handbook of teaching and policy* (pp. 42–80). New York, NY: Longman.

Good, T. L. (1988). Teacher expectations. In D. Berliner & B. Rosenshine (Eds.), *Talks to teachers* (pp. 159–200). New York, NY: Random House.

Good, T. L. (1996). Teaching effects and teacher evaluation. In J. Sikula (Ed.), *Handbook of research on teacher education* (pp. 617–665). New York, NY: Macmillan.

Good, T. L., & Brophy, J. E. (2008). *Looking in classrooms* (10th ed.). New York, NY: Longman.

Goodrich, H. (1997). Understanding rubrics. *Educational Leadership, 54*(4), 14–17.

Goodrich, J. M., Lonigan, C. J., & Farver, J. M. (2013). Do early literacy skills in children's first language promote development of skills in their second language? An experimental evaluation of transfer. *Journal of Educational Psychology*. doi: 10.1037/a0031780

Gordon, E. W. (1991). Human diversity and pluralism. *Educational Psychologist, 26*, 99–108.

Gordon, R., Kane, T. J., & Staiger, D. O. (2006). *Identifying effective teachers using performance on the job*. Washington, DC: The Hamilton Project—The Brookings Institute.

Gordon, T. (1981). Crippling our children with discipline. *Journal of Education, 163*, 228–243.

Goswami, U. (2004). Neuroscience, education, and special education. *British Journal of Special Education, 31*, 175–183.

Gottlieb, G., Wahlsten, D., & Lickliter, R. (2006). The significance of biology for human development: A developmental psychobiological systems view. In R. M. Lerner (Ed.), *Handbook of child psychology* (6th ed., Vol. 1: Theoretical models of human development, pp. 210–257). New York, NY: Wiley.

Graham, S. (1991). A review of attribution theory in achievement contexts. *Educational Psychology Review, 3*, 5–39.

Graham, S. (1996). How causal beliefs influence the academic and social motivation of African-American children. In G. G. Brannigan (Ed.), *The enlightened educator: Research adventures in the schools* (pp. 111–126). New York, NY: McGraw-Hill.

Graham, S. (1998). Self-blame and peer victimization in middle school: An attributional analysis. *Developmental Psychology, 34*, 587–599.

Graham, S., & Taylor, A. (2002). Ethnicity, gender, and the development of achievement values. In A. Wigfield & J. Eccles (Eds.), *Development of achievement motivation* (pp. 121–146). San Diego, CA: Academic Press.

Graham, S., & Weiner, B. (1996). Theories and principles of motivation. In D. Berliner & R. C. Calfee (Eds.), *Handbook of educational psychology* (pp. 63–84). New York, NY: Macmillan.

Gray, P. (2011). *Psychology* (6th ed.). New York, NY: Worth.

Gredler, M. E. (2005). *Learning and instruction: Theory into practice* (5th ed.). Boston, MA: Allyn & Bacon.

Gredler, M. E. (2009a). Hiding in plain sight: The stages of mastery/self-regulation in Vygotsky's cultural-historical theory. *Educational Psychologist, 44*, 1–19.

Gredler, M. E. (2009b). *Learning and instruction: Theory into practice* (6th ed.). Columbus, OH: Merrill.

Gredler, M. E. (2012). Understanding Vygotsky for the classroom: Is it too late? *Educational Psychology Review, 24*, 113–131.

Green, M., & Piel, J. A. (2010). *Theories of human development: A comparative approach* (2nd ed.). Boston, MA: Allyn & Bacon.

Greene, J. A., Muis, K. R., & Pieschl, S. (2010). The role of epistemic beliefs in students' self-regulated learning with computer-based learning environments: Conceptual and methodological issues. *Educational Psychologist, 45*, 245–257.

Greeno, J. G., Collins, A. M., & Resnick, L. B. (1996). Cognition and learning. In D. Berliner & R. Calfee (Eds.), *Handbook of educational psychology* (pp. 15–46). New York, NY: Macmillan.

Greenwald, A. G., Oakes, M. A., & Hoffman, H. G. (2003). Targets of discrimination: Effects of race on responses to weapons holders. *Journal of Experimental Social Psychology, 39*, 399–405.

Gregorc, A. F. (1982). *Gregorc Style Delineator: Development, technical, and administrative manual*. Maynard, MA: Gabriel Systems.

Greiff, S., Wüstenberg, S., Molnár, G., Fischer, A., Funke, J., & Csapó, B. (2013). Complex problem solving in educational contexts—something beyond g: Concept, assessment, measurement invariance, and construct validity. *Journal of Educational Psychology, 105*, 364–379. doi: 10.1037/a0031856

Griffins, P. E., & Gray, R. D. (2005). Discussion: Three ways to misunderstand developmental systems theory. *Biology and Philosophy, 20*, 417–425.

Griffith, J., Steptoe, A., & Cropley, M. (1999). An investigation of coping strategies associated with job stress in teachers. *British Journal of Educational Psychology, 69*, 517–531.

Grigorenko, E. L., Jarvin, L., Diffley, R., III, Goodyear, J., Shanahan, E. J., & Sternberg, R. J. (2009). Are SSATs and GPA enough? A theory-based approach to predicting academic success in secondary school. *Journal of Educational Psychology, 101*, 964–981.

Grigorenko, E. L., & Sternberg, R. J. (2001). Analytical, creative, and practical intelligence as predictors of self-reported adaptive functioning: A case study in Russia. *Intelligence, 29*, 57–73.

Grolnick, W. S., Gurland, S. T., Jacob, K. F., & DeCourcey, W. (2002). The development of self-determination in middle childhood and adolescence. In A. Wigfield & J. Eccles (Eds.), *Development of achievement motivation* (pp. 147–171). New York, NY: Academic Press.

Gronlund, N. E., & Brookhart, S. M. (2009). *Gronlund's writing instructional objectives* (8th ed.). Columbus, OH: Pearson.

Gröschner, A., Seidel, T., & Shavelson, R. S. (2013). Methods for studying teacher and teaching effectiveness. In J. Hattie & E. Anderman (Eds.), *International guide to student achievement*. New York, NY: Routledge.

Grossman, H., & Grossman, S. H. (1994). *Gender issues in education*. Boston, MA: Allyn & Bacon.

Grover, S., & Pea, R. (2013). Computational thinking in K–12: A review of the state of the field. *Educational Researcher, 42*, 38–43.

Guernsey, L. (2013, September 2). Very young programmers. *New York Times*. Retrieved from http://www.nytimes.com/2013/09/03/science/very-young-programmers.html

Guerra, N. G., Williams, K. R., & Sadek, S. (2011). Understanding bullying and victimization during childhood and adolescence: A mixed methods study. *Child Development, 82*, 295–310.

Guglielmi, R. S. (2008). Native language proficiency, English literacy, academic achievement, and occupational attainment in limited-English-proficient students: A latent growth modeling perspective. *Journal of Educational Psychology, 100*, 322–342.

Guglielmi, R. S. (2012, March 5). Math and science achievement in English language learners: Multivariate latent growth modeling of predictors, mediators, and moderators. *Journal of Educational Psychology, 104*, 580–602. doi: 10.1037/a0027378

Gunderson, E. A., Gripshover, S. J., Romero, C., Dweck, C. S., Goldin-Meadow, S., & Levine, S. C. (2013). Parent praise to 1- to 3-year-olds predicts children's motivational frameworks 5 years later. *Child Development, 84*(5), 1526–1541. doi: 10.1111/cdev.12064

Guo, J.-P., Pang, M. F., Yang, L.-Y., & Ding, Y. (2012). Learning from comparing multiple examples: On the dilemma of "similar" or "different." *Educational Psychology Review, 24*, 251–269.

Gurian, M., & Henley, P. (2001). *Boys and girls learn differently: A guide for teachers and parents*. San Francisco, CA: Jossey-Bass.

Guskey, T. R. (2011). Five obstacles to grading reform. *Educational Leadership, 69*(3), 17–21.

Guskey, T. R., & Bailey, J. M. (2001). *Developing grading and reporting systems for student learning*. Thousand Oaks, CA: Corwin Press.

Gut, J., Reimann, G., & Grob, A. (2013). A contextualized view on long-term predictors of academic performance. *Journal of Educational Psychology, 105*, 436–443. doi: 10.1037/a0031503

Guthrie, J. T., & Alao, S. (1997). Designing contexts to increase motivations of reading. *Educational Psychologist, 32*, 95–105.

Guthrie, J. T., Cox, K. E., Anderson, E., Harris, K., Mazzoni, S., & Rach, L. (1998). Principles of integrated instruction for engagement in reading. *Educational Psychology Review, 10*, 227–238.

Hacker, D. J., & Tenent, A. (2002). Implementing reciprocal teaching in the classroom: Overcoming obstacles and making modifications. *Journal of Educational Psychology, 94*, 699–718.

Haertel, E. H. (1999). Performance assessment and educational reform. *Phi Delta Kappan, 80*, 662–666.

Hafen, C. A., Allen, J. P., Mikami, A. Y., Gregory, A., Hamre, B., & Pianta, R. C. (2012). The pivotal role of adolescent autonomy in secondary school classrooms. *Journal of Youth and Adolescence, 41,* 245–255. doi 10.1007/s10964–011–9739–2

Hagborg, W. J. (1993). Rosenberg Self-Esteem Scale and Harter's Self-Perception Profile for Adolescents: A concurrent validity study. *Psychology in Schools, 30,* 132–136.

Hagemans, M. G., van der Meij, H., & de Jong, T. (2013). The effects of a concept map-based support tool on simulation-based inquiry learning. *Journal of Educational Psychology, 105,* 1–24. doi: 10.1037/a0029433

Haidt, J. (2012). *The righteous mind: Why good people are divided by politics and religion.* New York: Pantheon Books.

Haidt, J. (2013). Moral psychology for the twenty-first century. *Journal of Moral Education, 42,* 281–297. doi:10.1080/03057240.2013.817327

Haier, R. J., & Jung, R. E. (2008). Brain imaging studies of intelligence and creativity: What is the picture for education? *Roeper Review, 30,* 171–180.

Hakuta, K. (1986). *Mirror of language: The debate on bilingualism.* New York, NY: Basic Books.

Hakuta, K., & Garcia, E. E. (1989). Bilingualism and education. *American Psychologist, 44,* 374–379.

Haladyna, T. H. (2002). *Essentials of standardized achievement testing: Validity and accountability.* Boston, MA: Allyn & Bacon.

Haley, M. H., & Austin, T. Y. (2014). *Content-based second language teaching and learning: An interactive approach* (2nd ed.). Boston, MA: Pearson.

Halim, M. L., Ruble, D., Tamis-LeMonda, C., & Shrout, P. E. (2013). Rigidity in gender-typed behaviors in early childhood: A longitudinal study of ethnic minority children. *Child Development, 84,* 1269–1284.

Hall, L. J., Grundon, G. S., Pope, C., & Romero, A. B. (2010). Training paraprofessionals to use behavioral strategies when educating learners with autism spectrum disorders across environments. *Behavioral Interventions, 25,* 37–51.

Hall, V. C., Bailey, J., & Tillman, D. (1997). Can student-generated illustrations be worth ten thousand words? *Journal of Educational Psychology, 89,* 677–681.

Hallahan, D. P., & Kauffman, J. M. (2006). *Exceptional learners: Introduction to special education* (10th ed.). Boston, MA: Allyn & Bacon.

Hallahan, D. P., Kauffman, J. M., & Pullen, P. C. (2009). *Exceptional learners: Introduction to special education* (11th ed.). Boston, MA: Allyn & Bacon.

Hallahan, D. P., Kauffman, J. M., & Pullen, P. C. (2012). *Exceptional learners: An introduction to special education* (12th ed.). Boston, MA: Pearson.

Halpern, D. F., Benbow, C. P., Geary. D. C., Gur, R. C., Hyde, J. S., & Gernsbacher, M. A. (2007). The science of sex differences in science and mathematics. *Psychological Science in the Public Interest, 8,* 1–51.

Hamann, D. L., Baker, D. S., McAllister, P. A., & Bauer, W. I. (2000). Factors affecting university music students' perceptions of lesson quality and teaching effectiveness. *Journal of Research in Music Education, 48,* 102–113.

Hambrick, D. Z., Kane, M. J., & Engle, R. W. (2005). The role of working memory in higher-level cognition. In R. Sternberg & J. E. Pretz (Eds.), *Cognition and intelligence: Identifying the mechanisms of the mind* (pp. 104–121). New York, NY: Cambridge University Press.

Hamers, J. F., & Blanc, M. H. A. (2000). *Bilinguality and bilingualism* (2nd ed.). Cambridge, England: Cambridge University Press.

Hamilton, J. (2009). Multitasking teens may be muddling their brains. Retrieved from http://www.npr.org/templates/story/story.php?storyId=95524385

Hamman, D., Berthelot, J., Saia, J., & Crowley, E. (2000). Teachers' coaching of learning and its relation to students' strategic learning. *Journal of Educational Psychology, 92,* 342–348.

Hammer, C. S., Farkas, G., & Maczuga, S. (2010). The language and literacy development of Head Start children: A study using the family and child experiences survey database. *Language, Speech, and Hearing Services in Schools, 41,* 70–83.

Hammer, C. S., Lawrence, F. R., & Miccio, A. W. (2007). Bilingual children's language abilities and reading outcomes in Head Start and kindergarten. *Language, Speech and Hearing Services in Schools, 38,* 237–248.

Hamre, B. K., & Pianta, R. C. (2001). Early teacher–child relationships and the trajectory of children's school outcomes through eighth grade. *Child Development, 72,* 625–638.

Hanushek, E. A., Rivkin, S. G., & Kain, J. J. (2005). Teachers, schools and academic achievement. *Econometrica, 73,* 417–458.

Hapgood, S., Magnusson, S. J., & Palincsar, A. S. (2004). Teacher, text, and experience: A case of young children's scientific inquiry. *The Journal of the Learning Sciences, 13,* 455–505.

Harackiewicz, J. M., & Linnenbrink, E. A. (2005). Multiple achievement goals and multiple pathways for learning: The agenda and impact of Paul R. Pintrich. *Educational Psychologist, 40,* 75–84.

Harber, K. D., Gorman, J. L., Gengaro, F. P., Butisingh, S., Tsang, W., & Ouellette, R. (2012). Students' race and teachers' social support affect the positive feedback bias in public schools. *Journal of Educational Psychology.* doi: 10.1037/a0028110

Hardin, C. J. (2008). *Effective classroom management: Models and strategies for today's classrooms* (2nd ed.). Columbus, OH: Merrill/Prentice-Hall.

Hardman, M. L., Drew, C. J., & Egan, M. W. (2014). *Human exceptionality: Society, school, and family* (11th ed.). New York: Cengage.

Harklau, L., Losey, K. M., & Siegal, M. (Eds.). (1999). *Generation 1.5 Meet college composition: Issues in the teaching of writing to U.S.-educated learners of ESL.* Mahwah, NJ: Erlbaum.

Harp, S. F., & Mayer, R. E. (1998). How seductive details do their damage: A theory of cognitive interest in science learning. *Journal of Educational Psychology, 90,* 414–434.

Harris, J. R. (1998). *The nurture assumption: Why children turn out the way they do: Parents matter less than you think and peers matter more.* New York, NY: Free Press.

Harris, K. R. (1990). Developing self-regulated learners: The role of private speech and self-instruction. *Educational Psychologist, 25,* 35–50.

Harris, K. R., Alexander, P., & Graham, S. (2008). Michael Pressley's contributions to the history and future of strategies research. *Educational Psychologist, 43,* 86–96.

Harris, K. R., & Graham, S. (1996). Memo to constructivist: Skills count too. *Educational Leadership, 53* (5), 26–29.

Harris, K. R., Graham, S., & Pressley, M. (1992). Cognitive-behavioral approaches in reading and written language: Developing self-regulated learners. In N. N. Singh & I. L. Beale (Eds.), *Learning disabilities: Nature, theory, and treatment* (pp. 415–451). New York: Springer-Verlag.

Harris, K. R., & Pressley, M. (1991). The nature of cognitive strategy instruction: Interactive strategy construction. *Exceptional Children, 57,* 392–404.

Harris, M. A., Prior, J. C., & Koehoorn, M. (2008). Age at menarche in the Canadian population: Secular trends and relationship to adulthood BMI. *Journal of Adolescent Health, 43,* 548–554.

Harrower, J. K., & Dunlap, G. (2001). Including children with autism in general classrooms. *Behavior Modification, 25,* 762–784.

Harter, S. (1998). The development of self-representations. In N. Eisenberg (Ed.), *Handbook of child psychology: Vol. 3. Social, emotional, and personality development* (5th ed., pp. 553–618). New York, NY: Wiley.

Harter, S. (2003). The development of self-representation during childhood and adolescence. In M. R. Leary & J. P. Tangney (Eds.), *Handbook of self and identity* (pp. 610–642). New York, NY: Guilford.

Harter, S. (2006). The self. In W. Damon & R. M. Lerner (Series Eds.) *Social, emotional and personality development* (6th ed., pp. 646–718). New York, NY: Wiley.

Harter, S., & Whitesell, N. R. (2003). Beyond the debate: Why some adolescents report stable self-worth over time and situation, whereas others report changes in self-worth. *Journal of Personality, 71,* 1027–1058.

Hartley, B. L., & Sutton, R. M. (2013). A stereotype threat account of boys' academic underachievement. *Child Development, 84,* 1716–1733.

Hartocollis, A. (2013, Sept. 30). City unveils campaign to improve girls' self-esteem. *The New York Times.* Retrieved from http://www.nytimes.com/2013/10/01/nyregion/city-unveils-a-campaign-to-improve-girls-self-esteem.html

Hartshore, J. K., & Ullman, M. T. (2006). Why girls say "holded" more than boys. *Developmental Science, 9,* 21–32.

Hattie, J., & Timperley, H. (2007). The power of feedback. *Review of Educational Research, 77,* 81–112.

Haugland, S. W., & Wright, J. L. (1997). *Young children and technology: A world of discovery.* Boston, MA: Allyn & Bacon.

Hawkins, M. R. (2004). Researching English language and literacy development in schools. *Educational Researcher, 33*(3), 14–25.

Hayes, S. C., Rosenfarb, I., Wulfert, E., Munt, E. D., Korn, Z., & Zettle, R. D. (1985). Self-reinforcement effects: An artifact of social standard setting? *Journal of Applied Behavior Analysis, 18,* 201–214.

Hearn, S., Saulnier, G., Strayer, J., Glenham, M., Koopman, R., & Marcia, J. E. (2012). Between integrity and despair: Toward construct validation of Erikson's eighth stage. *Journal of Adult Development, 19,* 1–20.

Heath, S. B. (1989). Oral and literate traditions among black Americans living in poverty. *American Psychologist, 44,* 367–373.

Hecht, S. A., & Vagi, K. J. (2010). Sources of group and individual differences in emerging fraction skills. *Journal of Educational Psychology, 102,* 843–859.

Helms, J. E. (1995). An update of Helms's White and People of Color racial identity models. In J. G. Ponterotto, J. M. Casas, L. A. Suzuki, & C. M. Alexander (Eds.), *Handbook of multicultural counseling* (pp. 181–198). Thousand Oaks, CA: Sage.

Helwig, C. C., Arnold, M. L., Tan, D., & Boyd, D. (2003). Chinese adolescents' reasoning about democratic and authority-based decision making in peer, family, and school contexts. *Child Development, 74,* 783–800.

Henderson, M. (1996). *Helping your students get the most out of homework* [Brochure]. Chicago, IL: National Parent–Teacher Association.

Hennessey, M. N., Higley, K., & Chesnut, S. R. (2012). Persuasive pedagogy: A new paradigm for mathematics education. *Review of Educational Research, 24,* 187–204.

Henrich, C. C., Brookmeyer, K. A., Shrier, L. A., & Shahar, G. (2006). Supportive relationships and sexual risk behavior in adolescence: An ecological/transactional approach. *Journal of Pediatric Psychology, 31*, 286–297.

Henry, B. (2011, May 2). Personal communication.

Herbert, E. A. (1998). Design matters: How school environment affects children. *Educational Leadership, 56*(1), 69–71.

Herman, J., & Winters, L. (1994). Portfolio research: A slim collection. *Educational Leadership, 52*(2), 48–55.

Herman, M. (2004). Forced to choose: Some determinants of racial identification in multi-racial adolescents. *Child Development, 75*, 730–748.

Herron, A. (2013, December 10). Single-sex classrooms: Educators, students say the change makes a difference. *Winston-Salem Journal.* Retrieved from http://www.journalnow.com/news/local/article_f39deeb6–613c-11e3-be5c-0019bb30f31a.html

Hetherington, E. M. (2006). The influence of conflict, marital problem solving and parenting on children's adjustment in nondivorced, divorced and remarried families. In A. Clarke-Stewart & J. Dunn (Eds.), *Families count: Effects on child and adolescent development* (pp. 203–237). New York, NY: Cambridge University Press.

Hetherington, E. M., & Kelly, J. (2003). *For better or for worse: Divorce reconsidered.* New York, NY: Norton.

Hewstone, M. (1989). Changing stereotypes with disconfirming information. In D. Bar-Tal, C. Graumann, A. Kruglanski, & W. Stroebe (Eds.), *Stereotyping and prejudice: Changing conceptions* (pp. 207–223). New York, NY: Springer-Verlag.

Hickey, D. T. (2003). Engaged participation vs. marginal non-participation: A stridently sociocultural model of achievement motivation. *Elementary School Journal, 103*(4), 401–429.

Hickey, D. T., Kindfield, A. C. H., Horwitz, P., & Christie, M. A. (1999). Advancing educational theory by enhancing practice in a technology supported genetics learning environment. *Journal of Education, 181*, 25–55.

Hickey, D. T., Wolfe, E. W., & Kindfield, A. C. H. (2000). Assessing learning in a technology-supported genetics environment: Evidential and consequential validity issues. *Educational Assessment, 6*, 155–196.

Hidi, S., & Renninger, K. A. (2006). The four-phase model of interest development. *Educational Psychologist, 41*, 111–127.

Hidi, S., Renninger, K. A., & Krapp, A. (2004). Interest, a motivational variable that combines affective and cognitive functioning. In D. Y. Dai & R. J. Sternberg (Eds.), *Motivation, emotion, and cognition: Integrative perspectives on intellectual functioning and development* (pp. 89–115). Mahwah, NJ: Erlbaum.

Hiebert, E. H., & Mesmer, H. A. E. (2013). Upping the ante of text complexity in the Common Core State Standards: Examining its potential impact on young readers. *Educational Researcher, 42*, 44–51. doi: 10.3102/0013189X12459802

Hilgard, E. R. (1996). History of educational psychology. In R. Calfee & D. Berliner (Eds.), *Handbook of educational psychology* (pp. 990–1004). New York, NY: Macmillan.

Hill, E. L., & Khanem, F. (2009). The development of hand preference in children: The effect of task demands and links with manual dexterity. *Brain and Cognition, 71*, 99–107. doi:10.1016/j.bandc.2009.04.006

Hill, H. C., Rowan, B., & Ball, D. L. (2005). Effects of teachers' mathematics knowledge for teaching on student achievement. *American Educational Research Journal, 42*, 371–406.

Hindi, E. R., & Perry, N. (2007). Elementary teachers' application of Jean Piaget's theories of cognitive development during social studies curriculum debates in Arizona. *The Elementary School Journal, 108*, 64–79.

Hines, C. V., Cruickshank, D. R., & Kennedy, J. J. (1985). Teacher clarity and its relation to student achievement and satisfaction. *American Educational Research Journal, 22*, 87–99.

Hines, M. (2004). *Brain gender.* New York, NY: Oxford University Press.

Hinnant, J. B., O'Brien, M., & Ghazarian, S. R. (2009). The longitudinal relations of teacher expectations to achievement in the early school years. *Journal of Educational Psychology, 101*, 662–670.

Hinton, C., Miyamoto, K., & Della-Chiesa, B. (2008). Brain research, learning and emotions: Implications for education research, policy and practice. *European Journal of Education, 43*, 87–103.

Hipsky, S. (2011). *Differentiated literacy and language arts strategies for the elementary classroom.* Columbus, OH: Merrill.

Hiroto, D. S., & Seligman, M. E. P. (1975). Generality of learned helplessness in man. *Journal of Personality and Social Psychology, 31*, 311–327.

Hirsch, E. D., Jr. (1996). *The schools we need: Why we don't have them.* New York, NY: Doubleday.

Hirvikoski, T., Waaler, E., Alfredsson, J., Pihlgren, C., Holmström, A., Johnson, A., . . . Nordström, A. L. (2011). Reduced ADHD symptoms in adults with ADHD after structured skills training group: Results from a randomized controlled trial. *Behavioural Research and Therapy, 49*, 175–185.

Hmelo, C. E. (1998). Problem-based learning: Effects on the early acquisition of cognitive skill in medicine. *Journal of the Learning Sciences, 7*, 173–208.

Hmelo-Silver, C. E. (2004). Problem-based learning: What and how do students learn? *Educational Psychology Review, 16*, 235–266.

Hmelo-Silver, C. E., Ravit, G. D., & Chinn, C. A. (2007). Scaffolding and achievement in problem-based and inquiry learning: A response to Kirschner, Sweller, and Clark (2006). *Educational Psychologist, 42*, 99–107.

Hobbs, R. (2004). A review of school-based initiatives in media literacy education. *American Behavioral Scientist, 48*, 42–59.

Hoeffler, T. N., & Leutner, D. (2011). The role of spatial ability in learning from instructional animations—Evidence for an ability-as-compensator hypothesis. *Computers in Human Behavior, 27*, 209–216.

Hofer, M. (2010). Adolescents' development of individual interests: A product of multiple goal regulation? *Educational Psychologist, 45*(3), 149–166.

Hoff, E. (2006). How social contexts support and shape language development. *Developmental Review, 26*, 55–88.

Hofferth, S. L., & Sandberg, J. F. (2000). *Changes in American children's time, 1981–1997.* Ann Arbor, MI: University of Michigan Population Studies Center.

Hoffman, M. L. (2000). *Empathy and moral development.* New York, NY: Cambridge University Press.

Hoffman, M. L. (2001). A comprehensive theory of prosocial moral development. In A. Bohart & D. Stipek (Eds.), *Constructive and destructive behavior* (pp. 61–86). Washington, DC: American Psychological Association.

Hogan, T., Rabinowitz, M., & Craven, J. A., III. (2003). Representation in teaching: Inferences from research of expert and novice teachers. *Educational Psychologist, 38*, 235–247.

Hoge, D. R., Smit, E. K., & Hanson, S. L. (1990). School experiences predicting changes in self-esteem of sixth- and seventh-grade students. *Journal of Educational Psychology, 82*, 117–126.

Holahan, C., & Sears, R. (1995). *The gifted group in later maturity.* Stanford, CA: Stanford University Press.

Holzberger, D., Philipp, A., & Kunter, M. (2013). How teachers' self-efficacy is related to instructional quality: A longitudinal analysis. *Journal of Educational Psychology, 105*, 774–786. doi: 10.1037/a0032198

Hong, G., & Raudenbush, S. W. (2005). Effects of kindergarten retention policy on children's cognitive growth in reading and mathematics. *Educational Evaluation and Policy Analysis, 27*, 205–224.

Hong, J. S., & Garbarino, J. (2012). Risk and protective factors for homophobic bullying in schools: An application of the social–ecological framework. *Educational Psychology Review, 24*, 271–285.

Hoover-Dempsey, K. V., Battiato, A. C., Walker, J. M. T., Reed, R. P., DeJong, J. M., & Jones, K. P. (2001). Parental involvement in homework. *Educational Psychologist, 36*, 195–209.

Hopkins, M., Thompson, R. K., Linquanti, R., Hakuta, K., & August, D. (2013). Fully accounting for English learner performance: A key issue in ESEA reauthorization. *Educational Researcher, 42*(2), 101–108.

Horn, J. L. (1998). A basis for research on age differences in cognitive capabilities. In J. J. McArdle & R. W. Woodcock (Eds.), *Human cognitive theories in theory and practice* (pp. 57–87). Mahwah, NJ: Erlbaum.

Horovitz, B. (2002, April 22). Gen Y: A tough crowd to sell. *USA Today*, pp. B1–2.

Howe, M. J. A., Davidson, J. W., & Sloboda, J. A. (1998). Innate talents: Reality or myth? *Behavioral and Brain Sciences, 21*, 399–406.

Hsieh, P. P., & Kang, H. (2010). Attribution and self-efficacy and their interrelationship in the Korean EFL context. *Language Learning, 60*(3), 606–627.

Huang, C. (2012). Discriminant and criterion-related validity of achievement goals in predicting academic achievement: A meta-analysis. *Journal of Educational Psychology, 104*, 48–73. doi: 10.1037/a0026223

Hudley, C., Graham, S., & Taylor, A. (2007). Reducing aggressive behavior and increasing motivation in school: The evolution of an intervention to strengthen school adjustment. *Educational Psychologist, 42*, 251–260.

Hudley, C., & Novak, A. (2007). Environmental influences, the developing brain, and aggressive behavior. *Theory Into Practice, 46*, 121–129.

Huesmann, L. R., Moise-Titus, J., Podolski, C. P., & Eron, L. D. (2003). Longitudinal relations between children's exposure to TV violence and their aggressive and violent behavior in young adulthood: 1977–1992. *Developmental Psychology, 39*, 201–221.

Huguet, P., & Régner, I. (2007). Stereotype threat among schoolgirls in quasi-ordinary classroom circumstances. *Journal of Educational Psychology, 99*, 345–360.

Hulit, L., & Howard, M. (2006). *Born to talk: An introduction to speech and language development* (4th ed.). Boston, MA: Allyn & Bacon.

Hulleman, C. S., Godes, O., Hendricks, B. L., & Harackiewicz, J. M. (2010). Enhancing interest and performance with a utility value intervention. *Journal of Educational Psychology, 102*, 880–895.

Hung, D. W. L. (1999). Activity, apprenticeship, and epistemological appropriation: Implications from the writings of Michael Polanyi. *Educational Psychologist, 34*, 193–205.

Hunt, E. (2000). Let's hear it for crystallized intelligence. *Learning and Individual Differences, 12,* 123–129.

Hunt, J. McV. (1961). *Intelligence and experience.* New York, NY: Ronald.

Hunt, N., & Marshall, K. (2002). *Exceptional children and youth: An introduction to special education* (3rd ed.). Boston, MA: Houghton Mifflin.

Hunter, M. (1982). *Mastery teaching.* El Segundo, CA: TIP Publications.

Hurry, J., Nunes, T., Bryant, P., Pretzlik, U., Parker, M., Curno, C., & Midgley, L. (2005). Transforming research on morphology into teacher practice. *Research Papers in Education, 20*(2), 187–206.

Hutchinson, N. L. (2009). *Inclusion of exceptional learners in Canadian classrooms: A practical handbook for teachers* (3rd ed.). Toronto, Canada: Prentice Hall.

Hyman, I., Kay, B., Tabori, A., Weber, M., Mahon, M., & Cohen, I. (2006). Bullying: Theory, research and interventions about student victimization. In C. Evertson & C. S. Weinstein (Eds.), *Handbook for classroom management: Research, practice, and contemporary issues.* Mahwah, NJ: Erlbaum.

Idol, L. (2006). Toward inclusion of special education students in general education: A program evaluation of eight schools. *Remedial and Special Education, 27,* 77–94.

Individuals with Disabilities Education Act. (1997). Retrieved from http://www.ed.gov/policy/speced/guid/idea/idea2004.html

Individuals with Disabilities Education Act. (2004). Retrieved from http://www.ed.gov/

Inhelder, B., & Piaget, J. (1958). *The growth of logical thinking from childhood to adolescence: An essay on the construction of formal operational structures.* New York, NY: Basic Books.

Institute for Human and Machine Cognition. (2014). *Institute for Human and Machine Cognition Cmap Tools home page.* Dr. Alberto Cañas: Creator of Cmap Tools. Pensacola, FL: Author. Retrieved from http://cmap.ihmc.us

Iran-Nejad, A. (1990). Active and dynamic self-regulation of learning processes. *Review of Educational Research, 60,* 573–602.

Irvine, J. J. (1990). *Black students and school failure: Policies, practices, and prescriptions.* New York, NY: Praeger.

Irvine, J. J., & Armento, B. J. (2001). *Culturally responsive teaching: Lesson planning for elementary and middle grades.* New York, NY: McGraw-Hill.

Irvine, J. J., & Fraser, J. W. (1998, May). Warm demanders. *Education Week.* Retrieved from http://www.edweek.org/ew/ewstory.cfm?slug=35irvine.h17&keywords=Irvine

Jackson, L. A., von Eye, A., Biocca, F. A., Barbatsis, G., Zhao, Y., & Fitzgerald, H. E. (2006). Does home Internet use influence the academic performance of low-income children? *Developmental Psychology, 42,* 429–435.

Jacobs, J. E., Lanza, S., Osgood, D. W., Eccles, J. S., & Wigfield, A. (2002). Changes in children's self-competence and values: Gender and domain differences across grades one through twelve. *Child Development, 73,* 509–527.

Jaffee, S., & Hyde, J. S. (2000). Gender differences in moral orientation. *Psychological Bulletin, 126,* 703–726.

Jain, S., & Dowson, M. (2009). Mathematics anxiety as a function of multidimensional self-regulation and self-efficacy. *Contemporary Educational Psychology, 34,* 240–249.

James, W. (1890). *The principles of psychology* (Vol. 2). New York, NY: Holt.

James, W. (1912). *Talks to teachers on psychology: And to students on some of life's ideals.* New York, NY: Holt.

Jang, H., Kim, E. J., & Reeve, J. (2012). Longitudinal test of self-determination theory's motivation mediation model in a naturally occurring classroom context. *Journal of Educational Psychology, 104,* 1175–1188. doi: 10.1037/a0028089

Jang, H., Reeve, J., & Deci, E. L. (2010). Engaging students in learning activities: It is not autonomy support or structure but autonomy support and structure. *Journal of Educational Psychology, 102,* 588–600.

Jang, H., Reeve, J., Ryan, R. M., & Kim. A. (2009). Can self-determination theory explain what underlies the productive, satisfying learning experiences of collectivistically oriented Korean students? *Journal of Educational Psychology, 101,* 644–661.

Jarrett, R. (1995). Growing up poor: The family experiences of socially mobile youth in low-income African American neighborhoods. *Journal of Adolescent Research, 10,* 111–135.

Jarrold, C., Tam, H., Baddeley, A. D., & Harvey, C. E. (2011). How does processing affect storage in working memory tasks? Evidence for both domain-general and domain-specific effects. *Journal of Experimental Psychology: Learning, Memory, and Cognition, 37,* 688–705.

Jaswal, V. K., & Markman, E. M. (2001). Learning proper and common names in inferential versus ostensive contexts. *Child Development, 72,* 787–802.

Jensen, E. (2009). *Teaching with poverty in mind: What being poor does to kids' brains and what schools can do about it.* Alexandria, VA: Association for Supervision and Curriculum Development.

Jensen, L. A., Arnett, J. J., Feldman, S. S., & Cauffman, E. (2002). It's wrong but everybody does it: Academic dishonesty among high school and college students. *Contemporary Educational Psychology, 27,* 209–228.

Jerome, E. M., Hamre, B. K., & Pianta, R. C. (2009). Teacher–child relationships from kindergarten to sixth grade: Early childhood predictors of teacher-perceived conflict and closeness. *Social Development, 18*(4), 915–945.

Jia, Y., Way, N., Ling, G., Yoshikawa, H., Chen, X., & Hughes, D. (2009). The influence of student perceptions of school climate on socioemotional and academic adjustment: A comparison of Chinese and American adolescents. *Child Development, 80,* 1514–1530.

Jimenez, R. (2000). Literacy and identity development of Latina/o students who are successful English readers: Opportunities and obstacles. *American Educational Research Journal, 37,* 971–1000.

Jimerson, S. R. (1999). On the failure of failure: Examining the association between early grade retention and education and employment outcomes during late adolescence. *Journal of School Psychology, 37,* 243–272.

Jimerson, S. R., Anderson, G. E., & Whipple, A. D. (2002). Winning the battle and losing the war: Examining the relation between grade retention and dropping out of high school. *Psychology in the Schools, 39,* 441–457.

Jimerson, S. R., & Ferguson, P. (2007). A longitudinal study of grade retention: Academic and behavioral outcomes of retained students through adolescence. *School Psychology Quarterly, 22,* 314–339.

Jirout, J., & Klahr, D. (2012). Children's scientific curiosity: In search of an operational definition of an elusive concept. *Developmental Review, 32,* 125–160.

Jitendra, A. K., Star, J. R., Starosta, K., Leh J. M., Sood, S., Caskie, G., . . . Mack, T. R. (2009). Improving seventh grade students' learning of ratio and proportion: The role of schema-based instruction. *Contemporary Educational Psychology, 34,* 250–264.

Joët, G., Usher, E. L., & Bressoux, P. (2011). Sources of self-efficacy: An investigation of elementary school students in France. *Journal of Educational Psychology, 103,* 649–663. doi: 10.1037/a0024048

John-Steiner, V., & Mahn, H. (1996). Sociocultural approaches to learning and development: A Vygotskian framework. *Educational Psychologist, 31,* 191–206.

Johnson, A. (2003). Procedural memory and skill acquisition. In A. F. Healy & R. W. Proctor (Eds.), *Experimental psychology* (Vol. 4, pp. 499–523). New York, NY: Wiley.

Johnson, A. M., & Notah, D. J. (1999). Service learning: History, literature, review, and a pilot study of eighth graders. *The Elementary School Journal, 99,* 453–467.

Johnson, D. W., & Johnson, F. P. (2013). *Joining together: Group theory and group skills* (11th ed.). Boston, MA: Pearson.

Johnson, D. W., & Johnson, R. T. (1999a). *Learning together and alone: Cooperation, competition, and individualization* (5th ed.). Boston, MA: Allyn & Bacon.

Johnson, D. W., & Johnson, R. T. (1999b). The three Cs of school and classroom management. In H. J. Freiberg (Ed.), *Beyond behaviorism: Changing the classroom management paradigm* (pp. 119–144). Boston, MA: Allyn & Bacon.

Johnson, D. W., & Johnson, R. T. (2002). *Meaningful assessment: A meaningful and cooperative process.* Boston, MA: Allyn & Bacon.

Johnson, D. W., & Johnson, R. T. (2009a). An educational psychology success story: Social interdependence theory and cooperative learning. *Educational Researcher, 38,* 365–379.

Johnson, D. W., & Johnson, R. T. (2009b). Energizing learning: The instructional power of conflict. *Educational Researcher, 38,* 37–51. doi:10.3102/0013189X08330540

Johnson, D. W., Johnson, R. T., Dudley, B., Ward, M., & Magnuson, D. (1995). The impact of peer mediation training on the management of school and home conflicts. *American Educational Research Journal, 32,* 829–844.

Johnson, S. (2008, January 14). A childhood in poverty informs her teaching. *USA Today,* p. 7D.

Johnston, L. D., O'Malley, P. M., Bachman, J. G., & Schulenberg, J. E. (2013). *Monitoring the future: National survey results on drug use, 1975–2012: Volume I. Secondary students.* Ann Arbor, MI: The University of Michigan Institute for Social Research and the National Institute on Drug Abuse. Retrieved from http://www.monitoringthefuture.org//pubs/monographs/mtf-v011_2012.pdf

Jolly, J. L. (2008). Lew Terman: Genetic study of genius—Elementary school students. *Gifted Child Today, 31,* 27–33.

Jonassen, D. H. (2003). Designing research-based instruction for story problems. *Educational Psychology Review, 15,* 267–296.

Jonassen, D. H. (2011). Ask systems: Interrrogative access to multiple ways of thinking. *Education Technology Research and Development, 59,* 159–175.

Jones, D. C. (2004). Body image among adolescent girls and boys: A longitudinal study. *Developmental Psychology, 40,* 823–835.

Jones, M. G., & Gerig, T. M. (1994). Silent sixth-grade students: Characteristics, achievement, and teacher expectations. *Elementary School Journal, 95,* 169–182.

Jones, S. M., & Dindia, K. (2004). A meta-analytic perspective on sex equity in the classroom. *Review of Educational Research, 74,* 443–471.

Jones, V. (2015). *Practical classroom management* (2nd ed.). Boston, MA: Pearson.

Judd, T. (2013). Making sense of multitasking: Key behaviours. *Computers and Education, 63,* 358–367.

Jurbergs, N., Palcic, J., & Kelly, M. L. (2007). School-home notes with and without response cost: Increasing attention and academic performance in low-income children with attention deficit/hyperactivity disorder. *School Psychology Quarterly, 22,* 358–379.

Jurden, F. H. (1995). Individual differences in working memory and complex cognition. *Journal of Educational Psychology, 87,* 93–102.

Jussim, L. (2013). Teachers' expectations. In J. Hattie & E. Anderman (Eds.), *International guide to student achievement.* New York, NY: Routledge.

Jussim, L., & Harber, K. (2005). Teacher expectations and self-fulfilling prophecies: Knowns and unknowns; resolved and unresolved controversies. *Personality and Social Psychology Review, 9,* 131–135.

Jussim, L., Robustelli, S., & Cain, T. (2009). Teacher expectations and self-fulfilling prophecies. In A. Wigfield & K. Wentzel (Eds.), *Handbook of motivation at school* (pp. 349–380). Mahwah, NJ: Erlbaum.

Kagan, J. (1976). Commentary on reflective and impulsive children: Strategies of information processing underlying differences in problem solving. *Monograph of the Society for Research in Child Development, 41*(5) (Ser. No. 168).

Kagan, J., & Herschkowitz, N. (2005). *A young mind in a growing brain.* Mahwah, NJ: Erlbaum.

Kagan, S. (1994). *Cooperative learning.* San Juan Capistrano, CA: Kagan Cooperative Learning.

Kahneman, D. (2011). *Thinking, fast and slow.* New York: Farrar, Straus & Giroux.

Kail, R. (2000). Speed of processing: Developmental change and links to intelligence. *Journal of School Psychology, 38,* 51–61.

Kail, R., & Park, Y. (1994). Processing time, articulation time, and memory span. *Journal of Experimental Child Psychology, 57,* 281–291.

Kalogrides, D., & Loeb, L. (2013). Different teachers, different peers: The magnitude of student sorting within schools. *Educational Researcher, 42,* 304–316.

Kalyuga, S. (2011). Cognitive load theory: How many types of load does it really need? *Educational Psychology Review, 23,* 1–19.

Kalyuga, S., Chandler, P., Tuovinen, J., & Sweller, J. (2001). When problem solving is superior to studying worked examples. *Journal of Educational Psychology, 93,* 579–588.

Kalyuga, S., & Renkl, A. (2010). Expertise reversal effect and its instructional implications: Introduction to the special issue. *Instructional Science, 38,* 209–215.

Kalyuga, S., Rikers, R., & Paas, F. (2012). Educational implications of expertise reversal effects in learning and performance of complex cognitive and sensorimotor skills. *Educational Psychology Review, 24,* 313–337.

Kanaya, T., Scullin, M. H., & Ceci, S. J. (2003). The Flynn effect and U.S. policies: The impact of rising IQ scores on American society via mental retardation diagnoses. *American Psychologist, 58,* 1–13.

Kanazawa, S. (2010). Evolutionary psychology and intelligence research. *American Psychologist, 65*(4), 279–289.

Kantor, H., & Lowe, R. (1995). Class, race, and the emergence of federal education policy: From the New Deal to the Great Society. *Educational Researcher, 24*(3), 4–11.

Kaplan, A., & Maehr, M. L. (2007). The contributions and prospects of goal orientation theory. *Educational Psychology Review, 19,* 141–184.

Kaplan, J. S. (1991). *Beyond behavior modification* (2nd ed.). Austin, TX: Pro-Ed.

Kardash, C. M., & Howell, K. L. (2000). Effects of epistemological beliefs and topic-specific beliefs on undergraduates' cognitive and strategic processing of dual-positional text. *Journal of Educational Psychology, 92,* 524–535.

Karpicke, J. J., & Grimaldi, P. J. (2012). Retrieval-based learning: A perspective for enhancing meaningful learning. *Educational Psychology Review, 24,* 401–418.

Karpov, Y. V., & Bransford, J. D. (1995). L. S. Vygotsky and the doctrine of empirical and theoretical learning. *Educational Psychologist, 30,* 61–66.

Karpov, Y. V., & Haywood, H. C. (1998). Two ways to elaborate Vygotsky's concept of mediation implications for instruction. *American Psychologist, 53,* 27–36.

Katz, I., & Assor, A. (2007). When choice motivates and when it does not. *Educational Psychology Review, 19,* 429–442.

Katz, P. A. (2003). Racists or tolerant multiculturalists? How do they begin? *American Psychologist, 58,* 897–909.

Katz, S. R. (1999). Teaching in tensions: Latino immigrant youth, their teachers, and the structures of schooling. *Teachers College Record, 100*(4), 809–840.

Katzir, T., & Paré-Blagoev, J. (2006). Applying cognitive neuroscience research to education: The case of literacy. *Educational Psychologist, 4,* 53–74.

Kazdin, A. E. (2001). *Behavior modification in applied settings* (6th ed.). Belmont, CA: Wadsworth.

Kazdin, A. E. (2008). *The Kazdin method for parenting the defiant child.* Boston, MA: Houghton-Mifflin.

Keefe, J. W. (1982). Assessing student learning styles: An overview. In *Student learning styles and brain behavior.* Reston, VA: National Association of Secondary School Principals.

Keefe, J. W., & Monk, J. S. (1986). *Learning style profile examiner's manual.* Reston, VA: National Association of Secondary School Principals.

Keller, M., Neumann, K., & Fischer, H. E. (2013). Teacher enthusiasm and student learning. In J. Hattie & E. Anderman (Eds.), *International guide to student achievement.* New York, NY: Routledge.

Kemp, C., & Carter, M. (2006). The contribution of academic skills to the successful inclusion of children with disabilities. *Journal of Developmental and Physical Disabilities, 18,* 123–146.

Kempert, S., Saalbach, H., & Hardy, I. (2011). Cognitive benefits and costs of bilingualism in elementary school students: The case of mathematical word problems. *Journal of Educational Psychology, 103,* 547–561.

Kenney-Benson, G. A., Pomerantz, E. M., Ryan, A. M., & Patrick, H. (2006). Sex differences in math performance: The role of children's approach to school work. *Developmental Psychology, 42,* 11–26.

Kerckhoff, A. C. (1986). Effects of ability grouping in British secondary schools. *American Sociological Review, 51,* 842–858.

Keyser, V., & Barling, J. (1981). Determinants of children's self-efficacy beliefs in an academic environment. *Cognitive Therapy and Research, 5,* 29–40.

Kicken, W., Brand-Gruwel, S., van Merriënboer, J. J. G., & Slot, W. (2009). Design and evaluation of a development portfolio: How to improve students' self-directed learning skills. *Instructional Science, 37,* 453–473.

Kiewra, K. A. (1985). Investigating notetaking and review: A depth of processing alternative. *Educational Psychologist, 20,* 23–32.

Kiewra, K. A. (1989). A review of note-taking: The encoding storage paradigm and beyond. *Educational Psychology Review, 1,* 147–172.

Kiewra, K. A. (2002). How classroom teachers can help students learn and teach them how to learn. *Theory Into Practice, 41,* 71–80.

Kim, J., Schallert, D. L., & Kim, M. (2010). An integrative cultural view of achievement motivation: Parental and classroom predictors of children's goal orientations when learning mathematics in Korea. *Journal of Educational Psychology, 102,* 418–437.

Kim, J. S., & Guryan, J. (2010). The efficacy of a voluntary summer book reading intervention for low-income Latino children from language minority families. *Journal of Educational Psychology, 102,* 20–31.

Kim, J. S., & Quinn, D. M. (2013). The effects of summer reading on low-income children's literacy achievement from kindergarten to grade 8: A meta-analysis of classroom and home interventions. *Review of Educational Research, 83,* 386–431.

Kim, K. M. (1998). Korean children's perceptions of adult and peer authority and moral reasoning. *Developmental Psychology, 5,* 310–329.

Kindsvatter, R., Wilen, W., & Ishler, M. (1992). *Dynamics of effective teaching* (2nd ed.). New York, NY: Longman.

King, A. (1990). Enhancing peer interaction and learning in the classroom through reciprocal questioning. *American Educational Research Journal, 27,* 664–687.

King, A. (1994). Guiding knowledge construction in the classroom: Effects of teaching children how to question and how to explain. *American Educational Research Journal, 31,* 338–368.

King, A. (2002). Structuring peer interactions to promote high-level cognitive processing. *Theory Into Practice, 41,* 31–39.

Kingsley, T. L., & Tancock, S. M. (2014). Internet inquiry: Fundamental competencies for online research. *The Reading Teacher, 67,* 389–399.

Kirk, S. A., Gallagher, J. J., Anastasiow, N. J., & Coleman, M. R. (2006). *Educating exceptional children* (11th ed.). Boston, MA: Houghton Mifflin.

Kirschner, P. A., Sweller, J., & Clark, R. E. (2006). Why minimal guidance during instruction does not work: An analysis of the failure of constructivist, discovery, problem-based, experiential, and inquiry-based teaching. *Educational Psychologist, 41,* 75–86.

Kirschner, P. A., & van Merriënboer, J. J. G. (2013). "Do learners really know best" Urban legends in education. *Educational Psychologist, 48,* 169–183.

Kirsh, S. J. (2005). Cartoon violence and aggression in youth. *Aggression and Violent Behavior, 11,* 547–557.

Klahr, D., & Nigam, M. (2004). Equivalence of learning paths in early science instruction: Effects of direct instruction and discovery learning. *Psychological Science, 15,* 661–667.

Klassen, R. M. (2004). A cross-cultural investigation of the efficacy beliefs of South Asian immigrant and Anglo Canadian nonimmigrant early adolescents. *Journal of Educational Psychology, 96,* 731–742.

Klassen, R. M., & Chiu, M. M. (2010). Effects on teachers' self-efficacy and job satisfaction: Teacher gender, years of experience, and job stress. *Journal of Educational Psychology, 10,* 741–756. doi: 10.1037/a0019237

Klein, S. B. (2015). *Learning: Principles and applications* (7th ed.). Thousand Oaks, CA: Sage.

Klein, S. S., & Harris, A. H. (2007). A users guide to the Legacy Cycle. *Journal of Education and Human Development, 1*. Retrieved from http://www.scientificjournals.org/journals2007/articles/1088.pdf

Kleinfeld, J. (2005). Culture fuels boys learning problems. *Alaska Daily News*, p. B6.

Klinger, J., & Orosco, M. J. (2010). This issue: Response to intervention. *Theory Into Practice, 49*, 247–249.

Knapp, M., Turnbull, B. J., & Shields, P. M. (1990). New directions for educating children of poverty. *Educational Leadership, 48*(1), 4–9.

Knapp, M. S., & Woolverton, S. (2003). Social class and schooling. In J. A. Banks & C. A. Banks (Eds.), *Handbook of research on multicultural education*. San Francisco, CA: Jossey-Bass.

Kobayashi, K. (2005). What limits the encoding benefit of note-taking? A meta-analytic examination. *Contemporary Educational Psychology, 30*, 242–262. doi:10.1016/j.cedpsych.2004.10.001

Koehl, M., & Abrous, D. N. (2011). A new chapter in the field of memory: Adult hippocampal neurogenesis. *European Journal of Neuroscience, 33*, 1101–1114.

Kohlberg, L. (1963). The development of children's orientations toward moral order: Sequence in the development of moral thought. *Vita Humana, 6*, 11–33.

Kohlberg, L. (1975). The cognitive-developmental approach to moral education. *Phi Delta Kappan, 56*, 670–677.

Kohlberg, L. (1981). *The philosophy of moral development*. New York, NY: Harper & Row.

Kohn, A. (1993). Rewards versus learning: A response to Paul Chance. *Phi Delta Kappan, 74*, 783–787.

Kohn, A. (1996a). *Beyond discipline: From compliance to community*. Alexandria, VA: Association for Supervision and Curriculum Development.

Kohn, A. (1996b). By all available means: Cameron and Pierce's defense of extrinsic motivators. *Review of Educational Research, 66*, 1–4.

Kohn, A. (2005). Unconditional teaching. *Educational Leadership, 62*, 12–17.

Kohn, A. (2006). *The homework myth: Why our kids get too much of a bad thing*. Cambridge, MA: Da Capo Press.

Kokko, K., & Pulkkinen, L. (2000). Aggression in childhood and long-term unemployment in adulthood: A cycle of maladaptation and some protective factors. *Developmental Psychology, 36*, 463–472.

Kolata, G. (2013, September 2). Guesses and hype give way to data in study of education. *New York Times*. Retrieved from http://www.nytimes.com/2013/09/03/science/applying-new-rigor-in-studying-education.html

Kolb, G., & Whishaw, I. Q. (1998). Brain plasticity and behavior. In J. T. Spence, J. M. Darley, & D. J. Foss (Eds.), *Annual review of psychology* (pp. 43–64). Palo Alto, CA: Annual Reviews.

Komarraju, M., Karau, S. J., Schmeck, R. R., & Avdic, A. (2011). The Big Five personality traits, learning styles, and academic achievement. *Personality and Individual Differences, 51*, 472–477.

Koppelman, K. L. (2011). *Understanding human differences: Multicultural education for a diverse America* (3rd ed.). Boston, MA: Pearson.

Korf, R. (1999). Heuristic search. In R. Wilson & F. Keil (Eds.), *The MIT encyclopedia of the cognitive sciences* (pp. 372–373). Cambridge, MA: MIT Press.

Koriat, A., Goldsmith, M., & Pansky, A. (2000). Toward a psychology of memory accuracy. In S. Fiske (Ed.), *Annual review of psychology* (pp. 481–537). Palo Alto, CA: Annual Reviews.

Kornhaber, M., Fierros, E., & Veenema, S. (2004). *Multiple intelligences: Best ideas for research and practice*. Boston, MA: Allyn & Bacon.

Kosslyn, S. M., & Koenig, O. (1992). *Wet mind: The new cognitive neuroscience*. New York, NY: Free Press.

Kounin, J. S. (1970). *Discipline and group management in classrooms*. New York, NY: Holt, Rinehart & Winston.

Kozol, J. (2012). *Fire in the ashes: Twenty-five years among the poorest children in America*. New York, NY: Random House.

Kozulin, A. (1990). *Vygotsky's psychology: A biography of ideas*. Cambridge, MA: Harvard University Press.

Kozulin, A. (2003). Psychological tools and mediated learning. In A. Kouzlin, B. Gindis, V. Ageyev, & S. M. Miller (Eds.), *Vygotsky's educational theory in cultural context* (pp. 15–38). Cambridge, UK: Cambridge University Press.

Kozulin, A., Gindis, V. Ageyev, & S. M. Miller (Ed.). (2003). *Vygotsky's educational theory in cultural context*. Cambridge, UK: Cambridge University Press.

Kozulin, A., & Presseisen, B. Z. (1995). Mediated learning experience and psychological tools: Vygotsky's and Feuerstein's perspectives in a study of student learning. *Educational Psychologist, 30*, 67–75.

Krajcik, J., & Czerniak, C. (2007). *Teaching science in elementary and middle school classrooms: A project-based approach* (3rd ed.). Mahwah, NJ: Erlbaum.

Kratchovil, C. J. (2009). Current pharmacotherapy for ADHD. 2nd International Congress on ADHD. From Childhood to Adult Disease. May 21–24, 2009, Vienna, Austria. *Attention Deficit and Hyperactivity Disorders, 1*, 61.

Krathwohl, D. R., Bloom, B. S., & Masia, B. B. (1964). *Taxonomy of educational objectives. Handbook II: Affective domain*. New York, NY: David McKay.

Kratzig, G. P., & Arbuthnott, K. D. (2006). Perceptual learning style and learning proficiency: A test of the hypothesis. *Journal of Educational Psychology, 98*, 238–246.

Krauss, M. (1992). Statement of Michael Krauss, representing the Linguistic Society of America. In U.S. Senate, *Native American Languages Act of 1991: Hearing before the Select Committee on Indian Affairs* (pp. 18–22). Washington, DC: U.S. Government Printing Office.

Kreitzer, A. E., & Madaus, G. F. (1994). Empirical investigations of the hierarchical structure of the taxonomy. In L. W. Anderson & L. A. Sosniak (Eds.), *Bloom's taxonomy: A forty-year retrospective*. Ninety-third yearbook for the National Society for the Study of Education: Part II (pp. 64–81). Chicago, IL: University of Chicago Press.

Kroger, J. (2000). *Identity development: Adolescence through adulthood*. Thousand Oaks, CA: Sage.

Kroger, J., Martinussen, M., & Marcia, J. E. (2010). Identity status change during adolescence and young adulthood: A meta-analysis. *Journal of Adolescence, 33*, 683–698.

Kronholz, J. (2011). Challenging the gifted: Nuclear chemistry and Sartre draw the best and brightest to Reno. *Education Next, 11*(2), 1–8. Retrieved from http://educationnext.org/challenging-the-gifted/

Krumboltz, J. D., & Yeh, C. J. (1996). Competitive grading sabotages good teaching. *Phi Delta Kappan, 78*, 324–326.

Kuhn, D. (2007). Is direct instruction an answer to the right question? *Educational Psychologist, 42*, 109–113.

Kuhn, D., & Dean, D. (2004). Connecting scientific reasoning with casual inference. *Journal of Cognition and Development, 5*, 261–288.

Kuhn, D., & Franklin, S. (2006). The second decade: What develops (and how). In D. Kuhn & R. S. Siegler (Eds.), *Cognition, perception, and language* (6th ed., Vol. 2, pp. 953–993). New York, NY: Wiley.

Kuhn, D., Goh, W., Iordanou, K., & Shaenfield, D. (2008). Arguing on the computer: A microgenetic study of developing argument skills in a computer-supported environment. *Child Development, 79*, 1310–1328.

Kuklinski, M. R., & Weinstein, R. S. (2001). Classroom and developmental differences in a path model of teacher expectancy effects. *Child Development, 72*, 1554–1578.

Kulik, J. A., & Kulik, C. L. (1997). Ability grouping. In N. Colangelo & G. Davis (Eds.), *Handbook of gifted education* (2nd ed., pp. 230–242). Boston, MA: Allyn & Bacon.

Kumar, D. D., & Sherwood, R. D. (2007). Effect of problem-based simulation on the conceptual understanding of undergraduate science educational majors. *Journal of Science Education and Technology, 16*, 239–246.

Kyraciou, C. (1987). Teacher stress and burnout: An international review. *Educational Research, 29*, 146–151.

Lachter, J., Forster, K. I., & Ruthruff, K. I. (2004). Forty-five years after Broadbent (1958): Still no identification without attention. *Psychological Review, 111*, 880–913.

Ladson-Billings, G. (1990). Like lightning in a bottle: Attempting to capture the pedagogical excellence of successful teachers of Black students. *Qualitative Studies in Education, 3*, 335–344.

Ladson-Billings, G. (1992). Culturally relevant teaching: The key to making multicultural education work. In C. A. Grant (Ed.), *Research and multicultural education* (pp. 106–121). London: Falmer Press.

Ladson-Billings, G. (1994). *The dream keepers*. San Francisco, CA: Jossey-Bass.

Ladson-Billings, G. (1995). But that is just good teaching! The case for culturally relevant pedagogy. *Theory Into Practice, 34*, 161–165.

Ladson-Billings, G. (2004). Landing on the wrong note: The price we paid for Brown. *Educational Researcher, 33*(7), 3–13.

Ladson-Billings, G. (2006). From the achievement gap to the education debt: Understanding achievement in U.S. schools. *Educational Researcher, 35*(7), 3–12.

Lagattuta, K. H., Nucci, L., & Bosacki, S. L. (2010). Bridging theory of mind and the personal domain: Children's reasoning about resistance to parental control. *Child Development, 81*, 616–635.

Lahat, A., Helwig, C. C., & Zelazo, P. D. (2013). An event-related potential study of adolescents' and young adults' judgments of moral and social conventional violations. *Child Development, 84*, 955–969.

Lamb, M. E., & Lewis, C. (2005). The role of parent-child relationships in child development. In M. H. Bornstein & M. E. Lamb (Eds.), *Developmental science: An advanced textbook* (5th ed., pp. 429–468). Mahwah, NJ: Erlbaum.

Lambert, N. M. (1994). Seating arrangement in classrooms. *The International Encyclopedia of Education* (2nd ed., Vol. 9), pp. 5355–5359.

Landrum, T. J., & Kauffman, J. M. (2006). Behavioral approaches to classroom management. In C. M. Evertson & C. S. Weinstein (Eds.), *Handbook of classroom management: Research, practice, and contemporary issues*. Mahwah, NJ: Erlbaum.

Lane, K., Falk, K., & Wehby, J. (2006). Classroom management in special education classrooms and resource rooms. In C. M. Evertson & C. S. Weinstein (Eds.), *Handbook of classroom management: Research, practice, and contemporary issues* (pp. 439–460). Mahwah, NJ: Erlbaum.

Langan-Fox, J., Waycott, J. L., & Albert, K. (2000). Linear and graphic organizers: Properties and processing. *International Journal of Cognitive Ergonomics, 4*(1), 19–34.

Lashley, T. J., II, Matczynski, T. J., & Rowley, J. B. (2002). *Instructional models: Strategies for teaching in a diverse society* (2nd ed.). Belmont, CA: Wadsworth/Thomson Learning.

Lather, P. (2004). Scientific research in education: A critical perspective. *Journal of Curriculum and Supervision, 20,* 14–30.

Lave, J. (1988). *Cognition in practice: Mind, mathematics, and culture in everyday life.* New York, NY: Cambridge University Press.

Lave, J. (1997). The culture of acquisition and the practice of understanding. In D. Kirshner & J. A. Whitson (Eds.), *Situated cognition: Social, semiotic, and psychological perspectives* (pp. 17–35). Mahwah, NJ: Erlbaum.

Lave, J., & Wenger, E. (1991). *Situated learning: Legitimate peripheral participation.* Cambridge, MA: Cambridge University Press.

Lawson, M. A., & Lawson, H. A. (2013). New conceptual framework for student engagement research, policy, and practice. *Review of Educational Research, 83,* 432–479.

Leaper, C. (2002). Parenting girls and boys. In M. H. Bornstein (Ed.), *Handbook of parenting, Vol. 1: Children and parenting* (2nd ed., pp. 127–152). Mahwah, NJ: Erlbaum.

Leaper, C., & Smith, T. S. (2004). A meta-analytic review of gender variations in children's language use: Talkativeness, affiliative speech, and assertive speech. *Developmental Psychology, 40,* 993–1027.

Lee, A. Y., & Hutchinson, L. (1998). Improving learning from examples through reflection. *Journal of Experimental Psychology: Applied, 4,* 187–210.

Lee, C. (2008). Synthesis of research on the role of culture in learning among African American youth: The contributions of Asa G. Hilliard, III. *Review of Educational Research, 78,* 797–827.

Lee, J., & Shute, V. J. (2010). Personal and social-contextual factors in K–12 academic performance: An integrative perspective on student learning. *Educational Psychologist, 45,* 185–202.

Lee, K., Ng, E. L., & Ng, S. F. (2009). The contributions of working memory and executive functioning to problem representation and solution generation in algebraic word problems. *Journal of Educational Psychology, 101,* 373–387.

Lee, R. M. (2005). Resilience against discrimination: Ethnic identity and other-group orientation as protective factors for Korean Americans. *Journal of Counseling Psychology, 52,* 36–44.

Lee, S. J. (2008). Model minorities and perpetual foreigners: The impact of stereotyping on Asian American students. In M. Sadowski (Ed.), *Adolescents at school: Perspectives on youth, identity, and education* (2nd ed., pp. 75–85). Cambridge, MA: Harvard University Press.

Lee, S. J., Wong, N.-W. A., & Alvarez, A. N. (2008). The model minority and the perpetual foreigner: Stereotypes of Asian Americans. In N. Tewari & A. Alvarez (Eds.), *Asian American psychology: Current perspectives* (pp. 69–84). Boca Raton, FL: CRC Press.

Lefton, L. (1994). *Psychology* (5th ed.). Boston, MA: Allyn & Bacon.

Lehman, D. R., & Nisbett, R. E. (1990). A longitudinal study of the effects of undergraduate training on reasoning. *Developmental Psychology, 26,* 952–960.

Leinhardt, G. (2001). Instructional explanations: A commonplace for teaching and location for contrasts. In V. Richardson (Ed.), *Handbook of research on teaching* (4th ed., pp. 333–357). Washington, DC: American Educational Research Association.

LeMahieu, P., Gitomer, D. H., & Eresh, J. T. (1993). *Portfolios in large-scale assessment: Difficult but*

not impossible. Unpublished manuscript, University of Delaware.

Lemelson, R. (2003). Obsessive-compulsive disorder in Bali. *Transcultural Psychiatry, 40,* 377–408.

Lenhart, A. (2010). *Teens, cell phones and / texting: Text messages become the centerpiece communication.* Washington, DC: Pew Research Center. Retrieved from http://pewresearch.org/pubs/1572/teens-cell-phones-text-messages

Leong, D. J., & Bodrova, E. (2012). Assessing and scaffolding make-believe play. *Young Children, 67,* 28–32.

Lepper, M. R., & Greene, D. (1978). *The hidden costs of rewards: New perspectives on the psychology of human motivation.* Mahwah, NJ: Erlbaum.

Lepper, M. R., Keavney, M., & Drake, M. (1996). Intrinsic motivation and extrinsic reward: A commentary on Cameron and Pierce's meta-analysis. *Review of Educational Research, 66,* 5–32.

Lerner, R. M., Theokas, C., & Bobek, D. L. (2005). Concepts and theories of human development: Historical and contemporary dimensions. In M. H. Bornstein & M. E. Lamb (Eds.), *Developmental science: An advanced textbook* (5th ed., pp. 3–43). Mahwah, NJ: Erlbaum.

Lessow-Hurley, J. (2005). *The foundations of dual language education.* Boston, MA: Allyn & Bacon.

Leung, A. K.-Y., & Chiu, C.-Y. (2010). Multicultural experience, idea receptiveness, and creativity. *Journal of Cross-Cultural Psychology, 41,* 723–741.

Leung, A. K., Maddux, W. W., Galinsky, A. D., & Chiu, C. (2008). Multicultural experience enhances creativity: The when and how. *American Psychologist, 63,* 169–181.

LeVay, S., & Baldwin, J. (2012). *Human sexuality* (4th ed.). Sunderland, MA: Sinauer Associates.

Levin, J. R., & Nolan, J. F. (2000). *Principles of classroom management: A professional decision-making model.* Boston, MA: Allyn & Bacon.

Lewinsohn, P. M., Rohde, P., & Seeley, J. R. (1994). Psychological risk factors for future attempts. *Journal of Consulting and Clinical Psychology, 62,* 297–305.

Lewis, R. (2001). Classroom discipline and student responsibility: The students' view. *Teaching and Teacher Education, 17,* 307–319.

Lewis, T. J., Sugai, G., & Colvin, G. (1998). Reducing problem behavior through a school-wide system of effective behavioral support: Investigation of a school-wide social skills training program and contextual interventions. *School Psychology Review, 27,* 446–459.

Liben, L. S., & Bigler, R. S. (2002). The developmental course of gender differentiation: Conceptualizing, measuring, and evaluating constructs and pathways. *Monographs of the Society for Research in Child Development, 67*(2), 1–187.

Lillemyr, O. F., Søbstad, F., Marder, K., & Flowerday, T. (2011). A multicultural perspective on play and learning in primary school. *International Journal of Early Childhood, 43,* 43–65.

Lindberg, S. M., Hyde, J. S., Peterson, J. L., & Linn, M. C. (2010). New trends in gender and mathematics performance: A meta-analysis. *Psychological Bulletin, 136,* 1123–1135.

Lindsay, P. H., & Norman, D. A. (1977). *Human information processing: An introduction to psychology* (2nd ed.). New York, NY: Academic Press.

Linn, M. C., & Eylon, B. S. (2006). Science education: Integrating views of learning and instruction. In P. A. Alexander & P. H. Winne (Eds.), *Handbook of educational psychology* (2nd ed., pp. 511–544). Mahwah, NJ: Erlbaum.

Linn, R. L., Baker, E. L., & Betebenner, D. W. (2002). Accountability systems: Implications of

requirements of the No Child Left Behind Act of 2001. *Educational Researcher, 31*(6), 3–16.

Linn, R. L., & Miller, M. D. (2005). *Measurement and assessment in teaching* (9th ed.). Upper Saddle River, NJ: Prentice-Hall/Merrill.

Linnenbrink-Garcia, L., Middleton, M. J., Ciani, K. D., Easter, M. A., O'Keefe, P. A., & Zusho, A. (2012) The strength of the relation between performance-approach and performance-avoidance goal orientations: Theoretical, methodological, and instructional implications. *Educational Psychologist, 47,* 281–301. doi: 10.1080/00461520.2012.722515

Linnenbrink-Garcia, L., & Pekrun, R. (2011). Students' emotions and academic engagement: Introduction to the special issue. *Contemporary Educational Psychology, 36,* 1–3.

Lipscomb, L., Swanson, J., & West, A. (2012). Scaffolding. In M. Orey (Ed.), *Emerging Perspectives on Learning, Teaching, and Technology* (online journal). Retrieved from http://epltt.coe.uga.edu/index.php?title=Scaffolding

Liu, W. M., Ali, S. R., Soleck, G., Hopps, J., Dunston, K., & Pickett, T., Jr. (2004). Using social class in counseling psychology research. *Journal of Counseling Psychology, 51,* 3–18.

Lochman, J. E., & Wells, K. C. (2003). The Coping Power program for preadolescent aggressive boys and their parents: Effects at the one-year follow-up. *Journal of Consulting and Clinical Psychology, 72,* 571–578.

Locke, E. A., & Latham, G. P. (2002). Building a practically useful theory of goal setting and task motivation: A 35-year odyssey. *American Psychologist, 57,* 705–717.

Lockl, K., & Schneider, W. (2007). Knowledge about the mind: Links between theory of mind and later metamemory. *Child Development, 78,* 148–167.

Lonigan, C. J., Farver, J. M., Nakamoto, J., & Eppe, S. (2013). Developmental trajectories of preschool early literacy skills: A comparison of language-minority and monolingual-English children. *Developmental Psychology, 49,* 1943–1957.

Lorch, R. F., Lorch, E. P., Ritchey, K., McGovern, L., & Coleman, D. (2001). Effects of headings on text summarization. *Contemporary Educational Psychology, 26,* 171–191.

Loveless, T. (1998). The tracking and ability grouping debate. *Fordham Report, 2*(88), 1–27.

Loveless, T. (1999). Will tracking reform promote social equity? *Educational Leadership, 56*(7), 28–32.

Lowenstein, G. (1994). The psychology of curiosity: A review and reinterpretation. *Psychological Bulletin, 117,* 75–98.

Luckner, A. E., & Pianta, R. C. (2011). Teacher student interactions in fifth grade classrooms: Relations with children's peer behavior. *Journal of Applied Developmental Psychology, 32,* 257–266. doi:10.1016/j.appdev.2011.02.010

Luke, N., & Banerjee, R. (2013). Differentiated associations between childhood maltreatment experiences and social understanding: A meta-analysis and systematic review. *Developmental Review, 33,* 1–28.

Lyon, G. R., Shaywitz, S. E., & Shaywitz, B. A. (2003). A definition of dyslexia. *Annals of Dyslexia, 53,* 1–14.

Ma, X. (2013). The relation of teacher characteristics to student achievement. In J. Hattie & E. Anderman (Eds.), *International guide to of student achievement.* New York, NY: Routledge.

Maag, J. W., & Kemp, S. E. (2003). Behavioral intent of power and affiliation: Implications for functional analysis. *Remedial and Special Education, 24,* 57–64.

Mabry, L. (1999). Writing to the rubrics: Lingering effects of traditional standardized testing on direct writing assessment. *Phi Delta Kappan, 80,* 673–679.

Maccoby, E. E. (1998). *The two sexes: Growing up apart, coming together.* Cambridge, MA: Harvard University Press.

Mace, F. C., Belfiore, P. J., & Hutchinson, J. M. (2001). Operant theory and research on self-regulation. In B. Zimmerman & D. Schunk (Eds.), *Self-regulated learning and academic achievement: Theoretical perspectives* (2nd ed.). Mahwah, NJ: Erlbaum.

Macionis, J. J. (2003). *Sociology* (9th ed.). Upper Saddle River, NJ: Prentice-Hall.

Macionis, J. J. (2010). *Sociology* (13th ed.). Upper Saddle River, NJ: Prentice-Hall.

Macionis, J. J. (2013). *Society: The basics* (12th ed.). Upper Saddle River, NJ: Pearson.

Macrae, C. N., Milne, A. B., & Bodenhausen, C. V. (1994). Stereotypes as energy-saving devices: A peek inside the cognitive toolbox. *Journal of Personality and Social Psychology, 66,* 37–47.

Maddux, W. W., & Galinsky, A. D. (2009). Cultural borders and mental barriers: Living in and adapting to foreign cultures facilitates creativity. *Journal of Personality and Social Psychology, 96,* 1047–1061.

Maddux, W. W., & Leung, A. K.-Y., Chiu, C.-Y., & Galinsky, A. D. (2009). Toward a more complete understanding of the link between multicultural experience and creativity. *American Psychologist, 64,* 156–158. doi: 10.1037/a0014941

Madsen, C. H., Becker, W. C., Thomas, D. R., Koser, L., & Plager, E. (1968). An analysis of the reinforcing function of "sit down" commands. In R. K. Parker (Ed.), *Readings in educational psychology.* Boston, MA: Allyn & Bacon.

Madsen, K. (2003). The effect of accuracy of instruction, teacher delivery, and student attentiveness on musicians' evaluation of teacher effectiveness. *Journal of Research in Music Education, 51,* 38–51.

Maeda, Y., & Yoon, S. Y. (2012). A meta-analysis on gender differences in mental rotation ability measured by the Purdue Spatial Visualization Tests: Visualization of rotations (PSVT:R). *Educational Psychology Review, 25,* 69–94.

Mager, R. (1975). *Preparing instructional objectives* (2nd ed.). Palo Alto, CA: Fearon.

Mager, R. F. (1997). *Preparing instructional objectives: A critical tool in the development of effective instruction* (3rd ed.). Atlanta, GA: Center for Effective Performance.

Magnusson, S. J., & Palincsar, A. S. (1995). The learning environment as a site of science reform. *Theory Into Practice, 34,* 43–50.

Maguire, E. A., Gadian, D. G., Johnsrude, I. S., Good, C. D., Ashburner, J., Frackowiak, R. S., & Frith, C. D. (2000). Navigation-related structural change in the hippocampi of taxi drivers. *Proceedings of the National Academy of Science, USA, 97*(8), 4398–4403.

Major, B., & Schmader, T. (1998). Coping with stigma through psychological disengagement. In J. Swim & C. Stangor (Eds.), *Stigma: The target's perspective* (pp. 219–241). New York, NY: Academic Press.

Manning, B. H., & Payne, B. D. (1996). *Self-talk for teachers and students: Metacognitive strategies for personal and classroom use.* Boston, MA: Allyn & Bacon.

Manning, M. L., & Baruth, L. G. (1996). *Multicultural education of children and adolescents* (2nd ed.). Boston, MA: Allyn & Bacon.

Mantzicopoulos, P., & Morrison, D. (1992). Kindergarten retention: Academic and behavioral outcomes through the end of second grade. *American Educational Research Journal, 29,* 182–198.

Marchland, G., & Skinner, E. A. (2007). Motivational dynamics of children's academic help-seeking and concealment. *Journal of Educational Psychology, 99,* 65–82.

Marcia, J. E. (1991). Identity and self development. In R. Lerner, A. Peterson, & J. Brooks-Gunn (Eds.), *Encyclopedia of adolescence* (Vol. 1, pp. 107–123). New York, NY: Garland.

Marcia, J. E. (1994). The empirical study of ego identity. In H. Bosma, T. Graafsma, H. Grotebanc, & D. DeLivita (Eds.), *The identity and development.* Newbury Park, CA: Sage.

Marcia, J. E. (1999). Representational thought in ego identity, psychotherapy, and psychosocial development. In I. E. Sigel (Ed.), *Development of mental representation: Theories and applications* (pp. 391–414). Mahwah, NJ: Erlbaum.

Marcus, N., Cooper, M., & Sweller, J. (1996). Understanding instructions. *Journal of Educational Psychology, 88,* 49–63.

Marder, M., & Walkington, C. (2010). *Examining UTeach Outcomes: Classroom observations of UTeach graduates.* Retrieved from http://www.uteach-institute.org/images/uploads/marder_examining_uteach_outcomes.pdf

Marinova-Todd, S., Marshall, D., & Snow, C. (2000). Three misconceptions about age and L2 learning. *TESOL Quarterly, 34*(1), 9–34.

Markman, E. M. (1992). Constraints on word learning: Speculations about their nature, origins, and domain specificity. In M. Gunnar & M. Maratsos (Eds.), *Minnesota symposium on child psychology* (Vol. 25, pp. 59–101). Mahwah, NJ: Erlbaum.

Marks, A. K., Patton, F., & Coll, C. G. (2011). Being bicultural: A mixed-methods study of adolescents' implicitly and explicitly measured multiethnic identities. *Developmental Psychology, 47,* 270–288.

Markstrom-Adams, C. (1992). A consideration of intervening factors in adolescent identity formation. In G. R. Adams, R. Montemayor, & T. Gullotta (Eds.), *Advances in adolescent development: Vol. 4. Adolescent identity formation* (pp. 173–192). Newbury Park, CA: Sage.

Marsh, H. W., & Craven, R. (2002). The pivotal role of frames of reference in academic self-concept formation: The Big Fish Little Pond Effect. In F. Pajares & T. Urdan (Eds.), *Adolescence and Education* (Vol. II, pp. 83–123). Greenwich, CT: Information Age.

Marsh, H. W., Craven, R. G., & Martin, A. (2006). What is the nature of self-esteem: Unidimensional and multidimensional perspectives. In M. Kernis (Ed.), *Self-esteem: Issues and answers* (pp. 16–25). New York, NY: Psychology Press.

Marsh, H. W., & O'Mara, A. (2008). Reciprocal effects between academic self-concept, self-esteem, achievement, and attainment over seven adolescent years: Unidimensional and multidimensional perspectives of self-concept. *Personality and Social Psychology Bulletin, 34,* 542–552.

Marsh, H. W., Seaton M., Trautwein, U., Lüdtke, O., Hau, K. T., O'Mara, A. J., & Craven, R. G. (2008). The Big-fish–little-pond-effect stands up to critical scrutiny: Implications for theory, methodology, and future research. *Educational Psychology Review, 20,* 319–350.

Marsh, H. W., & Yeung, A. S. (1997). Coursework selection: Relation to academic self-concept and achievement. *American Educational Research Journal, 34,* 691–720.

Marshall, H. H. (Ed.). (1992). *Redefining student learning: Roots of educational change.* Norwood, NJ: Ablex.

Marshall, H. H. (1996). Implications of differentiating and understanding constructivist approaches. *Journal of Educational Psychology, 31,* 235–240.

Marshall, M. (2013). *Discipline without Stress® punishments or rewards: How teachers and parents promote responsibility & learning* (2nd ed.). Los Alamos, CA: Piper Press.

Martin, A. J., Liem, A. D., Mok, M. M. C., & Xu, J. (2012). Problem solving and immigrant student mathematics and science achievement: Multination findings from the Programme for International Student Assessment (PISA). *Journal of Educational Psychology, 104,* 1054–1073. doi: 10.1037/a0029152

Martin, A. J., & Marsh, H. W. (2009). Academic resilience and academic buoyancy: Multidimensional and hierarchical conceptual framing of causes, correlates and cognate constructs. *Oxford Review of Education, 35,* 353–370.

Martin, J. (2006). Social cultural perspectives in educational psychology. In P. A. Alexander & P. H. Winne (Eds.), *Handbook of educational psychology* (2nd ed., pp. 595–614). Mahwah, NJ: Erlbaum.

Martinez-Pons, M. (2002). A social cognitive view of parental influence on student academic self-regulation. *Theory Into Practice, 61,* 126–131.

Marvin, K. L., Rapp, J. T., Stenske, M. T., Rojas, N. R., Swanson, G. J., & Bartlett, S. M. (2010). Response repetition as an error-correction procedure for sight-word reading: A replication and extension. *Behavioral Interventions, 25,* 109–127.

Marzano, R. J., & Marzano, J. S. (2003, September). The key to classroom management. *Educational Leadership, 61*(1), 6–13.

Mascolo, M. F., & Fischer, K. W. (2005). Constructivist theories. In B. Hopkins (Ed.), *The Cambridge encyclopedia of child development.* New York, NY: Cambridge University Press.

Maslow, A. H. (1968). *Toward a psychology of being* (2nd ed.). New York, NY: Van Nostrand.

Maslow, A. H. (1970). *Motivation and personality* (2nd ed.). New York, NY: Harper and Row.

Mason, D. A., & Good, T. L. (1993). Effects of two-group and whole-class teaching on regrouped elementary students' mathematics achievement. *American Educational Research Journal, 30,* 328–360.

Mason, L. (2007). Introduction: Bridging the cognitive and sociocultural approaches in research on conceptual change: Is it possible? *Educational Psychologist, 42,* 1–7.

Masten, A. S. (2012). Risk and resilience in the educational success of homeless and highly mobile children: Introduction to the special section. *Educational Researcher, 41,* 363–365.

Matson, J. L., Matson, M. L., & Rivet, T. T. (2007). Social-skills treatments for children with autism spectrum disorders. *Behavior Modification, 31,* 682–707.

Matsumura, L. C., & Crosson, A. (2008). Classroom climate, rigorous instruction and curriculum, and students' interactions in urban middle schools. *The Elementary School Journal, 108,* 293–312.

Matsumura, L. C., Slater, S. C., & Crosson, A. (2008). Classroom climate, rigorous instruction and curriculum, and students' interactions in urban middle schools. *The Elementary School Journal, 108,* 293–312.

Matthews, G., Zeidner, M., & Roberts, R. D. (2002). *Emotional intelligence: Science and myth.* Cambridge, MA: MIT Press.

Matthews, J. S., Kizzie, K. T., Rowley, S. J., & Cortina, K. (2010). African Americans and boys: Understanding the literacy gap, tracing academic trajectories, and evaluating the role of learning-related skills. *Journal of Educational Psychology, 102,* 757–771.

Matthews, J. S., Ponitz, C. C., & Morrison, F. J. (2009). Early gender differences in self-regulation and academic achievement. *Journal of Educational Psychology, 101,* 689–704.

Maxwell, B., & Narvaez, D. (2013). Moral foundations theory and moral development and education. *Journal of Moral Education, 42*, 271–280. doi: 10.1080/03057240.2013.825582

Mayer, R. E. (1983). *Thinking, problem solving, cognition.* San Francisco, CA: Freeman.

Mayer, R. E. (1984). Twenty-five years of research on advance organizers. *Instructional Science, 8*, 133–169.

Mayer, R. E. (1996). Learners as information processors: Legacies and limitations of educational psychology's second metaphor. *Journal of Educational Psychology, 31*, 151–161.

Mayer, R. E. (2001). *Multimedia learning.* New York, NY: Cambridge University Press.

Mayer, R. E. (2004). Should there be a three-strikes rule against pure discovery learning: The case for guided methods of instruction. *American Psychologist, 59*, 14–19.

Mayer, R. E. (2005). Cognitive theory of multimedia learning. In R. E. Mayer (Ed.), *The Cambridge handbook of multimedia learning* (pp. 31–48). New York, NY: Cambridge University Press.

Mayer, R. E. (2008). *Learning and instruction* (2nd ed.). Columbus, OH: Merrill/Prentice-Hall.

Mayer, R. E. (2011). *Applying the science of learning.* Boston, MA: Pearson.

Mayer, R. E., & Gallini, J. K. (1990). When is an illustration worth ten thousand words? *Journal of Educational Psychology, 82*, 715–726.

Mayer, R. E., & Massa, L. J. (2003). Three facets of visual and verbal learners: Cognitive ability, cognitive style and learning preference. *Journal of Educational Psychology, 95*(4), 833–846.

Mayer, R. E., & Wittrock, M. C. (1996). Problem-solving transfer. In D. Berliner & R. Calfee (Eds.), *Handbook of educational psychology* (pp. 47–62). New York, NY: Macmillan.

Mayer, R. E., & Wittrock, M. C. (2006). Problem solving. In P. A. Alexander & P. H. Winne (Eds.), *Handbook of educational psychology* (2nd ed., pp. 287–303). Mahwah, NJ: Erlbaum.

Mayo Clinic. (2009). *Type 2 diabetes: Complications.* Retrieved from http://www.mayoclinic.com/health/type-2-diabetes/DS00585/DSECTION_complications

McAnarney, E. R. (2008). Adolescent brain development: Forging new links. *Journal of Adolescent Health, 42*, 321–323.

McCafferty, S. G. (2004). Introduction. *International Journal of Applied Linguistics, 14*(1), 1–6.

McCaslin, M., & Good, T. (1996). The informal curriculum. In D. Berliner & R. Calfee (Eds.), *Handbook of educational psychology* (pp. 622–670). New York, NY: Macmillan.

McCaslin, M., & Good, T. L. (1998). Moving beyond management as sheer compliance: Helping students to develop goal coordination strategies. *Educational Horizons, 76*, 169–176.

McCaslin, M., & Hickey, D. T. (2001). Self-regulated learning and academic achievement: A Vygotskian view. In B. Zimmerman & D. Schunk (Eds.), *Self-regulated learning and academic achievement: Theoretical perspectives* (2nd ed., pp. 227–252). Mahwah, NJ: Erlbaum.

McClelland, D. (1985). *Human motivation.* Glenview, IL: Scott, Foresman.

McCoach, D. B., Kehle, T. J., Bray, M. L., & Siegle, D. (2001). Best practices in the identification of gifted students with learning disabilities. *Psychology in the Schools, 38*, 403–411.

McCoy, A. R., & Reynolds, A. J. (1999). Grade retention and school performance: An extended investigation. *Journal of School Psychology, 37*, 273–298.

McDonnell, J., Hardman, M. L., & McDonnell, A. P. (2003). *Introduction to Persons with Moderate and Severe Disabilities: Educational and Social Issues*, 2nd Ed. Reprinted by permission of Pearson Education, Inc.

McEachin, A., & Polikoff, M. S. (2012). We are the 5%: Which schools would be held accountable under a proposed revision of the Elementary and Secondary Education Act? *Educational Researcher, 41*(7), 243–251.

McGoey, K. E., & DuPaul, G. J. (2000). Token reinforcement and response cost procedures: Reducing disruptive behavior of children with attention-deficit/hyperactivity disorder. *School Psychology Quarterly, 15*, 330–343.

McHugh, J. R., & Barlow, D. H. (2010). The dissemination and implementation of evidence-based psychological treatments: A review of current efforts. *American Psychologist, 65*(2), 73–84. doi:10.1037/a0018121

McKenzie, T. L., & Rushall, B. S. (1974). Effects of self-recording on attendance and performance in a competitive swimming training environment. *Journal of Applied Behavior Analysis, 7*, 199–206.

McKinley, J. C. (2011, January 24). Shot in the head, but getting back on his feet and on with his life. *New York Times*, p. A-16. Retrieved from http://www.nytimes.com/2011/01/24/us/24rehab.html?scp=7&sq=Houston%20rehabilitation&st=cse

McKown, C. (2005). Applying ecological theory to advance the science and practice of school-based prejudice reduction interventions. *Educational Psychologist, 40*, 177–189.

McLeod, S. A. (2010). *Kolb—learning styles.* Retrieved from http://www.simplypsychology.org/learning-kolb.html

McLoyd, V. C. (1998). Economic disadvantage and child development. *American Psychologist, 53*, 185–204.

McMillan, J. H. (2004). *Classroom assessment: Principles and practice for effective instruction* (3rd ed.). Boston, MA: Allyn & Bacon.

McNeely, C. A., Nonnemaker, J. M., & Blum, R. W. (2002). Promoting school connectedness: Evidence from the National Longitudinal Study of Adolescent Health. *Journal of School Health, 72*(4), 138–146.

McNeil, L. M., & Valenzuela, A. (2000). *The harmful impact of the TAAS system of testing in Texas: Beneath the accountability rhetoric.* Cambridge, MA: Harvard University Civil Rights Project. Retrieved from ID Number: www.law.harvard.edu/groups/civil-rights/testing.html

McTigue, E. M. (2009). Does multimedia learning theory extend to middle-school students? *Contemporary Educational Psychology, 34*, 143–153.

Meadows, S. (2006). *The child as a thinker* (2nd ed.). New York, NY: Routledge.

Mears, T. (1998, April 12). Saying 'Si' to Spanish. *Boston Globe.*

Mediascope. (1996). *National television violence study: Executive summary 1994–1995.* Studio City, CA: Author.

Medina, J. (2002, June 23). Groups say Regents Exam push immigrants to drop out. *The New York Times*, p. A28.

Meece, J. L., & Kurtz-Costes, B. (2001). Introduction: The schooling of ethnic minority children and youth. *Educational Psychologist, 36*, 1–7.

Meichenbaum, D. (1977). *Cognitive-behavior modifications: An integrative approach.* New York: Plenum Press.

Meijer, A. M., & van den Wittenboer, G. L. H. (2004). The joint contribution of sleep, intelligence and motivation to school performance. *Personality and Individual Differences, 37*, 95–106.

Melby-Lervåg, M., & Hulme, C. (2013). Is working memory training effective? A meta-analytic review. *Developmental Psychology, 49*, 270–291.

Melnick, S. A., & Meister, D. G. (2008). A comparison of beginning and experienced teacher concerns. *Education Research Quarterly, 31*(3), 39–56.

Mendle, J., & Ferrero, J. (2012). Detrimental psychological outcomes associated with pubertal timing in adolescent boys. *Developmental Review, 32*, 49–66.

Mendoza, E. M., & Johnson, K. O. (2000). Land of Plenty: Diversity as America's competitive edge in science, engineering, and technology. Washington, DC: Congressional Commission on the Advancement of Women and Minorities in Science, Engineering and Technology Development.

Mercer, N. (2013). The social brain, language, and goal-directed collective thinking: A social conception of cognition and its implications for understanding how we think, teach, and learn. *Educational Psychologist, 48*, 148–168.

Mertler, C. A., & Charles, C. M. (2005). *Introduction to educational research* (5th ed.). Boston, MA: Allyn & Bacon.

Merton, R. K. (1948). The self-fulfilling prophecy. *Antioch Review, 8*, 193–210.

Messick, S. (1975). The standard problem: Meaning and values in measurement and evaluation. *American Psychologist, 35*, 1012–1027.

MET Project. (2013, January). *Ensuring fair and reliable measures of teaching effectiveness: Culminating findings from the MET Projects' three-year study.* Seattle, WA: Bill and Melinda Gates Foundation.

Metcalfe, J., & Greene, M. J. (2007). Metacognition of agency. *Journal of Experimental Psychology: General, 136*, 184–199.

Metzler, C. W., Biglan, A., Rusby, J. C., & Sprague, J. R. (2001). Evaluation of a comprehensive behavior management program to improve school-wide positive behavior support. *Education and Treatment of Children, 24*(4), 448–470.

Mickelson, R. A., Bottia, M. C., & Lambert, R. (2013). Effects of school racial composition on K–12 mathematics outcomes: A metaregression analysis. *Review of Educational Research, 83*, 121–158.

Midgley, C., Kaplan, A., & Middleton, M. (2001). Performance-approach goals: Good for what, for whom, under what circumstances, and at what cost? *Journal of Educational Psychology, 93*, 77–86.

Midgley, C., Kaplan, A., Middleton, M., Maehr, M. L., Urdan, T., Anderman, L. H., . . . Roser, R. (1998). The development and validation of scales assessing students' achievement goal orientations. *Contemporary Educational Psychology, 23*, 113–131.

Miller, G. A. (1956). The magical number seven, plus or minus two: Some limits on our capacity for processing information. *Psychological Review, 63*, 81–97.

Miller, G. A., Galanter, E., & Pribram, K. H. (1960). *Plans and the structure of behavior.* New York, NY: Holt, Rinehart & Winston.

Miller, M. D., Linn, R. L., & Gronlund, N. E. (2013). *Measurement and assessment in teaching* (11th ed., p. 61). Upper Saddle River, NJ: Pearson.

Miller, N., & Harrington, H. J. (1993). Social categorization and intergroup acceptance: Principles for the development and design of cooperative learning teams. In R. Hertz-Lasarowitz & N. Miller (Eds.), *Interaction in cooperative groups: The theoretical anatomy of group learning* (pp. 203–227). New York, NY: Cambridge University Press.

Miller, P. H. (2011). *Theories of developmental psychology* (5th ed.). New York, NY: Worth.

Miller, R. B. (1962). Analysis and specification of behavior for training. In R. Glaser (Ed.), *Training research and education: Science edition.* New York, NY: Wiley.

Miller, G. A. (2005). Tips for getting children's attention. *Early Childhood Today, 19.*

Miller, S. A. (2009). Children's understanding of second-order mental statuses. *Psychological Bulletin, 135*, 749–773.

Milner, H. R. (2003). Teacher reflection and race in cultural contexts: History, meaning, and methods in teaching. *Theory Into Practice 42*(3), 173–180.

Milner, H. R. (2006). Classroom management in urban classrooms. In C. M. Evertson & C. S. Weinstein (Eds.), *Handbook of classroom management: Research, practice, and contemporary issues* (pp. 491–522). Mahwah, NJ: Erlbaum.

Milner, H. R., IV (2010). *Start where you are but don't stay there: Understanding diversity, opportunity gaps, and teaching in today's schools.* Cambridge, MA: Harvard Education Press.

Milner, H. R., IV (2013). Rethinking achievement gap talk in urban education. *Urban Education, 48,* 3–8.

Miranda, T. Z. (2008). Bilingual education for all students: Still standing after all these years. In L. S. Verplaetse & N. Migliacci (Eds.), *Inclusive pedagogy for English language learners: A handbook of research-informed practices* (pp. 257–275). New York, NY: Erlbaum.

Mitchell, M. (1993). Situational interest: Its multifaceted structure in the secondary school mathematics classroom. *Journal of Educational Psychology, 85,* 424–436.

Moll, L. C., Amanti, C., Neff, D., & Gonzalez, N. (1992). Funds of knowledge for teaching: Using a qualitative approach to connect homes and classrooms. *Theory Into Practice, 31,* 132–141.

Moller, A. C., Deci, E. L., & Ryan, R. M. (2006). Choice and ego-depletion: The moderating role of autonomy. *Personality and Social Psychology Bulletin, 32*(8), 1024–1036.

Möller, J., & Pohlmann, B. (2010). Achievement differences and self-concept differences: Stronger associations for above or below average students? *British Journal of Educational Psychology, 80,* 435–450.

Monroe, C. R., & Obidah, J. E. (2002, April). *The impact of cultural synchronization on a teacher's perceptions of disruption: A case study of an African American middle school classroom.* Paper presented at the American Educational Research Association, New Orleans, LA.

Montgomery, C., & Rupp, A. A. (2005). A meta-analysis for exploring diverse causes and effects of stress in teachers. *Canadian Journal of Education, 28,* 458–486.

Montrul, S. (2010). Dominant language transfer in adult second language learners and heritage speakers. *Second Language Research, 26,* 293–327.

Moore, M. K., & Meltzoff, A. N. (2004). Object permanence after a 24-hr delay and leaving the locale of disappearance: The role of memory, space, and identity. *Developmental Psychology, 40,* 606–620.

Moreno, M. A., Jelenchick, L., Koff, R., Eikoff, J., Diermyer, C., & Christakis, D. A. (2012). Internet use and multitasking among older adolescents: An experience sampling approach. *Computers in Human Behavior, 28,* 1097–1102.

Moreno, R., Ozogul, G., & Reisslein, M. (2011). Teaching with concrete and abstract visual representations: Effects on students' problem solving, problem representations, and learning perceptions. *Journal of Educational Psychology, 103,* 32–47.

Morin, V. A., & Miller, S. P. (1998). Teaching multiplication to middle school students with mental retardation. *Education & Treatment of Children, 21,* 22–36.

Morine-Dershimer, G. (2006). Instructional planning. In J. Cooper (Ed.), *Classroom teaching skills* (7th ed., pp. 20–54). Boston, MA: Houghton-Mifflin.

Morrow, L. M., & Weinstein, C. (1986). Encouraging voluntary reading: The impact of a literature program on children's use of library centers. *Reading Research Quarterly, 21,* 330–346.

Moshman, D. (1982). Exogenous, endogenous, and dialectical constructivism. *Developmental Review, 2,* 371–384.

Moshman, D. (1997). Pluralist rational constructivism. *Issues in Education: Contributions from Educational Psychology, 3,* 229–234.

Moskowitz, G., & Hayman, M. L. (1976). Successful strategies of inner-city teachers: A year-long study. *Journal of Educational Research, 69,* 283–289.

Mueller, C. M., & Dweck, C. S. (1998). Praise for intelligence can undermine children's motivation and performance. *Journal of Personality and Social Psychology, 75,* 33–52.

Muis, K. R., & Duffy, M. C. (2013). Epistemic climate and epistemic change: Instruction designed to change students' beliefs and learning strategies and improve achievement. *Journal of Educational Psychology, 105,* 213–225. doi: 10.1037/a0029690

Muis, K. R., & Franco, G. M. (2009). Epistemic beliefs: Setting the standards for self-regulated learning. *Contemporary Educational Psychology, 34,* 306–318.

Mullis, I. V. S., Martin, M. O., Gonzalez, E., & Kennedy, A. M. (2003). *PIRLS 2001 International report: IEA's study of reading literacy achievement in primary schools.* Chestnut Hill, MA: Boston College. Retrieved from http://timss.bc.edu/pirls2001i/PIRLS2001_Pubs_IR.html

Murayama, K., & Elliot, A. J. (2009). The joint influence of personal achievement goals and classroom goal structures on achievement-relevant outcomes. *Journal of Educational Psychology, 101,* 432–447.

Murdock, S. G., O'Neill, R. E., & Cunningham, E. (2005). A comparison of results and acceptability of functional behavioral assessment procedures with a group of middle school students with emotional/behavioral disorders (E/BD). *Journal of Behavioral Education, 14,* 5–18.

Murdock, T. A., & Anderman, E. M. (2006). Motivational perspectives on student cheating: Toward an integrated model of academic dishonesty. *Educational Psychologist, 42,* 129–145.

Murdock, T. B., Hale, N. M., & Weber, M. J. (2001). Predictors of cheating among early adolescents: Academic and social motivations. *Contemporary Educational Psychology, 26,* 96–115.

Murdock, T. B., & Miller, A. (2003). Teachers as sources of middle school students' motivational identity: Variable-centered and person-centered analytic approaches. *Elementary School Journal, 103,* 383–399.

Murphy, P. K., & Alexander, P. A. (2000). A motivated exploration of motivation terminology. *Contemporary Educational Psychology, 25,* 3–53.

Murphy, P. K., & Benton, S. L. (2010). The new frontier of educational neuropsychology: Unknown opportunities and unfulfilled hopes. *Contemporary Educational Psychology, 35,* 153–155.

Murphy, P. K., Wilkinson, I. A. G., Soter, A. O., Hennessey, M. N., & Alexander, J. F. (2009). Examining the effects of classroom discussion on students' comprehension of text: A meta-analysis. *Journal of Educational Psychology, 101,* 740–764.

Myers, D. G. (2005). *Exploring psychology* (6th ed. in modules). New York, NY: Worth.

Myers, D. G. (2010). *Psychology* (9th ed.). New York, NY: Worth.

Myers, I. B., & McCaulley, M. H. (1988). *Manual: A guide to the development and use of the Myers-Briggs Type Indicator.* Palo Alto, CA: Consulting Psychologists.

Nadler, J. T., & Clark, M. H. (2011). Stereotype threat: A meta-analysis comparing African Americans to Hispanic Americans. *Journal of Applied Social Psychology, 41,* 872–890.

NAGC. (2013). *Redefining giftedness for a new century: Shifting the paradigm.* Washington, DC: Author. Retrieved from www.nagc.org/index.aspx?id=6404

Nagengast, B., & Marsh, H. W. (2012). Big fish in little ponds aspire more: Mediation and cross-cultural generalizability of school-average ability effects on self-concept and career aspirations in science. *Journal of Educational Psychology, 4,* 1033–1053. doi: 10.1037/a0027697

National Alliance of Black School Educators. (2002). *Addressing over-representations of African American students in special education: The prereferral intervention process.* Arlington, VA: Council for Exceptional Education.

National Assessment of Educational Progress. (2013). *National Report Card.* Retrieved from http://nationsreportcard.gov/reading_math_2013/#/achievement-gaps

National Association for Gifted Children. (2013). *Redefining giftedness for a new century: Shifting the paradigm.* Washington, DC: Author. Retrieved from www.nagc.org/index.aspx?id=6404

National Center for Child Poverty. (2013). Child poverty. Retrieved from http://www.nccp.org/topics/childpoverty.html

National Center for Education Statistics. (2003). *Indicators of school crime and safety 2002.* Retrieved from http://nces.ed.gov/pubs2003/schoolcrime/6.asp?nav=1

National Center for Education Statistics. (2013). *Fast facts.* Retrieved from http://nces.ed.gov/FastFacts/display.asp?id=59

National Center for Homeless Education. (2013). Education for homeless children and youths program data collection summary. Washington, DC: NCHE, U.S. Department of Education. Retrieved from http://center.serve.org/nche/downloads/data-comp-0910-1112.pdf

National Children's Study. (2012). *What is bullying? 4 Types of bullying.* Retrieved from childrensstudymaine.com/health/what-is-bullying-4-types-of-bullying/

National Commission on Excellence in Education. (1983). *A nation at risk: The imperative for educational reform.* Washington, DC: Author. Retrieved from http://www.ed.gov/pubs/NatAtRisk/index.html

National Commission on Teaching and America's Future. (2003). *No dream denied: A pledge to America's children.* Washington, DC: Author.

National Federation of the Blind. (2010). *NFB nonvisual accessibility web certification granted to Instructure Learning Management System.* Retrieved from http://www.disabled-world.com/disability/accessibility/websitedesign/learning-management-system.php#ixzz1ZYiOqF56

National Institute of Child Health and Human Development (NICHD) Early Child Care Research Network. (2005a). *Child care and child development.* New York, NY: Guilford Press.

National Institute of Child Health and Human Development (NICHD) Early Child Care Research Network. (2005b). Pathways to reading: The role of oral language in the transition to reading. *Developmental Psychology, 41*(2), 428–442.

National Poverty Center. (2014). *Poverty in the United States: Frequently asked questions.* The University of Michigan, Gerald R. Ford School of Public Policy, Ann Arbor, MI. Retrieved from http://npc.umich.edu/poverty/

National Science Foundation. (2014). *Doctoral recipients by race, ethnicity, and citizenship, 2002–2012.* Retrieved from http://www.nsf.gov/statistics/sed/2012/pdf/tab19.pdf

National Science Foundation, Division of Science Resources Statistics. (2011). *Women, minorities, and persons with disabilities in science and engineering: 2011.* Special Report NSF 11–309. Arlington, VA. Retrieved from http://www.nsf.gov/statistics/wmpd/

National Service Learning Clearinghouse. (n.d.). *Service learning is. . . .* Retrieved from http://www.servicelearning.org/welcome_to_service-learning/service-learning_is/index.php

Navarro, R. L., Flores, L. Y., & Worthington, R. L. (2007). Mexican American middle school students' goal intentions in mathematics and science: A test of social cognitive career theory. *Journal of Counseling Psychology, 54,* 320–335.

Naveh-Benjamin, M. (1991). A comparison of training programs intended for different types of test-anxious students: Further support for an information-processing model. *Journal of Educational Psychology, 83,* 134–139.

Neisser, U., Boodoo, G., Bouchard, A., Boykin, W., Brody, N., Ceci, S. J., . . . Urbina, S. (1996). Intelligence: Knowns and unknowns. *American Psychologist, 51,* 77–101.

Nelson, C. A. (2001). The development and neural bases of face recognition. *Infant and Child Development, 10,* 3–18.

Nelson, J. R., & Roberts, M. L. (2000). Ongoing reciprocal teacher-student interactions involving disruptive behaviors in general education classrooms. *Journal of Emotional and Behavioral Disorders, 4,* 147–161.

Nelson, K., & Fivush, R. (2004). The emergence of autobiographical memory: A social cultural developmental theory. *Psychological Review, 111,* 486–511.

Nelson, T. O. (1996). Consciousness and metacognition. *American Psychologist, 51,* 102–116.

Nesbit, J. C., & Adesope, O. O. (2006). Learning with concept and knowledge maps: A meta-analysis. *Review of Educational Research, 76,* 413–448.

Neuman, S. B., & Roskos, K. A. (1997). Literacy knowledge in practice: Contexts of participation for young writers and readers. *Reading Research Quarterly, 32,* 10–32.

Neumeister, K. L. S., & Cramond, B. (2004). E. Paul Torrance (1915–2003). *American Psychologist, 59,* 179.

Neville, H. (2007, March). Experience shapes human brain development and function. *Paper presented at the biennial meeting of the Society for Research in Child Development,* Boston.

The New Teacher Project. (2013). *Perspectives of irreplaceable teachers: What America's best teachers think about teaching.* Brooklyn, NY: TNTP. Retrieved from http://tntp.org/assets/documents/TNTP_Perspectives_2013.pdf

New York City Department of Education. (2014). Scaffolding website. Retrieved from http://condor.admin.ccny.cuny.edu/~group4/

Newman, K. L., Samimy, K., & Romstedt, K. (2010). Developing a training program for secondary teachers of English language learners in Ohio. *Theory Into Practice, 49,* 152–161.

Nguyen, H.-H. D., & Ryan, A. M. (2008). Does stereotype threat affect test performance of minorities and women? A meta-analysis of experimental evidence. *Journal of Applied Psychology, 93,* 1314–1334.

Nhan, D. (2012). Interactive: State high school graduation rates by race, ethnicity. *National Journal.* Retrieved from www.Nationaljournal.Com/Thenextamerica/Education/Interactive-State-High-School-Graduation-Rates-By-Race-Ethnicity-20121130

Nicholls, J., Cobb, P., Wood, T., Yackel, E., & Patashnick, M. (1990). Assessing student's theories of success in mathematics: Individual and classroom differences. *Journal for Research in Mathematics Education, 21,* 109–122.

Nicholls, J. G., & Miller, A. (1984). Conceptions of ability and achievement motivation. In R. Ames & C. Ames (Eds.), *Research on motivation in education. Vol. 1: Student Motivation* (pp. 39–73). New York, NY: Academic Press.

Nielsen Company. (2010). *U.S. teen mobile report: Calling yesterday, texting today, using apps tomorrow.* New York, NY: Author. Retrieved from http://blog.nielsen.com/nielsenwire/online_mobile/u-s-teen-mobile-report-calling-yesterday-texting-today-using-apps-tomorrow/

Nieto, S., & Bode, P. (2012). *Affirming diversity: The sociopolitical context of multicultural education* (6th ed.). Boston, MA: Pearson.

Nitko, A. J., & Brookhart, S. M. (2011). *Educational assessment of students* (6th ed.). Boston, MA: Pearson.

No Child Left Behind Act. (2002). P.L. 107–110, Title IX, Part A, Section 9101 (22), p. 544, 20 U.S.C. 7802.

Noddings, N. (1990). Constructivism in mathematics education. In R. Davis, C. Maher, & N. Noddings (Eds.), *Constructivist views on the teaching and learning of mathematics* (pp. 7–18). *Monograph 4 of the National Council of Teachers of Mathematics.* Reston, VA: National Council of Teachers of Mathematics.

Noddings, N. (1995). Teaching themes of care. *Phi Delta Kappan, 76,* 675–679.

Noguera, P. (2005). The racial achievement gap: How can we assume an equity of outcomes. In L. Johnson, M. E. Finn, & R. Lewis (Eds.), *Urban education with an attitude.* Albany, NY: SUNY Press.

Nokes, J. D., Dole, J. A., & Hacker, D. J. (2007). Teaching high school students to use heuristics while reading historical texts. *Journal of Educational Psychology, 99,* 492–504.

Nokes-Malach, T. J., & Mestre, J. P. (2013). Toward a model of transfer as sense-making. *Educational Psychologist, 48,* 184–207, doi: 10.1080/00461520.2013.807556

Norbert, F. (2005). Research findings on early first language attrition: Implications for the discussion of critical periods in language acquisition. *Language Learning, 55*(3), 491–531.

Novotney, A. (2009). Dangerous distraction. *Monitor on Psychology, 40,* 32. Retrieved from http://www.apa.org/monitor/2009/02/dangerous.aspx

Novotney, A. (2011). Coed versus single-sex schools. *Monitor on Psychology, 42*(2), 58–62.

Nucci, L. P. (2001). *Education in the moral domain.* New York, NY: Cambridge Press.

Nucci, L. (2009). *Nice is not enough: Facilitating moral development.* Upper Saddle River, NJ: Pearson.

Nurmi, J. (2004). Socialization and self-development: Channeling, selection, adjustment, and reflection. In R. Lerner & L. Steinberg (Eds.), *Handbook of adolescent psychology* (2nd ed., pp. 85–124). New York, NY: Wiley.

Nussbaum, E. M. (2011). Argumentation, dialogue theory, and probability modeling: Alternative frameworks for argumentation research in education. *Educational Psychologist, 46,* 84–106, doi:10.1080/00461520.2011.558816

Nylund, D. (2000). *Treating Huckleberry Finn: A new narrative approach to working with kids diagnosed ADD/ADHD.* San Francisco: Jossey-Bass.

O'Boyle, M. W., & Gill, H. S. (1998). On the relevance of research findings in cognitive neuroscience to educational practice. *Educational Psychology Review, 10,* 397–410.

O'Connor, C. (1997). Dispositions toward (collective) struggle and educational resilience in the inner city: A case analysis of six African American high school students. *American Educational Research Journal, 34,* 593–629.

O'Donnell, A. M. (Ed.). (2002, Winter). Promoting thinking through peer learning. Special issue of *Theory Into Practice, 61*(1).

O'Donnell, A. M. (2006). The role of peers and group learning. In P. A. Alexander & P. H. Winne (Eds.), *Handbook of educational psychology* (2nd ed., pp. 781–802). Mahwah, NJ: Erlbaum.

O'Donnell, A. M., & O'Kelly, J. (1994). Learning from peers: Beyond the rhetoric of positive results. *Educational Psychology Review, 6,* 321–350.

O'Leary, K. D., & O'Leary, S. (Eds.). (1977). *Classroom management: The successful use of behavior modification* (2nd ed.). Elmsford, NY: Pergamon.

O'Leary, S. (1995). Parental discipline mistakes. *Current Directions in Psychological Science, 4,* 11–13.

O'Mara, A. J., Marsh, H. W., Craven, R. G., & Debus, R. L. (2006). Do self-concept interventions make a difference? A synergistic blend of construct validation and meta-analysis. *Educational Psychologist, 41,* 181–206.

O'Neil, J. (1990). Link between style, culture proves divisive. *Educational Leadership, 48*(2), 8.

Oakes, J. (1985). *Keeping track.* New Haven, CT: Yale University Press.

Oakes, J. (1990). *Multiplying inequities: The effects of race, social class, and tracking on opportunities to learn mathematics and science.* Santa Monica, CA: Rand.

Oakes, J. (1999). Promotion or retention: Which one is social? *Harvard Education Letter, 15*(1), 8.

Oakes, J., & Wells, A. S. (2002). Detracking for high student achievement. In L. Abbeduto (Ed.), *Taking sides: Clashing views and controversial issues in educational psychology* (2nd ed., pp. 26–30). Guilford, CT: McGraw-Hill Duskin.

OECD. (2007). *Understanding the brain: The birth of a learning science.* Paris: Author [OECD].

OECD. (2013). *PISA: Snapshot of performance in mathematics, reading and science.* Paris, France: Author. Retrieved from http://www.oecd.org/pisa/keyfindings/PISA-2012-results-snapshot-Volume-I-ENG.pdf

Ogbu, J. U. (1987). Variability in minority school performance: A problem in search of an explanation. *Anthropology and Education Quarterly, 18,* 312–334.

Ogbu, J. U. (1997). Understanding the school performance of urban blacks: Some essential background knowledge. In H. Walberg, O. Reyes, & R. P. Weissberg (Eds.), *Children and youth: Interdisciplinary perspectives* (pp. 190–240). Norwood, NJ: Ablex.

Okagaki, L. (2001). Triarchic model of minority children's school achievement. *Educational Psychologist, 36,* 9–20.

Okagaki, L. (2006). Ethnicity, learning. In P. Alexander & P. Winne (Eds.), *Handbook of educational psychology* (2nd ed., pp. 615–634). Mahwah, NJ: Erlbaum.

Olsen, L. (1988). *Crossing the schoolhouse border: Immigrant students and the California public schools.* San Francisco, CA: California Tomorrow.

Olson, D. R. (2004). The triumph of hope over experience in the search for "what works": A response to Slavin. *Educational Researcher, 33*(1), 24–26.

Olson, K. (2008). The wounded student. *Educational Leadership, 65*(6), 46–48.

Oosterhof, A. (2009). *Developing and using classroom assessments* (4th ed.). Columbus, OH: Pearson/Merrill.

Orange, C. (2000). *25 biggest mistakes teachers make and how to avoid them.* Thousand Oaks, CA: Corwin.

Orange, C. (2005). *44 smart strategies for avoiding classroom mistakes.* Thousand Oaks, CA: Corwin Press.

Organisation for Economic Co-operation and Development. (2007). *Understanding the brain: The birth of a learning science.* Paris: Author [OECD].

Organisation for Economic Co-operation and Development. (2013). *PISA: Snapshot of performance in mathematics, reading and science.* Paris, France: Author. Retrieved from http://www.oecd.org/pisa/keyfindings/PISA-2012-results-snapshot-Volume-I-ENG.pdf

Orlando, L., & Machado, A. (1996). In defense of Piaget's theory: A reply to 10 common criticisms. *Psychological Review, 103,* 143–164.

Ormrod, J. E. (2012). *Human learning* (6th ed.). Boston, MA: Pearson.

Ortony, A., Clore, G. L., & Collins, A. (1988). *The cognitive structure of emotions.* Cambridge, UK: Cambridge University Press.

Osborn, A. F. (1963). *Applied imagination* (3rd ed.). New York, NY: Scribner's.

Osborne, J. W., & Jones, B. D. (2011). Identification with academics and motivation to achieve in school: How the structure of the self influences academic outcomes. *Educational Psychology Review, 23,* 131–158.

Osborne, J. W., Tillman, D., & Holland, A. (2010). Stereotype threat and anxiety for disadvantaged minorities and women. In J. C. Cassady (Ed.), *Anxiety in schools: The causes, consequences, and solutions for academic anxieties* (pp. 119–137). New York: Peter Lang.

Osterman, K. F. (2000). Students' need for belonging in the school community. *Review of Educational Research, 70,* 323–367.

Ostrov, J. M., & Godleski, S. A. (2010). Toward an integrated gender-linked model of aggression subtypes in early and middle childhood. *Psychological Bulletin, 117,* 233–242.

Otto, B. (2010). *Language development in early childhood* (5th ed.). Columbus, OH: Merrill.

Ovando, C. J., & Collier, V. P. (1998). *Bilingual and ESL classrooms: Teaching in multicultural contexts* (2nd ed.). Boston, MA: McGraw-Hill.

Overton, W. F. (2006). Developmental psychology: Philosophy, concepts, and methodology. In R. M. Lerner (Ed.), *Handbook of child psychology: Vol. 1. Theoretical models of human development* (6th ed., pp. 18–88). New York, NY: Wiley.

Owens, R. E. (2010). *Language disorders: A functional approach to assessment and intervention* (5th ed.). Boston, MA: Allyn & Bacon.

Owens, R. E. (2012). *Language development: An introduction* (8th ed.). Boston, MA: Allyn & Bacon.

Ownston, R. D. (2012). Computer games and the quest to find their affordances for learning. *Educational Researcher, 41*(3), 105–106. doi: 10.3102/0013189X12439231

Pahlke, E., Shibley Hyde, J., & Mertz, J. E. (2013). The effects of single-sex compared with coeducational schooling on mathematics and science achievement: Data from Korea. *Journal of Educational Psychology, 105,* 444–452. doi: 10.1037/a0031857

Pai, Y., & Adler, S. A. (2001). *Cultural foundations of education* (3rd ed.). Upper Saddle River, NJ: Merrill.

Paik, E. S., & Schraw, G. (2013). Learning with animation and illusions of understanding. *Journal of Educational Psychology, 105,* 278–289.

Paivio, A. (1986). *Mental representations: A dual coding approach.* Oxford. England: Oxford University Press.

Paivio, A. (2006). *Mind and its evolution; a dual coding theoretical interpretation.* Mahwah, NJ: Erlbaum.

Pajares, F. (1997). Current directions in self-efficacy research. In M. L. Maehr & P. R. Pintrich (Eds.), *Advances in motivation and achievement* (Vol. 10, pp. 1–49). Greenwich, CT: JAI Press.

Pajares, F. (2000, April). *Seeking a culturally attentive educational psychology.* Paper presented at the annual meeting of the American Educational Research Association, New Orleans, LA. Retrieved from http://www.emory.edu/EDUCATION/mfp/AERA2000Discussant.html

Pajares, F. (2002). *Self-efficacy beliefs in academic contexts: An outline.* Retrieved from http://des.emory.edu/mfp/efftalk.html

Pajares, F. (2003). William James: Our father who begot us. In B. J. Zimmerman & D. H. Schunk (Eds.), *Educational psychology: A century of contributions* (pp. 41–64). Mahwah, NJ: Erlbaum.

Pajares, F. (2008). Self-efficacy information. Retrieved from http://www.des.emory.edu/mfp/banconversion.html

Pajares, F., & Schunk, D. H. (2001). Self-beliefs and school success: Self-efficacy, self-concept, and school achievement. In R. Riding & S. Rayner (Eds.), *Perception* (pp. 239–266). Westport, CT: Ablex.

Pajares, F., & Schunk, D. H. (2002). Self and self-belief in psychology and education: An historical perspective. In J. Aronson & D. Cordova (Eds.), *Psychology of education: Personal and interpersonal forces* (pp. 1–19). New York, NY: Academic Press.

Pajares, F., & Valiante, G. (1997). Influence of self-efficacy on elementary students' writing. *Journal of Educational Research, 90,* 353–360.

Palardy, G. (2013). High school socioeconomic segregation and student attainment. *American Educational Research Journal, 50,* 714–754.

Palincsar, A. S. (1986). The role of dialogue in providing scaffolded instruction. *Educational Psychologist, 26,* 73–98.

Palincsar, A. S. (1998). Social constructivist perspectives on teaching and learning. In J. T. Spence, J. M. Darley, & D. J. Foss (Eds.), *Annual Review of Psychology* (pp. 345–375). Palo Alto, CA: Annual Reviews.

Palincsar, A. S., & Brown, A. L. (1984). Reciprocal teaching of comprehension-fostering and monitoring activities. *Cognition and Instruction, 1,* 117–175.

Palincsar, A. S., & Brown, A. L. (1989). Classroom dialogues to promote self-regulated comprehension. In J. Brophy (Ed.), *Advances in research on teaching* (Vol. 1, pp. 35–67). Greenwich, CT: JAI Press.

Palincsar, A. S., & Herrenkohl, L. R. (2002). Designing collaborative learning contexts. *Theory Into Practice, 61,* 26–32.

Palincsar, A. S., Magnusson, S. J., Collins, K. M., & Cutter, J. (2001). Promoting deep understanding of science in students with disabilities in inclusion classrooms. *Learning Disabilities Quarterly, 24*(1), 15–32.

Palincsar, A. S., Magnusson, S. J., Marano, N., Ford, D., & Brown, N. (1998). Designing a community of practice: Principles and practices of the GIsML community. *Teaching and Teacher Education, 14,* 5–19.

Panitz, T. (1996). *A definition of collaborative vs cooperative learning.* Retrieved from http://www.londonmet.ac.uk/deliberations/collaborative-learning/panitz-paper.cfm

Papanikolaou, K., & Boubouka, M. (2010–2011). Promoting collaboration in a project-based e-learning context. *Journal of Research on Technology in Education, 43,* 135–155.

Papert, S. (1980). *Mindstorms: Children, computers, and powerful ideas.* New York, NY: Basic Books.

Papert, S. (1991). Situating constructionism. In I. Harel & S. Papert (Eds.), *Constructionism* (pp. 1–11). Norwood, NJ: Ablex.

Paris, S. G., & Ayres, L. R. (1994). *Becoming reflective students and teachers: With portfolios and authentic assessment.* Washington, DC: American Psychological Association.

Paris, S. G., Byrnes, J. P., & Paris, A. H. (2001). Constructing theories, identities, and actions of self-regulated learners. In B. J. Zimmerman & D. H. Schunk (Eds.), *Self-regulated learning and academic achievement: Theoretical perspectives* (2nd ed., pp. 253–287). Mahwah, NJ: Erlbaum.

Paris, S. G., & Cunningham, A. E. (1996). Children becoming students. In D. Berliner & R. Calfee

(Eds.), *Handbook of educational psychology* (pp. 117–146). New York, NY: Macmillan.

Park, G., Lubinski, D., & Benbow, C. P. (2013). When less is more: Effects of grade skipping on adult STEM productivity among mathematically precocious adolescents. *Journal of Educational Psychology, 105,* 176–198.

Parke, R. D., & Buriel, R. (2006). Socialization in the family: Ethnic and ecological perspectives. In W. Damon & N. Eisenberg (Eds.), *Handbook of child psychology* (5th ed., Vol. 3. Social, emotional, and personality development, pp. 553–618). New York, NY: Wiley.

Parker, W. C., & Hess, D. (2001). Teaching with and for discussion. *Teaching and Teacher Education, 17,* 273–289.

Pashler, H., McDaniel, M., Rohrer, D., & Bjork, R. (2009). Learning styles: Concepts and evidence. *Psychological Science in the Public Interest, 9,* 105–119.

Patall, E. A. (2013). Constructing motivation through choice, interest, and interestingness. *Journal of Educational Psychology, 105,* 522–534. Advance online publication. doi: 10.1037/a0030307

Pate, P. E., McGinnis, K., & Homestead, E. (1995). Creating coherence through curriculum integration. In M. Harmin (1994), *Inspiring active learning: A handbook for teachers* (pp. 62–70). Alexandria, VA: Association for Supervision and Curriculum Development.

Patterson, C. (1995). *Lesbian & gay parenting.* Retrieved from http://www.apa.org/pi/lgbt/resources/parenting.aspx

Patterson, G. R. (1997). Performance models for parenting: A social interactional perspective. In J. Grusec & L. Kuczynski (Eds.), *Parenting and the socialization of values: A handbook of contemporary theory* (pp. 193–235). New York, NY: Wiley.

Patton, D. U., Hong, J. S., Williams, A. B., & Allen-Meares, P. (2013). A review of research on school bullying among African American Youth: An ecological systems analysis. *Educational Psychology Review, 25,* 245–260.

Pauk, W., & Owens, R. J. Q. (2010). *How to study in college* (10th ed.). (Original work published 1962.) Florence, KY: Cengage Learning.

Paul, A. M. (2011, September 10). The trouble with homework. *New York Times,* Sunday Review Section, p. 6.

Paul, R., & Elder, L. (2014). *Critical thinking: Concepts and tools* (7th ed.). Dillon Beach, CA: Foundation for Critical Thinking.

Paulos, L. (2007). Multitasking madness. *Scholastic Choices, 23*(1), 10–13.

Pearl, R., Leung, M. C., Acker, R. V., Farmer, T. W., & Rodkin, P. C. (2007). Fourth- and fifth-grade teachers' awareness of their classrooms' social networks. *The Elementary School Journal, 108,* 25–39.

Pearson, B. Z., Fernandez, S. C., Lewedeg, V., & Oller, D. K. (1997). The relation of input factors to lexical learning by bilingual infants. *Applied Linguistics, 18,* 41–58.

Peebles, R., Harrison, S., McCown, K., Wilson, J., Borzekowski, D., & Lock, J. (2012). Voices of pro-ana and pro-mia: A qualitative analysis of reasons for entering and continuing pro-eating disorder website usage. *Journal of Adolescent Health, 50*(2), S62.

Pekrun, R., Elliot, A. J., & Maier, M. A. (2006). Achievement goals and discrete achievement emotions: A theoretical model and prospective test. *Journal of Educational Psychology, 98,* 583–597.

Pekrun, R., Goetz, T., Daniels, L. M., Stupinisky, R. H., & Perry, R. P. (2010). Boredom in achievement settings: Exploring control–value antecedents and performance outcomes of a neglected emotion. *Journal of Educational Psychology, 102,* 531–549.

Pekrun, R., Goetz, T., Titz, W., & Perry, R. P. (2002). Academic emotions in students' self-regulated learning and achievement. A program of qualitative and quantitative research. *Educational Psychologist, 37,* 91–105.

Pellegrini, A. D., Bartini, M., & Brooks, F. (1999). School bullies, victims, and aggressive victims: Factors relating to group affiliation and victimization in early adolescence. *Journal of Educational Psychology, 91,* 216–224.

Pellegrini, A. D., & Bohn, C. M. (2005). The role of recess in children's cognitive performance and school adjustment. *Educational Researcher, 34,* 13–19.

Pellegrini, A. D., Dupuis, D., & Smith, P. K. (2007). Play in evolution and development. *Developmental Review, 27,* 261–276.

Pellegrino, L. (2002). Cerebral palsy. In M. L. Batshaw (Ed.), *Children with disabilities.* Baltimore, MD: Brookes.

Pellis, S. (2006). The effects of orbital frontal cortex damage on the modulation of defensive responses by rats in playful and nonplayful social contexts. *Behavioral Neuroscience, 120,* 72–84.

Peng, S., & Lee, R. (1992, April). *Home variables, parent–child activities, and academic achievement: A study of 1988 eighth graders.* Paper presented at the annual meeting of the American Educational Research Association, San Francisco, CA.

Penuel, W. R., & Wertsch, J. V. (1995). Vygotsky and identity formation: A sociocultural approach. *Educational Psychologist, 30,* 83–92.

Peregoy, S. F., & Boyle, O. F. (2009). *Reading, writing, and learning in ESL: A resource book for teaching K–12 English learners* (5th ed.). Boston, MA: Allyn & Bacon/Pearson.

Perkins, D. N., Jay, E., & Tishman, S. (1993). New conceptions of thinking: From ontology to education. *Educational Psychologist, 28,* 67–85.

Perkins, D. N., & Salomon, G. (2012). Knowledge to go: A motivational and dispositional view of transfer. *Educational Psychologist, 47,* 248–258. doi: 10.1080/00461520.2012.693354

Perner, J. (2000). Memory and theory of mind. In E. Tulving & F. I. M. Craik (Eds.), *The Oxford handbook of memory* (pp. 297–312). New York, NY: Oxford University Press.

Perry, N. E. (1998). Young children's self-regulated learning and contexts that support it. *Journal of Educational Psychology, 90,* 715–729.

Perry, N. E., & Collie, R. J. (2011, April). *School climate and social and emotional learning: Predictors of early career teacher well-being and efficacy.* Paper presented at the annual meeting of the American Educational Research Association, New Orleans, LA.

Perry, N. E., & Drummond, L. (2002). Helping young students become self-regulated researchers and writers. *The Reading Teacher, 56,* 298–310.

Perry, N. E., Phillips, L., & Dowler, J. (2004). Examining features of tasks and their potential to promote self-regulated learning. *Teachers College Record, 106,* 1854–1878.

Perry, N. E., & Rahim, A. (2011). Studying self-regulated learning in classrooms. In B. Zimmerman & D. Schunk (Eds.), *Handbook of self-regulation of learning and performance* (pp. 122–136). New York, NY: Routledge.

Perry, N. E., VandeKamp, K. O., & Mercer, L. K. (2000, April). *Investigating teacher–student interactions that foster self-regulated learning.* In N. E. Perry (Chair), Symposium conducted at the meeting of the American Educational Research Association, New Orleans, LA.

Perry, N. E., VandeKamp, K. O., Mercer, L. K., & Nordby, C. J. (2002). Investigating teacher-student interactions that foster self-regulated learning. *Educational Psychologist, 37,* 5–15.

Peter, M., Glück, J., & Beiglböck, W. (2010). Map understanding as a developmental marker in childhood. *Journal of Individual Differences, 31,* 64–67.

Peters, M. P., & Bain, S. K. (2011). Bullying and victimization rates among gifted and high-achieving students. *Journal for the Education of the Gifted, 34,* 624–643.

Peterson, G. W., Cobas, J. A., Bush, J. R., Supple, A., & Wilson, S. M. (2004). Parent-youth relationships and the self-esteem of Chinese adolescents: Collectivism versus individualism. *Marriage & Family Review, 36,* 173–200.

Petitclerc, A., Boivin, M., Dionne, G., Zoccolillo, M., & Tremblay, R. E. (2009). Disregard for rules: The early development and predictors of a specific dimension of disruptive behavior disorders. *Journal of Child Psychology and Psychiatry, 50,* 1477–1484.

Petitto, L. A. (2009). New discoveries from the bilingual brain and mind across the life span: Implications for education. *Brain, Mind, and Education, 3,* 185–197.

Petitto, L. A., & Kovelman, I. (2003). The bilingual paradox: How signing-speaking bilingual children help us resolve bilingual issues and teach us about the brain's mechanisms underlying all language acquisition. *Language Learning, 8*(3), 5–18.

Petrill, S. A., & Wilkerson, B. (2000). Intelligence and achievement: A behavioral genetic perspective. *Educational Psychology Review, 12,* 185–199.

Peverly, S. T., Brobst, K., Graham, M., & Shaw, R. (2003). College adults are not good at self-regulation: A study on the relationship of self-regulation, note-taking, and test-taking. *Journal of Educational Psychology, 95,* 335–346.

Peverly, S. T., Ramaswamy, V., Brown, C., Sumowski, J., Alidoost, M., & Garner, J. (2007). What predicts skill in lecture note taking? *Journal of Educational Psychology, 99,* 167–180.

Pew Internet & American Life Project. (2013). Cell phone ownership. Retrieved from http://pewinternet.org/Reports/2012/Teens-and-smartphones/Cell-phone-ownership/Smartphones.aspx

Pfiffner, L., Barkley, R. A., & DuPaul, G. J. (2006). Treatment of ADHD in school settings. In R. A. Barkley (Ed.), *Attention-deficit hyperactivity disorder: A handbook for diagnosis and treatment* (3rd ed., pp. 547–588). New York, NY: Guilford.

Pfiffner, L. J., & O'Leary, S. G. (1987). The efficacy of all positive management as a function of the prior use of negative consequences. *Journal of Applied Behavior Analysis, 20,* 265–271.

Phillips, D. (1997). How, why, what, when, and where: Perspectives on constructivism and education. *Issues in Education: Contributions from Educational Psychology, 3,* 151–194.

Phillips, D., & Zimmerman, M. (1990). The developmental course of perceived competence and incompetence among competent children. In R. Sternberg & J. Kolligian (Eds.), *Competence considered* (pp. 41–66). New Haven, CT: Yale University Press.

Phinney, J. S. (1990). Ethnic identity in adolescents and adults: Review of research. *Psychological Bulletin, 108*(3), 499–514.

Phinney, J. S. (2003). Ethnic identity and acculturation. In K. Chun, P. Ball, & G. Marin (Eds.), *Acculturation: Advances in theory, measurement, and applied research* (pp. 63–81). Washington, DC: American Psychological Association.

Phinney, J. S., & Devich-Navarro, M. (1997). Variations in bicultural identification among African American

and Mexican American adolescents. *Journal of Research on Adolescence, 7,* 3–32.

Phye, G. D. (1992). Strategic transfer: A tool for academic problem solving. *Educational Psychology Review, 4,* 393–421.

Phye, G. D. (2001). Problem-solving instruction and problem-solving transfer: The correspondence issue. *Journal of Educational Psychology, 93,* 571–578.

Phye, G. D., & Sanders, C. E. (1994). Advice and feedback: Elements of practice for problem solving. *Contemporary Educational Psychology, 17,* 211–223.

Piaget, J. (1954). *The construction of reality in the child* (M. Cook, Trans.). New York, NY: Basic Books.

Piaget, J. (1962). *Comments on Vygotsky's critical remarks concerning "The language and thought of the child" and "Judgment and reasoning in the child."* Cambridge, MA: MIT Press.

Piaget, J. (1963). *Origins of intelligence in children.* New York, NY: Norton.

Piaget, J. (1964). Development and learning. In R. Ripple & V. Rockcastle (Eds.), *Piaget rediscovered* (pp. 7–20). Ithaca, NY: Cornell University Press.

Piaget, J. (1965). *The moral judgment of the child.* New York, NY: Free Press.

Piaget, J. (1969). *Science of education and the psychology of the child.* New York, NY: Viking.

Piaget, J. (1970a). Piaget's theory. In P. Mussen (Ed.), *Handbook of child psychology* (3rd ed.) (Vol. 1, pp. 703–732). New York, NY: Wiley.

Piaget, J. (1970b). *The science of education and the psychology of the child.* New York, NY: Orion Press.

Piaget, J. (1971). *Biology and knowledge.* Edinburgh, UK: Edinburgh Press.

Piaget, J. (1974). *Understanding causality* (D. Miles and M. Miles, Trans.). New York, NY: Norton.

Piaget, J. (1985). *The equilibrium of cognitive structures: The central problem of intellectual development* (T. Brown & K. L. Thampy, Trans.). Chicago, IL: University of Chicago Press.

Piaget, J. (1995). *Sociological studies.* New York, NY: Routledge. (Original work published 1965.)

Pianta, R. C., Belsky, J., Vandergrift, N., Houts, R., & Morrison, F. J. (2008). Classroom effects on children's achievement trajectories in elementary school. *American Educational Research Journal, 45,* 365–397.

Pianta, R. C., LaParo, K. M., & Hamre, B. K. (2008). *Classroom assessment scoring system manual: Pre-K.* Baltimore, MD: Brookes.

Piasta, S. B., Petscher, Y., & Justice, L. M. (2012). How many letters should preschoolers in public programs know? The diagnostic efficiency of various preschool letter-naming benchmarks for predicting first-grade literacy achievement. *Journal of Educational Psychology, 104,* 945–958. doi: 10.1037/a0027757

Pigge, F. L., & Marso, R. N. (1997). A seven-year longitudinal multi-factor assessment of teaching concerns development through preparation and early teaching. *Teaching and Teacher Education, 13,* 225–235.

Pinker, S. (2002). *The blank slate: The modern denial of human nature.* New York, NY: Penguin.

Pintrich, P. R. (2000). Educational psychology at the millennium: A look back and a look forward. *Educational Psychologist, 35,* 221–226.

Pintrich, P. R. (2003). A motivational science perspective on the role of student motivation in learning and teaching. *Journal of Educational Psychology, 95,* 667–686.

Pintrich, P. R., & De Groot, E. V. (1990). Motivational and self-regulated learning components of classroom academic performance. *Journal of Educational Psychology, 82,* 33–40.

Pintrich, P. R., Marx, R. W., & Boyle, R. A. (1993). Beyond cold conceptual change: The role of motivational beliefs and classroom contextual factors in the process of conceptual change. *Review of Educational Research, 63*, 167–199.

Pintrich, P. R., & Schunk, D. H. (2002). *Motivation in education: Research and applications* (2nd ed.). Boston, MA: Allyn & Bacon.

Pintrich, P. R., & Zusho, A. (2002). The development of academic self-regulation: The role of cognitive and motivational factors. In A. Wigfield & J. Eccles (Eds.), *Development of achievement motivation* (pp. 249–284). San Diego, CA: Academic Press.

Pinxten, M., De Fraine, B., Van Damme, J., & D'Haenens, E. (2010). Causal ordering of academic self-concept and achievement: Effects of type of achievement measure. *British Journal of Educational Psychology, 80*, 689–709.

Pisha, B., & Coyne, P. (2001). Smart for the start: The promise of universal design for learning. *Remedial and Special Education, 22*, 197–203.

Plant, E. A., & Peruche, B. M. (2005). The consequences of race for police officers' responses to criminal suspects. *Psychological Science, 16*, 180–183.

Plucker, J. A., Beghetto, R. A., & Dow, G. T. (2004). Why isn't creativity more important to educational psychologists? Potential pitfalls and future directions in creativity research. *Educational Psychology, 39*(2), 83–96.

Plummer, D. L., & Graziano, W. G. (1987). Impact of grade retention on the social development of elementary school children. *Developmental Psychology, 23*, 267–275.

Polson, P. G., & Jeffries, R. (1985). Instruction in general problem-solving skills: An analysis of four approaches. In J. Segal, S. Chipman, & R. Glaser (Eds.), *Thinking and learning skills* (Vol. 1, pp. 417–455). Mahwah, NJ: Erlbaum.

Ponitz, C. C., Rimm-Kaufman, S. E., Grimm, K. J., & Curby, T. W. (2009). Kindergarten classroom quality, behavioral engagement, and reading achievement. *School Psychology Review, 38*, 102–120.

Popham, W. J. (2005). *Classroom assessment: What teachers need to know* (4th ed.). Boston, MA: Allyn & Bacon.

Popham, W. J. (2008). *Classroom assessment: What teachers need to know* (5th ed.). Boston, MA: Allyn & Bacon.

Popham, W. J. (2014). *Classroom assessment: What teachers need to know* (7th ed.). Boston, MA: Allyn & Bacon.

Portes, A., & Hao, L. (1998). E pluribus unum: Bilingualism and loss of language in the second generation. *Sociology of Education, 71*, 269–294.

Posada, G., Jacobs, A., Richmond, M., Carbonell, O. A., Alzate, G., Bustamante, M. R., & Quiceno, J. (2002). Maternal care giving and infant security in two cultures. *Developmental Psychology, 38*, 67–78.

Posner, M. I. (1973). *Cognition: An introduction.* Glenview, IL: Scott, Foresman.

Potocki, A., Ecalle, J., & Magnan, A. (2013). Effect of computer-assisted comprehension training in less-skilled comprehenders in second grade: A one-year follow-up study. *Computers and Education, 63*, 131–140.

Prat-Sala, M., & Redford, P. (2010). The interplay between motivation, self-efficacy, and approaches to studying. *British Journal of Educational Psychology, 80*, 283–305.

Prawat, R. S. (1992). Teachers beliefs about teaching and learning: A constructivist perspective. *American Journal of Education, 100*, 354–395.

Prawat, R. S. (1996). Constructivism, modern and postmodern. *Issues in Education: Contributions from Educational Psychology, 3*, 215–226.

Preckel, T., Goetz, T., & Frenzel, A. (2010). Ability grouping of gifted students: Effects on academic self-concept and boredom. *British Journal of Educational Psychology, 80*, 451–472.

Premack, D. (1965). Reinforcement theory. In D. Levine (Ed.), *Nebraska symposium on motivation* (Vol. 13, pp. 123–180). Lincoln, NE: University of Nebraska Press.

Pressley, M. (1995). More about the development of self-regulation: Complex, long-term, and thoroughly social. *Educational Psychologist, 30*, 207–212.

Pressley, M. (1996, August). *Getting beyond whole language: Elementary reading instruction that makes sense in light of recent psychological research.* Paper presented at the annual meeting of the American Psychological Association, Toronto.

Pressley, M., & Harris, K. A. (2006). Cognitive strategies instruction: From basic research to classroom instruction. In P. A. Alexander & P. H. Winne (Eds.), *Handbook of educational psychology* (2nd ed., pp. 265–286). Mahwah, NJ: Erlbaum.

Pressley, M., Levin, J., & Delaney, H. D. (1982). The mnemonic keyword method. *Review of Research in Education, 52*, 61–91.

Pressley, M., Mohan, L., Raphael, L. M., & Fingeret, L. (2007). How does Bennett Woods Elementary School produce such high reading and writing achievement? *Journal of Educational Psychology, 99*, 221–240.

Pressley, M., Raphael, L., Gallagher, J. D., & DiBella, J. (2004). Providence St. Mel School: How a school that works for African American students works. *Journal of Educational Psychology, 96*(2), 216–235.

Pressley, M., & Roehrig, A. (2003). Educational psychology in the modern era: 1960 to the present. In B. J. Zimmerman & D. H. Schunk (Eds.), *Educational psychology: A century of contributions* (pp. 333–366). [A Project of Division 15 (Educational Psychology) of the American Psychological Association]. Mahwah, NJ: Erlbaum.

Pressley, M., & Woloshyn, V. (1995). *Cognitive strategy instruction that really improves children's academic performance.* Cambridge, MA: Brookline Books.

PREVNet. (2013). *Types of bullying: Bullying evolves throughout childhood.* Retrieved from prevnet.ca/bullying/types.

Price, L. F. (2005). The biology of risk taking. *Educational Leadership, 62*(7), 22–27.

Price, W. F., & Crapo, R. H. (2002). *Cross-cultural perspectives in introductory psychology* (4th ed.). Pacific Grove, CA: Wadsworth.

Proctor, C. P., August, D., Carlo, M. S., & Snow, C. (2006). The intriguing role of Spanish language vocabulary knowledge in predicting English reading comprehension. *Journal of Educational Psychology, 98*, 159–169.

Project Tomorrow. (2010). *The new 3 E's of education: Enabled, engaged, empowered. How today's students are leveraging emerging technologies for learning.* Irvine, CA: Author. Retrieved from http://www.tomorrow.org/about/team.html

Public Agenda Foundation. (1994). *First things first: What Americans expect from public schools.* New York, NY: Author.

Pugh, K. J., & Phillips, M. M. (2011). Helping students develop an appreciation for school content. *Theory Into Practice, 50*, 285–292.

Pulfrey, C., Darnon, C., & Butera, F. (2013). Autonomy and task performance: Explaining the impact of grades on intrinsic motivation. *Journal of Educational Psychology, 105*, 39–57. doi: 10.1037/a0029376

Puncochar, J., & Fox, P. W. (2004). Confidence in individual and group decision-making: When "Two Heads" are worse than one. *Journal of Educational Psychology, 96*, 582–591.

Puntambekar, S., & Hubscher, R. (2005). Tools for scaffolding students in a complex learning environment: What have we gained and what have we missed? *Educational Psychologist, 40*, 1–12.

Purdie, N., Hattie, J., & Carroll, A. (2002). A review of the research on interventions for Attention Deficit Hyperactivity Disorder: What works best? *Review of Educational Research, 72*, 61–99.

Putman, M., Smith, L. L., & Cassady, J. C. (2009). Promoting change through professional development: The place of teacher intentionality. *Literacy Research & Instruction, 48*, 207–220.

Puustinen, M., & Pulkkinen, L. (2001). Models of self-regulated learning: A review. *Scandinavian Journal of Educational Research, 45*, 269–286.

Pyke, A. A., & LeFevre, J. A. (2011). Calculator use need not undermine direct-access ability: The roles of retrieval, calculation, and calculator use in the acquisition of arithmetic facts. *Journal of Educational Psychology, 103*, 607–616

Rachlin, H. (1991). *Introduction to modern behaviorism* (3rd ed.). New York, NY: Freeman.

Rachlin, H. (2004). *The science of self-control.* Cambridge, MA: Harvard University Press.

Raffini, J. P. (1996). *150 Ways to increase intrinsic motivation in the classroom.* Boston, MA: Allyn & Bacon.

Raj, V., & Bell, M. A. (2010). Cognitive processes supporting episodic memory formation in childhood: The role of source memory, binding, and executive functioning. *Developmental Review, 30*, 384–402.

Ramirez, J. D., Yuen, S. D., & Ramey, D. R. (1991). *Final report: Longitudinal study of structured immersion strategy, early-exit, and late-exit transitional bilingual education programs for language-minority children.* San Mateo, CA: Aguirre International.

Ramon, I., Roache, J., & Romi, S. (2011). Coping styles as mediators of teachers' classroom management techniques. *Research in Education, 85*, 53–68.

Randi, J., & Corno, L. (2005). Teaching and learner variation, in Pedagogy—Learning from Teaching. *British Journal of Educational Psychology, Monograph Series, II*(3), 47–69.

Raudenbush, S. (1984). Magnitude of teacher expectancy effects on pupil IQ as a function of the credibility of expectancy induction: A synthesis of findings from 18 experiments. *Journal of Educational Psychology, 76*, 85–97.

Raudenbush, S. W. (2009). The *Brown* Legacy and the O'Connor Challenge: Transforming schools in the images of children's potential. *Educational Researcher, 38*, 169–180.

Raudsepp, E., & Haugh, G. P. (1977). *Creative growth games.* New York, NY: Harcourt Brace Jovanovich.

Rauscher, F. H., & Shaw, G. L. (1998). Key components of the Mozart effect. *Perceptual and Motor Skills, 86*, 835–841.

Rawson, K. A., & Dunlosky, J. (2012). When is practice testing most effective for improving the durability and efficiency of student learning? *Educational Psychology Review, 24*, 419–435.

Reardon, S. F. (2011). The widening academic achievement gap between the rich and the poor: New evidence and possible explanations. In R. Murnane & G. Duncan (Eds.), *Whither opportunity? Rising inequality and the uncertain life chances of low-income children.* New York: Russell Sage Foundation Press. See more at http://cepa.stanford.edu/content/widening-academic-achievement-gap-between-rich-and-poor-new-evidence-and-possible#sthash.gUtBj6hG.dpuf

Reder, L. M. (1996). Different research programs on metacognition: Are the boundaries imaginary? *Learning and Individual Differences, 8*, 383–390.

Reder, L. M., Park, H., & Kieffaber, P. D. (2009). Memory systems do not divide on consciousness: Reinterpreting memory in terms of activation and binding. *Psychological Bulletin, 135,* 23–49.

Reeve, J. (1996). *Motivating others: Nurturing inner motivational resources.* Boston, MA: Allyn & Bacon.

Reeve, J. (2002). Self-determination theory applied to educational settings. In E. L. Deci & R. M. Ryan (Eds.), *Handbook of self-determination research* (pp. 183–203). Rochester, NY: University of Rochester Press.

Reeve, J. (2009). Why teachers adopt a controlling motivating style toward students and how they can become more autonomy supportive. *Educational Psychologist, 44,* 159–175.

Reeve, J., & Jang, H. (2006a). Teachers as facilitators: What autonomy-supportive teachers do and why their students benefit. *Elementary School Journal, 106,* 225–236.

Reeve, J., & Jang, H. (2006b). What teachers say and do to support students' autonomy during a learning activity. *Journal of Educational Psychology, 98,* 209–218.

Reeve, J., Deci, E. L., & Ryan, R. M. (2004). *Self-determination theory: A dialectical framework for understanding the sociocultural influences on motivation and learning: Big theories revisited* (Vol. 4, pp. 31–59). Greenwich, CT: Information Age Press.

Reeve, J., Nix, G., & Hamm, D. (2003). The experience of self-determination in intrinsic motivation and the conundrum of choice. *Journal of Educational Psychology, 95,* 347–392.

Refugee Council USA. (2013). *History of the U.S. refugee resettlement program.* Washington, DC: Refugee Council USA. Retrieved from http://www.rcusa.org/index.php?page=history

Reich, J., Murnane, R., & Willett, J. (2012). The state of wiki usage in U.S. K–12 schools: Leveraging Web 2.0 data warehouses to assess quality and equity in online learning environments. *Educational Researcher, 41*(1), 7–17. doi: 10.3102/0013189X11427083

Reid, J. M., & Byrd, P. (1998). *Grammar in the composition classroom.* New York, NY: Heinle & Heinle Publisher.

Reimann, P., & Chi, M. T. H. (1989). Human expertise. In K. J. Gilhooly (Ed.), *Human and machine problem solving* (pp. 161–191). New York, NY: Plenum Press.

Reinke, W. M., & Herman, K. C. (2002a). A research agenda for school violence prevention. *American Psychologist, 57,* 796–797.

Reinke, W. M., & Herman, K. C. (2002b). Creating school environments that deter antisocial behaviors in youth. *Psychology in the Schools, 39,* 549–560.

Reis, S. M., Kaplan, S. N., Tomlinson, C. A., Westberg, K. L., Callahan, C. M., & Cooper, C. R. (2002). Equal does not mean identical. In L. Abbeduto (Ed.), *Taking sides: Clashing on controversial issues in educational psychology* (pp. 31–35). Guilford, CT: McGraw-Hill/Duskin.

Reis, S. M., & Renzulli, J. S. (2004). Current research on the social and emotional development of gifted and talented students: Good news and future possibilities. *Psychology in the Schools, 41,* published online in Wiley InterScience. Retrieved from www.interscience.wiley.com

Reis, S. M., & Renzulli, J. S. (2009). Myth 1: The gifted and talented constitute one single homogeneous group and giftedness is a way of being that stays in the person over time and experiences. *Gifted Child Quarterly, 53*(4), 233–235.

Reis, S. M., & Renzulli, J. S. (2010). Is there still a need for gifted education? An examination of current research. *Learning & Individual Differences, 20,* 308–317.

Reisberg, D., & Heuer, F. (1992). Remembering the details of emotional events. In E. Winograd & U. Neisser (Eds.), *Affect and accuracy in recall: Studies of "flashbulb" memories.* Cambridge, UK: Cambridge University Press.

Reiss, S. (2004). Multifaceted nature of intrinsic motivation: The theory of 16 basic desires. *Review of General Psychology, 8,* 179–193.

Render, G. F., Padilla, J. N. M., & Krank, H. M. (1989). What research really shows about assertive discipline. *Educational Leadership, 46*(6), 72–75.

Renninger, K. A. (2009). Interest and identity development in instruction: An inductive model. *Educational Psychologist, 44,* 105–118.

Renninger, K. A., & Hidi, S. (2011). Revisiting the conceptualization, measurement, and generation of interest. *Educational Psychologist, 46,* 168–184, doi: 10.1080/00461520.2011.587723

Renzulli, J. S. (2011). Theories, actions, and change: An academic journey in search of finding and developing high potential in young people. *Gifted Child Quarterly, 55,* 305–308.

Renzulli, J. S., & Reis, S. M. (2003). The schoolwide enrichment model: Developing creative and productive giftedness. In N. Colangelo & G. A. Davis (Eds.), *Handbook of gifted education* (pp. 184–203). Boston, MA: Allyn & Bacon.

Rescorla, R. A., & Wagner, A. R. (1972). A theory of Pavlovian conditioning: Variations in the effectiveness of reinforcement and nonreinforcement. In A. H. Black & W. F. Prokasy (Eds.), *Classical conditioning II* (pp. 64–99). New York, NY: Appleton-Century-Crofts.

Resnick, L. B. (1981). Instructional psychology. *Annual Review of Psychology, 32,* 659–704.

Reyes, M. R., Brackett, M. A., Rivers, S. E., White, M., & Salovey, P. (2012, March 5). Classroom emotional climate, student engagement, and academic achievement. *Journal of Educational Psychology, 104,* 700–712. doi: 10.1037/a0027268

Reynolds, C. R., & Shaywitz, S. E. (2009). Response to Intervention: Ready or not? Or, from wait-to-fail to watch-them-fail. *School Psychology Quarterly, 24,* 130–145.

Reznitskaya, A., & Gregory, M. (2013). Student thought and classroom language: Examining the mechanisms of change in dialogic teaching. *Educational Psychologist, 48,* 114–133. doi: 10.1080/00461520.2013.775898

Rhodes, R. A. (1997). *Community service and higher learning: Explorations of the caring self.* Albany, NY: State University of New York Press.

Rice, D., & Muller, C. (2013). Equity or marginalization? The high school course-taking of students labeled with a learning disability. *American Educational Research Journal, 50,* 656–682.

Rice, F. P., & Dolgin, K. G. (2002). *The adolescent: Development, relationships, and culture* (10th ed.). Boston, MA: Allyn & Bacon.

Rice, M. L. (1989). Children's language acquisition. *American Psychologist, 44,* 149–156.

Richell, R., Deakin, J., & Anderson, I. (2005). Effect of acute tryptophan depletion on the response to controllable and uncontrollable noise stress. *Biological Psychiatry, 57,* 295–300.

Rideout, V. J., Foehr, U. G., & Roberts, D. F. (2010, January). Generation M: Media in the lives of 8–18 year-olds. Kaiser Family Foundation. Retrieved from http://www.kff.org/entmedia/upload/8010.pdf

Rideout, V. J., Vandewater, E. A., & Wartella, E. A. (2003). *Zero to six: Electronic media in the lives of infants, toddlers, and preschoolers* (No. 3378). Menlo Park, CA: Henry J. Kaiser Family Foundation and the Children's Digital Media Centers (CDMC).

Riedesel, C. A., & Schwartz, J. E. (1999). *Essentials of elementary mathematics* (2nd ed.). Upper Saddle River, NJ: Pearson Education.

Rigby, K. (2012). Bullying in schools: Addressing desires, not only behaviours. *Educational Psychology Review, 24,* 339–348.

Rittle-Johnson, B., & Star, J. R. (2007). Does comparing solution methods facilitate conceptual and procedural knowledge? An experimental study on learning to solve equations. *Journal of Educational Psychology, 99,* 561–574.

Rivkin, S. G., Hanushek, E. A., & Kain, J. F. (2001). *Teachers, schools, and academic achievement.* Amherst, MA: Amherst College.

Rizzolatti, G., Fadiga, L., Gallese, V., & Fogassi, L. (1996). Premotor cortex and the recognition of motor actions. *Brain Research: Cognitive Brain Research, 3*(2), 131–141.

Robbins, S. B., Lauver, K., Davis, H. L., Davis, D., Langley, R., & Carlstrom, A. (2004). Psychosocial and study skill factors predict college outcomes? A meta-analysis. *Psychological Bulletin, 130,* 261–288.

Robbins, S. B., Le, L., & Lauver, K. (2005). Promoting successful college outcomes for all students: Reply to Weissberg and Owen (2005). *Psychological Bulletin, 131,* 410–411.

Roberge, M. M. (2002). California's Generation 1.5 immigrants: What experiences, characterisitcs, and needs do they bring to our English classes? *The CATESOL Journal, 14*(1), 107–129.

Roberson, D., Davidoff, J., Davies, I. R. L., & Shapiro, L. R. (2004). The development of color categories in two languages: A longitudinal study. *Journal of Experimental Psychology: General, 133,* 554–571.

Roberts, D. F., Foehr, U. G., & Rideout, V. (2005). *Generation M: Media in the lives of 8–18 year-olds.* Technical Reports 7250/7251. Menlo Park, CA: Kaiser Family foundation. Retrieved from http://www.kff.org/entmedia/7251.cfm

Roberts, D. S., Tingstrom, D. H., Olmi, D. J., & Bellipanni, K. D. (2008). Positive antecedent and consequent components in child compliance training. *Behavior Modification, 32,* 21–38.

Roberts, G., Mohammed, S. S., & Vaughn, S. (2010). Reading achievement across three language groups: Growth estimates for overall reading and reading subskills obtained with the early childhood longitudinal survey. *Journal of Educational Psychology, 102,* 668–686.

Robinson, A., & Clinkenbeard, P. R. (1998). Giftedness: An exceptionality examined. In J. T. Spence, J. M. Darley, & D. J. Foss (Eds.), *Annual review of psychology* (pp. 117–139). Palo Alto, CA: Annual Reviews.

Robinson, D. H. (1998). Graphic organizers as aids to test learning. *Reading Research and Instruction, 37,* 85–105.

Robinson, D. H., & Kiewra, K. A. (1995). Visual argument: Graphic outlines are superior to outlines in improving learning from text. *Journal of Educational Psychology, 87,* 455–467.

Robinson, J. P., & Espelage, D. L. (2012). Bullying explains only part of LGBTQ–heterosexual risk disparities: Implications for policy and practice. *Educational Researcher, 41,* 309–319.

Rodgers, R. F., Skowron, S., & Chabrol, H. (2011). Disordered eating and group membership among members of a pro-anorexic online community. *European Eating Disorders Review, 20,* 9–11.

Roediger, H. L., & Karpicke, J. D. (2006). The power of testing memory. *Perspectives on Psychological Science, 1,* 181–210.

Roeser, R. W., Peck, S. C., & Nasir, N. S. (2006). Self and identity processes in school motivation, learning, and achievement. In P. A. Alexander & P. H. Winne (Eds.), *Handbook of educational psychology* (2nd ed., pp. 391–424). Mahwah, NJ: Erlbaum.

Roeser, R. W., Schonert-Reichl, K. A., Jha, A., Cullen, M., Wallace, L., Wilensky, R., Oberle, E., Thomson, K., Taylor, C., & Harrison, J. (2013). Mindfulness training and reductions in teacher stress and burnout: Results from two randomized, waitlist-control field trials. *Journal of Educational Psychology, 105,* 787–804.

Rogers, C. R., & Freiberg, H. J. (1994). *Freedom to learn* (3rd ed.). Columbus, OH: Merrill.

Rogoff, B. (1990). *Apprenticeship in thinking: Cognitive development in social context.* New York, NY: Oxford University Press.

Rogoff, B. (1995). Observing sociocultural activity on three planes: Participatory appropriation, guided participation, and apprenticeship. In J. Wertsch, P. del Rio, & A. Alverez (Eds.), *Sociocultural studies of mind* (pp. 139–164). Cambridge, UK: Cambridge University Press.

Rogoff, B. (1998). Cognition as a collaborative process. In W. Damon (Series Ed.), D. Kuhn & R. S. Siegler (Vol. Eds.), *Handbook of child psychology: Vol. 2* (5th ed., pp. 679–744). New York, NY: Wiley.

Rogoff, B. (2003). *The cultural nature of human development.* New York, NY: Oxford University Press.

Rogoff, B., & Morelli, G. (1989). Perspectives on children's development from cultural psychology. *American Psychologist, 44,* 343–348.

Rogoff, B., Turkanis, C. G., & Bartlett, L. (2001). *Learning together: Children and adults in a school community.* New York, NY: Oxford.

Rohrkemper, M., & Corno, L. (1988). Success and failure on classroom tasks: Adaptive learning and classroom teaching. *Elementary School Journal, 88,* 297–312.

Roid, G. H. (2003). *Stanford-Binet Intelligence Scales, Fifth Edition.* Itasca, IL: Riverside.

Rojas, R., & Iglesias, A. (2013). The language growth of Spanish-speaking English language learners. *Child Development, 84,* 630–646.

Rolland, R. G. (2012). Synthesizing the evidence on classroom goal structures in middle and secondary schools: A meta-analysis and narrative review. *Review of Educational Research, 82,* 396–435.

Roorda, D. L., Koomen, H. M. Y., Spilt, J. L., & Oort, F. J. (2011). The influence of affective teacher–student relationships on students' school engagement and achievement: A meta-analytic approach. *Review of Educational Research, 81,* 493–529. doi: 10.3102/0034654311421793

Rosch, E. H. (1973). On the internal structure of perceptual and semantic categories. In T. Moore (Ed.), *Cognitive development and the acquisition of language* (pp. 111–144). New York, NY: Academic Press.

Roschelle, J. (2013). Special issue on CSCL: Discussion. *Educational Psychologist, 48,* 67–70. doi: 10.1080/00461520.2012.749445

Roschelle, J. M., Pea, R. D., Hoadley, C. M., Gordon, D. N., & Means, B. M. (2000, Fall/Winter). Changing how and what children learn in school with computer-based technologies. *Children and Computer Technology, 10*(2), 76–101.

Rosen, L. (2010). *Rewired: Understanding the iGeneration and the way they learn.* New York, NY: Palgrave Macmillan.

Rosenberg, M. (1979). *Conceiving the self.* New York, NY: Basic Books.

Rosenberg, M. S., Westling, D. L., & McLeskey, J. (2011). *Special education for today's teachers: An introduction.* Boston, MA: Allyn & Bacon/Pearson.

Rosenfeld, M., & Rosenfeld, S. (2004). Developing teacher sensitivities to individual learning differences. *Educational Psychology, 24,* 465–486.

Rosenshine, B. (1988). Explicit teaching. In D. Berliner & B. Rosenshine (Eds.), *Talks to teachers* (pp. 75–92). New York, NY: Random House.

Rosenshine, B., & Furst, N. (1973). The use of direct observation to study teaching. In R. Travers (Ed.), *Second handbook of research on teaching.* Chicago, IL: Rand McNally.

Rosenshine, B., & Meister, C. (1992, April). *The uses of scaffolds for teaching less structured academic tasks.* Paper presented at the annual meeting of the American Educational Research Association, San Francisco, CA.

Rosenshine, B., & Meister, C. (1994). Reciprocal teaching: A review of the research. *Review of Educational Research, 64,* 479–530.

Rosenshine, B., & Stevens, R. (1986). Teaching functions. In M. Wittrock (Ed.), *Handbook of research on teaching* (3rd ed., pp. 376–391). New York, NY: Macmillan.

Rosenthal, R. (1995). Critiquing Pygmalion: A 25-year perspective. *Current Directions in Psychological Science, 4,* 171–172.

Rosenthal, R., & Jacobson, L. (1968). *Pygmalion in the classroom.* New York, NY: Holt, Rinehart, Winston.

Roseth, C. J., Saltarelli, A. J., & Glass, C. R. (2011). Effects of face-to-face and computer-mediated constructive controversy on social interdependence, motivation, and achievement. *Journal of Educational Psychology, 103,* 804–820. doi: 10.1037/a0024213

Roskos, K., & Neuman, S. B. (1998). Play as an opportunity for literacy. In O. N. Saracho & B. Spodek (Eds.), *Multiple perspectives on play in early childhood education* (pp. 100–115). Albany, NY: State University of New York Press.

Ross, J. A., & Raphael, D. (1990). Communication and problem solving achievement in cooperative learning groups. *Journal of Curriculum Studies, 22,* 149–164.

Rotherham-Borus, M. J. (1994). Bicultural reference group orientations and adjustment. In M. Bernal & G. Knight (Eds.), *Ethnic identity* (pp. 81–102). Albany, NY: State University of New York Press.

Rowe, E. W., Kingsley, J. M., & Thompson, D. F. (2010). Predictive ability of the general ability index (GAI) versus the full scale IQ among gifted referrals. *School Psychology Quarterly, 25,* 119–128.

Rowe, M. B. (1974). Wait-time and rewards as instructional variables: Their influence on language, logic, and fate control. Part 1: Wait-time. *Journal of Research in Science Teaching, 11,* 81–94.

Rubie-Davies, C. M. (2010). Teacher expectations and perceptions of student attributes: Is there a relationship? *British Journal of Educational Psychology, 80,* 121–135.

Rubin, K. H., Coplan, R., Chen, X., Buskirk, A. A., & Wojslawowicz, J. C. (2005). Peer relationships in childhood. In M. H. Bornstein & M. E. Lamb (Eds.), *Developmental science: An advanced textbook* (pp. 469–512). Mahwah, NJ: Erlbaum.

Rubinsten, O., & Henik, A. (2006). Double dissociations of functions in developmental dyslexia and dyscalculia. *Journal of Educational Psychology, 98,* 854–867.

Ruble, D. N., Martin, C. L., & Berenbaum, S. A. (2006). Gender development. In *Handbook of child psychology* (Vol. 3, pp. 858–932). Hoboken, NJ: Wiley.

Rudolph, K. D., Lambert, S. F., Clark, A. G., & Kurlakowsky, K. D. (2001). Negotiating the transition to middle school: The role of self-regulatory processes. *Child Development, 72,* 926–946.

Rueda, R., & Moll, L. C. (1994). A sociocultural perspective on motivation. In F. O'Neil, Jr., & M. Drillings (Eds.), *Motivation: Theory and research* (pp. 117–137). Mahwah, NJ: Erlbaum.

Rummel, N., Levin, J. R., & Woodward, M. M. (2003). Do pictorial mnemonic text-learning aids give students something worth writing about? *Journal of Educational Psychology, 95,* 327–334.

Russell, M. K., & Airasian, P. W. (2012). *Classroom assessment: Concepts and applications* (7th ed.). New York, NY: McGraw-Hill.

Ryan, A. (2001). The peer group as a context for development of young adolescents' motivation and achievement. *Child Development, 72,* 1135–1150.

Ryan, K. E., & Ryan, A. M. (2005). Psychological processes underlying stereotype threat and standardized math test performance. *Educational Psychologist, 40,* 53–63.

Ryan, R. M., & Deci, E. L. (1996). When paradigms clash: Comments on Cameron and Pierce's claim that rewards do not undermine intrinsic motivation. *Review of Educational Research, 66,* 33–38.

Ryan, R. M., & Deci, E. L. (2000). Intrinsic and extrinsic motivation: Classic definitions and new directions. *Contemporary Educational Psychology, 25,* 54–67.

Sackett, P. R., Kuncel, N. R., Arneson, J. J., Cooper, S. R., & Waters, S. D. (2009). Does socioeconomic status explain the relationship between admissions tests and post-secondary academic performance? *Psychological Bulletin, 135,* 1–22.

Sadker, M., & Sadker, D. (2006). Questioning skills. In J. Cooper (Ed.), *Classroom teaching skills* (8th ed., pp. 104–150). Boston, MA: Houghton-Mifflin.

Sadker, M., Sadker, D., & Klein, S. (1991). The issue of gender in elementary and secondary education. *Review of Research in Education, 17,* 269–334.

Sagor, R. (2003). *Motivating students and teachers in an era of standards.* Alexandria, VA: Association for Supervision and Curriculum Development.

Sakiz, G., Pape, S., & Woolfolk Hoy, A. (2008, March). *Does teacher affective support matter? The role of affective support in middle school mathematics classrooms.* Paper presented at the annual meeting of the American Educational Research Association, New York, NY.

Salomon, G., & Perkins, D. N. (1989). Rocky roads to transfer: Re-thinking mechanisms of a neglected phenomenon. *Educational Psychologist, 24,* 113–142.

Sample Stanford Student Report in Score Report Sampler: Guide-Teaching and Learning Toward High Academic Standards for the Stanford Achievement Test Series (10th ed.). (Stanford 10). (2003). Upper Saddle River, NJ: NCS Pearson.

Sanders, W. L., & Rivers, J. C. (1996). *Cumulative and residual effects of teachers on student academic achievement.* Knoxville, TN: University of Tennessee Value-Added Research and Assessment Center.

Sarason, I. G. (1986). Test anxiety, worry, and cognitive interference. In R. Schwarzer (Ed.), *Self-related cognitions in anxiety and motivation* (pp. 19–34). Hillsdale, NJ: Erlbaum.

Sattler, J. M. (2001). *Assessment of children: Cognitive applications* (4th ed.). San Diego, CA: Jerome M. Sattler, Inc.

Sattler, J. M. (2008). *Assessment of children: Cognitive applications* (5th ed.). San Diego, CA: Sattler.

Sattler, J. M., & Hoge, R. D. (2006). *Assessment of children: Behavioral, social, and clinical foundations.* La Mesa, CA: Sattler.

Savage, R., Abrami, P. C., Piquette, N., Wood, E., Deleveaux, G., Sanghera-Sidhu, S., & Burgos, G. (2013). A (Pan-Canadian) cluster randomized control effectiveness trial of the ABRACADABRA Web-Based Literacy Program. *Journal of Educational Psychology, 105,* 310–328. doi: 10.1037/a0031025

Savage, T. V. (1999). *Teaching self-control through management and discipline.* Boston, MA: Allyn & Bacon.

Savin-Williams, R. C. (2006). Who's gay? Does it matter? *Current Directions in Psychological Science, 15*(1), 40–44.

Savin-Williams, R. C., & Vrangalova, Z. (2013). Mostly heterosexual as a distinct sexual orientation group: A systematic review of the empirical evidence. *Developmental Review, 33,* 58–88.

Sawyer, R. K. (2006). Introduction: The new science of learning. In R. K. Sawyer (Ed.), *The Cambridge handbook of the learning sciences* (pp. 1–16). New York, NY: Cambridge.

Saxe, G. B. (1999). Source of concepts: A cross cultural-developmental perspective. In E. K. Scholnick, K. Nelson, S. A. Gelman, & P. H. Miller (Eds.), *Conceptual development: Piaget's legacy* (pp. 253–267). Mahwah, NJ: Erlbaum.

Schacter, D. L., Gilbert, D. T., & Wenger, D. M. (2009). *Psychology.* New York, NY: Worth.

Schalke, D., Brunner, M., Geiser, C., Preckel, F., Keller, U., Spengler, M., & Martin, R. (2013). Stability and change in intelligence from age 12 to age 52: Results from the Luxembourg MAGRIP Study. *Developmental Psychology, 109,* 1529–1543. doi: 10.1037/a0030623

Scheibe, C., & Rogow, F. (2004). *12 basic principles for incorporating media literacy and critical thinking into any curriculum* (2nd ed.). Ithaca, NY: Project Look Sharp—Ithaca College.

Scherer, M. (1993). On savage inequalities: A conversation with Jonathan Kozol. *Educational Leadership, 50*(4), 4–9.

Scherer, M. (1999). The discipline of hope: A conversation with Herb Kohl. *Educational Leadership, 56*(1), 8–13.

Schiefele, U. (1991). Interest, learning, and motivation. *Educational Psychologist, 26,* 299–324.

Schmidt, H. G., van der Molen, H. T., te Winkel, W. W. R., & Wijnen, W. H. F. W. (2009). Constructivist, problem-based learning does work: A meta-analysis of curricular comparisons involving a single medical school. *Educational Psychologist, 44,* 227–249.

Schneider, W. (2004). Memory development in childhood. In U. Goswami (Ed.), *Blackwell handbook of childhood cognitive development* (pp. 236–256). Malden, MA: Blackwell.

Schneider, W., & Bjorklund, D. F. (1992). Expertise, aptitude, and strategic remembering. *Child Development, 63,* 416–473.

Schoen, R., & Canudas-Romo, V. (2006). Timing effects on divorce: 20th century experience in the United States. *Journal of Marriage and the Family, 68,* 749–758.

Schoenfeld, A. H. (1989). Teaching mathematical thinking and problem solving. In L. B. Resnick & L. E. Klopfer (Eds.), *Toward the thinking curriculum: Current cognitive research* (pp. 83–103). Alexandria, VA: ASCD.

Schoenfeld, A. H. (1994). *Mathematics thinking and problem solving.* Mahwah, NJ: Erlbaum.

Schoenfeld, A. H. (2011). *How we think: The theory of goal-oriented decision making and its educational applications.* New York, NY: Routledge.

Scholastic. (2011). *Planning for parent conferences.* New York, NY: Author. Retrieved from http://www2.scholastic.com/browse/article.jsp?id=4194

Schommer, M. (1997). The development of epistemological beliefs among secondary students: A longitudinal study. *Journal of Educational Psychology, 89,* 37–40.

Schommer-Aikins, M. (2002). An evolving theoretical framework for an epistemological belief system. In B. K. Hofer & P. R. Pintrich (Eds.), *Personal epistemology: The psychology of beliefs about knowledge and knowing* (pp. 103–118). Mahwah, NJ: Erlbaum.

Schraw, G. (2006). Knowledge: Structures and processes. In P. A. Alexander & P. H. Winne (Eds.), *Handbook of educational psychology* (2nd ed., pp. 825–847). Mahwah, NJ: Erlbaum.

Schraw, G., & Olafson, L. (2002). Teachers' epistemological world views and educational practices. *Issues in Education, 8,* 99–148.

Schunk, D. H. (1983). Ability versus effort attributional feedback: Different effects on self-efficacy and achievement. *Journal of Educational Psychology, 75,* 848–856.

Schunk, D. H. (1999). Social-self interaction and achievement behavior. *Educational Psychologist, 34,* p. 221.

Schunk, D. H. (2005). Self-regulated learning: The educational legacy of Paul R. Pintrich. *Educational Psychologist, 40,* 85–94.

Schunk, D. H. (2012). *Learning theories: An educational perspective* (6th ed.). Boston, MA: Allyn & Bacon/Pearson.

Schunk, D. H., Meece, J. L., & Pintrich, P. R. (2014). *Motivation in education: Theory, research, and applications* (4th ed.). Columbus, OH: Pearson.

Schutz, P. A., & Davis, H. A. (2000). Emotions and self-regulations during test-taking. *Educational Psychologist, 35,* 243–256.

Schwab, J. J. (1973). The Practical 3: Translation into curriculum. *School Review, 81,* 501–522.

Schwartz, B., Wasserman, E. A., & Robbins, S. J. (2002). *Psychology of learning and behavior* (5th ed.). New York, NY: Norton.

Schwarz, B. B., Neuman, Y., & Biezuner, S. (2000). Two wrongs may make a right . . . if they argue together! *Cognition and Instruction, 18,* 461–494.

Schwarzer, R., & Jerusalem, M. (1992). Advances in anxiety theory: A cognitive process approach. In K. A. Hagtvet & T. B. Johnsen (Eds.), *Advances in test anxiety research* (Vol. 7, pp. 2–31). Lisse, the Netherlands: Swetts & Zeitlinger.

Schweinle, A., Turner, J. C., & Meyer, D. K. (2008). Understanding young adolescents' optimal experiences in academic settings. *Journal of Experimental Education, 77,* 125–143.

Schworm, S., & Renkl, A. (2007). Learning argumentation skills through the use of prompts for self-explaining examples. *Journal of Educational Psychology, 99,* 285–295.

Scriven, M., & Paul, R. (2013). Defining critical thinking. Retrieved from http://www.criticalthinking.org/pages/defining-critical-thinking/410

Seaton, M., Marsh, H. W., & Craven, R. G. (2009). Earning its place as a pan-human theory: Universality of the Big-Fish-Little-Pond effect across 41 culturally and economically diverse countries. *Journal of Educational Psychology, 101,* 403–419.

Seligman, M. E. P. (1975). *Helplessness: On depression, development, and death.* San Francisco, CA: Freeman.

Seligman, M. E. P. (2006). *Learned optimism: How to change your mind and your life* (2nd ed.). New York, NY: Pocket Books.

Sénéchal, M., & LeFevre, J. A. (2002). Parental involvement in the development of children's reading skills: A five-year longitudinal study. *Child Development, 73,* 445–460.

Senghas, A., & Coppola, M. (2001). Children creating language: How Nicaraguan Sign Language acquired a spatial grammar. *Psychological Review, 96,* 323–328.

Senko, C., Hulleman, C. S., & Harackiewicz, J. M. (2011). Achievement goal theory at the crossroads: Old controversies, current challenges, and new directions, *Educational Psychologist, 46,* 26–47. doi: 10.1080/00461520.2011.538646

Serpell, R. (1993). Interface between sociocultural and psychological aspects of cognition. In E. Forman, N. Minick, & C. A. Stone (Eds.), *Contexts for learning: Sociocultural dynamics in children's development* (pp. 357–368). New York, NY: Oxford University Press.

Shaffer, D. W. (2010). *The Bicycle Helmets of "Amsterdam": Computer games and the problem of transfer* (Epistemic Games Group Working Paper No. 2010–01). Madison, WI: University of Wisconsin-Madison.

Shaffer, D. W., Hatfield, D., Svarovsky, G. N., Nash, P., Nulty, A., Bagley, E., . . . Mislevy, R. J. (2009). Epistemic network analysis: A prototype for 21st century assessment of learning. *International Journal of Learning Media, 1*(2), 33–53.

Shavelson, R. J. (1987). Planning. In M. Dunkin (Ed.), *The international encyclopedia of teaching and teacher education* (pp. 483–486). New York, NY: Pergamon Press.

Shayer, M. (2003). Not just Piaget; not just Vygotsky, and certainly not Vygotsky as alternative to Piaget *Learning and Instruction, 13,* 465–485.

Shaywitz, B. A., Shaywitz, S. E., Blachman, B. A., Pugh, K. R., Fulbright, R. K., Skudlarski, P., . . . Gore, J. C. (2004). Development of left occipitotemporal systems for skilled reading in children after a phonologically-based intervention. *Biological Psychiatry, 55,* 926–933.

Shechtman, Z., & Yaman, M. A. (2012). SEL as a component of a literature class to improve relationships, behavior, motivation, and content knowledge. *American Educational Research Journal, 49,* 546–567.

Sheets, R. H. (2005). *Diversity pedagogy: Examining the role of culture in the teaching-learning process.* Boston, MA: Allyn & Bacon.

Shepard, L. A., & Smith, M. L. (1988). Escalating academic demand in kindergarten: Counterproductive policies. *Elementary School Journal, 89*(2), 135–145.

Shepard, L. A., & Smith, M. L. (1989). Academic and emotional effects of kindergarten retention. In L. Shepard & M. Smith (Eds.), *Flunking grades: Research and policies on retention* (pp. 79–107). Philadelphia, PA: Falmer Press.

Sherman, D. K., Hartson, K. A., Binning, K. R., Purdie-Vaughns, V., Garcia, J., Taborsky-Barba, S., Nussbaum, A. D., & Cohen, G. L. (2013). Deflecting the trajectory and changing the narrative: How self-affirmation affects academic performance and motivation under identity threat. *Journal of Personality and Social Psychology, 104,* 591–618.

Sherwood, R. D. (2002). Problem-based multimedia software for middle grade science: Development issues and an initial field study. *Journal of Computers in Mathematics and Science Teaching, 21,* 147–165.

Shih, S. S. (2008). The relation of self-determination and achievement goals to Taiwanese eighth graders' behavioral and emotional engagement in schoolwork. *The Elementary School Journal, 108,* 313–334.

Shim, S. S., Cho, Y., & Cassady, J. C. (2012). Goal structures: The role of teachers' achievement goals and theories of intelligence. *The Journal of Experimental Education, 81,* 84–104.

Shim, S. S., Wang, C., & Cassady, J. C. (2013). Emotional well-being: The role of social achievement goals and self-esteem. *Personality and Individual Differences, 55,* 840–845.

Shonkoff, J. P. (2006). A promising opportunity for developmental and behavioral pediatrics at the interface of neuroscience, psychology, and social policy: Remarks on receiving the 2005 C. Anderson Aldrich Award. *Pediatrics, 118,* 2187–2191.

Shu, H., McBride-Chang, C., Wu, S., & Liu, H. (2006). Understanding Chinese developmental dyslexia: Morphological awareness as a core cognitive construct. *Journal of Educational Psychology, 98,* 122–133.

Shuell, T. J. (1996). Teaching and learning in a classroom context. In D. Berliner & R. Calfee (Eds.), *Handbook of educational psychology* (pp. 726–764). New York, NY: Macmillan.

Shute, V. J. (2008). Focus on formative feedback. *Review of Educational Research, 78,* 153–189.

Siddle Walker, V. (2001). African American teaching in the South: 1940–1960. *Review of Educational Research, 38,* 751–779.

Siegel, J., & Shaughnessy, M. F. (1994). Educating for understanding: An interview with Howard Gardner. *Phi Delta Kappan, 75,* 536–566.

Siegler, R. S. (1993). Adaptive and non-adaptive characteristics of low-income children's mathematical strategy use. In B. Penner (Ed.), *The challenge in mathematics and science education: Psychology's response* (pp. 341–366). Washington, DC: American Psychological Association.

Siegler, R. S. (1998). *Children's thinking* (3rd ed.). Upper Saddle River, NJ: Prentice-Hall.

Siegler, R. S. (2000). The rebirth of children's learning. *Child Development, 71,* 26–35.

Siegler, R. S. (2004). Turning memory development inside out. *Developmental Review, 24,* 469–475.

Siegler, R. S., & Alibali, M. W. (2005). *Children's thinking* (4th ed.). Upper Saddle River, NJ: Prentice-Hall.

Siegler, R. S., & Crowley, K. (1991). The microgenetic method: A direct means for studying cognitive development. *American Psychologist, 56,* 606–620.

Silverman, S. K. (2008, April, 11). Personal communication, Columbus, Ohio.

Simon, D. P., & Chase, W. G. (1973). Skill in chess. *American Scientist, 61,* 394–403.

Simon, H. A. (1995). The information-processing view of mind. *American Psychologist, 50,* 507–508.

Simon, T. (2010). Rewards and challenges of cognitive neuroscience studies of persons with intellectual and developmental disabilities. Special issue for the *American Journal on Intellectual and Developmental Disabilities, 115,* 79–82. doi:10.1352/1944-7558–115.2.79

Simonton, D. K. (2000). Creativity: Cognitive, personal, developmental, and social aspects. *American Psychologist, 55,* 151–158.

Simos, P. G., Fletcher, J. M., Sarkari, S., Billingsley-Marshall, R., Denton, C. A., & Papanicolaou, A. C. (2007). Intensive instruction affects brain magnetic activity associated with oral word reading in children with persistent reading disabilities. *Journal of Learning Disabilities, 40* (1), 37–48.

Sinatra, G. M., & Taasoobshirazi, G. (2011). Intentional conceptual change: The self-regulation of science learning. In B. Zimmerman & D. Schunk (Eds.), *Handbook of self-regulation of learning and performance* (pp. 203–216). New York, NY: Routledge.

Singley, K., & Anderson, J. R. (1989). *The transfer of cognitive skill.* Cambridge, MA: Harvard University Press.

Sio, U. N., & Ormerod, T. C. (2009). Does incubation enhance problem solving? A meta-analytic review. *Psychological Bulletin, 135,* 94–120.

Sirin, S. R. (2005). Socioeconomic status and academic achievement: A meta-analytic review of research. *Review of Educational Research, 75,* 417–453.

Skiba, R. J., Michael, R. S., Nardo, A. C., & Peterson, R. (2000). *The color of discipline: Sources of racial and gender disproportionality in school punishment* (Report #SRS1). Bloomington, IN: Indiana Education Policy Center.

Skibbe, L. E., Phillips, B. M., Day, S. L., Brophy-Herb, H. E., & Connor, C. M. (2012). Children's early literacy growth in relation to classmates' self-regulation. *Journal of Educational Psychology, 104,* 541–553. doi: 10.1037/a0029153

Skinner, B. F. (1950). Are theories of learning necessary? *Psychological Review, 57,* 193–216.

Skinner, B. F. (1953). *Science and human behavior.* New York, NY: Macmillan.

Skinner, B. F. (1989). The origins of cognitive thought. *American Psychologist, 44,* 13–18.

Slaby, R. G., Roedell, W. C., Arezzo, D., & Hendrix, K. (1995). *Early violence prevention.* Washington, DC: National Association for the Education of Young Children.

Slama, R. B. (2012). A longitudinal analysis of academic English proficiency outcomes for adolescent English language learners in the United States. *Journal of Educational Psychology, 104,* 265–285. doi: 10.1037/a0025861

Slater, L. (2002, February 3). The trouble with self-esteem. *The New York Times Magazine,* pp. 44–47.

Slavin, R. E. (1995). *Cooperative learning* (2nd ed.). Boston, MA: Allyn & Bacon.

Slavin, R. E. (2002). Evidence-based education policies: Transforming educational practice and research. *Educational Researcher, 31*(7), 15–21.

Smetana, J. G. (2000). Middle-class African American adolescents' and parents' conceptions of parental authority and parenting practices: A longitudinal investigation. *Child Development, 71,* 1672–1686.

Smith, C. S., & Hung, L.-C. (2008). Stereotype threat: Effects on education. *Social Psychology of Education, 11,* 243–257.

Smith, D. C., Tyler, N. C., & Smith, S. (2014). *Introduction to special education: New horizons.* Boston, MA: Pearson.

Smith, D. D. (2006). *Introduction to special education: Teaching in an age of opportunity* (5th ed.). Boston, MA: Allyn & Bacon.

Smith, D. D., & Tyler, N. C. (2010). *Introduction to special education: Making a difference* (7th ed.). Columbus, OH: Merrill.

Smith, D. G., Xiao, L., & Bechara, A. (2012). Decision making in children and adolescents: Impaired Iowa Gambling Task performance in early adolescence. *Developmental Psychology, 48,* 1180–1187. doi: 10.1037/a0026342

Smith, E. E., & Kosslyn, S. M. (2007). *Cognitive psychology: Mind and brain.* Upper Saddle River, NJ: Pearson/Prentice-Hall.

Smith, F. (1975). *Comprehension and learning: A conceptual framework for teachers.* New York, NY: Holt, Rinehart & Winston.

Smith, J. K., Smith, L. F., & De Lisi, R. (2001). *Natural classroom assessment: Designing seamless instruction and assessment.* Thousand Oaks, CA: Corwin Press.

Smith, J. L., Sansone, C., & White, P. H. (2007). The stereotyped task process: The role of interest and achievement motivation. *Journal of Educational Psychology, 88,* 99–114.

Smith, S. M., Glenberg, A., & Bjork, R. A. (1978). Environmental context and human memory. *Memory and Cognition, 6,* 342–353.

Snapp, M., & Woolfolk, A. E. (1973, March). *An examination of children in special education over a thirteen-year period.* Paper presented at the National Association of School Psychologists, 5th Annual Meeting, New York, NY.

Snow, C. E. (1993). Families as social contexts for literacy development. In C. Daiute (Ed.), *New directions for child development* (No. 61, pp. 11–24). San Francisco, CA: Jossey-Bass.

Snow, R. E. (1995). Pygmalion and intelligence. *Current Directions in Psychological Science, 4,* 169–171.

Snow, R. E., Corno, L., & Jackson, D. (1996). Individual differences in affective and cognitive functions. In D. Berliner & R. Calfee (Eds.), *Handbook of educational psychology* (pp. 243–310). New York, NY: Macmillan.

Snowman, J. (1984). Learning tactics and strategies. In G. Phye & T. Andre (Eds.), *Cognitive instructional psychology* (pp. 243–275). Orlando, FL: Academic Press.

Soares, D. A., Vannest, K. J., & Harrison, J. (2009). Computer aided self-monitoring to increase academic production and reduce self-injurious behavior in a child with autism. *Behavioral Interventions, 24,* 171–183.

Society for Research in Child Development. (2009). Young Hispanic children: Boosting opportunities for learning. *Society for Research in Child Development: Social Policy Report Briefs, 23*(2), 1–2.

Soemer, A., & Schwan, S. (2012). Visual mnemonics for language learning: Static pictures versus animated morphs. *Educational Psychology, 104,* 565–579.

Sokolove, S., Garrett, J., Sadker, D., & Sadker, M. (1986). Interpersonal communications skills. In J. Cooper (Ed.), *Classroom teaching skills: A handbook* (pp. 233–278). Lexington, MA: D. C. Heath.

Solomon, D., Watson, M. S., & Battistich, V. A. (2001). Teaching and schooling effects on moral/prosocial development. In V. Richardson (Ed.), *Handbook of research on teaching* (4th ed., pp. 566–603). Washington, DC: American Educational Research Association.

Son, L. K., & Simon, D. A. (2012). Distributed learning: Data, metacognition, and educational implications. *Educational Psychology Review, 24,* 379–399.

Soodak, L. C., & McCarthy, M. R. (2006). Classroom management in inclusive settings. In C. M. Evertson & C. S. Weinstein (Eds.), *Handbook of classroom management: Research, practice, and contemporary issues.* Mahwah, NJ: Erlbaum.

Sorhagen, N. S. (2013). Early teacher expectations disproportionately affect poor children's high school performance. *Journal of Educational Psychology, 105,* 465–477. doi: 10.1037/a0031754

Sotillo, S. M. (2002). Finding our voices, finding ourselves: Becoming bilingual and bicultural. In G. S. Boutte (Ed.), *Resounding voices: School experiences of people from diverse ethnic backgrounds* (pp. 275–307). Boston, MA: Allyn & Bacon.

Spearman, C. (1927). *The abilities of man: Their nature and measurement.* New York, NY: Macmillan.

Spencer, M. B., Noll, E., Stoltzfus, J., & Harpalani, V. (2001). Identity and school adjustment: Questioning the "Acting White" assumption. *Educational Psychologist, 36*(1), 21–30.

Spera, C. (2005). A review of the relationship among parenting practices, parenting styles, and adolescent school achievement. *Educational Psychology Review, 17,* 125–146.

Sperry, C. (2008). *Introducing Africa: A kit for teaching critical thinking and media literacy in the elementary grades.* Ithaca, NY: Project Look Sharp. Retrieved from http://www.ithaca.edu/looksharp/?action=introducingafrica

Spielberger, C. D., & Vagg, P. R. (1995). Test anxiety: A transactional process model. In C. D. Spielberger & P. R. Vagg (Eds.), *Test anxiety: Theory, assessment, and treatment* (pp. 3–14). Washington, DC: Taylor & Francis.

Spilt, J. L., Koomen, H. M. Y., & Thijs, J. T. (2011). Teacher wellbeing: The importance of teacher–student relationships. *Educational Psychology Review, 23,* 257–277.

Sprenger, M. (2005). Inside Amy's brain. *Educational Leadership, 62*(7), 28–32.

Sprenger, M. (2010). *Brain-based teaching in the digital age.* Alexandria, VA: Association for Supervision and Curriculum Development.

Stage, S. A., Jackson, H. G., Erickson M. J., Moscovitz, K. K., Bush, J. W., Violette, H. D., . . . Pious, C. (2008). A validity study of functionally-based behavioral consultation with students with emotional/behavioral disabilities. *School Psychology Quarterly, 23,* 327–353.

Stahl, S. A. (2002). Different strokes for different folks? In L. Abbeduto (Ed.), *Taking sides: Clashing on controversial issues in educational psychology* (pp. 98–107). Guilford, CT: McGraw-Hill/Duskin.

Stanford University. (2013). *The Protocol for Language Arts Teaching Observation (PLATO).* Retrieved from https://cset.stanford.edu/research/plato

Stanovich, K. E. (1992). *How to think straight about psychology* (3rd ed.). Glenview, IL: Scott, Foresman.

Star, J. R., & Rittle-Johnson, B. (2009). It pays to compare: An experimental study on computational estimation. *Journal of Experimental Child Psychology, 102,* 408–426.

Starko, A. J. (2014). *Creativity in the classroom: Schools of curious delight* (5th ed.). New York, NY: Routledge.

Stattin, H., Kerr, M, & Skoog, T. (2011). Early pubertal timing and girls' problem behavior: Integrating two hypotheses. *Journal of Youth and Adolescence, 40,* 1271–1287.

Steele, C. (1992). Race and the schooling of African-Americans. *Atlantic Monthly, 269*(4), 68–78.

Steele, C. M. (1997). A threat in the air: How stereotypes shape intellectual identity and performance. *American Psychologist, 52,* 613–629.

Steele, K. M., Bass, K. E., & Crook, M. D. (1999). The mystery of the Mozart effect: Failure to replicate. *Psychological Science, 10,* 366–368.

Stefanou, C. R., Perencevich, K. C., DiCintio, M., & Turner, J. C. (2004). Supporting autonomy in the classroom: Ways teachers encourage student decision making and ownership. *Educational Psychologist, 39,* 97–110.

Steffens, M. C., Jelenec, P., & Noack, P. (2010). On the leaky math pipeline: Comparing implicit math-gender stereotypes and math withdrawal in female and male children and adolescents. *Journal of Educational Psychology, 102,* 947–963.

Steinberg, L. (1998). Standards outside the classroom. In D. Ravitch (Ed.), *Brookings papers on educational policy* (pp. 319–358). Washington, DC: Brookings Institute.

Steinberg, L. (2005). *Adolescence* (7th ed.). New York, NY: McGraw-Hill.

Stemler, S. E., Sternberg, R. J., Grigorenko, E. L., Jarvin, L., & Sharpes, K. (2009). Using the theory of successful intelligence as a framework for developing assessments in AP physics. *Contemporary Educational Psychology, 34,* 195–209.

Sternberg, R. J. (1985). *Beyond IQ: A triarchic theory of human intelligence.* New York, NY: Cambridge University Press.

Sternberg, R. J. (1997). *Successful intelligence.* New York, NY: Plume.

Sternberg, R. J. (2000). *Handbook of human intelligence.* New York, NY: Cambridge University Press.

Sternberg, R. J. (2004). Culture and intelligence. *American Psychologist, 59,* 325–338.

Sternberg, R. J., & Davidson, J. (1982, June). The mind of the puzzler. *Psychology Today,* 37–44.

Sternberg, R. J., & Sternberg, K. (2012). *Cognitive psychology* (6th ed.). Belmont, CA: Wadsworth.

Stevenson, H. W., & Stigler, J. (1992). *The learning gap.* New York, NY: Summit Books.

Stewart, L., Henson, R., Kampe, K., Walsh, V., Turner, R., & Frith, U. (2003). Brain changes after learning to read and play music. *NeuroImage, 20*(1), 71–83.

Stice, E., & Shaw, H. (2004). Eating disorder prevention programs: A meta-analytic review. *Psychological Bulletin, 130,* 206–227.

Stiggins, J. (2002). Where is our assessment future and how can we get there? In R. W. Lissitz & W. D. Schafer (Eds.), *Meaningful assessment: A manageable and cooperative process.* Boston, MA: Allyn & Bacon.

Stiggins, R. J., & Chappuis, J. (2005). Using student-involved classroom assessment to close achievement gaps. *Theory Into Practice, 44,* 11–18.

Stinson, D. W. (2006). African American male adolescents, schooling (an mathematics): Deficiency, rejection, and achievement. *Review of Educational Research, 76,* 477–506.

Stipek, D. J. (1993). *Motivation to learn* (2nd ed.). Boston, MA: Allyn & Bacon.

Stipek, D. J. (2002). *Motivation to learn: Integrating theory and practice* (4th ed.). Boston, MA: Allyn & Bacon.

Stipek, D., de la Sota, A., & Weishaupt, L. (1999). Life lessons: An embedded classroom approach to preventing high-risk behaviors among preadolescents. *The Elementary School Journal, 99,* 433–451.

Stoeger, H., & Ziegler, A. (2011). Self-regulatory training through elementary-school students' homework completion. In B. Zimmerman & D. Schunk (Eds.), *Handbook of self-regulation of learning and performance* (pp. 87–101). New York, NY: Routledge.

Storch, S., & Whitehurst, G. (2002). Oral language and code-related precursors to reading: Evidence from a longitudinal structural model. *Developmental Psychology, 38,* 934–947.

Stormont, M., Stebbins, M. S., & Holliday, G. (2001). Characteristics and educational support needs of underrepresented gifted adolescents. *Psychology in the Schools, 38,* 413–423.

Stormshak, E. A., Bierman, K. L., Bruschi, C., Dodge, K. A., Coie, J. D., et al. (1999). The relation between behavior problems and peer preference in different classrooms. *Child Development, 70,* 169–182.

Story, M., & Stang, J. (2005). Nutrition needs of adolescents. In J. S. M. Story (Ed.), *Guidelines for adolescent nutritional services* (pp. 158–159). Minneapolis, MN: University of Minnesota Press.

Strom, P. S., & Strom, R. D. (2005). Cyberbullying by adolescents: A preliminary assessment. *The Educational Forum, 70*(1), 21–36.

Stumpf, H. (1995). Gender differences on test of cognitive abilities: Experimental design issues and empirical results. *Learning and Individual Differences, 7,* 275–288.

Südkamp, A., Kaiser, J., & Möller, J. (2012). Accuracy of teachers' judgments of students' academic achievement: A meta-analysis. *Journal of Educational Psychology, 104,* 743–762.

Suldo, S. M., Friedrich, A. A., White, T., Farmer, J., Minch, D., & Michalowski, J. (2009). Teacher support and adolescents' subjective well-being: A mixed-methods investigation. *School Psychology Review, 38,* 67–85.

Sullivan, M. A., & O'Leary, S. G. (1990). Maintenance following reward and cost token programs. *Behavior Therapy, 21,* 139–149.

Sulzer-Azaroff, B., & Mayer, G. R. (1986). *Achieving educational excellence using behavioral strategies.* New York, NY: Holt, Rinehart & Winston.

Sulzer-Azaroff, B., & Mayer, G. R. (1994). *Achieving educational excellence using behavioral strategies.* San Marcos, CA: Western Image.

Sung, E., & Mayer, R. E. (2013). Online multimedia learning with mobile devices and desktop computers: An experimental test of Clark's methods-not-media hypothesis. *Computers in Human Behavior, 29,* 639–647.

Sung, H.-Y., & Hwang, G.-J. (2013). A collaborative game-based learning approach to improving students' learning performance in science courses. *Computers and Education, 63,* 43–51.

Svoboda, J. S. (2001). Review of *Boys and Girls Learn Differently.* The Men's Resource Network. Retrieved from http://mensightmagazine.com/reviews/Svoboda/boysandgirls.htm

Swanson, H. L. (1990). The influence of metacognitive knowledge and aptitude on problem solving. *Journal of Educational Psychology, 82,* 306–314.

Swanson, H. L. (2001). Research on interventions for adolescents with learning disabilities: A meta-analysis of outcomes related to higher-order processing. *The Elementary School Journal, 101,* 332–348.

Swanson, H. L. (2011). Working memory, attention, and mathematical problem solving: A longitudinal study of elementary school children. *Journal of Educational Psychology, 103,* 821–837.

Swanson, H. L., & Jerman, O. (2006). Math disabilities: A selective meta-analysis of the literature. *Review of Educational Research, 76,* 249–274.

Swanson, H. L., Zheng, X. H., & Jerman, O. (2009). Working memory, short-term memory, and reading disabilities: A selective meta-analysis of the literature. *Journal of Learning Disabilities, 42,* 260–287.

Swanson, T. C. (2005). Providing structure for children with learning and behavior problems. *Intervention in School and Clinic, 40,* 182–187.

Swearer, S. M., Espelage, D. L., Vaillancourt, T., & Hymel, S. (2010). What can be done about school bullying? Linking research to educational practice. *Educational Researcher, 39,* 38–47.

Sweller, J., Kirschner, P. A., & Clark, R. E. (2007). Why minimally guided teaching techniques do not work: A reply to commentaries. *Educational Psychologist, 42,* 115–121.

Sweller, J., van Merriënboer, J. J. G., & Paas, F. G. W. C. (1998). Cognitive architecture and instructional design. *Educational Psychology Review, 10,* 251–296.

Sylvester, R. (2003). *A biological brain in a cultural classroom* (2nd ed.). Thousand Oaks, CA: Sage.

Sylvia, P. J., Henson, R. A., & Templin, J. L. (2009). Are the sources of interest the same for everyone? Using multilevel mixture models to explore individual differences in appraisal structures. *Cognition & Emotion, 23,* 1389–1406.

Synodi, E. (2010). Play in the kindergarten: The case of Norway, Sweden, New Zealand and Japan. *International Journal of Early Years Education, 18,* 185–200.

Syvertsen, A. K., Flanagan, C. A., & Stout, M. (2009). Code of silence: Students' perceptions of school climate and willingness to intervene in a peer's dangerous plan. *Journal of Educational Psychology, 101,* 219–232.

Talbot, M. (2002, February 24). Girls just want to be mean. *The New York Times Magazine,* pp. 24–291.

Tallal, P., & Miller, S. L. (2003). How the brain learns to read. *Middle Matters, 12*(1), 7.

Tamim, R. M., Bernard, R. M., Borokhovski, E., Abrami, P. C., & Schmid, R. F. (2011). What forty years of research says about the impact of technology on learning: A second-order meta-analysis and validation study. *Review of Educational Research, 81,* 4–28. doi: 10.3102/0034654310393361

Tang, Y., Zhang, W., Chen, K., Feng, S., Ji, Y., Shen, J., et al. (2006). Arithmetic processing in the brain shaped by culture. *Proceedings of the National Academy of Sciences USA, 103,* 10775–10780.

Taylor, E. (1998). Clinical foundation of hyperactivity research. *Behavioural Brain Research, 94,* 11–24.

Taylor, R. L., Richards, S. B., & Brady, M. P. (2005). *Mental retardation: Historical perspectives, current practices, and future directions.* Boston, MA: Allyn & Bacon.

TeachingWorks. (2014). *High-leverage practices.* Retrieved from http://www.teachingworks.org/work-of-teaching/high-leverage-practices

TenBrink, T. D. (2003). Assessment. In J. Cooper (Ed.), *Classroom teaching skills* (7th ed., pp. 311–353). Boston, MA: Houghton-Mifflin.

Tenenbaum, H. R., & Ruck, M. D. (2007). Are teachers' expectations different for racial minority than for European American students? A meta-analysis. *Journal of Educational Psychology, 99*, 253–273.

Terman, L. M., Baldwin, B. T., & Bronson, E. (1925). Mental and physical traits of a thousand gifted children. In L. M. Terman (Ed.), *Genetic studies of genius* (Vol. 1). Stanford, CA: Stanford University Press.

Terman, L. M., & Oden, M. H. (1947). The gifted child grows up. In L. M. Terman (Ed.), *Genetic studies of genius* (Vol. 4). Stanford, CA: Stanford University Press.

Terman, L. M., & Oden, M. H. (1959). The gifted group in mid-life. In L. M. Terman (Ed.), *Genetic studies of genius* (Vol. 5). Stanford, CA: Stanford University Press.

Tharp, R. G. (1989). Psychocultural variables and constants: Effects on teaching and learning in schools. *American Psychologist, 44*, 349–359.

Tharp, R. G., & Gallimore, R. (1988). *Rousing minds to life: Teaching, learning, and schooling in social context.* New York, NY: Cambridge University Press.

Theodore, L. A., Bray, M. A., Kehle, T. J., & Jenson, W. R. (2001). Randomization of group contingencies and reinforcers to reduce classroom disruptive behavior. *Journal of School Psychology, 39*, 267–277.

Thoman, D. B., Smith, J. L., Brown, E. R., Chase, J., & Lee, J. Y. K. (2013). Beyond performance: A motivational experiences model of stereotype threat. *Educational Psychology Review, 25*, 211–243.

Thomas, K. T., & Thomas, J. R. (2008). Principles of motor development for elementary school physical education. *The Elementary School Journal, 108*, 181–195.

Thome, J., & Reddy, D. P. (2009). The current status of research into attention deficit hyperactivity disorder: Proceedings of the 2nd International Congress on ADHD: From childhood to adult disease. *Attention Deficit Hyperactive Disorder, 1*, 165–174.

Thompson, G. (1991). *Teaching through themes.* New York, NY: Scholastic.

Thompson, G. (2008). Beneath the apathy. *Educational Leadership, 65*(6), 50–54.

Thompson, R. A., & Raikes, H. A. (2003). Toward the next quarter-century: Conceptual and methodological challenges for attachment theory. *Development and Psychopathology, 15*, 691–718.

Tierney, W. G. (1993). *Building communities of difference: Higher education in the twenty-first century.* Westport, CT: Bergin and Garvey.

Tingstrom, D. H., Sterling-Turner, H. E., & Wilczynski, S. M. (2006). The Good Behavior Game: 1962–2002. *Behavior Modification, 30*, 225–253.

Tobias, S. (2010). Generative learning theory, paradigm shifts, and constructivism in educational psychology: A tribute to Merl Wittrock. *Educational Psychologist, 45*, 51–54.

Tobler, N., & Stratton, H. (1997). Effectiveness of school-based drug prevention programs: A metaanalysis of the research. *Journal of Primary Prevention, 18*, 71–128.

Tollefson, N. (2000). Classroom applications of cognitive theories of motivation. *Education Psychology Review, 12*, 63–83.

Tomasello, M. (2006). Acquiring linguistic constructions. In D. Kuhn & R. S. Siegler (Eds.), *Handbook of child psychology: Vol. 2. Cognition, language, and perception* (6th ed., pp. 255–298). New York, NY: Wiley.

Tomasello, M., Kruger, A. C., & Ratner, H. H. (1993). Cultural learning. *Behavioral and Brain Sciences, 16*, 495–552.

Tomlinson, C. A. (2005a). Differentiating instruction. *Theory Into Practice, 44*(3)[entire issue].

Tomlinson, C. A. (2005b). Grading and differentiation: Paradox or good practice? *Theory Into Practice, 44*, 262–269.

Tomlinson-Keasey, C. (1990). Developing our intellectual resources for the 21st century: Educating the gifted. *Journal of Educational Psychology, 82*, 399–403.

Tomporowski, P., Davis, C. L., Miller, P. H., & Naglieri, J. A. (2008). Exercise and children's intelligence, cognitive and academic achievement. *Educational Psychology Review, 20*, 111–131.

Tools of the Mind. (2014). Brandon's play plans. Retrieved from http://www.toolsofthemind.org/curriculum/preschool/

Topping, K., Dekhinet, R., & Zeedyk, S. (2011). Hindrances for parents in enhancing child language. *Educational Psychology Review, 23*, 413–455.

Toppo, G. (2003, January 13). School violence hits lower grades: Experts who see violent behavior in younger kids blame parents, prenatal medical problems and an angry society; educators search for ways to cope. *USA Today.* Retrieved from http://www.usatoday.com/educate/college/education/articles/20030119.htm

Torrance, E. P. (1972). Predictive validity of the Torrance tests of creative thinking. *Journal of Creative Behavior, 6*, 236–262.

Torrance, E. P. (1986). Teaching creative and gifted learners. In M. Wittrock (Ed.), *Handbook of research on teaching* (3rd ed., pp. 630–647). New York, NY: Macmillan.

Torrance, E. P. (2000). A graphic assessment of the creativity of an eight-year-old. In *The Torrance Test of Creative Thinking.* Bensonville, IL: Scholastic Testing Service.

Torrance, E. P., & Hall, L. K. (1980). Assessing the future reaches of creative potential. *Journal of Creative Behavior, 14*, 1–19.

Toth, E., Klahr, D., & Chen, Z. (2000). Bridging research and practice: A cognitively based classroom intervention for teaching experimentation to elementary school children. *Cognition and Instruction, 18*, 423–459.

Trautwein, U. (2007). The homework–achievement relation reconsidered: Differentiating homework time, homework frequency, and homework effort. *Learning and Instruction, 17*, 372–388.

Trautwein, U., & Lüdtke, O. (2007). Students' self-reported effort and time on homework in six school subjects: Between-students differences and within-student variation. *Journal of Educational Psychology, 99*, 232–234.

Trautwein, U., Schnyder, I., Niggli, A., Neuman, M., & Lüdtke, O. (2009). Chameleon effects in homework research: The homework–achievement association depends on the measures used and the level of analysis chosen. *Contemporary Educational Psychology, 34*, 77–88.

Trebaticka, J., Paduchova, Z., Suba, J., et al. (2009). Markers of oxidative stress in ADHD and their modulation by Polyhenolic extract, Pycnogenal. From Childhood to Adult Disease. May 21–24, 2009, Vienna, Austria. *Attention Deficit and Hyperactivity Disorders, 1*, 33.

Trends in International Mathematics and Science Study (TIMSS). (1998). *Third International Mathematics and Science Study.* Washington, DC: National Center for Educational Statistics. Retrieved from http://nces.ed.gov/timss/

Trends in International Mathematics and Science Study (TIMSS). (2008). Fourth International Mathematics and Science Study. Retrieved from http://ncesed.gov/timss/

Trouilloud, D., Sarrazin, P., Bressoux, P., & Bois, J. (2006). Relation between teachers' early expectations and students' later perceived competence in physical education classes: Autonomy-supportive climate as a moderator. *Journal of Educational Psychology, 98*, 75–86.

Tsantis, L. A., Bewick, C. J., & Thouvenelle, S. (2003, November). Examining some common myths about computer use in the early years [Electronic Version]. *Beyond the Journal: Young Children on the Web,* pp. 1–9. Retrieved from http://journal.naeyc.org/btj/200311/CommonTechnoMyths.pdf

Tschannen-Moran, M., & Woolfolk Hoy, A. (2000). Collaborative learning: A memorable model. *The Teacher Educator, 36*, 148–165.

Tschannen-Moran, M., & Woolfolk Hoy, A. (2001). Teacher efficacy: Capturing an elusive construct. *Teaching and Teacher Education, 17*, 783–805.

Tschannen-Moran, M., Woolfolk Hoy, A., & Hoy, W. K. (1998). Teacher efficacy: Its meaning and measure. *Review of Educational Research, 68*, 202–248.

Tucker-Drob, E. M. (2009). Differentiation of cognitive abilities across the life span. *Developmental Psychology, 45*, 1097–1118.

Turkle, S. (2011). *Alone together: Why we expect more from technology and less from ourselves.* New York, NY: Basic Books.

Turner, J. C. (1997). Starting right: Strategies for engaging young literacy learners. In J. T. Guthrie & A. Wigfield (Eds.), *Reading engagement: Motivating readers through integrated instruction* (pp. 183–204). Newark, DE: International Reading Association.

Turner, J. C., & Paris, S. G. (1995). How literacy tasks influence students' motivation for literacy. *The Reading Teacher, 48*, 662–673.

Turner, J., Patrick, H., & Meyer, D. (2011). Engaging students in learning: A special issue dedicated to Jere Brophy. *Theory Into Practice, 50.*

Udell, W. (2007). Enhancing adolescent girls' argument skills in reasoning about personal and non-personal decisions. *Cognitive Development, 22*, 341–352.

Uline, C. L., & Johnson, J. F. (2005). Closing the achievement gap: What will it take? Special Issue of *Theory Into Practice, 44*(1), Winter.

Umbreit, J. (1995). Functional analysis of disruptive behavior in an inclusive classroom. *Journal of Early Intervention, 20*(1), 18–29.

UNICEF. (2012). *Measuring child poverty: Innocenti Report Card 10.* United Nations Children's Fund. Retrieved from http://www.unicef-irc.org/publications/pdf/rc10_eng.pdf

Unsworth, N., & Engle, R. W. (2005). Working memory capacity and fluid abilities: Examining the correlation between Operation Span and Raven. *Intelligence, 33*, 67–81.

Urdan, T. C., & Maehr, M. L. (1995). Beyond a two-goal theory of motivation and achievement: A case for social goals. *Review of Educational Research, 65*, 213–243.

U.S. Census Bureau. (2010a). *State and country quick facts.* Retrieved from http://quickfacts.census.gov/qfd/states/00000.html

U.S. Census Bureau. (2010b). *Hispanic population of the United States: Projections.* Retrieved from http://www.census.gov/population/www/socdemo/hispanic/hispanic_pop_presetation.html

U.S. Census Bureau. (2011a). *Children below poverty level by race and Hispanic origin.* Retrieved from http://www.census.gov/compendia/statab/2011/tables/11s0711.pdf

U.S. Census Bureau. (2011b). U.S. population projections 2010–2050. Retrieved from http://www.census.gov/population/www/projections/summarytables.html

U.S. Citizenship and Immigration Services. (2011). Home page. Retrieved from http://www.uscis.gov/portal/site/uscis

U.S. Department of Agriculture. (2013a). *Nutrition Assistance Program Report, September 2013 US Summary. National Data Bank (NDB), USDA/Food and Nutrition Service*. Washington, DC: Author.

U.S. Department of Agriculture. (2013b). *USDA Foods and Nutrition Service: Data and Statistics*. Retrieved from http://www.fns.usda.gov/sites/default/files/September%20performance%202013%20data.pdf

U.S. Department of Education. (2004). *26th Annual report to Congress on the implementation of the Individuals with Disabilities Act, 2005*. Washington, DC: Office of Special Education and Rehabilitative Services.

U.S. Department of Education. (2009, November). *Race to the Top Program: Executive summary*. U.S. Department of Education, Washington, D.C. Retrieved from http://www2.ed.gov/programs/racetothetop/executive-summary.pdf

U.S. Department of Education. (2010, March). *ESEA Blueprint for Reform*. Washington, DC: USDE, Office of Planning, Evaluation and Policy Development. Retrieved from http://www2.ed.gov/programs/racetothetop/index.html

U.S. Department of Education. (2011). *30th Annual report to Congress on the implementation of the Individuals with Disabilities Act, 2005*. Washington, DC: Office of Special Education and Rehabilitative Services.

Usher, E. L., & Pajares, F. (2009). Sources of self-efficacy in mathematics: A validation study. *Contemporary Educational Psychology, 34*, 89–101.

Uttal, D. H., Hand, L. L., & Newcombe, N. S. (2009, April). *Malleability of spatial cognition: Results of a meta-analysis*. Paper presented at the biennial meeting of the Society for Research in Child Development, Denver, CO.

Valentine, J. C., DuBois, D. L., & Cooper, H. (2004). The relations between self-beliefs and academic achievement: A systematic review. *Educational Psychologist, 39*, 111–133.

Valenzuela, A. (1999). *Subtractive schooling: U.S.–Mexican youth and the politics of caring*. Albany, NY: SUNY Press.

Valiente, C., Lemery-Chalfant, K., & Swanson, J. (2010). Prediction of kindergartners' academic achievement from their effortful control and emotionality: Evidence for direct and moderated relations. *Journal of Educational Psychology, 102*, 550–560.

van de Pol, J., Volman, M., & Beishuizen, J. (2010). Scaffolding in teacher–student interaction: A decade of research. *Educational Psychology Review, 22*, 271–296.

Van de Walle, J. A., Karp, K. S., & Bay-Williams, J. M. (2010). *Elementary and middle school mathematics: Teaching developmentally* (7th ed.). Boston, MA: Pearson.

van den Broek, P., Lorch, E. P., & Thurlow, R. (1996). Children's and adults' memory for television stories: The role of causal factors, story-grammar categories, and hierarchical level. *Child Development, 67*, 3010–3028.

van der Mass, H. L. J., Dolan, C. V., Grasman, R. P. P., Wicherts, J. M., Huizenga, H. M., & Raijmakers, M. E. J. (2006). A dynamic model of general intelligence: The positive manifold of intelligence by mutualism. *Psychological Review, 113*, 842–861.

van der Meij, J. (2012). Draw your physics homework? Art as a path to understanding in physics teaching. *American Educational Research Journal, 49*, 356–407. doi: 10.3102/0002831211435521

Van Der Veer, R. (2007). Vygotsky in context: 1900–1935. In H. Daniels, M. Cole, & J. V. Wertsch (Eds.), *The Cambridge companion to Vygotsky* (pp. 21–49). New York, NY: Cambridge University Press.

Van Dick, R., & Wagner, U. (2001). Stress and strain in teaching: A structural equation approach. *British Journal of Educational Psychology, 71*, 243–259.

van Driel, J. H., & Berry, A. (2012). Teacher professional development focusing on pedagogical content knowledge. *Educational Researcher, 41*, 26–28. doi: 10.3102/0013189X11431010

van Gelderen, A., Schoonen, R., Stoel, R. D., de Glopper, K., & Hulstijn, J. (2007). Development of adolescent reading comprehension in language 1 and language 2: A longitudinal analysis of constituent components. *Journal of Educational Psychology, 99*, 477–491.

van Gog, T., Paas, F., & Sweller, J. (2010). Cognitive load theory: Advances in research on worked examples, animations, and cognitive load measurement. *Educational Psychology Review, 22*, 375–378.

van Kraayenoord, C. E., Rice, D., Carroll, A., Fritz, E., Dillon, L., & Hill, A. (2001). *Attention deficit hyperactivity disorder: Impact and implications for Queensland*. Queensland, Australia: Queensland Disability Services. Retrieved from www.families.qld.gov.au

van Laar, C. (2000). The paradox of low academic achievement but high self-esteem in African American students: An attributional account. *Educational Psychology Review, 12*, 33–61.

Van Matre, J. C., Valentine, J. C., & Cooper, H. (2000). Effect of students' after-school activities on teachers' academic expectations. *Contemporary Educational Psychology, 25*, 167–183.

Van Merriënboer, J. J. G., & Sweller, J. (2005). Cognitive load and complex learning: Recent developments and future directions. *Educational Psychology Review, 17*, 147–177.

Van Meter, P. (2001). Drawing construction as a strategy for learning from text. *Journal of Educational Psychology, 93*, 129–140.

Van Meter, P., Yokoi, L., & Pressley, M. (1994). College students' theory of note-taking derived from their perceptions of note-taking. *Journal of Educational Psychology, 86*, 323–338.

Vandell, D. L. (2004). Early child care: The known and the unknown. *Merrill-Palmer Quarterly, 50*, 387–414.

Vandermass-Peler, M. (2002). Cultural variations in parental support of children's play. In W. J. Lonner, D. L. Dinnel, S. A. Hayes, & D. N. Sattler (Eds.), Online readings in psychology and culture (Unit 11, Chapter 3; Vol. 2007). Bellingham, WA: Center for Cross-Cultural Research, Western Washington University.

Vansteenkiste, M., Lens, W., & Deci, E. L. (2006). Intrinsic versus extrinsic goal contents in self-determination theory: Another look at the quality of academic motivation. *Educational Psychologist, 41*, 19–31.

Vansteenkiste, M., Simons, J., Lens, W., Sheldon, K. M., & Deci, E. L. (2004). Motivating learning, performance, and persistence: The synergistic role of intrinsic goals and autonomy-support. *Journal of Personality and Social Psychology, 87*, 246–260.

Varma, S., McCandliss, B. D., & Schwartz, D. L. (2008). Scientific and pragmatic challenges for bridging education and neuroscience. *Educational Researcher, 37*, 140–152.

Vasquez, J. A. (1990). Teaching to the distinctive traits of minority students. *The Clearing House, 63*, 299–304.

Vaughn, S., Levy, S., Coleman, M., & Bos, C. S. (2002). Reading instruction for students with LD and EBD: A synthesis of observation studies. *Journal of Special Education, 36*(1), 2–13.

Vecchio, G. M., Gerbino, M., Pastorelli, C., Del Bove, G., & Caprara, G. V. (2007). Multi-faceted self-efficacy beliefs as predictors of life satisfaction in late adolescence. *Personality and Individual Differences, 43*, 1807–1818.

Veenman, S. (1984). Perceived problems of beginning teachers. *Review of Educational Research, 54*, 143–178.

Veenman, S. (1997). Combination classes revisited. *Educational Research and Evaluation, 65*(4), 319–381.

Vélez, C. E., Wolchik, S. A., Tein, J. Y., & Sandler, I. (2011). Protecting children from the consequences of divorce: A longitudinal study of the effects of parenting on children's coping processes. *Child Development, 82*, 244–257. doi:10.1111/j.1467–8624.2010.01553.x

Vera, A. H., & Simon, H. A. (1993). Situated action: A symbolic interpretation. *Cognitive Science, 17*, 7–48.

Verhallen, M. J. A. J., Bus, A. G., & de Jong, M. T. (2006). The promise of multimedia stories for kindergarten children at risk. *Journal of Educational Psychology, 98*, 410–419.

Verplaetse, L. S., & Migliacci, N. (2008). Inclusive pedagogy: An introduction. In L. S. Verplaetse & N. Migliacci (Eds.), *Inclusive pedagogy for English language learners: A handbook of research-informed practices* (pp. 3–13). Mahwah, NJ: Erlbaum.

Vidal-Abarca, E., Mañá, A, & Gil, L. (2010). Individual differences for self-regulating task-oriented reading activities. *Journal of Educational Psychology, 102*, 817–826.

Vogt, M. E., Echevarría, J., & Short, D. J. (2010). *The SIOP® Model for teaching English-language arts to English learners*. Boston, MA: Pearson.

von Glasersfeld, E. (1997). Amplification of a constructivist perspective. *Issues in Education: Contributions from Educational Psychology, 3*, 203–210.

Vroom, V. (1964). *Work and motivation*. New York, NY: Wiley.

Vygotsky, L. S. (1978). *Mind in society: The development of higher mental process*. Cambridge, MA: Harvard University Press.

Vygotsky, L. S. (1986). *Thought and language*. Cambridge, MA: MIT Press.

Vygotsky, L. S. (1987a). The genetic roots of thinking and speech. In R. W. Rieber & A. S. Carton (Eds.), *Problems of general psychology, Vol. 1. Collected works* (pp. 101–120). New York, NY: Plenum. (Work originally published 1934)

Vygotsky, L. S. (1987b). *Problems of general psychology*. New York, NY: Plenum.

Vygotsky, L. S. (1987c). Thought and word. In R. W. Rieber & A. S. Carton (Eds.), *Collected works of L. S. Vygotsky: Vol. 1. Problems of general psychology* (pp. 243–285). New York, NY: Plenum. (Work originally published 1934)

Vygotsky, L. S. (1993). *The collected works of L. S. Vygotsky: Vol. 2* (J. Knox & C. Stevens, Trans.). New York, NY: Plenum.

Vygotsky, L. S. (1997). *Educational psychology* (R. Silverman, Trans.). Boca Raton, FL: St. Lucie.

Vygotsky, L. S. (1998). The problem of age. In R. W. Rieber (Ed.), *The collected works of L. S. Vygotsky: Vol. 5* (pp. 187–205). (M. J. Hall, Trans.). New York, NY: Plenum.

Wade, S. E., Schraw, G., Buxton, W. M., & Hayes, M. T. (1993). Seduction of the strategic reader: Effects of interest on strategies and recall. *Reading Research Quarterly, 28,* 3–24.

Wai, J., Lubinski, D., Benbow, C. P., & Steiger, J. H. (2010). Accomplishment in science, technology, engineering, and mathematics (stem) and its relation to stem educational dose: A 25-year longitudinal study. *Journal of Educational Psychology, 102,* 860–871. doi: 10.1037/a0019454

Waits, B. K., & Demana, F. (2000). Calculators in mathematics teaching and learning: Past, present, future. In M. J. Burke & F. R. Curcio (Eds.), *Learning mathematics for a new century: NCTM 2000 Yearbook* (pp. 51–66). Reston, VA: National Council of Teachers of Mathematics.

Walberg, H. J. (1990). Productive teaching and instruction: Assessing the knowledge base. *Phi Delta Kappan, 72,* 470–478.

Walker, J. E., Shea, T. M., & Bauer, A. M. (2004). *Behavior management: A practical approach for educators.* Upper Saddle River, NJ: Merrill/Prentice Hall.

Walker, V. S. (1996). *Their highest potential.* Chapel Hill: University of North Carolina Press.

Walls, M. L., & Whitbeck, L. B. (2011). Maturation, peer context, and indigenous girls' early-onset substance use. *Journal of Early Adolescence, 31(3),* 415–442.

Walqui, A. (2008). The development of teacher expertise to work with adolescent English learners: A model and a few priorities. In L. S. Verplaetse & N. Migliacci (Eds.), *Inclusive pedagogy for English language learners: A handbook of research-informed practices* (pp. 103–125). New York, NY: Erlbaum.

Wang, A. Y., & Thomas, M. H. (1995). Effects of keywords on long-term retention: Help or hindrance? *Journal of Educational Psychology, 87,* 468–475.

Wang, A. Y., Thomas, M. H., & Ouellette, J. A. (1992). Keyword mnemonic and retention of second-language vocabulary words. *Journal of Educational Psychology, 84,* 520–528.

Wanzek, J., et al. (2013). Extensive reading interventions for students with reading difficulties after grade 3. *Review of Educational Research, 83,* 163–195.

Ward, L. M. (2004). Wading through the stereotypes: Positive and negative associations between media use and Black adolescents' conception of self. *Developmental Psychology, 40,* 284–294.

Wares, A. (2013). An application of the theory of multiple intelligences in mathematics classrooms in the context of origami. *International Journal of Mathematics Education in Science and Technology, 44,* 122–131.

Warren, J. R., & Salimba, J. (2012). First- through eighth-grade retention rates for all 50 states: A new method and initial results. *Educational Researcher, 41(8),* 320–329. doi: 10.3102/0013189X12457813

Warren, J. S., Bohanon-Edmonson, H. M., Turnbull, A. P., Sailor, W., Wickham, D., Griggs, P., & Beech, S. E. (2006). School-wide positive behavior support: Addressing behavior problems that impede student learning. *Educational Psychology Review, 18,* 187–198.

Wartella, E., Rideout, V., Lajricella, A. R., & Connell, S. L. (2013). *Parenting in the age of digital technology: A national survey.* Evanston, IL: Center on Media and Human Development, Northwestern University.

Waterhouse, L. (2006). Multiple intelligences, the Mozart effect, and emotional intelligence: A critical review. *Educational Psychologist, 41,* 207–225.

Watson, J. B. (1919). *Psychology from the standpoint of a behaviorist.* Philadelphia: Lippincott.

Watt, H. M. G., & Richardson, P. W. (2013). Teacher motivation and student achievement outcomes. In J. A. C. Hattie & E. M. Anderman (Eds.), *The international guide to student achievement.* New York, NY: Routledge.

Waugh, C. K., & Gronlund, N. E. (2013). *Assessment of student achievement* (10th ed.). Columbus, OH: Pearson.

Waxman, S. R., & Lidz, J. L. (2006). Early word learning. In D. Kuhn & R. S. Siegler (Eds.), *Handbook of child psychology: Vol. 2. Cognition, perception, and language* (6th ed., pp. 299–335). New York, NY: Wiley.

Wayne, A. J., & Youngs, P. (2003). Teacher characteristics and student achievement gains: A review. *Review of Educational Research, 73,* 89–122.

Webb, N. M., Farivar, S. H., & Mastergeorge, A. M. (2002). Productive helping in cooperative groups. *Theory Into Practice, 41,* 13–20.

Webb, N. M., & Mastergeorge, A. M. (2003). The development of students' helping behavior and learning in peer-directed small groups. *Cognition and Instruction, 21,* 361–428.

Webb, N. M., & Palincsar, A. (1996). Group processes in the classroom. In D. C. Berliner & R. C. Calfee (Eds.), *Handbook of educational psychology* (pp. 841–876). New York, NY: Macmillan.

Wechsler, D. (2004). *The Wechsler intelligence scale for children—fourth edition.* London: Pearson Assessment.

Weil, E. (2008, March 2). Should boys and girls be taught separately? *The New York Times Magazine,* pp. 33–451.

Weiner, B. (1986). *An attributional theory of motivation and emotion.* New York, NY: Springer.

Weiner, B. (1994a). Ability versus effort revisited: The moral determinants of achievement evaluation and achievement as a moral system. *Educational Psychologist, 29,* 163–172.

Weiner, B. (1994b). Integrating social and persons theories of achievement striving. *Review of Educational Research, 64,* 557–575.

Weiner, B. (2000). Interpersonal and intrapersonal theories of motivation from an attributional perspective. *Educational Psychology Review, 12,* 1–14.

Weiner, B. (2010). The development of an attribution-based theory of motivation: A history of ideas. *Educational Psychologist, 45,* 28–36.

Weinert, F. E., & Helmke, A. (1995). Learning from wise mother nature or big brother instructor: The wrong choice as seen from an educational perspective. *Educational Psychologist, 30,* 135–143.

Weinstein, C. S. (1977). Modifying student behavior in an open classroom through changes in the physical design. *American Educational Research Journal, 14,* 249–262.

Weinstein, C. S. (1988). Preservice teachers' expectations about the first year of teaching. *Teachers and Teacher Education, 4,* 31–40.

Weinstein, C. S. (1999). Reflections on best practices and promising programs: Beyond assertive classroom discipline. In H. J. Freiberg (Ed.), *Beyond behaviorism: Changing the classroom management paradigm* (pp. 147–163). Boston, MA: Allyn & Bacon.

Weinstein, C. S., Curran, M., & Tomlinson-Clarke, S. (2003). Culturally responsive classroom management: Awareness into action. *Theory Into Practice, 42,* 269–276.

Weinstein, C. S., & Novodvorsky, I. (2015). *Middle and secondary classroom management: Lessons from research and practice* (5th ed.). New York, NY: McGraw-Hill.

Weinstein, C. S., & Romano, M. E. (2015). *Elementary classroom management* (6th ed.), New York: McGraw-Hill.

Weinstein, C. S., Romano, M. E., & Mignano, A. J. (2011). *Elementary classroom management: Lessons from research and practice* (5th ed.). New York, NY: McGraw-Hill.

Weinstein, R. S., Madison, S. M., & Kuklinski, M. R. (1995). Raising expectations in schools: Obstacles and opportunities for change. *American Educational Research Journal, 32,* 121–159.

Weisberg, R. W. (1993). *Creativity: Beyond the myth of genius.* New York, NY: Freeman.

Welsh, J. A., Nix, R. L., Blair, C., Bierman, K. L., & Nelson, K. E. (2010). The development of cognitive skills and gains in academic school readiness for children from low-income families. *Journal of Educational Psychology, 102,* 43–53.

Wenger, E. (1998). *Communities of practice: learning, meaning, and identity.* New York, NY: Cambridge University Press.

Wentzel, K. R. (2002). Are effective teachers like good parents? Teaching styles and student adjustment in early adolescence. *Child Development, 73,* 287–301.

Wentzel, K. R., Barry, C. M., & Caldwell, K. A. (2004). Friendships in middle school: Influences on motivation and school adjustment. *Journal of Educational Psychology, 96,* 195–203.

Werts, M. G., Culatta, A., & Tompkins, J. R. (2007). *Fundamentals of special education: What every teacher should know* (3rd ed.). Columbus, OH: Pearson/Allyn & Bacon-Merrill.

Wertsch, J. V. (1991). *Voices of the mind: A sociocultural approach to mediated action.* Cambridge, MA: Harvard University Press.

Wertsch, J. V. (2007). Mediation. In H. Daniels, M. Cole, & J. V. Wertsch (Eds.), *The Cambridge companion to Vygotsky* (pp. 178–192). New York, NY: Cambridge University Press.

Wertsch, J. V., & Tulviste, P. (1992). L. S. Vygotsky and contemporary developmental psychology. *Developmental Psychology, 28,* 548–557.

Westling, E., Andrews, J. A., Hampson, S. E., & Peterson, M. (2008). Pubertal timing and substance use: The effects of gender, parental monitoring and deviant peers. *Journal of Adolescent Health, 42,* 555–563.

Wheatley, K. F. (2002). The potential benefits of teacher efficacy doubts for educational reform. *Teaching and Teacher Education, 18,* 5–22.

Wheatley, K. F. (2005). The case for reconceptualizing teacher efficacy research. *Teaching and Teacher Education, 21,* 747–766.

Wheelock, A. (1992). *Crossing the tracks: How untracking can save America's schools.* New York, NY: The New Press.

Whitehead, A. N. (1929). *The aims of education.* New York, NY: Macmillan.

Whitehurst, G. J., Epstein, J. N., Angell, A. L., Payne, A. C., Crone, D. A., & Fischel, J. E. (1994). Outcomes of an emergent literacy program in Headstart. *Journal of Educational Psychology, 86,* 542–555.

Whitehurst, G. J., & Lonigan, C. J. (1998). Child development and emergent literacy. *Child Development, 69,* 845–872.

Wigfield, A., Byrnes, J. P., & Eccles, J. S. (2006). Development during early and middle adolescence. In P. A. Alexander & P. H. Winne (Eds.), *Handbook of educational psychology* (2nd ed., pp. 87–113). Mahwah, NJ: Erlbaum.

Wigfield, A., & Eccles, J. (1989). Test anxiety in elementary and secondary school students. *Educational Psychologist, 24,* 159–183.

Wigfield, A., & Eccles, J. (2002). The development of competence beliefs, expectancies of success, and achievement values from childhood through adolescence. In A. Wigfield & J. Eccles (Eds.), *Development of achievement motivation* (pp. 91–120). San Diego, CA: Academic Press.

Wigfield, A., Eccles, J., MacIver, D., Rueman, D., & Midgley, C. (1991). Transitions at early adolescence: Changes in children's domain-specific self-perceptions and general self-esteem across the transition to junior high school. *Developmental Psychology, 27,* 552–565.

Wigfield, A., Eccles, J. S., & Pintrich, P. R. (1996). Development between the ages of 11 and 25. In D. Berliner & R. Calfee (Eds.), *Handbook of educational psychology* (pp. 148–185). New York, NY: Macmillan.

Wigfield, A., & Wentzel, K. R. (2007). Introduction to motivation at school: Interventions that work. *Educational Psychologist, 42,* 191–196.

Wiggins, G. (1989). Teaching to the authentic test. *Educational Leadership, 46*(7), 41–47.

Wiggins, G. (1991). Standards, not standardization: Evoking quality student work. *Educational Leadership, 48*(5), 18–25.

Wiggins, G., & McTighe, J. (2006). *Understanding by Design* (2nd ed.). Columbus, OH: Pearson.

Wilkinson, G. R. (1988). Teacher stress and coping strategies—A study of Eastlake Comprehensive. *School Organization, 8,* 185–195.

Willcutt, E. G., Pennington, B. F., Boada, R., Ogline, J. S., Tunick, R. A., Chhabidas, N. A., & Olson, R. K. (2001). A comparison of the cognitive deficits in reading disability and attention-deficit/hyperactivity disorder. *Journal of Abnormal Psychology, 110,* 157–172.

William, D. (2010). Standardized testing and school accountability. *Educational Psychologist, 45,* 107–122.

Williams, T., & Williams, K. (2010). Self-efficacy and performance in mathematics: Reciprocal determinism in 33 nations. *Journal of Educational Psychology, 102,* 453–466.

Willingham, D. T. (2004). Reframing the mind. *Education Next, 4*(3), 19–24.

Willis, J. (2009). What brain research suggests for teaching reading strategies. *Educational Forum, 73,* 333–346.

Willoughby, T., Porter, L., Belsito, L., & Yearsley, T. (1999). Use of elaboration strategies by grades two, four, and six. *Elementary School Journal, 99,* 221–231.

Willower, D. J., Eidell, T. L., & Hoy, W. K. (1967). *The school and pupil control.* University Park, PA: The Pennsylvania State University.

Wilson, M. (2001). The case for sensorimotor coding in working memory. *Psychonomic Bulletin and Review, 8,* 44–57.

Wilson, M. (2002). Six views of embodied cognition. *Psychonomic Bulletin and Review, 9,* 625–636.

Wilson, M., & Trainin, G. (2007). First-grade students' motivation and achievement for reading, writing, and spelling. *Reading Psychology, 28,* 257–282.

Windschitl, M. (2002). Framing constructivism in practice as the negotiation of dilemmas: An analysis of the conceptual, pedagogical, cultural, and political challenges facing teachers. *Review of Educational Research, 72,* 131–175.

Winett, R. A., & Winkler, R. C. (1972). Current behavior modification in the classroom: Be still, be quiet, be docile. *Journal of Applied Behavior Analysis, 15,* 499–504.

Wink, J., & Putney, L. (2002). *A vision of Vygotsky.* Boston, MA: Allyn & Bacon.

Winne, P. H. (1995). Inherent details in self-regulated learning. *Educational Psychologist, 30,* 173–188.

Winne, P. H. (2001). Self-regulated learning viewed from models of information processing.

In B. J. Zimmerman & D. H. Schunk (Eds.), *Self-regulated learning and academic achievement: Theoretical perspectives* (2nd ed., pp. 153–189). Mahwah, NJ: Erlbaum.

Winne, P. H. (2011). A cognitive and metacognitive analysis of self-regulated learning. In B. Zimmerman & D. Schunk (Eds.), *Handbook of self-regulation of learning and performance* (pp. 15–32). New York, NY: Routledge.

Winne, P. H., & Hadwin, A. F. (1998). Studying as self-regulated learning. In D. J. Hacker, J. Dunlosky, & A. C. Graesser (Eds.), *Metacognition in educational theory and practice* (pp. 277–304). Mahwah, NJ: Erlbaum.

Winne, P. H., & Perry, N. E. (2000). Measuring self-regulated learning. In P. Pintrich, M. Boekaerts, & M. Zeidner (Eds.), *Handbook of self-regulation* (pp. 531–566). Orlando, FL: Academic Press.

Winner, E. (2000). The origins and ends of giftedness. *American Psychologist, 55,* 159–169.

Winner, E. (2003). Musical giftedness. *Bulletin of Psychology and the Arts, 4,* 1, 2–5.

Winsler, A., Carlton, M. P., & Barry, M. J. (2000). Age-related changes in preschool children's systematic use of private speech in a natural setting. *Journal of Child Language, 27,* 665–687.

Winsler, A., & Naglieri, J. A. (2003). Overt and covert verbal problem-solving strategies: Developmental trends in use, awareness, and relations with task performance in children age 5 to 17. *Child Development, 74,* 659–678.

Wittmaier, B. C. (1972). Test anxiety and study habits. *The Journal of Educational Research, 65,* 352–354.

Wittrock, M. C. (1982, March). *Educational implications of recent research on learning and memory.* Paper presented at the annual meeting of the American Educational Research Association, New York.

Wittrock, M. C. (Ed.). (1986). *Handbook of research on teaching* (3rd ed.). New York, NY: Macmillan.

Wittwer, J., & Renkl, A. (2010). How effective are instructional explanations in example-based learning? A meta-analytic review. *Educational Psychology Review, 22,* 393–409.

Wolf, M., Barzillai, M., Gottwald, S., Miller, L., Spencer, K., Norton, E., . . . Morris, R. (2009). The RAVE-O intervention: Connecting neuroscience to the classroom. *Mind, Brain, and Education, 3,* 84–93.

Wolfe, P. (2010). *Brain matters: Translating research into classroom practice* (2nd ed.). Alexandria, VA: Association for Supervision and Curriculum Development.

Wolfgang, C. H. (2009). *Solving discipline and classroom management problems* (7th ed.). Hoboken, NJ: Wiley & Sons.

Wong, H. K., & Wong, R. T. (2009). *The first days of school: How to be an effective teacher.* Mountain View, CA: Harry K. Wong Publications.

Wong, K. F., & Xiao, Y. (2010). Diversity and difference: Identity issues of Chinese heritage language learners from dialect backgrounds. *Heritage Language Journal, 7,* 153–187.

Wong, L. (1987). Reaction to research findings: Is the feeling of obviousness warranted? *Dissertation Abstracts International,* 48/12, 3709B. (University Microfilms #DA 8801059)

Wong, L. (2015). *Essential study skills* (8th ed.). Stamford, CT: Cengage.

Wood, D., Bruner, J., & Ross, S. (1976). The role of tutoring in problem solving. *British Journal of Psychology, 66,* 181–191.

Woodward, A., & Needham, A. (Eds.). (2009). *Learning and the infant mind.* New York, NY: Oxford University Press.

Woolfolk, A. E., & Brooks, D. (1983). Nonverbal communication in teaching. In E. Gordon (Ed.), *Review of research in education* (Vol. 10, pp. 103–150).

Washington, DC: American Educational Research Association.

Woolfolk, A. E., & Brooks, D. (1985). The influence of teachers' nonverbal behaviors on students' perceptions and performance. *Elementary School Journal, 85,* 514–528.

Woolfolk, A. E., & Hoy, W. K. (1990). Prospective teachers' sense of efficacy and beliefs about control. *Journal of Educational Psychology, 82,* 81–91.

Woolfolk, A. E., & Perry, N. E. (2015). *Child and adolescent development* (2nd ed.). Columbus, OH: Pearson.

Woolfolk, A. H., Winne, P. H., & Perry, N. E. (2006). The cycle of self-regulated learning, in *Educational psychology* (3rd Canadian ed., p. 307). Toronto, CA: Pearson.

Woolfolk Hoy, A. (2013). A reflection on the place of emotion in teaching and teacher education. In M. Newberry, A. Gallant, & P. Riley (Eds.), *Advances in research in education: Emotion and school: International perspectives on the function, process and products of the 'other' curriculum* (pp. 255–270). Bingley, UK: Emerald.

Woolfolk Hoy, A., & Burke-Spero, R. (2005). Changes in teacher efficacy during the early years of teaching: A comparison of four measures. *Teaching and Teacher Education, 21,* 343–356.

Woolfolk Hoy, A., Davis, H., & Pape, S. (2006). Teachers' knowledge, beliefs, and thinking. In P. A. Alexander & P. H Winne (Eds.), *Handbook of educational psychology* (2nd ed., pp. 715–737). Mahwah, NJ: Erlbaum.

Woolfolk Hoy, A., Demerath, P., & Pape, S. (2002). Teaching adolescents: Engaging developing selves. In T. Urdan & F. Pajares (Eds.), *Adolescence and education* (Vol. I, pp. 119–169). Greenwich, CT: Information Age Publishing.

Woolfolk Hoy, A., & Hoy, W. K. (2013). *Instructional leadership: A research-based guide to learning in schools* (4th ed.). Boston, MA: Pearson/Allyn & Bacon.

Woolfolk Hoy, A., Hoy, W. K., & Davis, H. (2009). Teachers' self-efficacy beliefs. In K. Wentzel & A. Wigfield (Eds.), *Handbook of motivation in school* (pp. 627–654). Mahwah, NJ: Erlbaum.

Woolfolk Hoy, A., & Murphy, P. K. (2001). Teaching educational psychology to the implicit mind. In R. Sternberg & B. Torff (Eds.), *Understanding and teaching the implicit mind* (pp. 145–185). Mahwah, NJ: Erlbaum.

Woolfolk Hoy, A., Pape, S., & Davis, H. (2006). Teachers' knowledge, beliefs, and thinking. In P. A. Alexander & P. H, Winne (Eds.), *Handbook of educational psychology* (2nd ed., pp. 715–737). Mahwah, NJ: Erlbaum.

Woolfolk Hoy, A., & Tschannen-Moran. M. (1999). Implications of cognitive approaches to peer learning for teacher education. In A. O'Donnell & A. King (Eds.), *Cognitive perspectives on peer learning* (pp. 257–284). Mahwah, NJ: Erlbaum.

Woolfolk Hoy, A., & Weinstein, C. S. (2006). Students' and teachers' perspectives about classroom management. In C. Evertson & C. S. Weinstein (Eds.), *Handbook for classroom management: Research, practice, and contemporary issues* (pp. 181–220). Mahwah, NJ: Erlbaum.

Wout, D., Dasco, H., Jackson, J., & Spencer, S. (2008). The many faces of stereotype threat: Group- and self-threat. *Journal of Experimental Social Psychology, 44,* 792–799.

Wouters, P., van Nimwegen, C., van Oostendrop, H., & van der Spek, E. D. (2013). A meta-analysis of the cognitive and motivational effects of serious games. *Journal of Educational Psychology, 105,* 249–265.

Wouters, S., De Fraine, B., Colpin, H., Van Damme, J., & Verschueren, K. (2012). The effect of track changes on the development of academic self-concept in high school: A dynamic test of the Big-Fish–Little-Pond Effect. *Journal of Educational Psychology, 3,* 793–805. doi: 10.1037/a0027732

Wu, W., West, S. G., & Hughes, J. N. (2010). Effect of grade retention in first grade on psychosocial outcomes. *Journal of Educational Psychology, 102,* 135–152.

Wu, X., Anderson, R. C., Nguyen-Jahiel, K., & Miller, B. (2013). Enhancing motivation and engagement through collaborative discussion. *Journal of Educational Psychology, 105,* 622–632. doi: 10.1037/a0032792

Xu, J., Coats, L. T., & Davidson, M. L. (2012). Promoting student interest in science: The perspectives of exemplary African American teachers. *American Educational Research Journal, 49,* 124–154. doi: 10.3102/0002831211426200

Yang, L., Shuai, L., Du, Q., et al. (2009). Atomoxetine and executive functioning in Chinese ADHD children. From Childhood to Adult Disease. May 21–24, 2009, Vienna, Austria. *Attention Deficit and Hyperactivity Disorders, 1,* 135.

Yarhouse, M. A. (2001). Sexual identity development: The influence of valuative frameworks on identity synthesis. *Psychotherapy, 38*(3), 331–341.

Yates, M., & Youniss, J. (1999). *Roots of civic identity: International perspectives on community service and activism in youth.* New York: Cambridge University Press.

Yell, M. L. (1990). The use of corporal punishment, suspension, expulsion, and timeout with behaviorally disordered students in public schools: Legal considerations. *Behavioral Disorders, 15,* 100–109.

Yerkes, R. M., & Dodson, J. D. (1908). The relation of strength of stimulus to rapidity of habit formation. *Journal of Comparative Neurology, 18,* 459–482.

Yough, M. (2010, August). *An intervention: Teaching candidates' beliefs and linguistic minority students.* Paper presented at the American Psychological Association Annual Convention, San Diego, CA.

Younger, M. R., & Warrington, M. (2006). Would Harry and Hermione have done better in single-sex teaching in coeducational secondary schools in the United Kingdom? *American Educational Research Journal, 43,* 579–620.

Youniss, J., & Yates, M. (1997). *Community service and social responsibility in youth.* Chicago, IL: University of Chicago Press.

Zeidner, M. (1995). Adaptive coping with test situations. *Educational Psychologist, 30,* 123–134.

Zeidner, M. (1998). *Test anxiety: The state of the art.* New York, NY: Plenum.

Zeidner, M., & Matthews, G. (2005). Evaluation anxiety: Current theory and research. In A. J. Elliot & C. S. Dweck (Eds.), *Handbook of competence and motivation* (pp. 141–163). New York: Guilford Press.

Zelli, A., Dodge, K. A., Lochman, J. E., & Laird, R. D. (1999). The distinction between beliefs legitimizing aggression and deviant processing of social cues: Testing measurement validity and the hypothesis that biased processing mediates the effects of beliefs on aggression. *Journal of Personality and Social Psychology, 77,* 150–166.

Zhang, L., & Sternberg, R. J. (2005). The threefold model of intellectual styles. *Educational Psychology Review, 17,* 1–53.

Zhou, Z., Peverly, S. T., Beohm, A. E., & Chongde, L. (2001). American and Chinese children's

understanding of distance, time, and speed interrelations. *Cognitive Development, 15,* 215–240.

Ziegler, A., & Heller, K. A. (2000). Effects of an attribution retraining with female students gifted in physics. *Journal for the Education of the Gifted, 23,* 217–243.

Zimmerman, B. J. (2002). Becoming a self-regulated learner. *Theory Into Practice, 41,* 64–70.

Zimmerman, B. (2011). Motivational sources and outcomes of self-regulated learning and performance. In B. Zimmerman & D. Schunk, (Eds.), *Handbook of self-regulation of learning and performance* (pp. 49–64). New York, NY: Routledge.

Zimmerman, B. J., & Schunk, D. H. (Eds.). (2001). *Self-regulated learning and academic achievement: Theoretical perspectives* (2nd ed.). Mahwah, NJ: Erlbaum.

Zimmerman, B. J., & Schunk, D. H. (2004). Self-regulating intellectual processes and outcomes: A social cognitive perspective. In D. Y. Dao & R. J. Sternberg (Eds.), *Motivation, emotion, and cognition: Integrative perspectives on intellectual functioning and development* (pp. 323–350). Mahwah, NJ: Erlbaum.

Zimmerman, B., & Schunk, D. (Eds.). (2011). *Handbook of self-regulation of learning and performance.* New York, NY: Routledge.

Zohar, D. (1998). An additive model of test anxiety: Role of exam-specific expectations. *Journal of Educational Psychology, 90,* 330–340.

Zusho, A., & Clayton, K. (2011). Culturalizing achievement goal theory and research. *Educational Psychologist, 46,* 239–260. doi: 10.1080/00461520.2011.614526

Subject Index